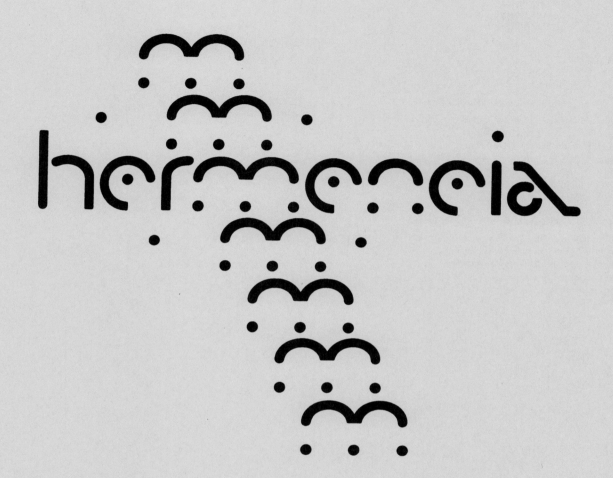

Matthew 8–20

A Commentary
by Ulrich Luz

Translation by
James E. Crouch

Edited by
Helmut Koester

**Fortress
Press**   Minneapolis

Matthew 8–20
A Commentary

Copyright © 2001 Augsburg Fortress
All rights reserved. Except for brief quotations in
critical articles or reviews, no part of this book may be
reproduced in any manner without prior written
permission from the publisher. Write: Permissions,
Augsburg Fortress, Box 1209, Minneapolis, MN
55440.

Cover and interior design by Kenneth Hiebert
Typesetting and page composition by
The HK Scriptorium

The Library of Congress has cataloged the first volume as follows:

Luz, Ulrich.
      [Evangelium nach Matthaus. English]
      Matthew : a commentary / Ulrich Luz ;
   translated by Wilhelm C. Linss.
         p.   cm.
      Translation of: Das Evangelium nach Matthaus.
      Bibliography: p.
      Includes index.
      Contents: v. [1]-7.
      ISBN 0-8066-2402-7
      1. Bible. N.T. Matthew—Commnetaries.   I. Title.
   BS2575.3.L8913   1989
   226'.207—dc19   89-383
                                              CIP

Matthew 8–20 ISBN 0-8006-6034-X

The paper used in this publication meets the minimum requirements of American National Standard
for Information Sciences—Permanence of paper for
Printed Library Materials, ANSI Z329.48–1984.

Manufactured in the U.S.A.   AF 1-6034

05   04   03   02   01   1   2   3   4   5   6   7   8   9   10

The Author

Ulrich Luz was born in 1938, and he studied theology in
Zürich and Göttingen under Hans Conzelmann, Eduard
Schweizer, and Gerhard Ebeling. He taught at the
International Christian University in Tokyo (1970–1971)
and at the University of Göttingen (1972–1980), and he
is now Professor of New Testament Studies at the
University of Bern in Switzerland. He received honorary
degrees from the universities of Leipzig, Budapest, and
Sibiu and served as president of the Societas Novi
Testamenti Studiorum in 1998. He is the author of
numerous books, including *Das Geschichtsverständnis des
Paulus* (1968), *Die Mitte des Neuen Testaments: Einheit und
Vielfalt neutestamentlich* (1983), *Matthew in History:
Interpretation, Influence and Effects* (1994), and *The
Theology of the Gospel of Matthew* (1995). He and his wife,
Salome Keller, have three children.

Contents
Matthew 8–20

■ **Commentary**

Indices

The name *Hermeneia,* Greek ἑρμηνεία, has been chosen as the title of the commentary series to which this volume belongs. The word *Hermeneia* has a rich background in the history of biblical interpretation as a term used in the ancient Greek-speaking world for the detailed, systematic exposition of a scriptural work. It is hoped that the series, like its name, will carry forward this old and venerable tradition. A second, entirely practical reason for selecting the name lies in the desire to avoid a long descriptive title and its inevitable acronym, or worse, an unpronounceable abbreviation.

The series is designed to be a critical and historical commentary to the Bible without arbitrary limits in size or scope. It will utilize the full range of philological and historical tools, including textual criticism (often slighted in modern commentaries), the methods of the history of tradition (including genre and prosodic analysis), and the history of religion.

Hermeneia is designed for the serious student of the Bible. It will make full use of ancient Semitic and classical languages; at the same time, English translations of all comparative materials—Greek, Latin, Canaanite, or Akkadian—will be supplied alongside the citation of the source in its original language. Insofar as possible, the aim is to provide the student or scholar with full critical discussion of each problem of interpretation and with the primary data upon which the discussion is based.

Hermeneia is designed to be international and interconfessional in the selection of authors; its editorial boards were formed with this end in view. Occasionally the series will offer translations of distinguished commentaries which originally appeared in languages other than English. Published volumes of the series will be revised continually, and eventually, new commentaries will replace older works in order to preserve the currency of the series. Commentaries are also being assigned for important literary works in the categories of apocryphal and pseudepigraphical works relating to the Old and New Testaments, including some of Essene or Gnostic authorship.

The editors of *Hermeneia* impose no systematic-theological perspective upon the series (directly, or indirectly by selection of authors). It is expected that authors will struggle to lay bare the ancient meaning of a biblical work or pericope. In this way the text's human relevance should become transparent, as is always the case in competent historical discourse. However, the series eschews for itself homiletical translation of the Bible.

The editors are heavily indebted to Augsburg Fortress for its energy and courage in taking up an expensive, long-term project, the rewards of which will accrue chiefly to the field of biblical scholarship.

The editor responsible for this volume is Helmut Koester of Harvard University.

Frank Moore Cross   *Helmut Koester*
For the Old Testament   For the New Testament
Editorial Board   Editorial Board

Reference Codes

1. Sources and Abbreviations

AB	Anchor Bible
ʾAbot R. Nat.	ʾAbot de Rabbi Nathan
Act. John	Acts of John
Act. Pet.	Acts of Peter
Acts Pet. 12 Apost.	Acts of Peter and the Twelve Apostles (NHC 6, 1)
ACW	Ancient Christian Writers: The Works of the Fathers in Translation (Westminster, Md.: Newman)
Adam and Eve	Books of Adam and Eve

Aeschylus

Pers.	Persae
ʾAg. Ber.	ʾAggadat Bereshit

Ambrose

De inc. dom. sac.	De incarnationis dominicae sacramento
Exhort. virg.	Exhortatio virginitatis
Fid.	De fide
In Luc.	In Lucam
Paen.	De paenitentia
Vid.	Liber de viduis
Virg.	De virginitate
AMNSU	Abeiten und Mitteilungen aus dem neutestamentlichen Seminar zu Uppsala

Anacreon

Od.	Odae
AnBib	Analecta biblica
ANET	Ancient Near Eastern Texts Relating to the Old Testament, ed. James B. Pritchard (3d ed.; Princeton: Princeton University Press, 1969)
ANF	Ante-Nicene Fathers
ANTJ	Arbeiten zum Neuen Testament und Judentum
Anton.	Antonianum
Apoc. Abr.	Apocalypse of Abraham
Apoc. Elijah	Apocalypse of Elijah
Apoc. Ezra	Apocalypse of Ezra
Apoc. Pet.	Apocalypse of Peter (NHC 7, 3)

Apollodorus

Bibl.	Bibliotheca

Apollonius of Rhodes

Argon.	Argonautica

Apuleius

Met.	Metamorphoses
ʿArak.	ʿArakin

Aratus

Phaen.	Phaenomena

Aristides

Apol.	Apologia

Aristophanes

Eq.	Equites

Aristotle

Eth. eud.	Ethica eudemia
Gen. an.	De generatione animalium
Probl.	Problemata

Artemidorus

Oneirocr.	Oneirocriticum
Asc. Isa.	Ascension of Isaiah
As. Mos.	Assumption of Moses
AsSeign	Assemblées du Seigneur
ASTI	Annual of the Swedish Theological Institute

Athanasius

Anton.	Vita Antonii
Contra Ar.	Contra Arianos
Epist.	Epistulae
Illud.	In illud: 'Omnia mihi tradita sunt . . .' (PG 25. 207–20)
Hom. sem.	Homilia de semente
AThANT	Abhandlungen zur Theologie des Alten und Neuen Testaments

Athenagoras

Suppl.	Supplicatio
ATR	Anglican Theological Review

Augustine

Bapt. Don.	De Baptismo contra Donatistas
Civ. D.	De civitate Dei
Conf.	Confessiones
Cons. ev.	De consensu evangelistarum
Contra Epist. Parmeniani	Contra Epistolan Parmeniani
Doctr. Chr.	De doctrina Christiana
Dono. pers.	De dono perseverantiae
Ep.	Epistulae
Expos. ad Rom.	Expositio ad Romanos inchoata
Faust.	Contra Faustum Manichaeum
Gaud.	Contra Gaudentius
Joh. ev. tract.	In Iohannis Evangelium tractatus
Quaest.	Quaestiones evangeliorum
Retract.	Retractationum
Sct. virg.	De sancta virginitate
Trin.	De trinitate
Util.	De utilitate credendi
AUSS	Andrews University Seminary Studies
b.	Babylonian Talmud tractate
BAC	Biblioteca de autores cristianos
BAGD	Walter Bauer, William F. Arndt, F. Wilbur Gingrinch, Frederick W. Danker, A Greek-English Lexicon of the New Testament (Chicago: University of Chicago Press, 1979)
Bar.	Baraita
2 Bar.	Syriac Apocalypse of Baruch
3 Bar.	Greek Apocalypse of Baruch

Barn.	*Epistle of Barnabas*	CBQMS	Catholic Biblical Quarterly Monograph Series
B. Batra	*Baba Batra*		
BBB	Bonner biblische Beiträge	CChr	Corpus Christianorum
BBE	Beiträge zur biblischen Exegese	CChr.SG	—Series Graeca
BCE	Before the Common Era	CChr.SL	—Series Latina
BDF	F. Blass, A. Debrunner, and Robert W. Funk, *A Greek Grammar of the New Testament* (Chicago: University of Chicago Press, 1961)	CD	Cairo (Genizah) text of the *Damascus Document*
		CE	the Common Era
		chap(s).	chapter(s)
Ber.	*Berakot*	Chrysostom	
BeO	*Bibbia e oriente*	*Adv. Jud.*	*Adversus Judaeos*
BEThL	Bibliotheca ephemeridum theologicarum lovaniensium	*Hom. adv. Jud.*	*Homilia adversus Judaeos*
		Hom in Act.	*In Acta Apostolorum homilia*
BEvTh	Beiträge zur evangelischen Theologie	*In Tit.*	*In epistolam ad Titum*
		In 1 Cor.	*In epistolam I ad Corinthios*
BFCTh	Beiträge zur Förderung christlicher Theologie	*Virg.*	*De virginitate*
		Cicero	
BGBE	Beiträge zur Geschichte der biblischen Exegese	*Divin.*	*De divinatione*
		Fin.	*De finibus bonorum et malorum*
BHH	*Biblisch-historisches Handwörterbuch*, Bo Reicke and Leonard Rost, eds. (Göttingen: Vandenhoeck & Ruprecht, 1962–79)	*Or.*	*Orationis*
		Clement of Alexandria	
		Exc. Theod.	*Excerpta ex Theodota*
		Paed.	*Paedagogus*
		Quis div. salv.	*Quis dives salvetur*
BHTh	Beiträge zur historischen Theologie	*Strom.*	*Stromata*
		CNT	Commentaire du Nouveau Testament
Bib	*Biblica*		
BibLeb	*Bibel und Leben*	ConNT	*Coniectanea Neotestamentica*
BKAT	Biblischer Kommentar: Altes Testament	*Const. ap.*	*Constitutiones apostolorum*
		Corp. Herm.	*Corpus Hermeticum*
BKV	Bibliothek der Kirchenväter (Kempten: Kösel; Munich: Kösee & Pustet)	CSCO	Corpus scriptorum Christianorum orientalium
		CSEL	Corpus scriptorum ecclesiasticorum latinorum
BLE	*Bulletin de littérature ecclésiastique*	*CTM*	*Concordia Theological Monthly*
B. Meṣ.	*Baba Meṣiʿa*	Cyprian	
B. Qam.	*Baba Qamma*	*Ep.*	*Epistulae*
BSac	*Bibliotheca Sacra*	*Hab. virg.*	*De habitu virginum*
BSKORK	*Bekenntnisschriften und Kirchenordnungen der nach Gottes Wort reformierten Kirche* (Zurich: Evangelischer Verlag, 1938)	*Unit. eccl.*	*De unitate ecclesiae*
		Cyril of Alexandria	
		Hom. div.	*Homiliae diversae*
		In Joh.	*In Joannis evangelium*
BSLK	*Bekenntnisschriften der evangelisch-lutherischen Kirche* (4th ed.; Göttingen: Vandenhoeck & Ruprecht, 1959)	*Matt.*	*Commentariorum in Matthaeum quae supersunt*
		Trin.	*De trinitate*
		Cyril of Jerusalem	
		Cat. myst.	*Catechesis mystagogica*
BTB	*Biblical Theology Bulletin*	*Der. ʾEr. Zuṭ.*	*Derek ʾEretz Zuṭa*
BU	Biblische Untersuchungen	*Did.*	*Didache*
BVC	*Bible et vie chrétienne*	*Didasc.*	*Didascalia Apostolorum*
BWANT	Beiträge zur Wissenschaft vom Alten und Neuen Testament	Dio Chrysosthom	
		Or.	*Orationes*
BZ	*Biblische Zeitschrift*	DJD	Discoveries in the Judaean Desert
BZNW	Beihefte zur *ZNW*		
c.	*circa*, approximately	DS	Heinrich Denzinger and Adolf Schönmetzer, eds., *Enchiridion symbolorum*
CA	*Confessio Augustana*		
CAF	*comicorum Atticorum Fragmenta*		
Catullus		*DThC*	*Dictionnaire de théologie catholique*
Carm.	*Carmina*	ed(s).	editor(s), edited by, edition
CBQ	*Catholic Biblical Quarterly*		

EDNT	*Exegetical Dictionary of the New Testament*, ed. Horst Balz and Gerhard Schneider (3 vols.; Grand Rapids: Eerdmans, 1990–93)	*Gos. Phil.*	*Gospel of Philip* (NHC 2, 3)
		Gos. Thom.	*Gospel of Thomas* (NHC 2, 2)
		Gos. Truth	*Gospel of Truth* (NHC 1, 3)
		Greg	*Gregorianum*
EHS	Europäische Hochschulschriften	Gregory the Great	
EKKNT	Evangelisch-katholischer Kommentar zum Neuen Testament	*Dial.*	*Dialogus*
		Epist.	*Registrum epistolarum*
		Hom. in ev.	*Homiliarum in evangelia*
1 Enoch	*Ethiopic Enoch*	Gregory of Nazianzus	
Epictetus		*Or.*	*Oratio*
Diss.	*Dissertationis*	GThA	Göttinger theologische Arbeiten
Epiphanius		*Ḥag.*	*Ḥagiga*
Haer.	*Adversus Haereses*	HbrMt	Hebrew text of Matthew of the Shem Tov (Ibn Shaprut), 14th century (cf. Howard in Short Titles)
Ep. or Epist.	*Epistula(e)*		
Ep. Apost.	*Epistula apostolorum*		
Ep. Arist.	*Epistle of Aristeas*	*Herm.*	*The Shepherd of Hermas*
Ep. Jer.	*Epistle of Jeremiah*	*Man.*	*Mandate*
Erub.	*Erubin*	*Sim.*	*Similitude*
Esth. Rab.	*Esther Rabbah*	*Vis.*	*Vision*
EstBib	*Estudios biblicos*	Hilary	
ET	English Translation	*Trin.*	*De trinitate*
EtB	Études bibliques	Hippolytus	
EThL	*Ephemerides theologicae lovanienses*	*Ref.*	*Refutatio omnium haeresium*
EThR	*Études théologiques et religieuses*	HKNT	Handkommentar zum Neuen Testament
EThSt	Erfurter theologische Studien		
Euripides		HNT	Handbuch zum Neuen Testament
Cret.	*Cretes*		
Heracl.	*Heraclidae*	*Hom.*	*Homilia*
Hipp.	*Hippolytus*	Homer	
Or.	*Orestes*	*Il.*	*Iliad*
Eusebius		*Hor.*	*Horayoth*
Ctr. Marc.	*Contra Marcellum*	Horace	
Dem. ev.	*Demonstratio evangelica*	*Carm.*	*Carmina (Odes)*
Hist. eccl.	*Historia Ecclesiastica*	*Sat.*	*Satirae*
In Ps.	*In Psalmi*	HThKNT	Herders theologischer Kommentar zum Neuen Testament
Praep. ev.	*Praeparatio evangelica*		
Theoph.	*Theophania*		
EvTh	*Evangelische Theologie*	*HTR*	*Harvard Theological Review*
ExpT	*Expository Times*	*HUCA*	*Hebrew Union College Annual*
FB	Forschung zur Bibel	*Ḥul.*	*Ḥullin*
FC	Fathers of the Church: A New Translation	Hyppolitus	
		Ref.	*Refutatio ombium haeresium*
fl.	flourished	Iamblichus	
frg(s)	fragment(s)	*Vit. Pyth.*	*Vita Pythagorae*
FRLANT	Forschungen zur Religion und Literatur des Alten und Neuen Testaments	ibid.	*ibidem*, in the same place
		ICC	International Critical Commentary
FTS	Frankfurter theologische Studien	idem	the same
FzB	Forschungen zur Bibel	Ignatius	
GCS	Griechische christliche Schriftsteller	*Eph.*	*Letter to the Ephesians*
		Rom.	*Letter to the Romans*
Gen. Rab.	*Genesis Rabbah*	*Int*	*Interpretation*
Giṭ.	*Giṭṭin*	Irenaeus	
GKC	*Gesenius' Hebrew Grammar*, ed. Emil Kautsch, trans. A. E. Cowley	*Epid.*	*Epideixes*
		Haer.	*Adversus haereses*
		JBL	*Journal of Biblical Literature*
GNT	Grundrisse zum Neuen Testament	Jerome	
		Dan.	*Commentariorum in Danielem*
Gos. Barth.	*Gospel of Bartholomew*	*Ep.*	*Epistulae*

Helv.	*Adversus Helvidium*	Macarius	
Jov.	*Adversus Jovinianum*	*Ep.*	*Epistles*
Pelag.	*Adversus Pelagium*	*Hom.*	*Homilies*
Tract. Ps.	*Tractatus de Psalmis*	*Mak.*	*Makkot*
JJS	*Journal of Jewish Studies*	*Mart. Isa.*	*Martyrdom of Isaiah*
John of Damascus		*Mart. Pol.*	*Martyrdom of Polycarp*
Hom. in trans.	*Homilia in transfigurationem domini*	*Mek.*	*Mekilta*
		Menaḥ.	*Menaḥot*
Jos. Asen.	*Joseph and Asenath*	Menander	
Josephus		*Sent.*	*Sententiae*
Ant.	*Antiquities of the Jews*	*Midr.*	*Midraš*
Ap.	*Contra Apionem*	MT	Masoretic text
Bell.	*Bellum Judaicum*	MThSt	Marburger theologische Studien
Vit.	*Vita*	*MThZ*	*Münchener theologische Zeitschrift*
JSHRZ	Jüdische Schriften aus hellenistisch-römischer Zeit	NCB	New Century Bible
		Ned.	*Nedarim*
JSNT	*Journal for the Study of the New Testament*	*Neot*	*Neotestamentica*
		NF	Neue Folge
JSNTSup	Journal for the Study of the New Testament Supplement Series	NHC	Nag Hammadi Codex
		NHS	Nag Hammadi Studies
JTS	*Journal of Theological Studies*	NIGTC	New International Greek Testament Commentary
Jub.	*Jubilees*		
Julian		n(n).	note(s)
Or.	*Orations*	no(s).	number(s)
Justin		Novatian	
Apol.	*Apologia*	*Trin.*	*De trinitate*
Dial.	*Dialogue with Trypho*	*NovT*	*Novum Testamentum*
KBANT	Kommentare und Beiträge zum Alten und Neuen Testament	NovTSup	Novum Testamentum Supplements
KEK	Kritisch-exegetischer Kommentar über das Neue Testament	NPNF	Nicene and Post-Nicene Fathers
		NR	Josef Neuner and Heinrich Roos, *The Teaching of the Catholic Church as Contained in Her Documents* (Karl Rahner, ed.; New York: Society of St. Paul, 1966)
Ker.	*Keritot*		
Ketub.	*Ketubot*		
Kil.	*Kil'ayim*		
KlT	Kleine Texte für Vorlesungen und Übungen		
KP	*Der Kleine Pauly Lexikon der Antike* (5 vols.; Stuttgart: Druckenmüller, 1964–75)	*NRTh*	*La nouvelle revue théologique*
		n.s.	new series
		NT	New Testament
Lam. Rab.	*Lamentations Rabbah*	NTAbh	Neutestamentliche Abhandlungen
LCC	Library of Christian Classics		
LCL	Loeb Classical Library	*NTApoc*	*New Testament Apocrypha*, 2 vols., by Edgar Hennecke and Wilhelm Schneemelcher (Philadelphia: Westminster, 1963–65)
LD	Lectio divina		
Lev. Rab.	*Leviticus Rabbah*		
LSJ	H. G. Liddell, R. Scott, H. S. Jones, and R. McKenzie, *A Greek–English Lexicon* (rev. ed.; Oxford: Clarendon, 1968)		
		NTD	Das Neue Testament Deutsch
		NTOA	Novum Testamentum et orbis antiquus
LThK	*Lexikon für Theologie und Kirche*	*NTS*	*New Testament Studies*
Lucian		OBO	Orbis biblicus et orientalis
Cyn.	*Cynicus*	*Odes Sol.*	*Odes of Solomon*
Dial. mort.	*Dialogi mortuorum*	*ʾOhol.*	*ʾOholot*
Eun.	*Eunuchus*	OLZ	Orientalistische Literaturzeitung
Fug.	*Fugitivi*	*Or.*	*Oratio*
Hermot.	*Hermotimus*	ʿ*Or.*	ʿ*Orlah*
Pergr. Mort.	*De morte Peregrini*	OrChr	Oriens christianus
Philops.	*Philopseudas*	OrChrA	Orientalia Christiana Analecta
Ver. hist.	*Verae historiae*	*OrChrP*	*Orientalia Christiana Periodica*
m.	Mishnah tractate		

Origen		Phileb.	Philebus
Cels.	Contra Celsum	Sym.	Symposium
Comm. in Rom.	Commentariorum in epistulam ad Romanos	Pliny the Elder	
		Hist. nat.	Naturalis historia
Exhor.	Exhortation to Martyrdom (Εἰς μαρτύριον προστρεπτικός)	Plutarch	
		Anton.	De Antonio
Hom. in 1. Reg.	In primum regnorum librum homiliae	Aud. Poet.	De audiendis poetis
		Quaest. Rom.	Quaestionis Romanae
Hom. in Cant.	Homilae in Canticum Canticorum	Ser. num. vind.	De sera numinis vindicta
Hom. in Jos.	Homilae in Joshua	Pollux	
Hom. in Lev.	Homilae in Leviticus	Onom.	Onomasticon
Hom. in Lucam	Homilae in Lucam	Porphyry	
Hom. in Num.	Homilae in Numeri	Vit. Pyth.	Vita Pythagorae
Princ.	De principiis	Ps.-Clement	Pseudo-Clement
OT	Old Testament	Ep. ad virg.	Epistula ad virgines
OTS	Oudtestamentische Studiën	1 Clem.	The First Epistle of Clement
p(p).	page(s)	2 Clem.	The Second Epistle of Clement
par.	parallel(s)	Hom.	Homilies
Pesaḥ.	Pesaḥim	Rec.	Recognitions
Pesiq. R.	Pesiqta Rabbati	Ps.-Clem. Hom.	Pseudoclementine Homilies
Pesiq. R. Kah.	Pesiqta de Rab Kahana	Ps.-Clem. Rec.	Pseudoclementine Recognitions
PG	Patrologia graeca = J. P. Migne, Patrologiae cursus completus, series graeca (162 vols.; Paris: Migne, 1857–66)	Ps.-Philo	
		Lib. ant. bib.	Liber antiquitatum biblicarum
		Ps. Sol.	Psalms of Solomon
		PW	Pauly-Wissowa, Real-encyclopädie der classischen Altertumswissenschaft
Philo			
Abr.	De Abrahamo		
Cher.	De cherubim	PWSup	Supplement to PW
Congr.	De congressu eruditiones gratia	1QapGen	Genesis Apocryphon from Qumran Cave 1
Decal.	De decalogo		
Deus imm.	Quod Deus sit immutabilis	1QH	Thanksgiving Hymns from Qumran Cave 1
Fug.	De fuga et inventione		
Leg. all.	Legum allegoriae	1QpHab	Pesher on Habakkuk from Qumran Cave 1
Leg. Gaj.	Legatio ad Gajum		
Migr. Abr.	De migratione Abrahami	1QS	Rule of the Community (Manual of Discipline) from Qumran Cave 1
Op. mun.	De opificio mundi		
Poster. C.	De posteritate Caini	3Q15	The Copper Scroll from Qumran Cave 3
Praem. poen.	De praemiis et poenis		
Q. Exod.	Quaestiones in Exodum	4QFlor	Florilegium (or Eschatological Midrashim) from Qumran Cave 4
Rer. div. her.	Quis rerum divinarum heres sit		
Som.	De somniis	4QpNah	Pesher on Nahum from Qumran Cave 4
Spec. leg.	De specialibus legibus		
Vit. con.	De vita contemplativa	4QpPs	Pesher on Psalms from Qumran Cave 4
Vit. Mos.	De vita Mosis		
Philostratus		4QTestim	Testimonia from Qumran Cave 4
Vit. Ap.	Vita Apollonii	11QMelch	Melchizedek from Qumran Cave 11
Phrynichus Arabius			
Ecl.	Eclogae	11QPsᵃ	The Psalms Scroll from Qumran Cave 11
Pirqe R. El.	Pirqe Rabbi Eliezer		
PJ	Palästina Jahrbuch	11QT	The Temple Scroll from Qumran Cave 11
PL	Patrologia latina = J.-P. Migne, Patrologiae cursus completus, series latina (217 vols.; Paris: Migne, 1844–55)	Q	Sayings Gospel Q
		QLk	Lukan Version of the Sayings Gospel
Plato		QMt	Matthean Version of the Sayings Gospel
Ap.	Apologia		
Gorg.	Gorgias	QD	Quaestiones disputatae
Leg.	Leges	Qidd.	Qiddušin
Phaedr.	Phaedrus		

Quintilian		Socrates	
Inst. orat.	*Institutio oratoria*	*Hist. eccl.*	*Historia ecclesiastica*
Rab.	*Rabbah* (following abbreviation for biblical book)	*Soph.*	*Sopherim*
		Sophocles	
RAC	*Reallexikon für Antike und Christentum*	*Ai.*	*Aiax*
		Ant.	*Antigone*
RB	*Revue biblique*	*Oed. Col.*	*Oedipus Coloneus*
RechBib	Recherches bibliques	*Oed. Tyr.*	*Oedipus Tyrannus*
RechSR	*Recherches de science religieuse*	SPAW	Sitzungsberichte der preussi-schen Akademie der
RevQ	*Revue de Qumran*		Wissenschaften
RGG	*Religion in Geschichte und Gegenwart*	SPAW.PH	—Philosophisch-Historische Klasse
RHPhR	*Revue d'histoire et de philosophie religieuses*	*StEv*	*Studia Evangelica*
RIDA	*Revue internationale des droits de l'antiquité*	*StPatr*	*Studia Patristica*
		Strabo	
RivB	*Rivista biblica*	*Geogr.*	*Geographia*
RNT	Regensburger Neues Testament	Str–B	Hermann L. Strack and Paul Billerbeck, *Kommentar zum Neuen*
Roš Haš.	*Roš Haššana*		*Testament aus Talmud und*
RThPh	*Revue de théologie et de philosophie*		*Midrasch* (4 vols.; 2d. ed.;
Šabb.	*Šabbat*		Munich: Beck, 1956)
Sanh.	*Sanhedrin*	*StTh*	*Studia Theologica*
SANT	Studien zum Alten und Neuen Testament	Suetonius	
		Aug.	*Divus Augustus*
SAQ	Sammlung ausgewählter kirchen- und dogmengeschichtlicher Quellenschriften	*Sukk.*	*Sukka*
		SUNT	Studien zur Umwelt des Neuen Testaments
SBB	Stuttgarter biblische Beiträge		
SBFLA	*Studii biblici franciscani liber annuus*	*s.v(v).*	*sub verbo* or *sub voce*, under the word(s) or entry(entries)
SBLSP	Society of Biblical Literature Seminar Papers	SVTP	Studia in Veteris Testamentii Pseudepigrapha
SBS	Stuttgarter Bibelstudien	*SZuṭaᶜ*	*Sipre Zuṭaᶜ*
SBT	Studies in Biblical Theology	*t.*	Tosephta tractate
SC	Sources chrétiennes	*Taᶜan.*	*Taᶜanit*
ScEs	*Science et esprit*	*T. Abr.*	*Testament of Abraham*
scil.	*scilicet*, namely: to be supplied or understood	*T. Adam*	*Testament of Adam*
		Tanch.	*Tanchumaʾ*
S. Deut.	*Sifre Deuteronomy*	*Teach. Silv.*	*Teachings of Sylvanus* (NHC 7, 4)
SEÅ	*Svensk exegetisk årsbok*	Tertullian	
Seneca		*Anim.*	*De anima*
Ben.	*De beneficiis*	*Bapt.*	*De baptismo*
Vita	*De vita beata*	*Carn.*	*De carne Christi*
Šeb.	*Šebiᶜit*	*Carnis*	*De carnis resurrectione*
Šeqal.	*Šeqalim*	*Cast.*	*De exhortatione castitatis*
Sextus		*Fuga*	*De fuga in persecutione*
Sent.	*Sententiae*	*Idol.*	*De idololatria*
Sib. Or.	*Sibylline Oracles*	*Marc.*	*Adversus Marcionem*
SJLA	Studies in Judaism in Late Antiquity	*Mon.*	*De monogamia*
		Or.	*De oratione*
SJT	*Scottish Journal of Theology*	*Paen.*	*De paenitentia*
S. Lev.	*Sifre Leviticus*	*Praescr. haer.*	*De praescriptione haereticorum*
SMHVL	Scripta minor K. humanistika vetenskapssamfundet i Lund	*Pud.*	*De pudicitia*
		Scorp.	*Scorpiace*
SNTSMS	Society for New Testament Studies Monograph Series	*Uxor.*	*Ad uxorum*
		Val.	*Contra Valentinianos*
SNTU A	Studien zum Neuen Testament und seiner Umwelt, Reihe A	*TDNT*	*Theological Dictionary of the New Testament,* Gerhard Kittel and
SNTU B	Studien zum Neuen Testament und seiner Umwelt, Reihe B		Gerhard Friedrich, eds. (Grand Rapids: Eerdmans, 1964–76)

Tg. Hos.	Targum on Hosea
Tg. Neof.	*Targum Neofiti I*
Tg. Onq.	*Targum Onqelos*
Tg. Yer. I	*Targum Yerushalmi I*
Tg. Yer. II	*Targum Yerushalmi II*
ThBei	*Theologische Beiträge*
ThBü	*Theologische Bücherei*
Thes. Steph.	H. Stephanus, *Thesaurus Graecae Linguae*
ThHKNT	Theologischer Handkommentar zum Neuen Testament
ThR	*Theologische Rundschau*
ThStK	*Theologische Studien und Kritiken*
ThZ	*Theologische Zeitschrift*
T. Job	*Testament of Job*
trans.	translator(s), translated by
TRE	*Theologische Realenzyklopädie* (Berlin: de Gruyter, 1977–)
TRev	*Theologische Revue*
Tri. Trac.	*Tripartite Tractate* (NHC 1, 5)
TS	*Theological Studies*
T. Sol.	*Testament of Solomon*
TTB	Topos—Taschenbücher
T. 12 Patr.	*Testaments of the Twelve Patriarchs*
T. Asher	*Testament of Asher*
T. Dan	*Testament of Dan*
T. Iss.	*Testament of Issachar*
T. Levi	*Testament of Levi*
T. Naph.	*Testament of Naphtali*
T. Reub.	*Testament of Reuben*
T. Sim.	*Testament of Simeon*
TU	Texte und Untersuchungen zur Geschichte der altchristlichen Literatur
TvT	*Tijdschrift voor theologie*
VC	*Vigiliae christianae*
VF	*Verkündigung und Forschung*
viz.	*videlicet*, namely
VT	*Vetus Testamentum*
v(v).	verse(s)
Virgil	
Aen.	*Aeneid*
Georg.	*Georgics*
WA	Martin Luther, *Kritische Gesamtausgabe* (= Weimar edition)
WMANT	Wissenschaftliche Monographien zum Alten und Neuen Testament
WuD	*Wort und Dienst*
WUNT	Wissenschaftliche Untersuchungen zum Neuen Testament
Xenophon	
Mem.	*Memorabilia*
y.	Jerusalem Talmud tractate
Yad.	*Yadayim*
Yeb.	*Yebamot*
ZDPV	*Zeitschrift des deutschen Palästina-Vereins*
ZKTh	*Zeitschrift für katholische Theologie*
ZNW	*Zeitschrift für die neutestamentliche Wissenschaft*
ZThK	*Zeitschrift für Theologie und Kirche*

2. Text-Critical Sigla

ℵ	Codex Sinaiticus
'A	Aquila (Greek translation of the Old Testament)
arab	Arabic
B	Codex Vaticanus
bo	Bohairic version
Byz.	Byzantine mss.
C	Codex Ephraemi
c	Colbertinus (Old Latin ms.)
co	Coptic versions (agreement of all Coptic versions)
Δ	Codex Sargallensis
D	Codex Bezae
f^1	family 1 of gospel minuscule manuscripts
f^{13}	family 13 of gospel minuscule manuscripts
it	Old Latin version
L	Codex Regius
lat	Latin manuscripts
LXX	Septuagint
𝔐	the Majority text
mae	Middle Egyptian Coptic textual witnesses
ms(s)	manuscript(s)
MT	Masoretic Text
Nestle[25]	Nestle-Aland, *Novum Testamentum Graece,* 25th ed., 1963
Nestle[26]	Nestle-Aland, *Novum Testamentum Graece,* 26th ed., 1979
P.	papyrus
P. Berol.	Berlin papyri
P. Leid.	Leiden papyri
P. Lond.	Greek papyri in the British Museum
P. Oxy.	Oxyrhynchus papyri
Σ	Symmachus (Greek translation of the Old Testament)
Sah.	Sahidic
sy^c	Curetonianus; four gospel manuscript in Old Syriac
sy^h	Heraclensis version (Syriac)
sy^p	Peshitta version (Syriac)
sy^s	four gospel Sinaitic manuscript in Old Syriac
Θ	Codex Koridethi
vg	Old Latin and Vulgate united textual reading
Vg	Vulgate
VL	Vetus Latina
W	Freer Codex

3. Short Titles of Commentaries, Studies, and Articles Often Cited

Abrahams, *Studies*
Israel Abrahams, *Studies in Pharisaism and the Gospels*, 2 vols. (1917; reprinted New York: Ktav, 1967).

Achelis–Flemming
Hans Achelis and Johannes Flemming, eds., *Die Syrische Didaskalia* (Leipzig: Hinrichs, 1904).

Afrahat
Aphraates (fl. 337–345), *Homilien: aus dem Syrischen übersetzt und erläutert* (ed. Georg Bert; Leipzig: Hinrichs, 1888).

Albright–Mann
W. F. Albright and C. S. Mann, *Matthew* (AB 26; Garden City, N.Y.: Doubleday, 1971).

Allen
Willoughby C. Allen, *A Critical and Exegetical Commentary on the Gospel According to St. Matthew* (ICC; 3d ed.; Edinburgh: T. & T. Clark, 1912).

Allison, "Divorce"
Dale C. Allison, "Divorce, Celibacy and Joseph (Mt 1:18-25 and 19)," *JSNT* 49 (1993) 3-10.

Annen, *Heil*
Franz Annen, *Heil für die Heiden* (FTS 20; Frankfurt: Knecht, 1976).

Anselm of Laon
Anselm of Laon (Pseudo-Anselm = Gottfried von Babion, 12th century), *Enarrationes in Matthaeum* (*PL* 162.1227–1500).

Arens, *HΛΘΟΝ-Sayings*
Eduardo Arens, *The HΛΘΟΝ-Sayings in the Synoptic Tradition* (OBO 10; Freiburg: Universitätsverlag, 1976).

Aretius
Benedictus Aretius (Marti) (c. 1522–74) *Commentarii in Domini nostri Jesu Christi Novum Testamentum* (Paris: Ioannem le Preux, 1607).

Arvedson, *Mysterium*
Tomas Arvedson, *Das Mysterium Christi: Eine Studie zu Mt 11,25-30* (AMNSU 7; Uppsala: Wretmans, 1937).

Bacon, *Studies*
Benjamin Wisner Bacon, *Studies in Matthew* (New York: Holt, Rinehart & Winston, 1930).

Bainton, "Liberty"
Roland H. Bainton, "Religious Liberty and the Parable of the Tares," in idem, *The Collected Papers in Church History*, vol. 1 (Boston: Beacon, 1962) 95–121.

Baltensweiler, *Verklärung*
Heinrich Baltensweiler, *Die Verklärung Jesu* (AThANT 33; Zurich: Zwingli, 1959).

Balthasar, *Ordensregeln*
Hans Urs von Balthasar, ed., *Die grossen Ordensregeln* (Menschen der Kirche in Zeugnis und Urkunde, NF 6; Einsiedeln: Benziger, 1974).

Barth, *CD*
Karl Barth, *Church Dogmatics*, 4 vols., ed. and trans. Geoffrey W. Bromiley and Thomas F. Torrance (2d ed.; Edinburgh: T. & T. Clark, 1975).

Barth, "Understanding"
Gerhard Barth, "Matthew's Understanding of the Law," in Bornkamm–Barth–Held, *Tradition and Interpretation*, 85–164.

Basil, *Regulae brevius*
Karl Suso Frank, ed. and trans., *Die Mönchsregeln: Basilius von Caesarea* (St. Ottilien: EOS, 1981).

Bauer, "Mt 19,12"
Walter Bauer, "Mt 19,12 und die alten Christen," in idem, *Aufsätze und kleine Schriften* (Tübingen: Mohr/Siebeck, 1967) 253–62.

Bayer, *Jesus' Predictions*
Hans F. Bayer, *Jesus' Predictions of Vindication and Resurrection* (WUNT 2/20; Tübingen: Mohr/Siebeck, 1986).

Beare
Francis Wright Beare, *The Gospel According to Matthew* (San Francisco: Harper & Row, 1981).

Bede
(Pseudo-) Beda Venerabilis (prior to 820), *In Matthaei Evangelium expositio* (*PL* 92.9–132).

Ben David, *Ökonomie*
Arye Ben David, *Talmudische Ökonomie* (Hildesheim: Olms, 1974).

Bengel
Johann Albrecht Bengel, *Gnomon Novi Testamenti* (Tübingen: Schramm, 1742).

Berg, *Rezeption*
Werner Berg, *Die Rezeption alttestamentlicher Motive im Neuen Testament–dargestellt an den Seewandelerzählungen* (Hochschul-Sammlung Theologie. Exegese 1; Freiburg: Hochschulverlag, 1979).

Berger, *Amenworte*
Klaus Berger, *Die Amenworte Jesu* (BZNW 39; Berlin: de Gruyter, 1970).

Berger, *Gesetzesauslegung*
Klaus Berger, *Die Gesetzesauslegung Jesu*, vol. 1: *Markus und Parallelen* (WMANT 40; Neukirchen-Vluyn: Neukirchener Verlag, 1972).

Berger, "Hartherzigkeit"
Klaus Berger, "Hartherzigkeit und Gottes Gesetz: Die Vorgeschichte des antijüdischen Vorwurfs in Mc 10,5," *ZNW* 61 (1970) 1–47.

Berger, "Messiastraditionen"
Klaus Berger, "Die königlichen Messiastraditionen des Neuen Testaments," *NTS* 20 (1973–74) 1–44.

Bert
See Afrahat.

Betz, "Eschatological Interpretation"
Otto Betz, "The Eschatological Interpretation of the Sinai Tradition in Qumran and in the New Testament," *RevQ* 6 (1967) 89–107.

Betz, "Felsenmann"
Otto Betz, "Felsenmann und Felsengemeinde," *ZNW* 48 (1957) 49–77.

Betz, "Krieg"
Otto Betz, "Jesu heiliger Krieg," *NovT* 2 (1957) 116–37.

Beyer, *Syntax*
Klaus Beyer, *Semitische Syntax im Neuen Testament*, vol. 1: *Satzlehre 1* (SUNT 1; 2d ed.; Göttingen: Vandenhoeck & Ruprecht, 1968).

Beza
Theodore von Beza (1516–1605), *Jesu Christi Novum Testamentum* (Geneva: Stephanus, 1582).

Black, *Approach*
Matthew Black, *An Aramaic Approach to the Gospels and Acts* (3d ed.; Oxford: Clarendon, 1967).

Blank, "Petrus und Petrusamt"
Josef Blank, "Petrus und Petrusamt im Neuen Testament," in *Papsttum*, 59–103.

Blinzler, *Brüder*
Josef Blinzler, *Die Brüder und Schwestern Jesu* (SBS 21; Stuttgart: Katholisches Bibelwerk, 1967).

Blinzler, "Εἰσὶν εὐνοῦχοι"
Josef Blinzler, "Εἰσὶν εὐνοῦχοι: zur Auslegung von Matt 19:12," *ZNW* 48 (1957) 254–70.

Bloch, *Atheism*
Ernst Bloch, *Atheism in Christianity* (New York: Herder and Herder, 1972).

Böcher, "Magie"
Otto Böcher, "Matthäus und die Magie," in Ludger Schenke, ed., *Studien zum Matthäusevangelium: Festschrift für Wilhelm Pesch* (SBS; Stuttgart: Katholisches Bibelwerk, 1988) 11–24.

Bonhoeffer, *Cost*
Dietrich Bonhoeffer, *The Cost of Discipleship*, trans. R. H. Fuller (New York: Macmillan, 1959).

Bonhoeffer, *Letters*
Dietrich Bonhoeffer, *Letters and Papers from Prison*, ed. Eberhard Bethge, trans. R. H. Fuller (New York: Macmillan, 1971).

Bonnard
Pierre Bonnard, *L'Évangile selon saint Matthieu* (CNT 1; 2d ed.; Neuchâtel: Delachaux & Niestlé, 1970).

Booth, *Laws of Purity*
Roger P. Booth, *Jesus and the Laws of Purity* (JSNTSup 13; Sheffield: JSOT, 1986).

Boring, *Sayings*
M. Eugene Boring, *Sayings of the Risen Jesus* (SNTSMS 46; Cambridge: Cambridge University Press, 1982).

Boring, "Unforgivable Sin"
M. Eugene Boring, "The Unforgivable Sin Logion Mark 3:28-29/Matt 12:31-32/Luke 12:10: Formal Analysis and History of the Tradition," *NovT* 18 (1976) 258–79.

Bornkamm, "End Expectation"
Günther Bornkamm, "End Expectation and Church in Matthew," in Bornkamm-Barth-Held, *Tradition and Interpretation*, 15–51.

Bornkamm, "Lösegewalt"
Günther Bornkamm, "Die Binde- und Lösegewalt in der Kirche des Matthäus," in idem, *Geschichte und Glaube* (BEvTh 53; Munich: Kaiser, 1971) 2.37–50.

Bornkamm, "Lohngedanke"
Günther Bornkamm, "Der Lohngedanke im Neuen Testament," in idem, *Studien zu Antike und Urchristentum* (BEvTh 28; Munich: Kaiser, 1959) 69–93.

Bornkamm-Barth-Held, *Tradition and Interpretation*
Günther Bornkamm, Gerhard Barth, and Heinz Joachim Held, *Tradition and Interpretation in Matthew*, trans. Percy Scott (Philadelphia: Westminster, 1972).

Bovon, *Lukas*
François Bovon, *Das Evangelium nach Lukas*, vol. 1: *Lukas 1,1-9,50* (EKKNT 3/1; Zurich: Benziger, 1989).

Brenz
Johannes Brenz (1499–1570), *In scriptum apostoli et evangelistae Matthaei de rebus gestis Domini Nostri Jesu Christi commentarius* (Tübingen: Mohard, 1567).

Breukelman, "Erklärung"
Frans H. Breukelman, "Eine Erklärung des Gleichnisses vom Schalksknecht," in *ΠΑΡΡΗΣΙΑ: Karl Barth zum achtzigsten Geburtstag am 10. Mai 1966* (Zurich: EVZ, 1966) 261–87.

Broer, "Parabel"
Ingo Broer, "Die Parabel vom Verzicht auf das Prinzip von Leistung und Gegenleistung (Mt 18,23-35)," in François Refoulé, ed., *À Cause de l'Évangile: Études sur les Synoptiques et les Actes: Offertes au P. Jacques Dupont, O.S.B. à l'occasion de son 70ᵉ anniversaire* (LD 123; Paris: Cerf, 1985) 145–64.

Broer, "Ringen"
Ingo Broer, "Das Ringen der Gemeinde um Israel. Exegetischer Versuch über Mt 19,28," in Rudolf Pesch and Rudolf Schnackenburg, eds., *Jesus und der Menschensohn: Für Anton Vögtle* (Freiburg: Herder, 1975) 148–65.

Brooks, *Community*
Stephenson H. Brooks, *Matthew's Community: The Evidence of His Special Sayings Material* (JSNTSup 16: Sheffield: JSOT, 1987).

Brown-Donfried-Reuman, *Peter*
Raymond E. Brown, Karl P. Donfried, and John Reumann, eds., *Peter in the New Testament* (Minneapolis: Augsburg, 1973).

Brown, *Miracles*
W. Norman Brown, *The Indian and Christian Miracles of Walking on the Water* (London: Open Court, 1928).

Bucer
Martin Bucer (1491–51), *Enarrationes perpetuae in Sacra quatuor Evangelia* (Argentoriati: Heruagium, 1530).

Bullinger
Heinrich Bullinger (1504–1575), *In Sacrosanctum Iesu Christi Domini nostri Evangelium secundum Matthaeum Commentariorum libri XII* (Zurich: Froschoverum, 1554).

Bultmann, *Exegetica*
Rudolf Bultmann, *Exegetica,* ed. Erich Dinkler (Tübingen: Mohr/Siebeck, 1967).

Bultmann, *History*
Rudolf Bultmann, *The History of the Synoptic Tradition* (2d ed.; New York: Harper & Row, 1968).

Burchard, "Senfkorn"
Christoph Burchard, "Senfkorn, Sauerteig, Schatz und Perle in Matthäus 13," *SNTU* A 13 (1989) 5–35.

Burchill, "Evangelical Counsels"
John Patrick Burchill, "Are There 'Evangelical Counsels' of Perpetual Continence and Poverty?" (Diss., Dominican House of Studies, Washington, 1975).

Burger, *Davidssohn*
Christoph Burger, *Jesus als Davidssohn* (FRLANT 98; Göttingen: Vandenhoeck & Ruprecht, 1970).

Burger, "Jesu Taten"
Christoph Burger, "Jesu Taten nach Matthäus 8 und 9," *ZThK* 70 (1973) 272–87.

Burgess, *History*
Joseph A. Burgess, *A History of the Exegesis of Matthew 16:17-19 from 1781 to 1965* (Ann Arbor: Edwards Brothers, 1976).

Calixtus
Georg Calixtus (1586–1656), *Quatuor Evangelicorum Scriptorum Concordia . . .* (Helmstedt: Mullerus, 1663).

Calovius
Abraham Calovius (1612–86), *Biblia Novi Testamenti illustrata,* vol. 1 (Dresden-Leipzig: Zimmermann, 1719).

Calvin
John Calvin (1509–64), *A Harmony of the Gospels: Matthew, Mark, and Luke,* 3 vols., ed. David W. Torrance and Thomas F. Torrance (Grand Rapids: Eerdmans, 1972).

Calvin, *Inst.*
John Calvin, *Institutio Christianae Religionis* (Lutetiis: Stephanus, 1553).

Cameron, *Violence*
Peter Scott Cameron, *Violence and the Kingdom: The Interpretation of Mt 11:12* (ANTJ 5; Frankfurt: Lang, 1984).

Cardenal, *Gospel*
Ernesto Cardenal, *The Gospel in Solentiname,* vol. 2 (Maryknoll: Orbis, 1978).

Catchpole, "John the Baptist"
David Catchpole, "John the Baptist, Jesus and the Parable of the Tares," *SJT* 31 (1978) 557–70.

Catchpole, "Reproof"
David Catchpole, "Reproof and Reconciliation in the Q Community: A Study of the Tradition-history of Mt 18:15-17, 21-22/Lk17:3-4," *SNTU* A 8 (1983) 79–89.

Catchpole, "Schaf"
David Catchpole, "Ein Schaf, eine Drachme und ein Israelit: Die Botschaft in Q," in Johannes Degenhardt, ed., *Die Freude an Gott, unsere Kraft:*

Festschrift für Otto Bernhard Knoch (Stuttgart: Katholisches Bibelwerk, 1991) 89–101.

Cerfaux, "Connaissance"
Lucien Cerfaux, "La connaissance des secrets du Royaume de Dieu d'après Mt 13,11 et par.," in idem, *Recueil,* 1962, 3.123–38.

Cerfaux, *Recueil,* 1962
Lucien Cerfaux, *Recueil Lucien Cerfaux,* vol. 3 (BEThL 18; Gembloux: Duculot, 1962).

Cerfaux, "Sources"
Lucien Cerfaux, "Les sources scripturaires de Mt 11,25-30," in *Recueil Lucien Cerfaux* (BEThL 71; rev. ed.; Louvain: Louvain University Press, 1985) 3.139–59.

Chilton, *God in Strength*
Bruce David Chilton, *God in Strength: Jesus' Announcement of the Kingdom* (SNTU B 1; Linz: SNTU, 1979).

Christ, *Sophia*
Felix Christ, *Jesus Sophia: Die Sophia-Christologie bei den Synoptikern* (AThANT 57; Zurich: Zwingli, 1970).

Christian of Stavelot
Christian of Stavelot (Christianus Druthmarus, d. 880), *Expositio in Matthaeum Evangelistam* (*PL* 106.1261–1504).

Chromatius
Chromatius of Aquileia (c. 400), *Tractatus in Matthaeum* (CChr.SL 9A; Turnholti, Brepols, 1974).

Claudel, *Confession*
Girard Claudel, *La confession de Pierre* (EtB n.s.10; Paris: Gabalda, 1988).

Cocceius
Johann Cocceius (1603–69), *Commentariolus sive notae breves in Matthaei Evangelium,* in *Opera* (Frankfurt, 1702) 4.1–43.

Colpe, "ὁ υἱὸς τοῦ ἀνϑρώπου"
Carston Colpe, "ὁ υἱὸς τοῦ ἀνϑρώπου," *TDNT* 8 (1972) 400–477.

Colpe, "Spruch"
Carsten Colpe, "Der Spruch von der Lästerung des Geistes," in Eduard Lohse, J. Christoph Burchard, and Bernt Schaller, eds., *Der Ruf Jesu und die Antwort der Gemeinde: Exegetische Untersuchungen Joachim Jeremias zum 70. Geburtstag gewidmet von seinen Schülern* (Göttingen: Vandenhoeck & Ruprecht, 1970) 63–79.

Concord, Book of
Theodore G. Tappert, ed., *The Book of Concord: The Confessions of the Evangelical Lutheran Church* (Philadelphia: Fortress, 1959).

Cotter, "Children"
Wendy J. Cotter, "Children Sitting in the Agora," *Forum* 5.2 (1989) 63–82.

Cramer, "Mt 18,10b"
Winfrid Cramer, "Mt 18,10b in frühsyrischer Deutung," *OrChr* 59 (1975) 130–46.

Crossan, *Finding*
John Dominic Crossan, *Finding Is the First Act: Trove Folktales and Jesus' Treasure Parable* (Semeia Studies; Philadelphia: Fortress, 1979).

Crossan, *Parables*
John Dominic Crossan, *In Parables: The Challenge of the Historical Jesus* (New York: Harper & Row, 1973).

Crossan, "Seed Parables"
John Dominic Crossan, "The Seed Parables of Jesus," *JBL* 92 (1973) 244–66.

Cullmann, *Peter*
Oscar Cullmann, *Peter: Disciple, Apostle, Martyr,* trans. Floyd V. Filson (2d ed.; Philadelphia: Westminster, 1962).

Cyril of Alexandria
Cyril of Alexandria (d. 444), *Commentariorum in Matthaeum quae supersunt* (*PG* 72.365–474).

Daffner, *Salome*
Hugo Daffner, *Salome: Ihre Gestalt in Geschichte und Kunst* (Munich: Schmidt, 1912).

Dahl, "Parables"
Nils Alstrup Dahl, "The Parables of Growth," *StTh* 5 (1952) 132–66.

Dalman, *Arbeit*
Gustaf Dalman, *Arbeit und Sitte in Palästina* (7 vols.; Gütersloh: Bertelsmann, 1928–39).

Dalman, *Grammatik*
Gustaf Dalman, *Grammatik des jüdisch-palästinischen Aramäisch* (2d ed., 1905; reprinted Darmstadt: Wissenschaftliche Buchgesellschaft, 1981).

Dalman, *Words*
Gustaf Dalman, *The Words of Jesus* (Edinburgh: T. & T. Clark, 1909).

Danby
Herbert Danby, *The Mishnah: Translated from the Hebrew with Introduction and Brief Explanatory Notes* (Oxford: Oxford University Press, 1933).

Daube, *New Testament*
David Daube, *The New Testament and Rabbinic Judaism* (London: Athlone, 1956).

Dauvillier, "Parabole"
Jean Dauvillier, "La parabole du trésor et les droits orientaux," *RIDA* 3/4 (1957) 107–15.

Davies, *Setting*
William David Davies, *The Setting of the Sermon on the Mount* (Cambridge: Cambridge University Press, 1966).

Davies–Allison
William David Davies and Dale C. Allison, *A Critical and Exegetical Commentary on the Gospel According to Saint Matthew* (ICC; Edinburgh: T. & T. Clark, 1991).

de Goedt, "Explication"
Michel de Goedt, "L'explication de la parabole de l'ivraie (Mt 13,36–43)," *RB* 66 (1959) 32–54.

Deissmann, *Light*
Adolf Deissmann, *Light from the Ancient East,* trans. L. R. M. Strachen (rev. ed.; New York: Doran, 1937).

Dell, "Matthäus 16,17-19"
August Dell, "Matthäus 16,17-19," *ZNW* 15 (1914) 1–49.

Denis, "Parabels"
Albert-Marie Denis, "De parabels over het koninkrijk (Mt 13)," *TvT* 1 (1961) 274–88.

Dermience, "Pericope"
Alice Dermience, "La pericope de la Cananéenne (Mt 15,21-28)," *EThL* 58 (1982) 25–49.

Derrett, *Law*
J. Duncan M. Derrett, *Law in the New Testament,* vol. 1 (London: Darton, Longman & Todd, 1970).

Deutsch, *Hidden Wisdom*
Celia Deutsch, *Hidden Wisdom and the Easy Yoke* (JSNTSup 18; Sheffield: JSOT, 1987).

Dewailly, "Parole"
L. M. Dewailly, "La parole sans œuvre (Mt 12,26)," in *Mélanges offerts à M. D. Chenu* (Bibliothèque Thomiste 37; Paris: Vrin, 1967) 203–19.

Dibelius, *Überlieferung*
Martin Dibelius, *Die urchristliche Überlieferung von Johannes dem Täufer* (FRLANT 15; Göttingen: Vandenhoeck & Ruprecht, 1911).

Dickson
David Dickson, *A Brief Exposition of the Evangel of Jesus Christ According to Matthew* (1647; reprinted Edinburgh: Banner of Truth Trust, 1981).

Didier, *Évangile*
M. Didier, ed., *L'Évangile selon Matthieu: Rédaction et théologie* (BEThL 29; Gembloux: Duculot, 1972).

Dinkler, "Jesu Wort"
Erich Dinkler, "Jesu Wort vom Kreuztragen," in idem, *Signum Crucis* (Tübingen: Mohr/Siebeck, 1967) 77–98.

Dionysius bar Salibi
Dionysius bar Salibi (d. 1171), *Commentarii in Evangelia,* 3 vols.; ed. I. Sedlacek and Arthur Vaschalde (Louvain: Durbecq, 1953).

Dionyius the Carthusian
Dionysius the Carthusian (d. 1471), *In quator Evangelistas enarrationes,* in *Opera,* vols. 11–14 (Tournai, 1896–1905).

Dodd, *Parables*
C. H. Dodd, *The Parables of the Kingdom* (1935; rev. ed.; London: Collins, 1961).

Donaldson, *Jesus*
Terence L. Donaldson, *Jesus on the Mountain: A Study in Matthean Theology* (JSNTSup 8; Sheffield: JSOT, 1985).

Drewermann, *Markusevangelium*
Eugen Drewermann, *Das Markusevangelium* (2 vols.; Olten: Walter, 1987–88).

Drewermann, *Tiefenpsychologie*
Eugen Drewermann, *Tiefenpsychologie und Exegese* (2 vols.; Olten: Walter, 1984–85).

Duling, "Son of David"
Dennis C. Duling, "The Therapeutic Son of David: An Element in Matthew's Christological Apologetic," *NTS* 24 (1977–78) 392–410.

Dungan, *Sayings*
David Dungan, *The Sayings of Jesus in the Churches of Paul* (Philadelphia: Fortress, 1971).

Dupont, "L'ambassade"
Jacques Dupont, "L'ambassade de Jean Baptiste," *NRTh* 83 (1961) 805-21, 943-59.

Dupont, *Béatitudes*
Jacques Dupont, *Les Béatitudes*, vol. 1: *Le problème littéraire;* vol. 2: *La bonne nouvelle;* vol. 3: *Les Évangelistes* (EtB; Paris: Gabalda, 1958-73).

Dupont, "Couple parabolique"
Jacques Dupont, "La couple parabolique du sénevé et du levain," in idem, *Études*, 2:609-23.

Dupont, *Études*
Jacques Dupont, *Études sur les Évangiles Synoptiques*, 2 vols., ed. Frans Neirynck (BEThL 70A, 70B; Louvain: Louvain University Press and Peeters, 1985).

Dupont, "Implications"
Jacques Dupont, "Les implications christologiques de la parabole de la brebis perdue," in idem, *Études*, 2.647-66.

Dupont, *Mariage*
Jacques Dupont, *Mariage et divorce dans L'Évangile* (Bruges: Desclee de Brouwer, 1959).

Dupont, "Nova et Vetera"
Jacques Dupont, "Nova et Vetera (Mt 13,52)" in idem, *Études*, 2.920-28.

Dupont, "Ouvriers de la onzième"
Jacques Dupont, "Les ouvriers de la onzième heure, Mt 20,1-16," *AsSeign* 56 (1974) 16-26.

Dupont, "Parabole"
Jacques Dupont, "La parabole de la brebis perdue (Mt 18,12-14; Lc 15,4-7)," in idem, *Études*, 2.624-46.

Dupont, "Point de vue"
Jacques Dupont, "Le point de vue de Matthieu dans le chapître des paraboles," in Didier, *Évangile*, 221-59.

Edwards, *Sign*
Richard Allen Edwards, *The Sign of Jonah in the Theology of the Evangelists and Q* (SBT 2/18; Naperville, Ill.: Allenson, 1971).

Ennulat, *Agreements*
Andreas Ennulat, *Die "Minor Agreements": Untersuchungen zu einer offenen Frage des synoptischen Problems* (WUNT 2/62; Tübingen: Mohr/Siebeck, 1994).

Ephraem Syrus
Ephraem Syrus (306-77), *Commentaire de l'Évangile Concordant ou Diatessaron,* trans. L. Leloir (SC 121; Paris: Cerf, 1966).

Episcopius
Simon Episcopius (1583-1643), *Notae breves in Matthaeum* (Amsterdam, 1665).

Epp-Fee, *New Testament Textual Criticism*
Eldon J. Epp and Godon D. Fee, eds., *New Testament Textual Criticism: Its Significance for Exegesis: Essays in Honor of Bruce M. Metzger* (Oxford: Clarendon, 1984).

Erasmus, *Adnotationes*
Desiderius Erasmus (1469-1536), *Opera Omnia*, vol. 6: *Novum Testamentum, cui, in hac Editione, subjectae sunt singulis paginis Adnotationes* (1705; reprint Hildesheim: Olms, 1962) 1-148.

Erasmus, *Paraphrasis*
Desiderius Erasmus, *Opera Omnia*, vol. 7: *In Evangelium Matthaei Paraphrasis* (reprint Hildesheim: Olms, 1962) 1-146.

Erlemann, *Bild Gottes*
Kurt Erlemann, *Das Bild Gottes in den synoptischen Gleichnissen* (BWANT 126; Stuttgart: Kohlhammer, 1988).

Euthymius Zigabenus
Euthymius Zigabenus (12th century), *Commentarius in quatuor Evangelia* (PG 129.107-766).

Ewald
Heinrich Ewald, *Die drei ersten Evangelien* (Göttingen: Dieterische Buchhandlung, 1850).

Faber Stapulensis
Faber Stapulensis (c. 1455-1536), *Comentarii initiatorii in quatuor Evangelia* (Basel: Andreae Cratandri, 1523).

Fabris
Rinaldo Fabris, *Matteo* (Commenti Biblici; Rome: Borla, 1982).

Fenton
John C. Fenton, *The Gospel of St. Matthew* (Baltimore: Penguin, 1964).

Field
Field, Frederick, ed. *Origenis Hexaplorum quae supersunt*, 2 vols. (Oxford: Clarendon, 1825; reprint Hildesheim: Olms, 1964).

Fiedler, *Sünder*
Peter Fiedler, *Jesus und die Sünder* (BBE 3; Frankfurt: Lang, 1976).

Flusser, *Gleichnisse*
David Flusser, *Die rabbinischen Gleichnisse und der Gleichniserzähler Jesus*, vol. 1 (Judaica et Christiana 4; Bern: Lang, 1981).

Flusser, *Jesus*
David Flusser, *Jesus* (New York: Herder and Herder, 1969).

Fong, *Crucem*
Maria Ko Ha Fong, *Crucem tollendo Christum sequi* (Münsterische Beiträge zur Theologie 52; Münster: Aschendorf, 1984).

France
R. T. France, *The Gospel According to Matthew* (Tyndale New Testament Commentaries 1; Grand Rapids: Eerdmans, 1985).

Frank, *Mönchsregeln*
See Basil.

Frankemölle, *Jahwebund*
Hubert Frankemölle, *Jahwebund und Kirche Christi* (NTAbh n.s. 10; Münster: Aschendorf, 1974).

Freedman-Simon
H. Freedman and Maurice Simon, eds., *Midrash Rabbah* (10 vols.; 3d ed.; London: Soncino, 1983).

Fridrichsen, "Péché"

Anton Fridrichsen, "Le péché contre le Saint-Esprit," *RHPhR* 3 (1923) 367–72.

Friedrich, *Gott im Bruder*

Johannes Friedrich, *Gott im Bruder? Eine methoden-kritische Untersuchung von Redaktion, Überlieferung und Tradition in Mt 25,31-46* (Calwer Theologische Monographien A7; Stuttgart: Calwer, 1977).

Friedrich, "Wortstatistik"

Johannes Friedrich, "Wortstatistik als Methode am Beispiel der Frage einer Sonderquelle im Matthäus-Evangelium," *ZNW* 76 (1985) 29–46.

Fritzsche

C. F. A. Fritzsche, *Evangelium Matthaei* (Leipzig: Sumtibus Frederici Fleischeri, 1826).

Fröhlich, *Formen*

Karlfried Fröhlich, *Formen der Auslegung von Matthäus 16,13-18 im lateinischen Mittelalter* (Tübingen: Fotodruck Präzis, 1963).

Fuchs, "Studie"

Albert Fuchs, "Entwicklungsgeschichtliche Studie zu Mk 1,29-31 par. Mt 8,14-15 par. Lk 4,38-39," *SNTU* A 6-7 (1981–82) 21-76.

Fuchs, *Untersuchungen*

Albert Fuchs, *Sprachliche Untersuchungen zu Matthäus und Lukas: Ein Beitrag zur Quellenkritik* (AnBib 49; Rome: Biblical Institute Press, 1971).

Gaechter

Paul Gaechter, *Das Matthäus-Evangelium* (Innsbruck: Tyrolia, 1963).

Galot, "Qu'il soit pour"

Jean Galot, "'Qu'il soit pour toi comme le païen et le publicain,'" *NRTh* 96 [= 106] (1974) 1009-30.

Gamba, "Eunuchia"

Giuseppe Gamba, "La 'eunuchia' per il Regno dei Cieli. Annotazione in margine a Matteo 19,10-12," *Salesianum* 42 (1980) 243–87.

García-Martínez, "Represión"

Florentino García-Martínez, "La represión fraterna en Qumrán y Mt 18,15-17," *Filología Neotestamentaria* 2 (1989) 23–40.

Gaston, "Beelzebul"

Lloyd Gaston, "Beelzebul," *ThZ* 18 (1962) 247–55.

Geist, *Menschensohn*

Heinz Geist, *Menschensohn und Gemeinde* (FzB 57; Würzburg: Echter, 1986).

Gerhardsson, "Seven Parables"

Birger Gerhardsson, "The Seven Parables in Matthew XIII," *NTS* 19 (1972–73) 16–37.

Gillmann, "Auslegung"

Franz Gillmann, "Zur scholastischen Auslegung von Mt 16,18," *Archiv für katholisches Kirchenrecht* 104 (1924) 41–53.

Ginzberg, *Legends*

Louis Ginzberg, *The Legends of the Jews,* 7 vols. (1913–28; reprinted Philadelphia: Jewish Publication Society of America, 1967–69).

Glynn, "Use"

Leo Edward Glynn, "The Use and Meaning of ἔλεος in Matthew" (Diss., Berkeley, 1971).

Gnilka

Joachim Gnilka, *Das Matthäusevangelium,* 2 vols. (HThKNT 1/1-2; Freiburg: Herder, 1986, 1988).

Gnilka, *Markus*

Joachim Gnilka, *Das Evangelium nach Markus,* 2 vols. (EKKNT 2/1-2; Zurich: Benziger, 1978–79).

Gnilka, *Verstockung*

Joachim Gnilka, *Die Verstockung Israels: Isaias 6,9-10 in der Theologie der Synoptiker* (SANT 3; Munich: Kösel, 1961).

Goulder, *Midrash*

M. D. Goulder, *Midrash and Lection in Matthew* (London: S.P.C.K., 1974).

Grässer, *Parusieverzögerung*

Erich Grässer, *Das Problem der Parusieverzögerung in den synoptischen Evangelien und in der Apostel-geschichte* (BZNW 22; 2d ed.; Berlin: Töpelmann, 1960).

Grimm, *Jesus*

Werner Grimm, *Jesus und das Danielbuch,* vol. 1: *Jesu Einspruch gegen das Offenbarungssystem Daniels (Mt 11,25-27; Lk 17,20-21)* (ANTJ 6/1; Frankfurt: Lang, 1984).

Grotius

Hugo Grotius (1583–1645), *Annotationes in Novum Testamentum,* 2 vols. (Groningen: Zuidema, 1826–27).

Grundmann

Walter Grundmann, *Das Evangelium nach Matthaeus* (ThHKNT1; Berlin: Evangelische Verlagsanstalt, 1968).

Guelich, "Not to Annul"

Robert A. Guelich, "Not to Annul the Law, Rather to Fulfill the Law and the Prophets" (Diss., Hamburg, 1967).

Gundry

Robert H. Gundry, *Matthew: A Commentary on His Literary and Theological Art* (Grand Rapids: Eerdmans, 1982).

Gundry, *Use*

Robert H. Gundry, *The Use of the Old Testament in St. Matthew's Gospel* (NovTSup 18, Leiden: Brill, 1967).

Hahn, *Mission*

Ferdinand Hahn, *Mission in the New Testament,* trans. Frank Clarke (SBT 47; Naperville, Ill.: Allenson, 1965).

Hahn, *Titles*

Ferdinand Hahn, *The Titles of Jesus in Christology: Their History in Early Christianity,* trans. H. Knight and G. Ogg (New York: World, 1969).

Hampel, *Menschensohn*

Volker Hampel, *Menschensohn und historischer Jesus* (Neukirchen-Vluyn: Neukirchener Verlag, 1990).

Hare, *Son of Man*

Douglas R. A. Hare, *The Son of Man Tradition* (Minneapolis: Fortress, 1990).

Hare, *Theme*

Douglas R. A. Hare, *The Theme of Jewish Persecution of Christians in the Gospel According to St. Matthew* (SNTSMS 6; Cambridge: Cambridge University Press, 1967).

Häring, *Law*

Bernhard Häring, *The Law of Christ: Moral Theology for Priests and Laity,* trans. Edwin G. Kaiser, 3 vols. (Westminster, Md.: Newman, 1961).

Harnack, *Christianity*

Adolf von Harnack, *What Is Christianity?* trans. T. B. Saunders (Fortress Texts in Modern Theology; Philadelphia: Fortress, 1986 [1900]).

Harnack, *Mission*

Adolf von Harnack, *The Mission and Expansion of Christianity in the First Three Centuries,* trans. James Moffatt (2d ed., 1908; reprinted New York: Harper, 1961).

Harnack, "Spruch"

Adolf von Harnack, "Der Spruch über Petrus als Felsen der Kirche (Mt 16,17f)," SPAW 1918, 637–54.

Harnack, "Zwei Worte"

Adolf von Harnack, "Zwei Worte Jesu," SPAW.PH 1907, 942–57.

Harnisch, *Gleichniserzählungen*

Wolfgang Harnisch, *Die Gleichniserzählungen Jesu* (Göttingen: Vandenhoeck & Ruprecht, 1985).

Heinemann, "Status"

Joseph H. Heinemann, "The Status of the Labourer in Jewish Law and Society in the Tannaitic Period," HUCA 25 (1954) 263–325.

Heising, *Botschaft*

Alkuin Heising, *Die Botschaft der Brotvermehrung* (SBS 15; Stuttgart: Katholisches Bibelwerk, 1966).

Held, "Matthew"

Heinz Joachim Held, "Matthew as Interpreter of the Miracle Stories," in Bornkamm–Barth–Held, *Tradition and Interpretation,* 165–299.

Hengel, *Leader*

Martin Hengel, *The Charismatic Leader and His Followers,* trans. James Greig (New York: Crossroad, 1981).

Hengel, *Zealots*

Martin Hengel, *The Zealots,* trans. D. Smith (Edinburgh: T. & T. Clark, 1989).

Heppe, *Dogmatik*

Heinrich Heppe, *Die Dogmatik der evangelisch-reformierten Kirche,* ed. Ernst Bizer (Neukirchen-Vluyn: Neukirchener Verlag, 1935).

Heuberger, "Sämann"

Josef Heuberger, "Sämann und Gottes Wort: Beitrag zu einer Geschichte der Auslegung des Sämannsgleichnisses in der griechischen Patristik" (Diss., Graz, 1979).

Heuberger, "Samenkörner"

Josef Heuberger, "Samenkörner des Sämanns auf griechischem Ackerboden," in Norbert Brox et al., eds., *Anfänge der Theologie: χαριστεῖον Johannes B. Bauer zum Jänner 1987* (Graz: Styria, 1987) 155–74.

Hezser, *Lohnmetaphorik*

Catherine Hezser, *Lohnmetaphorik und Arbeitswelt in Mt 20,1-16* (NTOA 15; Göttingen: Vandenhoeck & Ruprecht, 1990).

Higgins, *Son of Man*

A. J. B. Higgins, *The Son of Man in the Teaching of Jesus* (SNTSMS 39; Cambridge: Cambridge University Press, 1980).

Hilary

Hilary of Poitiers (c. 315–67), *In Evangelium Matthaei Commentarius* (PL 9.917–1078; cited according to Jean Doignon, ed.; SC 254. 258; Paris: Cerf, 1978–79).

Hill, "Δίκαιοι"

David Hill, "Δίκαιοι as quasi-technical term," NTS 11 (1964–66) 296–302.

Hirunuma, "Matthew 16:2b-3"

T. Hirunuma, "Matthew 16:2b-3," in Eldon Jay Epp and Gordon D. Fee, eds., *New Testament Textual Criticism: Its Significance for Exegesis: Essays in Honor of Bruce M. Metzger* (Oxford: Clarendon, 1981) 35–45.

Hoffmann, "Petrus-Primat"

Paul Hoffmann, "Der Petrus-Primat im Matthäus-evangelium," in Joachim Gnilka, ed., *Neues Testament und Kirche: für Rudolf Schnackenburg* (Freiburg: Herder, 1974) 94–114.

Hoffmann, *Studien*

Paul Hoffmann, *Studien zur Theologie der Logienquelle* (NTA NF 8; Münster: Aschendorf, 1972).

Hoh, "γραμματεύς"

Joseph Hoh, "Der christliche γραμματεύς," BZ 17 (1926) 256–69.

Holtzmann

H. J. Holtzmann, *Die Synoptiker* (HKNT 1/1; 3d ed.; Tübingen: Mohr/Siebeck, 1901).

Holtzmann, *Theologie*

H. J. Holtzmann, *Lehrbuch der neutestamentlichen Theologie,* 2 vols. (2d ed.; Tübingen: Mohr/Siebeck, 1911).

Hommel, "Tore"

Hildebrecht Hommel, "Die Tore des Hades," ZNW 80 (1989) 124–25.

Horbury, "Temple Tax"

William Horbury, "The Temple Tax," in Ernst Bammel and C. F. D. Moule, eds., *Jesus and the Politics of His Day* (Cambridge: Cambridge University Press, 1984) 265–86.

Howard

George Howard, *The Gospel of Matthew According to a Primitive Hebrew Text* (Macon, Ga.: Mercer University Press, 1987).

Hübner, *Gesetz*

Hans Hübner, *Das Gesetz in der synoptischen Tradition* (Witten: Luther, 1973).

Hummel, *Auseinandersetzung*

Reinhart Hummel, *Die Auseinandersetzung zwischen Kirche und Judentum im Matthäusevangelium* (BEvTh 33: Munich: Kaiser, 1963).

Hunzinger, "Bannpraxis"
Claus-Hunno Hunzinger, "Die jüdische Bannpraxis im neutestamentlichen Zeitalter" (Diss., Göttingen, 1954).

Hunzinger, "Bann II"
Claus-Hunno Hunzinger, "Bann II," *TRE* 5 (1980) 161–67.

Iersel, "Speisung"
B. M. F. van Iersel, "Die wunderbare Speisung und das Abendmahl in der synoptischen Tradition," *NovT* 7 (1964–65) 167–94.

Ishodad of Merv
Ishodad of Merv (d. 850), *The Commentaries*, vol. 1, ed. M. D. Gibson (Horae Semiticae 5; Cambridge: Cambridge University Press, 1911).

Jansen
Cornelius Jansen (1585–1638), *Tetrateuchus sive Commentarius in sancta Jesu Christi Evangelia* (Brussels: Francisci T'Serstevens, 1737).

Jastrow
Marcus Jastrow, *A Dictionary of the Targumim, the Talmud Babli and Yerushalmi, and the Midrashic Literature* (1903; reprinted New York: Judaica, 1989).

Jeremias, *Abba*
Joachim Jeremias, *Abba: Studien zur neutestamentlichen Theologie und Zeitgeschichte* (Göttingen: Vandenhoeck & Ruprecht, 1966).

Jeremias, *Golgotha*
Joachim Jeremias, *Golgotha* (Angelos Beiheft 1; Leipzig: Pfeiffer, 1926).

Jeremias, *Infant Baptism*
Joachim Jeremias, *Infant Baptism in the First Four Centuries*, trans. D. Cairns (London: SCM, 1960).

Jeremias, "Ἰωνᾶς"
Joachim Jeremias, "Ἰωνᾶς," *TDNT* 3 (1965) 406–10.

Jeremias, "Palästinakundliches"
Joachim Jeremias, "Palästinakundliches zum Gleichnis vom Sämann," *NTS* 13 (1966–67) 48–53.

Jeremias, *Parables*
Joachim Jeremias, *The Parables of Jesus*, trans. S. H. Hooke (rev. ed.; New York: Scribner's, 1972).

Jeremias, *Prayers*
Joachim Jeremias, *The Prayers of Jesus*, trans. John Bowden (Philadelphia: Fortress, 1978).

Jeremias, *Promise*
Joachim Jeremias, *Jesus' Promise to the Nations* (Philadelphia: Fortress, 1967).

Jeremias, "πύλη"
Joachim Jeremias, "πύλη," *TDNT* 6 (1968) 921–28.

Jeremias, *Theology*
Joachim Jeremias, *New Testament Theology*, trans. John Bowden (New York: Scribner's, 1971).

Jerome
Jerome [Hieronymus] (c. 340–420), *Commentariorum in Matthaeum libri IV* (CChr.SL 77; Turnholt: Brepols, 1959).

John Chrysostom
John Chrysostom (c. 354–407), *Commentarius in sanctum Matthaeum Evangelistam* (PG 57–58).

Jülicher, *Gleichnisreden*
Adolf Jülicher, *Die Gleichnisreden Jesu*, 2 vols. (1910; 2d ed.; reprinted: Darmstadt: Wissenschaftliche Buchgesellschaft, 1976).

Jüngel, *Paulus*
Eberhard Jüngel, *Paulus und Jesus* (Hermeneutische Untersuchungen zur Theologie 2; Tübingen: Mohr/Siebeck, 1962).

Kähler, "Kirchenleitung"
Christoph Kähler, "Kirchenleitung und Kirchenzucht nach Matthäus 18," in Karl Kertelge, Traugott Holtz, and Claus-Peter März, eds., *Christus Bezeugen: Festschrift Wolfgang Trilling zum 65. Geburtstag* (Leipzig: St. Benno, 1989) 136–45.

Kahlmeyer, *Seesturm*
Johannes Kahlmeyer, *Seesturm und Schiffbruch als Bild im antiken Schrifttum* (Hildesheim: Fikuart, 1934).

Kant, *Religion*
Immanuel Kant, *Religion Within the Limits of Reason Alone*, trans. T. M. Greene and H. H. Hudson (2d ed.; New York: Harper, 1960).

Karlstadt, *Reich Gotis*
Andreas Karlstadt, *Das reich Gotis leydet gewaldt und die gewaldrige nehmen oder rauben das selbig* (Wittenberg, 1521).

Käsemann, "Lukas 11,14-28"
Ernst Käsemann, "Lukas 11,14-28," in idem, *Exegetische Versuche und Besinnungen*, 2 vols. (Göttingen: Vandenhoeck & Ruprecht, 1965) 1.242–48.

Kasper, "Dienst"
Walter Kasper, "Dienst an der Einheit und Freiheit der Kirche," in Joseph Ratzinger, ed., *Dienst an der Einheit* (Düsseldorf: Patmos, 1978) 81–104.

Kasting, *Anfänge*
Heinrich Kasting, *Die Anfänge der urchristlichen Mission* (BEvTh 55; Munich: Kaiser, 1969).

Kierkegaard, *Training*
Søren Kierkegaard, *Training in Christianity*, trans. Walter Lowrie (1941; reprinted Princeton: Princeton University Press, 1957).

Kilpatrick, *Origins*
George D. Kilpatrick, *The Origins of the Gospel According to St. Matthew* (Oxford: Clarendon, 1946).

Kingsbury, "Figure of Jesus"
Jack Dean Kingsbury, "The Figure of Jesus in Matthew's Story: A Literary-Critical Probe," *JSNT* 21 (1984) 3–36.

Kingsbury, "Figure of Peter"
Jack Dean Kingsbury, "The Figure of Peter in Matthew's Gospel as a Theological Problem," *JBL* 98 (1979) 67–83.

Kingsbury, "Observations"
Jack Dean Kingsbury, "Observations on the 'Miracle Chapters' of Matthew 8–9," *CBQ* 40 (1978) 559–73.

Kingsbury, *Parables*
Jack Dean Kingsbury, *The Parables of Jesus in Matthew 13* (Richmond: John Knox, 1969).

Kingsbury, "Son of David"
Jack Dean Kingsbury, "The Title 'Son of David' in Matthew's Gospel," *JBL* 95 (1976) 591–602.

Klauck, *Allegorie*
Hans Josef Klauck, *Allegorie und Allegorese in synoptischen Gleichnistexten* (NTAbh NF 13; Münster: Aschendorff, 1978).

Kloppenborg, *Formation*
John S. Kloppenborg, *The Formation of Q: Trajectories in Ancient Wisdom Collections* (Philadelphia: Fortress, 1987).

Klostermann
Eric Klostermann, *Das Matthäusevangelium* (HNT 4; 2d ed.; Tübingen: Mohr/Siebeck, 1927).

Knabenbauer
Joseph Knabenbauer, *Commentarius in Evangelium secundum Matthaeum*, 2 vols. (Cursus scripturae sacrae 3/1–2; 3d ed.; Paris: Lithielleeux, 1922).

Kosch, *Gottesherrschaft*
Daniel Kosch, *Die Gottesherrschaft im Zeichen des Widerspruchs* (EHS 23/257; Bern: Lang, 1985).

Kraeling, *John the Baptist*
Carl H. Kraeling, *John the Baptist* (New York: Scribner's, 1951) 123–57.

Krämer, "Parabelrede"
M. Krämer, "Die Parabelrede in den synoptischen Evangelien," in Anton Bodem and Alois M. Kothgasser, eds., *Theologie und Leben: Festgabe für Georg Söll zum 70. Geburtstag* (Rome: Libreria Ateneo Salesiano, 1983) 31–53.

Krauss, *Archäologie*
Samuel Krauss, *Talmudische Archäologie*, 3 vols. (1910–12; reprinted Hildesheim: Olms, 1966).

Kümmel, *Heilsgeschehen*
Werner Georg Kümmel, *Heilsgeschehen und Geschichte*, 2 vols. (MThSt 3/16; Marburg: Elwert, 1965, 1978).

Künzel, *Studien*
Georg Künzel, *Studien zum Gemeindeverständnis des Matthäus-Evangeliums* (Calwer theologische Monographien 10; Stuttgart: Calwer Verlag, 1978).

Künzi, *Markus 9,1*
Martin Künzi, *Das Naherwartungslogion Markus 9,1 par.: Geschichte seiner Auslegung* (BGBE 21; Tübingen: Mohr/Siebeck, 1977).

Künzi, *Naherwartungslogion*
Martin Künzi, *Das Naherwartungslogion Matthäus 10,23: Geschichte seiner Auslegung* (BGBE 9; Tübingen: Mohr/Siebeck, 1970).

Lachs
Samuel Tobias Lachs, *A Rabbinic Commentary on the New Testament: The Gospels of Matthew, Mark, and Luke* (Hoboken, N.J.: Ktav, 1987).

Lagrange
M. J. Lagrange, *Évangile selon Saint Matthieu* (EtB; Paris: Gabalda, 1923).

Lambrecht, "Du bist Petrus"
Jan Lambrecht, "'Du bist Petrus,'" *SNTU* A 11 (1986) 5–32.

Lambrecht, "Parables"
Jan Lambrecht, "Parables in Mt 13," *TvT* 17 (1977) 25–47.

Lambrecht, *Treasure*
Jan Lambrecht, *Out of the Treasure: The Parables in the Gospel of Matthew* (Grand Rapids: Eerdmans, 1992).

Lampe, "Spiel"
Peter Lampe, "Das Spiel mit dem Petrus-Namen—Mt 16,18," *NTS* 25 (1978–79) 227–45.

Lange, *Erscheinen*
Joachim Lange, *Das Erscheinen des Auferstandenen im Evangelium nach Matthäus* (FB 11; Stuttgart: Katholisches Bibelwerk, 1973).

Lapide
Cornelius Lapide (= van den Steen) (d. 1687), *Commentarius in quatuor Evangelia: Argumentum in S. Matthaeum* (Antwerp: Meurstum, 1660).

Laufen, *Doppelüberlieferungen*
Rudolf Laufen, *Die Doppelüberlieferungen der Logienquelle und des Markusevangeliums* (BBB 54; Bonn: Hanstein, 1980).

Légasse, *Jésus*
Simon Légasse, *Jésus et l'enfant* (EtB; Paris: Gabalda, 1969).

Léon-Dufour, *Études*
Léon-Dufour, *Études d'Évangile* (Paris: Seuil, 1965).

Levine, *Dimensions*
Amy-Jill Levine, *The Social and Ethnic Dimensions of Matthean Salvation History* (Studies in the Bible and Early Christianity 14; Lewiston: Mellen, 1988).

Liber Graduum
Mihaly Kmosko, ed., *Liber Graduum* (Patrologia Syriaca 1/3; Paris: Firmin-Didot et socii, 1926).

Lightfoot
John Lightfoot (1602–75), *A Commentary on the New Testament from the Talmud and Hebraica*, vol. 2: *Matthew–Mark* (1859; reprinted Peabody, Mass.: Hendrikson, 1989).

Linnemann, *Parables*
Eta Linnemann, *Parables of Jesus,* trans. John Sturdy (New York: Harper & Row, 1966).

Linton, "Parable"
Olof Linton, "The Parable of the Children's Game," *NTS* 22 (1975–76) 159–79.

Liver, "Half-Shekel Offering"
J. Liver, "The Half-Shekel Offering in Biblical and Post-Biblical Literature," *HTR* 56 (1963) 173–98.

Lohfink, "Gleichnis"
Gerhard Lohfink, "Das Gleichnis vom Sämann," *BZ* NF 30 (1986) 36–69.

Lohfink, "Metaphorik"
Gerhard Lohfink, "Die Metaphorik der Aussaat im Gleichnis vom Sämann (Mk 4,3-9)," in *À Cause d'Évangile: Études sur les Synoptiques et les Actes: Offertes au P. Jacques Dupont, O.S.B. à l'occasion de son 70e anniversaire* (LD 123; Paris: Cerf, 1985) 211–28.

Lohmeyer
Ernst Lohmeyer, *Das Evangelium des Matthäus*, ed. Werner Schmauch (KEK Sonderband; 4th ed.; Göttingen: Vandenhoeck & Ruprecht, 1967).

Lohse, "σάββατον"
Eduard Lohse, "σάββατον κτλ," *TDNT* 7 (1971) 1–35.

Loisy
Alfred F. Loisy, *Les Évangiles Synoptiques*, 2 vols. (Paris; Ceffonds, 1907–8).

Lona, "In meinem Namen"
Horacio E. Lona, "'In meinem Namen versammelt': Mt 18,20 und liturgisches Handeln," *Archiv für Liturgiewissenschaft* 27 (1985) 373–404.

Löw, *Flora*
Immanuel Löw, *Die Flora der Juden*, 4 vols. (1924–34; reprinted Hildesheim: Olms, 1967).

Ludolphy, "Geschichte"
Ingetraut Ludolphy, "Zur Geschichte der Auslegung des Evangelium Infantium," in Erdmann Schott, ed., *Taufe und neue Existenz* (Berlin: Evangelische Verlagsanstalt, 1973) 71–86.

Ludwig, *Primatsworte*
Joseph Ludwig, *Die Primatsworte Mt 16,18. 19 in der altkirchlichen Exegese* (NTAbh 19/4; Münster: Aschendorff, 1952).

Lührmann, *Markusevangelium*
Dieter Lührmann, *Das Markusevangelium* (HNT 3; Tübingen: Mohr/Siebeck, 1987).

Lührmann, *Redaktion*
Dieter Lührmann, *Die Redaktion der Logienquelle* (WMANT 33; Neukirchen-Vluyn: Neukirchener, 1969).

Luther
Martin Luther (1483–1546), *D. Martin Luthers Evangelien-Auslegung*, 5 vols., ed. Erwin Mühlhaupt (Göttingen: Vandenhoeck & Ruprecht, 1964–73).

Luther, *WA* 38
Martin Luther, *Annotationes in aliquot capita Matthaei* in idem, *Werke*, vol. 38 (Weimar: Böhlau, 1912) (= Weimarer Ausgabe).

Luz, "Jünger"
Ulrich Luz, "Die Jünger im Matthäusevangelium," *ZNW* 62 (1971) 141–71, reprinted in Joachim Lange, ed., *Das Matthäus-Evangelium* (Wege der Forschung 525; Darmstadt: Wissenschaftliche Buchgesellschaft, 1980) 377–414.

Luz, *Matthew in History*
Ulrich Luz, *Matthew in History: Interpretation, Influence, and Effects* (Minneapolis: Fortress, 1994).

Luz, "Taumellolch"
Ulrich Luz, "Vom Taumellolch im Weizenfeld," in Hubert Frankemölle and Karl Kertelge, eds., *Vom Urchristentum zu Jesus: Für Joachim Gnilka* (Freiburg: Herder, 1989) 154–71.

Luz, "Wundergeschichten"
Ulrich Luz, "Die Wundergeschichten von Mt 8–9," in Gerald F. Hawthorne and Otto Betz, eds., *Tradition and Interpretation in the New Testament* (Grand Rapids: Eerdmans, 1987) 149–65.

Maldonat
Juan de Maldonado (1533–83), *Commentarii in quatuor Evangelistas*, vol. 1 (Johann Michael Raich, ed.; Moguntiae: Sumptibus Francisci Kirchheim, 1874).

Malherbe
Abraham J. Malherbe, ed., *The Cynic Epistles* (Sources for Biblical Study 12; Missoula, Mont.: Scholars Press, 1977).

Malina–Neyrey, *Names*
Bruce J. Malina and Jerome H. Neyrey, *Calling Jesus Names: The Social Value of Labels in Matthew* (Social Facets; Sonoma, Calif.: Polebridge, 1988).

Maloney, "Matthew 19:3-12"
Francis J. Maloney, "Matthew 19:3-12 and Celibacy: A Redactional and Form-Critical Study," *JSNT* 2 (1979) 42–60.

Manson, *Sayings*
T. W. Manson, *The Sayings of Jesus* (2d ed.; London: SCM, 1949).

Marchand, "Matthieu 18,20"
G. Marchand, "Matthieu 18,20 dans la tradition des six premiers siècles" (Diss., Gregoriana, Rome, 1958).

Marchel, *Abba*
Witold Marchel, *Abba, Père* (AnBib 19A; 2d ed.; Rome: Pontifical Biblical Institute Press, 1971).

Marco, "Las espigas arrancadas"
Mariano Herranz Marco, "Las espigas arrancadas en sábato (Mt 12,1-8 par.)," *EstBib* 28 (1969) 313–48.

Marguerat, *Jugement*
Daniel Marguerat, *Le Jugement dans l'Évangile de Matthieu* (Geneva: Labor et Fides, 1981).

Marquardt, *Privatleben*
Joachim Marquardt, *Das Privatleben der Römer* (1886; reprinted Darmstadt: Wissenschaftliche Buchgesellschaft, 1975).

Marshall, *Luke*
I. Howard Marshall, *The Gospel of Luke* (NIGTC; Grand Rapids: Eerdmans, 1978).

März, "Lk 12,54b-56"
Claus Peter März, "Lk 12,54b-56 par Mat 16,2b.3 und die Akoluthie der Redequelle," SNTU A 11 (1986) 83–96.

May, "Bann IV"
Georg May, "Bann IV," *TRE* 5 (1980) 170–82.

Mayser, *Grammatik*
Edwin Mayser, *Grammatik der griechischen Papyri aus der Ptolemärzeit* (Berlin: de Gruyter, 1970).

McDermott, "Mt 10:23"
John M. McDermott, "Mt 10:23 in Context," *BZ* NF 28 (1984) 230–40.

McGuckin, *Transfiguration*
John Anthony McGuckin, *The Transfiguration of Christ in Scripture and Tradition* (Studies in Bible and Early Christianity 9; Lewiston: Mellen, 1986).

McNeile
A. H. McNeile, *The Gospel According to St. Matthew* (1915; reprinted London: Macmillan, 1965).

Meier, "John the Baptist"
John P. Meier, "John the Baptist in Matthew's Gospel," *JBL* 99 (1980) 383–405.

Melancthon
Philip Melancthon (1497–1560), *Werke*, vol. 4: *Annotationes in Evangelium Matthaei iam recens in gratiam studiosorum editae,* ed. Robert Stupperich (Gütersloh: Bertelsmann, 1963).

Merklein, *Gottesherrschaft*
Helmut Merklein, *Die Gottesherrschaft als Handlungsprinzip* (FzB 34; 2d ed.; Würzburg: Echter Verlag, 1981).

Mertens, "L'hymne"
Herman Mertens, "L'hymne de jubilation chez les synoptiques" (Diss., Pontificia Universitas Gregoriana Roma, 1957).

Metzger, *Commentary*
Bruce M. Metzger, *A Textual Commentary on the Greek New Testament* (New York: United Bible Societies, 1971).

Meyer
H. A. W. Meyer, *Kritisch-exegetisches Handbuch über das Evangelium des Matthäus* (KEK 1/1; Göttingen: Vandenhoeck & Ruprecht, 1844).

Michaelis
Wilhelm Michaelis, *Das Evangelium nach Matthäus,* 2 vols. (Zurich: Zwingli, 1948–49).

Michel, "μικρός"
Otto Michel, "μικρός κτλ," *TDNT* 4 (1967) 648–59.

Mokrosch–Walz, *Mittelalter*
Reinhold Mokrosch and Herbert Walz, eds., *Mittelalter* (Kirchen- und Theologiegeschichte in Quellen 2; Neukirchen-Vluyn: Neukirchener, 1980).

Moltmann, *Church*
Jürgen Moltmann, *The Church in the Power of the Spirit,* trans. Margaret Kohl (New York: Harper & Row, 1977).

Mommsen, *Strafrecht*
Theodor Mommsen, *Römisches Strafrecht* (Leipzig: Duncker & Humblot, 1899).

Montefiore, *Gospels*
Claude Goldsmid Montefiore, *The Synoptic Gospels,* vol. 2 (1927; 2d ed.; reprinted New York: Ktav, 1968).

Montefiore, "Jesus"
Hugh Montefiore, "Jesus and the Temple Tax," *NTS* 10 (1963–64) 60–71.

Moore, *Judaism*
George Foot Moore, *Judaism in the First Centuries of the Christian Era,* 3 vols. (Cambridge: Harvard University Press, 1927–30).

Moore, "BIAZΩ"
Ernest Moore, "BIAZΩ, ΑΡΠΑΖΩ and Cognates in Josephus," *NTS* 21 (1974–75) 519–43.

Mora, *Signe*
Vincent Mora, *Le signe de Jonas* (Paris: Cerf, 1983).

Moule, "Mark 4:1-20"
C. F. D. Moule, "Mark 4:1-20 Yet Once More," in E. Earle Ellis and Max Wilcox, eds., *Neotestamentica et Semitica: Studies in Honour of Matthew Black* (Edinburgh: T. & T. Clark,1969), 95–113.

Moulton–Howard–Turner
James Hope Moulton, Wilbert Francis Howard, and Nigel Turner, *A Grammar of New Testament Greek,* 3 vols. (Edinburgh: T. & T. Clark, 1906–63).

Moulton–Milligan
James Hope Moulton and George Milligan, *The Vocabulary of the Greek Testament Illustrated from the Papyri and Other Non-literary Sources* (Grand Rapids: Eerdmans, 1949).

Musculus
Wolfgang Musculus (1497–1563), *In Evangelistam Matthaeum commentarii* (Basel: Heruagius, 1561).

Mussner, "Kairos"
Franz Mussner, "Der nicht erkannte Kairos (Mt 11,16-19/Lk 7,31-35)," *Bib* 40 (1959) 599–613.

Mussner, *Petrus und Paulus*
Franz Mussner, *Petrus und Paulus–Pole der Einheit* (QD 76; Freiburg: Herder, 1976).

Norden, *Agnostos Theos*
Eduard Norden, *Agnostos Theos* (1913; reprinted Darmstadt: Wissenschaftliche Buchgesellschaft, 1956).

Oepke, "Herrnspruch"
Albrecht Oepke, "Der Herrnspruch über die Kirche Mt 16,17-19 in der neuesten Forschung," *StTh* 2 (1950) 110–65.

Olshausen
Hermann Olshausen, *Biblical Commentary on the New Testament,* vol. 1 (New York: Sheldon, 1863).

Onasch, *Idee*
Konrad Onasch, *Die Idee der Metamorphosis (Verklärung) in den Liturgien, in der russischen Philosophie und im russischen Frömmigkeitsleben* (Danzig: Kloschies, 1944).

Opus imperfectum
Pseudo-Chrysostom (6th century, Arian), *Diatribe ad opus Imperfectum in Matthaeum* (*PL* 56.601–946).

Origen
Origen (185–254), *Matthäuserklärung,* 3 vols. (GCS Origenes 10, 11, 12; Leipzig: Heinrichs, 1935–41). For an English translation, see: *Commentary on the Gospel of Matthew,* in *The Ante-Nicene Fathers,* ed. Allen Menzies (Grand Rapids: Eerdmans, 1951), 10.411–512.

Orton, *Scribe*
David E. Orton, *The Understanding Scribe: Matthew and the Apocalyptical Ideal* (JSNTSup; Sheffield: Academic Press, 1989).

Otto, *Kingdom*
Rudolf Otto, *The Kingdom of God and the Son of Man: A Study in the History of Relgion,* trans. Floyd V. Filson and Bertram Lee Woolf (2d ed.; London: Lutterworth, 1951).

Papsttum
Papsttum als ökumenische Frage, edited by the Arbeitsgemeinschaft ökumenischer Universitätsinstitute (Mainz: Grünewald, 1979).

Paschasius Radbertus

Paschasius Radbertus (c. 790–859), *Expositio in Evangelium Matthaei* (PL 120.31–994).

Paschen, *Rein und Unrein*

Wilfried Paschen, *Rein und Unrein* (SANT 24; Munich: Kösel, 1970).

Patsch, "Abendmahlsterminologie"

Hermann Patsch, "Abendmahlsterminologie ausserhalb der Einsetzungsberichte," *ZNW* 62 (1971) 210–31.

Patte

Daniel Patte, *The Gospel According to Matthew: A Structural Commentary on Matthew's Faith* (Philadelphia: Fortress, 1986).

Paulus

Heinrich Eberhard Gottlob Paulus, *Philologisch-kritische und historische Commentar über die drey ersten Evangelien*, 4 vols. (Lübeck: Bohn, 1800–1808).

Per foramen

Per foramen acus. Il cristianesimo antico di fronte alla pericope evangelica del "giovane ricco" (Studia Patristica Mediolanensia 14; Milan: Vita e Pensiere, 1986).

Perrin, *Rediscovering*

Norman Perrin, *Rediscovering the Teaching of Jesus* (New York: Harper & Row, 1967).

Pesch, "Levi-Matthäus"

Rudolf Pesch, "Levi-Matthäus (Mc 2,14/Mt 9,9; 10,3): Ein Beitrag zur Lösung eines alten Problems," *ZNW* 59 (1968) 40–56.

Pesch, *Markusevangelium*

Rudolf Pesch, *Das Markusevangelium*, 2 vols. (HThKNT 2/1–2; Freiburg: Herder, 1976/77; 3d ed. with Supplement, 1980).

Pesch, *Simon-Petrus*

Rudolf Pesch, *Simon-Petrus* (Päpste und Papsttum; Stuttgart: Hiersemann, 1980).

Pesch, "Über die Autorität"

Rudolf Pesch, "Über die Autorität Jesu: Eine Rückfrage anhand des Bekenner- und Verleugnerspruchs Lk 12,8f par.," in Rudolf Schnackenburg, Josef Ernst, and Joachim Wanke, eds., *Die Kirche des Anfangs: Festschrift für Heinz Schürmann zum 65. Geburtstag* (EThSt 38; Leipzig: St. Benno, 1977) 25–55.

Pesch, *Matthäus*

Wilhelm Pesch, *Matthäus der Seelsorger* (SBS 2; Stuttgart: Katholisches Bibelwerk, 1966).

Pesch–Schnackenburg, *Jesus*

Rudolf Pesch and Rudolf Schnackenburg, eds., *Jesus und der Menschen bohn: für Anton Vögtle* (Freiburg: Herder, 1975).

Peter Chrysologus

Peter Chrysologus (c. 380–450), *Sermones* (PL 52.183–680). Cited according to G. Böhmer, trans., *Ausgewählte Predigten* (BKV 43. 15-140; Munich: Kösee & Pustet, 1923).

Peter of Laodicea

Peter of Laodicea (7th century), *Erklärung des Matthaeusevangeliums* (Beiträge zur Geschichte und Erklärung des Neuen Testaments 5; Leipzig: Durr, 1908).

du Plessis, *ΤΕΛΕΙΟΣ*

Paul Johannes du Plessis, *ΤΕΛΕΙΟΣ: The Idea of Perfection in the New Testament* (Kampen: Kok, 1959).

du Plessis, "Meaning"

J. G. du Plessis, "Pragmatic Meaning in Matthew 13,1-23," *Neot* 21 (1987) 33–56.

Plummer

Alfred Plummer, *An Exegetical Commentary on the Gospel According to St. Matthew* (2d ed.; London: Stock, 1910).

Polag, *Fragmenta*

Athanasius Polag, *Fragmenta Q* (Neukirchen-Vluyn: Neukirchener, 1979).

Rabanus

Rabanus Maurus (780–856), *Commentariorum in Matthaeum libri VIII* (PL 107.727–1156).

Ragaz, *Gleichnisse*

Leonhard Ragaz, *Die Gleichnisse Jesu: Seine soziale Botschaft* (Hamburg: Furche, 1971).

Reimarus

Charles H. Talbert, ed., *Reimarus: Fragments* (Philadelphia: Fortress, 1970).

Reiser, *Jesus*

Marius Reiser, *Jesus and Judgment: The Eschatological Proclamation in Its Jewish Context* (Minneapolis: Fortress, 1997).

Repo, "Fünf Brote"

Eero Repo, "Fünf Brote und zwei Fische," SNTU A 3 (1978) 99–113.

Reuss

Joseph Reuss, *Matthäus-Kommentare aus der griechischen Kirche* (TU 61; Berlin: Akademie-Verlag, 1957).[1]

Riesner, *Jesus*

Rainer Riesner, *Jesus als Lehrer* (WUNT 2/7; Tübingen: Mohr/Siebeck, 1981).

Riessler

Paul Riessler, *Altjüdisches Schrifttum ausserhalb der Bibel* (1927; reprinted Darmstadt: Wissenschaftliche Buchgesellschaft, 1966).

Rochais, *Récits*

Gerard Rochais, *Les récits de resurrection des morts dans le Nouveau Testament* (SNTSMS 40; Cambridge: Cambridge University Press, 1981).

---

[1]   Includes Apollinaris of Laodicea (d. c. 390), Theodore of Heraclea (d. c. 355), Theodore of Mopsuestia (c. 350-428), Theophilus of Alexandria (d. c. 410), Cyril of Alexandria (d. 444), Photius of Constantinople (820-91).

Roloff, *Kerygma*

Jürgen Roloff, *Das Kerygma und der irdische Jesus* (Göttingen: Vandenhoeck & Ruprecht, 1970).

Rordorf, *Sunday*

Willy Rordorf, *Sunday: The History of the Day of Rest and Worship in the Earliest Centuries of the Christian Churches* (Philadelphia: Westminster, 1968).

Rossé, *Ecclesiologia*

Gerard Rossé, *L'ecclesiologia di Matteo: Interpretazione di Mt 18,20* (Rome: Città Nuova, 1987).

Rothfuchs, *Erfüllungszitate*

Wilhelm Rothfuchs, *Die Erfüllungszitate des Matthäus-Evangeliums* (BWANT 88; Stuttgart: Kohlhammer, 1969).

de Ru, "Conception"

G. de Ru, "The Conception of Reward in the Teaching of Jesus," *NovT* 8 (1966) 202–22.

Rupert of Deutz

Rupert of Deutz (c. 1070–1129), *In Opus de gloria et honore Filii Hominis super Matthaeum* (*PL* 168.1307–1634).

Sabourin

Léopold Sabourin, *L'Évangile selon saint Matthieu et ses principaux parallèles* (Rome: Biblical Institute Press, 1978).

Sabugal, *Mesiánica*

S. Sabugal, *La embajada mesiánica del Bautista (Mt 11,2-6 par)* (Madrid: Systeco, 1980).

Salmeron

Alfonso Salmeron, *Commentarii in Evangelicam Historiam,* 11 vols. (Colonial Agrippinae: Apud Antonium Hierat et Ioan. Gymni, 1612).

Sand, *Evangelium*

Alexander Sand, *Das Evangelium nach Matthäus* (RNT; Regensburg: Pustet, 1986).

Sand, *Gesetz*

Alexander Sand, *Das Gesetz und die Propheten: Untersuchungen zur Theologie des Evangeliums nach Matthäus* (BU 11; Regensburg: Pustet, 1974).

Sand, *Reich Gottes*

Alexander Sand, *Reich Gottes und Eheverzicht im Evangelium nach Matthäus* (SBS 109; Stuttgart: Katholisches Bibelwerk, 1983).

Sato, "Q"

Migaku Sato, "Q und Prophetie" (Diss., Bern, 1984).

Schaff, *Sünde*

Philip Schaff, *Die Sünde wider den heiligen Geist* (Halle: Lippert, 1841).

Schenk, *Sprache*

Wolfgang Schenk, *Die Sprache des Matthäus: Die Test-Konstituenten in ihren makro- und mikro-strukturellen Relationen* (Göttingen: Vandenhoeck & Ruprecht, 1987).

Schlatter

Adolf Schlatter, *Der Evangelist Matthäus* (2d ed.; Stuttgart: Calwer Verlag, 1933; 1st ed. 1929).

Schlosser, *Règne de Dieu*

Jacques Schlosser, *Le règne de Dieu dans les dits de Jésus* (EtB; Paris: Gabalda, 1980).

Schmid

Josef Schmid, *Das Evangelium nach Matthäus* (RNT 1; Regensburg: Pustet, 1965; 1st ed. 1956).

Schmithals, *Markus*

Walter Schmithals, *Das Evangelium nach Markus* (Ökumenischer Taschenkommentar zum Neuen Testament 2/1; Gütersloh: Mohn, 1979).

Schnackenburg

Rudolf Schnackenburg, *Matthäusevangelium,* 2 vols. (Neue Echter Bibel 1/1–2; Würzburg: Echter Verlag, 1985–87).

Schnackenburg, "Petrus"

Rudolf Schnackenburg, "Petrus im Matthäus-evangelium," in *À Cause d'Évangile: Études sur les Synoptiques et les Actes: Offertes au P. Jacques Dupont, O.S.B. à l'occasion de son 70e anniversaire* (LD 123; Paris: Cerf, 1985), 107–25.

Schnider, "Gerechtigkeit"

Franz Schnider, "Von der Gerechtigkeit Gottes," *Kairos* 23 (1981) 88–95.

Schniewind

Julius Schniewind, *Das Evangelium nach Matthäus* (NTD 2; 8th ed.; Göttingen: Vandenhoeck & Ruprecht, 1956).

Schönle, *Johannes*

Volker Schönle, *Johannes, Jesus und die Juden: Die theologische Position des Mt und des Vf. der Logienquelle im Lichte von Mt 11* (Beiträge zur biblischen Exegese und Theologie 9; Frankfurt: Lang, 1982).

Schottroff, "Solidarity"

Luise Schottroff, "Human Solidarity and the Goodness of God: The Parable of the Workers in the Vineyard," in Willy Schottroff and Wolfgang Stegemann, eds., *God of the Lowly: Socio-Historical Interpretations of the Bible,* trans. M. J. O'Connell (Maryknoll: Orbis, 1984), 129–47.

Schottroff, "Volk"

Luise Schottroff, "Das geschundene Volk und die Arbeit in der Ernte: Gottes Volk nach dem Matthäusevangelium," in Luise and Willy Schottroff, eds., *Mitarbeiter der Schöpfung: Bibel und Arbeitswelt* (Munich: Kaiser, 1983) 149–206.

Schrenk, "βιάζομαι"

Gottlob Schrenk, "βιάζομαι κτλ," *TDNT* 1 (1964) 609–14.

Schulz, *Q*

Siegfried Schulz, *Q: Die Spruchquelle der Evangelisten* (Zurich: Theologischer Verlag, 1972).

Schürer–Vermes

Emil Schürer, *The History of the Jewish People in the Age of Jesus Christ,* 3 vols., ed. Geza Vermes, Fergus Millar, and Matthew Black, vols. 1–2; ed. Geza Vermes, Fergus Millar, and Martin Goodman, vol. 3 (rev. ed.; Edinburgh: T. & T. Clark, 1973–86).

Schürmann, *Gottes Reich*

Heinz Schürmann, *Gottes Reich–Jesu Geschick* (Freiburg: Herder, 1983).

Schürmann, *Lukasevangelium*
Heinz Schürmann, *Das Lukasevangelium: Erster Teil* (HThKNT 3/1; Freiburg: Herder, 1969).

Schürmann, "Redaktionsgeschichte"
Heinz Schürmann, "Zur Traditions- und Redaktionsgeschichte von Mt 10,23," in idem, *Untersuchungen,* 150–56.

Schürmann, *Untersuchungen*
Heinz Schürmann, *Traditionsgeschichtliche Untersuchungen zu den synoptischen Evangelien* (KBANT; Düsseldorf: Patmos, 1968).

Schwarz, *Jesus sprach*
Günther Schwarz, *"Und Jesus sprach": Untersuchungen zur aramäischen Urgestalt der Worte Jesu* (BWANT 118; Stuttgart: Kohlhammer, 1985).

Schweitzer, *Quest*
Albert Schweitzer, *The Quest of the Historical Jesus,* trans. William Montgomery (New York: Macmillan, 1948).

Schweizer, "Ob in der Stelle"
A. Schweizer, "Ob in der Stelle Matth 11,12 ein Lob oder ein Tadel enthalten sei?" *ThStK* 9 (1836) 90–122.

Schweizer
Eduard Schweizer, *The Good News According to Matthew,* trans. D. E. Green (Atlanta: John Knox, 1975).

Schweizer, *Mark*
Eduard Schweizer, *The Good News According to Mark,* trans. D. H. Madvig (Richmond: John Knox, 1970).

Schweizer, *Matthäus*
Eduard Schweizer, *Matthäus und seine Gemeinde* (SBS 71; Stuttgart: Katholisches Bibelwerk, 1974).

Schweizer, "Matthäus 12,1-8"
Eduard Schweizer, "Matthäus 12,1-8: Der Sabbat: Gebot und Geschenk," in *Glaube und Gerechtigkeit: in memoriam R. Gyllenberg,* ed. Jarmo Kiilunen et al. (Suomen Eksegeettisen Seuran julkaisuja 38; Helsinki: Finnische Exegetische Gesellschaft, 1983), 169–79.

Schweizer, "Ψυχή"
Eduard Schweizer, "Ψυχή κτλ," *TDNT* 9 (1974) 637–56.

Schweizer, "Sondertradition"
Eduard Schweizer, "Zur Sondertradition der Gleichnisse bei Matthäus," in idem, *Matthäus,* 98–105.

Scott, *Hear*
Bernard Brandon Scott, *Hear Then the Parable: A Commentary on the Parables of Jesus* (Minneapolis: Fortress, 1989).

Scroggs, "Communities"
Robin Scroggs, "The Earliest Christian Communities as Sectarian Movement," in Jacob Neusner, ed., *Christianity, Judaism and Other Greco-Roman Cults: Studies for Morton Smith at Sixty* (SJLA 12/2; Leiden: Brill, 1975) 1–23.

Segalla, "Il testo"
Giuseppe Segalla, "Il testo più antico sul celibato: Mt 19,11-12," *StPatr* 17 (1970) 121–37.

Segbroeck, "Jésus"
Frans van Segbroeck, "Jésus rejeté par sa patrie (Mt 13,54-58)," *Bib* 48 (1968) 167–98.

Segbroeck, "Scandale"
Frans van Segbroeck, "Le scandale de l'incroyance: La signification de Mt 13,35," *EThL* 41 (1965) 344–72.

Sheret, "Examination"
B. S. Sheret, "An Examination of Some Problems of the Language of St. Matthew's Gospel" (Diss., Oxford, 1971).

Simonetti, "Praecursor"
Manlio Simonetti, "Praecursor ad inferos: Una nota sull' interpretazione patristica di Matteo 11,3," *Augustinianum* 20 (1980) 367–82.

Spicq, *Dieu*
Ceslas Spicq, *Dieu et l'homme* (LD 29; Paris: Cerf, 1961).

Spicq, *Lexicon*
Ceslas Spicq, *Theological Lexicon of the New Testament* (Peabody, Mass.: Hendrickson, 1994).

Stählin, "σκάνδαλον"
Gustav Stählin, "σκάνδαλον κτλ," *TDNT* 7 (1971) 339–58.

Stanton, "Matthew 11:28-30"
Graham N. Stanton, "Matthew 11:28-30: Comfortable Words?" *ExpT* 94 (1982) 3–9.

Stehly, "Boudhisme"
Ralph Stehly, "Boudhisme et Nouveau Testament: À propos de la marche de Pierre sur l'eau (Matthieu 14,28s)," *RHPhR* 57 (1977) 433–37.

Stendahl, *School*
Krister Stendahl, *The School of St. Matthew* (Uppsala: Gleerup, 1954; rev. ed., Philadelphia: Fortress, 1968).

Strabo
Walafrid Strabo (attributed, 12th century), *Glossa Ordinaria* (PL 114.63–178).

Strauss, *Life*
David Friedrich Strauss, *The Life of Jesus Critically Examined,* trans. George Eliot (1848; reprinted Philadelphia: Fortress, 1973).

Strecker, *Weg*
Georg Strecker, *Der Weg der Gerichtigkeit: Untersuchungen zur Theologie des Matthäus* (FRLANT 82; Göttingen: Vandenhoeck & Ruprecht, 1962).

Streeter, *Gospels*
B. H. Streeter, *The Four Gospels* (London: Macmillan, 1924).

Strobel, "Kindertaufe"
August Strobel, "Säuglings- und Kindertaufe in der ältesten Kirche," in Otto Perels, ed., *Begründung und Gebrauch der heiligen Taufe* (Berlin: Lutherisches Verlagshaus, 1963) 7–69.

Stuhlmacher, *Evangelium*
Peter Stuhlmacher, *Das paulinische Evangelium*, vol. 1 (FRLANT 95; Göttingen: Vandenhoeck & Ruprecht, 1968).

Suggs, *Wisdom*
M. Jack Suggs, *Wisdom, Christology and Law in Matthew's Gospel* (Cambridge: Harvard University Press, 1970).

Sugranyes de Franch, *Études*
Ramon Sugranyes de Franch, *Études sur le droit paléstinien à l'époque Évangélique* (Arbeiten aus dem Juristischen Seminar der Universität Freiburg; Freiburg: Librairie de l'Université, 1946).

Theisohn, *Richter*
Johannes Theisohn, *Der auserwählte Richter: Untersuchung zum traditionsgeschichtlichen Ort der Menschensohngeschichte der Bilderreden des Äthiopischen Henoch* (SUNT 12; Göttingen: Vandenhoeck & Ruprecht, 1975).

Theissen, *Gospels in Context*
Gerd Theissen, *The Gospels in Context: Social and Political History in the Synoptic Tradition*, trans. Linda M. Maloney (Minneapolis: Fortress, 1991).

Theissen, *Miracle Stories*
Gerd Theissen, *The Miracle Stories of the Early Christian Tradition*, trans. Francis McDonagh (Philadelphia: Fortress, 1983).

Theissen, "Rohr"
Gerd Theissen, "Das 'schwankende Rohr' (Mt 11,7) und die Gründungsmünzen von Tiberias," *ZDPV* 101 (1986) 43–55.

Theissen, *Social Reality*
Gerd Theissen, *Social Reality and the Early Christians: Theology, Ethics and the World of the New Testament*, trans. Margaret Kohl (Minneapolis: Fortress, 1992).

Theissen, "Sozialkolorit"
Gerd Theissen, "Lokal- und Sozialkolorit in der Geschichte von der syrophönikischen Frau (Mk 7,24-30)," *ZNW* 75 (1984) 202–25. [ET: Theissen, *The Gospels in Context*, 61–80.]

Theophylactus
Theophylactus (d. c. 1108), *Ennaratio in Evangelium Matthaei* (*PG* 123.139–492).

Thoma–Lauer, *Gleichnisse*
Clemens Thoma and Simon Lauer, *Die Gleichnisse der Rabbinen*, vol. 1: *Pesiqta de Rav Kahana* (Judaica et Christiana 10; Bern: Lang, 1986).

Thomas Aquinas, *Catena*
Thomas Aquinas (1225–74), *Catena aurea in quatuor evangelia*, vol. 1: *Expositio in Matthaeum et Marcum* (Rome: Marietti, 1953). ET: *Catena Aurea: Commentary on the Four Gospels Collected out of the Works of the Fathers*, vol. 1, parts 1–3 on Matthew (Oxford: Parker, 1841).

Thomas Aquinas, *Lectura*
Thomas Aquinas, *Super Evangelium S. Matthaei Lectura* (5th ed.; Turin: Marietti, 1951).

Thomas Aquinas, *S. th.*
Thomas Aquinas, *Summa Theologica*, 5 vols. (BAC; Madrid: La Editorial Catolica, 1955–58).

Thompson, *Advice*
William G. Thompson, *Matthew's Advice to a Divided Community: Mt 17:22–18:35* (AnBib 44; Rome: Biblical Institute Press, 1970).

Thyen, *Studien*
Hartwig Thyen, *Studien zur Sündenvergebung* (FRLANT 96; Göttingen: Vandenhoeck & Ruprecht, 1970).

van Tilborg, *Leaders*
Sjef van Tilborg, *The Jewish Leaders in Matthew* (Leiden: Brill, 1972).

Tödt, *Son of Man*
Heinz Eduard Tödt, *The Son of Man in the Synoptic Tradition* (Philadelphia: Westminster, 1965).

Torrance, *School of Faith*
Thomas F. Torrance, ed., *The School of Faith: The Catechisms of the Reformed Church* (New York: Harper & Brothers, 1959).

Trilling, "Amt"
Wolfgang Trilling, "Amt und Amtsverständnis bei Matthäus," in Albert Descamps, ed., *Mélanges bibliques en hommage au R. P. Béda Rigaux* (Gembloux: Duculot, 1970) 29–44.

Trilling, *Evangelium*
Wolfgang Trilling, *Das Evangelium nach Matthäus* (Geisttische Schriftlesung; Düsseldorf: Patmos, 1963).

Trilling, *Hausordnung*
Wolfgang Trilling, *Hausordnung Gottes: Eine Auslegung von Matthäus 18* (Die Welt der Bibel/Kleinkommentare zur Heiligen Schrift; Düsseldorf: Patmos, 1960).

Trilling, *Israel*
Wolfgang Trilling, *Das wahre Israel: Studien zur Theologie des Matthäusevangeliums* (EThSt 7; 3d ed.; Leipzig: St. Benno, 1975).

Trilling, "Täufertradition"
Wolfgang Trilling, "Die Täufertradition bei Matthäus," *BZ* NF 3 (1959) 271–89, reprinted in idem, *Studien zur Jesusüberlieferung* (Stuttgarter biblische Aufsatzbände 1; Stuttgart: Katholisches Bibelwerk, 1988) 45–65.

Troeltsch, *Social Teaching*
Ernst Troeltsch, *The Social Teaching of the Christian Churches*, 2 vols. (Chicago: University of Chicago Press, 1981).

Uro, *Sheep*
Risto Uro, *Sheep Among the Wolves: A Study on the Mission Instructions of Q* (Annales academiae scientiarum Fennicae 47; Helsinki: Suomalainen Tiedeakatemia, 1987).

Valdés
Juan de Valdés, *Commentary upon the Gospel of Matthew*, trans. John B. Betts (London: Trübner, 1882).

Verseput, *Rejection*
  Donald Verseput, *The Rejection of the Humble
  Messianic King: A Study of the Composition of Matthew
  11–12* (Einleitung in die Heilige Schrift 23/291;
  Frankfurt: Lang, 1986).
Via, *Parables*
  Dan O. Via, *The Parables; Their Literary and
  Existential Dimension* (Philadelphia: Fortress Press,
  1967).
Vögtle, *Evangelium*
  Anton Vögtle, *Das Evangelium und die Evangelien*
  (KBANT; Düsseldorf: Patmos, 1971).
Vögtle, "Wunder"
  Anton Vögtle, "Wunder und Wort in urchristlicher
  Glaubenswerbung (Mt 11,2-5/Lk 7,18-23)," in
  idem, *Evangelium,* 219–42.
Vollenweider, *Freiheit*
  Samuel Vollenweider, *Freiheit als neue Schöpfung:
  Eine Untersuchung zur Eleutheria bei Paulus und in
  seiner Umwelt* (FRLANT 147; Göttingen:
  Vandenhoeck & Ruprecht, 1989).
Volz, *Eschatologie*
  Paul Volz, *Die Eschatologie der jüdischen Gemeinde im
  neutestamentlichen Zeitalter* (Tübingen:
  Mohr/Siebeck, 1934).
de Vries, "Entwicklung"
  Wilhelm de Vries, "Die Entwicklung des Primats in
  den ersten drei Jahrhunderten," in *Papsttum,*
  114–33.
Walker, *Heilsgeschichte*
  Rolf Walker, *Die Heilsgeschichte im ersten Evangelium*
  (FRLANT 91; Göttingen: Vandenhoeck &
  Ruprecht, 1967).
Wanke, *Kommentarworte*
  Joachim Wanke, *"Bezugs- und Kommentarworte" in
  den synoptischen Evangelien* (EThSt 44; Leipzig: St.
  Benno, 1981).
Weaver, *Discourse*
  Dorothy Jean Weaver, *The Missionary Discourse in
  the Gospel of Matthew: A Literary Critical Analysis*
  (JSNTSup 38; Sheffield: JSOT, 1990).
Weber, "Alltagswelt"
  Beate Weber, "Alltagswelt und Gottesreich," *BZ* NF
  37 (1993) 161–82.
Weber, *Economy*
  Max Weber, *Economy and Society,* trans. E. Fischoff
  et al. (Berkeley: University of California Press,
  1978).
Weder, *Gleichnisse*
  Hans Weder, *Die Gleichnisse Jesu als Metaphern*
  (FRLANT 120; Göttingen: Vandenhoeck &
  Ruprecht, 1978).
Wegner, *Hauptmann*
  Uwe Wegner, *Der Hauptmann von Kafarnaum (Mt
  7,28a; 8,5-10,13 par; Lk 7,1-10): Ein Beitrag zur Q-
  Forschung* (WUNT 2/14; Tübingen: Mohr/Siebeck,
  1985).
Weiser, *Knechtsgleichnisse*
  Alfons Weiser, *Die Knechtsgleichnisse der synoptischen
  Evangelien* (SANT 29; Munich: Kösel, 1971).

B. Weiss
  Bernhard Weiss, *Das Matthäus-Evangelium* (KEK
  1/1; Göttingen: Vandenhoeck & Ruprecht, 1898).
J. Weiss
  Johannes Weiss, *Das Matthäus-Evangelium* (2d ed.;
  Schriften des Neuen Testaments 1; Göttingen:
  Vandenhoeck & Ruprecht, 1907).
Weiss, *Predigt*
  Johannes Weiss, *Die Predigt Jesu vom Reiche Gottes*
  (1900; 3d ed.; reprinted Göttingen: Vandenhoeck
  & Ruprecht, 1964). [Contains material not in ET:
  Weiss, *Proclamation.*]
Weiss, *Proclamation*
  Johannes Weiss, *Jesus' Proclamation of the Kingdom of
  God,* trans. R. H. Hiers and D. L. Holland
  (Philadelphia: Fortress, 1971). [ET of the shorter,
  first edition of Weiss, *Predigt.*]
Weist, "Menschensohn"
  C. Weist, "Wer ist dieser Menschensohn? Die
  Geschichte der Exegese zum Menschensohn-
  begriff" (Diss., Vienna, 1972).
Wellhausen
  Julius Wellhausen, *Das Evangelium Matthaei*
  (Berlin: Reimer, 1904).
de Wette
  W. M. L. de Wette, *Das Neue Testament, griechisch
  mit kurzem Kommentar*, vol. 1 (Halle: Anton, 1887).
Wettstein
  Johann Jacob Wettstein, *Novum Testamentum
  Graecum*, vol. 1 (1751; reprinted Graz:
  Akademische Druck- und Verlagsanstalt, 1962).
Wilkens, "Redaktion"
  Wilhelm Wilkens, "Die Redaktion des
  Gleichniskapitels Mark. 4 durch Matth.," *ThZ* 20
  (1964) 305–27.
Wilson, *Sects*
  Bryan R. Wilson, *Religious Sects: A Sociological Study*
  (New York: McGraw-Hill, 1970).
Winter, "Matthew 11:27"
  Paul Winter, "Matthew 11:27 and Luke 10:22 from
  the First to the Fifth Century," *NovT* 1 (1956)
  112–48.
Wolzogen
  Johann Ludwig Wolzogen (1633–90), *Commentarius
  in Evangelium Matthaei* (Irenopolis, 1656).
Zahn
  Theodor Zahn, *Das Evangelium des Matthäus*
  (Kommentar zum Neuen Testament 1; Leipzig:
  Deichert, 1903).
Zahn, *Forschungen*
  Theodor Zahn, *Forschungen zur Geschichte des neutes-
  tamentlichen Kanons und der altkirchlichen Literatur,*
  6/2: *Brüder und Vettern Jesu* (Leipzig: Deichert,
  1900).
Zeller, "Bildlogik"
  Dieter Zeller, "Die Bildlogik des Gleichnisses Mt
  11,16f/Lk 7,31f," *ZNW* 68 (1977) 252–57.

Zeller, "Logion"

Dieter Zeller, "Das Logien Mt 8,11f/Lk 13,28f," *BZ* NF 15 (1971) 222–37; 16 (1972) 84–93.

Zeller, *Mahnsprüche*

Dieter Zeller, *Die weisheitlichen Mahnsprüche bei den Synoptikern* (FzB 17; Würzburg: Echter Verlag, 1977).

Zimmermann, "Struktur"

Heinrich Zimmermann, "Die innere Struktur der Kirche und das Petrusamt nach Mt 18," in Albert Brandenburg and Hans Jörg Urban, eds., *Petrus und Papst* (Münster: Aschendorff, 1977) 4–19.

Zinzendorf

Nicolaus Ludwig Graf von Zinzendorf, *Reden über die vier Evangelisten,* 3 vols., ed. G. Clemens (Barby: Theological Seminary, 1766–69).

Zmijewski, "Glaube"

Josef Zmijewski, "Der Glaube und seine Macht," in Josef Zmijewski and Ernst Nellessen, eds., *Begegnung mit dem Wort: Festschrift für Heinrich Zimmermann* (BBB 53; Bonn: Hanstein, 1980) 81–103.

Zumstein, *Condition*

Jean Zumstein, *La condition du croyant dans l'Évangile selon Matthieu* (OBO 16; Freiburg: Éditions universitaires; Göttingen: Vandenhoeck & Ruprecht, 1977).

Zwingli

Huldrych Zwingli, *Opera,* vol. 6.1: *Annotationes in Evangelium Matthaei,* ed. Melchior Schuler and Johannes Schulthess (Zurich: Schulthess, 1836).

This English edition of volume two is a translation of volume two and part of volume three of Professor Luz's German four-volume commentary on the Gospel of Matthew. It will be followed in the Hermeneia series by a third volume, based on the remaining chapters of volume three and all of volume four of the German work. The editors of Hermeneia decided to publish these volumes first, because an older English version of volume one of the German commentary has already been published. A revised edition of volume one will then be published, reflecting the author's changes and including full bibliographic information as well as indices for the entire work.

The English translation of the text of the Gospel of Matthew is based on the German translation by Professor Luz and reflects his exegetical decisions. Other biblical texts are usually quoted from the New Revised Standard Version. Quotations of Latin and Greek authors, except where noted, follow the texts and translations of the Loeb Classical Library or other standard editions. Translations from the Dead Sea Scrolls are normally from Geza Vermes, *The Dead Sea Scrolls in English* (3rd ed.; London and New York: Penguin, 1987).

The endpapers display the recto and verso of Oxyrhynchus 4403 (𝔓103, second to third century), Matthew 13:55-56 and 14:3-5, from *Oxyrhynchus Papyri* volume 64 (1997). Permission to reprint these images was granted by the Egypt Exploration Society, London.

Literature

Burger, "Jesu Taten."

Karl Gatzweiler, "Les récits de miracle dans L'Évangile selon saint Matthieu," in M. Didier, ed., *L'Évangile selon Matthieu: Rédaction et théologie* (BEThL 29; Gembloux: Duculot, 1972) 209–20.

Birger Gerhardsson, *The Mighty Acts of Jesus According to Matthew* (Scripta minora. K. Humanistiska Vetenskapssamfundet i Lund 5; Lund: Gleerup, 1979).

Held, "Matthew."

Rudolf and Martin Hengel, "Die Heilungen Jesu und medizinisches Denken," in Paul Christian and Dietrich Rössler, eds., *Medicus Viator: Fragen und Gedanken am Wege Richard Siebecks: eine Festgabe seiner Freunde und Schüler zum 75. Geburtstag* (Tübingen: Mohr/Siebeck, 1959) 331–61.

John M. Hull, *Hellenistic Magic and the Synoptic Tradition* (SBT 2/28; Naperville, Ill.: Allenson, 1974) 116–41.

Kingsbury, "Observations."

Simon Légasse, "Les miracles de Jésus selon Matthieu," in Xavier Léon-Dufour, ed., *Les Miracles de Jésus selon le Nouveau Testament* (Paris: Seuil, 1977) 227–49.

Hendrick van der Loos, *The Miracles of Jesus* (NovTSup 9; Leiden: Brill, 1965).

Luz, "Wundergeschichten."

Hermann Schlingensiepen, *Die Wunder des Neuen Testaments: Wege und Abwege ihrer Deutung in der alten Kirche bis zur Mitte des 5. Jahrhunderts* (BFCTh 2/28; Gütersloh: Bertelsmann, 1933) passim.

Theissen, *Miracle Stories.*

William G. Thompson, "Reflections on the Composition of Mt 8:1–9:34," *CBQ* (1971) 365–88.

Structure

Our section is the second main division within the major inclusion of 4:23–9:35. It is best divided into four subsections of almost equal length[1] that have certain key words in common: 8:1-17; 8:18–9:1;[2] 9:2-17; 9:18-35. It is difficult, however, to determine clear themes for them.

Held[3] sees in 8:1-17 the christological theme of the servant of God, in 8:18–9:17 the theme "Jesus as Lord of the church," in 9:18-34 the theme "faith." For Kingsbury the theme in 9:1-17 is the "separation from Israel."[4] Schniewind has put the entire section under his formulation of Jesus as "Messiah of the deed,"[5] but others have objected correctly that our text also contains two controversy stories that have no miracles (9:9-17). In recent studies, therefore, "church" has become important as the basic theme of our chapters.[6]

Although in almost all texts of our chapters Matthew puts the words of Jesus in the foreground and lets the narration recede into the background, he nevertheless tells stories and does not present themes. Narrative elements thus play the main role for his structure. Matthew 8:1-17 offers a self-contained unit: Jesus descends from the mountain; on the road he meets the leper; he goes into the city (8:5); and there he goes into the house (8:14). The same is true of 8:18–9:1: Jesus wants to avoid the mass of people (8:18); he goes to the other side of the lake (8:24-28) where he heals the demoniacs; and then he returns to his city (9:1). Matthew 9:2-34 is also a self-contained unit. A pericope is often closely connected in time with the preceding one (8:18, 28; 9:1, 14, 18, 31-32). Matthew is thus trying to offer a running narrative,[7] although he demonstrates a certain awkwardness in the process.[8] His treat-

---

1   Matthew 8:1-17 and 8:18–9:1 each have approximately 36 lines in Nestle; 9:2-17 has about 38 Nestle lines, 9:18-35 about 35 Nestle lines.

2   Verse 1 is transitional. Because of the geographical setting and the catchwords ἐμβαίνω εἰς τὸ πλοῖον (cf. 8:23) and διαπεράζω (cf. 8:18), v. 1a fits better with the preceding section. Verse 1b already indicates the location of the following story.

3   Held, "Matthew," 248–49.

4   "Observations," 568.

5   Julius Schniewind, *Das Evangelium nach Matthäus* (NTD 2; 8th ed.; Göttingen: Vandenhoeck & Ruprecht, 1956) 36, 106.

6   Burger, "Jesu Taten," 287; Georg Künzel, *Studien zum Gemeindeverständnis des Matthäus-Evangeliums*

(Calwer theologische Monographien A 10; Stuttgart: Calwer Verlag, 1978) 145–46.

7   Held ("Matthew," 225–46) notes that Matthew concentrates the miracle narratives in the conversations and plays down the narrative elements. However, he has overlooked the fact that Matthew was primarily interested in creating a narrative thread and not simply in using the stories as illustrations of various doctrines.

8   For example: the presence of the crowd (8:1) in combination with the command of silence (8:4); the presence of amazed "people" (8:27, different in Mark!) despite the absence of "other boats" in the storm (Mark 4:36); the herdsmen's report of "everything," "also what had happened to the demoniacs"

ment of the themes is much like a rope or a braid; it emphasizes first one strand, then another.[9] His strands run throughout the narrative. Thus the concept of discipleship that dominates 8:18-27 is anticipated in 8:1, 10 and appears again in 9:9, 27. The theme of faith (9:18-31) is prepared for in 8:10, 13 and 9:2. The controversy with Israel (9:2-17) is taken up again in 9:32-34. It is no accident that the title κύριος that dominates in 8:2-17 reappears in the story about disciples in 8:18-27. Thus in Matthew 8–9 secondary strands become main strands and main strands in turn become secondary strands.

At the same time the image of the braid indicates that the weaving together of Matthean themes in a narrative cord is directed toward a goal. At the end of chap. 9 the story of Jesus is no longer where it was at the beginning of chap. 8. That "Jesus' story" does not simply mean for Matthew a chronological-geographical sequence of events is clear from the monotony of strands that we see in this braid. The repetitions are intentional. Above all, the miracles of Jesus of which 4:23 already spoke are repeated, as are the idea of discipleship and the emerging conflicts with Israel's leaders. As is the case with the Gospel of Mark, Matthew tells a "theological" story of Jesus. He begins with the portrayal of the Messiah's activity among his people. The goal of this activity is to create a community of disciples (8:18-27) whom he will lead through the storm into gentile territory (8:28-34). How Jesus' activity creates discipleship is described once again in 9:9-13. At the same time all of chap. 9 illuminates how Jesus' activity leads to conflict in Israel that comes to a climax for the first time with the rupture of

9:32-34. It is now already clear that it is precisely this story of Jesus, of the community of disciples, and of Israel that chaps. 11–12 and chaps. 14–16 will continue.

In addition we would hazard the following conjecture: In chap. 8 we have the beginning of a story of Jesus on two levels. The surface structure of our text describes a succession of miracles and controversy dialogues that are geographically and chronologically connected. They are part of the story of Jesus with his people that will end with his execution and resurrection. It is a story of increasing conflict and of a rupture among the people. Beneath this surface level there is a deeper dimension. On this second level Matthew begins to tell the foundational story of his own church. It is a story that began with the activity of Jesus in Israel, that continued with the formation there of the community of disciples and with its separation from Israel, and that will end with its mission to the Gentiles. In the prologue we have already observed an example of this kind of story with two levels. On the surface it was a story of the infancy and the beginning of Jesus, but beneath the surface it was a prolepsis of the way the king of Israel and his people will go—from the city of David, Bethlehem, all the way to Galilee of the Gentiles.[10]

Sources

The arrangement of the individual texts in our section is different from that of Mark and Q, a feature that is strange, even unique. Matthew has combined two Markan sections (1:40—2:22; 4:35—5:43) and has supplemented them with Q material. He has not, however, used any sources other than Mark and Q.[11] While he has created something completely new from

---

(8:33) even though their herd was not even close (8:30); the reference to the faith of the paralytic's bearers, even though the episode of digging up the roof is missing (9:2), etc. Matthew is not a realistic and precise narrator!

9   Based on Matthew's use of various source strands, Burger ("Jesu Taten," 283) speaks of a "collage." However, this comparison does not grasp the intentionality of the Matthean narrative (cf. below).

10   Cf. vol. 1, I "Prelude (1:1–4:22)."

11   Because of the arrangement and of the minor agreements between Matthew and Luke, Schweizer (71–73) assumes that Matthew has used a compilation of Jesus' words and deeds that followed the Sermon on the Plain and that were used in the dispute with Israel. I find the thesis improbable! (1)

Matthew is aware of no other deeds of Jesus except those that are also in Q and Mark. (2) The arrangement reflects his redactional interests (cf. below) and is (3) conservative in comparison with the Gospel of Mark (cf. below); it is thus based on Mark 4. Since there are minor agreements in the use of all of the Markan material, they do not constitute a basis for a special explanation of Matthew 8–9. In my judgment they are either redactional improvements of Mark by Matthew and Luke or preredactional improvements of the Markan text—that is to say part of a slightly altered ("revised," second?) "edition" of Mark that Matthew and Luke used. Or they developed in oral tradition.

his sources, he has dealt cautiously with the arrangement of the material. He almost always maintains the order of the two Markan sections (with interruptions). In Q, Matt 8:5-10, 13 (= Luke 7:1-10) immediately followed the Sermon on the Plain and Matt 8:11-12 (= Luke 13:28-29) followed 7:22-23 (= Luke 13:26-27). Matthew omitted the section on the Baptist in Q (= Luke 7:18-35), but 8:19-22 (= Luke 9:57-62) is the second text in Q after the story of the centurion from Capernaum. Only at the end, in 9:27-34, did the evangelist depart from this conservative procedure and insert two texts from completely different contexts. We will need to pay particular attention to these changes.

These observations have an important implication for our understanding of Matthew. Matthew cannot have thought that he had found the correct, chronological course of the history of Jesus by combining stories from different sources or even with his bold duplication of two narratives in 9:27-34. Yet he depicts a chronological sequence of events and combines the individual stories chronologically and geographically. From a historical point of view, therefore, the chronological course of events is fictional. The evangelist must have been aware of that.[12] Therefore, source analysis also supports our thesis that the evangelist is interested in the inner, theological story of Jesus.

---

12 Probably the same is true of Mark who, e.g., puts the collection of parables in Mark 4 or the collection of stories in 4:35—5:43 into a chronological narrative thread.

The three stories of this section are closely connected with each other by means of the main words προσέρχομαι (vv. 2, 5), λέγων . . . κύριε (vv. 2, 5-6), ἅπτομαι with χείρ (vv. 3, 15), ὕπαγε (vv. 4, 13), the ἀκολουθέω of following Jesus (vv. 1, 10), the people (cf. also vv. 14-15), the authority of Jesus' word (λόγῳ vv. 8, 16), and the relation of all healing to Israel.[1] 4:23b summarizes the entire section: "he healed every sickness and every weakness among the people." The quotation in v. 17 with its catchword νόσος, which concludes and interprets this first section, also refers back to this summary.

---

1   For 8:1-4 this is derived from καθαρίζω and from v. 4; for 8:5-13 from the way the centurion is contrasted with Israel; for 8:14-17 from the formula quotation. This basic orientation is taken up again in 9:33b.

1.1 Jesus Heals a Leper (8:1-4)

Literature

Held, "Matthew," 213–15, 255–57.
For *additional literature* see above, II B on Matthew
8–9.

1	**But when he came down from the mountain, large crowds followed him.**
2	**And behold, a leper approached, fell down before him, and said,** **"Lord, if you will, you can make me clean."**
3	**And he stretched out his hand, touched him, and said,** **"I will; become clean!"** **And immediately his leprosy became clean.**
4	**And Jesus says to him, "See that you tell no one, but go, show yourself to the priest and offer the sacrifice that Moses commanded, for a witness to them."**

Analysis **Structure**

The little story is artfully constructed. Its midpoint at v. 3a is framed chiastically by the leper's request and Jesus' answer in vv. 2b and 3b (formulated as parallels: twice θέλω; three times καθαρίζω) and by the exposition and the acknowledgment of the healing in vv. 2a and 3c (λέπρος/λέπρα). The introduction in v. 1 is detailed, as is the concluding word of Jesus in v. 4 that receives special weight.

Sources

Except for the redactional[1] introduction in v. 1, the text comes from Mark 1:40-45. As is often the case, Matthew here abbreviates and thus makes the dialogue stand out more clearly. Notable are the numerous "minor agreements" with Luke 5:12-16.[2] They often correspond to Matthean and Lukan usage,[3] so that we could understand them if we had to[4] as improvements of Mark's text that the two evangelists made independently of each other. That suggestion leaves unexplained, however, why Matthew and Luke both omitted σπλαγχνισθείς (cf. Matt 9:36).[5] Thus we must ask whether at the time of Matthew there were different recensions of Mark. Mark 1:45 is omitted either because according to Matt 8:4 Jesus does not go to a lonely place as he does in Mark or because Matthew wanted to avoid having the healed man disobey Jesus. That Matthew uses Mark 1:44, 45a at the end of this main section in 9:30-31 is an example of his careful redaction that is faithful to the tradition![6]

Interpretation

■ **1** Verse 1 forms the transition from the Sermon on the Mount to the new story. Jesus descends from the mountain just as Moses once did from Sinai (cf. Exod 19:14; 32:1; 34:29).[7] Matthew closes the framework around the Sermon on the Mount and returns to the situation of 4:25. As they did there, the multitudes follow Jesus: They were with him on the mountain (7:28). The phrase "follow after" characterizes them as potential church, but the evangelist will not develop this thought until vv. 18-27.

■ **2** Then a leper[8] comes to Jesus, falls at his feet,[9] and addresses him with the majestic title "Lord" (κύριε). In

---

1. Cf. 4:25; 5:1 and vol. 1, Introduction 3.2 on ὄρος, ἀκολουθέω, ὄχλοι.

2. Verse 2: ἰδού, λέγων κύριε without ὅτι. Verse 3: the omission of σπλαγχνισθείς, the reversal of ἥψατο and αὐτοῦ, λέγων, θέλω without αὐτῷ, εὐθέως, the omission of Mark 1:43. Verse 4: the omission of μηδέν.

3. Cf. vol. 1, Introduction 3.2 on λέγων, κύριος, εὐθέως. On Matthew's downplaying of Jesus' emotions, cf. Allen, xxxi.

4. The number of such "independent" improvements in the space of two and a half verses makes this thesis problematic. Difficult is the omission of ὅτι in v. 2. It corresponds to Matthean but not necessarily to Lukan usage. Σπλαγχνίζομαι is important for Matthew (cf. 9:36; 20:34). That the Markan messianic secret is less prominent is, according to Andreas Ennulat, a feature of a deutero-Markan recension that Matthew and Luke used (*Agreements*, 425). Such a hypothesis cannot easily explain the rest of the minor agreements.

5. According to Gnilka (1.93), ὀργισθείς is the original reading, but this is text-critically improbable.

6. The conservative Matthew often later makes use of a Markan text that he had earlier omitted. It is an unusual and reverent process! In modern terms we might ask: Did Matthew have a "scrap file" in which he threw unused clippings from Mark for possible use later? His memory, which presumably functioned as a scrap file, must have been outstanding.

7. Cf. above, the analysis on 7:28-29.

8. Leprosy could include various kinds of skin diseases, including those that were more harmless. Cf. Pesch, *Markusevangelium* 1.142. Matthew certainly understood it, however, not to be a harmless skin disease, but the leprosy of which Leviticus 13–14 speaks and whose cure, according to the rabbis, is as difficult as is raising a person from the dead (Pesch, ibid., 1.143). That this is the first of his healing stories is also related to the difficulty of the case. Mark 1:29-31 would not have carried enough weight at the beginning of chaps. 8–9!

7:21-22 Matthew applied this title for the first time to Jesus as the lord of judgment. He is consistent in his use of the title. The disciples address Jesus this way (8:25; 14:28, 30; 16:22; 17:4; 18:21) as do the sick who come to the Lord for help (8:2, 6, 8; 9:28; 15:22, 25, 27; 17:15; 20:30-31, 33). The title does not appear on the lips of outsiders and is not simply polite speech.[10] From the perspective of this christological dimension the expression "if you will" becomes understandable. Everything depends on the sovereign will of Jesus who himself appears as the Lord who has his authority from God.[11]

■ **3** Stretching out one's hand, a common Old Testament expression[12] and a gesture that the miracle worker often makes in healing narratives,[13] means more in this case. Later Matthew will use this expression to symbolize the powerful protection under which the disciples of Jesus stand (cf. on 12:49). Jesus "wills," and his authority immediately heals the sick person. It is in keeping with Jesus' sovereignty that Matthew mentions no other emotion (cf. Mark 1:41a, 43a).[14]

■ **4** The final verse is not easy to understand. Contrary to his usual custom, Matthew makes use of Mark's command of silence, although he omits Mark's final v. 45 that is needed to make sense of the command. Presumably he wants to heighten the following command.[15] This, and only this, is what you are to do: Take your sacrifice[16] to the priest as is required by Leviticus

13–14. For Matthew it is important that the person who is healed keep the Torah of Moses at the command of Jesus (cf. 5:17-19!). The key word καθαρίζω ("to be clean") that is used three times also shows that we are now dealing with Israel and its law. Until modern times μαρτύριον ("testimony") was interpreted, probably incorrectly, as a sign of judgment on Israel;[17] but it is more likely that what is meant is a positive witness[18] initially for the priests, but then for all the people who are listening: As Israel's Messiah Jesus keeps the Torah.

Summary and History of Interpretation
Our little story thus shows a curious double quality. On the one hand, the leper addresses Jesus as "Lord" and falls at his feet. He acts, in other words, like a disciple, and Jesus stretches out his hand over him as he does over the disciples (12:49; 14:31). He thus becomes for the readers of the Gospel, who of course are also disciples, a figure with whom they can identify. On the other hand, we are clearly in Israel's space. The leper is a Jew, and Jesus commands him to keep the law. This is not a contradiction for Matthew, for he wants to show how Jesus heals "within the (holy) nation" (4:23) and how here someone who represents Israel finds his way to Jesus without being unfaithful to his people. The healed leper embodies, in a way, the basic unity between discipleship and Israel and is thus a witness for the people.

9   Cf. vol. 1 on 2:11: προσκυνέω.

10 On κύριε as a form of address cf. Geist, *Menschensohn*, 349–64.

11 As early as John Chrysostom it was noticed that the leper did not say to the Lord, "If you ask God . . . , you can make me clean."

12 More than eighty times in the LXX. For Matthew as well as for Mark it is improbable that this is an allusion to the miracles of Moses and Aaron in Egypt, where touching does not occur with the stretching out of the hand (contra Pesch, *Markusevangelium* 1.145). Cf. in addition Bovon, *Lukas* 1.239.

13 Cf. Theissen, *Miracle Stories*, 62–63, 92–93.

14 Bede (39) interprets the *maiestatis suae potestas* anti-heretically: "I will" is directed against the extreme Athanasian, Photinus; Jesus' command is directed against Arius, the touching against the Manichaeans.

15 On the basis of 12:16-21 Schweizer (211) points to the servant of God who neither cries out nor quarrels. However, *prior to* 12:16-21 who could have

understood this sporadic command of silence this way?

16 Δῶρον, frequently found in Matthew's Jewish-Christian special material (cf. 5:23-24;. 23:18-19), refers throughout Matthew, with the exception of 2:11 where it is plural, to sacrifice, as it does in the LXX text of Leviticus and Numbers.

17 John Chrysostom says, "not to improve them, nor to teach them, but . . . to accuse them, to 'convict' them"; similarly, e.g., Euthymius Zigabenus (281) and Maldonat (1.173).

18 Cf. 10:18; 24:14. At this point in the Matthean narrative the crisis in Israel has not yet happened.

The church's interpretation has repeatedly emphasized one side of this double nature, namely, how our story is transparent for Christian existence. The leper is a type of the believer who comes to Christ and receives a gift from him. As a rule his gift was understood figuratively; one is freed from "spiritual leprosy," from mortal sin.[19] Seldom was the physical and social dimension of Christ's help taken seriously.[20] Above all, little attention has been paid to the way this miracle of Jesus is related to the people of Israel. Usually one skirted v. 4 by claiming that Jesus was faithful to the law only until his death.[21] His obedience to the law is a sign of his humility[22] designed to stimulate us to gratitude.[23]

The history of interpretation thus shows that the second aspect of our text, Jesus' turning to Israel, was almost never taken seriously. Is there an overlooked potential meaning of our story here that might be mined today, in the aftermath of the Holocaust? Matthew's text requires caution. Our story is to be interpreted not in isolation but only as the beginning of the entire story that tells how Israel, after Jesus had turned to it, turned away from him. The original unity between Israel and Jesus' community of disciples will come unraveled in the Gospel of Matthew. Nevertheless, it may be that today we must make use of the potential meaning of Jesus' love for Israel that has been ignored in the history of interpretation. We can do this, however, only by critically and in a theologically responsible way working through the burden that the Matthean theology means here.

---

19 See, e.g., Augustine *Quaest.* App. 4 = 120 (leper = the one who does not keep the Sermon on the Mount); Euthymius Zigabenus, 280 (sin = leprosy of the soul); Calvin, *Harmony* 1.244; Lapide, 189: "*tropologice . . . peccatum mortale.*"

20 This is happening more frequently again since the rise of humanism (e.g., Erasmus, *Opera Omnia*, vol. 7: *In Evangelium Matthaei Paraphrasis* [reprint Hildesheim: Olms, 1962], 48; Beza, 35, and since the Enlightenment. Paulus (1.632) makes the noteworthy social-historical observation that the spread of leprosy is a result of poverty. The physical miracle is usually played down in classical interpretation—among others, by Luther (2.279), who suggests that miracles usually happen in the early period of a new teaching.

21 The literal cultic law has ended with Jesus' resurrection. (See, e.g., Thomas Aquinas, *Lectura*, no. 688.) It is frequently said that Christ lives according to the law, but his healings go beyond the law. (See, e.g., Anselm of Laon, *Enarrationes in Matthaeum* [*PL* 162.1227–1500] 1320.) Calovius (1.250) combines the two features: As the incarnate God, Jesus is lord of the law, but by virtue of his *officium* he kept even the ritual law.

22 Jerome on 8:4.

23 John Chrysostom (25.3–4 = *PG* 57.330–334) moves in this direction.

1.2 The Faith of the Centurion of Capernaum (8:5-13)

Literature

Chilton, *God in Strength*, 179–201.

Jacques Dupont, "Beaucoup viendront du levant et du couchant . . ." *ScEs* 19 (1967) 153–67.

Held, "Matthew," 193–97.

Paul Hoffmann, "Πάντες ἐργάται ἀδικίας: Redaktion und Tradition in Lc 13,22-30," *ZNW* 58 (1967) 188–214.

Jeremias, *Promise*, 55–60.

Kloppenborg, *Formation*, 117–21.

Marguerat, *Jugement*, 243–57.

Franz Schnider and Werner Stenger, *Johannes und die Synoptiker* (Biblische Handbibliothek 9; Munich: Kösel, 1971) 54–88.

Schulz, *Q*, 236–46.

Wegner, *Hauptmann*.

Zeller, "Das Logion Mt 8,11f/Lk 13,28f," *BZ* NF 15 (1971) 222–37; 16 (1972) 84–93.

For *additional literature* see above, II B on Matthew 8–9.

5 When he entered Capernaum, a centurion approached him, and asked him 6/ and said, "Lord, my son is lying at home lame, being horribly distressed." 7/ He says to him, "Shall I come and heal him?"[1] 8/ But the centurion answered and said, "Lord, I am not good enough to have you come under my roof; simply say it with a word, and my child will be healed. 9/ I also am a man under authority, and I have soldiers under me. I say to this one, 'Go!' and he goes, and to another, 'Come!' and he comes, and to my slave, 'Do this,' and he does it." 10/ But when Jesus heard that he marveled and said to those who were following him, "Amen, I tell you: I have not found such a great faith from anyone in Israel. But I say to you:

11 Many will come from east and west
 and will lie at the table with Abraham, Isaac
  and Jacob in the kingdom of heaven,

12 but the sons of the kingdom will be cast out into
  the outer darkness;
 there will be weeping and the gnashing of
  teeth there."

13 And Jesus said to the centurion, "Go, it will be for you even as you have believed." And the son was healed in that hour.

Analysis

Structure

Conversation dominates this most detailed of the miracle stories of the first section. For this reason it has often been described as a mixed form with the characteristics of an apophthegm and a miracle story. It is especially strange that in vv. 10-12 Jesus turns to the crowd that is following him and holds what amounts to a "discourse."[2] This is where the emphasis lies and the actual healing is secondary to it. The readers will note the catchword κύριε (occurring twice!) that reappears from the previous story. In the story itself the root πιστ- (vv. 10, 13) is especially important because it frames the decisive Jesus logion in vv. 11-12.

Sources

a. *Vv. 5-10, 13.* Verse 5a is reminiscent of Mark 2:1 that is going to be omitted later. Otherwise, the story comes from Q, where it appeared immediately after the Sermon on the Plain (Luke 7:1-10 after 6:20-49). In Q, along with a complex of material about the Baptist in Luke 7:18-35, it presumably belonged to a group of texts critical of Israel.[3] Only in the dialogue of vv. 8-10 = Luke 7:6b-9 is there a high number of verbal agreements.[4] Still, the dialogue makes sense only as part of a story that must have contained it from the beginning.[5] In Luke 7:2-6a the introduction is quite different. There the pious gentile centurion sends Jewish elders to Jesus as intermediaries. While Luke's text is highly redacted, Matthew presumably gives the Q text somewhat literally.[6] We may leave open here the question whether the Lukan introduc-

---

1 The short sentence is to be translated as a question. For one thing, it is only as a question that the ἐγώ makes sense in its emphatic position. For another, in the related story of 15:21-28 Jesus also rejects the request of the gentile woman.

2 Held, "Matthew," 196.

3 Kloppenborg, *Formation*, 119, 121.

4 Mattheisms are: ἀποκριθεὶς δέ, μόνον. Παρ᾽ οὐδενί (v. 10) is Matthean not for linguistic reasons but by virtue of its meaning. Cf. vol. 1, Introduction 3.2.

5 According to Manson (*Sayings*, 63), only the dialogue was in Q. However, the variant in John 4:46-54 also speaks against this view.

6 Mattheisms in vv. 5-7 are (cf. vol. 1, Introduction 3.2): προσέρχομαι, λέγων, κύριε, λέγει (historical present when Jesus speaks; cf. vol. 1, Introduction 3.1), perhaps βασανίζομαι, ἐλθών; in v. 13: ὑπάγω, πιστεύω, γενηθήτω, ὥρα ἐκείνη. For the analysis in detail cf. Wegner, *Hauptmann*, 91–276. On v. 13 cf. the similar formulations in 9:22; 15:28; 17:18 (also the healing of a child). The version in John 4:46-53 that is worded quite differently requires that we ask whether "that hour" (cf. John 4:52, 53) is part of the tradition. The Jewish healing from afar (*b. Ber.* 34b = Str-B 2.441) would support such a conclusion. In that case still another Matthean redactional term has been occasioned by the tradition.

tion 7:2-6a is due to a recension of Q (Q^Lk) or to Lukan redaction.[7] As a comparison with 15:28 shows, in v. 13 Matthew has worked quite independently.

b. *Vv. 11-12.* The most important Matthean change, however, is the insertion of the logion vv. 11-12, whose original position in Q is retained in Luke 13:28-29.[8] Matthew probably has taken over this logion from Q somewhat literally.[9] In my judgment the Matthean form, with its neat parallelism that contrasts with Luke 13:28-29 where the logion has been adapted to its context, is primary. Only τῶν οὐρανῶν ("of heaven") is clearly redactional. Luke shows that the typically Matthean formula about the weeping and the gnashing of teeth is traditional; thus Matthew found it in Q and has inserted it several times in his redaction (13:42, 50; 22:13; 24:51; 25:30). The same is probably true of τὸ σκότος τὸ ἐξώτερον ("the outer darkness") that is repeated in 22:13 and 25:30.[10] Everything speaks also for regarding υἱοὶ τῆς βασιλείας ("sons of the kingdom") as traditional, since in his context Luke has to change this saying to the second person. In 13:38 Matthew again uses the phrase redactionally. Perhaps the conservative Matthew has included three phrases from our saying in his list of preferred words. There can hardly be a clearer indication for the importance Matthew attaches to the saying!

Tradition History and Origin

a. *Verses 5-10, 13.* The Johannine recension of our story in John 4:46-53 is secondary and contributes nothing to the reconstruction of the history of the tradition. Like most healing narratives, this one may

have a historical kernel, especially since it appears to be a local tradition of Capernaum. However, as is the case with almost all such stories, here too it is impossible to say anything with certainty.

b. *Verses 11-12* form a judgment saying whose two parts neatly parallel one another. The emphasis is on the second part, the threat against the sons of the Kingdom, that is, against Israel. The logion takes up the traditional motifs of the Gentiles' eschatological pilgrimage to Zion[11] and of the eschatological banquet,[12] combines them, and uses them against Israel. The "shocking new element"[13] is that it uses against Israel the pilgrimage of the Gentiles of which the Old Testament-Jewish tradition as a rule spoke *ad majorem gloriam* of Israel. Now the "many" Gentiles will be accepted, but Israel will be excluded. Presumably the saying, much like that of John the Baptist in Matt 3:9-10, was a pointed threat rather than a prediction of something that is irrevocable.[14] It may well go back to Jesus.[15]

Interpretation

■ **5-6** As Jesus enters his hometown of Capernaum (4:13) he is accosted by a centurion, most likely a gentile commander of a company of a hundred men who was in the

---

7 Wegner (*Hauptmann,* 250–55) assumes that Matt 8:5-10, 13 = Q was further revised as special material prior to Luke.

8 Cf. vol. 1, II A 3.1 on 7:13-14.

9 The Q text of Matt 8:11-12 is a matter of controversy. Cf. Hoffmann, "Πάντες," 205–10; Chilton, *God in Strength,* 181–95.

10 The phrase might be traditional, since the Lukan ἐκβάλλω ἔξω is redactional. Cf. Luke 4:29; Acts 7:58; 9:40. With the catchword ἔξω Luke offers a connection to 13:25.

11 Zeller ("Logion," 222–37; 84–93) offers the best survey of the material. We have here not a direct Old Testament quote but a topos that is widespread in Jewish texts and could be used in various contexts.

12 Isa 25:6 is the basic passage. Cf. in addition *1 Enoch* 62.14; *2 Enoch* 42.3-14 Sokolov = Str–B 4.1138, n. 1; *m. ʾAbot* 3.17-18 (Akiba). For rabbinic sources see Str–B 4.1154–59.

13 Zeller, "Logion," 222–37; 84–93, 87.

14 Thus Sato ("Q," 138), who says that it also is uncertain whether originally all the people were addressed.

15 The conclusion is supported by the following: the parallels in Luke 14:16-24 and 11:31-32; the "inheritance" of John the Baptist (Matt 3:9-10!); the motif of the eschatological meal that is popular with Jesus; the Semitisms (with varying degrees of importance: parallelism; inclusive πολλοί = countless; υἱοὶ τῆς βασιλείας); and finally (only among others!) the criterion of dissimilarity. Chilton (*God in Strength,* 197–99) thinks that only v. 11 goes back to Jesus, while the pronouncement of judgment in v. 12 goes back only to Q. I see no real reasons, however, for a tradition history decomposition of the antithetical parallelism in vv. 11–12.

service of Herod Antipas.[16] He petitions Jesus on behalf of his son,[17] who is lying lame at home with what is clearly an acute and painful illness.[18]

■ **7** Jesus' answer, an astonished question, rejects the request, since as a Jew he cannot enter a Gentile's house.[19] Matthew is concerned to demonstrate that Jesus is faithful to the law.

■ **8-9** The gentile centurion affirms this concern by conceding that he is not good enough for the Lord to enter his house. He thereby expresses on the one hand his submission to the "Lord,"[20] while on the other hand accepting the reality that Jesus is a Jew and is sent to Israel. Still, he does not give up. For the second time he has called Jesus "Lord," that is, he has addressed him as a supplicant who expects everything from Jesus. "Simply say it with a word"[21] expresses the unlimited confidence in the authority of Jesus who can make sick people whole by means of his own word. It is not easy to interpret v. 9. We must proceed from the almost universally attested text $\upsilon\pi\grave{o}$ $\grave{\epsilon}\xi o\upsilon\sigma\acute{\iota}\alpha\nu$, not from a much easier reading, "with authority to command."[22] As far as the history of the tradition is concerned, the most attractive thesis is the assumption of a false Grecianizing of an Aramaic paratactic construction[23] in which the participle $\check{\epsilon}\chi\omega\nu$ would have corresponded to the main assertion, $\epsilon\grave{\iota}\mu\grave{\iota}$ $\upsilon\pi\grave{o}$ $\grave{\epsilon}\xi o\upsilon\sigma\acute{\iota}\alpha\nu$ ("I am under authority"), to a subordinate statement understood as concessive: Although I am only

a man in a subordinate position, I have soldiers under me whom I can command. This formulation corresponds precisely to that of a junior officer who, in contrast to the commander of a cohort,[24] has direct contact with the troops. On Matthew's level the text remains difficult. The idea may be implicit, but it certainly is not explicit: If even I, a minor officer, can give commands, how much more can you!

■ **10** The centurion's answer amazes Jesus. He turns to the crowd that since 8:1 has been following him, and he makes a short speech. Not in a single person in Israel has Jesus found such faith as this Gentile has. "Faith" means the unconditional confidence in Jesus' power to help—a confidence that refuses to be turned away. As is always the case in synoptic texts, here also Jesus is the one who characterizes a person's conduct as "faith." It is an exception when petitioners speak of their own faith. The sharp word is designed to prepare for vv. 11-12. The comment to the crowd that "follows" makes clear that the evangelist here consciously leaves the surface of the narrative and speaks on his deeper level. To this point Jesus has met few people; he has not yet had a single negative experience in Israel, yet v. 10 already assumes that Jesus' experience with Israel is going to be negative. The Matthean church knows that this is true both from the totality of the Jesus story and from its own experi-

---

16 Herod Antipas has his own troops (Josephus *Ant.* 18.113–14). Capernaum is a border town. On the organization of the Roman army, cf. T. R. S. Broughton in F. J. Foakes-Jackson and Kirsopp Lake, *The Beginnings of Christianity* (5 vols.; London: Macmillan, 1920–33) 5.427–29. A *centuria* that the centurion commands consists of one hundred men, the cohort ($\sigma\pi\epsilon\hat{\iota}\rho\alpha$) of six hundred men.

17 $\Pi\alpha\hat{\iota}\varsigma$ here means "son" and not "servant," a conclusion that eliminates the older interpretations that saw in our story an expression of solidarity between masters and servants. Reasons: (1) In v. 9 Matthew uses $\delta o\hat{\upsilon}\lambda o\varsigma$ for "slave"; (2) previously Matthew has used $\pi\alpha\hat{\iota}\varsigma$ with the meaning "child" (2:16); (3) in the related story of 17:14-21 $\pi\alpha\hat{\iota}\varsigma$ clearly means "son" (17:15, 18). Cf. also below, III A 1.3 on 12:18.

18 The narrator is not interested in medical precision; only in the severity of the case (cf. Luke 7:2; John 4:47). John 4:52 speaks of fever.

19 Cf. Acts 10:28; *m. ʾOhol.* 18.7 = Str-B 2.838.

20 This thought is very important for the ancient

church's interpretation. Cf. John Chrysostom (26.4 = *PG* 57.337), who understands $\check{\alpha}\nu\theta\rho\omega\pi o\varsigma$ in v. 9 to mean: "You are God, I am a human being."

21 $\Lambda\acute{o}\gamma\omega$ = *dativus instrumentalis*. The formulation is unusual both in Semitic and in Greek usage, and it places the emphasis on $\lambda\acute{o}\gamma o\varsigma$. (Cf., e.g., Phalaris *Ep.* 121.1 in Rudolf Hercher, ed., *Epistolographi Graeci* [Paris: Didot, 1873] 444.)

22 Thus sy^s according to Adalbert Merx, *Die vier kanonischen Evangelien nach ihrem ältesten bekannten Text*, vol. 2/1: *Erläuterungen. Das Evangelium Matthäus* (Berlin: Reimer, 1902) 136–37.

23 Wellhausen, 36; Beyer, 278; Jeremias, *Promise*, 30, n. 4.

24 Sy^s offers $\chi\iota\lambda\iota\acute{\alpha}\rho\chi\eta\varsigma$ as a variant reading in vv. 8 and 13. For this reason, if for no other, the reading in n. 22 above is secondary.

25 We find much the same phenomenon in 13:10-15 and 17:17. Cf. below, III B 2.1 on 13:10-12 and IV A 3.

26 The church's interpretation of this verse has been

10

ence in Israel. Thus vv. 10-12 have the character of a "signal" of what is to come.[25]

■ **11-12** The general logion in vv. 11-12 that is not related to the concrete situation anticipates what is to come. Its character as a signal is derived from the fact that overtones from these verses will be heard repeatedly throughout the entire gospel. Matthew has experienced both Israel's no to Jesus and the destruction of Jerusalem. He has seen many Gentiles turning to Jesus, and he challenges his own church to become involved in the gentile mission. The threatening word is for him also a prediction that exactly describes his own situation. The Gentiles from east and west will turn to the God of Israel. They will recline at the table with the patriarchs of Israel in the kingdom of God. The sons of the kingdom, however, will lose the "Kingdom" (cf. 21:43).[26] Darkness is their fate.[27] "Outer" expresses figuratively the exclusion from the banquet hall (cf. 22:13) and literally the infinite distance from the kingdom of God. "Weeping and gnashing of teeth" is the expression of horrible pain.[28] Matthew imagines the terror of hell to be very real, even if he does not elaborate on it conceptually.[29]

■ **13** With the concluding verse Jesus turns his attention back to the centurion. His faith has not been forgotten. Γενηθήτω is reminiscent of the Lord's Prayer (Matt 6:10) and shows how much for Matthew faith is the faith of prayer. Only now does Jesus grant the believing centurion his request. The statement is brief and to the point: In the same hour the child was healed.

Summary

Our story is multidimensional. Initially it is the story of a miracle. It is important for Matthew that it actually happened,[30] for it demonstrates the sovereignty of the Lord at whose mere word the boy immediately becomes well. Secondly, the miracle happens to a Gentile, but it does so in a section of the narrative that speaks of the miracles of Jesus in Israel. It is important for the evangelist that precisely this Gentile respects the law and Israel's priority in the history of salvation (cf. 15:21-28). However, this merely serves as the background for the "signal" in vv. 10-12. From the point of view of the community that is familiar with the end of the story of Jesus and that knows about the coming gentile mission, the centurion becomes the first member of the gentile church.[31] Jesus' prediction awakens the suspicion that later the Gentiles will come to the God of Israel, while Israel will remain on the outside.[32] At this point in the story our verses are an initial flash of lightning; salvation for the Gentiles will come only at the end of Jesus' activity on behalf of Israel. The evangelist will later explain how this happened. For the time being he moves on from his flash of lightning and returns to his theme, viz.,

surprisingly reserved, with the main interest by and large on vv. 7-9. One finds frequent references to Romans 11 such as that, e.g., by Musculus (196), who says that not all Jews are rejected.

27 "Darkness" is a frequent attribute of Sheol and of Gehenna. Cf. Str–B 4.1076–78; Gnilka, 1. 304.

28 We conclude this for κλαυθμός on the basis of 13:42, 50 (fire); 24:51 (cutting the servant into pieces); *1 Enoch* 108.3, 5 (crying/screaming from pain); *2 Enoch* 40.12 (weeping/complaining). One can gnash one's teeth on different occasions, but in the context it is to be interpreted as with κλαυθμός. Thus there is no need to think of hell's coldness (teeth chattering as when one shivers), of the rage of the condemned when they see the redeemed (cf. Luke 13:25-28; *4 Ezra* 7.83; *Midr. Qoh.* 1.15 = Str–B 4.1040), or of the "despairing remorse" of the condemned (Karl Heinrich Rengstorf, "βρύχω κτλ," *TDNT* 1 [1964] 642).

29 To a degree this has happened in the history of interpretation. The cold of hell (cf. n. 28) often was based on 24:19 (weeping from the heat, gnashing of teeth from the cold). The difficulty of combining the idea of fire with the "darkness outside" led to the idea of dark fire in, e.g., Maldonat, 178. Seldom has the expression been interpreted metaphorically, for the "weeping and gnashing and teeth" was useful as a proof text for the bodily resurrection (as, e.g., Jerome uses it).

30 It is thus not the case that our story is a historical-theological "parable" that Matthew uses to solve a "basic theological problem" (contra Frankemölle, *Jahwebund*, 113).

31 Thomas Aquinas, *Lectura* no. 694: *Centurio . . . praesidens ad salutem gentium.* He is the "Gentile Christians' ancestor in faith" (Franz Schnider and Werner Stenger, *Johannes und die Synoptiker* [Biblische Handbibliothek 9; Munich: Kösel, 1971] 76).

32 John the Baptist had already thus threatened that from stones God will raise up children *to Abraham* (3:9).

the miracles that Jesus performed in Israel. In that context the centurion of Capernaum is a marginal figure with a future perspective. However, this perspective is important for the readers in Matthew's church, for in the story of Jesus they recognize their own way. It is a way that, after Easter, leads them into conflict with Israel, out of Israel into the gentile world, and then in that world to the proclamation of the gospel to Gentiles.[33] At the same time, our story is significant for the church in yet in another direct way. It emphasizes the faith of the centurion and gives the readers courage in their own faith. The centurion becomes for them a figure with whom they can identify. The church's interpretation has always correctly understood it this way when the centurion became either the type of true humility[34] or a model of faith.[35] The story thus becomes transparent for the readers' own experience. The granting of the centurion's request becomes the promise to the church that lives by virtue of its Lord's support (28:20).

33   Cf. vol. 1, I 5.2.
34   See, e.g., John Chrysostom, 26.4 = *PG* 57.338; Jerome, 49; Walafrid Strabo, *Glossa Ordinaria* (*PL* 114.63–178) 113.

35   See, e.g., John Chrysostom, 26.2–3 = *PG* 57.335–36; Luther, *WA* 38, 467 (faith of a Gentile who is unworthy—as we are); Calvin 1.250–51.

1.3 Jesus Heals Peter's Mother-in-Law and Many Sick People (8:14-17)

Literature

Fuchs, "Studie," 21–76.

Held, "Matthew," 169–72.

Paul Lamarche, "La guérison de la belle-mère de Pierre et le genre littéraire des évangiles," *NRTh* 87 (1965) 515–26.

Xavier Léon-Dufour, "La guérison de la belle-mère de Simon-Pierre," in idem, *Études,* 125–48.

For *additional literature* see above, II B on Matthew 8–9.

14 When Jesus came into Peter's house, he saw his mother-in-law lying there with a fever. 15/ And he touched her hand, and the fever left her, and she got up and served him.

16 When it had gotten late they brought to him many who were demon-possessed, and he cast out the spirits with a word and healed all the sick,

17 so that what was said through the prophet Isaiah was fulfilled:
"He has taken away our weaknesses and carried away the diseases."

Analysis

Structure

The text consists of three parts: the healing of Peter's mother-in-law (vv. 14-15), the summary (v. 16), and the formula quotation (v. 17). The report of the healing is constructed in chiastic form around "he touched her hand." In the context the catchwords βέβλημαι and λόγῳ refer back to 8:5-13, the catchword ἅπτομαι with χείρ to 8:1-4. Προσήνεγκαν, δαιμονιζόμενοι, πάντας τοὺς κακῶς ἔχοντας, and ἐθεράπευσεν allude to 4:24, νόσος from the quotation in v. 17 to 4:23, the title verses of our pericope.

Source

The source is Mark 1:29-34. The most important characteristic of Matthew's treatment of his source is the

way he abbreviates it.[1] With the omission of several details the text becomes clearer and more transparent.[2] In spite of a few agreements with Luke, the text of Mark available to Matthew probably was not different from the one handed down to us.[3] Nowhere has the formula quotation from Isa 53:4 influenced the wording of the rest of the text; there is thus no indication that it might have been connected with the Markan text prior to Matthew.

The Formula Quotation

The *formula quotation* comes from Isa 53:4 and in its wording corresponds most closely to the Hebrew text. Among the Greek translations it has a certain affinity to Aquila. We do not have here a translation from the Hebrew by the evangelist himself;[4] the only word that fits exactly into the Matthean context, νόσος ("disease"), is found also in Aquila; in the rest of the quotation the language is hardly Matthean.[5] It most likely comes from a pre-Matthean collection or a redaction of Mark 1:32-34.[6]

Interpretation

■ **14-15** By tightening up the little story Matthew makes of it a pure Jesus story. The disciples disappear. No more requests are made of Jesus. He sees the sick woman, takes the initiative on his own, and heals her. After the healing, she serves only him. All biographical or novelistic interest is missing, even here where Peter's family is involved. The only thing that matters is Jesus' deed.

Of course, it was unavoidable that at least the history of interpretation would be interested in the more immediate circumstances, such as the location of Peter's house, the fact that as an apostle he obviously still owned a house, or his family relationships. From

---

1 Omitted are: Mark 1:29a (the connection with Mark 1:21-28 is superfluous); the names of the three disciples (the story of the call in 4:18-22 has long since happened in Matthew); the question to Jesus in Mark 1:30b; the redundant information about time and persons in Mark 1:32; the reference to the public in Mark 1:33; the command to the demons to be silent in Mark 1:34c. (After Matthew omitted the story of Mark 1:21-28, a command to silence would hardly have made sense, and it would have made difficult a smooth transition to the formula quotation.)

2 Mark's frequent changes of subject are reduced in vv. 14-15. In v. 16 the same weight is now placed quantitatively on the exorcistic and healing activity of Jesus that is reported with two verbs in v. 16b, c.

3 Contra Fuchs, "Studie." Ennulat (*Agreements,* 45, 47)

leaves the question open. It seems to me that only the omission of Mark 1:33 justifies the question whether Matthew and Luke had a different recension of Mark. However, independently of each other they also may have omitted this additional and unnecessary Markan comment.

4 Thus Rothfuchs, *Erfüllungszitate,* 71.

5 Ἀσθένεια is a *hapax legomenon* and quite unusual as a translation for חֳלִי. Βαστάζω (cf. Aquila Isa 53:11) appears two other times in the tradition.

6 Cf. vol. 1, I A 2.2: Excursus on the Formula Quotations: 3 "Wording and Origin of the Quotations."

the many questions discussed here, one from Bullinger is worth noting: "We see here that a married man was called by Christ as an apostle . . . Jerome concedes that all apostles were married except for John. Why then is it that the Roman popes took away the wives from the bishops and the other servants of the church?"[7] The question is supported with a reference to 1 Corinthians 9. As far as I have been able to see, at the time it was never taken up and answered by Catholic exegesis, although the traditions of the ancient church about Peter's wife and daughter[8] were frequently cited in the commentaries. The question still awaits an answer.[9]

■ **16** The summary that follows has a threefold function. For one thing, it makes clear to the reader that the miracle stories that have been told are only three examples of many healings that took place. It is for this reason that the evangelist here takes up once again the formulations of 4:23-24. For another, he is concerned to portray the absolute authority of Jesus. That is why Jesus here, in contrast to Mark's text, heals all the sick, and heals them, as he has already done in vv. 8 and 13, with his sovereign word. Finally, in this way Matthew can prepare for the formula quotation of v. 17.

■ **17** The formula quotation has often been overinterpreted. Given the context that speaks of the sovereign authority of Jesus the healer, ἔλαβεν and ἐβάστασεν can only mean "to take away" and "to carry away."[10] Αὐτός ("He") emphasizes Jesus' sovereign authority. The quotation thus shows how Jesus as Israel's Messiah heals with full authority among his people. It is important for Matthew that this corresponds to the plan of God predicted by the prophet. In this way the Isaiah quotation becomes a kind of interpretive word of the story of Jesus, much as 9:13 later does. There is, therefore, in the Matthean context no talk of the suffering of the servant of God. The quotation itself corresponds to the context in this regard. In contrast to 12:18-21, the word παῖς θεοῦ ("servant of God") does not appear here. Precisely that part of Isa 53:3-5 is used here that does not speak of the suffering of God's servant. Our quotation is an example of the way early Christian exegesis, like the Jewish exegesis of the time, sometimes quotes individual words of scripture without any regard for their context.

History of Interpretation

That this traditional exegetical practice often creates difficulties for exegesis today is connected with the classical, dogmatic interpretation of our quotation. For the exegesis of the ancient church, because of Isa 53:5 it was important that Christ took sins on himself.[11] The exegesis influenced by the Reformation liked to base its interpretation on the death on the cross: "God lets himself be driven out of the world onto the cross. He is powerless and weak in the world. . . . Mt. 8:17 makes it quite clear that Christ helps us, not by virtue of his omnipotence but by virtue of his weakness."[12] What Matthew actually says is closer to the opposite of this statement. Such interpretations subordinate the text to their own authority. At the same time, however, they do incorporate the individual text into the totality of Christian faith. They are legitimate if, and only if, the interpreters know that they—on their own theological responsibility and on the basis of their own understanding of faith—are making something new out of the text.

---

7   Bullinger, 200.

8   Clement of Alexandria *Strom.* 3.52-53; 7.63-64; Eusebius *Hist. eccl.* 3.30.

9   Schnackenburg, marginal note: "Why do Protestant theologians speak so little about the unmarried Paul?"

10   Held, "Matthew," 260-62. On λαμβάνω cf. 5:40; 15:26.

11   See, e.g., Chromatius of Aquileia, *Tractatus in*

Matthaeum 40.4 = 2.40 (CChr.SL 9A; Turnholti: Brepols, 1974). Zwingli (252) solves the problem by saying that Matthew is speaking of the lesser, but includes the greater in order to show that Christ is the physician of the soul *and* the body.

12   Dietrich Bonhoeffer, Letter of 16 July 1944, in Eberhard Bethge, ed., *Letters and Papers from Prison* (New York: Macmillan, 1971) 360.

The second section is held together with a geographical bracket. Jesus leaves his city of Capernaum to cross over to the other shore ($\pi\acute{\epsilon}\rho\alpha\nu$ 8:18), gets into the boat ($\dot{\epsilon}\mu\beta\alpha\acute{\iota}\nu\omega$ $\epsilon\dot{\iota}\varsigma$ $\tau\grave{o}$ $\pi\lambda o\hat{\iota}o\nu$, 8:23), and in 9:1a returns ($\dot{\epsilon}\mu\beta\alpha\acute{\iota}\nu\omega$ $\epsilon\dot{\iota}\varsigma$ $\pi\lambda o\hat{\iota}o\nu$, $\delta\iota\alpha\pi\epsilon\rho\acute{\alpha}\zeta\omega$). This geographical bracket contains two quite different pericopes, viz., the discipleship story (8:18-27) and the first of two miracle stories (8:28–9:1), that are followed in turn by another discipleship story (9:9-13). The external geographical structure and the internal structure, the succession of miracle stories and discipleship stories, overlay each other.

2.1 Following Jesus into the Storm (8:18-27)

Literature

Günther Bornkamm, "The Stilling of the Storm in the Gospel of Matthew," in Bornkamm–Barth–Held, *Tradition and Interpretation*, 52–57.

Maurice Casey, "The Jackals and the Son of Man," *JSNT* 12 (1985) 3–22.

Geist, *Menschensohn*, 251–56.

Kurt Goldammer, "Navis Ecclesiae," *ZNW* 40 (1941) 76–86.

Held, "Matthew," 200–204.

Hengel, *Leader*.

Earle Hilgert, *The Ship and Related Symbols in the New Testament* (Assen: Royal Vangorcum, 1962).

B. M. F. van Iersel and A. J. M. Linmans, "The Storm on the Lake," in Tjitze Baarda, A. F. J. Klijn, and W. C. van Unnik, eds., *Miscellanea Neotestamentica* (NovTSup 48; Leiden: Brill, 1978) 2.17–48.

Kahlmeyer, *Seesturm*.

Jack Dean Kingsbury, "On Following Jesus: The 'Eager' Scribe and the 'Reluctant' Disciple (Matthew 8:18-22)," *NTS* 34 (1988) 45–59.

Hans Günther Klemm, "Das Wort von der Selbstbestattung der Toten," *NTS* 16 (1969–70) 60–75.

Reinhard Kratz, *Auferweckung als Befreiung* (SBS 65; Stuttgart: Katholisches Bibelwerk, 1973) 37–56.

Xavier Léon-Dufour, "La tempête apaisée," in idem, *Études*, 153–82.

Schulz, *Q*, 434–42.

Schwarz, *Jesus sprach*, 91–97.

For *additional literature* see above, II B on Matthew 8–9.

18 But when Jesus saw a crowd around him, he commanded them to go over to the other shore. 19/ Then someone, a scribe, came up and said to him, "Master, I will follow you wherever you go." 20/ And Jesus says to him:
"The foxes have caves,
and the birds of the heaven have nests,
but the Son of Man does not have
anywhere to lay his head."
21 But another, one of the disciples, said to him, "Lord, allow me first to go away and to bury my father." 22/ But Jesus says to him, "Follow me, and let the dead bury their dead."
23 And when he got into the boat, his disciples followed him.
24 And behold, there was a great storm on the sea, so that the boat was swamped by the waves;
but he slept. 25/ Then they came to him, awakened him,
and said, "Lord, save! We are sinking!"
26 And he says to them, "How fearful you are,
you of little faith!"
Then he stood up and rebuked the winds and the sea.
And there was a great calm.
27 But the people were astonished and they said, "What kind of person is this that the winds and the sea obey him?"

Analysis

Structure

The pericope is a unit, defined by the catchwords "to go over/away" ($\dot{\alpha}\pi\acute{\epsilon}\rho\chi o\mu\alpha\iota$, vv. 18-19, 21), "to follow" ($\dot{\alpha}\kappa o\lambda o\upsilon\vartheta\acute{\epsilon}\omega$, vv. 19, 22-23), and "disciple" ($\mu\alpha\vartheta\eta\tau\acute{\eta}\varsigma$, vv. 21, 23). Jesus gives in v. 18 the order for the crossing that begins in v. 23 and is completed in v. 28a. Verses 19-22 come between the command of Jesus and its execution. The narrative of the stilling of the storm, vv. 23-27, is structured chiastically as a ring composition.[1] In the middle are the words of the disciples in v. 25b and of Jesus in v. 26a. Thus the great turning point takes place with v. 26. The words of the disciples and of Jesus, Jesus' "sleeping" and "rising," the "great storm" and the "great calm" all parallel each other antithetically. That the disciples follow in v. 23 is contrasted at the end in v. 27 with the reaction of the people. With its reference to the "people" ($\dot{\alpha}\nu\vartheta\rho\omega\pi o\iota$) this verse leaves the narrative's surface level, since Jesus has already left the people; only the disciples are with him. The pericope contains two

---

1 Cf. the graphic arrangement of the translation and Ennulat, *Agreements*, 141. Birger Gerhardsson (*The Mighty Acts of Jesus According to Matthew* [SMHVL 5; Lund: Gleerup, 1979] 53) counts eighty-three

syllables both in vv. 23-25 and in 26-27. The two main sections, vv. 18-22 and 23-27, also are of almost exactly equal length.

references back to 6:25-34 (τὰ πετεινὰ τοῦ οὐρανοῦ, ὀλιγόπιστος). Matt 14:22-33 has so many catchwords in common with vv. 23-27 that the second stilling of the storm will deepen and continue our story.[2]

Sources

The Markan story of the stilling of the storm in Mark 4:35-41 serves as the framework into which are inserted the two discipleship apophthegms from Q, Luke 9:57-60 = Matt 8:19-22. Combining pericopes this way is unusual for Matthew. Matthew has created v. 18 so that Jesus will be at the center of attention.[3] On the whole, vv. 19-22 agree with Luke 9:57-60. We cannot be certain of all the details in our reconstruction of Q. I think it is likely that εἷς γραμματεύς was already in Q.[4] In vv. 21-22 Matthew probably preserved the original position of ἀκολούθει μοι.[5] Since he could not use the command "but go and proclaim the kingdom of God" (Luke 9:60b) before they had all gotten into the boat, presumably he omitted it. Προσῆλθον (v. 19), the clarification τῶν μαθητῶν (v. 21),[6] and perhaps the two examples of personal address, διδάσκαλε (v. 19) and κύριε (v. 21), all come

from Matthew's hand.[7] The third discipleship episode, reported in Luke vv. 61-62, probably was not yet in Q.[8]

Verses 23-27 are a redactional reworking of Mark 4:36-41. Usually, but not always, the "minor agreements" with Luke 8:22-25 can be explained as the language of the two evangelists. They are unusually numerous. Did the two evangelists have a different edition of Mark?[9] In comparison with Mark, the Matthean version is more concise. Details that are not absolutely necessary are omitted; awkward formulations are avoided (cf. Matthew v. 23a with Mark 4:36a; Matthew v. 24b with Mark 4:37b, c; Matthew v. 26b with Mark 4:39). Mark's awkwardly situated v. 40 is located better in Matt 8:26a, where it constitutes the center of vv. 23-27. All the more striking in this polished, concise narrative is the concluding v. 27 with the ἄνθρωποι ("the people").[10]

Origin

The second discipleship apophthegm, vv. 21-22, may as a unit go back to an event in the life of Jesus. It is radical to the point of disrespect, and it does not con-

---

2   Ἐμβαίνω εἰς τὸ πλοῖον, εἰς τὸ πέραν, ὄχλος, κύματα, θάλασσα, κελεύω, κύριε σῶσον, ὀλιγόπιστος, ἄνεμος.

3   Ἐκέλευσεν! The participle ἰδών at the beginning (cf. vol. 1, Introduction 3.2) usually serves in Matthew to give the reason for an action.

4   That a (Jewish!) scribe wants to follow Jesus does not fit well in Matthew's concept. Cf. on 3:7; 5:20 and Matt 22:34-40. Mark 12:28-34 is different. Εἷς with the sense of an indefinite pronoun can be Matthean (9:18; 21:19; 26:69; 18:24?).

5   Luke puts the imperative first for two reasons: (1) because this order corresponds to the "discipleship story" genre, and (2) because the questioner would not even have made his request had there not been talk of a call. The Matthean sequence is *lectio difficilior*.

6   Cf. vol. 1, Introduction 3.2. By adding precision with τῶν μαθητῶν, Matthew explains why the questioner asks for permission: He was already a disciple and therefore does not first have to be called. In addition, an important connection to v. 23 is established.

7   Κύριος is the "leading word" of chap. 8, and it especially forms a connection with v. 25. For διδάσκαλος as a form of address from outsiders: 12:38, cf. 9:11; 17:24; in the tradition also 19:16; 22:16, 24, 36.

8   For the basis for this conclusion see Gnilka, 1.310, n. 3.

9   Προσελθόντες, λέγοντες and οἱ μαθηταὶ αὐτοῦ

may *also* (less clearly) be Lukan redaction, also δέ (v. 17/Luke v. 25) and the substitution of the historical present (v. 25/Luke v. 24). Ἐμβαίνω εἰς πλοῖον may come from Mark 4:1 for both evangelists. The omission of Mark 4:36a (a very awkward formulation!), of the "other boats" in Mark 4:36b (not necessary for the narrative), of γεμίζεσθαι τὸ πλοῖον in Mark 4:37c, of the "cushion" in Mark 4:38a (superfluous details), and of σιώπα and πεφίμωσο in Mark 4:39b (not an exorcism) are understandable, as is the plural ὑπακούουσιν in v. 27/Luke v. 25. Θάλασσα (v. 24) and λίμνη (Luke v. 23) correspond to a redactional formulation. Θαυμάζω may also be Matthean and Lukan redaction. Redaction is not evident in the omission of οὐ μέλει σοι (Mark 4:38c) and ἐκόπασεν ὁ ἄνεμος (Matt 14:32! Elsewhere Matthew emphasizes the literal agreements with 14:22-33). In addition, the plural ἄνεμοι in v. 27/Luke v. 25 is strange (does not correspond to Lukan redaction).

10   In addition to the terms mentioned in nn. 2, 3, 7, 9, Matthean are: ἀκολουθέω, μαθητής, ἰδού, σεισμός, σῴζω, ἄνθρωπος (cf. vol. 1, Introduction 3.2); the historical present with λέγει is Matthean (vol. 1, Introduction 3.1). Ὄχλον περὶ αὐτοῦ could come from Mark 3:32, but cf. Mark 4:36.

11   Cf. Carsten Colpe, "ὁ υἱὸς τοῦ ἀνθρώπου," *TDNT* 8 (1972) 403-4: Aram. בַּר אֱנָשׁ can only mean "I" when "a generic meaning . . . was apparent," thus, e.g., "I as a human being." The meaning then would be: The foxes and birds have a place to live, but I,

tain a general instruction that could have arisen after Easter as a rule of the church. By contrast, the logion in v. 20 can be separated from the first discipleship apophthegm. Whether it originated with Jesus is a question that depends on the Son of Man title. In my opinion, the saying may very well go back to Jesus, but it cannot be determined with certainty in which sense. We do not have to understand the word as a title. Jesus may simply be making a rhetorical point by referring to himself as a human being in contrast to the foxes and birds.[11] But if, as I think, he believed himself to be the coming Son of Man who is to judge the world, he may use the reference to intensify the contrast. Even the foxes and birds have what the coming world judge–Son of Man does not have.[12] In either case the saying does not speak of a presently active Son of Man who in fact or merely semantically must be distinguished from the future judge of the world. The *story of the stilling of the storm* is a post-Easter creation that was told in the colors of the Jonah story and that announces that Jesus is more than Jonah; he is for the church a protecting and saving deity.[13] Even prior to Mark it probably contained both a christological and a lesser soteriological-ecclesiological dimension.

Interpretation

■ **18** Jesus gives the order to leave for the other shore. To whom is his command directed? Is it principally directed to everybody, so that in the following verses two examples of reactions to Jesus are portrayed?[14] In that case our verses would indicate how a circle of disciples emerges from the people. Since, however, Matthew presupposes the existence of disciples beginning with 4:18-22 and 5:1,[15] he probably means what Mark means: Jesus and his disciples go away from the people.

■ **19-20** Before they leave, a scribe comes to Jesus and offers to follow him. The address, "teacher" ($\delta\iota\delta\acute{\alpha}\sigma\kappa\alpha\lambda\epsilon$), makes clear that he is not a disciple.[16] By means of a sharp paradox Jesus points out the difficulty of discipleship. The coming judge of the world, the Son of Man, does not even have on earth what the foxes and the birds of the heavens take for granted. Although Matthew seems to be familiar with a tradition about Jesus' permanent residence (4:12-13), he will describe Jesus as constantly on the move. The term $\acute{o}\,\upsilon\grave{\iota}\grave{o}\varsigma\,\tau o\hat{\upsilon}\,\grave{\alpha}\nu\vartheta\rho\acute{\omega}\pi o\upsilon$ appears here for the first time. Matthew uses it in a public statement of Jesus. Did the crowds that were listening understand it? It is not a Greek expression; as a translation of the Aramaic בַּר נָשׁ the doubled determinative Greek expression is unusual. There was in contemporary Judaism no general, widespread expectation of "the" coming Son of Man. It is probable only that Dan 7:13-14, where someone "like a son of man" is mentioned, was interpreted messianically in certain Jewish circles (cf. *1 Enoch* 70–71; 37–69); there it was expected that at the eschaton a "son of man" would come with the clouds of heavens. Be that as it may, for the crowds that were listening this expression was either linguistically strange and secretive, or it was nonsense, since Jesus obviously used the term to refer to himself. For Matthew's Christian readers, however, this expression was filled with everything that they already knew from the Christian tradition about Jesus' suffering, dying, rising, and especially about his coming as judge. Thus for the Christian readers this word of Jesus expressed a paradox, viz., that the one who is risen and who will come as

---

11 although I am a human being, have none . . .

12 Looking for an explanation of the logion by making a detour through Wisdom's homelessness (*1 Enoch* 42 and others!) as Gnilka does (1.311–12) is unnecessary. The logion speaks of the homelessness of Jesus, and the expression "Son of Man" (whether understood as a title or not) rhetorically intensifies its scandal. Its sharp edge should not be dulled by explaining it against the background of a given worldview.

13 Pesch, *Markusevangelium* 1.276.

14 William G. Thompson, "Reflections on the Composition of Mt 8:1–9:34," CBQ (1971) 365–88; 372.

15 In 8:1-17 Matthew has put Jesus in the center of the narrative and for this reason has never mentioned the disciples.

16 Jerome already noticed this in commenting on 8:21. Cf. correctly Jack Dean Kingsbury, "On Following Jesus: The 'Eager' Scribe and the 'Reluctant' Disciple (Matthew 8:18-22)," *NTS* 34 (1988) 45–59, 48–49: A Jewish scribe asks to be a pupil of Jesus according to Jewish custom but is taught by Jesus that something quite different is involved in discipleship.

the judge of the world had to live in absolute poverty and homelessness. Of course, the disciples in the Matthean story are not yet aware of this, but Jesus will repeatedly instruct them and lead them into the mystery of the fate of the Son of Man. In the final analysis, however, the crowds will not understand it.[17]

The point of the saying is thus the homelessness and absolute poverty of Jesus, who someday will judge the world. The immediate departure of Jesus, the repeated use of ἀπέρχομαι, and Jesus' expulsion from the land of the Gadarenes (8:34) show that Matthew understands Jesus to be literally homeless. Is that why even the cushion on which Jesus lays his head in the boat is missing (cf. Mark 4:38)? Jesus' poverty is also to be understood literally. The reader remembers 6:25-34,[18] where the issue was God's wonderful care for the poverty-stricken followers of Jesus.

History of Interpretation

The history of interpretation is worth considering, because it suppresses precisely this point. While it is strongly emphasized that the scribe was a "slave of money" and had unworthy intentions,[19] hardly anyone is aware anymore that discipleship is basically characterized by the demand of poverty.[20] The title "Son of Man" made it possible to put Jesus' poverty in a larger context and to claim that the Son of God Jesus has become a true human (= son of man) who demonstrates by his poverty that his kingdom is not

of this world.[21] However, the christological concentration also made it easier to avoid the real poverty. Protestant interpreters who have to offer a defense against the actual poverty of Catholic monks often emphasize that it is not the possession of houses, etc., that is contrary to the gospel but only one's attachment to them.[22] The interpretation that sees in the homeless Son of Man the "restlessly active one," who has "only work without rest," especially misses the mark.[23] So we have a stressed-out Jesus! Such observations should give us pause, because they are an indication of those areas where today we need to recapture the strangeness of Jesus.[24]

■ **21-22** The second person who meets Jesus before he leaves is a disciple who as such addresses Jesus as "Lord" (κύριος). His request is understandable. Before the departure he would like to bury his deceased father and thereby fulfill a pious duty that is of supreme importance in both Judaism[25] and Hellenism.[26] Measured by this yardstick, Jesus' answer can only have been absolutely shocking.[27] He formulates an oxymoron: "Let the dead make arrangements among themselves to bury themselves";[28] that is none of your business now! The word is scandalous,[29] especially when there is a death in the family, and we must not rush in too quickly to obscure its offensiveness. Augustine's beautiful line, *Amandus est generator, sed praeponendus est Creator* ("One should love the begetter but prefer the creator") can

---

17 Cf. below, the excursus at 16:21-28.

18 Τὰ πετεινὰ τοῦ οὐρανοῦ (6:26).

19 John Chrysostom, 27.2 = *PG* 57.346. Numerous comparisons have been made with Simon Magus.

20 *Liber Graduum* (Mihaly Kmosko, ed. [Patrologia Syriaca 1/3; Paris: Firmin-Didot et socii, 1926] 15.13 = 367) applies it to the celibate *perfecti*. With tortured arguments Lapide (197) defends the poverty of just some *religiosi* (the Franciscans) against Waldensians, Wycliffites, etc.

21 See, e.g., Bullinger, 84A. Cf. Luther, *WA* 38.469.

22 Martin Bucer (*Enarrationes perpetuae in Sacra quatuor Evangelia* [Argentorati: Heruagium, 1530] 91) says that houses are a gift of God; important is that one maintain the attitude of 1 Corinthians 7. W. Musculus (204) says the attachment of hearts to earthly riches is evil. Johannes Brenz (*In scriptum . . . Matthaei de rebus gestis . . . Jesu Christi commentarius* [Tübingen: Mohard, 1566] 386) recommends no dependence on earthly goods.

23 Reported by Schlatter, 286–87.

24 The examples from the history of interpretation show how the misinterpretation of Jesus would have to be turned around. J. Pöschl (in Anton Grabner-Haider, *Jesus N. Biblische Verfremdungen: Experimente jüngerer Schriftsteller* [Zurich: Benziger, 1972] 81–84) offers a good example of a misinterpretation of Matt 8:20: Jesus as an outsider, hitchhiker, shirking work.

25 For the sources see Str-B 1.487–89. In contemporary Judaism the OT commands were intensified. Burying one's relatives takes precedence over all Torah commandments (*m. Ber.* 3.1); the uncleanness of cadavers is restricted (Hengel, *Leader*, 9).

26 Hengel, *Leader*, 10; Wettstein, 1.352.

27 This is clear from the comparison with the call of Elisha, whom Elijah permits to take leave of father and mother (1 Kgs 19:20-21).

28 Carl Friedrich August Fritzsche, *Evangelium Matthaei* (Leipzig: Fleischer, 1826), 323.

29 "The ethical concept of filial piety was changed by Christ. His Church was a militant church. He had

only be spoken by someone who has a sense of what it means![30] Jesus, who also speaks positively about the commandment to honor one's parents (Mark 7:9-13), speaks here about making a break with the family for the sake of the kingdom of God—something that obviously he himself has done (Mark 3:31-35!), that he required of his followers (Luke 14:26), and that the post-Easter church repeatedly experienced (Mark 10:28-30; Matt 10:34-36). Such demands are scarcely reconcilable with the love commandment. They express the deep opposition that exists between the kingdom of God—including the kingdom of God proclaimed by Jesus—and the world. A follower who leaves everything and accepts Jesus' itinerant life and his work on behalf of the kingdom of God must live this opposition as a sign. Thus Jesus' call to discipleship is deeply serious and uncompromisingly radical, but there is also something inhuman about it.

History of Interpretation

The church's interpretation has felt this harshness and has repeatedly tried to mitigate it. It was thus often emphasized that there are many people to bury the dead but only a few who proclaim the kingdom of God.[31] In recent times the attempt has been made to soften the harshness with the aid of Aramaic so that the "undecided"[32] or even the people assigned as gravediggers[33] were responsible for burying the dead. Much more influential has been the suggestion that the first νεκρός refers to the spiritually dead. In that case the "dead" who are to bury "their dead" are the unbelievers, the sinners, and the Gentiles with whom one is not to have any dealings.[34] "Between believers and unbelievers the love among members of the family no longer applies,"[35] because the world obviously is "a kingdom of the dead" with which one does not want to have anything to do.[36] By understanding Jesus' oxymoron as a metaphor with a deeper meaning, the church's interpretation has generalized and thus also missed the sense of the saying.

How are we to judge such an interpretation in terms of the text? On the surface it is exegetically wrong. The logion is an oxymoron, not a metaphorical riddle. It does not invite us to discover a hidden meaning of "dead"; it is intended to shock and to alienate. The "dead" gravediggers are presumably not "spiritually" dead but really dead,[37] and the church's interpretation in my judgment changed the meaning of the logion and made it generally applicable. This harsh saying of Jesus was not intended to give general instructions about how people should act any more than the demand to give up

come not to send peace but a sword" (Montefiore, *Gospels*, 2.564).

30 *Sermo* 100.2 = *PL* 38.603.

31 The view is common, beginning with Origen fr 161 = 80. Origen already notes that this command appears "ἄτοπον . . . καὶ ἐναντίον."

32 Black, *Approach*, 208: מתינין = the waverers; מיתיהון = their dead.

33 F. Perles, "Zwei Übersetzungsfehler," *ZNW* 19 (1919–20) 96: לִמְקַבֵּר = the buried, inf. pe'al; לִמְקַבֵּר = the ones who bury, part. pa'el. Thus: "leave the dead to the gravediggers." Schwarz (*Jesus sprach*, 92–97) reports on further attempts and speaks about their motives with disarming frankness: "Is that (i.e., Jesus' gruffness) seriously conceivable? . . . Before we bring ourselves to ascribe to him this 'inhuman gruffness and lovelessness' we should examine whether it is not possible to trace the existing Greek wording back to a mistranslation" (92–93). This is simply a case of criticizing the subject matter under the cover of Aramaic linguistics!

34 The church's interpretation consistently advocates this explanation. Spiritually dead = sinners. See, e.g., Augustine *Civ. D.* 20.6 = NPNF 2.425; idem *Quaest.* App 6 = 121 ("*non credentes*"). Later it appears often. See, e.g., Brenz, 387 (Turks, hypocrites). The metaphorical interpretation of the first νεκρὸς as the spiritually dead is still widespread, despite Klemm ("Das Wort von der Selbstbestattung der Toten," *NTS* 16 [1969–70] 60–75).

35 Thomas Aquinas, *Lectura* no. 722 ("*retrahitur germanitatis affectus*"); Hilary (7.11 = SC 254.192) already offered a similar view: "Perfect faith is not bound by any ties to a secular duty that is mutually incumbent on people." This is the way those persons can talk who understand Christian faith as a διαπερᾶν ἀπὸ τῶν προσκαίρων ἐπὶ τὰ αἰώνια (Origen fr. 159 = GCS Origenes 12.79).

36 Bruno Bauer, *Kritik der evangelischen Geschichte der Synoptiker* (2 vols.; Frankfurt: Knecht, 1841) 2.50.

37 In the case of a metaphorical interpretation of νεκροί to mean spiritually dead, the saying could have its intended effect only if the metaphor were immediately obvious. That is, however, not the case. While it is an occasional Jewish metaphor, it always has to be explained: "people who in their lives are dead," etc. (Str–B 1.489; 3.652).

everything and to follow Jesus was a requirement for everybody. Instead, the followers of Jesus, itinerant prophets, were *specially* called to proclaim the kingdom of God, and along with this calling came blunt symbolic actions[38] that portray the deep divide between the kingdom of God and the world.

It is well known that early, perhaps even prior to Mark, "following" became a code word that, independent of actual wandering and radical poverty, was applied to *all* Christians. The impulse to generalize this logion too was thus given early on. We would like to know what Matthew himself, the evangelist of the love command, thought of our saying. He does not tell us here, but in 10:37 he gives some indication of what he is probably thinking. The issue is that one should not love one's own family *more* than Christ. This way of generalizing is, however, different from the church's interpretation in terms of the spiritually dead, i.e., the non-Christians. A church that used this saying to distinguish between itself and the "spiritually dead" world claimed out of hand that it was on the side of Jesus and the kingdom of God. Luther, who used the distinction between the first and the second tablets of the decalogue to interpret our text, had a strong sense of this: The hypocrites use the fourth commandment against the word of God. However, the church is also subject to the fourth commandment, the commandment to honor one's parents: "Thus they shout today, 'the church, the church! The fathers, the fathers!'"[39] Perhaps the church and its claims are also on the side of the fathers and of the kingdom of the world which one must reject, especially when the church *is convinced* that it is not spiritually dead.

To be sure, there are still questions about this saying of Jesus. Even when it is obvious that an oxymoron does not contain a general truth, and when it is clear that we have here a kind of prophetic symbolic action that is related to the special mission of discipleship rather than behavior that can be generalized, there is still a sense of unease. What kind of sign is this that is given right at the point at which one is called to piety and love? However, the question from Jesus back to us is: How often has it happened in the history of the church, and how often does it happen today, that persisting in one's traditional relations and structures—church, political, familial—that almost always is more comfortable than a change of life that involves poverty and homelessness, is dressed up with a reference to one's community obligations, even to the duties of love? The contrast between the "remaining" churches of the Reformation and the "departing" Anabaptist communities in the sixteenth century is only one example of this tension.[40] The questions—in both directions—should not be left unspoken.

■ **23-27** Jesus gets into the boat; his disciples follow him. The boat is involved in a great "quake." Matthew has chosen the word σεισμός because, for one thing, earthquakes belong to the tribulations of the end-time in which the community is living.[41] For another, σεισμός can more easily be transparent of an inner, psychic dimension than can the Markan λαῖλαψ.[42] The water symbolizes the power of death and darkness that threatens the disciples. Initially Matthew brings out the *christological dimension* of the narrative. Jesus sleeps while the waters are already covering the little boat. The image is not that of the superior human being who is always master of the situation,[43] but of the lord of nature who is master over its onslaught. The ancient church correctly spoke here of the deity of Jesus.[44]

■ **25** The disciples address him as "Lord," the Old Testament designation of God with which the church was familiar from its worship, and they use the prayer of supplication "save."[45] Σῴζω means salvation also from

38 Gnilka (1.314) correctly calls attention to OT symbolic actions such as Jer 16:1-9 that serve (admittedly not on an equal basis) as parallels.

39 Luther, *WA* 38.470.

40 Cf. vol. 1, II 2.2.5 on 5:38-42 "Summary."

41 Cf. 24:7; 27:54; Rev 6:12; 8:5; 11:13, 19; 16:18; *As. Mos.* 10.4; *2 Bar.* 70.8; Günther Bornkamm, "σείω κτλ," *TDNT* 7 (1971) 198.

42 Cf. 21:10; BAGD, *s.v.* σείω, 2; LSJ, *s.v.* σεισμός, 2 (σεισμὸς τοῦ σώματος!).

43 The "*audaces fortuna iuvat*" of ancient parallels on the sovereignty of Caesar and others in a storm

(Wettstein 1.353) influenced Rationalism's interpretation. See, e.g., Paulus, 1.347.

44 Cf. Gnilka, *Markus* 1.198, n. 35.

45 Cf. vol. 1, Introduction 4.2.1.

46 The *Opus imperfectum* 23 = 755 represents the entire interpretation of the ancient church when it emphasizes that alongside the allegorical interpretation the *simplicitas historiae* is still important (Pseudo-Chrysostom, *Diatriba ad opus Imperfectum in Matthaeum*; cited according to *PL* 56.601–946).

47 Beginning with Tertullian *Bapt.* 12 = ANF 3.675. Cf. the material in Goldammer, "Navis Ecclesiae," *ZNW*

the eschatological ἀπώλεια ("destruction") that one can hear behind ἀπολλύμεθα ("we are sinking"). The Lord responds to the prayer and with his word creates the great calm.

■ **27** The concluding verse that is decisive for Matthew also emphasizes the christological dimension. The ἄνθρωποι ("people") who ask who "this" is cannot be the disciples who have just addressed him as "Lord." Instead, the evangelist steps out of the story as it were and lets the people to whom his church proclaims the gospel speak as if they were reacting to Jesus' miracles. Jesus' miracles take place in the world's forum and are part of the proclamation. Verse 27 also shows that for Matthew the miracle's uniqueness cannot be surrendered, for that is what attracts people's attention. Thus our story is for him not only a portrayal of faith experiences in the form of a miracle story; it is a report about a miracle that actually happened that only in retrospect becomes transparent for what the church has experienced with the same Lord who performed it.[46]

The *soteriological-ecclesiological dimension* is added to the christological. From the ancient church[47] to the present[48] the boat has been interpreted as the "small ship of the church."

> This interpretation is not self-evident based on the ancient use of the term. Most frequent is the political use of the image of the ship to refer to the state.[49] In addition, in antiquity the ship is an image for life or

for the soul.[50] In Jewish texts the metaphor of the ship is less widespread than is that of the storm. The storm as something that is threatening, as danger and death, may come over both the individual and the entire community. In the context of the threatening storm one can also speak of the small ship as an image for life.[51] Only one solitary text speaks of the ship of Israel (*T. Naph.* 6.2-9). In any case, therefore, there is no connection between our text and a definite Jewish metaphor of the ship; and it does not make use of the ancient metaphor of the ship of state. Given the Hellenistic and Jewish parallels, the first thought would be of an individual interpretation (the "ship of life," etc.).[52] Still, in my judgment the claim that our text speaks of the little ship of the church is right. I base this conclusion, however, not on an established metaphorical meaning of the ship but on the Matthean ecclesiology that permits us to understand the "disciples" as the church. Thus presumably the metaphor of the "little ship of the church" was derived from our text because of the metaphorical meaning of the "storm" and of the transparency of the term "disciples" for the church. Later the comparison with the ancient metaphor of the ship of state confirmed the ecclesiological interpretation of the boat.

■ **24** The disciples' little ship is shaken and endangered in the storm. Σεισμός ("earthquake") and κύματα ("waves") do not have precise meanings; the readers must understand them in terms of their own experiences. The evangelist may especially have been thinking

---

40 (1941) 76–86, and Hugo Rahner, *Symbole der Kirche* (Salzburg: Müller, 1964) 304–60, 473–503 (Peter's little ship).

48 Bornkamm ("Stilling") has helped win acceptance for this interpretation. Most important is Kurt Goldammer, "Das Schiff der Kirche. Ein antiker Symbolbegriff aus der politischen Metaphorik in eschatologischer und ekklesiologischer Umdeutung," *ThZ* 6 (1950) 232–37.

49 Alcaeus fr. 46a D and 46b D (M. Treu, ed. [Munich: Heimeran, 1952] 40–41); fr. 119D = idem 42-43; Horace *Carm.* 1.34. For additional references see Hugo Rahner, *Symbole der Kirche* (Salzburg: Müller, 1964) 324-29; Kahlmeyer, *Seesturm*, 39–48; Goldammer, "Das Schiff der Kirche," 232–37.

50 Kahlmeyer, *Seesturm*, 19–22, 26–39 (26: "very rich material"). Examples for life = sea voyage, storm in the ship: Euripides *Or.* 340–44 (the fate of the rich); Euripides *Heracl.* 427–30 (the fate of the fugitives).

51 On the individual: Sir 33:2 (whoever despises the law is as in a storm); *Ep. Arist.* 251; *2 Bar.* 85.10-11

(harbor = death, end of the world); *4 Macc.* 7.1-3 (reason = steersman; sea of instincts; storm of afflictions); Philo, *Leg. all.* 3.223–24; 1QH 6.22-24 ("I was like a sailor on a ship in the raging of the sea"); 3.6 ("my soul like a ship"), 13–16 (ship); 7.4 (ship); 8.31; Ps 42:8. On the community: Ps 46:3-4, 93:3-4 (without a ship). For further references see Earle Hilgert, *The Ship and Related Symbols in the New Testament* (Assen: Royal Vangorcum, 1962) 26–39.

52 It is also always represented in the ancient church along with the ecclesiological interpretation. Examples: Origen *Hom. in Cant.* 3 = GCS 33.226. Ancient Christian artistic representations show the ship of life (on tombs!) and the little ship of the church. See Ulrike Weber, "Schiff," *Lexikon der christlichen Ikonographie* 4. 63. For the modern period cf. below, n. 56.

of the persecutions that came over his church (5:11-12; 10:16-39; 23:34-37). For him the central issue is the fear of the disciples, and for that reason the Lord first spoke to them.

■ **26** He calls their fear *little faith* and reminds the readers of the Gospel not only of the text about God's care, 6:25-33, but especially of their own faith—a faith that the disciples have now abandoned. "Little faith" also characterizes the situation of the church in Matthew's own day. What is this little faith? Is it faith without deeds?[53] For Matthew πίστις certainly is always active faith, but that is not the primary issue here. What constitutes little faith is, rather, that the disciples stop thinking about the power and presence of their Lord and then no longer *can* act. What our story conveys is that faith's strength consists of nothing but turning to the Lord and being supported by him.[54] Ecclesiologically, therefore, it bears witness to the presence of the Lord with his church "always, until the end of the world" (28:20).

Summary and History of Interpretation

We can, indeed we must, put our own *experiences* in our story and be understood anew "in" it. Only those who themselves are "in the ship" can understand it correctly.

> In the history of the text's interpretation its concrete application has a quite different appearance depending on the situation and the interpreter. I offer three examples: *Peter Chrysologus*, Bishop of Ravenna in the first half of the fifth century, discovered in our story the miracle of the Christianizing of Rome. The "foggy mists of the devils," "the storm clouds of the mobs," "the nations [swirling] like whirlpools," and "the sharp rocks of infidelity" were tamed by Christ, who made Christians of the Romans and granted peace to the church under Christian princes.[55] *August Hermann Francke* interpreted the text individualistically: Jesus "enters . . . the ship of our heart and orders it to leave the land of earthly life." Those who

(take) Jesus "into the ship (of their) heart and then unite (themselves) rightly with him" will "also be perfected with him."[56] In an impressive interpretation *Heinrich Schlier* speaks at the height of the church struggle of the seemingly calm and indifferent sea and the sudden "raging of the heathen and half-heathen storm" and then formulates in good Reformation manner: "Only where the church, because its heart has been enlightened and strengthened by the miracle of his word, no longer demands a miracle—there for certain the Lord rises up against the world and banishes its powers into his great stillness."[57]

The question is: Is our text open to *every* experience, and does it permit *every* interpretation, or does it also place limits on such interpretations and on putting oneself in the story? I would like to mention three limits that, based on Matthew's text, seem important to me: (1) Matthew sees faith as the center of the text. Faith lives from the reality that the risen Lord with his strength helps lift the doubter. There is no place in our text for experiences other than those in which faith has been changed by encountering the living Lord.[58] (2) Matthew speaks of an experience of the disciples, that is, an experience in a community. He is not interested in *merely* private edification and a "ship of the heart" understood only in this sense. (3) God's help and human struggle are intertwined. There is nothing passive about discipleship. Matthew has prefaced the experience of the stilling of the storm with a powerful statement about what is required from those who follow Jesus (19–22). What distinguishes little faith from unbelief is that little faith is the despair of these who have *risked* something with God. And it is precisely they who experience the Lord's power.

---

53 Léon-Dufour, "Tempête," 169–70.
54 Luther 2.298: "Little faith (holds on to) the Lord" and—in the sense of the Reformation's interpretation of the text—"his word."
55 *Sermones* 20 = FC 17.62.
56 Sermon of 1701 in Erhard Peschke, ed., *Werke in Auswahl*, (Witten: Luther, 1969) 339, 346.
57 *Das Schifflein der Kirche* (Theologische Existenz heute 23; Munich: Kaiser, 1935) 7, 20.
58 This would also apply, e.g., to Peter Chrysologus (above, n. 55).

2.2 The Two Demoniacs in Gadara (8:28—9:1)

Literature

Franz Annen, *Heil für die Heiden* (Frankfurter theologische Studien 20; Frankfurt: Knecht, 1976) 207–9.

Tjitze Baarda, "Gadarenes, Gerasenes, Gergesenes and the 'Diatessaron' Traditions," in Earl Ellis and Max Wilcox, eds., *Neotestamentica et Semitica: Studies in Honour of Matthew Black* (Edinburgh: T. and T. Clark, 1969) 181–97.

Jeanne Féliers, "L'exégèse de la pericope des porcs de Gérasa dans la patristique latine," *StPatr* 10 (1970) (= TU 107) 225–29.

Held, "Matthew," 172–75.

Rudolf Pesch, *Der Besessene von Gerasa* (SBS 56; Stuttgart: Katholisches Bibelwerk, 1972) 50–56.

For *additional literature* see above, II B on Matthew 8–9.

28 And when he came to the other shore, into the land of the Gadarenes, two demoniacs met him, coming out of the tombs. They were very violent so that no one was able to pass that way. 29/ And behold, they cried out and said, "What have we to do with you, Son of God? Have you come here to torture us before the time?" 30/ But far off from them a large herd of pigs was feeding. 31/ And the demons asked him and said, "If you cast us out, send us into the herd of pigs."

32 And he said to them: "Go!"

They came out and went away into the pigs. And behold, the entire herd rushed down the precipice into the sea, and they died in the water. 33/ But the herdsmen fled, went away into the city and reported everything, including what had happened to the demoniacs. 34/ And behold, the whole city came out to meet Jesus, and when they saw him they implored him to leave their region. 9.1/ He got into the ship and crossed over to the other side. And he came into his own city.

Analysis

Structure

In contrast to 8:1-4 or 8:14-15 this story is not told from the perspective of Jesus. He is the subject of actions only at the beginning (v. 28a), at the end (v. 9:1a), and especially in the middle (v. 32a). Otherwise everything comes indirectly to Jesus. How much Jesus is at the center of things is "mirrored" for the readers through the demoniacs, the demons, the herdsmen, and the people who come out of the city. The structure fits this pattern. With v. 32a at the center, the story is constructed chiastically with the aid of several inclusions: πέραν/διαπεράζω (vv. 28a/9.1a); ὑπαντάω/ὑπάντησις (vv. 28b/34a); δαιμονιζόμενοι (vv. 28b/33b); βοσκομένη/βόσκοντες (vv. 30/33a); ἀγέλη (vv. 30, 31b/32c). Several catchwords are taken over from the miracle stories in 8:1-17,[1] but hardly a single one from 8:18-27.

Source

The source, Mark 5:1-21a, is severely abridged, a factor that makes the story on the one hand simpler and clearer but on the other hand also less vivid.[2] Matthew is responsible for all of the changes.[3]

Interpretation

It is difficult to explain the story from the perspective of the evangelist. He has omitted so many details from his Markan source that one can hardly ask why in each individual case. A clear redactional tendency is not obvious. Is Wellhausen's judgment correct that the evangelist could not ignore "the offensive story," but also did not like it and therefore gave it "short shrift"?[4] The most curious feature is the omission of Mark 5:18-20. Thus the primary question for the interpretation is what Matthew was trying to do with his abridgment, or, perhaps, what it was about the Markan narrative that bothered him.

Let us look first at the *changes* Matthew makes in Mark's narrative. For him the story takes place near Gadara,[5] no

---

1 Verse 28 δαιμονιζόμενοι, cf. 4:24; 8:16; v. 31 ἐκβάλλω, cf. 8:16; v. 32 ὑπάγω, cf. 8:4, 13.

2 According to Matthew, in 8:29 the demoniacs are speaking, not the demons.

3 Favorite Matthean terms (cf. vol. 1, Introduction 3.2) are: v. 28: δαιμονίζομαι, λίαν, ὥστε, ἐκεῖνος; v. 29: ἰδού, ὧδε, καιρός; v. 32: ἰδουν; v. 33: ἀπέρχομαι, δαιμονίζομαι; v. 34: ἰδού, ἰδών, ὅπως, μεταβαίνω. The few minor agreements are all explainable as independent redaction by Matthew and Luke.

4 Wellhausen, 39. Cf. Trilling, *Israel*, 134–35.

5 Γαδαρηνῶν is probably the original reading in Matthew. Tjitze Baarda ("Gadarenes, Gerasenes, Gergesenes and the 'Diatessaron' Traditions," 181–97) points out that textually Gadara has especially strong roots in the Syriac tradition: syp, syh, the Byzantine text and part of the Caesarean text read "Gadarenes" in all the gospels. This reading presumably also stood in the Syriac Diatessaron. The Hebrew Matthew presumably reads Gergesa, with many MSS on Luke 8:26, 37 and few witnesses in Matthew (among others f1, 13).

longer in the region of Gerasa.[6] Both were well-known cities of the Decapolis. A Syrian like Matthew could definitely have known that the important trade center Gadara—also known as a center of philosophy—was only about six miles from the lake and had territory there[7]—something that was not true of Gerasa, located more than thirty miles from the lake. Gadara would also better fit the concept of the "biblical land"[8] than would Gerasa out on its periphery. However, the herd of pigs is another matter! The Jewish-Christian Matthew knows that a large herd of pigs does not belong in the holy land. According to the Bible, pigs were unclean animals (Lev 11:7) and were all the more taboo for the Jews because they were an important sacrificial animal in most Hellenistic cults.[9] Thus Matthew is probably not thinking of the biblical land in which the city was located. Instead, he corrects the Markan text according to his geographical knowledge without presumably even considering which "city" (πόλις, v. 34) in the land of the Gadarenes is meant.[10] It is probable that he regards as Gentiles not only the herdsmen but also the population of the city where they raised the alarm. The conclusion of the story then consists in the fact that the gentile population asks the Messiah of Israel to leave their area immediately. The time for the proclamation to the Gentiles has not yet come, but one could wish that Matthew had said that more clearly.

Other changes are even more difficult to explain. Why does Matthew speak of two demoniacs? The suggestion that one often reads to the effect that he wanted to make up for having eliminated Mark 1:23-28 is too risky.[11] He follows the same practice in 9:27-31 and 20:29-34 without having to replace something. Luke 24:4 (cf. Matt 26:60; Luke 7:18) shows that doubling characters is completely within the scope of a narrator's freedom.[12] Does Matthew eliminate the name "Legion" for political reasons, since the situation after 70 CE was delicate for a Jew(ish Christian)?

Why is the herd of pigs "far away" (v. 30)? So that Jesus will have nothing to do with unclean pigs? Or because the demoniacs are dangerous even for the pigs?[13] We do not know. Difficult finally is the insertion of πρὸ καιροῦ ("before the time") in v. 29. In the background may be the idea that the power of demons is limited to this eon.[14] Or does it indicate that it is not yet the time of the gentile mission? However, πρὸ καιροῦ also may be a simple prepositional phrase that means "prematurely."[15] Καιρός is not a technical term in Matthew for the eschaton. We should not place too much emphasis on this expression, therefore, and we may avoid a theological or salvation historical (over-?) interpretation.[16] Perhaps the demons simply want to live a little longer.

Most difficult to interpret, of course, are the massive abridgments. The abridgment of Mark 5:18-20 is obvious. Jesus' activity in the gentile country has no results. Obvious also is the omission of Mark 5:8-10. It makes the narrative's structure more severe. One can ask whether Matthew dislikes "demonistic" statements and thus wants to avoid them.[17] That he

6   If Gergesa were to be read in Mark 5:1 (Gnilka, *Markus,* 1.201), then, as he did in 15:39, Matthew would have avoided a completely unknown place-name.

7   According to Josephus (*Vit.* 42) the area of Tiberias borders that of Gadara and Hippos. Since the lake is the border with Hippos, this passage does not exclude the possibility that the area of Gadara at the southern shore extended to the lake (contra Pesch, *Markusevangelium* 1.285).

8   Cf. vol. 1 on 4:25.

9   *KP* 5.46.

10   If it is the somewhat distant major city of Gadara itself, the evangelist did not have a very precise image of what he was narrating (πᾶσα ἡ πόλις, v. 34). However, πόλις also may mean simply a fortified town. Cf. on Matt 9:1-8. On the formulation cf. 21:10.

11   Most recently Gundry, *Matthew,* 158.

12   Cf. Bultmann, *History,* 314–17, 449.

13   Rudolf Pesch, *Der Besessene von Gerasa* (SBS 56;

Stuttgart: Katholisches Bibelwerk, 1972) 53–54.

14   Cf. *1 Enoch* 16.1; 55.4; Str–B 4.527.

15   1 Macc 6:36; LSJ, *s.v.* καιρός, 3.1b.

16   Georg Strecker, in *Der Weg der Gerichtigkeit: Untersuchungen zur Theologie des Matthäus* (FRLANT 82; Göttingen: Vandenhoeck & Ruprecht, 1962) 88, interprets the term in terms of his understanding of history in Matthew: In Jesus' day the eschatological καιρός is not yet there. Annen (*Heil,* 209) has a similar interpretation.

17   Thus almost all the features that are important for a psychological interpretation of our story are missing in Matthew. Mark 5:1-20 is exceptionally well suited for such an interpretation, as the impressive exegesis by Eugen Drewermann (*Tiefenpsychologie und Exegese* [2 vols.; Olten: Walter, 1984–85] 2.247-77) makes clear. However, Matt 8:28-34 protects itself from such an exegesis. The people

abridges Mark 5:21-43 and Mark 9:14-27 in a similarly massive way, omits Mark 1:23-38 completely, and presents the saying of the return of the unclean spirits in 12:43-45 as a parable lends credence to the thesis. There is thus certainly some truth in it, although on the other hand Matthew is not silent about the fact that exorcisms happened, and he even emphasizes the authority of the disciples to cast out demons (10:1, 8). More importantly, the realistic descriptions of the demoniacs' condition are omitted (Mark 5:3-5); indeed, Matthew does not even mention that at the end they are well (Mark 5:15).[18] Obviously, for Matthew the demoniacs are not important in themselves. Their literary function is to "mirror" the power of the Son of God. The abridgments are in the service of a positive intention for the narrative.

Summary

The evangelist's report is short and to the point. Jesus travels over to the gentile eastern shore of the lake. Two "bad" demoniacs, who live in unclean tombs, confront him. Matthew does not spend time describing their condition. He reports nothing of the fruitless attempts to tame them, of their crying and self-mutilation. From the very beginning, his interest is concentrated on the encounter of the two men with Jesus. It is as if the demons already felt Jesus' power. They know that the Son of God will destroy them before their time is up. Therefore, for Matthew there is no conversation between the demons and Jesus. The Son of God simply does not let himself get drawn into a conversation. While they are screaming at him and asking that he at least let them continue to live in a far distant herd of pigs, Jesus is silent. He says only one thing: "Away with you!"[19] The evangelist could not have more effectively put Jesus at the center of the story.[20] John Chrysostom senses the power of Jesus well and "mirrors" it in literary form in the behavior of the demons: "They who kept others from passing are stopped at the sight of him who blocks their way."[21] The issue is Jesus and the power of his word.

The rest of the story describes the effect of this one word. The demons go into the pigs, the pigs plunge into the lake, and the demons (![22]) die. The terrified herdsmen run into the city and mobilize the entire population. They come to Jesus as if he were a prince.[23] They do not bring him into the city, however; instead, they ask the Messiah of Israel to leave their region. The evangelist does not say whether they do so out of anger over the loss of the pigs or from their fear of Jesus' divine power. The only thing that is clear is that Jesus leaves no trace among the gentile Gadarenes. We hear nothing more about the two who have been healed, no indication at all that they followed Jesus (cf. Mark 5:18-20), although the context would make that natural (Matt 8:18-27). Important only is that Jesus goes back across the lake to the heartland of Israel, because he is the Messiah of Israel who heals (4:23; 8:1-17).

---

are—somewhat overstated—little more than objects for the demonstration of the (unique!) power of the Son of God—a power that is not exactly paradigmatic for what a therapist does.

18   Thus Böcher, "Magie," 14–15.

19   As in 4:10 and 16:23, ὑπάγω here has the strong sense of "to go away." What is meant is that Jesus speaks a word of power, not that he makes a concession.

20   Gnilka (1.320) correctly speaks of a "christological concentration."

21   28.2 = PG 57.353.

22   Matthew intentionally formulates ἀπέθανον after ὥρμησεν (v. 32). That thereby the pigs died with the demons does not bother him (the Jew!). The interpretation of the ancient church offers many explanations: The world is to see how bad these demons were. A single saved person is worth much more than a herd of pigs. The pigs represent blasphemers who are destroyed, etc. Whoever is not satisfied with that explanation may take comfort in Wettstein (1.356): They could always still pickle the drowned pigs.

23   Schlatter (295) calls attention to Josephus *Ant.* 11.227; *Bell.* 7.100.

The third section contains few linking catchwords of its own. There are three controversy dialogues of Jesus with the scribes, the Pharisees, and the disciples of John. The third, the debate about fasting, takes place at the location of the second, the banquet with the publicans. The connection makes the dispute with Israel the dominant theme. That the existence of the church becomes visible in all three texts fits in with the theme. "To follow" (ἀκολουθέω, 8:19, 22-23; 9:9) and "disciple" (μαθηταί, 8:21, 23; 9:10, 14) are catchwords that connect with what has preceded. Alongside this dominant theme there is another: The narrator again leads his readers from a healing story to a discipleship story. One hears once again the narrative thread of 8:1-27.

For his sources, with 9:1b the evangelist returns to Mark 2 and thus further spins the thread that he had left lying in 8:4 and 8:16. He will not complete the Markan story of the Gadarenes that he has just told until vv. 18-26. We can scarcely say conclusively anymore why he chose to weave his material this way and not another. Probably—after the relatively low-key story of 8:28-34 that followed naturally the stilling of the storm—the narrative thread of Mark 2 was important for him, because it told of the resistance of Israel's leaders to Jesus. It is, as 9:33-34 demonstrates, such an essential thread in the Matthean fabric that the evangelist did not want to postpone it any longer. The three concluding healing miracles, 9:18-32, create then a positive contrast.

3.1 The Son of Man Forgives Sins (9:2-8)

Literature

Jacques Dupont, "Le paralytique pardonné (Mt 9,1-8)," NRTh 82 (1960) 940–58.
Heinrich Greeven, "Die Heilung des Gelähmten nach Matthäus," WuD 4 (1955) 65–78.
Held, "Matthew," 175–78, 270–71.
Hummel, Auseinandersetzung, 36–38.
Lange, Erscheinen, 55–64.
Frans Neirynck, "Les accords mineurs et la rédaction des Évangiles. L'épisode du paralytique (Mt IX 1-8/Lc V 17-26, par. Mc II 1-12)," EThL 50 (1974) 215–30.
Bo Reicke, "The Synoptic Reports on the Healing of the Paralytic: Matthew 9:1-8 with Parallels," in J. K. Elliott, ed., Studies in New Testament Language and Text: Essays in Honour of George D. Kilpatrick on the Occasion of his Sixty-fifth Birthday (NovTSup 44; Leiden: Brill, 1976) 319–29.
Sand, Gesetz, 64–68.
A. Vargas-Machuca, "El paralítico perdonado en la redación de Mateo (Mt 9,1-8)," EstBib 44 (1969) 15–43.
For additional literature see above, II B on Matthew 8–9.

2 And behold, they brought to him a lame man who was lying on a bed. And when Jesus saw their faith, he said to the lame man, "Take courage, my child, your sins are forgiven."
3 And behold, some of the scribes said to themselves, "This man blasphemes." 4/ And Jesus saw[1] their thoughts and said, "Why are you thinking evil things in your hearts? 5/ For what is easier to say, 'Your sins are forgiven,' or to say, 'Get up and walk around'? 6/ But so that you may see that the Son of Man has power on earth to forgive sins—" he then says to the lame man, "Get up,[2] take your bed, and go home!" 7/ And he got up and went away, to his house. 8/ But when the crowds saw it, they were afraid, and they praised God who gave people such power.

Analysis

Structure

The narrative has six parts: (1) The lame man is brought to Jesus, v. 2a (A); (2) Jesus speaks to the lame man, v. 2b, c (B); (3) Jesus' central discussion with the scribes, vv. 3a-6a (C); (4) Jesus speaks to the lame man, v. 6b, c (B´); (5) the lame man goes away under his own power, v. 7 (A´); (6) the concluding commentary of the crowds, v. 8 (D).

Again we have a ring composition with Jesus' comment to the scribe that stands out because of its length as the center. Parts 3 and 4 begin stereotypically with καὶ ἰδὼν ὁ Ἰησοῦς . . . αὐτῶν εἶπεν and reveal a characteristic of the narrative: Jesus stands alone in the center. Only he speaks in this story. Its most important expressions are ἀφίενται αἱ ἁμαρτίαι ("your sins are forgiven," vv. 2b, 5a, 6a) and ἐξουσία ("power," vv. 6a, 8b). Both appear in v. 6a. Here is the climax that is marked in Matthew very

[1] The typically Matthean ἰδών is more probable than is the more weakly attested reading εἰδώς that avoids saying that Jesus "sees" (invisible) thoughts. Cf. Metzger, Commentary, 24.

[2] The Mattheism ἐγερθείς is much better attested than is ἔγειρε that is inspired by the parallels in Mark and Luke.

clearly by the anacoluthon.[3] The conclusion, v. 8, is important, because it resumes the climax of v. 6a. Impressive are the many catchwords that Matthew takes over from 8:1-17. There is, by contrast, no connection to 8:28-34.

Source and Redaction

Mark's more wordy narrative, 2:1-12, is tightened up, leaving a clearer focus on the center—the person of Jesus and, in terms of content, vv. 3a-6a. Correspondingly, Matthew shortens primarily the beginning of the story. In the process even the colorful detail about the lame man's bearers digging through the roof is lost.[4] Their faith is illustrated only by the fact that they bring the lame man to Jesus.[5] Almost all of the changes correspond to Matthean language.[6] Conspicuous are the numerous minor agreements. In a number of places they can be explained as the independent redaction of Matthew and Luke, but in several places it is equally conceivable that Matthew and Luke used a (secondary?) recension of Mark that is somewhat different from our text of Mark.[7]

Interpretation

■ **2** Jesus is again in Capernaum, the city[8] in which he lives (cf. 4:13), after returning to Israel from the gentile area. The evangelist briefly reports that a lame man is carried to Jesus on his bed. Important is only what Jesus says to the sick man: "Child, your sins are now[9] forgiven." Θάρσει ("take courage") is an important word, because in Matthew, in contrast with Mark,[10] it occurs only on the lips of Jesus. The Christian readers who themselves have experienced the forgiveness of sins sense that the decisive experience, salvation, has come to this man. From the beginning the narrative is focused on forgiving sins. Sin separates the people from God; it also is the cause of sickness.[11] By dealing with the forgiveness of sins this story becomes transparent. All Christian readers can find themselves in it.

■ **3-5** The scribes are not introduced, nor do they engage in a dispute with Jesus; they only murmur inwardly. Matthew no longer reports why they think that Jesus

---

3   Matthew strengthens the anacoluthon with τότε.

4   This is not an indication of an old text form, contra Schlatter, 297.

5   Frans Neirynck, "Les accords mineurs et la rédaction des Évangiles," 215–30; 223–24.

6   The following are redactional (cf. vol. 1, Introduction 3.2): v.1: ἴδιος, πόλις; v.2: καὶ ἰδού, προσφέρω αὐτῷ, βάλλω. On θαρσέω cf. 9:22. Verse 3: καὶ ἰδού, ἐν ἑαυτοῖς; v. 4: καὶ ἰδών, ἐνθυμε-, πονηρός; v. 5: γάρ; v. 6: τότε, ἐγερθείς; v. 7: ἐγερθείς, ἀπέρχομαι; v. 8: ἰδὼν δέ, ὄχλοι, φοβέομαι, ἐξουσία. Matthean is also the avoidance of the Markan φέρω (v. 3), δύναμαι (v. 4), κράβατος (vv. 4, 9-12). On εὐθύς (vv. 8, 12) cf. vol. 1, Introduction 3.3.

7   Verse 2: καὶ ἰδού is Matthean and Lukan redaction. Verses 2, 6: κλίνη instead of the Markan κράβατος. One might expect that the popular (Latin and Aramaic loan word; modern Greek: bed = κρεβάτι!) and vulgar κράβατος (Phrynichus *Ecl.* 62 recommends instead σκίμπους = sofa [Phrynichus Arabius, *Phrynichi Eclogae nominum et verborum Atticorum* (Christian Augustus Lobeck, ed.; 1820; reprinted Hildesheim: Olms, 1965)]) would be replaced by the neutral generic term κλίνη. The preposition ἐπί in Matthew and Luke remains strange. Furthermore, Luke does not avoid the word elsewhere (Acts 5:15; 9:33!). Verses 2, 4: εἶπεν instead of λέγει. Matthean and Lukan redaction is possible (cf. Frans Neirynck, *The Minor Agreements of Matthew and Luke Against Mark* [BEThL 37;

Louvain: Louvain University Press, 1974] 223–25) but unusual in a saying of Jesus (cf. vol. 1, Introduction 3.1). Verse 5: omission of τῷ παραλυτικῷ and of καὶ ἆρον . . . σου; Matthean and Lukan redaction is likely. Verse 6: ἐπὶ τῆς γῆς ἀφιέναι ἁμαρτίας. The change in order can hardly be explained as redactional. Verse 7: ἀπῆλθεν εἰς τὸν οἶκον αὐτοῦ. Matthean redaction is conceivable. On Luke cf. 1:23. The large number of minor agreements in our text remains surprising.

8   Πόλις is used by Matthew (as by the other evangelists and Josephus) not in the sense of a Hellenistic city with a constitution but in the LXX sense. The LXX is not familiar with ἄστυ; πόλις is not used in the constitutional sense. In translating עיר, πόλις is any fortified settlement. In any case, we cannot conclude from the preference of Matthew and Luke for πόλις that they were city dwellers, contra Kilpatrick, *Origins*, 125.

9   Present: now, at this moment. The perfect ἀφέωνται (numerous MSS following Luke) emphasizes the enduring effect.

10 Mark 10:49 is omitted by Matthew because Jesus is not speaking. Does Matthew know already that he is going to omit the word in 9:28; 20:32, and does he therefore (twice!) use it earlier in 9:2, 22?

11 Lev 26:14-16; Deut 28:21-22; 2 Chr 21:15, 18-19; John 5:14; 9:2; 1 Cor 11:30. For rabbinic parallels see Str–B 1.495–96; for the literature see Pesch, *Markusevangelium*, 1.156, n. 16.

blasphemes. In Mark 2:7 their accusation was at least indirectly understandable. Obviously they believe that when Jesus grants God's (*passivum divinum!*) forgiveness of sins, he arbitrarily puts himself on the same level with God and claims divine prerogatives for himself. Matthew omits that concern. His Jewish-Christian readers, who are convinced that God himself acts in Jesus and who perhaps already are familiar with the Mishna's very restrictive regulations about blasphemy,[12] will no longer have understood why Jesus' granting of forgiveness of sins should be blasphemy. Thus in the eyes of the readers the scribes' reaction to Jesus is malicious. Matthew confirms the negative image of the scribes: Their thoughts are "evil." But from the very beginning Jesus is superior to them and can see through them. His question assumes that it is easier "to say, 'your sins are forgiven'" than "to say" that a lame man should get up and walk, for only the latter statement must be backed up with action.[13]

■ **6a** Verse 6 is the climax of the story. Jesus refers to himself as the Son of Man. The scribes are aware that he is speaking of himself, but for the church Jesus speaks as the eschatological judge of the world, the one for whom they are waiting. It is he who "on earth,"[14] that is, already now, forgives sins. The forgiveness of sins, which the church has also experienced, happens with the last judgment in mind. It does not eliminate the judgment of the Son of Man, but the forgiven sin is released in the last judgment.[15] After this climax, the granting of grace by the Son of Man, the sentence abruptly breaks off.[16]

■ **6b-7** Jesus now turns his attention again to the lame man in order to provide the practical proof. The scribes disappear from view. While one *can* understand Mark 2:12 to mean that they also ($\pi\acute{\alpha}\nu\tau\epsilon\varsigma$) share in praising God, that is not the case in Matthew; they are Jesus' enemies. Jesus commands the lame man to go home, and the latter faithfully does what he is commanded.[17] For Matthew the healed man's obedience is what is important. Demonstrating the miracle by carrying his bed is no longer necessary.

■ **8** Verse 8 turns the attention away from the lame man. The crowds are afraid. It is an attitude that is also typical of the disciples and that Jesus repeatedly overcomes by his personal attention (e.g., 10:26-28; 14:27, 30-31; 17:6-7). They praise God, not because of the miracle of Jesus but because he has given "people" the authority to forgive sins. $To\hat{\imath}\varsigma\ \grave{\alpha}\nu\vartheta\rho\acute{\omega}\pi o\iota\varsigma$ is notable after 9:6. The issue is not that Jesus is "another human being,"[18] but that the church has the authority to forgive sins.[19]

Forgiveness of Sins

The *forgiveness of sins* is an important Matthean theme. From the very beginning the evangelist had introduced the Son of God as the one who will save his people from their sins (1:21). The surprising ending of our story focuses attention once again on the $\grave{\epsilon}\xi ov\sigma\acute{\imath}\alpha$ ("power") of the Son of Man in v. 6a. It is the source of the church's $\grave{\epsilon}\xi ov\sigma\acute{\imath}\alpha$. Jesus later demonstrates that healing a sick person is more difficult only in the realm of "speaking"; much greater is the *act* of forgiving sins for which the healing is the indirect proof. Thus the healing points to the Son of Man's all-embracing authority. The catchword $\grave{\epsilon}\xi-ov\sigma\acute{\imath}\alpha$ appears again in 28:18. Part of the "all author-

---

12   *M. Sanh.* 7.5: The blasphemer is guilty only if he pronounces the name of God clearly.

13   At issue is the $\epsilon\grave{\imath}\pi\epsilon\hat{\imath}\nu$! Lapide (206) comments graphically that it is easier to write about the problems of the Tartars than about Italian problems, "*quia . . . ille a nemine falsitatis argui potest.*"

14   We should not attach too much significance to the change in the location of $\grave{\epsilon}\pi\grave{\imath}\ \tau\hat{\eta}\varsigma\ \gamma\hat{\eta}\varsigma$. The most we might say is that the proximity to $\grave{\epsilon}\xi ov\sigma\acute{\imath}\alpha$ forms a closer relationship with Matt 28:18. (Cf. Lange, *Erscheinen*, 64.)

15   Cf. 16:19; 18:18!

16   The public reader must pause here so that v. 6a can have an impact on the hearers. The anacoluthon is a rhetorical technique.

17   For the repetition of statements as a way to express

obedience see also 1:24-25; 2:13-14, 19-20.

18   Wolzogen, 264. Calvin (1.260–61) offers another variant of the christological interpretation of v. 8: The crowd is mistaken; God gives this authority only to the human being Christ. Similar is Lohmeyer's explanation, 169. Formerly this passage often was used as proof of a collective understanding of Son of Man. Cf., e.g., Weiss, 91; A. H. McNeile, *The Gospel According to St. Matthew* (1915; reprinted London: Macmillan, 1965) 116–17.

19   Jacques Dupont ("Le paralytique pardonné," 940–58; 952–58) and Heinrich Greeven ("Die Heilung des Gelähmten nach Matthäus," 65–78; 74–78) have given prominence to this interpretation; but cf. already Schlatter (301) and Bultmann

ity" that is given to the Exalted One "in heaven and on earth" is his authority to forgive sins "on earth." The church experiences it, for example, in the eucharist where the forgiveness of sins takes place (26:28). It also experiences it, however, in prayer, as the petition for forgiveness in the Lord's Prayer (6:12 + 14!) showed. At the same time it becomes clear there that God's forgiveness does not happen in isolation from human forgiving. Similarly, Matt 18:15-35 presents the reality of experienced and lived forgiveness as the basic order of the church. Ἐπὶ τῆς γῆς ("on earth") appears again in the two sayings about binding and loosing (16:19; 18:18).

Verse 9:8 thus reminds the church of what it itself has experienced and may now experience. And 9:6 reminds it of the origin of this experience. It is the authority of the Son "of Man" (= *Menschen*) that empowers the "human beings" (= *Menschen*) to forgive sins.

Summary

For Matthew the traditional Markan story becomes a fundamental expression of his own faith. If Mark had accentuated the traditional story of the healing of the lame man christologically and made of it a story about the authority of the Son of Man, then Matthew goes still further in speaking of what the authority of the Son of Man means for his church.[20] If the Son of Man is the one to whom all authority is given in heaven and on earth, that means that his authority is valid wherever he is with his own—always, until the end of the world. Thus for him our narrative not only calls attention to the spectacular presence of God back then in the Son of Man; at the same time it calls attention to the reality in which the Son of Man makes it possible for the church to live.

As is the case with most Matthean stories, this one is multidimensional. It is also significant in salvation-history terms because in it for the first time the enmity of the scribes toward Jesus is manifested. To be sure, the scribes disappear, and at the end Matthew concentrates totally on the positive reaction of the crowds. But they will—as enemies of Jesus—appear again (12:38; 15:1, etc.). At this point their enmity is still an isolated prelude, the significance of which only the continuation of Matthew's story will reveal.

History of Interpretation

The church's interpretation has sensed the basic dimension of our text. It also has discovered fundamental statements about its own faith in it, much as Matthew found his understanding of faith in the Markan text that came to him. Especially important are three dimensions.

1. Our text was connected with the *doctrine of the Trinity*. The question posed was: Why was it precisely as the "son of man" (= human being) that Jesus exercised the divine authority to forgive sins (cf. Mark 2:7)? This question is no mere wordplay. By making it clear that it was precisely the man Jesus who exercised this divine power,[21] the exegetes preserved the conviction that the forgiveness of sins is central to the saving work of the God-man. Our text thus shows that the Son "brought the divine authority down into his human nature because of his inseparable unity with it."[22] It formulates, therefore, the center of the soteriological content of the incarnation.

2. Although in Matthew the lame man is not at the center of the story, interpreters have justifiably made of him the *typical Christian*. They have heard in our text, for example, that God often does not directly

---

(*History*, 15–16). The interpretation of τοῖς ἀνθρώποις as a *dativus commodi* = for the benefit of human beings (Bengel, 64; Wolfgang Schenk, "'Den Menschen' Mt 9,8," *ZNW* 54 [1963] 275) is impossible because of 10:1; 21:23; 28:18.

20 Compared with Mark, this is a clarification but not a radical reinterpretation. With the insertion of Mark 2:5b-10 the story was already interpreted christologically, and the authority of the Son of Man became its focus. As a christological title in the Gospel of Mark, "Son of Man" has an "inclusive" dimension: The way of the Son of Man prefigures the way of the church.

21 Thomas Aquinas (*Lectura* no. 750) says impressively: *Ideo dicit hominis quia Dei est dimittere peccata*. Usually the interpretation was satisfied to maintain, e.g.,

with Hilary (8.6 = SC 254.201) that Jesus here acted as God.

22 Cyril of Alexandria fr. 103 also cited in Joseph Reuss, *Matthäus-Kommentare aus der griechischen Kirche* (TU 61; Berlin: Akademie-Verlag, 1957) 185–86. (The entire fragment is a classical formulation of Monophysite Christology.)

grant the petitions of the sick for physical health but gives them something much more important.[23] Even if Matthew does not want to devalue the healing's sign, it is entirely in keeping with his meaning that only liberation from sin is the basis of all true health.[24] The sixteenth-century reformers were not the first to see that the word of grace is what is fundamental: "The word went out and the miracle followed."[25]

3. Interesting is the way the exegesis of the sixteenth and seventeenth centuries made use of our text in the theological controversies of the day. In Luther's impressive interpretation the sinner who hears the gospel's word of forgiveness is contrasted with the "legalists and works people" for whom this word is untenable.[26] For all the interpreters of the Reformation this forgiveness became an expression of salvation by grace alone. The forgiveness of sins is based not on fasting or other worldy activity but alone on the *ministerium praedicationis Evangelii*.[27] "Thus the forgiveness of sins necessarily happens only by God's grace." Christ has called us not to

works of satisfaction but only to prayer.[28] Catholic exegesis suspected here a purely passive faith and polemicized correspondingly.[29] It recognized something that was important for Matthew, even if it did an injustice to the Protestant "heretics." The post-Reformation exegesis had seen especially clearly that, true to the evangelist's sense, our text is a basic text of the message of grace. Matthew and, mutatis mutandis, the exegetes of the Counter-Reformation remind us that grace does not simply make people passive; it lets them become, through their forgiveness of other people, an expression of the forgiving power of the Son of Man.

Our story's three basic types of interpretation have something in common. They mirror the freedom with which later interpreters use the stories that have been handed down to them in order to make them the language of their own faith. It is the same freedom that we have previously noticed in Matthew's own use of his tradition.

---

23   Peter Chrysologus (= *Sermo* 50).
24   Zwingli, 255: "One cannot speak of health where the causes of the illness have not been removed." From this it follows that everything we request of Christ is hypocrisy if the petition for forgiveness of sins is not included.
25   Ἐξῆλθε τὸ ῥῆμα καὶ τὸ θαῦμα ἐπηκολούθησεν (Cyril of Alexandria, above, n. 22).
26   Luther, *WA* 38.478.

27   Brenz, 393.
28   Musculus, 211. Cf. Calovius (257), who says that the text mentions not the bearers' love but their faith.
29   Lapide, 204; Maldonat, 190–92.

3.2 Jesus' Mercy on the Tax Collectors (9:9-13)

Literature

Bacon, *Studies*, 37–49.

Glynn, "Use," 56–71.

Guelich, "Not to Annul," 39–46.

David Hill, "The Use and Meaning of Hosea 6:6 in Matthew's Gospel," *NTS* 24 (1977–78) 107–19.

Hummel, *Auseinandersetzung*, 38–40, 97–99.

Mark Kiley, "Why 'Matthew' in Matt 9:9-13?" *Bib* 65 (1984) 347–51.

Pesch, "Levi-Matthäus," 40–56.

For *additional literature* see above, II B on Matthew 8–9.

9 And as Jesus was going on from there he saw a man named Matthew sitting at the custom house and says to him, "Follow me." And he got up and followed him. 10/ And it happened that he was reclining at the table in the house, and behold, many tax collectors and sinners came and reclined at the table with Jesus and his disciples. 11/ And when the Pharisees saw it, they said to his disciples, "Why does your teacher eat with the tax collectors and sinners?" 12/ But he heard it and said, "It is not the healthy who need the physician but the sick! 13/ But go and learn what it means: 'Mercy is what I want, and not sacrifice!' For I came not to call the righteous but sinners!"

Analysis

Structure

The narrative consists of the introductory call of Matthew (v. 9), the question of the Pharisees at the banquet (vv. 10-11), and Jesus' three-part answer (vv. 12-13). There is no direct connection with the preceding pericope, but with "to follow" (ἀκολουθέω, v. 9) and "disciples" (μαθηταί, vv. 10-11) there is probably a connection with 8:18-27. The same beginning[1] looks ahead to the similarly structured[2] story of 9:27-31 that also tells of Jesus' mercy with those who follow him.[3]

Source

The text is based on Mark 2:13-17. The linguistic changes are all redactional;[4] even the "minor agreements" with Luke 5:27-32 are all understandable as redaction.[5] The most significant changes of the Markan text, the name Matthew instead of Levi in v. 9 and the insertion of Hos 6:6 in v. 13, must be interpreted in the context of the evangelist's theology.

Interpretation

■ 9 According to the evangelist the next episode takes place as Jesus is leaving the place where the lame man was healed. He does not say, however, that Matthew was present at the healing;[6] instead, Jesus "saw" him sitting at the tax office. Thus the initiative for the call comes totally from Jesus. He speaks his word of command; Matthew immediately obeys. The historical present λέγει underscores the permanently valid element of Jesus' word.[7]

---

1   Παράγω/ἐκεῖθεν/ὁ Ἰησοῦς/ἀκολουθέω.

2   Also in 9:27-31 someone follows Jesus who goes into the house (vv. 10/28).

3   Ἔλεος, v. 13/ἐλεέω, v. 27.

4   Cf. vol. 1, Introduction 3.2. Matthean are: v. 9: ὁ Ἰησοῦς, ἐκεῖθεν, ἄνθρωπος defined by a participle, λεγόμενος with a name; v. 10: καὶ ἰδού; v. 11: ἰδών, διδάσκαλος as the way outsiders address Jesus (cf. on 8:19); v. 12: δέ; v. 13: πορευθείς with imperative; μαθητής, εἰ δὲ ἐγνώκειτε τί ἐστιν + Hos 6:6 (cf. 12:7), γάρ.

5   The omissions Matthew and Luke have in common are understandable as independent redaction: Mark v. 15c just hangs there; Mark v. 16a, b is superfluous after v. 15b and in any case is repeated word for word in the question of v. 16c. The redactional summary in Mark v. 13 has no function in either Matthew or Luke. Many details, among them especially the Markan lack of clarity about in whose house the dinner takes place (Luke: in Levi's house; Matthew: probably in Jesus' house) and the peculiar Markan "scribes of the Pharisees" (Matthew: Pharisees; Luke: Pharisees and scribes) show that Matthew and Luke redacted Mark independently from each other. Διὰ τί (instead of ὅτι) may be Matthean redaction (cf. 9:14). That is probably also true of εἶπεν, although Matthew likes to use the historical present with words of Jesus. Still, there are examples of the opposite: 9:2, 4; cf. 12:24 (after ἀκούσας).

6   In the interpretation of the ancient church and of modern conservatives the miracles of 8:1—9:8 play a large role in answering the question of why Matthew is just now being called. Jesus' grace is so great that he does not call people until they are able to accept him. Thus he does not call Matthew until he has heard and seen a great deal of Jesus.

7   Cf. vol. 1, Introduction 3.1.

Excursus: Matthew

Instead of Levi it is Matthew who is called. $M\alpha\vartheta\vartheta\alpha\hat{\iota}o\varsigma$, Aramaic מתי[8] or מתא,[9] is an abbreviation similar to Jannai, Zakkai, Jochai, or Nathai[10] and goes back to Mattaniah or Mattithiah (2 Kgs 24:17; Neh 8:4 = gift of Yahweh). Another abbreviation of the same name is $M\alpha\vartheta\vartheta\acute{\iota}\alpha\varsigma$.[11] Why did Matthew change the name Levi? From early times two competing explanations have been offered. According to one, Levi and Matthew are two names, for example, the name and surname, of the same person.[12] This is highly improbable, however, since with $\lambda\epsilon\gamma\acute{o}\mu\epsilon\nu o\varsigma$ ("named") Matthew wants to give a name, not a surname[13] and since there is scarcely any evidence for two different Aramaic[14] names for the same person.

The only the other possibility, and one that was seldom advocated[15] in the ancient church, is to assume that we are dealing with two different persons. In that case the evangelist has replaced the lesser-known Levi with Matthew, who was a member of the Twelve and to whom he refers in 10:3 as a tax collector. Why did he do this? One may conclude from the change that the circle of the Twelve was important for Matthew. It is obvious for him that in most places "the disciples" are the Twelve.[16] By identifying the disciples, who are transparent of his own community, with the earthly Jesus' unique circle of the Twelve, Matthew insists that discipleship always involves a relationship with the earthly Jesus and obedience to his commands.[17] That is also why he had characterized the gospel as $\epsilon\dot{v}\alpha\gamma\gamma\acute{\epsilon}\lambda\iota o\nu$ $\tau\hat{\eta}\varsigma$ $\beta\alpha\sigma\iota\lambda\epsilon\acute{\iota}\alpha\varsigma$, that is, as the earthly Jesus' proclamation of the kingdom of heaven.[18] And similarly in 27:56 he replaced the unknown Salome with the mother of the sons of Zebedee, who also appears in 20:20.[19] Here too a tradition is focused on the circle of the Twelve, a reality that has no significance for the question of the authorship of Matthew.

But why was it Matthew and not another member of the Twelve—for example, Thomas or Bartholomew—who was honored with this story of a call? Did it happen simply by accident?[20] Or because the name of Matthew had symbolic significance?[21] Or because Matthew was the ancestor and founding apostle of the area of the church in which our gospel is written?[22] That the author was so unfamiliar with the founding apostle of his own church that he had to provide him with a "foreign" call story speaks against this thesis. He does not know anything else to report about him. To me a more probable supposition is that it was still known of Matthew that he was a tax collector; therefore the story of Levi's call fit his situation. In short, it is improbable that the Matthean community venerated the apostle Matthew as its founding apostle and the guarantor of its tradition. It is next to

8   *B. Sanh.* 43a as the name of a disciple of Jesus.
9   On an inscription from Palmyra in Dalman, *Grammatik*, 178, n. 5.
10   For Jonathan, Zechariah, Jochanan, Nathaniah; further references in Dalman, *Grammatik*, 178–80. HbrMt offers מתתיה and then transcribes the Greek name.
11   Zahn, 371, n. 50.
12   Since Jerome (55) the dominant explanation has been that the other evangelists *propter verecundiam et honorem Mathei* kept silent about the publican's famous name and instead chose the tribal name Levi, while the modest Matthew did not have such compunctions and stood by his past. Among the many variants of this explanation is the suggestion that Matthew was a "circumcision name" (Gaechter, 290). For children born as Jews, however, there was no special circumcision name) or the name of honor given him at his call (Alfred Wikenhauser and Josef Schmid, *Einleitung in das Neue Testament* [6th ed.; Freiburg: Herder, 1973] 230) as a possibility.
13   Matthew uses $\lambda\epsilon\gamma\acute{o}\mu\epsilon\nu o\varsigma$ with names (2:23; 26:36; 27:16, 33) and $\acute{o}$ $\lambda\epsilon\gamma\acute{o}\mu\epsilon\nu o\varsigma$ with surnames (1:16; 4:18 etc.).
14   There are frequent cases of a Semitic and a Greek name together; two Semitic names occurred in such cases as a divorce and double marriage but are very unusual (contra Str-B 2.712).
15   Heracleon in Clement of Alexandria *Strom.* 4.9 = 71.3; Origen *Cels.* 1.62.
16   Strecker, *Weg*, 191–92; Pesch, "Levi-Matthäus," 50–53; Nikolaus Walter, "Zum Kirchenverständnis des Matthäus," *Theologische Versuche* 12 (1981) 27. However, in my judgment Matt 8:21-22 shows that it is not the case for Matthew that *every* $\mu\alpha\vartheta\eta\tau\acute{\eta}\varsigma$ is a member of the Twelve. In 8:21-22 not only is this not mentioned; also missing is the indispensable remark that the disciple had obeyed Jesus' prohibition of burying his father (contra Walter).
17   Luz, "Jünger," 142–43: Matthew's identification of the disciples with the Twelve is not in the service of a historicizing tendency.
18   Cf. the excursus on 4:23-25, vol. 1.
19   Pesch, "Levi-Matthäus," 54–55.
20   Beare, 225 ("at random").
21   Mark Kiley ("Why 'Matthew' in Matt 9:9-13?" *Bib* 65 [1984] 347–51) understands $M\alpha\vartheta\vartheta\alpha\hat{\iota}o\varsigma$ as the "learning one," cf. v. 13: $\mu\acute{\alpha}\vartheta\epsilon\tau\epsilon$. Nowhere else, however, do the names of the twelve disciples have symbolic meaning (with the exception of Matt 16:18, where Peter's name is explained).

impossible that the apostle Matthew wrote the gospel if he used Mark 2:14 as a source. As an explanation why our book became a εὐαγγέλιον κατὰ Μαϑϑαῖον, the best suggestion is still that it was a conclusion that later readers drew based on Matt 9:9.[23]

■ **10** is lying at the table[24] in the house. Whose house is it? Luke reports unambiguously (5:29) that Levi extended an invitation. Later that is how the church's interpreters consistently understood it and they interpreted Jesus' participation as an expression of his saving will and his humility.[25] What Matthew probably envisages is that Jesus, who had a residence in Capernaum (4:13; cf. 9:1), is "in the house" there (9:10, 28; 13:1, 36; 17:25)[26] and pays the temple tax where he lives. Whether the house belonged to Jesus, to Peter (cf. 8:14), or to someone else is of no concern to Matthew.[27] How is that to be reconciled with the many other places where he emphasizes that Jesus is constantly under way (for example, 8:19-20, 23, 28; 9:1; 11:1; 13:54; 15:21, 29; 16:13, etc.)? One is tempted to think of the analogy of later itinerant radicals who left their churches to go out on a mission and then returned to them.[28]

■ **11** The Pharisees see[29] that Jesus is eating with the despised and unclean tax collectors and with other crude sinners,[30] and therefore they reproach the disciples. "Teacher" is the designation for Christ used by outsiders.[31] "Your" reflects the separation between Pharisees and disciples and corresponds to the possessive "their synagogues." The scribes are no longer mentioned; they had their turn in 9:3-6. In 9:1-17 the evangelist is trying to sketch the gulf that opens up between Jesus and the different Jewish groups. Thus one pericope is dedicated to the scribes, one to the Pharisees, and one to the disciples of John.

■ **12** Jesus answers instead of the disciples. The image of the physician, for which there are Hellenistic parallels, shows that the Jewish-Christian Matthew no more shares the widespread scruples of Jews, for whom physicians were suspect because they were often unclean, than does the educated and genteel Jesus Sirach, and perhaps even Jesus himself.[32]

■ **13** Between the proverbial statement about the physician and the concluding logion Matthew inserts the quotation from Hos 6:6.[33] It is rather disturbing here and disrupts the context. Nothing has been said thus far about a sacrifice. Only by implication do the readers understand, since they know the Pharisees, that what Hosea here meant by "sacrifice" was directed at the Pharisaic purity Torah that made fellowship with tax collectors and sinners impossible.

From the early days it has been debated how the antithesis between mercy and sacrifice is to be understood. Two opposing possibilities are offered. Either

---

22 Fenton, 136; Pesch, "Levi-Matthäus," 41, 55–56.

23 Cf. also vol. 1, Introduction 5.7.

24 In contrast to the more open κατάκειμαι, ἀνάκειμαι usually has the technical meaning "to lie at table."

25 See, e.g., John Chrysostom, 30.2 = *PG* 57.363–64 (Christ wants to give good things); Peter of Laodicea, 94; Rabanus, 875 (an occasion to teach); Christian of Stavelot, 1336 (*humilitas*); Paschasius Radbertus, 372 (to grant grace).

26 In all the texts where Matthew uses ἐν τῇ οἰκίᾳ without any other attribute and in a narrative context with Jesus as the subject, Capernaum is at least possible as the place: 9:10, 28 after 9:1; 13:1, 36 (location on the lake); 17:25 after 24.

27 Cf. the analysis of Matt 4:12-17 in vol. 1. There may be old traditions that Jesus lived in Capernaum.

28 According to the synoptic tradition this was also true, e.g., of Peter who left home and yet kept his family (and his house).

29 As is usually the case, ἰδόντες is formulaic. Some

interpreters (e.g., Zahn, 373–74) think that such a banquet could not have been kept a secret in such a small place as Capernaum and that the Pharisees were waiting for the disciples at the door of the house. Well thought out!

30 It is improbable that Matthew was thinking here of the table fellowship with the Gentiles in the church (Hummel, *Auseinandersetzung*, 39; Gnilka, 1.332). The (traditional) text is formulated from a Jewish perspective. Table fellowship between Pharisees and עַם הָאָרֶץ is forbidden (Str-B 1.498–99).

31 Cf. above, n. 7 on 8:18-27.

32 Parallels in Wettstein, 1.358–59. On the Jewish skepticism toward physicians cf. Klaus Seybold and Ulrich Müller, *Sickness and Healing* (Nashville: Abingdon, 1981) 94–96. The "physician's praise" appears in Sir 38:1-15.

33 The LXX and B, among others, read in Hos 6:6 similar to the Targum ἤ = מִן. Cf. David Hill, "The Use and Meaning of Hosea 6:6 in Matthew's Gospel" (*NTS* 24 [1977–78] 107–19), 109.

one understands καὶ οὐ as an absolute antithesis, in which case sacrifice is rejected by Jesus (and by Hosea). Those in the ancient church who understood it this way were thinking that Hosea predicted the end of the cult in the new covenant.[34] The modern advocates of this interpretation assume that for Matthew the ceremonial law is abolished.[35] It is more probable, however, that καὶ οὐ should be interpreted comparatively in the sense of a *Hebraeorum idioma*[36] as a dialectical negation. Then it means: I desire mercy *more* than sacrifice. This was clearly the understanding of Hosea himself,[37] the Targum, and contemporary Jewish exegesis.[38] It also best fits the thought of Matthew himself, who did not abolish the cultic law but made it inferior to the love command (5:18-19; 5:23-24; 23:23-28). He understands Hos 6:6 in the sense of total obedience. If someone is not merciful toward the neighbor, all sacrifices avail nothing.[39] The cultic command cannot be separated from love, nor can it be opposed to it. For Matthew it is God's desire only under the sign of love. Jesus shows this by his practice.

This Hosea quotation is fundamental for the evangelist, and he will therefore repeat it in 12:7. Christologically it is to be understood as parenesis only in a secondary sense,[40] and it explains Jesus' behavior toward the tax collectors and sinners in the light of the Old Testament. Spoken to the Pharisees it means: Go and learn[41] that I fulfill the command of the prophet! It is thus formally a twofold explication of 5:17. It indicates what could be meant there by "and the prophets," and it confirms that for Matthew the fulfilling of the Law and the Prophets takes place primarily through Jesus' *behavior*. It is also a commentary on 5:20. With their objection the Pharisees show what inferior righteousness is; Jesus, on the contrary, shows what higher righteousness is.[42] That means more, however, than that Jesus gives his disciples an example. Instead, the entire Jesus story shows that his behavior results in mercy for the tax collectors, the sick, and the Gentiles. Thus beyond our pericope, in the context of Matthew 8–9, the quotation from Hos 6:6 is a kind of "explanatory word" of Jesus' healings. In them is manifested the mercy of which Hosea speaks. It is not by accident that from this point on the sick will address Jesus with ἐλέησον ("have mercy"; 9:27; 15:22; 17:15; 20:30-31). The parenetic dimension comes only after the christological dimension. Jesus "desires" mercy, a statement that agrees with the beatitude of Matt 5:7. The concluding sentence, taken from Mark, confirms then the priority of the christological interpretation over

---

34 Rarely advocated, because Hos 6:6b (LXX and Vg) is clearly comparative. Cf., however, Luther (WA 38.482), who explicitly against the patristic tradition interprets that only a justified person who loves can please God in all his deeds (including *labores* and *sacrificia*!). Johann Cocceius offers a different line of argument: *Tempus esse, in quo Deus sacrificia sit rejecturus* (*Commentariolus sive notae breves in Matthaei Evangelium*, in *Opera* [Frankfurt, 1702] 4.17). Lohmeyer's view is similar (173).

35 Strecker, *Weg*, 32.

36 Maldonat, 196; similarly, e.g., Calvin 1.265; Musculus, 232 ("*magis*"). This interpretation is advocated today primarily by those who affirm the basic validity of the law for Matthew; e.g., Barth, "Understanding," 82–83; Hummel, *Auseinandersetzung*, 43 ("priority").

37 Cf. Hos 6:6b.

38 *Tg. Hos.* 6:6 in Str-B 1.499. The usual rabbinic interpretation is based on Prov 21:3. The most important is that of Johanan ben Zakkai in ʾAbot R. Nat. 4 = Str-B 1.500: After the destruction of Jerusalem works of love "and not" sacrifice will become the basic possibility of expiation for Israel. Johanan bases the statement on Hos. 6:6 and obviously is not devaluing sacrifice. Matthew and Johanan emphasize the ethical dimension of the tradition on the basis of the prophetic heritage (and that of Jesus) independently of each other. Cf. vol. 1, Introduction 5.3.

39 Anselm of Laon, 1331: "God despises not sacrifices, but sacrifices without mercy"; Musculus, 233: "The error of the Jews is that they think that they serve by sacrifice alone (*ex opere operato*) without faith and love."

40 Guelich, "Not to Annul," 45–46; Glynn, "Use," 64–65; Held, "Matthew," 257–59.

41 Rabbinic expression צא למד (Str-B 1.499).

42 Glynn, "Use," 65–71.

43 Contra Pesch, *Markusevangelium*, 1.166. In my judgment this interpretation is philologically hardly possible, even if it would solve many of the difficulties posed by the content of the statement. Verse 13b is formulated parallel to v. 12; it is not that the healthy need the physician less than others do but that they need the physician not at all. Unlike καὶ οὐ, οὐκ ἀλλά cannot express a dialectical negation. This argument applies also to Mark 2:17 and to Matt 15:11 (cf. below, III C 2.2 on 15:7-11).

the parenetic one. Here the issue is not, as in the quotation of Hosea, that Jesus calls the sinners *more* than he calls the righteous; there is a real antithesis.[43] Although elsewhere he reckons with the existence of persons in Judaism who are actually righteous, to whom God is of course close, here he obviously does not give it much thought.[44]

---

44 Cf. 1:19; 13:17; 23:29, 35. Throughout the history of interpretation, confessional accents appear in the debate about whether the "righteous" are understood ironically. The reformers in general prefer the ironic interpretation (Luther, *WA* 38.483; Bullinger, 92), but they do so in connection with many interpreters of the ancient church (e.g., Cyril of Alexandria fr. 105 = Reuss, 187; Photius of Constantinople fr. 37 = Reuss, 287; John Chrysostom, 30.3 = *PG* 57.365; Jerome on this passage), while many Catholics point out that there actually were righteous persons such as, e.g., Joseph or Nathaniel (e.g., Lapide, 209; Maldonat, 196; cf. J. P. Migne, *Scripturae Sacrae Cursus Completus ex commentariis omnium . . . conflatus*, vol. 21 [Paris: Migne, 1840] 623–24).

3.3 The Bridegroom (9:14-17)

Literature

Franz Gerhard Cremer, *Die Fastenansage Jesu* (BBB 23; Bonn: Hanstein, 1965).

Idem, "'Die Söhne des Brautgemachs' (Mk 2,19 parr) in der griechischen und lateinischen Schrifterklärung," *BZ* 11 (1967) 246–53.

Idem, *Der Beitrag Augustins zur Auslegung des Fastenstreitgesprächs* (Études Augustiniennes; Paris: Institut d'études Augustiniennes, 1971).

Ferdinand Hahn, "Die Bildworte vom neuen Flicken und vom jungen Wein (Mk 2,21f. parr)," *EvTh* 31 (1971) 357–75.

Jürgen Roloff, *Das Kerygma und der irdische Jesus* (Göttingen: Vandenhoeck & Ruprecht, 1970) 235–37.

John A. Ziesler, "The Removal of the Bridegrooom: A Note on Mark 2:18-22 and Parallels," *NTS* 19 (1972–73) 190–94.

For *additional literature* see above, II B on Matthew 8–9.

14 **Then the disciples of John come to him and say, "Why do we and the Pharisees fast much,[1] but your disciples do not fast?" 15/ And Jesus said to them, "Can the wedding guests mourn as long as the bridegroom is with them? But days will come when the bridegroom is taken away from them, and then they will fast. 16/ But no one puts a patch of unfulled material on an old garment,**
    for the fullness tears from the garment, and a worse tear results.
17 **And they do not put young wine into old wineskins;**
    otherwise the wineskins are burst, the wine is spilled, and the wineskins are destroyed.
But they put young wine into new wineskins, and both are preserved."

Analysis

The next pericope is connected immediately by τότε. According to Matthew it still takes place at the banquet. It is divided into two parts, vv. 14-15 and vv. 16-17, that are not connected with each other in any recognizable way. In *vv. 14-15* Matthew smooths out a few awkward elements of the Markan text. Only the disciples of John come to Jesus, and they do so directly. Thus the Matthean pericope—and only the Matthean pericope—is a controversy story. Omitted are the complicated Markan introduction, Mark 2:18a, and the superfluous sentence in Mark 2:19c. The double logion in *vv. 16-17* has been changed only little from Mark. A few small peculiarities come from the Matthean redaction.[2] In the case of others we have to leave the question open.[3] The minor agreements with Luke are again noteworthy. Most, but not all, of them can be understood as the two evangelists' independent redaction of the Markan text.[4]

Interpretation

It is difficult to determine the Matthean accents in this pericope.

■ **14-15** Matthew omits the introductory Markan observation that the disciples of John and the Pharisees fast (Mark 2:18a). His readers know that the Pharisees recommend regular private fasting[5] and that John the Baptist was an ascetic (3:4; cf. 11:18). They probably also know that the Pharisees do not have "disciples." John's disciples advocate a concern of the Pharisees ("we and the Pharisees"). In contrast to 14:12 they appear here in the succession of Jewish opponents of Jesus who in 9:2-17 introduce the rupture between Jesus and Israel. That is noteworthy, because elsewhere Matthew closely identifies John the Baptist with Jesus.[6]

---

1 Πολλά (adv.) is unusual, because elsewhere Matthew avoids Mark's frequent adverbial usage (cf. vol. 1, Introduction 3.3). Since it is missing in Mark, it is likely the original text.

2 Cf. vol. 1, Introduction 3.2. Verse 14: τότε, προσέρχομαι with αὐτῷ, λέγων; v. 15: perhaps ἐφ᾽ ὅσον (cf. 25:40, 45); a reminiscence of Mark 2:19b?; v. 16: δέ, γάρ—the Markan formulation with εἰ δὲ μή (parallel to v. 22) is certainly original; v. 17: οὐδέ.

3 The parallelism between v. 16 and v. 17a-d is in places less clear in Matthew than in Mark—in contrast to the Matthean redaction elsewhere. In v. 16b the more fluent Matthean formulation is probably younger than the awkward Markan form. The conclusion καὶ ἀμφότεροι συντηροῦνται is special Matthean material, but it cannot clearly be shown to

be redactional.

4 The following may (!) be independent redaction: the omission of Mark v. 18a and v. 19c, ἀπὸ (τοῦ) ἱματίου v. 16b/Luke 5:36b (in a different place!), βάλλω or βλητέον v. 17d/Luke 5:38. Redaction is improbable in the case of ἐπιβάλλω v. 16a/Luke 5:36b, γέ v. 17b/Luke 5:37b, ἐκχέω or ἐκχύννομαι v. 17c/Luke 5:37c.

5 Str–B 2.242–43; *Did.* 8.1 (a church influenced by Matthew!): The hypocrites fast on Monday and Thursday.

6 Cf. 3:1-2, 15; 11:2-3, 18-19; 14:2, 12; 21:32.

Jesus' answer is not simple. For Matthew's readers the bridegroom is, of course, Christ (cf. 22:1-14; 25:1-13). Our text thus distinguishes two periods: the period of joy, when the bridegroom was with the wedding guests, and the period of mourning, when he will be absent. Does Matthew mean then that the time of Jesus' absence between resurrection and parousia is a time of mourning?[7] That fits poorly, however, with 28:20 and similar texts that interpret this time precisely as the time in which Jesus is present with his church. The two allegories 25:1-13 and 25:14-30 do indeed understand the present as a time of Jesus' absence; it is not, however, a time of mourning but of work and watchfulness. Or should we limit our understanding of "to mourn" ($\pi\epsilon\nu$-$\vartheta\dot{\epsilon}\omega$) to the imagery—wedding time is not mourning time? That would make things simpler; still, the readers will probably immediately understand the bridegroom to be Jesus.

It is clear, not least of all from the omission of $\dot{\epsilon}\nu$ $\dot{\epsilon}\kappa\epsilon\dot{\iota}\nu\eta$ $\tau\hat{\eta}$ $\dot{\eta}\mu\dot{\epsilon}\rho\alpha$ ("on that day"),[8] that in the time after Jesus' death the church fasts. However, we can base no theology of fasting on our text. One should not overload the text theologically at this point.[9] Matthew simply presupposes that the church fasts according to the will of Christ. In 6:16-18 he describes the spirit in which that is to happen. It may be that *Did.* 8.1 shows how it was actually done. That church is familiar with regular fasting on Wednesday and Friday.

■ **16-17** In contrast with Luke the double saying about the patch and the wine immediately follows the controversy dialogue. As was already the case in Mark, it remains unclear why the contrast between the old and the new is emphasized so much; both the Christian community and its opponents fast equally. Verse 17e says that the wine *and* the wineskins are preserved. Does Matthew reveal here an interest in what is old that would correspond, for example, to the fulfilling of the law by Jesus (5:17) or to the scribe who brings out of his treasure the old and the new (13:52)?[10] That is doubtful, since according to v. 17e it is the *new* wine and the *new* wineskins that are preserved! In my judgment the double saying thus most likely emphasizes the fundamental incompatibility of the old Israel, represented by the enemies of Jesus—the scribes, Pharisees, and disciples of John—with Jesus and the community of disciples. It may be that Matthew understood "both are preserved" to refer to the proclamation of Jesus and to its "container," the church. That, however, is only conjecture.

Summary and History of Interpretation

■ **2-17** The key to understanding vv. 16-17 is probably their position in the macrotext of Matt 9:2-17. When Jesus and his disciples ate with the tax collectors and sinners, affirming them rather than the righteous, their Jewish opponents reproached them for their freedom from fasting. Back then already the split between Jesus and Israel became visible. Jesus points out in his answer that his disciples are a new reality; they are sons of the bridegroom who are determined only by him and his presence or absence. Following three stories that speak of the beginning of a rupture between him and Israel's leaders, Jesus speaks in two basic parabolic sayings of

---

7   If one interprets the bridegroom metaphorically as Christ and the sons as the church, such an interpretation is almost unavoidable. John A. Ziesler ("The Removal of the Bridegrooom," 190–94; 192–93) avoids it by interpreting the sons in v. 15 as the Pharisees from whom the bridegroom is separated and who therefore must mourn. However, the Pharisees have always fasted!

8   Perhaps Matthew was thinking of a special Good Friday fasting.

9   Based on Matt 5:4, Strecker (*Weg,* 189) interprets mourning as an expression of the "distance from this eon" and the "waiting for the future basileia." Gnilka (1.336) connects this reference with the prophetic expectation of salvation (in among other places Isa 61:2-3) and is aware that "Christian fasting in Matthew . . . is oriented to the past insofar as it commemorates the death of Jesus, but is also eschatologically focused insofar as it expects the arrival of the basileia." Beautiful—and at the same time amazing what can be found in a text!

10   Gundry (171) points to Matt 5:17-20. Klauck (*Allegori,* 173) speaks here of an "interest in the positive values of the OT tradition."

the incompatibility of the old and the new. They point out that the "rupture" that has opened up in 9:2-15 is fundamental. There is here no connecting patch. Jesus is the new reality in Israel that can be preserved only in new wineskins. Instead of the difficult discussions about why the church's "old" fasting suddenly should be a new piece of cloth or new wine, my suggestion is that we relate the parabolic sayings not only to vv. 14-15 but to the entire section, vv. 2-15. The incompatibility of old and new thus refers to Jesus and to the people of Israel as defined by Pharisees and scribes. To be sure, it is not yet obvious at this stage of Matthew's story that the two forces are incompatible. The tension between the two has just been introduced with a few examples. That will become clear as the story continues. Our parabolic sayings thus point beyond the point at which the Matthean story has arrived, and they function as a signal.[11]

Thus by the context in which he has placed this very open double parable Matthew has indicated a direction for understanding it without precisely restricting it to a single exclusive meaning. The church's interpretation also has repeatedly found new ways to make concrete this open and "shimmering" text. Marcion understands the text to describe the relationship between the Old Testament and the gospel,[12] the *Gospel of Thomas* (logion 47), the impossibility of serving two masters. Augustine interprets it to refer to the fleshly senses and the new person, Origen to law and grace, Chromatius to the church and the perfidy of the "old" synagogue, Luther to the righteousness of the law and of faith.[13] Is there any concrete application that the text "prohibits"? Interpreting these parabolic sayings involves doing what Matthew himself did—filling the general images in one's own situation with new meaning based on one's own understanding of faith. Thus the possible new interpretations are limited not by the parabolic saying but by the context, that is, from the entirety of Matthew's theology. He makes a distinction between the synagogue or Israel, which he places in the old, and his law (or Bible), which belongs to the new because Jesus fulfills it (5:17). In this sense the interpretation of Chromatius, but not that of Marcion or of Origen, lies within the possibilities of meaning he suggests. Today, however, analogous to Chromatius, but not as he did, we will take into consideration not only the Gospel of Matthew but also the entirety of the Bible, when on the basis of our own faith we fill the old parabolic sayings with new meaning. Then we will have to rethink his separation between Israel and *its* (!) inheritance, the Bible and the law, and we will do so, for example, on the basis of Paul and in light of the tragic history of Christian-Jewish relations in the nineteen hundred years since Matthew—a history caused in part by the Christian understanding of the Bible.

---

11 If Jesus originally was thinking of "himself and his own" (Jülicher, *Gleichnisreden,* 2.197) or of "the dawning reign of God" (Ferdinand Hahn, "Die Bildworte vom neuen Flicken und vom jungen Wein," 357–75; 371), then Matthew is not far removed from the original meaning.

12 Tertullian *Marc.* 3.15.

13 Augustine *Sermo* 186 = *PL* 38.999–1000; Origen fr. 178 = 86; Chromatius, 46.3 = 2.88–89; Luther, *WA* 38.486.

Once again Matthew inserts the following miracles into a connected narrative thread. While the banquet with the tax collectors is still going on (9:10-17), the ἄρχων ("the ruler") appears. Jesus goes to the ruler's house (9:23) and then returns to the house where he usually stays (9:28, cf. 9:10). Two blind men follow him there. Just as they are leaving, the mute demoniac is brought to him (9:32). The four healing stories that make up our section are connected by a number of key words that they have in common.[1]

Ties to chap. 8 are also numerous.[2] All of the themes and many of the motifs of the preceding sections reappear in this concluding section. The theme of faith (9:22, 28-29) repeats 8:10, 13. The "following" of the blind men (9:27, cf. 19) reminds the reader of 8:18-27; 9:9. The scenery of this story (9:27) is that of 9:9-10. The girl's "sleeping" and "being raised" (9:24-25) corresponds to Jesus' behavior in the boat (8:25-26). The Christ-title, κύριος ("Lord"), in 9:28 picks up on the basic christological tenor of 8:2-25. The presence of the disciples (9:19) reminds the readers that we are dealing with the church in 8:18-27 and 9:8-15. The crowds announce again in 9:33 that the evangelist told about miracles of Jesus in Israel (cf. primarily 8:1-17). The

Pharisees' negative reaction in 9:34 is a reminder that in 9:2-17 a schism happened in Israel because of Jesus. The title "Concluding Miracles" is thus an expression not of a predicament but of the evangelist's desire to show and tie together once more all of the strands of his braid.[3] This part of the narrative results in the Pharisees' concluding rejection of Jesus (9:34) that will have consequences for the ongoing story (cf. 12:24!)

Our section is unusual as far as its sources are concerned. The first double story corresponds to Mark 5:21-43. That is not surprising, since in 8:23-34 Matthew has already used Mark 4:35–5:20. However, vv. 27-34 come from completely different contexts in Mark (10:46-52) and Q (Luke 11:14-15). Furthermore, both stories are repeated later (20:29-34; 12:22-24). Thus Matthew does something here that he previously had scarcely done with his sources. Why? 11:5-6 reveals the reason. The evangelist was concerned to give an example for each of the miracles that Jesus there enumerates for the disciples of John. Since he has thus far not had an appropriate story for the healing of the blind (τυφλοὶ ἀναβλέπουσιν) and mute (κωφοὶ ἀκούουσιν), he uses these two narratives here in anticipation.

---

1 Λαλέω (vv. 18, 33); ἄρχων (vv. 18, 23, 34); ἀκολουθέω (vv. 19, 27); πίστις/πιστεύω (vv. 22, 28-29); οἰκία (vv. 23, 28); ἐκβάλλω (vv. 25, 33-34); ὅλη ἡ γῆ ἐκείνη (vv. 26, 31 each time at the end of the pericope).

2 Προσκυνέω (8:2; 9:18); χείρ (8:3, 15; 9:18, 25); ἥψατο (8:3, 15; 9:29; cf. 20-21); σῴζω (8:25; 9:21-22); ὥρα ἐκείνη (8:13; 9:22); ἐλθών . . . εἰς τὴν οἰκίαν (8:14; 9:23, 28); δύω/κράζω/λέγων (8:28-29; 9:27); γενηθήτω (8:13; 9:29); ὅρα+μηδείς (8:4; 9:30); προσήνεγκαν (8:16; 9:32, cf. 9:2); ἐθαύμασαν (8:27; 9:33). Thus the entire section gives the readers the

impression that they are "familiar" with what they are reading.

3 Cf. above, II B Structure. The theme of faith is thus not *the* theme of our section (as Held ["Matthew," 248] with exclusion of vv. 32-34 claims) but *a* theme. It is missing in the story of the daughter of the ἄρχων (unlike Mark 5:36).

4.1 The Ruler's Daughter and the Hemorrhaging Woman (9:18-26)

Literature

Held, "Matthew," 178–81; 214–19.

Manfred Hutter, "Ein altorientalischer Bittgestus in Mt 9,20-22," *ZNW* 75 (1984) 133–35.

José O'Callaghan, "La variante *ΕΙΣ/ΕΛΘΩΝ* en Mt 9,18," *Bib* 62 (1981) 104–6.

Vernon K. Robbins, "The Woman Who Touched Jesus' Garment: Socio-rhetorical Analysis of the Synoptic Accounts," *NTS* 33 (1987) 502–15.

Gerard Rochais, *Les récits de résurrection des morts dans le Nouveau Testament* (SNTSMS 40; Cambridge: Cambridge University Press, 1981) 88–99.

For *additional literature* see above, II B on Matthew 8–9.

18 While he was saying this to them, behold, one[1] of the rulers[2] came, fell down before him, and said, "My daughter has just died. But come and lay your hand on her, and she will live." 19/ Then Jesus stood up and followed him and (also) his disciples. 20/ And behold, a woman who had been hemorrhaging for twelve years came up behind him and touched the tassels of his garment. 21/ For she said to herself, "If I just touch his garment, I am saved!" 22/ But Jesus turned around, saw her, and said, "Take courage, daughter, your faith has saved you!" And the woman was saved from that hour. 23/ When Jesus came to the ruler's house and saw the flute players and the noisy crowd, 24/ he said, "Go away. The girl[3] has not died; she is sleeping." And they laughed at him. 25/ When the crowd had been sent out, he went in, took her by the hand, and the girl got up. 26/ And this report went throughout that entire land.

Analysis

Structure

The text is divided into four small scenes, each of which has a different location: in the house of the banquet with the tax collectors (vv. 18-19), on the way (vv. 20-22), in front of the house of the ruler (vv. 23-25a), and—by no means separated from the others—in his house (v. 25b, c). Verse 26 is a concluding remark (cf. 8:27; 9:31). Except for the ruler, Jesus is the only one who speaks.[4] The second scene, vv. 20-22, stands out because of the catchword σῴζω ("to save"; three times). Jesus takes up the woman's thought (v. 21) with his comment, so that a type of rhetorical syllogism is created. Touching the garment is understood as faith (πίστις).[5]

Source

Notable is the number of instances where Matthew abbreviates Mark 5:21-43. One of the results of his omissions is that he loses the connection between the stories of the daughter of Jairus and of the woman with the hemorrhage. Since Jesus is now no longer detained by the woman, it is no longer the case that he arrives too late to heal the sick girl; she is dead from the beginning (9:18). The concluding notice in v. 26 about spreading the news has no basis in the Markan original, but it is not a completely independent creation of Matthew. He uses either Mark 1:28 or the concluding sentence of a deutero-Markan recension of Mark 5:21-43 that formed the source for

---

1   On the text-critical problem cf. José O'Callaghan, "La variante *ΕΙΣ/ΕΛΘΩΝ* en Mt 9,18," 104–6. Based on the external evidence the original text is *ΕΙΣΕΛΘΩΝ*. It is uncertain whether it is to be read as εἷς ἐλθῶν or as εἰσελθών. Although postpositive εἷς in the sense of τις is unusual for Matthew (or for that very reason!), εἷς ἐλθών is to be read. Most of the manuscripts that replaced ἐλθών with προσελθών and εἷς with τις understood it this way. Furthermore, in Mark 5:22 Matthew read εἷς.

2   Ἄρχων instead of Markan ἀρχισυνάγωγος. Is Matthew also thinking of a ruler of a synagogue? That is improbable, for the change has to be explained. Although an ἄρχων on occasion may also be an ἀρχισυνάγωγος (Wolfgang Schrage, "συναγωγή κτλ," *TDNT* 7 [1971] 845), as a rule ἄρχων is a municipal official. In Josephus the ἄρχοντες are the municipal leaders (*Bell.* 2.405, 407, 570).

     Ἄρχων was taken into Aramaic and Middle Hebrew as a loanword within the meaning "ruler," "municipal official" (אַרְכוֹן, cf. Samuel Krauss, *Griechische und lateinische Lehnwörter im Talmud, Midrasch und Targum* [2 vols.; 1898–99; reprinted Hildesheim: Olms, 1964] 129, and Marcus Jastrow, *A Dictionary of the Targumim, the Talmud Babli and Yerushalmi, and the Midrashic Literature* [New York: Judaica Press, 1989], *s.v.*). The translation "official" does not exactly convey the meaning, since the term means not necessarily a fixed municipal office but in a more general sense a leading position. The French "*un notable*" is a good translation (Bonnard, 134).

3   Phrynichus (*Ecl.* 73–74 = Christian Augustus Lobeck, ed., *Phrynichi Eclogae nominum et verborum Atticorum* [1820; reprinted Hildesheim: Olms, 1965]) criticizes a κοράσιον for being παράλογον (improper).

4   In Mark others also speak: the woman (ἔλεγεν; Matthew: ἔλεγεν ἐν ἑαυτῇ), the disciples, and people from the house of the ruler of the synagogue.

Matthew and Luke.[6] The "minor agreements" are quite numerous.[7] Our text is one of those synoptic texts that are clear indications of the existence of a deutero-Markan recension. The remaining Matthean peculiarities come from his editorial hand.[8]

Interpretation

■ **18-19** The text is brief, inexpressive, and retains only the essential elements. During the tax collectors' banquet, one of the rulers comes and does homage at the feet of Jesus.[9] It is no longer a ruler of a synagogue; it is some aristocratic person, perhaps a high official. The members of the church who are listening to the story could more easily identify with him than with the president of the synagogue that is hostile to them.[10] Unlike Mark 5:23, his child has just died. Thus the encounter

with the hemorrhaging woman does not delay an urgently needed healing, and, correspondingly, Matthew is not concerned to test and to deepen the ruler's faith (thus Mark 5:35-36). Instead, the miracle is heightened. The official throws himself at the feet of Jesus. He puts the request to Jesus in the way that Jesus will fulfill it in v. 25.[11] In the preceding stories Jesus' hand has become a symbolic word for his helping power (8:3, 15). The church knows that it too may stand under Jesus' outstretched hand, that is, in the realm of his powerful help (12:49; 14:31; 19:13-15). Thus this story becomes transparent for the church's own experience. Jesus immediately does what the ἄρχων asks.[12]

■ **20** On the way a woman comes to him. Matthew says nothing about her except that she has been bleeding

---

5   Vernon K. Robbins, "The Woman Who Touched Jesus' Garment," 506–7.

6   Cf. Luke 4:14b prior to the Lukan pericope parallel to Mark 6:1-6. A deutero-Markan concluding statement about spreading the report about Jesus would fit into the reduction of the "messianic secret" that Ennulat (*Agreements*, 425) regards as one of its (few) distinctive theological characteristics.

7   (1) Ἰδού . . . ἄρχων (v. 18, Luke 8:41); (2) θυγατήρ; and (3) perhaps the death that has already happened (v. 18, Luke 8:42?); (4) προσελθοῦσα ὄπισθεν ἥψατο τοῦ κρασπέδου (v. 20, Luke 8:44); (5) ἐλθὼν εἰς τὴν οἰκίαν (v. 23, Luke 8:51); (6) τῆς χειρὸς αὐτῆς (v. 25, Luke 8:54); (7) ἐξῆλθεν/φήμη/ὅλη (v. 26, Luke 4:14b); (8) various common omissions from Mark 5:23, 29, 33, 34, 41. Nos. 4 and 5 (elsewhere Luke says εἰσέρχομαι εἰς οἰκίαν) are not understandable as Lukan redaction; φήμη (no. 7) is a hapax legomenon for Matthew and Luke. As is the case in other texts, the minor agreements are more closely related to the Matthean than the Lukan redaction. That Luke would have used Matthew as a secondary source is improbable because of the different placement of nos. 5 and 7. Furthermore, the (insignificant) Lukan omissions would then be more difficult to understand. Bovon (*Lukas* 1.443) suggests a common oral tradition.

8   Cf. vol. 1, Introduction 3.2. Matthean are: v. 18: ἰδού, προσελθών, προσκυνέω, ἄρτι, τελευτάω. The introductory genitive absolute is inspired by Mark 5:35. Verse 19: ἐγερθείς; v. 20: ἰδού; γυνή with a participle (cf. 26:7) corresponds to ἄνθρωπος with a participle. On κράσπεδον cf. Mark 6:56. Verse 21: ἐν ἑαυτῇ, μόνον; v. 22: στρέφω (cf. 16:23 participle), ἰδών, ὥρα ἐκείνη (literally like 15:28; 17:18). On θαρσέω cf. 9:2. Verse 23: ἐλθών . . . εἰς τὴν οἰκίαν

as in 2:11; 8:14; 9:28; 17:25; v. 24: ἀναχωρέω, γάρ; v. 25: εἰσέρχομαι, ἐγείρω; v. 26: γῆ, ἐκεῖνος. Matthew avoids (cf. vol. 1, Introduction 3.3): πάλιν, θυγάτριον, εὐθύς, ξηραίνω, πολλά, εἰσπορεύομαι, ἀνίστημι, διαστέλλομαι, μηδείς. Without exception the abbreviations can be explained as Matthean redaction. Earlier the assumption of a Matthean tradition on precisely this story that was independent from Mark was quite widespread. Cf. still Walter Grundmann, *Das Evangelium nach Matthäus* (ThHKNT 1; Berlin: Evangelische Verlagsanstalt, 1968) 274; Bonnard, 134–35. It is, however, an unnecessary thesis. Cf. Rochais, *Récits*, 89–97.

9   Cf. vol. 1, I A 2.1 on 2:11.

10   In my judgment the omission of the name Jairus also serves this identification. Cf. 9:27-31 where the name Bartimaeus is missing.

11   V. 18: ἐλθών/ἐπίθες τὴν χεῖρα . . ./ζήσεται. V. 25: εἰσελθών/ἐκράτησεν τῆς χειρὸς αὐτῆς/καὶ ἠγέρθη.

12   Ἐγερθείς anticipates v. 25. That Jesus "follows" the ἄρχων is unusual. Ἠκολούθει is probably a "remnant" from Mark's omitted v. 24. The imperfect is *lectio difficilior* (contra Nestle[26]).

constantly for twelve years.[13] The Jewish-Christian readers of the gospel can imagine what she has experienced during the twelve years of her hemorrhaging and what that meant for her in terms of social and religious segregation. Why she comes to Jesus from the rear and is satisfied with touching his garment, the readers can only guess. It is probably from shyness because of the uncleanness[14] that she passes on to Jesus when she touches him. In short, the description of the woman and her problem is so brief that one does not get the impression that the evangelist has a special interest in her.[15] He does, on the other hand, mention that Jesus is wearing a garment with tassels; Jesus is presented as a pious Jew (cf. Num 15:38-40; Deut 22:12).[16]

■ **21** For Matthew it is important that the woman has an unlimited trust in Jesus' power; she hopes to be healed by touching his garment.[17] He has a positive opinion of this trust. By touching Jesus' garment, the woman has demonstrated faith.[18]

■ **22** Jesus turns around and looks at her. The crowd (Mark 5:24, 30-31) and the disciples (Mark 5:31) are no longer mentioned in our story; everything takes place solely between the woman and Jesus. Jesus, who looks into her heart and knows what she is doing, encourages her; her faith has saved her. With his omissions Matthew has made of the story a paradigm of his understanding of faith. Faith is something active; it risks unlimited trust in Jesus (cf. 14:28-29). Jesus responds to such risks, no matter how ambiguous they may be, and grants God's help (8:10, 13; 9:29; 15:28). On the human side, faith is risked prayer;[19] with his power God helps the ambiguous and weak human risktaking.[20] The healing that the woman experiences is transparent of much more, viz., salvation as every Christian experiences it in life with God (cf. 8:25-26). This story is paradigmatic, therefore, for healthy people also. "Saving" is something concrete. Since it thus also includes healing, Matthew talks about it in connection with actual healing. The saving and the healing go hand in hand, just as do faith and the woman's "magical" touching of the garment. However, the saving is more than the healing. Matthew expresses that first by relating that Jesus grants salvation to the woman because of her faith and only then by telling about the healing.[21] He expresses this also with his carefully chosen tenses. The unique healing that took place

---

13 $Αἱμορροοῦσα$ as in Lev 15:33.

14 Cf. *m. Zabim* 5.1, 6 = Str–B 1.520. Menstruating women are not allowed to participate in the Passover (Josephus *Bell.* 6.426).

15 Thus it probably is also not important for Matthew that Jesus or the church here accepts two women as Bovon (*Lukas*, 1.445) emphasizes for Luke.

16 $Κράσπεδον$ exists also in Aramaic as a loanword (כְּרוֹסְפְּדִין plural) for צִיצִת. The tassels, which are to remind the Jew of obedience to the law, are on the four corners of the garment and are normally three or four fingers in length (Str–B 4.281 in sections n and o).

17 Touching the garment and the tassels is a petitionary gesture. Cf. Zech 8:23; 1 Sam 15:27. For Eastern parallels see Manfred Hutter, "Ein altorientalischer Bittgestus in Mt 9,20-22," 133–35.

18 The Matthean abbreviations are often interpreted as designed to reduce the magical elements. See, e.g., John M. Hull, *Hellenistic Magic and the Synoptic Tradition* (SBT 2/28; Naperville: Allenson, 1974) 136: The woman "expects magic but instead is met by the healing grace of the Messianic Servant"; Birger Gerhardsson, *The Mighty Acts of Jesus According to Matthew* (Scripta minora. K. Humanistiska Vetenskapssamfundet i Lund 5; Lund: Gleerup,

1979) 47: "everything is at the conscious, personal level"; Böcher, "Magie," 15: "only the woman's superstitious hope, not . . . the successful way to magical healing." However, Matthew does not omit the "most magical" feature, viz., touching the hem of Jesus' garment. Verse 22 regards v. 21 positively, not critically ($σωθήσομαι/σέσωκεν$).

19 Luther 2.334: "There can no more be faith without prayer than fire without heat."

20 Calvin (1.272) sees here, not without justification, the scope of the story. The woman's faith is mixed with all kinds of mistakes and errors, but Christ does not criticize her; instead, he "graciously accepts her imperfect, weak faith."

21 The order is similar in 8:10 + 13, 26; 9:28-29; 15:24-28.

"in that hour"[22] is a concrete expression of the salvation by faith that is always real.[23]

■ **23** Jesus now comes to the house and there sees the flute players, who are indispensable in both Jewish and Greek funeral processions,[24] and the noisy people,[25] who for Matthew are probably the criers and mourners of Mark 5:38-39.

■ **24** The mourning stops abruptly. Jesus says that the child is not dead, only sleeping.[26] Of course, Jesus is not saying that she only appears to be dead.[27] Nor is he expressing the general doctrine that the hope of a future resurrection means that *every* death of a Christian is only sleep.[28] The statement intends to shock. Jesus speaks only of *this* dead girl, and he wants to call attention to his own power. For *him* this death is not a final death, because he is going to show that he has power over it. Of course, only the believing reader of the Gospel of Matthew understands this, certainly not the "noisy" crowd that laughs at him.

■ **25** Jesus throws them out. The raising is reported quite simply; it happens just as the ruler asked in v. 18. The disciples are not present; Matthew does not need witnesses for doubting readers. Nor does he demonstrate the raising by having the girl walk around and eat. The Aramaic awakening-word is missing. Matthew says simply that Jesus takes the girl's hand so that she was raised. This formulation—and only this formulation—becomes transparent of the church: It also stands under Jesus' protection, and it also some day will be raised by the risen one. Matthew's abridgment of the Markan story focuses the reader's attention on these associations.[29]

■ **26** The concluding statement in v. 26 shows that Matthew has no use for the Markan messianic secret.[30] The statement is part of the entire narrative thread of Matthew 8–9. At the end of the two chapters the statements about the effect of Jesus' miracles among the people are multiplied (vv. 26, 31; cf. 33, 35 πάσας!). Jesus' activity includes his entire nation. This prepares the way for the mission of the disciples in chap. 10, and it gives Jesus' rejection by the scribes, Pharisees, and disciples of John (9:2-17) its appropriate dimension.

Summary and History of Interpretation
Once again Matthew tells a Jesus story that is really understood only when it sheds light on and defines the church's own experiences with the risen Lord. It is

---

22 Ἀπὸ τῆς ὥρας ἐκείνης together with the aorist ἐσώθη emphasizes the one-time healing. In Matthew, miracle narratives are, in spite of their transparency, reports about unique events. For rabbinic linguistic analogies see Schlatter, 318.

23 Σέσωκεν (perfect) in v. 22b in contrast to ἐσώθη in v. 22c. On the intentional use of tenses in Matthew cf. vol. 1, Introduction 3.1.

24 Joachim Marquardt, *Das Privatleben der Römer* (1886; reprinted Darmstadt: Wissenschaftliche Buchgesellschaft, 1975) 351–52; Lucian *De luctu* 12.19. For further references see Wettstein 1.362–63; Jewish references: m. *Ketub.* 4.4 (even the poorest person in Israel provides two flute players and a mourning woman); Josephus *Bell.* 3.437.

25 Again an example of Matthew's conservative redaction. He does not want the crowd of Mark's narrative to disappear completely.

26 Sleep as a metaphor for death. Καθεύδω is seldom used this way. Cf. only Albrecht Oepke, "καθεύδω," *TDNT* 3 (1965) 432-33; BAGD, s.v. καθεύδω 2a (LXX!). This meaning is common with κοιμάομαι. Cf. modern Greek κοιμητήριο = graveyard and the formula common on Jewish tombstones in Rome: ἐν εἰρήνῃ ἡ κοίμησις αὐτοῦ (αὐτῆς).

27 This was the usual explanation in the Enlighten-

ment. Hermann Olshausen, e.g., speaks of a "trance" (*Biblical Commentary on the New Testament*, vol. 1 [New York: Sheldon, 1863] 390). Paulus (1.425–26, 439–40) reports on the danger of being buried alive, because burial in Palestine takes place very quickly after death. Even prior to the Enlightenment, interpreters pointed out that the crowd that is laughing at Jesus excludes such explanations. Cf., e.g., Theophylactus, 232 (they become witnesses for the miracle); Thomas Aquinas, *Lectura* no. 787; Zwingli, 261.

28 Thus, e.g., Origen fr. 185 = 88; Musculus, 249–50. By contrast Luther (2.338) says correctly that it is not a question of the "sleep of St. Michael in which one sleeps until the last day," but of the reality that Christ sees this death differently than do human beings: "Before you she is dead, but before me she sleeps."

29 Cf. Held, "Matthew," 179: "Abridgments are . . . a method of interpretation."

30 Mark 1:34c is also missing in Matthew. Rochais (*Récits*, 96) says that as a story of faith our text has general validity, and the messianic secret is not necessary.

appropriate, therefore, that the later church discovered in this story its own view of Christ and its own experiences with him.

a. From the perspective of faith in the Risen One our story had to receive new dimensions. It is less by individual raisings of the dead than by his own *resurrection* that Christ shows that death really is only sleep, viz., *recreatio ad vitam*.[31] Thus for Luther—not as a philosophy of life but as a testimony of faith—v. 24 becomes the center of the story. "Christ personally ridicules death . . . and calls it sleep." The story gives comfort to faith: "My tomb is (in reality) my bed . . . and I do not die; I sleep."[32] Ephraem the Syrian understands the christological scope of our story differently. It becomes what it was not directly in Matthew's gospel—a witness in advance of Jesus' death and resurrection.[33]

b. The interpreters have found their own experiences with the Risen One in our narrative in two ways. In the ancient church and the Middle Ages it was common to see the text as an *allegory of salvation history*. The hemorrhaging woman who comes to Jesus later and is healed first was interpreted as the gentile church, the daughter of the ruler of the synagogue as the synagogue. The order of the two miracles was then understood in the sense of Rom 11:25.[34] That made it possible to allegorize various details. The hemorrhage is idolatry; the woman's physicians (Mark 5:26) are the philosophers. The woman only touched Jesus' garment, because the Gentiles had no direct contact with the earthly Jesus. Jairus, the enlightener, is Moses. The flute players are the teachers of the law who lead the Jewish people astray. At this point, at the very latest, anti-Jewish undertones would then steal into the interpretations. The Jewish people are not a *turba credentium*, but a *turba tumultuantium*. "If the hands of the Jews that are covered with blood are not first cleansed" (cf. Matt. 9:25!), "their dead synagogue will not rise," writes Jerome,[35] in marked distinction from the text, and countless people copied it from him. As part of this interpretation, the "faith" of the ruler of the synagogue was always regarded as having less value than that of the hemorrhaging woman or even of the centurion of Capernaum.[36]

c. Alongside the salvation-history interpretation is the *personal* interpretation. In this case the listeners identify directly with the menstruating woman or with the girl or her father. The woman is an example of faith that believes against all hope.[37] Or she is an example of imperfect faith that believes that it can hide before Jesus.[38] The girl is the soul that died because of its sin.[39] Allegorically, the flute players are the flatterers; the people in the crowd are worldly thoughts.[40] Jesus' tunic represents the medicines of faith, the gospel, and the sacraments.[41] John Chrysostom identifies differently with the story. He contrasts the three disciples who enter the room (Mark 5:37) with the crowd that stays outside. His message is: Do not become mired in sadness because of death. Do not stay outside, as the people did, but go in, as Peter did. Come to the miracle of Christ that overcomes death![42]

Such interpretations have understood that Matthew's story is designed to make the hearers part of the story and to lead them to the living Christ who gives them faith (vv. 20-22) and who is for them the "one who conquers death"[43] (vv. 24-25). Viewed from Matthew's perspective, the *christological* scope is primary. Just as saving the hemorrhaging woman is more than simply healing her (although the latter is part of the former), so the resurrection story points to Christ's all-encompassing

31 Brenz, 406.
32 Luther, *WA* 38, 489.
33 Ephraem Syrus, 155.
34 Cf. Gnilka, *Markus*, 1.219–21. The ancient interpretation consistently inserts the statements missing in Matthew from Mark and Luke and even bases its comments in part directly on the Markan text. For good examples of salvation-history allegorizing see Jerome, 59–60; Hilary, 9.5–6 = SC 254.208–10; Ambrose *In Luc.* 6.54–64 = BKV 1/21.589–94; Bede, 48–49; Rabanus, 879–83; Strabo, 116–17; Paschasius Radbertus, 380–87; Thomas Aquinas, *Lectura* no. 778–86.
35 60.
36 Cf. Gnilka, *Markus* 1.220.
37 Bullinger, 94A.
38 Euthymius Zigabenus, 316.
39 See, e.g., Rabanus, 883–84; developed by Lapide, 214.
40 Thomas Aquinas, *Catena*, 1/1.353.
41 Brenz, 404.
42 31 = 436–49, especially 443, 447–48.
43 Schniewind, 121.

power to give life—a power that transcends the one-time event of the miracle.[44]

The *salvation-history* application (based primarily on the expression "ruler of the synagogue" that Matthew omits) is in this story of only indirect importance for Matthew. These two miracles also are among the Messiah's deeds on behalf of Israel that someday will reject him. More important for him is the readers' personal application of the story to their own faith and their own resurrection hope. To be sure, for modern readers a problem is that miracles are not available to us as much (or even at all) as tangible signs of the much more all-embracing power of Christ to give life, as indeed this raising of a dead person can make especially clear.[45] Our symbolic interpretation of the Matthean

miracle stories then easily becomes *only* a symbolic interpretation, and their testimony to the life-creating power of faith becomes a form of spiritualizing. By contrast, Matthew begins with the conviction that the miracles about which he tells really happened. Here exists—at least as far as raising the dead is concerned—a major difficulty for modern interpretation. Since, in my judgment, the experience of seeing a dead person brought back to life remains inconceivable for us, I see no solution to this problem.

---

44 Luther (sermon on Matt 9:18-26 = *WA* 11.205) states on Jesus' miraculous healings basically: *Omnia . . . miracula, quae fecit euserlich an leuten, sunt indicia beneficiorum, quae intus facit in animabus credentium.* This sentence goes to the heart of Matthew's under-

standing of miracles, not as an exhortation to internalize but in the sense that the miracles point to the living reality of Christ that transcends them.

45 Matt 10:8 assumes that dead will be brought back to life in the church too.

4.2 The Two Blind Men (9:27-31)

Literature

Burger, *Davidssohn*, 74–77.

Fuchs, *Untersuchungen*, 18–170.

Held, "Matthew," 219–25.

For *additional literature* see above, II B on Matthew 8–9.

27 **And as Jesus was going on from there two blind men followed him crying out and saying, "Have mercy on us, Son of David." 28/ But when he came into the house, the blind men came to him. And Jesus says to them, "Do you believe that I can do that?" They say to him, "Yes, Lord." 29/ Then he touched their eyes and said, "Let it happen to you according to your faith." 30/ And their eyes were opened. And Jesus admonished them and said, "See that no one knows it." 31/ But they went out and spread the news about him in that entire region.**

Analysis

Structure

The very brief and colorless nature of the story makes the detailed scenery stand out all the more. The blind men meet Jesus on the road (v. 27) and follow him into the house (v. 28), where they have to confirm again (v. 28) their request (v. 27). There are numerous ties to earlier stories. Most notable is the repetition of the scenery of 9:9-13 (παράγων ἐκεῖθεν, following after, going into the house). The number of the blind (two) is reminiscent of the two demoniacs who also cried out (δύο, κράζω, λέγοντες [8:28-29/9:27]). Reminiscent of 8:1-4 are δύναμαι, ἥψατο, and the command to silence introduced by

ὁρᾶτε μηδείς. In addition, Matthew takes up features that in 8:1-4 he had omitted from the Markan source, 1:40-45 (ἐμβριμάομαι, ἐξελθών + διαφημίζω Mark 1:43, 45). It is as if Matthew, in spite of shortening the material, would like to give up as little as possible of Mark! Verse 29b is reminiscent of the centurion of Capernaum (cf. 8:13). The conclusion (ἐν ὅλῃ τῇ γῇ ἐκείνῃ) is reminiscent of 9:26. In this way the story appears almost like a quilt[1] made of patches from earlier stories. Matthew thus consciously tells the story of blind Bartimaeus in a way designed to remind the reader of the preceding stories from chaps. 8–9. The reader is to sense that this is a "typical" healing of Jesus.

Source

The narrative comes exclusively from Mark 10:46-52,[2] except that in vv. 30b-31 Matthew makes use of the earlier omitted Mark 1:43. Matthew will bring up the story of the blind Bartimaeus again in 20:29-34 in a version that on the whole is closer to Mark. The changes are redactional.[3] At the most we might ask whether the version of the Markan text available to Matthew was slightly different from ours.[4] There is thus every reason to believe that the two duplications also come from him: One blind man becomes two, one story becomes two. More easily understandable is the duplication of the blind man that has its parallel in 8:28. It makes it easier to see the blind as types, strengthens the agreement with 11:5,[5] and corresponds with a law of popular storytelling.[6] The duplication of the story causes greater problems. Matthew

---

1 Klostermann (83) says that the story is "pieced together entirely from familiar patches."

2 Fuchs (*Untersuchungen*, 18-37) offers a detailed survey of the history of research.

3 According to vol. 1, Introduction 3.2, Matthean are: ἐκεῖθεν, ἐλθών (εἰς τὴν οἰκίαν cf. on 9:23), προσέρχομαι, ναί (cf. 13:51!), κύριε as an address of the supplicants, τότε, λέγων. Ἀκολουθέω (v. 27) anticipates Mark 10:52. Ὀφθαλμοί with ἀνοίγω (v. 30) is LXX language (more than fifteen times; Isa 35:5; 42:7 with τυφλοί).

4 Fuchs (*Untersuchungen*, 168–70) assumes a deutero-Mark, but the minor agreements are less numerous here than elsewhere. Matthean or Lukan redaction are λέγων (v. 27; 20:30; Luke 18:38); παράγω or παρέρχομαι (v. 27; 20:30, cf. 9:9; Luke 18:37). The omission of the name Bartimaeus and the address κύριε in miracle stories (v. 28; 20:33; Luke 18:41, cf. 8:2, Luke 5:12) can be explained as Matthean, but only with difficulty as Lukan redaction.

5 Our text is no more a reminder of the omitted

story, Mark 8:22-26, than 8:28-34 is of Mark 1:23-38. Only in 20:34 does Matthew use the "leftover" (Mark 8:23) ὄμμα. Of course, the reference to Matt 11:5-6 has only limited relevance, since we do not also have the case that two lepers are healed and two dead are raised.

6 Cf. the parallels from Matthew and Luke cited at 8:28 (above, II B 2.2) and the material in Bultmann (*History*, 314–17) on the popular use of the number two.

7 Missing in 9:27-31 are, among other things: the location at Jericho, the accompanying crowd, the statement that the blind men are sitting at the roadside, the crowd's rebuke, and Jesus' mercy. Missing in 20:29-34 are the faith motif and the command to silence. The features unique to the version in our text are due on the one hand to the fact that the context is different from that in Mark 10 and Matthew 20, on the other hand to the fact that Matthew is introducing motifs from earlier stories into our text. It is impossible that our text is a redac-

has to include the healing of a blind person before 11:5, but he could have simply included the story here and omitted it in chap. 20. Furthermore, he tells it in 20:29-34 so differently[7] that the reader has the impression that there are two different healings of blind people. But why does he speak both times of the healing of *two* blind men? It is clear that Matthew did not have our problems concerning historical truthfulness. That was made easier for him by the fact that doublets can be found repeatedly in the synoptic tradition.[8] For Matthew the truth of a gospel story obviously does not depend on historical faithfulness in detail. That is the only way to understand the freedom with which he was able to create a new narrative thread in chaps. 8–9 that is chronologically connected but historically fictitious.

Interpretation

■ **27** Two blind men follow Jesus as he walks by. The scene reminds the readers of 9:9-10; they know that again the issue is following Jesus. The two blind men have no names (in contrast to Mark 10:46; cf. Matt 9:18!), a fact that makes it easier to identify with them. In Matthew also "blindness" is used metaphorically. In the tradition, to be blind already means to lack understanding or to live in the darkness of the old eon.[9] Presumably in Mark the healings of the blind are to be read with such overtones. In the great Matthean discourse of woes the blindness of the Jewish leaders is recorded five times (23:16-28, cf. 15:14). In Matt 13:13-15 Jesus will declare Israel's blindness and deafness. Of course, the readers do not yet know all of this. They will, however, remember it later, especially when the evangelist again reports editorially on the healing of the blind (and the deaf) (12:22; 15:30-31; 20:30-31; 21:14). He introduces a motif here that he will repeat several times and that culminates in chap. 23 with the separation between the blind leaders of Israel and the Jesus who heals the blind. It is in this context that the plea for

mercy from Jesus, the Son of David, belongs.

Excursus:
Son of David in the Gospel of Matthew

Literature

Berger, "Messiastraditionen," 1–44.
Burger, *Davidssohn,* 72–106.
Duling, "Son of David," 392–410.
Frankemölle, *Jahwebund,* 167–70.
J. M. Gibbs, "Purpose and Pattern in Matthew's Use of the Title 'Son of David,'" *NTS* 10 (1963–64) 446–64.
Hummel, *Auseinandersetzung,* 116–22.
Kingsbury, "Son of David," 591–602.
W. R. G. Loader, "Son of David, Blindness and Duality in Matthew," *CBQ* 44 (1982) 570–85.
Brian M. Nolan, *The Royal Son of God: The Christology of Matthew 1–2 in the Setting of the Gospel* (OBO 23; Göttingen: Vandenhoeck & Ruprecht, 1979) 145–215.
Strecker, *Weg,* 118–20.
Alfred Suhl, "Der Davidssohn im Matthäus-Evangelium," *ZNW* 59 (1968) 57–81.

"Son of David" as a title of Christ is especially profiled in the Gospel of Matthew. On the one hand, scholarship has called attention in the *history of the tradition* to the expectation of the royal messianic Son of David that is documented sparsely in pre-Christian Judaism and more frequently in post-Christian Judaism.[10] On the other hand, it has been noticed that in Mark 10:47-48, and then especially in Matthew, "Son of David" is used by the sick, primarily by the blind, to address the miracle worker, Jesus (Mark 10:47-48; Matt 9:27; 20:30-31, cf. 12:23; 15:22; 21:15). That led to the question whether the Son of David of the gospels is an eschatological antitype of the first Son of David, viz., Solomon, the great sage and expert on things demonic.[11] The hypothesis is difficult, however, since according to Jewish tradition Solomon does not heal.[12] It may be more important

---

tional reworking of Matt 20:29-34 as Held ("Matthew," 219–20) claims; Matt 20:29-34 had not yet been written.

8 Cf. vol. 1, Introduction 1 F. The doublets that were created from the combination of Mark and Q are intentional, not accidental.

9 Cf. Wolfgang Schrage, "τυφλός κτλ," *TDNT* 8 (1972) 276–78; 281–82.

10 The expectation of a Davidic Messiah is widespread. However, the title "Son of David" is documented in

the pre-Christian period only in *Ps. Sol.* 17:21, then more frequently by the rabbis.

11 Berger, "Messiastraditionen," 3–9; For additional literature see Duling, "Son of David," 392–93, n. 4.

12 On Berger, "Messiastraditionen": The—quite scarce (certain only in *T. Sol.*!)—contemporary Jewish references to Solomon connect Solomon with exorcisms. That fits with Matt 12:23 and 15:22 but not at all with Mark 10:46-52 and the other Matthean references that speak comprehensively of Jesus' healing

that David himself was connected in Judaism with healings.[13] The miracles expected in the messianic age also provide a tradition-historical bridge to the gospels.[14] *Theologically* scholarship has regarded the Matthean Son of David primarily as the earthly figure of the past[15] in contrast to the κύριος (22:41-46), or as the Messiah of Israel who is then rejected by his people.[16]

In my judgment the Son of David title in the Gospel of Matthew must be explained primarily from the progression of the Gospel's narrative. The evangelist constructs his profile in three stages.

1. He introduces it in the "charter document" of chap. 1. In 1:2-16 he interprets it in terms of Jesus' descent from the royal line of David and thus not as an antitype of the "wise" Son of David, Solomon. Verses 1:18-25 describe how Jesus, despite his virgin birth, corresponds to this Jewish expectation. Jesus is truly the Messiah of Israel.[17]

2. In the main part of the Gospel, chaps. 8–20, Matthew describes the Son of David as Israel's healing Messiah. Here the title "Son of David" is connected *only* with miracle stories and almost exclusively with healings of the blind. The Messiah of Israel thus helps Israel with its blindness. It is significant that the title "Son of David" first occurs at the end of the miracle cycle of Matthew 8–9. The evangelist first *tells* how Jesus heals "in the holy nation" (4:23); only then does he have the blind call Jesus the Son of David. Thus for him chaps. 8 and 9 *tell* who the Son of David is. That is why the title also appears so often at the end of Jesus' public ministry in Israel in 20:30-31 and 21:9, 15. This is a correction of Israel's hope for the royal Messiah that Matthew takes up (chap. 1). Israel's Messiah is in reality the one who heals his people's sick (8:1–9:31), the healing servant of the Lord (8:17), the gracious king who heals the lame and

blind in the temple (21:1-15). The sick are Israelites. The two blind men in 9:27-31 represent, as it were, the answer of Israel to its Messiah that God wanted. In 12:22-24 Matthew again takes up the motif of blindness and contrasts the reaction of the true Israelites with that of the Pharisees. The Gentile-Canaanite woman's request that Israel's Son of David heal her daughter (15:21-28) merely underscores that Jesus is the Messiah of Israel. To summarize: In the tradition Matthew makes use of Mark 10:46-52,[18] but the primary interpretive framework for his understanding of the Davidic sonship is his own narrative, not a conception that existed prior to him in the history of the tradition.[19]

3. In the final part of his Gospel, Matthew establishes for his church, on the one hand, that the Son of David is more than just Israel's Messiah; he is the Lord of the world who is the church's companion and helper (22:41-46). He thereby develops what Israel's sick had already hinted when they called the Son of David "Lord" (9:27, 28; 15:22; 20:31-33; cf. 21:9). On the other hand, he sharply contrasts the lordship of Jesus, the Son of David, that the church recognizes with the continuing blindness of Israel's Pharisees and scribes (23:16-26). When confronted with the Son of David who heals the blind, the Pharisees become blind.[20] This perspective of Matthew's entire narrative is reminiscent of the healing of the blind man in John 9, that impressive chapter that ends by speaking in quite "Matthean" terms of the Pharisees' enduring blindness (John 9:41).

The Son of David title thus shows in an exemplary way how Matthew subordinates individual terms or concepts to his narrative. We do not do him justice when we ask systematically which title is dominant or

ministry (Duling, "Son of David," 393–99).

13 Josephus *Ant.* 6.166, 168.

14 Cf. Brian M. Nolan, *The Royal Son of God: The Christology of Matthew 1-2 in the Setting of the Gospel* (OBO 23; Göttingen: Vandenhoeck & Ruprecht, 1979) 165–66.

15 Bornkamm, "End Expectation," 33–34; Burger, *Davidssohn,* 89; Strecker, *Weg,* 119–20.

16 Walker, *Heilsgeschichte,* 129. Kingsbury ("Son of David," 601–2) emphasizes that the Son of David title in Matthew has a limited meaning and primarily serves the polemic against Israel. Hummel (*Auseinandersetzung,* 120) points out that Son of David was an important title precisely for Matthew's Pharisaic opponents.

17 Alfred Suhl ("Der Davidssohn im Matthäus-

Evangelium," *ZNW* 59 [1968] 57–81) regards Matt 1:23-24 as the decisive key for Matthew's concept of the Son of David: The Son of David is Immanuel (62–69, 75–81); when the sick call Jesus Son of David they are trying to obligate Jesus to fulfill his promise as Immanuel. In my judgment, however, we cannot say that in 1:18-25 Jesus' *Davidic sonship* is interpreted with Immanuel.

18 This is once again a case in which Matthew takes a relatively isolated statement of one of his theological fathers and considerably expands it. Cf. vol. 1, Introduction 4.1.

19 Cf. especially W. R. G. Loader, "Son of David, Blindness and Duality in Matthew" (*CBQ* 44 [1982] 570–85) 574–80.

20 J. M. Gibbs ("Purpose and Pattern in Matthew's Use

subordinate in his Christology.[21] Nor do we understand him when we ask what the theological concept is[22] according to which he makes use of the Son of David title. His intention becomes fully understandable only when we observe how the title changes in the course of the narrative and where he ends up in his narrative with the help of this title. To understand Matthew's Christology is to understand Matthew's *story* of Jesus.

■ **27** The blind men turn to Israel's Messiah, whom the evangelist thus far has described as a healer "among his people" (4:23). Ἐλέησον ἡμᾶς ("have mercy on us") is an expression that the church was familiar with from the Psalms and perhaps also from its worship.[23] It makes it easier to identify with the blind. As do the blind, so the church itself also turns to Jesus, who "desires mercy" (9:13).

■ **28** Jesus does not immediately comply with the request. The blind have to wait; their faith is tested again. As is the case in 8:8-10, 13, and 9:20-22, Matthew makes clear that faith precedes healing[24] and must be an active, constant faith.[25] The two blind men turn to Jesus as their "Lord" in the same way that the church does (8:25).

■ **29** The faith of the blind men becomes for the church a model of its own faith; Jesus' help gives the church itself courage. Thus the promise "let it happen to you according to your faith" (κατὰ τὴν πίστιν γενηθήτω ὑμῖν) also applies to the church itself. But can the church relate this saving help to itself? That Jesus heals sick people in a wonderful way is probably for the church the exception rather than the rule!

■ **30a** Two things are to be said here. For one thing, we must note the overtones and the symbolic dimension involved in the OT formulation "to open the eyes." Jesus certainly did not heal everyone, but he does open the eyes of all by giving his church faith in God the Father. For another, however, the experiences of concrete miracles of faith remain important for the church (cf. 17:19-20). To identify with the blind men in this story is by no means *merely* to spiritualize Jesus' promise; it is also to have the confidence that the Lord helps concretely in sickness and need. This story thus becomes transparent of the church's own confidence; at the same time, however, it becomes an important stage in the story of how Israel's Messiah leads the blind of Israel to sight through his healing love.

■ **30b-31** The command to silence and its immediate violation are difficult to interpret. To use a modern image: Matthew seems to have pulled from his scrap folder of unused Markan texts a useful clipping. At the end of his cycle of miracles he probably was glad to have the chance to emphasize the widespread effect of Jesus' healing activity in Israel. He thus makes clear that the Son of David is not a marginal figure in Israel, and he prepares for the summary description of the crowd's reaction in 9:33.

---

of the Title 'Son of David,'" *NTS* 10 [1963–64] 446–64) was the first to call attention to the significance of blindness for Jesus' story as Son of David.

21 Kingsbury ("Son of David") asks which christological titles are fundamental for Matthew and which are secondary.

22 Frankemölle (*Jahwebund,* 168) says that Matthew's leading "theological concept" for the Davidic sonship is that all messianic hopes are fulfilled in Jesus.

23 Cf. vol. 1, Introduction 4.2.1.

24 Hilary, 9.9 = SC 254.214: "Quia crediderant viderunt, non quia viderant crediderunt."

25 Luther 2.339: "Faith must be stubborn, enduring, without timidity, coarse, and shameless."

4.3 The Healing of a Dumb Demoniac (9:32-34)

32 **When they went out, behold, they brought him a dumb man who was demon-possessed.[1] 33/ When the demon was cast out, the dumb man began to speak. And the crowds were amazed and said, "Nothing like this has ever been seen in Israel!" 34/ But the Pharisees said, "By the ruler of demons he casts out the demons."[2]**

Analysis The brief miracle story again raises memories of earlier material, especially of 9:2-8, the only healing story in Matt 8:1—9:26 from which there were no reminiscences in vv. 27-31.[3] However, the emphasis lies not on the miracle but on Israel's reaction (vv. 33-34). The entire story is derived from Q (= Luke 11:14-15). Matthew will use it again with greater changes (12:22-23).[4] The twofold reaction to the miracles is already suggested in Q (Luke 11:14c, 15). Matthew has increased the positive reaction of the people;[5] for the Pharisees' negative reaction he uses what "some" people said in Q, Luke 11:15. Ἔλεγον comes from Mark 3:22. All the changes are Matthean redaction.[6]

Interpretation

■ 32 The programmatic story of the healing of the two blind men is followed by a double reaction of Israel. It is introduced by a short episode of the healing of a dumb demoniac.[7] Blindness and muteness appear together in the tradition[8] and in Matthew (12:22; 15:30-31). With this deed Jesus also fulfills the promises of Israel (11:5-6).

■ 34 The reaction is decisive. The Pharisees (as in 12:22, Matthew mentions them here because they are for him the most important of Jesus' opponents who appear in 9:2-17)[9] accuse Jesus of complicity with the devil.[10] The weighty accusation suggests the deep chasm that is going to open between them and Jesus.

■ 33 The reaction of the people is in sharp contrast. Θαυμάζω ("to be amazed") does not mean faith, but it probably does mean a basically positive reaction.[11] The people represent those persons who potentially accept Jesus.[12] At the same time, their reaction marks the limits of the ability to understand miracles "from the outside." For Matthew they are special events that are able to attract attention, but the crowds are only able to understand them externally. The deep dimension and the power of Jesus' miracles to influence their own lives remain hidden from them. That is revealed only in the encounter with Jesus himself that Matthew paraphrases with the catchwords "faith" (πίστις) and "to follow" (ἀκολουθέω). "In Israel" (Ἐν τῷ Ἰσραήλ) points once more to an important dimension of chaps. 8–9. Israel's Messiah performed his healings in and for his people Israel.

With this notice about Israel's divided reaction Matthew brings his first report of Jesus' deeds to a close. Similar notices will follow (12:22-24; 21:14-16). The final notice thus calls attention to the role that chaps. 8–9 play in the whole of the gospel. They introduce the division that the Messiah creates in his people and that will end with Israel's rejection of Jesus.[13]

---

1   Ἄνθρωπον (Nestle[26]) may well be a later addition that agrees with Matthew's diction. The shorter original text is attested not only by ℵ and B but also by parts of the other text families.

2   Verse 34 is missing in D and other witnesses. It is not only well attested; it is also indispensable to the composition of the section as the continuation of 9:1b-17 and the preparation for 10:25.

3   On ἰδοὺ προσήνεγκαν αὐτῷ cf. 9:2; on ὄχλοι, 9:8. The content of the reaction of the ὄχλοι is formulated by using the Markan text omitted in 9:8: οὐδέποτε, οὕτως. The conservative Matthew repeatedly makes use of "leftover" Markan expressions!

4   The assumption that Matthew used a special tradition (Schweizer, 231) is unnecessary. Matthew deals with Q just as he does with Mark 10:46-52.

5   Redactional are λέγων, φαίνω. Ἐν τῷ Ἰσραήλ takes up the content of the basic pronouncement of 8:1-

17 and corresponds to ἐν τῷ λαῷ in 4:23 and Son of David in 9:27. On οὐδέποτε, οὕτως cf. above, n. 3.

6   On ἰδού, προσφέρω αὐτῷ, δαιμονίζομαι, cf. vol. 1, Introduction 3.2. Ἐξέρχομαι (scil. out of the house of 9:28) and ἐκβάλλω (cf. 8:31!) anchor our story in the context.

7   Κωφός may mean mute or deaf; a person deaf from birth cannot speak. Here also there is a figurative meaning: "without knowledge," "dumb" (LSJ, s.v. 3c-5b).

8   Isa 29:18; 35:5; 42:18-19; 43:8.

9   Cf. vol. 1, I B 1.1 on 3:7-10: "Jewish Leaders."

10 Cf. below, III A 2 on 12:24.

11 8:27; 15:31; 27:14.

12 On the ὄχλοι, cf. vol. 1 on 4:25.

13 On the connection to Matthew's larger context cf. Luz, "Wundergeschichten," 152–58.

35   **And Jesus went about all the cities and villages, taught in their synagogues, proclaimed the gospel of the kingdom, and healed every disease and every infirmity.**

Interpretation

The circle comes to a close. With but small variations[1] the evangelist repeats 4:23. The readers look back on chaps. 5–9. They now know what the "gospel of the king-dom" is (chaps. 5–7) and how Israel's Messiah heals all diseases (chaps. 8–9). His activity encompasses all of the villages and cities of the region (cf. 9:26, 31); it is not something that takes place hidden in a corner of Israel. The OT coloring[2] is now in full relief. After chaps. 8–9 (8:17!) and 5–7 (5:17; 7:12!) the readers know that with his activity Jesus fulfills the Scriptures.

---

1   After 9:33-34 ὁ Ἰησοῦς is necessary. On τὰς πόλεις πάσας καὶ τὰς κώμας cf. Mark 6:56. Mark 6:56 has already been used in 9:20. In 14:34-36 Matthew omits v. 56a and uses it here in anticipation.

2   Cf. LXX Deut 7:15; 28:59-61; 2 Chr 21:15.

The Miracles of Israel's Messiah

Literature
See above, II B.

1. The Miracles as Part of the Story of Jesus

The dominant interpretation of the Matthean miracle narratives, represented by the work of Held,[1] has focused on their "themes," such as Christology, faith, discipleship, etc. The miracle stories were thus given a didactic character; they tended to become paradigms for certain themes of Christian doctrine. Such a tendency is deeply rooted in the modern, especially Protestant, interpretation of the miracles that is inclined to ask what the miracle stories mean independent of any question about the events themselves—indeed, to treat such a question as of secondary importance.[2] Our interpretation has shown that this approach is not completely wrong, but it is not sufficient. All Matthean stories intend to report actual events; in no way does the evangelist understand them as illustrations of theological themes. We have especially shown that they play a constitutive role in the Matthew's entire story of Jesus. It is no accident that Jesus begins his ministry in Israel with healings and miracles. The deeds of Jesus effect something. At the end of chap. 9 the story of Jesus is no longer where it was at the beginning of chap. 8. Matthew does not, as a skillful catechist, simply bring together a group of miracle stories that one can then interpret theologically; instead, he tells a coherent story that begins with miracles that Jesus performs on Israel's sick.[3] What Matthew gives us is not *doctrines* about faith and discipleship that are coded in a narrative way in the miracle stories but a narrative that reports how faith and discipleship *were established* by the Messiah's acts of mercy. In that sense the key to understanding the miracles is their *effect*—an effect that is reported in the stories themselves and in Matthew's entire narrative. That means that the language form of the miracle story is essential to what it wants to say and is not an accidental form of truths that could be stated differently.[4]

2. The Miracles of Jesus as an Expression of His Mercy

In terms of their content it is important that the series of miracle stories that Matthew brought together is composed almost exclusively of healing stories. They happened to people in Israel who were in need. The miracles meant for them a special experience that overcame the hopelessness of their need. Matthew himself has described this experience in OT terms as ἔλεος ("mercy"; 9:13 = Hos 6:6). Thus for him the story of Jesus begins with the mercy that Jesus shows to the people of Israel and with God's gracious acts. This mercy precedes everything else: the disciples' following, the people's astonished expectancy, the Pharisees' defaming comments, and the sending of the disciples. All of those things are, according to Matthew, only a reaction to Immanuel's activity.

3. The Transparency of the "Inclusive" Jesus Story

It is still true, of course, that these miracle reports have a kerygmatic function, even if they are not in an exclusive

---

1 Held, "Matthew," 246–96. Cf. Simon Légasse, "Les miracles de Jésus selon Matthieu," in Xavier Léon-Dufour, ed., *Les Miracles de Jésus selon le Nouveau Testament* (Paris: Seuil, 1977) 227–49; Kingsbury, "Observations."

2 Alfred Suhl, "Die Wunder Jesu. Ereignis und Überlieferung," in idem, ed., *Der Wunderbegriff im Neuen Testament* (Wege der Forschung 295; Darmstadt: Wissenschaftliche Buchgesellschaft, 1980) 500: In the New Testament hardly any miracle is transmitted for its own sake; instead its mention "stands . . . always in the service of an . . . intention that *is not focused on the miracle as such*" (italics mine). By contrast, in what follows we will emphasize precisely the unity of the miracle that happened and the experiences that result from its power—two realities

that *together* constitute the miracle.

3 In Held, "Matthew," the problem is that he is able to interpret the miracle stories completely independent of their location in the whole of the Matthean narrative.

4 Hans Weder, "Wunder Jesu und Wundergeschichten," *VF* 29 (1984) 49: The linguistic form of the miracle stories is irreplaceable and cannot be transformed into their intended "statement."

5 Held, "Matthew," 299.

6 Karl Barth (*CD*, 4/2.211), following W. Heitmüller, already speaks of the "transparent." Barth puts it well when he says of the miracle stories "that while Jesus does actually make *history* in the actions reported they are also *parables*" (218). From this perspective he is able to judge positively the church

sense "bearers of a message, of teaching or admonition."[5] I would propose the term "transparency"[6] for this kerygmatic function. In contrast to a directly didactic interpretation of the miracle stories as pure illustrations or symbolic stories, this concept tries to emphasize how the relationship between a report and one's own experience is irreversible. The report that is given explains, or even causes, the church's own experiences. The story about Jesus from the past has a material priority[7] over the church's own experiences. To the concept of "transparency," corresponds the concept of the "inclusive story" of Jesus[8]—a story that includes one's own experience and thus can be developed as "my" or "our" story.

Our exegesis has shown that the Matthean miracle stories become transparent in various ways. Depending on whether the community recognizes in them its own foundational story (inclusive story as "our" story) or whether they directly cause or illuminate experiences of individual Christians (inclusive story as "my" story), we could speak of "direct" or "indirect" transparency.

4. The Miracle Stories as the Church's Foundational Story (Indirect Transparency)

Several miracle stories were important primarily as a part of the entire Jesus story. The church recognizes that it owes its existence to the Messiah's merciful action in Israel (8:1-4, 14-17). It experiences how discipleship can result from God's action (8:18-22 after 8:1-17; 9:9-13 after 9:2-8; 9:27-31). In the disciples' dangerous crossing to the gentile shore it sees prefigured the story of its own journey from Israel to the Gentiles (8:23-34). It recognizes already in the Jesus story an example of how God's saving action pushes beyond Israel (8:5-13, 28-34). It sees how his story reveals the division in Israel which

then later determines its own story (9:32-34). It thus experiences Jesus' story as the foundation of its own story. In this way it also experiences the continuity of God's action before and after Easter, and it recognizes that the story of Jesus prefigures its own story. Thus it becomes indirectly transparent, that is, transparent through the mediation of a story.

5. The Miracle Stories as the Basis of Personal Experience (Direct Transparency)

However, the Matthean miracle stories were also in an immediate sense a prefiguration or model of the individual's own experiences. This is true first of all of the miracles themselves. The members of the community also experience and perform miracles like those reported of Jesus. Matthew 10:1, 8 will show that healings are constitutive of the disciples' mission, that is, are seen by Matthew as essential characteristics of the church.[9] In Matt 17:19-20 miracles are understood to be an expression of faith. At the same time this text shows that there were obviously problems in the Matthean community, since healings sometimes did not happen. Matthew does not make light of the problem; he admonishes them to have faith. However, the issue is not merely the experience of the miraculous. The physical healing of a blind man (9:27-31), for example, is but the kernel of what happens when blind people as whole persons are granted sight by Jesus and become his disciples. In other stories the subject has been guidance and protection from Jesus (8:23-27), faith (8:5-13, etc.), forgiveness of sins (9:2-8), or shedding light on the future resurrection from the dead (9:18-26). There it is not a question of symbolic or allegorical interpretation in the sense that the stories are speaking of anything other than what is on the surface; it is, rather, that the real experience

---

fathers' allegorical exegesis of the miracle stories.

7   Of course, this thesis is only valid generally and not in each individual case. The story of the stilling of the storm or the feeding stories, e.g., originated as symbolic encodings of personal experiences with the help of traditional (OT) motifs and stories. For other miracle stories, such as the summary reports or the healing miracles that Matthew doubled, it is evident that they have no direct relation to historical events. However, especially here it is clear that the story of Jesus is the presupposition for a secondary formation of miracle stories. This can

be shown also in the case of the feeding stories (Jesus' table-fellowship; Lord's Supper!).

8   Ulrich Luz, "Geschichte/Geschichtsschreibung/ Geschichtsphilosophie IV," *TRE* 12 (1984) 595–604, 596.

9   Cf. below, II C 2.1 on 10:7-8.

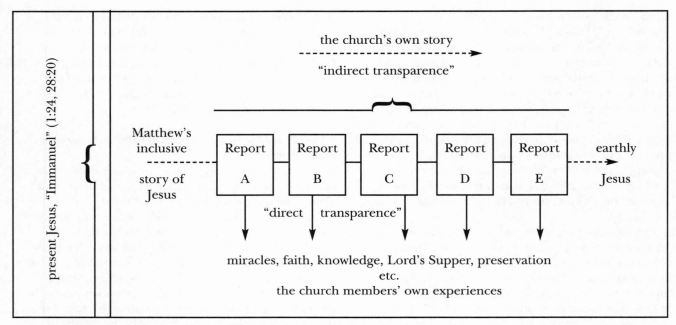

the church's own story
- ->
"indirect transparence"

Matthew's
inclusive
- - - - -   [Report A] [Report B] [Report C] [Report D] [Report E]   earthly
story of   Jesus
Jesus

"direct   transparence"

miracles, faith, knowledge, Lord's Supper, preservation
etc.
the church members' own experiences

present Jesus, "Immanuel" (1:24, 28:20)

Diagram 1

reported in each of them opens up a realm of experi-ence that is broader than what is simply reported.

6. The Matthean Miracle Stories as a Witness to Immanuel

Thus the reality of Jesus' miracles consists not only of the story that once happened but also of the present experience it directly or indirectly creates. It is in the experience of their effective power in the church's story of the community and in the individual lives of its members that they come to their whole reality. Christo-logically speaking: Jesus who performed miracles "back then" is for Matthew always the "Immanuel" (1:23-24) who is with his church always until the end of the world (28:20). Thus the experience that the miracles demon-strate their power in the lives of the church's members corresponds to the basic structure of Matthean Chris-

tology. We can present it graphically as in diagram 1 above.

It is in keeping with this understanding of the Matthean miracles that they cannot be understood from the outside. The evangelist leaves no room for misunder-standing in the way he uses the reaction of the crowds (9:33, cf. 12:23; 15:31; 21:15-16) to define the limits to understanding the miracles from the outside. Complete understanding is possible only for those who let the mir-acles lead them to faith, to discipleship, and to their own experience of the Lord. As is the case with the entire Gospel of Matthew, the Matthean miracle stories are designed not primarily to serve missionary proclamation[10] but to perform a function within the church.

---

10 Gottfried Schille (*Die urchristliche Wundertradition* [Arbeiten zur Theologie 1/29; Stuttgart: Calwer Verlag, 1967] 25–26) postulates this, e.g., for the pure genre of "miracle story," that, of course, is hardly to be found in the synoptic tradition. See Suhl (Alfred Suhl, "Die Wunder Jesu. Ereignis und Überlieferung," in idem, ed., *Der Wunderbegriff im*

Neuen Testament [Wege der Forschung 295; Darmstadt: Wissenschaftliche Buchgesellschaft, 1980] 502) for the original miracle tradition.

11 Cf., among other places, Deut 26:5-10 ("my father," "us"); Exod 20:2 ("who brought you out of Egypt"). In Deuteronomy Israel (at the time of Josiah) is immediately present at Sinai.

The view of reality in the miracle stories has precursors in the Old Testament where Israel's foundational story can become "our" or even "my" story.[11] However, the direct transparency of the miracle stories that leads the Christians to an analogous experience in their own lives of the Lord about whom they speak seems to be something different from the way the individual Israelites identified with their fathers—the bearers of Israel's foundational story. In the mystery religions the initiates also directly experience the fate of their god. In the mysteries, however, it is a question of an exclusively cultic experience to which a mythical "story" corresponds. In my judgment, actual and complete parallels are found only in the New Testament itself where prior to Matthew several miracle narratives were directly transparent of believers' own experiences (for example, Mark 4:35-41; 6:30-44, 45-52; 10:46-52). That is not surprising if the view of reality in the miracle stories corresponds to Christology.

On the Meaning of the Matthean Miracle Stories Today

We are part of a theological tradition that has repressed the miracles. This is especially true of Protestantism. As a whole, in our thinking the question of the reported miraculous event and the question of its meaning or its transparency have been almost completely separated from one another. The miracle's meaning has become quite independent of the reports about the miracles, while the fact of the miracle has become not only difficult but meaningless as well. Stated more concretely: Most people have no problem offering wonderful sermons on the kerygmatic meaning of miracle stories, but many have a problem with the events and experiences that underlie them. However, does not the truth of sermons depend on what happens in the story?

To understand our own situation better, let us take a brief historical review.

History of Interpretation

a. Miracles as Breaking Natural Laws

In intellectual history, our "emancipation" from the story as it was reported probably began primarily where the concept "miracle" has been understood in contrast to a particular understanding of nature and natural law. That did not happen for the first time with Spinoza, Descartes, or Lessing; it happened long before in the medieval tradition. For Thomas Aquinas the miracle takes place *praeter ordinem totius naturae creatae* ("outside the order of the entire created nature").[12] Since Thomas assumes that God himself is the first cause (*causa prima*) of all that is created and determines all of creation's causality,[13] it is in the final analysis *God* alone who can do miracles in the realm of the orders of creation that he has determined—not a creature that is always subject to the creator's order that is its destiny. When creatures—for example, humans or angels—act according to the order that God ordains for *them,* these are not miracles in the true sense.[14] Thomas interprets the miracles of Jesus as an expression of his divine nature[15] and thus principally designates them as something unique that is to be associated immediately with God himself. This corresponds basically to the understanding of miracles in both Protestant orthodoxy[16] and Catholicism.[17] Miracles are proof of God's activity.

---

12 Thomas Aquinas, *Summa Theologica* (5 vols.; BAC; Madrid: La Editoria Catolica, 1955–58) 1, q.110, a.4 corpus.

13 Thomas Aquinas (*S. th.* 1, q.105, a.6) compares God with the father of a family or a ruler who determines the *ordo domus* or *regni.*

14 In *S. th.* 1, q.110, a.4 Thomas rejects, e.g., the idea that angels can perform miracles. As angels and in their special angelic nature they are subject to their own order of creation. Thomas gives an example: It is of the nature of a stone that it falls to the ground. The human beings who can throw it in the air invalidate this order but do not thereby perform a miracle, since they are acting according to the order of *their* special nature.

15 *S. th.* 3, q.43 a.2 and 4.

16 Heinrich Heppe, *Die Dogmatik der evangelisch-reformierten Kirche,* ed. Ernst Bizer (Neukirchen-Vluyn: Neukirchener Verlag, 1935) 202. Cf., e.g., J. H. Heidegger, in the same book, 213: *Sed quod nulla creatura potest et quod Deus sine causis secundis operantibus ita facit solus . . . miraculum proprie dictum est.*

17 See Heinrich Denizinger and Adolf Schönmetzer, eds., *Enchiridion symbolorum* (36th ed.; Barcinone: Herder, 1976), hereafter abbreviated as DS: DS no. 3009 (= 1790); no. 3034 (= 1813) = Vaticanum 1 (*miraculis divinam religionis christianae originem rite probari*). Josef Neuner and Heinrich Roos, *The Teaching of the Catholic Church as Contained in Her*

The counterattack of the modern era was bound to follow. The meaning of the rationalist critique of miracles is not that it denied that the majority of Jesus' miracles happened. In my judgment, in its opposition to theology its meaning lay deeper. By explaining miracles as natural events and affirming their historical reality, it deprived them of their theological meaning, for only that which *cannot* be explained in the realm of secular laws (*causae secundae*) can on the basis of orthodox thinking direct attention to God. Thus understood, by means of modern, scientific thought the miracle of necessity lost its theological significance. This is true both of the legend that has become unhistorical and of the miracle whose possibility has been "explained."[18] The problem changes little when the reality of miracles is moved from the realm of the physical into the realm of the psychological.[19] To its credit this approach reopens access to the *human* and religious reality of miracles that Rationalism removed, but calling attention to psyche and feeling says nothing at all about the theological relevance of this reality.

b. Miracles as a Religious Interpretation of the Totality of Reality

The attempts to understand all of human reality as miracle appear to me to be theologically more important because they are in keeping with a different concept of God. This probably becomes most distinct in Spinoza, who connects God precisely with the "works which we recognize clearly and distinctly," that is, with the perfection of natural law and not with the things that appear

to be exceptions to it. Spinoza understands such exceptions as examples of remaining human ignorance.[20] Among the reformers there are similar tendencies. They claim that God indeed is the Lord of all creation. "That a kernel of wheat or any other kind of plant should come from the earth is as great a miracle as if God were still giving manna from heaven today."[21] Indeed, God holds back on miracles so that the "ordinary" will not be contemptible.[22] Schleiermacher's proposal has been especially influential in Protestantism. He understands the miracle as belonging to the natural order and understands it as the religious interpretation of "happenings." "To present all events in the world as the actions of a god is religion."[23] The difficulty with this expansion of the concept of miracle is that it also de facto renders meaningless the question about the events related in the biblical miracle stories. If *everything* is miraculous and *every event* points to God, then a "miracle" has no advantage over a nonmiraculous event, and the theological meaning of events or "miracles" is exclusively a matter of interpretation. The question is whether people, as religious persons or believers, *understand* an event as a miracle. *What* they understand as miracle is in the last analysis immaterial.

c. The Discrepancy Between Kerygma and History

It is not surprising, therefore, that in modern New Testament scholarship throughout all denominations the primary question is the question of the miracle's kerygmatic *meaning*. To be sure, Protestants go further here and claim that the true miracle is the forgiveness of sins

Documents, ed. Karl Rahner (New York: Mercier, 1967) no. 66 (Pius X: "wholly sure signs of the divine origin of the Christian religion").

18 Lessing's basic thesis that "accidental truths of history" (which include God's miracles) "can never become the proof of necessary truths of reason" would have to be applied consistently not only to the miracles that happened in the past (about which we have only reports) but to all miracles and leads, in my judgment, to a basic impossibility of proving a truth from the occurrence of miracles. (See "On the Proof of the Spirit and of Power," in *Lessing's Theological Writings*, ed. Henry Chadwick [Stanford: Stanford University Press, 1957] 53.)

19 Drewermann, *Tiefenpsychologie* 2.64, 239–40.

20 Benedictus de Spinoza, *Tractatus Theologo-Politicus*,

trans. Samuel Shirley (Leiden: Brill, 1989) 124–25.

21 Luther, Sermon from 1525, WA 16.301.

22 Cf. Ulrich Mann, *Das Wunderbare: Wunder, Segen und Engel* (Handbuch Systematischer Theologie 17; Gütersloh: Mohn, 1979) 26–27.

23 Friedrich Schleiermacher, *On Religion: Speeches to Its Cultured Despisers*, trans. Richard Crouter (Cambridge: Cambridge University Press, 1988) 105.

24 Cf., e.g., Luther, *Promotionsdisputation* of F. Bachofen, 1534, WA 39 2.236; Sermon from 1535, WA 41.19.

25 Rudolf Bultmann, "The Question of Wonder," in idem, *Faith and Understanding* (Philadelphia: Fortress, 1987) 260.

26 Paradigmatic for Mark: Karl Kertelge, *Die Wunder Jesu im Markus-evangelium* (SANT 23; Munich:

and faith. Taking up this Reformation thesis,[24] Bultmann can say that what is actually theologically important is precisely the ambiguity of miracles.[25] Most of the more recent miracle scholarship has been occupied with redaction-critical questions, that is, with the meaning of the miracles for the evangelists' faith and theology.[26] What is reported can be rendered unimportant amazingly quickly by simply asking what it means. Günter Klein says, for example, on Matt 8:5-13 that "the narrator has amazingly little interest" in the fact "of the healing from a distance," and this corresponds with his statement about Jesus himself to the effect that we can "be sure that for him his potential deeds of power had no overriding significance."[27] Walter Schmithals understands the miracle stories of the Gospel of Mark as metaphorical stories of a gifted narrator who unfolds the kerygma of Christ in story form. He cannot and does not want to ask "what . . . he may have had as traditions or historical reminiscences."[28] Schmithals is the most consistent representative of the modern Protestant understanding of miracles. Only hesitatingly does Catholic exegesis follow the radical Protestant disregard of the question about what really happened.[29] The question cannot be eliminated, especially in the pastorate. Pastors who interpret miracle narratives are repeatedly asked by students and members of their churches: "But what really happened?"

Result: Our own situation is characterized by a separation between the question of the (historical or physical) event and its (theological) meaning. The event threatens to become meaningless, the meaning groundless. This situation is rather discouraging, for no "existentialist interpretation . . . (can) take the place of the human question about the real presuppositions of faith."[30] In a religion that does not, like the Indian religion, understand itself to be a "religion of the eternal law of the world," but that makes the world "dependent on the actions of . . . a personal God who is infinitely superior to it,"[31] the question must be asked about the particular *event* that constitutes faith. If it does not do so, this religion surrenders its self. What impulses can the Matthean miracle stories give in this situation?

d. The Trajectory of the Matthean Miracle Stories

For Matthew, Jesus' miracles are special deeds that break through the normal experience of reality. But what experience of reality do they offer? From Matthew's perspective, it is a mistake to think here of laws of nature.[32] It is not the natural law that is broken by the deeds of the Son of David; it is human suffering, human fear, threat, and blindness. It is not the power of the law of nature that is broken but the power of the devil (cf. Matt 9:34; 12:22-30). The miracles point not to the boundaries of causality but (with Jesus) to the end of the world ruled by sickness and suffering in the kingdom of God, or (with Matthew) to the Christ who as "God with us" contradicts this world. That something "special" happens in Jesus' miracles is fundamentally important, not because one can patch together a proof for God from a so-called breaking of natural laws, but because the deeds of Jesus contradict what suffering human beings experience in the world. The deeds of Jesus thus are designed to speak not about natural law but about Israel's suffer-

Kösel, 1970); Ludger Schenke, *Die Wundererzählungen des Markusevangeliums* (SBB; Stuttgart: Katholisches Bibelwerk, 1974); Dietrich-Alex Koch, *Die Bedeutung der Wundererzählungen für die Christologie des Markusevangeliums* (BZNW 42; Berlin: de Gruyter, 1975); for Matthew: Held, "Matthew"; for Luke: Ulrich Busse, *Die Wunder des Propheten Jesus* (FB 24; Stuttgart, Katholisches Bibelwerk, 1977).

27 Günter Klein, "Wunderglaube und Neues Testament," in idem, *Ärgernisse* (Munich: Kaiser, 1970) 45, 52.

28 Walter Schmithals, *Das Evangelium nach Markus* (Ökumenischer Taschenkommentar zum Neuen Testament 2/1; Gütersloh: Mohn, 1979) 44.

29 Cf., e.g., the cautious criticism of Karl Kertelge, *Die*

Wunder Jesu im Markus-evangelium (SANT 23; Munich: Kösel, 1970) 203–8.

30 Björn Schilling, "Die Frage nach der Entstehung der synoptischen Wundergeschichten in der deutschen neutestamentlichen Forschung," *SEÅ* 35 (1970) 61–78, 78.

31 Helmuth von Glasenapp, *Die fünf grossen Religionen* (Düsseldorf: Diederich, 1952) 1–2, as the basic definition of the religions east and west of the Hindukush.

32 Cf. Hans Georg Fritzsche, *Lehrbuch der Dogmatik* (Göttingen: Vandenhoeck & Ruprecht, 1964) 1.140–45; Gerhard Ebeling, *Dogmatik des christlichen Glaubens* (Tübingen: Mohr/Siebeck, 1979) 1.332, 2.462.

ing and the everyday experiences of suffering people. They describe experiences that human beings normally do *not* have.[33] The decisive question thus is not the abstract question about whether miracles are conceivable,[34] but the concrete question about the reality of *special* experiences of salvation, help, and wholeness in the midst of a world dominated by disaster, alienation, and suffering.

> It seems to me that a helpful beginning point for dealing with the Matthean miracle stories is Augustine's understanding of miracles. He understands miracle not in contrast to natural law but as the experience of what is unusual and surprising.[35] Helpful also is Barth's concept of the "extraordinary." The "extraordinary" points to the kingdom of God that is opposed to the world and within the world is that which is "alien, marvelous, inconceivable."[36]

The "special" element in the Matthean miracle stories is related to Christology. They tell how God was and is at work with Jesus and "with us." Through them Matthew tells the readers how the earthly Jesus is with his church "always, until the end of the world" (28:20). The question about the truth of the Matthean miracle stories thus confronts us concretely as a question about our *own* experiences of salvation. Do we have in our life "special" experiences of Christ like those described in the miracle stories: healing, protection, receiving sight, forgiveness of sins, the gift of life? However, even their presence or absence does not yet determine the truth of the miracle stories. They are, after all, *stories*, and as such they are designed to make something happen. The question then is: Do these miracle stories have the power to break through the everyday suffering in the world and to lead us to such experiences? At the very latest the *general*, ideological question about the possibility of miracles here becomes the *existential* question of whether we will permit them to move us. Matthew paraphrases this movement as "to get into the boat," "to enter the house," "to follow," in short, as the risk that Jesus identifies as faith (9:22). To understand the miracle stories christologically as stories of the activity of Jesus who is both past and present is to lay claim to the activity of Jesus about which they tell as *help* for oneself. They become understandable only when we let ourselves be thus moved by them. It is not from the outside but only in our own relationship to Jesus that they reveal their meaning to us. Their truth is thus not simply something that they possess in themselves (for example, as scientifically "nevertheless" possible events). Instead, they *demonstrate* their truth by encouraging analogous experiences of life and salvation and by making such experiences happen. They are not simply reports of events that have happened; they are events that want to happen again in our understanding. In this sense they are "transparent."

33 For this reason Schleiermacher's interpretation of the miracle as a religious term for "event," as much as is theologically correct in it, misses precisely the decisive element in the synoptic miracle narratives (*On Religion: Speeches to Its Cultured Despisers*). The world is not—or to a large degree not—simply "wonderful"; it is characterized by suffering, illness, anxiety, and need. What counters these experiences is precisely the "special" element of the miracles of Jesus.

34 With the help of psychology, parapsychology, psychosomatic insights, the academic study of religions, and medicine, probably all of the synoptic healing miracles and exorcisms are conceivable (which does not mean that historically they all happened). It is a different matter with nature miracles and raisings of the dead that at the present time probably have to be described as not (not yet?) conceivable.

35 "Miraculum voco, quidquid arduum aut insolitum supra spem vel facultatem mirantis apparet" (*Util.* 16.34 = CSEL 25/1 43.16–17).

36 *CD* 4/2.215. With regard to the world, Barth describes the miracles as "alien," in terms of analogies and natural laws loosely as "relatively miraculous" (212). Cf. the helpful positive comments in the entire section, 209–47.

Literature

Yoshito Anno, "The Mission to Israel in Matthew: The Intention of Matthew 10:5b-6 Considered in the Light of the Religio-Political Background" (Diss., Chicago, 1984).

F. W. Beare, "The Mission of the Disciples and the Mission Charge: Matthew 10 and Parallels," *JBL* 89 (1970) 1–13.

Dietrich Bonhoeffer, *The Cost of Discipleship* (New York: Macmillan, 1969) 221–46.

Boring, *Sayings,* 141–50, 158–69, 208–12.

Brooks, *Community,* 47–57.

Schuyler Brown, "The Mission to Israel in Matthew's Central Section," *ZNW* 69 (1978) 73–90.

H. J. B. Combrink, "Structural Analysis of Mt 9:35-11:1," *Neot* 11 (1977) 98–114.

Dungan, *Sayings,* 41–75.

Goulder, *Midrash,* 338–53.

Hahn, *Mission,* 120–28.

Harnack, *Mission,* 36–42.

Kloppenborg, *Formation,* 190–203, 206–16.

Lange, *Erscheinen,* 250–60.

Akira Ogawa, *L'histoire de Jésus chez Matthieu: La signification de l'histoire pour la théologie matthéenne* (EHS 23/116; Frankfurt: Lang, 1979) 234–40.

Hiltrud Stadtland-Neumann, *Evangelische Radikalismen in der Sicht Calvins: Sein Verständnis der Bergpredigt und der Aussendungsrede (Mt 10)* (Beiträge zur Geschichte und Lehre der reformierten Kirche 24; Neukirchen-Vluyn: Neukirchener, 1966) 42–49.

Jirair S. Tashjian, "The Social Setting of the Mission Charge in Q" (Diss., Claremont, 1987).

Uro, *Sheep.*

Weaver, *Discourse.*

Position in the Gospel

The second discourse is also carefully incorporated into the structure of the gospel, although it does not exhibit the careful ring composition that we find in the Sermon on the Mount. Only 9:35 corresponds to 11:1b, and 10:1 corresponds to 11:1a.

The linkage of the discourse's content to earlier material is clear. The charge to the disciples in 10:7b to preach corresponds to the proclamation of Jesus in 4:17. The charge to heal in 10:8 is reminiscent of some of the deeds of Jesus reported in chaps. 8–9.[1] The sending of the disciples to Israel (10:5-6, 23; 11:1) corresponds to Jesus' activity in Israel (4:23; chaps. 8–9). Jesus' healing in 9:35c corresponds to the authority that is given to the disciples (10:1c). The disciples' behavior and fate correspond to the commands of the Sermon on the Mount. The disciples are defenseless (10:10, 16, cf. 5:38-42), poor (10:9-14, cf. 6:19-34), and persecuted (10:16-23, 38-39, cf. 5:10-12). They are under God's care (10:28-31, cf. 6:25, 31) and do not need to worry (10:19, cf. 6:25-34). Thus Matthew makes clear that the mission given to the disciples is no different from Jesus' own mission, just as their authority and their fate are no different from those of Jesus. The content of their proclamation corresponds to their lifestyle.

Matthew 11:1-7 takes up the narrative thread of chaps. 8–9 without a break. Matthew is able to do this because he does not report that Jesus sent the disciples out (as in Mark 6:7-13, 30 or Luke 10:1, 17-20). When the discourse is completed it is not the disciples who go away, having been sent out, but Jesus himself (11:1b).[2] Reading the concluding statement in 11:1, this discourse, like the other Matthean discourses, has no immediate function in the narrative thread. Since it has no direct consequences, it is as if Jesus has simply spoken it into thin air. Thus 11:1-7 takes up the narrative thread where Matthew had left it in chap. 9, which explains why there are so many references in 11:1-7 back to chaps. 3–9.[3] In view of what follows in the Matthean report we

---

1   Cf. 8:16-17; 9:35; 9:18-26; 8:1-4; 8:28-34; 9:32-34.

2   Patte, 138–39, concludes from this fact that the organization of the Gospel of Matthew is not narrative but didactic and then, with the help of the contrasts in the text, he analyzes the themes Matthew deals with. Incorrectly! He fails to recognize that the narrative parts of Matthew (i.e., of chaps. 8–9, 11–12, etc.) are complete units into which this discourse of Jesus, like others, is inserted, and he treats the Matthean discourse and narrative sections as the same kind of literature. Matthew himself intend-ed—as he indicates with the conclusions of the discourses—to give the discourses a special position *within* the narrative.

3   Matthew 11:3 refers to 3:11b, 11:5a-d to the miracles in chaps. 8–9, the end of 11:5 and 6 to the macarisms 5:3 (-12), 11:7 to 3:1, 5.

can understand the sending discourse as a preview of coming events. The next main section, chaps. 12–16, tells of the separation between the disciples and Israel and thus makes clear the meaning of the saying about sheep among wolves (10:16). Israel's opposition and the new family of disciples (cf. 10:25, 34-37) will be the subject of the following section. Jesus faces the burden of the cross and the loss of his life. Even in its details, chap. 10 sounds themes of later sections. Texts that from the perspective of the entire narrative are previews of what is to come are, for example, 10:6 (cf. 15:24; 28:18-20), 10:15 (cf. 11:20-24), 10:17-22 (cf. 24:9-14), 10:25 (cf. 12:22-30), 10:38-39 (cf. 16:16-21; 27:31-56), 10:40-42 (cf. 18:1-14; 25:31-46).

That Matthew here interrupts the flow of his narrative with a second discourse has several meanings. At the earliest possible place following the first gathering of a group of disciples, Jesus instructs the disciples about the task and shape of discipleship. He thus applies ecclesiologically what he has thus far done and taught. That the discourse has no immediate consequences within the story of Matthew and is, as it were, spoken into thin air, is an indication that it is designed to be meaningful beyond the unique historical situation of that time. The numerous allusions to the future story or words of Jesus not only serve the didactic purpose of heightening the interest through anticipation and repetition, they especially show that Jesus is master of this story and in his words and deeds will remain true to himself.

Structure

Outlining the structure of our discourse is not easy. Clearly recognizable is (1) *the narrative introduction in 9:36—10:5a*. It begins in the same way as the narrative introduction of the Sermon on the Mount,[4] but is then more detailed. In addition to the list of the apostles (10:1-4), it contains two logia important for the interpretation of the discourse (9:36, 37-38) that are heard again in the discourse itself. The actual discourse is to be divided into two main parts[5] of approximately equal length.

(2) *The first main section* is *10:5b-23*. As does the second part, it ends with an amen word with $o\vec{v} \mu\eta$ (vv. 23, 42). The catchword "Israel" ($\mathit{I}\sigma\rho\alpha\eta\lambda$) forms an inclusion (vv. 6, 23). The unit is divided into the two subsections, *vv. 5b-15* and *16[6]-23*, each of which contains at its beginning the catchwords "I send" ($\dot{\alpha}\pi o\sigma\tau\acute{\epsilon}\lambda\lambda\omega$) and "sheep" ($\pi\rho\acute{o}\beta\alpha\tau o\nu$; vv. 5-6, 16) that are anticipated in the introduction (9:36; 10:2a). Both conclude with a reference to the judgment in the form of an amen saying (vv. 15, 23). In the first section, imperatives are dominant, in the second, future tenses. The first section contains the actual mission commands, the second speaks of the persecution that is part of the mission.

(3) *The second main section, 10:24-42,* cannot be organized unequivocally. *Verses 24-25* have a key function. They connect the fate of the disciples with that of the master with whom they are members of the same household. For this reason vv. 34-39 are best understood around the theme of whether one is attached to Jesus or to the "members of the household" ($o\dot{\iota}\kappa\iota\alpha\kappa\acute{o}\iota$, vv. 25, 36) to which one has previously belonged. Jesus' appearance means a severing of one's previous household relationships (vv. 34-36; three times $\kappa\alpha\tau\acute{\alpha}$), for the attachment to him must take precedence over everything else (vv. 37-39; three times "is not worthy of me," $o\dot{v}\kappa \ \ddot{\epsilon}\sigma\tau\iota\nu \ \mu o\nu \ \ddot{\alpha}\xi\iota o\varsigma$, seven times "me," $\mu o\nu, \dot{\epsilon}\mu\acute{\epsilon}$) and leads to suffering. *Verses 26-33* are characterized by the catchword "to fear" ($\varphi o\beta\acute{\epsilon}o\mu\alpha\iota$) and are designed to encourage the proclaimers. For reasons of their content, vv. 32-33 belong

---

4   After 4:23 par. and 9:35 cf. 5:1 par. and 9:36: $\dot{\iota}\delta\grave{\omega}\nu$ $\delta\grave{\epsilon} \ \tau o\grave{\upsilon}\varsigma \ \ddot{o}\chi\lambda o\upsilon\varsigma$. See similarly Terence J. Keegan, "Introductory Formulae for Matthean Discourse," *CBQ* 44 (1982) 428–29.

5   Jean Radermakers (*Au fil de l'Évangile selon saint Matthieu* [2 vols.; Heverlee-Louvain: Institut d'études théologiques, 1972] 135–47), H. J. B. Combrink ("Structural Analysis of Mt 9:35-11:1," *Neot* 11 [1977] 98–114, 109–11), and N. W. Lund (*Chiasmus in the New Testament* [Chapel Hill: University of North Carolina Press, 1942] 262–71) suggest a division of vv. 5-42 into five sections that

are arranged chiastically (5-15/34-42; 16-23/26-33) around the center 24-25. It is not clear, however, that the sections A and E or B and D linguistically correspond to one another. Rainer Riesner ("Der Aufbau der Reden im Matthäus-Evangelium," *ThBei* 9 [1978] 176) regards the two main sections as 10:1(!)-16 and 17-42. My own suggestion owes much to the observations of Weaver, *Discourse,* 71–126.

6   For formal reasons (inclusion with vv. 5-6) v. 16 could be assigned to the preceding section. Because of its content, however, it belongs to vv. 17-23. Furthermore, the image changes in v. 16.

to this unit. They make clear which proclamation was meant in vv. 26-31. Both sections emphasize the christological foundation of vv. 24-25 ($\lambda \acute{\epsilon} \gamma \omega \ \acute{\upsilon} \mu \hat{\iota} \nu$, vv. 27, 32-33; $\mathring{\eta} \lambda \vartheta o \nu$ vv. 34-35, $\acute{\epsilon} \mu \acute{\epsilon}$, vv. 37-39, 40a, $\grave{\alpha} \mu \mathring{\eta} \nu \ \lambda \acute{\epsilon} \gamma \omega \ \acute{\upsilon} \mu \hat{\iota} \nu$, v. 42). A promise to the disciples and those in solidarity with them concludes the discourse (*vv. 40-42*).

The most important difference between the two main sections consists in their *temporal structures*. The first main section is framed by the two sayings that limit the disciples' mission to Israel (10:5-6, 23). In addition, there are in this main section sayings that indicate that it is speaking of the mission in Israel (vv. 17-18, cf. 16). Our interpretation will have to show whether the readers of the Gospel of Matthew understood the words to be speaking to their own present. In the second section, by contrast, nothing is limited to Israel; here the church can understand everything that Jesus says as spoken directly to its own situation.

Sources

The relationship to *the sources* is complex. As with all of the discourses, the disciples discourse is a composition consciously composed by the evangelist. There are disciple sendings in Mark (6:7-13, 30-31) and in Q (Luke 10:2-16). The placement of the disciples discourse is suggested by both sources relatively but not absolutely. In his use of Mark, Matthew had proceeded as far as Mark 5:43 (= Matt 9:26), but in the verse that frames chaps. 5–9 (4:23 = 9:35) he had already used formulations from Mark 6:6. From Q he had moved Luke 9:57-60 to an earlier place (= Matt 8:19-22) so that Luke 10:2-16 would now come next. In both sources, however, there are still omitted materials (Mark 2:23-4:34; 6:1-6a; Q = Luke 7:18-35). The evangelist thus generally follows his sources faithfully, but the exact placement of the disciples discourse is his own free choice. He wants the disciples discourse to appear immediately after the cycle of Jesus' deeds (Matthew 8–9).

There is similar freedom in the way Matthew arranges the details. The introduction, 9:36—10:4, is not only especially long, but also especially independent. Matthew frames a logion from the sending discourse (9:37-38 = Luke 10:2 Q) and the introduction to the Markan sending discourse (10:1 = Mark 6:7) with two Markan units that come from different contexts (9:36 = Mark 6:34?; 10:2-4 = Mark 3:16-19). Unlike the Sermon on the Mount, only in a very loose sense does the sending discourse of Q provide the total framework: 10:7-16 and the conclusion 10:40 (= Luke 10:16 Q) correspond to it. At the beginning (10:7-16) Matthew follows textually the sending discourse of his sources. In the process he freely rearranges the Q material that goes beyond the common kernel of the two sending discourses (Mark 6:8-11; Luke 10:4-12 Q), or he moves it to other sections of his gospel.[7] In 10:17-39 he adds additional material to the sending discourse of his sources (much as he does in 13:24-52; 18:10-35; 24:37-25:46). The first traditional unit comes from Mark (10:17-22 = Mark 13:9-13), the later material mostly from Q.[8] The evangelist doubles the Markan unit, as he does in other cases[9] (Mark 13:9-13 = Matt 10:17-22 and 24:9-14). The material that comes from Q is given essentially in the order of the source. Matthew goes through the source and excerpts what thematically fits his own discourse. This also is a procedure with which we are familiar from other discourses.[10] In places that are decisive for his composition he adds material from special traditions (10:5-6, 23, 24-25, 41-42, cf., e.g., 5:17-19; 18:20; 23:8-11). It is noteworthy that Matthew frequently makes use of his sources this same way in other discourses. This is in my judgment a convincing confirmation of the two-source theory that our analysis

---

7   He consistently deals this way with Q. Only in the Sermon on the Mount does Matthew follow the outline of the Sermon on the Plain of Q (because no Markan counterpart exists). By contrast, in Matthew 23 he follows the structure of Q only minimally. The outline of Luke 17:22-37 is partially destroyed by Matthew, that of Luke 12:39-59 completely.

8   Similar instances in which Matthew concludes with Q material after material from other sources are Matt 5:25-26 (after 5:23-24 = special material of Matthew), Matt 5:38-48 (after the "primary" antitheses), and Matt 13:31-33 (after 13:24-30), but

Matthew can also use a different approach. Even more important is that in all the discourses, with the exception of the Sermon on the Mount, the first part comes from Mark.

9   Cf. vol. 1, Introduction I F and the commentary on 9:27-31.

10   Cf. vol. 1, II A 3 and Vincent Taylor, "The Original Order of Q," in Angus J. B. Higgens, ed., *New Testament Essays: Studies in Memory of Thomas Walter Manson* (Manchester: Manchester University Press, 1959) 246–69.

presupposes.[11] In general, in spite of the careful way he treats his sources, he creates a new discourse with a clearly recognizable, new profile.

Addressees

The discourse is addressed to the "twelve disciples" (10:1; 11:1) to whom Matthew can also refer as the "twelve apostles" (10:2). The use of both terms, "apostles" and "disciples," reveals a problem. "Disciples" is a term that is transparent of the community. The "apostles" by contrast are a unique entity from the church's beginnings. For whom is the discourse intended? Is it meant for the apostles of the beginning period or basically for the church?

The difficulty facing the interpreter lies in the fact that Matthew here appears to make no distinction at all. Sayings that can apply only to the beginning period (10:5-6, 23), sayings that clearly suggest a past situation (e.g., 10:17-18), and sayings that are always valid alternate with one another without an indication anywhere from the evangelist that the validity of the sayings is limited. By not distinguishing between the "transparent" disciples and the "past" apostles he shows that he wants to see past and present together. Not until the history of interpretation did it become important to distinguish between the two. Distinguishing between them was a way to confine to the beginning period of the church those sayings that contradicted one's own church situation.[12] Another advantage of limiting the validity of the sending discourse to the apostles is that individual sayings thus did not have to be applied to the entire church but could be limited to those who held an office. Here too the discourse's challenge is considerably toned down.[13] By contrast, Matthew seems to make such simple distinctions impossible.

A second, related difficulty is that a number of the sayings of the sending discourse speak to the so-called wandering charismatics, that is, to itinerant disciples (10:5-6, 9-14, 23, 40), while others are directed expressly to settled Christians (10:41-42). Most of the sayings can be applied to wandering charismatics and to settled members of the community without distinction. Again, however, Matthew does not appear to make a distinction. The addressees are always the same.

Verses 40-42 give us information about the situation of the Matthean church. It has close contact with wandering charismatics.[14] According to v. 42 even ordinary members of the church are on the road. The use of μικροί for itinerant members of the church in 10:42 and for Christians in general in chap. 18 shows that Matthew does not fundamentally distinguish between them. The same is true of other texts. Matthew applies 6:25-33 to the entire church—a text that originally spoke of the wandering charismatics. The content of the perfection that according to Matt 5:48 is the goal for the entire church is, according to 19:21, that the "rich young man" sell all his possessions and become Jesus' follower, that is, a wandering charismatic. That most likely corresponds to the historical reality. We should avoid making a fundamental distinction between itinerant and settled Christians.[15] Acts 13:2-3 gives an example of settled Christians becoming wandering charismatics, while *Didache* 12–13 gives instructions for the wandering charismatics who would settle down. If we regard the relationship between settled Christians and wandering charismatics as fluid, then it is understandable why Matthew can address in our discourse the entire church as potential wandering charismatics. With their preaching they vicariously fulfill the mission given to the

---

11 An example of the difficulty of other hypotheses is that Goulder (*Midrash*) is forced to assume that Matthew deals differently with different kinds of Markan material. He paraphrases the discourse material by expanding it (345–47 on 10:7-15, 347–53 for the midrashlike expansion 10:23-42), while he consistently rigorously abbreviates the Markan narrative material. Even 10:17-22, 38-39 do not expand the Markan source. Furthermore, the redactional vocabulary is relatively minor in the so-called midrashlike additions to Mark.

12 Cf. below, nn. 24, 30, 39, 69 on Matt 10:5-15.

13 This reduction is made frequently with 9:37. The laborers are the teachers or preachers (e.g., Dionysius bar Salibi, *Commentarii in Evangelia*, 3 vols., ed. I. Sedlacek, and Arthur Vaschalde

[Louvain: Durbecq, 1953] 208; Christian of Stavelot, 1343B). In the Lima Document "Ministry" 9 (*Baptism, Eucharist, and Ministry* [Geneva: World Council of Churches, 1982] 21) Matt 10:1-8 is used as one of the biblical foundations for the ordained (!) ministry ("The church has never been without persons holding specific authority and responsibility").

14 Cf. vol. 1, Introduction 5.2.

15 Ulrich Luz, "Die Kirche und ihr Geld im Neuen Testament," in Wolfgang Lienemann, ed., *Die Finanzen der Kirche* (Munich: Kaiser, 1989) 535–37.

entire church, while the church is in solidarity with "its" wandering radicals (10:10, 40-42). Itinerant radicalism is a special possibility of Christian perfection (19:16-30). In my judgment, this is the only way to understand why Matthew does not change the addressees in our chapter, even though he speaks to wandering radicals and to settled believers.

Our interpretation will take seriously what the discourse's location in the gospel has demonstrated. Having been granted the same authority as Jesus, the disciples have the same mission to heal and to proclaim as does their master. They correspond in their life to the εὐαγγέλιον τῆι βασιλείαι of Jesus, the Sermon on the Mount, and will suffer the same fate as Jesus. That all speaks in favor of attributing fundamental ecclesiological significance to the sending discourse. In it Matthew extends the ministry of Jesus into the church. In it Matthew speaks of the church as the figure of Jesus. *For this reason we are calling it disciples discourse rather than sending discourse.* The concept of "disciple" (μαϑητής) frames the discourse at the beginning (9:37; 10:1), in the middle (10:24-25), and at the end (10:42; 11:1). Of course, this basic thesis will have to prove itself in the interpretation of the historicizing and limiting verses that appear to be valid only for a certain time or for a certain group of the church.

The two sections 9:36-38 and 10:1-5a have no catchwords in common and are also different in content. The list of the names of the apostles in 10:2-4 at first looks like an excursus that became necessary because Matthew transposes the Markan sequence of the text and has to append Mark 3:13-19 as a necessary presupposition for Mark 6:7-13. The interpretation will show that that is not *only* the case: An implicit connection between their contents underlies both sections.

1.1 The Task: The People's Suffering (9:36-38)

For *literature* see above, II C on Matt 9:36—11:1.

36   When he saw the crowds, he had compassion for them, because they were harassed and beaten down, like "sheep who have no shepherd." 37/ Then he says to his disciples: "The harvest is great, but there are (only) few laborers. 38/ Ask therefore the Lord of the harvest to send out laborers into his harvest."

Analysis   Matthew again begins a new major section not with a caesura but with a transition.[1] Verse 36a immediately follows the preceding summary. We will be able to see how important the following *v. 36b, c* is for Matthew only from the source analysis: Mark 6:34a-c is moved up from the feeding narrative to this point. Σκύλλω is a word from a Markan section (Mark 5:35) that had been omitted from 9:18-26 but that the "conservative" Matthew did not want to lose.[2] Most of the other

changes in v. 36 are redactional.[3] *Verses 37-38* contain, after a Matthean introduction,[4] the first logion of Q's sending discourse (Luke 10:2) without changes.[5] "Laborer" (ἐργάτης) is a connecting link to 10:10. Because of its eschatological understanding of the disciples' preaching activity, this logion could come from Jesus.[6]

Interpretation

■ **36** The disciples discourse begins with compassion for the people without a shepherd. Matthew thus makes clear that discipleship is fundamentally related to the people, that is, its mission. The *church* is *eo ipso* a missionary community in the sense of proclamation by works, signs, and words. Σκύλλω means "to torment," "to oppress," ῥίπτω "to throw on the ground," passive "to be prostrate, depressed." The "sheep who have no shepherd" is an Old Testament expression that occurs several times;[7] it should not be restricted to the sense of an individual Old Testament text. However, it is clear from the Old Testament language that one is thinking of the people of Israel.[8] The open formulation permits a variety of understandings of need.[9] For Matthew obviously the entire nation is in need. The stories of the sick told in chaps. 8 and 9 are representative of all the people. The singular ποιμήν ("shepherd") does not suggest a direct polemic against the Jewish leaders.[10] On the basis of 2:6 the most natural assumption is that Matthew

---

1   Cf. vol. 1, Introduction 1 on the difficulties related to Matthew's outline.

2   Σκύλλω is a Matthean and Markan hapax legomenon. Cf. also n. 3 on 9:32-34.

3   On ὁράω (ἰδών), δέ, ὄχλος plural, ὡσεί, cf. vol. 1, Introduction 3.2. Also redactional is ῥίπτω (cf. 15:30; 27:5). Σπλαγχνίζομαι περί is neither redactional, nor LXX language, nor good Greek (BDF § 229 [2]).

4   Cf. on τότε, λέγω with the dative vol. 1, Introduction 3.2, on the historical present with λέγω vol. 1, Introduction 3.1.

5   It was probably Luke who changed the word order ἐργάτης ἐκβάλῃ. Cf. Paul Hoffmann, *Studien zur Theologie der Logienquelle* (NTA NF 8; Münster: Aschendorf, 1972) 263.

6   Hahn (*Mission*, 40, n. 3), e.g., argues for authenticity. Others advocate a Q formation. Uro (*Sheep*, 208–9), e.g., attributes it to the optimistic perspective of the gentile mission. Jirair S. Tashijian ("The Social Setting of the Mission Charge in Q" [Diss.,

Claremont, 1987] 220) correctly notes that the early stages of the mission discourse do not yet anticipate a negative reaction from Israel.

7   Num 27:17; 3 Βασ 22:17; 2 Chr 18:16; Jdt 11:19; Ezek 34:5.

8   Cf. the resumption of the image in 10:6.

9   Based on the end of 9:35 and 10:1 one will initially think of the affliction that Israel's sick brought to Jesus in Matthew 8–9. Looking back on Matthew 8–9 from the perspective of 9:36 reveals that the sick and the demon-possessed represent the people of Israel.

10   This is a frequent interpretation based on Zech 11:16-17. There is, however, no allusion here to that text. There is no reference to bad shepherds in 9:36.

11   Uro (*Sheep*, 201) provides Old Testament and Jewish material. In a marginal note in his *Matthäusevangelium*, Schnackenburg interprets it, however, in terms of an understanding of mission that was developing in the primitive church. Relevant here would be not only John 4:36-38 but

is thinking of Jesus himself as a shepherd. He thus begins his disciples discourse by calling attention to grace—Jesus' mercy toward God's people.

■ **37-38** The disciples' task will be to heal Israel's affliction. In the Old Testament and Judaism the image of harvest is definitely associated with judgment.[11] In the sayings source a strongly eschatological tone probably resonated. The gathering of Israel for the kingdom of God by means of the disciples' proclamation is an eschatological event. Matthew was also familiar with this eschatological outlook (3:12; 13:39); for him also in the proclamation of the disciples a degree of judgment happens in advance (10:13-15, cf. 34-36). By contrast, the harvest laborers[12] in 13:39, 41 (cf. 24:31) are the angels of the Son of Man and not the disciples. The images of mission as harvest and of the coming of the Son of Man as harvest are juxtaposed in Matthew without being connected. Our saying was important for the evangelist not only because of its eschatological perspective, but also because he was thus able to place at the beginning of his disciples discourse an admonition to prayer (cf. Acts 13:1-3). As we have seen already in the Sermon on the Mount, prayer is for him the basis of the disciples' missionary existence. The disciples' discourse thus begins by looking to the Lord of the harvest whose work the disciples will do; it ends by referring to him who is present in those who are sent (10:40).

Summary

The juxtaposition of the images of the shepherd and the harvest that are so different leaves the reader somewhat uncertain. The positive element, mercy, dominates the image of the shepherd. In the image of the harvest another element resonates: the threat of judgment. Matthew does not remove the uncertainty; he lets the two images stand side by side without connecting them. Something of this ambivalence will also be felt in the charge to the disciples in 10:7-15. We are confronted here by one of the major problems in understanding the entire gospel: How are the merciful shepherd and the Lord of judgment—Son of Man—to be understood together?

---

also the Pauline usage of $\kappa\alpha\rho\pi\delta i$. However, the use of the image elsewhere in Matthew contradicts this view. Important for the decision on this question is whether Matthew expected an imminent parousia (a view that I would affirm).

12 However, Matthew does not use the term $\dot{\epsilon}\rho\gamma\dot{\alpha}\tau\eta\varsigma$, which comes from the missionary language and anticipates 10:10. Paul gives evidence of the same usage—strangely enough, always to refer to his opponents (2 Cor 11:13; Phil 3:2). Cf. n. 44 on 10:5-15.

1.2 The Commissioned (10:1-5a)

Literature

Antonio Salerno, "Un nuovo aspetto del primato di Pietro in Mt 10,2 e 16,18-19," *RivB* 28 (1980) 435–39.

For *additional literature* see above, II C on Matt 9:36-11:1.

1   **And he called his twelve disciples together and gave them authority over the unclean spirits, to cast them out, and to heal every sickness and every weakness.**

2   **But these are the names of the twelve apostles: first Simon, who is called Peter, and his brother Andrew, and James, the son of Zebedee, and his brother John,**

3   **Philip and Bartholomew, Thomas and Matthew, the tax collector, James, the son of Alphaeus, and Thaddaeus,[1]**

4   **Simon the Cananaean[2] and Judas of Iscariot[3] who also betrayed him.**

5   **These twelve Jesus sent out and commanded them:**

Analysis

Structure

The list of apostles in vv. 2-4 is framed by the authorization and sending of the twelve (vv. 1-2a, 5).[4] The wording of the authority in v. 1b, c goes back to 4:23 and 9:35. In addition, Matthew uses catchwords from 9:6, 8 (ἐξουσία) and 8:16 (πνεῦμα, ἐκβάλλω). Ἔδωκεν ἐξουσίαν anticipates the key christological text of 28:18. Together with 11:1 δώδεκα μαθηταί constitutes an inclusion. The compositional bracketing that Matthew achieves with the introductory verse is thus very intensive.

Source

Verse 1 is largely redactional.[5] Even the agreements with Luke 9:1 do not contradict this observation.[6] Verses 2-4 correspond to the list of the twelve in Mark 3:16-19. The opening words in v. 2a are probably redactional.[7] Changing the location of Andrew in the list makes v. 2b-e a reminiscence of the calling of the disciples in 4:18-22.[8] After this emphatic reminder, Matthew structures the list so that the apostles are listed in pairs. The introduction to the discourse in v. 5a, formulated along the lines of Mark 6:7-8, is also redactional. The other changes in the Markan source also are redactional.[9]

Interpretation

■ **1, 2, 5** Jesus responds to Israel's suffering by calling the twelve disciples to himself. The word δώδεκα ("twelve") appears three times in short intervals (vv. 1, 2, 5). Matthew knows that the twelve disciples correspond to the twelve tribes of Israel (19:28).[10] Thus the section

---

1   Is Λεββαῖος (with parts of the Western tradition and Origen) or Θαδδαῖος (with the most important Alexandrian MSS and parts of the Western tradition) original? Most MSS harmonize the two names and understand one as the surname of the other. The witnesses for Θαδδαῖος are weightier. According to McNeile (132), Λεββαῖος comes from the Hebrew לֵב = heart, Θαδδαῖος from the Aramaic תַּדְיָא = breast. Dalman (*Words,* 50) thinks of the Greek name Θεῦδας and understands Λεββαῖος as the corresponding Aramaic name. The matter remains puzzling.

2   Very many MSS read Κανανίτης; they obviously understand the designation to be a *nomen gentilicium* (as, e.g., Ἱεροσολυμίτης).

3   The variants fluctuate between Ἰσκαριώθ (thus also Mark and Luke), Σκαριώτης (D etc.; from Hebrew סכר: Piel = hand over [very rare] or from *sicarius* [dagger bearer] or from שקר = lie, cheat?) and Ἰσκαριώτης (the most important witnesses and Matt 26:14). This reading is not only the best attested; it also conforms to the Matthean tendency of a limited Grecianizing of Aramaisms. Cf. vol. 1, Introduction 3.3, n. 98.

4   Δώδεκα (v. 1); ἀπόστολοι (v. 2a); δώδεκα ἀπέστειλεν (v. 5a).

5   Mark 3:13 and 6:7 are in the background. On μαθητής, ὥστε, θεραπεύω, μαλακία, νόσος cf. vol. 1, Introduction 3.2; on the participle and aorist, vol. 1, Introduction 3.1. On the bracketings cf. above II C, "Position in the Gospel." Προσκαλεσάμενος τοὺς . . . μαθητάς (cf. 15:32) is a redactional Markan formula taken over by Matthew.

6   Luke also has a preference for the aorist, νόσος (plural!), and θεραπεύω. The different order of the bestowal of authority and the sending (Luke 9:2//Matt 10:5) is obvious. The minor agreements are so numerous, however, that one may ask whether the original Q introduction to the sending discourse is to be found behind Matt 10:1 and Luke 9:1 (Uro, *Sheep,* 74–75).

7   To be sure, this cannot be proved linguistically, but leaving out the Markan bestowal of the names (Mark 3:16b, 17b) corresponds to the omission of a report about the *appointment* of the twelve (Mark 3:16a: ἐποίησεν). Ὄνομα comes from Mark 3:16-17, ἀπόστολος from Mark 6:30.

8   With the exception of πρῶτος, all the words of v. 2b-e appear in 4:18, 21. Luke 6:14 also changes the location of "his brother Andrew." Was this the reading in the Markan text that was available to the two evangelists, or did Luke, who had to add Andrew

9:36—10:6 is entirely about Israel. Matthew presupposes that Jesus has twelve disciples, but unlike Mark 3:13-15 he says nothing about the institution of the circle of the twelve. His concern here is not with its historical constitution, but with the authorization by Jesus that determines the church's entire activity. The disciples share in his own authority; that is made clear by the references back to 4:23, 9:35, and 8:16. As 28:18-20 will underscore, their power is an expression of the power of the Lord who remains with his church. Matthew is thus not simply interested in giving a report about the beginnings of the church. In all probability that is why in 10:1 he uses the word that is transparent of the present, $\mu\alpha\vartheta\eta\tau\alpha\acute{\iota}$ ("disciples"), instead of $\grave{\alpha}\pi\acute{o}\sigma\tau o\lambda o\iota$ ("apostles").[11] On the other hand, he uses the apostles to interpret the disciples and with the number "twelve" also indicates that he is speaking of the twelve disciples of Jesus back then. Matthew thus presents the mission of the twelve as the prototype of the continuing mission of the church.

The authority of the disciples to perform miracles—mentioned here alone and in vv. 7-8 along with the charge to preach—is eminently important for the formation of the church. If miracles are regarded as a peculiarity that was necessary only at the beginning of the church's history because uneducated fishermen had to proclaim a new truth to the entire world,[12] then we have missed, or at least repressed, something that is fundamental for Matthew.

■ **2a** The circle of the apostles had already been identified with the twelve in Mark (6:7, 30) prior to Matthew, and alongside Matthew the identification also appears in Revelation and in Luke. In contrast to Revelation, however, Matthew is not interested in the heavenly nature of the apostolic church (Rev 21:14), and in contrast to Luke he is less interested in the continuity of tradition that is assured by the testimony of the twelve apostles.[13] Along with the following list of names, the term $\grave{\alpha}\pi\acute{o}\sigma\tau o\lambda o\varsigma$ enables him to connect discipleship with the earthly Jesus.[14] Likewise, it is *Jesus'* message ("gospel of the kingdom"; $\varepsilon\grave{\upsilon}\alpha\gamma\gamma\acute{\varepsilon}\lambda\iota o\nu$ $\tau\hat{\eta}\varsigma$ $\beta\alpha\sigma\iota\lambda\varepsilon\acute{\iota}\alpha\varsigma$!) that the disciples proclaim, *his* miracles that they continue, and *his* presence that defines them (10:40, cf. 28:16-20). Mentioning the twelve apostles is a reminder that the exalted one is the earthly one.

■ **2b-4** From a literary perspective the list of names is an instructive incidental observation. In general, the changes in the Markan source are easily understandable. The list begins with the four disciples whose call was reported in Matt 4:18-22. Matthew says no more about renaming Peter and the sons of Zebedee (Mark 3:16-17) than he does about the establishment of the circle of the twelve. Simon is Peter from the beginning.[15] Probably the surname "sons of thunder" no longer played a role in his community. Matthew is, clearly based on 9:9, the tax collector. The surnames of Simon and Judas remain difficult to explain. On "Cananaean" ($K\alpha\nu\alpha\nu\alpha\hat{\iota}o\varsigma$) we can surmise that the evangelist was not thinking of the place-name Cana[16] or of the biblical Canaanites (= $X\alpha\nu\alpha\nu\alpha\hat{\iota}o\varsigma$) but, as Luke translates in Luke 6:15 and Acts 1:13, of the zealous one,[17] Simon the Zealot. Obviously his readers did not need a translation. The evangelist understood "of Iscariot" ($\dot{I}\sigma\kappa\alpha\rho\iota\acute{\omega}\tau\eta\varsigma$) proba-

---

after 5:1-11, edit it independently of Matthew?

9   Verse 2: On ὁ λεγόμενος cf. vol. 1, Introduction 3:2. On the position of the apposition cf. vol. 1, I A 3.2 on 4:18-22, n. 1. Verse 3: on ὁ τελώνης cf. 9:9; on Ἰσκαριώτης cf. 26:14. Verse 4: on παραδούς cf. 27:3-4. The change in the order of Thomas and Matthew remains unclear.

10   Since Origen (fr. 195 I = GCS Origenes 12.94) there has been speculation about further symbolism of the number twelve: 12 legions of angels, 12 hours of the day, 12 as the perfect number (3 × 4!), 12 patriarchs, 12 stones in the Jordan river (Joshua 4), a combination of Trinity and the 4 areas of the world, etc. The symbolism in Rabanus (Thomas Aquinas, *Catena* 1.162 = ET 1.363) is especially prolific.

11   Μαθητής is a key word at the beginning, in the center (vv. 24-25), and at the conclusion (v. 42; 11:1) of the disciples discourse.

12   Cf. Maldonat, 210; Bullinger, 97B.

13   Unlike the church's interpretation since Origen (fr. 194 = GCS Origenes 12.93), who says that Matthew explicitly names the twelve apostles to distinguish them from the false apostles.

14   Cf. Luz, "Jünger," 142–43, 145 and above, n. 16 on Matt 9:9-13.

15   4:18; 8:14 in contrast to Mark. Σίμων occurs in Matthew only as direct address (16:17; 17:25).

16   In which case we would expect Καναῖος or something similar.

17   Cf. Hebrew/Aramaic קנא = to be zealous.

bly in the sense of a *nomen gentilicium*: the man from "Iscaria."[18] That is the most likely explanation for a writer who probably was not familiar with Hebrew but knew the Greek noun formation.[19] The most difficult element is the word "first" (πρῶτος) before Peter that corresponds neither to 4:18-22, nor to the Markan source, nor to Matthew's customary language.

History of Interpretation

The Vulgate translates: *Primus Simon.* For the church's interpretation the term has always meant that Peter was the first one called. One frequently finds the idea that Peter's *meritum* also caused him to be at the head of the list.[20] That enabled a connection with 16:18, but seldom was a line drawn beyond Peter to the papacy.[21] It was not until the sixteenth century that the text became the object of major controversy.

Following, for example, John Chrysostom, many Protestants interpret it to refer to the time of the call, not to Peter's special qualities.[22] However, the question then remained why πρῶτος is mentioned at all. That Peter was the first one called in 4:18-20 and is first in 10:2 does not need to be mentioned explicitly. Furthermore, at the other extreme Judas is always placed at the end of the list because he was unworthy.[23] The question repeatedly asked by Catholics is whether Peter's *dignitas* can be excluded from 10:2.[24] A number of Protestants have conceded a possible "merit" for Peter but deny that it might have any legal significance for the Roman pope.[25] By contrast, during the time of the Counter-Reformation, many Catholic interpreters[26] wanted to find in our text "the subordination of the apostles, bishops, and all believers under the one head," the pope.[27]

18　Cf., e.g., Πατριώτης, Ἡρακλειώτης, Κωρυκιώτης, Μασσαλιώτης, Πηλουσιώτης, Σικελιώτης, Ἀφαμιώτης. Cf. Eduard Schwyzer, *Griechische Grammatik* (3 vols.; Handbuch der klassischen Altertumswissenschaft 2/1; vol. 1, 5th ed. [1977]; vol. 2, ed. Albert Debrunner [1950]; vol. 3 ed. D. Georgacas [1953]; Munich: Beck, 1950–77) 1.500, and Wilhelm Dittenberger, "Ethnica und Verwandtes," *Hermes* 41 (1906) 181–88.

19　Matthew was not aware that Ἰσκαριώθ might come from אִישׁ קְרִיּוֹת (= a man from the Judean place, Kerioth; cf. Josh 15:25) (thus obviously John 14:22 D!); the article ὁ then would not be necessary.

20　The concept of "*meritum*" appears since Jerome, 63. Cf., e.g., Paschasius Radbertus, 403 ("*in meritis primus*" with reference to Matt 16:18); Euthymius Zigabenus, 324 (although Peter is younger than his brother Andrew, he is superior to him in stability).

21　Most clearly in Albertus Magnus, *In Evangelium secundum Matthaeum Iuculenta expositio,* vols. 20–21: *Opera Omnia* (Adolphe Borgnet, ed.; Paris: Ludicoricum Vives, 1893–94) 443: "Petrus . . . dicatur primus. Non tamen dicitur Andreas secundus . . . sed omnes secundi sunt Petro ad iurisdictionem: quia non unus sub alio, sed omnes sub Petro." By contrast, Augustine interprets our text much differently in relation to Matt 16:18: Peter is the first apostle because of Matt 16:18, but the rock is Peter's confession, i.e., actually Christ himself (in *Joh. ev. tract.* 124.5 = FC 92.89).

22　See, e.g., Zwingli, 263; Calovius, 265 (*principatus ordinis*). John Chrysostom (32.3 = *PG* 57. 380) says that Mark lists the apostles according to their worthiness, Matthew without order.

23　Cornelius Jansen (1585–1638), *Tetrateuchus sive*

Commentarius in sancta Jesu Christi Evangelia (Brussels: Francisci T'Serstevens, 1737) 91.

24　Maldonat, 211. Maldonat's opponents based their argument primarily on the different order of the apostles in the various New Testament lists. Beza (43) incites the special wrath of Maldonat by asking whether perhaps πρῶτος, which is not followed by any other number, might be a later gloss for the purpose of stabilizing the papacy. However, few followed his lead.

25　See, e.g., Calvin 1.290. Cocceius (18) interprets the "primacy" of Peter typologically and thus approaches Matthew's understanding: The special revelation to and temptations of Peter show him as "ὑπόδειγμα lapsorum, gratia ipsius (*scil.* Jesu) conservatorum." Bengel (116) asks sharply: "*Primus . . . inter apostolos, non supra apostolos; . . . quid hoc ad papam Romanum?*"

26　Maldonat (210–11) regrets that in his time even many Catholics interpreted the text incorrectly.

27　The quotation is from Lapide, 219. Alfonso Salmeron (*Commentarii in Evangelicam Historiam* [11 vols.; Coloniae Agrippinae: Apud Antonium Hierat, et Ioan. Gymni, 1612], 4/2.13 = 4.341–42) says that because the *primus* is not followed by *secundus*, etc., the absolute primacy of Peter is meant. Robert Bellarmine (*De summo pontifice* [Sedan, 1619] 1/18 = 123–26) says that it cannot be the time of the call, because Andrew was called before the younger Peter and that it cannot be because of Peter's personal virtue, because the virtue of the married Peter was less than that of the celibate John.

Leaving the overinterpretation of the confessional controversies, we return to the text. Peter was the first one called. Why is that underscored with πρῶτοί? We can offer an answer only on the basis of later texts.[28] That answer will be that Peter, the first to be called by Jesus, is especially important for Matthew, because Peter can show in an exemplary way that discipleship basically means nothing more than becoming part of the one-time story of Jesus with his disciples back then. However, πρῶτος implies neither a special ecclesiastical competence or office of Peter,[29] nor a special succession in the later church. Rather, in Peter the "power" (ἐξουσία) that Jesus gives to *all* disciples becomes clear in a *special* way.

■ **5a** The actual introduction to the discourse, v. 5a, is clearly related to vv. 1-4. Jesus sent out those twelve to whom he had given authority over demons and illnesses and whose names have just been mentioned. Thus Jesus first gives the disciples his authority; only then does he send them out. With its connection to vv. 1-4 the discourse also receives its clear place in the *story* of Jesus. In what follows we have not simply timeless instructions about mission but a charge of Jesus to his disciples at a definite point in his story. What the disciples *always* are to do is rooted in a mission given by Jesus back then.

---

28   Cf. the excursus "Peter in the Gospel of Matthew" at 16:13-20.

29   Sand (*Evangelium,* 218) is of a different opinion. He says that the group of four who are listed first has "a special significance for the constitution of the church" that "justifies a rudimentary structure of 'offices' that already exists in the Matthean community." Unfortunately he offers no evidence. We can only warn against such claims made at a theologically controversial sensitive place.

2.1 The Mission (10:5b-15)

Literature

Roman Bartnicki, "Tätigkeit der Jünger nach Mt,5b-6," *BZ* 31 (1987) 250–56.

Schuyler Brown, "The Two-fold Representation of the Mission in Matthew's Gospel," *StTh* 31 (1977) 21–32.

Lucien Cerfaux, "La mission apostolique des Douze et sa portée eschatologique," in *Mélanges Eugène Tisserant* (Città del Vaticano: Biblioteca apostolica vaticana, 1964) 43–66.

Martino Conti, "Fondamenti Biblici della povertà nel ministero apostolica (Mt 10,9-10)," *Anton* 46 (1971) 393–426.

Hubert Frankemölle, *Jahwebund*, 123–30.

Idem, "Zur Theologie der Mission im Matthäusevangelium," in Karl Kertelge, ed., *Mission im Neuen Testament* (QD 93; Freiburg: Herder, 1982) 93–129.

A. E. Harvey, "'The Workman Is Worthy of His Hire': Fortunes of a Proverb in the Early Church," *NovT* 24 (1982) 209–21.

Hoffmann, *Studien*, 254–84, 287–304, 312–31.

Laufen, *Doppelüberlieferungen*, 201–95.

Levine, *Dimensions*, 13–57.

Heinz Schürmann, "Mt 10,5b-6 und die Vorgeschichte des synoptischen Aussendungsberichtes," in idem, *Untersuchungen*, 137–49.

Schulz, *Q*, 404–19.

Trilling, *Israel*, 99–105.

Zumstein, *Condition*, 429–35.

For *additional literature* on the disciples discourse see above, II C.

5b	**"Do not go on the way to the Gentiles, and do not enter a city of the Samaritans.**
6	**Go rather to the lost sheep of the house of Israel.**
7	**But go and proclaim: 'The Kingdom of Heaven has come near.'**
8	**Heal the weak, raise the dead, cleanse lepers, cast out demons. You received freely, give freely.**
9	**Do not take gold, silver, or small change[1] in your girdles,**
10	**no bag on the way, not two undergarments, no shoes, and no staff, for the laborer is worthy of his food.**
11	**When you enter any city or village, inquire who is worthy in it, and stay there until you leave.**
12	**But when you enter a house, greet it.**
13	**And if the house is worthy of it let your peace come on it. But if it is not worthy, let your peace return to you.**
14	**And whoever does not receive you and does not listen to your words— Go out of the house or that city and shake the dust from your feet.**
15	**Amen, I say to you: It will be more tolerable for the land of Sodom and Gomorra on the day of judgment than for that city.**

Analysis

Structure

The commands of Jesus recall first of all his own activity. Like Jesus (9:37) the disciples are to care for Israel's sheep (10:6). They are to carry his proclamation (4:17) further (10:7) and perform (10:8) his deeds (8:1-4, 17, 28-34; 9:18-26, 32-35). The text consists entirely of imperative sentences; only the concluding amen saying in v. 15 changes this basic structure and provides a definite caesura. *Verses 5b-6* contain a double prohibition in parallel form and a simple but correspondingly longer command. *Verses 7-8* command the disciples to preach and to heal. The preaching is defined with a statement of its content, and the healing is made specific with three exemplary imperatives. The brief final sentence with the double δωρεάν ("freely") is rhetorically effective. The sevenfold prohibition against accumulating things follows in *vv. 9-10*. Each of the middle members has an additional definition with εἰς resulting in a double sentence with mirrored symmetry. Again an unusual sentence follows containing the word ἐργάτης ("laborer"), familiar from 9:37-38, and that begins with the key word ἄξιος ("worthy")—a term that is repeated in vv. 11-13 (and in vv. 37-38) in close sequence. The structure of *vv. 11-13* is not completely clear. Presumably v. 11 describes how the disciples are to find a suitable host in the city or village that they enter. Verses 12 and 13a then speak of entering an individual house and of the positive reception there. Verses 13b-14 describe in much more detail how the disciples are to leave the house and the city when they do not find a friendly reception. Thus the first part, vv. 11-13a, speaks in two stages of entering (εἰσέλθητε/εἰσερχόμενοι), the second part—taking the house and the city together—of leaving (ἐξερχό-μενοι, v. 14b). The change in direction takes place between v. 13a and v. 13b (parallel formulation!).

---

1 Χαλκός = νομισμάτιον λεπτόν (Pollux *Onom.* 9.92). Pollux points to common phrases such as οὐκ ἔχω χαλκόν or ὀφείλω χαλκόν. Χαλκός is in this sense non-Attic. Atticists say χαλκίον (Pollux *Onom.* 9.90).

Sources[2]

Matthew combines Mark 6:8-11 and Q = Luke 10:4-12 into a new text. He is more likely to follow whichever source has the more detailed wording, and he takes some liberties especially with Q in wording and placement. Verses 5-6 and the end of 8 are special material. In detail:

Verses 5b-6: The logion, which in my judgment is not redactional,[3] has come to Matthew either from his special material or from Q[Mt], but Matthew is probably responsible for the placement.[4]

Verses 7-8: Matthew himself formulates the mission charge patterned loosely after Luke 10:9 and Mark 3:15; 6:13.[5] By so doing he makes concrete in terms of 4:17 the charge to preach, and in terms of Matthew 8–9 he makes concrete the charge to heal. The end of v. 8 formulates the Matthean understanding of vv. 9-10. We can no longer say whether the short sentence was already (in Q[Mt]?) transmitted.

Verses 9-10: Matthew formulates an equipment regulation that is almost as long as that of Mark 6:8-9 but in content approaches the severity of the short rule of Q = Luke 10:4a.[6] However, while Luke 10:4 is a rule about *possessing*, Matt 10:9-10 is formulated as a prohibition against *acquiring*. Appropriately, the Old Testament triad "gold-silver-small change," unknown in Mark and Q, is listed first.[7] Linguistically, neither it nor the verb κτάομαι ("to acquire") is Matthean. Since, however, the prohibition against earning money by means of preaching and healings corresponds with the scope of v. 8e and the statement about the laborer in v. 10b that was moved here by Matthew, the entire reworking is most likely Matthean. Τροφή ("food" instead of "wages" [μισθός]) is also probably from Matthew's hand.[8]

Verses 11-14: Instead of the two logia about entering a house (Luke 10:5-7) and a city (Luke 10:8-11), Matthew formulates a single saying. The possibility of a positive reception is mentioned only briefly (the corresponding Q material had already been used in part in vv. 7-8) so that, as is often the case in Matthew, the idea of judgment is dominant. Therefore, Luke is probably closer to the wording of Q. The editing is for the most part Matthean, even if not everything can be conclusively demonstrated on linguistic grounds.[9]

Verse 15 generally[10] corresponds to Q = Luke 10:12.

Origin

In their various versions the sayings give us a glimpse into the history of early Christian itinerant radicalism and show how it developed in the first century and adapted to changing circumstances. However, early Christian itinerant radicalism is understandable only

---

2   Q texts in Athanasius Polag, *Fragmenta Q* (Neukirchen-Vluyn: Neukirchener Verlag, 1979) 44–46, and in Laufen, *Doppelüberlieferungen*, 245; detailed reconstruction also in Hoffmann, *Studien*, 263–84.

3   Contra Heinrich Kasting, *Die Anfänge der urchristlichen Mission* (BEvTh 55; Munich: Kaiser, 1969) 113–14; Frankemölle, *Jahwebund*, 129–30; Uro, *Sheep*, 54–56; Gnilka 1.362. In my judgment there is not enough redactional vocabulary (πορεύομαι, πρόβατον, ἀπόλλυμι, cf. vol. 1, Introduction 3.2 and 4:15) to support the conclusion. Well documented is Trilling's view (*Israel*, 99–101) that 10:5b-6 is a traditional, complete logion, while in 15:24 Matthew has reused part of this logion and fitted it into a new context.

4   Cf. the compositionally important references to 9:33, 36; 10:16. Schürmann ("Vorgeschichte," 139) assumes that Matthew has placed the word here also because he has moved Luke 10:3 (sheep!) to a later point. His thesis that the logion stood in Q, between Luke 10:7 and 8, is a mere postulate. Schürmann believes that Luke has replaced it with the pericope of the Samaritan village in 9:51-56 (141–49).

5   Matthew omits ἐφ᾽ ὑμᾶς from Luke 10:9 (adaptation

to 3:2; 4:17). Πορευόμενοι establishes the connection with v. 6. Κηρύσσειν and θεραπεύειν are catchwords from 9:35.

6   Matthew takes over the catchwords πήρα, χαλκός, εἰς τὴν ζώνην, εἰς ὁδόν, δύο χιτῶνες, and ῥάβδος from Mark 6:8-9, πήρα and ὑπόδημα from Q = Luke 10:4. Ἄργυρος also may have stood in Q. Cf. Luke 9:3.

7   Exod 25:3. Also Num 31:22; Josh 6:19, 24; 1 Chr 22:14; 29:2; Dan 2:35, 45 in connection with other metals.

8   *Μισθός* is in Matthew the reward at the last judgment. On *τροφή* cf. vol. 1, Introduction 3.2.

9   Mark's influence is decisive in v. 11b and v. 14a. Probably Matthean redaction are: v. 11: κώμη (from 9:35), ἐξετάζω (cf. 2:8), ἄξιος (key word of chap. 10, taken over from Luke 10:7 = Q); v. 14: λόγοι (cf. for Jesus: 7:24-28). Is ἀσπάζομαι (v. 12) a reminiscence of the omitted part of the verse Luke 10:4b = Q?

10   Matthean are (cf. vol. 1, Introduction 3.2) ἀμήν, γῆ, ἡμέρα κρίσεως. Γομόρρων is a secondary (cf. 11:24!) and understandable addition to the Q text, but it is not completely appropriate, since in Genesis 19 it is only the Sodomites who were not hospitable.

as a continuation of the disciples' itinerant life with Jesus. For precisely this reason we may be relatively optimistic about the authenticity of most of the logia. Jesus is the initiator of a movement of itinerant charismatics.[11] Jesus' call to discipleship is to be understood as a commissioning to join him in an itinerant life of proclaiming the kingdom of God.[12] From this perspective the sending is, as it were, the crux of discipleship and is thoroughly appropriate for Jesus. That our logia have been handed down in duplicate and have often been changed also confirms that they are quite old. In particular, the equipment regulation of Luke 10:4 is formulated so radically that all of the gospels were forced to modify it explicitly.[13] Mark has adapted it by permitting staff and sandals (6:8-9). Luke has partly invalidated it (22:35-36). Matthew has changed it into a rule about acquiring. In short, we may conclude that most of the logia of Luke 10:2-12 and Matt 10:9-16 come from Jesus. It is also possible that a one-time sending of the disciples by Jesus is historical. Along with additions like Matt 10:8e and 10b, we can say that Luke 10:12 and Matt 10:15 (presumably in Q a secondary creation based on Luke 10:14)[14] and Matt 10:5-6 do not go back to Jesus. With its harsh *no* even against the Samaritans, its appearance only in Matthew, and its "technical" use of the term "lost" (cf. Luke 19:10 and 1 Cor 1:18 among others), this saying is most at home in a Jewish-Christian church that separated itself from the gentile mission and saw its own task to be solely the proclamation to Israel.[15]

Interpretation

Few gospel texts let us feel the distance between their original situation and our own time as clearly as does this text. That is due on the one hand to the changed church situation. The text speaks of itinerant radicals who, dirt poor and without an established residence, roam through the countryside. We live in a church that has at its disposal stable institutions, buildings, and salaries. The distance is created on the other hand primarily by vv. 5-6, Jesus' command to the apostles to go only to Israel, that would seem to be long obsolete. It is not surprising, therefore, if in parts of the history of interpretation the dominant opinion has been that this text is concerned not with generally valid instructions for Christian mission but with something unique, something obsolete,[16] as if it were a missionary "trial mission"[17] that after Easter was then replaced by a definitive form. With this text the question of the enduring validity of the individual instructions is especially acute.

11   Gerd Theissen, "The Wandering Radicals," in idem, *Social Reality,* 45: "Probably more of the sayings must be 'suspected' of being genuine than many a modern skeptic would like to think."

12   Hengel, *Leader,* 74–75.

13   Admittedly, no small difficulty lies in the tension between the image of Jesus as "glutton and winebibber" (Matt 11:19) and the severity of the equipment regulation. Uro (*Sheep,* 133) attributes it, therefore, to a later ascetic radicalizing of the Jesus movement in Q. On the other hand, the fact of the homelessness of Jesus (demand to follow him!) is well established, and Matt 10:9 fits well other radical demands that Jesus placed on his followers (e.g., Luke 9:60; 14:26-27). There is no direct contradiction, since Matt 10:9 does not contain a regulation about food; cf. Luke 10:7. We must also distinguish between fundamental asceticism and prophetic symbolic action, to which, in my judgment, the equipment regulation belongs.

14   Cf. Lührmann, *Redaktion,* 62–63.

15   This saying is hardly ever attributed to Jesus today. Still, an argument on its behalf could be that throughout early Christianity the gentile mission was regarded as an innovation and was never understood as something that had been commanded by the earthly Jesus (cf. Matt 28:16-20; Luke 24:47; Acts 10; Gal 1:16). However, this is also an argument against its authenticity. Where gentile mission was not an issue anyway, it also does not have to be explicitly prohibited. The main argument for not attributing the word to Jesus, however, is the command not to go to the Samaritans that, in my judgment, contradicts such texts as Luke 10:30-35.

16   Calvin 1.289; Bucer, 103D ("*temporaria*"); Dickson, 125, calls it a "temporary commandment."

17   Augustus Neander, *The Life of Jesus Christ in Its Historical Connexion and Historical Development* (trans. from 4th German ed.; New York: Harper & Brothers, 1870) 257. Bengel (70) compares the mission with the internship of theology students who then return to the "*schola.*"

18   The expression does not mean: through a gentile area. ὁδός plus a geographical term in the genitive case means "way to": 4:15; Ἰερ 2:18; Exod 13:17.

19   It is improbable, at least for Matthew, that undetermined πόλις = מדינה is a Semitizing term for province (thus Jeremias, *Promise,* 19, n. 5), since πόλις in the meaning "city" is a key word in Matt 10:5-23 (6 times).

20   For a detailed collection of material see Str–B 1. 538–60.

■ **5b-6** After the disciples have received their authority from Jesus, he sends them on their way. They are not to take a road that leads to the Gentiles.[18] Even more remarkable is that they also are not to go into Samaritan cities,[19] for there are in the gospels several texts that indicate that Jesus was much more open toward the Samaritans than were most Jews of the day[20] (Luke 9:51-56; 10:30-35; 17:11-19; John 4). The lost sheep of the house of Israel[21] who are contrasted with the Gentiles and Samaritans are not (partitively) the sinners, outcasts, and marginalized in Israel but (explicatively) all Israel.[22] Matthew puts this saying emphatically at the beginning. It sounds harsh even for early Christian ears, for at the time of the Gospel of Matthew the gentile mission was successful and was being carried out by many churches. Nevertheless, there are no limitations placed on it, as, for example, by adding νῦν ("now"). It corresponds to Jesus' own mission to Israel as described in Matthew 8–9. In 15:24 the evangelist will again take up the traditional v. 6 and apply it redactionally to the mission of Jesus: I am sent *only* to the lost sheep of the house of Israel. Again the formulation is harshly exclusive.[23] In comparison with this statement, the mission command to go to all ἔθνη (28:19) takes a different course. How are we to understand the two texts together?

A *historical interpretation* of the difference between Matt 10:5-6 and Matt 28:16-20 assumes either that there were two distinct stages of the activity of Jesus,[24] or that one of the two texts, viz., Matt 28:16-20, is post-Easter,[25] or, finally, that both texts are post-Easter and perhaps come from different churches or periods. In any case, a historical explanation cannot

replace an interpretation of the *content* of the sayings. We must ask: How did Matthew understand the juxtaposition of the two texts whose tension he has created with "a certain subtlety"[26]? There are the following possibilities.

a. Matt 10:5-6 does not mean a mission to Israel at all. This is the approach of the classical allegorical interpretation that related the prohibition of the Samaritan mission to the heresies and the prohibition of the gentile mission to heathen doctrines, to philosophy, or to heathen festivals, and especially to the theater.[27] "Israel" means the true Israel, viz., the church. This way out of the dilemma is impossible. Even the presuppositions of the church's allegorical exegesis make it problematic, since the allegorical approach usually tries to deepen the literal meaning, not replace it.

b. An explanation based on the history of the church: In the Matthean church there is a particularistic Jewish-Christian wing. Another group in the community also wants to evangelize the Gentiles (cf. v. 18). With the context and the mission command the evangelist is trying to strengthen the position of those who claim that the gentile mission is a legitimate possibility even for the Matthean community.[28] That is, however, an unsatisfactory explanation. Are we to assume that Matt 10:5b-6 is valid only for his community, but not for the rest of the church, and only until further notice?

c. 10:5-6 applies only to the Twelve, while the great commission is for the entire church.[29] That explanation is also completely unsatisfactory. With the exception of Judas, the mission command is directed to the same disciples as is 10:5-6.

All other interpretations assume that vv. 5-6 are valid only for the time of Jesus. Matthew thus regarded the disciples' mission limited to Israel as a thing of

---

21 LXX language! Cf. Herbert Preisker and Siegfried Schulz, "πρόβατον κτλ," *TDNT* 6 (1968) 689, 690. Οἶκοι Ἰσραήλ appears frequently in the LXX.

22 The macrotext also supports this interpretation: 4:23; 9:35! On the basis of 9:37-38, Levine (*Dimensions,* 56–57) emphasizes the social aspect and says that the issue is the sheep, not their shepherd.

23 Οὐκ . . . εἰ μή. The πρῶτον of Mark 7:27 is omitted.

24 See, e.g., Schlatter, 798; Zahn, 712 ("a preliminary exercise").

25 Klostermann, 232; Manson, *Sayings,* 180. Harnack (*Mission,* 43, n. 1) says that 10:23 (along with 10:5-6) "precludes the hypothesis that the speech of Jesus referred merely to a provisional mission."

26 Harnack, *Mission,* 40, n. 2.

27 See, e.g., *Didasc.* 13 = 72 Achelis-Flemming (Hans Achelis and Johannes Flemming, eds., *Die Syrische Didaskalia* [Leipzig: Hinrichs, 1904]); Hilary, 10.3 = SC 254.218.

28 Primarily Schuyler Brown, "The Two-fold Representation of the Mission in Matthew's Gospel" (*StTh* 31 [1977] 21–32) 30–32. Cf. idem, "The Matthean Community and the Gentile Mission," *NovT* 22 (1980) 215–21.

29 Goulder, *Midrash,* 343.

the past.[30] What is clearly correct about this view is that vv. 5-6 locate the sending discourse in the narrative thread of the Gospel of Matthew. Similarly, in other discourses narrative insertions such as 13:36a and 24:1-3a serve to locate the discourse in the macrotext of the Matthean narrative. As far as the content is concerned, what is at issue here is that the disciples are to assume the mission of Jesus. And up to this point—with the exception of 8:28-34—Jesus has not crossed the borders of Israel. In 15:24, when the crisis in Israel has become so intense that he is forced to "withdraw" into gentile territory, Jesus will again speak of his exclusive mission to Israel. However, we do not find a basically different orientation until 28:19-20. Then the disciples are to make disciples of πάντα τὰ ἔϑνη ("all the Gentiles"). The two catchwords πορεύομαι and ἔϑνη show that 28:19 in all probability consciously refers to 10:5-6.

We are confronted with two questions. In the first place, what is the meaning of the mission of Jesus and his disciples to Israel? It could be here a case of fulfilling biblical promises.[31] In any case, the biblical language of the verse would support this view.[32] The second question is more difficult. How is 10:5-6 related to the mission command in 28:19-20? It is a question that includes the issue of the meaning of Matthew's entire narrative.

Two interpretations are possible. First of all, we may interpret the mission of the disciples to all ἔϑνη as an *expansion* of their mission only to Israel. The Matthean paradigm would be that of two concentric circles. Israel stands in the center, the nations are arranged around it.[33] Ἔϑνη in 28:19 would have to be translated as "nations" so that Israel remains the center of the circle and also can continue to be addressed by the message of Jesus. Verses 5-6 would then be "preserved" in the mission command and would underscore the continuity of the post-Easter community with Jesus and with Israel.[34] A second possibility, however, is that we interpret the sending of the disciples to all ἔϑνη as a *cancellation* of their exclusive mission to Israel. In this case Matthew would be advocating a substitutionary view. The gentile church would replace Israel (cf. 21:43). Then ἔϑνη would have to be translated as "Gentiles." According to 28:19-20 there would, at least in principle, no longer be a mission of the disciples to Israel. Verses 5-6 would not be preserved in the mission command but would be "canceled" by it. In this case vv. 5-6 would prepare for the idea of Israel's guilt. Although Jesus himself and his disciples came exclusively to Israel, it has rejected Jesus.[35] We cannot yet choose between the two alternatives, but two items suggest the second interpretation. For one thing, it is noteworthy that the formulation of vv. 5-6 is exclusive and particularistic. Thus the mission command appears as something new that has not already been given by Jesus—as a change of direction. For another, the deliberate reference of 28:19 to 10:5-6 suggests that ἔϑνη is to be interpreted the same way in

30   This interpretation is as old as Tertullian (*Fuga* 6.1 = CChr.SL 2.1142), who limits the text to the apostles. Jerome (65) distinguishes between the time before and after the resurrection. Today it has a number of advocates. See, e.g., Strecker, *Weg*, 196; Günther Bornkamm, "Der Auferstandene und der Irdische: Mt 28,16-20," in Erich Dinkler, ed., *Zeit und Geschichte: Dankesgabe an Rudolf Bultmann zum 80. Geburtstag* (Tübingen: Mohr/Siebeck, 1964) 181–82; Anton Vögtle, "Das christologische und ekklesiologische Anliegen von Mt 28,18-20," in idem, *Evangelium*, 266. Cf. also above, n. 16 and below, n. 71.

31   Kasting, *Anfänge*, 113.

32   Cf. above, n. 21 and Frankemölle, *Jahwebund*, 128, n. 227.

33   See, e.g., Kilpatrick, *Origins*, 122–23; Hahn, *Mission*, 127; Frankemölle, *Jahwebund*, 121 (ἔϑνη = nations in 28:19 is contrasted not with Israel but with the community of the disciples immediately after Easter); idem, "Zur Theologie der Mission im

Matthäusevangelium," in Karl Kertelge, ed., *Mission im Neuen Testament* (QD 93; Freiburg: Herder, 1982) 93–129, 124; Roman Bartnicki, "Der Bereich Tätigkeit der Jünger nach Mt 10,5b-6," *BZ* 31 (1987) 155–56; Gnilka 1.362–63; Levine, *Dimensions*, 46.

34   Frankemölle, *Jahwebund*, 142.

35   This interpretation also has roots in the ancient church. It appears wherever interpreters refer to the mission model of Acts (in which the message was first preached in the synagogue) and to the guilt of the Jews: e.g., Origen fr. 197 = GCS Origenes 12.95; Cyril of Alexandria (*Commentariorum in Matthaeum quae supersunt* [*PG* 72.365–474]) fr. 113 = Reuss, 190; Gregory the Great *Hom. in ev.* 4.1 = *PL* 76.1089. More recent advocates are, e.g., Trilling, *Israel*, 103. Walker (*Heilsgeschichte*, 63) says that "the rebellion . . . of the people is ignited by the salvation which is aimed at it alone," Yoshito Anno ("The Mission to Israel in Matthew: The Intention of Matthew 10:5b-6 Considered in the Light of the Religio-Political Background" [Diss., Chicago, 1984]

both places. In our text, however, it is clear that ἔθνη means the Gentiles in contrast to Israel and not the nations including Israel.[36]

■ **7, 8a-d** In the following charge to preach and to heal, one already no longer senses any kind of temporal limitation. The charge to preach, given to the disciples, is the same as that of John the Baptist (3:2) and Jesus (4:17, cf. 9:35). Even after Easter the disciples proclaim not the kerygma of the suffering and risen Christ but Jesus' own message (28:20). That the message is here described in terms of the nearness of God's rule is not an indication that Matthew reckoned with a distant parousia. The kingdom of God is primarily the setting for the ethical proclamation of Jesus.[37] Alongside the preaching mission the charge to heal is equally important. The three examples of healing the sick take up stories from Matthew 8–9 and correspond in part to the formulations of 11:5. Healings and proclamation are closely related. With the healings the crowds are made aware that something extraordinary is happening in Israel (9:33). They demonstrate to John the Baptist that Jesus is the coming one (11:2-6). In Jesus' miracles the church also recognizes its own experiences and thus experiences the powerful help of its Lord. The mission to heal and the proclamation are thus essentially related so that the message does not become mere ethical exhortation but includes concrete experiences of salvation—indeed, of healing. It is no accident that prior to his disciples discourse Matthew has spoken of the disciples' ἐξουσία ("power"; 10:1) and has put programmatically at the beginning the command to heal that is

mentioned somewhat incidentally in the sayings source (Luke 10:9).

History of Interpretation

Problems arose here for later Christians, because the experience of miracles was often denied them (cf. already 17:19-20). It may be that the problems are already visible when in the transmission of the text there is the tendency to reduce the number of the four miracle commands. John Chrysostom provides good evidence of these difficulties. It is only with a great deal of effort that he can claim the model of the apostles for the priests and teachers of his time. For him the virtues (10:9-10!) that the proclaimers are to exhibit are more important than the miracles. Miracles are often dubious, "fantastic deception or otherwise very suspicious," as the example of the Corinthians demonstrates.[38] The greatest miracle is the freedom from sin. John Chrysostom is an example of a process of displacement that usually has taken place implicitly. The important thing about our text became what doctrine the apostles are to preach; all of v. 8 is minimized or even ignored.[39] It has remained that way in most Western churches until the present.[40] For Matthew, however, experiences of miracles are constitutive of faith, just as Jesus' miraculous deeds are of his activity. They make grace—that is, what the disciples have received "freely"—concrete. They are emergency cases of a faith that certainly is not limited to them (cf. 9:22, 29-30; 17:19-20), and they are experienced answer to prayer (cf. 8:25; 9:27). In Matthew's view the loss of such experiences cannot simply be irrelevant.

In my judgment v. 8 also poses an important question to the modern church. It is not yet answered with

---

325–37) that Israel's guilt becomes even greater after Jesus sent the disciples only to it.

36   If the second interpretation is correct, the question is still open about *when* the change from the Israel mission to the gentile mission takes place. On the surface of the Matthean narrative Easter constitutes the great caesura. However, many of the sayings taken over by Matthew (e.g., 5:11-12; 10:17-18, 23 or 23:34-39) indicate that after Easter Matthew's church did initially pursue a mission to Israel. At the level of the church's own history, therefore, that we have called "indirect transparency" (cf. above on the summary of chaps. 8–9), the transition takes place at a later time. Has it already taken place? Or is Matthew writing his gospel in order to cause it? Cf. on this matter vol. 1, Introduction 5.2.

37   Cf. vol. 1, on 3:2 ("βασιλεία τῶν οὐρανῶν"), on 4:17, and the excursus following 4:25.

38   32.6-8 = *PG* 57.384–388. The quotation is from 57.387.

39   Luther, *WA* 38.495. Additional examples of suppressing v. 8: For Thomas Aquinas (*Lectura*, no. 818), once faith has been acknowledged, miracles are no longer necessary. For Jerome (65) the miracles are important because the apostles were uneducated and incapable of speaking eloquently and needed "reinforcement"; Christian of Stavelot (26 = 1346C) and Faber Stapulensis (44B-C) are primarily interested in the spiritually/mentally "sick" and "dead."

40   Is it an accident that in the conversation of the peasants of Solentiname the discussion of Luke 9:1-2 is

the observation that we can experience love today as miracle,[41] but neither is the simple exhortation to obey the Matthean command to heal satisfactory. Jesus healed and cast out demons, because those deeds were for him signs of the inbreaking kingdom of God. Matthew tells about that and passes it on to his church as part of its mission, because he has learned from Jesus that "sickness . . . (contradicts) the saving will of the creator God, who wants life and not death," and that in the final analysis, therefore, we cannot simply accept it.[42] Is, however, this radical view the whole truth of the gospel? It can also be very unloving and ungracious for those who have to bear the burden of illnesses and disabilities. Is becoming well the only form of liberation from illness, or can it also be a form of healing, for example, to recognize in an illness some meaning, perhaps even an opportunity? We will have to pose such questions not only *from* Matthew and Jesus but also *to* them when we attempt to make concrete the command to heal the sick as a call to pray, perhaps to lay hands on the sick, but also to pastoral care and to service.

■ **8e, 10b** Verses 8e and 10b indicate a new emphasis. Matthew has framed the old equipment regulation with two short proverbial statements. The brief sentence "you received freely, give freely," tying the disciples' gifts to the gift of Jesus,[43] on the surface appears to be in tension with the proverbial sentence of v. 10b[44] that the laborer is to receive his food. The tension is removed, however, when we observe that Matthew has replaced the μισθόι ("wages") that he found in his source with

τροφή ("food").[45] In this case the reworking is polemical: The laborer is to receive only food, no salary.[46] The ancient sentence is thereby protected against a possible misunderstanding. The meaning is that financial compensation for the messengers of the gospel or performing miracles for pay are completely out of the question.

■ **9-10** This also determines the interpretation of the equipment regulation in vv. 9-10a. Κτήσεσθε ("acquire," "take") must be understood literally. The issue is not possessions—whether an itinerant charismatic might leave something at home is not the question; it is that one is to accept no compensation for preaching and performing miracles, except for food which God will provide through the churches and other people (cf. 6:26). This is the only way to understand the prominent position of money and the plerophorous enumeration of gold, silver, and small change in the belt.[47] The sequence probably involves a graduation: You are not to accept the smallest coin for your labor! Admittedly the following enumeration of the bag for provisions,[48] the two undergarments, the shoes, and the staff does not fit well. It is difficult to imagine payment in produce that would consist of a staff or a bag for provisions. Since κτάομαι is a somewhat general verb and can also mean approximately "to get for oneself," the old equipment regulation most likely has influenced v. 10 so that it also refers to what one is not to take on the journey. Thus two things

focused on the healing (Ernesto Cardenal, *The Gospel in Solentiname*, vol. 2 [Maryknoll: Orbis, 1978] 142–46)?

41 Thus Gnilka 1.371. According to Matthew, however, more is at stake. We should remember here not only the fundamental significance of the charismatic movement but, e.g., also the fundamental importance for the *church* (!) of the therapeutic mission, e.g., of Eugen Drewermann.

42 Klaus Seybold and Ulrich B. Müller, *Sickness and Healing*, trans. Douglas W. Stott (Nashville: Abingdon, 1981) 191.

43 Important is not only the imperative "give freely," but also the reminder of the receiving (Zumstein, *Condition*, 435). Gustaf Dalman (*Jesus-Jeshua: Studies in the Gospels* [1929; reprinted New York: Ktav, 1971] 226) cites proverbial parallels to Matt 10:8e.

44 The parallels in A. E. Harvey ("'The Workman Is Worthy of His Hire': Fortunes of a Proverb in the Early Church," *NovT* 24 [1982] 209–21, 211, n. 9) are, admittedly, not literal.

45 1 Tim 5:18 quotes the saying (as γραφή!) with μισθός. The *Didache*, a work influenced by Matthew, offers in 13:1 a version that agrees with Matthew. Paul is familiar with the apostolic privilege of support and does not claim it for himself (1 Corinthians 9). There the catchwords ἐργάζομαι (vv. 6, 13) and μισθός (vv. 17-18) appear. In 2 Cor 11:13 the (ψευδ-)ἀπόστολοι, against whom Paul boasts that he has not accepted money from the Corinthians (2 Cor 11:7: δωρεάν!), are ἐργάται δόλιοι. It is quite possible that Paul knew the saying in its Q form.

46 HbrMt inserts: "accept no payment."

47 Money was kept in the belt (Str-B 1.565; Wettstein 1.368-69).

48 Πήρα is a general word for the bag for provisions (Suidas, 4.126 [Ada Adler, ed., *Suidae Lexicon* (5 vols.; Leipzig: Teubner, 1928–38)]): θήκη τῶν ἄρτων), and, unless there is some indication from the context, does not mean the beggar's sack, e.g.,

are important for Matthew: first, that the proclamation of the gospel is not to be a business, and then—taking up the Q tradition—that a person who has made arrangements in advance for food, is on the road in good shoes,[49] strides along in normal clothing,[50] and is armed with a staff against attacks[51] cannot proclaim the king-

dom of God. For Matthew, poverty and defenselessness belong to the proclamation of the gospel.[52]

In the old equipment regulation of the *sayings source* the proclamation of the messengers was connected to demonstrative poverty and defenselessness. Even the most necessary things were forbidden. Without shoes one lives below the minimum for existence.[53] That

---

of the Cynic (Wilhelm Michaelis, "πήρα," *TDNT* 6 [1968] 119).

49 By contrast with σανδάλιον (Mark 6:9) ὑπόδημα is a generic term for shoe (Pollux *Onom.* 7.80–94). Σανδάλια (with only a sole and straps for tying) belong to the λεπτὰ ὑποδήματα (7.86), in addition to which there are also ὑποδήματα κοιλά with leather on the top and boots that go up to the calves. Ὑπόδημα is preferably the "entire" shoe. Pollux notes in 7.84: Τὰ δὲ μὴ κοιλὰ αὐτὸ μόνον ἀποχρῶν (a misuse) ἐστιν εἰπεῖν ὑποδήματα. There does not have to be a contradiction with Mark then if one understands ὑποδήματα only as shoes with leather on top. More natural—and to be assumed for Q—is a general prohibition of shoes.

50 Wearing an undergarment under the upper garment or the cloak is normal with Jews: Josephus *Ant.* 17.135–36 (ἐντὸς χιτών of a [royal] slave); Str-B 1.566; Samuel Krauss, *Talmudische Archäologie* (3 vols.; 1910–12; reprinted Hildesheim: Olm, 1966), 1.523, n. 47 and 593, nn. 466–67 (cases of more than one כְּתֹנֶת). It is hardly a matter of prohibiting special luxury; for obvious reasons undergarments can serve only in a limited way to demonstrate one's wealth. However, cf. Krauss, *Archäologie* 1.161. Important are *b. Besa* 32b = Str-B 1.566 (some say: whoever has only one shirt has no life) and the references to a lack of clothing in extreme situations in Krauss, *Archäologie* 1.135. Jews, Greeks, and Romans also designate as "naked" (nakedness is to be avoided under all circumstances!) people who have only an undergarment (Krauss, *Archäologie* 1.128; Albrecht Oepke, "γυμνός κτλ," *TDNT* 1 [1964] 773–74). For Romans, wearing a woolen *tunica interior* under the tunic is normal. For outdoor wear there is, in addition, the toga (Marquardt, *Privatleben* 2.552–53). For the most part the Cynic philosophers wear no undergarments as a sign of the simple life (Lucian *Cyn.* 20); Epictetus *Discourses* 3.22.45–47 (ἕν τριβωνάριον [worn out cloak] = γυμνός); Diogenes Laertius, 6.13 (Antisthenes doubles his cloak and wears only the one garment).

51 ῥάβδος is a general word for sticks of all kinds. The prohibition of a staff is quite unusual, since one

never was safe against attacks, dogs, and similar dangers. For this reason even itinerant Essenes carry a weapon, although they have the reputation of being peace-loving (Josephus *Bell.* 2.125–34). The same is true of Cynic philosophers (Carl Schneider, "ῥάβδος κτλ," *TDNT* 6 [1968] 969, n. 21) and itinerant rabbis (*Gen. Rab.* 100.2 [end] on 49:33: the equipment for the dead indicates that slippers and (!) shoes, and staff are the normal equipment of a rabbi on the road). Cf. in addition Schneider, n. 22. On the staff as a weapon see Krauss, *Archäologie* 2.312. Not having a staff is a very unusual sign, probably of defenselessness. It is understandable that it quickly was again permitted (Mark 6:8, cf. 1 Cor 4:21).

52 The prohibition against earning money with the Torah was valid also for the rabbis (*m. ʾAbot* 1.13; 4.5; *b. Ned.* 62a = Str-B 1.562). At a later date individual regulations were necessary for the payment of teachers (among others), for supervising children, grammar lessons, or as support for the poor (Str-B 1.563 d). The difference is that the rabbinic regulations applied only to the misuse of the Torah for profit and that poverty as such was never constitutive for teaching the Torah as it was among the Christian itinerant charismatics for proclaiming the kingdom of God.

53 Cf. *b. Besa* 32b, above, n. 51. Mourners, people who are under the ban or are fasting, and the entire nation on the Day of Atonement go barefoot (Krauss, *Archäologie* 1.183–84), but not outside of the villages (Str-B 1.569). To have no shoes is an expression of extreme poverty: *b. Šabb.* 129a = Str-B 1.568 (it is better to sell the beam of the house than to have no shoes; only starving is worse); *b. Šabb.* 152a = Str-B 1.568 (whoever has no shoes is not a human being). For additional references see Krauss, *Archäologie* 1.184. On the condition of the roads in the orient, cf. Krauss, *Archäologie* 2.323–24.

corresponded, however, to the gospel that was being proclaimed—the good news for the poor (Q = Luke 6:20), the defenselessness (Q = Luke 6:29), the love of one's enemies (Q = Luke 6:27-28), the break with all earthly relatives (Q = Luke 14:26), and living alone for the kingdom of God (Q = Luke 12:31). The equipment regulation[54] presumably had nothing to do with the holiness of the messengers[55] and definitely nothing at all to do with the idea that the messengers should travel lightly, because they would find hospitality anyway in friendly houses![56] The issue is, rather, demonstrative, shocking poverty and defenselessness that is appropriate to the kingdom of God. It is a confirming sign for the proclamation[57] and is best understood as analogous to prophetic symbolic actions.[58]

The *Matthean interpretation* is in no way a "cold" invalidation of this rule. There is no parallel to Luke 22:36 in Matthew. Indeed, he had already emphasized the basic significance of poverty for the life of a Christian in 6:19-34.[59] The rule of poverty remains valid as the command of Jesus for Matthew's own present and with "do not take gold, silver, or small change," he merely gives it an emphasis—the prohibition of earning and begging—that because of the experience with wandering charismatics

obviously was of special importance for his own present. Religious begging was common at the time and was repeatedly portrayed as a great evil.[60] In order not to discredit themselves, the messengers of Jesus had to be fundamentally different. Furthermore, people had obviously had quite different experiences with traveling Christians.[61] There probably were current reasons why Matthew made of the regulation a rule against acquiring. That does not change the reality, however, that for Matthew poverty is a fundamental part of the gospel and of the existence of a disciple. In that regard the disciples are like their master (8:20).

History of Interpretation

The question of what we should do with this equipment regulation today is especially difficult, since this rule was already being interpreted differently, softened (Mark 6:8-9), and eliminated (Luke 22:36) in the gospels. Paul and other missionaries in the Diaspora carried out their mission differently. Furthermore, the difference between the various ages is especially great here. In place of the early Christian itinerant charismatics without (solid!) shoes there are now Christian pastors, employed and

---

54 Migaku Sato ("Q und Prophetie" [Diss., Bern, 1984] 311) speaks pointedly of "disarmament."

55 According to *m. Ber.* 9.5 one is to come to the temple mount with veiled head and without staff, shoes, bag, and dust on the feet, is not to spit there or use it as a shortcut. Schniewind (129) thus interprets the regulation to mean that one should be "like the worshippers." Hoffmann (*Studien*, 323-24) correctly objects to this view, since the parallel is only partial.

56 Calvin 1.293–94. Dungan (*Sayings*, 68) similarly explains the Matthean text as a "'non-provision' passage" and says that the disciples can assume that they will be taken care of by the brothers. It is the same with the Essenes in Josephus *Bell.* 2.124–26. Gottfried Schille (*Frei zu neuen Aufgaben* [Berlin: Evangelische Verlagsanstalt, 1986] 63–69) offers an original suggestion: One can go barefoot only in cities, where the mission in the houses also will take place (v. 13). Q is post-Markan and presupposes an urban situation. That is not the case, however! Even in ancient cities, where the streets were not always paved, people did not go barefoot.

57 Martino Conti, "Fondamenti Biblici della povertà nel ministero apostolica (Mt 10,9-10)," *Anton* 46 (1971) 393–426, 425 ("*dovute credenziali*").

58 A similar, if not completely identical, symbolic

action is found in Isa 20:2-4, where Isaiah is barefoot and "naked," i.e., wearing an undergarment. Cf. also *Mart. Isa.* 2.10–11 that speaks of poverty in the wilderness as a prophetic sign against injustice.

59 Cf. vol. 1, II A 2.4, 2.4.1, 2.4.2 on 6:31-34, and below, IV C 3 on 19:16-30.

60 Among the numerous references are, e.g., Lucian *Fug.* 14-21 (Cynics); Apuleius *Met.* 8.24-30 (*Dea Syria*); Juvenal, 6.542-91 (Jewish, Chaldean, and other interpreters of dreams and sellers of horoscopes). For a Syriac inscription from Kefr-Hauar see Deissmann, *Light*, 109 (*Dea Syria*). Especially instructive as a parallel to vv. 11-15 from the opposite perspective is Menander *Sent.* 43 (trans. according to Krauss, *Archäologie* 3.26): "Do not grant hospitality to the priest. . . . If you invite (him) . . . to enter your house: at entering he blesses you, at leaving he . . . curses"; he puts the food into a bag for his family and still curses!

61 Itinerant Christian beggars: Paul defends himself against the pseudo-apostles who (perhaps in the name of the apostolic right of support?) fleece the congregations (2 Cor 11:6-13; 12:13, 17). *Did.* 11.5–6, 9, 12 (close to Matthew!) has to defend against greedy itinerant apostles and prophets and says that the community should entertain them only

with a car. So much has changed in the course of history that here too changes are probably unavoidable. On the other hand, it is noteworthy that—without exception!—all of the changes have weakened the regulation. The history of the text's influence will illustrate the problems.

a. In the dominant *church interpretation* the attempts to soften the regulation began where there were differences among the individual gospel texts. Of course Peter and Paul went round in cloak and shoes.[62] A staff is allowed for walking but not for hitting.[63] Going barefoot is good for toughening; walking in sandals is less troublesome than is walking in high shoes.[64] Several times it was "discovered" that it was possible to add a δύο before ὑποδήματα so that the only thing prohibited is taking a second pair of shoes.[65] The text lent itself well to polemics against opponents of the church who allegedly lived in luxury and lived the life of a vagabond.[66] The allegorical interpretation, which discovered much in the details that is theologically sound, is by and large also a way of evading the text's severity.[67] In the context of the two-tiered ethics, living without possessions is a *consi-*

lium for priests and bishops but not a *praeceptum*.[68] Hermeneutically interesting is the attempt to attribute the discrepancies among the individual gospel texts to the meanings of the *words*, while the *basic* meaning lying behind the words is the same in all the gospels.[69] Our texts are then concerned with warning against pride and avarice and with trust in God.[70] The center of the texts is shifted from concrete matters to the question of one's attitude. Similar is the attempt to declare that the concrete form of this command is valid only for the beginning period of the first apostolic mission.[71] Olshausen makes it easy for himself: "The details given must not be too much pressed but must be taken in all the freedom in which the apostles themselves received them."[72]

b. Seldom do we find *literal obedience* to the equipment regulation—even less so than with the commands of the Sermon on the Mount. The itinerant brothers of the pseudo-Clementine letters *Ad virgines*, whose life is strongly influenced by Matthew 10, are first of all ascetics, that is, celibate. Their major concern is not poverty, but whether they will accept hos-

three days; then they should work. For the journey they should get only provisions, no money (cf. Matt 10:10b!); a prophet who demands money is a pseudo-prophet. *Herm. Man.* 11.12 offers similar advice. Lucian tells how the former Cynic and later Christian Peregrinus became rich (*Pergr. Mort.* 11–16). Cf. also Julian *Or.* 7.224B (*Oeuvres complètes,* ed. Gabriel Rochefort [Paris: Société d'édition "Les Belles Lettres," 1963] 2.70).

62 Bullinger, 99A.

63 Zwingli, 266, Lapide, 226.

64 Jerome, 66 (according to Plato's advice!); Lapide (225) praises sandals for their practicality.

65 Maldonat, 215; Jansen, 93; Paul Schanz, *Commentar über das Evangelium des heiligen Matthäus* (Freiburg: Herder, 1879) 289–90. Paulus (4.291–92) says that one should not accept shoes as a gift (μὴ κτήσεσθε)!

66 Eusebius *Hist. eccl.* 5.18.7 (Apollonius against the Montanists); Luther, *WA* 38.497 (with the aid of 2 Tim 3:6 Luther is principally opposed to itinerant preachers); Musculus, 286; Bullinger, 998 (is against papal luxury and papal delegates who do not even travel on foot anymore); Cocceius, 18 (opposes sellers of indulgences).

67 Examples of allegorical interpretation are: *to go barefoot*: Augustine (*Cons. ev.* 2.30 [75]): without worry; Christian of Stavelot, 26 = 1347A: no covering up of the gospel; *to own only one chiton*: Hilary, 10.5 = SC 254.220–21: to put on only Christ; Apollinaris of Laodicea fr. 47 = Reuss, 14: not to put on Christ and the old man; *no staff*: Ambrose *In Luc.* 7.60-61 =

BKV 1/21.651–52: the spirit of punishment; Maldonat, 215 on Mark 6:8: the staff of Moses for performing miracles; Hilary, 10.5 = SC 254.220–21: the root of Jesse.

68 Thomas Aquinas *S. th.* 2/2, q.185, a.6 corpus and ad 2.

69 Lapide, 224: the *substantia* of the text has to be distinguished from the *modus praecise ad litteram*, viz., protecting the mind against greed; similarly Luther, *WA* 38.496.

70 Usually the text is interpreted, parallel to 6:25-34, as a warning against *sollicitudo* (common since John Chrysostom, 32.7 = *PG* 57.382). Admonitions to moderation are also widespread: e.g., Theophylactus, 237 (τροφή, not τρυφή [luxury]). Zwingli (265) recommends the middle way between Anabaptist renunciation of salary and papal accumulation of riches: moderation.

71 Cf. above, n. 30. Calvin (1.289, 293–94) is a prominent advocate of the view that the text refers only to the initial sending of the apostles; thus not all servants of the word are to be subject to the norm of Matthew 10. The argument had already played a role in the Middle Ages for the inquisitors in the fight against the itinerant radicals (cf. Georg Schmitz-Valckenberg, *Grundlehren katharischer Sekten des 13. Jahrhunderts* [Veröffentlichungen des Grabmann-Instituts, NF 11; Munich: Schöningh, 1971] 66, 74).

72 400, on the basis of the differences among the synoptic versions.

pitality from women on their wanderings.[73] The letters take it for granted that they have possessions at home.[74] They differ from pagan religious beggars by not dishonoring the gospel in the presence of blasphemous Gentiles.[75] The equipment regulation plays a major role then with the itinerant preachers of the High Middle Ages[76] and later with the mendicant orders. It is said that Francis of Assisi threw away his shoes after hearing the gospel text Matt 10:9-10.[77] Our equipment regulation is at the center of the first rule of St. Francis[78] but no longer in the second. It is even more important for the Waldensians. It is a special command for preachers who enter the *via apostolica*.[79]

c. An actual paradigmatic case for applying our rule would be the question of *church salaries*. The findings are largely negative in the history of interpretation. In accordance with Matt 10:10b the following formula has found a degree of acceptance. The support is to come from the people, the reward from God.[80] *Ps-Clem. Hom.* 3.71 offers a concrete case: Paying support to a bishop who is poor is not sin, but only if he is poor.[81] John Chrysostom confesses openly, although not without pangs of conscience, that he owns shoes and a second garment.[82] Thomas Aquinas and Luther are in agreement that preachers must be free of worldly worries but may not be greedy.[83] According to Zwingli and Musculus the pastor must not have more than physical necessities and clothing.[84] This rule is later relaxed: It does not basically matter whether a servant of the gospel is rich and lives by his own means or whether he is poor and is supported by his brothers.[85] The Anabaptist preachers did not receive a fixed salary but were supported by the members of the congregation.[86] The question of the pastor's salary was a controversial issue in the disputations; the preachers defended their salary on the basis of Luke 10:7b.[87]

Our text plays no role in the modern discussion of ecclesiastical salaries and the form of the churches. The statement, rather moderate when measured by Matt 10:9, that "the rights of a university education and social standing mean nothing to those who have become messengers of Jesus" appears characteristically in a book that is regarded as radical.[88] Any sympathy the itinerant charismatics enjoy is only secret.[89]

73   1.10–11; 2.1–5 = ANF 8.58–59, 61–62.

74   *Ad virgines* 2.1 = ANF 61.1.10–11 warns against idleness.

75   *Ad virgines* 2.6.3 = ANF 62.

76   Herbert Grundmann, *Religiöse Bewegungen im Mittelalter* (2d. ed.; Hildesheim: Olms, 1961) 17, 21. Cf. the description of Robert of Arbrissel in Johannes von Walter, *Die ersten Wanderprediger Frankreichs*, vol. 1: *Robert von Arbrissel* (Studien zur Geschichte der Theologie und Kirche 9/3; Leipzig: Dieterich, 1903) 128: barefoot, rough clothing, tattered penitential clothing.

77   Werner Goez, "Franciscus von Assisi," *TRE* 11 (1983) 299–307, 300; Kajetan Esser, *Anfänge und ursprüngliche Zielsetzungen des Ordens der Minderbrüder* (Studia et documenta Franciscana 4; Leiden: Brill, 1966) 119.

78   *Regula non bullata* no. 14. On the prohibition of money cf. no. 8, printed in Hans Urs von Balthasar, *Die grossen Ordensregeln* (Menschen der Kirche in Zeugnis und Urkunde, NF 6; Einsiedeln: Benziger, 1974) 300, 295–96.

79   Reinhold Mokrosch and Herbert Walz, eds., *Mittelalter* (Kirchen- und Theologiegeschichte in Quellen 2; Neukirchen-Vluyn: Neukirchener Verlag, 1980) 119; Kurt Victor Selge, *Die ersten Waldenser* (Arbeiten zur Kirchengeschichte 37; Berlin: de Gruyter, 1967) 1.49–50, 116–17.

80   Augustine *Sermo* 46.5 = CChr.SL 41.533; John Chrysostom, according to Lapide, 226.

81   Luke 10:7 is here cited. Origen also understands the compensation given to coworkers in the church as support of the poor. Cf. 16.21 on Matt 21:12 = GCS Origenes 10. 546: no riches, $\mu\acute{o}\nu o\nu$ $\delta\iota\alpha\zeta\widehat{\eta}\nu$.

82   32.6 = *PG* 57.385.

83   Thomas Aquinas *S. th.* 3, q.40 a.3 corpus (affirmed is *terrenorum possessio*, rejected is *nimia . . . sollicitudo*); Luther, *WA* 38.496 (*licet vivere de Euangelio* even with a family; rejected is *avaricia, fastus et luxus*).

84   Cf. Zwingli, above, n. 70. Musculus, 289: only living expenses and clothing, *corporalis necessitas*.

85   Calvin (1.293) is of the opinion that one can leave gold, silver, bag, etc. at home. Zinzendorf (2.717–18) sees various possibilities: Proclaimers can live from their possessions and even do good things with them; they may have part-time employment; one of the Christian "siblings" gives support, or it "resolves itself."

86   "Schleitheimer Bekenntnis" 5 in Heinold Fast, ed., *Der linke Flügel der Reformation* (Bremen: Schünemann, 1962) 65. In the seventeenth century Luke 10:7b ($\mu\iota\sigma\vartheta\acute{o}\varsigma$!) was already being used to justify the church tax (in Kleve, 1662 and 1687). Cf. Friedrich Giese, *Deutsches Kirchensteuerrecht* (Stuttgart: Enke, 1910) 27–28.

87   Heinold Fast, *Heinrich Bullinger und die Täufer* (Schriftenreihe des Mennonitischen Geschichtsvereins 7; Weierhof: Pfalz, 1959) 25, 143; Zofingen Colloquy of 1532 = Quellen zur Geschichte der Täufer. Schweiz 4.221.

88   Bonhoeffer, *Cost,* 186.

Kierkegaard's experience remains typical. After he had concluded on the basis of our text that the salary of clergy employed by the state is "directly contrary to Christ's ordinance" and that there is literally not a single honest priest, he once shared this opinion with Bishop Mynster. "To my surprise Bishop Mynster replied, 'Yes, there is something in that.' I had not really expected this answer; for though this was said, to be sure, in private, yet on this point Bishop Mynster was usually prudence itself."[90]

Our text is among the most suppressed statements of the gospels. Is it to be laid *ad acta*? Or how is its meaning to be claimed in a changed situation? We postpone this question until our summary.

■ **11-15** The following five verses belong together. Matthew probably intended that the disciples upon entering a village or a city should first make inquiries among the inhabitants about suitable places to stay. Thus they are not just to go to the first possible house but from the beginning are to avoid "bad" houses. The sayings source was much less concerned here.[91] The Matthean text may reflect experiences of ambiguous and difficult missionary situations. Only after these inquiries are they to enter the house. Early (cf. Mark 6:10) problematic experiences with missionaries may lie behind the command to stay in the quarters once one has occupied them (v. 11c). One should not look around for a better place to stay or give the impression of instability.

■ **12-13** When entering the house, they are to extend the greeting of peace. This is not the everyday Semitic greeting of שָׁלוֹם (Shalom) but a special blessing that spreads

something of the material presence of God's salvation over the house and can also be withdrawn. Behind this formulation was perhaps originally the thought of the *Tg. Isa.* 52.7 that speaks of the revelation of the kingdom of God and of eschatological peace.[92] The decisive question is whether the chosen house really proves to be worthy. The reaction of its inhabitants must correspond to the peace given to them. Initially this is demonstrated simply by whether they do or do not receive the messengers of Jesus.

■ **14** If they do not, then they no longer live in the realm of God's eschatological peace. Therefore the messengers leave the house and the city and terminate all fellowship with them. That is the meaning of the symbolic action of shaking the dust from the feet.[93] It is neither a symbolic discharge of responsibility,[94] nor a curse, nor a pronouncement of judgment; it is an execution of judgment.[95] When the peace of God returns to the messengers and they break off fellowship, then the house or the city lies outside the saving sphere of God's peace. The issue of salvation or disaster is finally decided in the encounter with the disciples of Jesus.

■ **15** The judgment word of v. 15 simply seals what has already happened. In the final judgment it will be better for the notoriously sinful region of Sodom and Gomorra[96] than for this city. The solemn "amen" and

---

89   Cf. Gerd Theissen, *Sociology of Early Palestinian Christianity* (Philadelphia: Fortress, 1978) 125, n. 40.

90   "The Instant 7, 8," in Kierkegaard's *Attack Upon "Christendom"* (Princeton: Princeton University Press, 1944) 228, 230.

91   Cf. Hoffmann, *Studien,* 273.

92   Text in Str-B 3.8.

93   The shaking of the dust from the feet is probably a spontaneously created prophetic symbolic action, thus a parallel to Neh 5:13 (shaking out the garment!) and not a copy. The (later) rabbinical conviction that gentile land is unclean (references in Str-B 1.571) did not lead to a rite of shaking off the dust; this has been created (!) by Billerbeck. The meaning of the symbolic action is the demonstrative termination of all fellowship. Cf. Acts 13:51; 18:6.

94   Examples: Erasmus (*Paraphrasis,* 60): The messengers testify that they have not received any earthly advantage from this house. Or the messengers emphasize the effort they have made on behalf of this house (a view widespread since Jerome).

95   Luise Schottroff and Wolfgang Stegemann, *Jesus and the Hope of the Poor* (Maryknoll: Orbis, 1986) 50: "The messengers do not see themselves as judges." Indeed, they proclaim the love of one's enemies. On the contrary! They may indeed make no decision about God's judgment, but since they are bearers of the saving sphere of the eschatological peace that returns to them, they become instruments of judgment.

96   Sodom and Gomorra are regarded as models of sinfulness: Str-B 1.571-76.

the biblical language of the saying[97] intensify the seriousness and the inescapability.

History of Interpretation

The Syriac Book of Stages, the *Liber Graduum*, offers in its fifth homily, "Concerning the Milk of the Little Ones," an interpretation of our text that can reveal a fundamental problem with the content of the text. The entire Book of Stages distinguishes between the commands for the perfect and the commands for the beginners or ordinary Christians, for example, the "milk of the little ones." Surprisingly, it applies our commands for the wandering charismatics not to the perfect but to the "little ones." "Because they were (*scil.* still) children in the truth, . . . they were afraid to go to the Gentiles." Those who are little and unstable greet no one on the road, and they shake the dust from their feet. The little ones go only to the worthy, "so that their spirit might not suffer harm." The perfect, however, say that "God sends us to the nations, not to righteous sheep." They spend the night with sinners and tax collectors just as Jesus himself did. If someone does not receive them, instead of shaking the dust from their feet, they pray for those who persecute them.[98] Zwingli also asks whether this command of Jesus could not destroy the sinners and the weak instead of encouraging them.[99]

Whoever deals with the command of Jesus in v. 14 has to ask whether and how it can be governed by love. To shake the dust from one's feet in the name of God can inwardly be an act of weakness and self-protection on the part of people who do not dare to expose themselves to what is foreign and new. Outwardly it can be an act of extreme self-absolutizing and of lovelessness and not a sign of God. Here lies a danger of this text. On the other hand, a church that is no longer able to shake the dust from its feet because it has its cathedrals and palaces next to the houses of those who do not receive its message, testifies less to the truth of God than to its own lack of freedom. To the princely housed but unfree church, our word asks whether it is still capable of confronting people with binding decisions as did the homeless but free Son of Man and his disciples.

Summary and Meaning for Today

The message of the entire text is that the authority and the lifestyle of Jesus that come from his mission are entrusted completely to his disciples. They represent him in their defenselessness, homelessness, and in their poverty. To live as a disciple is to live as Jesus does. That is why telling about this Jesus is so important for Matthew. Jesus' way of living is a prophetic sign that embodies the truth of his message of the kingdom of God. The message is thus destroyed for Matthew if the life of the messengers is not "right." Of whom is Matthew speaking here? Jesus' "mission instruction" was initially directed to the itinerant charismatics, to those who followed him in the literal sense of the word. Does that mean that this text speaks of a special kind of discipleship? Matthew is writing for a settled community, but he makes no distinction between the "twelve apostles" of the beginning and the disciples who are transparent of the entire church. We have surmised that for him the missionary proclamation is a task of the *entire* church and, correspondingly, that living as an itinerant charismatic is a way of life for each member of the church. Since the defenselessness and poverty of the messengers make concrete some of the commands of the Sermon on the Mount (cf. 5:38-42; 6:25-34), it probably is safe to say that all in freedom should do as much as they can on the way to righteousness. In any case, the community identifies to a great degree with the itinerant charismatics and their mission.

How can we transfer that into the present? First of all, we must consider the rest of the New Testament. Such things as Paul's renunciation of the apostolic claim for support, abandoning the traditional style of itinerant radicalism in the great urban centers of Greece and Asia Minor, and certainly the transition to the missionary proclamation of the local churches in the later period reveal that there was a great deal of freedom in dealing with Jesus' commands. That may be even more true for our own Western European situation, where the

---

97 On γῆ with a geographical designation cf. vol. 1. Introduction 3.2. Ἡμέρα κρίσεως is a postbiblical-Jewish expression (*Ps. Sol.* 15:12; Jdt 16:17; *4 Ezra* 7.102, 113; 12.34; for rabbinical material see Schlatter, 335).

98 Mihaly Kmosko, ed., *Liber Graduum,* 101–38; quotations 107, 127, 134. Homily 30 on the command-

ments of faith and love also assigns 10:5 to the (lower) commandments of faith (*Liber Graduum,* 895).

99 267. Both Zwingli and Bullinger (100B) argue against casually leaving the church on the basis of this passage (against the Anabaptists).

Christian national churches in a complex way have become a factor and ferment of society as a whole. On the other hand, the history of interpretation has demonstrated drastically that just about anything has been repressed and excused by "all the freedom"[100] of Jesus. It is part of the basic *orientation* of the Gospel of Matthew that "gospel" means the *binding* commands of Jesus. Proclamation means that these commands take shape in the works (5:16) and in the life of the proclaimers. It may be that Matthew would fundamentally deny the claim of our Western European churches to proclaim the "gospel of the kingdom," not because of their preaching, or because they do not uncritically take over *his* form of the church, but because they no longer go in the *direction* that he indicates and scarcely demonstrate anymore in their own life signs of the poverty, the homelessness, and the powerlessness that would make recognizable the "higher righteousness" and with it the gospel.

I am of the opinion that what is at stake here, just as in the Sermon on the Mount,[101] is risktaking in two ways. On the one hand, the *entire* institution of the church, including all of its members and office bearers, is challenged to take small but intentional and active steps in the direction of greater poverty and powerlessness, of greater wholeness of its proclamation and distance from the world—and to do so in such a way that the existing form of the churches is not simply negated but changed.[102] There is no *evangelical* legitimacy of a national-church reality, only a practical "legitimacy"! On the other hand, it is indispensable for the entire church that *in* it (not alongside it!) individual groups and communities raise up on behalf of the entire church signs of radical homelessness, nonviolence, poverty, and holistic proclamation.

---

100 Olshausen, 400.
101 Cf. vol. 1, II A 2.2.5 on 5:38-42 (Summary), II A 2.5 on 7:12 (Summary), and the concluding reflections on the practice of the Sermon on the Mount today.
102 Cf. on this subject the suggestions in Ulrich Luz, "Die Kirche und ihr Geld im Neuen Testament," in Wolfgang Lienemann, ed., *Die Finanzen der Kirche* (Munich: Kaiser, 1989) 554.

2.2 The Persecution of the Disciples (10:16-23)

Literature

Ernst Bammel, "Matthäus 10,23," *StTh* 15 (1961) 79–92.

Barry S. Crawford, "Near Expectation in the Sayings of Jesus," *JBL* 101 (1982) 225–44.

Jacques Dupont, "'Vous n'auriez pas achevé les villes d'Israël avant que le fils de l'homme ne vienne' (Mat 10,23)," *NovT* 2 (1958) 228–44.

André Feuillet, "Les origines et la signification de Mt 10,23," *CBQ* 23 (1961) 182–98.

Geist, *Menschensohn*, 227–38.

Charles H. Giblin, "Theological Perspective and Matthew 10:23b," *TS* 29 (1968) 637–61.

Grässer, *Parusieverzögerung*, 137–41.

Volker Hampel, "'Ihr werdet mit den Städten Israels nicht zu Ende kommen': Eine exegetische Studie über Matthäus 10,23," *ThZ* 45 (1989) 1–31.

Hare, *Theme*, 96–114.

Werner Georg Kümmel, "Die Naherwartung in der Verkündigung Jesu," in idem, *Heilsgeschehen*, 1.457–70.

Künzi, *Naherwartungslogion*.

Lange, *Erscheinen*, 252–60.

McDermott, "Mt 10:23," 230–40.

Bo Reicke, "A Test of Synoptic Relationships: Matthew 10,17-23 and 24, 9-14 with Parallels," in William R. Farmer, ed., *New Synoptic Studies* (Macon: Mercer University Press, 1983) 209–29.

Léopold Sabourin, "'You will not have gone through All the Towns of Israel, Before the Son of Man Comes' (Mat 10:23b)," *BTB* 7 (1977) 5–11.

Heinz Schürmann, "Zur Traditions- und Redaktionsgeschichte von Mt 10,23," in idem, *Untersuchungen*, 150–56.

Schweitzer, *Quest*, 326–66.

Anton Vögtle, "Exegetische Erwägungen über das Wissen und Selbstbewußtsein Jesu," in idem, *Evangelium*, 296–344.

For *additional literature* on the disciples discourse see above, II C.

16   Behold, I send you as sheep in the midst of
   wolves; become, therefore, as wise as the serpents and as pure as the doves.
17   Beware of people!
   for they will deliver you up to councils,
   and in their synagogues they will scourge
   you,
18   and before governors and kings you will be
   led
   for my sake
   as a testimony to them and to the Gentiles.
19   But when they hand you over do not worry
   how or what you shall speak,
   for it will be given you at that hour
   what you shall speak.
20   For you are not the ones who are speaking,
   but it is the spirit of your father speaking
   through you.
21   But brother will deliver brother to death,
   and the father his child;
   and children will rise up against their parents
   and kill them.
22   And you will be hated by all for my name's sake.
   But whoever endures to the end will be saved.
23   But when they persecute you in this city,[1] flee to
   the next.
   For amen, I say to you:
   You will not complete the cities of Israel until the
   Son of Man comes.

Analysis

Structure

The section consists of an introductory sentence (v. 16) with the catchwords ἀποστέλλω ("to send") and πρόβατον ("sheep") from 10:5-6,[2] a concluding sentence (v. 23b-d) introduced (as was v. 15) by ἀμὴν λέγω ὑμῖν ("amen, I say to you") that speaks of judgment, and the intervening sentences vv. 17-23a. Thus on the one hand to a degree the section parallels vv. 5-15. On the other hand, however, v. 23 also points back to vv. 5-6 (πόλις, Ἰσραήλ) so that the inclusion vv. 5-6/23 frames the entire first main section of the discourse. The intervening sentences consist of an introductory imperative (v. 17a), two pronouncement statements introduced by the future tense of παραδί-δωμι ("to deliver"; vv. 17b-18, 21-22), and two statements of instructions for behavior introduced by ὅταν δέ ("But when"; vv. 19-20, 23a). The concluding v. 23b supports the instruction of v. 23a with a word of comfort much as the encouragement of vv. 19b, c-20 does with v. 19a, b. The determinative catchword of the section, παραδίδωμι, reveals that our section, although closely connected with vv. 5-15, has a different theme.

Sources

Verse 16a comes from the sending discourse of Q (= Luke 10:3). Matthew has saved it until this point

---

1   The long text "and when they persecute you in the next, then flee (again) to another" (primarily Western MSS but also Q, f[1.13] and Origen) reveals the effort to interpret the advice to flee as a fundamentally valid command.

2   Cf. above, II C.

because it serves as an appropriate introduction to the section on persecution. *Verse 16b is missing in Q.* Since similar comparisons appear in Jewish texts,[3] and since only the defenselessness and innocence of the dove, not the serpent's craftiness, fit into Matthean theology, it is better to assume here a pre-Matthean addition (Q[Mt]?) rather than Matthean redaction. Only *v. 17a* may be a redactional introduction.[4] *Verses 17b-22* are moved up from Mark 13:9-13.[5] *Καὶ τοῖς ἔθνεσιν* in v. 18b corresponds to the Markan *καὶ εἰς πάντα τὰ ἔθνη* of 13:10.[6] For reasons of content Matthew has omitted (cf. 10:5-6!) the rest of this verse that speaks of the gentile mission. In addition, vv. 18-20 have a parallel in Q (Luke 12:11-12) that has clearly influenced our text. It immediately follows the section Q = Luke 12:2-9 that Matthew will use for vv. 26-33.[7] Matthew has taken from it *μὴ μεριμνήσητε* ("do not worry") with which he creates one of the frequently occurring reminiscences in chap. 10 of Matt 6:25-34. Here, as in his use of Mark 13:9-13, it is clear that Matthew is surveying those parts of his sources that he has not yet used. In v. 17 *μαστιγόω* ("scourge") is redactional. Along with "in their synagogues" and the motif of persecution from city to city (v. 23a), this verb looks forward to 23:34 where Matthew again will take up the theme of the persecution of the messengers of Christ in Israel and will pronounce a sharp judgment on Israel. The reference to the "father" in v. 20 is also redactional. *Verse 23* is special Matthean material. Worth considering is the suggestion that the logion comes from Q, or more likely from Q[Mt], where it could have

appeared after Q = Luke 12:11-12; the structure of the two sayings is very similar.[8] It has recently been suggested that the verse could come completely or partially from Matthew.[9] In my judgment, however, there is not enough linguistic evidence to support such a thesis.[10] In any case it was Matthew who inserted the logion; important for him in the process were the catchword connection *τέλος/τελέω* ("end," "complete") in vv. 22/23 and the compositional references to vv. 5-6, 14-15, and 19.

Tradition History and Origin

Originally, there were four individual logia:

a. *Matt 10:16a* reflects the situation of persecution in only general terms. There are no compelling reasons to deny this saying to Jesus.

b. *Matt 10:17b-20* (= Mark 13:9, 11; Luke 12:11-12) is an originally self-contained logion that in the course of the history of tradition increasingly emphasized the disciples' situation of persecution. It may well have originated as a prophetic word assuring the spirit to the post-Easter church engaged in mission in Israel.[11]

c. *Matt 10:21-22* (= Mark 13:12-13), like Matt 10:34-36, is influenced by Mic 7:6. The change from the third (v. 21) to the second person plural (v. 22) is like that in vv. 17-18. The saying probably was formed in the post-Easter community. Whether a kernel of this tradition goes back to Jesus will be discussed in connection with Matt 10:34-36.

d. The circumstances of the tradition of *Matt 10:23* are complex. Controversial are: (1) whether the

---

3   Cf. below, nn. 27–28.

4   Cf. Matt 6:1; 7:15; 16:11-12.

5   Bo Reicke ("A Test of Synoptic Relationships," 213) regards this strange (not unique!) procedure of Matthew as "too artificial" and assumes that Matt 10:17-22 and 24:9-13 (just as the other synoptic parallels) are in literary-critical terms independent variants of the same Jesus tradition.

6   Schweizer (242) argues that since Matthew did not read punctuation marks in his Markan text, he perhaps thought that the end of the Markan sentence did not come until after *ἔθνη* (Mark 13:10). Of course, in that case the asymmetrical connection *εἰς μαρτύριον αὐτοῖς καὶ εἰς . . .* would become difficult. Matt 24:14 also shows that Matthew read it differently.

7   Matthew omits Q = Luke 12:10, because he will combine it in 12:32 with the corresponding Markan parallel.

8   Thus especially Heinz Schürmann, "Zur Traditions-

und Redaktionsgeschichte von Mt 10,23," 150–56. In my opinion, a position after Q = Luke 10:12 (*vox πόλις*) or the assumption that it is special material would be just as possible.

9   Frankemölle (*Jahwebund*, 130) as a possibility; McDermott ("Mt 10:23," 230–40, 236–40) for v. 23b; Gnilka 1.374–75.

10   Redactional are: *διώκω, πόλις, ἀμὴν (γὰρ) λέγω ὑμῖν, ἔως,* cf. vol. 1, Introduction 3.2. Not redactional are: *τελέω* (used redactionally by Matthew in a different way), the motif of flight *ἐν τῇ πόλει ταύτῃ* after 10:14-15 that is somewhat surprising (after v. 14 *ἐκείνη* would be expected) and *ἕτερος* with the article (cf. 6:24).

11   Cf. Pesch, *Markusevangelium* 2.287.

logion is a unity or whether v. 23a is secondary and provides a situation for v. 23b, and (2) its origin.

Concerning (1): I would vote for the unity of all of v. 23. Οὐ μὴ τελέσητε τὰς πόλεις τοῦ Ἰσραήλ (v. 23b) presupposes something—if not v. 23a, then a different statement that later would have been replaced by v. 23a.[12] The former is the simpler assumption. Ἐν τῇ πόλει ταύτῃ (v. 23a) again presupposes something. In the present context it probably refers back to vv. 14-15.[13] Perhaps originally the actual city was meant to which the speaker alluded.[14] The formal parallels to v. 23b also tend to support the verse's unity.[15]

Concerning (2): Even if we assume that the logion was a unity, we cannot automatically decide the question of authenticity in favor of the early church. The existence of the unfulfilled prophecy in v. 23b is not a convincing argument for authenticity; such a statement could also go back to an early Christian prophet.[16] The formal parallels to amen sayings with οὐ μή do not constitute an argument against authenticity.[17] In my judgment, the suggestion that Jesus would not have advised flight instead of confession is also not convincing.[18] Our interpretation will show that the focus of the saying lies not in limiting the mission of the disciples to Israel but in the comfort that the imminent arrival of the Son of Man provides. This focus is basically in harmony with Jesus' proclamation.[19] Thus the decision will have to be based on whether we think that the situation of the persecution of the disciples in Israel presupposed in v. 23a is conceivable during the activity of Jesus. Usually a negative answer is given, but this negative answer for its part is based on the negative decision about numerous other sayings whose authenticity is similarly uncertain (for example, Luke 10:10-11; Matt 10:16a, 28, 34-36, 38, 39; 11:20-23; 23:37-39). Since we

---

12 Especially Werner Georg Kümmel ("Die Naherwartung," 1.466–67) has argued that it is not a unity. He claims that τελέω (v. 23b) cannot mean "to come to an end with" (as it is offered, e.g., in the Zurich translation) and that v. 23b therefore does not fit v. 23a—that τελέω means "to bring to an end," "to complete," "to execute." Even objects whose execution or completion were not in the intention of the subject can be connected with τελέω. LSJ (s.v. τελέω, 1.7) notes, e.g., πόνος, βίος, νοῦσος. The problem lies not in the "singular" meaning of the *word* τελέω but in the abbreviated figure of speech possible in Greek that Kümmel did not recognize, viz., the "omission of the noun that can be supplied from the context" (Mayser, *Grammatik* 2/1.20). It is not the towns of Israel that will be "completed," but the mission to them. Kümmel did not recognize this stylistic device and attempted to translate literally. He thus arrived at the "singular" German translation "to come to an end with" (*zu Ende kommen mit*).

13 Anton Vögtle ("Exegetische Erwägungen über das Wissen und Selbstbewußtsein Jesu," 330–31) assumes that the (for him secondary) v. 23a was formulated on the basis of v. 14.

14 Jeremias (*Promise*, 20, n. 4) regards the awkward demonstrative pronoun ταύτῃ as a Semitism (pleonastic Aramaic demonstrative pronoun). However, in Aramaic "the one—the other" is usually paraphrased with the same pronoun (Dalman, *Grammatik*, 114–15). Ἕτερος for "another" is common in popular Koine (James Hope Moulton and George Milligan, *The Vocabulary of the Greek Testament Illustrated from the Papyri and Other Non-literary Sources* [Grand Rapids: Eerdmans, 1949] 257).

15 Related to v. 23b are other logia introduced by ἀμὴν λέγω ὑμῖν that also terminate a prediction, made negative with οὐ μή, with an ἕως sentence (Mark 9:1; 13:30; 14:25; cf. Matt 5:18, 26; 23:39; John 13:38 and vol. 1, II A 2.1 on 5:17-20, "Structure"). Of these sayings Mark 14:25 and 13:30 are not understandable apart from their preceding context; Matt 5:26; 23:39; and John 13:38 are the literary conclusions of more comprehensive texts; only Matt 5:18 and Mark 9:1 are originally isolated logia. Matt 17:20 is not relevant here since the structure of this logion is different (contra McDermott, "Mt 10:23," 238–39).

16 Carston Colpe ("ὁ υἱὸς τοῦ ἀνθρώπου," *TDNT* 8 [1972] 400–477, 436–37) claims that the community would not have handed down an erroneous prediction of Jesus. However, it has done that in the case of Mark 14:25. Furthermore, the later church was never offended by this prediction.

17 Cf. above, n. 15. Mark 14:25 certainly, Matt 5:25-26 probably are genuine Jesus sayings (contra Boring, *Sayings*, 209; Barry S. Crawford, "Near Expectation in the Sayings of Jesus," 225–44, 242–43).

18 Differently Boring, *Sayings*, 210. The difference between leaving a town (10:14) and fleeing from it is not all that great.

19 Limiting the disciples to the cities of Israel will become programmatic only if one reads our logion together with 10:5-6 (contra Tödt, *Son of Man*, 60). Volker Hampel ("'Ihr werdet mit den Städten Israels nicht zu Ende kommen,'" 24-27) argues that it came from Jesus.

can conclude from relatively secure logia that there were at the very least conflicts within families (Luke 14:26), with Jewish opponents (for example, Luke 11:15-20), and a possible trial situation (Luke 12:8-9); and since the sending of the disciples by Jesus as such is probable; and since Jesus' conscious anticipation of his own death presupposes that he expected to be persecuted; we can say at the very least that it is not impossible that the entire logion comes from Jesus.

Interpretation

This section of the text fluctuates in its time structures. In the Matthean narrative it is part of the sending of the disciples during the life of Jesus, but even the interpreters of the ancient church noted that many of Jesus' statements were fulfilled only after Easter.[20] Modern interpretation often questions whether our text must be limited to the time of the Matthean church's mission to Israel, which from Matthew's perspective is already a time of the past.[21] It is claimed that Matthew repeated it in a different form in the context of the gentile mission of his day (24:9-14) and that especially v. 23, referring back to vv. 5-6, makes a pronouncement that may no longer have been relevant for the Matthean church. However, the literal repetitions from vv. 18 and 22 in 24:9, 13-14 show that the sending of the disciples to Israel "back then" must have a meaning for the gentile mission of the church in the present. The anticipation of the end in 10:22b shows that we cannot simply distin-guish between "past" mission to Israel and "eschatological" mission to Gentiles. Furthermore, the end of v. 18 even refers to the Gentiles. For this reason our text has been understood "typologically," so that the church's *entire* mission is rooted directly in the sending by Jesus.[22] Since a decision between the alternatives of past and present is impossible, the question is how the *past* situation of the sending of the disciples to Israel has for Matthew a basic, typological significance.

■ **16a** Verse 16a introduces a new theme. The coexistence of sheep and wolves raises the specter of experiences of violence. The eschatological peace in which wolf and sheep will live together in harmony (Isa 11:6; 65:25) is not yet a reality. In Old Testament and Jewish tradition sheep and wolves often appear together in descriptions of Israel's situation among the nations.[23] Now for Jesus or the earliest church to describe the situation of the disciples *in Israel* this way is to change the image so that it shocks and prepares for vv. 18-23. In the towns of Israel the disciples experience not only rejection (vv. 14-15) but violence. For their part they are to be defenseless as sheep who do not want "even in their thoughts to take revenge on their persecutors."[24] That corresponds to the Sermon on the Mount (5:38-48), forgoing the protective staff (10:10), and the greeting of peace (10:12-13). The readers who have been reading the gospel from the beginning know that the dangerous

20   Origen, 12.16 = GCS Origenes10.106–7; John Chrysostom, 33.3 = *PG* 57.391.

21   Walker, *Heilsgeschichte*, 77 ("'retrospective' Israel text"); Lange, *Erscheinen*, 254 ("historicizing"). Strecker (*Weg*, 41) sees the transition from the sending of the disciples to the description of the church's fate as lying between vv. 16 and 17. In v. 23, that appears to fit better with vv. 5-16, along with Knabenbauer (1.455) and Johannes Munck (*Paul and the Salvation of Mankind* [Atlanta: Knox, 1977] 256, n. 1) Strecker then has to interpret the πόλεις τοῦ Ἰσραήλ as the Hellenistic cities of the Diaspora, in which Jews also resided, in order to save the direct reference to the present. A different kind of salvation-historical division distinguishes between the church's "continuing situation," described in the sending discourse (Willi Marxsen, *Mark the Evangelist* [Nashville: Abingdon, 1969] 202–3) and the still future eschaton that is described in chap. 24 (similarly Grässer, *Parusieverzögerung*, 139).

22   Zumstein, *Condition*, 444 (then there is no principal difference between the interpretation of 10:17-22 and 24:9-14); similarly Schuyler Brown, "The Mission to Israel in Matthew's Central Section," *ZNW* 69 (1978) 73–90, 74, 90 ("transparency"); Charles H. Giblin, "Theological Perspective and Matthew 10:23b," 637–61, 654–61 (the mission of the twelve disciples is representative of the mission of the entire church which is understood as the work of the Christ).

23   Herbert Preisker and Siegfried Schulz, "πρόβατον κτλ," *TDNT* 6 (1968) 690; sheep in contrast to wolves: *1 Enoch* 89.55; *4 Ezra* 5:18; *Tanch.* 32b = Str-B 1. 574; *Esth. Rab.* 10.11 on 9:2 (the sheep that is preserved among 70 wolves).

24   Basil, *Regulae brevius* 245 (Karl Suso Frank, ed. and trans., *Die Mönchsregeln: Basilius von Caesarea* [St. Ottilien: EOS, 1981] 327).

situation of the Christians as sheep among wolves is not limited to the first mission in Israel. In 7:15 the evangelist had described their own experiences with the false prophets this way.[25] The sequence of vv. 7-15 and v. 16 makes clear from the beginning that Jesus' charge to preach leads to conflicts. Thus the emphatic ἐγώ ("I") is important. Jesus himself has sent the disciples into this situation, and from the beginning he is in charge of it.[26] It does not come as a surprise for the disciples.

■ **16b** General directions for behavior follow: Be wise as serpents and pure as doves. It is difficult to see how the two are related. The dove was for Greeks and Jews a model of integrity, defenselessness, and purity.[27] As early as Gen 3:1 the serpent is considered as crafty (עָרוּם, LXX: φρόνιμος). There is a Jewish text that also brings the cunning serpent and the pure dove together, but it does so in antithesis.[28] The dove's simple purity fits well with the sheep's nonviolence, but the serpent's craftiness poses a problem. Without other indications in the text, it cannot automatically be connected with the obedience of the "wise" in parables (7:24-27; 25:1-12) or timely flight in persecutions (10:23a!).[29] We should not press this general wisdom exhortation to be cunning, and we especially should not read too much into it theologically.

History of Interpretation
The church's interpreters have had difficulties with the serpent's cunning ever since in the name of the

simplicity of the orthodox dove the fathers had to defend themselves against the alleged cunning of the gnostic serpent.[30] In many different ways people make of it a Christian image. One often finds the claim, borrowed from ancient literature, that the snake when attacked coils up and protects its head with its body. In the same way the "clever" Christians should protect their "head," by which was meant faith or Christ.[31] Other interpreters see the serpent's cunning in a dialectic with the dove's simple purity[32] that later gave rise to the postulate of a "middle way" "between the intelligent use of humans and relationships" and "simple-hearted dedication to a great cause."[33] Karl Barth sets the "harmlessness of the dove" over the "diplomacy" of the "serpent's shrewdness."[34] In each case the interpreter's own understanding of the world of the interpreter finds here its battleground!

■ **17-20** The logion of vv. 17b-20 leads us into the complex time structure of our text. Matthew moves from the generally formulated "beware of people" (v. 17a) to a general understanding of the saying: All unbelievers are dangerous (vv. 17b-18). However, the traditional logion speaks only of the danger coming from Jews. Συνέδριον does not yet have the technical meaning of a Jewish

25 Προσέχετε ἀπό . . . intensifies this reference to 7:15.
26 Cf. John Chrysostom, 33.1 = *PG* 57.388 ("that no one should think that they had to suffer these afflictions because of the powerlessness of their lord").
27 Heinrich Greeven, "περιστερά κτλ," *TDNT* 6 (1968) 65, 67. Ἀκέραιος is frequently parallel to ἁπλοῦς (Wettstein 1.371).
28 *Midr. Cant.* 2.14 (101a) = Str-B 1.574-75. (Before God Israel is תָּמִים as a dove, among the Gentiles cunning as a serpent.) In other texts Israel is compared with a dove but not with a serpent.
29 Jerome's explanation (69: *per prudentiam devitent insidias*) is later applied to v. 23a, e.g., by Maldonat, 218; Calvin 1.298 (the serpents are intent on flight); Bullinger, 101A (not to stumble carelessly into dangers); Olshausen, 405.
30 Tertullian *Scorp.* 15 = ANF 3.648; idem *Val.* 2-3 = CChr.SL 1.754-55 (the dove as a symbol of the Christians; the serpent as the robber of the divine image and the animal who trades in secrets); for the Ophites cf. Epiphanius *Haer.* 37.7.6 = GCS 31.60.
31 Since Origen (fr. 202 = GCS Origenes 12.97) this explanation has been repeated frequently. The fourth quality of the serpents in Physiologus 11 (Ursula Treu, trans., *Physiologus: Naturkunde in frühchristlicher Deutung* [2d ed.; Berlin: Union, 1981] 26) was influential. Cf. Virgil *Georg.* 3.422-24.
32 See, e.g., Gregory the Great *Pastoral Rule* 3.11 = NPNF Second Series 12.33 (the serpent's shrewdness makes the dove's simplicity alert, and the dove's simplicity mitigates the serpent's shrewdness; both are bad in excess); *Opus imperfectum* 24 = 57; Luther, WA 38.499 (cautious toward insidious people, sincere toward good people).
33 J. Weiss, 309. Bernhard Häring, *The Law of Christ: Moral Theology for Priest and Laity* (3 vols.; Westminster, Md.: Newman, 1966-67) 2.500: Cleverness of serpents and sincerity of doves correspond to the tension of being "in the world" but not "of the world."
34 Barth, *CD* 4/3.630-31.

Sanhedrin with seventy-one or twenty-three members,[35] but refers generally to the court of justice.[36] The scourging in synagogues refers to the punishment of thirty-nine lashes with the whip that, according to the Mishna, was imposed by a court of three men for severe transgressions of the law and was executed by the synagogue servant.[37] In New Testament literature ἡγεμών almost always has the meaning "governor." Βασιλεῖς will make the readers think of client-kings such as Agrippa I. The trial of Paul in Acts is an example. It shows that the logion does not absolutely have to be interpreted from the Palestinian situation, but that, on the other hand, that situation is nowhere clearly exceeded.[38] As in 23:34, where Matthew will refer back to 10:17, 23, he is most likely dealing with experiences that the church had in the past mission to Israel. Ἕνεκεν ἐμοῦ and εἰς μαρτύριον αὐτοῖς ("for my sake" and "as a testimony to them") make clear that these persecutions came about only as the result of the proclamation. As in 8:4 and 24:14, μαρτύριον refers not to the testimony before the court against the governors and kings, but to the witnessing before them. By αὐτοῖς the governors and kings are meant, perhaps also those who "hand over" and "scourge." Καὶ τοῖς ἔθνεσιν ("and to the Gentiles") follows somewhat awkwardly, because at least the governors were also Gentiles. With this somewhat belated addition Matthew wants to move outside the framework of the disciples' preaching to the Jews (vv. 5-6, 23) and to remind the readers of what they themselves are experiencing in the present—a subject of which Matthew will later speak (cf. 24:9-14; 28:18-20).

There is, therefore, a complex mixing of various levels of time. From the very beginning it is clear that Matthew is not speaking about experiences of the disciples during the lifetime of Jesus. The Matthean Jesus looks into the future. However, he speaks not of the readers' present but of the past when they were still under the jurisdiction of the synagogue and were being scourged. Yet v. 17a and the end of v.18 make clear that these past events are typical; the experiences of the mission to Israel will be repeated in the gentile mission (cf. 24:9-10, 14). Thus vv. 17-18 speak *indirectly* to the present; the past history of the proclamation in Israel has the continuing character of personal address. In addition, a third level of time becomes indirectly visible. Παραδίδωμι ("to deliver") reminds each reader of the passion of Jesus. The passion narrative of Jesus also contained a handing over to the Sanhedrin, a scourging,[39] and a rendering of accounts to the governor. In this way the readers are prepared to see that the suffering of the proclaimers means that they accept Jesus' own fate (cf. 10:24-25). Thus the three levels of time correspond to each other typologically. In each period the experiences of the earlier are repeated.

■ **19-20** Verses 19-20 follow with the promise that belongs to vv. 17-18: God[40] will give the disciples the spirit. Behind this promise is the experience of early Christian prophecy. In a trial situation all disciples will have the prophetic gift. At the same time that affliction will be the eschatological hour of the bestowal of the spirit. That it is called the "spirit of your father" underscores the divine love. In a way our logion is an early stage in the direction of the Johannine idea of the

---

35   *M. Sanh.* 1.6.

36   As in Philo and Josephus. Cf. Eduard Lohse, "συνέδριον," *TDNT* 7 (1971) 861–62. Lohse points out that, in Greek also, συνέδριον in a nontechnical sense may designate a court of justice.

37   Cf. 2 Cor 11:24; Jewish: *m. Mak.* 3.12; Str–B 3.527–30. We do not know how much these later regulations of the Mishna were applied to Christians in the synagogues of the first century. Thus from the synagogue punishment of scourging we cannot definitely conclude that the Christians were punished because of transgression of the Law.

Cf. Hare, *Theme*, 44–46.

38   Hare (*Theme*, 108) interprets v. 17 to refer to Jewish, v. 18 to gentile persecutions. Καὶ τοῖς ἔθνεσιν would then equal καὶ τοῖς λοιποῖς ἔθνεσιν. That is not impossible, but it is more difficult in view of v. 23 and the emphatic resumption of the gentile mission in 24:9-14! 23:34-36 speaks explicitly and 5:11-12 (12b!) implicitly of persecutions by Jews.

39   In 27:26 designated with the Latin word φραγελλόω, corresponding to the Roman trial before Pilate but in 20:19 with μαστιγόω.

40   *Passivum divinum.*

Paraclete.[41] However, what makes it special in the context of the Gospel of Matthew is that it is not embedded in a general and comprehensive discourse about the spirit. Matthew rarely speaks of the spirit, and when he does it is usually in connection with Jesus (1:18, 20; 3:16; 4:1; 12:18, 28). He downplays the idea of the bestowal of the spirit on Christians in favor of the idea of the presence of Jesus with his community (18:20; 28:20). Except for the baptismal formula in 28:19 (cf. 3:11), this is the only place where the spirit is promised to the disciples. It is clear that Matthew is thinking here, in the midst of persecution, of a very special, supportive experience of God.

History of Interpretation

■ **17-20** In the history of interpretation a certain reserve toward this promise is frequently evident. Augustine applies the text to the preacher's everyday situation and then has to defend himself against the suggestion that one would no longer engage in sermon preparation. However, preparation by prayer is more important than rhetorical preparation.[42] Thomas Aquinas appeals to John Chrysostom in warning that God's promise is valid for the preacher only if he has no time for preparation; "he must not tempt God when he has time for reflection." Rejecting antirational thoughts is especially important for him. The difference between the spirit of God and the spirit of the devil is that the former does not suspend the *ratio* ("reason").[43] The reserve toward the spirit is especially poignant in the Reformed tradition, where the main concern is that the preachers would neglect the study of the Bible because of the promise of the spirit.[44] Those who, like the apostles, are uneducated are urged as a substitute to listen diligently to sermons and to engage in careful study of the catechism.[45] It is perhaps not accidental that there is no reference to our text in most confessional writings; the only time it appears is in connection with the inspiration of the scriptures.[46]

In the perspective of Matthew's understanding of discipleship it was certainly appropriate to expand the promise of this text beyond the situation of a trial. Indeed, there has often been the tendency to suppress the *special* experience of the prophetic spirit and the *concrete* support in times of crisis in favor of the general presence of the spirit. The history of interpretation here offers important examples of what especially the churches of the Reformation have lost by their "generalization" of the spirit, although such a development was theologically essential. The Matthean text, which with its almost singular use of the word "spirit" puts the accent on a very specific experience, becomes here a question to the reader.

■ **21-22** Matthew takes over the logion about family dissension from Mark with no changes. That he speaks of it again in 10:34-36, also on the basis of Mic 7:6, shows how important this experience is for him. As in 23:34-36 he even says that the believers will be killed.[47] When the Jewish-Christian church speaks here of its brothers and fathers, it is clear that experiences from the mission (διὰ τὸ ὄνομά μου) to *Israel*[48] lie behind the logion. However, the statement that "you will be hated by *all*" (cf. 24:9!) is an indication that these experiences have general validity. Matthew also includes in our text the promise to those who endure to the end (of the world).[49] Together

---

41 Cf. especially John 15:26 (the Paraclete's testimony in a trial situation!).

42 *Doctr. Chr.* 4.15.32 = FC 4.198.

43 *Lectura* no. 847 (quotation), 849.

44 Cf., e.g., Zwingli, 269 (human *iudicium* and *opera* are necessary); Bucer, 106B (study of the scriptures); Musculus, 304 (whoever neglects the study of scripture does not speak by the Holy Spirit); Cocceius, 19 (the promise applies only to those who make an effort to study the scriptures).

45 Brenz, 427.

46 *"Confessio Helvetica posterior"* 1 = *BSKORK* 223.19. = Arthur C. Cochrane, ed., *Reformed Confessions of the 16th Century* (Philadelphia: Westminster, 1966) 224–25.

47 On the persecution of the Matthean community by Judaism, cf. Hare, *Theme,* 19–129 passim; Gal 4:29; 6:12; 1 Thess 2:15-16, etc.

48 Of the Jewish parallels that speak of eschatological divisions and struggles, *Jub.* 23.16, 19; *4 Ezra* 6.24; *2 Bar.* 70.1-3; *m. Sota* 9.15; *b. Sanh.* 97a (= Str–B 1.586) do not deal with struggles in the family. *1 Enoch* 56.7 speaks only of the destruction of families; 99.5 speaks of the murder of infants by hunger, and only *1 Enoch* 100.2 compares directly with our text. The historical experiences that were derived from Mic 7:6 clearly remake the apocalyptic topos.

49 The translation "whoever endures to the last" (εἰς τέλος adverbially; BAGD, s.v. τέλος, 1dγ) is linguistically possible. However, analogous to 24:13 (between 24:6 and 14) εἰς τέλος can refer only to

with 10:23b, this anticipation of the end shows that the evangelist was not thinking of divorcing the community's past mission to Israel from its eschatological expectation and of contrasting it with the eschatological gentile mission (24:9-14) as a historical experience.[50] Instead, the *entire* time of the disciples' mission stands under the sign of the end.

■ **23** Verse 23 is a well-known *crux interpretum*. We must distinguish among (a) the original meaning, (b) the pre-Matthean interpretation, and (c) how the evangelist might have understood the saying.

a. Since we have not been certain about its authenticity, we are able to offer only very cautious conjectures about the meaning of the logion for *Jesus*. In contrast to Luke 17:26-27, the issue is not that the Son of Man will come suddenly, but soon. Nevertheless, it is not the philosophical concept of the near expectation that is at the center; instead, the coming of the Son of Man—as with other statements about the near expectation in apocalyptic texts and perhaps even in Jesus (Mark 14:25)—is personal address and comfort for those who are under attack.[51] The comfort is derived from the imminence of his coming.[52] The emphasis lies not on the command to flee (23a), but on the comfort in those situations in which one has to flee (23b)[53] from one town of Israel[54] to the next. Albert

Schweitzer (*Quest*) made our logion the starting point of his thesis that Jesus expected the kingdom of God to come during the mission of his disciples in Galilee. My own hypothesis differs from Schweitzer's not in principle, but only in the fact that I do not claim to know that much. We can say nothing about an original connection of our logion with Jesus' sending of the disciples, since its position in Matthew 10 is secondary.[55] Also conceivable, for example, as a *Sitz im Leben* would be a farewell statement of Jesus that would speak of the continuing proclamation of the kingdom of God after his execution. In any case, if our logion does go back to Jesus it must belong to the last period of time before his death, when the resistance against the proclamation of the kingdom of God in Israel was already public.

b. The interpretation of our logion in the *pre-Matthean tradition* is also very uncertain, since we could make a clear statement only if it were in the context of Q or Q^Mt. Through the connection with Luke 12:11-12 the comforting element would be intensified. The imminent expectation and the central significance of the coming Son of Man would fit well in the sayings source. The persecutions are not further identified; the text gives no indication whether they are part of the eschatological afflictions.[56] It fits well in the situation of the post-Easter Palestinian itinerant radicalism.

---

the end of the world. Then the only remaining choice is to interpret the brief sentence either as piously preserved traditional material or as a witness to Matthew's near expectation of the end. At least some of his contemporaries will experience the end.

50   Contra Marxsen, *Mark the Evangelist,* see above, n. 21. On the Matthean near expectation cf. the excursus at Matthew 24.

51   Texts that presuppose that Jesus expected an imminent end are Luke 12:49-50, Mark 14:25, formulations with ἐγγίζειν, and (uncertain) Mark 9:1 and Luke 12:54-56. Admittedly, the nearness of the end is often the presupposition and not the scope of such sayings.

52   Gerhard Delling, "τέλος κτλ," *TDNT* 8 (1972) 60, n. 20: "The point . . . is not the time of the parousia but the promise to the afflicted." No! The promise consists precisely in the nearness of the time. False is the interpretation of Josef Schmid (*Das Evangelium nach Matthäus* [RNT 1; Regensburg: Pustet, 1965] 181) that de facto eliminates the near expectation (for the missionaries there will "always be a refuge in time of persecution") or of Zahn

(405: they will "not fail to find an Israelite city"). The comfort comes not from the large number of Israelite cities but from the imminent arrival of the Son of Man.

53   One even has to ask whether the imperative φεύγετε is not to be understood originally in the sense of a Semitizing conditional clause: "if they persecute you . . . and you have to flee into another town." Cf. the references to Semitic conditional clauses with the imperative in Klaus Beyer, *Semitische Syntax im Neuen Testament*, vol. 1: *Satzlehre 1* (SUNT 1; 2d ed.; Göttingen: Vandenhoeck & Ruprecht, 1968) 251.

54   Πόλις = עִיר = fortified settlement. Cf. n. 8 on Matt 9:1-8.

55   Those who believe that Jesus identified himself directly or indirectly as the Son of Man cannot, like Schweitzer, assume a coming (of another!) Son of Man during Jesus' lifetime.

56   Contra Heinz Schürmann, "Zur Traditions- und Redaktionsgeschichte von Mt 10,23," 150–56, 153 with n. 17; and Ernst Bammel, "Matthäus 10,23," 79–92. The text gives no basis for any such conclusions.

History of Interpretation

Our text confronts us with the problem that Jesus was mistaken in his belief that the eschaton was imminent. Even if it does not go back to Jesus, it is still true that early Christian prophets in the name of the exalted Lord accepted, emphasized, and even set a temporal limit to Jesus' expectation (cf. Mark 9:1). However, this is only a modern problem, since the ancient church scarcely noticed it.[57] It appears for the first time almost incidentally in Hermann Samuel Reimarus,[58] and it has found its most pronounced form in the studies of Albert Schweitzer and Martin Werner.[59] It is astonishing how little exegesis has dealt with this fundamental problem. Many exegetes, and not only Catholic exegetes, obviously still apply the principle: What a saying may not mean, it does not mean.[60] Especially in the Protestant scholarship of the nineteenth and twentieth centuries, declaring that the logion was not genuine has been a way of avoiding the problem.[61] Even the systematic theologians punish this uncomfortable logion by neglecting it.[62]

Prior to the Enlightenment, the history of interpretation did not acknowledge this problem. The exegetical interest was focused largely—and incorrectly—on v. 23a and thus on the question whether a Christian is permitted to flee. It was repeatedly emphasized that flight would have to be in the service of spreading the gospel.[63] For many marginal groups such as Anabaptists, Puritans, or Huguenots, flight became the way of preserving and promulgating the gospel.[64] Those who thought more rigorously on this point interpreted the admonition to flee only as permission, or they limited it to the time of the apostles.[65] Since Augustine, it has been determined, in reference to Matt 10:23, when a shepherd could leave his flock. The primary consideration was that the congregations should not be without shepherds.[66]

Less attention was given to v. 23b. Various "escapes" made it possible to claim that there simply was no problem. One was able to interpret the cities of Israel allegorically to refer to the cities of the new Israel, that is, to see them as a reference to the gentile

---

57   Martin Werner (*Die Entstehung des christlichen Dogmas* [Bern: Haupt, 1941] 72–73, n. 112) understands the lack of traces of Matt 10:23b in the second century to be an indication of the church's embarrassment. Künzi (*Naherwartungslogion,* 127–29) correctly argues against this view.

58   The concern of Reimarus, "Concerning the Intention of Jesus and His Teaching (Disciples?)," in *Reimarus,* 2 § 8 = 148. However, his main concern is not this problem but the demonstration that Jesus understood his Messiahship politically.

59   Schweitzer, *Quest;* Werner, *Die Entstehung des christlichen Dogmas,* above, n. 57.

60   Cf. the report by Künzi, *Naherwartungslogion,* 125–34, 148–58.

61   Why can one cope with the error of an anonymous early Christian prophet of Jesus so much more easily than with an error of Jesus?

62   Karl Barth's *Church Dogmatics* mentions only v. 23a. Matt 10:23b is mentioned by: Helmut Thielicke, *The Evangelical Faith,* vol. 2: *The Doctrine of God and of Christ* (Grand Rapids: Eerdmans, 1974) 133 ("*praesens aeternum*" [!] of Jesus); Michael Schmaus, *Katholische Dogmatik* 4/2 (Munich: Hueber, 1959) 150 (an inner historical interpretation in the sense of nn. 69–72 below). Otherwise, I have found nothing in modern dogmatics.

63   Especially since Jerome, 70: "tribulationis occasio . . . euangelii seminarium."

64   Cf. Barth, *CD* 4/3.626.

65   Clement of Alexandria *Strom.* 4.76.1-2 = ANF 2.423

(flight as a relative command so that the Christian does not become the cause for the persecutor to do something evil); similarly the martyr Mark of Arethusa in Gregory of Nazianzus *Or.* 4 (*ad Julianum tributorum ex aequatorem*) 87–89 = BKV 1/59, 126–29; Tertullian *Fuga* 6 = CChr.SL 2.1142–44 (one-time permission only for the apostles to flee from Israel for the sake of the gentile mission); idem, *Uxor.* 1.3 = ANF 4.40 (flight is a concession for the weak); Origen in Künzi, *Naherwartungslogion,* 18 (flight = permission). Often flight is also interpreted as advice for the purpose of sparing the persecutors or in order not to tempt God. The Donatist Gaudentius categorically rejects the flight of officeholders. Augustine responds by appealing to Matt 10:23 (*Contra Gaudentius* 1.16 [17]-1.17 [18] = CSEL 53. 211–13).

66   Augustine, *Ep. 228* to Honoratus 2 = FC 32.142. (if only an office bearer is persecuted, he is to flee, provided the church is not thereby abandoned; if all are persecuted, he is to remain); Thomas Aquinas *S. th.* 2/2, q.185, a.5 (when the salvation of the flock requires the presence of the shepherd, he must remain).

mission.[67] Or one could understand the mission to Israel, for example, in the sense of Rom 11:11-24 as a missionary activity that would continue concurrently with the gentile mission until the end of the world.[68] One was able to interpret the coming of the Son of Man to be Jesus' presence during his lifetime,[69] his resurrection,[70] the help of the spirit,[71] or the judgment on Jerusalem in the year 70.[72] These ways of avoiding the problem could also be combined. The difficulties of the logia exist only if the coming of the Son of Man is interpreted to refer to the parousia and at the same time the "cities of Israel" refer exclusively to the initial proclamation in them during the time of Jesus or the primitive church. That never happened in the ancient church. However, it seems to me that those who today make use of the escape mechanisms of the ancient church have to accept the charge that they are guilty of "evasion."[73]

c. Does *Matthew*'s own interpretation of our logion provide a way out of the difficulties? Here again clear statements are very difficult. Since the evangelist did not change the saying given to him, our interpretation depends exclusively on the context. Matthew spoke in vv. 16-22 of the persecutions of the disciples in Israel. Following v. 22, v. 23 shows the consequences that everyone's hatred has for the disciples. Not only the spirit (v. 20) but especially the imminent coming of the Son of Man comforts the persecuted disciples. Thus the perspective that dominates our section is the same as that of 24:9-36, and the transparency of the situation of the past mission to Israel for the present situation of the gentile mission becomes clear once again. It is also worth considering whether for Matthew the disciples' flight might have been an expression of their commitment to non-resistance (cf. vv. 10, 16a, b).[74]

However, the *connection with vv. 5-6* presents diffi-

culties. It is only in light of vv. 5-6 that the admonition to the disciples to flee into another city of Israel appears to restrict their flight to the cities of Israel. Then, however, difficulties arise for both possibilities for interpreting the mission to Israel that we considered earlier.[75] If the mission to Israel is still a reality in Matthew's own day, then v. 23 cannot be interpreted in terms of vv. 5-6 in spite of the catchwords that they have in common, "city" ($\pi\acute{o}\lambda\iota\varsigma$) and Israel, for the church's mission is now *also* to the Gentiles and no longer exclusively to the cities of Israel.[76] However, this difficulty is minor in comparison with the one we have with the other interpretation. If we understand the Israel mission and the gentile mission in the sense of 21:43 as two successive epochs and the history of the Matthean church in such a way that it is in the process of reorienting itself from the mission to Israel to that to the Gentiles,[77] then our logion simply is no longer "true." The church's mission and persecution in Israel were terminated not by the coming of the Son of Man but by the command of the risen Lord to go to the Gentiles. Then Matthew's basic problem would have had to be—even with the differences in time—the same as our problem today. What came was not the Son of Man, but the history of the church. The text does not indicate whether or how Matthew thought about this problem.

If with the first interpretation the problem concerns "only" the failure of the near expectation and the elimination of the exclusivity of the mission to Israel (vv. 5-6), with the second interpretation v. 23 becomes "false." Are there ways out of the dilemma? Was *Matthew* thinking of the Hellenistic cities with

67 Rupert of Deutz, *In Opus de gloria et honore Filii Hominis super Matthaeum* (PL 168.1307–1634) 1496.
68 Hilary, 10.14 = SC 254.232–33.
69 John Chrysostom (34.1 = *PG* 57.397) (persecutions prior to Jesus' passion) and the Greek exegesis dependent on him. Latin exegesis interprets predominantly in terms of the (de facto distant) parousia (Künzi, *Naherwartungslogion*, 166).
70 Especially in medieval exegesis. See Künzi, *Naherwartungslogion*, 168 and more recently Levine, *Dimensions*, 51.
71 Since Calvin 1.302.
72 Since Bullinger, 1028 (scattering of Israel as the Son of Man's punishment).
73 Thus André Feuillet ("Les origines et la signification de Mt 10,23," 182–98, 187) against Jacques

Dupont ("'Vous n'auriez pas achevé les villes d'Israël avant que le fils de l'homme ne vienne' (Mat 10,23)," 241–43) (only the reunion of the disciples with the earthly Son of Man Jesus is meant). Feuillet himself is probably guilty of an "*échappatoire*." Following J. A. T. Robinson he claims that Jesus spoke in an imprecise way that was later applied to the parousia.
74 Basil (*Regulae brevius* 244) interprets on the basis of Matt 5:39. Cf. also the flight of the Arians from Constantinople under Theodosius in Socrates *Hist. eccl.* 5.7 = *PG* 67.573, 576.
75 Cf. the two possibilities above, II C 2.1 on 10:5b-6.
76 Gnilka (1.379) speaks of the mission to Israel as a "continuing task."
77 Cf. vol. 1, Introduction 5.2.

their Jewish Diaspora?[78] Then 21:43 would refer only to the Judaism of Palestine. It seems more likely to me that for Matthew not only 10:5-6 but also 10:23 were corrected by the Great Commission.[79] However, in 28:18-20 there are reminiscences only of 10:5-6, not of 10:23, so that this can only be postulated.

Verse 23 remains difficult in the framework of the Gospel of Matthew. At the very least the difficulties should not be ignored. We assume, therefore, that our logion in part was no longer valid for Matthew. However, its enduring significance lies for him in the reality that the church was constantly hated and persecuted in the world and rested its hope on the coming of the Son of Man.

Summary

The central point of the whole text is Matthew's conviction that proclaiming the kingdom, including following Jesus, *of necessity* involves suffering. For this reason the church's experiences in the mission to Israel that are expressed with the aid of Mark 13:9-13 are given a fundamental significance. Luther correctly translates the spirit of v. 22: "And you *must* be hated by everybody." On this point there is a deep convergence between

Matthew and Paul.[80] The "apostolate" is "essentially—not merely fortuitously— . . . active suffering and . . . suffering activity."[81] In vv. 24-25 Matthew will indicate the christological basis of this conviction; in vv. 26-39 he will develop it.

The deepest problem posed by this text is that often today—especially in the first world countries—the church that glibly talks about suffering does not suffer, although according to Matthew suffering is a *necessary* consequence of the proclamation and of Jesus' lifestyle. Individuals who suffer *in* the church, such as, for example, Kierkegaard, are not able to compensate for the *church*'s lack of suffering; they can only call attention to it. To understand our text means, therefore, to ask with John Chrysostom where the "practice field" for training in suffering might be. Is it only the life of the individual as, for example, Job's struggle can demonstrate?[82] Or does the church itself also provide a field for practice? In his critical response to Thomas Müntzer, Konrad Grebel thus comments, for example, about the sheep among wolves: "Moreover, the gospel and its adherents are not to be protected by the sword, nor [should] they [protect] themselves."[83]

78 Cf. above, n. 21.
79 Geist, *Menschensohn*, 231: Matthew sees "in retrospect a certain salvation-historical phase."
80 Cf., e.g., 2 Cor 4:10-11 or 1 Cor 15:31.
81 Jürgen Moltmann, *The Church in the Power of the Spirit* (New York: Harper & Row, 1977) 361.
82 John Chrysostom, 33.6 = *PG* 57. 95–96 (395: "practice field").

83 Leland Harder, ed., *The Sources of Swiss Anabaptism: The Grebel Letters and Related Documents* (Scottsdale, Pa.: Herald, 1985) 290.

3. The Suffering of the Disciples in Following Jesus (10:24-42)

3.1 As the Master, so the Disciples (10:24-25)

Literature

Lloyd Gaston, "Beelzebul," *ThZ* 18 (1962) 247-55.

Jülicher, *Gleichnisreden* 1.44-50.

Meinrad Limbeck, "Beelzebul—eine ursprüngliche Selbstbezeichnung Jesu?" in Helmut Feld and Josef Nolte, eds., *Wort Gottes in der Zeit: Festschrift Karl Hermann Schelkle zum 65. Geburtstag* (Düsseldorf: Patmos, 1973) 31-42.

E. C. B. MacLaurin, "Beelzeboul," *NovT* 20 (1978) 156-60.

Rainer Riesner, *Jesus als Lehrer* (WUNT 2/7; Tübingen: Mohr/Siebeck, 1981) 256-59.

Schulz, *Q*, 449-51.

Wanke, *Kommentarworte*, 21-26.

For *additional literature* on the disciples discourse see above, II C.

24 No disciple is more than the master
    and no servant more than his lord.
25 It is enough for a disciple to be as his teacher[1]
    and a servant as his lord.
If they have called the master of the house
    Beezeboul,[2]
    how much more the members of his
    household?

Analysis

Structure

The saying constitutes the transition from the first to the second main section of the discourse. The framing catchword $\mu\alpha\vartheta\eta\tau\acute{\eta}\varsigma$ ("disciple," 10:1, 42; 11:1) appears again in the center of the discourse. The theme of "persecution" is resumed from vv. 16-23 and christologically deepened. At the same time, the catchword $o\grave{\iota}\kappa\iota\alpha\kappa\acute{o}\varsigma$ ("member of a household") sounds the theme of the destruction of the old community and of the creation of the new community forged in persecution—a theme that will become especially important for vv. 34-42. The saying is clearly structured by two parallelisms and a concluding sentence. With the final sentence (v. 25c, d) a generally valid gnome is applied to Jesus' situation.[3]

Source

There is a shorter parallel in the Sermon on the Plain, Luke 6:40. John uses the saying twice (13:16; 15:20). It is frequently assigned to Q,[4] but one can prove neither the supplements as Matthean,[5] nor the abbreviations as Lukan. The Johannine parallels suggest that at least v. 24b (and also v. 25b) are pre-Matthean. Does v. 25c, d come from Matthew? It is improbable, since not until later (12:22-27) does Matthew give the Beelzebul pericope that is needed to understand it. Thus in all probability the long form is a special tradition taken over by Matthew.

Origin

The formulation "it is enough for the servant to be as the lord" corresponds to a Jewish proverb.[6] Its recollection presumably explains the dative in v. 25a that deviates from the nominatives of vv. 24a, b and 25b. The parallel between pupil and servant[7] and different (also with differing degrees of probability!) Semitisms[8] point to a Jewish-Christian milieu. The entire logion probably arose in a Jewish-Christian community that was familiar with traditions such as Matt 12:22-27 or those about the new family of Jesus

---

1 Ἀρκετόν + dative + ἵνα is not usual in Greek and corresponds exactly to the formulation דַּיּוֹ ... שֶׁ of the rabbinical proverb cited below in n. 6.

2 Βεεζεβούλ (ℵ, B also in 12:24, 27) is the most difficult reading. Was it improved to agree with the (correct?) Βεελζεβούλ and with the Old Testament Βεελζεβούβ (2 Kgs 1:2-6)? However, Βεελζεβούλ also could have been written by a Greek copyist in order to avoid the unusual letter combination -λζ- (Gaston, "Beelzebul," 247). The early and broad Christian witnesses to Βεελζεβούλ (*T. Sol.*, Valentinians, Origen; cf. Gaston, "Beelzebul," 250) could support this view.

3 According to Jülicher (*Gleichnisreden* 2.45) we have here a "perfect parable" with application. Scarcely! The disciples are themselves also μαθηταί (and δοῦλοι), and Jesus is διδάσκαλος (and κύριος). It is not that a parable is transferred to its referent; rather, a general truth is applied to a special case.

4 Schulz, *Q*, 449-51; Heinz Schürmann, *Lukasevangelium*, 1.364-72; Gnilka, 1.374.

5 On the Matthean parallelisms cf. vol. 1, Introduction 3.1. Κύριοι (profane or as title for Jesus with the exception of direct address) and πόσῳ μᾶλλον are not Mattheisms (contra Gundry, 195); the redactional term οἰκοδεσπότης (vol. 1, Introduction 3.2) appears elsewhere only in parables.

6 References in Str-B 1.578.

7 From Elijah's disciples to the pupils of the rabbis, pupils were at the same time servants (Karl Heinrich Rengstorf, "μανθάνω κτλ," *TDNT* 4 (1967) 428-29, 434. Cf. Josephus *Ant.* 8.354: Elisha as μαθητὴς καὶ διάκονος.

8 Julius Wellhausen (*Einleitung in die drei ersten Evangelien* [2d ed.; Berlin: Reimer, 1911] 12) understands the nominative of v. 25b as a Semiticizing hyperbaton; Black (*Approach*, 129) understands the aorist ἐπεκάλεσαν in the sense of a Semitic perfect. Perhaps the saying was based on an Aramaic play on words such as between בְּעֵיל בֵּיתָא (lord of the

(Mark 10:29-30; 3:31-35). Parts of the saying can be attributed to Jesus only if one is willing to accept quite complicated and unprovable literary-critical operations.[9]

Interpretation

■ **24** "These things are matters more for meditation than for explanation, for they are sufficiently clear in themselves," writes Calvin on this text.[10] The explanations may indeed be brief. The readers of the Gospel of Matthew could not understand the terms μαθητής ("disciple") and διδάσκαλος ("teacher") simply as neutral, general terms, for they immediately understood themselves as disciples who had *one* teacher (23:8). They were also familiar with κύριος ("master") as the way Jesus was addressed in worship.[11] In the case of δοῦλος ("servant"), the religious tradition of this word in Judaism[12] and the many parables of Jesus that speak of servants facilitated the reference to the readers. Thus the general and obvious sentence of vv. 24, 25a, b[13] was for them from the very beginning more than a pleasant generalization. Even metaphorically they understood it as a statement about them, although the explicit application does not follow until v. 25c, d.

Those who come to our saying from Matt 10:17-22 will immediately make associations to the parallel between disciple and master. The disciples will be "handed over" (vv. 17, 19, 21), scourged (v. 17), led before governors (v. 18), and killed (v. 21) like the master. The preceding context recalled the passion of Jesus, but the basic formulation οὐκ ἔστιν leads beyond vv. 17-22. It is finally clear to the reader that those were not special experiences of the missionaries to Israel. Instead, suffering and persecution are necessary experiences for all disciples because they *must* be like the master. Thus vv. 24-25 are the "switching point" in our discourse where the particularity of the past mission to Israel that characterized vv. 5-23 is finally abandoned. The sending discourse becomes the disciples discourse. It is now clear that the special experiences of suffering during the mission to Israel were a necessary expression of discipleship.

■ **25c, d** By contrast, the application of the saying in v. 25c, d is limited. Jesus has been given the surname[14] Beelzebul (cf. 12:22-27).

Beelzebul, which means something like "lord of the (heavenly) dwelling" or "lord of the temple," is probably the original name of the Baal of Ekron, familiar only from the New Testament and later Christian as well as Ugaritic texts and that was "cacophonized" in 2 Kgs 1:2-16 into בַּעַל זְבוּב (= lord of the flies).[15] The name is not found in Jewish

---

house) and בְּעִיל זְבוּל. זְבוּל, which means (admittedly it is found only in Hebrew) "heavenly dwelling," "temple," showing a certain closeness to "house." However, a direct translation of בְּעִיל זְבוּל with οἰκοδεσπότης is hardly possible (contra E. C. B. MacLaurin, "Beelzeboul," 156–60). For additional possible Semitisms see Riesner, *Jesus,* 258. The weightiest factor, it seems to me, is the Semitic proverb, mentioned above in n. 6.

9 Riesner (*Jesus,* 257–58) assumes that Matthew has combined two original sayings of Jesus (24a + 25a; 24b + 25b) and added 25c, d.
10 1.303.
11 Cf. vol. 1, Introduction 4.2.1.
12 Δουλεύειν (τῷ κυρίῳ!) is a term for worship in the LXX; individuals or groups are "servants of God" (usually παῖς in Greek).
13 Wettstein (1.373) contrasts a Greek thesis with this: πολλοὶ μαθηταὶ κρείσσονες διδασκάλων. Such a sentence is hardly conceivable in the system of Jewish teaching that is focused on tradition. To be

sure, there are no direct Jewish parallels to Matt 10:24a. He makes it clear that in the Jewish context independence is not a goal—that a disciple basically remains obligated to his teacher's tradition and is obligated to obey and serve him during his discipleship.
14 Ἐπικαλέω with double accusative means to give a surname. As Euthymius Zigabenus (340) already observed, this applies to Matt 12:22-27 only *cum grano salis.*
15 For the Ugaritic material see MacLaurin, "Beelzeboul," 156–60. Ernst Jenni ("Baal-Sebub," *BHH* 1 [1962] 175–76) interprets זְבוּל on the basis of the Ugaritic texts as "grandeur." However, the Middle-Hebrew זְבוּל suggests instead (heavenly) dwelling, temple, or heaven. Since the word appears relatively seldom, the lack of an Aramaic equivalent is of little consequence. We must regard as abandoned earlier explanations, such as זֶבֶל (sewage, compost) or דְּבָבָא (enemy), which must operate with

texts, except in a single text of magic.[16] However, that does not mean that it was not preserved in the tradition. According to New Testament tradition (Matt 12:24 par., cf. 9:34) and later texts,[17] he is the ruler of the demons, as Ashmedai is in late rabbinic texts.[18] He is probably to be distinguished from the devil. It is strange that he appears in the New Testament under his real name and not in the form of 2 Kings 1 as in those parts of the textual tradition where Hebrew was known.[19] However, the names of gentile gods do not necessarily have to be bowdlerized. The relative difficulty of this explanation is less than that of other explanations.[20]

In the tradition the Beelzebul accusation belongs together with the exorcisms of Jesus (12:22-27). The disciples also had been charged to perform exorcisms (10:1, 8). Thus the members of the church experienced and expected the same accusations as their Lord. The context makes our logion concrete for the evangelist and the readers of the Gospel of Matthew. Verses 24-25 help the disciples understand that their suffering (vv. 17-22)

is the same as that of the Lord and master. Verse 25c, d looks ahead to the following section that will speak of the division in the families (vv. 34-37) and the new community in Jesus' name (vv. 40-42). While "teacher" and "servant" emphasize primarily the subordination under Jesus, "member of the household" suggests the relationship with him.[21] The idea of the new family of God whose head is Jesus (cf. 12:46-50) surfaces.[22]

Summary

Jesus' suffering is the basic model for the fate of his disciples. It originates in the mission he gives them; everything Jesus says to the disciples in this discourse becomes understandable in terms of his own way. Of special importance is the element of comfort the entire story of Jesus brings to the disciples' suffering. It takes place not only in the master's footsteps; it stands at the same time under the perspective of his own resurrection. Thus Thomas Aquinas spoke not incorrectly of the "gift of suffering for Christ."[23] Matthew clearly understands the reference to the suffering of Jesus as a word of comfort, for he continues in v. 26: "*Therefore*, do not be afraid."

radical changes in the pointing or even in the consonants.

16 Richard Reitzenstein, *Poimandres* (Leipzig: Teubner, 1904) 75–76. The numerous references of the *T. Sol.* usually are considered Christian.

17 Hippolytus *Ref.* 6.34.1 (of the Valentinians); *T. Sol.* 3.6.

18 Str–B 4.510–13.

19 Sy[s.p]; Jerome (Vg); also in a few VL MSS.

20 Gaston ("Beelzebul," 252–55) assumes that Jesus' own claim to be "lord of the house" (i.e., of the temple) was the occasion of the Beelzebul accusation by the Pharisees. Of course, there is no documentation. Furthermore, Matt 12:24 par. does not fit well with this explanation, but it does fit quite well with

the role of Beelzebul in magic for which *T. Sol.* and the text, *Poimandres,* give evidence. According to Meinrad Limbeck ("Beelzebul—eine ursprüngliche Selbstbezeichnung Jesu?" 31–42) Beelzebul is not a Jewish designation for the devil but a designation of Jesus (cf. v. 25c!) designed to disqualify him. Its relation to 2 Kgs 1:2-16 remains unclear. The Jewish reference, above n. 16, is then also difficult.

21 Οἰκιακός means not so much "members of the household" as "family members or relatives" (BAGD, *s.v.*).

22 The church's interpreters often refer to John 15:15 (φίλοι instead of δοῦλοι) as a parallel. Cf. John Chrysostom, 34.1 = *PG* 57.399.

23 *Lectura* no. 861.

3.2 Proclamation Without Fear (10:26-33)

Literature

A. J. B. Higgins, "'Menschensohn' oder 'ich' in Q: Lk 12,8-9/Mt 10,32-33?" in Pesch and Schnackenburg, *Jesus,* 117–23.

Kloppenborg, *Formation,* 208–16.

Werner Georg Kümmel, "Das Verhalten Jesus gegenüber und das Verhalten des Menschensohns: Markus 8,38 par und Lukas 12,8f par. Matthäus 10,32f," in Pesch and Schnackenburg, *Jesus,* 210–24.

Sergio Pagani, "Le versioni latine africane del Nuovo Testamento: Considerazioni su Mt 10,32-33 in Tertulliano e Cipriano," *BeO* 20 (1978) 255–70.

Rudolf Pesch, "Über die Autorität Jesu: Eine Rückfrage anhand des Bekenner- und Verleugnerspruchs Lk 12,8f par.," in Rudolf Schnackenburg, Josef Ernst, and Joachim Wanke, eds., *Die Kirche des Anfangs: Festschrift für Heinz Schürmann zum 65. Geburtstag* (EThSt 38; Leipzig: St. Benno, 1977) 25–55.

Sato, *"Q,"* 144–45, 174–75, 274–77.

Schulz, *Q,* 66–76, 157–61, 461–65.

Wanke, *Kommentarworte,* 66–74.

Zeller, *Mahnsprüche,* 94–101.

For *additional literature* on the disciples discourse see above, II C.

26 Therefore, do not be afraid of them.
There is nothing concealed
that will not be revealed,
and (nothing) hidden
that will not be known.

27 What I say to you in the dark
say in the light.
And what you hear in the ear
proclaim on the housetops.

28 And do not be afraid of those
who can kill the body but cannot kill the soul,
but fear rather the one
who is able to destroy both the body and soul
in hell.

29 Are not two sparrows sold for an as?
And one of them will not fall to the earth

30 without your father.
—But with you even the hairs of your head
are counted.—

31 Therefore, do not be afraid.
You are worth more than many sparrows.

32 For everyone who will confess me before people,
I will also confess before my father in heaven.

33 But everyone who denies me before people,
I will also deny before my father in heaven.

Analysis

Structure

Verses 26-31 are composed in the form of a ring. The antithetical double logion of v. 28 stands in the middle ("do not fear"—"but rather fear"), surrounded by the two sayings, vv. 26b-27b and vv. 29-30, and the framing sentences, v. 26a and v. 31 ("therefore do not be afraid"). The concluding v. 31 carries extra weight, because v. 31b also takes up v. 29. Formally v. 30 attracts attention as a parenthetical remark. With its catchword πατήρ ("father"), v. 29b is also a bridge to the concluding logion in vv. 32-33. Formally and in its content the latter is independent, but it belongs to this section which it concludes with a reference to the last judgment, similar to verses 15, 23, 39 at the conclusion of vv. 6-14, 16-22, 34-38.

Sources

The section stems, as does 10:34-36 and probably also partially 10:19-20, from the disciple sayings of Q (= Luke 12:2-9). The introduction, v. 26a, is redactional.[1] The restructuring of v. 27 also comes from Matthew's hand. In place of the announcement that the hidden proclamation of the disciples will be revealed there is the charge to the disciples to proclaim publicly the hidden proclamation of Jesus.[2] However, Matthew may well transmit vv. 28-31 generally in the form of Q. He is responsible for only insignificant stylistic changes.[3] In vv. 32-33 he replaced "Son of Man" with "I" and "God's angels" with "my father in heaven."[4] In this way Matthew achieves an excellent parallelism between v. 32 and v. 33.

---

1 Cf. vol. 1, Introduction 3.2 under οὖν, φοβέομαι. The (categorical, BDF § 337 [3]) imperative aorist is redactional. The imperative present φοβεῖσθε, vv. 28, 31, is Q text.

2 Linguistically the proof is difficult. The imperative aorist (cf. above, n. 1) and ἀκούω (cf. vol. 1, Introduction 3.2) are Matthean. The most important argument is the context of the instruction to the disciples in vv. 26-31. Ἀνθ᾽ ὧν, πρός are Lukan redaction in v. 3. Ἐν τοῖς ταμιείοις might be Q text in opposition to ἐπὶ τῶν δωμάτων. The opposite

position is advocated by Wanke, *Kommentarworte,* 67.

3 Contra Polag, *Fragmenta,* 58. Δέ, μᾶλλον (v. 28), οὖν (v. 31) are to be understood as Matthean redaction; cf. vol. 1, Introduction 3.2. Furthermore, the singular πωλεῖται (v. 29) is Matthean. Πεσεῖται ἐπις τὴν γῆν ἄνευ τοῦ πατρὸς ὑμῶν (v. 29) is probably traditional in spite of its redactional Lukan linguistic coloring, because the corresponding Lukan formulation is very clearly redactional.

4 On οὖν, κἀγώ, πατὴρ ἐν τοῖς οὐρανοῖς cf. vol. 1, Introduction 3.2. Probably λέγω (δὲ?) ὑμῖν (Luke

Origin

We are dealing with three originally independent sayings: vv. 26b-27, 28-31, 32-33. *Verses 26b-27* consists of a wisdom gnome ("whatever is hidden will eventually come to light") and its application to the disciples' proclamation. Taken by itself—and Mark 4:22 shows that the word at one time was independent—v. 26b also is a maxim.[5] It was related by v. 27 = Luke 12:3 to the proclamation of the disciples. It is difficult to say whether the future tenses ἀκουσθήσεται and κηρυχθήσεται originally were applied to the present, viz., to the church's proclamation,[6] or eschatologically, viz., to the final judgment.[7] It seems to me that for Q at the latest the context (Luke 12:8-9!) makes the eschatological interpretation more probable. One can conceive of the origin in different ways. Either Jesus has taken over a common maxim and applied it to his proclamation, in which case Luke 12:2-3, similar to the parables of contrast, would emphasize the difference between the present hiddenness and the revealing at a later time. Or an early Christian prophet has taken over a maxim or a saying of Jesus[8] and applied

it to the proclamation of the disciples in order to encourage those who proclaim the kingdom of God "in private" by focusing attention on its eschatological revelation.[9] A clear decision is hardly possible.

In my judgment, *vv. 28-31* are a unified logion[10] except for the secondarily inserted proverbial[11] comment in v. 30. It is formally a hortatory saying in wisdom style,[12] in structure very artistic with prohibition and command separated by argumentation and concluding with an imperative; it is not capable of further decomposition. In content it is only superficially an exhortation; the real aim of the saying is to encourage the disciples on the basis of v. 29. Almost nothing more can be said about the origin of the logion.

Verses 32-33, a two-part Son of Man saying, are difficult to assign to a traditional genre. In reaction against its common understanding as a prophetic "sentence of holy law,"[13] its wisdom structure has been especially emphasized.[14] In my judgment, there

---

12:8) was omitted by Matthew (Pesch, "Über die Autorität Jesu," 30-33). Ἐνώπιον (Luke 12:9) is more clearly redactional than ἔμπροσθεν in Matthew. Ἀρνηθήσεται in Luke 12:9 is very difficult. Is here still a recollection that the saying originally was not a Son of Man saying (Philipp Vielhauer, "Gottesreich und Menschensohn in der Verkündigung Jesu," in idem, *Aufsätze zum Neuen Testament* [ThBü 31; Munich: Kaiser, 1965] 77)? In my judgment it is more likely that Luke wanted to avoid the clumsy ὃς ἂν ἀρνήσηταί με . . . καὶ ὁ υἱὸς τοῦ ἀνθρώπου ἀρνήσεται αὐτόν and to shorten the formulation in the second part of the parallelism. The Lukan formulation (with ἐνώπιον τῶν ἀγγέλων τοῦ θεοῦ) does not understand ἀρνηθήσεται as a *passivum divinum*. It is disputed whether originally υἱὸς τοῦ ἀνθρώπου or "I" was read. The decision is connected with one's judgment about the entire Son of Man question. I assume that υἱὸς τοῦ ἀνθρώπου was original and thus follow, among others, A. J. B. Higgins ("'Menschensohn' oder 'ich' in Q: Lk 12,8-9/Mt 10,32-33?" in Pesch and Schnackenburg, *Jesus*, 117-23).

5 Mark 4:22 and *Gos. Thom.* 5-6 demonstrate the independence of Luke 12:2. Bultmann (*History*, 95) calls attention to the proverb, "The sun will bring it to light." Proverbial parallels: Sophocles fr. 301 (A. C. Pearson, ed., *The Fragments of Sophocles* [Cambridge: Cambridge University Press, 1917] 1.217) = Aulus Gellius, *Noctes Atticae* 12.11 (T. E. Page, ed.; vol. 2; LCL; Cambridge: Harvard

University Press, 1948) 394; Sophocles *Ai.* 646-47; *Oed. Tyr.* 1213; *Oed. Col.* 1454; Euripides *Hipp.* 1051; Aelianus fr. 62; Menander *Sent.* 639, 829, 839, ed. Siegfried Jäkel [Leipzig: Teubner, 1864] 70, 80-81 (time will reveal it, or something similar); *m. ʾAbot* 2.5 (Hillel: Each word will be heard at the end).

6 Thus, e.g., Kloppenborg, *Formation,* 210-11. Q = Luke 12:2-3 is already then an indirect "exhortation to bold preaching" that Matthew with his reformulation simply would have made clearer.

7 Thus, e.g., Hoffmann, *Studien,* 132: "eschatological rehabilitation of the group and its message."

8 Thus Sato, "Q," 245.

9 Cf. Schulz, *Q,* 464.

10 The attempts at decomposition, e.g., by Zeller (*Mahnsprüche,* 95-96) and similarly by Gnilka (1.390) (original unit: vv. 29, 31b; very early supplements, vv. 28, 30, 31a), are in my judgment not convincing, as is already revealed by Zeller's many reservations.

11 Cf. 1 Sam 14:45; 2 Sam 14:11; 1 Kgs 1:52; Luke 21:18; Acts 27:34.

12 Kloppenborg, *Formation,* 208-9 (with a reference to the parallel 4 Macc 13:14-15); Sato, "Q," 174-75. Exact formal parallels for this formally complex text, however, are not available.

13 Since Ernst Käsemann, "Sentences of Holy Law in the New Testament," in idem, *New Testament Questions of Today* (Philadelphia: Fortress, 1969) 77-78.

14 Cf. Klaus Berger, "Zu den sogenannten Sätzen heili-

is no such thing as a prophetic genre of sentences of holy law,[15] but on the other hand our saying is by no means a wisdom saying. The authoritative "I" that speaks in Luke 12:8-9 is not characteristic of wisdom thinking and is more reminiscent of the prophetic figures of the Bible.[16] Of course, the judgments of researchers on the origin of the saying mirror their various positions on the Son of Man question. In my judgment, the differentiation between the "I" of Jesus and the Son of Man cannot be explained satisfactorily if we assume that the saying was created in the church. I can well imagine a situation of judgment such as that presupposed by the logion in the events leading up to Jesus' passion. I thus conclude that the logion goes back to Jesus. The oldest form is that of Q; Mark 8:38 is completely secondary.[17]

Interpretation

This section deals with overcoming fear during persecution. The foundation is laid in vv. 24-25. The disciples know that their fate will be no different from that of their master and that they therefore (οὖν) do not have to fear "those" who mistreat and vilify them before a court of law.[18]

■ **26** Verse 26 offers an additional argument. How it is to be understood has been debated from ancient times.

The question is: *When* will what is hidden be revealed? In history or at the last judgment? Is the comfort for the disciples in the ultimately unavoidable success of their cause in the course of time, or is it in its final disclosure in the last judgment?

History of Interpretation

■ **26-27** Two circumstances later made it tempting to interpret the verse to refer to the revelation of truth in the course of time. One of them was the remembrance of the well-known Greek proverb about time bringing the truth to light,[19] the other the conditions surrounding the post-Constantinian church whose proclamation was both public and recognized. Thus v. 26b often was interpreted historically to mean that the hidden proclamation of Jesus is presently heard by everyone.[20] The word of comfort then is: Do not be afraid—the temptation is temporary. "When the gospel is revealed, the hostility will cease."[21] Then, to be sure, it becomes difficult to understand the church in Matthew's sense fundamentally as a suffering church. Kierkegaard has formulated this difficulty the most harshly: "Where all are Christians, even the free-thinkers, the situation is as follows: Calling oneself a Christian is the means whereby one protects oneself against all possible inconveniences and discomforts."[22] The comfort that emerges from this interpre-

gen Rechts," *NTS* 17 (1970/71) 26, 33–34, 39–40.

15   Cf. the modification of Berger's thesis by Sato ("Q," 264–78), who says that the general idea of the *talio* is used in various ways both in wisdom and in prophecy. One could speak of a "sentence of law" at most in the metaphorical sense.

16   Sato ("Q," 276) points especially to analogies in Jeremiah, e.g., 26:16-19; 38:6-13; 39:15-18; 43:1-7. One's attitude toward the prophet is at the same time obedience or disobedience toward Yahweh.

17   Although the opposition of ὁμολογέω and ἀρνέομαι later, especially in the context of martyrdom, became part of the church's technical language (cf. Werner Georg Kümmel, "Das Verhalten Jesus," 218), in comparison with the Markan ἐπαισχύνομαι it is original. Ἐπαισχύνομαι is language of the church (Colpe, "ὁ υἱὸς τοῦ ἀνθρώπου," 447, n. 331) and conforms to the expansion τοὺς ἐμοὺς λόγους (cf. Rom 1:16; 2 Tim 1:8; Pesch, "Über die Autorität Jesu," 36). The Aramaism ὁμολογέω ἐν (BDF § 220 [1]; BAGD, *s.v.* ὁμολογέω, 4) also indicates the age of this reading. Other elements of Mark 8:38 are also secondary: ἐν τῇ γενεᾷ . . . ἁμαρτωλῷ likewise expands the focus beyond the situation of judgment. Concepts from Mark 13:24-27 appear at the end of v. 38 (ἔρχεσθαι, δόξα). Cf. Dan 7:13; *1 Enoch*

61.8, 10 (glory, angel). Only the generalizing πᾶς in Matt 10:32 (not in Matt 10:33!) may have been added secondarily in Q.

18   Weaver (*Discourse,* 107) claims that αὐτούς refers to the subject of vv. 17-23, 25b.

19   Cf. above, n. 5. John Chrysostom (34.1 = *PG* 57.399: "time will reveal everything") and Euthymius Zigabenus (340), e.g., recall this idea. Already Bullinger (1038) cites Sophocles (above, n. 5).

20   See, e.g., John Chrysostom, 34.1 = *PG* 57.399 ("all will call you saviors and benefactors of the globe"); Erasmus, *Paraphrasis* 62 ("*aliquando*"); Calvin 1.305 ("a little later"); Maldonat, 221; Olshausen, 408 ("disclosure of all the mysteries in the church by the Spirit").

21   Klostermann, 90.

22   Newspaper article of March 21, 1855 = Walter Lowrie, ed., *Kierkegaard's Attack upon "Christendom"* (Princeton: Princeton University Press, 1944) 27.

tation of v. 26b would be confirmed by history in the most impressive way. But is it the correct interpretation? Alongside the interpretation that applied the saying to history, from ancient times there have been those who understood it in terms of the last judgment, as Thomas a Celano has formulated it most impressively in his *Dies irae*: "*Quidquid latet apparebit, nil inultum remanebit.*"[23] If one understands v. 26b to refer to God's revelation of truth in the last judgment, then the text becomes foreign to the world of today's readers. It is not easy for most people today to find comfort and a reason for fearlessness in the thought that God will reveal his truth in the final judgment by letting the Son of Man confess those who are his and condemn the others (vv. 32-33).

I find it probable that Matthew intends to be understood in this latter sense. Of course, that cannot be proved, especially since the evangelist parenetically reworked the eschatological commentary saying Q = Luke 12:3. We can only point out that presumably in Q the future tenses of Luke 12:2-3 already were understood eschatologically and that the Matthean context is full of references to the last judgment (10:15, 23, 28-31, 32-33, 39, 41-42) so that from that perspective this interpretation makes sense for the readers.

■ **27** However, the way the text continues must have surprised them. The evangelist changes the promise of Luke 12:3 (Q) into an exhortation. The disciples should already act in the present in a way that is appropriate to the final revelation that takes place in the last judgment.

Thus v. 27 says what the eschaton means for the proclamation. You are to preach publicly, from the flat roofs[24] of Palestinian houses, so that everyone can hear.[25] Such parenetic accentuations are typical of the evangelist, who constantly is concerned that the disciples should conform to the coming kingdom of heaven by seeking its righteousness (cf. 6:33). Since, at the very latest in 10:24-25, the sending discourse has become a general disciples discourse, *all* members of the community know that this charge to proclaim is addressed to them.

■ **28** Verses 28-31 sharpen this charge. The challenge not to fear[26] those who can kill only the body belongs to the tradition of martyrdom parenesis.[27] Such a saying shows, just as do the direct references (5:11-12; 10:17-22; 22:6; 23:34-36), that the community was being persecuted and faced the possibility of martyrdom. The distinction between the body humans can kill and the soul they cannot kill reflects the influence of Greek dichotomous anthropology on wide circles of Judaism.[28] What is important is that the Greek concept of the immortal soul is not taken over here. God can also destroy the soul in hell. The Gehinnom is understood here not in the sense of later rabbinic Judaism as an intermediate[29] but as the final place of punishment. The punishment for the wicked consists in their complete destruction, body and soul.[30]

---

23   "What is hidden will appear, nothing will go unavenged." Thomas a Celano *Dies irae* 6.2, in Karl Langosch, *Hymnen und Vagantenlieder: Lateinische Lyrik des Mittelalters mit deutschen Versen* (2d ed.; Darmstadt: Wissenschaftliche Buchgesellschaft, 1958) 86–89. The following, e.g., interpret it as referring to the last judgment: Jerome, 70; Hilary, 10.16 = SC 254.234; Theodor of Mopsuestia fr. 55 = Reuss, 114; Cyril of Alexandria fr. 123 = Reuss, 193. Many interpreters combine the two interpretations.

24   According to Jerome's information (*Ep.* 106.63 = CSEL 55.278), δῶμα (house, room) is used in the oriental provinces in the sense of "*tectum*" (roof).

25   According to *Tanch.* 243b = Str-B 1.580, the synagogue servant blows the horn on Friday before the beginning of the Sabbath from the highest roof of the city.

26   Φοβέομαι ἀπό appears in the OT but is not a clear Semitism (BAGD, s.v., 1a); φοβέομαι ἀπὸ προσώπου would be characteristic of the LXX. However, it does conform to the LXX that the call to fear God

in v. 28b is formulated without ἀπό. The LXX never says ἀπό in connection with θεός or κύριος.

27   2 Macc 6:30 (suffering κατὰ τὸ σῶμα, joy κατὰ ψυχήν from the fear of God); 4 *Macc* 13.13-15 (surrendering the bodies; preservation of the soul from eternal torture; no fear of him who thinks he is able to kill); for additional sources see Zeller, *Mahnsprüche*, 96–100. Greek sources, e.g., are: Epictetus *Diss.* 2.2.15 (humans can kill but not harm); 3.13.17 (the person is not killed; only the σωμάτιον); (Ps) Themistius, *Orations* 12 (Glanville Downey, ed.; 3 vols.; Leipzig: Teubner, 1965–74) 3.140–41 (you kill the body, the soul will fly away).

28   Albert Dihle and Eduard Lohse, "ψυχή κτλ," *TDNT* 9 (1974) 632–34, 636–37.

29   Cf. vol. 1, II 2.2.1 (on 5:21-26), n. 19.

30   Especially close to Matt 10:28 are: *1 Enoch* 22.13 (the souls of the sinners will not be raised on the day of judgment); *1 Enoch* 108.3 (along with their eternal torture, reference is made to killing the spirits); *b. Ros Has.* 16b.34 (= Str-B 4.1033 = *t. Sanh.*

History of Interpretation

■ **28** Our text does not intend to make statements about anthropological questions or about life after death. With the help of such statements Matthew wants to encourage the church. Nevertheless, it was unavoidable that in the history of interpretation our text became a *locus "inter primos religionis nostrae"*[31] for the immortality of the soul. The text strengthens the general conviction that the body will disappear after death. It is only a "mask" of the soul.[32] Sensual love will come to an end with the body.[33] What dies is then "only" the body; the real death is "being without the one who has said, 'I am the life.'"[34] The idea of the resurrection of the body is combined with the idea of the immortality of the soul.[35] The difficult statement that God "can destroy body and soul" in hell can then be interpreted in two ways: He *can* destroy the soul, but he doesn't do it.[36] Or the "destroying"—it does not say "killing"—is that God turns over the soul to eternal torture.[37] None of these statements, which influenced Christian faith so decisively for centuries, is presupposed in our text. The text is aware of no immortal soul, but it does know that the "soul," in contrast to the body, is removed from the person's control. It leaves open the question how the relationship of the visible "body" ($\sigma\hat{\omega}\mu\alpha$) and the invisible "soul" ($\psi\upsilon\chi\acute{\eta}$) is to be understood. Also open is how it conceives of life after death. On the positive side we can say that it offers no support for a devaluation of the bodily as an unreal self.

It is not the devil but God who destroys body and soul in hell.[38] God is to be feared. The "fear of God" is a familiar demand in the Old Testament-Jewish tradition that permits various possibilities of accentuation.[39] In our text "fear of God" suggests the punishing, judging God who has unlimited power. The thought that human beings are determined heteronomously through the fear of God is still distant. In most Jewish texts, fear of God and love of God are close together; the two converge in obedience to his will.[40] Our text is especially ill-suited to contrast a Jewish God of fear and a Christian God of love. It is more the case that independently of each other in Judaism and in Christianity the question of the relationship of loving God and fearing God was raised.[41] Our text makes it clear that theologically the idea of the fear of God is connected with the sovereignty of God. The comfort for the disciples lies not in the indestructibility of a human kernel of the soul but in the power of God. From the perspective of the power of God, human power is limited to the visible body and does not encompass the entire human self, the "soul."

13.4–5: Sinful Israelites are tortured for twelve months in Sheol, then body and soul are destroyed and they become dust, in contrast to sectarians, apostates, Epicureans, etc., who are tortured eternally). For additional sources see Paul Volz, *Die Eschatologie der jüdischen Gemeinde im neutestamentlichen Zeitalter* (Tübingen: Mohr/Siebeck, 1934) 321.

31 Bullinger, 104A.

32 John Chrysostom, 34.5 = *PG* 57.404. Cf. also Novatian *Trin.* 25 = CChr.SL 4.143.

33 John Chrysostom 34.4 = *PG* 57.403.

34 Origen fr. 209 = GCS Origenes 12.100.

35 See, e.g., Zwingli, 271; John Calvin, *Institutio Christianae Religionis* (Lutetiis: Stephanus, 1553) 3.25.7. The connection with the idea of the immortal soul takes place, e.g., according to Bullinger (104A), in such a way that the resurrection refers *only* to the body that will then be reunited with its soul for the last judgment. This is the general conviction of Protestant orthodoxy.

36 Musculus, 310.

37 Lagrange, 208 ($\dot{\alpha}\pi o\lambda\acute{\epsilon}\sigma\alpha\iota$ = *rendre misérable*"); Gaechter, 343. As a rule, the orthodox commentaries understand the suffering of the soul in hell metaphorically as its "death."

38 Thus, e.g., Lührmann, *Redaktion*, 50; John P. Meier, *Matthew* (New Testament Message 3; Wilmington, Del.: Glazier, 1981) 112. There is no reference to the devil in the entire text. Already Justin (*Apol.* 1.19) and Irenaeus (*Haer.* 3.18.5) interpret it in reference to God.

39 Cf. Günther Wanke, "$\varphi o\beta\acute{\epsilon}\omega$ $\kappa\tau\lambda$," *TDNT* 9 (1974) 201–3, and Horst Balz, ibid., 205–7. Basic possibilities of accentuation are: fear of God as obedience (the Elohist, Deuteronomy, legal Psalms, *T. 12 Patr.*, rabbinical texts); fear of God as knowledge of God and corresponding behavior (wisdom); fear of God as trust and relationship with God (Psalms); fear of God as fear of the epiphany (apocalyptic texts).

40 Beginning with Deut 10:12, 20; 13:5. Cf. Deut 6:5//13.

41 *B. Sota* 31a and par. in Str–B 2.112–13 (the love of God is superior to the fear of God); *y. Ber.* 9.14b.40 and par. in Str–B 4.338–39 (Pharisees out of fear and Pharisees out of love); 1 John 4:16-18 (fear is rejected, not the fear of God).

■ **29-31** However, the idea of the power of God is immediately intensified. The powerful God is "your father," who cares even for sparrows. Sparrows were a common article on the market,[42] by far the cheapest bird,[43] the poultry of the poor.[44] The Roman *as* is a common coin; for two *as* one can buy a daily ration of bread.[45] The text is thus deliberately formulated as exaggeration. Not a single[46] sparrow will become a hunter's prey apart from the will of God. God's power over his creatures is experienced by the church just as intensively and tangibly as his care in the promise of Matt 6:26.[47] The move from the sparrows to human beings is almost humorous. In order to equal the value of a human being, many sparrows are needed![48] The intervening thought in v. 30 formulates a similar idea with the example of the hairs that in Jewish texts also illustrate God's care.[49] A single hair is a very insignificant part of the entire person.

Summary and History of Interpretation

■ **28-31** God, the lord over body and soul, is a loving father. In its suffering the church is supported by him, much as it is in 10:20 by his spirit and in 28:20 by the Lord. God's power and God's love belong closely together. They establish fear of God and liberate from the fear of humans.

Our text has become extraordinarily influential as the classic proof text of dogmatic theology's *locus de providentia*. Normally it is cited in connection with discussions of the *providentia Dei specialis*,[50] that is, that providence of God that relates, beyond the orders and laws of nature, to each individual human act and to each event. "Nothing happens to us by accident and without the will of our best-of-all heavenly father."[51] Of course, such sentences are speculative in themselves, and they can justify everything as willed by God.[52] If we understand the providence of God as

42 They appear in Diocletian's maximum tariff and are being sold in bunches of 10 pieces (Deissmann, *Light,* 273–74). For that reason alone one should not think of sacrifice (contra Str-B 1.582).

43 Deissmann, *Light,* 274. The Mishna (*Kar.* 1.7) states that the price of a pair of doves (a sacrificial animal!) is ¼ of a silver denarius up to 1 gold denarius.

44 *Lev. Rab.* 3.1 on 2:1 quotes as a proverb: Whoever rents a garden, eats birds (צִיפָּרִים; in LXX, צִפּוֹר is often translated with στρουθίον). Cf. in addition *b. Ber.* 57b (meat of birds is bad for sick people); *Lam. Rab.* 3.6 on 3:17 (80 kinds of bird brain at a banquet).

45 Ἀσσάριον, from the Latin adjective *assarius,* is not a diminutive form but the common transliteration of "as" into Greek. The value is stated in the literature variously as 1/24 or 1/16 of a denarius. Daniel Sperber (*Roman Palestine 200–400: Money and Prices* [Bar-Ilan Studies in Near Eastern Languages and Culture 28; Ramat-Gan: Bar-Ilan University, 1974] 157) assumes that under Antigonus (40–37 BCE) the Jewish system of coinage was adapted to the Roman system so that one *as* would equal 1/16 of a denarius. In the texts of the Mishna the older system of coinage is retained. *M. Pe' a* 8.7 prescribes the daily ration to be given to a wandering poor person to be bread in the value of one *pundion* (= 2 *as*), so that the price for two sparrows would approximate the cost of bread for one meal.

46 Ἔν . . . οὖν may be a Semitism (BDF § 302 [1]).

47 Related is *y. Šeb.* 9.38d.22 and par. in Str-B 1.582–83 (no bird perishes without heaven). Still more closely

related formally is Q = Luke 12:24/Matt 6:26 with common catchwords that appeared quite close together in Q (Luke 12:7, 24), διαφέρετε with the genitive, ὑμεῖς, πατὴρ ὑμῶν. Did Luke 12:24 Q influence our text, or does Q contain a secondary adaptation of both texts to each other?

48 Jeremias (*New Testament Theology,* 184) wants πολλά to be understood inclusively: all the sparrows (of the world). Julius Wellhausen, *Das Evangelium Matthaei* (Berlin: Reimer, 1904) assumes a mistranslation from the Aramaic (50): You are much better than sparrows (cf. Matt 6:26!). Both are unnecessary.

49 Str-B 1.584 and the texts cited above in n. 11.

50 Calvin *Inst.* 1.16.4–5; the Concord formula, *Solida Declaratio* 11.4 = *Book of Concord,* 617; Heinrich Schmid, *The Doctrinal Theology of the Evangelical Lutheran Church* (reprinted Minneapolis: Augsburg, 1961) 180, 190; Hans Joachim Kraus, *Reich Gottes: Reich der Freiheit: Grundriss systematischer Theologie* (Neukirchen-Vluyn: Neukirchener Verlag, 1975) 209 ("*providentia Dei specialissima*").

51 *Confessio Belgica* (1561) 13 = BSKORK 124 = Arthur C. Cochrane, ed., *Reformed Confessions of the 16th Century* (Philadelphia: Westminster, 1966) 197. Cf. "Heidelberg Catechism 1" = BSKORK 149 = Torrance, *School of Faith,* 69: ". . . so preserve me that without the will of my Father in heaven not a hair can fall from my head: indeed, all things must minister to my salvation."

52 An example: Cyprian (*Ep.* 59.5 = FC 51.177) appeals to Matt 10:29 to defend the legitimacy of bishops.

a theorem, then it must be questioned at each death and each war, even each time that a sparrow flies into a snare. However, the tradition usually knew that this is not the meaning of such statements about providence. After Zwingli had asked whether robbery and betrayal happen according to the will of God, he answers: Such a question "is the best argument that I do not yet know God. For I am wanting to . . . measure God with *my* foot, namely, the law under which *I* live."[53] And the *Confessio Belgica* says on the same problem: "It is sufficient for us to be Christ's disciples, in order to learn only what he himself teaches us by his word."[54] On the entire subject of the special providence of God we must say the same thing that is to be understood as an example in the classic New Testament text on the topic, Matt 10:29-31: The right "use of the divine providence" is, "to comfort us in the greatest dangers," with the assurance that "this God truly is our father,"[55] but not to speculate about the order of the universe.

That also clearly describes the "use" of our verses. Based on Christ, they intend to give assurance of God's faithfulness in a crisis situation. If we separate them from Christ and from concretely experienced need, they become religious whitewashing that does not take seriously the world's reality, because it transgresses the limits of the mystery of God.

Interpretation

■ **32-33** The saying about confessing and denying Jesus concluded the section already in Q. The Matthean reworking emphasizes that God, the lord of judgment, is none other than the heavenly father who cares for his own and to whom they pray because he is their father (cf. 6:5-14). The knowledge about the heavenly father becomes the decisive element of our section that will then be effectively contrasted with the break with the earthly fathers (10:35, 37). The main emphasis is on v. 32. The issue is comfort for the suffering disciples. The

all-decisive revelation (v. 26!) takes place in the judgment when Jesus will confess his confessors. That means more than that Jesus acts as a witness in court,[56] and also more than that he intercedes for his disciples in the sense of the early concept of the Paraclete.[57] The passage 7:21-23 has already made it clear that Jesus is the lord of the judgment. His "confessing" before the court is an irrevocable statement of judgment (cf. 7:23). Whether the Lord then will say "I have never known you!" (7:23) or "Come, you blessed of my father!" (25:34) is a decision about death and life. For the first time in our chapter Matthew speaks here of the rescue of the disciples in judgment. He knows that it is not self-evident. The possibility of condemnation remains for the disciples,[58] if the fear of others overwhelms them and they no longer publicly stand with Jesus. However, Matthew also knows that being rescued in the judgment is an act of grace. Jesus carries his disciples by the authority which he grants them (10:1), by his promise, by his own model of life (10:24-25), and by his references to the father who stands over the judgment. Ὁμολογεῖν still has here the general sense of "to say yes, to agree, to stand publicly with someone" and is not yet thinking of special situations of judgment or confession.

History of Interpretation

■ **32-33** The subject was a matter of intense discussion in the history of interpretation. Ὁμολογεῖν was a term that lent itself to the special concerns of every period and to the special accents of every understanding of faith. Initially our text was a classical martyrdom text. The *homologia* was confessing Christ before the judges and witnessing with one's own life.[59] Later, the correct doctrine that would distinguish genuine from false Christians became more important. Now the right confession is that Christ is

---

53 Zwingli, 272.
54 Ibid. (above, n. 51).
55 Bullinger, 104B.
56 Tödt, *Son of Man,* 90. But how could Matthew have distinguished between Jesus' roles as witness (= "I") and judge (= "Son of Man" in, e.g., 25:31)?
57 Cf., e.g., Rom 8:34; 1 John 2:1.
58 Pesch ("Über die Autorität Jesu," 32) wants to distinguish between the future ὁμολογήσει and the subjunctive aorist ἀρνήσηται and relates the latter to the past denial of Jesus by the persecutors in v. 25b. However, the tenses are often used *promiscue*

59

(BDF § 380 [2]). More probable (on the basis of 26:70, 72 and Matthew's general understanding of judgment) is that v. 33 is to be understood as a possibility that threatens the church.

59 Examples: 2 Tim 2:12 (earliest use of our text in a fictitious farewell letter of the imprisoned Paul!); *Acta Acacii* 3.5; *Martyrdom of Irenaeus* 3.3 (= Gustav Krüger, *Ausgewählte Märtyrerakten* [Sammlung ausgewählter kirchen- und dogmengeschichtlicher Quellenschriften NF 3; Tübingen: Mohr/Siebeck, 1929] 59, 103); Origen *Exhortatio* 34 = LCC 2.417; Tertullian *Scorp.* 9 = ANF 3.642; *Fuga* 7.2 = CSEL

God.[60] In the Reformation the personal relationship to Christ, that is, the personal element of ὁμολογεῖν, became important. The confession of Christ excludes the use of other instruments of salvation, such as the intercession of the saints or trust in "papal masses."[61] The thought, already central in the texts of martyrdom, that the confession has to take place publicly also becomes extremely important; there is no quiet confessing in the hidden recesses of the heart.[62] Throughout the entire history of interpretation there is the thought that confession is to take place not only with words but also with the practice of the Christians.[63] Confession demands the *entire* person;[64] the text is to become part of everyday life. Not only martyrs, or pastors and teachers who have to be public advocates of correct doctrine, but every Christian is called to confess.[65] Also interesting is the—philologically flawed—attempt to interpret the prepositional construction ὁμολογέω ἐν mystically in terms of the relationship with Christ that makes confessing possible in the first place.[66]

Such attempts demonstrate how from the entire perspective of Christian faith new accents repeatedly shine out in an old text. The question is not only to what degree they are exegetically "justified." In its historical development Christian faith creates for itself in the individual texts of the Bible a *potential of meaning that transcends the original meaning.* Guided by the center of their own faith in Christ and not simply by the original meaning of a text, interpreters may attempt, in conversation with the interpretations of fathers, sisters, and brothers, in their own theological responsibility for the present to distinguish between legitimate and illegitimate interpretations. However, the interpreter must inquire of the original meaning of the text what *directions* it points out for later discoveries and what correcting questions it poses to them.[67]

For Matthew's understanding of confession the connection between proclamation and life appears to be decisive. As far as its content is concerned, the disciples' proclamation must be the proclamation of Christ (ἐν ἐμοί). For Matthew the confession "to me" involves "everything I have commanded you" (28:20). All of chap. 10 also makes clear that *existence* in conformity with Jesus is a part of confessing (10:7-14, 17-22, 24-25, 38-39), that is, poverty, defenselessness, and suffering on behalf of Jesus. Confessing and denying Jesus before a court of law is only a condensed expression of what must determine the entire life of all Christians "before people."

Summary

■ **26-33** Modern readers have difficulties with this text. The comfort Matthew offers the church no longer seems to provide comfort. Neither the idea of the power of God, who can destroy body and soul in hell, nor the idea of the last judgment of the Son of Man, who not only pardons but also condemns, nor the idea of God's providence, that too often seems to fail even with the sparrows, can easily be affirmed. It is tempting—and in the history of interpretation it has happened not infrequently—to meet the text on a level that does not correspond to its scope, viz., on the level of a philosophical discussion of theological statements about the beyond, the judgment, or providence. By contrast, it is important that the text speaks first of all of a *mission*, namely, the mission to engage in fearless and public proclamation. This mission encompasses all of life and leads to a "sheep existence" for the disciples in defenselessness

---

76.29 (*quomodo confitebitur fugiens?*); Cyprian *Ep.* 58.3–4 = FC 51.164–65; Hans v. Campenhausen, "Das Bekenntnis im Urchristentum," in idem, *Urchristliches und Altkirchliches* (Tübingen: Mohr/Siebeck, 1979) 222–23; Sergio Pagani, "Le versioni latine africane del Nuovo Testamento: Considerazioni su Mt 10,32-33 in Tertulliano e Cipriano," *BeO* 20 (1978) 255–70, 266.

60 Cyril of Alexandria fr. 125 = Reuss, 193.

61 Musculus, 315; Bullinger, 105B.

62 Cf. Calvin 1.308–9 and idem, *Excuse à messieurs les Nicodémites* (Corpus Reformatorum 34; Brunsvigae: Schwetschke, 1867) 589–614, especially 594, 603–4.

63 For the first time *2 Clem.* 3.4 in referring to Matthew: "But how do we confess him? By doing what he says."

64 Barth, *CD* 4/1.777: The confession is "not a special action of the Christian, all that is demanded is that he should be what he is."

65 Zwingli, 273 ("qui ministri publici non sunt . . . confiteri debent . . . non ore solum, sed et corde et factis, imo tota vita").

66 Origen fr. 213 = 102; Tertullian *Scorp.* 9 = ANF 3.642.

67 On the "sense of direction" of biblical texts, cf. vol. 1, at the end of I B 1.1 on 3:13-17: "History of Interpretation and Summary"; the concluding pages of vol. 1 on the reflections on the practice of the Sermon on the Mount today; and Ulrich Luz, "Erwägungen zur sachgemässen Interpretation neutestamentlicher Texte," *EvTh* 42 (1982) 504.

and suffering. Thus Matthew does not want to stimulate *general* reflection on theological problems but an uncompromising and courageous proclamation of "everything I have commanded you" (28:20). Only in obedience to this commission is it possible to reflect appropriately on the theological questions raised in our text.

They are concentrated on God. It is obvious that our text does not ignore God's dark side. He destroys body and soul in hell (v. 28d) and confronts even the church with the possibility of an annihilating judgment (v. 33). Thus, first of all, the correct relations are established. God does not meet the observer here as an object of reflection; instead, as the Lord he meets those to whom he has given a mission. The question up for debate is not whether God's providence really functions or whether God's annihilating judgment can be reconciled with his love, but the question of God's judgment about the fulfilling of his commission. God's dark aspects in this text serve initially to emphasize this point. They lead away from speculations about God and the course of the world just as they do from the question about whose confession of Jesus is the correct one. They pose exclusively the question of one's *own* courage and one's *own*

confession before human beings. The dark statements about God have an activating power, perhaps even a liberating effect.

However, they give the impression that they are not connected with those statements that bear the greatest weight. God, who also can condemn the church, is the father of Jesus (vv. 32-33). The God who can destroy people in hell is "with them" and preserves them. The dark background makes the promise greater. It is precisely the one who has the power to destroy who promises his love to the disciples. It is clear that this is not meant to be an image of God that is subject to calculation. Matthew does not claim that no sparrows fall to the ground and certainly not that the disciples will be spared suffering and need. The key to understanding lies in the person of Jesus. The fatherhood of God is intertwined with him. He whose discipleship will lead to the cross and to the loss of life (10:38-39) says that all of the hairs on one's head are counted. That means that only discipleship is the place where the idea of providence and the fatherhood of God can be spelled out and practiced. Matthew knows nothing of a place that would allow us to discuss abstractly the activity of the father and judge of the world.

3.3 Division of Families and Cross (10:34-39)

Literature

Arens, *ΗΛΘΟΝ-Sayings,* 64–90.

Karen A. Barta, "Mission and Discipleship in Matthew: A Redaction-Critical Study of Mt 10:34" (Diss., Milwaukee, 1980).

Matthew Black, "Uncomfortable Words III: The Violent Word," *ExpT* 81 (1969/70) 115–18.

Gerhard Dautzenberg, *Sein Leben bewahren* (SANT 14; Munich: Kösel, 1966), 51–67.

Dinkler, "Jesu Wort," 77–98.

Fong, *Crucem.*

C. Frings, "Untersuchungen zu den Texten vom Kreuztragen in der Synopse" (Diss., Gregoriana Roma, 1971).

Augustin George, "Qui veut sauver sa vie la perdra; qui perd sa vie la sauvera," *BVC* 83 (1968) 11–24.

Richard Koolmeister, "Selbstverleugnung, Kreuzaufnahme und Nachfolge: eine historische Studie über Mt 16,24," in *Charisteria I. Kopp* (Papers of the Estonian Theological Society in Exile 7; Stockholm, 1954) 64–94.

Laufen, *Doppelüberlieferungen,* 315–42.

Johannes Schneider, "Σταυρός κτλ," *TDNT* 7 (1971) 577–79.

Anselm Schulz, *Nachfolgen und Nachahmen* (SANT 6; Munich: Kösel, 1962) 79–97.

Schulz, *Q,* 258-60, 430-33, 444–49.

Schweizer, "Ψυχη," 642–45.

Robert Tannehill, *The Sword of His Mouth* (Semeia S 1; Philadelphia: Fortress, 1975) 140–44.

Marciano Vidal, "Seguimiento de Cristo y evangelización (Mt 10,34-39)," *Salmanticensis* 18 (1971) 289–312.

Wanke, *Kommentarworte,* 76–81.

For *additional literature* on the disciples discourse see above, II C.

34 **Do not think that I came to bring peace on the earth.**
I came not to bring peace but the sword.

35 **For I came**
    to make a man hostile against his father
    and a daughter against her mother
    and a daughter-in-law against her mother-in-law,

36 **and the members of one's own household are one's enemies.**

37 Whoever loves father or mother more than me
    is not worthy of me.
    And whoever loves son or daughter more than me
    is not worthy of me.

38 And whoever does not take his cross and follow me
    is not worthy of me.

39 Whoever finds his life will lose it,
    and whoever has lost his life for my sake will find it.

Analysis

Structure

Verses 34-36 deal with the sending of Jesus, vv. 37-39 with that of the followers. With the threefold ἦλθον ("I came") and the threefold κατά, the structure of vv. 34-36 is rhetorically effective. Additional rhetorically important words are βαλεῖν εἰρήνην (twice), ἄνθρωπος ("bring peace," twice), and the αὐτοῦ/αὐτῆς (twice each), that concludes the last four segments. Πατήρ, μήτηρ and θυγατήρ ("father," "mother," "daughter") are the bridge to the next unit, *vv. 37-39.* There a relative clause (v. 38a) is framed by two sets of parallel participial clauses. The first three members end with οὐκ ἔστιν μου ἄξιος ("is not worthy of me"), the final two with a future tense + αὐτήν. The last segment, v. 39b, is somewhat longer; the pattern is broken by the addition of ἕνεκεν ἐμοῦ ("for my sake") that calls attention to the first-person pronouns. Six times μου or ἐμέ appear before ἕνεκεν ἐμοῦ. The formal unity of these logia is thus immense. At the same time, catchwords appear in the text that connect it with the entire discourse: εἰρήνη ("peace"; v. 34, cf. v. 13), οἰκιακοί ("members of one's household"; v. 36, cf. v. 25), ὑπέρ with accusative ("worthy"; v. 37, cf. v. 24), ἄξιος (v. 37-38, cf. vv. 10-13).

Sources

Both groups of logia probably stem from Q. However, in both cases there are uncertainties.

1. *Verses 34-36* have their parallel in Luke 12:51-53. Luke 12:51-59 is a Q section in which there is a conspicuous lack of agreement in wording. In v. 34 the amount of redaction is uncertain.[1] The repeated "I came" in vv. 34b/35a is most certainly redactional.[2] After that Luke is expanded by the introduction in 12:52, Matthew by the concluding v. 36. Luke 12:53 and Matthew vv. 35-36 allude to Mic 7:6. Matthew is

---

1 Difficult is (a) the relationship to 5:17, which is strongly shaped by the redaction. Are 5:17 and 10:34 redactional, or is 10:34 the "model," according to which Matthew has formed 5:17? Difficult is (b) the relationship to Luke 12:49-53. Verse 34 contains reminiscences of Luke 12:49 that Matthew presumably omitted from Q (ἦλθον, βαλεῖν ἐπὶ τὴν

γῆν). Does that support the view that Matthew has newly formulated v. 34 using Q = Luke 12:49 as his model? However, on the other hand, Luke 12:51 is also strongly shaped by redaction (παραγίνομαι, διαμερισ-, perhaps δοκεῖτε ὅτι, οὐχί - ἀλλά). The upshot is: *non liquet.*

2 On the intensification of the parallelism, cf. vol. 1,

probably further from the LXX wording than Luke, but in v. 36 he still accepts Mic 7:6d. The Masoretic Text (MT) of Mic 7:6d might be the basis for "members of one's household." Since Matthew already used the same text in v. 21 without unifying it, it is improbable that he changed the wording.[3] However, the Lukan text also, especially the six opposing pairs in 12:53 and the three against two in v. 52 that does not fit with six pairs, cannot entirely be attributed to redaction. Result: The evangelists most probably received the logion in a different form in Q^{Mt} and Q^{Lk}.

2. The three old logia, *vv. 37-39*, appear together not only in Q = Luke 14:26-27, but partly also in Mark (8:34-35) and John (12:25-26) and constituted a very old group of sayings.[4] Presumably Luke has deferred the logion about sacrificing one's life until 17:33 in the eschatological discourse in order to emphasize the suffering of the disciples that corresponds to the suffering of the Son of Man (17:25).[5] In *v. 37* "is not worthy of me" comes from Matthew, who is concerned not with the process of becoming a disciple but with the verification of discipleship. Probably the formulation "loves . . . more than me" with its attractive parallelism is Matthean,[6] while from Luke come εἴ τις ἔρχεται πρός με in Luke 14:26, perhaps the expansion of the family members to include brothers and sisters, and almost certainly ἔτι τε καὶ τὴν ψυχὴν

αὐτοῦ, a reminiscence of the Q verse Matthew 10:39 (= Luke 17:33!) that was "moved" from this location.[7] In *v. 38* "follow" instead of "come" and the final phrase with "worthy" is more likely Matthean, βαστάζει and ἑαυτοῦ more likely Lukan.[8] In *v. 39* the formally striking addition "for my sake" (cf. Mark 8:35/Matt 16:25) is almost certainly Matthean, while decisions are difficult with the remaining special features.[9]

3. The evangelist Matthew is responsible for the *placement* of the two groups of sayings; in this part of the disciples discourse, he does his composing quite independently.[10]

Tradition History and Origin

It is uncertain whether *vv. 34-36* is a unitary logion or whether an old logion, v. 34, was later explained by the apocalyptic Old Testament saying about family dissension, vv. 35-36.[11] I am inclined to argue for the unity of the saying, because the puzzling word about "bringing the sword" needs an explanation, and that is given in vv. 35-36. If this is correct, then the popular claim is no longer possible that v. 34 could come from Jesus, while vv. 35-36 are the church's expansion.[12] Of course, it is possible that the church, which in Mark 13:12 also used Mic 7:6 to interpret its own situation, has created the saying. However, since Mic 7:6 already played a role in Judaism in the description

Introduction 3.1. On the repetition of key words, cf. vol. 1, Introduction 1D.

3 Schulz (*Q*, 258) regards Luke v. 52 as redactional, Polag (*Fragmenta*, 64) its omission by Matthew.

4 Wanke (*Kommentarworte*, 79–81) regards v. 39 as an old commentary word that in the parenesis clarified the demand of discipleship.

5 Cf. below the reminiscence in Luke 14:26 and Laufen, *Doppelüberlieferungen*, 315–21.

6 On ἄξιος in the final position cf. vol. 1, Introduction 3.2, on the parallelism, vol. 1, Introduction 3.1. Φιλέω is no more Matthean redaction than μισέω is Lukan redaction. However, ὑπὲρ ἐμέ connects v. 37 with v. 24.

7 On ἔρχομαι πρός . . . cf. Luke 6:47; 7:7; on ἔτι τε καί, Acts 21:28. Ἑαυτοῦ is Lukan. On the list of family members we must ask: Did Matthew with omissions improve the parallelism, or did Luke expand the list? On behalf of the latter view it should be noted that in Luke 18:29 the wives but not the husbands are mentioned. Does the Lukan redaction advocate a "male" perspective (Elisabeth Schüssler-Fiorenza, *In Memory of Her* [New York: Crossroad, 1983] 145–46)?

8 On ἀκολουθέω cf. vol. 1, Introduction 3.2. The striking ὀπίσω recalls the Semitizing Q formulation

ἔρχομαι ὀπίσω. On ἄξιος (Matthew) / μαθητής (Luke): Unnecessary and complicated is the assumption of a translation variant from the Aramaic that works with the unusual East Aramaic word שׁוּלְיָא = apprentice (instead of תַּלְמִיד) and the quite different שָׁוֵי = of equal value (T. W. Manson, *The Teaching of Jesus* [Cambridge: Cambridge University Press, 1963] 237–41).

9 Ζητέω, περιποιέομαι, and ζωογονέω may be Lukan, but εὑρίσκω (cf. vol. 1 Introduction 3.2 and 16:25b) might also be Matthean.

10 Luke 12:2-9 (Q) and Luke 12:11-12 (Q) were used previously by Matthew (10:26-33, 17-19). He used Luke 12:22-34 (Q) already in the Sermon on the Mount. Luke 12:39-46 (Q) was obviously already being held for the eschatological discourse. Luke 12:49-50 (Q?) did not fit in the disciples discourse at all. Thus for the "excerpting" Matthew, Luke 12:51-53 Q was the next piece.

11 Thus, e.g., Sato, "Q," 295, Gnilka 1.394.

12 Arens (*ΗΛΘΟΝ-Sayings*, 84–86) believes that v. 34b may have come from Jesus. Structurally the saying then would correspond to Mark 2:27b. Franz Mussner ("Wege zum Selbstbewusstsein Jesu," *BZ*

of the end-time,[13] and since Jesus caused dissension at least in his own family (Mark 3:31-35), it may also be a saying of Jesus.[14] *Non liquet:* Both possibilities are to be considered in the interpretation.

With *vv. 37-39* it is at least not disputed that we have here three independent individual sayings. While vv. 37 and 39 are usually attributed to Jesus, the question is quite controversial in the case of v. 38. Here also the problems are to be considered in connection with the interpretation.

Interpretation

■ **34-36** The sword saying is difficult. Its content is "dangerous and almost unbearable"[15] and seems "more appropriate to the Qur'an than to the Gospels."[16] It does not fit well with the greeting of peace that the disciples are to bring into the houses (10:13) and with the image of the disciples as peacemakers (5:9, cf. Mark 9:50). It is more appropriate for the Christ of the Apocalypse who carries the sword in his mouth (Rev 1:16; 2:12, 16; 19:15, 21). Is Jesus caught in a contradiction here, because he himself could not "carry out his extreme ethical teaching"[17]?

History of Interpretation

■ **34-36** The history of interpretation shows two tendencies. According to some (not ecclesiastical-orthodox) interpreters, we have here traces of an originally by no means peaceful revolutionary Jesus.

According to Reimarus, the disciples understood Jesus to be the one who would "redeem the people of Israel from temporal servitude" and only after his death "changed their previous doctrine of his teaching and deeds."[18] Here begins the unceasing chain of attempts to understand Jesus as a political revolutionary. More recent representatives are, for example, K. Kautsky, R. Eisler, or S. G. F. Brandon.[19] E. Bloch sees the belligerent side of Jesus quite differently. For him the content of the great advent is love and the kingdom of peace, but

where the background is not so much that of the realized Kingdom as that of the divisions and decisions of the last days of separation and crisis, Jesus' preaching is far tougher than that of all his prophetic predecessors, with their *Olam-ha-shalom.* There is not much talk then of loving one's enemies; the scene is rather one of unexpected spiritual warfare,[20]

and Jesus finally was correctly understood and executed as an insurgent. According to Bloch, the difference between Jesus and Bar Kochba is not that Jesus was politically more harmless, but rather that he presented himself not as a fighter for a restoration of the Davidic kingdom but as "the new eschatological Exodus, overthrowing all things from their beginning to their end: the *Exodus into God as man.*"[21]

By comparison, the theological interpretation of our text sounds much more harmless.

The inner *peace* of Christ is contrasted with the world's external peace. It is only the latter that Jesus rejects in order to lead to the true peace of the heart. Brenz's formulation is a classic example. First one has to understand the peace of the kingdom of Christ

in contrast to earthly kingdoms. . . . Second: What is said concerning the peace of the kingdom of Christ is to be understood of the peace of one's conscience, of the pacification that through Christ was created between God and the human race. Whoever recognizes this pacification can lack

---

NF 12 [1968] 166) attributes v. 34 to Jesus, because the church would not have formed a word so capable of being misunderstood politically. The argument is not compelling. Only if one separates v. 34 from vv. 35-36 and understands μάχαιρα as sword, does the saying become political.

13 *M. Sota* 9.15 = Str-B 1.586.

14 The claim that Jesus never cited Old Testament texts (an actual quotation doesn't even exist) is a *petitio principii.*

15 Brenz, 438.

16 Matthew Black, "Uncomfortable Words III," 115.

17 Joseph Klausner, *Jesus of Nazareth* (New York: Macmillan, 1953) 395.

18 Reimarus, 128–29.

19 Karl Kautsky, *Foundations of Christianity* (New York: Monthly Review Press, 1972) 365; Robert Eisler, *ΙΗΣΟΥΣ ΒΑΣΙΛΕΥΣ ΟΥ ΒΑΣΙΛΕΥΣΑΣ* (Heidelberg: Winter, 1930) 2.254-71; S. G. F. Brandon, *Jesus and the Zealots* (New York: Scribner's, 1967) 321.

20 Ernst Bloch, *Atheism in Christianity* (New York: Herder and Herder, 1972) 136.

21 Ibid., 137.

nothing and has peace even in the midst of wars and in the temptations of this world.[22]

Thus true peace is the peace among the children of peace, that is, in the church.[23] Not infrequently this brings about a devaluing of secular-political peace.[24] The saying was used to demarcate the church against the *world*. One may not make friends with the enemies of God.[25] In the allegorical interpretation a widespread explanation is that the "mother" and the "mother-in-law" of v. 35 refer to the synagogue.[26] Since the Reformation the distinction between "passive" and "active" sword has became important. The former is meant in our text,[27] that is, "not a sword that the disciples are to use, but the sword that is drawn and used against them."[28] The saying is then almost always understood to express result and not purpose. Christ came not *in order* to bring the sword, but the coming of Christ resulted in dissensions and struggles. They are caused by the world's evil.[29] The saying was then used to justify the spiritual battle against *heretics*.[30] In questions of doctrine one may make no concessions for the sake of external peace.[31] Following Heb 4:12 and Eph 6:17, the sword that Jesus brings is frequently interpreted to be the sword of the word of God or of the spirit.[32] Then there is no longer any reason not to interpret the saying in terms of a person's internal spiritual battle. Jesus has brought to earth, for example, the battle between flesh and spirit.[33] The Gnostics interpret it as the battle between the person's kernel of pneuma and matter.[34] In more modern thinking it is the "inner struggle for truth."[35]

Interpretation

■ **34** We turn now to the interpretation of the text, after which we will try to take a position on the various possible meanings raised in the history of interpretation. Verse 34 formulates an antithesis. It is directed presumably against the expectation of a messianic prince of peace that was widespread in contemporary Judaism.[36] While "to cast peace" is a Semitic term,[37] using "I cast" with "sword" is linguistically quite unusual.

■ **35-36** The unusual formulation and the unusual statement demand an explanation that is given in v. 35 with language from Mic 7:6. Jesus uses the "short sword" or "saber"[38] to "sever" the families.[39] In contrast to Rev 6:4, the explanation of "sword" does not suggest war. "Peace" ($\epsilon\iota\rho\eta\nu\eta$ = שָׁלוֹם) is more than the opposite of "war." The split in the families is carried out drastically, in extreme formulations.[40] The three appearances of "against" and the location of "hostile" early in the sentence intensify the enmity that the mission of Jesus creates in families.

22 Brenz, 438–39. Similarly, e.g., Faber Stapulensis, 47 (101: *pax coelestis . . . in corda fidelium*); Dickson, 136.

23 In *Ps.-Clem. Rec.* 2.26–31 the contradiction between Matt 5:9 and 10:34 is discussed: Matt 5:9 refers to the believers, Matt 10:34 to the unbelievers who reject the doctrine. Pseudo-Chrysostom, *Diatribe ad opus Imperfectum in Matthaeum* (PL 56.601–946) 26 = 767: *pax bona . . . inter fideles . . . pax mala . . . inter infideles*.

24 Bullinger (106A) claims that even "bloodthirsty soldiers, ambitious people, vicious people," etc. accept secular peace. Salmeron (9.54 = 9.425 [1]) says that secular peace is *infida, inconstans atque perniciosa*.

25 Cyril of Alexandria fr. 126 = Reuss, 193.

26 Bede, 55; Anselm of Laon, 1347B; Paschasius Radbertus, 432; Dionysius bar Salibi, 297 = 2.220.

27 Luther, *WA* 38.509.

28 Barth, *CD* 4/3.625.

29 Luther, *WA* 38.509; Calvin 1.310 following John Chrysostom 35.1 = *PG* 57.406.

30 See, e.g., Cyril of Alexandria against Nestorius: third letter to Nestorius = FC 76.80.

31 Musculus, 317.

32 See, e.g., Origen fr. 214 = GCS Origenes 12.102; Tertullian *Marc.* 3.14.4–5; Hilary, 10.23 = SC 254.242 (preaching the gospel); Augustine *Quaest.*

App. 3 = 120.

33 Origen fr. 214 = GCS Origenes 12.102. Cf. Erasmus, *Paraphrasis* 63F: the sword cuts the lusts out of the heart.

34 *Pistis Sophia* 116.

35 Ewald, 250.

36 Isa 9:5-6; 11:5-10; Mal 3:23-24 (the coming Elijah will bring together the families); *2 Bar.* 73.

37 Str–B 1.586.

38 Μάχαιρα is the large knife (LSJ, *s.v.* 1), as a weapon the saber or the short sword, in distinction from the large broad sword (= ῥομφαία). Ξίφος (seldom in the LXX, never in the NT), the most general term. All three words can be used generally for "sword." The figurative use of μάχαιρα is very rare in the LXX (Wilhelm Michaelis, "μάχαιρα," *TDNT* 4 [1967] 525), later somewhat more frequent (e.g., in the NT: Rom 8:35; Eph 6:17; cf. BAGD, *s.v.* μάχαιρα, 2).

39 As the context vv. 35-36 shows, both expressions are to be understood metaphorically here. Διχάζω and μάχαιρα go together just as the general διαμερίζω and διαμερισμός do in Luke 12:52-53.

40 Cf. Tannehill, *Sword*, 142.

41 *Jub.* 23.16, 19-20; *1 Enoch* 100.2; *4 Ezra* 6.24; *m. Sota*

Behind the language are not only traditions but, as v. 37 shows, experiences of the church that, as, for example, 8:21-22 shows, Jesus and his message caused. In comparison with the tradition, the saying creates a feeling of estrangement. It is even greater because one may relate the dissension in the families to the Jewish topos of the struggle of families and friends in the eschaton. One expected such divisions in Judaism for the time *before* the coming of the Messiah and understood them as an expression of the last triumph of sin and evil.[41] In our saying they are connected with the coming of Christ. It is precisely the mission of Christ that will bring the horrors of the eschaton.

It is easiest to interpret this saying in the context of the *church*. In the background then are the experiences of divisions in the family intimated also in Mark 13:12 and caused by the proclamation of Jesus. With the aid of Mic 7:6 they are understood as predicted events of the eschaton. As there, but differently from Luke 12:52-53, the issue is the alienation of the younger generation from the older ones; presumably the believing sons and daughters struggled with their parents. However, in contrast to Mic 7:6, all negative tones are missing. The disobedience of the children is not bemoaned or condemned. Instead, it is caused by the coming of Jesus[42] and corresponds then to God's will.[43]

Matt 10:34-36 can also be understood as a *saying of Jesus*. Then it is to be seen together on the one hand with the saying about fire in Luke 12:49 and on the other with the saying about the hatred of the followers toward their family members in Luke 14:26. The harsh saying about the members of the household who will be separated in the eschaton (Luke 17:34-35)—a saying that has no parallel—indirectly belongs here as well. Jesus speaks in these sayings about judgment and the break with the world signified by the coming of the kingdom of God and thus his mission as well. He himself has made the break with his family (Mark 3:31-35) and demands it also of his followers. God's kingdom means not only that radical love

breaks out; it means at the same time a break with the world whose expression among the followers is the renunciation of possessions, vocation, and family. It is not a narrow political interpretation of this saying, describing Jesus as a revolutionary, that is in keeping with the basic structure of the proclamation of Jesus, but probably an eschatological interpretation somewhat along the lines of Bloch's understanding that makes him part of the dawning of the radically different kingdom of God.[44]

For *Matthew* the christological aspect is initially important. "I came" three times emphasizes that the disciples' suffering is a direct part of the sending of Jesus. With a common catchword ("members of one's household") v. 36 is connected to the christological introit of vv. 24-25. According to Matthew the church lives in the eschaton of which the divisions in the families are a part.[45] In their content vv. 34-36 heighten the tension of vv. 26-31, since here the "enemies" are one's closest family members. It will become clear, not on the basis of the word "sword" that is used metaphorically here but on the basis of vv. 38-39, that the persecution of the church is a matter of life and death. At the same time v. 36 indirectly contains a positive statement. The disciples know that they are "members of the household" of Jesus (v. 25!).

Summary

■ **34-36** From our interpretation and the history of the text's interpretation we can say on the one hand *negatively* that our saying does not reveal a revolutionary Jesus. Jesus did not come to bring to the earth a political rebellion against Rome. The immediate context, vv. 35-36, makes this interpretation impossible. On the other hand, Jesus did not come simply to bring about an inner struggle in people. What is at issue here is an actual altercation, not only among people generally but reaching into the closest circle of the family—something that with the

9.15; *b. Sanh.* 97a (Str–B 1.586). Cf. additional texts at Matt 10:16-23, n. 48.

42   Ἦλθον with infinitive has here (as in Mark 1:24, 2:17, 10:45, Luke 12:43, 19:10, Matt 5:17) the meaning of purpose and not of result.

43   Thus the logion has nothing to do with the political question of war and peace. It seems to me that Klaus Wengst (*Pax Romana and the Peace of Jesus Christ* [Philadelphia: Fortress, 1987] 62) is wrong. He believes that Matt 10:34 speaks against a domes-

tication of Jesus' activity by the anti-Zealot peace party.

44   To be sure, it is probably not the case that the concept of "holy war" is behind the topos of the division of families, as Otto Betz assumed ("Jesu Heiliger Krieg," *NovT* 2 [1958] 116–37, 129–30).

45   Cf. vol. 1, II A 3.2 on 7:15-23 (on Matthew's view that the false prophets are a sign of the eschaton) and vol. 3 on 24:10-12.

close family and clan ties in the Near East was no small matter! We must look *positively* for the meaning of the saying between these two impossible possibilities. The coming of Jesus and his message of the kingdom of God are at odds with familial and societal ties. It is the disciples' greeting of *peace* that causes the split (cf. vv. 12-14). And it is the rejection of the greeting of peace that seals the split with unheard-of sharpness (cf. v. 15). As a result of this division the disciples are to suffer (cf. vv. 17-23; vv. 38-39 after v. 37). To this degree the line of interpretation formulated by the Reformation approaches the sense of the text. Passive acceptance is the only possible response to the violence that results from the divisions caused by the gospel—the text speaks of no other violence. *Indirectly* our saying also has political significance. The message of ultimate peace, of the reversal of secular rule, and of the love of God for the underprivileged has a political dimension and evokes the resistance of all those who defend power and privileges. For them, the disciples whose life corresponds to this message and who abandon the structures of the world are not pleasant figures.

The history of interpretation also points indirectly to the place where we might find the meaning of our saying for today. The word was at least also internalized; discovering its true or false political dimensions became the concern of people outside exegesis. As a rule, in today's Western society Christianity is no longer the basis for divisions in the family but, from a social perspective, the common basis of sons and fathers, daughters and mothers, families, national churches and states—or at least the common basis *desired* by mothers and fathers. The divisions are primarily something one *talks* about. This breach between the gospel's original effect and Christianity's thoroughgoing self-evidence in today's society is, in my judgment, our saying's true *scandalon*.

Interpretation

■ **37** Verse 37 helps us recognize where the evangelist

Matthew stands on the long road from an original radical eschatology to Christianity as a fermenting agent in today's Western society. The comparative element is characteristic for his version of the saying about hating one's own family. Matthew basically affirms familial love (15:3-6; 19:19), but a conflict may arise between discipleship to Christ and loyalty to one's family. When that happens, one must love Christ *more*. Basically that has the same practical meaning that we also find in Epictetus: "One must value the good higher than any kinship."[46] It corresponds to the Matthean *way* to perfection (5:20, 48). On the other hand, the final clause, "is not worthy of me," is not formulated comparatively. As the use of "worthy" in 10:11-13; 22:8 and the context (vv. 32-33, 40-42) make clear, Matthew is thinking in the framework of the last judgment that will also include the disciples and that will end only in a yes or in a no.

The original saying of Jesus was formulated in a more radical, viz., in an antithetical, way. It was a condition for becoming a disciple: "Whoever does not hate father and mother . . . cannot be my disciple." For our understanding of the word, the obvious statement that it does not mean hatred in the sense of a psychic emotion[47] is of less importance than the statement that Jesus pronounced the disciple's rejection of the family with the strongest possible word, "hate," and its condition in the most basic form possible.[48] Discipleship as a special ministry in the proclamation of the kingdom of God and attachments to one's family obviously were irreconcilable for him (cf. Luke 9:60; Mark 1:20).

History of Interpretation

■ **37** The history of interpretation has essentially continued along the lines laid out by Matthew. There is an *ordo* of love: God, father, mother, children. Only in the case of *necessitas* should the commandment to love one's parents be transgressed.[49] The first table of the Ten Commandments basically takes precedence

46 Epictetus *Diss.* 3.3.6. This also agrees with Jewish practice. Cf. Josephus *Ant.* 11.145–47 (in Ezra's day those living in mixed marriages divorce their wives for the sake of the law); *Bell.* 2.134 (the Essenes are allowed to support their relatives only with the consent of the supervisors); *b. Yeb.* 5b *Bar.* = Str–B 1.587 (keeping the sabbath holy as a duty toward

God takes precedence over honoring the parents).
47 Otto Michel, "μισέω," *TDNT* 4 (1967) 690.
48 One can compare statements about the holiness of Levi: Deut 33:9; 4QTestim 15–17 (Levi no longer knows his family); and Exod 32:27, 29 (killing family members who worship the golden calf).
49 Jerome, 74.

over the second, at the beginning of which is the command to love one's parents.[50] The fourth commandment can be diminished only if the parents keep us from doing God's will.[51] That is, in any case, not what normally happens in discipleship, but an "ethical borderline case" that may not be generalized. It is something done by "prophetic people" who have "special . . . tasks." The practice of loving less consists then not of hate and controversy, but perhaps also of a "distancing . . . in all peace and even in mutual understanding."[52] Luther warns against making this Jesus saying a pretext for living out one's adolescent rebellion.[53]

In my judgment, all of this follows the lines laid down by Matthew. The accents are shifted only where the command to honor one's parents, the second most important of the commandments, is emphasized above everything else.[54] In the Lutheran tradition the context of the two kingdoms doctrine later becomes important. The command to honor one's parents is part of the "bourgeoisie life." The Christian obeys it in all cases and is "emancipated" from it only inwardly.[55] We find the main points of an ethic of intention already in Calvin, who argues against monasticism's special way and thus puts the entire weight on the *willingness* to obey God more. "Thus, true abnegation, which the Lord asks of His people, is sited not so much in deed (*in actu*, as they say), but in intention (*in affectione*)."[56]

The original radicality of Jesus' command is preserved most clearly in the sign-like radical lifestyle of monasticism. Leaving the family is characteristic of the perfect way; remaining with one's parents is the sign of the "secondary way."[57] Parents, brothers, relatives, possessions, one's own life are, according to Macarius, part of what goes on in the world; the "lonely life" must be related solely to the love of Christ.[58]

The Gospel of Matthew stands between the basic demand to make a break with the world and the simple internal willingness to do so. It does not merely abandon the "old" commandment to honor one's parents. If in the antitheses the Old Testament commandments of the Decalogue were intensified and thus at the same time changed and preserved, here the fourth commandment is superseded and in cases of conflict thus relativized. Thereby Matthew, without explicitly saying it in the text, raises principally the possibility of deciding conflicts on the basis of love.

■ **38-39** Verses 38-39 once again shift the focus. They speak no longer of the relationship of the disciples to other people but of the consequences this has, including the break with one's own family, for one's own life.

Original Meaning

■ **38** The question of the *original meaning of the saying about carrying the cross* is a matter of great controversy.[59] It is intertwined with the question of whether it is a saying of Jesus. The following possibilities of interpretation compete with one another:

1. The expression "to take the cross" is connected directly to the Roman custom that condemned persons have to carry their cross themselves to the place of execution. In this case the saying refers to the execution facing the followers and means literally that all followers have to go to their own execution. The willingness to die is thus made the condition of discipleship.[60] This interpretation has the following two difficulties.

a. The sequence "to take the cross—to follow me" seems illogical, since execution is the consequence of following. This difficulty disappears when one consid-

50 Luther, *WA* 38.511: "*Prima tabula est supra secundam . . . Deus supra creaturas*."

51 Cyril of Jerusalem *Cat.* 7.15 = FC 61.178; Thomas Aquinas *S. th.* 2/2, q.26, a.7 ad 1.

52 Barth, *CD* 3/4.262, 264, 265.

53 Luther, *WA* 38.511.

54 Musculus, 319–20: After Christ there immediately follows the command about the parents. If we want to love Christ in a special way above the members of the family, *necesse erit, ut eos diligamus*.

55 Zinzendorf 2.757.

56 Calvin 1.315. On the rootedness of the ethics of intention in the theology of the Reformation, cf. vol. 1, II A (concluding the History of Interpretation section).

57 *Liber Graduum* 19.9 = 467.

58 Macarius *Hom.* 45.1 = George A Malony, ed. and trans., *Pseudo-Macarius: The Fifty Spiritual Homilies and the Great Letter* (New York: Paulist, 1992) 226–27.

59 For a good survey of the possible interpretations see Johannes Schneider, 577–79, and Fong, *Crucem*, 14–25.

60 Thus, e.g., Schürmann, *Lukasevangelium*, 1.542–43; cf. Gnilka, 1.398; J. Gwyn Griffiths, "The Disciple's Cross," *NTS* 16 (1969/70) 358–64 (Jesus as a nonviolent opponent of Rome).

ers that the condemned takes up ($\lambda\alpha\mu\beta\acute{\alpha}\nu\epsilon\iota$) the cross at the beginning of the road to execution.[61] All of discipleship is then understood as the way to execution. Such an understanding is made easier by the fact that in antiquity the walk of the condemned to the place of crucifixion often received a great deal of attention.[62]

b. Can we assume that Jesus or the church really reckoned with the special form of execution reserved for political criminals, that is, with the "death of a Zealot"?[63] That is quite conceivable, for execution by crucifixion was by far the most widespread form of the "intensified death penalty," since other forms, as, for example, the sentence *ad bestias,* were not always an option.[64] It was not limited to political crimes.[65]

2. The expression "to take the cross" is to be understood figuratively in the sense of "to suffer, to have pain." If the saying should go back to Jesus, the coincidence with his own death by crucifixion would initially be accidental.[66] This interpretation is quite difficult. There are indeed a few scattered references for the metaphorical use of "cross" in Latin,[67] but not in Greek or in Semitic languages. Without an indication to that effect in the context, no one would have understood the meaning of such a metaphor. Furthermore, the unique illustration of "taking" the cross would not be explained.

3. The cross is understood in the sense of Ezek 9:4-6[68] as *taw,* that is, as a sign for Yahweh. To "take the cross" is then an act of sealing.[69] In support of this view is the fact that early Christian baptism also was understood as a sealing[70] and that Clement of Alexandria seems to interpret our passage to refer to baptism.[71] However, there are no other witnesses for the claim that Jesus had "tattooed" his disciples. After Easter the formulation with $\sigma\tau\alpha\nu\rho\acute{o}\varsigma$ (not, for exam-

---

61 Jeremias, *Theology,* 242, following Anton Fridrichsen, "Ordet om a baere sit kors," in *Gamle Spor og Nye Veier Tydninger og Tegninger* (Festschrift Lyder Brun; Kristiania, 1922) 17–34. Luke is the first to speak of *carrying* the cross, which is the language of all non-Christian parallels and which corresponds to the suffering of the Christian (Luke 9:23: $\kappa\alpha\vartheta'$ $\dot{\eta}\mu\acute{\epsilon}\rho\alpha\nu$). Q and Matthew speak, uniquely in comparison with the parallels, of *taking up* the cross (cf. Mark 8:34: $\alpha\check{\iota}\rho\omega$).

62 The rabbis compare the way of Isaac, who, according to Gen 22:6, carries the wood for the sacrifice, with the way of a person to be crucified (*Gen. Rab.* 56 [36c]; *Pesiq. R.* 31 [143b] in Str–B 1.587). Artemidorus *Oneirocr.* 2.56 ($\sigma\tau\alpha\nu\rho\acute{o}\nu$ . . . $\beta\alpha\sigma\tau\acute{\alpha}$-$\zeta\epsilon\iota\nu$); Plutarch *Ser. num. vind.* 9 = 2.554B ($\check{\epsilon}\kappa\alpha\sigma\tau\sigma\varsigma$ . . . $\dot{\epsilon}\kappa\varphi\acute{\epsilon}\rho\epsilon\iota$ $\tau\grave{o}\nu$ $\dot{\epsilon}\alpha\nu\tau\sigma\hat{\nu}$ $\sigma\tau\alpha\nu\rho\acute{o}\nu$); Cicero *Divin.* 1.26 (*furcam ferens*) speak in the literal sense of the way to execution.

63 Hengel (*Zealots,* 260, n. 151) thinks that Jesus has taken over a Zealot formula from general linguistic usage. There is, however, no evidence for such a formula.

64 Theodor Mommsen, *Römisches Strafrecht* (Leipzig: Duncker & Humblot, 1899), especially 917–24: crucifixion, drowning, burning, leading *ad bestias* are among the forms of intensified capital punishment (*summa supplicia*) in contrast to the "simple" execution by the sword. For practical reasons the other forms of intensified capital punishment could not be applied in general and were reduced in favor of execution by crucifixion.

65 In the *Sentenciae* of Paulus the grounds for crucifixion are, among others: murder, magic of the worst kind, serious perjury, desecration of graves, prophecy *de salute dominorum,* kidnapping (Martin

Hengel, "Mors turpissima crucis," in Johannes Friedrich, Wolfgang Pöhlmann and Peter Stuhlmacher, eds., *Rechtfertigung: Festschrift für Ernst Käsemann zum 70. Geburtstag* [Tübingen: Mohr/Siebeck, 1976] 146; cf. also the list in Mommsen, *Strafrecht,* 1045). According to Hengel (*Zealots,* 32–33), crucifixion is more a class-related punishment for *peregrini* and *humiliores* than a punishment for political crimes.

66 As a saying of Jesus, e.g., Sand, *Evangelium,* 231 ("willingness to follow into suffering [not into martyrdom]"); Josef Ernst, *Anfänge der Christologie* (SBS 57; Stuttgart: Katholisches Bibelwerk, 1972) 140 ("in general . . . self-denial"; cf. the version of Mark 8:34!).

67 The references in Hengel ("Mors turpissima crucis," 165–66) are of little use. The comparisons are not relevant (Philo *Poster. C.* 61; *Som.* 2.213; cf. Plato *Phaedr.* 83cd: the soul is fastened by lust as with a nail to the body). There remain some rhetorical metaphors (Seneca *Vita* 19.3 [*cruces = cupiditates*]; Cicero *Fin.* 5.84 [*crux = dolor*]) and poetic (Catullus *Carm.* 99.4 for the suffering of love). The remaining references Hengel lists all refer to literal crosses used in execution. Result: The figurative meaning of cross as suffering that is self-evident to the advocates of this interpretation is by no means self-evident, even on the basis of the few Latin parallels.

68 Cf. *Ps. Sol.* 15.6–9; Rev 7:2-8; 14:9-12.

69 Dinkler, "Jesu Wort."

70 2 Cor 1:22. Cf. Rom 4:11; *Hermas, Sim.* 9.16.3–4.

71 *Strom.* 7.79.5 = ANF 2.546: $\dot{\epsilon}\grave{\alpha}\nu$ $\mu\grave{\eta}$ $\tau\grave{o}$ $\sigma\eta\mu\epsilon\hat{\iota}o\nu$ $\beta\alpha\sigma\tau\acute{\alpha}\sigma\eta\tau\epsilon$. Cf. Erich Dinkler, "Kreuzzeichen und Kreuz," in idem, *Signum Crucis* (Tübingen: Mohr/Siebeck, 1967) 43–44. Admittedly, Clement often uses $\sigma\eta\mu\epsilon\hat{\iota}o\nu$ to mean cross without referring to

ple, σφραγίς or σημεῖον) would make it more natural to think of the cross of Jesus. It also is difficult that the Jewish references for the *taw* sign come almost exclusively from ossuaries or from necropolises.[72] Thus only the custom of decorating grave sites with the Yahweh sign is well attested, while there is no direct evidence for a Jewish rite of sealing with the *taw* sign.[73]

To conclude, in my judgment the second interpretation fails because of the impossibility of interpreting "to take the cross" generally as "to suffer"; the third fails because of its too-narrow historical basis. The first interpretation is by far the most probable. Entering the way of the cross is a matter of being ready for martyrdom as a condition of discipleship.

Does the logion go back to Jesus? The external evidence could speak in favor of it. The saying is attested in Q, in Mark, and in John (12:26). Furthermore, on the basis of this saying one can understand the Pauline "existential" meaning of the cross (cf., for example, Gal 6:14). However, those are not yet the decisive factors. If the logion goes back to Jesus, one has to assume that he clearly reckoned with his own violent death. Given today's understanding, this is conceivable, especially just before his passion. In addition, he also would have had to expect a similar fate for his disciples. This also cannot simply be excluded, for example, in view of Luke 12:8-9 and Matt 10:39.[74] Assuming that the church formulated the logion also involves difficulties. Right after the violent *death* of Jesus, "cross" cannot have been a general metaphor for suffering. In his own way Mark shows this by reformulating the logion so that it may be interpreted in this manner (Mark 8:34). However, speaking of the willingness to die as a condition of discipleship was of little topical interest, since it was clear that the martyrdom of the disciples was more likely the exception rather than the rule.[75] Furthermore, if it were a formulation of the church we would more likely expect a christological formulation that would have spoken of taking up the cross *of Jesus*. Result: Difficulties remain with any view, but they seem to be least in assuming that it is a saying of Jesus.

The *church* combined our logion with that about

the surrender of one's life (Matt 10:39/Mark 8:35). That also supports the idea that it was understood at first in the literal sense of death. Thus in the early period for some time death by execution was understood as the end point of the way of the cross. Ignatius still attests to this.[76] A new understanding of the logion is for the first time probable for Mark. His formulation is no longer conditional, but parenetic, and he puts self-denial first. The context of his gospel, that is, his concept of the discipleship of suffering in Mark 8:27-10:52 (but not yet the semantic meaning of the expression αἴρω τὸν σταυρὸν αὐτοῦ!), makes it clear that he understands carrying one's cross to mean the discipleship of suffering.

Matthew presupposes the Markan understanding of the discipleship of suffering. That the disciples discourse, beginning as early as v. 16, has suffering for Jesus' sake as its theme shows how important this is for him. Suffering is the necessary consequence of the proclamation and the necessary form of discipleship. Therefore, Matthew is thinking here not so much of the actual experiences of his church but of Christ. Suffering and persecution are the master's lifestyle (vv. 24-25). It is demonstrated in persecutions, trials, family strife, and, finally, in martyrdom. Since it is the freely chosen lifestyle of Jesus, "taking" the cross is not simply accepting everything that happens, but an active lifestyle of suffering that the disciples have to demonstrate for the coming judgment. There they will show themselves to be "worthy" of Jesus.

■ **39** Verse 39 carries the thought further and lets the charge to the disciples conclude with a promise. Those who lose their life will find it. What is meant here by "life"? The church's interpretation somewhat unanimously distinguishes between the earthly life that one

---

baptism. Cf. *Quis div. salv.* 8.2; *Strom.* 6.87.2; *Exc. Theod.* 42.2; 43.1 = GCS 17.120.

72   Erich Dinkler ("Kreuzzeichen und Kreuz," in idem, *Signum Crucis* [Tübingen: Mohr/Siebeck, 1967]) 49–52.

73   Dinkler ("Jesu Wort," 90) only points to the anointing of the priests with the letter "X."

74   Cf. the references in the analysis of II C 2.2 (repeat-

ed here for the reader's convenience: Luke 10:10-11; Matt 10:16a, 28, 34-36, 38, 39; 11:20-23; 23:37-39]).

75   Called to my attention by Chr. Riniker, to whom I owe much in the interpretation of this verse.

76   Ignatius *Rom.* 4.2; 5.3. Fong (*Crucem,* 32) assumes the influence of Matt 10:38/Luke 14:27.

loses and the eternal life that one receives.[77] This is right to a certain extent. On the basis of the biblical usage[78] the expression ψυχὴν ἀπολλύναι means in v. 39b death, in v. 39a—as in 10:28—the loss of life in hell. The verb "to find," new in Matthew, makes clear in contrast to "to seek" (Luke 17:33) or "wanting . . . to save" (Mark 8:35) that at issue is something that one cannot procure for oneself, but only receive; it fits well with life after death in v. 39b but not well in content with v. 39a.[79] Thus Matthew is thinking of death and eternal life. At the same time, however, the logion makes clear that "life" is a single and indivisible reality.[80] Earthly and eternal life are here not designated as ψυχή in a wordplay with a term that means two completely different things.[81] Instead, "life" means a single indivisible reality that God grants humans. True "life" is not what human beings acquire for themselves, but what God will grant them precisely through *death*. The precise parallelism of the two parts of the verse intensifies the character of life as a gift of God that is promised as continuing only through its opposite. The scope of the verse is the promise for those who for Jesus' sake surrender their life (v. 39b),[82] not such things as the exhortation to a special effort, to

asceticism,[83] to courage,[84] or to preserving one's honor.[85] Thus, while v. 38 speaks of the suffering of Jesus' disciple, presumably in the sense of Mark's discipleship of suffering, v. 39 deals with its most extreme form, martyrdom, and places it under Jesus' promise without making it a condition of being a disciple. In this way v. 39 takes up something of the original radical and later mitigated meaning of the logion of taking the cross.

History of Interpretation

■ **38-39** In Matthew the two sayings do not only speak of martyrdom; they put its beginning in the life of the disciples. Martyrdom is the high point of suffering for Christ, its concentration (not its borderline case!). The history of interpretation corresponds in part to this perspective.[86] Martyrdom and other forms of suffering appear side by side.

> In the ancient church, prior to the changed situation under Constantine, the dominant interpretation of our text understood it in terms of *martyrdom*.[87] The faithful die "not in mild fevers and in beds but as martyrs when you take up your cross and follow the Lord."[88] The sword of the Lord "was brought not to

---

77 See, e.g., Origen fr. 217 = GCS Origenes 12. 03; Cyril of Alexandria fr. 128 = Reuss, 194; Euthymius Zigabenus, 345, etc.

78 Lev 7:20-21, 25, 27; 17:10; 20:6; 23:30; 1 Macc 9:2. עָבַד נֶפֶשׁ always contains the element of losing by one's own choice. Cf. Karl Georg Kuhn, *Der tannaitische Midrasch Sifre zu Numeri* (Rabbinische Texte 2/3; Stuttgart: Kohlhammer, 1959) 505.

79 Cf. Schweizer, "Ψυχή κτλ," 643. A more accurate formulation is that of Matt 16:25: ὅς . . . θέλη τὴν ψυχὴν . . . σῶσαι. The Matthean linguistic usage is perhaps inspired by the LXX; cf. Ιερ 45:2; 46:18 (ἔσται ἡ ψυχὴ αὐτοῦ εἰς εὕρεμα = he will live).

80 Gerhard Dautzenberg (*Sein Leben bewahren*, 66–67) therefore translates it as "existence"; Albright-Mann (129) as "self." Schweizer ("Ψυχή," 638) says that ψυχή contains, in contrast to ζωή, an individual note and expresses at the same time the attachment of life to the body.

81 Maldonat, 223: "similibus ambiguis vocabulis."

82 Gregory the Great (*Hom. in ev.* 32.4 = PL 76.1235 [inspired by John 12:24?]) says impressively: A farmer cannot keep grain in the barn where it will sooner or later spoil but can preserve it only by sowing it into the soil.

83 Thus the Jewish parallels *b. Tamid* 66a; *b. Ber.* 63b =

Str–B 1.587–88.

84 Thus the ancient parallels in the *cohortatio* of the general's speech (Johannes B. Bauer, "'Wer sein Leben retten will . . .' Mk 8,35 Parr.," in Josef Blinzler, Otto Kuss, and Franz Mussner, eds., *Neutestamentliche Aufsätze: Festschrift für Prof. Josef Schmid zum 70. Geburtstag* [Regensburg: Pustet, 1963] 7–10). Already John Chrysostom (55.2 = PG 57.543) uses the reference to the general as a homiletical means.

85 Plato (*Crito* 48b) has Socrates advocate the principle that it is not living that is worth striving for but living well. Epictetus (*Diss.* 4.1.165) says that Socrates could not be saved αἰσχρῶς but ἀποθνῄσκων σῴζεται.

86 On this Richard Koolmeister, "Selbstverleugnung, Kreuzaufnahme und Nachfolge: eine historische Studie über Mt 16,24," in *Charisteria I. Kopp* (Papers of the Estonian Theological Society in Exile 7; Stockholm, 1954) 64–94; Fong, *Crucem*.

87 Cf., e.g., Tertullian *Scorp.* 11 = ANF 3.644 (on v. 39); Irenaeus *Haer.* 3.18.4 (on Matt 16:24-25); John Chrysostom, 55.2 = PG 57.542 (on 16:24).

88 Tertullian *Anim.* 55.5 = CChr.SL 2.863.

heaven, but to the earth." Following this rule Tertullian interprets the entire section of vv. 34-39 in terms of martyrdom.[89] Martyrdom was the ultimate example of the cross; beyond that, however, the Christian's entire existence shall be in the shape of the cross. The demand in Mark 8:34 par. Matt 16:24 to deny oneself, but also frequently cited Pauline texts, such as Gal 2:20 or 6:14, meant that "every thought . . . every word and every deed" must be put under the sign of self-denial and of the cross.[90]

There are many witnesses for the *milder interpretation* of our saying. Cross means "not the wood," but "patience in cases of injustice and mistreatment, struggles, sweat and suffering, denial and emptying of the world."[91] Cross means any suffering: "In speaking of the cross, I am thinking not of the wood, but of suffering. Furthermore, the cross is found in Britain, in India, and in every part of the earth." This statement comes not from a modern figure, but from Jerome.[92] In Clement and Origen the carrying of the cross is combined with their view of Christian perfection.[93] Thus "every deed of the perfect person is a testimony to Christ Jesus" and everyone who abstains from sin takes up the cross.[94] Even one's own body can have the form and shape of the cross.[95] Thus there are many forms and shapes of carrying of the cross. Among them are also the special ascetic lifestyles of monasticism. The monk is "cross-bearer" ($\sigma\tau\alpha\upsilon\rho o\phi\delta\rho o\varsigma$) par excellence.[96] The saying about carrying the cross refers to the *perfecti* or to the unmarried itinerant ascetics in Syria.[97] Carrying the cross refers to the renunciation of possessions: How can I follow Christ if I am loaded down with gold?[98] The saying about losing one's life also was interpreted in terms of the renunciation of possessions.[99]

Summary

In this colorful enumeration of attempts to make concrete our saying in the church's interpretation, there were also some that clearly deviated from what Matthew

said. The question is: Which concrete interpretations does the text itself legitimate? How can we establish boundaries? We attempt here to determine more closely the *direction* and the *boundaries* of the text on the basis of Matthean theology as a whole.

1. The issue for Matthew is a conscious willingness[100] to suffer, culminating in martyrdom. While that involves an active behavior of the disciples themselves, it is *not an ascetic exercise for its own sake*. Here lies the first of the restrictions to be placed on the text's application. We come especially close to such a problematic interpretation where the cross is applied to the relationship of persons to themselves. On the basis of Matt 10:39, suffering for Christ's sake is an expression not of self-improvement, but of love.

> Gnosticism probably gives us a case of transgressing the boundaries. Here taking one's cross meant to take off the world, to leave behind the world of matter.[101] In Clement the true Gnostic by attaching little value to everything fleshly hates father and mother and in so doing carries the cross.[102] For the ascetic ideal "to carry the cross" meant to deny one's own will, the lusts, the love of life, and one's own body.[103] The *Imitatio Christi* of Thomas à Kempis understands "the way of the holy cross" and "daily dying" as a method of achieving true inner peace. "You must endure patiently if you wish to have inner peace and gain eternal life."[104] In a letter to Eustochius Jerome equates the cross with the renunciation of marriage. "For no soldier goes with a wife to battle."[105] In general, however, the history of interpretation has been able to distinguish with amazing acuteness: "One . . . tortures his flesh for empty glory. . . . He appears to carry the cross but does not follow the Lord."[106] Cocceius states it clearly: "But we must receive it from the hand of God, but not make it for ourselves."[107]

89   Tertullian *Scorp.* (above, n. 87) 10 = ANF 3.644.
90   Origen 12.24 = GCS Origenes 10.124.
91   Dionysius bar Salibi, 297 = 2.220.
92   Jerome *Tract. Ps.* 95.10 = CChr.SL 78.154.
93   Fong, *Crucem*, 43–61.
94   Origen 12.24 = GCS Origenes 10.124–25.
95   Tertullian *Idol.* 12 = ANF 3.68.
96   Basil in Fong, *Crucem*, 100. Cf., e.g., his detailed interpretation of Matt 16:24 in the *Regulae fusius* 8.1 (= Frank, *Mönchsregeln*, 105–6).
97   *Liber Graduum* 30.26 = 924; Ps.-Clement *Ad virg.* 2.5.4 = ANF 8.62.
98   Jerome *Ep.* 14.6 = NPNF Second Series 6.16.

99   Afrahat, *Homilies* 6.
100   The catchword of readiness appears frequently. See, e.g., *Opus imperfectum* 26 = 769 ("paratus . . . ad omne periculum"); Calvin 1.314.
101   Fong, *Crucem*, 36–37.
102   *Strom.* 7.59.5-7 = ANF 2.546.
103   Euthymius Zigabenus, 473 (on 16:24).
104   Thomas à Kempis *The Imitation of Christ* 2.12.3–4 [Macon, Ga.: Mercer University Press, 1989] 48–49).
105   *Ep.* 22.21 = NPNF Second Series 6.31.
106   Strabo, 120.
107   19.

2. A second boundary that on the basis of Matthew's holistic understanding of Christian faith is not to be transgressed is the *exclusive spiritualizing* of the cross that often accompanies the ascetic interpretation.

> Forfeiting one's ψυχή ("soul/life") in v. 39 has obviously opened the way for this interpretation. Hilary interprets the cross to be the *mortificatio* of the body with its sins and lusts, the loss of the ψυχή to be "despising things present."[108] Tauler speaks of laying aside all worry that is alien to God.[109] Dionysius the Carthusian interprets the cross to be the "pain of repentance, the crucifixion of vices and lusts," while "life" is the "joys of the world."[110]

3. Finally, it seems to me that understanding carrying the cross as *purely passive acceptance* of injustice and misery is difficult in view of the basic Matthean thought of active obedience to Jesus' commands.

Brenz speaks of *adversa tolerare*.[111] Thomas à Kempis is aware: "You will find that you always must experience some suffering."[112] On the other hand, J. Smolik asks whether "we Christians have not contributed to a sacralizing of the status quo through our understanding of the cross," by understanding the toleration of misery and injustice "as a Christian virtue rather than as sin."[113] By contrast in his influential hymn "'Come, follow me,' the Savior spake," Johann Scheffler already correctly placed our verses under the call to battle: "For those who bear the battle's strain/The crown of heav'nly life obtain."[114] Here it is understood that bearing the cross is for Matthew a *practice* for which the disciples must give account in the judgment, where it will be revealed whether they were "worthy."

---

108 10.26 (on Matt 10:39) = SC 254.248.
109 "Sermon on Matt 6:33," printed in Mokrosch-Walz, *Mittelalter*, 184.
110 132.
111 445.
112 Kempis, *Imitation*.
113 Josef Smolik, "Die Revolution des Kreuzes," *Communio Viatorum* 11 (1968) 233–34.

114 "'Come, follow me,' the Savior spake," *Lutheran Book of Worship* (Minneapolis: Augsburg, 1978) 455, stanza 5.

3.4 Hospitality for the Disciples (10:40-42)

Literature

Johannes Friedrich, *Gott im Bruder? Eine methodenkritische Untersuchung von Redaktion, Überlieferung und Tradition in Mt 25,31-46* (Calwer Theologische Monographien A7; Stuttgart: Calwer Verlag, 1977) 87–108.

David Hill, "Δίκαιοι as Quasi-technical Term," *NTS* 11 (1964/66) 296–302.

Simon Légasse, *Jésus et l'enfant* (EtB; Paris: Gabalda, 1969) 76–85.

Michel, "μικρός."

Schulz, *Q,* 457–59.

Marciano Vidal, "La 'Recompensa' como motivación del comportamiento moral cristiano," *Salmanticensis* 19 (1972) 261–78.

For *additional literature* on the disciples discourse see above, II C.

40   Whoever receives you receives me
     And whoever receives me, receives the one who sent me.
41   Whoever receives a prophet because it is a prophet
         will receive a prophet's reward.
     And whoever receives a righteous person because it is a righteous person
         will receive a righteous person's reward.
42   And whoever gives one of these little ones even only a cup of cool water to drink because it is a disciple,
     Amen, I say to you:
         He will not lose his reward.

Analysis   **Structure**

The careful structuring of the preceding section is continued. Four participial sentences (vv. 40-41) are followed by a general relative sentence that is emphasized and that serves as a conclusion (v. 42). The length of the sentences increases; v. 42 clearly has, as the longest sentence and because of the "Amen, I say to you," a concluding position. From vv. 37-39 the first-person pronoun is taken over (three times in v. 40), from vv. 38-39 λαμβάνω (two times in v. 41) and

ἀπόλλυμι (v. 42). The lead word in vv. 40-41 is δέχομαι (six times), in vv. 41-42 it is εἰς ὄνομα with the genitive (three times) and μισθόι (three times). Προφήτης, δίκαιος, and εἰς τῶν μικρῶν τούτων are a descending series. Δέχομαι also forms a connection with v. 14, but now the focus is no longer on the itinerant disciples but on the settled brothers.

Sources

Verse 40 has parallels in Luke 10:16, Mark 9:37 (= Matt 18:5) and John 13:20,[1] v. 42 in Mark 9:41. Verse 41 is Matthean special material. According to the two-source theory, in v. 40 Matthew has reached back to the conclusion of the sending discourse of Q (Luke 10:16) but has supplemented it with Mark 9:37-41, which he later almost completely omits. For formal reasons the Markan pericope of the strange exorcist (Mark 9:38-40) did not fit his discourse; at the same time its content was probably also disturbing for the church-minded evangelist, as a comparison of 12:30 with Mark 9:40 shows. Thus v. 40 is a new version of Luke 10:16 that Matthew, following Mark 9:37, has related to the reception of the disciples. Opinions vary on *v. 41.* I find improbable that it is Matthean redaction, although this is linguistically possible.[2] However, the designation "righteous" for a special group of Christian itinerant disciples is not Matthean. The almost technical expressions "a prophet's reward" and "a righteous person's reward" are also striking.[3] Here Matthew has taken over a Jewish-Christian logion. Also difficult is *v. 42.* Does it come from Mark 9:41, or is it an older variant of the Markan verse? Εἶς τῶν μικρῶν τούτων ("one of these little ones") could be tradition, since it also occurs in Mark 9:42 and supplements the catchword connection with Mark 9:37-50.[4] It is also uncertain whether εἰς ὄνομα μαθητοῦ ("because it is a disciple") is an old Semitism[5] or a redactional adaptation to v. 41.

---

1   Cf. also Ignatius *Eph.* 6.1; *Did.* 11.4.

2   Cf. vol. 1, Introduction 3.2, *s.v.* δίκαιος, λαμβάνω, μισθός, προφήτης. Do the logia in v. 40 (δέχομαι) and v. 42 (εἰς ὄνομα, μισθός) influence the formulation of the material? Lührmann (*Redaktion,* 111) attributes it to Q^Mt, Schweizer (164) to the church's subsequent formulation, Gundry (202) and Gnilka (1.400) to Matthean redaction (as a substitute for Mark 9:38-40).

3   While the combination of prophets and righteous persons occurs only in Matthew, in the two other texts (13:17 and 23:29) it is related to the OT

period. Did Matthew here again take over an expression from the tradition and then make use of it redactionally? Cf. also *T. Dan* 2.3 (in a longer list).

4   Cf. Schweizer, *The Good News According to Mark,* 196–97.

5   Cf. Str-B 1.590–91. The corresponding form is בְּשֵׁם not בִּמְקוֹם. The former means "instead of, on behalf of," the latter "in the tradition of" (Hans Kosmala, "In My Name," *ASTI* 5 [1966/67] 89–93). The conditional relative sentence also is (as in Mark 9:41) a Semitism, but οὐ μή with the subjunctive aorist is "vulgar Koine" (BDF § 365 [2]).

Unlike μόνον,[6] ψυχροῦ is hardly redactional. Thus there are several reasons for assuming an old, independent tradition as a source for v. 42 and not simply Mark 9:41. Also uncertain is who is responsible for the combination of the sayings. Did Matthew already find v. 41 (42) in his copy of Q in combination with v. 40? For theological reasons one would like to assume that it was he who connected v. 42 to vv. 40-41. However, there are no reasons other than theological to draw such a conclusion. Verse 42 corresponds to Matthew's understanding of the church.

Origin

If the sending of the disciples goes back to Jesus, we cannot exclude the possibility of the same for v. 40. In all probability v. 41 already presupposes post-Easter church structures. We cannot be any more certain about the origin of v. 42 than we can about its earliest meaning. I find it more probable that the verse from the very beginning spoke of the hospitality toward disciples than that it originally dealt with children.[7]

Interpretation

■ **40** The disciples discourse ends with promises of salvation. First Matthew returns to the situation of wandering that had not really been the subject since v. 16. For the itinerant disciples who are addressed, Jesus' saying is a concluding encouragement. In them Jesus himself confronts the people, and in Jesus God confronts them. The common fate shared by the disciples and their master, which has been accentuated since v. 24 in terms of suffering, is now seen from its positive side. In the background are the Jewish emissary law[8] (an emissary represents with full authority the one who commis-

sioned him) and the high regard for teachers in the rabbinic tradition.[9] For whom is this encouragement meant, in Matthew's understanding?

> The question has been debated since ancient times. Our saying was very widespread even in early Christianity. Ignatius applied it to the bishop (*Eph.* 6.1); the *Didache* to the apostles, as the itinerant preachers are generally called there (11.4, cf. 12.1); *1 Clement* to the apostles, who then appointed bishops and deacons in the cities and villages (42.1, 4). From this point it was then connected with the idea of apostolic succession.[10] Later it was applied to the papacy[11] and, by contrast, to the church as a whole.[12] In the exegesis of the Reformation our verse was applied primarily to the office of preaching.[13]

While it is true that Matthew spoke of the sending of the twelve apostles in v. 5 (cf. 11:1), the whole discourse has made clear that they are transparent of the disciples. The concluding v. 42 that interprets the "you" addressed there as "one of these little ones" confirms this. In Matthew's view every Christian participates in the church's missionary proclamation. Thus Jesus' promise applies to everyone.

■ **41-42** In vv. 41-42 Matthew offers a threefold example of this "you." In place of the presence of God, there is the eschatological promise of heavenly reward.

> ■ **41** The *pre-Matthean v. 41* is a conditional assurance of salvation[14] for the reception of prophets and righteous persons. "Prophets" is to be understood in the sense of 23:34 as itinerant prophets. More difficult is the question about who the "righteous" are. Although there are neither Jewish nor Christian direct sources for the use,[15] the reference to a special "righteous person's reward" makes it probable that they also are

---

6   On μόνον cf. vol. 1, Introduction 3.2, *s.v.*

7   Friedrich (*Gott im Bruder,* 98–100) offers good reasons against interpreting the saying to refer to hospitality toward children (= μικροί). One would have to assume the existence of widespread begging on the part of wandering children!

8   *M. Ber.* 5.5; *b. Qidd.* 41b = Str–B 1.590. Figuratively *Tanch.* 52b = Klostermann, 93 (commandments as ambassadors of God). Cf. Acts 9:4: "Why do you persecute me?"

9   *B. Ber.* 63b; *b. Ketub.* 11b; *Num. Rab.* 22 (192d); *Mek. Exod.* 18:12 (67a); *b. Sanh.* 110a (all in Str–B 1.589–90).

10   Cyprian *Ep.* 66.4 = FC 51.226 (with Luke 10:16); Vatican II Constitution on the Church, 7 = NR no. 463.

11   Council of Constantinople 869/70; canon 21 *contra Photium* = DS[36] no. 661.

12   Augustine *In Joh. ev. tract.* 89.2 = NPNF 7.358 (only those Gentiles who have not heard the proclamation of the church have an excuse for the sin of unbelief).

13   Luther *WA* 38.514: *nobis praedicantibus est gloria et consolatio*; Catechismus Genevensis no. 307 = BSKORK 34.40ff. = Torrance, *School of Faith,* 53; Confession de foy (1559) no. 25 = BSKORK 72.10ff. = Arthur C. Cochrane, ed., *Reformed Confessions of the 16th Century* (Philadelphia: Westminster, 1966) 153; Calvin, *Inst.* 4.3.3 (on Luke 10:16).

14   Klaus Berger, *Formgeschichte des Neuen Testaments* (Heidelberg: Quelle und Meyer, 1984) 167–68.

15   Individuals such as Noah, Abraham, Abel, Joseph,

a special group of pious persons,[16] perhaps wandering ascetics who were not prophets and for whom there is no further evidence in the Matthean church. Our verse thus shows the circumstances of an earlier time.[17] It gives us a glimpse into the structure of early Christian itinerant radicalism.[18] It promises a special reward for receiving a prophet or a righteous person—the reward that awaits the prophet and the righteous person in the eschaton.[19] The scope of our logion is that for the minimal service of hospitality it promises the immensely great reward that the prophets and righteous will receive in the eschaton. This interpretation is confirmed by the genre of the assurance of salvation and the future tense $\lambda\acute{\eta}\mu\psi\epsilon\tau\alpha\iota$ ("he will receive").[20] Our logion thus assumes that there are different heavenly "classes of reward," but it immediately changes the idea by promising a far greater reward than has been earned.

Verse 41 only partly corresponds to what Matthew wants to say. With the addition of v. 42, which puts the "little ones" on the level of the prophets and righteous, the latter are stripped of their special status. For Matthew "the righteous" are all Christians who are on the way to perfection (5:20, 48). Their righteousness will appear in the last judgment (13:43, 49; 25:37, 46). Nowhere else does he apply this designation to the

Christians. Nor does he elsewhere like to use the idea of a graduated reward.[21]

The question of whether there are *gradus meriti* or *dignitatis* became an important issue in the post-Reformation theological controversies. The Catholic side affirmed it; the Protestant side did not deny it,[22] but emphasized that God's reward is measured *ad . . . liberalitatem*.[23] This idea of a reward beyond what is owed, which is already in the pre-Matthean v. 41, is especially emphasized by the evangelist in the concluding v. 42.

■ **42** In v. 42 the evangelist sets a new accent. Not only the reception of prophets and righteous, but even the reception of "one of these little ones," is under the promise of heavenly reward. This traditional expression will be important to him later in his church discourse (18:6-14). In Judaism the socially weak,[24] the childish and immature,[25] and the pious[26] can be designated as "little ones." In early Christianity the term is used in Mark 9:42 to refer to ordinary, insignificant Christians.[27] Matthew, who creates a deliberate contrast to the "special" prophets and righteous, has understood the term the same way. Ordinary Christians are just as important as the prophets and righteous. We will meet a similar

---

etc. can be designated as "righteous" (Jewish sources: Gottlob Schrenk, "$\delta\acute{\iota}\kappa\alpha\iota\varsigma$," *TDNT* 2 [1964] 186; Benno Przybylski, *Righteousness in Matthew and His World of Thought* [SNTSMS 41; Cambridge: Cambridge University Press, 1980] 44-45; Christian sources: Matt 1:19; 23:35; Luke 2:25).

16 Hill, "$\Delta\acute{\iota}\kappa\alpha\iota\iota$."

17 Trilling, "Amt," 38–39. Eduard Meyer (*Ursprung und Anfänge des Christentums* [3 vols.; 1923–25; reprinted Darmstadt: Wissenschaftliche Buchgesellschaft, 1962] 1.143, n. 1) assumes the existence of a church order consisting of three levels: prophets, tested Christians, and ordinary disciples. Others, such as McNeile (150) and Gundry (203), reckon with four groups, including the apostles of v. 40. The analogy to 1 Cor 12:28 where the "teachers" would correspond to the "righteous" is immediately obvious. However, such an analysis does not take seriously the tradition-historical relationships. The text has a complicated history prior to Matthew. Whether there still was in his own community a *special* class of "righteous" remains questionable on the basis of his own usage of $\delta\acute{\iota}\kappa\alpha\iota\varsigma$.

18 The *Opus imperfectum* 26 = 770–71 is still aware of this. The prophets and righteous persons are the *propter Deum peregrinante(s)*.

19 Gregory the Great *Hom. in ev.* 20.12 = *PL* 76.1165: participation in a prophet's heavenly reward.

20 Precisely this speaks against Hill's interpretation ("$\Delta\acute{\iota}\kappa\alpha\iota\iota$," 299) according to which the text is speaking of the reward that a prophet and a righteous person gives, i.e., prophecy and instruction.

21 Marguerat, *Jugement*, 44. He is, however, familiar with it. Cf. vol. 1, II A 2.1 on 5:17-19.

22 Maldonat, 224; Bullinger, 108B (*nemo . . . pius negat . . . esse mercedem* but *non tanquam debitum . . . sed tanquam gratiam*).

23 *Confessio Helvetica posterior* 16 = BSKORK 248 = Cochrane, *Reformed Confessions of the 16th Century*, 260.

24 Michel, "$M\iota\kappa\rho\acute{\varsigma}$," 648–49; Schlatter, 353 (opposites: sons of the little ones, sons of kings).

25 For disciples of learned men see Str-B 1.592; Michel, "$\mu\iota\kappa\rho\acute{\varsigma}$," 649–50.

26 *2 Bar.* 48.19.

27 That is the point of Mark 9:42: Offending the little ones results in drastic punishment. Similarly in our logion: the "insignificant" Christian corresponds to the negligible service of love; the contrasting promise of an immensely great reward is rhetorically effective.

nonhierarchic familial understanding of the church in 18:1-14 and 23:8-12. Also important for Matthew is the idea of a reward of grace. Μόνον ("even only") is probably to be related to ποτήριον ψυχροῦ ("a cup of cold water").[28] The interpretation of the ancient church correctly emphasizes that anyone, even the poor, can fulfill this condition.[29] At issue here is not a merit that is earned but a completely disproportionate reward for a simple act of goodwill.[30] The modest gift of a cup of cold water[31] takes place εἰς ὄνομα μαθητοῦ ("because it is a disciple"). It is thus not a matter of a general praise of hospitality, not "gentile acts of kindness,"[32] but of receiving a disciple qua disciple. It is not certain who the receivers are. On the basis of vv. 11-14 one might think of non-Christian houses,[33] but non-Christians are not reading the Gospel of Matthew. Resident Christians who stay at home hear our verses speak to them. At the conclusion they are encouraged to hospitality and solidarity with the wandering ones.[34] For the wandering "little ones" the verse is a promise. They may be assured that their coming is a precious gift for those who receive them—a gift containing a heavenly reward. They are bearers of a heavenly promise and thus in spite of all their suffering may fulfill their mission with joy.

Summary

Thus at its conclusion the discourse returns to its beginning. Once again the focus is on the itinerant disciples. Once again it becomes clear that the settled Christians are connected with the task of the wandering ones. As in other discourses this discourse also ends with a reference to the judgment. However, after so much earlier talk of suffering, it is not threatening but promising.[35] Above all, however, it is made clear to those who stay at home what a blessing the wandering brothers are for them. An encounter with Christ, indeed, with God, and a heavenly reward are promised to those who stand in solidarity with them.

---

28   In the Gospel of Matthew μόνον appears after nouns (5:47; 21:19) but before verbs (three times).

29   Jerome, 76 (cold water does not even require wood for cooking); Luther, *WA* 38.516 (rhetorically one cannot make the service smaller than it is here).

30   Macarius *Ep.* 2 = BKV 1/10.387: "immeasurable philanthropy (of God)."

31   Ψυχρόν (*scil.* ὕδωρ) is the customary expression for cold water, cf. BAGD, *s.v.* 1b.

32   Luther, *WA* 38.516.

33   In this sense our text is the closest parallel to 25:31-46 and at the same time the strongest argument for interpreting the "least of the brothers" as Christian missionaries.

34   Cf. Euthymius Zigabenus, 345: Christ "opens for the disciples the houses of the faithful."

35   Weaver (*Discourse,* 123) describes vv. 40-42 as a positive counterpart to v. 15.

1   **And it happened, when Jesus had finished his commands to the twelve disciples,[1] he went from there to teach and to preach in their cities.**

Analysis   The conclusion of the discourse follows the customary scheme.[2] It consists totally of redaction.[3] Verse 1a refers back to 10:1, v. 1b to 9:35. The conclusion is a transition.[4] At the same time v. 1b sets the general scene for the following chapters.

Interpretation

The only deviation from the customary concluding scheme is διατάσσων τοῖς δώδεκα μαθηταῖς ("commands to the twelve disciples"). This discourse was thus a disciples discourse; it was not meant for the people. It is Jesus' command; its obligation is again emphasized. Verse 1b returns to Jesus' activity in "their" towns (cf. 9:35). Matthew resumes the narrative thread where he had left it in 9:35. Thus no sending report follows; the disciples will not preach until after Easter. Instead, Matthew continues to tell the story of Jesus' activity in Israel, which with increasing clarity becomes a story of tensions and divisions.

---

1   On τελέω with the participle, cf. BDF § 414 (2).
2   Cf. vol. 1, II A 3.4 on 7:28-29.
3   Cf. vol. 1, Introduction 3.2 on γίνομαι, τελέω, μαθητής, μεταβαίνω ἐκεῖθεν, διδάσκω, κηρύσσω, πόλις; on τοῦ with the infinitive cf. vol. 1, Introduction 3.1. Only the hapax legomenon διατάσσω is unique.
4   Cf. vol. 1, Introduction 1 on difficulties of determining the structure, 3.

The Basic Message of the Disciples Discourse

Our initial question was whether Matthew's disciples discourse had a fundamental ecclesiological meaning, or whether instead it contained instructions relevant only to a past epoch, viz., the time of the church's Israel mission, or whether it was intended only for one part of the church, viz., the itinerant charismatics. Our interpretation has demonstrated that the logia in vv. 5-6 (and 23) that are exclusively related to the mission to Israel served to incorporate the discourse into the narrative thread of the Gospel of Matthew. However, the past mission of the disciples to Israel turned out to be the model for the church's mission. Matthew understood the call to mission as the task of the entire church and life as an itinerant missionary to be a possibility of obedience for every Christian.[1] Thus our *thesis* is: *The disciples discourse is the fundamental ecclesiological text of the Gospel of Matthew*. It shows how the disciples assume Jesus' preaching mission and his authority and how their life is influenced by Jesus' own fate and by the Sermon on the Mount, Jesus' gospel of the kingdom of God.

What are the basic characteristics of Matthew's understanding of the church in the disciples discourse? First of all we may say that the church is formed after the pattern of Christ. It is formed after the pattern of Christ, however, not by visibly representing the spiritual reality of the crucified and risen Christ as the mysterious body of Christ but by continuing the life and the mission of the *earthly* Jesus after his death. Matthew, for whom the risen Lord is no other than the earthly Jesus (28:20), also thinks of the church in terms of the earthly Jesus. In this regard he differs from those New Testament authors who derive their understanding of the church from the risen Lord.[2] Thus for Matthew the church is patterned after Jesus, as he expresses it in the central logion of 10:24-25. What does that mean?

1. The church *depends on Jesus' compassion* (9:36) and thus on grace. This dimension is alluded to relatively briefly at the beginning of the discourse. The church depends on prayer to the Lord (9:37). It receives Jesus'

own authority (10:1, cf. 40). For this reason the disciples also represent the absent Lord (10:40).

2. The church *accepts Jesus' mission to the world*. Preaching (10:7, 27, 32, cf. 4:17) and healing (10:1, 8, cf. 4:23; 9:35) are thereby of equal importance. While Jesus' proclamation has primarily an ethical accent in Matthew, the charge to heal means that the preaching of the disciples is embedded in a concrete experience of salvation. This twofold mission of Jesus, preaching and healing, is directed beyond the church to the world that is the realm of the Son of Man (cf. 13:38, 41). To be the church is from the very beginning (10:52!) to be sent.

3. The church *takes over Jesus' lifestyle*. This characteristic, along with the next, is probably the most important for the Matthean understanding of the church. It is noteworthy that the disciples discourse is almost exclusively a discourse about the behavior and the fate of the disciples. That corresponds to the Matthean Christology. Matthew tells the story of Jesus as the story of the obedient Son of God who fulfills all righteousness (3:15), the Law and the Prophets (5:17). It also corresponds to the Matthean understanding of preaching. The light which the disciples are in the world consists not so much in their words as in their works, which they are to let shine and for whose sake people will praise the Father in heaven (5:14-16). That is why Matthew deals so expressly with the practical side of discipleship. The disciples discourse especially emphasizes the following characteristic behaviors: itinerancy (1:5-6, 11, 14, 16, 23, 40-42), poverty (10:8b-10, cf. 40-42), and defenselessness (10:10, 16, 38-39). They are essential for the church, because they correspond to the behavior of Jesus and thus to his preaching.

4. The next main characteristic is that the church *shares Jesus' suffering*. The fate of the disciples is none other than that of the master (10:24-25). The charge to preach brings them into deadly danger (10:27-31). The stages of the passion narrative are clearly remembered or anticipated (10:17-19, 38-39). Even the experience of the divisions in the families is rooted in Jesus' sending (10:34-37). Matthew does not wonder why the mission of

---

1   Cf. above, II C on the "addressees."
2   That is especially true for the understanding of the church as the body of Christ that in connection with Platonic concepts later became determinative

for the distinction between heavenly and earthly church (Ignatius, Hippolytus, Origen, etc.).

Jesus leads to suffering; according to his experience that is just the way it is. He is thinking not of suffering in general but of the suffering that derives from the world's *no* to Jesus, from the hatred "by all for my name's sake" (cf. 10:22). The church does not seek out suffering; it is simply unavoidable because Jesus suffered, and the disciples are to be like him in everything. For this reason Matthew is able to connect suffering with the term ἀκολουθεῖν ("to follow after," 10:38). If the disciples do not suffer, they obviously have not been like Jesus in their preaching and in their practice.

5. The church *is moving toward the judgment of Jesus.* The judgment that the messengers carry out symbolically against the cities of Israel and with which they threaten them (10:14-15) is also awaiting the messengers. This perspective becomes important in the concluding part of the discourse (10:32-33, 37-39, 40-42). The disciples know that the judge is none other than Immanuel, the Son of Man Jesus, who will judge them in the might of his father (10:29-30, 32-33). The disciples discourse thus places the church in the tension between being authorized by Jesus and carried by the Father on the one hand and, on the other, the judgment in which their behavior and their life must be tested before the Son of Man and the Father. It is this tension that makes possible the dynamic that lies in Matthew's understanding of the church. Church is not simply church; it *becomes* church by proving its authority and its mission in its obedience and in its suffering.

6. The *key ecclesiological term* of our discourse is μαθητής ("disciple") that appears at the beginning (9:37, 10:1), in the middle (10:24-25), and at the end (10:42; 11:1) of the discourse. With Matthew it has the status of a fundamental ecclesiological concept. It reveals a *personal understanding of church*: What is set before the disciples who constitute the church is not the "church" as an intellectual or institutional entity but solely the Lord. It reveals a *democratic-familial understanding of the church*: The concept of disciple has no room for basic distinctions within the church; in mission and authority it makes all disciples equal (cf. 23:8-10). It

reveals a *dynamic understanding of the church*: Discipleship is lived and suffered obedience on the way with Jesus. That, and only that, is the "essence" of the church. Chap. 13 and chap. 18 will develop and expand these lines of thought.

Reflections on the Meaning of the Disciples Discourse Today

The disciples discourse of the Gospel of Matthew opens at many points a deep division between what in Matthew's eyes church should be as lived discipleship and what it has been in its history or is today. "Poverty," "defenselessness," "itinerancy," or "suffering" indicate something of this division. Nevertheless, the significance of the disciples discourse is, in my judgment, not simply that it prescribes a different form for the modern church. As clearly as a particular practice is determinative for the church's existence or nonexistence, Matthew makes equally clear that this practice cannot simply be the same, unchanged, in every situation; when the situation changes the practice also changes. Such things as the changes in the equipment regulation or the experiences of the post-Easter mission that are integrated into the disciples discourse make that clear. Here too when considering what practice will determine the essence of the church, the best way to formulate what the evangelist intended will be to follow the "sense of direction"[3] that the texts lay out. In my judgment, to formulate the sense of direction of the Matthean disciples discourse we must begin at a more fundamental level than we did with the statements of the individual texts, viz., with the basic implications of the concept of disciple for the understanding of the church. We will try to approach it from a perspective different from that of the dominant theological tradition that understands the earthly church in terms of the invisible church and thus christologically in terms of the Risen One. In different ways this tradition has had a lasting influence on both the Protestant and Catholic churches.

In keeping with the Augsburg Confession *Protestant ecclesiology* is in the habit of defining the visible church as "an assembly of all believers among whom the Gospel

---

3   Cf. Ulrich Luz, "Vom Sinn biblischer Texte," in Horst Georg Pöhlmann, ed., *Worin besteht der Sinn des Lebens?* (Festschrift Milan Machovec; Gütersloh: Mohn, 1985) 86.

is preached in its purity and the holy sacraments are administered according to the Gospel."[4] Gospel and sacraments are the only *notae* that in the world's ambiguity are constitutive for the visible church. Similarly Calvin says: That "God's word is flawlessly preached . . . and the sacraments are administered as Christ has instituted them" are the two "*symbola*" of the visible church.[5]

A number of concerns are combined in this Protestant thesis. In keeping with the doctrine of justification the true church in the world cannot be recognized by what people make of it or do with and for it but only by what God gives it. The visible church is constituted only by the gifts of God entrusted to it. A related emphasis is a demarcation that especially Calvin but also Luther[6] clearly enunciated. The visible church is not recognized by its own holiness or righteousness. Instead, the "illusion of a perfect holiness" destroys the church, and "thoughtless zeal for righteousness" becomes sin when fellowship is broken with those whose life does not correspond to the doctrine.[7] Calvin reacts here against the Donatists, Cathari, and Wycliffites, but also against the Anabaptists of his own day.

In my judgment, however, the Protestant definition is not able to produce a real distinction between true and false visible church; at the most it can protect itself from overly hasty and self-absolutizing distinctions. Calvin already saw the problem clearly. What happens when the word of God has been obscured for centuries in the church? Who decides which word of the church corresponds to the gospel? Even in the administration of the sacraments, mistakes can creep in. Who determines whether they are peripheral or whether they destroy the proper administration of the sacraments?[8] One could say: Word and sacrament are *notae* of the *concept* of the visible church, but whether the church's reality corresponds to this concept is an open question.[9] Above all the question remains: Of what does the *congregatio sanctorum*, of which the Augsburg Confession speaks, actually consist? In the Protestant tradition for a number of reasons the central idea has become that of the *corpus permixtum* that is the visible church. However, that makes the church's holiness an attribute that can only be accepted on faith. Is that enough? It is no accident that in various writings Luther has increased the number of the *notae ecclesiae* and, for example, in "Von Conciliis und Kirchen" made suffering and persecution a *nota ecclesiae*.[10] In the Reformed tradition after Calvin the *disciplina* or the *oboedientia* became a third *nota ecclesiae*.[11] It was the first time in the Protestant tradition that the idea of obedience, so important for Matthew, was taken up in a particular refraction.

The problem posed by the Protestant tradition is, in my judgment, as follows: When one defines the visible church only in terms of the divine gifts that constitute it and completely ignores the form of the church in which these gifts are present, one is in danger of a kind of ecclesiological docetism. The true, visible church to whom word and sacrament are given can then be separated from the actual form of the church.[12] How the church appears and what it does is in the final analysis irrelevant as long as word and sacrament take place. The understanding of the visible church is then an ideal without any power to influence the actual church.[13] Church always remains church of the sinners.

The *Catholic ecclesiology* also understands church in the Augustinian tradition in the tension between visible

---

4   *Confessio Augustana* 7 = BSLK, 61 = *Book of Concord*, 32.

5   Calvin *Inst.* 4.1.9, 8.

6   Cf. sermon from 1531: There is no greater sinner than the church; it is holy only to the degree that it asks for forgiveness (*WA* 34, 1.276.7ff.).

7   *Inst.* 4.1.13.

8   Cf. *Inst.* 4.1.12.

9   Cf. Dietrich Bonhoeffer (*The Communion of Saints* [New York: Harper & Row, 1963] 89) speaks against theoretically deriving a doctrine of the church from faith: "What is conceptually necessary is not for that reason real."

10 "Von den Konziliis und Kirchen," *WA* 50.628–43.

11 Cf. already Calvin in a letter to Sadolet in idem, *Opera Selecta*, 5 vols., ed. Peter Barth (Munich:

Kaiser, 1926) 1.467. On the Reformed orthodoxy, cf. Heppe, *Dogmatik*, 541–42 (Locus 27, n. 19).

12 Calvin (*Inst.* 4.1.1) introduces the church as *externum subsidium* of faith only to speak immediately (*Inst.* 4.1.2–3) and against his intention of the invisible church. In the Lutheran and Reformed "normal dogmatic works" of H. Schmid and H. Heppe the church is discussed as the next-to-last subject, immediately before eschatology but after the sacraments.

13 Am I permitted here to offer my own (Zwinglian!) tradition as an especially good example? Since the visible church is born solely from the word, its form and its practice are among the external things that the Christian magistrate can regulate.

and invisible church. Its difference from Protestant ecclesiology is that the true church is visible not only in word and sacrament but also in the institution of the church. The supranatural fellowship becomes visible in the visible teaching office, in the visible priestly office, in the visible office of the shepherd, and in the entire visible body of the church.[14] The Second Vatican Council's Constitution on the Church identifies the church confessed in the creed with the Catholic church led by Peter's successors and the bishops.[15] The true church is the Catholic church. While a Protestant understanding of the church is in danger of separating the actual, visible church from the true church and of excluding it from its reflections ("docetism"), a Catholic understanding of the church is more likely to correspond to an incarnation Christology. The church carries in itself the traits of both the incarnate one and the Risen One. It is visible-invisible as is the Son of God.[16] Thus the visible and the invisible church are mysteriously connected just as are the two natures of Christ. The problem with this combination is that the visible church, to the degree that it is formally identical with the invisible church, becomes a reality that is beyond change.[17] A view of the church understood in terms of the Risen One, that is, the two natures of Christ, always appears to have a static quality.

By contrast, Matthew's reflection on the church begins at a point that in both Protestant and Catholic dogmatics is considered not in a discussion of the nature of the church but elsewhere—usually in the doctrine of sanctification, or in ethics, or not at all.[18] It begins with *discipleship*. Matthew understands the church in terms of its *authority* and its *mission*. For him, therefore, the decisive characteristics of the church are its deeds of obedience, righteousness, love, and the consequences of these deeds—hostility, suffering, and death. In comparison with the Protestant tradition Matthew achieves something essential. He puts his characteristics of the church in the midst of the world's concreteness but also in its contentiousness. He understands the church precisely in the terms that the Protestant tradition appears to separate from it, viz., in terms of its existence in the world. The appearance of an ecclesiological docetism so frequent in the Protestant tradition is here from the outset impossible.[19] Matthew's impulse has in common with a Catholic understanding of the church that he also speaks of the actual church which exists in the world. He differs, however, in his dynamic view of the church. It is church never simply as it is but in its obedience and in its deeds. It is not in control of its own existence as church but must always test its gifts and its mission in its obedience. Thus the church is not church independent of its obedience and its deeds. It "is" not simply church,

---

14 A design of the First Vatican Council on a Constitution on the Church, 4 = NR no. 389.

15 Constitution on the Church 1.8 = NR no. 411.

16 Michael Schmaus, *Katholische Dogmatik* 3/1 (Munich: Hueber, 1958) 400–401; Hermann Lais, *Dogmatik* (Kevelaer: Butzon und Bercker, 1972) 2.64 ("analogue to the divine-human essence of Jesus"). Cf. Karl Rahner, "Membership in the Church According to the Teaching of Pius XII's Encyclical *Mystici Corporis Christi*," in idem, *Theological Investigations* (Baltimore: Helicon, 1963) 2.86–87. The formulations take their inspiration from the encyclical *Mystici Corporis* of 1943.

17 "According to this concept the church believes in itself (Schmaus)" (A. Adam, "Kirche III," *RGG* 3 [1959] 1311).

18 There are, of course, churches and fellowships that understand themselves in terms of discipleship. Probably on the list are de facto the medieval poverty movements (Waldensians, Franciscans, Wycliffites), the Anabaptists and their descendants

(cf. "Disciples of Christ"!). If I understand them correctly, however, one of their characteristics is that they—justifiably—did not develop a *doctrine* of the church as discipleship but spoke almost solely of the church's practice. This is, in my judgment, one of the reasons why in the late-medieval Franciscan theology it was so easy to subordinate the Franciscan movement to the traditional Augustinian ecclesiology and thus to integrate it into the church at large.

19 I am aware that I share here the concern of Moltmann, *Church,* 342: "We cannot therefore merely give the marks of the church bearings that tend in an inward direction, understanding them in the light of word and sacrament; we must to the same degree give them an outward direction and see them in reference to the world." Moltmann pursues this theme in pp. 342–61 in terms of the church's unity, catholicity, holiness, and apostolicity.

but it *becomes* church by verifying in its deeds the mission and the authority entrusted to it.

Thus in comparison with the Protestant understanding of the church, Matthew offers the chance to speak of the church concretely and in terms of the world. In comparison with the Catholic understanding of the church, he offers the chance to speak of the church dynamically and without any self-absolutizing. Both are possible, because Matthew ties the church to the concrete human being, Jesus, whose *story* he *tells*. Church—Jesus' discipleship—does not simply exist; it *becomes* when Jesus, who heals among his people, shares his authority with the disciples. Church—Jesus' discipleship—does not simply exist; it *remains*, when this Jesus is with it in various ways, always until the end of the world, and helps it when its own faith is not sufficient. Church—Jesus' discipleship—does not simply exist; it *will appear* as that which it should be, when the Son of Man Jesus separates out of his kingdom sheep and goats in order to remind all one last time that God alone judges what has been true church. It thus happens that the church cannot *define* its own churchness, whether beyond its concrete reality in that which it proclaims, or whether in its concrete reality in what it is as institution. It can only *demonstrate* its churchness in its decisions, in its deeds of righteousness and love, and in the consequences that these deeds can have for it. However, these issues are at the disposal not of the church but solely of the one who one day will judge it.

> Matthew's understanding of the church is to be clarified in the face of *two inquiries*. One question is whether in the final analysis the true church is here not to be recognized in human deeds. Then the church would be nothing more than the result of human activity, and the degree to which it is authentically church could be determined by how resolute or radical it is. This would be an ecclesiological form of righteousness by works. In my judgment, it is foreign to Matthew's thought, not only because the disciples receive their authority and their mission as a gift, nor simply because Jesus must constantly help them in their obedience, but primarily because the idea of judgment deprives the church of the possibility of passing judgment on its own churchness. The church can do nothing more than prove itself in obedience and then turn over to Jesus the world-judge the issue of what it has been. Thus it is precisely the idea of judgment—correctly understood—that renders impossible any righteousness based on works.
>
> However, that raises a second question. Does this disciples ecclesiology not mean the exclusion of any possibility of a *nota ecclesiae* that helps us recognize where the visible church actually *is*? If on the one hand Matthew merely suggests the direction in which the obedience to Jesus' mission is to take shape in the church without, however, defining, for example, how much poverty, healing gifts, defenselessness, or suffering is required for a church actually to be the church, and if on the other hand it is God alone who judges the deeds of the disciples, does that not mean in the final analysis that the visible church is in principle hidden, just as the good seed is hidden among the weeds? This possibility would bring Matthew again close to Protestant ecclesiology. To be sure, it would likely be only an apparent similarity, since for Matthew Jesus' way of *life* and obedience to his commands is a "*nota*" *ecclesiae*. It is simply something that cannot be made quantitatively unambiguous.

Following the "direction" of the Matthean idea that the way to perfection is a way on which the church *goes*, we can say that for Matthew the visible church's decisive *nota* is *going on a way*. A church that is not on the way and that does not commit all its energies to obedience to its Lord is for Matthew no church. That may well be the meaning of Matthew's statement that the true family of Jesus are those who do the will of the Father (Matt 12:50).

Literature

Martin Dibelius, *Die urchristliche Überlieferung von Johannes dem Täufer* (FRLANT 15; Göttingen: Vandenhoeck & Ruprecht, 1911) 6–39.

Richard A. Edwards, "Matthew's Use of Q in Chapter Eleven," in Joel Delobel, ed., *Logia: les paroles de Jesus: Mémorial Joseph Coppens* (BEThL 59; Louvain: Peeters, 1982) 257–75.

Paul Hoffmann, *Studien,* 190–233.

Kraeling, *John the Baptist,* 123–57.

John P. Meier, "John the Baptist in Matthew's Gospel," *JBL* 99 (1980) 383–405.

Schönle, *Johannes.*

Trilling, "Täufertradition," 45–65 (= *BZ* NF 3 [1959] 271–89).

Verseput, *Rejection.*

Walter Wink, *John the Baptist in the Gospel Tradition* (SNTSMS 7; London: Cambridge University Press, 1968) 27–41.

Chapter 11 not only concludes the gospel's first main section, it is also a transition to the second.[1] In vv. 5-6 and 21, 23 it refers back to Jesus' miraculous deeds of chaps. 8–9. Especially in its second part with, for example, the catchwords γενεὰ αὕτη, κρίσις, and υἱὸς τοῦ ἀνθρώπου ("this generation," "judgment," "Son of Man"), it looks ahead to chap. 12.

There are difficulties involved in determining the internal structure of Matthew 11. We can say, of course, that Matthew is here adding material from Q that he thus far has been unable to use. Then Matthew 11 would be simply a collection of addenda.[2] The suggestion, however, does not do justice to Matthew's narrative skill. The chapter is primarily (vv. 7-30) a discourse of Jesus to the multitudes, but Matthew has not characterized it as one of his five discourses. Unlike those discourses, this material has no clear theme, but it is functionally incorporated into the narrative thread.

It is divided into two parts, vv. 2-19 and vv. 20-30. The narrator's comment in v. 20 is a new beginning. The following section, vv. 20-30, is divided into two antithetical parts: negatively, the announcement of judgment on the Galilean cities in vv. 21-24 and, positively, the Savior's call to the laboring and heavy laden among the people (vv. 28-30). Thus the situation is still open; the invitation is still being extended to all Israel. That is the conclusion that Jesus (and the narrator Matthew) draw at the end of the first part of his story. The Savior's call is preceded by the so-called cry of jubilation (vv. 25-27), one of the gospel's fundamental christological texts. It will turn out to have numerous points of connection throughout the gospel. In it Matthew for the first time brings together his book's view of Christ and prepares the way for further basic texts such as 16:16-17 and 28:16-20.

The preceding part of the discourse on John, vv. 2-19, prepares for the announcement of judgment. Jesus speaks of the mission of John the Baptist and makes it clear that he is Elijah's forerunner (vv. 10 and 14 with a concluding attention-evoking formula in v. 15). The parable of the children at play (vv. 16-19) contains a final warning. The crowds that initially were open toward John (vv. 7-9) have now become "this generation" that rejects Jesus and his Elijah, John (vv. 16-19). Verses 7-15 prepare and intensify the accusation; Israel rejects its own Elijah just as it does Jesus. Finally, the introductory section, vv. 2-6, prepares for vv. 7-15 and at the same time leads to the discourse on judgment. The "works of Christ" intensify the judgment on an Israel that is not brought to repentance by these powerful deeds (vv. 20-24).

We may say, therefore, that Matthew 11 is the concluding discourse of the Messiah Jesus to his people Israel after his initial activity. It is as if Jesus were drawing the consequences of chaps. 8–10. If they do not lead to repentance, John, the last prophetic witness, and the deeds of the Christ become the accusing witness. However, the invitation to the entire nation is still open. Chapters 12–16 will portray how the people respond to it.[3]

---

1 Cf. vol. 1, Introduction 1 on chaps. 12–28.

2 Schmid on 11:2—13:53: "loosely connected pieces" (188).

3 Verseput (*Rejection,* 2–3) thinks along these same lines, but he does not recognize the importance that chap. 11 has in its own right, because from the very beginning he reads it under the influence of chap. 12. "The chosen nation falls under judgment, while a new family of God appears" (2).

1.1 The Baptist's Inquiry (11:2-6)

Literature

Dupont, "L'ambassade," 805–21, 943–59.

Augustin George, "Paroles de Jésus sur les miracles (Mt 11,5.21; 12,27.28 et par.)," in Jacques Dupont, ed., *Jésus aux origines de la christologie* (BEThL 40; Louvain: Louvain University Press, 1975) 283–301.

Werner Georg Kümmel, "Jesu Antwort an Johannes den Täufer: Ein Beispiel zum Methodenproblem in der Jesusforschung," in idem, *Heilsgeschehen* 2.177–200.

Cesare Marcheselli Casale, "'Andate e annunciate a Giovanni ciò che udite e vedete' (Mt 11,4; Lc 7,22)," in *Testimonium Christi: scritti in onore di Jacques Dupont* (Brescia: Paideia, 1985) 257–88.

Rudolf Pesch, *Jesu ureigene Taten?* (QD 52; Freiburg: Herder, 1970) 36–44.

Sabugal, *Mesiánica.*

Sato, "Q," 138–40.

Daniel Sheerin, "St. John the Baptist in the Lower World," *VC* 30 (1976) 1–22.

Simonetti, "Praecursor," 367–82.

Stuhlmacher, *Evangelium* 1.218–25.

Vögtle, "Wunder," 219–42.

For *additional literature* on Matthew 11 see above, II D.

2   **But John, who had heard in prison of the deeds of the Christ, sent his disciples to say to him: 3/ "Are you the one who will come, or should[1] we expect another?" 4/ And Jesus answered and said to them: "Go and tell John what you hear and see:**

5   **The blind see again**
        and the lame walk,
    the lepers are cleansed
        and the deaf hear,
        and the dead are raised,
        and poor people have the gospel
            preached to them,

6   **and happy is the one who takes no offense at me."**

Analysis   **Structure**

The text consists of a question from John (vv. 2-3) and a (longer) answer of Jesus (vv. 4-6). This answer is well structured. Verse 5 consists of six short clauses. The first two pairs, connected by καί, stand asyndetically side by side; each of the last two brief clauses is introduced by "and." Verse 6 also begins with καί; the emphasis lies on this overlong concluding sentence. Formally and in terms of its content the text is connected with its context. John's question reminds the reader that in 3:11 he had spoken of the one who was to come who would baptize with fire. The verb ἔρχομαι also connects with what follows. Not only is Jesus the one who is to come; John also had to "come" as Elijah (v. 14). "Works" are mentioned again in v. 19. The list of miracles in v. 5 especially reminds the readers of what they have previously read in Matthew 8–9. For each of the five miracles there is an example in these chapters, viz., the healing of the blind (9:27-31) and of the lame (9:2-8), the cleansing of a leper (8:1-4), the healing of a deaf person (9:32-34), and the raising of a dead person (9:18-26). The preaching of the gospel to the poor is reminiscent of the Sermon on the Mount (cf. 5:3).

Redaction and Source

Matthew now goes back to the Q text of Luke 7:18-35 after he has used the sending discourse in chap 10. Matthew has formed the introduction in v. 2.[2] "Another" in v. 3 is probably Matthean.[3] Luke 7:20-21 is completely Lukan, as is the introduction in Luke 7:18. The transposition of "see" and "hear" in v. 22 is perhaps also Lukan; for Luke what is visible, viz., the miracles, is a decisive indication of God's action. Q has probably formulated the hearing and seeing in the present tense. The Lukan aorist corresponds to the redactional v. 21.

Origin

The first question is whether the text can be analyzed further in terms of its tradition history. If so, the scene is an illustration of an old logion (of Jesus or the church) that contained either only v. 5 or vv. 5-6. Depending on one's answer to this first question, the second question, that of historicity, applies either to the entire scene or only to the older logion. There is no scholarly consensus on either question.

1. Except for one point the text gives the impression of *unity*. The only difficulty that might justify a tradition-history decomposition of the text[4] lies in the fact that Jesus does not give a direct answer to the Baptist's question. He speaks not of himself but in general terms of the present time of salvation. How-

---

1   Subjunctive present, cf. BDF § 366 (1).

2   On ἀκούσας, ἔργον, Χριστός, and πέμψας, cf. vol. 1, Introduction 3.2. Δεσμωτήριον is a hapax legomenon, but it presupposes the situation of 4:12. What the Baptist hears, according to Matthew, are Jesus' deeds reported by Matthew in chaps. 8–9.

3   Cf. vol. 1, Introduction 3.2. In Matthew ἕτερος with-out the article often means "another." Luke would not have omitted what clearly is for him a favorite word, ἕτερος.

4   Examples of such decompositions are Bultmann, *History,* 23; Schürmann, *Lukasevangelium* 1.413–14; Sato, "Q," 141.

ever, the question is whether the formal unevenness is not to be interpreted as an expression of the intention of the text (cf. our interpretation below). If one assumes that the burden of proof for the tradition-history decomposition of a text is on those who affirm it, then we must first attempt to interpret the text as a unity. Only if the entire text cannot be interpreted meaningfully in its historical context are we permitted, assuming there are no formal indications for so doing, to decompose the text. Only in the case of the macarism in v. 6 would I like to leave open the possibility that it is a later application and generalization of Jesus' answer. It appears to be directed not exclusively to John and his disciples, and its warning tone is a poor response to John's positive question. On the other hand, the question of the disciples of John requires a statement about Jesus' person that is not given at all in v. 5 but follows—here also indirectly—in v. 6. *Non liquet.*

2. On the question of *authenticity* the scholarly disagreement is quite large. The pericope is a favorite example for discussions about the criteria of authenticity. The most important arguments for attributing the saying to the church[5] are: (a) The Baptist, who expected God or the Son of Man to come as an eschatological judge with fire, would not have been able to ask such a question of Jesus who was active on earth as a human being.[6] (b) We must ask whether the list of miracles in v. 5 that is not only descriptive but also prophetically interpreted would be conceivable coming from Jesus.[7] (c) If the saying came from Jesus, it would be strange that the exorcisms, which are so important for Jesus himself, are not mentioned.[8]

In my judgment the second and third objections can be overcome. To say that it was not Jesus but only the church after him that interpreted his ministry in the light of biblical prophecy is a *petitio principii.* The exorcisms need not be excluded as is shown, for example, by the healing of the dumb demoniac (Luke 11:14). The first objection, on the other hand, carries a great deal of weight.

In my judgment the contradictory theses produced

by scholarship show how difficult is the attempt to explain the apophthegm as a creation of the church. Is the point to present the Baptist "as a witness to the messiahship of Jesus"?[9] But the Baptist does not bear witness to anything. Is it to deal with the "uncertainty of the community"?[10] Why then are the disciples not the questioners (cf., for example, Mark 8:27-30!)? Why the roundabout way through the Baptist's disciples that made of the Baptist, who otherwise was highly regarded by the early church as Elijah, a doubter and thus a "dangerous example not to be followed by Christians"?[11] Or is the saying a polemic against the non-Christian disciples of the Baptist? But the text does not report that Jesus' answer convinced the Baptist. Is the pericope designed to prove to disciples of the Baptist that Jesus and not the Baptist is the true eschatological prophet?[12] This thesis presupposes that John the Baptist, who probably did not perform any miracles, was regarded by his disciples as an eschatological prophet—a hazardous assumption! Or was the purpose to challenge undecided disciples of the Baptist to join the Jesus community?[13] But a remaining difficulty here is that Jesus' miracles do *not* demonstrate that he is the Son of Man whom the Baptist expected. The reference to Jesus' miracles could hardly have been very convincing for the followers of the Baptist. It would make more sense to me to imagine that our pericope resulted from the church's inner-Christian christological reflection on the relationship between the apocalyptic messianic hope of the Baptists and its own confession to Jesus Christ.[14] But why then does the question come from the disciples of the Baptist? In short, the difficulties in finding a convincing *Sitz im Leben* in the church for the formation of this apophthegm carry their own weight and speak against the thesis that it was formed by the church.

---

5   Forcefully advocated by Augustin George, "Paroles de Jésus sur les miracles (Mt 11,5.21; 12,27.28 et par.)," 283–301; Rudolf Pesch, *Jesu ureigene Taten?*, 36–44; Stuhlmacher, *Evangelium*; and especially Vögtle, "Wunder."

6   Kraeling, *John the Baptist,* 127.

7   Hoffmann, *Studien,* 211; Sato ("Q," 143) claims that even with the beatitudes the reference to Isa 61:1 belongs to the oldest church tradition. Cf. vol. 1, II A 1.2 on "tradition history."

8   See, e.g., Gnilka, 1.410; Vögtle, "Wunder," 233–34; Sato, "Q," 143 (the exorcisms are missing because

they do not occur in the OT).

9   Bultmann, *History,* 23.

10   Sand, *Evangelium,* 238.

11   Gundry, 207.

12   Stuhlmacher, *Evangelium,* 220; Sabugal, *Embajada,* 130–32, 200–201 (for Q).

13   See, e.g., Schürmann, *Lukasevangelium* 1.413.

14   Following Kraeling, *John the Baptist,* 128–31.

An argument in favor of the historicity[15] is that after Easter the idea of a doubting John the Baptist would be singular—not impossible but certainly difficult to conceive.[16] Our pericope may well preserve the reminiscence, no doubt historically accurate, that the relationship of the Baptist to Jesus was at best ambivalent. Only such a situation can explain why after the death of the Baptist some of his disciples became followers of Jesus while others did not. In addition, the criterion of coherence (cf. Luke 11:31-32; Mark 2:19, and especially Luke 10:23-24) supports the argument for historicity.[17] The indirectness with which Jesus makes his claim also is typical of him. Still, none of these arguments is conclusive.

The upshot for me is: We can accept John's question and the entire accompanying episode as historically authentic if, and only if: (a) John expected not God but the Son of Man as the one who was to come; (b) Jesus understood his own ministry as that of the coming world-judge–Son of Man; and (c) Jesus also said this to his disciples (so that John might have heard about it). I regard this as possible. To be sure, then it would become an important witness for how Jesus understood his miracles at the dawning of the kingdom of God.

Interpretation: Jesus

John the Baptist—whether already in prison or not we do not know—asks Jesus through his disciples whether he is the coming Son of Man whom he had proclaimed (cf. 3:11-12). The Baptist may have heard that Jesus spoke to his disciples about the judgment by fire (Luke 12:49) and about his way as the Son of Man. The most natural explanation for his question is that the Baptist previously had not thought of this as a possibility,[18] but had begun to wonder because of the reports about Jesus.[19] Jesus avoids answering his ques-

tion directly and instead indirectly points to the time of salvation experienced in his healing miracles, which he may already be interpreting with Old Testament prophetic images. He also spoke in a similar way in Mark 2:19 of the wedding time and in Luke 10:23-24 of the time of salvation that prophets and kings had longed to see and to hear. In Luke 11:20 he sees the finger of God and the kingdom of God at work in his exorcisms. That is all that he says to the disciples of John. If the concluding beatitude also comes from him, then he continues: The question of who the coming one is cannot be decided theoretically. Here personal decisions are necessary for or against Jesus' claim. The healings of the time of salvation should help in making this decision.

Interpretation: Matthew

■ **2** The evangelist Matthew tells how John, who had been imprisoned even before the beginning of Jesus' activity in Galilee (4:12), heard in prison of the "works of the Christ." The works include Jesus' words and deeds—everything that is reported in Matthew 5–9.[20] In Matthew ὁ Χριστός is to be understood as a title in the sense of "Israel's Messiah" and parallel to "Son of David."[21] As with the Son of David title, the Christ title must be interpreted in Matthew on the basis of the gospel's *narrative*. In the prologue he had introduced him as Israel's promised Messiah (1:1, 16-17; 2:4). Who this Messiah is becomes clear only in the story the evangelist tells. He had come to his people in the preaching to the poor (Matthew 5-7) and in the healing miracles (Matthew 8-9).

---

15 Forcefully argued by Werner Georg Kümmel, "Jesu Antwort an Johannes den Täufer," 2.177–200. Cf. also Walter Wink, "Jesus' Reply to John," *Forum* 5 (1989) 126–27.

16 Dibelius, *Überlieferung,* 37.

17 Cf. the catchwords ἰδεῖν-ἀκούειν. However, one cannot automatically understand Matt 11:2-6 as a post-Easter development of the Jesus saying in Luke 10:23-24 as, e.g., Vögtle does ("Wunder," 240–42). The points of contact are only the already-mentioned catchwords and the macarism that in content is quite different.

18 Pointedly advocated by David Friedrich Strauss, *The Life of Jesus Critically Examined* (1848; reprinted Philadelphia: Fortress, 1973) 1.221–35; August Neander, *The Life of Jesus Christ* (New York: Harper

& Brothers, 1850) 57–61.

19 Then it would historically not be the case that the Baptist for some reason began to doubt Jesus' messiahship, as has often been claimed in the history of interpretation, but the opposite. The Baptist heard about Jesus and then began to wonder: Could Jesus be the "coming one"?

20 There are in Judaism no particular concepts of "messianic deeds." One did not expect the Messiah to perform miracles of healing. The expression ἔργα τοῦ Χριστοῦ is a Matthean creation and is to be interpreted on Matthew's terms.

21 Cf. the excursus on υἱὸς Δαυίδ above, at 9:27-31.

■ **3** Through his disciples John sends a message to Jesus in Galilee.[22] Various Old Testament texts have been suggested as lying behind the question "Are you the one who is to come?"[23] However, this expression is not associated with a particular messianic hope. Matthew is probably thinking of John's saying about the stronger one "who comes after him" (3:11), that is, of the Son of Man.[24] That means that here, as in the reference in 3:11 to the one who will judge by fire, we must also think of Jesus' future coming as world-judge–Son of Man. It is no accident that in chaps. 11 and 12, where the judgment on Israel first appears on the horizon, the evangelist speaks more frequently of the coming Son of Man (11:19; 12:32, 40).

History of Interpretation

■ **3** Why does the Baptist, who—for both the church and the evangelist!—had proclaimed Jesus as the coming one, suddenly become a doubter? The question angers Luther.[25] "Most of what I can find written about this gospel deals with the question of whether St. John did not know that Jesus is the rightful Christ; but that is an unnecessary question, and it is of no great consequence."[26] In the ancient church Tertullian, among others, dared to say that John had doubted Jesus' messiahship,[27] but he encountered unanimous and indignant protest. The usual answer was that John had asked Jesus not for his own sake but for that of his disciples.[28] Beginning with Origen

a number of interpreters have understood "the one who will come" with a future meaning and have interpreted John's question just before his own death as asking whether Jesus also would come into the underworld so that John could proclaim him as the forerunner there also after his death.[29] Since the Enlightenment, Protestant exegesis has again taken seriously the possibility that John genuinely doubted. Depending on one's theological position, the interpretations have gone in different directions. Some found it to be understandable that even brave men would experience all kinds of doubts and anxieties in a prison cell.[30] Another was confident that doubt is part of a prophet's "religious condition."[31] Widespread is the thesis of the Baptist's messianic impatience whose doubts came simply from the fact that Jesus delayed his messianic revelation too long.[32] It was said that such impatience would also be understandable in a prison cell! At the same time, it was said, there are obvious pedagogical reasons why Jesus delayed. He wanted first to win the hearts of the people.[33] Knabenbauer announces, not without pride, that in his time "practically all" Protestants believed that John doubted Jesus' messiahship, while the Catholics attempted to remove from him any shadow of doubt.[34]

Interpretation

■ **3** There is no indication that Matthew would have seen John's doubt as a problem.[35] However, since in his entire gospel he strongly Christianizes the Baptist,[36] precisely

---

22 Πέμπω διά is not necessarily a Semitism; it is equally possible in Greek (cf. Moulton-Milligan, *s.v.* πέμπω; on the absolute use πέμπω cf. Wettstein on this text).

23 Among others, the following have been suggested: Ps. 118:26 (cf. Matt 21:9; 23:39); Isa 59:20; Hab 2:3; Gen 49:10 (with προσδοκία; the Targum interprets it messianically: Dupont, "L'ambassade," 816); Zech 9:9 (cf. Matt 21:5); 14:5.

24 Cf. vol. 1, I B 1.1 on 3:11-12. Perhaps one may also associate with it Dan 7:13 and the widespread Maranatha.

25 On the history of interpretation cf. Dupont, "L'ambassade," 806–13; Sabugal, *Mesiánica*, 5–27; Simonetti, "Praecursor."

26 Luther 2.372.

27 *Marc.* 4.18 = CSEL 47.477–78; *Bapt.* 10 = ANF 3.673–74.

28 Origen fr. 220.2 = GCS Origenes 12.165; John Chrysostom 36.2 = *PG* 57.414; Augustine, *Sermo* 66.33–34 = *PL* 38.432.

29 Since Origen *Hom. in 1 Reg.* 28.3-25 = GCS Origenes 4.290.30–32. In the West this interpretation was spread through Jerome (77–78); idem *Ep.* 121.1 *ad Algasiam* = CSEL 56.5 on the basis of the translation in the Vulgate "*qui venturus es*" (future). Cf. Daniel Sheerin, "St. John the Baptist in the Lower World," 1–22, 7–17; later material in Simonetti, "Praecursor," 372–82.

30 See, e.g., Olshausen, 417–18 (in the "gloomy prison at Machaerus . . . a dark hour"); Meyer, 218 ("psychologically . . . understandable"); Lightfoot, 191 ("why am I so long detained in prison?").

31 Zahn, 417–18.

32 Paulus 1.694–99; Weiss, 214.

33 Paulus 1.696.

34 1.476.

35 Or did he understand the "reed that is moved by the wind" (v. 7) to refer to John's doubt? That is hardly to be assumed.

36 Cf. vol. 1, I B 1.1 on 3:1-2, 11-12 and I B 3.1 on 3:17 and below, II D 1.2 on 11:11-15 from Matthew's per-

in his gospel John's question is somewhat strange. Do we have here simply traditional material passed along unthinkingly? Or is the basic aspect of John's question important for Matthew? Are people to approach Jesus as openly as John (and his disciples!) in order to give Jesus an occasion for talking about his activity? In that case the skeptical crowds are compared with John's disciples after they have left (vv. 7-19). Then John and his disciples would be important not so much as individual figures but as representatives of that part of Israel that was favorable toward Jesus. However, none of that is stated explicitly.

■ **4-5** In his answer Jesus calls the questioners' attention to their own experiences: "what you hear and see." "Hearing" is mentioned first and along with the end of v. 5 ("poor have the gospel preached to them") chiastically forms a bracket around Jesus' miracles. Putting hearing first corresponds to the location of the Sermon on the Mount before chaps. 8–9. Unlike Luke 7:21 Matthew does not find it necessary to have John's disciples immediately experience Jesus' miracles; the reports of chaps. 8–9 that are here summarized are sufficient for him. That shows that Matthew is thinking more of the situation of the disciples (who were present) or his readers (who have read chaps. 8–9) than "historically" of the situation of John's disciples. In its content the summary is clearly based on the report of chaps. 8–9,[37] but in its formulation and structure it is just as clearly influenced by prophetic state-

ments of hope. Several OT passages lie in the background, especially Isa 61:1 ($\epsilon\dot{\upsilon}\alpha\gamma\gamma\epsilon\lambda\dot{\iota}\sigma\alpha\sigma\vartheta\alpha\iota$ $\pi\tau\omega\chi\hat{o}\hat{\iota}\varsigma$, $\tau\upsilon\phi\lambda\hat{o}\hat{\iota}\varsigma$ $\dot{\alpha}\nu\dot{\alpha}\beta\lambda\epsilon\psi\iota\nu$); Isa 29:18-19 ($\dot{\alpha}\kappa\omega\dot{\upsilon}\sigma\omega\nu\tau\alpha\iota$ ... $\kappa\omega\phi\omega\dot{\iota}$, $\tau\upsilon\phi\lambda\hat{\omega}\nu$ ... $\pi\tau\omega\chi\omega\dot{\iota}$);[38] Isa 35:5-6 (... $\tau\upsilon\phi\lambda\hat{\omega}\nu$, ... $\kappa\omega\phi\hat{\omega}\nu$ $\dot{\alpha}\kappa\omega\dot{\upsilon}\sigma\omega\nu\tau\alpha\iota$, $\chi\omega\lambda\dot{o}\varsigma$); Isa 42:18 ($\kappa\omega\phi\omega\dot{\iota}$ $\dot{\alpha}\kappa\omega\dot{\upsilon}\sigma\alpha\tau\epsilon$, $\tau\upsilon\phi\lambda\omega\dot{\iota}$ $\dot{\alpha}\nu\alpha\beta\lambda\dot{\epsilon}\psi\alpha\tau\epsilon$), and in addition perhaps the healings of lepers and the raising of the dead in the time of Elijah and Elisha (1 Kgs 17:17-24; 2 Kgs 4:18-37; 5:1-27).

> The hope is widespread in *Judaism*[39] that in the new eon or in the messianic time all diseases and distresses will disappear. The thought is that the new eon will correspond to the time at Sinai[40] or to the time of Elijah.[41] Late texts are able to cite Isa 35:5-6 for this hope.[42] God, Israel's physician, will remove the diseases.[43] There are no Jewish texts that say that the Messiah will heal. It is expected that eschatological prophets will repeat miracles from the time of the exodus but no healings.[44] The Qumran text 11QMelch, which interprets the messenger of joy of Isa 61:1 to be the eschatological prophet, does not speak of miracles. Therefore, we should not base an interpretation of the pericope on the hope for an eschatological prophet.[45]

Jesus' answer evades the question of John's disciples. He responds to their question about the *person* of Jesus by referring to the present *time* of salvation that the questioners may experience. Not only Jesus' miracles but (especially) the proclamation of the gospel to the poor

---

spective, III C 1.2 on 14:1-2, and IV A 2 on 17:10-13. Cf. in addition Trilling, "Täufertradition," 63–65.

37   Cf. above, Analysis: Structure. Already in the Q tradition the important thing was that they were miracles *of Jesus*. That is demonstrated by the "unbiblical" use of the healing of lepers and of the raising of the dead. Furthermore, Q also begins with a healing story (Luke 7:1-10) as an example. In his composition Matthew here follows Q.

38   Both texts thus provide the framework for Matt 11:5. It is thus premature to make Isa 61:1 (and the hope for an eschatological prophet that is perhaps [!] connected with it) one-sidedly the "overriding theme" of Jesus' answer, contra Stuhlmacher, *Evangelium* 219; Werner Grimm, *Die Verkündigung Jesu und Deuterojesaia* (ANTJ 1; Frankfurt: Lang, 1976) 128–29.

39   Cf. especially Hoffmann, *Studien,* 206–8 and Cesare

Marcheselli Casale, "'Andate e annunciate a Giovanni ciò che udite e vedete' (Mt 11,4; Lc 7,22)," 269–78.

40   Str–B 1.594-95.

41   *Pesiq.* 76a. 13 = Str–B 1.594 (c. 300).

42   *Tanch.* B § 7 (24a) = Str–B 1.594; *b. Sanh.* 91b (= ibid.)

43   See, e.g., *Jub.* 23.30; cf. *1 Enoch* 96.3; *2 Bar.* 29.7; for good parallels from Jewish prayers see Joseph Heinemann, *Prayer in the Talmud* (Studia Judaica 9; Berlin: de Gruyter, 1977) 58.

44   Josephus *Bell.* 2.259-62; 7.438-40; *Ant.* 20.97-99.

45   Cf. Stuhlmacher, above, n. 38.

(cf. 5:3) belong to the time of salvation. He thus does not apply a given messianic expectation to himself.

■ **6** Only in the concluding macarism of v. 6 is the person of Jesus mentioned explicitly. Σκανδαλίζω, a late Jewish and Christian word, means "to set a trap," "to erect an obstacle," then more generally "to give offense," "to lead to ruin," "to seduce to sin." Ἐν designates the person or thing through which the offense comes.[46] In Matthew (and Mark), the word is used of the final abandoning of Jesus in the passion (26:31, 33) and in the end-time (24:10). Our text looks ahead to these texts and to 13:57; 15:12. The general formulation in the third person shows that more is involved than a warning to John's disciples.[47] Instead, here at the conclusion is the christological-parenetic point of our text that is fundamental for the evangelist. He is concerned not that one should have the right knowledge about Jesus but that one not reject the experiences of salvation to which Jesus extends an invitation. These experiences of salvation make a claim; they require a decision for or against Jesus.[48] It is for just this reason that the evangelist, after Jesus' healing ministry in Israel (chaps. 8–9), had Jesus give the disciples the task of confronting Israel with a decision (chap. 10).

Summary

First of all, the meaning of our text must be determined on the basis of Matthew's entire story. After the programmatic proclamation and the miracles of Israel's Messiah, Israel must respond to the question of who Jesus truly is. It can respond not by formulating a correct messianic answer but only by actually becoming part of the *story* of Jesus and by letting the story bring it to a life decision about Jesus. Our text is a model of how Matthew takes christological titles and concepts into his story of Jesus and subordinates them to it. It is a model of what is called *narrative Christology* and of how it lays a claim on people. Thus Matthew uses the Baptist and his disciples to show the way of understanding "on which the disciples also had to go and on which the people should go."[49] What is important is that one become part of the story, the deeds of the Christ. No "abstract" christological answer can replace this participation in the story of the Christ. The Baptist and his disciples demonstrate positively the possibility of salvation for Israel.[50] The continuation of the story will then clarify, in the form of prophetic warnings whose central figure is once again John the Baptist, the negative possibility—Israel's *no*.

---

46   BAGD, *s.v.* σκανδαλίζω, 1b.

47   Sabugal (*Embajada*, 49–55, cf. 76) claims that we have here polemics and mission directed toward disciples of the Baptist and Pharisaic Judaism. In my judgment the Matthean churches did not have direct contact with John's disciples; cf. vol. 1, I B 1.2, n. 7. Only in the context of Matthew's story of Jesus is v. 6 an (indirect) missionary appeal to Israel.

48   By not reporting the Baptist's reaction and by ending the text with the warning macarism, Matthew emphasizes the model call to decision.

49   Schmid, 189.

50   If the text comes from Jesus it also shows that the design of a Jesus narrative in the form of a *gospel* has an internal justification from Jesus himself.

1.2 Elijah Returned and His Call to Decision (11:7-15)

Literature

Betz, "Eschatological Interpretation," 89–107.

Idem, "Krieg."

Cameron, *Violence.*

David Catchpole, "On Doing Violence to the Kingdom," *Irish Biblical Studies* 3 (1981) 77–92.

Frederick W. Danker, "Luke 16:16—An Opposition Logion?" *JBL* 77 (1958) 231–43.

Harnack, "Zwei Worte," 942–57.

Hoffmann, *Studien,* 50–79.

Karlstadt, *Reich Gotis.*

Kloppenborg, *Formation,* 108–17.

Kosch, *Gottesherrschaft.*

Werner Georg Kümmel, "'Das Gesetz und die Propheten gehen bis Johannes'—Lukas 16,16 im Zusammenhang der heilsgeschichtlichen Theologie der Lukasschriften," in idem, *Heilsgeschehen* 2.75–86.

Merklein, *Gottesherrschaft,* 80–95.

Moore, "*BIAZΩ,*" 519–43.

Schlosser, *Règne de Dieu* 1.155–67, 2.509–39.

Gottlob Schrenk, "βιάζομαι κτλ," *TDNT* 1 (1964) 609–14.

Schulz, *Q,* 229–36, 261–67.

A. Schweizer, "Ob in der Stelle Matth 11,12 ein Lob oder ein Tadel enthalten sei?" *ThStK* 9 (1836) 90–122.

Theissen, "Rohr," 43–55.

Wanke, *Kommentarworte,* 31–35.

Weiss, *Predigt,* 192–97.

For *additional literature* on Matthew 11 cf. above, II D.

7 **But when they went away, Jesus began to say to the crowds about John:**
"Why[1] did you go out into the wilderness?
To see a reed shaken by the wind?

8 **But why did you go out?**
To see a man in soft clothes?
Behold, those who wear soft clothes are in the royal palaces.

9 **But why did you go out?**
To see a prophet?

10 **Yes, I tell you, even more than a prophet!**
This is he of whom it stands written:
'Behold, I send my messenger before you
Who will prepare your way before you.'

11 **Amen, I say to you:**
Among those born of women there has arisen no one greater than John the Baptist,
but the smallest in the kingdom of heaven is greater than he.

12 **But from the days of John the Baptist until now the kingdom of heaven suffers violence, and violent people take it away.**

13 **All the prophets and the Law prophesied until John,**

14 **and if you are willing to accept it: He is Elijah who is to come. 15/ Whoever has ears shall hear!**

Analysis

Structure

Verse 7a introduces a longer discourse of Jesus that is interrupted only in v. 20a with a brief observation. Verses 7b-10 are a clearly structured first unit, introduced by three parallel rhetorical questions and concluded by a scripture quotation that in turn is introduced by a definition ("this is he"). Verse 14 brings a further definition with "he is." Verses 7-10 and vv. 11-14 constitute two sections, the second of which is quite unstructured. A formulaic call to hear in v. 15 concludes the first main section.

Sources

In continuation of *vv. 2-6, vv. 7-11* come from Q = Luke 7:24-28. Here Matthew hardly changes the wording.[2] On the other hand, *vv. 14-15* are completely redactional.[3]

There is a great deal of uncertainty about *vv. 12-13.* The logion is usually ascribed to Q,[4] but there are a number of reasons for our uncertainty. Luke 16:16-18 is not in a Q context and cannot be located in Q in a way that makes sense. There are also difficulties in reconstructing the Q wording in Matt 5:18, 32 = Luke 16:17-18. In all three sayings one must assume an

---

1   *Τί* can also be translated as "what?" Then the infinitives θεάσασθαι and ἰδεῖν are in each case part of the first question. A definite decision is not possible. The word order προφήτην ἰδεῖν in v. 9a (thus ℵ*, B¹ etc.; Luke 7:26 is different) supports the translation offered above, while the reverse order, given in Nestle²⁶, permits both translations. Did the majority of the witnesses adapt Matthew to Luke? Or did some witnesses try to eliminate the ambiguity? It may have come from a literal translation from the Aramaic. There rhetorical questions introduced with מָה are normal; מָה is not translated. Thus the

Aramaic original might have meant: "Did you perhaps . . . go out in order to see a reed shaken by the wind?" cf. Beyer, *Syntax,* 100–101, n. 7.

2   Redactional are: in *v. 7a* πορεύομαι, in *v. 10* ἐγώ (with LXX). The changes in Luke 7:25b are Lukan. In v. 11, τοῦ βαπτιστοῦ, τῶν οὐρανῶν, and perhaps ἀμήν are redactional. Cf. vol. 1, Introduction 3.2.

3   Εἰ θέλεις (-ετε) + infinitive: 4/0/0; αὐτός ἐστιν: cf. 16:20. Μέλλω: cf. vol. 1, Introduction 3.2 and 16:27. The short version of the formulaic call to hear in v. 15 corresponds to 13:9, 43.

unusually large amount of redaction for both evangelists so that the number of words they have in common is minimal.[5] I will not try to reconstruct a possible Q wording. Matthew is probably responsible for: (1) in v. 12a ἀπὸ δὲ τῶν ἡμερῶν Ἰωάννου τοῦ βαπτιστοῦ ἕως ἄρτι;[6] (2) in v. 13 πάντες and ἐπροφήτευσαν;[7] the order of "prophets" and "law" remains unclear; (3) the change in order of Luke 16:16a (= Matt 11:13) and Luke 16:16b, c (= Matt 11:12).[8] In the traditional logion the first half was perhaps something like Luke 16:16a and the second half probably contained βασιλεία . . . βιάζεται καὶ βιασταὶ ἁρπάζουσιν αὐτήν.

Tradition History and Origin

Verses 7b-9 constitute a homogeneous three-part saying of Jesus that ends with the overly long concluding sentence v. 9c that is introduced by an emphatic "Yes, I tell you." It is a unity; only v. 8c might be an explanatory gloss that was inserted before Matthew. The aorist "Why *did* you go out?" might indicate that John's activity is already in the past. Then the saying would have been created by Jesus—just as Matthew reports it—when John was in prison or already executed. Later the church deepened and interpreted it

in two ways in v. 10 and vv. 11-14. The scripture quotation in *v. 10* is probably the church's addition.[9] *Verse 11* is an originally independent, unitary logion whose two parts are related to each other in strict antithetical parallelism.[10] In the context of Q it is a "commentary" on vv. 7-9.[11] In my judgment its content indicates that it probably comes from the church's tradition (cf. the interpretation, below). The "violence saying" of *vv. 12-13* was a "'disturbing' tradition."[12] Luke especially seems not to have understood the meaning of ἁρπάζω any longer. That suggests that the saying is quite old.[13]

Interpretation

■ **7-9** Jesus now turns to the crowds. He begins his discourse on John the Baptist with three well-crafted rhetorical questions designed to win the agreement of the hearers: "You certainly did not go out into the wilderness to see a reed shaken by the wind?" The wilderness is first of all the place where, along the Jordan, one may find reeds. The wilderness is a place where in those days one could find people in splendid apparel in the royal winter palaces.[14] The hearers agree; they

---

4   Luke 16:16 is in a small block of sayings about the law (Luke 16:16-18) that was not created by Luke, since it does not fit into the main scope of Luke 16.

5   Cf. vol. 1, II A 2.1 on 5:17-20, "Sources and Origin" and II A 2.2.3 on 5:31-32.

6   Cf. vol. 1, Introduction 3.2 on ἀπό, ἡμέρα, ἕως, ἄρτι. On ἡμέραι with the genitive of the person cf. in addition 2:1; 23:30; on ἀπό-ἕως cf. 1:17 redactional (three times); 26:29 redactional; 27:45 redactional; on the entire statement cf. Matt 3:1.

7   On προφητεύω cf. 7:22. Verse 13 corresponds to Matthew's understanding of the scripture (formula quotations!). On the other hand, however, Luke 16:16a corresponds to the exegetically usual (Lukan?) periodization of history so that we cannot be certain.

8   For formal reasons (common catchwords!) Matt 11:12 follows 11:11 well; Matt 11:13 prepares for the redactional v. 14. In an originally independent logion the Matthean order would not be understandable.

9   Only in the temptation story, which is very late in the history of tradition, are there other scripture quotations in Q introduced by γέγραπται.

10   Because of its content many regard v. 11b as secondary. The apparently contradictory judgments on John the Baptist could then be explained diachronically as a correction (thus, e.g., Bultmann, *History,*

165; Ferdinand Hahn, *The Titles of Jesus in Christology* [New York: World, 1969] 367; Gnilka 1.419). However, the antithetical parallels between v. 11a and b are very close: μείζων - μικρότερος ἐν γεννητοῖς γυναικῶν - ἐν τῇ βασιλείᾳ . . . The otherwise banal ἐν γεννητοῖς γυναικῶν especially requires a parallel. Such a smooth parallelism must not be decomposed into stages of tradition simply because of the content. Rhetorically v. 11a is quite conceivable as a preparation that intensifies and emphasizes the negative statement of 11b about the Baptist (Schlosser, *Règne de Dieu* 1.160). This also eliminates the need to find in v. 11a the original conclusion of vv. 7b-9 (e.g., Dibelius, *Überlieferung,* 12; Bultmann, *History,* 165). By the way, the logia 78 (= vv. 7-8) and 46 (= v. 11) of the *Gospel of Thomas* already speak against this view.

11   Wanke, *Kommentarworte,* 34.

12   Kosch, *Gottesherrschaft,* 47.

13   On the other hand, asking for an Aramaic original text is not helpful here; there is no unambiguous and direct possibility of a retranslation. This is shown by Dalman (*Words,* 141–42) and Black (*Approach,* 211, n. 2: "a notoriously *unheilbare St.*"); and, contrary to their intention, Daube (*New Testament,* 285–92) and Schwarz (*Jesus sprach,* 256–60).

14   Contra Theissen, "Rohr," 43. One thinks, e.g., of Herod's palaces in Jericho, Cyprus, Masada.

indeed went to the wilderness—the old, biblical place of revelation[15]—because they hoped to see a prophet. To this point Jesus is in full agreement with his listeners.

Agreement creates the basis for approvals that may remain unspoken. It has been often asked whether such approvals do not stand behind the images of our text. Of themselves, they are relatively banal. Any amount of reeds can be found in the wilderness along the Jordan. Does it simply mean that people do not go out into the wilderness for "something common"?[16] The second image, on the other hand, of a person in soft clothing appears not to fit, because it comes from a completely different area of life. It is tempting to interpret it figuratively in contrast to John's character. The ascetic John in his camel's hair is the opposite of a courtier in soft clothes. Must we interpret the first image of the reed figuratively too? One might think of an inability to form independent judgments,[17] or of an easy conformity that shows a lack of character[18] along the lines of Aesop's well-known fable of the reed and the oak,[19] or in a more general sense of weakness. These are qualities that one certainly could not attribute to John the Baptist, especially after his confrontation with the tetrarch Herod. In addition, we can ask whether both images do not contain hidden allusions to Herod Antipas. It is certainly possible with "one person" (singular!) "in soft clothing," and Theissen has pointed out that Herod Antipas, in his first period until c. 26 CE after the founding of Tiberias, had coins imprinted with the personal emblem of a reed.[20] Is it thus underground ridicule among his subjects—black humor about an unpopular ruler whom one could not criticize directly? Then the meaning would be: You did not go out to see *this* (well-known!) windbag and sissy! That is entirely possible. Then the generalizing interpretation of the addition of v. 8c about the royal palaces would be on the mark.[21] And the approval that Jesus evoked from his listeners with his rhetorical questions would be underground!

However, this is not yet the scope of the logion. It is in v. 9c that Jesus says emphatically that John is more than a prophet. Here he presumably distances himself from his hearers without furnishing a clear and useful formula for determining who John actually was. Jesus' saying may have caused his listeners, who at first smiled approvingly, to do some more thinking about what he said. Someone who is more than a prophet deserves special obedience.

■ **10-11** The next two verses make more precise the meaning of the vague "more than a prophet." Both the pre-Matthean layers of tradition and Matthew himself betray the need for a more exact description of the Baptist. That is the purpose of the quotation in v. 10 from Mal 3:1, supplemented by reminiscences of Exod 23:20,[22] that was widely applied to the Baptist in early Christianity (Mark 1:2; Luke 1:17, 76).[23] It is important that already in Mal 3:23-24 and later in early Judaism beginning with Sir 48:10 it was applied to the return of Elijah. In v. 14 Matthew will explicitly retain this widely known interpretation. The second explanation, the old commentary in v. 11, is difficult. The main problem is how Matthew combines the statement that the smallest in the kingdom of heaven is greater than the Baptist

15 Werner Schmauch, *Orte der Offenbarung und der Offenbarungsort im Neuen Testament* (Göttingen: Vandenhoeck & Ruprecht, 1956) 27–47.

16 [Literally: "everyday matter"] Klostermann, 96; Schönle, *Johannes,* 67.

17 Cf. Lucian *Hermot.,* 68: whoever is not capable of judgment is like "a reed . . . that bends in every wind even if only a little breeze is blowing and moving it."

18 Schweizer, 260: "weather vane"; Meier, "John the Baptist," 393: "vacillating crowd-pleaser."

19 Cf. Theissen, "Rohr," 44–45. Later the rabbis were also familiar with the fable (*b. Ta*ᶜ*an.* 20b *Bar.* = Str-B 1.598; Flusser, *Gleichnisse,* 1.52.

20 Theissen, "Rohr," 45–49.

21 Just as the interpretation in the *Gos. Thom.* 78: "your

kings and great ones."

22 Ἀποστέλλω (Malachi: ἐξαποστέλλω) and πρὸ προσώπου σου come from Exod 23:20. Σου (Malachi: μου) makes it formally possible that the reference is to the Messiah (instead of to God).

23 That this quotation is quite old is shown by the fact that its second half in v. 11c is based not on the LXX text but on the MT. The MT, along with Symmachus and Theodotion, reads the piel פִּנָּה = to prepare (the way), the LXX the qal פָּנָה = ἐπιβλέψεται (to look for). The connection of Mal 3:1 with Exod 23:20 also is an indication that it is old, for it is presumably already Jewish (Stendahl, *School,* 50. Cf. *Exod. Rab.* 32 [93d] in Str-B 1.597).

with his own frequently visible tendency to Christianize the Baptist and to connect him with the kingdom of God.[24]

Tradition

■ **11** Even as a traditional logion v. 11 offers a number of difficulties. Verse 11a is clear. Among the created, perishable human beings[25] God has not raised up[26] anyone greater than John the Baptist. In terms of content the thought here is less of the course of John's life[27] than of his mission and the content of his preaching. Difficult is v. 11b. Is "the smallest," "the least" ($\mu\iota\kappa\rho\acute{o}\tau\epsilon\rho\sigma\varsigma$) to be understood as comparative or superlative? In the former case one can think of Jesus who is younger[28] or less honored than his master, John.[29] However, "in the kingdom of God," which because of its position and as a contrast to "among those born of women" probably is attributive to "the smallest" ($\mu\iota\kappa\rho\acute{o}\tau\epsilon\rho\sigma\varsigma$), would argue against this view. $M\iota\kappa\rho\acute{o}\tau\epsilon\rho\sigma\iota$ in the kingdom of God does not mean "younger" (in the world). It thus would be better to interpret the logion in a general sense. Ὁ $\mu\iota\kappa\rho\acute{o}\tau\epsilon\rho\sigma\varsigma$ is presumably a superlative, thus: "the least in the kingdom of God."[30]

How is the phrase "*in the kingdom of God*" to be interpreted? (a) The classic interpretation understands it to refer to the kingdom of God that is present since Jesus, that is, the church. It leads to the general thesis: "the

least Christian is . . . as a Christian more than the greatest Jew."[31] The church fathers justified this view by appealing to regeneration, to relationship of Christians to God as their father, to baptism or to the Holy Spirit.[32] However, this interpretation is difficult, since the members of the church also are born of women. And who in the church would be "the least"? With this interpretation one would at least have to assume that the church created the saying. If we assume that it came from Jesus, then one might (b) think of the presently dawning kingdom of God that Jesus promises, for example, to the poor (= the least!). However, then the formulation "in" the kingdom of God is very difficult. Or does it mean (c) the future reign of God that one will "enter" and in which God's judgment will determine the ranking?[33] The present tense $\dot{\epsilon}\sigma\tau\acute{\iota}\nu$ makes this interpretation problematic. Furthermore, as a practical matter it excludes John—perhaps unintentionally—from the future kingdom. In my judgment, the formulaic "in the kingdom" ($\dot{\epsilon}\nu$ $\tau\hat{\eta}$ $\beta\alpha\sigma\iota\lambda\epsilon\acute{\iota}\alpha$) suggests that the saying originated in the church. The need to determine the Baptist's place in the history of salvation was greatest in the church, even if our logion's statement does not correspond to the otherwise prevailing tendency to Christianize the Baptist,[34] for it makes John part of the old world and not of the new eon whose nucleus is the church. From this perspec-

---

24 Cf. especially Trilling, "Täufertradition," and Walter Wink, *John the Baptist in the Gospel Tradition* (SNTSMS 7; London: Cambridge University Press, 1968) 27–41.

25 Biblicism; cf. e.g., Job 14:1; 15:14; 25:4; Jewish: 1QH 13.14; 18.12–13, 16, 23.

26 Biblicism; cf. Judg 2:16; 3:9; 1 Kgs 11:14, 23. *Passivum divinum!*

27 Classically Cyril of Jerusalem *Cat.* 3.6 = FC 61.111–12 (asceticism); Peter Chrysologus *sermo* 127 = *PL* 52.549 (*sanctitas, iustitia, virginitas, pudicitia, castitas, poenitentia*).

28 This is a possible but rare meaning of $\mu\iota\kappa\rho\sigma\varsigma$: LSJ, *s.v. $\mu\iota\kappa\rho\sigma\varsigma$, 2.2.*

29 This was a frequent interpretation in the ancient church. See, e.g., John Chrysostom, 37.2 = *PG* 57.421; *Opus imperfectum* 27 = 775; Luther, *WA* 38.519. By contrast Calvin (2.7) applies it to all servants of the gospel, an interpretation that is still held today. Cf. Franz Dibelius, "Zwei Worte Jesu," *ZNW* 11 (1910) 190–92; Oscar Cullmann, "Ὁ ὀπίσω

$\mu\sigma\upsilon$ ἐρχόμενος," in idem, *Vorträge und Aufsätze 1925–1962* (Tübingen: Mohr/Siebeck, 1966) 173–72; Suggs, *Wisdom*, 46–47; Hoffmann, *Studien*, 221–24; Schlosser, *Règne de Dieu* 1.165.

30 As in modern Greek: article + comparative = superlative.

31 Wellhausen, 54.

32 Cyril of Alexandria fr. 136 = Reuss, 196; Theodore of Heraclea fr. 75 = Reuss, 76–77.

33 See, e.g., McNeile, 154. The Jewish background of the question for the great or little one could support this interpretation. The texts distinguish between this and the future world (*Midr. Ruth* 1.17 [128a]; *b. B. Mes.* 85b; *Pesiq. R.* 83 [198b] in Str-B 1.598); further passages in Lachs, 193, n. 8. However, the logion contains no temporal distinctions.

34 P. Hoffmann (marginal comment): It also does not fit Q this way.

tive it is not necessary to interpret "in the kingdom of heaven" as present or future. We concede that a precise interpretation of the logion remains difficult.

■ **12-13** The original meaning of the "violence saying" that follows is one of the greatest riddles of the exegesis of the Synoptics. More than eighty years ago Harnack wrote: "There are few sayings of Jesus over which such a flood of explanations has been poured in various combinations and whose understanding still has remained so uncertain."[35] That is still true today.

We begin with lexical considerations. In Greek βιάζομαι is part of the contrast "volunteer—coerce," and in my judgment it almost always contains a negative element.[36] Most common is the middle with the active meaning ("to use force, to do violence, to overwhelm"). The corresponding passive is also frequently documented.[37] The intransitive middle used as an absolute ("to act violently") is less frequent.[38] I have never seen an example of the intransitive middle in the positive sense.[39] Βιαστής ("violent person") is a very rare, late word that always carries negative connotations.[40] Ἁρπάζω ("to rob, carry off, abduct, tear out, plunder, seize quickly") may be used in numerous ways. The negative meaning is predominant, especially in connection with a word of the stem βια-.[41] We now turn to the types of interpretation that have influenced the history of interpretation:

History of Interpretation

It has long been the custom to organize the types of interpretation in terms of whether they give the verb βιάζομαι (1) a middle-intransitive or (2) a passive meaning and whether they understand v. 12a in a (a) positive or (b) negative sense. The result is that there are three types of interpretation:[42]

1a. *Middle-intransitive interpretation.* Since John the Baptist the kingdom of God is breaking in irresistibly,[43] and the people, that is, the followers of Jesus, seize it eagerly.[44] However, this interpretation of v. 12b can be made to agree with the meaning of ἁρπάζω only with difficulty, with βιαστής scarcely, and with the combination of the two not at all. Therefore, it was suggested that v. 12b be understood antithetically: The kingdom of God is breaking in irresistibly, *but* there are violent people who rob it.[45] However, it is difficult to understand v. 12b that is introduced by καί as an antithetical parallelism; furthermore, βιασταί seems to take up the verb βιάζομαι with the same meaning. The advantage of the middle–intransitive interpretation would be that it

---

35 "Zwei Worte," 947.

36 Cf. the lexicographers. Hesychius β 590 defines βιάζεται as βιαίως κρατεῖται. Pollux *Onom.* 1.110 relates the verb to storm and waves; 6.132: βιάζομαι is the perversion of ἰσχύς, just as deceit is the perversion of wisdom; cf. 8.7. Moore ("*BIAZΩ*," 534) says as a result of the linguistic usage in Josephus: "The direct employment of physical violence is almost invariably implied in their usage." Other important connotations in Josephus are: βιά(ζομαι) happens against the will of the person involved and without any legal basis (Moore, "*BIAZΩ*," 535–36).

37 LSJ, *s.v.*, 1/1.

38 See Moore ("*BIAZΩ*," 520) on Josephus. For Hellenistic sources see Schrenk, "βιάζομαι," 610, n. 3 [609, n. 3] (about Ananke, a flood, about the rage of Ares).

39 Epictetus *Diss.* 4.7.20–21, the text most frequently cited to support this usage, is in my judgment to be understood as passive. The often-quoted text Exod 19:24 also has a negative meaning. When the Israelites "crowd" onto Mount Sinai, God will destroy them. Betz ("Eschatological Interpretation," 99) sees in this OT text the biblical background for Matt 11:12-13.

40 Hesychius β 594: γυναῖκας βιάζεται. For additional

(scarce) secular sources see Schrenk, "βιάζομαι," 613. Only the antiquated noun βιατάς that appears frequently in Pindar has a positive meaning ("strong, courageous"), but one should not automatically identify it with βιαστής.

41 Frequent in Josephus (Moore, "*BIAZΩ*," 530–34). Cf. Pollux, 5.60.

42 The combination 1b. makes no sense.

43 The interpretation as a middle is widespread especially in Protestantism since Melanchthon. Cf. Cameron, *Violence,* 55–56. More recent advocates have been Harnack ("Zwei Worte," 952–55), Manson (*Sayings,* 134), Betz ("Eschatological Interpretation," 103), or Merklein (*Gottesherrschaft,* 83).

44 Verse 12b was interpreted positively in the ancient church beginning with Irenaeus (*Haer.* 4.37.7: μετὰ σπουδῆς) and Clement of Alexandria (*Quis div. salv.* 21.3: βιαίως, μᾶλλον δέ; βεβαίως [!]). Similarly today, e.g., Merklein says that the basileia demands "new, forceful, extraordinary actions" (*Gottesherrschaft,* 89). Βιασταί are "people who are determined for anything" (82).

45 This is the interpretation, e.g., of Betz ("Eschatological Interpretation," 103) and Kosch (*Gottesherrschaft,* 26). Frederick W. Danker ("Luke 16:16—An Opposition Logion?" *JBL* 77 [1958] 236–37, 240),

follows naturally the previous sentence of Luke 16:16a. With John the Baptist the time of Law and Prophets is at an end, and now something new, the kingdom of God, irresistibly breaks in. It is impossible, however, by virtue of the meaning of βιάζομαι.

2a. *Passive-positive interpretation.* Violence is inflicted on the kingdom of God by the hearers of the word, that is, it is violently coveted.[46] The second sentence, v. 12b, was usually interpreted positively. People overcome all obstacles that separate them from the kingdom of God—with repentance, asceticism, earnest hearing of the word, etc. Albert Schweitzer's interpretation belongs to the same basic type. The kingdom of God is compelled, that is, "it is the host of penitents which is wringing it from God, so that it may now come at any moment."[47] This type of interpretation also ignores the negative connotations of βιάζομαι/βιαστής and has to contend with the difficulty that v. 12b can hardly be understood in a positive sense.

2b. *Passive-negative interpretation.* The kingdom of God suffers violence; violent people take possession of it.[48] The representatives of this interpretation usually think of the Zealots, often also of the Jewish opponents of Jesus or of John the Baptist. Its difficulty is that the first sentence, Luke 16:16a, does not fit well. After the statement about the time of Law

and Prophets one expects a positive statement about the kingdom of God and not one about "an unpleasant side effect of the new age."[49] However, the negative statement in v. 12b goes well with the equally negative v. 12a.

■ **12-13** The decision can only be made on the basis of the (straightforward!) linguistic meaning of βιάζομαι and therefore must be made in favor of the third interpretation. Since John the Baptist, violence has been done to the kingdom of God. Then v. 12b secretively explains by whom. A frequent suggestion is the Zealots, a view that is supported by the Jewish texts that speak of the Zealot attempts to compel the end of the world.[50] In my judgment, however, we should not think of the Zealots in general, since there had been Zealots since long before John the Baptist. One might think at most of overzealous followers of the Baptist and of Jesus who seize the kingdom of God, for example, people from Zealot circles.[51] However, it is most natural to think of the opponents of John and Jesus who take away the kingdom by force.[52] The general formulation includes both political opponents (Herod Antipas!) and the religious establishment. Their opposition weighs heavily on Jesus. It is directed against the kingdom of God itself. Q = Luke 16:16a poses a difficulty for this interpretation. It is possible that this sentence is designed to empha-

---

Jeremias (*Theology,* 112), and Schlosser (*Règne de Dieu* 2.522) attempt to avoid the difficulty of having a positive and a negative statement stand so harshly side by side by understanding v. 12b as Jesus' use of a Pharisaic accusation. The Pharisees accuse Jesus' disciples of being βιασταί who usurp what is holy. But what is the use of merely quoting an accusation that Jesus then does not refute?

46   This interpretation is the most widespread in the ancient church and was also taken over by the reformers. More recent forceful advocates are scarce, but one of them is Schniewind, 145 (the urgent arrival of the end for which the Pharisees hope has actually happened).

47   *Quest,* 357 [404]. In support of this interpretation are the numerous late and anti-Zealot Jewish statements that the coming of the Messiah can be hastened by repentance, keeping the commandments, the study of the Torah, etc. (Str–B 1.599–60 but never with verbs that contain an element of violence or force).

48   Karlstadt (*Reich Gotis*) was the first advocate of this type of interpretation. It later found some followers again in the eighteenth century and was advocated so convincingly by A. Schweizer that it has become the most popular one until today. More recent

forceful advocates: are J. Weiss (*Predigt*) and Schrenk ("βιάζομαι").

49   Harnack, "Zwei Worte," 951.

50   *Midr. Cant.* 2.7 (99a) and the other texts mentioned by Str–B 1.599.

51   Thus, e.g., Judas Iscariot or the people of John 6:15. There is no evidence that John had Zealot followers. In the history of interpretation this interpretation has given rise in the modern period to indirect polemics in, e.g., A. Schweizer, who spoke of "the Zealotism in the form of Anabaptism in the time of the Reformation" ("Ob in der Stelle," 113). J. Weiss (*Predigt,* 196) speaks of "fanatics." Ferdinand Christian Baur locates this text, which he regards as a creation of the Jewish-Christian church, in a historical context: The perpetrators of violence are the missionaries to the Gentiles who do violence to the kingdom of God (*Kritische Untersuchungen über die kanonischen Evangelien* [Tübingen: Fues, 1847] 616 n).

52   Ἁρπάζω in this interpretation cannot mean "to rob" in the sense of "to abduct," "to seize," but only "to remove," "to lead away." That corresponds well to 13:19 redactional ("to rob" = to destroy the fruit of the proclamation).

size the eschatological and illegal character of the violence. Until John the Law and Prophets were observed, but from then on, in the end-time, the opposition to the kingdom of God erupts "with force, i.e., . . . illegally."[53] Then the background of Matt 11:12-13 would be not the concept of the persecution of the righteous or the general idea of a holy war but rather the eschatological affliction or the eschatological struggle of evil against good.[54] However, only conjectures are possible here.

Matthew

■ **11-14** If we try to understand the tense interplay of statements about John's exaltation and lowliness in vv. 11-14 at the level of the Gospel of Matthew, we must be careful about exaggerations. The goal of Matthew's thought lies in v. 14. John is the Elijah who was predicted by the prophets (cf. vv. 10, 13!). On the one hand, he is one of the prophets who made predictions;[55] on the other he is more than they, viz., the promised Elijah. There is here a certain imbalance in the way John is classified. Matthew emphasizes that John proclaims the kingdom of God (3:2), although he does not perform its signs (11:2-6). But, as the evangelist has already indicated (4:12; 11:2) and will again report (14:3-12), he also experiences the violence that is done to the kingdom of God. His suffering serves as a prelude to the fate of Jesus. However, it is this fate that both of them have in common with the prophets. To suffer violence is the fate of prophets (21:33-39; 23:29-37). Thus John is, although a proclaimer of the kingdom of God, at the same time the last prophet (v. 13).[56] Appropriately, according to old Jewish sources, the returning Elijah will have prophetic tasks.[57] As Elijah-who-has-returned John is, as it were, the personified continuity between the kingdom of God and the prophets of Israel who prophesied about Jesus.[58]

If we begin with the idea that John is the connecting link between Israel and the kingdom of God, then it is no insurmountable difficulty that in vv. 11-13 Matthew has combined various statements about him.[59] The traditional v. 11b introduces an intervening thought that is not along the lines of what Matthew actually wants to say. He really does not want to exclude John fundamentally from the kingdom of God, even though he does not let him share in its miracles (11:2-6, cf. 13:16-17) and its joy (9:14-15; 11:18-19). Of course, the least in the kingdom of heaven is greater than he. What is especially true, however, is that John, Jesus, and the disciples suffer the same violence when the kingdom of God dawns. Matthew must not "necessarily retract"[60] v. 11b, but he does have to secure it. He does that with v. 12 that again brings John together with the kingdom of God.[61] Verses 18-19 will carry this idea further. Thus in v. 12 Matthew gives, as if it were a parenthetical thought, his own basic idea that the kingdom of God leads every prophet and proclaimer into suffering. Suffering is at the same time testimony. And so the Baptist, who is nothing less than the returned Elijah, becomes a witness against an Israel that rejects the kingdom of God. This prepares the way for the preaching of judgment in vv. 16-24.

---

53 A. Schweizer, "Ob in der Stelle," 118. I agree with him that the original meaning of Luke 16:16a is by no means that the time of Law and Prophets is ended and abolished. In my judgment that would be inconceivable for Q also.

54 Cf. 1QpHab. 2.6; 4QpPs. 37, 2.14 (the violent ones עָרִיצִים toward the covenant [in the end-time]); 1QH 2.11–12, 21, 25–29 (war of the violent against the pious); in Q cf. Luke 12:50, 51-53, further David Catchpole, "On Doing Violence to the Kingdom," *Irish Biblical Studies* 3 (1981) 77–92, 80; Betz, "Krieg," 128–29. (Betz is thinking of the struggle between God and Belial and also sees the evil spirits in the violent persons.)

55 As a rule ἕως is used inclusively in Matthew. Cf. 1:17; 2:15; 20:8; 23:35; 27:8.

56 If ἕως is to be interpreted inclusively in v. 12, then it also has to be interpreted inclusively in v. 13. However, ἕως cannot designate the content of the prophecy.

57 Cf. *Tg. Mal.* 3:23 (prophet!); Sir 48:10 (ἐλεγμοί); Str–B 4.785 (Elijah as proclaimer).

58 Thus one cannot say that the Baptist stands "over against the prophets and the law and together with Jesus" (Meier, "John the Baptist," 403).

59 Matthew is not aware of the modern academic question whether the Baptist belongs to the old or the new eon.

60 Schönle, *Johannes,* 127.

61 As a rule the temporal ἀπό is inclusive in Matthew. Cf. 1:17; 19:8; 20:8; 23:35; 24:21; 27:45 and Trilling, "Täufertradition," 52–53.

■ **13** Verse 13 prepares the main thought.[62] Skipping vv. 11b-12, $\gamma\acute{\alpha}\rho$ probably refers back to v. 11a and carries it further. "All" ($\pi\acute{\alpha}\nu\tau\epsilon\varsigma$) emphasizes Matthew's basic and comprehensive claim to the prophetic witness as it is also expressed in the formula quotations. John is one of the prophets[63] who have prophesied. However, the last prophet, John, is more than a prophet.

■ **14** What the portrayal in 3:4[64] and the quotation of v. 10 indicated, v. 14 now makes explicit: John is the returned Elijah. Matthew emphasizes this in order to give weight to his testimony and his call to Israel (and indirectly to the church!) to repent. Israel faces the decision whether it will accept him. Matthew's story will show that it will reject John, its Elijah, and the Son of Man Jesus, its Messiah.

■ **15** The warning call in v. 15 is intended to make the people aware of this basic decision. Viewed from the end of Matthew's story, it sounds like a warning signal before Israel's missed decision.

Summary and History of Interpretation

The interpretation has made clear that our text primarily serves a function in the macrotext. Its purpose is not to give instruction about John or about the kingdom of God but to show how Jesus lays claim on John the Baptist, Israel's Elijah, in order to call the people with final urgency to decision. Thus the text prepares for the coming crisis. Matthew creates it with the help of traditional individual sayings about John that he uses without completely exhausting their meaning and that had their own independent influence both before him in the church and after him. The greatest difficulties in interpreting the sayings for the present happen when one focuses simply on the individual sayings that Matthew used and not on the entire unit in the macrotext. Since the difficulties are greatest for the section's theologically central logion, the "violence saying," we will use it as an example.[65]

Sometimes Jesus' sayings convey the impression that they are simply linguistic hulls that throughout the history of their interpretation have repeatedly been filled with totally new meaning. This impression is especially strong in the case of the violence saying. Presumably the evangelist Matthew did not completely exhaust the meaning of the traditional saying. It is so obscure that an exegete is reluctant to suggest one's own original meaning, reconstructed with many questions and uncertainties, as the norm and standard of new actualizations, for example, in preaching. Within the biblical material Luke is probably the first who in 16:16 filled the linguistic hull that he received with completely new meaning.

In the later history of the saying's interpretation, in certain churches and epochs, basic understandings of the gospel are reflected. Characteristic of the ancient church, especially in the East, is the ascetic interpretation associated primarily with v. 12b. To "rob" the kingdom is not simply to renounce idolatry and the old ethic[66] but to want to possess by virtue what we have not received by nature.[67] The "ones who rob" are those who oppress themselves by force.[68] Alongside this interpretation, in the Middle Ages there was often the salvation-history interpretation that came from Hilary.[69] The

---

62 Thus we may not follow the tradition and interpret v. 13 as part of the "violence saying" but, following Matthew's thinking, we must understand it as a preparation for the main scope of v. 14 after the "*accessoire*" (Loisy, 1.673), vv. 11b-12.

63 Matthew puts the prophets first and lets the law follow in order to make clear that he is here interested in the predictive function of both. Cf. Berger, *Gesetzesauslegung*, 223–24.

64 Cf. vol. 1, I B 1.1 on 3:4.

65 Cameron (*Violence*) reviews the history of interpretation.

66 Cyril of Alexandria fr. 139 = Reuss, 197.

67 Jerome, 80.

68 *Qui affligunt seipsos violenter* (Dionysius bar Salibi 2.226). Matthew 11:12 appears at the end of an Egyptian history of the saints (*Apophthegmata Patrum* 1152 = Bonifaz Miller, *Weisung der Väter* [Freiburg: Lambertus, 1965] 399) along with the statement: "Thus it is good that because of God one treat one's self violently in everything." [*Trans.*: Benedicta Ward plays down the element of violence in her ET: "Truly it is good to constrain oneself for God's sake." *The Wisdom of the Desert Fathers: The 'Apophthegmata Patrum'* (The Anonymous Series; Fairacres, Oxford: SLG Press, 1975) 26.]

69 11.7 = SC 254.260.

believing Gentiles rob Israel of the kingdom of God. Karlstadt argued against the ancient church's ascetic interpretation. He was the first and for two centuries the only person to interpret force as evil and hostile to God: "In temptation and persecution God's kingdom becomes witty, intelligent, strong, and extremely great and much."[70] With this interpretation Karlstadt is able not only to refute what he regarded as the ancient church's Pelagian interpretation but also to comfort churches of the Reformation that were persecuted and under attack and to include among the evil people of violence the "most high pontifex." However, the "normal" Protestant interpretation is different. While structurally the same as that of the ancient church, it understands both the kingdom of God and violence in a new sense. At issue now is the preaching of the gospel; the text speaks of the "fruit of the word," and the violent persons are those "who hear and hear in such a way that nothing can hold them back."[71] "To rob" is to desire grace *avidissime*; "violence" is the *ardor audiendi*.[72] Again the hull of the saying is filled with a new basic understanding of the gospel. Two more examples from more recent times: For the pious liberal Johannes Weiss it is "blasphemous to use violence on God's reign . . . instead of waiting obediently, humbly, and faithfully until it will please God to establish his reign."[73] What is important for Eduard Schweizer, coming from dialectical theology,

is that the presence of the kingdom stands "already under the sign of the cross" and means "oppression, assault, suffering."[74]

What has happened here? In each of these cases, from the hull of the violence saying a new meaning has arisen that was based on an interpreter's or a church's understanding of faith. In each of these cases, it is not the text alone that participated in producing this meaning but also the interpreter, who again acted not alone but in conversation with other interpreters and as a member of the church. And in each of these cases the interpreter's conversation partner was not simply the individual text but, as it were, the whole believed Christ as the one who gives and demands, who is crucified and risen.[75] He is the most important agent in bringing new meaning to a text. He fills the hulls of the sayings. Thus already in the Gospel of Matthew the individual texts derive their meaning from Matthew's entire story of Christ and from the Matthean Christ. At the same time, however, this Christ always lives only in and from the hulls, the received texts, whose meaning he constantly changes, and in and from the story that these texts tell.

---

70 Karlstadt, *Reich Gotis* (no page numbers; at the top of the third page from the end).
71 Luther, *WA* 38.519.
72 Bullinger, 111B, 112A.
73 *Predigt*, 196.
74 262.
75 In the case of Matt 11:12-13 the regulating power of the individual text is relatively small and the innovating power of the "whole Christ," who accompanies the church throughout the history of interpretation, is relatively large, because early on the meaning of the individual text (already in Luke?) was dimmed and because several later new actualizations are more pregnant and powerful than the biblical one in Matthew. One may regret this in a church, which lives from the *perspicuitas* of the scripture, or one may rejoice over Christ's power of innovation. Important is that Matt 11:12-13 is in a sense an extreme case. With most texts the clarity of the traditional meaning and thus the weight of the individual text as one of the powers that produces new meaning is greater than in this case.

1.3 This Stubborn Generation (11:16-19)

Literature

Arens, *HΛΘON-Sayings*, 221–43.

Fred W. Burnett, *The Testament of Jesus-Sophia: A Redaction-Critical Study of the Eschatological Discourse in Matthew* (Washington: University Press of America, 1981) 81–94.

Christ, *Sophia*, 63–80.

Cotter, "Children," 63–82.

Flusser, *Gleichnisse*, 151–55.

Hoffmann, *Studien*, 224–31.

Jülicher, *Gleichnisreden* 2.23–36.

Légasse, *Jésus*, 289–317.

Ragnar Leivestad, "An Interpretation of Matt 11:19," *JBL* 71 (1952) 179–81.

Linton, "Parable," 159–79.

Lührmann, *Redaktion,* 29–31.

Mussner, "Kairos," 599–613.

Antonio Orbe, "El Hijo del hombre come y bebe (Mt 11,19; Lc 7,34)," *Greg* 58 (1977) 523–55.

Rainer Russ, ". . . Und ihr habt nicht getanzt," in idem, ed., *Gott bei den Tänzern und Narren* (Trier: Paulinus, 1980) 55–73.

Harald Sahlin, "Traditionskritische Bemerkungen zu zwei Evangelienperikopen," *StTh* 33 (1979) 69–84.

Sato, "Q," 179–83.

Schulz, *Q,* 379–86.

Suggs, *Wisdom,* 33–58.

Wanke, *Kommentarworte,* 35–40.

Zeller, "Bildlogik," 252–57.

For *additional literature* on Matthew 11 see above, II D.

16 "But with what shall I compare this generation? It is like children who sit in the market places and call to the others;[1] 17/ they say: 'We played the flute for you, and you did not dance!

We have sung the mourning song, And you did not beat your chests.'

18 For John came neither eating nor drinking, and they say: 'He has a demon!'

19 The Son of Man has come eating and drinking, and they say: 'Behold, the man is a glutton and a drunkard, the friend of tax-collectors and sinners.'" And wisdom was justified because of her works.[2]

Analysis

Structure

The section consists of a short parable and a word of interpretation. Λέγουσιν ("they say"), repeated three times, helps to relate the interpretation to the parable. The statements of the interpretive word in vv. 18-19d about John and Jesus are formally parallel, but the greater length of the criticism directed at Jesus and the use of "Son of Man" instead of the name show where the emphasis lies. Verse 19e gives the impression of being an unrelated afterthought, but with the catchword ἔργα ("works") it looks back to v. 2. The brief sentence is best understood as the narrator's commentary.

Source and Redaction

The section comes from Q, where it is the continuation of 11:7-11 = Luke 7:24-28.[3] While the wording is in general in agreement, for the most part we cannot decide the individual questions with any certainty. I would regard as Matthean: in v. 16 the reduction of the Lukan double question,[4] λέγουσιν three times in vv. 17-19,[5] in vv. 18-19 ἦλθεν instead of ἐλήλυθεν,[6] and in v. 19e ἔργων.[7] The remaining differences are most likely due to Lukan redaction, although κόπτω/κλαίω remains quite difficult.[8]

---

1 Ἑταίροις in a number of witnesses is a typical Itacism. It is not well attested, but Linton ("Parable," 166) correctly points out that the addition αὐτῶν that is found in many MSS actually only fits the variant ἑταίροις, so that the number of witnesses that *meant* "companions" perhaps is increased.

2 That most witnesses read τέκνων along with Luke 7:35 shows that the Lukan ecclesiological interpretation was more easily understood than was the Matthean christological interpretation. Since the Vulgate and the *textus receptus* also read τέκνων, ἔργων has hardly ever been interpreted.

3 Luke 7:29-30 is redactional.

4 Cf. 13:31, different from Mark 4:30 and Luke 13:18. However, it remains strange that Matthew even introduces a parable with a question.

5 Matthew emphasizes the parallelism (three times λέγουσιν).

6 Cf. 17:12 (different Mark 9:13); 21:32.

7 Cf. 11:2. Thus we can dismiss the once popular explanation of the difference between Matthew and Luke as translation variants of the Aramaic עבדי; furthermore, the translation of עבדא (servant) by τέκνον would be more than strange.

8 The idea that κόπτω was "too Palestinian" for the readers of Luke (Schürmann, *Lukasevangelium* 1.424, n. 115) is refuted by Luke 8:52; 23:27.

Origin and Transmission

In the opinion of most interpreters the parable of vv. 16-17 and the interpretation of vv. 18-19 do not quite fit together.[9] The parable, vv. 16-17, is generally attributed to Jesus, since there are no convincing reasons not to do so. The interpretation, vv. 18-19, is usually considered as a creation of the church. A problem with that view is that without an explanation no one understands why "this generation" can be compared with the playing children. The colorful palette of suggested interpretations that scholarship offers for this parable (cf. below) speaks volumes. The parable needs a commentary; why should the one offered in vv. 18-19 not be the original? I find it probable that v. 19e was a secondary addition. It is not an originally independent logion,[10] nor is it a proverb,[11] but an expansion that presupposes vv. 16-19d.[12] It has nothing to do with the generation that rejects Jesus, but here the Q community contrasts itself as "children of wisdom" with the generation of Israel that rejects Jesus.

Interpretation: Jesus

■ **16-19** The question of the original meaning of the parable has long been a *crux interpretum*. There are three basic possibilities:

a. The most widespread interpretation understands "this generation" to be the children *addressed* in v. 17. They are called to play wedding, but they do not want to dance. They are called to play funeral, but they do not want to beat their breasts as if they were in mourning. They are *passive, obstinate, killjoys* who simply do not want to get involved in anything. Here lies then the *tertium comparationis* for "this generation." It is stupid;[13] it does not want to do anything.[14] What is it that it does not want? Here one must insert something. Without the referent this parable is not understandable.

With this interpretation, however, the introduction in v. 16a is not only imprecise, as is often the case in Jewish parables, but even distorted, for it explicitly compares this generation with the children who are speaking.[15] In contrast to the introduction, this first interpretation that compares John and Jesus with the children who are speaking, is attractive. It provides the chance for a lovely allegory—a chance eagerly used by the church's interpretation. John mourns, while Jesus introduces the wedding joy of the kingdom of God with his flute playing.[16] Then, however, another difficulty arises. In vv. 18-19 the order of the players is reversed—Jesus is the joyful one, John the mournful! Lesser difficulties are offered by a differ-

---

9   One assigned John (allegorically!) to the mourning, Jesus to the flute playing, and then it was discovered that the order of the two is reversed in vv. 17 and 18-19. It was claimed that the disharmony of the children among themselves (ἀλλήλοις) does not fit well the two clear parties of vv. 18-19 with John and Jesus on one side, their opponents on the other, and that v. 19e does not fit as an interpretation of the parable anyway. Examples for such argumentation: Klostermann, 99; Schulz, *Q*, 381; Hoffmann, *Studien*, 227–30; Arens, *ΗΛΘΟΝ-Sayings*, 22–23; Gnilka 1.423.

10   Contra Christ (*Jesus Sophia*, 63–75), who tacitly presupposes this every bit as much as he does that v. 19e came from Jesus.

11   Thus Ragnar Leivestad ("An Interpretation of Matt 11:19," *JBL* 71 [1952] 179–81) in the sense of: "Wisdom is known by deeds." However, there is no documentation, and Leivestad also cannot explain the change to τέκνα, which is for him secondary.

12   The second wisdom text of Q, Luke 11:49-51, is also a secondary addition. Thus in terms of the history of the tradition the wisdom statements in Q are secondary. Cf. Kloppenborg, *Formation*, 143–44. The third wisdom text in Q, Luke 13:34-35, which also concludes a Q section, also supports this conclusion.

13   The scarce and late rabbinical parallels interpret it in this direction: *b. Sanh.* 103a (Rab Papa) = Str-B 1.604; *Midrash ekah rabbati*, 12th proömium, according to Zeller, "Bildlogik," 256; also Aesop's fable 11 (August Hausrath, ed., *Corpus fabularum Aesopicarum* [Bibliotheca scriptorum Graecorum et Romanorum Teubneriana; Leipzig: Teubner, 1959] 17), widely known in antiquity (Cotter, "Children," 69–70), of the fish who do not want to dance to the flute.

14   See, e.g., Schürmann, *Lukasevangelium* 1.424: "who could not be moved . . . by anything" and "each time reacted negatively"; Bonnard, 164 "décidé à ne pas 'entrer dans le jeu'"; Zeller, "Bildlogik," 256: "that Israel did not want to hear God's call"; Gundry, 212 ("stubbornness of 'this generation'").

15   Thus Harald Sahlin ("Traditionskritische Bemerkungen zu zwei Evangelienperikopen," *StTh* 33 [1979] 69–84, 78–79) changes it (in Aramaic!). It is, of course, correct that there are in Matthew as well as in Judaism *imprecise* introductions to parables (e.g., Matt 13:45; 22:2; 25:1; cf. already Grotius 1.341; Jeremias, *Parables*, 100–102; Verseput, *Rejection* (105), but this introduction does not use just any characteristic theme word from the parable but the only one that is downright wrong.

16   Cf. Knabenbauer 1.502; Légasse, *Jésus*, 295–96.

ent type of allegorical interpretation that understands the children who are calling out to be not only John and Jesus but also Israel's pious, for example, the prophets.[17]

b. The second type of solution compares this generation not with the children addressed but with the children who are calling out.[18] Once again without a referent the parable is not at all understandable. If one includes vv. 18-19, John and Jesus represent the children who are addressed. But how? Do his opponents summon John, the harsh preacher of repentance, to "messianic joy," and Jesus, the joyful wedding celebrant, to mourning?[19] But John "did not dance to their flutes"; Jesus "did not grieve to their laments."[20] While this interpretation is indeed correct as far as the parable's introduction is concerned, it is artificial. In order to make it "more natural," J. Jeremias resorted to the help of a Palestinian expert who obviously is also familiar with Palestinian children. The children who are doing the speaking are the lazy ones who want to remain sitting. They give the exhausting part—the dancing and the mourning—to their playmates.[21] What Jesus then says to this generation is: "You just want to give orders." This interpretation has no problems with the parable's introduction and sequence, but beyond that it has serious problems. The major problem is that vv. 18-19 speak not of the Jews' expectation of John and Jesus but of their reaction to them.

c. The third type of solution begins with the observation that "this generation" is compared not with a group of children but with *all*.[22] Some children want to play wedding, the others funeral, and they cannot agree. One can then understand the *tertium comparationis* in different ways. One can focus on the *lost chance to play* as the point of comparison. If they do not agree, they cannot play. The point is "the play that was rained out"[23] or, more theologically, the "missed kairos."[24] This interpretation is attractive,[25] but it has the disadvantage that precisely the scope is not stated by the parable's narrator. In my judgment it would be better—as the parable's introduction also suggests—to begin with the children. Then the *tertium comparationis* could be the childish capriciousness,[26] the "fickle willfulness that never wants whatever it is that is offered."[27] This suggestion is compatible with the (imprecise but not wrong) introduction to the parable. The image is also imprecise, for it is not said that different children suggest the different games. It also depends on an interpretation. One must explain wherein this generation's capriciousness lies. However, it has the advantage that it does not tempt us to put John and Jesus allegorically in the parable, for *all* children belong to "this generation."

Thus far the interpretation has not actually made use of the *opposition between the two games* (playing wedding/playing funeral). Dance and mourning are traditional opposites.[28] The criticisms the Jews level against John and Jesus also are opposites. What they criticize John for is precisely what they want Jesus to do. In my judgment, the point of comparison lies not in the children's character but in their conflicting

---

17 See, e.g., Paschasius Radbertus, 443–44 (prophets and apostles against *omne genus Iudaeorum*); Strabo, 121 (the *humiles spiritu* in Israel); Albertus Magnus, 489; Thomas Aquinas, *Lectura* no. 936 (David as "cantor" for Israel; dancing = spiritual joy; mourning = repentance).

18 To my knowledge first advocated by Euthymius Zigabenus, 356.

19 Holtzmann, *Synoptiker,* 67. Similar, only a little less colorful, is Linton ("Parable," 177): "They asked both John and Jesus to observe traditional customs."

20 Meyer, 223.

21 Jeremias, *Parables,* 161. The expert is E. F. F. Bishop, *Jesus of Palestine* (London: Lutterworth, 1955). Cotter ("Children," 67–68) offers a new variant of this interpretation: καθήμενοι, ἐν ἀγορᾷ, and προσφονεῖν refer to "the world of judicial courts"; "this generation" is like childish judges. But are the linguistic parallels really clear enough so that the dissonance between the childish play and the imitated adult world is recognizable?

22 Thus already Maldonat (236), who on this text offers quite modern principles of parable interpretation that anticipate Jülicher: "In parabolis non personae personis, non partes partibus, sed totum negotium toti negotio comparetur."

23 [Literally "hailed." *Trans.*] The formulation is Zeller's ("Bildlogik," 254).

24 The title of Mussner's essay: "Der nicht erkannte Kairos." This interpretation is substantially represented by, e.g., Dibelius (*Überlieferung,* 17) and Hoffmann (*Studien,* 226).

25 It is the only interpretation that can be understood without the explanation of vv. 18-19.

26 Cf. the parallels in Epictetus *Diss.* 3.15.5–7 (the changeable character of children's play); 4.7.5 (thoughtlessness of children at play).

27 Jülicher, *Gleichnisreden* 2.32, similarly Mussner, "Kairos," 606; Schmid, 194.

28 Cf. Eccl 3:4 (a time to mourn, a time to dance); Sir 22:6 (music is not appropriate for mourning); Prov

wishes. The parable thus best corresponds to the interpretation that is necessary anyway. The same opposition also characterizes the criticisms the Jews make against John and Jesus. Matthew also calls attention to the parallel with the threefold λέγουσιν. Jesus says: Like children at play you do not know what you really want![29] You want *everything*, and you cannot agree on anything. Beneath the surface it may be: Your contradictions reveal that in the final analysis you do not want at all!

As a *result*, it seems clear to me that the parable and the interpretation belong together. The origin of the entire text is still an open question. The Son of Man title is what makes it difficult to attribute it to Jesus. "Son of Man" is to be understood here as a title. If we may assume that in Aramaic "son of man" used alone is not a simple equivalent for "I," but means "I" with a generalizing connotation ("I" as human; a human being such as I),[30] then a nontitular "son of man" simply does *not* fit here where Jesus speaks only of John and himself.[31] On the other hand, the title "Son of Man" fits very well because it sharpens the accusation against this generation. He whom you call a glutton and drunkard is precisely the one who will come as judge of the world! There are now three possible explanations for the origin of vv. 16-19c. Those who believe—as I do—that Jesus already regarded himself as the coming Son of Man are forced by this logion to deal with the difficulty that vv. 18-19 can only be understood as a public reproach. Did Jesus speak publicly of himself as the Son of Man?[32] That is the case with a number of syn-

optic sayings about the present activity of the Son of Man, at least some of which *can* go back to Jesus.[33] Or we can assume, in the second place, that an original I-saying of Jesus was later rhetorically sharpened with the Son of Man title. The rhetorical thrust of the text might support this possibility. Although vv. 18-19 want to present Jesus and John as parallels, the use of the Son of Man title puts Jesus above John. The third possibility is that the entire text, vv. 16-19d, is a creation of the church. A problem with this view is that at least the accusation that Jesus is a glutton and drunkard goes back in substance to the time of Jesus. Result: vv. 16-19d *may* indeed come from Jesus.

Interpretation: Matthew

■ **16a** The adversative particle δέ is the first sign for a marked mood shift in Jesus' discourse. Not until v. 18 will its reason be clear. "This generation" has rejected John the Baptist, who had come to Israel as Elijah at the dawning of the kingdom of God (vv. 12-14). Γενεὰ αὕτη here does not mean, as the Greek might suggest, "this race," viz., Israel, but "this generation," viz., the contemporaries of John and Jesus.[34] This conclusion is based, on the one hand, on the biblical and Jewish usage behind Matthew,[35] on the other hand on parallel passages,[36] and, finally, on the context. Verse 12 had spoken of the *time* of John and Jesus. Within the framework of his story Matthew thus thinks first of all of Jesus' con-

---

25:20; Zech 12:10 LXX (κατορχέομαι - κόπτομαι); 1 Macc 9:41; Ovid *Heroides* 12.137-42.

29 Cf. John Chrysostom, 37.4 = *PG* 57.424 (Jewish self-contradiction); Olshausen 427: "one part desires this, and the other that"; Loisy, 1.697: The Jews "se contredisent eux-mêmes dans les jugements qu'ils portent sur Jean et sur Jésus."

30 Colpe, "ὁ υἱὸς τοῦ ἀνθρώπου," 403-4 (with references). It is, therefore, a puzzle to me why the same Colpe (432) can propose for Matt 11:19: "Now there comes one who eats and drinks . . ." בַּר נָשָׁא here means precisely Jesus in distinction from other people!

31 Contra Bultmann, *History*, 155.

32 Cf. Sato, "Q," 181.

33 Cf. Luke 9:58; 11:30; 12:10; Mark 2:10, 28; Luke 19:10. Of the group Luke 9:58 is, in my judgment, most likely genuine, perhaps also Luke 11:30 and Mark 2:10. In each of the three sayings Luke 7:34-35, 9:58, and 11:30 a certain feature of the activity of Jesus familiar to the hearers (eating and drink-

ing, homelessness, preaching repentance) functions *rhetorically* as a "means of identification" that makes clear to the hearers who is meant by the Son of Man (indicated by Chr. Riniker).

34 With Légasse (*Jésus*, 302-6) and Verseput (*Rejection*, 106-7) and contra Max Meinertz, "'Dieses Geschlecht' im Neuen Testament," *BZ* NF 1 (1957) 283-89 (for Meinertz the negative moral accent of γενεά is primary).

35 Hebrew דּוֹר means primarily "human age, generation"; this meaning is transferred to the term γενεά in the LXX. Cf., e.g., Jer 8:3; Ps 95:10; *Jub.* 23.15-16, 22 ("this generation," *scil.* the [evil] generation of the end-time); 1QpHab 2.7 (הַדּוֹר הָאַחֲרוֹם).

36 23:36; 24:34 (always with the attribute αὕτη); 1:17 (4 times). However, Matthew's linguistic usage is not unified. In other texts the temporal nuance recedes and the qualitative (attribute: πονηρά) is in the foreground (e.g., 12:39, 45), without excluding in each case the other nuance.

temporaries. However, the use of the word γενεά in 12:39-45 and especially in 23:36 will show that the Israel back then was no exception.

■ **16-19** The Matthean Jesus thus compares his contemporaries with the children at play. The interpretation in vv. 18-19 is clearer than the parable itself. The twofold ἦλθεν ("came") connects John the Baptist and Jesus with each other. Both are rejected and suffer the same fate. The double criticism conveys the impression of Israel's hardness. At the same time, however, the greater length of v. 19a-d and the nature of the criticism make clear the superiority of Jesus. The criticism that Jesus is a glutton and drunkard and a friend of the tax collectors and sinners goes to the heart of the mission of Jesus. While many people probably praised John's asceticism, "glutton" and "drunkard" traditionally are negatively loaded words.[37] Matthew has already illustrated the accusation in 9:10-13 where Jesus' opponents—there they are Pharisees—reject the mercy of Israel's Messiah. Primarily, however, it is the Son of Man title that makes clear how catastrophic their criticism is. The "Son of Man" comes—and with this title Matthew always thinks of Jesus who will some day rise and judge the world[38]—and Israel misunderstands him as a "human being," who carouses and drinks.[39] The twofold ἄνθρωπος ("man") is not a redundancy,[40] but a pregnant play on words. "This generation" misunderstands the coming Son of Man Jesus as a man!

■ **19e** In this brief concluding sentence Matthew has introduced a significant change. Wisdom was justified not, as in Q, by[41] her children but because of[42] her works. The hypostatized wisdom is in Judaism an expression of God's beneficial rule that forms the world (Prov 8:22-31), directs history (Wisdom 10–12), and fills human beings. She can pass into humans (Wis 7:27) and can have humans as children (Prov 8:32-33; Sir 4:11). In Q the community of the Son of Man set itself against all those who rejected John and Jesus. The divine wisdom, whose emissaries John and Jesus are (cf. Luke 11:49), was justified by the church. When Matthew now substitutes wisdom's "works" for her "children," our verse indirectly receives a christological meaning. While one can understand wisdom also as the power of God that stands *behind* Jesus and John and acts through them as "friends of God and prophets" (Wis 7:27), Matthew is probably taking up the thread of 11:2. Wisdom's works are the miracles of healing and the preaching of Christ—and not of John—in Israel. Verse 19e is for him a commentary only on v. 19a-d and not, as in Q, on vv. 18-19. Thus presumably Jesus and wisdom are indirectly[43] identified.[44] In my judgment we may not regard this identification as a conscious theological new creation. Matthew never identifies Jesus directly with the divine wisdom; he simply presupposes their identity.[45] He does not stop to think about the christological consequences that this identification, widespread in early Christianity, might have and that are illustrated, for example, by John 1:1-18; Phil 2:6-11; Col 1:15-20, etc., viz., preexistence and the idea of incarnation. Nevertheless, with v. 19e he

---

37 On φάγος cf. φαγονέω = to be fat, lazy. While οἰνοπότης may be neutral, cf. Prov 23:20. However, I do not think, as is often assumed, that the comparison with Deut 21:20 plays a role in our text. The formulation is too different. For Hellenistic parallels see Cotter, "Children," 75–76.

38 Cf. above on 8:20; 9:6; on Q cf. Hoffmann, *Studien,* 149. For Matthew we must completely abandon the idea of differing semantic meanings of the title in the three "groups" of Son of Man sayings.

39 Cf. below, IV A 1, the excursus on the Son of Man in the Gospel of Matthew, 4.

40 McNeile, 158.

41 Ἀπό = ὑπό with the passive: BAGD, s.v. ἀπό, V 6.

42 BAGD, s.v. ἀπό, V 6.

43 Similarly 11:28-30 where one could speak of a func-

tional identity of Jesus and wisdom (cf. below, vv. 28-30: Matthew) and 23:34 where σοφία is replaced by ἐγώ.

44 Thus, among others, Suggs, *Wisdom,* esp. 57; Fred W. Burnett, *The Testament of Jesus-Sophia: A Redaction-Critical Study of the Eschatological Discourse in Matthew* (Washington: University Press of America, 1981) 88–92. Verseput (*Rejection,* 116–17) remains skeptical.

45 Thus the incarnation of divine wisdom in Jesus ("Wisdom has 'become flesh and dwelled among us'"; Suggs, *Wisdom,* 57) is *not* the center of Matthean Christology. Matt 11:19e remains an additional comment with which Matthew wants to call attention to the foundational character of the *deeds* of the Christ about which he tells in his book.

takes a further step[46] in the direction of increasing Jesus' majesty. While in Q the divine wisdom puts John and Jesus as her emissaries on the same level, Matthew intimates his special majesty. Jesus' deeds are the works of God's wisdom. The story of the deeds of Christ that Matthew tells contradicts in the clearest language all of Israel's rejection and criticisms.

Summary and History of Interpretation

Our text derives its meaning primarily from the macrotext of Matthew's story. It is Jesus' first reaction to his contemporaries' growing rejection. While in Q it also indicated something of the church's own position toward the Israel that rejects Jesus (Luke 7:35), a similar dimension can barely be seen in the Matthean version. Therefore the history of the text's interpretation concentrated primarily on the question of the text's meaning without uncovering many possibilities of applying that meaning.[47] When interpreters identified with any figures in the text, it was with Jesus—significantly and regrettably never with "this generation"! A number of interpreters mention experiences similar to that of Jesus. Luther states, for example: Where the gospel is proclaimed, the world says "no" in all possible ways, even if the "no" is only for show.[48] Seldom did our text play a role in the discussion of fasting and asceticism.[49]

Since the evangelist used the text within his Jesus story as an indictment of the *former* generation and did not apply it to the situation of his own church, the question of its *not-yet-exhausted potential meaning* is especially clear here. I offer an example that is especially important today. Since Matthew saw the Baptist and Jesus as one, the question has rarely been asked what it means that Jesus ate and drank and John did not. And also in the history of interpretation only occasionally has the behavior of both been positively affirmed in terms of divine pedagogy.[50] The *joy* of the kingdom of God, and thus the opposition between John and Jesus, has not received independent attention. In this direction our text contains other little-used potential meanings. Two quite different examples from the history of interpretation, typically both from songs, are:

> Grace is dancing.
> I want to play the flute; dance, all of you! Amen.
> I want to sing a song of mourning; grieve, all of
>   you! Amen.
>
> . . .
>
> The twelfth number is dancing above. Amen.
> The dancer belongs to the universe. Amen.
> Whoever does not dance does not understand
>   what is happening.[51]

And:

> "I danced for the scribe and the Pharisee,
> but they would not dance and they would not
>   follow me.
> I danced for the fishermen, for James and John,
> and they came with me and the dance went on.
>
> . . .
>
> I am the Lord of the dance," said he.[52]

---

46   The Son of Man title in v. 19a was already such a step.

47   Rainer Russ ". . . Und ihr habt nicht getanzt," 71, n. 1: The text (*scil.* Luke 7:32-33) does not appear in the Sunday pericopes. Matt 11:16-17 has "also been removed from the weekday *Lectio continua*."

48   He refers (*WA* 38.522) to his experiences with the "Papists": "First we were reprimanded as 'the devil's hypocrites' when we were celibate, then, after we married, as 'carnal.'" He thinks that all of that happened simply because his opponents rejected the proclamation of the gospel. Brenz (462) points out that whenever the gospel is truly preached *tot dissidia oriuntur*.

49   Cf. Antonio Orbe, "El Hijo del hombre come y bebe (Mt 11,19; Lc 7,34)," 524–33 (Valentinus, Irenaeus).

50   Impressive is the image of the hunter chosen by John Chrysostom, 37.3 = *PG* 57. 423. As hunters surround the game from two sides in order to capture it, in order to win Israel God offered it on the one hand the way of asceticism and on the other the way of sociability.

51   *Act. John* 95.11-17 (Valentinian?).

52   "Lord of the Dance," in *Hymns for Now* (St. Louis: Concordia, 1967).

2.1 Woes on the Cities of Israel (11:20-24)

Literature

Joseph Comber, "The Composition and Literary Characteristics of Matth 11:20-24," *CBQ* 39 (1977) 497–504.

Marguerat, *Jugement,* 259–64.

Franz Mussner, "Gab es eine 'galiläische Krise'?" in Paul Hoffmann, Norbert Brox, and Wilhelm Pesch, eds., *Orientierung an Jesus: zur Theologie der Synoptiker: für Josef Schmid* (Freiburg: Herder, 1973), 238–52.

Lorenz Oberlinner, *Todeserwartung und Todesgewissheit Jesu* (SBB 10; Stuttgart: Katholisches Bibelwerk, 1980) 86–93.

George M. Soares-Prabhu, "De usu textus Mathaei 11,20-24 apud exegetas posttridentinos usque ad annum 1663" (Diss., Roma [Gregoriana], 1952).

Theissen, *Gospels,* 43–59.

For *additional literature* on Matthew 11 see above, II D.

20 **Then he began to reproach the cities in which many of his mighty deeds had happened, because they had not repented:**

21 **"Woe to you, Chorazin, woe to you, Bethsaida! For if the mighty deeds had happened in Tyre and Sidon that have happened in you, they would have repented long ago in sackcloth and ashes.**

22 **Truly[1] I say to you: It will be more tolerable for Tyre and Sidon on the day of judgment than for you.**

23 **And you, Capernaum! Will you be exalted to heaven? (No,) you will descend to Hades.[2] For if in Sodom the mighty deeds had happened that have happened in you, it would still be standing today.**

24 **Truly I say to you: It will be more tolerable for the land of Sodom on the day of judgment than for you."**

2 The Appeal to Israel: Judgment and Invitation (11:20-30)

Analysis

Structure

The text consists of an introduction (v. 20) and two parallel words of judgment. The introduction contains catchwords found in the following verses (ἐγένετο, δυνάμεις, μετενόησαν). Each of the two judgment sayings contains a word of reproach (vv. 21, 23) consisting of a woe and its reason and a word of threat (vv. 22, 24). Since their parallelism is otherwise almost exact,[3] the extra material in v. 23b, c (μὴ . . . καταβήσῃ) is especially noticeable.

Source

Matthew has written v. 20 by using terms from the following sayings.[4] The rest of the text comes from Q. It probably belonged originally in the context of the sending discourse (Luke 10:13-15). Presumably a Q redactor had used v. 12 (that simply varies v. 14) to link the old threat-word, Luke 10:13-14, with the preceding sending of the messengers into a city (Luke 10:8-11).[5] As a second word of judgment, Q probably contained only the lapidary saying against Capernaum, Luke 10:15, that corresponds to the Matthean "excess" in v. 23b, c. Matthew has then expanded the word of judgment against Capernaum to parallel the first one.[6] Only the end of v. 23, ἔμεινεν . . . σήμερον,[7] and ἡμέρα κρίσεως[8] in vv. 22, 24 are new in content and redactional. Matthew gives here a classic example of tradition-oriented redaction!

Origin

Do the two judgment sayings go back to Jesus? The decision must not be influenced here by a distaste for the idea of judgment. One can say anyway against its authenticity that there are no other reports of miracles of Jesus in Chorazin and that the woes in Luke 11:39-48 probably also were secondarily expanded by the unconditional announcement of judgment in

---

1 On the basis of LXX linguistic usage πλήν (actually adversative: nevertheless) can be a formula of solemn affirmation, esp. with oaths: "yes," "certainly," "indeed" (Berger, *Amenworte,* 79–80; Schenk, *Sprache,* 411–12).

2 We should probably read καταβήσῃ and not καταβιβασθήσῃ that presumably is an adaptation to the passive form ὑψωθήσῃ.

3 Including the striking ὑμῖν in v. 24. Unlike v. 21 only one city is addressed. In v. 24, in comparison with 10:15, καὶ Γομόρρων is missing, thus preserving the parallel to the *one* city, Capernaum.

4 In addition, Matthean are: τότε, πόλις, perhaps

πλεῖστος in first position (cf. 21:8). On τότε ἤρξατο cf. 4:17; 16:21.

5 Lührmann, *Redaktion,* 62–63.

6 With ὑμῖν in v. 24 the imitation is especially clear. Matthew loves parallelisms!

7 On μέχρι τῆς σήμερον cf. 28:15.

8 On the Matthean preference for parallelisms cf. vol. 1, Introduction 3.1. Λέγω ὑμῖν in v. 22 could be Matthean; cf. vol. 1, Introduction 3.2. The omission of καθήμενοι (Luke, v. 13) is difficult to judge since wearing sackcloth and sitting on sacks are both documented for mourning and penance; cf. Schlatter, 379.

Luke 11:49-51.[9] Those are two admittedly weak arguments in favor of the view that the sayings were created by the church. On the other hand, the probably genuine sayings in Luke 11:31-32 and 13:28-29 that are similar in content can support the claim that they originated with Jesus. In them also in the judgment the Gentiles are favored over Israel. However, the difference is that our sayings sound more definitive and unconditional than the threat in Luke 13:28-29 and the accusation in Luke 11:31-32. Nevertheless, as I see it, at least with the saying against Chorazin and Bethsaida, the arguments in favor of authenticity carry more weight than do those against.[10] With the saying against Capernaum that has a stronger Old Testament coloring it is more likely that the church created it.[11] Perhaps this saying was formulated by early Christian prophets in connection with their unsuccessful mission to Israel.

Interpretation

■ **20-24** The entire text, but especially the introductory v. 20, evokes memories. It was said in 9:35 that Jesus taught and healed in all of Israel's cities and villages. In 4:17 Jesus had begun his preaching with the word μετανοεῖτε ("repent") as John the Baptist had in 3:2. This happened after Jesus had settled in Capernaum (4:13). Especially numerous in our text, the penultimate pericope of the first main section, are the reminiscences of 4:12-17,[12] the penultimate pericope of the prologue. And one is reminded immediately of Matt 10:11-15, Jesus' instructions to the twelve disciples about their mission in a city. It ends with the saying of judgment in v. 15 that corresponds exactly to v. 24. The mighty deeds (vv. 21, 23) resume at least in content Jesus' summary of his

deeds in v. 5 and thus indirectly chaps. 8–9. All this prevents us from taking vv. 20-24 lightly and interpreting them "merely" as woes against a few cities. Then there is another consideration: For the reader of the gospel, these harsh woes of Jesus must come as a surprise. In narrative terms they are incorrectly located, since there have been no reports of miracles of Jesus in Chorazin and Bethsaida. To be sure, in Jesus' "own" city (9:1), Capernaum, many miracles happened (8:5-17; 9:1-34), but on the basis of the Matthean story one can certainly not say that all of Capernaum had rejected Jesus. Thus the readers will have understood these woes primarily proleptically. They, Jewish-Christians in Syria, who have experienced an unsuccessful mission to Israel in their former homeland of Palestine, know that Israel has not repented! They understand these sayings of judgment by Jesus as a prediction of the judgment on Israel at the end of the Jesus story.[13] Therefore, the end of 11:23 looks ahead linguistically to Matt 28:15, just as Matt 11:25-30 will be similar to Matt 28:16-20.

Thus our text has fundamental meaning as the conclusion of an entire main section of the gospel. It not only indicates that the first phase of Jesus' activity in Galilee has reached a preliminary ending; it "signals" in an exemplary way that Jesus' ministry in Israel will end with the judgment on Israel. Because of the evangelist's expansion of the sayings of judgment and the strict parallelism, they carry even more weight. Also important is the way the two woes intensified and heightened. After Chorazin and Bethsaida[14] comes Capernaum, *the* city of

---

9   Sato, "Q," 199.

10   On the genuineness of 11:21-22 Hahn (*Mission*, 27) argues, e.g., that such an antithetical use of the OT is possible only for Jesus; Franz Mussner ("Gab es eine 'galiläische Krise'?" 238–52, 244) sees it as evidence for the "Galilean crisis" in the life of Jesus; Schweizer, 266; Gnilka (1.430) argues that the provocative tone fits Jesus. That no Christian communities are presupposed for Tyre and Sidon also supports the view that the saying is quite old (Theissen, *Gospels in Context*, 52).

11   On the other hand, would they (after Easter) have located Jesus' rejection precisely in "his" city of Capernaum?

12   Cf. especially Marguerat, *Jugement*, 264.

13   Joseph Comber ("The Composition and Literary

Characteristics of Matt 11:20-24," 497–504, 503) thinks that this text reveals "a new stage" in the relationship of Jesus to Israel.

14   Chorazin is located about two miles north of the lake, Bethsaida east of the point where the Jordan flows into the lake. Bethsaida was expanded before 2 CE by Philip and renamed Julias in honor of the daughter of Augustus (Josephus *Ant.* 18.28; *Bell.* 2.168). Since Julias participated in the Jewish War, the population was Jewish (Josephus *Vit.* 398-406). Cf. Schürer-Vermes 2.171-72.

Jesus. On the other side Sodom, the exemplary town of wickedness,[15] follows Tyre and Sidon—cities that in the Old Testament were pilloried for their wealth and arrogance. The second woe against Capernaum receives greater weight from its greater length and its solemn biblical language. While the contrast of climbing to heaven and falling into the underworld is a widespread rhetorical topos,[16] here it is formulated in deliberate similarity to the word of judgment against Nebuchadrezzar in Isa 14:13-15. The doubling and repetition of vv. 21-22 in vv. 23-24 make the entire unit solemn and weighty.

How definitive is the judgment announced to the Galilean towns? Οὐαί ("woe") is a strong expression of complaint.[17] However, the ὅτι clause does not yet explain the reason for the complaint but only the pronouncement of judgment that follows in vv. 22, 24 with its total reversal of conditions. Thus our question is to be answered not on the basis of οὐαί ("woe") but only on the basis of vv. 22, 24.[18] The two threat-words are provocatively sharply formulated. Both times the cities of Israel are contrasted with gentile cities.[19] As in 8:11-12 the traditional biblical values are turned upside down. Pronouncements of judgment against Israel take the place of the biblical oracles against the foreign nations.[20] In the judgment it will be better for the Gentiles than for the cities of Galilee. Every hearer of that word would have "regarded the Tyrians and Sidonians as wicked despisers of God"![21] "Day of judgment" makes it clear that the evangelist is looking forward to the eschatological day of judgment. Thus the biblical image from Isa 14:13, 15 in the reproach against Capernaum probably

also becomes an announcement that is to be taken literally. Capernaum will fall into Hades;[22] it will suffer the same fate as Nebuchadrezzar did earlier. Thus the judgment is irrevocable. Of course, this has to be interpreted within the context of Matthew's entire narrative. The Matthean Jesus will continue to heal and to teach in the cities and villages of Galilee (chaps. 12–15). The judgment is first pronounced, and then the further course of the Matthean story will confirm the pronouncement. From this perspective our text has a signal function, just as does 8:11-12.

In what does the guilt of the Galilean cities consist? Why should they have repented in sackcloth and ashes?[23] Interpreters have attempted to draw all kinds of conclusions from the formulation "will you be exalted to heaven," in my judgment to no avail. The issue here is not that these cities are self-righteous or have a false awareness of their own election.[24] It is simply that they did not recognize the "mighty deeds" that Jesus performed as a call to repentance. Δυνάμεις are the healings of Jesus as unusual, spectacular mighty deeds (cf. 7:22; 13:54, 58; 14:2). Along with the entire synoptic tradition Matthew is not of the opinion that they clarify who Jesus is (cf. 12:38-40; 16:1-4). However, they lead to astonishment and to the *question* who this extraordinary Jesus is (9:33; 12:23). To have experienced these mighty deeds without being brought to repentance by them is worse than all the sins of Sidon, Tyre, and Sodom. In

---

15 Cf. Isa 1:9-10; Lam 4:6-16; Ezek 16:46-56; *Jub.* 20.5; *T. Naph.* 3.4; *3 Macc.* 2.5; Str-B 1.572-74.

16 Cf. Amos 9:2; Obad 4; Ezek 28:2-8; 31:14; *Ps. Sol.* 1.5; Ovid *Tristia* 1.2.19.

17 After the LXX, the biblical-Hebrew distinction between the lament for the dead or its prophetic use (הוֹי) and the cry of fear or complaint (אוֹי) has little effect in Greek.

18 Contra Verseput, *Rejection*, 122–24.

19 Cf. in the OT Ezek 16:44-58, where Samaria and Sodom (!) are against Jerusalem. Comparable also is the series of the oracles against foreign nations in Amos 1:3—2:16 that ends in sayings of judgment against Judah and Israel.

20 Against Tyre and Sidon: Isa 23; Ezek 26-28; Joel 4:4; Zech 9:2-4.

21 Calvin 2.15.

22 It is probable that ᾅδης = שְׁאוֹל has the neutral meaning of the realm of the dead rather than negative meaning of the place of damnation. Cf. below, III C 3.3 Gates of Hades (on Matt 16:18).

23 Cf. vol. 1, II A 231 on 6:16-18 with nn. 64, 65.

24 Schweizer's comment (267) is descriptive but fanciful: Capernaum enjoyed "having the famous prophet Jesus living among them." Based on the opposition Israel/Gentiles (which he interprets quite subjectively) Patte (163) says that they are "privileged" Israelites who regard their exaltation to heaven as guaranteed. Fenton (184) says in an especially edifying way: "Capernaum's impenitence comes from pride, which attempts to make itself like God." Most interesting here is the need of com-

this way the miracles of Jesus can become in Matthew the basis for the complaint.[25]

Summary and History of Interpretation

Although our text appears at a decisive location in the Gospel of Matthew, it has attracted little attention in the history of interpretation. It could have been used effectively in polemics against an unbelieving Judaism but was scarcely used that way.[26] Frequently it was the occasion for reflections on predestination and prescience, since Christ seemed to foresee that the Tyrians and Sidonians would believe. Frequently it also was the occasion for differentiating in the dispensing of grace. In contrast to the Phoenician cities that had only heard about Jesus, the Galileans were also granted the special grace that is present in Christ's activity.[27] However, the ancient authors already warn against overloading the text dogmatically.[28] The possibilities of parenetic interpretation are very limited. Then the commentators saw that even worse punishment would have to threaten their own churches, since indeed Germany, for example, had heard the gospel for centuries and not, like the Galilean towns, for only two years![29]

In more recent times the commentaries provide primarily "factual" information about such things as the geographical location of Chorazin. Are these signs that the text causes some embarrassment?

Gaechter appeals to Old Testament traditions in still speaking naively of "moral collective guilt" while Beare cannot imagine a proceeding "*en masse*" in the final judgment.[30] J. Weiss defends Jesus and at the same time indirectly limits the significance of the text. In the "powerful sense of the overwhelming importance of his mission" Jesus is "shattered by the horrible fate" that threatens the Galilean cities, but he is not "offended . . . because they do not want to hear him."[31]

The most difficult substantive problem lies not with the pronouncement of judgment as such. In my opinion God's judgment is at the center of Jesus' proclamation of the kingdom of God and keeps it from becoming a message of harmless love. The problem lies rather in the definitiveness of this pronouncement of judgment. For Matthew it lies in the fact that he transmits it in the framework of a story that tells how the kingdom of God is taken from Israel (cf. 21:43). And if we should be dealing here with words of Jesus, then for the sake of the kingdom of God we would have to insist even against him on the difference between a *threat* of judgment that can give wings to people (cf. Luke 16:1-8!) and a *prediction* of judgment that closes the doors to them.

---

mentators to explain something, while for Matthew the rejection of Jesus is sufficient reason for the condemnation.

25 This is an aspect that Held ("Matthew") completely neglects. Held does not interpret the Matthean miracle narratives on the basis of their function in the macrotext. Cf. Luz, "Wundergeschichten," 150.

26 Augustine *Dono pers*. 9 = 22–23 (= *PL* 45.1005–6) speaks in passing of the unbelief of the Jews for which they themselves are guilty.

27 Cf. Lapide, 250; George M. Soares-Prabhu, "De usu textus Mathaei 11,20-24 apud exegetas posttridenti-

nos usque ad annum 1663," esp. 120–24.

28 Calvin 2.15 ("subtle questions about God's secret plans"); Maldonat, 238 ("not necessary for explaining this passage").

29 Bullinger, 114B. Luther (*WA* 38.523) formulates forcefully *Nihil horribilius quam verbum Dei habere et negligere*. John Chrysostom 37.5 = *PG* 57.425 thinks back to the mission situation and accuses his hearers of lacking hospitality.

30 Gaechter, 373; Beare, 264.

31 319–20.

2.2 The Son's Invitation to the Toiling and Heavy-Laden (11:25-30)

Literature

Arvedson, *Mysterium.*

Hans Dieter Betz, "The Logion of the Easy Yoke and of Rest (Mt 11:28-30)," *JBL* 86 (1967) 10–24.

Lucien Cerfaux, "Les sources scripturaires de Mt 11,25-30," in idem, *Recueil* 3.139–59.

Idem, "L'évangile de Jean et le 'logion johannique' des synoptiques," ibid., 161–74.

Christ, *Jesus Sophia,* 81–119.

Deutsch, *Hidden Wisdom.*

Jacques Dupont, "Les 'simples' (petayim) dans la Bible et à Qumrân. À propos des νήπιοι de Mt 11,25; Lc 10,21," in idem, *Études* 2.583–91.

Idem, *Béatitudes,* 521–37.

André Feuillet, "Jésus et la sagesse divine d'après les évangiles synoptiques," *RB* 62 (1955) 161–96.

Hubert Frankemölle, "Die Offenbarung an die Unmündigen: Pragmatische Impulse aus Mt 11,25f," in idem, *Biblische Handlungsanweisungen* (Mainz: Grünewald, 1983) 80–108.

Werner Grimm, "Der Dank für die empfangene Offenbarung bei Jesus und Josephus," *BZ* NF 17 (1973) 249–57.

Idem, *Jesus,* 3–69.

Idem, *Weil ich dich liebe: Die Verkündigung Jesu und Deuterojesaia* (ANTJ 1; Frankfurt: Lang, 1976) 102–11.

Walter Grundmann, "Die NHΠIOI in der urchristlichen Paränese," *NTS* 5 (1958/59) 188–205.

Adolf von Harnack, *Sprüche und Reden Jesu: Beiträge zur Einleitung in das Neue Testament* (Leipzig: Hinrichs, 1907) 2.189–216.

Hoffmann, *Studien,* 104–42.

A. F. J. Klijn, "Matthew 11:25/Lk 10:21," in Epp and Fee, *New Testament Textual Criticism,* 3–14.

Künzel, Studien, 84–94.

Lange, *Erscheinen,* 152–67.

Simon Légasse, "La révélation aux NHΠIOI," *RB* 67 (1960) 321–48.

Idem, *Jésus,* 122–85.

Idem, "Le logion sur le Fils révélateur (Mt 11,27 par. Lc 10,22)," in Joseph Coppens, ed., *La notion biblique de Dieu* (BEThL 41; Louvain: Louvain University Press, 1985) 245–74.

Ulrich Luck, "Weisheit und Christologie in Mt 11,25-30," *WuD* 13 (1975) 35–51.

Witold Marchel, *Abba, Père* (AnBib 19A; 2d ed.; Rome: Pontifical Biblical Institute, 1971) 142–67.

Mertens, "L'hymne."

Norden, *Agnostos Theos,* 277–308.

L. Randellini, "L'inno di giubilo: Mt 11,25-30; Lc 10,20-24," *RivB* 22 (1974) 183–235.

Schulz, *Q,* 213–28.

Heinrich Schumacher, *Die Selbstoffenbarung Jesu bei Mat 11,27 (Luc 10,22)* (Freiburg: Herder, 1912).

Stanton, "Matthew 11:28-30."

Strecker, *Weg,* 172–75.

Suggs, *Wisdom,* 71–108.

Winter, "Matthew 11:27."

Zumstein, *Condition,* 130–52.

On the history of interpretation

Athanasius, *In illud.:* "Omnia mihi tradita sunt . . ." *PG* 25.207–20.

Gustav Adolf Benrath, *Wyclifs Bibelkommentar* (Arbeiten zur Kirchengeschichte 36; Berlin: de Gruyter, 1966) 236–42.

Albert Houssiau, "L'exégèse de Matthieu XI,27B selon saint Irénée," *EThL* 29 (1953) 328–54.

Irenaeus *Haer.* 4.6.

Kierkegaard, *Training in Christianity,* 11–72.

Juan Ochagavia, *Visibile Patris Filius: A Study of Irenaeus' Teaching on Revelation and Tradition* (OrChrA 171; Rome: Pont. Institutum Orientalium Studiorum, 1964) 62–70.

Antonio Orbe, "La revelación del Hijo por el Padre según San Ireneo (*Adv. haer.* IV 6)," *Greg* 51 (1970) 5–86.

For *additional literature* on Matthew 11 see above, II D.

25	At that time Jesus answered and said: "I praise you, Father, Lord of heaven and earth, that you hid these things from the wise and intelligent and revealed it to the simple people.
26	Yes, Father, for thus it became pleasing before you.
27	Everything was delivered to me by my Father, and no one knows[1] the Son except the

---

1   On the basis of the overwhelming tradition of the early church fathers from Justin (*Apol.* 1.63.3, 13) to Eusebius, Adolf von Harnack (*Sprüche und Reden Jesu* 2.195–201) and Winter ("Matthew 11:27," 135–40) surmise that ἔγνω instead of γινώσκει stood in the original text (Harnack: only in Luke 10:22 = Q). Irenaeus (*Haer.* 4.6.1) forcefully argues for the present tense and surmises that behind the variant ἔγνω lies heretical exegesis that did not know what to do with a knowledge of God in the

Father,[2]
            and no one knows the Father except the Son,
            and everyone to whom the Son wills to
            reveal it.
28   Come to me all who are toiling and burdened,
            I will give you rest.
29   Take my yoke on you and learn from me
            that[3] I am friendly and humble in heart,
        and you will find rest for your souls.
30   For my yoke is gentle and my burden is light."

Analysis

Structure

The text stands in sharp contrast to the woes pronounced on the Galilean cities. Matthew bridges it with a connecting introduction but without a change of addressees. The following prayer and the invitation of Jesus are formulated in exalted language with many repeated catchwords and parallelisms. The introduction is followed by two four-part sayings and one six-part saying. The first, the prayer of thanks in vv. 25-26, follows the scheme a b b´ a´ with antithetical parallelism in the middle members and the connecting catchword πατήρ in a and a´. The second logion, the word of revelation in v. 27, is connected to the first with the catchwords πατήρ and ἀποκαλύπτω and is structured on the scheme a b b´ c. The keyword πατήρ connects the first three clauses, the keyword υἱός the clauses 2-4. The third logion, vv. 28-30, has no catchwords linking it to the others. Its scheme is formally a b c d b´ a´. Parallel are the stem φορτ- in a and a´, the stem ἀναπαυ- in b and b´ and, in addition, ζυγός in c and a´. Only v. 29b (= member d) is not linked by catchwords. Syntactically, an exhortation (a, c) is followed twice by a promise (b, b´). A substantiation brings the entire unit to a close (a´). The ὅτι clause in v. 29b (member d) is also not syntactically anchored in the logion.

Noteworthy are the connections to other texts. Πατήρ and οὐρανός/γῆ are reminiscent of the Lord's Prayer, οὐρανός, γη, (πάντα) (παρ)εδόθη, ὁ υἱός and also μανθάνω-μαθητεύω of 28:18-19. Υἱός, πατήρ, and ἀποκαλύπτω are reminiscent of 16:16-17. All three texts are key Matthean texts. The connections

---

Old Testament. However, since Justin also is a witness for the present tense in the unabbreviated quotation in *Dial.* 100.1, it cannot simply be an antiheretical countercorrection. The compound word ἐπιγινώσκει appears for the first time in Eusebius (*Ctr. Marc.* 1.1.6) and in Cyril of Jerusalem (*Cat. myst.* 4.7; 6.6). We cannot simply dismiss the reading of the church fathers with the popular claim that their quotations were free and inexact, for on three points they are quite constant. They generally avoid (1) the Matthean compound ἐπιγινώσκω in favor of the (Lukan!) simple verb and (2) the Lukan formulation τίς ἐστιν, and they (3) frequently cite the aorist instead of the present tense. The first two points correspond to the Q text. The aorist is not the original text of Matthew or Luke; that is clear from the very clear manuscript tradition. Should we assume a quite firm oral tradition? It may be that the aorist is an attempt to exclude the unsuitable ingressive nuance that clings to the Greek γιγνώσκω. Γιγνώσκω initially means (like the Latin *nosco*) "to get to know, to experience, to perceive." The aorist corresponds to the Latin *novi* and emphasizes the perfect "knowing" that prevails between Father and Son after the "delivering" of "everything" (v. 27a); cf. Gal 4:9, etc. Or is the aorist an adaptation to παρεδόθη?

2   Verses 27b and c are in reverse order in most of the church fathers prior to Clement of Alexandria (Irenaeus is an exception) and also frequently later but seldom in the manuscript tradition (Winter, "Matthew 11:27," 113-15, 140-43). The change in order shifts the accent. In the Nestle[26] text the content of the Son's revelation seems to be primarily the mystery of the Father. In the variant, the emphasis is primarily on the mystery of the Son. In my judgment we should again not seriously consider declaring the reverse order to be the original Matthean or Lukan text against the testimony of almost all mss. Unlike Irenaeus (above, n. 1!) I see no dogmatic reasons for a certain order but rather stylistic reasons. Verse 27c follows v. 27a better than v. 27b does: The delivery (of knowledge) to the Son means that only the Son knows the Father. Verse 27d follows v. 27c well (then it is not only the Son who knows the Father but also the νήπιοι), but follows v. 27b less well (because then the "knowledge" of the Father and of the people appear side by side). Is the variant reading of the church fathers an attempt to improve the difficult transition from v. 27a to 27b? This difficulty also might have led to the omission of v. 27b in the Latin codex a. However, that is by no means the original text (contra Winter, "Matthew 11:27," 129-34). For their help with nn. 1 and 2 I thank the coworkers of the Institut für Neutestamentliche Textforschung in Münster.

3   Ὅτι can be translated as "that" or as "because." Against most of the more recent authors but with, among others, Strecker (*Weg*, 174) I prefer "that." Μανθάνω is found with an object also in 9:13; 24:32. Cf. also *Εσθηρ* 1:1n; *Barn.* 9.7; Philo *Leg. all.*

with the immediate context also are close. Ἐν ἐκείνῳ τῷ καιρῷ and ἀποκριθείς[4] refer in content to the preceding text. The same introduction connects our text with 12:1-8. Thus we have the picture of a key text at the end of the first main section that stands out because of its cross-references to other texts and that at the same time is connected with the immediately preceding context and leads to the next text without a break.

Source and Redaction

Verses 25-27 come from Q = Luke 10:21-22, presumably as a continuation of Q Luke 10:13-16 (cf. Matt 11:20-24). The introduction is redactional in both gospels, so one can only assume that in Q the logia also were introduced. Otherwise there are few differences in the wording.[5] The wisdom saying of *vv. 28-30* is missing in Luke; there is no reason to assume that Luke omitted it. It comes from Matthew's special material. Given its content it is probable that it was Matthew who added it to vv. 25-27. It shows Mattheisms especially in v. 29b; it may be that Matthew created this part of the text that is not linked to the context by catchwords.[6] It is also conceivable that he has inserted πάντες in v. 28a and that there and in v. 30 he inserted the image of the burden.[7] Thus we might conjecture as tradition a five-part saying without synonyms, in which two impera-tives, each with promise, were concluded by a substantiation:

> Come to me, you who labor,
>> and I will give you *rest*.
> Take my *yoke* upon you,
>> and you will find *rest* for your souls,
>> for my *yoke* is kindhearted.

Tradition History and Origin

It is an assured result of research that Matt 11:25-30 is not a unitary text but that we have here three logia. While frequently, especially in the history of religions school, a three-part scheme has been postulated consisting of praise, soliloquy of the revealer (reception of gnosis), and invitation,[8] the parallels cited have not been convincing.[9] Above all it became clear that methodologically literary-critical analysis must take precedence over form criticism and the history of religions. In terms of form and origin the three logia are to be evaluated differently:

1. *Verses 25-26* are a Todah, a prayer of thanksgiving or praise as we know them from the Psalter (cf. especially Psalms 9, 138; Sir 51:1-12) and especially from the songs of praise from Qumran.[10] What is notable in comparison with the Qumran texts is not only the brevity but also the fact that Jesus praises God not for himself but for the experiences of others. For this reason a number of authors have spoken of a prayer in

---

3.51; LSJ, *s.v.* III 3; Moulton-Milligan, *s.v.* Sir 8:9 is different.

4   Ἀποκριθείς is found only in 22:1 (cf. 12:38) at the beginning of a pericope, and there also it serves to connect the following pericope with the preceding one.

5   The simple verbs κρύπτω, ἐπιγινώσκω, and οὐδέ probably are Matthean (cf. vol. 1, Introduction n. 92 and 3.2, and II A 3.2, [401] n. 3). On the other hand, τίς ἐστιν is Lukan, as is the avoiding of the stylistically awkward doubling of the verb in Matthew v. 27b, c.

6   Perhaps with v. 29aβ καὶ μάθετε ἀπ᾽ ἐμοῦ. Cf. Künzel, *Studien,* 90–91, similarly Légasse, *Jésus,* 132–35 and Stanton, "Matthew 11:28-30." This is linguistically possible; cf. according to vol. 1, Introduction 3.2 the typical Matthean terms δεῦτε, πᾶς, κἀγώ, μανθάνω, πραΰς, εὑρίσκω, γάρ. From the content it is even probable; cf. 5:5, 8; 18:4; 21:5; 23:12. It is also formally probable; cf. the absence of linking catchwords. In my judgment further suggestions for Matthean redaction (Gundry [219] claims that the entire logion of vv. 28-30 is redactional) cannot be linguistically justified.

7   Künzel, *Studien,* 89; cf. Dupont, *Béatitudes* 3.526. While φορτίζω and ἐλαφρός are hapax legomena,

φορτίον occurs again in 23:4. There Matthew has added βαρέα, an exact counterpart to φορτίον ἐλαφρόν in v. 30. The image of the burden is missing in the wisdom contexts that generally influence Matt 11:28-30.

8   Norden, *Agnostos Theos,* 277–308 (with a reference to Sirach 51; *Odes Sol.* 33; *Corp. Herm.* 1.27–32 and others); Martin Dibelius, *From Tradition to Gospel* (New York: Scribner's, 1935), 279–83. Arvedson (*Mysterium*) develops this thesis further and reduces the threefold formal scheme to two parts that correspond to the liturgy of a mystery celebration of the enthronement of Christ. With different argumentation Cerfaux ("Sources") claims that the constant wisdom-apocalyptic reference to scripture speaks for the unity of the text and its origin with Jesus.

9   Sirach 51 is not a unified text; cf. 11QPsa 21.11–17 = Sir 51:13-20. Actual substantive parallels exist only between Matt 11:28-30 and Sir 51:23-29. Norden's other parallels (*Agnostos Theos*) are not close and are already different in their structure. Cf. below, n. 108.

10 An especially close parallel is 1QH 7.26–33: "I thank Thee, O Lord, for Thou hast enlightened me through Thy truth. In Thy marvellous mysteries . . . Thou hast granted me knowledge." Part of the for-

form only; the verse is essentially a "sermon,"[11] or an instruction. This suggestion at least accurately reflects the church's interest in transmitting the tradition. Verses 25-26 are usually and justifiably attributed to Jesus. Not only the form but also the language are Semitizing.[12] The content of the praise fits Jesus.

2. *Verse 27* is an unusual logion that has its closest parallels in the Gospel of John.[13] It is formally unusual, because between v. 27a and b there is a transition from the first to the third person. Thus there are no parallels in the Gospel of John to the *entire* logion. The indications for a Semitic linguistic background are not unambiguous.[14] Primarily because of its content, most authors here correctly assume that the church created the saying. Jesus scarcely spoke of the "Son," nor did he speak of the mutual and exclusive knowledge of the Father and the Son.[15] In my judgment the logion cannot stand alone; πάντα in v. 27a presupposes something. Because of the catchwords it has in common with vv. 25-26, we best understand it as a commentary on vv. 25-26. It explains how the revelation to the νήπιοι takes place.[16]

3. The "savior's call" in *vv. 28-30* has its closest parallels in Jewish wisdom invitations.[17] If one assumes the Matthean redaction as suggested above, there are no longer specific Jesus traits in the basic material. The well-rounded logion offers no reason for further tradition-historical decomposition.[18] It can be a quotation from a Jewish wisdom writing, but it can equally well be a Christian creation.[19]

Interpretation

Bullinger described our text as the "vein and source . . . of the most holy gospel and the entire mystery of Christ," Lagrange as the "most precious pearl" of the Gospel of Matthew.[20] Why? We quote a classical interpretation of our text:

> You must believe . . . in the one and only Son of God, our Lord Jesus Christ, God, begotten of God, life, begotten of life, light, begotten of light. He is similar

---

mal scheme is the introduction with אוֹדְכָה אֲדוֹנִי כִּי (1QH 7.26) = ἐξομολογήσομαί σοι, κύριε, ὅτι (= ψ 137:1). On the form cf. Günter Morawe, *Aufbau und Abgrenzung der Loblieder von Qumran* (Theologische Arbeiten 16; Berlin: Evangelische Verlagsanstalt, 1961) esp. 29–37; James M. Robinson, "Die Hodajot-Formel in Gebet und Hymnus des Frühchristentums," in Walther Eltester, ed., *Apophoreta: Festschrift für Ernst Haenchen* (BZNW 30; Berlin: Töpelmann, 1964) 194–201. HbrMt uses here שבח that is popular also in the Targums. In such texts it is clear that he does not represent an "original text" (contra Howard, 225 and passim).

11 Martin Dibelius, *From Tradition to Gospel* (New York: Scribner's, 1935) 281; Schulz, *Q*, 215.

12 Ἐξομολογοῦμαι is Semitic; in Greek formulation one would expect the future that is usual in the LXX. On ὁ πατήρ as a substitute for the vocative cf. BDF § 147 (3). On the Jewish parallels to κύριε τοῦ οὐρανοῦ καὶ τῆς γῆς, σοφοὶ καὶ συνετοί, εὐδοκία ἐγένετο ἔμπροσθέν σου, cf. below on vv. 25-26 from Jesus' perspective.

13 Cf. below, nn. 92, 97.

14 Jeremias (*Prayers*, 46–48) calls attention to: (1) the asyndeton in v. 27a; (2) οὐδεὶς . . . εἰ μή = only (but cf. Beyer, *Syntax*, 110–11: no direct Semitism); (3) the repetition of the verb; (4) the parataxis; (5) the parallelism of v. 27b, c as a circumlocution of the reciprocal pronoun "one another" that is not found in Semitic languages. None of these is convincing proof for original Semitic language. Furthermore,

no. 5 presupposes a certain (not compelling) interpretation of the logion. According to Dalman (*Words*, 284, n. 1) Aramaic מן with the passive (= ὑπό) is rare.

15 Only few authors are of a different opinion. See, e.g., Jeremias, *Prayers*, 47–52 (v. 27b, c is a comparison); Marchel, *Abba*, 147–52 (the cry of jubilation reveals for the first time Jesus' mystery of Son and Father, but it happened only after Peter's confession at Caesarea Philippi); Mertens, "L'hymne," 46–49 (closeness to other synoptic texts).

16 Πάντα refers back to ταῦτα.

17 Cf. below, "Wisdom Saying" on the interpretation of vv. 28-30.

18 Contra Werner Grimm (*Weil ich dich liebe*, 104–5), who separates Matt 11:28 as a "messianic call" (ibid., 108) that was influenced by Isa 55:1-2.

19 The strongest indication for an original Semitic formulation is that there is in v. 29c a formulation from Jer 6:16 MT (the LXX is different). Of course, that the saying originated with Jesus cannot be conclusively excluded.

20 Bullinger, 115; Lagrange, 226.

in everything to the Begetter. Not in time has he become, but he was born before all eternity, eternally from the Father in an incomprehensible manner. He is the wisdom of God and the personal, essential power and righteousness. . . . He is lacking nothing of the divine glory. He knows the Begetter as he is known by the Begetter. To say it briefly, think of the word that is written in the gospels: "No one knows the Son except the Father, and no one knows the Father except the Son."[21]

History of Interpretation

From the ancient church up to the Catholic exegesis at the beginning of our century our text was interpreted in trinitarian terms. It played an essential role in support of the doctrine of the trinity, especially in its anti-Arian form. Since the history of its interpretations has not yet been written, only a few accents can be sketched as examples.

Irenaeus (*Haer.* 4.6) attacks the gnostic and Marcionite exegesis that interpreted the text in terms of the Son who for the first time revealed the previously unknown Father.[22] For him the Son is the preexistent Word who has been at work since the creation.[23] It is an interpretation that is the basis of all later exegesis. Since that time the preexistence of Christ is connected with Matt 11:27.[24]

Our text became important for the interpretation of the trinity in the Arian controversy. On the basis of

11:27 the Arians denied the eternal divinity of Christ, because there must have been a time when not yet "everything was delivered to" Christ.[25] If I see it correctly, two possibilities of interpretation are visible in the orthodox interpretation.

1. Like Irenaeus, most of the fathers think of the preexistent Son of God. Power and knowledge of God are then assigned to the divine, not to the human Jesus. Our text is a classic witness to the essential divinity of Christ.[26] "Only the divine nature of trinity knows itself."[27] The process of the mutual knowledge of Father and Son must be fundamentally distinguished from any human knowing.[28] In his own way Augustine understood the concept of the trinity as a process of thinking and revealing. The Son, God's eternal Word, is at the same time (here Augustine is not so far from the text!) God's wisdom in which the deity knows itself and at the end enlightens human beings.[29] In the opinion of many fathers our text speaks of the *aeterna generatio* of the trinity—thus of that inner-trinitarian ground of all historical salvation that lets Albertus Magnus in a well-known image compare the Father with the sun and the Son with the light. The sun brings forth light; it has given everything to the light. Indeed, it is the light that in the final analysis alone enlightens human beings.[30]

2. By contrast, in arguing against the Arians Athanasius (*Illud.*) relates the "delivery of everything" in v. 27a not to the preexistent mediator of creation but—apparently in misunderstanding, but in my judgment deeper and also much more biblically—to the

21 Cyril of Jerusalem *Cat.* 4.7 = NPNF Second Series 7.21.
22 There are few direct sources. Cf. Albert Houssiau, "L'exégèse de Matthieu XI,27B selon saint Irénée," 328–54, 329–32; Antonio Orbe, "La revelación del Hijo por el Padre según San Ireneo," 7–15. Simon interprets gnostically in *Ps.-Clem. Hom.* 17.4.3–4; 18.4.2–5; 18.15 (with refutation by Peter) and Clement of Alexandria *Paed.* 1.20.2–3 = ANF 2.214. According to Tertullian (*Marc.* 4.25.1 = CSEL 47.503) Marcion interprets it to refer to the previously hidden God
23 *Haer.* 4.6.3 = ANF 1.468.
24 See, e.g., Tertullian *Marc.* 2.27.5 = CSEL 47.373; Athanasius, *Contra Ar.* 3.35 = NPNF Second Series 4.413 (the Son as logos and wisdom); *Ps.-Clem. Rec.* 2.48 (in this way Moses and the prophets proclaim him).
25 Athanasius *Illud.* 1 = 209.
26 Tertullian *Marc.* 2.27.5 = CSEL 47.373 (*ipse erat Deus*); Gregory of Nyssa *Contra Eunomium* 2.28 =

Werner Jaeger, ed. (2 vols.; 1921; reprinted Leiden: Brill, 1960) 322–23 (the Son *is* in the Father and vice versa); cf. later Thomas Aquinas, *Lectura* no. 965 (*aequalitas, consubstantialitas*); Jansen, 113 (*maiestas Patri aequalis*). Combined with 1 Cor 2:10-11 (the Spirit searches the depths of God) our text becomes the witness for the inner-trinitarian knowledge of God (Basil *Contra Eunomium* 1.14 = SC 299.220).
27 Cyril of Alexandria fr. 148 = Reuss, 200, cf. Hilary *De Trinitate* 2.6–7 = FC 25.39–42 (every human word is too weak for the knowledge of the Father and the Son that is meant here).
28 Thus Origen *Princ.* 1.2.8 = GCS 22.38; 2.4.3 = GCS 131; Cyril of Alexandria *Trin.* 11 = *PG* 75.1161.
29 *Trin.* 7.3 (4) = FC 45.225.
30 Albertus Magnus, 498–99; cf. Jansen, 112 (*aeterna generatio*); Calovius, 281 (*communicatio divinae maiestatis hypostatica*).

moment when the eternal Logos became incarnate. Then when Christ "became what he (previously) was not, everything was given to him."[31] Everything is delivered not to the God Christ but to the human Jesus. More precisely: Everything is delivered to the God-man Jesus. Otherwise the "giving" would be an act of creation before time.[32] The incarnate Son who alone knows the Father (v. 27b) cannot be a creature.[33] Athanasius is concerned with soteriology. Verse 27a does not make abstract christological statements about the God Jesus but is immediately related to redemption. God has delivered everything to the *One who has become human* so that he might save the human person. The attempt to understand Matt 11:27a-c simply as a statement about the divinity of Jesus is like trying to separate the light from the sun.[34] In the Middle Ages the attempt was made to combine the two approaches. Dionysius the Carthusian states, for example, that in accordance with his divine nature the entire fullness and perfection of the deity was "delivered" to Christ from eternity; in accordance with his human nature the authority over all things created was given to him at the incarnation.[35]

However, the history of interpretation shows not only the classical doctrine of the trinity but also its collapse. It begins with Hugo Grotius and J. L. Wolzogen. Grotius is brief in his exegesis of our text: It refers to the decisions of the divine plan of salvation that the Son knows. Thus Jesus knows that one comes to the knowledge of God only through faith and to faith only through awareness of sin and repentance.[36] Calovius immediately clearly understood what it is that Grotius does *not* say.

He is not talking about the *person* of Christ, his nature and thus the trinity.[37] Wolzogen already grasps the point more sharply. The issue is Christ's *knowledge*, his insight into the Father's plan of salvation. This means the end of the classical doctrine of the trinity.[38] Instead of the second person of the trinity one has a human being to whom is granted a special *knowledge* or *experience* of God. And that is what our text says, especially for the critical Protestant exegetes of the nineteenth century. Here the divinity of Jesus is as it were subjectivized and replaced by Jesus' consciousness of God.

Again a few examples must suffice. F. C. Baur understands Jesus' consciousness of God ethically. "The one who speaks as Jesus does in the Sermon on the Mount . . . must also have in himself the consciousness that he can speak this way only as God's ambassador. The same consciousness is expressed . . . in Matt 11:25-26, only here it is more immediate and personal."[39] R. Rothe speaks of a moral rather than a metaphysical equality of Jesus with God,[40] P. Wernle of his familiarity with the Father.[41] J. Weiss emphasizes more strongly Jesus' religious experience. What is at issue is the mystery of his personality. "God's wonderful plan of salvation became clear to him as a sudden inspiration . . . , God's innermost essence revealed itself to him." Such a "blessed momentary vision of God" makes one lonely. "No one suspects anything of the mystery of his soul: No one knows the Son . . . only few are called to experience the mys-

---

31 Athanasius *Illud.* 213.
32 "For if the creation were meant, then he had nothing before the creation and seems to get something more from the creation. But far be it to think that!" (*Illud.* 3 = 213).
33 Athanasius *Contra Ar.* 2.22 = NPNF Second Series 4.360; 4.16 = NPNF Second Series 4.439.
34 Athanasius *Illud.* 3 = 216.
35 144.
36 1.349: Christ speaks "de decretis Divinae dispensationis" which the Son alone knows ("conscius ipsi solu est Filius").
37 281.
38 Wolzogen (282) writes for those who know Latin (the others need not understand it!): "Eccur vero Christus sic loqueretur, si ipse esset idem ille Deus summus, qui Pater est? Quid ipsi Pater sive dare,

sive revelare potuit, quod non ipse jam antea habuerit out sciverit? Quid etiam Pater humanae Christi naturae dare out revelare potuit, si cum secunda Trinitatis persona, a qua omnia habuit ac scivit, conjuncta & arctissime coaluit?"
39 Ferdinand Christian Baur, *Vorlesungen über neutestamentliche Theologie* (1864; reprinted Darmstadt: Wissenschaftliche Buchgesellschaft, 1973) 114.
40 Richard Rothe, *Dogmatik*, 2/1 (Daniel Schenkel, ed.; Heidelberg: Mohr, 1870) 89, also p. 91 in reference to Matt 11:27: "Such a knowledge of God and such a conformity with his will (is) possible only in the real community with God as it perfects itself as unity with him." Thus the unity of the Son with the Father is "still in the process of becoming."
41 Paul Wernle, *Jesus* (2d ed.; Tübingen: Mohr/ Siebeck, 1916): "to act with the Father's attitude"

tery."[42] Holtzmann sees in Matt 11:25-27 the "triumphant self-awareness" of the "religious genius" that breaks forth "out of the depths of his inner life."[43] For Harnack—a subjectivistic variant of Augustine!—Jesus' *knowledge* of God is decisive. "The knowledge of God is the sphere of his divine sonship . . . Jesus is convinced that he knows God as no one before him."[44] Such a question naturally leads to the biographical question of how this special knowledge of God originated. Ritschl referred here to Jesus' vision at his baptism.[45]

That brings us to our century. The question of the Son's consciousness and of Jesus' religion has largely disappeared from the exegesis of Matt 11:25-27, because v. 27 is no longer attributed to Jesus, and vv. 25-26 do not permit a direct answer to this question. One scarcely asks anymore about the trinitarian dimensions of this "pearl" of the Gospel of Matthew. One factor in this development is that in Protestant exegesis the conservative wing tries to defend the authenticity of the saying and thus its Semitic character. Then, of course, one is miles away from the doctrine of the trinity and in content close to the questions of the nineteenth century.[46] In Catholicism the classical interpretations of our word

seem to have moved over into dogmatics,[47] in Protestantism often not even that.[48] The "source" of the traditional faith[49] has silently dried up; nothing is said in exegesis about its loss.[50] Today Protestantism is admonished by Fundamentalism: "'No one knows the Father except the Son and every one to whom the Son desires to reveal it' . . . We confess the gospel that the eternal Son of God became human in the historical Jesus of Nazareth and at the same time remained God. . . . Therefore the false doctrine must be rejected that Jesus was merely a human being."[51]

The exegesis of our text must reflect on the history of this loss. What connects it with the church's trinitarian interpretation? Can our text still and again become a "source" of faith?

Interpretation: Jesus

■ **25b, 26** The doxology of vv. 25-26 is to be interpreted first of all as a prayer of Jesus. It is addressed to the Father and the Lord (v. 25b), a combination characteristic of Jesus. "Father" is Jesus' favorite way of addressing God.[52] To it he adds "lord of heaven and earth." As the

(327). Cf. also B. Weiss, 227: Decisive is not "superhuman consciousness," but "that his will . . . completely agrees with that of his Father."

42 J. Weiss, 322–23.

43 Holtzmann, *Theologie* 1.345, 341.

44 Harnack, 137–38.

45 Albrecht Ritschl, *Die christliche Lehre von der Rechtfertigung und Versöhnung* (Bonn: Marcus, 1900) 2.96–97. Cf. similarly today Jeremias, *Theology*, 61.

46 J. Jeremias (cf. below on "The Son" and n. 77) is the best example of how one can completely misunderstand this text when one wants to save its genuineness at any cost!

47 Cf. Michael Schmaus, *Katholische Dogmatik* (6th ed.; Munich: Hueber, 1960) 1.390 (trinitarian); Karl Adam, *Jesus Christus* (3d ed.; Augsburg: Haas und Grabherr, 1934) 206–11 (206: "What content does his consciousness of being the Son enclose?").

48 No reference in Emil Brunner, Paul Tillich, Gerhard Ebeling, Hans-Joachim Kraus; a brief mention in Barth *CD* 4/2.344, 759.

49 Cf. above, n. 20.

50 A notable exception is the emphatically trinitarian monograph by Heinrich Schumacher (*Die Selbstoffenbarung Jesu bei Mat 11,27 (Luc 10,22)*. Otherwise, the trinitarian dimension of our text appears

only in surreptitious reminiscences such as, e.g., in Marchel (*Abba*, 160–61: *une vrai égalité, voire identité de connaissance*); Mertens ("L'hymne," 72: *nature divine du fils*); Trilling, *Evangelium* (1.256: "in the depth . . . he is equal to the Father"); Gaechter (381: "identity of the same I" of Jesus as human being and Son of God).

51 The Düsseldorf declaration of the confessing movement *"Kein anderes Evangelium"* [No Other Gospel] of 1967, cited according to H. W. Krumwiede, ed., *Neuzeit* (2 vols.; Kirchen- und Theologiegeschichte in Quellen 4/1, 2; Neukirchen-Vluyn: Neukirchener Verlag, 1979–80) 2.210.

52 Cf. vol. 1, II A 2.3.3 on 6:9b.

third petition of the Lord's Prayer also says, God is not only creator but lord of history who, according to Tob 7:17 and 1QapGen 22:16, grants blessing and joy.

Here Jesus speaks in the language of Jewish prayer[53] and makes clear how little for him the address "Father" differs from the traditional language of Jewish prayer.[54] The address corresponds to the conclusion of the praise in v. 26. Here also the address "indeed,[55] Father"[56] is combined with a traditional Jewish prayer formula: "this became your gracious will."[57] Alongside the address as Father this prayer formula again stresses the absolute sovereignty of God's love. Thus the two forms of address show how Jesus consciously focuses attention on God, the loving Father and Lord. He is at the center of attention. All human salvation is determined in his will.[58]

■ **25c, d** Jesus states the reason for his praise in an antithetical parallelism. Jesus, of course, does not thank God that he has not chosen the wise; only that he has revealed himself to the simple, while he remained closed to the wise. Rhetorically effective, the two brief antithetical sentences stand in a popular Semitizing parataxis.[59] The praise contains no element of resignation. God, the Lord of heaven and earth, is not a failure with the wise![60]

However, both deliberations call attention to what is decisive in our text: the antithetical opposition of wise and simple. The "wise" are various groups in Judaism, depending on the context and the situation: Israel's wisdom teachers, wisdom's "pupils," the followers of apocalyptic groups,[61] the members of the sect and next to them the special class of the wise in Qumran,[62] and above all the scribes.[63] In the course of time the early Jewish usage became "more technical." The "wise" are a certain group, a class that is separate from "ordinary people." However, the general use of the term without an article and the parallel with the nontechnical συνετοί advise against attempts to think here only of certain groups of people such as, for example, the scribes.[64] The term includes all who in Israel are "wise" or who consider themselves to be such, the entire religious aristocracy. The opposite term νήπιος contains a double nuance. Literally it means "infant, child"; figuratively it means "immature, minor." In the Hebrew פֶּתִי, which we must assume to be the Semitic equivalent,[65] the negative nuance is stronger. As a translation νήπιος can simply

---

53 Except for Tob 7:17AB, 1QapGen 22.16 and the *Tefilla* quoted by Jeremias, *Theology,* 187–88, there are no exact parallels. Cf., however, the similar formulation "lord of heaven" (Dan 2:37), "God of heaven and earth" (2 Esdr 5:11), "God of heaven" (with ἐξομολογεῖσθαι ψ. 135:26), "Yahweh, God of heaven and God of earth" (Gen 24:3, cf. 7); for further references see A. F. J. Klijn, "Matthew 11:25/Lk 10:21," 3–14, 5. Widespread among the rabbis is "Lord of the world" (Str–B 2.176).

54 Cf. vol. 1, II A 2.3.3 at the end of the "interpretation" of 6:9b.

55 Ναί with the emphatic repetition of one's own statement (BAGD *s.v.,* 3) probably corresponds not to אָמֵן but to the Aramaic אִין, הֵין.

56 The choice of the Aramaizing translation ὁ πατήρ was made here for rhythmic reasons (after the short ναί) as was the πάτερ (after the long ἐξομολογοῦμαί σοι) in v. 25b. The Greek translation of this prayer is—as in the case of the Lord's Prayer—very artistic.

57 Cf. Matt 18:14 (in a similar context). A Jewish (not OT) correspondence is: יְהִי רָצוֹן מִלְּפָנֶיךָ. Cf. Dalman, *Words,* 211.

58 When Calvin (2.21–23) here brings predestination into play, it corresponds to the text's theocentric

orientation. We are to "acknowledge His will as the highest wisdom and righteousness" (23) and learn from it that God's grace is unmerited. However, this does not lead "to anxious questions about the sign from which" one can "be certain of the secret counsel of God"; it leads to Christ, the ground of the assurance of salvation (v. 27!).

59 Cf. Isa 12:1; Rom 6:17 and Beyer, *Syntax,* 259–86; Moulton–Howard–Turner 3.342; Mayser, *Grammatik,* 1/3.184–86.

60 Michaelis, 2.131.

61 Dan 12:3; *1 Enoch* 104.12; 4 Ezra 12:38; *2 Bar.* 28.1.

62 Ulrich Wilckens, "σοφία κτλ," *TDNT* 7 (1971) 505: In Qumran there is a double linguistic usage. חכמי are the members of the sect and a special group of the wise.

63 Sir 38:24-39:11; Josephus (e.g., *Ant.* 20.264), Qumran (above, n. 62) are stages on the way to rabbinic linguistic usage where חָכָם widely has become the technical designation of honor of the rabbinic scholar. Further material in Wilckens, "σοφία κτλ," 496–507.

64 Verseput (*Rejection,* 137) for Matthew: broad reference.

65 In the LXX νήπιος is used for עוֹלָל = infant and for פֶּתִי, simple. The opposition "wise" and the parallels

mean "simpleminded, uneducated, stupid."[66] The expression is strong. The Father has revealed himself precisely not to those who ordinarily lay claim to him but to the simple people. Who are these simple people? Here again we must look for an open interpretation. The Father does not reveal himself to the religious elite, whether of apocalyptic, Essene, or scribal type. Jesus will probably be thinking of his listeners: the women, the Galileans, the poor people on the land who have neither the time nor the possibility of going to school to the "wise." The "*Am ha arez*" are best identified with the νή-πιοι.[67] The doxology is part of Jesus' proclamation of the kingdom of God that brings God first of all[68] to Israel's poor, simple, and déclassé. The indefinite ταῦτα is thus best understood as a reference to the kingdom of God.

Jewish Tradition
The expression "wise and understanding" is reminiscent of the Bible (LXX: Prov 16:21; Dan 1:4; cf. Sir 16:28). How then does Jesus' experience relate to the Old Testament and Jewish tradition? Many exegetes emphasize here Jesus' uniqueness. Do we have here an *"unicum" au sein de la pensée biblique*?[69] Especially noticeable is the contrast with Dan 2:20-23, a prayer

of praise from Daniel who thanks God that he gives his wisdom to the wise, and with which Matt 11:25-26 has a number of words in common.[70] Grimm understands Jesus' prayer as a deliberate "objection to Daniel's system of revelation."[71]

It cannot be denied that Jesus contradicts a broad stream of apocalyptic, Essene, and rabbinic thinking. For the apocalypticists wisdom and the mysteries of the future are hidden (cf. *1 Enoch* 42) and are revealed by the seer (for example, *1 Enoch* 103.2) to the few who are wise (4 Ezra 12:36-38; 14:26; *2 Bar.* 46.2-5; 48.3). For the Essenes the mysteries of God are hidden from humans (1QS 11.6); God reveals them only to the members of the sect. For the rabbis wisdom is connected with Torah and study[72] and thus is not for everyone. Corresponding to the idea of wisdom's hiddenness is the Jewish revelation of wisdom to the few and the call to intensive study. However, even in wisdom texts the accents are different. While here also wisdom is hidden (Job 28:12-23; Bar 3:15-4:4; Sir 1:4-9) since it is with God and only he can give it, he has given it to Israel (Bar 3:37; Sir 24:3-17), and therefore it calls its children in Israel to itself (Bar 4:1-4; Sir 4:18-22). Wisdom's appeals to the ἀπαίδευ-τοι (Prov 8:5; Sir 51:23) and to those who lack understanding (Prov 9:4; cf. Wis 9:4-5) are possible because God's wisdom is accessible in Israel. Finally, other

---

(cf. below, nn. 66–67) show that one must begin with רֵדָ. Cf. Légasse, *Jésus,* 168–76. On the other hand, HbrMt has secondarily עֲנִיֵּי.

66   Wis 12:24; 15:14 alongside ἄφρων. Here a difference also appears between Matt 11:25-26 and the similar, but conceptually much more Greek, Pauline parallel text of 1 Cor 1:18-25; 3:1-4, 18-23. In Paul νήπιοι are those who are not *yet* mature in contrast to the τέλειοι. The opposite of σοφοί are the μωροί (1 Cor 1:25, 27; 3:18) who substantively but not terminologically correspond to the νήπιοι in our text. Walter Grundmann ("Die *NHΠIOI* in der urchristlichen Paränese," 188–205) calls attention to the peculiarity of our passage also in comparison with the use of νήπιος in Heb 5:13; Eph 4:14, etc. There is no dependence of Paul on Matt 11:25-27.

67   Cf. 4QpNah 3.5 (the פְּתָאֵי אֶפְרַיִם are the nonmembers of the sect who are led astray by the Pharisees; the pious hope that they will join the community); 11QPs 154 (= col. xviii) 4.7 (the פּוֹתָאִים are the people to whom the sect preaches); John 7:49.

68   Perhaps one may point to the absence of the definite article with σοφῶν καὶ συνετῶν.

69   Simon Légasse, "La révélation aux *NHΠIOI*," 321–48, 341.

70   Especially to Theodotion: θεὸς τοῦ οὐρανοῦ, σοφία,

σύνεσις, ἀποκαλύπτω, ἀπόκρυφα, ἐξομολογοῦμαι. The analogies were often observed, e.g., by Cerfaux ("Sources," 140–45), Werner Grimm ("Der Dank für die empfangene Offenbarung bei Jesus und Josephus," 252–54), idem (*Jésus,* 25–69), L. Randellini ("L'inno di giubilo: Mt 11,25-30; Lc 10,20-24," 199–201), Hubert Frankemölle ("Die Offenbarung an die Unmündigen," 91–95).

71   The title of his book: *Einspruch gegen das Offenbarungssystem Daniels!* It is possible that our text consciously refers to Dan 2:20-23, at least in its Greek version.

72   Cf. *m. ʾAbot* 2.7 ("the more study of the Law the more life; the more schooling the more wisdom" [ET: Danby, 448]); *Midr. Qoh.* 1.7 (Str–B 1.661): God has given wisdom not to the foolish but to the wise (Dan 2:21!) so that it will be spoken of in the synagogues and not in theaters and bathhouses.

tones emerge in the law piety of the Psalms: "The testimony of the Lord . . . makes the simple wise" (Ps 19:8, cf. 119:130). Therefore the "simple" know that they are in God's hand (Ps 116:6).[73] The pious of Qumran can take up this positive view of the "simple" and once call themselves the "simple of Judah."[74] Here we are in substance close to Matt 11:25-26, although the antithetical formulation of the prayer of Jesus points beyond the Jewish context. However, that is also true of the prophetic protest against the high-handed wisdom of the mighty whom the holy one of Israel opposes with his "no" (Isa 5:21; 29:14-19; Jer 9:22-23). Thus it is precisely in his antithesis to the prevailing stream of Jewish piety that Jesus, who contrasts the simple people with the wise of Israel and grants them God's revelation, lives out of biblical roots.

Church Tradition

■ **27** The post-Easter church now adds a commentary to this saying of Jesus. It explains ταῦτα ("these things") and holds fast to the place where God's revelation takes place for it. Important for it in vv. 25-26 is what the Father has "delivered" to the Son and what the latter has made known to those who are his. Thus vv. 25-26 speak not of general revealed truths but of what has happened through Jesus. The emphasis lies on v. 27d, where again the revelation to human beings is mentioned.[75] The νή-πιοι ("immature") are now those to whom the Son will reveal it, that is, the church. There is thus in v. 27, along with the christological, an ecclesiological concentration of vv. 25-26. At the same time it means a narrowing.[76] Now it no longer speaks of all of Israel's simple but of the church. These "simple" again have their special knowledge. They know of the mystery of the Father and the Son. Thus v. 27 brings God's revelation to the νή-πιοι structurally closer to the apocalyptic texts and the texts of Qumran where the issue also was a special group of people and their knowledge. At the same time, however, v. 27a-c makes christological and theological statements of great depth that are much more than a mere preparation for v. 27d.

The interpretation is contentious. The following are difficult:

1. the meaning of the absolute ὁ υἱός ("the son") in v. 27b-d,
2. the question of what has been "delivered" to Jesus in v. 27a, and
3. the meaning of γινώσκειν ("to know") and the reciprocal statement of knowledge in v. 27b, c. The first two questions are connected.

The Son

On 1: "The Son" as an absolute term occurs elsewhere in the New Testament in Mark 13:32/Matt 24:36 and 1 Cor 15:28 as well as in Hebrews and frequently in the Gospel of John. Scholarship makes a distinction between this title and "Son of God" and attempts to explain it in terms of its own history of religions background. Thus far a consensus has not emerged. There are in essence three opposing attempts.

a. The attempt of J. Jeremias to take a *comparison* as the starting point is appropriate only for our logion (and John 5:19-20).[77] He claims that it spoke originally not of *the* son but of *a* son. A father and a son know each other. A son is entrusted with everything by his father when, for example, he becomes his father's apprentice. In my judgment we can eliminate this attempt. The logion shows no trace of a comparison. Furthermore, v. 27d would not be understandable in a comparison, and the exclusivity of the Father-Son relationship in v. 27b, c would be difficult to understand.[78] Jeremias wants to save the saying for Jesus and an Aramaic original at any cost, even at the cost of changing the wording and of completely changing the meaning.

b. More helpful is the attempt to derive our text—along with 1 Cor 15:28 and Mark 13:32—from the *Son of Man Christology*.[79] The absolute use of "the Son," influenced by wisdom, would take the place of "Son of Man." Then one could understand v. 17a against the background of Dan 7:14; it would speak of the transfer of power to the Son. P. Hoffmann has attached a bold hypothesis to this derivation. He

---

73   Cf. Wis 10:21 (wisdom opens the mouth of the mute and makes the language of infants understandable).

74   1QpHab 12.4. Cf. 1QH 2.9: the teacher becomes good sense for the simple.

75   Hoffmann, *Studien*, 108–9.

76   Cf. the similar consequences of the addition of Matt

5:11-12 to the original three beatitudes (vol. 1, II A 1.2 on the history of the transmission).

77   *Prayers*, 48–52; *Theology*, 59–61.

78   Why should *only* a father know his son and *only* a son know his father?

79   Cf. primarily Eduard Schweizer, "υἱός κτλ," TDNT 8 (1972) 370–73.

claims that Jesus has been identified with the Son of Man for the first time in our logion—that it is the Easter kerygma of the Q community that Jesus was exalted to be the Son of Man.[80] A problem with this view is that one does not *have* to interpret the $\pi\acute{\alpha}\nu\tau\alpha$ $\mu o\iota$ $\pi\alpha\rho\epsilon\delta\acute{o}\vartheta\eta$ ("everything was delivered to me") in v. 27a in terms of Daniel 7.[81] Verse 27b and c appear to have no parallels in the realm of the Son of Man Christology.[82] It is not understandable why—especially in the sayings source with its Son of Man Christology—"the Son" takes the place of "Son of Man." In my judgment we must ask differently in all three texts how far motifs of the Son of Man Christology have influenced the sayings, but we will not be able to explain the expression "the Son" on this basis.

c. The third suggestion attempts to derive the title "the Son" from the Jewish *preexistent wisdom*.[83] Indeed, much in v. 27 is reminiscent of the figure of wisdom. Human beings cannot know the hidden wisdom on their own; God knows wisdom; wisdom knows God.[84] This derivation would fit the "wisdom" context in vv. 25-26. "Everything was delivered to me" would then have to be understood primarily as the transmission of knowledge, that is, as a "process of tradition." However, what is difficult with this thesis is that Q elsewhere does not seem to know an identification of Christ and wisdom. Difficult also is that

the (feminine!) wisdom is nowhere called "the Son" in the sources.

In my judgment we cannot provide a history of religions derivation for the title "the Son." In almost all texts the polarity of "the Son" and "the Father" is constitutive. It is thus "the Father" who rhetorically—and not in terms of the history of religions—requires "the Son" as his opposite.[85] Furthermore, in most of the other NT texts it is demonstrable and presupposed that Jesus is God's son.[86] Thus what is meant is *the Son of God*. What is *said*, however, in rhetorical polarity to "the Father" is "the Son."

If one proceeds in the interpretation of our text from its rhetorical structure, what it makes clear above all is the uniqueness and special character of the relationship of Father and Son. "Father" and "Son" designates a special, close, and unique relationship. From the beginning a person is "son" in relation to his father and "father" in relation to his son. The relationship to the father is not something that is additional, accidental in the son and vice versa.[87] While it is true that what normally determines the relationship of a father to his son is a presupposition for the rhetorical figure of our text,[88] it does not simply speak figuratively. Rather, the Father is God

---

80 *Studien*, 139–42.

81 The formulation $\dot{\epsilon}\delta\acute{o}\vartheta\eta$ $\alpha\grave{\upsilon}\tau\tilde{\omega}$ $\dot{\epsilon}\xi o\upsilon\sigma\acute{\iota}\alpha$ does not support this interpretation, especially since the detour also is frequently taken to it by way of Matt 28:18.

82 Simon Légasse ("Le logion sur le Fils révélateur," 255) calls attention to *1 Enoch* 49.2 (the spirit of wisdom, insight, and teaching dwells in the elect) and 46.3 (the Son of Man reveals everything that is hidden, for God has chosen him), but these passages clarify neither the exclusivity nor the mutuality of knowing in v. 27b, c.

83 Cf. in different ways especially André Feuillet, "Jésus et la sagesse divine d' après les évangiles synoptiques," 161–96, 179–84; Christ, *Sophia*, 87–91, and Suggs, *Wisdom*, 89–95. In *Sophia*, Christ already identifies the earthly Jesus with wisdom without ever justifying it. Suggs makes the detour over the righteous son of God of wisdom 2:4-5. In my judgment, in this way he arrives only at a "typical figure" (p. 93) and not at the unique figure of *the* Son in Matt 11:27.

84 Cf. especially Wis 8:9; 9:1, 4, 9; John 1:18. For additional sources see Christ, *Sophia*, 89.

85 A linguistic parallel is *Mek. Exod.* on 12:1 = Jakob Winter and August Wünsche, *Mechiltha: ein tannaitischer Midrash zu Exodus* (Leipzig: Hinrichs,

1909) 3–4: Elijah demanded the honor of the father and not of the son, Jonah demanded the honor of the son and not of the father, Jeremiah demanded the honor of the father and the son. This text also is an ad hoc rhetorical creation of an absolute "the Father" and an absolute "the Son" that presupposes God's and Israel's sonship of God.

86 That can be postulated only for Mark 13:32 and our text.

87 It would be different if instead of "Son" something like "young person" had been used. Then the relationship to the father would be something accidental.

88 A secular example is given in Tob 5:2א: Tobias says about his future father-in-law, Raguel, who at the time was still unknown to him: $A\grave{\upsilon}\tau\grave{o}\varsigma$ $o\grave{\upsilon}$ $\gamma\iota\nu\acute{\omega}\sigma\kappa\epsilon\iota$ $\mu\epsilon$ $\kappa\alpha\grave{\iota}$ $\dot{\epsilon}\gamma\grave{\omega}$ $o\grave{\upsilon}$ $\gamma\iota\nu\acute{\omega}\sigma\kappa\omega$ $\alpha\grave{\upsilon}\tau\acute{o}\nu$.

from the beginning, and again the Son is Jesus from the beginning. The definite article also indicates that here "the Father" and "the Son" are used in actual discourse.[89] That there are also earthly fathers and sons makes at least somewhat understandable and expressible what otherwise would be completely unrecognizable and unutterable, viz., God's actual fatherhood and the actual sonship of Jesus.

■ **27a** *On 2:* Two possibilities exist for the interpretation of παραδίδοσθαι ("to deliver") in v. 27a.

a. With the main stream of the church's interpretation one can understand the πάντα ("everything") in terms of the power that is transferred to Jesus.[90] Then one can interpret πάντα comprehensively: "the heavenly, the earthly, and that which is under the earth."[91] This reading best corresponds with the trinitarian interpretation of our text. Matt 28:18 as a parallel supports this interpretation.[92] From a history of religions perspective it corresponds to the Son of Man Christology. Verse 27a then means that already now, in earthly humility, all power was given to the Son of Man.[93] However, πάντα has also been understood more narrowly and interpreted with soteriological interest to refer, for example, to the people whom the Son is to lead to the Father,[94] to the church where the rule of Christ is presently visible,[95] or to Jesus' authority in his activity.[96] However, there is no suggestion of a narrowing-down in πάντα ("everything").

b. In many more recent interpretations it is not the power transferred to Jesus that stands in the foreground but his wisdom, the knowledge of the Father. The heavenly mysteries have been entrusted to Jesus by the Father.[97] The most important argument in support of this interpretation is the context. Both vv. 25-26 and v. 27b-d speak of knowing and revelation. Verse 27a gives then a direct reason for v. 27b and c. If all knowledge is given to the Son by the Father, then Father and Son can recognize each other mutually as equals. The verb παραδίδωμι ("to deliver") is not a very strong argument for this interpretation. While it is used as a *terminus technicus* for "to pass on tradition" in Jewish and also in Hellenistic secular and religious texts,[98] it always means "horizontal" tradition to later generations and not heavenly revelation from above.[99]

The general term πάντα supports the first, but the context decisively supports the second interpretation. The latter argument is stronger. Since v. 27 was designed as a commentary on vv. 25-26, v. 27a probably refers back to the revelation that was mentioned there. To be sure, more is at issue in Matt 28:18, viz., all "power" in heaven and on earth. Matthew presumably has formed that verse redactionally by taking up the traditional logion of 11:27 and consciously expanding it.[100]

Reciprocity

On 3: Today there are two contrasting interpretations of the mutual knowing of Matt 22:27b and c: an "Old Testament" and a "mystical" interpretation. Both differ from the Greek "theoretical" understanding of knowing.

89 Cf. Eph 3:15: The fatherhood of God is derived not from earthly fathers but ἐξ οὗ (*scil.* God) πᾶσα πατριὰ . . . ὀνομάζεται.

90 Cf. above on the history of interpretation. Among more recent advocates see, e.g., Marchel (*Abba*, 159); Schulz (*Q*, 222); Hoffmann (*Studien*, 120–21).

91 *Opus imperfectum* 28 = 777–78.

92 Already Olshausen, 433; W. M. L. de Wette, *Das Neue Testament, griechisch mit kurzem Kommentar* (Halle: Anton, 1887) 1.73. John 3:35 and 13:3 also belong here. Cf. 5:26; 10:29.

93 Hoffmann, *Studien*, 121–22; Schweizer, 272.

94 Jerome, 86; Bede, 59. Cf. John 17:2.

95 Luther 2.426 (Sermon from 1546).

96 Maldonat, 240: *potestas gubernandi servandique homines*; John Chrysostom 38.2 = *PG* 57.430: the ability to cast out demons as an expression of the divinity of Jesus.

97 Thus already Hilary, 11.12 = SC 254.266; more recently, e.g., Norden, *Agnostos*, 290–91 (secret teaching in a mystical sense); Wellhausen, 57 (παράδοσις directly from God); Lucien Cerfaux, "L'évangile de Jean et le 'logion johannique' des synoptiques," 3.162–63; Deutsch, *Hidden Wisdom*, 33–34 (secret knowledge about the Father). Close to this interpretation are John 5:20; 7:16, 28-29; 8:19, 38; 12:49.

98 BAGD, *s.v.*, 3.

99 With this interpretation one must either understand παραδίδωμι metaphorically or interpret it in the sense of "to give" (= δίδωμι). Cf. Matt 13:11.

100 Lange, *Erscheinen*, 209, 488 (with a different interpretation of 11:27).

a. The Old Testament interpretation points out that "knowing" in the Bible is always something concrete and whole, an experience, a being close. When God's own "knowing" is the subject, the idea of election is associated with it, for God calls those whom he knows and loves.[101] When the subject is the human knowledge of God, the idea of acknowledging, of obedience is associated with it.[102] Thus the mutual knowledge of Father and Son is in reality asymmetric.[103] The Father has chosen the Son, the Son has acknowledged the Father in obedience.[104] The unity of Father and Son—if one can speak of unity at all—is in this interpretation a unity of the will.

> Although this type of interpretation fits today's biblical-theological landscape, it is difficult. The difficulty is not that reciprocal statements are missing in all Old Testament texts, or that knowledge of the Father and the Son according to 11:25-26 certainly also contains a noetic element. That the Father communicates the divine plan of salvation to the Son who then reveals it to his own is quite compatible with the Old Testament interpretation.[105] However, the two identical present tenses ἐπιγινώσκει ("knows") are difficult. They do not support the view that the text speaks of the earlier divine election and the Son's subsequent response to it. The translator then would have had to misunderstand our logion in a thoroughgoing "mystical" sense. However, the greatest—and in my judgment insurmountable—difficulty of this interpretation

lies in the exclusivity of the knowledge that is at issue. For it does not say that the Father has "chosen" only the Son—this may sound harsh, but it is still possible—but that *only* the Father has "chosen" the Son. That is nonsense; who else would have chosen the Son? And it also does not say that the Son acknowledges only the Father but that *only* the Son "acknowledges" the Father. That is not nonsense, but it is quite discouraging for the church that is called to obedience. From the failure of the Old Testament interpretation we can learn that every interpretation of Matt 11:27 has to pass the test of the exclusivity of the relationship of Father and Son.[106]

b. The "mystical" interpretation[107] began with the mystical statements of reciprocity. Our text then describes Jesus' *unio* with the Father that takes place in the mutual recognition of their nature. Naturally, John 10:14-15 was understood to be related: "I know my own and my own know me, as the Father knows me and I know the Father." In addition, reference has been made to Gal 4:9; 1 Cor 8:3; 13:12 and several more or less close parallels from "Hellenistic mysticism."[108]

> This interpretation has become quite unfashionable in the tide of attacks on the so-called early Christian mysticism that have been inspired by dialectical theology. People have demonstrated basic Old Testament elements in Paul's understanding of the knowledge of

101 Cf. Jer 1:5; Amos 3:2; Hos 13:5, etc.

102 Hos 4:1; Isa 11:2 (par. fear of God); Jer 22:16 (par. right and justice for the miserable and poor), etc.

103 There are hardly any reciprocal statements; at most one could point to Exod 33:12-13: Because God knows Moses, Moses also wants to know God's plans.

104 This type of interpretation is advocated, e.g., by Jacques Dupont, *Gnosis: La Connaissance Religieuse dans les Epîtres de Saint Paul* (2d ed.; Universitas Catholica Lovaniensis, Diss. 2/40; Louvain: Nauwelaerts, 1960) 61–62; Hahn, *Titles*, 310–11; Schweizer, "υἱός κτλ," 373; Sand, *Evangelium*, 252.

105 On the basis of apocalyptic parallels Hoffmann (*Studien*, 128–30) emphasizes—as Maldonat (241) already does before him—the noetic element in knowing. To know God means to recognize his plans. In rabbinic Judaism the noetic element is strengthened. To know God is to know his Law, i.e., to be wise.

106 Hoffmann, *Studien*, 123: The reciprocity is subordi-

nated to the exclusivity of the knowledge of Father and Son.

107 Classically advocated by Norden, *Agnostos Theos*, 303–7; Arvedson, *Mysterium*, 152–57.

108 *Corp. Herm.* 1 (*Poimandres*) 31–32 (no reciprocal statement); 10 (key); 15 (God γνωρίζει καὶ θέλει γνωρίζεσθαι); *Odes Sol.* 7.12–13 (no reciprocal statement); 8.12 (no reciprocal statement); *Gos. Thom.* 3 ("When you come to know yourselves, then you will become known; and you will realize that it is you who are the sons of the living Father"; is this dependent on 11:27?); *Tri. Trac.* 87.15–16 (the Son is the gnosis of the Father whom he wanted them to recognize); *Lond.* 122.50 quoted in Wilhelm Bousset, *Kyrios Christos* (New York: Abingdon, 1970) 165 ("I know you, Hermes, and you know me. I am you, and you are I"—but this deals with magical practices); a later Isis magical papyrus (in Norden, *Agnostos Theos*, 291). With some distance the closest parallel is offered by the (mystical pantheistic) Ekhnaton hymn = *ANET*, 371 (John A. Wilson,

God[109] and at least asserted the same for John 10:14-15. They have emphasized the fundamental differences between the New Testament and neighboring texts, especially the Odes of Solomon and the *Corpus Hermeticum*.[110] However, since for the most part they have no longer recognized that even in the mystical relationship with God there remains a difference between God and the mystic, for reasons understandable in the history of theology the tendency has been to throw out the baby with the bathwater.

It appears to me to be incontestable that in a number of mystical texts statements appear that are related to 11:27b, c. In addition to the few statements of reciprocity it is important to examine the larger conceptual world of such texts. The *Sapientia Salomonis* says in good wisdom fashion that wisdom is inaccessible to humans (9:17), but in Wisdom 8 she is an "initiate in the knowledge of God" (8:4). Whoever is akin to wisdom wins immortality (8:17). Formally this is the Old Testament concept of knowledge. To know means taking part, experience, love, acknowledging. At the same time, however, it involves much more. To know God means that wisdom, "the mirror of divine reality," "passes into holy souls" (7:26-27). Only the person who is so graced is able to know God, "for God loves nothing so much as the one who lives with wisdom" (7:28). Thus to know God means fellowship with God and, by intimation, equality of essence. This language is mystical and at the same time indicates the milieu in which texts like Matt 11:27 could originate. We find similar tones in *the writings of Philo*. The highest degree of knowledge of God, reserved for the "one who sees God," who has left the world of the senses and the world of reason, is the mystical experience of God in which like is known by like, light by light (*Spec. leg.* 1.42), sun by sun, God by God (*Praem. poen.* 45). Here also the concept of knowledge is un-Greek; Philo paraphrases it with images not only of seeing but also of eating and drinking, of rest, of love (*Rer. div. her.* 79; *Fug.* 137–38; *Som.* 2.232). Here one sees God. Pure rays of full light stream over the one who is carried up by intense longing to the pinnacle of pure spirit so that the spiritual eye is blinded (*Op. mun.* 71). God comes to meet Abraham, the vision-

ary, who has set out toward God. "Therefore it does not say that the wise saw God but that 'God appeared' to the wise" (*Abr.* 79–80). "Only those who are granted a realization of God by God achieve . . . the truth" (*Praem. poen.* 46) when God himself shows himself to the yearning eye of the spirit. We have here the beginning impulses of deification and also of statements of reciprocity, but at the same time the character of the knowledge of God as absolute grace is not eliminated. In the final analysis, all knowledge is God's own knowledge, and human knowledge exists only as knowing that is granted.[111]

I think that the way was prepared for the statement of our verse in the milieu of mystical transformation of Old Testament faith. The knowledge here spoken of is knowledge of like by like. The Son to whom the Father "has delivered" all knowledge is known by him and knows him.[112] Thus knowledge of God is God's own knowledge in God. Just as the "seers of God" in Philo are fundamentally different from sensuous people and spirit people, in v. 27 the knowledge of God by the Son is a non-sensory, divine knowledge. Just as in the mystical statements, here also the knowledge of God comes from God alone. And just as there, the being of the one who knows is not an act that could be separated from the self. The Son is Son by knowing the Father. There are, of course, great differences that give our statement an unmistakable original character. Here nothing is said, as there is especially in Philo, of achieving wisdom by moving out of the sensory world to the spiritual pinnacle; the movement is instead one-directional from the Father to the Son and then from him to humans. The sequence of the parts of the verse, including the order of v. 27b and c, is irreversible. Furthermore, in v. 27 the Son—and only the Son—assumes the role of the one united with wisdom or of the perfect "mystic." The subject is exclusively Christ and not a mystical relationship that is foundational for everyone. In any case, v. 27d does not, as

---

trans.): "Thou art in my heart/ And there is no other that knows thee/ Save thy son Nefer-kheperu-Re Wa-en-Re/ For thou hast made him well-versed in thy plans and in thy strength."

109 Cf. Dupont, *Gnosis*, 61–62 passim.

110 See, e.g., Rudolf Schnackenburg, *The Gospel According to St. John*, 3 vols. (New York: Crossroad, 1987) 2.298.

111 Ὁ δὲ δεικνὺς ἕκαστα ὁ μόνος ἐπιστήμων θεός (*Migr. Abr.* 40).

112 The way from Philo to Origen is not far. In *Princ.* 2.4.3 Origen reflects on the difference between (sensory) seeing and γινώσκειν that alone befits the perfect spiritual nature of the Father and the Son (= GCS 22.131).

does John 10:14b, absorb the believers into an analogous relationship to the Father but uses the term ἀποκαλύ-πτω ("to reveal") that is different from γινώσκω ("to know"). The knowledge that is "revealed" to them by a free decision of the Son is not the same as the knowledge that is given to the Son as it were "naturally"—observe the present tense ἐπιγινώσκει—by the Father. Therefore, part of what is revealed to them is not only the knowledge of the mystery of the Father but also the knowledge of the mystery of the revealer, the Son.

Matthew

■ **25-27** The evangelist Matthew has scarcely changed the text. By introducing the unit with ἐν ἐκείνῳ τῷ καιρῷ ("at that time") and ἀποκριθείς ("answered") he has connected it closely with the preceding material. Jesus' doxology is his counterpoint to the woe pronounced on the Galilean cities. Alongside the word of judgment comes as counterpoint the thanks for the call of the church out of the ranks of the "simple people." Ταῦτα ("these things") is now to be interpreted from the context and refers to the meaning of the whole story of Jesus in Israel.[113] There is no distinction to be made in Matthew between "Son" and "Son of God" (cf. 28:19). Thus v. 27 reminds the reader of the baptismal story where God revealed through the Spirit that Jesus is God's Son (3:17). It is reminiscent also of 1:21-23 and 2:15 where through God himself—viz., through the angel or the scripture—the mystery of Jesus' sonship of God became known.[114] It prepares the way for 16:16-17, the revelation of the divine sonship to Peter, and for 17:5, the transfiguration. Verses 26:63-64 and 27:43 will show how Israel's wise (high priests, scribes, and elders) fail to recognize Jesus' sonship and thus finally reveal their unbelief. Verse 27a is also reminiscent, although literal

references are almost completely absent,[115] of the temptation story, where Satan wanted to deliver supreme power to the Son of God. And above all it looks ahead to 28:18-20, where not only has God given all power in heaven and on earth to the Son, but at the same time Jesus reveals this to his own.

Summary and History of Interpretation

The interpretation makes clear that the tendency of v. 27 justifies the later trinitarian interpretation. In this verse the post-Easter church was reflecting on the fundamental *theological* meaning of the salvation that the νήπιοι experienced through Jesus. The doctrine of the trinity shares with our text the concern to anchor this salvation in God and in the Son. In the Son and his revelation God himself is at work.[116] The exclusive formulation of the mutual knowledge then means: The Son belongs essentially, not merely accidentally,[117] on the side of the Father. Without Jesus God's divinity is not conceivable. Without the Father there is no way to Jesus. Both belong together. God becomes understandable only as the gift of the Son, only by revelation. Thus the issue in 11:27 is what the Son *is* and not what he thinks of himself. Our interpretation has tried to make clear why the reduction of the trinitarian reflection to a question of Jesus' self-consciousness does not correspond to what the text intends to instigate.

Now that is not all that can be said for us today. We cannot turn back the clock on the reality that in our century the doctrine of the trinity has disappeared from the interpretation of our text without a struggle. It may well be that the trinity in its classical form today really is passé or at the very most is understandable for the "wise" but not for the νήπιοι, the simple people. To attempt to recapture it in its pristine state might there-

---

113 Deutsch, *Hidden Wisdom*, 29: "The person of Jesus, . . . his deeds, . . . their significance."

114 Cf. vol. 1, I A 1.3 on 1:22-23, I A 2.2 on 2:15, and I B 1.2 on 3:17 "Son of God."

115 Only: Ταῦτά σοι πάντα δώσω (4:9).

116 Sebastian Franck (*Paradoxa*, ed. Edward J. Furcha [Lewiston: Mellen, 1986] 25–26) formulates excellently as his conclusion on Matt 11:27: "To sum up: God himself has to be everything in a person. What he himself is or does not do, love, plead or know in us, is sin. . . . Indeed, no one can know, love, ask, etc., God except God himself."

117 Cf. *Gos. Thom.* 61: "I am he who exists from the Undivided. I was given some of the things of my Father." Marchel (*Abba*, 160) formulates on the basis of the present tenses: "Il ne s'agit pas d'une connaissance acquise . . . mais bien d'une connaissance permanente."

fore be directly contrary to the intention of our text. Nevertheless, its original intention must provide the direction for dealing with our text today. It calls the reader to understand that one cannot comprehend God apart from Jesus. Matthew is concerned that Jesus is "Immanuel," that is, *God* with us. When one does not direct to Jesus the question about *God*, one misses both him and the experience of God that the text intends for people. In our modern time there are enough examples of such a general belief in God or of a purely "human" Jesus piety.

We conclude with a look at two differently accentuated interpretations in the history of the text's interpretation that might serve "corrective functions" today. One is the *mystical interpretation* that has existed throughout the entire history of the church. I offer two examples. After the conclusion he draws from 11:27d, Dionysius the Carthusian formulates in a kind of postscript (*postremo*) that the trinity cannot be recognized *ex lumine naturali*. He asks how the knowledge of God, brought about by the revelation of the Son, can be realized in life and says that it happens when we let go of ourselves "in order to be united (*uniamur*) with God as one who, as far as his essence is concerned, is incomprehensible and who will continue to be unknown."[118] In this *postremo* both God's *prae* and his enduring mystery are preserved in the *unio*.[119] In the sermon *Haec est vita aeterna* Meister Eckhart formulates on our text: "Ergo if a man is to know God, and therein consists his eternal bliss, he must be with Christ the only Son of the Father. If ye would be blest, ye must be the only Son; not many sons: one Son . . . And hence if ye are one with Christ ye are the sole issue with the eternal Word."[120] Here also something essential from our text is incorporated. Blessedness consists in the knowledge of God;[121] Christ is prior to our knowledge; this is not a natural process but is dependent on the word. In both interpretations v. 27d, the revelation by the Son, is deepened and made concrete by a mystical experi-

ence without calling into question the irreversible flow from God to the human being that our text sets. In vv. 28-30 Matthew himself will not offer a mystical application of the knowledge of the Father and the Son, but these two examples may help to temper the fear of the mystical potential of our text.

The second interpretation is the *parenetic*, for which we have a specially good example in Pietism. Here the weight of the interpretation returns to v. 25. Now the νήπιοι are at the foreground but no longer as the "foolish" who are the human beings, as was the case with Jesus, but as the simple whom they are to become. Zinzendorf says that a Christian "must regain something of the attitude of children that a two-year-old child has." This means not stupidity but a "happy, childlike, simple nature," dying "to superfluous reflection, to musing on truths of the heart" and the "blessed simplicity," "in which we know what we want, because we know nothing but what we hear from him." If one does not become a child this way, then with the Christians "the old patriarchal life-style emerges again," and it does so even worse than before.[122] The "humility" of 11:29 makes this clear. There is scarcely a text with which Zinzendorf was as intensively occupied as this one. In his hermeneutical work *Christus der Kern Heiliger Schrift* [Christ the Nucleus of Holy Scripture] A. H. Francke cites our text in dealing with the application of Christology which as "external science" is still by no means understood. "But you must humble yourself before God as a child and must begin all your Bible reading in humble knowledge of your inability with most sincere and fervent prayer and sighing to God." One must recognize one's sin and misery as a heavy burden and thus *become* a νήπιος. Francke calls out to the "wise" theologian: *multi sunt theologi gloriae, pauci crucis.*[123] Here our text is applied parenetically.

Interpretation

■ **28-30** The tradition-history development of Matt 11:25-30 was similar to that of the Beatitudes.[124] In the sayings

---

118 145.

119 Thus in the "*unio*" the difference between God and the human being is not eliminated.

120 Franz Pfeiffer, *Meister Eckhart* (London: Watkins, 1947) 128.

121 Cf. Origen *Comm. in Joh.* 1.16: in the definitive apokatastasis, *everyone* "will see God, being formed in the knowledge of the Father—as now only the Son has known the Father—in order to become altogether in a perfect way his sons" (= GCS 10.20).

122 Zinzendorf 2.799, 804, 800.

123 *Christus der Kern Heiliger Schrift* (1702), in *Werke in*

Auswahl, ed. Erhard Peschke (Witten: Luther, 1969) 235, 245, 247.

124 Cf. vol. 1, II A 1.2 on the history of the transmission, and the summary.

125 Here, as everywhere in the book of Wisdom, it is not wisdom who is speaking but the teacher in wisdom's name. In Sir 51:23 also, unlike Proverbs 8–9, Sir 14:19ff., and the *Teachings of Silvanus,* it is not wisdom but her teacher who is speaking.

source the originally "open" Beatitudes were interpreted christologically, and their proclamation of grace was related to the church under persecution. The process of ethicizing began then before and in Matthew. Grace is not simply cheap, self-evident grace; it is connected with a human attitude and human practice. Matthew's addition of vv. 28-30 shows in our text this beginning stage of "ethicizing." Here (also) the issue is that the νήπιοι prove themselves by their *behavior* (11:29-30). Corresponding to this shift in accent is the development in the history of interpretation from the interpretation of the reformers and Orthodoxy to Pietism. Textually this development meant a displacement of the accent to vv. 29-30; in terms of content it meant a shift to application and parenesis. As with the Sermon on the Mount, now again the question will be whether the grace of which vv. 25-27 speak is thus not destroyed. We will need to examine this fundamental question with the interpretation of vv. 28-30.

Wisdom Saying

An invitation of wisdom is, from a tradition-history perspective, the basis of verses 28 and 30. Therefore, our verses are first of all to be interpreted against their wisdom background. The closest analogies are Sir 51:23-29; 24:19-22; cf. Sir 6:18-37; Wis 6:11-16.[125] Older examples are Prov 8:1-21, 32-36; 9:4-6, newer ones the *Teach. Silv.* 89.5-13 and *Odes Sol.* 33.6-13. In form these texts are often an actual invitation, a challenge and a promise, but the structure does not correspond to a fixed formal scheme. Thus our text, for example, ends not with the promise but with the reason. In these texts and other related wisdom texts appear numerous motifs of our text. Wisdom or her teacher turns to the uneducated (Sir 51:23), to those who lack intelligence (*Teach. Silv.* 89.7), to those who desire her (Sir 24:19) or *toil* for her.[126] Since the goal of wisdom is always praxis, "to toil" for wisdom means a life in obedience and righteousness. The image of the *yoke* is widespread in the Bible and Judaism, initially in the secular sense. Thus one speaks of the yoke of foreign domination, of slavery,

of fate, or of the "human yoke." Then a religious linguistic usage also evolved. Sirach speaks of the "yoke of wisdom" (Sir 6:24; 51:26). Since in Sirach 24 wisdom was identified with the Torah, that means nothing more than the "yoke of the commandments," or of the Torah, a widespread Jewish expression.[127] Also related are the terms "yoke of God" (Jer 2:20; 5:5; *2 Enoch* 34.1-2) or "yoke of the kingdom of God."

The thought is widespread that humans will find "rest" in wisdom (Sir 6:28; 51:27, cf. 24:7). This image, originally connected with the promise of occupying the land, was later given an eschatological meaning by the prophets, and in Philo and Gnosticism it became a symbol for the absolutely transcendent salvation.[128] It is difficult to decide in any given situation how much salvation history, eschatology, and transcendence is involved. In wisdom even the simple experiences of the preacher can play a role, so that wisdom always goes about with quietness and superiority, folly with noise and shouting (Eccl 9:17). It is helpful to look at other images connected with achieving wisdom. In the Proverbs and in Sirach it is the quenching of thirst and stilling of hunger (Prov 9:4-5; Sir 24:20-22; 51:24; cf. 15:3), joy (Sir 6:28; 15:6), the garment of honor and the crown (Sir 6:31, cf. 7:16-18). These images indicate that one should not limit the gifts of wisdom to the eschaton. What is meant is that life with wisdom or with the law here and now brings joy, fulfillment, freedom, rest, clarity, and power. For this reason the yoke of wisdom is a *benevolent yoke*. There are also parallels to this view in our wisdom texts. Sir 51:26 emphasizes that wisdom is near and may be found. Those who love her can see her easily, for she seeks those who are worthy of her and appears to them in their paths (Wis 6:12, 16). Those who begin early will have no difficulty (Wis 6:14). She can be bought for nothing (Sir 51:25). For the fool she is a rough road, but the wise person who serves her need make only a little effort and will eat of her fruit on the very next day (Sir 6:19-20).

It is with these statements that—for us!—the problem of interpretation lies. Why is the way of wisdom and of law—the "effort" she demands—an easy way? Must we speak here of a paradox?[129] Probably this is necessary only from a Christian standpoint. For a Jew who enters

---

126 *Κοπιάω* means "to become tired" or "to toil." The second meaning predominates in the wisdom parallels: "to exert oneself" (for wisdom). Cf. Wis 6:14; Sir 24:34; 33:18; Wis 9:10; 10:17. Σιρ 51:27 speaks of the efforts of wisdom for her sons.

127 Cf. *2 Bar.* 41:3; for rabbinic references see Str–B 1.608 b, c.

128 Cf. Exod 33:14; Deut 12:9-10; Isa 14:3; 32:18; Jer 6:16 (= Matt 11:29b); 2 Thess 1:7; Rev 14:13; Heb 3:11-4:11; *Gos. Thom.* 90; *Corp. Herm.* 13.20; Dupont, *Béatitudes* 3.527–28.

129 Deutsch, *Hidden Wisdom,* 117, 137.

the marriage with wisdom by living in the law and obeying it this obedience is joy and fulfillment.

Matthew

■ **28-30** In Matthew Jesus calls in wisdom's stead. Only the Son is the way to God. Functionally at least Matthew identified him with wisdom.[130] However, in my judgment here, as in 11:19 and 23:34, that is not the decisive Matthean statement but only its presupposition. The central statement is rather that Jesus "is friendly and humble of heart" (v. 29a). Nevertheless, the closeness of Jesus to wisdom sets an important basic tone for our logion. Since Jesus is inserted without interruption into the house of wisdom, a continuity to the law is also given with which Judaism identified wisdom. If in v. 29 Matthew calls the νήπιοι to the way of learning, this continuity is strengthened.[131] As in Judaism, μανθάνω means something practical, the learning of a behavior.

Jesus calls: Come to me, *all*. After the emerging crisis in Israel (11:7-19) and after the woes pronounced on the Galilean cities (11:20-24), that is an important accent. Access to God is still open for all Israel. As the gospel story continues it will show how Israel responds. Κοπιάω means "to labor (in physical or mental work)." Neither the context of the Gospel of Matthew nor the wisdom background of the word[132] nor the imperatives that follow in v. 29 support the "passive" translation "*mühselig*" (weary, toilsome), widespread since Luther.[133] Then the passive participle πεφορτισμένοι is to be understood not as an interpretation but as a continuation of κοπιῶντες. What does the "burden" mean? In the con-

text of the gospel we cannot avoid interpreting it on the basis of 23:4. It is the scribes and Pharisees who bind difficult burdens on people that they themselves do not carry. Thus the tradition he received is given an anti-Pharisee accent by the evangelist.[134] If this interpretation is correct, our logion still addresses the entire nation of Israel, not simply the disciples.[135] Why is the Pharisaic interpretation of the law a burden? One must direct a similar question to Acts 15:10. There one can give an answer, because a Gentile-Christian author has put the word about the "yoke" into Peter's mouth—a yoke "that neither our fathers nor we have been able to bear." However, with the Jewish-Christian Matthew the answer is not easy, since his Jesus commands that one keep the whole law with all iotas and dots (5:18-19). Why then is the law heavy when it is interpreted and imposed by the Pharisees but when Jesus commands it a "mild yoke" and a "light burden"?

History of Interpretation: φορτίον ἐλαφρόν ("light Garden")

The church's interpretation has attempted many answers. The Christian cliché of the Torah as a collection of many confusing and senseless individual commandments has made it difficult to understand the text (as well as Judaism).[136] Such an interpretation was significantly reinforced by the Enlightenment. Here the fullness "of Pharisaic regulations and ceremonies" was every bit as cumbersome as the Chris-

---

130 This is emphasized by, among others, Christ (*Sophia*, 116–17: the savior's call is presumably already from Jesus); Suggs (*Wisdom*, 96); Deutsch (*Hidden Wisdom*, 130–31: Jesus is the teacher of wisdom and is wisdom).

131 Ulrich Luck ("Weisheit und Christologie in Mt 11,25-30," 35–51) interprets the entire text in the framework of wisdom, but he emphasizes that through the knowledge of *the Son* this framework is decisively revalued (49). In my judgment that is correct for vv. 25-27, while it is more likely that from vv. 28-30 the entire text again strongly receives wisdom accents.

132 Cf. above, n. 126. The only Matthean parallel is 6:28 where it refers to physical labor.

133 Cf. by contrast the Vulgate: "*laboratis*"; "Zwingli"

(the Froschau Bible, 1531): "those who work"; the *Einheitsübersetzung*: "you who toil"; New English Bible (1961): "whose work is hard."

134 Künzel, *Studien*, 89; Deutsch, *Hidden Wisdom*, 43.

135 Contra Dupont, *Béatitudes* 3.530 and Stanton, "Matthew 11:28-30," 7 (in vv. 25-27 the νήπιοι are the disciples); both undervalue the πάντες and the meaning of the Matthean macrotext that tells the story of Jesus with Israel.

136 Cf., e.g., Michaelis 2.136: "The Pharisaic interpretation" entices the people "into a maze of scruples." The interpretation of the ancient church had already prepared the way for this tendency. Cf., e.g., Jerome, 87; Strabo, 123. Paschasius Radbertus (454) points out that the law of Christ is aware of only two precepts (the double commandment of love).

tian yoke "of dogmas and secret doctrines."[137] Kant thus understood the easy yoke of Christ as the moral law of the mature person. It consists of the duties that everyone "can regard as imposed on him by himself and through his own reason; and that yoke he therefore . . . takes upon himself freely." Therefore "only the moral laws . . ." are "divine commands."[138] Basically Kant's answer is not so far removed from the classical Christian answer. Thomas Aquinas, for example, tried to achieve a balance between Matt 5:19 and the antitheses on the one hand and Matt 11:28 on the other by claiming that the ceremonial law was invalidated and at the same time by stating that Christ added little to the natural law.[139] Thus the heavy burden is the Jewish law, the easy yoke is the *lex evangelica*. On a deeper level Maldonat[140] sees four reasons why the Jewish law is a hard yoke: (1) the infinite . . . number of precepts that exceed the natural law; (2) the penalties for transgressing the law that are based on a spirit of fear and servitude; (3) the coercion in the law and the free expression of love in the gospel; and (4) the gift of the Holy Spirit that is lacking in the old covenant. The most perceptive response, however, is probably that of Augustine: "Whatever is hard in what is demanded of us, love makes easy."[141]

Interpretation

■ **30** The answer would be easy for Matthew if, like the later Epistle of James and the ancient church, he had abolished the ceremonial law and identified the will of God with the "rational" natural law. We have rejected this possibility in our interpretation of Matt 5:17-20.[142] Jesus did not proclaim a different or less strict Torah than the Old Testament law. His invitation also consists of imperatives. "His" yoke must not be interpreted in opposition to the Torah, which he has come to fulfill.

■ **29** That the yoke is pleasant and the burden is easy is connected for Matthew with Jesus who imposes them. Did he think of the didactic qualities of Jesus the teacher who, unlike the rabbis, is patient with his pupils and does not punish quickly and harshly?[143] However, "humble in heart" is much more than a didactic qualification, and πραΰς ("friendly") is a poor contrast to the Judaism that, for example, praises Hillel because of his leniency in comparison with Shammai.[144] Or is Jesus πραΰς because he "enters the ranks of sinners, submits to baptism and so, on behalf of sinners goes the way of the cross"?[145] We must begin with the meaning of the two terms. Πραΰς and ταπεινός ("humble") are already linked in the Old Testament (Isa 26:6; Zeph 3:12; cf. Prov 16:19).[146] The connection of ταπεινός with the dative of relation τῇ καρδίᾳ ("in heart") is also biblical (Dan 3:87 LXX). In Greek ταπεινός has a generally negative connotation. In the Old Testament the word moves into the circle of meaning of עָנִי/עָנָו and thus can receive a positive meaning: God chooses the lowly. The dative τῇ καρδίᾳ internalizes the lowliness. One may think

137 Paulus 2.704.

138 Kant, *Religion*, 167, note.

139 *S. th.* 1/2 q.107, a.4.

140 241–42.

141 Augustine *Sermo* 96.1 = *PL* 38.584; similarly Dionysius bar Salibi 2.231.

142 Cf. vol. 1, II A 2.1 on 5:17 "History of Interpretation"; interpretation of 5:17-19; Ulrich Luz, "Die Erfüllung des Gesetzes bei Matthäus," *ZThK* 75 (1978) 424–26.

143 This is not a new interpretation. Cf. Theodore of Mopsuestia fr. 67 = Reuss, 118: forbearance and patience characterize Jesus; Cyril of Alexandria fr. 150 = Reuss, 201: ἐν ἁπλοῖς ῥήμασιν. More recent interpreters understand it in contrast to Jewish teachers. Zahn (443) says, e.g., in the anti-Jewish jargon of his time: Jesus is "not an unmerciful and arrogant master . . . as were the teachers of the law in his day." Schlatter (387) asserts that the teachers are "perfectionists" since they also "advocate the divine wrath." And Jesus doesn't? It is amazing how

a basically anti-Jewish attitude can blur the vision of otherwise competent scholars. Montefiore (*Gospels*, 2.610) justifiably complains about "the German Protestant explanations"!

144 *B. Sabb.* 30b, 31a; *b. Sota* 48b; and other sources (also for other rabbis) in Str-B 1.198–99. On the humility of Moses see *b. Ned.* 38a. According to Josephus (*Ant.* 13.294) the Pharisees are lenient in their punishment.

145 Barth, "Understanding," 148, n. 2.

146 Cf. *Pesiq. R.* 5.44a (in Walter Grundmann, "ταπεινός κτλ," *TDNT* 8 [1972] 14): Saul becomes king because he is עניו ושפל רוח. In early Christianity the two stems are connected in 2 Cor 10:1; Col 3:12; Eph 4:2; *1 Clem.* 30.8; Ignatius *Eph.* 10.2; *Herm. Man.* 11.8 = 43.8. Often ἡσύχιος or ἐπιεικής is added.

both of a condition (emotionally "down")[147] and an attitude ("humble").[148] The other texts in which the stem occurs in Matthew (18:4; 23:11-12; cf. 18:10; 20:26-28; 23:8-10) demonstrate that the issue is the humble attitude. What is meant is that human attitude that in love retreats into the background for the sake of the other.[149] Πραΰς in Matthew also means an attitude as it is expressed in the entry of the king who rides on a donkey to Jerusalem (Matt 21:5) and as it is praised as happy in 5:5: "humble," "kind."[150] In addition, when one considers that μάθετε ὅτι probably means "to learn *that*,"[151] then it becomes clear that Matthew is thinking here of the example of Jesus who himself embodies the will of the Father in his life and thus fulfills the law. Jesus himself is "kind" toward human beings as the two following stories in Matt 12:1-14 make clear. He is humble and free of violence as the passion narrative best shows. Matthew probably is also thinking here no differently than does a Jew who connects humility with learning the Torah and regards it as a decisive quality of a teacher. His anti-Jewish front is expressed only in his opinion that the Pharisees and scribes in practice are not humble but love the best places, respectful salutations, and titles (23:5-7). Jesus, on the other hand, lives what he teaches,[152] and it is precisely the example that he gives—according to Matthew in distinction from the Pharisees (23:4!)—that makes his yoke "kind and light."[153] Whether he thought,

as did Augustine,[154] that the love that is *always* the guide and canon for weighing the regulations of the law (Matt 23:23!) makes possible a new, free, and thus "unburdened" obedience is difficult to say. In addition, one probably must think of the "rest" that he promises. The power of the Father is delivered to the Son of God, and he, the demanding and obedient one, wants to accompany his church to the end of the world (28:18-20). And, finally, for Matthew the future of the kingdom of God (cf. Matt 5:3-12) also belongs to the "rest" that Jesus promises.

Summary and History of Interpretation

The later interpreters of Matt 11:28-30 tried to find new applications for the text. When we select a few lines from the history of its interpretation, a constant issue is the question of the limits and legitimacy of these applications.

1. The question has repeatedly been asked what it might mean "to labor and be burdened." The "normal" church interpretation in all ages has referred to the burden of sin and of the law.[155] Impressive is a long excursus from Erasmus, well hidden in the *Annotationes,* about the burdens that the Catholic church and its dignitaries imposed on the people.[156] Instead of the burden of the law, Paul Tillich speaks of the burden of religion and of the man who "labors and toils under the religious demand to believe things he

---

147 Thus ψ 33:19 (ταπεινοὶ τῷ πνεύματι).

148 Cf. *T. Reub.* 6.10 (humility toward Levi); *T. Jos.* 6.2 (prayer and fasting); *T. Dan* 6.9 (ἀληθής, μακρόθυμος, πρᾷος; the text is possibly a Christian interpretation of Matt 11:29). For the rabbis humility is a decisive virtue and a special presupposition for understanding the Torah: *m. ʾAbot* 6.5 (Torah is acquired through humility); ʾAbot R. Nat. 11; *Tanch.* כי תבא 24b (Torah resides with the humble) and additional texts in Str–B 1.192–93.

149 Zinzendorf repeatedly dealt with humility and arrived at remarkable formulations: Humility is not dwelling on the misery of sin, for "the savior," who was sinless, "had nothing humiliating in himself" (2.872). Humility also is not self-hatred, but only: "he did not take time to think of himself, to become vainglorious about his person and performance" (2.874). "Not to be pleased with oneself, to expedite the good so quickly that the left hand does not know what the right hand is doing, not to take time to think about past good deeds, because one has

immediately another object—that is what it means to learn humility from the savior" (2.873).

150 Cf. vol. 1, II A 1.2 on 5:5.

151 Cf. above, n. 3.

152 The old interpretation of our text in *T. Dan* 6.9 (above, n. 148) continues: ἐκδιδάσκων διὰ τῶν ἔργων τὸν νόμον κυρίου.

153 Kierkegaard (*Training*, 41, 53) effectively shows how Jesus' example can be *grace*: In training for Christianity, the "tremendous halt . . . which is the condition for the very existence of faith" (43) can originate only through him whom it cost his life but not by a "fashionable man in a silk gown, with a pleasant and sonorous voice" (41).

154 Cf. above, n. 141. An argument in support of this view would be the (not explicit) interpretation of the "mild yoke" with ἔλεος in 12:7.

155 See, e.g., Origen fr. 245 = 114; Jerome, 86; Luther, WA 38.527 (the attack from the Law); Bucer, 113, Jansen, 113, etc.

156 63–64 (from 1525).

cannot believe."[157] Finally, the peasants of Solentiname relate the text to "the burden of exploited people."[158] In the history of the church they have a predecessor in Luther who, because of his "passive" translation, "burdened," was open to expanding the term to include all tribulations including "hunger, poverty, shame, or other affliction."[159] The text was thus expanded. If one begins with the limitless love of Christ, then it is clear that no struggle and no burden may be excluded from his "savior's call" and that the task of modern interpretation is on the basis of this love constantly to discover and to take seriously where troubles and burdens are in new situations. Thus the text was understood as a message of *grace*.

2. This applies especially to the exegesis influenced by the Reformation. Luther calls out: *O ingens et opulenta misericordia tam dulciter vocantis ad sese peccatores miseros!*[160] The "all" (v. 28) is repeatedly emphasized. In his impressive interpretation Brenz repeats the word *omnes* ten times in only seven lines.[161] The text took on great influence, because it was used in the Zwinglian and Anglican liturgy as the invitation to the Lord's Supper.[162] To be sure, it was sometimes difficult for the interpreters to discover the promised grace concretely in the present, especially when they put the main emphasis on the burden of sin. An example: "It is sufficient in this life that we find rest

for our souls, although our bodies be troubled."[163] If grace is promised only for the future, then the text has no more motivating force in the present. Therefore, E. Bloch warns about our text: Jesus "is anything but an artful dodger into invisible inwardness, or a sort of quartermaster for a totally transcendent heavenly Kingdom."[164]

3. In the history of interpretation it has never been completely forgotten that our text has a *parenetical scope* in Matthew—that he even parenetically intensifies the "call of praise" into life. Beginning with *1 Clem.* 16.17[165] and *T. Dan* 6.9 its center has been seen in humility. Harnack speaks of the second-century Christian triad πραΰτης, ἐπιείκεια, ταπεινοφροσύνη ("friendliness," "gentleness," "humility").[166] Centers of focus in the history of interpretation have been Augustine,[167] monasticism,[168] and Wycliffe. It may be that the latter is especially close to Matthew, because he understands yoke of Jesus to be the *lex evangelica* and emphasizes that humility always requires concrete deeds.[169] Usually in the history of interpretation humility has been identified with discipleship or following Jesus on the way to the cross.[170] Sometimes ascetic demands were connected with humility such as, for example, mortifying one's self[171] or martyrdom in a situation of persecution.[172] On the whole, however, the opposite tone prevailed. The

---

157 Paul Tillich, "The Yoke of Religion," in idem, *The Shaking of the Foundations* (New York: Scribner's, 1948) 97.

158 Cardenal, *Gospel* 2.14.

159 2.415 (Sermon from 1517).

160 *WA* 38.526. Calvin (*Inst.* 3.4.3; 3.12.7) bases his interpretation of the savior's call on Isa 61:1-2.

161 471.

162 Stanton, "Matthew 11:28-30," 4; Fritz Schmidt-Clausing, *Zwinglis liturgische Formulare* (Frankfurt: Lembeck, 1970) 26. Cf. also Luther's "Large Catechism" (BSLK, 721 = *Book of Concord,* 454); "Formula of Concord" (BSLK, 996 = *Book of Concord,* 582: the "true and worthy communicants . . . are those timid, perturbed Christians, weak in faith").

163 Dickson, 158. Cf. Zwingli, 283: Rest and peace for the consciences. Of course, this and similar interpretations often were inspired by Pauline statements about the suffering of the apostle or of Christians (e.g., 1 Cor 4:9-13; 2 Cor 1:3-11; 4:7-15, etc.).

164 *Atheism*, 129–30.

165 "If the Lord was so humble-minded (ἐταπεινοφρόνησεν), what are we to do who through him have come under the yoke of his favor?"

166 Adolf von Harnack, "Sanftmut, Huld und Demut in

der alten Kirche," in *Festgabe für Julius Kaftan zu seinem 70. Geburtstage* (Tübingen: Mohr/Siebeck, 1920) 121; cf. 118: Πραΰς is one of the most common words in early Christian literature.

167 Cf. Otto Schaffner, *Christliche Demut: Des hl. Augustin Lehre von der Humilitas* (Cassiciacum 17; Würzburg: Augustinus, 1959) e.g., 129–31.

168 Cf. Gregory of Nazianzus *Or.* 14.4 = BKV 1/59. 275–76; Albert Dihle, "Demut," *RAC* 3 (1957) 765–71.

169 Wycliffe (354–62) with worthy admonitions to "us theologians" who evade the humility demanded by scripture with, e.g., allegorical interpretation or by distinguishing between *consilia* and *praecepta* (357). However, this is *superbia*; without active (!) humility there is no understanding of the scripture.

170 See, e.g., Calvin 2.26: soldiers of the cross.

171 *Herm. Sim.* 7.4 = 66.4: Simple repentance is not enough; what is needed is βασανίσαι τὴν ἑαυτοῦ ψυχήν.

172 Origen *Exhor.* 32 = LCC 2.414.

yoke of Christ consists not of a special asceticism, not in special fasting, but in loving one's neighbor and disdaining wealth.[173] Especially impressive is Augustine's formulation: "If you want to be great, begin with the least. If you want to erect a high building, think first of the foundation of humility. . . . Whoever digs a foundation must go down very deep."[174] In his polemic against the many monastic rules, Luther says with similar impressiveness: "Learn, learn, learn to be friendly (*mitis*), and you have performed infinite works."[175]

Matthew has combined the basic christological text of vv. 25-27 with a parenetic appeal (vv. 28-30). Therefore, the decisive direction of the text seems to lie for him in the *combination* of grace and parenesis. If the knowledge of Christ is separated from the parenesis, it becomes an abstract doctrine or a religious experience with no consequences. If the parenesis is separated from Christology, it becomes merely a religious or ascetic exercise. Matthew, on the other hand, in this text at the end of the first main part, presents us with a type of summary of his ethical Christology or christological ethics. He is concerned with the Son of God to whom alone the Father imparted himself and who alone imparts himself and the Father. Thus the focus is on the Son of God whose mystery Matthew alluded to in the prologue and revealed for the first time in the baptism story. The Father becomes recognizable in him alone. However, this Son of God travels a *way* on earth. He goes a way of obedience and humility from the temptation to the passion. The revelation of the Father and the Son happens when, and only when, the Son of God calls his own to follow him on the *way* of obedience. Revelation, salvation, knowledge of God happen in life, in concrete praxis, not prior to and outside it. In order to make that clear, Matthew combines the cry of jubilation of the Son of God with the savior's call. For him grace and praxis belong together as the content and form of the same substance. Whoever begins the way of the Son of God receives his revelation, and those to whom the Son reveals himself are already on the way. Therefore, the way of the obedient Son of God, about which Matthew tells and to which he extends an invitation, and the revelation of the mystery of the Father and the Son are for him one and the same thing.

---

173 John Chrysostom, 46.4 = *PG* 57.480–81.
174 Augustine *Sermo* 69.2 = *PL* 38.441; cf. *Sermo* 117.17 = *PL* 38.671: "If you would like to understand God's height, then first understand his humility."
175 *WA* 38.528.

This main section tells of Jesus' "retreat" in the face of the attacks from Israel's hostile leaders. Three times such a retreat is characterized by the word ἀναχωρέω ("to withdraw"; 12:15; 14:13; 15:21); twice it is expressed differently (13:36a; 16:4b). In each instance a debate with Israel's leaders precedes the withdrawal. The section consists of three parts. The prelude in chap. 12 is characterized by controversies and polemics. Its structure parallels that of chap. 11. A description of Jesus' miracles (12:1-21; cf. 11:2-6) is followed by a warning discourse (12:22-37; cf. 11:2-19) and finally a pronouncement of judgment to Israel (12:38-45; cf. 11:20-24) that is contrasted with a pronouncement of salvation to the church (12:46-50; cf. 11:25-30). The parable discourse, chap. 13:1-53, unlike the Sermon on the Mount and the disciples discourse, is structured as narrative. It contains numerous new beginnings and interruptions and, in its center 13:36, another withdrawal of Jesus "into the house" where he begins an instruction only for the disciples. The narrative section that follows, 13:53-16:20, has three parts. Here the guiding themes (controversies, withdrawals, symbolic scenes with disciples, confessions) are especially numerous.[1] With the confession scene of 16:13-20 a conclusion of this main section is reached. At the same time, this text is closely linked to the following with inclusions.[2] Here, as in the transitional section 4:12-22 and in the transitional chap. 11, it is clear that the narrator Matthew does not sharply separate his main sections but permits them to flow into one another.

One can also see the kinship of the main sections in the numerous resumptions of motifs and themes from chaps. 12–13 and from the transitional chap. 11 in 13:53—16:20. In reading the material the reader has a feeling of déjà vu and is constantly reminded of what is already known. We note several examples arranged in terms of Jesus' conversation partner in each case:[3]

Jesus and his opponents:
11:20-24; 14:2
    (cf. 13:54-58):   rejection of δυνάμεις

12:38-39; 16:1-2, 4:	demand for signs
11:6; 13:57; 15:12:	σκανδαλίζεσθαι of Jesus' opponents
12:22-24; 15:14, 30, cf. 9:27-31:	healings of blind—blindness of the opponents

Jesus and the people:
12:15; 14:14, 35-36; 15:29-31, cf. 8:16-17:	healing summaries
11:5; 15:30:	deaf, lame, blind
11:21-22; 15:21:	mighty deeds in Tyre and Sidon
12:15; 14:13; 15:21, cf. 16:4c:	Jesus' "retreats" from Israel

Jesus and John the Baptist:
11:12, 18-19; 14:3-12, cf. 17:12:	hostility toward John
11:2-4; 14:12:	John's disciples and Jesus

Jesus and the church:
11:25-27; 16:16-18, cf. 14:33	revelation of the Son of God
13:10-23, 36ff.; 15:11-20, cf. 17:19-20:	instruction of the disciples

If we look at the surface of the narrative, we again have, as with chaps. 8 and 9, the impression of a musical piece in which a number of themes and motifs are repeated. The image of a "braid" in which a narrative strand repeatedly comes to the surface is also helpful here. The repetitions are a narrative device by which Matthew creates the impression of his story's connectedness and inevitability.[4] In many cases they deal directly with the deep structure of the Matthean story.[5] They call the reader's attention to what the real issue is: the separation of the disciples of Jesus from Israel, the founding of the church, and its way to the Gentiles.

---

1   Cf. below, introduction to 13:53—16:20 (III C).
2   Cf. below, III C 3.3 Analysis.
3   Only in those cases where the Matthean redaction has created or intensified the references.
4   Cf. the remarks of J. C. Anderson, "Double and

Triple Stories: The Implied Reader and Redundancy in Matthew," *Semeia* 31 (1985) esp. 82–85.
5   Cf. above, II B and below, III C and IV (introduction to 16:21—20:34).

Literature

Robert A. Guelich, "Not to Annul," 46–64.

Eduard Lohse, "σάββατον."

Willy Rordorf, *Sunday: The History of the Day of Rest and Worship in the Earliest Centuries of the Christian Churches* (Philadelphia: Westminster, 1968) 54–75.

Verseput, *Rejection,* 155–206.

The section is homogenous. As is often the case in Matthew, it consists of three scenes.[1] The first two scenes, 12:1-8 and 9-14, take place on the same Sabbath, first in the field, then in the synagogue. The participants are the same: Jesus and the Pharisees. A reaction of the Pharisees to both incidents is not reported until 12:14. They want to destroy Jesus. The two scenes are linked with the catchwords σάββατον ("sabbath"; vv. 1, 2, 5, 8, 10, 11, 12) and ἔξεστιν ("it is permitted"; vv. 2, 4, 10, 12). They are also structured alike. With ὁ δὲ εἶπεν αὐτοῖς ("but he said to them") Jesus responds to an objection of the Pharisees with a long answer (vv. 3-8, 11-12). The final scene with the formula quotation, 12:15-21, is like a counterpoint to the conflicts. After the Pharisees decide he must die, Jesus withdraws—the important catchword ἀνεχώρησεν ("he withdrew") appears (cf. 14:13; 15:21). The crowds follow him. Jesus' healing—12:9-14 gave another example—benefits all the people.[2]

From here on Matthew follows the thread of his Markan source, beginning at Mark 2:23, without essential changes in order. Q material and special material are inserted into the Markan thread. With the exception of 12:22-45 and 24:37-51 there will no longer be larger connected Q units.

1.1   The Disciples Are Hungry on the Sabbath (12:1-8)

Literature

Hermann Aichinger, "Quellenkritische Untersuchung der Perikope vom Ährenraufen am Sabbat Mk 2,23-28 par Mt 12,1-8 par Lk 6,1-5," in Albert Fuchs, ed., *Jesus in der Verkündigung der Kirche* (SNTU A 1; Freistadt: Fuchs, 1976) 110–53.

Pierre Benoit, "Les épis arrachés (Mt 12,1-8 et par.)," *SBFLA* 13 (1962/63) 76–92.

D. M. Cohn-Sherbok, "An Analysis of Jesus' Arguments Concerning the Plucking of Grain on the Sabbath," *JSNT* 2 (1979) 31–41.

Glynn, "Use," Part 4.

Hübner, *Gesetz,* 113–28.

Hummel, *Auseinandersetzung,* 40–44, 97–103.

Etan Levine, "The Sabbath Controversy According to Matthew," *NTS* 22 (1975/76) 480–83.

Mariano Herranz Marco, "Las espigas arrancadas en sábato (Mt 12,1-8 par.)," *EstBib* 28 (1969) 313–48.

Benjamin Murmelstein, "Jesu Gang durch die Saatfelder," *Angelos* 3 (1930) 111–20.

Vernon K. Robbins, "Plucking Grains on the Sabbath," in Burton L. Mack and Vernon K. Robbins, *Patterns of Persuasion* (Sonoma, Calif.: Polebridge, 1989) 107–41.

Ed Parish Sanders, "Priorités et dépendances dans la tradition synoptique," *RechSR* 60 (1972) 519–40.

Luise Schottroff and Wolfgang Stegemann, "The Sabbath Was Made for Man: The Interpretation of Mark 2:23-28," in Willy Schottroff and Wolfgang Stegemann, eds., *God of the Lowly: Socio-Historical Interpretations of the Bible* (Maryknoll, N.Y.: Orbis, 1984) 118–28.

Schweizer, "Matthäus 12,1-8," 169–79.

For *additional literature* on Matt 12:1-21 see above, III A 1.

1 At that time Jesus went through the grain fields on the Sabbath; but his disciples were hungry and began to pluck ears of grain and to eat. **2** But the Pharisees who saw that said to him: "Look, your disciples are doing what it is not permitted to do on the Sabbath." **3** But he said to them: "Have you not read what David and his companions did when he was hungry 4/ that[3] he went into the house of God and they ate the loaves of showbread that neither he nor his companions were permitted to eat but only the priests? **5** Or have you not read in the law that the priests profane the Sabbath in the temple on the Sabbath and are guiltless? 6/ But I say to you: Something greater than the temple is here. **7** But if you had understood what it means, 'I desire mercy and not sacrifice,' you would not have condemned the guiltless. **8** For the Son of Man is lord of the Sabbath."

---

1   Cf. vol. 1, Introduction (Structuring of Shorter Sections, C).

2   Θεραπεύω: connecting catchword in vv. 10/15.

3   Πῶς is here best translated as "that." Cf. Moulton-Milligan, 561; Wolfgang Schenk, *EDNT* 3 (1993) 203.

Analysis **Structure**

The pericope is self-contained. After a short statement of the situation (v. 1), the Pharisees formulate an accusation. In v. 3 Jesus begins the answer that makes up the main part of the pericope. It is artistically structured. After a double οὐκ ἀνέγνωτε ("Have you not read?" vv. 3, 5) that in each case introduces a biblical argument in the form of a question, the conclusion follows in v. 7: You did not recognize; otherwise you would have acted differently. With the rhetorically gripping address, the stress lies on v. 7. Verse 8 is an appended christological argument. With the repetition of σάββατον, ἔξεστιν, ἱερεύς and ἀναίτιος ("Sabbath," "it is permitted," "priest," "guiltless"), the pericope is inwardly tied together. Verse 7a refers back to 9:13. The Pharisees and the Son of Man are the great antagonists of all of chapter 12 (cf. vv. 14, 24, 38; vv. 32, 40).

Redaction and Sources

The comparison of the three synoptic parallels is complicated, because there are in our text an unusual number of agreements between Matthew and Luke. Matthew has the longest text; the verses 5-7 in the place of Mark 2:27 are his special material. Luke has the shortest text; Mark 2:27 is missing in Luke also. Must we assume Luke to be the oldest text because he presents the smallest common denominator of all

three gospels?[4] Or must we proceed on the assumption that Matthew is the oldest text?[5] However, it is very difficult to declare, for example, the error "Abiathar" in Mark 2:26 as secondary or—in the second case—to understand why Mark would have omitted the Jewish-sounding verses Matt 12:5-6 but would have added v. 27 which is (externally?) just as Jewish. In general we have here confirmation of the hypothesis that Matthew has smoothed out and improved the Markan text.[6] Some of the "minor agreements" can be explained as independent Matthean and Lukan redaction: for example, the inversion of "on the Sabbath" in v. 2//Luke 6:2,[7] the omission of the ambiguous probable Latinism, ὁδὸν ποιεῖν in v. 1//Luke 6:1,[8] or the omission of "at the time of the high priest Abiathar."[9] However, εἶπεν (v. 3),[10] the omission of οὐδέποτε,[11] the omission of χρείαν ἔσχεν (v. 3),[12] and the plural μόνοι (v. 4)[13] can hardly be explained in this way. If we do not want to assume that Matthew and Luke used two different sources,[14] we have to assume the existence of a recension of Mark that is somewhat different from and presumably later than our text of Mark.[15] The most difficult question is why Matthew and Luke did not transmit Mark 2:27. There are several possible explanations, none of which is entirely satisfactory. From the oral tradition Matthew and Luke may have known that Mark 2:27 with its

---

4   Thus Ed Parish Sanders, "Priorités et dépendances dans la tradition synoptique," 519–40, 534–35.

5   Mariano Herranz Marco, "Las espigas arrancadas," 313–22 (only Matt 12:7 is redactional; Mark 2:27 is a substitute for Matt 12:5-6); Pierre Benoit, "Les épis arrachés (Mt 12,1-8 et par.)," 76–92, 81–87, 90–92 (Matthew—and partly Luke—represent the oldest tradition, although they are literarily secondary); C. S. Mann, *Mark* (AB 27; Garden City, N.Y.: Doubleday, 1986) 237 (Griesbach hypothesis).

6   Stylistic improvements are in v. 1: Matthew avoids the Markan ἐγένετο with a finite verb or an infinitive (cf. Mark 1:9 par.; 4:4 par.); τίλλειν, in terms of content the most important statement, depends on ἤρξαντο; in v. 2: εἶπαν (assimilation of the tenses); in vv. 2/3: δέ (twice); in vv. 3/4: twice μετά (assimilation of the preposition). Matthean language is: πορεύομαι, ἰδών, ἰδού, οὐδέ; cf. vol. 1, Introduction 3.2.

7   The more precise statement is appropriate for biblically literate interpreters: Deut 23:26 permits ears of grain to be plucked but not on the Sabbath.

8   Ὀδὸ(ν)ποιεῖν can mean: "to clear a way for oneself" and (Latin *iter facere*) "to wander, travel." In the first case (which in my judgment is improbable in spite of Marco, "Las espigas arrancadas," 338–39) the

transgression in Mark would be that the disciples pulled off ears of grain in order to clear for themselves a path through the field.

9   The statement is wrong. According to 1 Sam 21:2, Ahimelech, the father of Abiathar, was priest in Nob. However, when we assume independent Matthean and Lukan redaction, we must explain why both evangelists omit the statement rather than correct it. Schmid (75) points out that Matthew and Luke relatively often omit unfamiliar names.

10   Matthew tends to use the historical present with sayings of Jesus. Cf. vol. 1, Introduction 3.1.

11   A favorite word in Matthew; cf. esp. 21:16, 42.

12   Cf. Mark 2:17; 11:3; 14:63 with their parallels. The phrase would have fit well the Matthean emphasis on the disciples' hunger (Ennulat, *Agreements*, 79).

13   *Μόνον* would be the Matthean redaction.

14   Thus Hübner, *Gesetz*, 117–19 (Q and Mark are the sources of Matthew and Luke). However, then one must explain the cases where Matthew and Luke did not follow Mark even though their own language or theology would have made it natural to do so. Then the differences between Matthew and Luke are made difficult.

15   Hermann Aichinger ("Quellenkritische Untersuchung der Perikope vom Ährenraufen am Sabbat

special introduction is an addition to the original core of Mark 2:23-26.[16] For Matthew it is true that Mark 2:27 would have disturbed his coherent line of thought (cf. interpretation).[17] The suggestion that Matthew and Luke had available a deutero-Markan recension without Mark 2:27 is also possible, but it does not explain any of the difficulties here. The attempt to explain the omission in terms of the content of the verse has not been convincing.[18] There simply is no satisfying explanation.

Verses 5-7 are an additional argument that supplements the not very sound argument about David in vv. 3-4. Linguistically, vv. 5-6 are to a large extent, but not completely, redactional.[19] Matthean redaction is v. 7 with the Hosea quotation that is already known from 9:13.[20] It has often been claimed that vv. 5-6 are a traditional argument from a Jewish-Christian community with v. 7 as Matthean redaction.[21] However, the interpretation will demonstrate that vv. 5-7 create a coherent train of thought that probably as a whole is to be attributed to the evangelist.[22] Therefore, I also do not regard v. 6 as an originally independent saying of Jesus[23] but as a Matthean sentence that is formally patterned after 12:41-42.[24]

Interpretation

The pericope is closely connected with 11:25-30 both formally with the same beginning of "at that time" and in terms of content. The story of the conflicts in Israel that had begun in chaps. 9 and 11 continues without interruption. In terms of 11:25-30 the Pharisees are among the "wise and understanding," from whom God has withheld the truth, while the disciples represent the νήπιοι ("simple people").[25] "Mercy" (v. 7) will unfold what was meant by the "kind yoke."

■ **1** In v. 1, the exposition, Matthew emphasizes the disciples' hunger. He thereby does not simply intend to accommodate the situation of the disciples to that of David (v. 3); with a view to the Jewish discussion about the Sabbath commandment he wants to say that the disciples transgressed it not wantonly but out of need. That Matthew explicitly says that the disciples ate is perhaps more than simply an obvious narrative detail. Jewish-Christian readers know that eating well belongs to the Sabbath celebration.[26] Plucking ears of grain is thus at most the minimum to which the disciples are entitled on the Sabbath.

■ **2** The Pharisees, who at the beginning of the Jewish opposition to Jesus appear alone as the opponents,[27] protest the disciples' behavior.[28] Plucking ears of grain was regarded as part of the process of harvesting, one of

---

Mk 2,23-28 par Mt 12,1-8 par Lk 6,1-5," 141–53) and Ennulat (*Agreements,* 84) advocate a deutero-Mark hypothesis because the majority of the agreements are an improvement in language or content.

16 However, Mark 2:28 was presumably added still later, viz., by the author of the pre-Markan collection of controversy stories, and was taken over by Matthew and Luke.

17 Cf. below on v. 7.

18 Based on its content, the exegetes have made quite contradictory statements. Depending on the interpretation, Mark 2:27 is too liberal, not christological enough, too much or too little Jewish, etc.

19 Perhaps redactional are: ἤ before a question (cf. 26:53), ἀναγινώσκω with a quotation from scripture (cf. 19:4; 21:16; but here in receiving v. 3 = Mark 2:25), νόμος, λέγω δὲ ὑμῖν, ὧδε (cf. vol. 1, Introduction 3.2). Βεβηλόω is LXX language.

20 On γινώσκω, cf. vol. 1 Introduction 3.2, on τί ἐστιν and the quotation, 9:13, on καταδικάζω, 12:37.

21 Bultmann, *History,* 16; Barth, "Understanding," 82–83. Cf. similarly vol. 1, Introduction 4.2.2.

22 Of course, the argument in v. 5 can in itself be traditional, but that can hardly be the case for the self-contained line of argument of vv. 5-7.

23 Schweizer, "Matthäus 12,1-8," 171.

24 Without a prior word about the temple v. 6 would not be understandable. 12:41d, 42d confirm that such "'greater-than' logia" have a concluding function but are not independent.

25 Rupert of Deutz, 1525.

26 One is to hallow the Sabbath with eating and drinking and study of the Torah (*b. Pesah.* 68b *Bar.* = Str–B 1.611). This tradition goes back to Rabbi Jehoshua ben Chanania, who says explicitly: "The joy of a festival day is . . . a commandment." A clean garment also belongs to the Sabbath joy (*Midr. Cant.* 5:16 [121b] = Str–B 1.611). Fasting on the Sabbath is prohibited (Lohse, "σάββατον," 16). Cf. the wealth of material in Str–B 1.611-15. Noteworthy is that unlike good eating, participation in the synagogue service is not regarded as a commandment.

27 Cf. vol. 1, I B 1.1 on 3:7-10 (Jewish Leaders). Matthew likes to combine Jesus' opponents in groups of two. In 12:1-37 Matthew lets only the Pharisees appear in action (cf. also 9:32-34). According to Matthew, the opposition to Jesus begins with the Pharisees.

28 That is emphasized by Matthew. Cf. the accusation against the innocent at the end of v. 7 and the adap-

the main categories of work forbidden on the Sabbath;[29] on other days it would have been allowed.[30]

■ **3-4** Jesus gives a threefold answer. His first argument comes from the story of David's visit to the priest Ahimelech in Nob (1 Sam 21:1-7). As in Mark it is formulated with a view toward its application to Jesus. David does not ask the priest; he is a sovereign agent. He does not receive the showbread; he simply eats it. There is no longer any talk of the sexual abstinence of David's companions. They are more active participants than in Mark. Chapter 21 of 1 Samuel does not mention the Sabbath, but one may conclude from Lev 24:8 that the story must have taken place on the Sabbath if the showbread was prepared. That is at least what the rabbinic exegesis—which in various ways is concerned to exonerate David from blame—presupposes. One excuse is similar to that in Matthew: David and his people ate the sacred loaves because they were hungry.[31] The rabbis regard hunger as life-threatening, and a life-threatening situation had always taken precedence over keeping the Sabbath commandment.[32] That is how the rabbis later absolved David and it is how the Matthean Jesus absolves his disciples. Thus that is all rabbinically correct, except for a single

point. One cannot justify a halakah with a (haggadic) example.[33] As v. 7 shows, however, Matthew's intention is not to define a possible exception for a marginal situation but to establish an interpretive *principle* for the law. His line of argument is thus for Jewish ears still incomplete.

■ **5-6** Therefore, a further argument follows in vv. 5-6: The Sabbath sacrifices commanded in the Bible (Num 28:9-10) invalidate the Sabbath commandment.[34] That is true even in the strict Sabbath halakah of the Essenes.[35] For the rabbis it is fundamental that obligations tied to a certain time supersede the Sabbath command.[36] However, the argument is not simply an example of the principle that the Sabbath command had to be transgressed for other reasons as well, for Jesus now continues with a kind of *qal wahomer* conclusion: Something greater than the temple is here. What is greater than the temple? In my judgment one obscures Matthew's train of thought when one skips too quickly over the neuter μεῖζον ("something greater") and interprets v. 6 christologically.[37] Jesus does not say that he is greater than the temple, nor may we simply insert here the concept of the kingdom of God.[38] Instead, in the context

---

tation of the example of David. David and his companions are treated equally (ἔφαγον instead of: ἔφαγεν . . . καὶ ἔδωκεν).

29 *M. Sabb.* 7.2. The plucking is regarded as forbidden according to the late text *y. Sabb.* 7.9b.67 = Str-B 1.617. However, *b. Sabb.* 128a, also a late text, specifies and mitigates for just our case: "One may pinch with the hand and eat but not with a tool; one may crush and eat something . . . with the fingertips" (cf. Luke 6:1).

30 Cf. above, n. 7. Later, in *b. B. Mes.* 87b, this permission was limited to the owner's day laborers. Our text is not yet aware of this.

31 *Yalkut* on 1 Sam. 21:5, § 130; *b. Menah.* 95b/96a. For all of the material see Benjamin Murmelstein, "Jesu Gang durch die Saatfelder," 111–120, 112–15; Str-B 1.618–19.

32 *M. Yoma* 8.6. Additional material is in Lohse, "σάββατον," 14–15. In actuality this principle had been observed since the time of the Maccabean period. The texts cited above in n. 31 demonstrate that one could interpret the principle of the life-threatening situation very broadly (at least in justifying David's behavior!).

33 Cf. Daube, *New Testament,* 67–71; D. M. Cohn-Sherbok, "An Analysis of Jesus' Arguments Concerning

the Plucking of Grain on the Sabbath," 33–36.

34 It is quite unnecessary and, given the general formulation in vv. 5-6, also not obvious to think with Etan Levine ("The Sabbath Controversy According to Matthew," 480–83) of the עמר (cut ears of grain) of Lev 23:10-14 that, according to *m. Menah.* 10.1, 3, also could be harvested on the Sabbath.

35 CD 11.18; *Jub.* 50.10–11.

36 This applies, e.g., to circumcision, to commands in connection with the calendar, to the "temple service," to the Passover (already in Hillel, cf. Lohse, "σάββατον," 10, n. 63), to the tabernacles. Cf. especially *b. Sabb.* 130–37 and the material in Str-B 1.620–22; Lachs, 198.

37 Already C, L, Δ, et al. read μείζων. Similarly, e.g., Sand, *Evangelium,* 155; Gnilka 1.444. However, the neuters in 12:41-42 also, in my judgment, are not to be directly interpreted christologically. Cf. below, III A 2.2 on 12:41-42.

38 Thus Schweizer, "Matthäus 12,1-8," 171.

what is "greater than the temple" is an open question. In my judgment the following verse gives a further explanation here. With the word θυσία it takes up again the idea of sacrifice on the Sabbath and supersedes it with "mercy." "For if one is allowed to violate the Sabbath because of sacrifice, how much more must it be allowed because of mercy for those who are suffering, for mercy is more acceptable to God than is sacrifice."[39] Thus what is greater than the temple is mercy, which in Jesus' interpretation of the will of God has become the greatest thing. In Matthew's own time the destruction of the temple was probably an indication for him of how accurately Jesus had interpreted the will of God. At that time rabbis also, citing Hos 6:6 and Prov 21:3, formulated similar principles.[40] Of course, for Matthew mercy is not only a substitute for the sacrificial cult that was no longer possible after 70 CE but truly *more*.[41] Mercy is the center of God's will, which Jesus fulfills with his behavior (5:17; 9:13). He demands it of the Pharisees. At the same time, in v. 7 he reproaches them by quoting Hos 6:6. They could have recognized this from their own scripture! Thus v. 7 is in the context of the argumentation, not an ethical principle that is directed to the church[42]—that is clear from the direct address to the Pharisees. Our suggestion that one understand v. 7 as an interpretation and as an anti-Pharisaic intensification of the μεῖζον ("something greater") of v. 6 has the advantage of being

able to explain Matt 12:3-7 as a unified train of thought.[43] As in 9:13, where the quotation of Hos 6:6 that is important to Matthew has already appeared once, we must interpret the negation in the Hosea quotation dialectically and not antithetically. God wants mercy *more* than sacrifice. Jesus does not intend to abolish the laws of sacrifice; otherwise neither his own argument *with* them in v. 5 nor the comparative μεῖζον in v. 6 would make sense. The Pharisees who knew their scripture would have had to behave differently toward the disciples if they had comprehended what this "greater" is. Thus Jesus is thinking here neither directly of the disciples' behavior,[44] nor of his own,[45] nor of God's mercy[46] that stands above everything, but of the idea that the Pharisees should have been merciful toward the hungering disciples. Then they would have fulfilled the chief demand in the Torah, "justice, mercy, and faith" (23:23), and, as vv. 3-6 made clear, not also have approved a transgression of the Sabbath command. If this is correct, then the disciples' hunger receives a substantively central meaning far beyond the fact that, according to Jewish principles, it excuses a transgression of the Sabbath command. The hungering ones become the standard of the mercy that God desires and thus in the final analysis also the standard for correct fulfillment of the Sab-

---

39   Knabenbauer 1.529; similarly Akira Ogawa, *L'histoire de Jésus chez Matthieu: La signification de l'histoire pour la théologie matthéenne* (EHS 23.116; Frankfurt: Lang, 1979) 126–27.

40   Especially Johanan ben Zakkai, above on 9:9-13 (p. 34, n. 38).

41   *Deut. Rab.* 5 (201d) = Str-B 1.500 is formally similar, but it offers a different argument: Charitableness is greater than sacrifice, because its atoning power is greater.

42   See, e.g., Hummel, *Auseinandersetzung*, 43–44 (v. 7 "has in mind Matthew's church that performs charitable deeds on the Sabbath"); Hill, "Hosea 6:6," 116 ("concerned . . . with the Church of Matthew's own day").

43   The proposed interpretation by Roloff (*Kerygma*, 76–78) is artificial: David has broken the order of the temple (v. 3-4); the priests in the temple have broken the law of the Sabbath (v. 5-6); therefore Jesus who ("in the same way as David") is more than the temple is also lord of the Sabbath. Thus vv. 5-6

would then have the task of putting Jesus on the same level as David! Formally interesting is the suggestion of Vernon K. Robbins ("Plucking Grains on the Sabbath," in Burton L. Mack and Vernon K. Robbins, 132–39), who assumes a series of different rhetorical arguments (vv. 3-4 ἐκ παραδείγματος, v. 5 based on an analogy, v. 6 based on a comparison [πρὸς τί], v. 7 ἐκ κρίσεως).

44   Correctly Barth, "Understanding," 82–83 ("the disciples have not exactly kept the moral law by plucking the ears of corn").

45   Thus Roloff, *Kerygma*, 76: Jesus gave the disciples permission to pluck ears of grain. However, there is nothing to that effect in the text! Unlike 9:13, Hos 6:6 is not applied christologicaly here but polemically and, indirectly, parenetically. Different also are Guelich ("Not to Annul," 53: God is at work with his mercy in Christ) and Verseput (*Rejection*, 169–73; 173: "the humble Saviour").

46   Barth, "Understanding," 83 ("because God himself is . . . merciful, he wants us to be merciful").

bath.[47] Thus understood, mercy is the center of the will of God which Jesus proclaims and is more than the temple.

■ **8** In the first and the sixth antitheses, with his sovereign "but I say to you," Jesus had already contrasted love as the center of God's will with the Torah of Moses without abolishing the latter. Matthew expresses the same sovereignty of Jesus here in v. 8 with the words from Mark 2:28: The Son of Man is lord of the Sabbath. The Son of Man is Jesus, who for Jewish ears claims an authority here that he does not have. For the readers of the gospel he will someday rise up and judge the world, that is, Pharisees and disciples. For them v. 8 demonstrates that in v. 7 the issue was not a general principle of love, nor was it human autonomy toward the Sabbath commandment as such;[48] it was the will of the Father, finally and compellingly formulated by Jesus—the will of the biblical God that also includes the Sabbath command. There is a tension in our text similar to that of Matt 5:17-48.[49] Jesus does not contradict the Torah in its depth, but it is by virtue of his absolute sovereignty that he does not contradict it.

Summary

The Matthean community presumably observed the Sabbath. Verse 24:20 shows that this probably was done with consistency. Those who pray that the tribulation will not happen on the Sabbath show they are not willing to abandon the Sabbath command, even when their lives are in danger.[50] Mercy as the standard for dealing with Sabbath and purity commandments—that was probably the praxis of the Matthean community that it had learned from the Son of Man, Jesus. Thus the issue is not that parts of the Torah, viz., the ceremonial law, are annulled,[51] but that the entire Torah is subordinate to its own center, mercy (Hos 6:6). Matthew's entire argumentation is in its depth very Jewish, but it has a new foundation. It is based on the reality that through the *Son of Man* Jesus the biblical command of mercy becomes the greatest command—greater than the temple.[52] It is precisely on *this* basis that it does not discard the Jewish faith but participates in the Jewish Sabbath discussion about when the Sabbath command must give way before the principle to protect life.[53] It engages in the Jewish Sabbath discussion so deeply that one must say: If it had

---

47   Luise Schottroff and Wolfgang Stegemann, "The Sabbath Was Made for Man: The Interpretation of Mark 2:23-28," 125. Cf. Calvin 2.28: "As if [the Sabbath] were ordained so that hungry men should perish sooner than relieve their hunger." Clear also is Zwingli, "Von Erkiesen und Fryheit der Spysen," in *Zwingli Hauptschriften: Der Prediger* (Zurich: Zwingli, 1940) 1.17: "Note well that need surpasses and breaks not only the human but the divine law." We might add: Precisely this "breaking" can be the center of God's law!

48   The recently popular misinterpretation of ὁ υἱὸς τοῦ ἀνϑρώπου as meaning every human being, inspired by the juxtaposition of Mark 2:27 and 28, goes back to Grotius (1.358) and Wolzogen (285).

49   Cf. vol. 1, II A 2.1 on 5:17-20 (Summary), II A 2.2.

50   Cf. Schweizer, "Matthäus 12,1-8," 174.

51   Strecker (*Weg,* 32–33) advocates most forcefully the thesis that for Matthew the ceremonial law was abolished and that only the moral law remained in force. Walker (*Heilsgeschichte,* 139) offers similar arguments. Opposing this view are Glynn ("Use and Meaning," 98); Hummel (*Auseinandersetzung,* 38–45; 45: "a valid . . . halakah about the Sabbath, contradicts that of the Pharisees"); Geist (*Menschensohn,* 313–14). Cf. also vol. 1, II A 2.1 on 5:17-19. On the

theological and intellectual roots of this interpretation, cf. below, nn. 61–63.

52   Thus what is specific to Matthew in comparison with Judaism is in v. 8. Based on this verse the church's interpreters say, not incorrectly, that the *God* Christ is the lord of the Sabbath. See, e.g., Calovius (285) against the interpretation of Grotius cited above in n. 48.

53   It is no accident that precisely with our text Irenaeus (*Haer.* 4.8–9) demonstrates the unity of the two testaments. Cf. 4.9.2 on 12:6: "But with things that are not connected or that even . . . are at odds with each other one does not speak of more or less."

regarded the Sabbath as simply an outdated and abolished ceremonial law, it could have saved itself a number of intellectual detours, and it could have said it more succinctly. It also probably knows that the Sabbath "is a precious *gift* in (God's) treasury."[54] It has a deep affinity to the *social* basis of the biblical Sabbath commandment. As in Deut 5:14-15, the Sabbath exists for the poor, the hungry, or the slaves. Within Judaism Matthew represents a radically different position from that of the Essenes who during the Sabbath left a "living human being" lying in a "water hole" or "any other place," if saving the person was possible only with a ladder or a rope.[55] The Matthean community *fundamentally* subordinates the Sabbath command to the love command. Because of Jesus it thus takes a step that no other group in Judaism took. However, it also has Jewish relatives, for example, the Hillelites, who allowed those who mourn to be comforted on the Sabbath and sick people to be visited.[56] It represents, in a manner of speaking, the extreme example of a way of interpreting the Torah that has also become increasingly important in Judaism, precisely with Hillelite Pharisaism.[57]

History of Interpretation

The interpretation of our text is largely uninteresting until the Reformation, since the impression prevailed that this text was important primarily for Jesus' own time and not for the post-Easter church in which the Sabbath was no longer observed. From the history of interpretation after the Reformation I note two points.

1. *Law and gospel.* For the reformers our text was connected with the dialectic of law and gospel, each time with a different accent. *Luther* interprets in terms of *salvation history*: "It is finished with Moses and your thing."[58] Christ has liberated people from God's order, because he himself is God. People may do with the temple and Sabbath as they wish, but if they make of it a law, it is sin![59] *Zwingli* and *Melancthon* take from the ancient church and from humanism the *distinction between ceremonial and moral law.* "The lord has freed us from the law of the external traditions."[60] Calvin, basically influenced in his thinking by the Old Testament, warns: "Those who think that Christ was here abrogating the Sabbath for good are, as I think, mistaken."[61]

The issue is, rather, its *right use,* viz., its use on the *principle of love.* Of all the reformers Calvin is closest to Matthew.[62] After the Reformation, following roots in the ancient church[63] and humanism,[64] our text is interpreted in the sense of Zwingli and Melancthon in terms of the contrast between ceremonial and moral law,[65] an interpretation that has remained important from the time of the early Enlightenment until today.[66] It has its essential root there in the early Enlightenment and its thought based on natural law.

2. *Keeping Sunday holy.* What role did our text play for the question of hallowing the Sunday and of physical labor on Sunday? The answer to this question must be: almost none.[67] We may not forget that for

---

54   *b. Sabb.* 10b.

55   CD 11.16–17.

56   Cf. *b. Sabb.* 12a.

57   Hugh Montefiore (*Rabbinic Literature and Gospel Teachings* [1930; reprinted New York: Ktav, 1970] 242) says of v. 7 that it is "sound Rabbinic doctrine . . . at its best . . . and not very unusual." The statement is not completely incorrect, but it is probably exaggerated!

58   *WA* 38.532. Of the biblical Sabbath command Luther can say: It "does . . . not concern us Christians. It is an entirely external matter, like the other ordinances of the Old Testament" (*Large Catechism* = BSLK, 580 = *Book of Concord,* 376).

59   Sermon from 1534 = 2.433.

60   Zwingli, 283. Cf. Melancthon, 175–76: "Lex de sabbato sanctificando, si litteram spectes, caeremoniale est, et si spiritum, morale."

61   2.30.

62   Cf. vol. 1, II A 2.1 on 5:17-20.

63   In substance this is the distinction that Irenaeus makes between the Mosaic *praecepta servitutis,* that have a predictive or pedagogic function, and the *lex Christi.*

64   Erasmus (*Paraphrasis,* 71) speaks of *quaedam instituta* like food, clothes, fasting, feast days that are not in and of themselves good but only if they are not used *superstitiose* but lead to *pietas.* Melanchthon (175–76; above, n. 60) speaks similarly.

65   Cf. Cocceius, 22 on v. 7 (*iugum legis ceremonialis-studium amoris*); Grotius 1.356 (the love commandment is always superior to the ceremonial law), similarly Wolzogen, 285.

66   Cf. above, n. 51.

67   Calixtus (160) concludes indirectly from our text that one may do on Sunday that "which, without damage and harm for humans cannot be omitted."

the Christian church, in contrast to Judaism, the central focus of Sunday has never been resting from physical labor but the worship service. Indeed, the Sabbath is abolished. It is not part of the order of creation, but it was later given to the Jews with all other sacrificial laws because of their hardness of heart,[68] while God himself never rests in his care for the world.[69] The New Testament texts important for the understanding of the Sabbath in the ancient church were Col 2:16-17 and Heb 3:7-4:11, not Matthew 12 and other synoptic texts. The Christians are to "celebrate the Sabbath constantly"[70] and not simply cease from labor one day a week; they are to renounce the works of the world and to become free for spiritual works.[71] The story of David and Ahimelech becomes then quite consistently in the ancient church a type of the "spiritual" celebration, of the Lord's Supper.[72] Thus, unlike Jesus and Matthew, one basically abandoned the Jewish Sabbath.[73] The Sunday labor laws that were later authoritative for Christianity come from the heathen (!) Constantine and have only gradually interested and occupied the church.[74] In the view of the reformers the Sunday rest is a remnant of the order "from ancient times,"[75] useful for the furtherance of the worship life of the church and for the Christian education of the common people and beyond that, on the human level, important for those who do physical work all week.[76] The situation is different only where the ordinance of the day of rest, completely contrary to the tradition of the ancient church, again is given the dignity of an order of natural law. That was the case later in both of the major Western confessions.[77] On this basis then "halakic" consequences of our text again became possible. In both confessional traditions Matt 12:5 was thus understood to mean that the pastor or priest must in any case do the necessary work for the worship service, *etiamsi servilia sint*.[78]

The history of the text's interpretation confronts us initially with a basic problem in the history of theology. Our churches are not heirs of the Jewish Christianity that is faithful to the law—for example, of Matthew—but of the Gentile Christianity that is free of the law and for whom the Sabbath commandment was no longer valid. Neither Jesus' nor Matthew's faithfulness to the Sabbath commandment and to the Jewish law is directly binding for us. Sunday is not the Christian Sabbath. What does Jesus' renewal of the Sabbath have to say to us today about mercy as the center of the life that God wills? I would suggest that in place of the Mosaic law that is no longer ours we put our traditional Christian or Gentile-Christian ordinances. Among them is also the traditional day of rest. From Matthew's perspective this law is not simply to be abolished but to be lived on the principle of mercy. In my judgment there are clear decisions from the perspective of our text. Work on Sunday, for example, that today is required primarily for economic reasons, is to a great degree unmerciful and destructive of the well-being of people, if it regularly destroys the *common* rest, for example, of families with their children. Mercy is more than profit and growth! However, in the sense of the text the decisions must be made from love and the well-being of the people. The traditional laws, such as those about keeping Sunday holy, are to help in making those decisions.

---

68 Justin *Dial.* 18.2; 19.6; 43.1, etc.

69 *Didascalia* 26 = Achelis-Flemming, 137.

70 Justin *Dial.* 12.3.

71 Origen *Hom. in Num.* 23.4 = GCS Origenes 7. 215, 34–216, 13.

72 Rordorf, *Sunday,* 114–15.

73 Luther formulates in the *Large Catechism* that one hallows the Sunday "not when we sit behind the stove and refrain from external work, or deck ourselves with garlands and dress up in our best clothes, but . . . when we occupy ourselves with God's word and exercise ourselves in it" (BSLK, 582 = *Book of Concord,* 377).

74 Cf. the analysis of the imperial laws about days of rest and their ecclesial reception in Rordorf, *Sunday,* 162–73.

75 Luther, *Large Catechism* = BSLK, 582 = *Book of Concord,* 376.

76 Luther, *Large Catechism* = BSLK, 580–81 = *Book of Concord,* 376; *Geneva Catechism,* BSRK 132–33 = Torrance, *School of Faith,* 31.

77 For the Protestant side cf., e.g., the Westminster Confession 21.7 = BSRK 589–90 = *The Confession of Faith* (Edinburgh: Publications Committee of the Free Presbyterian Church of Scotland, 1967) 95, for the Roman Catholic side the *Catechismus Romanus* 3/4 q.22.

78 Dickson, 120; *Catechismus Romanus* 3/4 q.22 (quotation).

1.2 The Healing of a Disabled Man on the Sabbath (12:9-14)

Cf. the literature above, III A 1 on Matt 12:1-21.

9   **And when he went away from there, he came into their synagogue.**

10   **And behold, (there was) a man with a rigid hand.**
      And they asked him and said, "Is one permitted to heal[1] on the Sabbath" so that they might accuse him.

11   **But he said to them: "Who among you will be the person who has a single sheep, and if it falls into a pit on the Sabbath will not grasp it and lift it out? 12/ How much more than a sheep is a person? Therefore, one may do good on the Sabbath."**

13   **Then he said to the man: "Stretch out your hand."**
      And he stretched it out, and it became whole again, like the other.

14   **But the Pharisees went out and took counsel against him to destroy him.**

Analysis   **Structure**

The story is composed in ring form around the image of the sheep in the pit according to the scheme A B C D´ B´ A´.[2] A and A´ are the introduction and conclusion. Jesus enters "their" synagogue (v. 9); the Pharisees go out (v. 14). B and B´, and C and C´ correspond to each other not only in content but also with catchwords.[3] The controversy with the Pharisees now is completely at the center; the healing is moved to the end. Thus the genre of our story clearly becomes that of a controversy dialogue. At the end the Pharisees, who have accompanied Jesus since 12:2 and are not separately introduced in our story, go away.[4] Thus this concluding note refers to the entire section 12:1-13. With the immediate temporal connection in v. 9a, with various common catchwords, and with an almost parallel structure[5] Matthew has also made clear that 12:1-8 and 12:9-14 are a related pair of stories.

Sources and Origin

Matthew achieves this rounded structure by stylistically reworking[6] and tightening[7] the healing story of Mark 3:1-6. Matthew further inserts an additional argument of Jesus into the center of the story (vv. 11-12a). These verses are traditional and show linguistically a Semitic background.[8] The example of the domestic animal that has fallen into the pit, a "model case" in Jewish Sabbath interpretation,[9] may have been used in the debate about the Sabbath practice in which the Aramaic-speaking church was engaged; it also appears in the Lukan story of the healing of the man with dropsy (Luke 14:5). What is new here is that in v. 12a it is no longer simply an example but is surpassed and intensified with a comparison between

---

1   I read θεραπεύειν with B, C, *l*, et al.; θεραπεῦσαι (Nestle[26]) is an adaptation to Luke 14:3.

2   Cf. Ennulat, *Agreements*, 85–86.

3   B, B´: Ἄνθρωπος, χείρ; C, C´: ἔξεστιν τοῖς σάββασιν. Thus to explain this formulation it is not necessary to refer back to Luke 14:3 (contra Gundry, 226).

4   The Herodians are missing, in contrast to 22:16, because Matthew has only the Pharisees appear in these first conflicts of Jesus with Judaism. Cf. above, n. 28 on 12:1-8.

5   Exposition 12:1, 10a; the opponents' question 12:2, 10b; Jesus' answer (ὁ δὲ εἶπεν αὐτοῖς . . .) 12:3-8, 11-12. Formally vv. 5-7 and 11-12 are structured alike; a Jewish analogy 12:5, 11; surpassing 12:6, 12a; concrete action on the basis of love 12:7, 12b.

6   *Verse 9*: Μεταβὰς ἐκεῖθεν creates the connection to 12:1-8. Cf. 11:1; 15:29. Πάλιν is missing because Matthew has omitted Mark 1:21-28. Cf. also vol. 1, Introduction 3.3. *Verse 10a*: The formulation is extremely brief. On the Markan ξηραίνω cf. vol. 1, Introduction 3.3. Ἐπερωτάω, in itself a term that Matthew avoids, is almost always used by Matthew for hostile questions. Cf. Schenk, *Sprache*, 261. By letting the opponents ask the question about what is permitted on the Sabbath, Matthew creates the

parallel between C and C´. *Verse 13*: The awkward Markan repetition of χείρ is avoided. *Verse 14*: On the Markan εὐθύς cf. vol. 1, Introduction 3.3; on the Latinism συμβούλιον λαμβάνειν = *consilium capere*, vol. 1, Introduction 3.2, *s.v.* λαμβάνω.

7   The structure becomes clearer in Matthew because Jesus does not turn to the sick person until v. 13 (Mark 3:3 is different).

8   The relative clause has a conditional meaning. Τίς . . . ἄνθρωπος ὅς corresponds to the Hebrew מִי־הָאִישׁ אֲשֶׁר with the conditional meaning "if someone has a single sheep . . ." The NT examples differ from the Semitic examples given by Beyer (*Syntax*, 290–91) in that a forceful ἐξ ὑμῶν is added to the introductory question, and the main clause is formulated not as an imperative but as a rhetorical question; cf. Matt 6:27; 7:9-10; Luke 11:5-7; 14:28; 15:4, 8; 17:7-10. Is this a favorite way Jesus spoke in short parables, which the church then transferred to other areas? Since, however, our text is not a parable but a halakic analogy, we may not simply assume that we are dealing with Jesus' *ipsissima vox*, contra Heinrich Greeven, "'Wer unter euch . . . ?'" *WuD* 3 (1952) 95–96, 101.

9   Cf. below, n. 14.

a sheep and a human being. Since this πόσῳ-μᾶλλον ("how much more") conclusion corresponds in substance to the love commandment that is central for Matthew, v. 12a may be Matthean.[10] Missing from Mark 3:5 is not only the wrath of Jesus but also the hardening of the opponents, as is also the case elsewhere in Matthew (cf. Mark 1:43 par.; Mark 6:52; 8:17 par.).

Interpretation

■ **9-10** Immediately after the plucking of the ears of grain, Jesus enters "their" synagogue. It is probably not, as might be suggested by the context, the synagogue of the Pharisees but, as elsewhere, the synagogue of the Jews.[11] Matthew writes here from the perspective of his readers or of his church that no longer belongs to the synagogue. Presumably there—but that is of no importance to the narrator—Jesus sees a man who can no longer move his hand.[12] Matthew tells nothing of the encounter between the man and Jesus; he is interested in the conflict with the Pharisaic opponents. From the perspective of Matthew, who already knows how the entire story will turn out and for whom the Pharisees are the center of the Judaism that is hostile toward the church,[13] the fronts are straightaway clear. The opponents obviously already know that Jesus will heal on the Sabbath, and they ask only in order to have legal grounds for accusing him.

■ **11** Jesus' answer begins with a concrete situation that was often discussed in Judaism: Is it permitted to save an animal that has fallen into a pit on the Sabbath? The Essenes answered this question with a categorical no; the later rabbis obviously regarded that as harsh and developed a subtle mediating solution: One may help the animal, but it must come out of the pit by itself.[14] However, it is important that Jesus precisely does not refer to such a "semiliberal" Sabbath practice. He asks rhetorically: "Who among you will not pull out his sheep?" and thus presupposes an obvious, noncontroversial practice. He speaks of a practice of farmers who have sheep and not of a halakah of scholars. It may be that we can catch a glimpse here of a non-Essenic but also non-rabbinic Sabbath practice[15] among Galilean farmers. Furthermore, Jesus speaks of a man who has *one* sheep. In both Greek and Aramaic in the course of linguistic development the numeral "one" also assumed the meaning of the indefinite article. That is, however, seldom the case in Matthew, especially when ἕν is placed after the noun. As in Nathan's fable in 2 Sam 12:3, Matthew certainly was thinking of a poor man's only sheep.[16] It may be that we have in our logion one of the few indications that (of course, not the Gospel of Matthew) some of Matthew's traditions are formulated from the perspective of Palestine's rural poor environment.[17] Since the poor peasant

---

10   Hummel, *Auseinandersetzung,* 44 (the form is analogous to 6:26; 10:31). The πόσῳ-μᾶλλον conclusion presupposes v. 12b (= Mark!).

11   Cf. vol. 1, II on 4:23.

12   There have been varied attempts to diagnose the illness medically, from the "normal solution" of atrophy (e.g., Gaechter, 393) through the empathetic theory in Albertus Magnus, 518 (by using his hand too intensively and as a result of the dryness of the lime the mason [cf. below at n. 21] has acquired a "drying out of the nerves") to the psychological explanation of Drewermann (*Markusevangelium,* 1.282), "in depth psychology . . . a hysterical symptom." Linguistically, ξηρός permits the conclusion that the hand was stiff and could no longer be moved. Cf. 3 Βασ 13:4; *T. Sim.* 2.12–13.

13   Cf. vol. 1, I B 1.1 on 3:7-10 (Jewish Leaders).

14   CD 11.13–14, cf. 16; *b. Sabb.* 128b = Str–B 1.629 (one may put blankets and padding under the animal and feed it, but it must come out by itself).

15   Οὐχὶ κρατήσει καὶ ἐγερεῖ presupposes that one

actively takes the sheep out, i.e., that one does more than put padding and cushions under him (cf. above, n. 14).

16   We can, therefore, reject not only those explanations that are based on a general love of animals (e.g., Lohmeyer, 185; Gaechter, 394) but especially the widespread anti-Jewish explanation that is found in the church's tradition beginning with Jerome (90) and Bede (61) that, viz., the Pharisees save their sheep on the Sabbath because they are greedy (cf. Albertus Magnus, 518; Thomas Aquinas, *Lectura* no. 988; Erasmus, *Paraphrasis,* 71). A trace of this view appears in Schlatter (400): "The traditional ethics valued property highly, but withheld love from the human being."

17   Cf. vol. 1, II A 3.3 on 7:24-27 (Analysis). Luke 14:5 speaks not of a single animal, and also not of a sheep but of an ox.

is dependent on his only sheep, he will obviously save it.

■ **12** For Matthew, however, the Sabbath practice of the small farmer is not in itself a convincing argument. He continues with a conclusion from the smaller to the greater. The common denominator between the two must be drawn from v. 12b. Thus in v. 12 Matthew argues on a different level, viz., in terms of the love that for him is the center of the divine will. From this love it becomes clear what is to be done on the Sabbath—if even for a sheep, how much more for a human being! Here it becomes clear that "mercy" is fundamentally more than sacrifice and Sabbath. It becomes clear what it means for Matthew that the entire Law and the Prophets "depend" on the double commandment of love (22:40) and what the function of the "weighty" commandments is in comparison with the others (cf. 23:23).[18] Thus *formally* v. 12b is a halakah,[19] viz., the basic rule of the Matthean church's Sabbath practice. In its *content*, however, it is concerned with a *fundamental* subordination of the Sabbath commandment under love. While it is true that it is not abolished but remains the will of God, the cases where it may be or even must be transgressed can no longer be regulated as halakah as one does with animals who fall into a pit. It is therefore certainly no accident that the Jewish-Christian Matthew has omitted Mark 3:4's reference to "saving lives." A life-threatening situation or saving a life was for the scribes the "borderline" that made possible a transgression of the Sabbath commandment,[20] but that is not the issue. Love cannot be limited. While rabbinically saving a life is a boundary for the Sabbath commandment, in Matthew love becomes the commandment's center. For Matthew this center is not something that is foreign to the Jewish law. Instead of waiting to show that in the pericope of the double commandment (22:34-40), he shows it also in our pericope by letting Jesus use the *Sabbath* practice of the common people as an argument.

■ **13** Verse 12 is the high point of the pericope. Verse 13 gives a brief, concise report on the healing of the man.

Jesus commands, the man obeys, and his hand is restored. Matthew seems to have as little interest in him here as he does in the exposition of v. 10a. It is Jesus who is important to him. His action is a concrete example of what it means to do good on the Sabbath. The primary concern here is not the miracle of healing; it is that the healing is a concrete example of love.

■ **14** Even more important to him is what Jesus' Sabbath healing leads to. The Pharisees leave Jesus and his disciples, go out, and decide to kill Jesus. The expression "to make a decision" ($\sigma\upsilon\mu\beta\omicron\acute{\upsilon}\lambda\iota\omicron\nu$ $\lambda\alpha\mu\beta\acute{\alpha}\nu\epsilon\iota\nu$) functions as a signal. It points ahead to the passion narrative where again exclusively Jesus' opponents will make their decisions (27:1, 7; 28:12, cf. 22:15). For the first time in the gospel the end of the Jesus story, the passion, comes explicitly into view. Matthew and his readers know more here than do the followers of Jesus in the story. They know that the death sentence of the Pharisees is final and that it achieved its goal. They also know that the schism in the nation of Israel can no longer be healed. Our verse lives from this knowledge; it is from it that the verse receives its terrible darkness. It also indirectly reminds the church that is reading the Gospel of Matthew that this decision to kill Jesus has created a permanent distance between the community and the Pharisees. Figuratively, the Pharisees "went out."

Summary and History of Interpretation

Thus our story first of all wants to put on record *ethically* what Jesus' commandment for the Sabbath is, or even how the biblical Sabbath commandment is seen in the light of mercy. To apply it in a concrete situation is to seek people with "withered hands" (or hearts) who because of the Sabbath (or other religious laws) cannot be healed (or become whole). To apply it is to discover where and how mercy is more than sacrifice, or how God's law is fulfilled in its depth precisely by love.

Two examples from the history of the text's interpretation that may not be obvious for the exegete: Jerome lifts from the *Gospel of the Hebrews* the passage

---

18 Verseput, *Rejection,* 183–84.

19 Hummel, *Auseinandersetzung,* 45.

20 In Judaism healing on the Sabbath is permitted when there is a threat to life, and the principle may be "expanded" (one may, e.g., in certain cases eat or drink something as medication that is normally for-

bidden on the Sabbath). Cf. the material in Str–B 1.623-29.

that the man was a "mason, [who] earned his living with his hands" and asked Jesus to keep him from having to "beg disgracefully for food."[21] Customarily the exegesis—in a sense correctly—characterizes this as a later legendary embellishment that somewhat helped the Jewish-Christians behind the *Gospel of the Hebrews* to adapt the scandal of Jesus' Sabbath transgression to the Jewish borderline principle of the life-threatening situation. It does not *have* to be seen this way. One also may say that the *Gospel of the Hebrews* is an attempt at a narrative application of our text. It tries to describe more clearly the "withered hand" in order to give a concrete example of love. "To help people help themselves" is by no means an outdated expression of love.

The other example: When E. Drewermann diagnoses the withered hand in terms of depth psychology,[22] the exegete will and must scowl at such an overburdening of the text. However, one may also see it differently. It may be an attempt to use a "modern" diagnosis to get *modern* people to become aware of their psychic and physical rigidity and to ask the pious among them to what degree it is religion that prevents a healing so that they can no longer "'grasp' their own life 'with their hands.'"[23] Not that the evangelists would have described the man of Mark 3:1-6 par. that way! This exegesis is also in reality an application that helps recently born readers of Matthew to discover the withered hands in the realm of their own experience.

In addition, the text wants to *remind the Matthean church of its own history in Israel.* It wants to remind them that Jesus created a crisis for traditional Jewish religiosity by placing love provocatively at its center. Not that this would have meant in Matthew's understanding "the end of Judaism"[24]! D. Flusser[25] calls attention to the fact that a healing on the Sabbath by means of a word, without physical labor, need not be regarded as a violation of the law.[26] However, one could have safely postponed the healing of a disabled person to the next day or at least have carried it out discreetly outside the synagogue. That is obviously not what Jesus wanted. He wanted to challenge Israel's traditional religious identity,[27] to create a stumbling block, even a provocation in the name of love.[28] The Pharisees—and under their leadership, Israel—are according to Matthew those who did not accept this challenge of love and thus failed to understand their own law. According to him, this led to Jesus' death and to the separation of the community of Jesus from the larger part of Israel. In the final analysis the church owes its identity to these provocations of love by Jesus. And that in turn becomes a challenge to her.

It is thus not accidental and not wrong that in the history of this text's interpretation the *christological and salvation-history dimension of our text* was repeatedly discovered, usually under the signature of allegorical interpretation. Already the Valentinian author of the *Gospel of Truth,* one of the many Christian Gnostics who understood grace in an especially profound way, gave thanks that the Son worked even on the Sabbath for the sheep that had fallen into the pit and that he brought it out of the pit, for it is not appropriate that salvation should rest on the Sabbath.[29] Our story was given a salvation-history interpretation especially in the Middle Ages. The withered hand symbolizes the fall into sin from which there is no healing in the synagogue but only by the hand of Christ stretched out on the cross.[30] A lovely deepening of our story in light of the *entire* gospel! But only as long as it does not lead to the assurance that one *possesses* salvation while the synagogue remains in its own "avarice."[31] In terms of the text one would have to say pointedly that Christ's hand, stretched out on the cross, is effective by repeatedly and provocatively reminding his church of love in its *own* religious laws.

---

21 Jerome, 90.
22 Cf. above, n. 12.
23 Drewermann, *Markusevangelium* 1.283.
24 Leonhard Goppelt, *Christentum und Judentum im ersten und zweiten Jahrhundert* (Gütersloh: Bertelsmann, 1954) 47.
25 Flusser, *Jesus,* 49.
26 Thus already Athanasius *Hom. sem.* 16 = *PG* 28.168.
27 Since the exile the Sabbath was understood as a special characteristic of Israel and as basic for its identity. Cf. Lohse, "σάββατον," 5, 8.
28 Flusser (*Jesus,* 48) speaks in an understated way of "pedagogic attacks against the hypocrites."
29 *Gos. Truth* = NHC I 32, 18–25.
30 Jerome, 90; Christian of Stavelot, 1364; Strabo, 124; Thomas Aquinas, *Lectura* no. 985, etc.
31 Cf. above, n. 16.

1.3 The Healing Son of God (12:15-21)

Literature

O. Lamar Cope, *Matthew: A Scribe Trained for the Kingdom of Heaven* (CBQMS 5; Washington, D.C.: Catholic Biblical Association of America, 1976) 32–52.

John Grindel, "Matthew 12:18-21," *CBQ* 29 (1967) 110–15.

Gundry, *Use*, 110–16.

Barnabas Lindars, *New Testament Apologetic* (Philadelphia: Westminster, 1961) 144–52.

Jerome Neyrey, "The Thematic Use of Isaiah 42:1-4 in Matthew 12," *Bib* 63 (1982) 457–73.

Rothfuchs, *Erfüllungszitate*, 72–77.

Stendahl, *School*, 107–15.

For *additional literature* see above, III A 1 on Matt 12:1-21.

15	But when Jesus became aware of it, he withdrew from there. And many[1] followed him, and he healed them all,
16	and he warned them sharply that they should not make him known, 17/ so that that might be fulfilled which was spoken through Isaiah the prophet:
18	"Behold, my child[2] whom I have chosen, my beloved with whom my soul was pleased. I will lay my spirit on him, and he will proclaim judgment to the Gentiles.
19	He will neither quarrel nor shout, and no one will hear his voice in the streets.
20	A crushed reed he will not break, And a glowing wick he will not extinguish until he brings judgment to victory.
21	And the Gentiles will hope in[3] his name."

Analysis

Structure

The pericope begins with a description of the situation in four brief main clauses (vv. 15-16). They form the basis for a long formula quotation (vv. 18-21) in which God himself is speaking. Its five pairs are formulated in part in parallelisms (v. 18a, b; v. 19a, b; v. 20a, b). The quotation begins with God speaking in the first person (v. 18a-c) and then moves immediately to statements about the παῖς ("child"; vv. 18d-20), the last of which is concluded by a temporal clause (v. 20c). The independent final sentence in v. 21 has a new subject ("the Gentiles") that sets it apart. Verse 18d has a proleptic effect, because it anticipates the two catchwords κρίσις and ἔθνη ("judgment" and "Gentiles") that are important for the concluding sentences, vv. 20c and 21.

Sources

For the formulation of the introduction, vv. 15-16, Matthew returns to the healing summary of Mark 3:7-12 but uses only part of it.[4] The introduction, v. 15a, is largely redactional.[5] The wording of the formula quotation from Isa 42:1-4 agrees neither with the MT nor with the LXX. Again there are two basic hypotheses.[6] Either Matthew has taken over this quotation from a source, or he (or his "school") has produced his own targum-like text. However, the textual problems cannot be discussed apart from the problems associated with the contents.

Interpretation

■ **15** The new pericope is closely connected to the preceding one. Jesus sees through the plans of the Pharisees. He is not a plaything for their conspiracies. That he retreats is neither flight nor a sign of fear. It is important that many people follow him but not the Pharisees. This foreshadows the later withdrawals of Jesus that lead to the formation of a church in Israel (14:13; 15:21).[7] As in 8:16, Jesus heals *all* the sick; the healing of 12:9-14 is exemplary for Jesus' entire activity.

■ **16** He orders the sick not to make him known. In Mark this command was given to the spirits and was related to Jesus' divine sonship. Matthew has no interest in most of the material that is associated with the Markan messianic secret. The idea that the demons are aware of Jesus' divine sonship must be "simply distasteful and

---

1. In my judgment ὄχλοι is a secondary addition on the basis of the similar expressions in 4:25; 8:1; 19:2; cf. 20:29.

2. Cf. below on v. 18.

3. Possible also is the translation: by means of his name (instrumental dative).

4. Not used are the statement about the origin of the people (Mark 3:7b-8a), because Matthew has already used it in 4:25, and the notice of the boat in Mark 3:9 that does not fit in Matthew. In addition, some of the details of the healing activity of Jesus in Mark 3:10b and, what is most interesting in content, the

confession of the demons in Mark 3:11 are missing. In this way Matthew works much as he did in 8:16 with Mark 1:32-34.

5. On δέ, γνούς, ἀναχωρέω, ἐκεῖθεν, cf. vol. 1, Introduction 3.2. Verse 15a is patterned after v. 9a and connects with the preceding pericope.

6. Cf. the excursus The Formula Quotations § 3, vol. 1, I A 2.2.

7. Strabo (125), Albertus Magnus (520), and again today Gundry (228) differ: Jesus' retreat is an example of the flight from one town into the next that is commanded the disciples in 10:23.

offensive"[8] for Matthew, who understood that sonship in terms of Jesus' obedience to the will of the Father; as agents of the devil the demons are completely disobedient to God! That Matthew mentions the command to silence here at all must be connected with the idea that it is an expression of the hiddenness and the "silence" that according to v. 19a are marks of the παῖς ϑεοῦ ("child of God").

■ **18-21** However, the bridge from v. 16 to the formula quotation is narrow; compared to the narrative introduction, the quotation is a far-reaching thematic overhang. If it is true that prior to Matthew it was not yet connected with Mark 3:7-12, then we must say that Matthew did not add the formula quotation from Isaiah 42 here because he spoke of the command to silence; it was the other way around: Because Matthew wanted to use this long and important formula quotation here in the middle of his gospel and at the point in his narrative where the separation from Israel begins, he retained the Markan command to silence in order to have at least a small bridge to the quotation. The entire weight lies, therefore, on the quotation.

> In various ways the formula quotation is a special case. It is the longest quotation Matthew has used. At the same time, it is the quotation that is the least well anchored in context, vocabulary,[9] and content. The point of contact for the quotation is Jesus' command of silence in v. 16 to those who have been healed, while v. 19 speaks of the silence of *Jesus*! While with most of the other formula quotations either the entire quotation is interpreted by the context[10] or at least can be supplemented without difficulty from the context,[11] Matthew 12:18-21 contains a whole series of

statements about the "servant" of God that go far beyond the context. The result of these observations is that the text poses a problem for our general thesis[12] that the formula quotations were worked out by scribes in the Matthean community before Matthew but in connection with the materials to which they now belong in Matthew.

As far as the *content* is concerned, there seem to be two alternatives. Either the quotation is connected with the context in only one point, viz., at the command to silence in vv. 16 and 19, or it is at the center of the gospel an encoding of the entire Jesus story that far surpasses the immediate context but is never explicit. From a tradition-history perspective the alternatives are: Either Matthew has taken over the wording of the quotation essentially from the tradition, as he probably did with the other formula quotations,[13] or he has formed it himself in view of the entirety of his story of Jesus.[14] The two first basic alternatives and the two second basic alternatives have an affinity with each other. With both alternatives there are mediating solutions.

■ **18-21** *Wording and tradition history.* Unfortunately, the problems are more complicated here than with any other formula quotation. Matt 12:18-21 as a whole is closest to the *Masoretic text* of Isa 42:1-4. One could understand vv. 19b, 20a and in part v. 18a, b (ἠρέτισα, ὁ ἀγαπητός) and v. 20b (τυφόμενον) as free translations of the MT. Ἀπαγγελεῖ in v. 18d may correspond to the Targum.[15] Verse 21 corresponds to the LXX almost literally; in v. 18a (παῖς), v. 19 (οὐδέ) and v. 20a (συντετριμμένον) we must reckon with its influence. With the two most difficult problems it is possible (but not necessary!) that errors in writing[16] are a factor. The omission of Isa 42:4a and the combination of Isa 42:3c and 4b in v. 20c may be caused by

Analysis

8 Wilhelm Wrede, *The Messianic Secret* (Greenwood, Conn.: Attic, 1971) 155.

9 There is no connection whatever with the immediate context; only with 3:17; 17:5. Comparable here is only the quotation in Matt 2:18 that, however, is clear in the context. In all other formula quotations the quotation is connected with the context at least by one, often by several, verbal bridges (cf. especially 1:23; 4:15-16; 27:9-10).

10 Matt 1:23; 2:6, 15, 23; 8:17; 13:35; 27:9-10.

11 Matt 2:18; 4:15-16 (here with an added meaning: Galilee = "Gentile country"); 21:5, cf. 3:3; 13:14-15.

12 Cf. vol. 1, I A 2.2 The Formula Quotations § 3.

13 Pointedly: Lindars, 148, 151; Strecker, *Weg,* 67-70; vol. 1, I A 2.2 The Formula Quotations § 3.

14 Pointedly advocated by Barth ("Understanding,"

125–28); Rothfuchs (*Erfüllungszitate,* 72–77); widely also Gundry (*Use,* 111–16). Stendahl (*School,* 109–15) advocates a mediating position: The Matthean school did not simply formulate freely but selected existing textual variants on the basis of its own theological intentions. However, that is improbable. Cf. vol. 1, I A 2.2 The Formula Quotations, n. 28.

15 יגלי = he will reveal.

16 It is probably also due to a scribal error that the LXX Isa 42:4c offers the remarkable ΤΩΟΝΟΜΑΤΙ-ΑΥΤΟΥ instead of ΤΩΝΟΜΩΑΥΤΟΥ. A similar error occurred in 2 Παρ 6:16; Exod 16:4A and ψ 118:165 (John Grindel, "Matthew 12:18-21," 110–15, 112). This assumption appears as early as Maldonat (251).

a haplography (two times מִשְׁפָּט/κρίσις).[17] In the case of ἐρίσει one has assumed the Aramaic stem רב that in Hebrew means "to quarrel, to fight," in East-Aramaic "to make noise, to shout,"[18] but this assumption is very difficult.[19] Εἰς νῖκος cannot be explained on the basis of any OT text.[20] At least for ἐρίσει and εἰς νῖκος, perhaps also elsewhere, we must assume a *spontaneous, targum-like translation ad sensum.*

It took place presumably in Christian circles, but it is not clear at what stage in the history of tradition. A *redactional reworking* of the quotation is quite possible in v. 21. As he did in 4:4 and 13:14-15, Matthew may have supplemented from the LXX the quotation that he received.[21] It is also possible for v. 18a, b with the (only partial) assimilation to the voice at the baptism and transfiguration (Matt 3:17; 17:5). Why, however, has Matthew not consistently carried out the assimilation? Most of all: Why instead of saying υἱός does he stay with the christological παῖς that for him is singular? Other alleged redactional changes in the text seem quite improbable to me.[22] Except for v. 21, therefore, in all cases it seems to me more probable that the wording of Isa 42:1-4 was changed for the sake of the christological interpretation prior to Matthew. Thus among such pre-Matthean christologically conditioned clarifications are perhaps the partial adaptations to the voice at Jesus' baptism[23] in v. 18, the proclaiming word ἀπαγγέλλω, and εἰς νῖκος

in v. 20. Given the christological interpretation, the reserve toward the LXX text that interprets the text collectively of Israel is understandable.[24] Thus prior to Matthew there probably were not only "mechanical" changes in the text but also some that were determined by the content.

Because of the weak connection with the Matthean context, I would assume for this formula quotation, unlike the other formula quotations, a pre-Matthean christological *testimonium* that late in the process was connected, perhaps by Matthew himself, with the summary of Mark 3:7-12.

Interpretation

■ **18-21** *Content.* Why does Matthew bring such a long quotation here? If he had been concerned *only* with the quiet and secret activity of Jesus,[25] v. 19 would have sufficed as a quotation. Therefore, we must try to interpret the entire quotation in the context of the gospel. The quotation of Isa 42:1-4 is concerned not merely with the single feature of the withdrawal of Jesus and the command to silence in vv. 15-16; instead, the passage "paints the whole Christ."[26] Thus Matthew inserts the quotation, because at this point in his gospel he wants to use the Bible to remind his readers of the entirety of the story of Christ.

17 Thus already Jerome *Ep.* 121.2.6 *ad Algasiam* = CSEL 56.10. However, it was not a case of simple haplography, since ἕως ἄν possibly comes from Isa 42:4b but ἐκβάλη from Isa 42:3c.

18 Stendahl, *School,* 111.

19 There is no Aramaic dialect in which both meanings are documented together. The Hebrew ריב means the lawsuit, the Greek ἐρίζω means quarrel, rivalry, or at most a dispute.

20 MT and LXX: "to the truth." Maldonat (250) surmised an Aramaic זָכוּתָא (thus the Peshitta on Matt 12:20) that may mean "acquittal, innocence, kindness, victory," but not really "truth." Karl Elliger (*Deuterojesaja* [2d ed.; Biblischer Kommentar 11/1; Neukirchen: Neukirchener Verlag, 1989] 215) points out that לאמת means "to reality" and thus in content is not far removed from εἰς νῖκος.

21 Two stages in the history of the tradition of vv. 18-20/21 are assumed by Schlatter (402); Bacon (*Studies,* 475); Kilpatrick (*Origins,* 94); Joachim Jeremias ("παῖς θεοῦ," *TDNT* 5 [1967] 700); and Schweizer (281). Against this view one might cite at most the dative τῷ ὀνόματι that differs from the LXX (but is classical).

22 Barth ("Understanding," 126) regards ἡρέτισα as Matthean. While it appears occasionally in the LXX

as a translation of בחר, it is a hapax legomenon in the NT. To declare the free translation ἐν ταῖς πλατείαις as Matthew's adaptation to the context (Barth, "Understanding," 127; Rothfuchs, *Erfüllungszitate,* 75) is more than risky, since Matthew never mentions streets in connection with Jesus' activity. Of similar difficulty is the Matthean origin of ἐκβάλλειν (Rothfuchs, *Erfüllungszitate,* 76) that Matthew likes to use but mostly for demons.

23 Jeremias ("παῖς θεοῦ," 701) even assumes, on the basis of John 1:34, that Isa 42:1 was originally quoted by the voice at the baptism.

24 Cf. especially Isa 42:1a, b: Ἰακώβ, Ἰσραήλ. The *Tg. Jonathan* interprets it messianically.

25 Thus Strecker, *Weg,* 69–70 ("special situation of Jesus' *bios*").

26 Luther, *WA* 38.535.

But of what specifically does he want to remind them? It is amazing how differently the exegetes explain Matthew's interest in Isa 42:1-4. J. Weiss, for example, emphasizes Jesus' "modesty and quiet reserve."[27] For G. Barth, his "humility and lowliness" are "especially" important,[28] for R. Walker the proclamation to the Gentiles.[29] The interpretation is difficult, because the wording of the quotation is so open that one often cannot say which associations Matthew intends for the readers and where the arbitrariness of the interpretation begins. We will attempt to trace the associations intended by Matthew in the knowledge that often there are no controls for the process and that the quotation, at least in Matthew's understanding, was intended primarily to permit associations and not limit them.

■ **18** God himself calls attention to his παῖς ("child") with the word of the Bible. Παῖς in Greek usually means child,[30] much less often servant.[31] That is true also for the NT and Matthew.[32] His readers will have understood our text in light of the story of the baptism, and they probably thought: Now there is talk in "biblical" language of the Son of God of whom that story spoke.[33] Thus there is in Matthew no more than elsewhere in the

New Testament a special "servant of God Christology." Instead, he is aware only of a Son of God Christology[34] of which he speaks differently here only once in a quotation from the Bible. "Beloved" and "well pleased" point the reader literally to the baptism story (3:17). The LXX expression αἱρετίζω[35] "to choose, adopt" recalls the substance of the story. There also Jesus is endowed with the Spirit (3:16), an event of which the prophet speaks prophetically in the future tense. In the exorcisms about which Matthew tells in the second part of our chapter Jesus proves to his opponents, the Pharisees, that he possesses the Spirit (12:28, cf. 32).[36] Thus in a sense the Isaiah quotation transports the reader back to the beginning of the Jesus story, where likewise God himself had revealed to the people who Jesus is. In the temptation narrative that followed, Matthew had interpreted Jesus' divine sonship by his obedience. Precisely that is what the words from Isaiah in vv. 19-20 also want to do. However, before that happens there is the remarkably abrupt statement of 18d: "He will proclaim κρίσις to the Gentiles."[37] The meaning of κρίσις is an old *crux interpretum*. Our choices are "right, justice"[38] and "judg-

---

27 J. Weiss, 326.

28 Barth, "Understanding," 128.

29 Walker, *Heilsgeschichte*, 78 ("Gentiles-Savior-secret").

30 Referring to descent (where the opposite is father or parents) or referring to age. The word is gender-neutral. It is used more rarely for "servant, slave" and then emphasizes, in contrast to δοῦλος, belonging to a *familia* rather than the relationship of dependence that might be regarded as unjust (cf. for the LXX, Karl Heinrich Rengstorf, "δοῦλος κτλ," *TDNT* 2 [1964] 266). Hellenistic Judaism "is inclined to understand the παῖς θεοῦ as *God's child*" (Jeremias, "παῖς θεοῦ,"684). Wis 2:18 and 5:5 speak, therefore, of the "Son" even when influenced by Isaiah 53 (in 2:13 παῖ is synonymous). Cf. also the variant readings in the translations of 4 Ezra 13:32, 37, 52; 14:9 (Son: lat, syr, sah; servant or young man: arab).

31 Similarly Latin *puer*, modern Greek παιδί, German *Knabe/Knappe*.

32 Cf. above, n. 17 on 8:5-13. With the exception of 14:2 (Herod's παῖδες), this is always the case with Matthew. In 24:49 he formulates redactionally συνδούλους instead of παῖδας καὶ ... παιδίσκας.

33 Apart from Matt 12:18 a christological παῖς θεοῦ appears in the NT only in Acts 3:13, 26; 4:25, 27.

Here too it is a linguistic variation. Luke has the earliest apostles proclaim the risen one in the holy city Jerusalem in biblical language as God's servant.

34 Its center, the idea of obedience (cf. vol. 1, I B 1.2 on 3:17; I B 2 on 4:5-7 and on the History of Interpretation and Summary) is also in content close to the Wisdom of Solomon (cf. above, n. 30).

35 Translation of בחר. Cf. בחירי in Isa 42:1.

36 Jerome Neyrey ("The Thematic Use of Isaiah 42:1-4 in Matthew 12," 457–73) and Cope (*Matthew*, 32–46) correctly call attention to the quotation's close connections to the following context, 12:22 through (in my judgment) 12:45. Without accepting all of their views, in what follows I will make use of some of their observations.

37 Our text does not indicate whether ἔθνη is to be translated as "Gentiles" or "nations."

38 This interpretation has its precursors in the post-Reformation exegesis where the forensic/eschatological meaning is increasingly lost. Cf. Bullinger, 120 (the righteousness in the gospel, i.e., the forgiveness of sins); Musculus, 340 (*doctrina et cognitio veritatis*). Since the Enlightenment it is ethicized (cf. Paulus 2.80: "what is right, how one ought to act"; Fritzsche, 429: *quod fieri par est*) and generalized (cf. Georg Fohrer, *Das Buch Jesaja* [Zürcher Bibelkom-

ment."[39] Now in secular Greek κρίσις never means "justice,"[40] and Matthew also has used the word thus far only for the final judgment and will continue to do so.[41] That is all the more important, since κρίσις is a key word that connects our text with the following text (cf. vv. 36, 41-42). In the Hebrew text of Isa 42:1 מִשְׁפָּט also means the divine judgment, but this judgment now no longer contains disaster but salvation for Israel.[42] Thus κρίσις probably means "judgment." Verses 20c, 21 will indicate that this judgment of God may turn out to be positive for the Gentiles. Verses 41-42 will place negative limits on it: But it will be different for "this generation."[43] Verse 18d is abrupt, because Jesus thus far has not yet proclaimed God's beneficial judgment to the Gentiles but has been active only in Israel.[44] Thus v. 18d breaks out of the time frame of the Jesus story and signals[45] ahead to its goal. Therefore, it is repeated at the end of the quotation (vv. 20d, 21).

■ **19** Verses 19-20 speak of the Son's behavior. Since the text indicates only negatively what is meant in v. 19 and speaks figuratively in v. 20, it leaves a great deal of room for the readers to make their own associations. Contrary to a popular interpretation,[46] ἐρίζω and κραυγάζω (v. 19a) cannot be understood under the general concept of striving for justice.[47] The meaning is first of all indicated by v. 16. Jesus' command to silence points to his own "hiddenness." Of what does this hiddenness consist in his larger story? The church's interpretation formulated dualistically is that Jesus does not seek empty, worldly fame.[48] However, "not to quarrel and not to shout" points in a different direction. The Son of God is characterized by peace.[49] May we perhaps think of Jesus' nonviolence in his passion? Or may we think of the quiet that according to 11:28-29 the peaceful and humble Son of God will grant?[50] Verse 19b goes further. Does it *only* mean Jesus' retreat—in 12:22 Jesus will begin to raise his voice again in Israel!—or may we also understand it to mean that nobody *listens* to him, that is, that Jesus is rejected by most of the people in Israel?[51] Then, for example, 12:22-37, 38-42 or 13:53-58 would be an illustration of what is meant. It must remain an open question.

■ **20a, b** As in Deutero-Isaiah, the crushed reed and the smoking wick are also open images, not fixed metaphors or references to proverbs. A crushed reed is worthless trash; an oil lamp's smoking wick has to be extinguished and cut or replaced. The Son of God, Jesus, does not do that. What does he do? Obviously he preserves what is crushed and lets imperfect light shine.[52] What does that mean?

History of Interpretation

It is no accident that it was just at v. 20 that the ancient church's allegorical interpretation blossomed. Allegorical interpretation was repeatedly the attempt

mentar; Zurich: Zwingli, 1964] 2.47, 49: "truth," "knowledge of faith," "religious truth") without ever becoming the dominant interpretation.

39 Neutral, in the sense of acquittal or of conviction. Cf., e.g., John Chrysostom 40.2 = *PG* 57.441 (conviction); Augustine *Civ. D.* 20.30 = FC 14.336 (neutral); Hilary, 12.10 = SC 254.276 (acquittal). The classical Catholic interpretation is in the middle: κρίσις = *lex evangelica*, i.e., the measure by which Christ will judge (Jansen, 118; Lapide, 260; Maldonat, 249).

40 Only in the LXX as a translation of מִשְׁפָּט, which occasionally has this special meaning.

41 Matthew 23:23 is the only exception of this linguistic usage.

42 Karl Elliger, *Deuterojesaja* (2d ed.; BKAT 11/1; Neukirchen: Neukirchener Verlag, 1989) 53–54, 206–7.

43 Thus exactly the opposite of Deutero-Isaiah!

44 Cf. by way of example 8:11-12; 10:18.

45 Cf. vol. 1, Introduction 1 J.

46 Stendahl, *School*, 111–12; Rothfuchs, *Erfüllungszitate*, 74; Verseput, *Rejection*, 198–99.

47 Ceslas Spicq (*Theological Lexicon of the New Testament* [Peabody, Mass.: Hendrickson, 1994] 2.70) understands ἐρίζω as referring most likely to "disputes between rabbis" and "personal rivalries"; Allen (131) notes on κραυγάζω the clamor in a theater, the barking of a dog, the calling of a drunk, in short: "discordant forms of utterance" and not the cry for justice!

48 See, e.g., Theophylactus, 266; Dionysius the Carthusian, 151.

49 Christian of Stavelot (1365) says nicely, *Pacem portabit ore et opere*.

50 In support of this view is the observation that 11:25-30 and 12:18-21 deal with the Son of God and his behavior.

51 Ἀκούω would then have to mean "to obey" (LSJ, *s.v.*, II 2; BAGD, *s.v.*, 4). Given this interpretation, the frequently made connection with Matt 7:13-14 in the church's exegesis has its relative right: Those

to open up for a text fields of application and concrete usages. "Morally" it was said, for example, that the crushed reed and the smoking wick are sinners suffering under the burden of sin, or believers whose faith is weak and uncertain.[53] They are people with a repentant and humble heart.[54] Calvin says pointedly: "Are they not all like half-broken reeds?" Christ condescends to our weakness, and we are dependent on his kindness.[55] The "mystical" interpretation thinks in terms of salvation history. The crushed reed or smoking wick are Jews and Gentiles, whereby any meaning can be assigned. The Gentiles are like the smoking wick, because their natural knowledge of God is extinguished.[56] However, the smoking wick also may refer to the few Jews who believe in Christ and their *igniculum fidei*.[57] Christ has patience with Jews and Gentiles until the judgment.[58]

The text gives the readers the freedom to apply to themselves the images of the reed and the wick in light of Matthew's story of Jesus. Important for him is the basic *christological* direction that he gives with the help of these images. They show Christ's πραΰτης, his patience, nonviolence, peacefulness, kindness, and love. They show that Christ "did not respond in kind when he was reviled, did not threaten when he suffered."[59] They show the Christ who practices the Sermon on the Mount, the nonviolent, gracious king of Matthew 21.

■ **20c** The quotation ends with two concentrated sentences. Verse 20c cites the divine future perspective. This nonviolent, loving Son of God will lead God's judgment to victory. We should think here less of Jesus' resurrection than of his judging as the Son of Man. That it is precisely the nonviolent, loving, obedient one—who has rejected the temptation to rule the world (Matt 4:8-

10), who will execute judgment on the world in God's name—is simply an unaccountable miracle of God that stands as the final perspective on the way of Jesus. In v. 20c God himself intimates this perspective in the biblical word.

■ **21** Just as incalculable is the promise that concludes the quotation in v. 21. God's judgment means the hope of the Gentiles. At the end of his Jesus story Matthew will make this "signal" concrete (Matt 28:16-20). With the last two sentences he opens the eyes of his readers for God's future, and he gives to his Jesus story what in terms of God's word is the right perspective.

Summary

Two points seem important to me about this central text.

First, with this exceptionally long formula quotation that goes beyond the scope of the context Matthew opens the eyes of his readers to the entirety of the story of Jesus. From the beginning of his gospel he told it as the story of the Son of God and Immanuel. Only those who remember that in Jesus God himself is "with us" understand his story. At its end Jesus will have all power in heaven and on earth and will send his disciples to the Gentiles. Only those who know that Jesus' way of obedience has such a future will correctly understand the depths into which it leads. Our text wants to open the readers of the gospel to this perspective. To illustrate: The story of Jesus, who is increasingly persecuted and threatened as he travels through Israel, is like an excursion in bad weather under low-lying clouds. Our text

who are on the "broad street" do not hear Jesus' voice (since Origen fr. 258 = 119).

52   Luther (*WA* 38.540) tries to translate the negative statements into positive ones: not to break = to solidify, to strengthen; not to extinguish = to light, to enlighten.

53   Jerome (91) is frequently quoted: "Whoever does not extend a hand to the sinner and does not bear the burden of a brother breaks a crushed reed. And whoever despises the moderate flame of faith in the little ones extinguishes a smoking wick." Concrete applications: Bullinger, 120: reed = frivolous and unstable people; smoke = people with major crimes; Dionysius the Carthusian, 151: crushed reed = corruption from sins; glowing wick = insignificant intellectual light.

54   Luther, *WA* 38.539.

55   2.37.

56   Rabanus, 925.

57   Albertus Magnus, 523.

58   Augustine *Civ. D.* 20.30 = FC 24.336 (Jesus does not destroy his Jewish persecutors but gives them another chance before the last judgment); Hilary, 12.10 = SC 254.276 (the Gentiles are not broken or extinguished but preserved for salvation).

59   Rabanus, 925.

wants to pull aside the layer of clouds for a moment so that the sky—in substance, the true, divine perspective of the sad story of the obedience of Jesus—becomes visible again. Only then does it become understandable, for only those who know about heaven understand the world. Only those who know about God's future understand the present. That is clear especially in vv. 18, 20c-21.

Second, the story of Jesus, to the degree that it takes place under the layer of clouds, is a story of gentleness, of mercy, of nonviolence, and of love. Twice in 12:1-14 Matthew has illustrated the πραΰτης and ταπεινότης ("friendliness" and "humility") of Jesus (11:29). They are expressed also in his command of silence to those who are healed (v. 16), as vv. 19-20b intimate. After the situation in Israel has come to a head and Jesus' death has been decided for the first time, he is concerned to emphasize once again his obedience to God and his graciousness toward people. Jesus is stubbornly, literally, and without compromise obedient to the will of the Father as it is proclaimed in the Sermon on the Mount. The text wants to say that this is the will of God and that God's judgment comes to victory in this way—and only in this way![60]

---

60   Yet we should not fail to observe that the continuation of the story in Matt 12:22-45 provides a strange contrast to this central view of Jesus. Instead of the silent and defenseless Son there is the Jesus who pronounces judgment, who talks constantly and "finishes off" his Jewish opponents—in a sense, the anticipated judge!

Literature

H. Benedict Green, "Matthew 12,22-50 and Parallels: An Alternative to Matthean Conflation," in Christopher Mark Tuckett, ed., *Synoptic Studies* (JSNTSup 7; Sheffield: JSOT, 1984) 157–76.

Hummel, *Auseinandersetzung*, 122–28.

Jülicher, *Gleichnisreden* 2.214–40.

Bruce J. Malina and Jerome H. Neyrey, *Calling Jesus Names: The Social Value of Labels in Matthew* (Social Facets; Sonoma, Calif.: Polebridge, 1988) 3–67.

Verseput, *Rejection*.

The second part of the chapter also consists of three sections, albeit of very unequal length: vv. 22-37, 38-45, 46-50. It consists mainly of a long judgment discourse of Jesus to the Pharisees, interrupted in vv. 31, 38 by apophthegmatic insertions (vv. 25-45). After the conflict between Jesus and his opponents has broken out (chap. 11) and Jesus' death has appeared for the first time as an issue (12:14), our section makes clear how Jesus reacts to his opponents. The final pericope again assumes a special place; the Pharisaic opponents are no longer there, while the ὄχλοι remain (vv. 23, 46).

2.1   Beelzebul and God's Spirit (12:22-37)

Literature

Athanasius *Epistula 4 ad Serapionem*, BKV 1/13.471–97.

Augustine *Sermo* 71 = *PL* 38.445–67.

Boring, "Unforgivable Sin," 258–79.

Colpe, "Spruch," 63–79.

Dewailly, "Parole," 203–19.

B. Rod Doyle, "A Concern of the Evangelist: Pharisees in Matthew 12," *Australian Biblical Review* 34 (1986) 17–34.

Gottfried Fitzer, "Die Sünde wider den Heiligen Geist," *ThZ* 13 (1957) 161–82.

David Flusser, "Die Sünde gegen den heiligen Geist," in Ernst Ludwig Ehrlich and Bertold Klappert, eds., *Wie gut sind deine Zelte, Jaakow: Festschrift zum 60. Geburtstag von Reinhold Mayer* (Gerlingen: Bleicher, 1986) 139–44.

Fridrichsen, "Péché," 367–72.

Albert Fuchs, *Die Entwicklung der Beelzebulkontroverse bei den Synoptikern: traditionsgeschichtliche und redaktionsgeschichtliche Untersuchung zu Mk 3,22-27 und Parallelen* (SNTU B 5; Linz: SNTU, 1980).

Jülicher, *Gleichnisreden* 2.116–28.

Käsemann, "Lukas 11,14-28," 1.242–48.

Klauck, *Allegorie*, 174–84.

Kloppenborg, *Formation*, 121–26.

Laufen, *Doppelüberlieferungen*, 126–55.

Simon Légasse, "L'homme fort' de Luc 11,21f," *NovT* 5 (1962) 5–9.

Evald Lövestam, *Spiritus Blasphemia* (Scripta minora. K. humanistiska vetenskapssamfundet i Lund 1966/67:1; Lund: Gleerup, 1968).

Eugène Mangenot, "Blasphème contre le Saint-Esprit," *DThC* 2 (1905) 910–16.

Frans Neirynck, "Mt 12,25a/Lc 11,17a et la rédaction des Évangiles," *EThL* 62 (1986) 122–33.

Vernon K. Robbins, "Rhetorical Composition and the Beelzebul Controversy," in Burton L. Mack and Vernon K. Robbins, *Patterns of Persuasion* (Sonoma, Calif.: Polebridge, 1989) 161–93.

Sato, "Q," 132–36.

Schaff, *Sünde*.

Schürmann, *Gottes Reich*, 104–8.

Schulz, *Q*, 203–13, 246–50, 316–20.

Tödt, *Son of Man*, 118–20, 312–18.

Wanke, *Kommentarworte*, 26–31, 51–56, 70–75.

W. M. L. de Wette, *Über die Sünde wider den heiligen Geist* (Berlin, 1819).

Hans-Theo Wrege, *Die Überlieferungsgeschichte der Bergpredigt* (WUNT 9; Tübingen: Mohr/Siebeck, 1968) 164–80.

For *additional literature* on Matt 12:22-50 see above, III A 2.

22	Then a blind and deaf demoniac was brought to him, and he healed him so that the deaf man spoke and saw.
23	And all the crowds were beside themselves and said: "Could this be the Son of David?"
24	But the Pharisees who heard it said: "He casts the demons out[1] by Beezebul,[2] the ruler of the demons!"
25	But he knew their thoughts and said to them: "Every kingdom that is divided against itself becomes desolate, and every city or house that is divided against itself will not stand.

26	And if Satan casts out Satan,
	    he was divided against himself;
	        how then will his kingdom remain standing?

27	And if I cast out demons by Beelzebub,
	    by whom do your sons cast them out?
	        Therefore they will be your judges.

---

1   The construction with οὐκ . . . εἰ μή is Semitizing and serves to emphasize something. Cf. Beyer, *Syntax*, 129–31.

2   On the text-critical problem cf. n. 2 on 10:24-25.

28	But if I cast out demons by the Spirit of God,
	    the kingdom of God has (already) come to
	        you.

29	Or how can someone enter the house of the
	        strong man and rob his possessions,
	if he does not first bind the strong man?
	    And then he will plunder his house.

30	Whoever is not with me is against me,
	    and whoever does not gather with me
	        scatters.

31	Therefore I say to you:
	Every sin and blasphemy will be forgiven people,
	    but the blasphemy of the Spirit will not be
	        forgiven.

32	And whoever says a word against the Son of Man,
	    will be forgiven;
	    but whoever speaks against the Holy Spirit,
	        will not be forgiven, neither in this eon
	        nor in the future eon.

33	Either assume[3] that the tree is good, then (you
	        must also assume)
	    that its fruit (is) good,[4]
	or assume that the tree is useless, then (you
	        must also assume)
	    that its fruit (is) useless,
	for the tree is known by its fruit.

34	Brood of vipers! How can you speak good when
	        you are evil?
	    For the mouth speaks of that of which the
	        heart is full.

35	The good person brings good things from the
	        good treasure;
	and the evil person brings from the evil treasure
	        evil.

36	But I say to you: For every useless[5] word that people will speak they will give account on the day of judgment;
37	for of your words you will be justified, and of your words you will be condemned."
Analysis	**Structure**

A short exorcism (vv. 22-24) introduces the following discourse of Jesus. It names the persons who are present: Jesus, the Pharisees, and the people. Through v. 45 Jesus argues with the Pharisees; the people will not be mentioned again until v. 46. The discourse is

held together by three key words, all of which refer back to preceding texts: κατά,[6] ἐκβάλλω,[7] and πνεῦμα.[8] Its first part, vv. 25-30, consists of short sayings: vv. 25-26, 27, 28, 29, 30. After the arguments in vv. 25-26 and 27, v. 28 is the real "counterdefinition" to the thesis that the Pharisees pose in v. 24. Διὰ τοῦτο λέγω ὑμῖν (v. 31) is a new beginning leading the dispute to its climax that in the second part of the discourse, vv. 31-37, lies in the two sayings compositions of vv. 31-32 and vv. 33-37. Both contain a solemn λέγω ὑμῖν (vv. 31a, 36a) and end with a reference to the condemnation in the last judgment (vv. 32d, e, 36-37). Verses 31-32 and 33-37 are related to each other by the catchwords λόγος and ἄνθρωποι. Matthew has structured the individual sayings in well-crafted parallelisms and connected them with catch-words. Verses 25-26 consist of three members: two parallel images in v. 25 and the application in v. 26.[9] Verse 27 is a three-member disputation saying that, together with v. 28, forms an antithetical parallelism.[10] Verse 29 is again a two-member disputation saying with question and answer. We find an additional antithetical parallelism in vv. 31-32.[11] Verses 33-37 also consist of numerous antithetical parallelisms (v. 33a/b; v. 35a/b; v. 37a/b) and pairs of opposites. In addition, the rhetorical questions are conspicuous; three are introduced by πῶς (vv. 26, 29, 34). Thus we have the impression of a rhetorically formulated section in which Jesus' arguments pepper the opponents with blow after blow, with the antitheses dominating. They come to a climax in the opposites devil and Spirit of God. Truly, heavy guns against the Pharisees! The rhetorical art of the entire section is outstanding.[12]

Sources, Tradition History, and Origin

According to the simplest and most common assumption,[13] in the Beelzebul controversy Matthew has com-

---

3	Ποιεῖν = to assume (the case): LSJ, *s.v.*, A VI. This is also possible in Aramaic; cf. Black, *Approach*, 302.
4	On the translation cf. Beyer, *Syntax*, 254–55; Black, *Approach*, 202–3 ("a Semitic conditional parataxis").
5	Semitizing *casus pendens* taken up in the main clause with αὐτοῦ, cf. vol. 1, Introduction 3.2.
6	Matthew 12:25-32 five times, cf. 12:14.
7	Matthew 12:24-35 seven times, cf. 12:20.
8	Verses 28, 31, 32, cf. v. 18.
9	Connecting catchwords: πᾶσα . . . μερισθεῖσα καθ᾽ ἑαυτῆς, βασιλεία, σταθήσεται (each twice); ἑαυτοῦ

	and μερίζω even three times.
10	Thus results the pregnant pair of opposites: Beelzebul and Spirit of God. The parallelism is emphasized by the identical sounding introduction εἰ . . . ἐκβάλλω τὰ δαιμόνια.
11	It is a double antithetical parallelism. Verse 32a takes up v. 31aβ, v. 32b v. 31b. Both members of v. 32 go beyond v. 31: v. 32a with "Son of Man," v. 32b with the full-sounding conclusion "neither in this eon nor in the future eon."
12	Vernon K. Robbins ("Rhetorical Composition and

bined the Markan text 3:22-30[14] that follows Mark 3:7-12 with the Q text Luke 11:14-23. In so doing he essentially followed the order of Q.[15] Apart from some insertions and changes in order, Matt 12:22-45 is a coherent Q unit (= Luke 11:14-32), the final larger coherent Q unit before the eschatological discourse. The individual subdivisions are as follows:

■ **22-24** a. The section begins with the introductory *exorcism, vv. 22-24* from Q = Luke 11:14-15. Matthew omits Mark 3:20-21 just as Luke does. Since the Griesbach hypothesis that regards Mark as the latest gospel is improbable both in its entirety and in its details,[16] the only remaining possibilities are that either Matthew and Luke independently of one another avoided[17] the offensive verse or that they used a Markan recension that did so. In 9:32-34 Matthew had already told of the exorcism once.[18] Unlike the previous occasion, he here formulates rather freely.[19]

As in 9:32-34 the people and their leaders react differently to the exorcism; in keeping with the narrative thread of all of chap. 12 the Pharisees play the negative role. Matthew has sharpened the opponents' accusation in v. 24b.[20] The exorcism is so brief and without its own point that early on it must have served as the exposition of what follows.

■ **25-30** b. In the *controversy dialogue of vv. 25-30* Matthew combines Mark 3:24-27 with Q = Luke 11:17-23. For his part Luke has not been influenced by Mark. The logia transmitted in Mark and Q are identical only in part. In the double parabolic saying of *vv. 25-26* Matthew not only has some of his favorite words;[21] he especially has better parallelisms and a longer text than does Luke. Did he expand the Q text according to Mark 3:24-26, or did Luke abbreviate so that the Markan parallel would give an indication of the age of the Matthean text? It is not simply an

---

the Beelzebul Controversy," 185) notes that the section contains almost all the steps that, according to Hermogenes, are necessary for a complete rhetorical argument.

13 Deviating from this common assumption, Albert Fuchs, in an extensive monograph (*Die Entwicklung der Beelzebulkontroverse bei den Synoptikern: traditionsgeschichtliche und redaktionsgeschichtliche Untersuchung zu Mk 3,22-27 und Parallelen*) advocates the thesis that an editor of Mark (Deutero-Mark) has worked the Q material into the Markan text prior to Matthew and Luke. Fuchs wants to show on the one hand that the deviations from the Markan text common to Matthew and Luke go back to Deutero-Mark. On the other hand, he does not give up the Q hypothesis. In my judgment the two assumptions make each other alternately unnecessary. I see in Deutero-Mark a helpful attempt to understand the "minor agreements" between Matthew and Luke in terms of the *Markan* text. However, the Beelzebul pericope is a special case, because these agreements are incomparably greater than usual, since there is a Q variant that was used directly by Matthew and Luke. Cf. the overview in Ennulat, *Agreements*, 5–10.

14 Mark 3:13-19 was used already in Matt 10:1-4.

15 He will bring Q = Luke 10:23-24 in 13:16-17; Q = Luke 11:1-4, 9-13 appeared already in the Sermon on the Mount. From other Q material, Luke 11:14-23 follows the sending discourse (Luke 10:1-16, 21-22). Then follows Q = Luke 11:29-32, 24-26 = Matt 12:38-45.

16 Would Mark the "*epitomator*" have added to his sources such a derogatory statement about Jesus from the lips of his followers (ἐξέστη = "he has lost his senses," Mark 3:21)? William R. Farmer (*The Synoptic Problem* [Dillsboro, N.C.: Western Carolina Uni-

versity Press, 1976] 163–64) points out that ἐξίστα-μαι is not used so negatively by Mark elsewhere and therefore interprets it neutrally. However, the negative linguistic usage is well documented in secular Greek (cf. BAGD, *s.v.*, 2). That alone explains why Jesus' family wanted to bring him home, and also why so many text witnesses of Mark 3:21 toned down the text. Cf. Gnilka, *Markus* 1.148, n. 22.

17 Is ἐξίσταντο in v. 23, found only here in Matthew, a reminiscence of Mark 3:21?

18 Cf. above, II B 4.3 Analysis. On the problem of the narrative doublets cf. the analysis of Matt 9:27-31.

19 Matthean are: τότε, προσφέρω + αὐτῷ, δαιμονί-ζομαι, τυφλός, θεραπεύω, ὥστε with infinitive, πᾶς, μήτι, οὗτός ἐστιν, υἱὸς Δαυίδ, ἀκούσας. Cf. vol. 1, Introduction 3.2. The readers are not to notice that Matthew uses the same miracle story from Q twice. That is why he is also a *blind* man in Matthew!

20 On οὐκ . . . εἰ μή cf. 14:17; 15:24.

21 On ἐνθύμησις cf. 9:4, on πᾶς, πόλις, κατά (keyword in 12:14-32!), πῶς, οὖν, vol. 1, Introduction 3.2.

either-or decision.[22] The introduction in v. 25aα shows in part Matthean influence.[23] *Verses 27-28* are missing in Mark, but they show a great deal of agreement with Luke vv. 19-20; only πνεύματι ϑεοῦ ("by the spirit of God") in v. 28a is redactional.[24] *Verse 29* corresponds almost literally[25] to Mark 3:27. Whether the parallel Luke 11:21-22 is an "independent variant"[26] or comes from Q[27] is a controversial issue. Mark and Matthew speak of breaking into a strong man's house, Luke 11:21-22 of the attack "of the stronger one" against his fortress. Both the image and the wording[28] are secondary in Luke. Nevertheless, it is in my view a Q logion that has been strongly reworked by Luke. It is improbable that Matthew and Luke independently of one another would have expanded the same logion at the same place but not in the same place as Mark.[29] Finally, *v. 30* again agrees literally with Luke 11:23.

What was the oldest nucleus of the controversy dialogue? It may be that vv. 25-26 originally followed the exorcism. In support of this view is the retention of vv. 25-26 in Mark and Q as well as their position at the beginning in both sources.[30] Or it may be that the logion in v. 27 = Luke 11:19 that is retained only in Q was the original answer of Jesus to the Beelzebul accusation. This view is supported by the fact that v. 27 speaks of Beelzebul and not, as do vv. 25-26, of Satan, and that v. 27 actually responds to the accusation of Jesus' opponents on v. 24, while vv. 25-26 at least linguistically speak of something else, viz., the division of Satan within himself. The arguments for the second hypothesis appear stronger to me. In addi-

tion, vv. 25-26 par. are notable in language and content—in language because the construction of a conditional clause in the aorist tense (thus Luke 11:18) with a subsequent main clause in the future tense expresses a *real* case[31] that, however, because it is a hypothetical assumption, has to be understood as a condition contrary to fact.[32] In content, vv. 25-26 are difficult, because Jesus, according to his own claims, destroyed the kingdom of Satan (cf. Luke 10:18; Mark 3:27), yet in this logion he emphatically presupposes with a rhetorical question the continuing existence of Satan's kingdom. I suspect that Q = Luke 11:17-18 originally did not belong to the context of the Beelzebul controversy. It may be that the division of Satan's kingdom referred originally to Jesus' victory over him that becomes visible in the exorcisms and not to the hypothetical and rather absurd case that in Jesus' exorcisms Satan could act against himself. Then the saying, much like Mark 3:27, originally indirectly referred *christologically* to the new thing that takes place in Jesus. Only later with its insertion into the Beelzebul controversy was it downgraded to a hypothetical *formally* logical argument.

I thus picture the growth of the controversy dialogue as follows: Added to the original nucleus Q = Luke 11:14-15, 19 was first of all the formally similar, originally independent logion Q = Luke 11:20, then the saying Q = Luke 11:21-22 that is related in content (perhaps in the formulation of Mark 3:27), and finally the call to decision Q = Luke 11:23. Because it speaks of the devil, the logion Q = Luke 11:17-18 could not be added at the end of the composition but had to be

---

22   Luke has misunderstood the image of Matt v. 25b. He understood "house" as a building and then compressed the entire image in light of that understanding. Therefore, v. 25c (without πόλις ἤ) comes from Q. In v. 26a Matthew probably has expanded the brief Q logion with "if Satan casts out Satan" according to Mark 3:23b, 26a and, as far as the content is concerned, better integrated it into the context. Obviously Luke had the same need and therefore added v. 18c as a gloss.

23   It is reminiscent of 9:4 from whence ἐνθύμησις is derived. It is noteworthy that 9:2-8 and 12:31-32 speak of blasphemy, of the Son of Man, and of forgiveness of sins (cf. vv. 31-32). Frans Neirynck ("Mt 12,25a/Lc 11,17a et la rédaction des Évangiles," 122–33) would like to assume (in my view incorrectly) that no Q text exists at all for this introduction but that it comes from independent Matthean/ Lukan redaction.

24   Πνεῦμα recalls v. 18 and prepares for vv. 31-32. Cf. Schlosser, *Règne de Dieu* 1.132–34, contra Käse-

mann, "Lukas 11,14-28," 244 (Luke writes LXX language); Schürmann, *Gottes Reich,* 106.

25   Only the interrogative form, introduced by πῶς, is redactional, corresponding to vv. 26, 34.

26   Lührmann, *Redaktion,* 33.

27   Simon Légasse, "L'homme fort' de Luc 11,21f," 5–9 (extensive Lukan redaction that wants to show Jesus overcoming wealth).

28   Along with some Lukanisms, the LXX language of Luke 11:21-22 is especially striking. Cf. I. Howard Marshall, *The Gospel of Luke* (New International Greek Testament Commentary; Grand Rapids: Eerdmans, 1978) 476–77.

29   Laufen, *Doppelüberlieferungen,* 130–31.

30   It could speak against this view that Matthew v. 25a and Luke v. 17a offer an unnecessary new beginning with εἰδώς.

31   Cf. BDF § 372 1c with (2).

32   A condition contrary to fact can indeed be formulated without ἄν, but the tense is imperfect or

fit in at the beginning of the already existing composition. In my judgment, the logia are all originally independent. Verses 28 and 29, as well as vv. 25-26, could go back to Jesus in their presumably original form, while we are scarcely able to make statements about the controversy dialogue in vv. 22-24, 27[33] and about v. 30.

■ **31-32** c. The *saying about the blasphemy of the Spirit, vv. 31-32* = Mark 3:28-29 and Luke 12:10, appears in Q in the context of the persecution logia of Luke 12:2-12, in Mark in the Beelzebul discourse. Both contexts are awkward. In the Markan Beelzebul debate the logion is suspended in the air, because there had been no prior mention of the Spirit; in Luke 12:10 one expects after Luke 12:8-9 that it would be the sin against the Son of Man that is unforgivable.[34] The wording also differs considerably. In Mark the issue is human blasphemies and sins (subjective genitive), in Q evil talk against the Son of Man [German: *Menschen* vs. *Menschen-sohn.—Trans.*]. Matthew witnesses to both wordings by offering in v. 31 a shortened version of Mark 3:28-29a and in v. 32a-c the wording of Q = Luke 12:10. From Matthew's editorial hand come especially the introduction, v. 31a,[35] the conclusion of v. 32d,[36] and perhaps κατά in v. 32.[37]

Difficult is the question of the earliest available wording. Many scholars regard the Markan text as earlier,[38] just as many the Q text.[39] In my judgment,

more of the evidence supports the Q text. It contains clearer Aramaisms,[40] and formally it shows a closed parallelism, while Mark 3:28-29 makes a more diffuse impression. In addition, in content the Q text is clearly the *lectio difficilior*. However, the reconstruction of the history of the tradition and statements about the origin remain extremely difficult. We must resort to arguments based on the content, and in the final analysis we can ask only which hypothesis offers the lesser difficulties.

The interpretation of the logion in Q usually begins by contrasting two periods—the time of the earthly Jesus, that is, of the Son of Man, and the time of the Spirit. What was said *earlier*, against Jesus, is forgiven, but what is said *now*, against his messengers who as prophets have God's Spirit, is unforgivable.[41] With a titular understanding of Son of Man, the logion could have been created in the Q community to answer the question why the messengers of Jesus "in spite of the rejection that Jesus experienced in Israel now" turn "again to the people."[42] In that case Acts 3:17-19 would be substantively parallel. However, the main difficulty of this thesis, in my view, is not that the verbs of our logion do not distinguish between two periods,[43] but that nowhere else does Q distinguish this way between the past of Jesus and the present and then designate the "past" Jesus as "Son of Man." For Q the Son of Man Jesus is the *present*

---

aorist, hardly present or future. Cf. BDF § 360 (4); Moulton–Howard–Turner 3.93.

33 Since according to Matt 10:25 both the lord of the house and his disciples were called Beelzebul, such a debate could have taken place in the time of Jesus or later in the church.

34 Is Luke 12:10 simply externally added to 12:8-9 *ad vocem* "Son of Man," or is v. 10 a "commentary" designed to actualize and perhaps correct vv. 8-9 in the situation after Easter when the Son of Man is no longer present (thus Wanke, *Kommentarworte*, 75)? As far as the content is concerned, it would be easier to assume that the Q community "corrected" Luke 12:10 with Luke 12:8-9 than vice versa!

35 Διὰ τοῦτο, πᾶς; cf. vol. 1, Introduction 3.2.

36 The reference to the two eons may be occasioned by the Markan αἰωνίου ἁμαρτήματος.

37 Nothing more can be said with certainty. The construction of the two halves of Luke 12:10 probably is already adapted (partly already in Q?) to Luke 12:8-9.

38 See, e.g., Wellhausen, 62; Manson, *Sayings*, 109–10; Colpe, "Spruch," 66–75 (far-reaching); Boring, "Unforgivable Sin," 274–79 (a pre-Markan original form).

39 See, e.g., Fridrichsen, "Péché," 371; Ernst Percy, *Die*

Botschaft Jesu (Lund: Gleerup, 1953) 253–56; Gottfried Fitzer, "Die Sünde wider den Heiligen Geist," *ThZ* 13 (1957) 176–82 (every blasphemy will be forgiven *the* Son of Man); Tödt, *Son of Man*, 314–18; Berger, *Amenworte*, 40.

40 "To say a word against" (cf. Dan 7:25; Black, *Approach*, 194–95); a conditional relative clause put first (Beyer, *Syntax*, 178); *casus pendens* (Black, *Approach*, 53 [not a clear Semitism]).

41 Thus, e.g., Fridrichsen, "Péché," 369 (citing 2 Cor 5:16 and John 16:8); Schlatter, 410; Günther Bornkamm, "End Expectation," 34; Tödt, *Son of Man*, 118–19.

42 Hoffmann, *Studien*, 151. Then, however, the emphasis should lie on Luke 12:10a and not on 12:10b.

43 Contra Sato ("Q," 135). As soon as the saying is formulated as a saying of Jesus, e.g., in the context of the Matthean or Lukan story of Jesus, the periods of time can no longer be distinguished, because one cannot have Jesus himself look back on the blaspheming of the Son of Man that took place during his lifetime!

exalted coming judge of the world! I hardly believe, therefore, that the logion was *created* in Q with this wording. Did the Q community take over an Aramaic saying that did not understand "son of man" as a title? In that case the saying originally meant that God will forgive those who speak against a human being,[44] but not those who speak against the Holy Spirit.[45] Q would have retained the wording but not the meaning. The Greek text that was transmitted to Mark would be a paraphrase that approached the original meaning but replaced the misleading "Son of Man" with the plural.[46] However, I think it most probable that in Q the already traditional logion was, without much theological reflection, simply added *ad vocem* "Son of Man" to Luke 12:8-9. Is the Aramaic saying that was not understood as a title a saying of Jesus?[47] That is a difficult assumption. Elsewhere Jesus spoke hardly at all of the Holy Spirit. Elsewhere he did not take lightly evil words spoken against people (cf. Matt 5:21-22, 23-24). In my judgment it is easiest to assign the saying, not yet understood with a titular meaning, to the Aramaic-speaking community, but this is simply the "solution" that least offers difficulties.

■ **33-35** d. The concluding piece from Q (= Luke 6:43-45), *vv. 33-35*, of the tree and the fruit, Matthew had already used at the corresponding place in the Sermon on the Mount (Matt 7:16-20). At that time he was able to use only part of it so that there was still some unused material (Q = Luke 6:45). This time he brings it in more literally and completely; he omits only Q = Luke 6:44b (= Matt 7:16a). Except for one change in order,[48] he follows the order of Q (= Luke). Also to be attributed to Matthew are: the imperative challenge to the opponents in v. 33 related to the situation of the dispute: ἢ ποιήσατε . . ., ("either assume . . ."), the address "brood of vipers" in v. 34aα that is reminiscent of 3:7, with the following half verse 34aβ,[49] and a few minor details in vv. 34b-35.[50] The Q piece as a whole is a unit and consists of an image (Luke 6:43-44) and its application (Luke 6:45, perhaps originally without 45c?). We can say nothing conclusive about its origin.[51]

■ **36-37** e. The *concluding verses 36-37* are probably redactional.[52]

Interpretation

■ **22-24** The narrator begins a new unit that has no recognizable connection to the preceding story. A deaf and blind demoniac is brought to Jesus. The reader remembers earlier stories: 9:27-31; 9:32-34. Matthew reports the healing as briefly as possible. As in 9:32-34, the reaction of the people is divided, but it goes beyond 9:33-34. If there the crowds were astonished, here "all the crowds are beside themselves." If there they only note that something unique is happening in Israel, here it begins to dawn on them that Jesus might actually be the Son of David. The people suspect—but no more than that—their Messiah.[53] The Pharisees, on the other hand, sharpen their rejection: Jesus is in the service of Beelzebul;[54] he makes use of satanic powers; he performs black magic.

---

44   For sources for Aramaic נַשׁ בַּר = human being see Geza Vermes, "Der Gebrauch von בַּר נָשָׁא/בַּר נָשׁ im Jüdisch-Aramäischen," in Black, *Approach*, 316–18 (undetermined), 323 (determined).

45   Thus already Grotius 1.375–76.

46   It may be that the translation of "speak against" with βλασφημέω caused "the sons of men" to be moved in the saying. In the LXX (not in Greek!) βλασφημ- always implies a reference to God so that βλασφημεῖν εἰς τοὺς υἱοὺς τῶν ἀνθρώπων was no longer appropriate.

47   Sato ("Q," 135) is thinking of a situation similar to the one presupposed in Mark 3:22-30: One may rail at Jesus as a human being but not as an exorcist and bearer of the Spirit of God! However, nowhere else has Jesus drawn a distinction between himself as God's representative and himself as a private person and indicated that by "Son of Man." Luke 12:8-9 sounds much different!

48   Matthew moves Luke 6:45c forward where it now appears as v. 34b after the addition 12:34a. That made possible for Matthew a better connection of vv. 36-37.

49   On ἀγαθός, πονηρός cf. vol. 1, Introduction 3.2, ον πῶς 12:26, 29; on πονηροὶ ὄντες 7:11.

50   Ἐκβάλλειν is a keyword in 12:20-35. In v. 35b Matthew adds ἄνθρωπος and θησουρός for the sake of clarity and of the parallelism. The plural ἀγαθά or πονηρά corresponds to the plural λόγοι in v. 37.

51   Cf. vol. 1, II A 3.2 on 7:15-23 with n. 12.

52   On λέγω δὲ ὑμῖν, πᾶς, ῥῆμα, ἄνθρωποι, ἀποδίδωμι, ἡμέρα κρίσεως, γάρ cf. vol. 1, Introduction 3.2, on ἀργός cf. 20:3, 6, on καταδικάζω 12:7.

53   Μήτι requires a negative or at most an open answer; cf. BAGD, *s.v.* Here a positive nuance must be implied, since the Pharisees formulate their accusation in response to it (ἀκούσαντες!). On the Son of David title cf. the excursus at 9:27-31.

54   On οὐκ . . . εἰ μή cf. above, n. 2; on Beelzebul cf. above on the interpretation of 10:25.

Such an accusation is common about religious charismatics.[55] Historically it is the first of a long series of Jewish testimonies that reject Jesus because of magic.[56] It deeply perverts what Jesus is about by claiming that precisely the Jesus who was far removed from any magic and who used his power to work miracles in the service of suffering humanity should act in the name of the devil! His opponents see at work in the figure of Jesus the devil himself, whose rule Jesus saw broken by the coming of the kingdom of God (cf. v. 28-29)! Thus labeled, Jesus' exorcisms evoke fear instead of liberating. His opponents say no to Jesus with the devil's help, that is, with the help of the greatest possible "metaphysical" power. Now no more bridges can be built.

■ **25-30** That Jesus knows the thoughts of the Pharisees is on the surface of the story not important, since the Pharisees have verbalized their thoughts. Fundamentally what Matthew wants to say is that Jesus sees through his opponents. In the debate in which he now engages he is absolutely sovereign and superior. He initially takes up the Pharisees' accusation indirectly and in vv. 25-27 demonstrates its absurdity in two logia. Not until vv. 28-29 will he pose a counterthesis against it.

■ **25-26** Verses 25-27 consist of two images with an application. It is obvious that neither a kingdom, a family,[57] nor—as Matthew adds in natural association—a city can endure if it is divided. Experiences in civil wars, for example, confirm this and have also been frequently expressed.[58] Thus an experience with which the readers are familiar prepares them for the application in v. 26. If in the exorcisms of Jesus, Satan (through his instrument Jesus) casts out Satan (in the demons who are his followers), he is internally divided, and his kingdom will no longer endure. But that is absurd! "Here he showed how absurd it was of them to suppose an alliance with Beelzebul for the destruction of Satan's kingdom."[59] The logic is formally convincing if it is obvious to us that the kingdom of the devil is intact and if we exclude the possibility that the miracles that Jesus performs for people are the devil's especially cunning tricks.

■ **27** The next argument is connected immediately with "and." It is also rhetorically effective. If Jesus casts out demons in the name of the devil, what then do your own exorcists do? According to Matthew he is speaking of exorcists from the ranks of the Pharisees.[60] It is presupposed that demon exorcisms were recognized not only on the level of popular piety but also "officially" in Judaism. That was generally true,[61] even if one could not easily delineate the boundary between exorcisms and magic, which was punishable by death.[62] Since Jesus did not use magical techniques, according to the norms of the Mishnah he could of course compare himself with recognized Jewish exorcists. From this argument it also follows that, without denying their own "children," the Pharisees cannot accuse Jesus of doing the devil's work. They would condemn their own people.

Verses 25-26 and v. 27 are more rhetorical than material arguments. Rabbinically speaking they are "straws."[63] They simply raise the question of what Jesus' exorcisms are if they are not works of the devil. Verses 28-29 make this clear.

---

55 Theissen (*Miracle Stories*, 272) calls attention to Apollonius of Tyana, Simon (Magus!), Pythagoras, Empedocles, and even Eliezer ben Hyrcanus (Str–B 1.127–28).

56 Justin *Dial.* 69.7. The Jewish references are collected in Joseph Klausner, *Jesus of Nazareth* (New York: Macmillan, 1953) 18–28; Str–B 1.38–39, 84–85, 631. Therefore, healings in the name of Jesus (by Jewish Christians) were later strictly rejected (Str–B 1.36).

57 BAGD, *s.v.* οἰκία 2. Simply on the basis of the image of the "family" there can be here no knowledge of the original meaning of Beelzebul as "master of the house" (cf. nn. 15, 20 on 10:24-25); contra Zahn, 458.

58 Cf. biblically, e.g., Dan 2:41-42; 11:4; Jewish, *Der. ʾEr. Zuṭ.* 5 = Str–B 1.635 (a house in which there are

factions is destroyed); classically Sophocles *Ant.* 672–74 (anarchy destroys cities); Plutarch *Aud. Poet.* 2.23E (cities in dispute); Cicero *Fin.* 1.18 = 58 (state in unrest, house in discord), etc.

59 Weiss, *Proclamation*, 77.

60 According to Luke = Q, Jewish exorcists in general.

61 On exorcisms in Judaism cf. Klaus Thraede, "Exorzismus," *RAC* 7 (1969) 56–58. Among the skilled exorcists are not only Father Abraham (1QapGen 20.28–29) but also such authorities as Johanan ben Zakkai and Simeon bar Yohai (Str–B 4.534–35).

62 *M. Sanh.* 7.4.

63 Jülicher (*Gleichnisreden* 2.232) speaks of an "intolerable" sequence in vv. 27, 28, because for all practical purposes Jesus concedes that the Jewish exorcists

■ **28** Δέ signifies an antithetical new beginning. In contrast to other exorcists, in Jesus to whom God has given his Spirit (cf. v. 18) the kingdom of God is involved. In a rhetorically effective way Matthew twice sets "God" against the devil.[64] Jesus' exorcisms indicate that the kingdom of God has come to "you," that is, also to the Pharisees. In spite of the unusual word φϑάνω ("has already come")[65] that was transmitted to the evangelist, we may not interpret our passage in the macrotext of the gospel as basically different from "the kingdom of God has come near" (4:17; 10:7); there was talk there also of exorcisms (4:24; 10:8).[66] In Matthew the kingdom of God reaches the people without being exhausted in what occurs in the miracles and exorcisms, in the proclamation of the gospel, and especially in the new practice of righteousness (6:33). It is present, but it retains its transcendence or its future. Thus there is no contradiction with 4:17 and 10:7, even if those texts emphasize above all the temporal aspect, the *near* future, while our text emphasizes the beginning that is already present and perhaps also the spatial aspect of the kingdom of God. In contrast to the accusation of the Pharisees and to what the Jewish exorcists also do, Matthew thus emphasizes that Jesus' exorcisms are a realm of experience where something completely new and qualitatively different appears. Of course, that can no longer be made evident with rhetorical conclusions, because for all prac-

tical purposes the Jewish exorcists do the same thing. Here the demand of faith comes into play, to which we can respond only by making decisions (cf. v. 30). Between v. 27 and v. 28 there is a qualitative leap. Through v. 27 the arguments were rational-rhetorical; from v. 28 on they become content-oriented and christological. Through v. 27 the opponents actually should have to agree; to vv. 28-29 they can only say "no," because they have a different understanding of the kingdom of God and of the person of Jesus. However, we must surmise that this qualitative leap remained hidden from Matthew himself.[67] The image of the strong man that now follows has a different character from the "rhetorical" parable of v. 25.

■ **29** Jesus speaks of a break-in into a "strong man's" house. A "strong man" is, for example, a hero, a king's attendant, or even a robber.[68] The image is biblically prefigured in Isa 49:24-25 to which the definite article, "*the* strong man," may refer. There the "strong one" is the enemy of God from whom God rescues his children.[69] "Binding" also awakens associations. In the end-time God's adversaries, above all the devil himself, will be

---

have the powers of the kingdom of God. Cf. the discussion of Johanan ben Zakkai with a Gentile about the charge of magic at the cleansing with the ashes of the red cow, *Pesiq.* 40a = Str–B 4.524. Johanan argues that the Gentiles do the same thing and is therefore accused by his disciples of using a "straw," i.e., a superficial argument.

64 The unusual βασιλεία τοῦ ϑεοῦ is not simply tradition; it is used by the evangelist very effectively, cf. Patte, 177; Gundry, 235.

65 Classically, φϑάνω means "to precede," "to be ahead of." In Koine Greek and the LXX it also means "to arrive," "to reach," "to arrive at," "to extend to." Cf. Moulton-Milligan, *s.v.*, 2; BAGD, *s.v.*, 2. The word is synonymous with the classical ἀφικνεῖσϑαι, not with ἐγγίζειν. Its basic meaning is that the goal has been reached and not merely almost reached. When the subject is a spatial concept that cannot move, φϑάνειν means: "to extend to, to reach." Cf., e.g., the tree that reaches to the sky in Dan 4:8, 17, 19Θ. This meaning might resonate in 12:28 for the

βασιλεία that in Matthew also has a spatial dimension.

66 In Matthew the accent may (but does not have to!) be somewhat different than it is in the church's oldest tradition. There one must ask why the Aramaic verb for "to come," that we do not know for a certainty (Dalman, *Words,* 107 מְטָא), was translated with φϑάνω and not, e.g., with ἐγγίζω. It may be that the present aspect may have been more important in an earlier time than it was in the Matthean context for which the formulation of J. Weiss (*Proclamation,* 129) that the kingdom of God is "at the door" is not at all bad.

67 That we are aware of it is possible because of the post-Enlightenment distinction between fact and meaning. On the consequences of this hiddenness in Matthew cf. below on the summary and history of interpretation of 12:22-37.

68 Schlatter, 407.

69 To be sure, LXX Isa 49:24-25 translates גִּבּוֹר with γίγας, because ἰσχυρός is often used of God in the

bound.[70] Thus the choice of words is probably not accidental; Jesus could also have spoken, for example, of a "mighty one" and of the "victory" over him (cf. Luke 11:21-22). Probably σκεῦοι is also not accidental. A "vessel" is a frequent metaphor for the human body.[71] In short, the image focuses the associations in a certain direction. Jesus suggests that the devil is already bound; only then can one enter his house and liberate people who are ruled by him. Later interpretations have expanded this metaphorical imagery into a full-blown allegory.[72] What is important, however, is not that in many details it goes beyond Matthew but that a complete allegorical interpretation changes the character of the whole. One cannot decode this saying by setting equal signs and then "knowing" what each metaphor means. What Jesus here intimates is not yet accessible to simple knowing. While it is true that the rhetorical question can be answered easily, the text does not furnish a key for its translation into the real world. It remains in dim light and permits in the hearers only a glimmer of the unheard-of event that has now happened.[73] It is something that one cannot simply know, but one can only respond to it by committing one's life. Precisely that is what is meant by the concluding v. 30.

■ **30** Verse 30 is a call to decision[74] (not an additional argument)[75] that is directed to open and undecided people and not to the opponents of Jesus, who have already reached a decision. As an interpretation of the challenges to faith in vv. 28-29 it is necessary and appropriate. "To gather" is reminiscent of the harvest, of a shepherd and his flock, or of the hope that God will again gather his scattered people.[76] "To scatter" is a negative thing. One smashes objects in pieces with a hammer, the victor scatters the army of one who is vanquished, or the enemies scatter Israel among the nations.[77] The Jews who were grounded in the Bible probably thought most naturally of the "gathering" of the nation of Israel that was hoped for from God and

---

Bible. The image left its mark on *Ps. Sol.* 5.3 (ἀνὴρ δυνατός). It may be that Isa 53:12 also is an influence (LXX: τῶν ἰσχυρῶν μεριεῖ [cf. vv. 25-26!] σκῦλα [cf. Luke 11:21-22!]).

70 Binding the devil: *1 Enoch* 10.4-5; *Jub.* 48.15, 18; *T. Levi* 18.12; Rev 20:2-3; binding the evil ones: *1 Enoch* 69.27-28 (binding the sinners and deceivers by the Son of Man); binding the demons in the endtime: *1 Enoch* 54.3-5 (of Azazel's army); *Jub.* 10.7; cf. Klauck, *Allegorie*, 181, n. 168.

71 Christian Maurer, "σκεῦος," *TDNT* 7 (1971) 358-59; Klauck, *Allegorie*, 181, n. 172. *T. Naph.* 8.6: "The devil will inhabit him (*scil.* the evil man) as his own vessel."

72 Even Luke 11:22 speaks of the ἰσχυρότερος and probably is thinking of Jesus; cf. Luke 3:16. The allegorizing continues in the church's interpretation: The strong one is the devil (e.g., Origen fr. 268 = 121; Thomas Aquinas, *Lectura* no. 1018); the house is the world (e.g., Jerome, 94; Theodore of Mopsuestia fr. 68 = Reuss, 119); the vessels are the people (e.g., Irenaeus *Haer.* 3.8.2; Jerome, 94; Theodore of Mopsuestia fr. 68 = Reuss, 119). Other suggestions: The strong one is sin; the house is the person's body (Origen fr. 267 = 121); the vessels are the demons (e.g., Photius of Constantinople fr. 50 = Reuss, 296). Luther (*WA* 38.544-45) interprets the entire text *consilio mystico* of Christ who conquered Satan not by force but by his death and liberated the human being who is like a good horse who is being ridden by a robber.

73 Jesus presumably put his exorcisms in the context of the eschatological struggle against Satan and his kingdom. Cf. Jeremias, *Theology*, 93-94. A parallel to Matt 11:29 is Luke 10:18, where, indirectly, the victory over Satan is also indicated: "I saw Satan fall like lightning from heaven."

74 The parallels listed by Str-B 1.635-36 offer nothing by way of content. Cf., however, Cicero *Or.* 41 (*Pro Quinto Ligario*) 11 (31): For us all are opponents except those who are with us; for Caesar all are his to the degree that they are not against him (cf. Mark 9:40).

75 The ancient church usually interpreted v. 30 to refer the devil and said that the works of the devil who scatters and Christ who gathers are not compatible. That is why Christ first had to conquer the "strong one." Cf. Jerome, 94; John Chrysostom, 41.3 = *PG* 57.448, etc.

76 Harvest: Matt 3:12, cf. 9:38; 13:28-29, 39; shepherd: Isa 40:11; Ezek 34:13; God will gather Israel: 1 Bar 4:37; *Ps. Sol.* 11.2; 17.44; *Shemone Ezre Ber.* 10 = Str-B 4.212; the Messiah will gather Israel: *Ps. Sol.* 17.26, cf. Matt 23:37; 24:31, etc.

77 To demolish: Ιερ 28:20-22; God scatters Israel: Ιερ 9:16; cf. Sir 48:15; bad shepherds scatter the sheep: Ιερ 23:1-2; the enemies scatter Israel and Judah: Zech 1:19, 21.

that surprisingly was fulfilled in Jesus' ministry.[78] The readers of the Gospel of Matthew thought that in Jesus God is "with us" (1:23; 28:20), while discipleship, on the other hand, consists of being "with him" (cf. 12:3-4) until death (cf. 26:29, 36, 40, 51, 69, 71).[79] Our verse will turn out to have been a "signal"[80] when the readers in the passion narrative come across the prophetic statement that "the sheep of the flock will be scattered" (26:31). In its context our saying means: With Jesus there is no neutrality and distance.[81] One can only come to him with one's whole life—or one has missed him and stands on the side of God's enemies.

History of Interpretation

Since Cyprian, v. 30 is interpreted ecclesiologically: "Whoever gathers elsewhere, outside the church, destroys the church of Christ." "When Christ is with us, but the heretics are not with us, then the heretics certainly are against Christ."[82] This interpretation appears also in Augustine. He resolves the tension between Matt 12:30 and Mark 9:40 as follows: Mark 9:40 means that the Catholic church concedes the use of the sacraments to the heretics, but Matt 12:30 is superior, for the separation from the Catholic church is against Christ.[83] In general, this application has not become very influential in the history of interpretation, because v. 30 was almost always interpreted as an argument rather than as a call to decision.[84] In the Reformation Musculus defends himself by arguing that whoever does not accept the "tyranny of the Roman Pope" and the "open errors" in the church is not a "*desertor ecclesiae*." As far as the text is concerned, it is important on the basis of Matthew's understanding of the church that he puts the accent in v. 30b on "gathering." By gathering one demonstrates that one belongs to Christ. "Those bishops who today do not gather (people) into the kingdom of God do not belong to Christ."[85] The church is not simply identical with the Christ who has been given to it; it has to prove the gift it has been given!

■ **31-32** The second part of the judgment discourse begins with vv. 31-32. As elsewhere,[86] διὰ τοῦτο ("therefore") introduces a concluding consequence with a threatening character. Λέγω ὑμῖν ("I say to you") intensifies the solemn character. The well-known logion of the blasphemy against the Spirit follows. It is formulated with special urgency in Matthew, because the harsh οὐκ ἀφεθήσεται ("will not be forgiven") appears twice. What does it mean? Augustine confesses that this may be the most difficult and most important question in the Bible.[87] There are questions on two levels. First, the exegetical question is: Of what does the blasphemy against the Spirit consist? The texts do not elaborate on it but presuppose that it is understood. The question becomes especially difficult when it is contrasted with speech against the Son of Man that can be forgiven. Second, the theological question is: Is there a limit to grace? Does this sentence not contradict the boundless love of God—thus the center of the proclamation of Jesus—and therefore also the conviction of the boundless power of the Holy Spirit?

History of Interpretation

The exegetical problem appeared important because it contained numerous questions about dogmatic issues. Among them are the question of the classification of sins, the question of the eternity of the punishments in hell, the question of purgatory, the question of the possibility of repentance. Since the ancient church countless special treatises[88] and, in classical dogmatics, the *locus de blasphemia Spiritus Sancti* dealt with it. Thus we have the rare case that a difficult Bible passage "produced" a dogmatic *locus*. However, the theological industriousness had more than theoretical reasons. We are aware from many biographies how in the course of church history sensible and pious people were tortured by the fear that they had committed the unforgivable sin against the

---

78 Cf. especially Ezek 28:25; 29:13, where both verbs occur.
79 Cf. vol. 1, I A 1.3 on 1:23.
80 Cf. vol. 1, Introduction 1J.
81 Bengel, 83: "Non valet neutralitas in regno Dei." Cf. John Charles Ryle, *Expository Thoughts on the Gospels: St. Matthew* (1856; reprinted Edinburgh: Banner of Truth Trust, 1986) 130: In religion there is no average according to the motto: "not as bad as others," "but . . . not saints."
82 Cyprian *Unit. eccl.* 6 = FC 36.100–1; idem, *Ep.* 75.14 (from Firmilian) = FC 51.305.

83 *Cons. ev.* 4.5 = 400.
84 Cf. above, n. 76.
85 Musculus, 345.
86 13:13; 21:43; 23:34.
87 *Sermo* 71.8 = 449.
88 Schaff (*Sünde*, 1–2) counts 26 monographs for German-speaking Protestantism between 1619 and 1824! Eugène Mangenot ("Blasphème contre le Saint-Esprit," 910–16) offers an overview of the classic ancient and Catholic interpretations.

Holy Spirit.[89] Today the sin against the Holy Spirit has largely disappeared from dogmatics. However, it still shows up in the case histories of religious people in psychiatric clinics.

In the history of interpretation we can observe three classical types of interpretation among which in the course of time there has been some partial mixing.

1. An interpretation that one might call the "trinitarian" interpretation is associated especially with *Athanasius* (*Epistula 4*). The Spirit is the essence of the divine Logos (4 = 474). The blasphemy of the Son of Man is a blasphemy only of the *human* Jesus, such as that, for example, of the Nazarenes (Matt 13:54) (20 = 493) or "this generation" (Matt 11:19).[90] However, exorcisms are *divine* works of Jesus; the Pharisees "denied . . . his divinity and sought refuge with the devil" (22 = 496). The blasphemy of the Spirit is thus the denial of the divinity of Christ by non-Christians,[91] Jews,[92] or heretics in spite of God's public works.[93]

2. As far as I know, the second basic type goes back to *Origen*. He interprets the blasphemy against the Spirit as the "*sin of Christians.*" Origen proceeds from the idea that the Spirit dwells not in everyone but only in Christians and therefore can be blasphemed only by them.[94] This interpretation of our passage was combined with the interpretation of Heb 6:4-6

and 1 John 5:16-17. It has become the church's dominant interpretation. Unless one wanted to identify the sin against the Holy Spirit absolutely with mortal sin,[95] one had to limit and to define it. The sin against the Holy Spirit is apostasy from the faith to the degree that it is done with malice, with full knowledge of the truth, and from contempt of grace in the church.[96] The reformers,[97] Protestant orthodoxy,[98] and the Catholic theology of the Counter-Reformation[99] have taken over this definition with only negligible new accents. This limitation and precise definition of the sin against the Holy Spirit had a twofold consequence. On the one hand, it served to ease consciences, because it became a special sin. On the other hand, it now became tangible so that all could ask whether they had not perhaps committed it and were eternally condemned.

3. The third interpretation, that of Augustine in *Sermo* 71, is actually a modification of the second interpretation. For Augustine also the issue is apostasy from faith, cutting oneself off from the source of forgiveness (34 = 464). However, two new accents are clear. In the first place, the *ecclesiological dimension* of the sin against the Holy Spirit is important for Augustine. It is committed by those who "with unrepentant heart resist the unity of the church" (36 = 465), for the Spirit is granted only in the church (37 = 466).[100] Then—here we encounter an accent that more often

---

89 Impressive examples: the biography of the former Protestant Francesco Spiera (sixteenth century) in Schaff, *Sünde,* 173–210; the letters of the Bern Pietist Samuel Schumacher (1695) to A. H. Francke and to his father in Rudolf Dellsperger, *Die Anfänge des Pietismus in Bern* (Arbeiten zur Geschichte des Pietismus 22; Göttingen: Vandenhoeck & Ruprecht, 1984) 185–88.

90 Theophylactus (269) and Juan de Valdés (*Commentary upon the Gospel of Matthew,* trans. John B. Betts [London: Trübner, 1882] 227), e.g., refer to Matt 11:19.

91 Athanasius (*Epistula 4* 12 = 483) argues correctly against Origen (cf. below) that he cannot explain why the Pharisees, i.e., precisely those who are not Christians, commit the sin against the Holy Spirit.

92 Thus, e.g., W. M. L. de Wette (*Über die Sünde wider den heiligen Geist,* 23–24) with anti-Semitic tones: As punishment for the Jewish rulers Jerusalem, "this seat of unbelief and stubbornness," and the land of Israel, which has become desolate and unfruitful, is cursed "and its rejected miserable sons languish in oppression and disgrace."

93 Similar to Athanasius, e.g., Theodore of Heraclea fr. 86 = Reuss, 81; Cyril of Alexandria fr. 156–57 = Reuss, 203; Basil in *Regula brevius* 273= *PG* 31.1076;

Zwingli, 290–91.

94 *Princ.* 1.3.7.

95 Thus for all practical purposes in Maldonat, 255.

96 Dionysius the Carthusian, 154 ("ex certa malitia, ex impugnatione agnitae veritatis, ex invidentia fraternae gratiae"). Cf. similarly Thomas Aquinas *S. th.* 2/2, q.14, a.1 Sed contra; a.2 Sed Contra and Corpus.

97 Luther, 442–50 (sermon from 1528 = WA 28.10–20): those who reject the forgiveness of sins granted by the Spirit cannot receive the forgiveness of sins; ibid., 450; Calvin *Inst.* 3.3.21–22.

98 Cf. primarily Heppe, *Dogmatik,* 258–59, 284–90 (*Locus de peccato* with sources, nn. 27–32). A distinctively Reformed idea was anchoring this sin in the will of God: God does not *will* to forgive it. For Lutheranism cf. Heinrich Schmid, *The Doctrinal Theology of the Evangelical Lutheran Church* (Minneapolis: Augsburg, 1961) 254, 256–57.

99 The image of Bellarmine (*De sacramento poenitentiae* 2.16, in Knabenbauer, 1.551) is beautiful: Those who commit the sin against the Holy Spirit are like sick persons who refuse to take the only medicine that can heal them.

100 Cf. *Sermo in Monte* 1.22 (75) = *PL* 34.1267.

than not was later rejected—Augustine said that only at death was it determined whether someone had committed the sin against the Holy Spirit (21 = 456; cf. 37 = 466). Therefore, one may not despair about godless persons, for as long as they live they have the chance to find the way (back) to the Catholic church.[101] The consequence for the interpretation of our text is that Augustine explicitly and against the opinion of most people maintains that the Pharisees can*not* have committed the sin against the Holy Spirit.[102]

The history of interpretation makes clear a double problem. One of them is the dogmatic problem. Olshausen formulates it with the observation that our Bible word is "for dogmatics the main proof text for the doctrine of eternal punishment."[103] This is certainly implied in our word, but is such a statement, established as "doctrine," defensible in light of God's limitless love? It is not surprising that a great deal of emotional distress is caused by such a doctrine. The other problem lies in the function of this saying. It was able to be used quite well for condemning heretics and thus for justifying oneself, not last of all in its Augustinian application to the church. The list of those whom church authorities with its help have consigned into eternal darkness is impressive and reaches from Simon Magus[104] over the Arians[105] to the "Papists and rabble who willfully oppose our teaching."[106] Our text even had to serve as proof for purgatory.[107] This is not at all pleasant. Can exegesis protect our saying from its own history of interpretation?

Interpretation: Church

The saying takes up the Jewish distinction between forgivable and unforgivable sins.[108] Of course, the formulation "to speak against the Holy Spirit" is almost unique in the Jewish context.[109] If we do not want to assume that the saying means a blasphemy of biblical prophecy (but what could be the occasion for that?), we must think of the Spirit of God who was given to the early Christian communities and missionaries. They have formulated the logion out of the certainty that they possess the Spirit of God. From the Spirit they have an authority that is not merely human, and thus they themselves become unassailable.[110] Who is able to distinguish between them as human beings and as bearers of the Spirit? Thus the logion enjoins the "suprahuman" importance of their message.[111] Those who reject it "resist" "obstinately" "the Holy Spirit" (Acts 7:51). The logion betrays a part of the immense claim that the messengers of Jesus made on behalf of their message. As soon as "Son of Man" was understood as a title, that message could not be questioned—not even on the authority of Jesus.

101 *Retract.* 1.18 = CSEL 36.93–94.
102 *Sermo in Monte* 1.22(75) = *PL* 34.1267 (in the context of an interpretation of the sixth antithesis!).
103 411. Not without reason, our passage is also cited repeatedly as proof against Origen's statements about universal reconciliation. See, e.g., Athanasius, *Fragmenta in Matthaeum, PG* 27.1384.
104 Ambrose *Paen.* 2.4 = CSEL 73.172–75.
105 Athanasius (*Epist. 4*, 22 = 496), the Athanasian interpretation of the blasphemy of the Spirit in terms of the denial of the divinity of Jesus was "tailored" to the Arians; Leo the Great *Sermo* 75.4 = FC 93.333.
106 Luther 2.447.
107 Augustine (*Civ. D.* 21.24 = NPNF 2.470), Gregory the Great (*Dialogues* 4.39 = FC 39.243), and others concluded from the formulation "neither in this eon nor in the coming eon" that sins other than the one against the Spirit could be forgiven in the future eon, i.e., in purgatory. Cf. also Concilium Lugdunense 1 in DS36 no. 838. Luther (WA 38.547–48) disputed this conclusion. For a counter-polemic see Maldonat, 255–56.
108 Cf. Moore, *Judaism*, 1.465–67; Str–B 1.636–38: Those who deny God, blaspheme the Torah, and despise circumcision find no forgiveness. *M. Sanh.* 10.1 adds: those who deny the resurrection of the dead or are "Epicureans." *2 Enoch* 59–60: those who violate a soul (noteworthy: even the soul of an animal!). ʾ*Abot R. Nat.* 39 = 58b (trans. J. Goldin [1955], 161): those who repeatedly sin and repent or who sin with the intention to repent.
109 Cf. just by way of example *1 Enoch* 67.10: "to deny the spirit of the Lord." In *1 Enoch* 20.6 (only in Greek), Saraqâêl is set over those who sin ἐπὶ τῷ πνεύματι. David Flusser ("Die Sünde gegen den heiligen Geist," 143–44) interprets this as meaning blasphemy against God. However, he does so with the help of difficult conjectures. Important is CD 5.11–12 where defilements of the Holy Spirit are paralleled with blasphemies against the regulations of the covenant. Evald Lövestam (*Spiritus Blasphemia* [Scripta minora. K. humanistiska vetenskapssamfundet i Lund 1966/67:1; Lund: Gleerup, 1968] 26–31) calls attention to Ps 106:33; Isa 63:10.
110 The use of the logion in *Did.* 11.7 illustrates the difficulties that arose from this also for the churches: One may not test or judge a prophet who speaks in the Spirit. Only external criteria such as a prophet's lifestyle remain for judging. Cf. also *Gos. Barth.* 5.2–4 (= NTApoc 1.502): Everyone who decrees against any man who serves my Father has blasphemed against the Holy Spirit.

Interpretation: Matthew

In Matthew the warning against blaspheming the Spirit is strengthened by repetition and by the solemn conclusion "neither in this age nor in the one to come." From the context it is clear that by accusing Jesus of casting out demons in the name of the devil the Pharisees blaspheme not only Jesus but Jesus as the bearer of the Spirit (v. 18) who works through the Spirit of God (v. 28). Jesus' pronouncement thus applies to them: Your sin is not abolished—by God[112]—for all eternity. However, what then about the distinction between the Son of Man and the Spirit, since it is Jesus whom the Pharisees blaspheme?[113] I must confess that none of the interpretations that I have found in the literature[114] satisfy me. The most honest approach is the information that Matthew here simply preserves the wording he had received and that v. 32a for him was probably "*d'importance secondaire.*"[115]

Summary

■ **31-32** Looking back at the history of interpretation, the Athanasian understanding of the blasphemy of the Spirit as a deliberate denial of the divinity of Jesus by non-Christians and heretics comes closer to the text than does the interpretation of Origen or Augustine as a specific sin of Christians for which a "second repentance" is impossible. In Matthew (and Mark) it is the Pharisees who spoke this blasphemy. We have surmised that for the early period it was the high claims of Christian missionary preaching that prompted our saying. Given this understanding there is no exegetical basis for the uncertainty of Christians about the weight of their own sin. Zwingli's saying applies to them: "If they have repentance" (that is, if they are uncertain about themselves), "they have the Spirit."[116] As long as one has the knowledge and consciousness of sin, one has not blasphemed the Holy Spirit; the sin against the Spirit is fundamentally unrecognizable.[117] However, not all of the problems that this saying poses are solved yet. The history of its interpretation gives pause. That it has repeatedly been used to support one's *own* claims to truth, to absolutize one's (own!) church, and to destroy the church's opponents[118] has to raise the question whether it actually is a good expression of the gospel of *God*'s rule and *God*'s love. The Matthean evidence confirms such reservations. The evangelist has Jesus use this word as a blow against "the" evil Pharisees, who historically were not at all so evil, but who in retrospect became for the rejected and persecuted Matthean community what they are today in the Gospel of Matthew. What happened here is quite different from what was meant in the Sermon on the Mount by the Jesus whose commandments his disciples are to proclaim and to live until the end of the world!

111 Kloppenborg, *Formation,* 213: "Warning . . . that opposition invites disastrous consequences." Thereby no means appealing—story of Ananias and Sapphira can illustrate the consequences. Cf. Acts 5:9.

112 *Passivum divinum.*

113 The addition of an οὐκ in v. 32a by B is understandable.

114 A sample: J. Weiss (329) separates the Spirit from Jesus "as a private person," Zahn (462) from Jesus "as a human being," France (R. T. France, *The Gospel According to Matthew* [Tyndale New Testament Commentaries 1; Grand Rapids: Eerdmans, 1985] 210) from the "incognito character of Jesus' ministry." Colpe ("Spruch," 76) is of the opinion that here the knowledge of the original meaning of Son of Man is gradually being lost and the title is becoming "the designation of Christ as the true human being." However, Matthew knows that the way of the Son of Man will go through death and resurrection to the judgment of the world. Verseput (*Rejection,* 239) distinguishes between Jesus as a person and his saving work in the Spirit, Schweizer (288) between the mere "report about the Son of Man" and the deeds of the Spirit that are actually happening. Verse 12:30 speaks against this!

115 Marguerat, *Jugement,* 104.

116 425.

117 Luther 2.449–50: "It would be . . . a new kind of sin against the Holy Spirit if one did not want to believe in forgiveness."

118 Not without bitterness (and not without relevant experiences!) Drewermann (*Markusevangelium,* 1.319) formulates: "In the final analysis it is even the Holy Spirit himself who forbids the freedom (*scil.,* for truth), so that anyone who wants to challenge the widespread fraud is accused of having an 'evil spirit.'"

Thus I would like to criticize this saying on the basis of the history of interpretation. It produced scarcely any fruit of love.[119] Admittedly there is also an evangelical concern in our saying. It is concerned that forgiveness not become automatic and that God's holiness be maintained before the human "claim" on forgiveness. However, it is obviously dangerous to express this concern with the help of the Holy Spirit, because it makes it too easy to claim the Holy Spirit exclusively for the church. And in personal interpretations the blasphemy against the Holy Spirit too often became the instrument with which a strong, religiously characterized superego killed a weak ego. In my judgment, with this saying the negative consequences outweigh its positive potential. I personally would not choose it as a sermon text except for a sermon *against* the text in the service of an examination of its consequences.

■ **33-37** The final section again focuses on the accusation against the Pharisees. It consists of a parabolic saying (v. 33), its application[120] (vv. 34-35), and a concluding word (vv. 36-37) addressed to the Pharisees but having general validity.

■ **33** The image of the tree and its fruits is familiar to the readers from 7:16-18; the metaphor "fruit" is generally known.[121] In contrast to 7:16, Matthew here stays with the image.[122] The fruits are "unusable" and not, as in 7:17, "evil." The meaning of the image is evident: If one sees good fruit, one will say that the tree is good or vice versa, for only on the basis of the fruit can one recognize the value of a tree.

■ **34** The application follows in v. 34 with a drumroll. The Baptist had already called the Pharisees and Sadducees a "brood of vipers." Jesus takes up his words[123]

and will repeat them once more in 23:33. What have the Pharisees done to deserve them? Matthew's opinion is that their evil words against Jesus show that they are evil through and through. A well-known sentence documents this: From the mouth one can know something about the heart.[124] The conviction that words reveal something of a person's essence was widespread. In early Christianity it provides the basis both for Mark 7:21 par. ("out of a man's heart come evil thoughts, fornication, theft, etc.") and for the widespread polemic against heretics that sees a connection between their false doctrine and their moral evil (for example, Tit 1:10-11; *Did.* 11.8, etc.).

■ **35** Verse 35 develops v. 34b for good and evil persons. "Treasury" is used metaphorically in a number of ways;[125] the thought is of the fullness of goodness or malice of a good or evil person. The high point of the section is in vv. 34-35. Here is Jesus' first direct attack against his opponents.[126] Are the Pharisees already condemned? Augustine thought not;[127] most interpreters correctly say yes. Of course, Matthew *knows* that the Pharisees will continue to pursue their goal, the death of Jesus. His whole story is for him a confirmation of their evil. While Jesus will continue to argue with them and be concerned about them, it will be without success. That will make clear for Matthew how evil they are.

■ **36-37** Verses 36-37 bring the section to a close. Jesus does continue to speak to the Pharisees, but in v. 36 he formulates a generally valid sentence in the third person. Verse 37 sharpens this sentence as a warning, in the traditional "you" of the wisdom saying, to the individual

119 Cf. vol. 1, Introduction 6 (thesis 2.5).

120 Luke 6:45a, b/Matt 12:35 is not an image (thus Schürmann [*Lukasevangelium*, 1.378] of the "good or bad master of the house" with his harvest stored) but a substantive statement that contains a familiar metaphor ($\vartheta\eta\sigma\alpha\nu\rho\acute{o}\varsigma$).

121 Cf. vol. 1, II A 3.2 on 7:16b with nn. 28–29, 33, 71–72.

122 Thus the controversial question in the interpretation of the ancient church whether it is Jesus who is meant with the tree (thus, e.g., John Chrysostom, 42.1 = *PG* 57.451; Hilary, 12.18 = SC 254.284) or the Pharisees (thus, e.g., Augustine *Sermo in monte* 2.24 [79] = *PL* 34.1305–6) is posed incorrectly. In v. 34 the image is *applied* to the Pharisees.

123 Similarly already in 7:19, cf. vol. 1 II A 3.2 with n. 36.

124 $\Sigma\iota\rho$ 27:6, *T. Naph.* 2.6 ("as his heart, so also is his mouth . . . as his soul, so also is his word"); for rabbinical material from the interpretation of Gen 37:4 see Str–B 1.639.

125 Most frequently the treasure in heaven is the opposite of earthly possessions; cf. vol. 1, II A 2.4.1 on 6:19-20 with n. 29. Cf. in addition, e.g., *T. Asher* 1.9 (treasure of counsel); 4 Ezra 6:5 (treasures of faith); Plato *Phileb.* 15e; Philo *Congr.* 127 (treasure of wisdom); morally: Philo *Fug.* 79 (treasure of evil or good); *Sib. Or.* 5.184; further material in BAGD, *s.v.*, 1b, 2bγ.

126 Verseput, *Rejection*, 242.

127 Cf. above, n. 123.

member of the church.[128] In contrast to λόγος ("word"), ῥῆμα has a narrower sense and means the "spoken word."[129] When referring to persons ἀργός, actually ἀ-εργός, means "unemployed, lazy"; when referring to things it means "unproductive, useless."[130] That corresponds to Matthean usage (cf. 20:3, 6). To look for a Semitic "original" simply makes our understanding of the word more difficult and less clear.[131] The meaning of the Greek text is extremely precise, and it furthermore eases the contradiction that in 7:15-20 the fruits are deeds, but in 12:33-35 they are words. Every word must lead to a deed, otherwise it is ἀργός, without effect. It is precisely that for which the human words are scrutinized in the judgment.[132] Thus only superficially is our saying the kind of general warning against talkativeness that is also found in wisdom and Hellenistic literature.[133] In the Gospel of Matthew it has a more pregnant meaning. On the day of judgment human words are asked whether they have produced deeds, and in Matthew that means essentially whether they have produced love. That is true for the Pharisees and their words that they spoke about Jesus, but it also is true for the church and its speaking and acting. Here for the first time[134] the Pharisees are a negative example that is used "productively" to warn the church.

Summary and History of Interpretation

■ **22-37** Thus the meaning of this text lies first of all in the context of the Matthean narrative. In the dispute with the Jewish leaders that has come to a provisional climax our text is Jesus' accusation and response to his opponents' maliciousness. At the same time it is an announcement of the divine judgment of whose reality the readers are aware, since they know the end of the Jesus story and at the same time that of the history of Israel[135] with the destruction of the temple in the year 70. It is a strength of the Gospel of Matthew that it does not simply comfort its church with the knowledge that God's judgment has taken place on the evil words of the Pharisees but that it lets this knowledge immediately become a warning to that church. She also can be condemned on the basis of her ineffective words!

We can illustrate the uneasiness that the text nevertheless causes with a passage from a late writing of Luther that in more modern editions is usually treated with embarrassed silence. In response to the question about what the preacher may learn from our Bible text, Luther answers that we want to "believe that our Lord Jesus Christ is truthful who said of the Jews who did not accept but crucified him: 'you are a bunch of snakes and children of the devil.'" Then using our text Luther confirms in the name of Jesus anti-Semitic horror stories of his own time: "However, it all coincides with the judgment of Christ which declares that they are venomous, bitter, vindictive, malicious snakes, assassins, and children of the devil, who secretly sting and work harm. . . . That is why I would like to see them where there are no Christians."[136] Thus the Matthean stylizing of Jesus' harsh judgment on the Pharisees becomes in Luther the theological legitimation for believing all possible malicious rumors—words!—about the Jews. A dangerous phenomenon, because it has been repeated numerous times in history!

And now unfortunately it must be acknowledged that the *ground* for such phenomena lies in the New Testament texts themselves. I am thinking not only of extreme sayings such as Matt 12:31-32 that in the name of the Spirit declare one's own standpoint to be beyond question but of the entire text and especially of the understanding of miracle hidden in it. Those who see miracles

---

128 The second-person singular requires neither that we assume the existence of a traditional individual saying (Schweizer, 285–86; the redactional integration in the context is too strong for that) nor that we postulate a proverb (Klostermann, 111) for which there is no evidence.

129 Dewailly, "La parole," 205.

130 Spicq, *Lexicon* 1.195–98; Dewailly "La parole," 206–9. Thus ἀργός means exactly what Jerome (96) as the first of many said, *sine utilitate et loquentis . . . et audientis.*

131 See, e.g., Schwarz, *Jesus sprach,* 270–73 (בָּטִיל = idle,

worthless, invalid).

132 It is an exact parallel in content to James 2:20 (πίστις . . . ἀργή).

133 Cf. Plutarch *De garullitate* 2.502–15.

134 Cf. especially the interpretation of chap. 23.

135 In Matthew's understanding!

136 "On the Jews and Their Lies," in *Luther's Works* (Philadelphia: Fortress, 1971) 47.277.

as a visible and clear manifestation of the divinity of Christ on earth, who understand miracles in such a way that in them *formally* the limits of human power are breached and supernatural might is claimed,[137] must react indignantly to the rejection of such power. Indirectly our text teaches that such a formal understanding of miracle ends in an aporia. Obviously one may ascribe *formally* such miracles just as well to the devil as to God.[138] With the "half-believing" reaction of the people in v. 23 Matthew himself intimates that mere openness here does not yet lead to the goal.[139] He also knows that faith and unfaith must come into play with Jesus' miracles. Historical facts *alone* are not yet a sufficient reason for faith.

> In the text and in the history of its interpretation the difficulty in dealing with v. 27 becomes visible. That Jesus concedes at least rhetorically that the "sons of the Pharisees" do the same as he does becomes a scandal when his miracles are understood christologically as works of the deity. Then the Jewish exorcisms must also be works of the deity! Therefore, the church's interpretation for centuries has almost unanimously interpreted "your sons" (v. 27) to mean the apostles who, although also Jews, were primarily apostles of Jesus.[140] In modern times, by contrast, the correctly understood text was then rejected, because it "misunderstands the ambiguity of all mere fact" and remains "in the horizon of history of religions comparisons."[141] In my view, however, on the basis of Jesus we must come to a new view of the ancient

church's understanding of miracle not only in regard to its worldview but also in regard to its christological content. "The true and real God" exercises "in his deeds no greater power" than the Jewish exorcists also do.[142] The Jesus story also is an ambiguous, ambivalent story and by no means a clear revelation of the deity of God. Our text betrays this, so to speak, not intentionally but between the lines. Signs such as the healing of a blind and mute person are real signs, but in their worldview they remain ambivalent. Jesus' victory over Satan is shown not because it reveals a special power but because in Jesus' miracles love happens on behalf of suffering people.[143] A qualitative leap remains between the philosophical ambivalence of these signs (cf. vv. 22-27!) and the coming of the kingdom of God (cf. v. 28!).

Matthew has not seen this leap. He could not see it. Therefore he had to accuse the Pharisees of sinning against the Holy Spirit because of their malicious stubbornness toward God's activity. In so doing he has changed God's love that shines forth in Jesus' miracles into its opposite. Today we can see this qualitative leap. Therefore, in spite of Matthew we are not permitted to label as unbelievers people who reject what simply appears to be evidence of God's activity in provable miracles, be they Jews or non-Jews.

---

137 Cf. above, at the conclusion of chaps. 8–9: On the Meaning of the Matthean Miracle Stories Today, a.

138 Malina and Neyrey (*Calling*, 42) speak culturally-anthropologically of a "normal Mediterranean accusation in such circumstances" and—historically as a generalization—of a "witchcraft-label." Rudolf Bultmann ("The Question of Wonder," in *Faith and Understanding* [London: SCM, 1969] 260) says that as provable events miracles "are not secured against being explained as demonic activities."

139 In his story the amazed and friendly ὄχλοι frequently become the λαός that rejects Jesus (27:25; cf. already 13:10-17).

140 From John Chrysostom, 41.2 = *PG* 57.446–47; Jerome, 93 (as a possibility); Hilary, 12.15 = SC 254.280 up to Beza, 56 and Maldonat, 251.

141 Käsemann, "Lukas 11,14-28," 244.

142 Cf. Athanasius *Epist. 4* 15 = 486–87.

143 Cf. above, conclusion of chaps. 8–9, On the Meaning of the Matthean Miracle Stories Today.

2.2 The Sign of Jonah and the Return of the Demons (12:38-45)

Literature

Bayer, *Jesus' Predictions,* 110–45.

Wolfgang Bittner, *Jesu Zeichen im Johannesevangelium* (WUNT 2/26; Tübingen: Mohr/Siebeck, 1987) 28–74.

Dietrich Correns, "Jona und Salomo," in Wilfred Haubeck and Michael Bachmann, eds., *Wort in der Zeit: Neutestamentliche Studien: Festgabe für Karl Heinrich Rengstorf zum 75. Geburtstag* (Leiden: Brill, 1980) 86–94.

Edwards, *Sign.*

Geist, *Menschensohn,* 275–90.

Higgins, *Son of Man,* 90–113.

Jeremias, "Ἰωνᾶς."

Kloppenborg, *Formation,* 126–34.

Laufen, *Doppelüberlieferungen,* 139–47.

Lührmann, *Redaktion,* 34–43.

Paul W. Meyer, "The Gentile Mission in Q," *JBL* 89 (1970) 405–17.

Mora, *Signe.*

Henrik Samuel Nyberg, "Zum grammatischen Verständnis von Matth. 12,44-45," *Arbeiten und Mitteilungen aus dem neutestamentlichen Seminar zu Uppsala* 4 (1936) 22–35.

Sato, "Q," 150–51, 281–84.

Götz Schmitt, "Das Zeichen des Jona," *ZNW* 669 (1978) 123–29.

Schulz, *Q,* 250–57, 476–80.

Paul Seidelin, "Das Jonaszeichen," *StTh* 5 (1952) 119–31.

Tödt, *Son of Man,* 52–54, 211–14.

Anton Vögtle, "Der Spruch vom Jonaszeichen," in idem, *Evangelium,* 103–36.

Wanke, *Kommentarworte,* 56–60.

For *additional literature* cf. above, III A 2 on Matt 12:22-50.

38 **Then some of the scribes and Pharisees answered him and said: "Master, we want to see a sign from you." 39/ But he answered and said to them:**
"An evil and adulterous generation demands a sign, and it will be given only the sign of the prophet Jonah.
40 **For as Jonah was in the belly of the sea monster three days and three nights,**
so will the Son of Man be in the heart of the earth three days and three nights.

41 **The people of Nineveh will rise in the judgment with this generation and will condemn it,**
because they repented at the preaching of Jonah,
and behold, more than Jonah is here!
42 **The queen of the south will be raised at the judgment with this generation and will condemn it,**
because she came from the ends of the earth to hear the wisdom of Solomon,
and behold, more than Solomon is here!
43 **But when an unclean spirit goes out from a person, it roams through dry areas seeking rest and does not find it. 44/ Then it says 'I will return to my house from whence I came.' And when it comes, it finds it empty, swept and decorated. 45/ Then it goes and takes with it seven other spirits, more evil than it is, and they move in and live there; and at the end it is worse with that person than at the beginning. Thus it will also be with this evil generation."**

Analysis

Structure

After a short intervention by the Jewish opponents (v. 38) Jesus begins a further series of judgment words. It has three parts. Verses 39-40 contain the riddle of the sign of Jonah that is explained in v. 40a-b, c-d with a biblical comparison largely formulated in parallels. Matthew 16:1-4 will repeat this section in places almost word for word. Thus our text belongs to the doublets that are intentionally created in the Gospel of Matthew.[1] Verses 41-42 are two parallel logia connected with v. 39 by the catchwords Jonah and γενεά ("generation"). Emphasized is the catchword κρίσις ("judgment") that is connected to v. 36. The third section, vv. 43-45, confuses the readers. In a context that was speaking of exorcisms, they will perceive the text first of all as a somewhat puzzling ghost story. Not until the end of v. 45 do they realize to their surprise that Jesus was formulating a parable. Ἀνάπαυσιν . . . οὐχ εὑρίσκει ("does not find rest") is a negative parallel to 11:29c. Γενεὰ πονηρά ("evil generation") at the end of v. 45 refers back to the beginning, v. 39, and frames the entire text.

---

1   In a synchronic reading of the gospel we may not make a distinction between the doublets that, according to literary criticism, are newly created by Matthew (e.g., 9:32-34 and 12:22-24) and the doublets that he took over when using the double traditions in Mark and Q and may even have accentuated.

Source

Our text comes from Q (= Luke 11:29-32, 24-26). The first part of the demand for a sign also has a parallel in Mark 8:11-12 (= Matt 16:1-4). The introduction is strongly redacted by both evangelists.[2] In Luke 11:29a the demand of the Pharisees and scribes for a sign is missing. The redactionally located notice in Luke 11:16 suggests that the demand for a sign stood in Q but that the scribes and Pharisees come from Matthew. The uniqueness of the introduction in Mark and Luke is that the Pharisees as opponents *tempt* Jesus by demanding a sign *from heaven*. Verse 39a also is strongly redacted;[3] Matthew has edited his Q source in v. 39 and his Mark text in 16:2a, 4 so that they sound alike. Except for the addition of $\tau o\hat{v}$ $\pi\rho o\phi\acute{\eta}\tau o v$ ("of the prophet"), v. 39b agrees with the Q text. In v. 40 Matthew goes his own way; only the basic structure of Matthew, v. 40, and Luke, v. 30, agrees. Although Matthean redaction cannot be proved linguistically,[4] it seems clear that Luke 11:30 offers the Q text. Luke certainly would have taken over the christological text of Matthew, v. 40, had he known it. In Q, Luke 11:30 was most likely followed by the saying about the queen of the south (Luke 11:31/Matt 12:42). Matthew probably put the Jonah saying, Q = Luke 11:32, first in order to have a better connection with vv. 39-40.[5] In vv. 41-42 he has retained the Q text literally. The Q text of the

"relapse saying," Luke 11:24-26//Matt 12:43-45 also is preserved very well.[6] In Q it followed Luke 11:23 in the Beelzebul controversy. The Matthean change in order is connected with the new interpretation. The brief concluding sentence at the end of v. 45, which makes the saying a parable for "this generation," goes back to him.[7]

Tradition History and Origin

We begin by observing that there were three originally independent units: vv. 38-40, vv. 41-42, vv. 43-45.[8]

1. The little pericope of the *sign of Jonah, vv. 38-40*, is extremely difficult and controversial. In the history of tradition, how did the pericope Luke 11:29-32, which obviously is not unified, come into existence? For Q = Luke 11:29-30 there are three possibilities:
a. Luke 11:29-30 is an original unit.[9]
b. The oldest nucleus was Luke 11:29; v. 30 is an interpretation of the sign of Jonah added secondarily.[10]
c. The oldest version did not speak of the sign of Jonah at all but corresponded to the nucleus of Mark 8:11-12 = Luke 11:29a-c.[11] With this solution it is an open question whether:
(1) in the Q tradition first the sign of Jonah, Luke 11:29d, was added as an exception and then v. 30

---

2   According to vol. 1, Introduction 3.2, redactional in v. 38 are: $\tau\acute{o}\tau\epsilon$, $\grave{\alpha}\pi o\kappa\rho\acute{\iota}\nu o\mu\alpha\iota$, $\gamma\rho\alpha\mu\mu\alpha\tau\epsilon\hat{\iota}\varsigma$ $\kappa\alpha\iota$; $\Phi\alpha\rho\iota\sigma\alpha\hat{\iota}o\iota$ (opponents in groups of two: vol. 1, I B 1.1 Jewish Leaders), $\lambda\acute{\epsilon}\gamma\omega\nu$, $\delta\iota\delta\acute{\alpha}\sigma\kappa\alpha\lambda o\varsigma$ (as an address by outsiders, cf. n. 16 on 8:18-27), perhaps $\vartheta\acute{\epsilon}\lambda\omega$, $\dot{o}\rho\acute{\alpha}\omega$.

3   Cf. vol. 1, Introduction 3.2 on $\dot{o}$ $\delta\grave{\epsilon}$ $\grave{\alpha}\pi o\kappa\rho\iota\vartheta\epsilon\grave{\iota}\varsigma$ $\epsilon\hat{\iota}\pi\epsilon\nu$. $Mo\iota\chi\alpha\lambda\acute{\iota}\varsigma$ could be formed according to Mark 8:38.

4   Matthean is $\ddot{\omega}\sigma\pi\epsilon\rho$ $\gamma\acute{\alpha}\rho$ and the agreement of the quotation with the LXX. A number of scholars assume the existence of two independent recensions of Q in Luke 11:30/Matt 12:40. The content gives no reason for questioning the Matthean character of v. 40.

5   Or has Luke secondarily created in vv. 29-32 a framing with $\check{I}\omega\nu\hat{\alpha}\varsigma$? In this case, Luke would create the chronological order of Solomon and Jonah, in the other case, which in my judgment is more probable, it would have been the ordering principle of the two logia in Q. Dietrich Correns ("Jona und Salomo," 86–94) assumes an influence of the fasting liturgy in *m. Ta an.* 2.4, where first Jonah, then Solomon are mentioned and therefore regards the Matthean order as original.

6   Presumably Matthean are $\delta\acute{\epsilon}$ in v. 43 and $\tau\acute{o}\tau\epsilon$ in v. 44.

7   Preferred Matthean vocabulary (vol. 1, Introduction 3.2): $O\ddot{v}\tau\omega\varsigma$ ($\check{\epsilon}\sigma\tau\alpha\iota$), $\pi o\nu\eta\rho\acute{o}\varsigma$. $\Gamma\epsilon\nu\epsilon\grave{\alpha}$ $\pi o\nu\eta\rho\acute{\alpha}$: inclusion with v. 39.

8   Higgins (*Son of Man*, 105) reckons with an original unit of vv. 38-42. However, the two logia, vv. 41-42, were originally independent, because (a) only v. 41 but not v. 42 is thematically connected with vv. 38-40, and because (b) they are missing in Mark 8:11-13.

9   See, e.g., Marshall, *Luke,* 486; Bayer, *Jesus' Predictions,* 131 (as a saying of Jesus, possibly with Luke 11:31-32); Philipp Vielhauer, "Jesus und der Menschensohn," in idem, *Aufsätze zum Neuen Testament* (ThBü 31; Munich: Kaiser, 1965) 112 (probably as the church's creation).

10   See, e.g., Schürmann, *Gottes Reich,* 164; Wanke, *Kommentarworte,* 57; Kloppenborg, *Formation,* 130 (for Kloppenborg both the omission of the sign of Jonah in Mark 8:11-12 and its commentary in Q = Luke 11:30 are a secondary attempt to remove difficulties).

11   See, e.g., Lührmann, *Redaktion,* 42; Edwards, *Sign,* 79–80; Pesch, *Markusevangelium* 1.409; Geist,

as its explanation,[12] or whether the reverse was true, that

(2) an old logion, Luke 11:30, was added to the rejection of signs by means of the later transitional expression εἰ μὴ τὸ σημεῖον Ἰωνᾶ, Luke 11:29d.[13] Luke 11:30 may (but need not) have been an independent logion like Luke 17:24, 26-27, 28-30.

I can imagine the solutions a and c(2) but not b or c(1), according to which Luke 11:29a-d once existed without Luke 11:30. It is not only for us today that Luke 11:29a-d is not understandable without further explanation but also for the Jewish hearers of that time.[14] Luke 11:29 would be a riddle, but a riddle that gives absolutely no clue to its solution is not a σημεῖον that is able to make a statement; it is simply speech that makes no sense. The advantage of solution a is that it is the simplest.

Thus we face the question of the relation of the Q version to Mark 8:11-12 in the history of the tradition. There the sign of Jonah is missing; Jesus unconditionally refuses the demand for a sign from heaven. On the one hand, it is quite conceivable if the sign of Jonah that, especially for gentile readers, made almost no sense was later omitted, and the text became a clear and unmistakable rejection of the demand for a sign. On the other hand, the Markan

abbreviated oath εἰ δοθήσεται is Semitizing. However, it also may be LXX language.[15] Clearly secondary in Mark is the temptation motif, perhaps also the clarification of the sign with "from heaven," because it explains of what the temptation consists.[16] In my judgment, Mark 8:11-12 is on the whole more likely later and either a very old simplification of the Q tradition or an independent parallel tradition.[17] All of these considerations favor solution a. However, the origin of the traditional unit, Luke 11:29-30, is still unclear. The only somewhat noncontroversial matter is that in its substance the rejection of the demand for a sign goes back to Jesus.[18] Whether that is true also for the presumably oldest unit of the tradition, Luke 11:29-30, can be decided only on the basis of the interpretation.

2. *Verses 41-42*: In my judgment the *two threat-sayings, Q = Luke 11:31-32*, have most likely been added to Luke 11:29-30 as interpretive "commentaries."[19] Formally, the addition is connected to the catchwords Νινευῖται ("Ninevites") and γενεὰ αὕτη ("this generation"; vv. 30, 29).[20] The "commentary" then fits best if Luke 11:30b deals with the preaching of the "present" Son of Man to "this generation," that corresponds to the "proclamation" (κήρυγμα) of Jonah to the Ninevites. Luke 11:31 (Solomon!) is intrusive; this shows that the double logion Luke 11:31-32 was originally independent. Against attributing the two Semi-

---

Menschensohn, 279–80; Paul W. Meyer, "The Gentile Mission in Q," *JBL* 89 (1970) 405–17, 407 (an early Christian prophet introduces the reference to the prophet to the Gentiles, Jonah, as a sign of judgment against Israel). Götz Schmitt ("Das Zeichen des Jona," *ZNW* 669 [1978] 123–29, 128) advocates this thesis in an interesting variant: The sign of Jonah is the τέρας of a crying stone that proclaims the destruction of Jerusalem, as it is announced in *The Lives of the Prophets* 10.10–11 (only in the recensions B, C, D). However, this connection of the well-known motif of the speaking stone (cf. Hab 2:11 and Wettstein 1.788–89 on Luke 19:40) with Jonah is so unique that I am not able to assume that it was known at that time.

12 This would mean that solution 2 would then be the second stage of the development of the tradition within the Q circle. Cf., e.g., Edwards, *Sign*, 85.

13 Sato, "Q," 283.

14 Cf. below on the "original meaning."

15 Cf., e.g., Num 14:20; 32:11; Deut 1:35; 1 *Βασ* 3:14; 14:45; 28:10 and elsewhere; altogether about 38 times in the LXX. The "unambiguous Hebraism" (BDF § 454 [5]) thus comes from the LXX and occurs as a biblicism in Aramaic only in the Targumim (Moulton–Howard–Turner 2.469). On the

other hand, the formulation at the end of Luke 11:29 (εἰ μή . . .) also is Semitizing. Cf. Colpe, "ὁ υἱὸς τοῦ ἀνθρώπου," 449, n. 349. If it is a Septuagintism, then Sato's argument ("Q," 282) is invalid to the effect that the negation with εἰ that is assumed to be original could not have had an expansion with εἰ μή next to it.

16 Edwards, *Sign*, 76.

17 It seems to be almost a dogma in scholarship today that Jesus could not have rejected a sign unconditionally on one occasion but formulated this rejection on another occasion with the "sign of Jonah" that essentially means the same thing. Why not?

18 Cf. also 1 Cor 1:22.

19 Wanke, *Kommentarworte*, 58–59.

20 Contra Lührmann (*Redaktion*, 41), who, proceeding from the tradition-history thesis 3(a), understands Luke 11:30 as a late "redactional bracket" between Luke 11:29 and 31-32.

tizing logia[21] to Jesus is at most their content. The judgment on Israel seems to be definitive, while Jesus called Israel to repentance until the end of his activity. However, as in Luke 13:28-29 and perhaps also in Luke 10:13-14, one may understand the words also as a final, urgent appeal to Israel.

3. The *"relapse saying,"* vv. 43-45c, is a unity. Concerning its origin, we can determine only that it must go back to a Semitic tradition.[22]

Interpretation

■ **38** The scribes now join the Pharisees, who are the main opponents of Jesus in chap. 12. We may not ask where they suddenly come from; for the evangelist it is clear from the perspective of his time that they belong with the Pharisees and are generally identified with them (cf. 23:2-29). They respond to Jesus' long judgment discourse by demanding a sign. Σημεῖον is an open term that is used rather formally in the tradition. A "sign" is usually something visible by which one can clearly identify something,[23] for example, a seal, a symbolic action, a miracle, a sign from heaven, a physical characteristic. Special "signs" in the biblical and Jewish tradition are God's Exodus miracles and prophetic symbolic actions. Thus signs are not simply identical with miracles (δύναμις, τέρας). They can but do not have to be miracles.

What does Matthew understand as a "sign"? Except for the two pericopes about the demand for a sign, the word occurs almost exclusively in connection with the parousia of the Son of Man in the eschatological discourse of chap. 24.[24] As in the entire synoptic tradition, it is never used for "miracle." Furthermore, Jesus had already performed many miracles, including miracles in the presence of the Pharisees and scribes.[25] After declaring the exorcism of the deaf and blind person to be satanic, they demand something other than simply another miracle. In the similarly formulated parallel text of 16:1 Matthew speaks of a "sign from heaven"[26] that the Pharisees and scribes demand in order to "tempt" Jesus. There the reader is reminded of the temptation story with the miracles of bread and flight. Although Matthew does not change the formulations of the source, he probably is thinking here also of a special sign that makes clear Jesus' identity. Thus the issue here is probably not the prophetic signs of authentication such as one finds in the Bible and for which one was permitted to ask.[27] It is also more than the legitimating miracles of eschatological prophets.[28] After all of the negative things that the readers of the gospel have already heard about the Pharisees, they will regard their demand as impermissible; the peremptory "we want to see a sign from you" also supports this view.[29]

---

21 Βασιλίσσα νότου = the queen of the south without an article is Semitizing (cf. *status constructus!*); ἀναστῆναι μετά = to dispute is not a Semitism (against Black, *Approach,* 134); cf. below n. 60.

22 Henrik Samuel Nyberg ("Zum grammatischen Verständnis von Matth. 12,44-45," 29–35) and Beyer (*Syntax,* 285–86) argue that a Semitic background is probable on the basis of the parataxis with conditional meaning. See, e.g., v. 44: "when he comes and finds . . . the house."

23 Cf. Linton, "Parable"; Karl Heinrich Rengstorf, "σημεῖον κτλ," *TDNT* 7 (1971) esp. 204–6, 213–16, 220, 224–25.

24 Cf. especially 24:3 (signs of your parousia), 30 (σημεῖον τοῦ υἱοῦ τοῦ ἀνθρώπου ἐν οὐρανῷ).

25 In the church's interpretation it is occasionally understood as an expression of the unbelief of the Pharisees and scribes that, after so many miracles of Jesus have already happened, they still demand "signs." See, e.g., *Opus imperfectum* 30 = 787; Thomas Aquinas, *Lectura* no. 1047; Calvin 2.57.

26 The expression is not technical. The immediate background is probably provided by the cosmic signs that apocalypticism expects for the end-time: *Sib. Or.* 3.786–806; 4 Ezra 4:52; 6:12, 20; 7:26-27; 8:63; 9:1, 6; cf. 5:1-13; 6:13-27; 7:39-42; Rev 12:1, 3; 15:1. Rabbinic material: *b. B. Mes.* 59b = Str–B 1.127 (a *bath qol*); *S. Deut.* 13.2 § 83–84 = Str–B 1.726–27 (stars). Jerome (96–97) refers to Samuel, 1 Sam 12:18 (thunder) and Elijah, 1 Kgs 18:38 (fire from heaven).

27 Cf., e.g., Deut 13:1-2; 1 Sam 10:1-7; 1 Kgs 13:3, 2 Kgs 19:29; 20:8-11; Isa 7:10-16; rabbinic material: *b. Sanh.* 98a = Str–B 1.640–41. For the Matthean redaction that shows its understanding of signs most clearly in 24:3, 30 the issue is therefore more than the legitimation of an (eschatological) prophet, which Wolfgang Bittner regards as the original demand for a sign (*Jesu Zeichen im Johannesevangelium,* 51–53).

28 Cf. Josephus *Bell.* 2.259, 262 (the Egyptian); *Ant.* 18.85–87 (the Samaritan); 20.97–99 (Theudas;

■ **39-40** Jesus' answer is correspondingly harsh. Only an evil and adulterous "generation"[30] demands a sign. By designating the Pharisees and scribes as "generation," the evangelist generalizes their behavior without identifying them explicitly with the entire nation of Israel.[31] In Matthew πονηρός ("evil") carries the weight of that which God condemns in the final judgment (7:17-18; 12:34-35; 13:38, 49). Μοιχαλίς[32] ("adulterous") reminds the reader of the biblical image of adultery[33] that represents the breaking of the covenant with God (Hos 3:1; Ezek 16:38; 23:45. Cf. Isa 57:3-9; Jer 13:26-27; Hosea 1-3). Truly God[34] will give this generation the sign of Jonah.[35] What does that mean?

■ **40** Matthew's explanation follows in v. 40. It refers to what was most important for every Jew in the story of Jonah: his rescue from the belly of the fish after three days and nights.[36] Jonah 2:1 is quoted literally.[37] The parallel between the fates of Jonah and Jesus is all the more clear since the psalm in Jonah 2 already interpreted the belly of the fish with the aid of mythical images of death.[38] Jonah's rescue from the fish is a rescue from death. In Jewish thought three days is a symbolic number. "God leaves the righteous no longer than three days

in distress."[39] The same thing that happened to Jonah will happen with the Son of Man. Our saying is a distinctively typical Matthean Son of Man saying. The Son of Man Jesus is for Matthew the one whose story he tells in his gospel—the story of his living, suffering, and dying—of his resurrection, exaltation, and parousia.[40] The Son of Man Jesus is "in the heart of the earth," that is, probably in the grave; Jesus' descent into hell, important in the church's interpretation, would be singular in the synoptic tradition and is therefore more improbable, although we cannot rule it out.[41] Matthew does not enunciate the idea of the resurrection, but it has to be present. One can neither recall the story of Jonah without also being reminded of the prophet's rescue nor as a Jew speak of the "three days" without thinking that after this period God intervenes on behalf of his righteous ones. Matthew 27:62-63 takes up our text again. There Matthew speaks again of Jesus' resurrection "after three days." The Pharisees of all people tell Pilate that Jesus had previously announced it. There is for Matthew no tension between the "three days and three nights" and the "third day," for in 27:64 he repeats "after three days" as "until the third day," his usual expression for the time of the resur-

---

29 crossing the Jordan); John 6:30-31 (manna). Unlike the question of the disciples in 24:3 ("Tell us . . ."), it is a question of the *performing* of a cosmic sign by Jesus.

30 Our text says nothing about the question of whether γενεά more likely means temporally the contemporaries of Jesus or ethnically the race, i.e., the nation. It is best to interpret it, therefore, on the basis of 11:16; cf. above on Matthew's understanding of 11:16.

31 Thus we may not with Günther Baumbach (*Das Verständnis des Bösen in den synoptischen Evangelien* [Theologische Arbeiten 19; Berlin: Evangelische Verlagsanstalt, 1963] 87) narrow the expression to the scribes and Pharisees.

32 Only here and at 16:4.

33 Thus it does not mean that the Pharisees or Jews were literally adulterers. What one can read on this question in Schlatter (415) is so explicitly anti-Semitic that one cannot "punish" it with silence.

34 *Passivum divinum.*

35 As far as its meaning is concerned, the exception is an emphatic affirmation. Cf. Arnulf Kuschke, "Das Idiom der 'relativen Negation' im NT," *ZNW* 43 (1950/51) 263.

36 Jeremias ("Ἰωνᾶς," 409): On the basis of Jewish tra-

dition the rescue of Jonah from the belly of the sea monster must be considered as *the* miracle that happened to Jonah. Only in connection with it is the word "sign" used once in the Jewish world (*Pirqe R. El.* 10 = Str–B 1.644–46, there 646). Cf. the (mostly late) material in Str–B 1.643–47.

37 The LXX corresponds here to the MT.

38 Jonah 2:3-4: ἐκ κοιλίας ᾅδου; εἰς βάθη καρδίας θαλάσσης; 2:6: ἄβυσσος . . . ἐσχάτη. Cf. from the Jewish Jonah tradition *Pirqe R. El.* 10 in Str–B 1.646: "You are called the one who kills and makes alive: behold, my soul is close to death." Cf. especially Paul Seidelin, "Das Jonaszeichen," *StTh* 5 (1952) 119–31, 123, 125.

39 *Yalqut* on Josh 2:16 § 12 in Str–B 1.647. Biblically: Gen 42:17-18; Exod 19:11, 16; Hos 6:2; further Old Testament and Jewish references in Karl Lehmann, *Auferweckt am dritten Tag nach der Schrift* (QD 38; Freiburg: Herder, 1968) 180–81, 262–72.

40 Cf. the excursus on Son of Man below at 16:21-28 (Son of Man in Matthew's Narrative).

41 In any case, we cannot, as many ancient interpreters did, understand ἐν τῇ καρδίᾳ τῆς γῆς to refer to the descent into hell because the grave is on the earth's surface. This would misunderstand the symbolic character of the expression. Klostermann

rection.[42] He has little interest in the exact interval,[43] so important is it for him that Jonah, "the prophet," typologically prefigures in his fate the *event* of Jesus' death and resurrection. Thus they are the "sign" that God will give this generation. However, they will be signs for Israel in a paradoxical sense. Israel will be guilty of the death of Jesus and thus bring about the promised sign. In Jesus' resurrection God will then reverse the evil that Israel has done. And just this becomes the "sign," but not the sign *for* Israel; it is rather a sign that Israel rejects and that thus becomes a sign *against* Israel.[44] In 27:64 the high priests and Pharisees speak of the "deception" of the resurrection and reject it. Verses 28:11-15 then show that it is precisely the rescue of Jesus from death that keeps "the Jews" "to the present day" in unbelief. Thus the resurrection of Jesus will seal the unbelief of Israel; that is why one must speak in Matthew's sense of a σκάνδαλον ("stumbling block") of the resurrection.[45] However, the Lord's response to Israel's unbelief will be his call to the Gentiles (28:16-20). When our text follows the sign of Jonah with the testimony of two Gentiles against Israel (12:41-42), it signals in advance this great turning of God's way from Israel to the Gentiles. Thus our text is the first prelude of the Matthean passion and Easter story and also a first response of Jesus to the decision of the Pharisees in 12:14 to kill Jesus.

Original Meaning

The question of the original meaning of the sign of Jonah is difficult. In the older text, Luke 11:30, the focus is not on Jonah in the sea monster but on Jonah in Nineveh. The Jewish Jonah tradition has dealt little with this part of the Jonah story. Neither from Luke 11:30 nor from the Jewish image of Jonah does it become clear how Jonah became a sign for the Ninevites. The following main suggestions are advocated.

1. The sign of Jonah refers to *Jonah's preaching of repentance* or that of the earthly Son of Man, Jesus.[46] Thus there is no other sign than the preaching. That it is the preaching of the Son of Man, that is, of the coming judge of the world Jesus, strengthens the threatening character of this "sign." The later commentary in Luke 11:32 supports this interpretation. In its favor is that Jesus' proclamation and Jonah's preaching of repentance in Ninevah actually do parallel each other. What speaks against it is not that preaching cannot be a "sign" in the ordinary sense of the word. If the sign of Jonah is intended to be a "non-sign," then the concept of "sign" is alien. What does speak against this interpretation is the future ἔσται in Luke 11:30, but this argument is really conclusive only in the Greek text, not in the Aramaic.[47]

---

(111) and Tödt (*Son of Man*, 213) think of the *descensus ad inferos* not in the specifically christological sense. The church's interpretation is divided on this point. While the majority of interpreters since Irenaeus (*Haer.* 5.31.1) think of the *descensus ad inferos* in the sense of the creed, the interpretation that the expression refers to the sojourn of Jesus in the grave has always been able to maintain itself through the influence of John Chrysostom, 43.2 = *PG* 57.458.

42 For a Jew the day begins with sunset so that with part of Friday, the Sabbath, and the night from the Sabbath to Sunday one arrives at three "days." Of course, "three nights" is still wrong. However, "day and night" is a common Hebrew expression for a calendar day, since יוֹם primarily meant daylight time in contrast to the night. Cf., e.g., Gen 7:4; 1 Sam 30:12-13.

43 The ancient church's exegesis has expended a great deal of effort here and has come up with some unusual suggestions: *Didasc.* 21 = Achelis-Flemming,

106 (Good Friday's darkness counts as one night) or Afrahat 12.5 = Bert, 189 (Afrahat begins counting with the "death" of Jesus in the last supper).

44 Verseput, *Rejection,* 276: "The only sign . . . will be the reversal of Israel's murderous rejection of Jesus in the resurrection. This . . . is not a sign to evoke faith, but a confirmation of God's wrath" on Israel.

45 *Quod est signum Jonae!? Scandalum crucis!* (*Opus imperfectum* 30 = 788). No! We violate Matthew when we read him in the light of 1 Cor 1:18-25.

46 See, e.g., Manson, *Sayings,* 90–91; Schulz, *Q,* 255–56; Kloppenborg, *Formation,* 132–33; Geist, *Menschensohn,* 281. The interpretation goes back to Rationalism. Cf., e.g., Paulus 2.116; de Wette, 79–80.

47 One frequently reads that in Greek the future ἔσται is gnomic after the ambiguous future δοθήσεται. However, after the aorist ἐγένετο and in contrast to τῇ γενεᾷ ταύτῃ, the future ἔσται is quite unusual.

2. The sign of Jonah is, as later in Matthew, the *miraculous rescue of Jonah from the belly of the fish.*[48] It is the Jewish parallels that primarily support this view.[49] Also in its favor is that this interpretation is the only one that uses the word "sign" in the usual way. Against it is that in the Jewish Jonah tradition Jonah's rescue did not become a sign for the Ninevites, who were not even present.[50] It also would remain very unclear how the risen Son of Man is to become a sign "for this generation." Does this refer to the parousia when the Son of Man, rescued by God from death, will be revealed to all peoples?[51] However, that cannot all be derived from Luke 11:30b alone without any knowledge of Matt 12:40, unless one already knows of the resurrection and the parousia. Then, however, Luke 11:30 is a creation of the church, as is assumed by many advocates of this interpretation. In my judgment, it is not probable as a creation of the church, because in the image Jonah's rescue did not become a sign for the Ninevites.[52] Only the *new* formulation of Matthew in v. 40a makes it possible, but here Jonah is no longer a sign for the Ninevites.

3. The sign consists not in something that Jonah or the Son of Man did or experienced, but *they themselves are* the sign. The genitive σημεῖον Ἰωνᾶ ("sign of Jonah") is to be understood not as a subjective genitive but as an appositive or epexegetical genitive. Just as Jonah was sent to announce judgment to Ninevah, so the "Son of Man" will be the eschatological judge or witness expected by Jesus' hearers.[53] Thus the meaning of the sign of Jonah is: The only "sign" remaining for this generation is the judge of the world himself. In favor of this interpretation is the formulation ἐγένετο ὁ Ἰωνᾶς . . . σημεῖον ("became Jonas a sign," Luke 11:30). In Old Testament terms the prophets themselves can be understood as signs.[54] The word "sign" is also alien with this interpretation, but at least Matthew speaks later of the eschatological "sign of the Son of Man" (24:30) and thus presupposes such an alien understanding of "sign." Against this interpretation is that we can establish no real correspondence between Jonah, the preacher of judgment, and the coming Son of Man, who himself brings the judgment.[55] The Ninevites escaped the judgment that Jonah preached—something that "this generation" will no longer be able to do at the coming of the Son of Man.[56]

In my judgment, this argument against the third interpretation is strong. The first interpretation remains for me the least improbable.[57] The question of the origin of Luke 11:29-30 cannot be clearly determined on the basis of the interpretation. It depends in my view exclusively on one's total view of the Son of Man problem.[58]

■ **41-42** The thought of the "Son of Man" leads Matthew farther to the last judgment.[59] There the Ninevites will rise up[60] and condemn "this generation." In my opinion, the word has less to do with the Jewish conception of the eschatological pilgrimage of the nations to Zion than with the idea that the righteous will judge the world on

---

48   See, e.g., Jeremias, "Ἰωνᾶς," 409; Marshall, *Luke,* 485; Bayer, *Jesus' Predictions,* 138; Mora, *Signe,* 40–41.

49   Cf. above, n. 36.

50   While the sailors (*Pirqe R. El.* 10 = Str–B 1.646) and Jonah's οἰκεῖοι (3 Macc. 6.8) become aware of Jonah's rescue, the Ninevites never do. Nor is Bayer's reminder helpful (*Jesus' Predictions,* 135) that Ninevah means "fish," that it has a fish as a coat of arms and was founded by a fish god. "The tale of a sojourn in the belly of a fish must have proven most overwhelming to the Ninevites"! However, neither the Old Testament text nor the Jewish tradition seems to be aware of this fact that is of such interest to a student of local color.

51   Thus Anton Vögtle, "Der Spruch vom Jonaszeichen," 130.

52   Is it correct for Q, where Luke 12:31-32 was added? Thus, e.g., Mora, *Signe,* 57–69: The sign of Jonah will be that in the judgment the risen Son of Man will make the converted Gentiles accusers of this generation.

53   E.g., Bultmann, *History,* 117–18; Tödt, *Son of Man,* 53; Lührmann, *Redaktion,* 40; Sato, *"Q,"* 283.

54   Cf. Isa 8:18; Ezek 12:6; *Jub.* 4.24.

55   In my judgment we could solve this problem only if we assume with Higgins (*Son of Man,* 103) that Luke 11:32 explains exactly this incongruence: ("here is more than Jonah," viz., the Son of Man–world-judge). However, Luke 11:32 is not an original part of the pericope of the sign of Jonah. Cf. above, n. 8.

56   Sato ("Q," 283) speaks of an intentional inconsistency. Is that a solution born of a predicament? Or may one refer to Tob 14:4, 8 where it is presupposed that the judgment on Ninevah really happened? Cf. Josephus *Ant.* 9.214.

57   It fits the tradition-historical hypothesis 1 favored above. In this case the parallel to Luke 17:24, 26-27, 28-30 is only formal.

58   Cf. above on Jesus' understanding of 11:16-19.

59   According to 12:36 κρίσις means the last judgment.

60   The issue is not, as, e.g., in Mark 14:57, the rising up to bring an accusation in a court of law (contra

God's behalf or with God.[61] Similar to Matt 8:11-12 and 11:21-24, what is shocking is that Israel's expectation is reversed. The gentile Ninevites assume the place of the righteous, while this generation of Israel sits in defendant's chair and is condemned.[62] Its guilt consists in, and only in, its rejection of Jesus. The text does not say what the "more" is that happens with Jesus in comparison to the proclamation of Jonah. The church's interpretation thought here of a number of things: Jonah is prophet, Christ is Messiah and Son of God; Christ has performed miracles, Jonah has not; Jonah remained alive in the sea monster, Christ died in the heart of the earth; Jonah preached to the Ninevites only once, Christ to Israel countless times.[63] None of this is wrong; what is most important is that Matthew does not formulate here a "dogmatic" christological sentence but points "openly" to what in Christ happens with Israel. Israel could experience the "more"; Matthew tells about it in his story. The parallel saying about the queen of the south[64] is reminiscent of 1 Kgs 10:1-13. In the Jewish tradition Solomon is the paradigmatic sage. He knows all proverbs, the demons, nature, even the Torah.[65] Again

the saying leaves room for many considerations about what the "more" with Jesus might be. The usual explanation in the church's interpretation was that Solomon's wisdom is concerned with earthly things, Christ with heavenly ones.[66] Knowledgeable readers will also remember that in 11:28-30 Jesus had taken over the function of divine wisdom,[67] but again that is not emphasized. It is important for the evangelist that in these sayings Gentiles are mentioned twice. Both of them—the Ninevites and the Queen of Sheba—look ahead as a double "signal" to the church's future gentile mission after Easter.[68]

■ 43-45 Matthew concludes the section with the strange saying about the return of the unclean spirits. It is argued whether it was originally an exorcistic instruction[69] or a parable.[70] In my judgment the latter comes not from the text but from the general human need to apply a Bible text ethically and the modern need to remove Jesus as far as possible from historically conditioned exorcistic practices.[71] The text itself contains no indications of an illustrative dimension,[72] but it also con-

BAGD, s.v. ἀνίστημι, 2c) but the general resurrection of the dead, as in Dan 12:2; *1 Enoch* 22; 51.1-2; Rev 20:12, etc. In my view, the variation in v. 42 with ἐγείρω shows that clearly.

61   Dan 7:22, LXX; Wis 3:8; *Jub.* 24.29; *1 Enoch* 95.3, cf. 96.1, 98.12; Str-B 4.1103-4.

62   In great unanimity and contrary to the meaning of κατακρίνω, many exegetes conclude that the Ninevites and the Queen of Sheba will not condemn Israel but simply accuse it; thus Beza, 58 ("*suo . . . exemplo*"); Grotius 1.382–83 (witnesses, accuser). Today, e.g., cf. Allen, 140; Schmid, 215; Eduard Lohse, "Σολομών," *TDNT* 7 (1971) 465; Sand, *Evangelium,* 267; Schnackenburg, 1.114 ("shaming examples"); Verseput, *Rejection,* 268 ("condemn" in quotation marks). God or the Son of Man has to remain the judge! Thus the sharpness of the reversal of the traditional Israelite expectation of judgment is tempered.

63   Cf., e.g., Jerome, 98; Strabo, 128; Lapide, 269.

64   Νότος = יָמִין. Wellhausen (65) points out that our text may be the earliest reference (or the origin) for locating the Queen of Sheba in Yemen.

65   Lohse, "Σολομών," 462–63.

66   See, e.g., Euthymius Zigabenus, 389; Lapide, 270. Zwingli (427) elaborates nicely: While the Queen of Sheba undertook a long journey to Solomon, of

Christ it holds that: "I come to you, I pursue you, I bring you heavenly wisdom, and you despise and reject me."

67   However, the parallel verse 41 shows that this idea is not in the foreground. Jesus is not identified with "prophecy."

68   The church's allegorical interpretation took this up by interpreting the Queen of Sheba as the gentile church, Solomon as Christ (e.g., Origen fr. 277 = 124; Hilary, 12.20 = SC 254.288; similarly Strabo, 128; Thomas Aquinas, *Lectura* no. 1058).

69   Otto Böcher, *Christus Exorcista* (BWANT 96; Stuttgart: Kohlhammer, 1972) 17 ("Summary of ancient demonology").

70   More recently, e.g., Jülicher, *Gleichnisreden* 2.238; Bultmann, *History,* 164; Jeremias, *Parables,* 197–98.

71   J. Weiss (331) says engagingly, e.g., "that these things have for him (*scil.,* Jesus) just as much reality as the children's playing. . . . Also a certain mocking tone is unavoidable"!

72   Grotius (1.383) regards the text not as a parable but as a picture-like logion with a moral meaning. Cf. 2 Peter 2:20; Dio Chrysostom *Or.* 5.22 = 94D (at the cleansing of the soul which is like a place filled with evil beasts [= lusts], it happens that when people relax their efforts they are overwhelmed and destroyed by the remaining lusts). Apart from the

tains no instruction for performing exorcisms.[73] Thus it may have been originally a piece of exorcistic folk wisdom, a "demonological" formulation of the experience that every relapse into illness is worse than its first phase,[74] and, connected with it, an expression of the fear of the return of evil spirits. Our text may already have been interpreted as an illustration in Q, following the call to decision in Luke 11:23. With Christ there are only *total* decisions and no halfway measures, no neutrality,[75] no "empty spaces."[76] It is clear that for Matthew the text is a parable, applicable to "this evil generation" (end of v. 45).

We look first at the image. It is based on the widespread concept that the "possessed person" is a house of demons or of the devil.[77] An exorcised demon is homeless, it wanders about in uninhabited places, and—thus Matthew formulates in an uncanny remembrance of 11:29—it "finds no rest." If on returning to its old home it finds the house uninhabited,[78] swept, and decorated (the first participle notes the presupposition for reoccupying the house, the second and the third describe how attractive it is in contrast to the waterless desert), the demon will return with seven others, that is, a superior demonic force,[79] and again occupy its old dwelling, so that it is now worse than ever for the one who was tem-porarily healed. The evangelist applies this scope to the "evil" generation of Israel that rejects Jesus. His goal is clear. If they reject Jesus, it will be worse for Israel than before. According to vv. 41-42 Matthew is thinking of the last judgment. There will be repeated references to it in his story, such as the announcement of the destruction of Jerusalem as the king's punishment for rejecting Jesus' messengers in the parable of the wedding feast (22:7) or the terrible story of the death of Judas (27:3-9). At the present, however, none of that has become reality, but Jesus' efforts to win Israel continue. Still, the reader of the gospel knows that Jesus' predictions will come true and that therefore the signs for Israel indicate that a storm is approaching. The catastrophic end of "this generation" is foreshadowed.

History of Interpretation

The text does not permit a thoroughgoing *salvation-history allegorizing*, such as later became customary. Thus attempts were made to determine more closely when Israel's demons were cast out. Was it the time of Moses in the wilderness,[80] the "purifying" time of the exile,[81] or the present, viz., Israel's generally positive response to John the Baptist and, in the beginning, also to Jesus?[82] None of these possibilities is convincing. Also arbitrary in terms of the text and not suggested by available metaphors is the widespread interpretation of the "waterless places" as

---

fact that in Jewish thought the demons also cause vices (sources in Gnilka 1.467), the text offers no basis for an ethical interpretation.

73 As, e.g., Josephus *Ant.* 8.47 (μηκετ᾿ εἰς αὐτὸν ἐπαν-ήξειν); Mark 9:25 (μηκέτι εἰσέλϑῃι εἰς αὐτόν); cf. on this Pesch, *Markusevangelium*, 2.94.

74 Wettstein 1.397. Cf. also the Arabic proverbs in Bultmann, *History,* 164.

75 Kloppenborg, *Formation,* 127.

76 Gnilka, 1.469 (on Matthew). Schulz (*Q,* 479) sees in the Q text a devaluation of Jewish exorcists who do not cast out the demons eschatologically, i.e., they do it only temporarily. However, Matt 12:27 par. does not make that distinction.

77 *T. Naph.* 8:6 (the devil inhabits the evil person); *b. Hul.* 105b; *b. Git.* 52a = Str–B 1.652. Cf. also the NT statements of the indwelling of the Spirit of God: Rom 8:9; 1 Cor 6:19; Eph 2:21-22. The closest parallel is the late *Midr. Prov.* 24:31 (quoted according to Kloppenborg, *Formation,* 127): "A king went into the steppe and found dining rooms and large rooms and dwelt in them. Thus it is with the evil impulse:

if it does not find the words of the Law ruling (in the heart), you cannot drive it out of your heart."

78 Σχολάζω (to have leisure for) with places = to be empty.

79 Euthymius Zigabenus, 389; Maldonat, 281: "*Septem . . . pro multis.*" *T. Reub.* 2.1–3.8 speaks of the seven spirits of the senses and the corresponding seven spirits of error.

80 Thus the normal type of church interpretation since Jerome, 99; Hilary, 12.22 = SC 254.290, 292; Apollinaris of Laodicea fr. 74 = Reuss, 22; Cyril of Alexandria fr. 163 = Reuss, 205–6.

81 Thus in modern times, e.g., in Grotius 1.384–85; Wolzogen, 294; Olshausen, 469.

82 See, e.g., Zahn, 472; Plummer, 184 (John the Baptist); Gaechter, 420; Rinaldo Fabris, *Matteo* (Commenti Biblici; Rome: Borla, 1982) 284. The difficulty with this interpretation, which still is the most likely, is that Jesus has just presupposed his own ministry in Israel in v. 43a, and already in the first main clause of the "parable" in v. 43b he speaks of the demon wandering in the waterless

referring to the Gentiles or to the individual Gentile.[83]

The history of interpretation shows in a depressing way how each announcement of judgment is perverted as soon as it becomes a contemplation of the judgment that came over others by those who themselves are not affected by it. It was particularly bad for the "heretics" of all kinds who—once having deserted the recognized truth—became hopelessly possessed and incurably lost.[84] This text has especially been interpreted in a massively anti-Jewish and anti-Semitic manner. We cite two especially depressing testimonies from the rather lengthy gallery of anti-Jewish witnesses. In his first sermon about the Jews John Chrysostom begins with this text and warns his Christians:

> Thus you gather with possessed people, with people in whom so many unclean spirits live, with people who have been raised among murders and destruction, and you are not overcome with horror? Should you greet them and speak with them or should you not rather flee from them as from disease and pestilence of the whole earth? For what vices have they not committed? How often and how long have they not been accused by the prophets?[85]

To these words we add a modern interpretation: "After their return (*scil.*, from the exile), the Jews appear in greater purity than they ever did before. But instead of idolatry the more dangerous Pharisaism returned; and this was, after all, the same spirit of idolatry in different forms."[86] Jülicher already has said what is necessary on this matter: "Poor taste" that, as he believes, "is not Matthew's fault."[87]

In my judgment, more positive theological powers of the text appear in another branch of the history of interpretation. It was able to be interpreted not only in salvation history but also in *individual parenetic* terms. Then the unclean spirit is sin, and the house is the human heart.[88] The text then becomes a warning to the church: A relapse into one's earlier sin is the worst thing that can happen.[89] The higher one is, for example, as a priest or a monk, the deeper one can fall.[90] Zwingli sums up: "Thus the one whom Christ has once rescued by his grace from Satan's bonds must be alert and must pray intensively that he is not overtaken again by his former vices and come into temptation. Satan does not sleep."[91] "This evil generation" becomes here "productive" as a negative example against which the church should actively and effectively protect itself. Thus the church still faces the obstacle of Israel. This dimension of the history of interpretation is in complete harmony with what Matthew does—while not in this text, in the whole of his gospel—with the negative example of Israel.

Summary

■ **38-45** Does Matthew not share some of the guilt for the harsh anti-Jewish and antiheretical consequences of his text? His Christ narrative appears to be headed toward a catastrophe of which it can only be asked whether it is a catastrophe for all Israel or only for its leaders and whether it is a total catastrophe of Israel or only of the "evil generation" of that day. The reason for this catastrophe is that Matthew can conceive of a no to Christ, the Son of God promised by the prophets, only as a guilty no. Jesus' miracles among his people were for Matthew so obvious that one cannot reject them without guilt.[92] If in addition the Jewish leaders still demand a "sign" that makes God's activity in Jesus even clearer, then they become tempters (16:1) and thus guilty. Jesus

wilderness, something that cannot be interpreted allegorically at all.

83 See, e.g., Hilary, 12.22–23 = SC 254. 293; Anselm of Laon, 1367; Dionysius the Carthusian, 158.

84 Maldonat, 261: The worst heretics are those who fell away from the Catholic faith; the worst Catholics are the monks who deserted their order; Lapide (271) is thinking of the apostate Judas Iscariot and later apostates from Nestorius and Pelagius down to Luther and Menno Simons.

85 *Hom. adv. Jud.* 1.6 = *PG* 48.852.

86 Olshausen, 469.

87 Jülicher, *Gleichnisreden*, 2.237.

88 Formulated classically already by Valentinus in Clement of Alexandria *Strom.* 2.114.3–6 = FC 85.232: With the heart it is much as it is with an inn

that all kinds of people treat disrespectfully, because the house does not belong to them. "The heart also, unless it takes care in advance, experiences something similar, being unpurified and a home for many spiritual powers."

89 Since Jerome (100) an "entry" for the parenetic interpretation was the interpretation of the seven spirits as the seven cardinal vices. Examples for the parenetic interpretation: John Chrysostom, 43.4 = *PG* 57.461 referring to John 5:14 ("sin no more so that even worse things will not happen to you"); Augustine *Quaest.* 1.8 = 12 (*cupiditas, neglegentia*); Euthymius Zigabenus, 392; Theophylactus, 276.

90 Augustine according to Maldonat, 261.

91 Zwingli, 297.

92 Cf. the summary on 12:22-37, above.

can respond to such an unreasonable demand only by announcing the "sign" of cross and resurrection. It is the last, deepest sign of God for salvation even for Israel, but it does not make God unambiguous and at one's disposal. Matthew looks back on the rest of Israel's history with Jesus; this showed him that deepest sign and how in Israel God's last sign of salvation became a sign of disaster.

Precisely this is Matthew's accusation against Israel and—even more than his—of some parts of the later history of interpretation through which they themselves become guilty. Why? In their history the Christians have taken possession of God's sign of grace, which consists in the death and resurrection of Jesus, and have made of it a sign of destruction that demonstrates Israel's ruin. However, a "sign" that in this way puts God at one's disposal is part of what Jesus rejected when it was demanded of him. For Zwingli in his interpretation of our text the word was the most powerful sign. "Those who demand signs after the truth is proclaimed show that in reality they resist the truth."[93] The history of our text's influence teaches that the word of proclamation also can become a misused sign, viz., when it is no longer received as a gift but becomes a possession, a theological position by means of which one can condemn others. Then the sign refused by Jesus, or the paradoxical sign that consists of Jesus' dying and rising, becomes a "known" sign, a theological standard that even decides where the demons are most destructive. Matthew already moved in this wrong direction by reinterpreting christologically Jesus' "non-sign" and especially by interpreting Jesus' resurrection, similar to his miracles, as a public sign from God, whose rejection by the Jews demonstrates the height of their maliciousness.[94] In my judgment, today we must, contrary to Matthew, explore the hiddenness even of the resurrection of Jesus that remains a miracle available to no one—not even, indeed, especially not, to faith.[95] Or, expressed in terms of tradition history: While the issue for Matthew was to interpret the *paradoxical sign of Jonah as the resurrection of Jesus*, today's issue must be to interpret anew the *resurrection of Jesus* as a *paradoxical "sign of Jonah" that is not at our disposal*—that is, as a gift of God that remains *his* gift and *his* mystery. Christologically that means for me that the majesty of God is so deeply hidden in the human and crucified Son of God that the only response to the guilt of the human refusal to recognize God in Christ can be a renewed proclamation of grace. With Matthew, however, there is a limit to grace, as there also is in the church's interpretation, where the sign of the resurrection that the church possesses becomes the canon of its judgment on Israel or on heretics. Here we must ask whether someday the Son of Man, in the light of this church that possesses the signs, will reverse the Christian expectations of judgment[96] so that in the last judgment, for example, Jews will assume the role of the Ninevites, and the Christians, who for so long possessed the Jonah sign of the resurrection, will be condemned on the basis of what they have done with this sign.

---

93   Zwingli, 294–95.
94   Cf. the interpretation of 27:62-66; 28:11-15.
95   A marginal comment of Rudolf Schnackenburg: "The resurrection of Jesus remains a mystery under the cover of faith."
96   Cf. above on vv. 41-42.

2.3 Jesus' True Family (12:46-50)

Literature

Agostino Ceruti, "L'interpretazione del testo di S. Matteo 12,46-50 nei Padri," *Marianum* 19 (1957) 185–221.

For *additional literature* see above, III A 2 on Matt 12:22-50.

46   **While he was still speaking to the crowds, behold, his mother and his brothers stood outside wanting to speak to him. 47/ But someone said to him: "Behold, your mother and your brothers are standing outside wanting to speak to you."[1]**

48   **But he answered and said to the one who had told him:**
        "Who is my mother? And who are my brothers?"

49   **And he held his hand over his disciples and said:**
        "Behold, here is my mother and my brothers!

50   **For whoever does the will of my father in heaven, that one is my brother and sister and mother."**

Analysis

Structure

The short text is quite stereotypical. After a brief connection to the preceding unit in v. 46a, μήτηρ and ἀδελφοί with possessive pronouns are repeated five times, ἰδού three times, ἔξω (ἔστηκα), ζητοῦντες . . . λαλῆσαι and the question τίς ἐστιν (τίνες εἰσίν) twice. Between them are short introductions to the direct speech around which our pericope is structured. Verse 46 is exposition, the information to Jesus follows in v. 47 that in turn is followed in vv. 48-50 by Jesus' answer, that, as is often the case in apothegms, dominates. It begins with a question, is interrupted

with a gesture of Jesus, and ends in v. 50 with a general concluding sentence. There remain finally two brief sentences that are not repeated. Precisely for that reason the reader notices them: "and he held his hand over his disciples" (v. 49a) and: "The one who does the will of my father in heaven . . ." (v. 50a). We noted the first sentence already, because of the gesture that interrupted Jesus' answer. The second is a general response that goes beyond the concrete situation. The emphasis of the pericope is on these two brief sentences.

Source and Redaction

Matthew has created this tight form by rigorously shortening the much more lively story in Mark 3:31-35. He omitted everything that did not fit into his formal scheme (Mark 3:31b, 32a, 34a). Almost all his linguistic changes correspond to his redactional style.[2] Two minor agreements are difficult.[3] Only ἐκτείνας τὴν χεῖρα ("and he held his hand") in v. 49a is linguistically unusual, but it has an exact parallel in 14:31.

Interpretation

■ **46** While Jesus is still speaking to the crowds, whom the evangelist last mentioned in v. 23,[4] something new takes place. Jesus' mother and brothers[5] are standing "outside." Since nothing was previously said of a house, the location is left hanging; not until 13:1 will Matthew refer again to the house.[6] "Outside" evokes for the reader the impression of a distance between Jesus and

---

1   Verse 47 is missing in ℵ B and other witnesses. Verse 48 probably presupposes the verse. I am more inclined to think that an erroneous omission occurred through haplography rather than that an original short version of the text was expanded on the basis of the parallels.

2   Verse 46: the genitive absolute is rare in Matthew, but ἔτι αὐτοῦ λαλοῦντος is a biblicism (about 12 times in the LXX) and also an unused leftover from Mark 5:35; cf. Matt 17:5; 26:47 (= Mark). Verse 49: on ἐκτείνας τὴν χεῖρα cf. 8:3; 12:13; 14:31 (redaction), different in content is 26:51; the expression comes from the LXX. On ὄχλοι, ἰδού (after the genitive absolute: Schenk, *Sprache*, 297), ὁ δὲ ἀποκριθεὶς εἶπεν, μαθηταί, θέλημα (πατρός), πατὴρ . . . ἐν τοῖς οὐρανοῖς cf. vol. 1, Introduction 3.2.

3   Ἑστήκασιν in v. 47c may be Matthean redaction (repetition of v. 46c) but hardly Lukan redaction; ὁ δὲ ἀποκριθεὶς εἶπεν in v. 48a is good Matthean style but hardly Lukan. The remaining minor agree-

ments are not significant or can be explained from the redaction.

4   On the basis of 12:23 the crowds neither prefigure the gentile church (thus Gundry, 248) nor are they the evangelist's indirect attempt to present all of the people, together with the Pharisees and scribes, as "this evil generation" (thus Verseput, *Rejection*, 283); they are relatively neutral, not (yet) followers of Jesus.

5   Of course, the question of Jesus' siblings has engaged the history of interpretation for this text also. For now we will set it aside (cf. below, History of Interpretation on 13:53-58).

6   Perhaps for Matthew the house did not suit the ὄχλοι as hearers. Cf. 13:36.

his relatives—an impression that the brief narrative will confirm. They want to speak to him. Matthew formulates their intention neutrally and blandly after he omits the strong Markan statement that Jesus' family wants to take home their "crazy" son (Mark 3:21). Thus the issue here is not a polemic against Jesus' family.[7]

■ **47-49** Someone tells Jesus what has happened. The repetition has a *ritardando* effect; it increases the tension. Jesus responds with a question. He asks the obvious: Who are my mother and my brothers? What looks to be obvious increases the surprise that his answer brings. It is introduced with a gesture. Jesus stretches out his hand over his disciples. The appearance of the disciples is a surprise to the reader; they have not been mentioned since v. 2 and are not really needed in this pericope. With Jesus' gesture Matthew calls special attention to them. In the tradition the gesture of stretching out the hand has many connotations. It can indicate the need for help (cf. 12:13), hostility (cf. 26:51), attention,[8] including God's attention,[9] or—very frequently in the LXX—his power and his judgment.[10] In Matthew it indicates in the healing narrative of 8:1-4 Jesus' loving and powerful attention to the sick person (8:3),[11] in the symbol-laden story of the sinking Peter his protective power (14:31). In our story also it is probably not simply that on the surface Jesus points to the disciples,[12] but rather that the disciples stand under the protection of their Lord.[13] Thus v. 49 describes as it were the "indicative" side of the disciples' life. They stand under the protection of the one who is with them always until the end of the world (28:20). Matthew reinterprets the Markan peri-

cope that spoke here of all the people (Mark 3:32a, 34a) and makes of it a paradigmatic portrayal of *discipleship*. The disciples, not those who stand outside, are Jesus' "mother" and "brothers." For ἀδελφός he makes use of an expanded meaning of the word. For Jews "brother" is one who belongs to the nation of Israel; for Christians it refers to a member of the community. Surprising is only that Jesus speaks of the disciples as "my" brothers. However, designating the disciples as Jesus' brothers is peculiar to Matthew (28:10, cf. 25:40; 23:8).[14] With "my mother" there is no expanded meaning in the current usage of which the evangelist can make use. Here the story he received had the effect of creating language. Obviously the mother of Jesus, accompanied by her sons, has come looking for Jesus, while his sisters, according to custom, stayed at home.[15] Expanding the meaning of "mother" was made possible on the one hand by the early tendency to understand the church as "family," where there were, infrequently enough, also mothers (Mark 10:30; Rom 16:13; 1 Tim 5:2), and on the other hand probably by the women in the churches who could identify with this term. Still, "sister," also used by Matthew in v. 50, is a more appropriate term.[16] In short, the true family of Jesus is his church that stands under his protection.

■ **50** Verse 50 goes further and extends the focus beyond the time of Jesus. Everyone who does the will of the Father belongs to Jesus' family. Two things are impor-

---

7   Thus Pesch (*Markusevangelium,* 1.224) for the original pericope.

8   See, e.g., Gen 48:14 (blessing); *Jos. Asen.* 12.8; 19.10.

9   Adam and Eve 37.4.

10 The LXX especially in Ezekiel but also in Jeremiah and Zephaniah.

11 Cf. n. 12 on 8:1-4.

12 Thus BAGD, *s.v.* ἐκτείνω, 1.

13 The LXX, by whose language Matthew is influenced, uses the prepositions with ἐκτείνω τὴν χεῖρα very consciously. While πρός almost always means the gesture of prayer to God, ἐπί is used when a mighty one (God, Moses, Aaron, the king) stretches out his hand. Ἐπί designates then the realm over which the mighty one has power (e.g., the sea, the land of Egypt, the inhabitants of the

land, a people); sometimes it tends to have the meaning "against."

14 Outside of Matthew, in the gospels only in John 20:17. Cf. in addition Rom 8:29; Heb 2:11-12.

15 Of course, it also corresponds to the underlying event that "father" is missing. Joseph, the father of Jesus, probably died early. This also corresponds to the theological language of Matthew: God alone is father (cf. 23:9 and also the negative finding in Mark 10:30).

16 Ἀδελφή appeared already in Mark 3:35 but not in Mark 3:32 where in my judgment only a Western variant is present, with Metzger (*Commentary,* 82, additional comment). Μήτηρ is put last in v. 50 because the women had been mentioned with ἀδελφή, scarcely because Mary already enjoyed a

tant in this "definition"[17] of being a disciple. In the first place, Matthew here makes clear the second, the "imperative" side of being a disciple. To be a disciple of Jesus means to do the will of the heavenly Father that Jesus has proclaimed. Jesus himself lived this will as an example (26:42). The church prays for it in the Lord's Prayer (6:10); it is the mission proclamation of the community (cf. 28:20), and someday the Son of Man will base his judgment on it (7:21-23). To be a Christian means obedience, action. However, the obedience is not simply to a heteronomous power but to the Father who is with his Son (1:23) and in him with his church (28:20). The content of the will of the Father has its center in love, that is, in the relationship of the members of the community to one another as brother, sister, and mother. In the second place, the time structure of discipleship is important. To be a disciple is on the one hand to be with Jesus and to stand under his protection. This is where the emphasis lies in v. 49, and this also maintains the continuing tie to the past history of Jesus. On the other hand, discipleship happens in the present, where obedience toward the will of the Father is to shine (cf. 5:16). That is brought to expression in the general formulation of v. 50.

Summary and History of Interpretation[18]

As is often the case, the significance of our story lies on two levels. On one level it depends "narratologically" on its position in the gospel. After Jesus' long judgment discourse on Israel in 12:22-45, Matthew wanted to present a positive countermodel. In this sense the structure of 12:22-50 corresponds to that of 11:7-30 with its positive concluding text, 11:25-30. Through the activity of Jesus, his true family, the church, has come into existence in Israel, while the other part of Israel is heading for destruction. Thus in several onsets, Matthew describes in chaps. 11–12 the division that came about as a result of Jesus' activity in Israel.

> In the history of interpretation this level of meaning has found its continuation in the ancient church's so-called mystical interpretation, that is, in the *salvation-history allegory*. Jesus' mother and brothers "in the flesh" represent here Israel or the synagogue; "outside" means outside the church.[19] With different accents and in different categories this interpretation takes up something of what Matthew wanted to say in the framework of his entire story. However, the church's allegorization was no more interested in disparaging the family of Jesus than was Matthew.

At the same time our story makes a "direct" statement for the present. It too becomes clearer from the history of interpretation.

> The history of the text's interpretation dealt primarily not with its positive but with its *negative* statement. The issue for the interpretation was why Jesus "slaps in the face" his own family and especially "his dear mother, the holy virgin."[20] It was increasingly difficult to harmonize this with the church's positive family ethics and especially with the increasing veneration of Mary. Gnostics, Marcionites, and later Manichaeans found in our text proof that Jesus was not born of earthly parents, that is, of the flesh.[21] Tertullian correctly points out that the birth of Jesus is not at issue here. For him the unbelief of the family of Jesus—not only of his brothers but at that time also of his mother—is the decisive reason for Jesus' negative response.[22] In a somewhat weaker form John Chrysostom and interpreters who follow him criticize Mary and the family of Jesus. They show vanity ($\kappa\varepsilon\nu o\delta o\xi\iota\alpha$), pride ($\varphi\iota\lambda o\tau\iota\mu\iota\alpha$), lack of understanding, and obtrusiveness. They cannot wait until Jesus has finished his sermon, and they want to demonstrate their

special esteem at that time (thus Schnackenburg 1.116).

17 Trilling, *Israel*, 30.

18 On the history of interpretation in the ancient church, cf. the beautiful essay by Agostino Ceruti ("L'interpretazione del testo di S. Matteo 12,46-50 nei Padri," 185–221), a summary of his dissertation that was not available to me: "L'interpretazione del testo Mt 12,46-50 nei Padri" (Rome, 1950).

19 Already Tertullian *Carn.* 7 = CSEL 70.212, and Origen fr. 281 = 126 (the soul that gives birth to the will of the father is Christ's mother); in addition,

e.g., Jerome, 101; Hilary, 12.24 = SC 254.295; Gregory the Great *Hom. in ev.* 3.1–2 = *PL* 76.1086.

20 Luther 2.459 (= Sermon from 1528).

21 Reported by Tertullian *Carn.* 7 = CSEL 70.208–11; *Marc.* 4.19.6–13 = CSEL 47.482–83; Augustine *Faust.* 7 = CSEL 25.302–05; Ephraem Syrus, 201. There are also the church's echoes of this interpretation, viz., wherever the divinity of Jesus is especially emphasized, e.g., *Opus imperfectum* 30 = 791: *Nescio parentes in mundo.*

22 Tertullian *Carn.* 7 = CSEL 70.211; *Marc.* 4.19.13 = CSEL 47.481; indirectly also Ambrose *In Luc.* 6.37 =

authority over Jesus before all the people.[23] For Augustine and others the issue is that a "*carnalis affectus*" must never hinder Jesus' spiritual works or his own mission.[24] Jesus shows here that he is faithful to his own word, Matt 10:37.[25] Since the end of the ancient period the antithesis "fleshly-spiritual" dominates the history of interpretation.[26] "Spiritual" relatives of Jesus are those who do God's will. The relationship of spiritual to bodily kinship is not antithetical but comparative, and the former is to be preferred.[27] Since Augustine's day, among Jesus' spiritual relatives are Mary, the exemplary obedient one,[28] or also the brothers of Jesus, who in reality with all good intention wanted to free Jesus from the hands of his opponents, the Pharisees.[29] Thus every shadow is removed from the holy family.

On this point the Reformation meant a freedom to be able to see again the *positive* statement in the text. Zwingli observes a greater freedom among the ancients to speak of the weaknesses of the saints than in his own day, "when we today regard the saints as gods."[30] Especially impressive is Luther's interpretation, whose veneration for Mary is certainly beyond dispute. For him the issue of our text is putting obedience toward God over all "authority, father and mother, indeed even (the) Christian church."[31] Musculus formulates the *parenetic* scope of our story: "Do not believe that this beatitude refers only to the disciples. . . . For *everyone* who does the will of my father in heaven is himself my brother, my sister and mother. Therefore, if you also do this, you also will be brother, sister, and mother to Christ."[32]

Musculus has captured exactly what the text wanted to say directly to the Christian churches in their own time: "You also" have the chance to become Jesus' sister or brother! Thus the text does not statically contrast the church with the Pharisees; instead the scope is parenetic. The new "definition" of Jesus' family challenges the church to do the will of the Father. However, the parenetic scope contains at the same time an element of grace and of promise. The disciples stand under Jesus' protective hand. To do the will of the Father means the chance to be close to the Lord. Protected and obedient, his disciples are no longer strangers; they are "neighbors": brothers, sisters, mothers.

BKV 1/21.581: They should not have stayed outside!

23   John Chrysostom, 44.1 = *PG* 57.464–65; Euthymius Zigabenus, 392–93; Theophylactus, 276 ("φιλόδοξος . . . καὶ ἀνθρωπίνη γνώμη"); Peter of Laodicea, 144.

24   Augustine *Sermo* 25.3 on Matt 12:41-50 = *PL* 46.934 with the often useful admonition "audiant matres, ne impediant carnali affectu bona opera filiorum."

25   Basil *Regulae brevius* 188 = *PG* 31.1207; Ambrose *In Luc.* 6.36 = BKV 1/21.581; Jerome *Ep.*14 (*ad Heliodorum*) 3 = NPNF second series 6.14.

26   See, e.g., Thomas Aquinas, *Lectura* no. 1075 (*generatio caelestis*); Dionysius the Carthusian, 159 (*conceptio spiritualis*); Lapide, 272.

27   See, e.g., Origen fr. 282 = 126; Ambrose *In Luc.* 6.38 = BKV 1/21.582; Anselm of Laon, 1368; Bengel, 144.

28   Augustine *Joh. ev. tract.* 10.3 = NPNF 7.70. 170; idem *Sct. virg.* 3.5 = CSEL 44.237, 239; *Opus imperfectum* 30 = 791.

29   Lapide, 272.

30   Zwingli, 297.

31   Luther 2.462. In Luther's interpretation the question of Mary's "vindication" is no longer asked.

32   Musculus, 355.

B   The Parables Discourse (13:1-53)

Literature

Burchard, "Senfkorn," 5-35.

D. A. Carson, "The ὅμοιος Word-Group as Introduction to some Matthean Parables," *NTS* 31 (1985) 277-82.

Crossan, "Seed Parables," 244-66.

Dahl, "Parables," 132-66.

Denis, "Parabels," 274-88.

Dupont, "Point de vue," 221-59.

Friedrich, "Wortstatistik," 29-46.

Gerhardsson, "Seven Parables," 16-37.

Kingsbury, *Parables*.

Krämer, "Parabelrede," 31-53.

Lambrecht, "Parables," 25-47.

Louis Marin, "Essai d'analyse structurale d'un récit-parabole. Matthieu 13,1-23," *EThR* 46 (1971) 35-74.

Christian Mellon, "La Parabole: Manière de parler, manière d'entendre," *RechSR* 61 (1973) 49-63.

Gary A. Phillips, "History and Text: The Reader in Context in Matthew's Parables Discourse," in SBLSP 1983, 415-37 (= *Semeia* 31 [1985] 111-38).

Jean Pirot, *Paraboles et allégories Évangéliques* (Paris: Lethielleux, 1949) 91-160.

du Plessis, "Meaning," 33-56.

Schweizer, "Sondertradition," 98-105.

Segbroeck, "Scandale," 344-72.

W. Vorster, "The Structure of Matthew 13," *Neot* 11 (1977) 130-38.

Stephen L. Wailes, *Medieval Allegories of Jesus' Parables* (Berkeley: University of California Press, 1987).

Weder, *Gleichnisse*, 99-147.

David Wenham, "The Structure of Matthew 13," *NTS* 25 (1978/79) 516-22.

Wilkens, "Redaktion," 305-27.

Position in the Gospel

As with the other discourses, Matthew's narrative is not advanced by this discourse; instead, at its conclusion the narrative thread takes up exactly where it left off.[1] In that sense, this discourse is also a manifesto to the readers that interrupts the narrative. However, it has one peculiarity that distinguishes it from all other discourses: It is repeatedly interrupted by statements about the situation and by new beginnings (vv. 10-11a, 24aα, 31aα, 33aα, 34-37aα, 51-52aα). Sometimes it is addressed to the people, sometimes to the disciples. Jesus carries on brief scholarly dialogues with the disciples. Thus in a very special way this discourse is itself a narrative. Even provisional observations indicate that these statements about the situation and new beginnings are important to the evangelist: the information about the place in 13:1—"Jesus comes out of the house"—and about the hearers in 13:2—"large crowds gathered around him"—appears suddenly without any advance preparation, or it is redundant and is thus obtrusive for the readers.[2] Equally important then are changes in the persons addressed and the location in v. 10 and v. 36 that refer to vv. 1-2. The "speaking in parables" (v. 3a) also appears again later (vv. 10, 34-35).

Correspondingly, the preceding narrative section prepares almost exclusively for the discourse's situational intervening texts, and in the following section it is almost exclusively those that leave an echo. In 13:34-35 the readers remember the negative part of Jesus' cry of jubilation: "You have hidden it from the wise and understanding" (11:25). That the disciples understand or should understand is not only a main theme of the parables discourse; it is also recalled in the following narrative section (16:12; 17:13, cf. 15:10). The Pharisees, on the other hand, "heard the word," but "were offended" at it (15:12, cf. 13:19, 21, 23). By contrast, the connection of the discourse's *content* with the context is weak. It is especially important that—unlike Mark 3:23—the keyword παραβολαί ("parables") has not previously been used. The speaking ἐν παραβολαῖς (vv. 3, 10, 13, 34-35) is completely new. While the "message of the kingdom of Heaven" has been proclaimed (4:17, 23; 9:35; cf. 10:7), the kingdom of heaven itself was never the subject of the reflection. Also new is the theme of understanding.[3] Nor had Matthew mentioned previously the hardening of the hearts (unlike Mark 3:5).

---

1   With the catchwords μήτηρ, ἀδελφοί, ἀδελφαί 13:53-58 is directly linked with 12:46-50. The hostile Nazarenes and the family of Jesus belong together. The problem becomes clearest in people's attitude to Jesus: positive both in chaps. 11-12 and chaps. 14-16, while in the parables discourse itself the people do not understand and are hardened. Cf. in addition below on the summary of the parables discourse (Basic Message of the Parables Discourse) and III C (Jesus' Withdrawal from Israel and the Origin of the Church).

2   Cf. below on 13:2.

3   Συνίημι: keyword in Matt 13 (six times); prior to chap. 13: never.

In short, the parables discourse is structured as a narrative, even though it does not advance the main thread of Matthew's story. What position then does this curious "narrative within the narrative" hold in the total gospel? We must wait for the interpretation to answer the question.[4]

According to Kingsbury, Matthew 13 is the "turning point" of the entire Gospel of Matthew.[5] After the Jews have rejected Jesus as the Messiah and inaugurator of God's eschatological kingdom in chaps. 11–12, in chap. 13 Jesus turns against them. He asserts that they are blind and without understanding (13:13), and he now turns to his disciples, the church (cf. especially 13:36-37). This interpretation agrees with the basic meaning of 13:36 as the decisive break within the parables discourse. What speaks against it, however, is that already in 12:22-45, indeed even in 11:16-24, judgment was the dominant theme. After the turning point nothing has changed. In chap. 13 Jesus still addresses the people, and they are still open toward him. In Matthew the turning point obviously takes place in stages; Furthermore, the discourse of chap. 13 is not simply an "ordinary" part of the gospel's narrative thread.

Structure

Types

Scholarship has not arrived at a unanimous presentation of the structure of Matthew 13. If we base the arrangement primarily on formal criteria,[6] there are three basic types.

1. A *two-part model with a caesura after v. 23*.[7] The chapter then consists of two parallel parts with the following structure: public teaching in parables (vv. 3-9, 24-33); purpose of parables (vv. 10-17, 34-35); interpretation of parables for the disciples [with further parables] (vv. 18-23, 36-52).[8]

2. A *two-part model with a caesura at v. 36*.[9] Then the chapter consists of a public teaching in parables at the lake—that, however, is interrupted in vv. 10-23 by an instruction for the disciples—and an instruction of the disciples in the house.[10]

3. A *model of inclusion*.[11] The introductory and concluding notes, vv. 2, 53 and vv. 3-9, 51-52, the only two parables that do *not* deal with the kingdom of heaven,[12] provide the framework.[13] A number of advocates of this model do not carry it out consistently but see two parallel strands within the inclusion, each of which contains a disciples instruction on the meaning of the parables (10-17, 34-36), an interpretation of a parable for the disciples (18-23, 37-43), and three parables (24-33, 44-50).[14]

Narrative Interruptions

For the disposition we must take into account the discourse's two large narrative interruptions, vv. 10-11a and vv. 34-37a. They are connected with a change of hearers; the second interruption also brings a change in location. In addition, the new narrative beginnings

---

4   Cf. below, the summary at the conclusion of III B on the basic message of the parables discourse, esp. A: The Parables Discourse as Part of the Jesus Story.

5   Kingsbury, *Parables,* 130.

6   Denis ("Parabels"), e.g., arranges the material in terms of its content: Matthew 13 tells a continuing *story* of the *basileia* from its founding (13:3-23) through its present (13:24-46) to its completion (13:47-50). The difficulties appear in many places. Matthew 13:19-23 (= 3-9), e.g., also speaks of present problems; 13:28-30, 40-43 also speak of the basileia's completion.

7   Segbroeck, "Scandale," 352–54; Dupont, "Point de vue," 231–32; cf. Louis Marin, "Essai d'analyse structurale d'un récit-parabole. Matthieu 13,1-23," *EThR* 46 (1971) 50–54.

8   The most important disadvantages of this model: The break in the narrative in vv. 34-37a is not used effectively. Verses 44-52 are "left hanging."

9   Lohmeyer, 190–91; Wilkens, "Redaktion," passim, esp. 306–7, 319–21, 324–27; Kingsbury, *Parables,* 12–16; W. Vorster, "The Structure of Matthew 13,"

Neot 11 (1977) 130–38; Lambrecht, "Parabels"; Gnilka 1.474–75; Sand, *Evangelium,* 276–77; Burchard, "Senfkorn," 6–19.

10 The most important disadvantage of this model: It is difficult to accommodate the disciples' instruction of vv. 10-23 that is inserted into the first part.

11 David Wenham, "The Structure of Matthew 13," 516–18 (complete model of inclusion: frame parable 3-9, 52; understanding 10-23, 51; three parables 24-33, 44-50; center 34-43); similarly Rainer Riesner, "Der Aufbau der Reden im Matthäus-Evangelium," *ThBei* 9 (1978) 177–78. In both models vv. 18-23 and vv. 37-43 are not easy to accommodate. Similarly Gerhardsson ("Seven Parables," 27) for Matthew.

12 Pointed out by Stanley D. Toussaint, "The Introductory and Concluding Parables of Matthew Thirteen," *BSac* 121 (1964) 351–55.

13 The most important disadvantages of this model: the great narrative interruption, vv. 34-37a, and the different hearers (vv. 24-33: the people; vv. 44-50: the disciples) are not taken seriously enough.

14 Thus France, 216; similarly Gundry, 250–51.

in vv. 24, 31, 33, 51 are important. Numerous stylistic features also indicate a very artful construction. We observe:

1. *Keywords*. "parable": 12 times, 11 of them in vv. 3-36; 5 times "in parables"; "kingdom": 12 times, 8 times with "of the heaven"; "to hear": 13 times, 12 of them in vv. 9-23; "to speak": 6 times in 13:3-34, 13 times in 12:22-13:34; "to understand": 6 times.

2. *Inclusions*. The entire chapter: vv. 3/53 the beginning and end of the parables; vv. 3b-9/52 parables that do not deal with the kingdom of heaven ("parables about parables");[15] vv. 10-23/52 not understanding-understanding. In the first part, vv. 1-36a, there are the following inclusions: vv. 1/36aβ (leaving/entering the house); vv. 2/36aα (the crowd gathers/Jesus leaves the crowd); vv. 3/34 (λαλεῖν . . . ἐν παραβολαῖς . . . [αὐτοῖς]). In the second part, vv. 36b-52, there is an inclusion formed by vv. 40-43/49-50 (interpretations of the parables of the weeds or fishnet, with numerous common formulations).

3. *Repetitions and agreements*. The most important are: vv. 1-3a, 36: introducing the section dealing with the people or the disciples (inclusions at the same time!); vv. 10-11, 36b-37 καὶ προσ(ελθόντες) οἱ μαθηταί . . . ὁ δὲ ἀποκριθεὶς εἶπεν ("and the disciples came . . . but he answered"); vv. 14, 35 introductory phrase for the formula quotation or variation in Jesus' direct address; vv. 24, 31, 33 ἄλλην παραβολὴν παρέθηκεν αὐτοῖς ("he set another parable before them"); vv. 31, 33, 44, 45, 47 ὁμοία ἐστὶν ἡ βασιλεία τῶν οὐρανῶν ("the kingdom of heaven is like . . ."); vv. 9, 43 the call to watchfulness "let the one who has ears hear."

Which structural model best does justice to the evidence? As with the Sermon on the Mount there are many inclusions, but unlike that situation these do not lead to a clear center. In my judgment we must begin with the major narrative interruption of vv. 34-37a, which parallels the introduction to the entire discourse in vv. 1-3a, for the narrative passages determine the direct speech. Thus we begin basically with the second structural model and see in the discourse two main sections: vv. 1-36a and vv. 36b-52, each of which contains four parables.[16] This arrangement is confirmed by the

threefold inclusion around the first main section and the simple inclusion around the second main section. It also fits in with this arrangement that the first main part has its own keywords—"to speak," "to hear," "parable" (λαλέω, ἀκούω, παραβολή), which in the second part are scarcely important at all. Thus chap. 13 is a two-part discourse that is framed in whole and in part by inclusions. The two "marginal parables" of unequal length about understanding parables (vv. 3-23, 51-52) are also part of this arrangement. On both sides of the center, vv. 34-37a, there are two parallel strands, one of which begins with the parable of the weeds, the other with its interpretation (vv. 24-30, 37-43). They are followed by brief parables of the kingdom of God with identical introductions (vv. 31-33, 44-50). The structure of the first main section offers special difficulties. An address to the disciples is inserted into it (vv. 10-23). This insertion ends with the new beginning in v. 24 "and he put another parable before them" that implies that Jesus now is speaking again to "them" (cf. vv. 13, 14), that is, to the crowd. The repetition of this new beginning in vv. 31, 33 is not really necessary, but it serves to hold together the section vv. 24-33.[17]

Unlike the first structural model that favors a parenetic interpretation of the discourse,[18] with our structural model the arrangement of the discourse in Matthew's *story* is basic for the interpretation. The entire discourse reflects how Jesus turns from the people and to the disciples. This happens in two stages, viz., provisionally in vv. 10-23 and definitively in vv. 36-52. In the first instructions to the disciples, Jesus explains why the people, unlike the disciples, do not understand the parables "presented" to them (vv. 10-17). The following explanation of the parable of the fourfold field (vv. 18-23) deepens what it means "not to understand" and "to understand." Obviously bearing fruit is what is decisive for understanding. Matthew concludes Jesus' public address with a formula quotation. That the people do not understand what is hidden is in agreement with the

---

15 Gundry, 250.

16 The much discussed number seven of the Matthean parables came about only because it was not noticed that in Matthew's sense v. 52 is also a parable.

17 In the second part the identical introductions to parables with πάλιν in vv. 44, 45, 47 have the same function.

18 Cf. esp. Dupont, "Point de vue," 240: Both main sections come to a climax in a parenesis (vv. 18-23, 37-50); the new beginning in v. 36-37 is irrelevant.

19 Cf. n. 11 on 9:36—11:1.

20 Gerhardsson ("Seven Parables," 16, 28) postulates differently a second source alongside Mark, a "tract of seven parables," that understands the six para-

words of the prophet (vv. 34-35). The second part of the discourse leads the disciples into further understanding. It begins with the explanation of a parable that Jesus has told publicly and thus clarifies the difference between the people and the understanding disciples (vv. 37-43). The scope of this section is parenetic. It is significant that twice the judgment of the Son of Man as a perspective of Christian action comes into view (vv. 40-43, 49). As the parable of the field already indicated, our chapter has a double conclusion: here the people who do not understand (vv. 34-35), there the disciples who do understand (v. 51).

Sources

The parables discourse is a well-rounded and splendidly composed Matthean unit. That it is at the same time a collection of traditions from various sources is intimated on the synchronic level only by individual asymmetries in the composition. Part of this unevenness is that the two parables Matt 13:31-32, 33 are not explained in the disciples' section and that the double parable of the treasure and of the pearl stand somewhat "isolated" in the disciples' section. What Matthew is trying to do with them is not explained.

Matthew was able to take over one of the two large Markan discourses (Mark 4:1-34). In Mark also it follows the pericope about Jesus' true relatives (Mark 3:31-35 = Matt 12:46-50). He follows his usual procedure[19] and expands a Markan discourse before him with Q and traditions from his special material.[20]

On the Details

The parable of the fourfold field is expanded in its intervening piece, vv. 10-18, with a logion from the otherwise missing logia complex of Mark 4:21-25 (v. 12 = Mark 4:25)[21] and with one from Q (Luke 10:23-24 = vv. 16-17). The parable of the weeds in the wheat field (vv. 24-30) appears in place of the Markan parable of the seed growing by itself (Mark 4:26-29). It has been surmised that it comes from a (written?) collection of five larger parables, all of which begin with ὡμοιώθη ("it is like")[22] and deal with the separation that will take place in judgment.[23] I find it more probable for many of the parables claimed for this collection that on the basis of oral tradition they were put into written form for the first time by Matthew.[24] The detailed analysis will show that most of these parables demonstrate an above-average number of redactional particularities. The parable of the mustard seed in vv. 31-32 is found in Mark (4:30-32) and in Q, in the latter with the parable of the leaven (Luke 13:18-21). Therefore, Matthew has inserted it also here (13:33). The conclusion of the main section at the lake, vv. 34-35, follows Mark 4:33-34. That means that the entire

---

bles after the parable of the sower as meditations on the different possibilities of the soil in Matt 13:3-9. He correlates 13:24-30 with v. 4; 13:31-33 with vv. 5-6; 13:44-46 with v. 7; and 13:47-48 with v. 8 (ibid., 18–25). Unfortunately he does not offer any literary critical arguments and is satisfied by saying that he can interpret his "source" independently of the Matthean redaction that destroys its structure. My conclusion: That an exegete can interpret a source that he has "discovered" is not reason enough to conclude that it actually existed.

21   The other logia of Mark 4:21-25 have doublets in Q and are offered by Matthew only once and in a different location: Mark 4:21 = Luke 11:33Q = Matt 5:15; Mark 4:22 = Luke 12:2Q = Matt 10:26; Mark 4:24 = Luke 6:38Q = Matt 7:2. The call to watchfulness in Mark 4:23 appears in a similar way in Matt 13:43.

22   D. A. Carson ("The ὅμοιος Word-Group as Introduction to some Matthean Parables," 277–82) attempts to interpret the different introductions to the parables in Matthew in terms of their content. He assigns those with the passive of ὁμοιόω to the eschatologically accentuated parables, those with ὅμοιος . . . to the non-eschatological parables. However, his attempt is not fully successful. Matthew 13:47-50 and 20:1-16 are introduced by ὅμοιος and are accentuated eschatologically.

23   Schweizer, "Sondertradition," 99–100; cf. Friedrich, "Wortstatistik," 38–42; vol. 1, Introduction 2. Characteristic for the introduction to a parable is ὡμοιώθη + kingdom of God + ἀνθρώπῳ + an attribute (13:24; 18:23; 22:2; cf. 20:1; 25:1).

24   Βασιλεία τῶν οὐρανῶν and ἄνθρωπος with a substantive or participial attribute are Matthean; cf. vol. 1, Introduction 3.2. Only ὁμοιόω, which Matthew avoids at Mark 4:30 and Luke 13:20, is not Matthean. Friedrich ("Wortstatistik") focuses only on the traditional character of the parables and also counts 13:47-48; 25:31-46 as part of this collection.

concluding scene with the instruction of the disciples in the house (vv. 36-52) is an addition to Mark that Matthew has created. The interpretation of the parable of the weeds in vv. 36-43 is redactional.[25] The fol- lowing three parables of the treasure, of the pearl, and of the fishnet probably are derived from an oral special tradition,[26] likewise the small concluding parable of the householder in 13:52. However, the introduction is probably redactional. Cf. below, the excursus on the Matthean interpretation at the end of III B 3.4, 2. The Parables of the Kingdom of Heaven.

---

25 Cf. the analysis of 13:36-43 below, III B 3.1.
26 Schweizer ("Sondertradition," 98–99) would like to ascribe the five small parables of Matthew 13 that begin with ὁμοία ἐστὶν ἡ βασιλεία τῶν οὐρανῶν (13:31, 33, 44, 45, 47) to a pre-Matthean tradition.

1   **On that day Jesus went out of the house[1] and sat down[2] beside the sea. 2/ And large crowds gathered with him, so that he got into a boat and sat down; and the whole crowd stood on the beach. 3a/ And he spoke many things to them in parables and said:**

Analysis   The introduction to the parables discourse is brief. It establishes a close temporal connection to the preceding scene "on that day" (ἐν ἐκείνῃ τῇ ἡμέρᾳ) but leads Jesus to a new stage. The hearers, the people, are reintroduced. Verses 1-2a correspond to v. 36a where the scenery again will change. That Jesus is described twice as sitting contrasts with the crowd's standing. Verse 3a is a general comment on Jesus' speaking in parables that corresponds to vv. 10, 13, 34, 53. As far as sources are concerned, in v. 1 Matthew loosely follows Mark 4:1a, in vv. 2 and 3a more closely Mark 4:1b-2. The evangelist is presumably[3] responsible for reworking the source.[4]

Interpretation

■ **1** The narrative continues without a temporal interruption. The house that Jesus leaves has not been previously mentioned; only in retrospect does the reader notice that the previous story obviously took place in a house. Since the connection to what precedes is not very smooth, the readers "stumble" over the house, and they notice it. Jesus sits down by the lake of Gennesaret that thus far in Matthew has played a role as the place where the disciples were called (4:18) and where the community of disciples had its first experiences with Jesus (8:24-27).

■ **2** Once again large crowds gather with him. In the course of the Matthean story they are, of course, Jews.[5] The readers are surprised here too, because since 12:23

they are assuming that the crowds are present. Why do they have to gather again? Either the evangelist is simply careless about the external scenery of his book, because its "internal story," that is, the separation of the community of disciples from Israel, is the only thing that is important for him, or he includes the casual details as a stylistic way of calling attention to the "internal scenery." Be that as it may, the readers are startled and thus pay attention to the stage and the ("new-old") hearers. The large crowds and the open-air scene go together. Jesus gets into the boat. The readers are thus reminded of the stilling of the storm,[6] where the disciples began the way of discipleship. In the Gospel of Matthew the ship always implies a certain distance from the crowds (cf. also 14:13; 15:39). It is not explicitly said that the disciples are with Jesus in the ship, but it is presumably presupposed, as their question in v. 10 shows. It is appropriate that Jesus sits while the people stand. In antiquity as a rule the teacher sits.[7] With the standing of the people we should probably think less of standing in a temple or a synagogue than of the family of Jesus "standing outside" (12:46-47). Chapter 13 will show how the people occupy the place of those who stand outside.

■ **3** Jesus now begins to speak to the people. Matthew avoids the Markan "teaching" and chooses for Jesus' speaking the open verb λαλέω ("to speak"). It is not only his desire to emphasize linguistically the connection to chap. 12[8] that influences him; in his own usage διδάσκειν ("to teach") is close to the interpretation of the law and to ethical proclamation, and it often takes place in the synagogue.[9] The parables discourse deals

---

1   Τῆς οἰκίας is missing in D, it, sy⁸ because of the difficult connection to chap. 12.
2   Κάθημαι = to sit down: BAGD, s.v., 2.
3   The minor agreement πολλοί (cf. Luke 8:4, sing. πολλοῦ) agrees with Matthean and Lukan redaction; the absence of teaching in parables also in Luke (but cf. Luke 5:3) is connected with the fact that he shrinks the entire Markan parable discourse into a single parable.
4   On ἡμέρα, ἐξέρχομαι, ὄχλοι πολλοί, ἕστηκα, λαλέω cf. vol. 1, Introduction 3.2. Ἐν ἐκείνῃ τῇ ἡμέρᾳ (cf. 3:1; 22:23) may come from Mark 4:35 (Matt 8:18 is different). Ἐπὶ τὸν αἰγιαλόν is repeated in v. 48. Εἱστήκει and ἐλάλησεν refer back to 12:46-47.

5   Thus we may not see the crowds as a direct prefiguring of the church—the *corpus permixtum*—contra Gundry, 251. Verses 10-16 and 34-36a already contradict this view.
6   Cf. 8:23: Ἐμβάντι αὐτῷ εἰς τό πλοῖον.
7   Cf. also 5:1; 15:29; 23:2; 24:3; Carl Schneider, "κάθημαι κτλ," *TDNT* 3 (1965) 443.
8   Cf. 12:22, 34, 36, 46, 47.
9   Cf. vol. 1, II (excursus following 4:25).

with neither of these. What does "speaking in parables" mean? While Matthew has previously used images and parables, he has never used the word "parable." In his gospel it is concentrated in 13:1-36; the section 21:28-22:14 is an additional focal point for "parable." Outside these sections it occurs only three times. Thus in 13:1-36 Matthew will unfold what parables are for him. We begin with the general meaning of the word. In biblical usage, corresponding to the Hebrew מָשָׁל, the word means "illustration, saying, fable, proverb, riddle." In Greek it means more narrowly "comparison," in rhetoric "parable." Then we make a first observation: Matthew designates parables as παραβολαί primarily when they are public and directed to all the people.[10] Our chapter will successively show the further dimensions of παραβολαί.[11]

---

10 Kingsbury, *Parables*, 31: "Enigmatic form of speech directed primarily at outsiders."
11 Cf. the excursus on the Matthean parable interpretation below, III B 3.4, 1. Overview.

2.1 The Seed in the Fourfold Field: On Understanding the Parables (13:3b-23)

Literature

Cerfaux, "Connaissance" 3.123–38.

Crossan, "Seed Parables."

Gustaf Dalman, "Viererlei Acker," *PJ* 22 (1926) 120–32.

Christian Dietzfelbinger, "Das Gleichnis vom ausgestreuten Samen," in Eduard Lohse, J. Christoph Burchard, and Bernt Schaller, eds., *Der Ruf Jesu und die Antwort der Gemeinde: Exegetische Untersuchungen Joachim Jeremias zum 70. Geburtstag gewidmet von seinen Schülern* (Göttingen: Vandenhoeck & Ruprecht, 1970) 80–93.

Drewermann, *Tiefenpsychologie* 2.739–46.

Jacques Dupont, "La parabole du semeur," in idem, *Études* 1.236–58.

Birger Gerhardsson, "The Parable of the Sower and Its Interpretation," *NTS* 14 (1967–68) 165–93.

Gnilka, *Die Verstockung Israels: Isaias 6,9-10 in der Theologie der Synoptiker* (SANT 3; Munich: Kösel, 1961) 90–115.

Idem, "Das Verstockungsproblem nach Matthäus 13,13-15," in Willehad Paul Eckert, Nathan Peter Levinson, and Martin Stohr, eds., *Antijudaismus im Neuen Testament?* (Munich: Kaiser, 1967) 119–28.

Ferdinand Hahn, "Das Gleichnis von der ausgestreuten Saat und seine Deutung (Mk 4,3-8.14-20)," in Ernest Best and R. McLean Wilson, eds., *Text and Interpretation: Studies in the New Testament Presented to Matthew Black* (Cambridge: Cambridge University Press, 1979) 133–42.

Heuberger, "Sämann."

Idem, "Samenkörner," 155–74.

Jeremias, "Palästinakundliches," 48–53.

Jülicher, *Gleichnisreden* 2.514–38.

Klauck, *Allegorie*, 186–209, 242–55.

Heinz-Wolfgang Kuhn, *Ältere Sammlungen im Markusevangelium* (SUNT 8; Göttingen: Vandenhoeck & Ruprecht, 1971) 112–22.

Xavier Léon-Dufour, "La parabole du semeur," in idem, *Études*, 256–301.

Lohfink, "Metaphorik," 211–28.

Idem, "Gleichnis," 36–69.

Luther 3.117–32 (on Luke 8:4-18).

Marguerat, *Jugement*, 415–24.

Christian Mellon, "La parabole, manière de parler, manière d'entendre," *RechSR* 61 (1973) 49–63.

Moule, "Mark 4:1-20," 95–113.

P. B. Payne, "The Authenticity of the Parable of the Sower and Its Interpretation," in R. T. France and David Wenham, eds., *Gospel Perspectives* (Sheffield: JSOT, 1980) 1.163–207.

2 The Discourse to the People (13:3b-35)

Antonio Quacquarelli, *Il triplice frutto della vita christiana: 100. 60. 30 (Matteo 13,8 nelle diverse interpretazioni)* (Rome: Coletti, 1953).

Dan O. Via, "Matthew on the Understandability of the Parables," *JBL* 84 (1965) 430–32.

David Wenham, "The Interpretation of the Parable of the Sower," *NTS* 20 (1974) 299–318.

K. D. White, "The Parable of the Sower," *JTS* n.s. 15 (1964) 300–307.

Zumstein, *Condition*, 206–12.

For *additional literature* on the parables discourse see above, III B.

3b/ "Behold, a sower went out to sow. 4/ And when he sowed, some [seed] fell on the way. The birds came and ate it. 5/ But other [seed] fell on the rocky ground, where it did not have much soil. It came up immediately, because it had no deep soil; 6/ but when the sun rose it was scorched and it dried out, because it had no root. 7/ But other [seed] fell in the thorns; the thorns grew and choked[1] it. 8/ But other [seed] fell on good soil and brought fruit, one[2] a hundred, another sixty, (still) another thirty. 9/ Whoever has ears shall hear."

10 And the disciples came and said to him: "Why do you speak to them in parables?"
11/ But he answered and said to them:
"Because it is given to you to know the secrets of the kingdom of heaven;
but to them it is not given.

12 For to the one who has it will be given, and he will have abundance;
but whoever does not have, even what he has will be taken away.

13 That is why I speak to them in parables, because they
see and yet do not see
and hear and yet do not hear
and also do not understand.

14 And in them the prophecy of Isaiah is fulfilled which says:
'Hearing you will hear and not understand.
Seeing you will see and not see (anything).

15 For the heart of this people was made impervious,
and with their hears they became hard of hearing,
and they have closed their eyes
so that they might not see with their eyes
and hear with their ears

---

1 Ἔπνιξαν. Ἀπέπνιξαν (Nestle[25]) could be harmonization with Luke. It is not a minor agreement.

2 The relative pronoun instead of the article with ὁ μέν—ὁ δέ is frequent in the Koine (BDF § 250).

and understand with their heart
and turn back,
and I will heal them.'[3]

16   But happy are your eyes, because they see,
and your ears, because they hear!
17   Amen, I say to you:
Many prophets and righteous people longed
to see what you see, and they did not see it,
and to hear what you hear, and they did not
hear it.
18   You, therefore, hear the parable of the sower:
19/ with everyone who hears the word of the
kingdom and does not understand,[4] the evil one
comes and seizes what is sowed in his heart.
That is what is sowed 'on the way.' 20/ But the
one 'sowed on the rocky ground' is the one who
hears the word and immediately receives it with
joy. 21/ But he has no root in himself and is a
person of this world; when there is distress or
persecution because of the word, he is immediately led astray. 22/ But the one sown 'among
the thorns' is the one who hears the word, and
the care of the world and the deceit of wealth
choke the word, and he becomes unfruitful.
23/ But the one sowed 'on the good ground' is
the one who hears and understands the word,
who then also brings fruit and does, 'the one a
hundred, the other sixty, (still) another thirty.'"

Analysis

Structure

The parable of the fourfold field consists of three
parts of unequal length. The actual parable (vv. 3b-9)
and its explanation for the disciples (vv. 18-23) correspond to one another. The parable is interpreted line
by line, and in each case a piece from the corresponding passage is quoted. The middle part is the longest
(vv. 10-17). After the disciples' question (v. 10), Jesus'
answer is divided into two parts, vv. 11-12 and vv. 13-
17. Verse 11 functions as a title: "to you" (ὑμῖν) are
given the secrets of the kingdom of heaven," "to

them" (ἐκείνοις) not. Verse 12 adds a supporting
argument. In vv. 13-17 what is indicated in the title is
carried out in chiastic order. Jesus speaks to "them"
in parables—at the same time the disciples' question
in v. 10 is taken up and answered—because they do
not understand (vv. 13-15). "Your" eyes and ears, on
the other hand, are declared happy, because they see
and hear (vv. 16-17). The repetition of "to hear," "to
see," "eyes," "ears," (ἀκούειν, βλέπειν, ἰδεῖν, ὀφθαλμοί, and ὦτα) links the two parts together. The non-
seeing and non-hearing crowds and the seeing and
hearing disciples are contrasted. With this contrast
the emphasis lies on the first, negative half. The disciples' question in v. 10 aimed at this contrast, and in
vv. 14-15 Jesus himself (a unique procedure in the
Gospel of Matthew) affirms its main statement with a
scripture quotation. It is introduced similarly to a formula quotation and looks ahead to the concluding
formula quotation of the first part of the discourse in
v. 35. Then vv. 14-15 also stand exactly in the center
of the entire text.

Redaction and Sources

a. *Verses 3b-9* are a reworking of Mark 4:3-9 with only
negligible redactional interventions.[5] The most
important is the descending order of the numbers in
v. 8 that has been newly introduced by Matthew. It
corresponds with the parable of the talents in 25:15.
A few "minor agreements" are difficult to explain
redactionally.[6]

b. *Verses 10-17:* The first part, *vv. 10-13*, is based on
Mark 4:10-12.[7] Verse 12 has been moved here from
Mark 4:25; it is the last of the logia from Mark 4:21-25
not previously used by Matthew.[8] After the insertion
of v. 12, the redactional v. 13a takes up the disciples'

---

3   This result is made obvious by καί, thus the indicative: BDF § 442 (8). Cf. Matt 5:25; Luke 14:8-9;
Mayser, *Grammatik* 2/1.253.
4   The construction in Greek borders on being incorrect. Matthew wanted (a) to use *casus pendens* as he
does in vv. 20, 22, 23 and (b) with a genitive
absolute to suppress the difficulty that in Mark the
seed is both the word and the hearers; cf. below,
interpretation of v. 19. Matthew often uses the genitive absolute, even when the possibility of connecting the participle to a relationship word exists. Cf.
vol. 1, Introduction 3.1.
5   Redactional are: in v. 3 the purposive infinitive with
τοῦ, in vv. 5-8 and v. 8 μέν/δέ, in v. 5 εὐθέως, in v. 6
the genitive absolute before a main verb (B. S.
Sheret, "An Examination of Some Problems of the

Language of St. Matthew's Gospel" [Diss., Oxford,
1971] 229–30), in vv. 7-8 ἐπί (also corresponds to
Ιερ 4:3); cf. vol. 1, Introduction 3.1 and 3.2.
Matthew and Luke abbreviated Mark 4:8 in different ways. The short form of the call to watchfulness
in v. 9 corresponds to 11:15; 13:43.
6   Noticeable are the absence of ἀκούετε in Mark 4:3
(did Matthew destroy the inclusion Mark 4:3, 9?)
and of καὶ ἐγένετο in Mark 4:4 (does not correspond to Lukan redaction).
7   Redactional are: in v. 10a προσελθόντες οἱ μαθηταί (cf. vol. 1, Introduction 3.2); v. 10b (cf. vv. 3, 13,
33-34); in v. 11a ὁ δὲ ἀποκριθεὶς εἶπεν; in v. 11b
τῶν οὐρανῶν; in v. 13 διὰ τοῦτο, οὐδέ, cf. vol. 1,
Introduction 3.2.
8   The redactional addition καὶ περισσευθήσεται (cf.

question of v. 10b[9] and at the same time the "in parables" (ἐν παραβολαῖς) that was omitted from Mark 4:11b. In Matthew v. 13b-d is only an allusion to Isa 6:9-10 in the neat parallelism that is characteristic of him. Notable is a series of Matthean/Lukan agreements in vv. 10-13, especially the change of the complicated Markan "those who were around him with the twelve" to "the disciples" (οἱ μαθηταί), along with "to you it is given to know the mysteries of the kingdom" (ὑμῖν δέδοται γνῶναι τὰ μυστήρια τῆς βασιλείας), the omission of "everything comes" (τὰ πάντα γίνεται; Mark 4:11c) and of Mark 4:13aα, b, as well as the abbreviation of the (in Matthew first) use of Isa 6:9-10 by omitting the μήποτε clause of Mark 4:12c. They not only simplify and smooth the Markan text; they avoid the Markan lack of understanding on the part of the disciples and emphasize the disciples' knowing. They cannot be completely explained as independent Matthean and Lukan redaction.[10] For me the most probable explanation is a deutero-Markan reworking of the Markan text that in general reduces the disciples' lack of understanding in Mark.[11]

Verses 14-15 are difficult. We have an introductory phrase that is in part non-Matthean[12] and a quotation that corresponds almost exactly to the LXX. That is exactly the reverse of what we find with most other formula quotations. For this reason many authors

regard the "doubled" quotation in vv. 14-15 as a post-Matthean gloss.[13] In my judgment the thesis creates more difficulties than it solves. Nowhere are vv. 14-15 omitted in the textual tradition. The introductory phrase of v. 14a[14] can be understood almost completely as Matthean. Matthew had to keep three things in mind here: (1) Jesus himself formulates a quotation; it is not a commentary from Matthew, the narrator. (2) With the hardening of Israel we are dealing, as in 2:17 and 27:9, with a "negative" occurrence that, while it indeed is predicted in scripture, does not happen for the purpose (ἵνα!) of fulfilling the scripture. (3) Matthew wanted to create a connection to Isaiah's prophecy in 15:7-9 where the issue again is Israel's hard heart, its understanding, and then the interpretation of a parable.[15] Verses 14b-15 add the entire quotation of Isa 6:9-10 (almost) literally according to LXX. Formally the LXX text fits well in the Matthean redaction.[16] As was the case, for example, with Matt 1:23, it was Matthew and not a scribe in the community who, based on his knowledge of Isaiah LXX,[17] formulated the well-known quotation about the hardening of the heart. As elsewhere, he follows an allusion to the text with its complete wording.[18] In this way it receives greater emphasis. Notably Luke also later adds the full LXX wording of Isa 6:9-10 that is identical to Matthew—to be sure, not until Acts 28:26-27. However, the common wording—with a

---

vol. 1, Introduction 3.2) corresponds to the repetition in 25:29.

9   It is formulated redactionally—not freely but using Mark 4:2 and especially 4:33. That is the origin of λαλέω that in Matthew takes the place of the Markan διδάσκω and becomes a keyword in the first main part of Matthew 13.

10 Γνῶναι comes from Mark 4:13, a verse omitted by Matthew and Luke, and is used by Matthew and Luke in a positive statement about the disciples. Here is revealed, in my judgment, a deliberate tendency (in a possible Deutero-Markan recension?). The plural μυστήρια might correspond to the Matthean tendency to "intellectualize" (cf. below on v. 23), but it is inexplicable as Lukan redaction. The omission of the μήποτε clause could be independent redaction: Matthew abbreviates in v. 13. Luke maintains the thesis of the ἄγνοια of the Jews at the time of Jesus (pointed out by P. Hoffmann). In any case, not all of the minor agreements (and certainly not the very large number) can be explained by independent redaction.

11 Ennulat, *Agreements,* 122, 128, 425; Cerfaux ("Connaissance," 126–28) assumes a source common to Matthew, Mark, and Luke, Gundry (255) Matthean influence on Luke, Bovon (*Lukas* 1.405) the

influence of oral tradition.

12 Ἀναπληρόω and προφητεία are hapax legomena. Why did Matthew not adapt them more to the introductory phrase in the formula quotations?

13 See, e.g., Stendahl, *School,* 131–32; Strecker, *Weg,* 70, n. 3; Gnilka, *Verstockung,* 103–5; contra Segbroeck, "Scandale," 349–51.

14 The variety among the introductions to the quotations that for various reasons could not be stylized as formula quotations is quite large in Matthew. Cf., e.g., 2:5; 3:3; 11:10; 15:7; 21:42; 22:31.

15 Common keywords and motifs: ἐπροφήτευσεν . . . Ἡσαΐαι (15:7); καρδία (15:8); ἀκούετε καὶ συνίετε (15:10); προσελθόντες οἱ μαθηταί; ἀκούσαντες τὸν λόγον ἐσκανδαλίσθησαν (15:12, cf. 13:19, 21!); the image of planting (15:13, cf. 13:3-9); the request for an explanation of the "parable" (15:15). Unexplained on this basis remains only ἀναπληρόω instead of the simple πληρόω.

16 Cf. vol. 1, I A 2.2 (excursus on the formula quotations, 3).

17 Cf. vol. 1, I A 2.2 (excursus on the formula quotations, 2).

18 21:2-5; 27:3-10; 27:35 Δ, Θ. Cf. 1 Peter 2:4-6. Matt 27:35 Δ, Θ shows that a post-Matthean gloss proba-

small common omission in comparison to the normal LXX text—comes not from a secondary recension of Mark that Luke also would have used[19] but from the LXX. Both evangelists have a great, but not necessarily the same, interest in Isa 6:9-10. They both bring the complete quotation but in different places.

Verses 16-17 are a Q logion (= Luke 10:23-24) and probably a genuine saying of Jesus. It is the last word from the context of the sending in Q that Matthew has not yet used. In its first half he expanded and altered it redactionally[20] in order to create a closer relation to vv. 14-15. In v. 17 the "righteous" come from him.

c. In *vv. 18-23* the deviations from Mark also can only be partially explained as redactional. Along with the omission of Mark 4, 13aβ, b, unusual are "in the heart" (ἐν τῇ καρδίᾳ) in v. 19 (cf. Luke 8:12, 15) and the construction. Luke 8:14-15 and Matthew, vv. 19-23, use οὗτος that takes up the *casus pendens*. The Matthean version with its consistent use of the singular improves the quite awkward Markan text 4:15-20 more consistently than does Luke. Did a deutero-Markan redactor first improve[21] Mark, and did Matthew then again rework the style[22] of that construction that is retained in Luke? We clearly find Matthean redaction especially in vv. 19 and 23, where the double "understand" (συνιείς) is most important.[23]

History of Interpretation

"Fourfold is the arable field—how is your heart tilled?" Thus begins a stanza of the well-known old folk song "Listen you men and let me tell you." The stanza indicates how our parable was interpreted during many centuries in preaching and popular piety. The preacher's interest was parenesis, that of the hearer, searching the conscience. The determining factor was the allegorical interpretation of the parable in Matt 13:18-23 par. The threefold failure of those who heard the word—the others usually are not even mentioned!—set the basic tone. It is gloomy. There are many warnings: of the winged demons,[24] of the stony heart,[25] of the deception of riches, of gluttony,[26] of becoming people with "asphalt hearts" who just barely function,[27] or of the birds "from the realm of mere intellect" that pick away the seed of the kingdom of God.[28] In the sermons are mirrored the problems of each time and each preacher. No wonder that in the face of so many warnings Luther found this parable to be *satis terribili(s)*.[29] The gospel bears fruit only in a very few! Only a woeful fourth of the people are saved![30] At fault is "not the sower but the soil . . . , i.e., the soul that does not pay attention."[31] The question that was repeatedly asked was: "To which of the hearers do I belong?" Bonhoeffer characterized this question as "legalistic-pietistic."[32] Does this interpretation or its evaluation reflect what the text says? The question is especially urgent because—with the allegorical interpretation of vv. 18-23—it seems to be anchored in the Bible itself.

---

bly would have received a "stylistically authentic" introduction to the quotation.

19 Cf. Ennulat, *Agreements*, 127–28. Unfavorable for such an explanation of the minor agreements is also that the preceding short version of the quotation in Matthew, v. 13b, c par. Luke 8:10b is quite different.

20 Cf. the correspondence between Matthew, v. 16 and v. 13: Ὅτι . . . βλέπουσιν . . . ἀκούουσιν. Ὀφθαλμοί (tradition) and ὦτα connect with v. 15. Uncertain is only whether the participial formulation οἱ βλέποντες in Luke 10:23 is not perhaps Lukan. In any case, important for Matthew is *that* the disciples hear and see, for Q *what* they hear and see (Schulz, *Q*, 419). The position of ὑμῶν before αὐτοῖς in v. 13 is also Matthean. On δίκαιοι cf. vol. 1, Introduction 3.2 (3 times with προφῆται). The rest remains uncertain.

21 David Wenham ("The Interpretation of the Parable of the Sower," 299–318, 305–18) assumes that behind all three gospels is a basic writing with regular *casus pendens*. In this view the explanation of the Markan text is the most difficult. Wenham himself says: "The result of his stylistic change was rather unfortunate" (312).

22 The *casus pendens* taken up with οὗτος is Matthean but not Lukan. Cf. vol. 1, Introduction 3.1, n. 93.

23 The genitive absolute in v. 19 remains difficult. Cf. above, n. 4.

24 *Opus imperfectum* 31 = 793; Strabo, 130; Dionysius the Carthusian, 160.

25 Zwingli, 300.

26 John Chrysostom, 44.5 = *PG* 57.470–72. By the way, it is significant that in *Hom.* 44 this great preacher interprets only vv. 19-22 but not v. 23!

27 Helmut Thielicke, *Das Bilderbuch Gottes* (Stuttgart: Quell, 1957) 68.

28 Leonhard Ragaz, *Die Gleichnisse Jesu: Seine soziale Botschaft* (Hamburg: Furche, 1971) 133.

29 Sermon on Luke 8:5ff. (1517), *WA* 1.134 = Luther 3.117.

30 Theophylactus, 280; Euthymius Zigabenus, 397; Musculus, 356.

The ancient church's *parenetic interpretation* has indeed been the basic type of the church's exegesis of our text down to the present. With its enumerations in vv. 19-23 it calls for people who "by the grace of God strive for a better life," "as if someone wants to move a large rock . . . to a given place." Such a person "will strain all sinews to that end," for "the life of the pious on earth is a struggle" against the constantly emerging weeds that continually must be pulled out. This is the formulation of the reformer Zwingli,[33] someone who certainly is not suspected of works righteousness. Many of the church's interpreters speak in a similar way.

■ **8, 23** In the service of parenesis was also the *allegorical interpretation of the various fruits in vv. 8, 23* that was widespread since the ancient church. Irenaeus already combined our verses with the idea of the various dwellings in the father's heavenly house from John 14:2.[34] Since Origen, interpreters have spoken of the "three orders" of Christians at different levels of perfection.[35] The leading point of view was always the dualism "spiritual-worldly" or, with different accents, the freedom from sexual concupiscence.[36] At the top of the list Origen put the martyrs as people with a hundredfold fruit, and then he followed them with the "virginal people" and the widows.[37] Of course, after the end of martyrdom in the fourth century the "virginal" clerics and the members of orders moved to the top of the list ahead of widows and married people.[38] It conformed with monastic ideals when the anachorites ranked before the cenobitic monks and

the married Christians.[39] When the reformers met such orders of rank,[40] they combated them early on.[41] They spoke of the various "states" to which masters, servants, men, women, single, married, etc. belong. In all "states" good works are demanded; no "state" is in itself a good work.[42] Therefore, one should not despise the "ordinary people" in the church; God loves them just as much as the others.[43] The exegesis of the Counter-Reformation, on the other hand, maintained that there is at least a different reward for different stages of perfection. However, what the stages of perfection are is not a question of truth but of usefulness about which the preacher is to decide in the parenesis.[44] In this way the exegesis of the Counter-Reformation may have understood the concerns of the church fathers, who never argued about the different classifications but amicably and peacefully passed them on side by side.

Alongside the parenetic interpretation, there was no shortage of attempts in the history of interpretation to give the parable a different accent so that the divine grace came more clearly to expression.

a. The *christological allegorizing of the sower*—in itself widespread—was able to be used repeatedly in the service of this concern. Already the *Odes of Solomon* have the savior say, "I sowed my fruits in hearts and transformed them through myself" (17:13). Cyril of Alexandria emphasizes: "He himself it is who sows everything good, and we are *his* field; every spiritual fruit comes through him and from him."[45] With many

31 John Chrysostom, 44.3 = *PG* 57.468.
32 Dietrich Bonhoeffer, "Letter to R. Grunow," in idem, *Gesammelte Schriften* (Munich: Kaiser, 1959) 2.590.
33 300–301.
34 *Haer.* 5.36.2.
35 Fr. 296 = 132. On the entire subject, along with Antonio Quacquarelli (*Il triplice frutto della vita christiana: 100. 60. 30 [Matteo 13,8 nelle diverse interpretazioni]*) cf. esp. the two studies by Heuberger ("Sämann," and "Samenkörner").
36 Dionysius the Carthusian, 162: "*a carnalibus ad spiritualia*," "*continentia virginalis*"; cf. Knabenbauer 1.581.
37 *Hom. in Jos.* 2.1 = SC 71.118. Cf. already *Exhor.* 49 = LCC 2.428. Cf. in addition Cyprian *Hab. virg.* 21 = FC 36. 48–49; Augustine *Quaest.* 1.9 = 13; Thomas Aquinas, *Lectura* no. 1093.
38 First with Athanasius *Ep. ad Ammonium* = Hugo Koch, *Quellen zur Geschichte der Askese und des Mönchtums in der alten Kirche* (SAQ NF 6; Tübingen:

Mohr/Siebeck, 1933) 51. Cf. Heuberger, "Sämann," 314–15; further in Jerome, 106; in more detail idem, *Jov.* 1.3 = *PL* 23.222–23.
39 Theophylactus, 380 and HebrMt. on the passage.
40 Even Luther (3.121) advocates it in his sermon of 1517—of course, with the condition that the person is more important than all work and merit.
41 On Luther, cf. Loewenich, *Luther,* 36–37, furthermore Calvin 2.73.
42 Luther 3.126–27 (Sermon of 1528). Luther says there very soberly that chastity is essentially a question of biological vitality and not of virtue.
43 Calvin 2.73; Musculus, 364 (*non minus charus est, qui trigecuplum, eo qui centuplum habet*).
44 Lapide, 280–81; Maldonat, 274: *Parabolam ad mores nostros alii (scil.,* the fathers) *aliter, omnes utiliter accommodarunt.*
45 Cyril of Alexandria *Hom. 41 in Luke* = CSCO 140.69 (quoted according to Heuberger, "Samenkörner," 157, n. 3).

other authors Thomas Aquinas gives the sower's "going out" a trinitarian interpretation as the going out of the Son from the Father.[46] Thus is secured the grace of God through Christ that precedes all human application.

b. The *interpretation influenced by the Reformation* puts the accent on grace in differing ways. For Luther the parable is not so much a parable of the soil or of the human heart but of the seed or of "good fortune and bad fortune *verbi*."[47] He especially criticizes the enthusiasts' and Donatists' contempt for the external word. The truth of the divine word depends not on its efficacy; the word remains true even where it does not bring fruit, that is, even in the Protestant national churches.[48] Thus the parable becomes a comfort for preachers who might despair at the success of their sowing.[49] Thus in the interpretation influenced by the Reformation more frequently than elsewhere the sower is identified not only with Christ but with every preacher.[50] Other accentuations of grace are also possible in the Reformation tradition. For Melancthon the scattered word is the *principium iustificationis*.[51] Calovius emphasizes against a broad stream of the ancient church's interpretation that the "root" (v. 21) is the faith and not the will of a person.[52] However, on the whole it must be said of the post-Reformation interpretation and preaching that the basic parenetic tone is as unbroken as it ever was. Only the accents change. The issue is now no longer the practice of abstinence but the practice of hearing the sermon and the human response to it in the Christian life.

c. *Historical-critical research* has produced an interpretation of our parable that in many regards is close to the approach of the reformers. Its basis is the attempt to distinguish the original parable of Jesus from the primitive church's allegorical interpretation. Unencumbered by this allegorical interpretation it recognized in the original parable a parable of contrast. In the midst of present failures, the hearers can nevertheless be confident that the kingdom of God will prevail.[53] Or: As a confident sower Jesus counts on a rich harvest.[54] In the history of theology Jesus,

the sower who is not discouraged, is the historical variant of the preacher who is comforted by the interpretation of the Reformation. The interpretation of our parable as a parable of contrast is indirectly rooted in Reformation theology. At the same time it corresponds—in a generalized way—with a deep need of people today. People living in resignation, who are "choked" by the burden of their duties and the demands of everyday life are to learn to see beyond their own failures the "unconditional promise of God."[55] The preacher's encouragement in the Reformation's interpretation and Jesus the confident sower of historical criticism become in today's psychological interpretation the encouragement of *every* person. "Admittedly, our 'fruit' is not visible and our 'success' is not demonstrable, but what we give to God is never worn out . . . , what we submit to him is never destroyed."[56] Historical-critical and psychological exegesis join hands here. Both have their roots in the traditions of the Reformation.

The interpretation will have to show whether these attempts to find a "theology of grace" in the parable of the sower can be anchored in the text or whether the assumption that our text is "legalistic-pietistic" is correct.

Interpretation

■ **3-9** Since Matthew gives his own interpretation of the parable in vv. 18-23, we make initially only a few observations on the parable's imagery and on the original meaning. It is noteworthy how much is not mentioned. Is the soil rich or poor, damp or dry, level or hilly?[57] Is it the early sowing in autumn or the late sowing in early winter after the first rain?[58] We do not know, because nothing is said about plowing. Nor is anything said about the weather conditions, which are just as important for the result as is the condition of the soil.

■ **3** Only what is important for the interpretation is reported. The parable mentions the sower but is not further concerned about him.

46 *Lectura* no. 1085.
47 Sermon from 1525, *WA* 17/1.46.
48 Luther, *WA* 38.553–54, similarly Musculus, 360.
49 Luther, Sermon from 1524, *WA* 15.426.
50 Bullinger, 133A; Brenz, 505; Musculus, 360.
51 177.
52 299.
53 C. H. Dodd, *The Parables of the Kingdom* (1935; reprinted London: Collins, 1961) 135–36.
54 Jeremias, *Parables*, 150–51.
55 Drewermann, *Markusevangelium* 1.326–27, cf. 332–33.
56 Drewermann, *Tiefenpsychologie*, 745.
57 Of interest, e.g., to Columella *De re rustica* 2.2 (vol. 1; Will Richter, ed.; Munich: Artemis, 1981).
58 Jeremias ("Palästinakundliches," 49) according to E. Schneller: In the early sowing the seed is sowed before the rain on the unplowed field. Then the seed is plowed under along with all of the weeds that have dried out during the summer. In the late sowing a first plowing is done during the rainy season. Then one lets the weeds that have grown already dry out, sows the seed, and then once more plows everything under. This description is not sup-

■ **4** At v. 4 the scattered seed becomes the subject. Some of it falls on the edge of the path.[59] The farmer, of course, does not intentionally throw the seed on the way. He will not plow it under; then the birds would not be able to pick at the seed.[60] The narrator describes something here that in sowing can probably never be completely avoided.

■ **5-6** Some seeds fall on rocky ground. In many places in the Palestinian hill country the layer of topsoil over the rock is thin but not yet eroded, so that one sows on it.[61] This seed sprouts, but it is dried out by the sun and withers.[62]

■ **7** Other seeds fall among the thorns. Literally understood that means that the dried-up thorn plants of the preceding year are still standing in the field that has not yet been plowed so that one actually does sow "into" them. Then the field would still be unplowed at the sowing. We cannot be positive about this; it is also possible that we have here a case of breviloquence and that the sower sows in the pre-plowed field where later weeds will also grow.[63] In any case the much debated question about whether in the parable the sowed field is already plowed is not important for understanding the parable—

the seed is in any case plowed under *after* the sowing!

■ **8** It is a different matter with the second question about the parable's imagery that is strongly debated in scholarship: Is the hundred-, sixty-, or thirtyfold yield that grows on the good soil a realistic statement, or is there an intentional assumption of a surprisingly large yield? This question is connected with a second: Do the numbers refer to the yield of the entire field or to the individual seed? The second question can be answered clearly for Matthew. He contrasts individual groups of seed with ἅ μέν . . . ἄλλα δέ; only the seed sowed on the good soil brings fruit. That also the interpretation of vv. 18-23 where the issue is the seed sowed into the different kinds of soil. Thus the figures cannot refer to the total yield of the field,[64] but only to the seed in the good soil. It is simplest to relate the numbers to the controllable number of kernels that come from an individual seed.[65] Then they are realistic.[66]

For Matthew, therefore, it is not a parable of contrast. The idea of an abundant yield in spite of many adversities is far from him. Various additional observations sup-

ported by the testimony of a Jordanian agronomist in K. D. White, "The Parable of the Sower," *JTS* n.s. 15 (1964) 300–307, who says that he has never observed the first method. Jeremias ("Palästinakundliches") and, with more reserve, Gustaf Dalman (*Arbeit und Sitte in Palästina* [7 vols.; Gütersloh: Bertelsmann, 1928–39] 2.179–84, 194–96) think of an early sowing (one plowing after sowing) as a rule for Palestine. However, there are also other sources (Dalman, *Arbeit* 2.191, 195; in the OT, e.g., Isa 28:24). Klauck (*Allegorie,* 190–91) thinks of two plowings. That, in any case, is what the ancient authors recommend (Marcus Terentius Varro *Rerum rusticarum* 1.29.2 [Jacques Heurgon, ed.; Paris: Société d'Édition "Les Belles Lettres," 1978]; cf. Columella, *De re rustica* 2.4; Pliny the Elder, *Hist. nat.* 18.8 = 45), as well as modern advisers (Dalman, *Arbeit* 2.179–80) and perhaps also Jer 4:3.

59   Thus BAGD, *s.v.* παρά, III 1b. The preposition παρά (also Mark; not ἐπί) does not suggest that the farmer sows on the path that later will be plowed over.

60   Against Dalman, "Viererlei Acker," 120–32, 121–23; Jeremias, *Parables,* 11–12. In the parable in *Jub.* 11.11 the birds of Mastema eat the seed of the entire field before it is plowed.

61   Dalman, *Arbeit* 2.15–16. According to *m. Kil.* 7.1 the soil has to be three fingers deep in order to be worked.

62   Much as in a seed pan. The seeds sprout faster in it because they are warmer in the shallow layer of dirt. However, the seeds need more water.

63   Be it because the seeds of the weeds previously plowed under also sprout or because the stock of seeds was not completely clean.

64   Only then are they unrealistically high. Arye Ben David (*Talmudische Ökonomie* [Hildesheim: Olms, 1974] 1.104–5) speaks of four- to ninefold yield; especially good fields bring a ten- to fifteenfold yield. Cf. similarly Klauck, *Allegorie,* 191. Pliny the Elder (*Hist. nat.* 18.21 = 94), who cites examples of very great fertility, tells of a 150-fold yield in Africa, similarly Varro (*Rerum rusticarum* 1.44.2) of a hundredfold yield in Africa and near Gadara, but he does so with reservations ("*dicunt*").

65   Verse 8 clearly supports this view: ἄλλα (σπέρματα) . . . ὁ δ μέν. It speaks of the seed that brings fruit.

66   Dalman (*Arbeit* 2.243) reckons with 15–40 grains for ears with four rows, Sonnen (in Dalman, ibid.) with 60–70 grains per ear of wheat; with barley, Dalman (252) reckons with 36–66 kernels. Ancient representations and modern experiments come to an aver-

port this view. First, there is the descending series of the figures in v. 8[67]—hundred, sixty, thirty—that would ruin the point of the contrast between the present time of failures and the "abundant" yield that nevertheless results. Second, it is important that in Matthew this parable is not a parable of the kingdom of God, even though he transmits a great many parables as parables of the kingdom of God. Important in the third place is that the parable does not intend to emphasize the great difficulties that a farmer encounters while sowing. It is not the case that three-fourths of all the seed is lost! Only a little falls on the way, depending on how carefully the farmer sows. Also with the thorns, how much of the yield is lost depends on the farmer himself. Jeremiah had long since given the correct advice about what to do when a field is filled with weeds: plow the fallow land first and do not sow among the thorns (Jer 4:3)! In any case, the parable does not deal with abundant "failure and resistance" that confronts a farmer in the "bleak wasteland."[68] And finally, fourth, it is important to remember that v. 8 speaks of the yield of the individual kernel of seed. That does not interest a "normal" farmer; he is concerned about the field's total yield.[69] The so-called parable of the sower is not told from the perspective of the sower, who disappears after v. 3; it is concerned with the seed or the field. Only that interests Matthew, Mark, and the allegorical interpreter of the parable before them.

■ **9** They are concerned to contrast various types of soil in the interest of parenesis, as the evangelist indicates with his call to watchfulness in v. 9. In other words: The Matthean (and the Markan) version of our parable is composed completely with a view to its interpretation. The question is whether this was so from the beginning.

Original Meaning

How the original form of our text looked is a matter of great controversy. A series of controversial preliminary questions come together into the main question about the meaning of the original parable.

1. *Is the story a parable or a similitude?* The past tense supports the view that it is a parable but not conclusively.[70] Against the view that it is a parable is the observation that it tells not about a special event but about what happens to every farmer when sowing in the Palestinian hill country. The aorist tenses of our text are not part of a continuing narrative; four times it begins anew. Instead of a story we have different kinds of experiences in the same activity—sowing. In my view our text is a fourfold similitude.[71] Only a tradition-historical decomposition could make of it a parable.

2. *Is the story a parable of the kingdom of God?* In none of the gospels is it directly designated as such. Even the metaphors of the images themselves do not point in this direction.[72] Thus initially everything contradicts this very widespread thesis.

3. *Is the allegorical interpretation of Mark 4:13-20 secondary to the parable itself?* Clearly the interpretation demonstrates many linguistic contacts with the language of early Christian mission.[73] Less convincing are the Semitisms that are supposed to be in the parable but not in the interpretation.[74] It becomes extremely difficult to extract a scope of the parable that differs from the interpretation. Here the attempts at interpretation have been so diverse that

---

age of 30 grains (Lohfink, "Gleichnis," 53, nn. 66–67). In view of these relatively low figures, Lohfink ("Gleichnis," 53–57, with numerous ancient references) reckons with side shoots, i.e., that the main stalk can branch off under the surface at the lowest knot and then bring forth an average of two to five stalks. Pliny the Elder (*Hist. nat.* 18.21 = 95) knows of such a branched-out kind of wheat known as "*centigranium.*" Further references from Herodotus, Theophrastus, and Strabo are in P. B. Payne, "The Authenticity of the Parable of the Sower and Its Interpretation," 1.163–207, 185.

67   Cf. similarly Matt 25:15.
68   Jeremias, *Parables,* 150.
69   Midrash Rabbah on the Song of Songs 7.3 § 3 (=H. Freedman and Maurice Simon, eds., *Midrash Rabbah* [10 vols.; 3d ed.; London: Soncino, 1983] 9.283): One measures the wheat before sowing and then

again after threshing. However, one may not conclude from this that it has to be that way in our parable, but one must ask why it is not!

70   Cf., e.g., Matt 13:33, 47-48.
71   Thus, e.g., Ferdinand Hahn, "Das Gleichnis von der ausgestreuten Saat und seine Deutung (Mk 4,3-8.14-20)," 133–42, 134 ; Lohfink, "Gleichnis," 50–57.
72   Cf. below on vv. 20-23.
73   Cf. esp. Jeremias, *Parables,* 77–78; Klauck, *Allegorie,* 203–4.
74   The ἔν (= רחַ + number = . . . -fold) in Mark 4:8 *and* 20, which is avoided by Matthew and Luke and very

many scholars regard the original meaning of the parable as unknowable.[75] For the time being we will leave the question open.

4. Can Mark 4:3-8 be decomposed in terms of the history of its tradition? There are here different attempts, all of which begin by recognizing that the individual sections of the parable are of unequal length. Especially the section concerning rocky ground in Mark 4:5-6 is unusually long. In their details the reconstructions of the original version are quite different.[76] In all cases shortening the parable increases the distance between it and its interpretation—probably an unstated purpose of the exercise! In the process the reconstructed original version in every case corresponds amazingly to the interpretation of the parable given by the reconstruction. I do not want to deny that in oral tradition there are widespread accentuations and changes of a traditional narrative skeleton for the sake of each interpretation and application; however, the same sort of thing obviously also happened to these scholars for the sake of *their* interpretation! In any case, there is nothing in the text that compels a given decomposition.

That brings us to the main question: What was the *original meaning* of the parable? We can first of all distinguish between two basic types of interpretations.

a. According to the first basic type[77] the *emphasis*

lies solely on the conclusion, that is, on the rich yield of the seed on good soil. The three prior negative examples then either have only a literary function—they are to heighten the tension and to strengthen the impression of the conclusion[78]—or they represent the difficulties that the proclamation of the kingdom of God encounters.[79] The parable then serves to encourage the hearer that the kingdom of God has begun already or that Jesus' proclamation will achieve its goal.[80] This type of interpretation tends to emphasize the extraordinary wealth of the harvest. The element of contrast nearly always plays a constitutive role. Most of the time the parable is understood as a parable of the kingdom of God.

b. According to the second type of interpretation our parable is a *self-reflection of Jesus the preacher on the success and failure of his proclamation.* Here the emphasis lies equally on the three negative sections and on the positive concluding section; the text has the character of a meditation. As does every teacher, the proclaimer of the word of God has to "reckon with defeats."[81] "Many words (are) spoken in the wind."[82] Only "when it is endangered (does the) meaning of the mission" of Jesus prevail.[83] With this interpretation the parable can be (but does not have to be!) understood as a parable of the kingdom of God: "The Kingdom of God is here already, and opposition has broken out against it everywhere."[84] This

many witnesses, is a clear Semitism. Cf. Dan 3:19; *Tg. Onq. Gen. 26:12*; Black, *Approach*, 124. There is nothing in the parable's interpretation that corresponds to $\kappa\alpha\rho\pi\grave{o}\nu$ $\delta\iota\delta\acute{o}\nu\alpha\iota$ = נָתַן פְּרִי (Mark 4:8), but it also appears in the LXX. In the Markan parable there are, corresponding to the narrative style, no hypotaxises and participles; in the interpretation there are a few, but there is also a Semitizing parataxis in Mark 4:20 (Beyer, *Syntax,* 266–67). The evidence is not very impressive.

75 E.g., Bultmann, *History,* 199–200; Eta Linnemann, *Parables of Jesus* (New York: Harper & Row, 1966) 117, 181–82; Heinz-Wolfgang Kuhn, *Ältere Sammlungen im Markusevangelium* (SUNT 8; Göttingen: Vandenhoeck & Ruprecht, 1971) 112.

76 Cf., e.g., Crossan, *Parables,* 40–42; Klauck, *Allegorie,* 186–89 (original version according to the rule of three: three parallel stanzas with three verbs each; a final stanza with three levels of yield); Weder, *Gleichnisse,* 101–2, 108; Lohfink, "Gleichnis," 37–46 (original version with increasing length of the individual members). Plausible is only that Mark 4:5-6 is abundant.

77 On its place in the history of theology cf. above on the History of Interpretation, a–c.

78 Weder, *Gleichnisse,* 109. Cf. the Jotham fable in

Judg 9:7-15.

79 Examples: The kingdom of God will prevail despite the catastrophe of John the Baptist (Dodd, *Parables,* 136), despite the failures of Jesus himself (Dahl, "Parables," 154). The sower is not to despair "in spite of every failure and opposition" (Jeremias, *Parables,* 150).

80 Cf. above, History of Interpretation. Wherever seed is sown "it is certain that it will bring fruit" (Weder, *Gleichnisse,* 109). "The germ for the overwhelming success in the future has already been established" (Klauck, *Allegorie,* 196). "The Basileia . . . comes already at the sowing" (Lohfink, "Gleichnis," 66).

81 Jülicher, *Gleichnisreden* 2.536. Similarly Krämer, "Parabelrede," 39: Failures are unavoidable.

82 J. Weiss, 108.

83 Christian Dietzfelbinger, "Das Gleichnis vom ausgestreuten Samen," 92.

84 Schweizer, *Mark,* 91.

type of interpretation often (but not always) tends to emphasize the first three cases where the seed is lost and to interpret each of them individually.

The advocates of both types of interpretation regard the allegorical interpretation of Mark 4:13-20 as a secondary creation of the church. In the first case it means a major dislocation of the original meaning; in the second it is more a matter of making it concrete. One crosses over the boundary to allegory when the parable presents in detail the reasons "for the sake of which his [*scil.*, Jesus'] activity did" not "succeed,"[85] that is, when the individual statements about the seed are interpreted. The question, however, is whether this was not from the beginning the intention of the fourfold parable. The negative examples chosen are strange. A field's yield depends in the first place on its location and the general quality of the soil, in the second on the weather conditions, and then on the incidence of pests, etc. A good farmer will make every effort not to sow on the path; he also knows the places where his field has rocky subsoil. One gets at the thornbushes by repeated pre-plowing and by weeding.[86] It seems to me that the hearers of the story must have noticed that precisely *these* kinds of losses are mentioned. In addition, in each individual verse we come across "existing images"[87] that from the very beginning directed the hearers' associations in a given direction.[88] They do not suggest a parable of the kingdom of God. In my judgment these conventional metaphors determined the choice of examples. Even Jülicher asked whether this so-called model parable did not have allegorical

characteristics.[89] I can understand him only too well. Along with others[90] I assume that the fourfold parable of the seed was meant exactly as it was interpreted in Mark 4:13-20. From the beginning it was a "parable about parables,"[91] or *a meditation about the various hearers of Jesus' proclamation.* The interpretation fits the original character of the fourfold parable exactly. If we assume that it was formulated by the early church,[92] then the question about whether our parable originated with Jesus is completely open. The interpretation in Mark 4:13-20 *may* be accurate even while being later than an original parable of Jesus.[93] However, both the parable and the interpretation also *may* have originated in the church.[94]

With a glance at the history of interpretation we formulate a *result*: The modern interpretation of our text as a parable of the kingdom of God and of contrast that corresponds in substance with the Reformation's theology of grace and at the same time takes up the need of today's people to escape the hopelessness of their own efforts and designs does not correspond to the parable. In my view the attempt to separate Jesus from the parenesis of the early church in our text has failed. Thus the question is unavoidable: How are we to deal with this parenesis that strikes many as being "legalistic"?

Interpretation

■ **10** After Jesus' first parable the disciples come to him—Matthew no longer appears to be thinking of the boat.

---

85 Jülicher, *Gleichnisreden* 2.537.
86 The narrator obviously is willing to put up with the impression of an "unusually bad farmer" (John Drury, "The Sower, the Vineyard, and the Place of Allegory in the Interpretation of Mark's Parables," *JTS* n.s. 24 [1973] 370).
87 Hahn, "Gleichnis," 139. What is meant is pre-formed, conventional metaphors.
88 Cf. below on vv. 20-23.
89 *Gleichnisreden* 2.537-38.
90 See, e.g., Birger Gerhardsson, "The Parable of the Sower and Its Interpretation," 165–93, 187; Moule, "Mark 4:1-20," 109–10; Flusser, *Gleichnisse*, 63, 122, 125; Schmithals, *Markus* 1.229–30; Payne, "The Authenticity of the Parable of the Sower and Its Interpretation," 1.163–207, 168–86. Pesch (*Markusevangelium* 1.234) also comes close to this interpretation. Krämer ("Parabelrede," 40–43) offers a fanciful interpretation of the three negative images on the level of Jesus as the (stubborn) Pharisees, the (initially enthusiastic) people, and the rich.

91 Moule, "Mark 4:1-20," 108.
92 Supporting this view are not so much the individual terms (cf. above, n. 73) as the situations that are presupposed: temptation, persecution (Mark 4:17), delusion of riches (Mark 4:18), the general "desire for other things" (ibid.), and the formulation of the initial enthusiasm and the lack of roots that presupposes a longer time period (Mark 4:16-17).
93 With a short introductory sentence (e.g., "with the hearers of the proclamation it is as with . . .") and with the help of the numerous conventional metaphors, the fourfold parable could be understood well even without an interpretation. Cf. *Gos. Thom.* 9, Justin *Dial.* 125.1.
94 This is a classic case where the "criterion of dissimilarity" fails. The "similarity" between Jesus and the church does not exclude a text's authenticity.

Their question goes back to v. 3 (πολλὰ ἐν παραβολαῖς) and is, compared with Mark 4:10, very precise. It has to do with the reason for the parables discourse for the crowd (αὐτοῖς). Jesus' answer in v. 11 appears to create a deep rift between the people (ἐκείνοις) and the disciples (ὑμῖν). The disciples are declared to be blessed because they see (vv. 16-17); the people, on the other hand, are cast down into the abyss of not understanding. This is a surprise for the readers of the gospel. What did the people, who thus far have listened faithfully to Jesus and have reacted positively to him, do to deserve this "rejection"? Is Jesus not unfair here? If the people cannot understand the mysteries of the kingdom, then Jesus should speak more clearly! The readers are overcome by the uneasy feeling that everything happens here according to God's predestination and that the people really cannot do anything about it.

Our section is a prime example that the Gospel of Matthew sometimes does not reveal itself if it is read only on the level of "story." Its macrotext is transparent of the church's historical experience.[95] It teaches her to understand how what she herself has experienced in her history—the no of the majority of Israel and her own separation from the nation—has already taken place with Jesus. The people's lack of understanding is, as it were, predetermined for Matthew from the end of the story—both the story of Jesus and that of his community.[96] Already Mark 4:10-12, the source behind our section, was an attempt to understand this lack of understanding of Israel in the present. Matthew takes up this attempt and carries it further.

■ 11 The knowledge of the mysteries of the kingdom has been given to the disciples by God.[97] With this sentence the readers will remember 11:25-27, especially 11:27d, the Son's revelation to his own. What mysteries are

thought of? "Secrets of the kingdom of heaven" is probably to be interpreted in Matthew as analogous to the expressions "gospel of the kingdom" and "word of the kingdom" (v. 19).[98] It is everything that Jesus teaches in parables.[99] Later, in the eschatological discourse of 24:32-50, γινώσκω ("to know") is used as a keyword.[100] That suggests that the "mysteries" at issue here also include the eschatological dimension of the parables. Most of all, however, Jesus' parable interpretation in our chapter is concerned with ethical exhortations. In contrast to Jewish apocalypticism, whose understanding of "parable" has influenced Mark 4:11 and also Matthew,[101] the "mysteries" that are revealed to people are not only heavenly and otherworldly; they have a solid this-worldly practical dimension. In contrast to Mark 4:11, the plural indicates that it is not only *the* mystery of Christ. Thus the entire wealth of the teaching of Jesus is "given" to the disciples, and that means that it is revealed through Jesus' instruction.

To "them," on the other hand, it is not given. The text does not say what the people have done wrong. If we do not simply want to speak in general terms of the people's "unbelief," we may indirectly conclude from the interpretation of the parable in vv. 18-23 that the issue there is that with the help of the allegories the community of disciples learns to apply the various types of field to itself. Thus the hearers should have applied the parable to themselves and should have asked themselves how they themselves receive the "word of the kingdom." To understand parables in Matthew's sense is, like David with Nathan's parable, to hear the words: "You are the man!" (2 Sam 12:7).

---

95   Cf. above, II B Summary on the transparency of the miracle stories.

96   Gundry (255) interprets it differently: The people are the false Christians in the sense of Matt 13:36-43. However, that contradicts Gundry's interpretation of the people elsewhere as potential church. The ecclesiological-parenetic dimension of the text does not appear until vv. 18-23.

97   *Passivum divinum.*

98   Cf. below on v. 19.

99   Zumstein, *Condition,* 208: the themes of the para-

bles; Marguerat, *Jugement,* 417: "infléchissement didactique."

100 Five times, four of them in parables.

101 On the heavenly and future mysteries in apocalypticism that are revealed to the seer by means of encoded speech and visions (parabolic discourses: *1 Enoch* 38.1 and often; similitudes: *4 Ezra* 4.3, 47 etc.) and interpreted by an angel, cf. Maxime Hermaniuk, *La parabole évangélique* (Bruges-Louvain: Desclee de Brouwer, 1947) 124–53; Cerfaux, "Connaissance," 130–33; Klauck, *Allegorie,* 75–88.

■ **12** An early Christian wandering logion[102] and proverb, added here by Matthew, that originally complained that the rich always get richer and the poor always get poorer,[103] suggests a reason and at the same time the perspective of Jesus' answer: "God gives no static possessions."[104] What do the disciples "have"? Obviously they have what according to v. 11 was "given" to them: the beginning understanding of the kingdom of God.[105] What "will be given" to them? Here one naturally thinks initially of the growing understanding (cf. vv. 19-23, 36-52) and living,[106] which the unique teacher Jesus mediates by his instruction and his support. At the very latest one sees in 25:29 that there is also an eschatological dimension in our logion: The abundance will result in the "joy of the Lord" (25:21, 23). The eschatological dimension is even clearer on the other side. What will be taken away from the one who has not? There is a Matthean logion that—presumably suggested by our logion[107]—takes up again the opposition of ἀρθήσεται and δοθήσεται: "Therefore I tell you, the kingdom of God will be taken away from you and given to another people that produces its fruits" (21:43).[108] Thus it is not the case that Jesus from now on will no longer speak to the people—he will continue to do so— but that Israel will lose its election because it does not accept Jesus' preaching.[109]

■ **13** After this perspective Jesus again takes up the question of v. 10 and answers it. He speaks to the people in parables because they see and yet do not see.[110] Israel's failure to see and to hear is for Matthew an established fact. It is not caused by Jesus' parables;[111] it is more the case that Jesus speaks in parables in "response"[112] to this lack of understanding. Or to put it even better: In the parables discourse the peoples' lack of understanding is condensed in narrative form.[113] On the other hand, the parables discourse is not explicitly designated as "punishment" for Israel's lack of understanding.[114] The parables have only a negative function in the face of Israel's hardening. They do not remove it. Of course, it is Israel, not Jesus, who is responsible for this.[115] Looking ahead to the various types of hearers in the explanation, Matthew holds that the people do not "understand" (cf. vv. 19, 23).

> Thus Matthew takes over the apocalyptic and Markan understanding of "parable" as encoded, riddling speech. He does not, however, have a coherent "theory of parables."[116] In 21:45-46 the Jewish leaders "knew" (ἔγνωσαν) that "the parables" were about them, but they drew the wrong conclusions from this knowledge. In our text, on the other hand, following Mark it is precisely the not knowing that is characteristic of the people. What is clear is only that while the parables do not *create* understanding (only Jesus the "interpreter" effects that), they do maintain the boundary between those who understand and those who do not.

---

102   In Matt 25:29 the logion has a pre-Matthean anchor in the parable of the talents. Καὶ περισσευθήσεται in both texts is a redactional addition. Cf. vol. 1, Introduction 3.2.

103   Cf. Prov 9:9; 11:24; 15:6; *4 Ezra* 7.25; *Midr. Qoh.* 1.7 = Str-B 1.661 (parable on the theme *on ne prête qu'aux riches* = French proverb); Martial, 5.81; Juvenal, 3.24–25, 204–22; Terentius *Phormio* 1.1.7–8 (= Jules Marouzeau, ed. [Paris: "Belles Lettres," 1947] 2.119).

104   Schniewind, 167.

105   Cf. Jerome, 103: *fides* but not yet *virtutes*; Photius of Constantinople fr. 57 = Reuss, 300: προαίρεσις, σπουδή; Theophylactus, 280: the one who has is the ζητῶν. Thomas Aquinas (*Lectura* no. 1102-6) systematizes *desiderium, studium, caritas, fides* and at the same time warns that nobody can attain eternal glory *ex puris naturalibus*.

106   Cf. 5:20: περισσεύσῃ ὑμῶν ἡ δικαιοσύνη.

107   Trilling, *Israel*, 58.

108   Cf. 13:8, 23.

109   Hilary, 13.2 = SC 254.296: The Jews will lose the law.

110   Διὰ τοῦτο points forward as it does in 24:44 and is continued by ὅτι.

111   Thus Mark with purposive ἵνα.

112   Klauck, *Allegorie,* 252. Wilkens, "Redaktion," 312: the hardening is not the goal but the reason for speaking in parables.

113   Burchard ("Senfkorn," 10) puts it well: "The parables discourse is not the continuation of preaching by other means but the dramatized rupture of communication."

114   Thus Gnilka, *Verstockung,* 103; Lambrecht, "Parables," 34; Klauck, *Allegorie,* 252.

115   Segbroeck ("Scandale," 347) says sharply: It is "l'intention de Matthieu de bien établir la responsabilité des Juifs." Of course, Matthew does not say that directly here yet.

116   Correct Kingsbury, *Parables,* 49–51.

■ **14-15** Israel's lack of seeing is so important for Matthew that he wanted to document it with Isa 6:9-10, the classical scripture quotation[117] that in primitive Christianity helped explain Israel's failure to believe. As in 4:15-16 and 21:42 he wanted to understand the way of election from Israel to the Gentiles as God's way that had been predicted in the scriptures. Isaiah's prophecy is completely fulfilled in "them," the unbelieving people. And now Matthew simply lets the scripture speak. *It* says what is incomprehensibly harsh: The heart of God's people became "fat," "impermeable"; they "closed" their eyes. The purposive μήποτε ("so that")[118] probably is to be related to Israel and not to God. Israel has closed its ears and eyes in order not to come to understand and to turn.[119] Μήποτε maintains Israel's guilt and not God's predestination. If Israel were to repent, then God would truly heal it![120]

■ **16-17** Verse 16 brings an abrupt change in tone and content. Matthew begins anew with a disciples' beatitude. Ὑμῶν is put first emphatically, even contrary to normal style. The Isaiah quotation is so to speak turned on its head. In place of the people's closed eyes and blocked ears are the seeing of the eyes and the hearing of the ears of the disciples. The formulation is intentionally detailed so that the contrast to vv. 14-15 will be obvious. What do the disciples see and hear? The reader remembers 11:4. They "see" the healings that belong to the promised and longed-for[121] time of salvation. They "hear" the "gospel of the kingdom." As in v. 13, seeing and hearing are not simply identical to understanding,[122] but they are associated with it. "Seeing eyes" and "hearing ears" are the basis on which understanding can grow. The disciples *are* not understanding people, but they *become* such through Jesus' instruction. Does all of this apply only to the historical disciples of Jesus who were eyewitnesses of his activity and hearers of his preaching? Initially yes, but not only to them. It is important that Matthew has replaced "kings" (Luke 10:24) with "righteous," for the Christians of the Matthean church themselves are not "kings," but they are "prophets" and "righteous" (10:41; 23:34, cf. 37). Therefore, the Old Testament believers who hoped correspond to the church that, in the form of the disciples of Jesus, is permitted to participate in the time of salvation itself.[123]

■ **18** After exuberantly blessing the disciples, Jesus brings them back to reality in v. 18. He takes up again the parable of the sower.[124] He suppresses Mark's reproach of the disciples; indeed, the disciples are not without understanding. However, it is now important that they not only hear externally as do the crowds, but that from now on they let Jesus' instruction lead them to "understanding" (cf. 13:36-52; 15:10, 12-20; 16:5–17:13). That happens first of all by having Jesus explain our parable's many "conventional metaphors." Formally he makes use of the allegorical interpretation of visions that is frequent in apocalyptic literature and for which there is some scattered evidence also in rabbinic

---

117 Cf. John 12:39-40; Acts 28:26-27.

118 *Μήποτε* that in Mark perhaps (!) means "perhaps" has a purposive meaning in seven cases in Matthew ("in order that it might not") and expresses a feeling of concern; in the sentence it introduces there is something feared, something negative. Only in 25:9 does it introduce a main clause, but here too with a negative meaning.

119 The church fathers almost always interpret it this way, and probably correctly, for that is the only way that a Matthean view comes about that is coherent with replacing Mark's ἵνα with ὅτι (v. 13). John Chrysostom (45.2 = *PG* 58.473) and the tradition that depends on him add: It is a subtle wink that God will actually heal them if they repent. Cf. below, n. 120.

120 Similar to Matt 5:25 the indicative may have the function of emphasizing the reality of the final clause; 5:25: so that your opponent does not turn you over to the judge . . . and you—actually—are thrown into prison! Cf. above, n. 3.

121 Cf. *Ps. Sol.* 17:44 ("blessed are those who live in those days") and in Gottfried Quell and Siegfried Schulz, "σπέρμα κτλ," *TDNT* 7 (1971) 537, 544; Lohfink, "Metaphorik," 223–24.

122 Contra Strecker, *Weg*, 197.

123 Correctly observed by du Plessis, "Meaning," 51: Verses 16-17, with their "vivid directness" turn to the implied reader.

124 Cf. 13:36: παραβολὴ τῶν ζιζανίων. That, of course, does not mean the parable that "the sower" (Christ) has told; contra Gundry, 258.

Judaism.[125] With the sowing of the seed one naturally thinks first of all of the widespread metaphoric of the sowing of the word. It is especially common in Greek sources,[126] but it is also found occasionally in Jewish texts.[127] In Mark's text there is some obscurity, because the seed initially is the word (Mark 4:14), but then, beginning in v. 16, it is the people who have heard the word. Presumably this is only a "popular carelessness"[128] required by the material from which no further conclusions are to be drawn.[129]

■ **19** Matthew formulates somewhat more clearly in v. 19 by avoiding an explicit identification of the seed with the proclaimed word, but he does so at the cost of a rather unwieldy participial construction. However, he also does not completely avoid the difficulties.[130] Thus for him the seeds are, as in v. 38, primarily the people who hear the word. He thereby uses another Jewish image—God plants his nation or human beings in general in the world. To be sure, there is some variety in his application.[131] In all

later interpretations Matthew consistently uses the singular ($ο\mathring{υ}τος$). The issue is the individual who hears the "word of the kingdom." This formulation corresponds to his "gospel of the kingdom" (4:23; 9:35; 24:15) and means the earthly Jesus' proclamation of the kingdom of God.[132] With the first type of person he adds, "and does not understand." Only the last type of person will hear "and understand" (v. 23). With this framing Matthew indicates that the "understanding" that in vv. 13-14 he denied the crowds who were only listening is for him a central concern in our text. We will have to return to this in v. 23. Thus with the first type of person the devil[133] steals the sown word. Both the image, that the devil is portrayed as a bird,[134] and the substance, that the devil especially likes to accost new converts,[135] were presumably known to the readers of the gospel.

■ **20-21** Familiar images also appear in vv. 20-21. While in Jewish wisdom texts the wise person is likened to a tree that stands at the stream and has solid roots, the

---

125 Klauck, *Allegorie*, 201. Rabbinical allegorizing of parables, e.g., Str–B 1.664–65; also *Deut. Rab.* 11.6 (in Schlatter, 433–34).

126 The material is found in Klauck, *Allegorie*, 192–94; for additional material see above, n. 121.

127 *4 Ezra* 9.31 (I sow my law in you; it shall bring forth fruit); *4 Ezra* 8.6 (seed for the heart; fruit); morally: Hos 10:12 (justice); *T. Levi* 13.6 (good/evil); *4 Ezra* 4.29–32 (evil/good).

128 Jülicher, *Gleichnisreden* 2.533. Similar inconsistencies also occur elsewhere. Cf., e.g., *Midr. Qoh.* 5.10.28a in Str–B 1.665 (in the parable the person is at the same time the tenant and the rent produced by the lease); Matt 13:24-30 (the church appears again in the growing grain or weeds but also in the questioning servants); Col 1:6, 10 (the gospel or the members of the church bear fruit); *Herm. Sim.* 9.20.1–3 = 98.1–3 (the thistles are at the same time the rich and what keeps them from entering the kingdom of God).

129 Euthymius Zigabenus (403) attempts to explain them linguistically with the doubled possibility of an object of "sowing": $σπείρεται$ $καὶ$ $ὁ$ $σπόρος$ . . . $σπείρεται$ $καὶ$ $ἡ$ $γῆ$. Lohfink ("Metaphorik," 225) absolutizes: a Jewish metaphoric (God's sowing of the people in the original parable [cf. below, n. 131]) is superimposed on a Greek metaphoric (cf. above, n. 126).

130 Since in v. 19b the seed is eaten, it cannot be the hearing person, in spite of the masculine $ο\mathring{υ}τος$.

131 For this reason Lohfink ("Metaphorik," 225–27)

wants to find the parable's original meaning in the announcement of the eschatological renewal of the people of God. Arguing against this view are the following: (1) There is no reason to relate the sower to God. (2) Except for Jer 31:27 (and *1 Enoch* 62.8) the OT uses for this motif the image of planting and not of sowing. (3) $Σπείρω$ with the people as the object is used in the OT usually in the sense of "scattering" (= $διασπείρω$). Comparable, however, are *4 Ezra* 5.48 and 9.41 (individual people are sown into the world).

132 Cf. vol. 1 on 4:23-25 (Excursus: Preaching, Teaching, and Gospel in Matthew).

133 Different from 5:39; 6:13 but presumably as in 13:38. Ὁ $πονηρός$ = the devil appears very seldom in Jewish sources (cf. only *b. B. Batra* 16a in Günther Harder, "$πονηρός$," *TDNT* 6 [1968] 552 n. 40) but more frequently in the NT (1 John!; Eph 6:16).

134 *Jub.* 11.11–12 (Mastema sends ravens and birds that eat the seed). Cf. *Apoc. Abr.* 13.3–7 (Azazel as an unclean bird). For additional material see Klauck, *Allegorie*, 201.

135 *T. Job* passim, esp. 6–8; *Jos. Asen.* 12.9–11; 1 Tim 3:6; cf. 1 Pet 5:8.

godless and the doubter are like a tree without roots that quickly withers.[136] The text here uses this image and fills it out of the church's experiences. Many new converts receive the word "with joy" (cf. 1 Thess 1:6) but live in the here and now.[137] "Persecution" is an experience that the Matthean church had to endure, especially at the hands of Jewish enemies (5:10-12; 10:23; 23:34). The evangelist will not speak again of "affliction" until his eschatological discourse (24:9, 21, 29), where it will also include the enmity of the Gentiles. Thus it is wrong to separate the "affliction" Matthew means from the tribulations of the end-time.[138] The persecutions also belong to the end-time,[139] and the interpretation of chap. 24 will show that the Matthean church understands itself as living in the end-time. Matthew also understands the apostasy of the "here-and-now people" as an experience of the end-time (cf. 24:10). The eschatological perspective also makes understandable to a certain degree the strict dualism that prevails in our interpretation. Satan himself appears; and even with the second and third types of people, where the seed at least sprouts and grows some, the evangelist is not interested in intermediate tones. The only thing important to him is that none of the three bears fruit.

■ **22** The seed sown among the thorns is another image that in Judaism makes possible many associations about evil.[140] The connection with wealth and business may even be rooted in catechetical tradition.[141] The readers of the Gospel of Matthew are immediately reminded of 6:19-34 that dealt first with riches and then with worrying. In the Sermon on the Mount where the section on riches was placed immediately after the central part on prayer, in the sending discourse where the members of the church are addressed as potential itinerant radicals, and here where the warning against riches is the only direct ethical exhortation, it is clear how central this warning is for Matthew.[142] The "fraud" that wealth is means most likely the objective danger that riches represent as a part of this world.[143] The "worry" about the "world,"[144] which is usually given a one-sided emphasis in the interpretations,[145] is the subjective aspect, the relationship to wealth. At the conclusion the negative perspective again dominates. This person remains without fruit. Again there are no intermediate tones.

■ **23** The positive conclusion finally comes after all the negative examples. There are also people with whom the seed falls on good soil. These are the people who understand the word. Matthew will still show a number of times how the disciples come to "understanding"

---

136 Positive sources: Jer 17:8; Ezek 31:2-5; Ps 1:3; cf. Job 14:8-9; negative sources: Sir 40:15 (the root of the ungodly comes upon sheer rock); Wis 4:3-4 (the roots of the ungodly have no depth); cf. Isa 40:24; Sir 23:25. In Christian literature *Herm. Sim.* 9 is quite close: 9.1.6 = 78.6; 9.21 = 98 (doubters are like plants that wither in the sun [= ϑλῖψις]).

137 Πρόσκαιρος in contrast to αἰώνιος; cf. *4 Macc.* 15.2, 8, 23; *Jos. Asen.* 12.15; *T. Abr.* l.R. 14.15; 2 Cor 4:18. Luther's translation *wetterwendisch* (weather capricious)—a word coined by Luther that Bauer (BAGD, *s.v.*) took over with the meaning "fickle like the weather"—misses the eschatological nuance.

138 Contra Strecker, *Weg*, 44; with Kingsbury, *Parables*, 57–58.

139 Cf. the eschatological dimension of 10:23; 23:34.

140 Thorns and thistles are a common biblical image for disaster. Cf. Gen 3:18; Jer 12:13 (to sow wheat, to harvest thorns); Nah 1:10 (opponent of God). For further sources see Klauck, *Allegorie*, 195–96.

141 Cf. *Herm. Sim.* 9.1.1 = 78.1; 9.19.1 = 97.1: thorns

and thistles = rich people and business people.

142 Cf. vol. 1, II A 2.4.1 on 6:19-24 (Summary); 2.4.2 on 6:25-34 (Summary); above, II B 2.1 on 8:18-20; II C Addressees; II C 2.1 on 10:8-10; II C: The Basic Message of the Disciples Discourse; below, III B 3.2 on 13:44-46; IV A 1 Self-denial; IV C 3 on 19:16-30.

143 Ἀπάτη = "deceit" (vg: *fallacia*); however, it may also mean "lust" (it b c g h q: *voluptas*). We cannot be certain one way or the other. Luke 8:14, which omits ἀπάτη and adds ἡδοναὶ τοῦ βίου, probably understood it in the second sense.

144 Objective genitive or genitive of quality (worldly worry).

145 Clement of Alexandria *Quis div. salv.* 11.2. The church fathers, for whom the warning against bonding with riches plays a prominent role most of the time, generalize on the basis of Luke (φιληδονία, μέριμναι βιωτικαί, ἐπιθυμίαι κόσμου). Cf. Heuberger, "Sämann," 241–83. Luther (3.120) internalizes and interprets it to mean *amor sui*.

through Jesus (15:10; 16:12; 17:13).[146] There is understanding only through him. The texts show that understanding is first of all a matter of the head. It is a parable (13:19-23), a rebuke (15:10), or a riddle-like saying (16:12; 17:12), that is, a teaching that the disciples understand with the help of Jesus. However, our text goes farther and is therefore virtually the fundamental text of Matthean hermeneutics. Understanding is connected with bearing fruit[147] and, as Matthew here introduces, with "doing."[148] Hearing, understanding, and doing go together for him, as they do in Judaism.[149] Understanding the word of the kingdom is possible only for the one who combines it with obedience and practice.[150] That is obviously here for Matthew the meaning of the allegory. It is not, as with apocalyptic visions, a matter of decoding mysteries that, given the numerous "common images," are not all that mysterious; the allegory is for him the linguistic device for relating the parable to the hearers. The disciples are to understand that they *themselves*[151] are the issue, and not until they have understood that have they understood. Understanding leads into one's own life and thus to the fruits. That is why Matthew intentionally did not say that the "rocks people" and the "thorn people" "understand."[152] Their understanding would not be different from that of the false prophets who say "Lord, Lord" with a great deal of "understanding," but do not bear the fruit that the lord demands (7:16-23). That the fruit is a hundred-, sixty-, or thirtyfold means obviously in Matthew's sense that it is varied in size, similar to, for example, the parable of the talents in Matt 25:20, 22. Here even the degrees in the exegesis of the ancient church can appeal to Matthew with some (but only partial) justification. However, these differentiations change the total positive image no more than does the partial growth of ears of corn in vv. 20-22 change the negative image. Matthew paints in black and white. He is concerned with the *that* of the fruit, not with the *how much*.

Summary

The parable of the fourfold field reflects the situation of the Matthean church. It is concerned not simply with the problems of the new converts,[153] but with the life of the entire community in the time before the end. The disciples are to relate the parable of the fourfold field to themselves and thus come to understanding. From the perspective of the text the self-critical question "O human, how is it with your heart?" is necessary and correct. One comes to understand our text by asking about one's own fruits. In the interpretation of Matt 13:19-23 there is a healthy element of self-criticism. Matthew obviously believes that there are people in the church who are not at all touched by the word of the kingdom and some in whom the word is stunted before it bears fruit. His church is not permitted to believe that in its bosom salvation is guaranteed. For that very reason it is to rouse itself and to let itself be moved. That corresponds to the image of the community in 13:36-43[154] and to the guest without a wedding garment in 22:11-14. It also corresponds to the entire powerful perspective of

146 On συνιέναι in Matthew see Barth, "Understanding," 105–11 (understanding as the *condition* for bearing fruit); Luz, "Jünger," 148–51 (the disciples understand the teaching of Jesus but are of little faith). Strecker (*Weg*, 228–29) correctly emphasizes the inseparability of understanding and doing but may go too far when he considers whether συνιέναι is still a mental process and not rather a "chiffre of the true Christian being."

147 Δή is here providing emphasis rather than giving a reason. Cf. BAGD, *s.v.*, 1.

148 Ποιεῖν in connection with fruits: Matt 3:8, 10; 7:17-19; 13:26 and above all 21:43.

149 Cf. 7:24, 26 and vol. 1, II A 3.3 on 7:24-27, n. 6.

150 Simon Episcopius, *Notae breves in Matthaeum* (Amsterdam, 1665), 81: "non intellectus . . . actus, sed voluntatis." One should say: *Et intellectus et voluntatis!*

151 Therefore Drewermann (*Tiefenpsychologie*, 716–21) is basically right when he says that a psychological hermeneutics serves to open up such texts. Cf. 2 Sam 12:7!

152 Contra Gnilka, 1.486.

153 Thus correctly Kingsbury, *Parables*, 54–55.

154 The relationship between vv. 18-23 and 36-43 is indicated by various catchwords: σπείρω, αἰών, σκάνδαλον, πονηρός, βασιλεία.

24:37-25:46. Matthew is not self-assured and self-satisfied, nor should his readers be.

None of the attempts in the history of interpretation to interpret our text in terms of grace[155] in any way came as close to it as did its classical parenetic interpretation. We thus return to our beginning question: Is it "legalistic-pietistic"? I would like to focus the question on the problem of the certainty of salvation. On what may the church rely? Obviously it can*not* be sure that at the end all of its members will belong to those who bear fruit and who thus can be justified before the judge of the world. However, it can depend on Jesus. He is "with them" (cf. 28:20) in this parables chapter. He pronounces them blessed for their hearing and seeing. And he makes this beatitude come true by explaining the parable to them as a teacher and accepting them as it were into his school of life. That is what it means for Jesus to teach the disciples in the house (vv. 36-53). He also unlocks for them the fate of the people of Israel who do not hear and do not understand. That it is granted to the church to understand Israel's lack of understanding as a warning for itself is a positive power. Here also is a suggestion for dealing with the black-and-white contrast that dominates our text. We can and probably must ask whether this dualistic evaluation of people really agrees with God's truth. We can and must ask whether the futile attempts, for example, of those who could not resist the pressure of persecution or of wealth really are of no value, while even the thirtyfold fruit of a hearer and doer is 100 percent positive. Our text was deadly, and may become so again, when one is confident that the first three types of soil mean "the others," for example, Israel or the marginal members of a Christian society. Then the text is distorted. It does not intend to instruct generally about "the" human being and certainly not to lead to confidence in one's own fruitfulness. It is correctly understood only when the hearers understand it *self-critically* as a question to themselves.

Thus one's own fruits to which the text summons are not reliable. They do not guarantee salvation, even though they will be tested in the judgment. However, that testing does not make our text "legalistic," because Jesus who calls the church to bear fruit is reliable and remains with his church until the end of the world (28:20).

---

155 Cf. above, on the History of Interpretation.

2.2 The Tares in the Wheat Field (13:24-30)

Literature

Philippe Bacq and Odile Ribadeau Dumas, "Reading a Parable: The Good Wheat and the Tares (Mt 13)," *Lumen Vitae* 39 (1984) 181–94.

Bainton, "Liberty" 1.95–121.

Gerhard Barth, "Auseinandersetzungen um die Kirchenzucht im Umkreis des Matthäusevangeliums," *ZNW* 69 (1978) 158–77.

Catchpole, "John the Baptist," 557–70.

José Corell, "La parábola de la cizaña y su explicación," *Escritos del vedat* 2 (1972) 3–51.

Michel de Goedt, "L'explication de la parabole de l'ivraie (Mt 13,36-43)," *RB* 66 (1959) 32–54.

Friedrich, *Gott im Bruder,* 66–87.

Geist, *Menschensohn,* 74–104.

Joachim Jeremias, "Die Deutung des Gleichnisses vom Unkraut unter dem Weizen (Mt 13,36-43)," in idem, *Abba,* 261–65.

Jülicher, *Gleichnisreden* 2.546–63.

Jüngel, *Paulus,* 145–49.

Luz, "Taumellolch," 154–71.

Daniel Marguerat, "L'église et le monde en Matthieu 13,36-43," *RThPh* 110 (1978) 111–29.

Idem, *Jugement,* 436–46.

Charles W. F. Smith, "The Mixed State of the Church in Matthew's Gospel," *JBL* 82 (1963) 149–68.

Theisohn, *Richter,* 182–201.

Trilling, *Israel,* 124–27, 151–54.

Anton Vögtle, "Das christologische und ekklesiologische Anliegen von Mt 28,18-20," in idem, *Evangelium,* 253–72.

For *additional literature* on the parables discourse see above, III B.

24 He set another parable before them and said: "The kingdom of heaven is like[1] a man who sowed good seed in his field. 25/ But while people were sleeping his enemy[2] came and sowed tares among the wheat and went away. 26/ But when the stalks began to sprout and to bear fruit the tares also appeared. 27/ But the servants of the house master came and said to him: 'Master, did you not sow good seed in your field? Whence does it now have tares?' 28/ But he said to them: 'An enemy[3] did this.' But the servants said to him: 'Do you want us to go away and gather it?' 29/ But he said: 'No, lest in gathering the tares you should root up the wheat with them. 30/ Let both grow together until the harvest. And at the harvest time I will say to the reapers: First gather the tares together and tie them in bundles to burn them, but gather the wheat into my barn.'"

Analysis

Structure

The brief introduction (v. 24a) connects our parable with the two following parables (vv. 31a, 33a). The theme of sowing is the same as in the preceding parable; the catchwords ἀγρός, σπέρμα, and σπείρω appear again. Quite strange for the reader is that the interpretation in vv. 37-43 is separated from the parable; it takes place later in the house. The story itself is divided into two parts, the exposition in vv. 24-26 and the householder's conversation with the servants in vv. 27-30. The first part of this conversation, vv. 27-28a, simply repeats in question and answer the two parts of the exposition, that is, the "sowing" of the "good seed" "in the field" (vv. 24b, 27b) and the deed of the "enemy" (vv. 25a, 28a). The second part, vv. 28b-30, leads to the master's overly long answer. There are a number of strange features. More than half of this narrative consists of a discussion in which nothing happens. The temporal structure is complicated. Along with the time of sowing and the time of growing the time of harvest also appears, but it is only anticipated in the direct speech of the house master. The long answer of the house master in vv. 29-30 contains a speech within the speech, viz., what the house master will say at the appropriate time to the reapers. Thus the story is a drama with three acts in which the last act is simply announced.[4] Several details appear to be unmediated or inconsistent. The farmer who (obviously himself!) sows (v. 24) becomes

---

1 Semitizing aorist instead of confective present: BDF § 333; GKC 312 = § 106, 2c (Hebrew perfect of "experiential fact").

2 Putting the possessive pronoun first is possible only in Greek. Sheret ("Examination," 315) counts in Matthew only 29 places among 291 cases where the third-person possessive pronoun appears before the noun. Thus the correct translation is not on the basis of Semitic language, "an enemy of his" (thus Jeremias, *Parables,* 224) but as above. Presumably the article, based on the interpretation, is to be explained: *the* enemy = the devil.

3 Ἐχθρός may be a noun or an adjective. Ἄνθρωπος with a noun is customary in Greek. Cf. BAGD *s.v.,* 3aε. It is not necessary to assume a Semitism (contra Black, *Approach,* 106).

4 Therefore the "dialogue parable" of Luke 13:6-9, or the similar rabbinical dialogue parable of the lessee in *Pesiq. R. Kah.* app. 1B (in Clemens Thoma and Simon Lauer, *Die Gleichnisse der Rabbinen,* vol. 1: *Pesiqta de Rav Kahana* [Judaica et Christiana 10; Bern: Lang, 1986] no. 76 = 321), is not an authentic parallel.

a "house master" with many servants. However, he will conduct the harvest not with them but with "reapers" (v. 30a). Elementary narrative laws of parables, such as linearity and the smallest possible number of participating persons,[5] seem to be violated in this story. As with many parables it contains an element of surprise, viz., the nocturnal action of the enemy.[6] That, however, is not, as is often the case, the scope of the story[7] but the beginning of a "question-and-answer session" with a long explanation from the house master about what he intends to do. The house master formulates his answer at the end with the words of John the Baptist (cf. Matt 3:12). Jülicher found "this form of presentation" to be lacking "any analogy within the discourses of Jesus."[8] It is in any case very strange.

Source

The parable stands in the place of the Markan parable of the seed growing by itself (Mark 4:26-29) that is missing in Luke as well. The reminiscences of this story are striking. In the same order are ἄνθρωπος, καθεύδω, βλαστά(ν)ω, χόρτος, σῖτος, θερισμός. One can read our story as a counterstory to Mark 4:26-29: A man sowed *good* seed. However, while he was sleeping, instead of the seed sprouting an evil enemy came . . . Was this counterstory created by Matthew?[9] It is not impossible, but in my judgment it is more likely

improbable, since linguistically it is largely traditional and only reformulated by Matthew.[10] If the story is traditional, then either Matthew added allusions to Mark 4:26-29 when he located it here, or it was it told in the Matthean church as a critical variant of the parable of the seed growing by itself. Both possibilities are conceivable. It is less probable that Matthew found it in his copy of Mark in place of Mark 4:26-29.[11]

Tradition History and Origin

The story is curious, even if it is not contradictory.[12] It actually invites tradition-history attempts at decomposition. Since there are no actual breaks, decisions are difficult. Either one has (a) attempted to remove the evil enemy from the narrative (perhaps vv. 25, 27, 28a).[13] This would leave as the kernel the contrast between the growth of wheat and weeds now and their separation at the harvest. Or one can (b) regard the master's detailed answer looking to the harvest as secondary (v. 30).[14] In that case, the parable, similar to 13:3-8, does not explicitly look forward to the coming judgment. Or one can (c) combine both solutions.[15] It would be good if we had an exact parallel to the parable of the fishnet that Matthew has already felt to be a parallel parable. However, that is not the case with most of the suggested solutions.[16] We can get rid of *all* of the aforementioned irregular-

---

5   Bultmann, *History,* 187–88.

6   Jeremias (*Parables,* 224) has a special explanation of this surprise that itself is surprising, because it is in my judgment without analogy in the parables of Jesus. He claims that Jesus made use of an actual event.

7   Klaus Berger, *Formgeschichte des Neuen Testaments* (Heidelberg: Quelle & Meyer, 1984) 54: In parables "the *point* . . . (has) the structure . . . 'Think about it! Something like this can also happen.'" That is true of the householder's instruction not to let the darnel be weeded but not of the enemy's surprising behavior.

8   Jülicher, *Gleichnisreden* 2.559.

9   Thus Gundry (261) speaks of a redactional mixing between Mark 4:26-29 and Mark 4:3-9. Also Goulder (*Midrash,* 367–69) thinks of a Matthean creation.

10   Matthean are: the introduction in v. 24aα (ἄλλος, λέγων), also in v. 24 τῶν οὐρανῶν, ἄνθρωπος + participle; in v. 25 δέ, ἀπέρχομαι (?); in v. 26 δέ, τότε, perhaps καρπὸν ποιέω, φαίνομαι; in v. 27 προσελθόντες . . . εἶπον, κύριε, οὖν; in v. 28 δέ, οὖν, ἀπελθών (?); in v. 29 φημί, μήποτε (?); in v. 30 ἕως, ἐρῶ, πρῶτον, συνάγω, πρὸς τό with the infinitive. Cf. vol. 1, Introduction 3.2.

11   That Matthew and Luke both *omit* Mark 4:26-29 is

even a "major agreement." Matthew offers a substitute, however, while Luke leaves out the entire section Mark 4:26-34 and replaces it with 8:19-21.

12   The most difficult is καρπὸν ἐποίησεν in v. 26, because the period of growth seems to be broken. However, it is understandable in the story also if one understands the aorist like ἐβλάστησεν ingressively (contra Weder, *Gleichnisse,* 121, n. 120).

13   J. Weiss, 334; Wilfred L. Knox, The *Sources of the Synoptic Gospels,* vol. 2: *St. Luke and St. Matthew* (Cambridge: Cambridge University Press, 1957) 130.

14   See, e.g., Jüngel, *Paulus,* 148. Especially radically Kingsbury, *Parables,* 65; vv. 24b-26 are the kernel of the pre-Matthean parable.

15   Schweizer, 303 (vv. 25, 27-28a and in part v. 30 are secondary); similarly Beare, 304–6; Weder, *Gleichnisse,* 122 (two stages of church editing; vv. 24, 26 and 30b, c may be original as a story); Catchpole, "John the Baptist," 563–69 (vv. 24b, 26b . . . 30b are original).

16   The parable of the fishnet is formulated in v. 48 from the standpoint of the "harvest," while the parable of the weeds looks ahead to the future harvest.

ities only by completely reformulating parts of it. All of these suggestions assume that there was at one time an original parable. It is simply that its reconstruction is so obviously difficult—just as difficult as if only the Matthean version of the story of the great banquet in 22:1-14 had been preserved. Most people see it as a warning against premature separation and an encouragement to be patient until the harvest. God will execute the separation in his time![17] The disciples are not living under the "compulsion to produce a 'pure' community of the righteous."[18] Indeed, Jesus himself has established his own community of the "true Israel." This popular "anti-Essene" interpretation of the original parable is possible only if the decomposition is not too radical and if at least some of the anticipation of the harvest in v. 30, that is so difficult for the narrative, is original. Then, however, the parable remains *formally* strange.[19] Furthermore, it presupposes that the story-half of the parable is plausible "agriculturally," so that what the house master says to the servants makes sense to the hearers. Since that is very questionable,[20] other interpretations have been suggested.[21] Result: If there was an original parable, we can hardly recognize its meaning anymore.

There is, however, a fundamentally different possibility of interpretation according to which the allusions to Mark 4:26-29 are not secondary but from the beginning are a basic part of the story. In this case it was formed in the church to deepen or critically expand Mark 4:26-29. We then do not need to decompose it at all in terms of the history of its tradition, since from the beginning it was a concisely formulated and consistent, strongly allegorical story.[22] It reformulates the story of Mark 4:26-29 in light of the experience that, even though the kingdom of God has been "sown," evil continues to be real and effective, and it attempts to understand the "interim period with its specific . . . problems" on the basis of the "beginning and especially the completion of the *basileia*."[23] While the Matthean interpretation in vv. 37-43 remains secondary to the parable, it is then an accentuation in the framework of the allegorical interpretive potential that the story provided from the beginning.[24] This explanation is seductive because it is so simple. I prefer it, therefore, without being able to prove it.

Interpretation

■ **24** We deal only with the story here, since Matthew will present his interpretation in vv. 37-43. The kingdom of heaven is like a sower who sowed good seed in the field. The apparently superfluous "good" prepares for the surprise that follows.

■ **25** In the night his enemy came and sowed darnel seeds in it. Ζιζάνια,[25] "darnel," is widespread throughout the entire Middle East and is often regarded as a degeneration or as a bewitched form of wheat.[26] Contrary to Jerome's opinion,[27] with its narrow leaves it can be distinguished from wheat not only in its mature stage but also while it is growing.[28] Its poison comes from a fungus that is frequently found in it.

■ **26-27** When the wheat grows and begins to ripen, the darnel also becomes visible. Servants appear who ask the farmer—now a householder—the completely superfluous question whether he had not sowed good seed and what the source of the darnel is. The question is unnecessary, especially since the servants do not ask why there is so much darnel. Who is surprised when in a field of grain the unavoidable darnel appears?

17 Jeremias, *Parables,* 226–27; similarly, e.g., Dodd, *Parables,* 38 (as a response to the objection that the kingdom of God cannot come as long as there is sin in Israel); Herbert Braun, *Spätjüdisch-häretischer und frühchristlicher Radikalismus* (2 vols.; BHTh 24; Tübingen: Mohr/Siebeck, 1957) 2.59 (referring to Matt 7:1-2); Bonnard, 198, 204; de Goedt, "Explication," 54 (against the impatience of Jesus' disciples).

18 Weder, *Gleichnisse,* 125.

19 Unless one writes it partly anew, as, e.g., Catchpole ("John the Baptist," 569) or Weder (*Gleichnisse,* 125).

20 Cf. the interpretation below on vv. 28-30.

21 Catchpole ("John the Baptist," 569-70), e.g., understands the original parable as it is decomposed by him as a warning to the "*corpus permixtum*" of Israel: The divine judgment on the people will definitely come with the harvest.

22 Manson, *Sayings,* 193; Klauck, *Allegorie,* 226–27.

23 Peter Dschulnigg, *Rabbinische Gleichnisse und das Neue Testament* (Judaica et Christiana 12; Bern and New York: Lang, 1988) 496. Dschulnigg understands the text without tradition-historical decomposition as a parable of Jesus that makes clear "various stages of the basileia."

24 The allegorical interpretation would then fit the received story just as well as it does in Mark 4:3-8, 13-20.

25 Semitic loan word. Cf. Luz, "Taumellolch," 156; Greek αἷρα = *lolium temulentum.*

26 Dalman, *Arbeit* 2.249; Luz, "Taumellolch," 156.

27 112.

28 Luz, "Taumellolch," 156 n. 11.

■ **28** Even more surprising is the house master's answer. He obviously knows that an evil enemy has done it. However, what enemy would come across this idea and then would have enough darnel seed ready to scatter it in the dark of night![29] It is more likely that someone would cut the ripe grain secretly[30] in the night or set fire to the field. On the other hand, the servants' suggestion that they weed the darnel out of the field is understandable, for that indeed is what one would normally do.[31]

■ **29** However, the master does not want that done lest the wheat is pulled out with the darnel. Thus the parable does not intend to portray the usual farming procedure.

■ **30** That becomes especially clear at the end. The reapers, not the questioning servants, will first collect the darnel, tie it in sheaves, and burn it. Normally it is the other way around: The darnel that had not been weeded out would be dropped to the ground by the reapers and later gathered as chicken feed or burned.[32]

It is thus an unusual kind of farming about which the hearers of the parable would have had their own ideas! What makes those ideas even easier is that several expressions easily lend themselves to metaphorical interpretation. It is true of sowing and bearing fruit and of the enemy who in Jewish texts often means the devil,[33] while the householder symbolizes God,[34] the servants the righteous. The juxtaposition of weeds and wheat in Jewish parables frequently represents the nations and Israel.[35] The harvest is a widespread image for judgment;[36] "uprooting" also is frequently used this way in the tradition.[37] It is also appropriate in this context that the darnel stalks first are gathered and burned, for according to Jewish expectation in the final tribulations or in the annihilating judgment the evil will be destroyed and the righteous preserved.[38] Appropriate finally is the distinction between the questioning servants, that is, the believers, and the reapers, who assume the role of the punishing angels.[39] In short, the church may have seen in our narrative a riddle parable[40] whose improbable features it interpreted with the aid of familiar metaphors. It may have related it perhaps to its relationship to that part of Israel that did not believe in Christ, which then, in contrast to the Jewish parables,[41] appears in the image of the darnel. Jesus' proclamation has aroused enmity in Israel. However, one must not prematurely force the separation from the part of Israel that is hostile to Jesus. God's judgment will bring it. I find it more probable, however, that prior to Matthew the narrative was related to the church itself and spoke of the appearance of evil *within* the community. This then is the scope for Matthew himself.[42]

29 Who would keep darnel seeds at home? The flowery Middle Eastern story, repeatedly cited since Dalman (*Arbeit* 2.308–9), of a man who supposedly sowed reed grass in his neighbor's field simply shows how well one can tell stories in the Middle East.

30 *S. Deut.* 43 on 11:17-18 (*Der tannaitische Midrasch Sifre Deuteronomium,* trans. Hans Bietenhard [Bern: Lang, 1984] 158–59).

31 Thus for Arab Palestine Dalman, *Arbeit* 2.323–25. The exception cited there confirms the rule.

32 Immanuel Löw, *Die Flora der Juden* (4 vols.; 1924–34; reprinted Hildesheim: Olms, 1967) 1.726; Dalman, *Arbeit* 2.325, 327.

33 *T. Dan* 6.3; *3 Bar.* 13.2; *T. Job* 47.10; *Apoc. Mos.* 2, 7, 25, 28.

34 Thus also in the closely related parable of the tree of life and the tree of death, *Pesiq. R. Kah.* app. 1B, cf. above, n. 4.

35 Sources in Luz, "Taumellolch," 157, n. 19. *Num. Rab.* 4 (141b) = Str–B 1.667 and *Ag. Ber.* 23 (=

Buber, 48, quoted in Flusser, *Gleichnisse,* 135) contrast darnel and wheat with each other.

36 Cf. n. 11 on 9:36-38 and Klauck, *Allegorie,* 223–24.

37 Cf. Weder, *Gleichnisse,* 121–22, n. 123.

38 Cf. Volz, *Eschatologie,* 157–58, 304–05 and Revelation 19–20.

39 Cf. *1 Enoch* 53.3–5; 54.6; *As. Mos.* 10.2; Str–B 1.672, 974; Volz, *Eschatologie,* 276–77, 303–4.

40 De Goedt, "Explication," 52: "De la parabole-énigme à l'allégorie, la distance n'est pas grande."

41 Cf. above, n. 35.

42 Daniel Marguerat ("L'église et le monde en Matthieu 13,36-43," 127–28) correctly cites 1QS 3.13–4.26 as a general parallel. There also the stable side-by-side of good and evil until the final judgment is utilized parenetically by the author.

At the very latest for Matthew and for those of his readers who knew the parable in Mark 4:26-29, the reminders of it were important. It is especially noteworthy that in our story the motif of sleeping is used differently. While in Mark 4:26-29 sleeping is a natural and inconsequential matter, here the evil enemy comes while the people are sleeping.[43] Matthew had already mentioned the householder and his servants in 10:24-25. The subject is Christ and his disciples. That is also why the servants address him as "Lord." At the burning (κατακαίω) of the weeds and the gathering of the wheat into the barns (συνάγειν τὸν σῖτον εἰς τὴν ἀποθήκην) they thought of John the Baptist's preaching of judgment in 3:12. Thus once again Jesus takes up a saying of the Baptist.[44] In short, for the readers of the gospel the story has two levels. What is its referent? Because of the context, Matt 13:1-3, they may initially have thought of their life together with "unbelieving" Israel.[45] However, this—perhaps traditional—interpretation was no longer fitting, for in the meantime the wheat, the church, had to separate from the darnel, the synagogue.[46] Therefore, in the house away from the people Matthew will give his readers, or Jesus will give his disciples, a new interpretation.

---

43 Cf. the negative setting of καθεύδω in Mark 13:36, 1 Thess 5:6, and in the Gethsemane pericope. Matthew (and the tradition before him) exhort to watchfulness (24:42; 25:13; cf. 26:38, 40). Does one sense here some of the church's uneasiness with Mark 4:26-29? Christians should not sleep but be watchful, for "your adversary the devil prowls around, like a roaring lion" (1 Pet 5:8).

44 Cf. vol. 1, II A 3.2 on 7:19, n. 36.
45 Proposed by Wilkens ("Redaktion," 318–19) and Kingsbury (Parables, 72–76).
46 Cf. vol. 1, Introduction 5.3.

2.3 Mustard Seed and Leaven (13:31-33)

Literature

Jacques Dupont, "Les paraboles du séneve et du levain (Mt 13,31-33; Lc 13,18-21)," in idem, *Études* 2.592–608.

Idem, "Couple parabolique," 609–23.

Claus-Hunno Hunzinger, "σίναπι," *TDNT* 7 (1971) 287–91.

Jülicher, *Gleichnisreden* 2.569–81.

Klauck, *Allegorie*, 210–18.

F. Kogler, *Das Doppelgleichnis vom Senfkorn und vom Sauerteig in seiner traditionsgeschichtlichen Entwicklung* (FzB 59; Würzburg: Echter Verlag, 1988).

Otto Kuss, "Zur Senfkornparabel," in idem, *Auslegung und Verkündigung* (Regensburg: Pustet, 1963) 1.78–84.

Idem, "Zum Sinngehalt des Doppelgleichnisses von Senfkorn und Sauerteig," in idem, *Auslegung und Verkündigung* (Regensburg: Pustet, 1963) 1.85–97.

Laufen, *Doppelüberlieferungen*, 174–200.

Bernhard Schultze, "Die ekklesiologische Bedeutung des Gleichnisses vom Senfkorn," *OrChrP* 27 (1961) 362–86.

Schulz, *Q*, 298–309.

For *additional literature* on the parables discourse see above, III B.

31 He put another parable before them and said:
"The kingdom of heaven is like a mustard seed
which a man took and sowed in his field;
32   although it is the smallest[1] of all seeds,
            when it has grown
        it is the largest of the vegetable plants and
        becomes a tree,
            so that the birds of the heaven come
            and settle in its branches."[2]
33 He spoke[3] to them another parable:
"The kingdom of heaven is like leaven
    that a woman took and hid in three measures of flour
until it was completely leavened."

Analysis

Structure

The two short parables of the mustard seed and leaven bring to a close Jesus' public parables discourse. The parable of the mustard seed stays with the theme of the preceding seed parable and is connected to it with several catchwords.[4] The introduction to the parable is also the same as in 13:24. In the parable of the leaven it is varied. The two parables have parallel constructions in their first parts but not in their conclusions.

Sources

Both parables come from Q.[5] The Q text is transmitted rather literally in Luke 13:18-21. The introductions in v. 31a and v. 33a are redactional.[6] Matthew also found the *mustard seed parable* in Mark 4:30-32. For the central part, v. 32a-c, he relies on Mark; in the beginning and the end he follows Q with negligible changes.[7] In the *leaven parable* Matthew differs from Q only by the omission of the rhetorical introductory question and by τῶν οὐρανῶν.

Tradition History

The Markan and the Q versions of the *parable of the mustard seed* differ in a number of points. Which version is older? In my judgment the following is clear: In Mark the contrast between the "smallest of all seeds on the earth" and the "largest of all vegetable plants" is emphasized, while in Q it is simply presupposed by implication with the image of the tiny mus-

---

1   In New Testament language the comparative has largely taken over the meaning of the superlative as well without a way of distinguishing between the two meanings (BDF §§ 60, 244).

2   Κατασκηνόω (= "to settle, rest, tent, take residence") does not necessarily mean here "to build a nest" (certainly not in Mark 4:32!).

3   The best-attested reading here is ἐλάλησεν and in v. 31 παρέθηκεν. If this corresponds to the original text, then Matthew has given up the precise parallelism of the parable introductions in v. 33 and with ἐλάλησεν has already created a bridge to v. 34.

4   Ἄνθρωπος, σπείρω, ἐν τῷ ἀγρῷ αὐτοῦ, σπέρμα.

5   Franz Kogler (*Das Doppelgleichnis vom Senfkorn und vom Sauerteig in seiner traditionsgeschichtlichen Entwicklung*) rejects Q as a source and assumes

instead a deutero-Markan recension as the sole source of Matthew/Luke. Apart from the difficulties of explaining what would then be the redactional placement of Luke 13:18-21, the thesis generally fails because the so-called overlapping texts (double traditions from Mark and Q) manifest a *significantly* larger number of minor agreements that then would require special explanation. Cf. Ennulat, *Agreements*, 10.

6   Παρατίθημι with λόγος, νόμος etc. is LXX language.

7   Matthean are: the introduction in v. 31a, the omission of the rhetorical introductory questions, ἐν τῷ ἀγρῷ αὐτοῦ (cf. v. 24), μέν - δέ (cf. vol. 1, Introduction 3.2), αὐξάνω in the passive (cf. Mark 4:8).

tard seed. Here the Markan version is clearly secondary, because its accents disrupt the construction of the parable.[8] For this reason δένδρον in Q is also original.[9] Less clear is the main question. The Q text is a *parable* that tells about a sower; Mark 4:30-32 is a *similitude* that compares the kingdom of God with a mustard seed. In the Markan version the contrast between the smallest seed and the expansively portrayed largest vegetable plant is explicitly emphasized; it is contained in the Q parable only implicitly by the image of the mustard seed. Is the Q text secondary because the original mustard seed similitude was adapted to the leaven parable (Luke 13:20-21)? Or did the parable become a similitude in the pre-Markan tradition because the narrator wanted to mention explicitly the contrast between a tiny mustard seed and a large plant?[10] Nothing is provable here. It seems to me that the argument for the higher age of the form of the parable in Q is weightier.[11] Finally, the biblical allusion at the end is unclear. In Mark 4:32 it is most like Ezek 17:23, in Q Dan 4:18 (= 4:21Θ). In any case it is not a literal quotation. It can no longer be determined which is the older version. It is even possible that the biblical allusion as a whole is a secondary accretion; *Gos. Thom.* 20 does not know it. One could say on its behalf, however, that it is similarly transmitted in Mark and Q. Thus on the whole Q is older than the Markan version. The *similitude of the leaven* has been formulated as a parable and at the very least contains no obvious biblical allusion. It cannot be further decomposed. The absence of a biblical allusion in the parable of the leaven and the Markan tradition that offers only the mustard seed similitude speak in favor of the view that the two texts probably were not originally a double parable.[12] The consensus is that both texts go back to Jesus.

History of Interpretation

Our two parables do not have an allegorical interpretation in the Gospel of Matthew. That made it all the easier for the interpretation of the ancient church to search out its mysteries. Its basic principle can be formulated as follows: "There are three ways we may assume the kingdom of heaven, either Christ himself . . . or the present church . . . or . . . the gospel."[13] The mustard seed or leaven then represents Jesus, the Christ who is present in the church as his body, or the logos. The remaining features of the parables are able to be grouped allegorically in various ways around this central theme. In the history of interpretation two basic types of understanding are exposed: an ecclesiological and an individual interpretation. They were not mutually exclusive but supplemented each other.

a. *Ecclesiological interpretations.* The basic experience was that of the expansion of the church—an expansion that was perceived to be miraculous. Here Christ is usually the sower with whom the church had its beginning. "Attica and the philosophy of the Greeks that is wonderfully suited for argumentation were covered up by the greatness of a gospel that was at home in the country."[14] The "smallest of all religions" became "the . . . universal church of the entire world."[15] Augustine formulates the image of the church as the moon: almost invisible in the sky at the new moon, then finally round and full and cannot be ignored.[16] The spreading kingdom of God is thus the church. Luther says bluntly: "The church is the Kingdom of God, because all other secular kingdoms fight against her, (she) who is alone, and weak, and despised, and nothing, but they do not conquer her. Instead, in the end she conquers all kingdoms and

---

8   Mark 4:32 repeats ὅταν σπαρῇ and adds the explanation μικρότερον . . . in the neuter. In addition, γῆ in Mark 4:31a and b thus receives a different meaning. However, the pre-Markan text also spoke of growth (ἀναβαίνει/καὶ ποιεῖ κλάδους μεγάλους).

9   Καὶ ποιεῖ κλάδους μεγάλους in Mark 4:32b is then necessary as a transition to the biblical allusion given in the tradition.

10 In my judgment, we do not have to assume a difference in content between the Markan and the Q versions. Perhaps it was only necessary to explain to a non-farmer, e.g., a city dweller, what is special about a mustard seed.

11 Similarly Dupont ("Couple parabolique," 2.618–19) says that the mention in Mark of how tiny the mustard seed is has led to the form of the similitude.

12 That is supported by the *Gospel of Thomas,* which transmits the two parables separately in logia 20 and 96. Dupont, "Couple parabolique," 614–23 offers a counterthesis.

13 Paschasius Radbertus, 496.

14 Euthymius Zigabenus, 408.

15 Faber Stapulensis, 61b (132).

16 In Maldonat, 276.

17 *WA* 38.563.

converts them to herself. . . ."[17] Not all that differently Maldonat triumphs: "Once the church was in the state, now the state is in the church,"[18] for, after all, kings sit on its branches! A Catholic even tried to use the parable of the mustard seed to win non-Catholics to the papacy, which at the beginning "in the rest of the church" (*scil.*, apart from Rome) was present only "as a germ." Today, he argued, this germ has become the tree that requires a decision, since, of course, several trees cannot have grown "from the tiny mustard seed"![19] In the parable of the leaven the woman could be identified with the church that lets the gospel work as leaven in the world.[20] The three measures of flour were then popularly interpreted as the three sons of Noah or the nations that descended from them.[21] There is something triumphalistic about all of these interpretations. The ecclesiological interpretation changed its character when the church was no longer a small, inconspicuous flock needing encouragement[22] but an established, powerful institution that one could not simply dismiss by referring to it *verbally* as "mustard seed." Quite apart from the naïveté with which for centuries the church and kingdom of God have been identified, there are other reasons for being horrified. Even for Bengel the catchword "tree" could be an obvious reference to the time of Constantine,[23] but it loses its joyful character today in the time of shrinking and dying national churches. The church—a sick and dying mustard bush? Is *this* church still the kingdom of God?

b. *Individual interpretations.* The starting point here is the interpretation of the mustard seed to refer to Christ as Logos that has been common since Ire-naeus.[24] Frequently we also find the mustard seed or the leaven identified with the proclaimed word, the doctrine of the church, or the gospel.[25] The mustard seed can also be identified with faith, as Matt 17:20 naturally suggests.[26] Augustine advocates an ethical interpretation of the leaven as love.[27] In this type of interpretation the earth into which the mustard seed is planted, is, for example, the inner person;[28] and the birds that are sitting on the branches of the tree are not so much the nations or kings as "the souls that contemplate what is heavenly."[29] Above all, the three measures of flour in the parable of the leaven offered many opportunities to think of a person's various parts, the most obvious of which was the popular division into body, senses, and reason.[30] Educated Platonists thought here of lust, courage, and reason.[31] Or Augustine thinks of the heart, soul, and strength of the שְׁמַע יִשְׂרָאֵל.[32] The goal of the leavening process is uniting the human powers under the rule of God, perhaps mediated by reason. This interpretation doubtless contains a great deal of potential for the individual application of the parables. Its problem lies again in the definition of the kingdom of God. Here for all practical purposes it is identified with the individual, for it is "in you" (Luke 17:21). It thus loses not only its eschatological but also its cosmic dimension.

In modern times two other approaches appear that at least in part are to be understood as correctives to the previous interpretations.

c. *Cosmopolitical approaches.* Attempts to overcome the narrow focus of the ecclesiological interpretation and

18 Maldonat, 277.

19 Bernhard Schultze, "Die ekklesiologische Bedeutung des Gleichnisses vom Senfkorn," 362–86, 371–72, 383, and passim.

20 Origen fr. 302 = 135; Jerome, 109–10; Ambrose *In Luc.* 7.191 = BKV 1/21.727.

21 Origen fr. 302; Lapide, 284 (Asia, Africa, Europe); somewhat differently Theodore of Mopsuestia fr. 74 = 121 (Jews, Samaritans, Greeks).

22 Ephraem Syrus (207) formulates as the scope: Do not be afraid, you small flock!

23 Bengel, 90.

24 Fr. 29 (= W. Wigan Harvey, ed.; 1857) 2.494. Cf. Clement of Alexandria *Paed.* 1.11 (96.1–2) = FC 23. 85.

25 See, e.g., the Gnostic Markos in Irenaeus *Haer.* 1.13.2; John Chrysostom 46.2 = *PG* 58.478; Jerome, 108–9 (*praedicatio*); Euthymius Zigabenus, 408–9; Theophylactus, 285 (κήρυγμα, λόγος τῆς πίστεως); Brenz, 514; Maldonat, 276 (gospel, *doctrina evangelica*).

26 Ambrose *In Luc.* 7.177 = BKV 1/21.718; Augustine, *Quaest.* 1.11 (*fervor fidei*); idem, *Sermo* App. 87 and 88 = *PL* 39.1913–14. According to him (88.1 = 1914) and Luther (*WA* 38.665, on 17:20) faith and kingdom of heaven are interchangeable.

27 *Quaest.* 1.12 = 14.

28 Markos in Irenaeus *Haer.* 1.13.2.

29 Dionysius the Carthusian, 165.

30 See, e.g., Origen fr. 302 = 135; Ambrose *In Luc.* 7.191 = BKV 1/21.727.

31 See, e.g., Jerome, 109 (τὸ λογιστικόν, τὸ θυμικόν, τὸ ἐπιθυμητικόν); Theophylactus, 285; Paschasius Radbertus, 500. Thomas Aquinas (*Lectura* no. 1163–69) offers a collection of all possible interpretations.

32 *Quaest.* 1.12 = 14.

to regain the kingdom of God whose breadth surpasses the church have been different approaches to a cosmopolitical interpretation in modern times. One such attempt in Catholicism is the church's claim to "leaven" the world. "Through the messianic kingdom all of life's practices and conditions, both private and public, all institutions, courts of justice, trade relations, and all businesses are, in a manner of speaking, permeated and consecrated by a new color—by religion, justice, and holiness."[33] Similar sounds are made in liberal Protestantism, although without such ecclesiastical claims. The kingdom of God must "extend over the entire nation and permeate all of its national life."[34] "The Christian must live in the world, for the leaven cannot work without contact." Thus human life in all areas—work and play, religion and leisure, politics and trade, science and art, must be permeated "by the penetrating action of Christian morality and Christian ideals."[35] A compelling formulation that avoids both an ecclesiastical and an individual narrowing of our texts is offered by a peasant in Solentiname who speaks—nota bene—not of political actions but of the word of God as mustard seed and then says: The "tree is the transformation of the world."[36] Questions remain. Above all: Is there a difference between the future kingdom of *God* and a renewed world?

d. *Approaches to eschatological interpretations.* Around the turn of the century in the history of religions school there was the recognition that the kingdom of God is a future, otherworldly reality, the end of the present world—in any case, not the church and also not God's power that "comes to the individual and enters into his soul."[37] Corresponding exegetically to the new insight of the history of religions school is the interpretation of our parables as parables of *contrast* and not of growth.[38] What is important for A. Schweitzer in the growth of the mustard seed is "not the natural but the miraculous."[39] J. Weiss applies the

comfort subjectively to Jesus himself. He [Jesus] knows only implausible beginnings of the kingdom of God but looks forward imperturbably to its complete victory. Important for Weiss is above all the "unwavering confidence of Jesus" in his "success," that will "someday exceed all expectations."[40] J. Jeremias understands these texts as a rhetorical means of taking the wind out of the sails of hearers' doubts about Jesus' mission. "This wretched band, comprising so many disreputable characters . . . God's miraculous power" will "cause . . . to swell into the mighty host of the people of God in the Messianic Age."[41]

What does the understanding of the kingdom of God in the history of religions school have to do with our texts? As J. Weiss already recognized,[42] the texts are awkward for the basic thesis of the history of religions school, since the idea of organic growth is deeply anchored in their images, and the entire history of the church's interpretation went in other directions. They could almost be used as major witnesses against the history of religions school. According to them the kingdom of God comes not as a cosmic eruption, not "with much show of power and glory," but "unnoticed" and in secret.[43] Their basic idea appeared to be that the kingdom of God is a "principle that permeates (the world or the Jewish people?)."[44] Loisy, who knows that the issue in the parable is "*l'avènement du royaume, non la communauté chrétienne,*" surmises that the idea of growth may have already been important for the evangelists.[45] According to Grässer, because of the delay of the parousia the parables of contrast very early became parables of growth in the church, and they did so differently in each of the gospels and in Q.[46]

As much as these eschatological approaches raise legitimate questions about the immanent ecclesiological, individual, and cosmopolitical interpretation of our parables, they also reveal their own difficulties. An

---

33 Knabenbauer 1.592–93.
34 B. Weiss, 261.
35 Plummer, 194–95.
36 Cardenal, *Gospel* 2.51.
37 Harnack, *Christianity,* 56 (end of the third lecture).
38 Weiss, *Predigt,* 48–49.
39 *Quest,* 356. This statement is the basis of an oft-repeated assertion that "the Oriental mind" (Jeremias, *Parables,* 148–49) regarded the sprouting and growing of seed not as a natural process but as a miracle. This assertion is inspired by, among others, 1 Corinthians 15; 1 Clement 23–24; John 12:24, but not by ancient secular texts. Kuss, "Zur Senfkorn-parabel," 78–80 and "Zum Sinngehalt," 91–94)

40 Weiss, *Predigt,* 83. That Jesus believes not in the kingdom of God but in its overwhelming success is, based on Weiss's own presuppositions, inconsistent.
41 *Parables,* 149. The idea of growth is here too—implicitly—present.
42 *Predigt,* 48, 82.
43 Plummer, 194.
44 Wellhausen, 70. Cf. B. Weiss, 261.
45 Loisy, 1.771; cf. 772.
46 Grässer, *Parusieverzögerung,* 141–42.

picks apart the basis of "proof."

absolutely understood contrast obviously destroys the possibility of discovering a *relation* between beginning and end in our parables. Yet that is precisely what is important in the images. The small mustard seed becomes the large tree; the little leaven becomes the entire mass of dough. At the same time relation means that the kingdom of God is not simply something that is totally different from the present reality. At some point Jesus' own experiences, and later those of the church or of the individual, must be inserted into this relation. The question is: Where? At the beginning? Or at the end? Or in between?

Interpretation

■ **31** We look first at the images. The mustard seed is proverbially small.[47] While black mustard seeds (*brassica nigra*) have a diameter of little more than one millimeter,[48] the shrub may reach a height of two or three meters and thus, while it is not a large tree, it is one of the largest vegetable plants (v. 32). Its leaves are cooked as greens; its kernels serve as spice, as medicine, and as food for the birds.[49] The Mishna regards the black mustard as a field plant and not a garden plant, but in Palestine, as elsewhere, it probably was planted in the garden.[50] Somewhat strangely, a person sowed "a" (single) mustard seed in his field. The reader is reminded of the preceding parable (13:24), but here it is obviously not a matter of sowing and harvesting but of a characteristic of "the" mustard seed with which the kingdom of God is compared.

■ **32** Matthew calls attention explicitly, as does Mark, to the difference in size between the seed and the fully grown shrub. Thus the choice of the image is not accidental; not just any seed can take the place of the mustard seed. The parable's conclusion is exuberant: The

birds of the air come and sit in its branches. The readers will not find that impossible, for birds like to eat mustard seeds.[51] However, the biblical language directs their attention beyond the level of the image and reminds them of the biblical images for God's coming kingdom.

■ **31-32** What associations does the parable evoke for the hearers? We will have to distinguish between the original hearers and those in the Matthean church.

Jesus' original hearers were probably surprised above all by the choice of images. A mustard seed is not an object of comparison for the kingdom of God[52] that is to usher in God's triumph over his enemies and the freedom of his people Israel. That the kingdom of God is compared with a large tree is understandable, for the tree is a biblical image for a kingdom.[53] In Ezek 17:22-24 the proud cedar is used as an image for the future restoration of the kingdom of Israel. The real surprise of the parable is that Jesus takes his images not from the mountains of Lebanon but from the vegetable garden—that he speaks not of the largest tree but of the smallest seed. Thus it really is "the beginning that counts."[54] With this beginning the parable says: Something different from what you expect will become God's biblical tree! To what does this different beginning refer? The frequent supposition that Jesus speaks here of his own activity is certainly correct. The kingdom of God is at work not with heavenly armies but with earthly disciples—not in the victory over the Romans but in hidden exorcisms and healings. Precisely this inconspicuous beginning will have an unexpected result. Thus the contrast opposes not the idea of growth but the conceptions of the kingdom of God that to this point have been prevalent in Israel. Here indeed there is a fundamental difference from all triumphalist hopes for the kingdom of God.

47 Str–B 1.669; Claus-Hunno Hunzinger, "σίναπι," 287–91, 288; proverbial sources in Löw, *Flora*, 522.

48 Löw, *Flora*, 521. The weight of about 750 seeds is approximately 1 gram.

49 Dalman, *Arbeit* 2.293–94.

50 *M. Kil.* 3.2; *t. Kil.* 2.8 = Str–B 1.669, differently Pliny the Elder *Hist. nat.* 20.236.

51 According to Maldonat (277), who, as a Spaniard, must know.

52 Paschasius Radbertus (495) has sensed this well:

"Mira et ineffabilis comparatio: ecce grano sinapis comparata est tota coelestis magnitudo."

53 Ezek 17:2-10, 22-24; 31:3-18; Dan 4:7-12, 17-23; ancient Near Eastern material in Friedrich Schmidtke, "Baum," *RAC* 2 (1954) 9.

54 Jüngel, *Paulus*, 153.

Matthew

For the readers of the Gospel of Matthew the image of the mustard seed is no longer a surprise. They are long since familiar with Jesus' images from the tradition. In reading the gospel they have just come from the parable of the weeds. Since Jesus will not explain our parable, they will understand it in light of Jesus' explanation of the parable of the darnel. Therefore, they probably understand the "person" who sows as the Son of Man, and the "field" as the world.[55] Since there is no evil seed in the parable of the mustard seed, they most likely will have understood it as a positive contrast to the parable of the darnel.[56] It can give hope to the church. They undoubtedly know about the inconspicuous beginning of the Son of Man, his death in Israel, and his disciples' persecuted and harassed existence. For them, therefore, the weight shifts to the end, the promise of the greatness and fullness of the future kingdom of God. It is conceivable that the "coming" and "settling" of the birds reminded the members of the community of the Gentiles coming together in the eschaton—the very Gentiles whom they are to evangelize. The metaphor "birds = Gentiles" can in any case be documented.[57] Thus it may be that in Matthew the beginning of the gentile mission in the present is connected with the hope of the coming kingdom of God.[58] That does not mean, however, that the kingdom of God is anticipated in the church; that is excluded by the interpretation of the parable of the darnel in the wheat field that follows (vv. 37-43). The brief transitional ὅταν δὲ αὐξηθῇ by no means implies that the church thinks it can achieve or accelerate it by its

own missionary program. No more is said than: What Jesus the Son of Man did and what his disciples do on his behalf is the beginning of the great thing that God will grant—the kingdom of God!

■ **33** The image of the leaven comes from the kitchen. The use of leaven [literally "sourdough"—*Trans.*] is common among Jews and Greeks when baking bread. The housewife took it from old dough, bought it in the bakery, or made it herself.[59] The formulation "hid" is somewhat strange; the readers would more likely expect a description of kneading. Especially unusual is the amount of flour. Three measures is the equivalent of almost 40 liters, enough for a meal for more than 150 persons or for approximately 110 pounds of bread.[60] Thus the text does not describe what a farmer's wife ordinarily does. For the hearers of *Jesus* this image probably was again a great surprise. Leaven is not one of the metaphors that demonstrates a relationship to the kingdom of God. In fact, the Passover rituals would lead one to think of something negative. What is leavened is to be removed during the Passover celebration and is useless for sacrifice.[61] However, this association is probably not at all important, for Jesus is speaking not of the Passover but of baking bread. The scope is probably not the smallness of leaven; nothing is said about that in the text, and, in any case, for forty liters of flour almost four pounds of leaven [sourdough] are needed.[62] For something tiny that changes all of the dough the image of salt

---

55 Jacques Dupont, "Les paraboles du séneve et du levain (Mt 13,31-33; Lc 13,18-21)" 2.592–608, 605; Gundry, 266.

56 Weder, *Gleichnisse,* 136.

57 *1 Enoch* 90.30, 33, 37; *Midr. Ps.* 104.13 = Buber, 222a, quoted by T. W. Manson, *The Teaching of Jesus* (Cambridge: Cambridge University Press, 1963) 133.

58 If it is true that the Matthean church is just *beginning* the gentile mission (cf. vol. 1, Introduction 5.2), the tree in which the "Gentiles" settle is an expression of the *hope* but not yet of their present reality. If, on the other hand, the Matthean church has been engaged in gentile mission for some time, then church experiences and eschaton move closer together.

59 On its production cf. Krauss, *Archäologie* 1.99 and 458; Pliny the Elder *Hist. nat.* 18.102–3.

60 Josephus *Ant.* 9.85: 1 measure (Aramaic סְאָתָא, Hebrew סְאָה) corresponds to 1 1/2 Roman *modii* (= c. 13 liter); Dalman, *Arbeit,* 4.120.

61 Exod 12:15-20; 23:18; 34:25; Lev 2:11; 6:10; cf. 1 Cor 5:6-8. In Gal 5:9 and Matt 16:6 leaven is something infectious, evil. Lohmeyer (221) therefore sees a "contrast to the view of the Jewish . . . cult." However, along with other negative uses of the metaphor of leaven, there are also positive ones. Cf. Philo *Spec. leg.* 2.185-86 (perfect nourishment; leaven as a symbol of rising and of joy) and below nn. 20–21 on 16:5-12.

62 Pliny the Elder (*Hist. nat.* 18.103) calculates 2 pounds as 2 ½ *modii* (= 22 liters).

would have been more appropriate. The issue is rather that leaven is hidden in the flour but irresistibly leavens a large amount of flour.[63] Thus it is with the kingdom of God. Once the "leaven" is in it, an irresistible process leads to excessive fullness. In this parable the idea of "growth" is more central than it is in the parable of the mustard seed; in my view its closest parallel is the parable of the seed growing by itself. Where *Matthew's church* found its own experiences in this parable is not easy to say. Since the little word ἐνέκρυψεν ("hid") is not only deliberately formulated by Matthew but also anchored in the context (cf. vv. 35, 44), it is most likely the church's view that what she repeatedly experienced was the hiddenness of the truth. The hiddenness of the truth in the parables (v. 35) and the hiddenness of the treasure in the field (v. 44) corresponds to the "hidden" leaven. The church has the task of uncovering the hidden truth by word and deed (10:26-27, cf. 5:13-16). In so doing it leavens the world.

Summary

■ **31-33** Where then is the church's place in this movement at the end of which is the kingdom of God? Only a negative answer is clear. The Matthean church has not triumphed; it has not yet embodied the tree with the many birds or the dough leavened by the gospel. The future of the kingdom of heaven remains for it the *hope* in God himself. In this regard the church differs from numerous triumphalist, especially ecclesiological, interpretations of a later time. In the context of Matthew 13 we may not forget that Matthew most clearly connects the kingdom of God with *judgment* that will also come over the church. However, how did it see the relationship between itself and the coming kingdom of God? Again a negative answer stands out: It is not defined by our parables. It is clear that the church has something to do with the mustard seed sown by the Son of Man and with the leaven that is leavening, but it is not said that the church is the beginning of the kingdom of God, let

alone its historical embodiment. At most we might say that the church has something to do with the *movement* of growth, the *process* of leavening the dough. In the images of Matt 5:13-16, the church is the light that shines and the salt that seasons. And along the way it is carried by the hope that at the end the large tree will be a nesting place for all people and the enormous amount of dough will be nourishment for many. If one were to ask Matthew what the church's deeds and experiences have to do with the future of the kingdom of God, he might answer, much as Augustine later did,[64] by referring to love.

In light of the "triumphalist" and "ecclesiastical" history of interpretation that has preceded us, today we must, in my judgment, clearly give a different accent. What can be experienced by the gospel as signs of hope today, in a post-Auschwitz world full of hunger and injustice that is facing frightening human-made ecological catastrophes, is mustard seed and leaven. That these signs could be the beginning of God's kingdom can be neither experienced nor predicted, is simply God's surprising promise. Especially the figure of the church corresponds *at best* to the mustard seed and leaven, not to the tree and the leavened dough. It may be that the christological exegesis of the mustard seed parable in the ancient church reminds us most clearly that and why it is so. Hilary sees Christ himself as the mustard seed that was sown in the field and killed and buried and in precisely *this* way surpassed all the glory of others.[65] In light of the entire New Testament Hilary recalled the cross in order to understand the mustard seed. Only on this basis is it understandable why the mustard seed (and not the tree) determines the form of the church until the coming of the kingdom of God. Once the interpretation has understood that, it will be able to make use profitably of many aspects of the history of interpretation. The "eschatological" interpretations put on record that the kingdom of God is promised to human beings but not created by them. The "individual" interpretations

---

63   It is not clear whether a biblical allusion is associated here, similar to the conclusion of the parable of the mustard seed. In Gen 18:6 Sarah had used 3 seahs (= measures) of flour for the messengers of God. Cf. Judg 6:19; 1 Sam 1:24 (1 ephah = 3 measures).

64   Cf. above, n. 27.

65   Hilary, 13.4 = 298; Augustine *Sermo* 88 App. = *PL* 39.1915. For additional representatives of this type see Stephen L. Wailes, *Medieval Allegories of Jesus' Parables* (Berkeley: University of California Press, 1987) 112-13.

not only narrowly define the kingdom of God in terms of the individual; they can show how the future kingdom of God wants to move the individual in the present. Or the "cosmopolitical" interpretations are not only an expression of ecclesiastical imperialism; they can become reminders that the kingdom of God will be more extensive and greater than the perfect church.

2.4 Conclusion of the Public Discourse (13:34-35)

Literature

See above, III B.

34 Jesus said all of this in parables to the crowds, and without a parable he said nothing to them,

35 so that it was fulfilled what was spoken by the prophet Isaiah:[1]
"I will open my mouth in parables,
I will utter what has been hidden from the beginning."[2]

Analysis Verses 34-35 bring the public discourse to a close emphatically with a formula quotation. Here Matthew reaches back to vv. 2-3 and vv. 10, 13. Verse 34 is an abbreviated and tightened[3] rendering of Mark 4:33-34. In the *formula quotation* from Ps. 78:2 the first part, v. 35b, corresponds to the LXX; only the LXX offered the plural ἐν παραβολαῖς ("in parables") that is important to Matthew. Verse 35c corresponds to no known biblical text, and it also is not Matthean language.[4] In comparison with other text forms, v. 35c sounds more basic. What is "hidden" suggests—unlike "riddles" (Ps. 78:2 MT)—the hidden mysteries of God that are preserved in heaven for the future,[5] while ἀπὸ καταβολῆς suggests the "beginning of the world." Does the quotation come from a Christian apocalyptic milieu where—much like Mark 4:11 par.—the parables were understood as enigmatic encodings of God's heavenly mysteries?

Interpretation

Matthew summarizes. Everything that Jesus has said thus far to the people was in parables. With the parables it becomes clear that the people did not let Jesus lead them to understanding. Israel's lack of understanding is such a weighty matter that Matthew uses a formula quotation to show how Jesus' parables discourse corresponds to God's will, even as does the way of God's light to the Gentiles (cf. 4:15-16). The quotation itself is clear in its first half. "In parables" is again to be understood with the secondary accent of "enigmatic discourse."[6] Its second half is more difficult, because it seems to speak of the *revelation* of that which was hidden from beginning.[7] However, that is probably not the way Matthew understood it. While "that which is hidden from the beginning" is, as in 25:34, understood to be the preexistent kingdom of God, the rare word ἐρεύγομαι hardly means "to reveal," but quite externally "to make noise," "to expel," "to express."[8] Therefore, it is more probable that ἐρεύγομαι in v. 35c parallels v. 35b and refers only to the exposure of what is hidden. However, the people do not understand what Jesus has said.[9] Only the disciples understand, and Jesus now withdraws with

---

1   Ἠσαΐου is only weakly attested by, among others, ℵ* Θ f1, 13, but it is clearly the *lectio difficilior*, since the quotation comes from Ps. 78:2. A similar error of Matthew, also corrected by copyists, appears in 27:9. The omission of Ἠσαΐου is a simple and appropriate correction, for the temple singer Asaph was considered a prophet (cf. 1 Chr 25:2; 2 Chr 29:30 and Stendahl, *School*, 118). When Porphyry noticed Matthew's error, Jerome (*Tract. Ps.* 77 = CChr.SL 78. 66–67) had to defend himself with a text-critical conjecture that he repeats in revised version in his Matthew commentary (110–11). He said that the original text read "Asaph" and that a copyist who did not know this prophet corrected it to "Isaiah." Nestle[26] follows here the external attestation of the text. Cf. Metzger, *Commentary*, 33. Cf. on the entire subject the important comments by Segbroeck ("Scandale," 360–64).

2   It is unclear whether τοῦ κόσμου was added by the majority of witnesses in analogy to the nine other passages in the NT with sequence of words or whether the longer text was shortened to agree with the OT wording. I find the former more probable, since καταβολή does not correspond to the LXX.

3   Mark 4:33b is omitted, also Mark 4:34b, because in

Matthew the entire following major section, vv. 36-52, takes its place.

4   Ἐρεύγομαι is a hapax legomenon; ἀπὸ καταβολῆς (κόσμου) appears also in 25:34. Κεκρυμμένα and the composite ἐνέκρυψεν in v. 33 are not assimilated to each other.

5   Cf., e.g., *1 Enoch* 43.3; 46.3.

6   Cf. above on the interpretation of 13:1-3, 13:14-17, and below, the excursus On the Matthean Parable Interpretation, 1 Overview.

7   Strecker (*Weg*, 71–72) sees in this an indication that the traditional quotation originated independently from its present context. Kingsbury (*Parables*, 89–90) relates the second part of the quotation to the disciples to whom God declares what is hidden. According to Wilkens ("Redaktion," 320) Matthew is interested only in the catchword παραβολαί.

8   As, e.g., the roaring of a lion or the raging of the sea; cf. LSJ, *s.v.*

9   Similarly Schmid, 223; Segbroeck, "Scandale," 360.

them into the house. The people stay outside. The readers ask themselves once again[10] what evil thing the people have done to deserve this abrupt about-face of Jesus. On the level of the text of Matthew 13 we have to say: nothing. That is what demonstrates that our chapter's narrative skeleton is an anticipation that is out ahead of Matthew's story of Jesus. However, the readers of the Gospel of Matthew know that the people also helped bring Jesus to the cross and that they then repeatedly rejected his messengers. That is here presupposed and reflected.

---

10 Cf. above, III B 2.1 on 13:10.

3.1 The Interpretation of the Story of the Tares (13:36-43)

Literature

See above, III B 2.2 on Matt 13:24-30 and III B on the parables discourse.

36 **Then he left the crowds and came into the house. And his disciples came to him and said: "Explain to us the parable of the tares in the field."**
37/ But he answered and said:
"The one who sows the good seed is the Son of Man;
38 **the field is the world;**
the good seed, those are the sons of the kingdom;
the tares are the sons of the evil one;
39 **the enemy who sowed them is the devil;**
the harvest is the end of the age;
the reapers are angels.
40 **Now as the tares are gathered and burned in the fire,[1] so will it be at the end of the age. 41/ The Son of Man will send out his angels, and they will gather from his kingdom all who give offense and who act against the Law, 42/ and they will throw them into the oven of fire; there will be there wailing and gnashing of teeth. 43/ Then the righteous will shine like the sun in the kingdom of their father. Those who have ears shall hear!"**

Analysis **Structure**

The brief, unconnected main clause in v. 36a carries a great deal of weight. It refers back to 13:1-2.[2] The disciples' question followed by Jesus' answer has its counterpart in v. 51 where Jesus asks and the disciples answer. The explanation itself is divided into two unequal parts: vv. 37-39 is a stereotypically formulated, lexical interpretive catalog of individual terms that has its formal parallels in Jewish and Christian texts.[3] Verses 40-43 are a "little apocalypse"[4] that is

introduced by a comparison. It ends with the call to watchfulness that stood already at the beginning of Jesus' discourse to the people (cf. v. 9). Noteworthy in this little apocalypse are: (1) the close contacts with the conclusion of the parable of the fishnet in 13:49-50,[5] and (2) the numerous terms it has in common with 25:31-46.[6]

Sources

It is clear and largely uncontested that this interpretation is secondary to vv. 24-30. It is selective. Not interpreted are the sleeping of the people, the servants, their conversation with the master, the ripe grain, the bundles, and the barn. Above all, what in the story itself is decisive, viz., the waiting until the end, plays no role. The little apocalypse interprets only v. 30b, c. Controversial is whether the entire interpretation, or only part of it, comes from Matthew.[7] The advocates of the second hypothesis repeatedly begin with the (in my judgment only apparently) unbalanced juxtaposition of church and world in our text. For their part they are not of one mind.[8] Some think that the interpretive catalog in vv. 37-39 is a church tradition that Matthew has actualized with the little apocalypse.[9] Others think that the little apocalypse, perhaps in the wording of vv. 49-50, is traditional and that Matthew formulated vv. 37-39 as an introduction to it.[10] I think that both parts of the interpretation come from Matthew. It is linguistically possible. In vv. 37-39 the list of the terms to be interpreted is of course already given from vv. 24-30. Furthermore, there are numerous Mattheisms.[11] Linguistically, vv.

---

1   *Κατακαίω* is better attested than *καίω* and is therefore original. This formulation thus corresponds to v. 30 and 3:12.
2   Double inclusion, cf. above, III B Structure.
3   Luz, "Taumellolch," 159, n. 26.
4   Jeremias, *Parables*, 81, cf. de Goedt, "Explication," 43.
5   *Οὕτως ἔσται ἐν τῇ συντελείᾳ τοῦ αἰῶνος . . . καὶ βαλοῦσιν αὐτοὺς εἰς τὴν κάμινον τοῦ πυρός· ἐκεῖ ἔσται ὁ κλαυθμὸς καὶ ὁ βρυγμὸς τῶν ὀδόντων.* In addition *ἄγγελοι, δίκαιοι.*
6   Friedrich, *Gott im Bruder,* 66–67.
7   Thus especially Joachim Jeremias, "Die Deutung des Gleichnisses vom Unkraut unter dem Weizen (Mt 13,36-43)," in idem, *Abba,* 261–65.
8   Friedrich (*Gott im Bruder,* 67–82) is especially con-

servative and claims that only vv. 36-37a and 43b come entirely from Matthew. Friedrich comes to his result by considering only the vocabulary but not the relation to the context. He furthermore excludes all the terms that come from the parable. However, how could one have explained the parable without them?
9   See, e.g., Schweizer, 309; Crossan, "Seed Parables," 260; Weder, *Gleichnisse,* 124; de Goedt, "Explication," 41.
10 See, e.g., Klostermann, 123; Flusser, *Gleichnisse,* 64, 109; Trilling, *Israel,* 125; in detail Theisohn (*Richter,* 190–201) who speaks of the influence of the parabolic discourses of *1 Enoch* on the traditional piece in 13:49-50.
11 *Οὗτοι* (after *casus pendens*), *κόσμος, υἱοὶ τῆς*

40-43 are almost completely Matthean.[12] Two observations are especially important: (a) In both parts of the interpretation there is a linguistic reference back to 8:12, viz., υἱοὶ τῆς βασιλείας ("sons of the kingdom") in v. 38 and the formula of weeping and gnashing of teeth in v. 42; (b) The terms that are not interpreted in vv. 37-39 are at the same time those that are irrelevant for the "little apocalypse" in vv. 40-43. The two parts are thus formed from one casting, that is, probably by Matthew. The introduction in v. 36 is unquestionably Matthean.[13]

Interpretation

■ **36** Jesus leaves the crowds who have been listening to him to this point and with the disciples goes back into the house from which he had come in 13:1. He will now instruct the disciples. Understanding comes not through a supernatural process of revelation; it happens when the "only teacher," Jesus (cf. 23:8), teaches the disciples. Discipleship means continuous "school" with Jesus—instruction *and* schooling for life. Matthew cites the parable of the darnel according to its negative point, the weeds, because in what follows the important thing is the warning.

■ **37-39** The lexical interpretive catalog of vv. 37-39 prepares for the application in vv. 40-43. The sower is the Son of Man. That does not mean the earthly Jesus in distinction from the judge of the world; v. 41 will make clear that the Son of Man has in his hand not only the sowing but also the harvest and thus the entire history of the world. In Matthew the Son of Man is the Lord of judgment who accompanies the church on its entire way through lowliness, suffering, and resurrection.[14] The field is the world. In 5:14 the disciples were the light of the world. Jesus announces here a universal claim for his message. Thus the field is not the church. This idea is impossible for Matthew not only from a literary point of view, since at this point in his story of Jesus, where the disciples are not yet definitively constituted as a special "community," there is as yet no church. It is above all impossible also in substance, because for him who concludes his gospel with the great commission, church always exists only in its mission to the world. Unlike the parable of the field,[15] the seed is the sons of the kingdom. The expression is reminiscent of 8:12. There it referred to the Israelites. Here it is left open who will be the "sons of the kingdom"; the entire Gospel of Matthew tells how, instead of the Israelites, the "Gentiles" (ἔθνη) who bear fruit (cf. 21:43) will become the "sons of the kingdom." The darnel seeds are the "sons of the evil." Whether τοῦ πονηροῦ is to be interpreted as masculine or neuter must remain open.[16] The enemy is the devil whom Matthew believes to be at work, as at 13:19, in the present when the seed is sown. The harvest is the end of time, as Matthew formulates it with a common Jewish expression.[17] The reapers are the angels of judgment

---

βασιλείας (cf. 8:12); πονηρός, διάβολος (in distinction from τοῦ πονηροῦ), συντέλεια αἰῶνος. Cf. vol. 1, Introduction 3.2.

12 Matthean are (cf. vol. 1, Introduction 3.2): Οὖν, συντέλεια τοῦ αἰῶνος, ὥσπερ—οὕτως (ἔσται), σκάνδαλον, ἀνομία, βάλλω, πυρός as st. c., τότε, δίκαιος, πατήρ. On the kingdom of the Son of Man cf. 16:28; 20:21; in addition, 19:28; 25:31, 34 (βασιλεύς); 26:64. Ἀποστελεῖ τοὺς ἀγγέλους αὐτοῦ corresponds literally to 24:31, cf. 16:27; on σκάνδαλον cf. 16:23; 24:10, on ἐκεῖ ἔσται ὁ κλαυθμὸς καὶ βρυγμὸς τῶν ὀδόντων cf. above, II B 1.2 on the sources of 8:11-12, on βασιλεία τοῦ πατρός 26:29, on the comparison with the sun 17:2; on the apocalyptic call 11:15; 13:9. The numerous LXXisms of these verses also fit well in Matthew: Ποιεῖν ἀνομίαν, cf. Mal 3:19; Ps. 36:1 [37:1]; κάμινος τοῦ πυρός, cf. Dan 3:6; 4 Macc 16.21, etc.; shining of the righteous like the sun, cf. Dan 12:3; Judg 5:31; Mal 3:20; Sir 50:7.

13 Redactional are (cf. vol. 1, Introduction 3.2): Τότε,

προσέρχομαι . . . αὐτῷ, μαθηταί, λέγων, ὁ δὲ ἀποκριθεὶς εἶπεν. Matt 13:18 is the only other place in the NT where a parable is named.

14 Cf. Geist, *Menschensohn,* 103 and below, IV A 1 the excursus on the Son of Man, 4: "Son of Man" in Matthew's narrative. The issue is not the contrast between the time of the earthly Son of Man (v. 37) and the coming judge of the world (v. 41); the Son of Man title includes all of the activity of Jesus and thus also the "post-Easter activity of the risen Lord." That is shown by the expression "kingdom of the Son of Man" (referring to the present).

15 In the history of interpretation based on Mark 4:14/Matt 13:19 the seed is often interpreted as referring to the word. Cf., e.g., Tertullian *Praescr. haer.* 31 = ANF 3.258.

16 On the basis of Jewish usage both are possible. Cf. expressions such as "sons of Belial" (4QFlor. 1.8) or "men of the evil one" (Prov 28:5). In favor of a neuter understanding is the contrast to the "substantive" formulation υἱοὶ τῆς βασιλείας and the

who are important in Judaism precisely in the circle of the Son of Man expectation.[18]

History of Interpretation

Matthew does not interpret other expressions of the parable allegorically, but later the church's interpretation did. It has, for example, interpreted the sleeping people as the church's bad shepherds, teachers, pastors, church leaders.[19] The servants, whose zeal is often highly praised in the history of interpretation, are, for example, the proclaimers of the word.[20] Such additional allegorical interpretation is not forbidden by the text. On the contrary, it serves to sharpen the parenesis, just as do the Matthean allegories in the "catalog of interpretation." To say it in a "reversal" of Jülicher's classic parable theory: Here it is the individual allegorical interpretations that prepare the soil that permits Matthew to formulate a topical parenetic *scope* of the story. As with 13:19-23, here also the allegorization serves to apply the text to the listeners themselves.[21]

Interpretation

■ **40** After the preparatory interpretations of the various details, in vv. 40-43 Matthew formulates his own concern. No longer is the issue for him waiting and the separation of wheat and darnel but judgment as such. In keeping with the title (v. 36) the emphasis falls on the negative side that is broadly described. As that house master will gather the darnel at the harvest and have it "burned with fire" (cf. 3:12), so will it happen to the sons of the evil one at the end of time.

■ **41** As in 24:31 the Son of Man will send out his angels. There and in *Did.* 10.5 the gathering of the elect is the decisive event, but here it is the destruction of the evil ones. They are "offense" ($\tau\grave{\alpha}$ $\sigma\kappa\acute{\alpha}\nu\delta\alpha\lambda\alpha$) and "doers of lawlessness." The latter expression is suggested directly by 7:23, indirectly by the Bible,[22] and means all who do not hold fast to the biblical law that has its apex in the love commandment. As in 7:15-23, for Matthew practice rather than correct doctrine is what is decisive in the judgment. The $\sigma\kappa\acute{\alpha}\nu\delta\alpha\lambda\alpha$ are more difficult to interpret. In the Bible the expression[23] always refers to things and not to people.[24] In 18:6-7 Matthew will warn against leading the little ones astray and will speak of the necessity of the $\sigma\kappa\acute{\alpha}\nu\delta\alpha\lambda\alpha$. The expression shows how much Matthew is implicitly thinking of the church and the dangers to which it is exposed. The "kingdom of the Son of Man" corresponds to the "field," and thus is the world.[25] Unlike 16:28; 20:21 (cf. 25:31, 34) it is here not something that will come only with the parousia but something that already exists in the world. It is the reign of the exalted one over heaven and earth that he now makes visible primarily through the proclamation and the life of his disciples (28:16-20!).[26] Negatively we must say that the "field" and "the kingdom of the Son of Man" are not the church[27] as a special space within the world. Naturally the Matthean interpretation *points in*

---

linguistic differentiation between $\pi o\nu\eta\rho\acute{o}\varsigma$ and $\delta\iota\acute{\alpha}\beta o\lambda o\varsigma$. In favor of the masculine understanding is the preceding text 13:19.

17 Cf. Luz, "Taumellolch," 160, n. 32; Str–B 1.167; Schlatter, 445; Dalman, *Words*, 155.

18 Cf. above, n. 39 on 13:24-30.

19 See, e.g., John Chrysostom, 46.1 = *PG* 58.475 (presiders); Jerome, 112 (*magistri*); Luther 2.467 (proclaimers).

20 Zwingli, 302.

21 Cf. above on 13:23.

22 Ἀνομία with $\pi o\iota\acute{e}\omega$ is frequent in LXX especially in Ezekiel (c. 10 times); in LXX Pss οἱ ἐργαζόμενοι τὴν ἀνομίαν is like a formula. Cf. also vol. 1, II A 3.2 on 7:15-23, n. 10.

23 In Greek the word is documented only with the meaning "snare." In the LXX it contains, following the Hebrew כשל = to stumble, the conceptual field of "striking against" that can then also be used metaphorically. Cf. Ps. 140:9 [141:9] τὰ σκάνδαλα (snares) τῶν ἐργαζομένων τὴν ἀνομίαν; Zeph 1:3 Σ;

Ezek 14:3 Ἀ; Ps. 30:11 Ἀ (texts in Gustav Stählin, "σκάνδαλον κτλ," *TDNT* 7 [1971] 343–44).

24 Stählin ("σκάνδαλον," 344) points to Zeph 1:3 Σ where τὰ σκάνδαλα means the idols.

25 Especially Vögtle ("Das christologische und ekklesiologische Anliegen von Mt 28,18-20," in idem, *Evangelium*, 253–72, 267–71) on the basis of Matt 28:18-20; similarly, e.g., Strecker, *Weg*, 218–19; Kingsbury, *Parables*, 97; Trilling, *Israel*, 126; Dupont, "Point de vue," 229; Russell Pregeant, *Christology Beyond Dogma: Matthew's Christ in Process Hermeneutic* (Semeia Supplements 7; Philadelphia: Fortress, 1978) 109–12.

26 Apart from 28:16-20, 26:64 is also to be cited as a parallel: "Ἀπ᾽ ἄρτι you will see the Son of Man seated . . ."

27 Thus, e.g., Jülicher, *Gleichnisreden* 2.555–56; Schmid, 224–26; Bornkamm, "End-Expectation," 19, 44–45; Charles W. F. Smith, "The Mixed State of the Church in Matthew's Gospel," *JBL* 82 (1963) 153 ("the problem of the church in the world . . .

the *direction* of the church, but he does not define it statically as, for example, a space separate from the world in which good and evil are still temporarily together; instead, he understands it dynamically as a community that practices and proclaims Jesus' commandments. Precisely that is also his goal for "all nations" whom the disciples are to teach "everything" that Jesus "has commanded" (28:20). Thus Matthew's concern is not a definition of what the church *is*, but that the church that now lives and acts in the kingdom of the Son of Man, in the world, *becomes*[28] what it should be, viz., a community of righteous ones who some day will shine in the kingdom of the Father.

Thus in our text the church is not the topic of discussion but the one to whom the Matthean exhortation is addressed. The text is parenetic. The disciples in the house are to take care that they do not belong to the "ones who give offense" (σκάνδαλα) and the doers of lawlessness who are inside and outside the church.

■ **42** For this reason there follows in v. 42 the drastic reference to the oven of fire—a biblical expression for judgment[29]—and the "wailing and gnashing of teeth" that Matthew likes to use.[30]

■ **43** The promise to the righteous in v. 43 that again makes use of biblical language and Jewish concepts[31] appears rather brief after the extensive statements about the fate of the unrighteous. The "kingdom of the Father" is to be distinguished from the kingdom of the Son of Man; after the destruction of all the evil ones, the kingdom of the Son of Man is changed into the kingdom of the Father.[32] Matthew ends the interpretation with his well-known summons to alertness—what Jesus has explained is central to the life of the disciples!

Summary

The evangelist has accentuated in two ways the story that was already understood allegorically when he received it. He has given it a clear universalistic horizon: The *world* is the kingdom of the Son of Man. He has power in the entire world; in the world he claims obedience. If in the pre-Matthean church the story of the darnel was applied to the church's relationship with Israel,[33] the changed situation is obvious. The separation from Israel is now complete; the church is beginning the gentile mission. Now the world becomes its field of endeavor.[34] At the same time Matthew sharpens the scope of the story *inward,* to the church. Its situation is basically no different from that of the world which it calls to obedience to the commandments of Jesus. The community is also still awaiting the judgment of the Son of Man. It too will be asked about the fruits it bears. In this way the story becomes inwardly an exhortation and warning for the church.

Thus our story has found a new profile in a new situation. The evangelist has given it a new accent. For him its meaning obviously was not simply something established; it could be changed. He was set in motion in this process by the Risen One himself in whom he believed and who brought him to the proclamation to the Gentiles and to calling his churches to an accounting. The old story functioned as a kind of matrix that gave rise to new meaning. But what determined this new meaning? There are three factors. First of all, there is of course the existing matrix and its potential for meaning. In this case the traditional text is not simply a mere "verbal husk,"[35] but a story rich in potential applications contained especially in the existing metaphors.[36] In the

---

turns out to be that of the world in the church"); Marguerat, *Jugement,* 440, 445–46 (the church *in mission*).

28 Cf. the basic discussion above, following II C 4 on the "reflections on the meaning of the disciples discourse today." On this basis the *goal* of the Matthean statements is the same as in 22:11-14, although there the issue is not the world but those who have responded to God's invitation, i.e., the church.

29 On the formulation cf. Dan 3:6-22 (six times!); on the content *1 Enoch* 10.6; on the formulation and the content *1 Enoch* 98.3 (literal parallel). Cf. in

addition vol. 1, II A 2.2.1 on 5:22, n. 18.

30 Cf. above, II B 1.2 on 8:11-12.

31 Dan 12:3 Θ; *1 Enoch* 39.7; 104.2; formal parallels Sir 43:4; 50:7; *Ep. Jer.* 66; Matt 17:2.

32 Cf. 1 Cor 15:24-28!

33 Cf. above on 13:30.

34 Cf. vol. 1, Introduction 5.2.

35 Cf. above, II D 1.2: Summary and History of Interpretation.

36 One cannot say, however, that the original meaning of the text regulates its application. In Matthew's case he was not able to distinguish between the original meaning and the meaning of the text given

second place, *Matthew's situation* had an *innovative* effect. Here we have mentioned the separation from Israel that had already happened, the gentile mission, and the need to admonish the church. A new situation has led to a new accentuation of the text. In the third place, the *entirety of the Matthean understanding of Christ* was a creative force. The meaning that our story received in Matthew corresponds in astonishing measure to his Christology and his basic understanding of the gospel. Let us remember: Christ is the exalted Lord of the whole world who is identical with the earthly Jesus and who accompanies his church and gives it a missionary task for the entire world; the gospel consists of the commandments of Jesus; the church is an obedient band of disciples whose obedience will be weighed by the judge of the world. Thus one can say that the risen Lord as Matthew understands him is the standard for the new interpretation; he regulates the potential meanings that are hidden in the matrix of the old story. And now for Matthew the risen Lord is not a diffuse and unclear spirit-Christ but the earthly one whose story Matthew is telling us.[37] That is to say: It is not simply his subjective faith or his own spiritual vision of Christ that regulates new applications of the text in a new situation but the way of the earthly Jesus and his commandments. A personal element, of course, remains here—corresponding to the risen Lord is the theology of his witnesses. But what determines the Matthean image of Christ is the continuing listening to all the commandments of the one teacher, Jesus, and the orientation toward his paradigmatic basic story.

History of Interpretation

The same thing happens again in the later interpretations and applications of our text. The Risen One opened up in new situations new meaning for the potential of the old matrix of the text. The biblical text, even in its fixed and canonized form, has not restricted the freedom of the Risen One to create new meaning in new situations; indeed, it made it possible. Here also the standard for the new actualization was not the individual text but the risen Lord Jesus Christ as a whole as he was understood and believed by the church or by the individual interpreter.[38] The question is whether this standard is sufficiently clear to make clear theological judgments possible in light of the wide-ranging history of our text's interpretation. Or does the opening up of new potential meanings as we observe it already in the New Testament and certainly in the history of influence mean *arbitrary* freedom in the name of a Christ who is *simply* the external reflection of one's own faith? Of great significance here is precisely the basic Matthean christological approach that the exalted Christ is none other than the earthly Jesus and that all faith is to be measured against his commands.

One can classify the church's interpretations according to whether they understand the field as
1. the individual person,
2. the church, or
3. the world,
and whether the darnel seed is related
   a. dogmatically to heresy or
   b. ethically to evil.

The combinations of 2 with a and b are especially frequent, since the issue here was the problem of the "pure church" and how to deal with heresy, that is, two fundamental problems that have accompanied the church throughout its entire history. It is thus not surprising that in the history of our text's interpretation basic questions of ecclesiology have constantly appeared. Ethical interpretations (1b) are scarce, interpretations in terms of the world (3) even scarcer.

The Problem of the Pure Church (Interpretation 2b)

As early as Calistus our text was important for justifying the readmission of sinners in the church. He is reported to have said: "Let the darnel and the grain grow together, that is, the sinners in the church."[39]

---

to him in his community tradition. For us there is the additional factor that the original meaning and the original author of our text are no longer discernible with sufficient certainty.

37   Cf. vol. 1, I A 1.3 on 1:18-25, Summary.

38   If what regulates the interpretation is the (original) meaning of the individual text rather than the

Christ who is believed in the present, as, e.g., is the case in modern scholarly interpretation, we may at most achieve a (more or less) *correct* interpretation but not one that is *true* that can claim to declare what is valid in and for the present.

39   Hippolytus *Ref.* 9.20 = ANF 5.131.

The text later became important in the controversy with Novatianists and Donatists who wanted to keep the church, or at least the clergy, free of mortal sinners. Even if there are weeds in the church, says Cyprian, we should not leave it, for our task is to be sure that we ourselves are wheat.[40] Origen also points out that there were Jebusites in Jerusalem too, that is, in the church.[41] Augustine's statement on the subject was especially pronounced. He is not completely against church discipline, but he is aware that he lives in a church with a great many weeds. We should not pull out the weeds, so that the wheat will not be pulled out at the same time. Only if this danger does not exist, that is, if the wheat is firmly rooted, should one pull out the weeds.[42] Where the sickness is too great only pain and sighing remain[43] and at least removing the evil from one's own heart. The theologians of the Reformation saw the problems of the ancient church returning. In the Reformation and post-Reformation interpretations the definition of the church as *corpus permixtum* appeared. "In the church evil people and hypocrites will always be mixed with good and true Christians."[44] Luther compares the church with a person who cannot get along without his body, "the filthy bag."[45] There is church only "hidden under the great mass . . . of the godless."[46] Nevertheless the reformers did not dispense with church discipline. It is simply relative. Calvin understands our text as a comfort for pastors who with their church discipline "will not succeed in cleansing the Church completely from all defilement," and Zinzendorf later admonishes the "brothers and sisters" to take care that "the field of Jesus Christ bear as few weeds as possible," but an "institution . . . without spots and wrinkles" (Eph 5:27!) is not possible.[47]

It is a long way from Matthew's small minority community to the *corpus permixtum* of the reformers. One may argue that the reformers' theological solution is consistent. When the national church, that in its place can scarcely be distinguished from the world, has taken the place of the minority church, then it *must* be—even in Matthew's sense—a *corpus permixtum*. Nevertheless there is, in my judgment, precisely in such a situation the danger that Matthew's concern will be lost. His purpose was to exhort the members of the church to be wheat and not darnel. Important for him was movement, the growth of fruits, being able to stand in the judgment. That there definitely was church discipline in his community is clear from 18:15-18. I think that whenever—especially in a national church—the designation of the church as a *corpus permixtum* is not only a description but becomes a basic definition of the nature of the church, then the danger exists that such a definition cripples the church on its way of obedience and does not help it on its way. The *essence* of the church according to Matthew is not that it is a *corpus permixtum*. While it is true that the church in *reality* is (still!) a *corpus permixtum*, its task is to become wheat and not darnel.

Dealing with Heretics (Interpretation 2a)

It is understandable that the darnel that confuses people was interpreted as heresy. As the wheat was sowed prior to the darnel, so also the true doctrine came first, but heresy was "introduced later, foreign and inauthentic."[48] In interpreting our text Luther speaks of the painful experience that "where God builds a church, the devil also wants to have a chapel or a tavern."[49] What instructions about dealing with heretics did our text give? It appeared to take a "liberal" position, but from the very beginning the problem arose about how to combine it with other texts, especially with antiheretical texts in the letters. Thus one looked for compromises. John Chrysostom was of the opinion that one may, even should, excommunicate and silence heretics, but under no circumstances should one kill them, for then one would prevent God from giving them the chance to repent.[50] Theophylactus exemplifies: If one had killed the tax collector, Matthew, we would not have his

40 *Ep.* 54.3 = FC 51.132–33; cf. *Ep.* 55.25 = FC 51.150.
41 Origen *Hom. in Jos.* 21.1 = GCS 30.428–29.
42 Augustine *Contra Epistolam Parmeniani* 3.2.13 = CSEL 51.115.
43 Augustine *Contra Epistolam Parmeniani* 3.2.14 = CSEL 51.116.
44 Bucer, 126c.
45 Luther 2.474.
46 Apology of the Augsburg Confession 7 = BSLK 237–39 = *Book of Concord*, 170–72; the quotation is on p. 171. Similarly Luther, *WA* 38.566 ("Ecclesiam plenam semper fore sectis, scandalis, malis");

Cocceius, 26; Calovius, 300 (*necessitas scandalorum*).
47 Calvin 2.76; Zinzendorf 2.944.
48 Tertullian *Praescr. haer.* 31 = ANF 3.258, cf. Jerome, 112; John Chrysostom 46.1 = *PG* 58.476. Following Augustine (*Retract.* 2.28) most medieval exegetes interpreted it to refer to the heretics *and* the evil ones. Already in the NT the heretics were morally disparaged.
49 Luther, *WA* 38.558.
50 46.2 = *PG* 58.477.

gospel today![51] Of great influence was the restriction that the weeds were permitted to grow so that the wheat would not be endangered. Where weeds could be removed without danger to the wheat, one should do it.[52] By turning the reason that the house master gave the servants into a restriction the tendency of the story was decisively altered. Thus Thomas Aquinas was able to justify religious wars in the interest of the wheat,[53] and with the help of our text a sixteenth-century inquisitor was able to legitimate the Inquisition by saying that at the edge of the field one could "pull out two or three, on occasion six or eight or even ten or twelve, indeed, even a hundred weeds without damaging the wheat."[54] In reality this leads to intolerance as soon as one is in the definite majority. The exegesis of the Counter-Reformation was of the opinion that if the pope says that in pulling out the weeds the wheat would also suffer damage, then one must leave the weeds alone.[55] However, the reformers' view of the problem was not fundamentally different. Luther asks: Does *sinite utraque crescere* (let both grow) mean that one should let even the pope and the monasteries grow? He rejects that decisively and says that the saying does not want to affirm papacy and heresy but to comfort the church and exhort it to be patient. The only new feature in the interpretation of the reformers is that a fundamental distinction was made between the task of the state and that of the church. The church fights with the weapon of the word. "The heretics and rebels . . . may grumble in the corner, but you should not let them come to the chancel, to the pulpit, to the altar."[56] For the secular power, however, "allow both to grow" (*sinite utraque crescere*) does not apply. The task of the secular power is "physically to punish blasphemy, false doctrine, heresies and their followers."[57]

Humanists were the first to offer a basically different view. Erasmus demands that the possibility of repentance must be left open for the heretics, fundamentally and without limitation.[58] With an appeal to our text Sebastian Castellio and Jacob Acontius make a basic claim on behalf of tolerance.[59] Since the Enlightenment there has been an increasing sense that the history of post-Constantinian Christianity was a burden. "Anathemas were pronounced not against individuals but against nations. . . . Thus it happened that the darnel was pulled out with the wheat, innocent with guilty, even more: that the wheat was often regarded as darnel."[60] For H. E. G. Paulus our parable demands fundamental tolerance. "In the realm of morality, no one should by force put himself in charge of someone else's behavior. Each individual according to his individual conviction!"[61]

In light of our parable L. Ragaz describes two potentially mistaken ways for the church: the frequently used way of narrowness and the much more rarely used, but in modern Protestantism frequently trod, way of relativism. By contrast the parable's quintessence is: "It is not we who possess the truth but God . . . Only he."[62] The observation captures something central. The Matthean parable places the division alone and exclusively in the hand of the judge of the world and makes subordinate to him all the plants in his field, including and especially the church. From this perspective one will not only reject killing heretics physically, as was done in the past, but also question the institution of excommunication and the church's magisterial office. A church that in the name of a truth that it believes to possess absolutely condemns or excommunicates people as heretics must be asked whether it spiritually kills "erring people." In my judgment, from Matthew we must say that a church can judge and excommunicate only when it is willing to put its own possession of truth and its own practice just as seriously under the judgment of the world judge. No church can exercise church discipline or

---

51   285.

52   Cf. Augustine above, nn. 42–43; in addition, John Chrysostom 46.2 = *PG* 58.477; Thomas Aquinas, *Lectura* no. 1149; Maldonat, 275.

53   *S. th.* 2/2 q.10, a.8 corpus (not to convert them but so they would not be an obstacle to faith).

54   Bainton, "Liberty," 106.

55   Maldonat, 275; Lapide, 286.

56   2.481 (Sermon from 1546).

57   Melancthon, *Epist.* 7, no. 1494 = *Corpus Reformatorum* 3.199–200; similarly also Luther after 1531; cf. *Hauspostille* of 1544, *WA* 52.134–35 and Bainton, "Liberty," 112–13. Calvin (*Refutatio Errorum*

Michaelis Serveti [*Opera* 8. 472; Brunsvigae: Schwetschke, 1870]) advocates the Augustinian position: "toleranda esse mala admonet quae sine pernicie corrigi nequeunt."

58   *Paraphrasis*, 80.

59   Bainton, "Liberty," 117–18; Gustav Adolf Benrath, in Carl Andresen, ed., *Handbuch der Dogmen- und Theologiegeschichte* (3 vols.; Göttingen: Vandenhoeck & Ruprecht, 1980–84) 3.40, 43.

60   Grotius 1.410, similarly already Cocceius, 26.

61   Paulus 2.222.

62   Ragaz, *Gleichnisse*, 149, 151 (quotation).

doctrinal condemnation as does the judge of the world, that is, finally and forever.[63] On the other hand, however, where a church does not even exercise church discipline any longer as a sign and for the sake of love and where the "inner pluralism"[64] relativizes any binding truth, one can ask whether such a church is going anywhere at all and whether it can claim as a church to represent truth at all.

Ethical Interpretations (Interpretation 1b, 2b)

In view of the interpretations thus far described, Episcopius energetically appeals for order. The issue in this parable is not to describe the "*status ecclesiae*" or to discuss the problem of heretics. Instead, the scope is solely ethical. In light of the coming judgment the gospel demands "a sincere attitude and a conversion of one's whole life."[65] The Enlightenment man, H. E. G. Paulus, also says sharply that the real scope of the parable is not tolerance but practical good deeds.[66] Often the field is here identified with the individual. Both weeds and wheat exist in the individual—not, however, unchangeably as fleshly matter and divine spirit,[67] but combined with the idea of free will: "If you want to do so, you can change and become wheat!"[68]

The ethical interpretation is Matthean. Applying it to the individual (as with the story of the fourfold field) or (as in Matt 13:36-43) to the church were never mutually exclusive alternatives in the history of interpretation. Here the preachers can and should choose according to the situation. The only important thing is that the hearers and readers understand the text as an open question to them. Both the church and the individual bear in themselves the possibility of wheat and the possibility of tares.[69]

The World as the Field (Interpretation 3)

This dimension of the text has been recognized only sporadically in the history of interpretation.[70] Interpretations that applied it to realities within the church remained predominant. That approach corresponded with the Matthean text to the degree that the text intends not to identify theoretically the church and the world but to arouse and exhort the church with its parenesis of judgment. In Matthew's understanding, of what does the church's *prae* ("advantage") toward the world consist if the world is the kingdom of the Son of Man and if in the final judgment the church's members are asked just like everyone else whether in their deeds they were wheat or darnel? Matthew, who in his interpretation says nothing about the church, nevertheless gives a very precise answer to this question. It is: The advantage that Jesus' disciples have is that Jesus takes them into the house and explains everything to them. It is, therefore, that they understand what they and the world have to look forward to and that they know what they have to do. And—their advantage is that they do not have to go their way alone but are instructed and accompanied by Jesus. Thus v. 36, which is reminiscent of this reality, is not simply an irrelevant transitional remark but is of great theological consequence.

63 On the tension with 16:19; 18:18 that might occur here, cf. the interpretation of 18:18.

64 The catchword ("inner pluralism" = *Binnenpluralismus*) comes from *Christsein gestalten,* commissioned by the Council of the Evangelical Church in Germany (4th ed.; Gütersloh: Mohn,1986) 80. It is probably no accident that here my Catholic partner P. Hoffmann in a marginal comment regards "symbolic" church discipline as "nonsense" and calls for "new modalities of conflict resolution," while as a Protestant Christian and member of a Swiss Reformed church in which doctrinal or ethical conflicts can no longer even arise, since individuals are free to believe and act as they please (unless the "openness" of the national church is endangered!), I put the accent differently. Both of us have been negatively influenced by our churches!

65 86.

66 2.218–19.

67 Clement of Alexandria *Exc. Theod.* 53.1 = GCS 17.124 (darnel = flesh).

68 Athanasius *Hom. sem.* 5 = *PG* 28.149. Interpreting the field in terms of the individual are also Origen (10.2 = GCS Origenes 10.2); Jerome (*Pelag.* 1.13 = FC 53.247–8); Theophylactus (284); Rabanus (947) and Zwingli (429–30).

69 That is why Matthew did not interpret the servants allegorically as the disciples. Had he done so, their place on the side of the Son of Man would have been unambiguous.

70 For example: Origen (10.2 = GCS Origenes 10.2), Thomas Aquinas (*Lectura* no. 1134), and Albertus Magnus (562) interpret it to refer to the *processio* of the word into the world at the creation. Thomas Aquinas (*S. th.* 2/2 q.64, a.2) applies the text secularly to the problem of capital punishment (if the wheat is not endangered and it is useful for society as a whole, it is permitted).

3.2 Of the Treasure in the Field and of the Pearl (13:44-46)

Literature

Tullio Aurelio, *Disclosures in den Gleichnissen Jesu* (Regensburger Studien zur Theologie 8; Frankfurt: Lang, 1977) 145–54.

F. Cochini, *Un discorso sulla scrittura per Greci, Guidei, Gnostici e Cristiani* (Studi Storico-Religiosi 5; L'Aquila, 1981) 105–33.

Crossan, *Finding.*

Dauvillier, "Parabole," 107–15.

B. Dehandschutter, "La parabole de la perle (Mt 13,45-46) et l'Évangile selon Thomas," *EThL* 55 (1979) 243–65.

Derrett, *Law* 1.1–16.

Jacques Dupont, "Les paraboles du trésor et de la perle," in idem, *Études* 2.908–19.

Jeffrey A. Gibbs, "Parables of Atonement and Assurance: Matthew 13:44-46," *CTM* 51 (1987) 19–43.

Otto Glombitza, "Der Perlenkaufmann," *NTS* 7 (1960/61) 153–61.

Jülicher, *Gleichnisreden* 2.581–85.

Linnemann, *Parables.*

Merklein, *Gottesherrschaft,* 64–69.

Ragaz, *Gleichnisse,* 116–24.

Scott, *Hear,* 389–403.

Hermann Usener, "Die Perle: Aus der Geschichte eines Bildes," in *Theologische Abhandlungen Carl v. Weizsäcker zu seinem siebzigsten Geburtstag, 11 Dezember 1982, gewidmet von Adolf Harnack* (Freiburg: Mohr, 1892) 203–13.

Constantine Vona, "La margarita pretiosa nella interpretazione di alcuni scrittori ecclesiastice," *Divinitas* 1 (1957) 118–60.

For *additional literature* on the parables discourse see above, III B.

44   The kingdom of heaven is like a treasure hidden in a field:
      A man found it, hid it,

and from joy he goes and sells (everything)[1]
      he has and buys that field.

45   Again the kingdom of heaven is like a merchant seeking beautiful pearls:

46   But he found one valuable pearl,
      went away and sold[2] everything he had
      and bought it.

Analysis

Structure and Source

Apart from minor variations,[3] the two short parables are structured formally alike. After a title (= "*thema*") in vv. 44a and 45, the story (= "*rhema*") begins in vv. 44b and 46 with εὑρών ("found") and connected finite verbs. They differ in that in v. 45 the kingdom of God is compared not with the pearl, as one might have expected, but with the merchant. Linguistically, both parables have a number of favorite Matthean terms.[4] Since Matthew never formulates completely new parables elsewhere, it is probable that he has taken them over from the oral tradition and himself committed them to writing for the first time. In the context of the discourse, the relationship to vv. 36-43 and vv. 47-50 is relatively weak, but there are probably clear reminiscences of vv. 31-33. The parable introductions in vv. 31, 33, 44, 45, the syntactic structure of the four parables, and a number of terms are identical.[5]

Tradition History and Origin

The written version that Matthew has created is so brief that little more than the bare narrative skeleton is transmitted. Thus we are not able to decompose the two parables; on the other hand, we may not exclude the possibility that earlier narrators in the church accentuated it differently or told it in more detail. The parallels in the *Gospel of Thomas* (logia 76 and 109) are of no help in reconstructing the history of the tradition; they are secondary, based in part on other traditions, and completely gnostic.[6] It is also

---

1. Πάντα is text-critically uncertain. Given the many synoptic parallels, it may be a later addition, but the short text is documented almost exclusively by B.

2. The awkward perfect appears, because the aorist of the old verb πέρνημι (postclassical present = πιπράσκω) even then was already obsolete. Cf. the references in LSJ, s.v.

3. The most important difference is that v. 46 tells the story in the past tense, v. 44c, d in the present. Other differences result from the different subject. Cf. below, n. 7.

4. Favorite Matthean terms (cf. vol. 1, Introduction 3.2) are: Ὅμοιος, βασιλεία τῶν οὐρανῶν, ϑησαυρός, κρύπτω, ἀγρός, ἄνϑρωπος, χαρά, ὑπάγω, πάντα ὅσα, ἐκεῖνος, δέ, πάλιν, ἀπελϑών. On πωλέω with ϑησαυρός cf. 19:21 and Mark 10:21, on

ἔμπορος cf. 22:5 (the older version in Luke 14:18 speaks of the *purchase* of a field!); on πολύτιμος cf. 26:7 variant reading, on (πιπράσκω) πάντα ὅσα ἔχει cf. 18:25. Gundry (275–79) assumes the Matthean formulation of both parables on the basis of 18:25; 19:21; 22:5, but a high number of Matthean preferred terms is also usual when Matthew himself writes something for the first time.

5. Structure: parable introduction + dative + relative clause with participle and finite verbs that follow. Additional common catchwords with 13:31-32: ἐν τῷ ἀγρῷ, ἄνϑρωπος; with 13:33: κρύπτ- (13:44 twice!).

6. B. Dehandschutter, "La parabole de la perle (Mt 13,45-46) et l'Évangile selon Thomas," 243–65.

uncertain whether the two parables were told as a double parable before Matthew or whether Matthew first combined them.[7] The story of the treasure in the field is a variant of a motif that is common in countless popular narratives and fairy tales;[8] there appear to be scarcely any close parallels to the parable of the pearl merchant. That has nothing to say, however, about whether the parables came from Jesus. That he used a widespread popular subject is just as possible as that he created a new parable.

Interpretation

The interpretation of these two short parables appears to be simple, but the Matthean context already presents difficulties. They do not fit well between the interpretation of the parable of the tares and the parable of the fishnet. We cannot blame the arrangement on a source. The claim that a "field" also appears in the parable of the treasure[9] is somewhat superficial. The two parables are clear but open-ended in their imagery; the transfer to the referent is correspondingly difficult.

■ **44** Widespread in antiquity is not only the popular idea that one might discover a treasure somewhere in a field or in a ruin[10] but also stories in which a farmer or laborer finds a treasure in his own or another's field and thus makes his fortune. The many parallels give us the chance to discover the *special* arrangement of the motifs in our story as well as the narrative elements that were freely chosen and thus to trace the narrator's intention.

Horace alludes to it: "If only I could accidentally find a pot of gold, like the hireling who discovered the treasure and bought and ploughed in his own right the field where he found it! Hercules was a good friend to him!"[11]

His commentator Porphyrio calls this story a well-known "*fabula*" and mentions that the lucky man in spite of his wealth continued to plow and work the field faithfully.[12] Apollonius of Tyana buys for a poor pious man with four marriageable daughters a field with a treasure.[13] In two Jewish variants of our story the poor man finds the treasure in his own field.[14] As a parable there is the story of the heir who sold his weed-infested field for a pittance; then when the buyer worked in it, he found a treasure (or a spring).[15] The story is known also as a difficult legal problem: To whom does the discovered treasure belong? Persian law answered that it belonged to the king.[16] Wise judges like the legendary King Kazia or philosophers like Apollonius of Tyana find more humane solutions. When King Kazia had to render judgment at a trial, he married the son of the finder and buyer of the field with the daughter of the seller; in the same situation Alexander the Great would have had the two litigants killed and would have confiscated the treasure.[17] Apollonius determines which of the two contestants is the better person and gives the treasure to him.[18] In Roman law the "treasure in the field" was a model case of a legal debate. It ended

7 In my judgment we can hardly draw definite conclusions from the *Gospel of Thomas* that is secondary here. The remaining differences are not significant and result for the most part from the subject: The treasure must be hidden, while the merchant must look for pearls. Πιπράσκω refers to larger business transactions (Schenk, *Sprache*, 11) and fits well with the merchant. Most significant is the nonagreement of the "theme" that in v. 44 is a thing ("treasure") and in vv. 45-46 a person ("merchant"). However, is that more than a stylistic variation of Matthew? Result: an original double parable is at least possible.

8 Cf. Crossan, *Finding*, esp. 53–71.

9 David Hill, *The Gospel of Matthew* (NCB; London: Marshall, Morgan, and Scott, 1972) 237.

10 Cf., e.g., the copper scroll from Qumran (3Q15), a list of 64 treasures (hidden during the Jewish war?).

11 *Sat.* 2.6.10–13 (Casper J. Kraemer Jr., trans., *The Complete Works of Horace* [New York: Random House, 1936] 71).

12 Alfred Holder, ed., *Pomponi Porfyrionis commentum in Horatium Flaccum* (Ad Aeni Pontem: Wagner, 1894) 313. Persius also alludes to it (*Saturarum liber* 2.10–12, ed. Wendell Vernon Clausen [Oxford: Clarendon, 1956]).

13 Philostratus *Vit. Ap.* 6.39.

14 First: Philo *Deus imm.* 91 (as an example for an unexpected discovery of knowledge). Second, *y. Hor.* 3.4.7 = 48a.44–62 (G. Wevers, trans., 1984, 99–100); *Lev. Rab.* 5.4 (Freedman-Simon 4.66–67); *Deut. Rab.* 4.8 (Freedman-Simon 6.97–98) (as a reward for benevolence toward the rabbis).

15 *Mek.* on Exod 14:5 (2 variants: spring and treasure with gold and pearls); *Midr. Qoh.* 4.13 (116a) = Str-B 1.674; *Pesiq. R. Kah.* 11.7 = Thoma-Lauer, *Gleichnisse* 1.181 and elsewhere. As a rule the parable is interpreted in salvation-history terms, i.e., of the pharaoh who let Israel leave Egypt.

16 *B. B. Mes.* 28b.

17 *Y. B. Mes.* 2.8c.39 and elsewhere = Str–B 1.674. In the later Jewish legend of the converted Ninevites

finally with the decision that the buyer of a field also acquires the treasure as long as the previous owner did not know about it.[19] Jewish law seems to have followed a similar practice.[20]

The material shows that the narrator of the parables has selected a definite "option." The field, and along with it the treasure, belonged not to the finder but to a stranger. That this person was the patron or lessor the parable does not say, any more than it says that the finder was a poor day laborer.[21] *First of all* [22] the man finds the treasure and thus has an improbable chance—the kind of chance about which people normally only dream. Finding the treasure is thus not the reward for hard work or charity, as it is in other variations of the story. Thus far, however, only the parable's exposition—one might say its *"thema"*—has been given. Now the actual story, the *"rhema,"* begins with the finite verbs in v. 44b. Thus the emphasis lies neither on the "immeasurably high value" of the treasure[23]—that is already clear from the subject!—nor on the joy of the lucky finder[24]

that is mentioned only in the first parable. Important is rather what the man now does. Here too the narrator can choose among various options. The man could, for example, have stolen the treasure secretly.[25] Or he could have obeyed the law and have had his discovery announced in order to find out who the owner was.[26] However, he covers it up again. That was clever, for nobody is to discover his find in the intervening time until the purchase of the field has been completed. Whether his action was legal or moral does not interest the narrator.[27] Then he bought the field. Here too the narrator would have had other options. The man could have withdrawn his money from the bank, sold a part of his possessions, or borrowed money. He does none of those, but he "sells everything he has." This variation is not accidental, especially since it is repeated in the following parable. Everything is obviously pointed toward this goal. That is why the man must first find the treasure, and that is why he must cover it up again. The

---

both renounce the treasure and the heirs of the original owner are able to be located (Louis Ginzberg, *The Legends of the Jews* [7 vols.; 1913–28; reprinted Philadelphia: Jewish Publication Society of America, 1967–69] 4.251; 6.351).

18 Philostratus *Vit. Ap.* 2.39.

19 Paulus *Digesta* 41.2, 3.3 (in George Francis Hill, *Treasure-Ttrove: The Law and Practise of Antiquity* [London: Milford, 1934] 8–11; Derrett, *Law*, 3, n. 1). It is presupposed that the owner can no longer be determined. Hill (*Treasure-Trove*, 27) and Dauvillier ("Parabole," 109) cite the older Hadrianic law: The finder gets only half; prior to Hadrian the state may have claimed the find.

20 Dauvillier ("Parabole," 111) calls attention to *m. Qidd.* 1.5 (movable goods are acquired with real estate); Derrett (*Law*) offers a more complicated argument: A movable object is acquired when one lifts it or picks it up (cf., e.g., *m. Qidd.* 1.4–5). He explains the hiding of the treasure by saying that the work of a hired laborer or renter belongs to the patron who pays the wage. Thus the man in Matt 13:44 could have picked up the treasure only in the name of his patron (cf. especially *b. B. Mes.* 10a); he must, therefore, have been a day laborer or a hired laborer. However, none of that interests the text. Derrett's legal argumentation is, moreover, questionable. Cf. Crossan, *Finding,* 91.

21 The narrator of the parable is not interested, as, e.g., Horace is, in the social aspect that a poor

wretch has come upon great fortune. Besides, the man has so much to sell that he was able to buy the field from the proceeds, and the pearl merchant in the parallel parable is not poor anyway.

22 Cf. the title of Crossan's book: *Finding Is the First Act.*

23 Jülicher, *Gleichnisreden* 2.585.

24 Jeremias, *Parables*, 200–201, cf. Schweizer, 311.

25 In that case he really would have been openly immoral, and Crossan's interpretation would be correct that the man left not only his possessions for the sake of the kingdom of God but also his old morality (*Finding*, 75, 93, 106, 112–13). However, here the immoral element in the man's behavior remains unemphasized. Crossan's interpretation fails with the parallel parable of the pearl where nothing immoral happens.

26 Every found object, from three coins on top of each other on up, must be announced publicly (*m. B. Mes.* 2.2). Also to be announced are: money in a bag, a pile of money; cf. Crossan, *Finding,* 92. Cf. the Ninevites above, n. 17.

27 In my judgment, legal and moral deliberations are just as far removed from the parable as they are, e.g., in Luke 16:1-8; 18:1-8.

issue for the narrator is the "deliberate risk" of the finder who gives up "everything else in order to gain the Kingdom of Heaven."[28]

The parable shows how the narrator from the repertory of possibilities in an existing story chooses the one suitable to him. The choice is determined by the subject matter, the kingdom of God. Since the issue is the kingdom of God, it is inconceivable, for example, that the finder would have been the longtime owner of the field,[29] and it is just as inconceivable that the finder would have spent, for example, only a part of his possessions for this treasure.

■ **45-46** In a similar way the imagery of the following parable of the pearl merchant is also determined by its subject matter. Ἔμπορος is the "wholesale dealer" who exports and imports.[30] As a rule pearls were imported from India. Since the time of Alexander the Great they had been in fashion and were considered as the essence of luxury.[31] In Jewish religious language the pearl could be used in various ways as an image for something priceless, for example, for the Torah,[32] for Israel,[33] for an appropriate thought,[34] or, much like the treasure, as an expression of God's abundant reward for the pious.[35] In

contrast to the parable of the treasure, however, this narrative may have been created by Jesus.[36] The theme of the story is a pearl merchant. He finds a very costly pearl. That it is *one* pearl is not irrelevant;[37] it is necessary because of the referent, the kingdom of God.[38] Again the parable is not interested in the details of the purchase, such as whether the merchant paid a realistic price for the pearl; nor is it concerned about whether he could sell it again afterwards. Important is only that the merchant "went away and sold everything he had" in order to buy the pearl. The pearl merchant now has only this one pearl for which he has given everything. That is obviously the issue for the narrator.

■ **44-46** Thus the two parables want to underscore human action in view of the opportunity presented by the kingdom of heaven. Of what does it consist? By saying twice "he sold everything he had" Matthew certainly has thought beyond the imagery very concretely of the renunciation of possessions that was part of the discipleship of the itinerant radicals.[39] He had in mind here the statement of Mark 10:21.[40] We have already met the demand to renounce earthly treasures in 6:19-34 in the center of the Sermon on the Mount[41] and have under-

28 Linnemann, *Parables*, 103; Flusser, *Gleichnisse*, 131; cf. Tullio Aurelio, *Disclosures in den Gleichnissen Jesu*, 150. We should not speak of "sacrifice" or "renunciation" (Schlatter, 446); these concepts are too religiously or ascetically loaded.

29 The gnostic author of *Gos. Thom.* 109 can formulate in this way, for the pneuma kernel is in the Gnostic long before he even attains to gnosis.

30 BAGD, *s.v.*

31 Friedrich Hauck, "μαργαρίτη," *TDNT* 4 (1967) 472, esp. nn. 4–6.

32 *Pesiq. R. Kah.* 12.11 = Thoma-Lauer, *Gleichnisse*, 191.

33 *Ag. Ber.* 68 = Buber, 133 (cited by Flusser, *Gleichnisse*, 131).

34 Str-B 1.447–48.

35 Cf. *b. Sabb.* 119a = Str-B 1.675. In *Exod. Rab.* 20.9 on 13:17 (= Freedman-Simon 3. 250) a parable of a stupid owner of pearls is told as a variant to the parable of the heir (cf. above, n. 15).

36 In my view, there are no Jewish parallels on the subject; the parable of the seaman who abandons his entire cargo in a storm in order to reach the rich city (*T. Job* 18:6-8) is a *substantive* parallel.

37 Thus it is not a literal rendering of an Aramaic indefinite article חד.

38 In the preceding parable εἷς was superfluous, since

one does not find several treasures; with the merchant who buys many pearls, εἷς is necessary in order to stress the surpassing value of this one pearl. With a christological interpretation of the pearl merchant, recently suggested again by Jeffrey A. Gibbs ("Parables of Atonement and Assurance: Matthew 13:44-46," 19–43, 27–38) and Burchard ("Senf korn," 23–30), this feature cannot be interpreted. Why does the Son of Man Jesus by his death save only *one* pearl and sell all the others?

39 Correctly Jacques Dupont, "Les paraboles du trésor et de la perle," in idem, *Études* 2.918. Here the referent, i.e., life, intrudes into the image and makes the formulation a metaphor.

40 Common words: ὑπάγω, πωλέω, ὅσα ἔχεις.

41 Cf. vol. 1, II A 2.4.1 on 6:19-24 (Summary) and II A 2.4.2 on 6:25-34 (Summary, etc.).

42 Cf. above, II C on addressees, II C 2.1 on 10:8-10, II C on the basic message of the disciples discourse, III B 2.1 on 13:22 and below, IV A 1 on self-denial and IV C 3 on 19:16-30.

43 Cf. the similar formulations in 18:25.

44 *Act. Pet.* 20 = NTApoc 2.303; *Act. John* 109 = NTApoc 2.256.

stood the disciples discourse of chap. 10 *also* as a reminder of the way of poverty in discipleship which is basically demanded of the entire church.[42] In the story of the rich young man the idea will occur once more, again in connection with the catchword "treasure" (19:21). Matthew understands the renunciation of possessions as a part of the church's *way* to perfection that is shaped by love. I do not thereby intend to say that Matthew speaks here *only* of the renunciation of possessions as a response to the kingdom of heaven. In the parables "selling everything" *also* has an illustrative metaphorical dimension and means more than it says.[43] In view of the formulations and of the importance of the renunciation of possessions in the entire gospel, however, it is not conceivable that the imagery should be strictly separated from the referent (something that Matthew never does in his allegorizing parable interpretation!) so that it did *not* speak here of the renunciation of possessions.

Summary and History of Interpretation

It is thus clear how Matthew intended for the two parables to be applied. Nevertheless, in the church's interpretation they have a rich history that in part emphasized quite different accents. Most of the time the various tendencies included rather than excluded one other.

Christological Interpretations

Early on Christ became the pearl and the treasure.[44] That could be unfolded, for example, in a salvation-history approach. The treasure hidden in the field is the Christ who is hidden in the scriptures.[45] Like the diligent pearl merchant who sought many pearls, Israel had taken great pains with the law, but it was all in vain.[46] Therefore, salvation was taken away from Israel, as the field was taken from the farmer.[47] The christological interpretation of the parable of the pearl made frequent use of ancient legends about the pearl's origin. The purple mussel "drinks the heavenly dew and the beams of the sun and the moon and the stars and thus generates the pearl out of the light from above."[48] What was more suggestive than to interpret it as the incarnate one who was generated by God in the virgin?[49] As is the pearl, so Christ is *"lapis ex carnibus genitus."*[50] Using this interpretation of the parable of the pearl or also the treasure hidden in the field, many interpreters recall that Christ's divinity is hidden in the flesh.[51] Certainly such interpretations are not exegetically correct, but they do develop the New Testament insight that Jesus' parables after his death could be transmitted only by making the teller of parables himself the content of the parables.

But it is not the interpretation of the treasure and the pearl as Christ that characterizes most interpretations. Instead, the opinion of most interpreters is expressed by Maldonat: "The kingdom of heaven, I think, one must . . . as in the preceding parables assume as faith, the gospel, or the evangelical doctrine."[52] Beginning here, one can put the accent either on the promise of salvation or on the exhortation.

The Promise of Salvation

What does the treasure or the pearl mean here? Following Dionysius the Areopagite, Thomas Aquinas speaks of the truth that grants unity,[53] Brenz of the

---

45 Irenaeus *Haer.* 4.26.1.

46 Hilary, 13.8 = 302; Luther, *WA* 38.567.

47 Origen, 10.6 = GCS Origenes 10.6.

48 Physiologus, 44 (Ursula Treu, trans., *Physiologus: Naturkunde in frühchristlicher Deutung* [2d ed.; Berlin: Union, 1981] 86); cf. already Pliny the Elder *Hist. nat.* 9.54.107. From here it is understandable why in Gnosticism and among the Mandaeans and Manichaeans the pearl became a widespread image for the soul.

49 Especially impressive in Ephraem Syrus, *Sermo* 148 (in Armand Benjamin Caillau and Marie Nicolas Silvestre Guillon, eds., *Collectio selecta SS Ecclesiae Patrum* 37 [Paris: Méquignon-Havard, 1834] 186–213). Hermann Usener ("Die Perle: Aus der Geschichte eines Bildes," in *Theologische Abhand-*

lungen Carl v. Weizsäcker zu seinem siebzigsten Geburtstag, 11 Dezember 1982, gewidmet von Adolf Harnack [Freiburg: Mohr, 1892] 206–7) points out that here Christ parallels Aphrodite, who according to the ancient view was also born from a mussel.

50 Ephraem Syrus, *Sermo* 8 = 192.

51 Cf. Clement of Alexandria *Paed.* 2.12 (118.5) (the "clear and pure Jesus, [the] seeing eye in the flesh, [the] transparent logos for whose sake the flesh is costly"); Dionysius the Carthusian, 169; Lapide, 287 (*deitas in humanitate*).

52 279. Cf., e.g., Theodore of Mopsuestia fr. 75 = Reuss, 121 (Kerygma); Jerome, 113 (*scientia Salvatoris*; the Bible); Bullinger, 128AB; Brenz, 517–18, 519 (gospel).

53 *Lectura* no. 1193.

forgiveness of sins,[54] Zinzendorf of the "universal reality" that makes "healthy" and "blessed," viz., the message of the martyr Jesus through his blood,[55] Ragaz of the "miracle" and of the "happiness," "when . . . the one thing comes."[56] In modern—almost solely Protestant—exegesis this interpretation of the parables as referring to grace appears again in an unusual variation when one subjectively regards "the great joy, surpassing all measure" as the scope of the parables[57] or when one objectively puts in the foreground the "greater value" of the rule of God that "obviously" affects human action.[58] In my judgment, the presupposition of the two parables here becomes their scope. While the parables certainly make such an application possible, one should recognize first of all that this is an application and not exegesis. Then, in the second place, one should ask why for Matthew the renunciation of possessions obviously is not "obvious." Third, one should recognize how much one's own Protestant background determines such reinterpretations.

The Exhortation

The classical church interpretation also gave great weight to exhortation. Frequently quoted parallel texts are Matt 10:37-39 or the example of Paul, who regarded all previous things as "refuse" (Phil 3:8) when compared with the gospel. Usually the renunciation of possessions is removed from the center, and the exhortation is generalized. The issue is not simply renouncing possessions but renouncing "with joy" and being "eager in doing good."[59] Baronius formulates forcefully, for example, that it is important to be

"businesspeople" and not "idlers" in view of the kingdom of God.[60] Luther's brief, purely parenetical interpretation is especially impressive. He derives from our parables pointedly that nobody is a Christian who believes himself or herself to be more than someone who is in the process of *becoming* a Christian. "*Stare in via Dei est retrogredi*"[61] (to stand still on God's way is to go backwards). Others warn against "riches, delights, honours, and comforts of the world"[62] or issue a call to strive for heaven.[63] On the whole, it is noteworthy how much in the history of interpretation the spiritual forms of "renouncing the world" have pushed the real renunciation of possessions into the background.

The main point of the two parables is so clear in Matthew that Jesus does not have to interpret it for his disciples. It is all the more striking that the exhortation to renounce possessions almost disappeared from the history of interpretation and that many other statements moved to the foreground. Certainly, *all* of these statements are important and valuable, and most of them are not completely beyond the potential meaning of these parables or at least the parables of Jesus in general. Nevertheless, it is worth noting that "the warning against riches" that is "the only direct ethical exhortation" of our entire chapter[64] once again was not heard in the history of interpretation. What shall we say to this? Matthew himself has said it already: "The care of the world and the deceit of riches choke the word" (13:22).

54 518.

55 2.979–80.

56 *Gleichnisse*, 120.

57 Cf. Jeremias, *Parables*, 201 and above, n. 24.

58 Jüngel, *Paulus*, 143, 145; cf. Ernst Fuchs, "Was wird in der Exegese interpretiert?" in idem, *Zur Frage nach dem historischen Jesus* (Tübingen: Mohr/ Siebeck, 1960) 292 ("Jesus . . . grants" to the hearers that they risk everything when "they receive his word"); Weder, *Gleichnisse*, 141 (the "rule of God as *agens* . . . [the] hearer as *reagens*").

59 John Chrysostom 47.2 = *PG* 58.483–84.

60 In Knabenbauer 1.600: "Negotiatores, non otiatores."

61 WA 38.568 following Bernard of Clairvaux. Then follows: "*Igitur, qui Christianus est, non est Christianus, hoc est, que se putat* factum *Christianum, cum sit tantum* fiendus *Christianus, ille nihil est*" (emphases not in the original).

62 Calvin 2.83.

63 Gregory the Great *Hom. in ev.* 11.1 = *PL* 76.1114.

64 Quotation from the interpretation of 13:22 above.

3.3 On the Dragnet (13:47-50)

Literature

Franz Dunkel, "Die Fischerei am See Genesareth und das N.T.," *Bib* 5 (1924) 375–90.

Jülicher, *Gleichnisreden* 2.563–69.

W. G. Morrice, "The Parable of the Dragnet and the Gospel of Thomas," *ExpT* 95 (1983/84) 269–73.

For *additional literature* see above, III B 2.2 on Matt 13:24-30 and III B on Matthew 13.

47   **Again, the kingdom of heaven is like a dragnet that was thrown into the sea and gathered (fish) of every kind. 48/ When it was full, they pulled it onto the shore and sat down; they gathered the good into vessels but threw out what was not usable. 49/ Thus it will be at the end of the age. The angels will come out and separate the evil from the midst of the righteous 50/ and throw them into the oven of fire; weeping and gnashing of teeth will be there.**

Analysis   **Structure**

The parable of the dragnet begins like that of the pearl and almost like those of the mustard seed, the leaven, and the treasure. It is also structured as they are. After an introductory statement of the theme with a participial designation (v. 47), the brief narrative begins in v. 48 with a relative clause and continues with finite verbs. The interpretation in vv. 49-50 refers only to v. 48. It has a great deal of similarity with the interpretation of the parable of the darnel: Verses 49-50 correspond to vv. 40-43. Unlike those verses, it does not say what happens to the good. Thus the announcements of judgment in 13:40-43 and 13:49-50 frame the intervening parables. Some of the vocabulary also agrees with 13:24-30.[1] In addition, our text is especially connected to three texts. The parable of vv. 47-48 is reminiscent of the scene that introduces the entire chapter, 13:1-2 (θάλασσα,

καθίζω, συνάγω, ἐπὶ τὸν αἰγιαλόν). The contrast καλός/σαπρός recalls the saying about the tree and its fruits in 7:17-18 and 12:33. Relatively numerous also are the verbal connections to the description of the judgment of the world in 25:31-46 (συνάγω, καθίζω, ἀφορίζω, δίκαιος, πῦρ).

Redaction and Source

The interpretation in vv. 49-50 seems to me to be completely redactional just as vv. 40-43 were.[2] Except for the hapax legomena σαγήνη, ἀναβιβάζω and ἄγγος that are conditioned by the material, the parable is also largely redactional.[3] Should we assume it to be a story invented by the evangelist?[4] That is unlikely, not only because Matthew nowhere invents parables, but also parable and interpretation do not fit together as well as they do with the parable of the darnel. There is nothing in the image of sorting fish that corresponds to the fire of judgment.[5] I find it most probable, therefore, that Matthew has taken over the dragnet parable in vv. 47-48 from oral tradition and has put it in writing; for the interpretation of vv. 49-50 he has offered a variation of his own interpretation of the darnel parable in vv. 40-43. An "interpretive catalog" such as the one in vv. 37-39 was here neither necessary nor possible; the parable is too short and lacks clearly interpretable metaphors. Thus for Matthew the two parables were a pair. They are not, however, an original double parable but are considerably different. In 13:24-30 the time factor, viz., the waiting until the harvest, is decisive; here it plays no role. The pericope at 13:24-30 portrays an extremely improbable case from farming; here we have a completely normal and everyday example from fishing. The text at 13:24-30 is a temporally more complex, three-step process; this text speaks only of the "harvest" of the fish.

---

1   Συνάγω, συλλέγω, καλός; cf. ἀνὰ μέσον/ἐκ μέσου.

2   Cf. analysis 2 on 13:36-43. On ἐξέρχομαι, δίκαιοι, πονηροί cf. vol. 1, Introduction 3.2. Ἀφορίζω (esp. the future tense) and (ἐκ) μέσου are LXX language. On βάλλω cf. below, n. 3. On the relations to the context, esp. to 13:36-43 and 25:31-46, cf. above, section 1. Theisohn (*Richter*, 190–201) and Friedrich (*Gott im Bruder*, 82–85) regard vv. 49-50 as traditional. Cf. above, nn. 8 and 10 on 13:36-43.

3   On βάλλω, πληρόω cf. vol. 1, Introduction 3.2. More important are the contacts with 12:33; 13:1-2, 24-30, 40-43; 25:31-32; cf. above, section 1. On the eschatological "throwing out" cf. 3:10; 5:13; 7:19; 8:12; 18:8; 22:13; 25:30. Decisive is that the parable is formulated with a view to the redactional interpretation. Cf. below on vv. 47-48.

4   Thus Goulder (*Midrash*, 374) and Gundry (279), who see the impetus to the creation of the parable in the saying about fishing for people (Matt 4:19).

5   The useless fish are thrown back into the lake! They remain alive while the "good" fish end up in the frying pan!

Tradition History and Origin

Can vv. 47-48 be decomposed in traditional historical terms? The variant in *Gos. Thom.* 8 is of no help here; it is clearly secondary. The parable there deals with an especially costly fish that corresponds to gnosis; it was influenced by Matt 13:45-46. Since Matthew is probably the first to put the story in writing, as with Matt 13:44, 45-46 there is little that we can determine about different accents it may have had with earlier narrators or with Jesus.[6] In general it is probable that it goes back to Jesus.

History of Interpretation

The story of the net has always stood in the shadow of the story of the darnel and was interpreted under its influence. As with that parable, this one also, especially in the interpretations influenced by the Reformation, became a portrayal of the church as a *corpus permixtum* of good and evil people.[7] And, as with the former, so also with this one, this interpretation was made possible by shifting the viewpoint from the end to the beginning, from the kingdom of God to the church. Indeed, in its imagery it even offered the chance to establish the church directly in the parable. In the allegorical interpretation the church corresponded to the net[8] that contained all kinds of fish, for example, fish from all nations.[9] Thus the eschatological parable became a parable of the history of missions. The fishers not mentioned in it were then forthwith introduced and identified with the "fishers of people" (Matt 4:19), the apostles and their successors.[10] More recent interpretations also are often influenced by the story of the darnel. From that story, for example, one introduces a time factor. The

expulsion of all evil ones will take place "not before the final consummation."[11] Or the "afterwards" of the separation and the "before" of the gathering are contrasted, in which case the before is decisive: "for where no fish are caught, one cannot sort them."[12] Then the emphasis is put on the now: "Now people are given 'space for a decision.'"[13] With such interpretations the last judgment is forgotten or becomes marginal. Then modern exegesis can extract itself from this theologically and philosophically difficult dilemma by claiming that Matthew is the first to be interested in judgment and that he ignores the element of the "gathering"[14]—that Jesus himself accentuated the parable differently. It is amazing what can be surmised with a hypothetically reconstructed Jesus text! However, we know nothing about Jesus' original version. In view of the results of the analysis, the only thing left for us to do is interpret the Matthean text.

Interpretation

■ **47-48** The text is severe. As in the preceding parables, here too the theme is stated first, in v. 47. Then in v. 48 the story itself (the "*rhema*") is told in finite verbs. Thus v. 47 is, as it were, the subject; in v. 48 the predicates follow. Matthew thus does not speak of gathering and separating but of separating what already had been gathered in the net. That corresponds exactly to his own interpretation that refers only to the conclusion. That the image is formed with the interpretation of vv. 49-50 in mind is shown in the way Matthew formulates the theme impersonally with the catchword σαγήνη and then in v. 48 introduces a personal but not mentioned subject, viz.,

---

6   Following Rudolf Otto (*The Kingdom of God and the Son of Man* [London: Lutterworth, 1951] 127), Manson (*Sayings,* 197–98) and Schweizer (313) assume that the original parable contained only v. 47. Behind it is a greater interest in the fishnet in which the different fish are mingled than in the final stage in which the good fish are in the container and the bad on the garbage dump. At least they are aware that such an interest fits badly the parable's present text! W. G. Morrice ("The Parable of the Dragnet and the Gospel of Thomas," 269–73) sees the scope of the original parable (for him also only 13:47) in universalism (ἐκ παντὸς γένους!) in contrast to limiting the proclamation to Israel.

7   Luther, *WA* 38.569 (against Donatists, followers of

Müntzer); Calvin 2.83; Brenz, 520–21.

8   See, e.g., Gregory the Great *Hom. in ev.* 11.4 = *PL* 76.1116; Strabo, 134; Thomas Aquinas, *Lectura* no. 1197 (alongside the interpretation in terms of doctrine); Olshausen, 499 ("the Kingdom of God . . . according to its actual appearance").

9   Thomas Aquinas, *Lectura* no. 1197; Theophylactus, 292.

10   See, e.g., Theophylactus, 289; Lapide, 288.

11   Jülicher, *Gleichnisreden* 2.567; cf. Dahl, "Parables," 151.

12   Jüngel, *Paulus,* 146; cf. Weder (*Gleichnisse,* 144), who says that the issue is the "unconditional character" of the gathering and the "obviousness" of the separation.

13   Gnilka 1.510.

"they," that is, the fishermen. Why this awkwardness? Their sorting and throwing away, described with finite verbs, corresponds to the activity of the angels in vv. 49-50. However, nothing that the angels do corresponds to the casting of the net and the fishing of the title.[15] Obviously Matthew did not want to evoke any associations with the "fishers of people" and therefore has formulated the parable impersonally "about the dragnet." He also does not say, unlike v. 30, where the useless fish are thrown. The reason is clear. They are not thrown into the fire! In short, once more Matthew has formulated the parable in terms of his interpretation.

A σαγήνη is a dragnet. Dragnets at the lake of Gennesaret are, according to modern descriptions, from about 250 to 450 meters long and about 2 meters wide. A rope is fastened at each end. Weights are hung from one of the long sides so that it sinks; the other is furnished with cork or light wood so that it floats. The dragnet is taken out by boat and then pulled to land.[16] Fishnet and fishing were not conventional metaphors,[17] but there are a few formulations that might catch the attention of the listeners and readers. Ἐκ παντὸς γένους is in content superfluous, but it prepares for v. 48b where the readers will discover that it means the useful and useless fish. Πληρόω is not only in our gospel but already in Judaism a theologically loaded word; it may be that behind the superficial meaning there is the thought of the completion of the time determined by God or of the measure determined by God.[18] While it could be taken for granted that a fisher, after pulling in the net, would sit down, sort the catch, and eliminate inedible or unclean[19] fish, the sitting of the fishers may be reminiscent of the sitting of the Son of Man-world-judge (19:28; 25:31; 26:64) and of the Lord and Lamb of God exalted to the right hand of God (cf., e.g., Col 3:1; Eph 1:20;

Revelation 4–5 passim). The readers will still have in mind the contrasting pair καλός ("good") and σαπρός ("unusable") from the image of the trees with their fruit; there the thought was of people's works or words (7:16-20; 12:33). The unusual throwing "out"—at the lake of Gennesaret the fishers are themselves outdoors—awakens associations with other judgment texts in the gospel.[20] Thus the readers sense that the text has an underlying meaning; this time it is not the images themselves but the consciously chosen formulations that create this impression.[21] Above all, they will remember the introductory scene to the whole discourse. There at the "lake" (13:1-2) stood a large crowd "gathered" "on the shore" while Jesus "sat" in the boat and spoke in parables. It is as if our parable took up that introductory scene and commented on it. The readers know that this speaking of Jesus caused the separation between the people and the disciples. As the following interpretation makes clear, the separation parallels the last judgment. Thus, although the Son of Man does not appear in it explicitly, our parable has an underlying christological meaning. What Jesus has already caused will be repeated in the judgment.

■ **49-50** Thus the readers are prepared for the following interpretation. They know it already from vv. 40-43. The issue in this parable of the kingdom of heaven is the final judgment. This time the Son of Man is not directly mentioned; the image did not permit that. That the issue in the judgment is how one lives, praxis, becomes clear through the contrasting pair πονηροί–δίκαιοι ("evil–righteous"). As in 13:24-30 what the devil has sown is first removed from the field of the Son of Man, so here, corresponding to Jewish ideas about judg-

---

14 Weder, *Gleichnisse,* 146.

15 Later exegetes were thinking here of the mission of the church. Cf. above, nn. 4 and 10.

16 Cf. the descriptions in Lagrange, 279; Franz Dunkel, "Die Fischerei am See Genesareth und das N.T.," *Bib* 5 (1924) 375–90, 377–79; Dalman, *Arbeit* 6.348–50.

17 Str–B 1.675 notes only that the pious live by the Torah as the fish live from water. Flusser (*Gleichnisse* 1.37) is not aware of any rabbinic parallels.

18 Cf. Gerhard Delling, "πληρόω κτλ," *TDNT* 6 (1968) 288; Rainer Stuhlmann, *Das eschatologische Mass im*

Neuen Testament (FRLANT 132; Göttingen: Vandenhoeck & Ruprecht, 1983) 189, 191–92.

19 Cf. Lev 11:10-12; Deut 14:9-10.

20 Cf. above, n. 3.

21 It is noteworthy that, except for βάλλω (with a completely different usage) and θάλασσα, nothing is reminiscent of 4:18-22. Especially the word ἁλιεύς is missing; the expressions for "net" are different there. Matthew could easily have created reminders had it—and with it the subject matter of 4:18-22, viz., the mission—been important to him. Thus for

ment,[22] the evil ones are removed from the midst of the righteous. Here too the world, with good and evil people in it, is the world of the Son of Man or of God. It is not that the righteous are transferred by the angels into heaven but that the evil are removed from the earth. This time nothing is said about the fate of the righteous, for the emphasis of the parable is exclusively on the warning.

Summary

Once again the church did not appear in this parable. Contrary to what was thought in the ancient church, it is not identical with the dragnet.[23] Here also the church is not an existing entity but a church in the process of becoming. The church is to see itself in the disciples to whom Jesus speaks with this story. In the parable it belongs to the fish along with the rest of the people. And this is the decisive point where the parable does not apply. While fish are by nature clean or unclean, edible or inedible, people determine by their deeds whether they "are good kinds and worthy of the containers"[24]—or not. Where the disciples someday will be lies in their own hands!

In this chapter Jesus taught them to understand what will happen to the people who are standing on the shore. He explained to them the future and the purchase price of the kingdom of God, and now he ends with a warning appeal: Praxis will show where true church has existed.[25] The reference to the annihilating judgment that the church can also face is intended to move it to action rather than to make it anxious and to paralyze it.

him at least the saying about fishing for people in 4:19 is not a key to this parable.

22 Cf. above, n. 38 on 13:24-30.

23 Cf. above, n. 8.

24 Origen, 10.11 = GCS Origenes 10.12. The decisive contrast is not φύσις but προαίρεσις.

25 To this degree Maldonat (280) is absolutely right in the positive thesis when he emphasizes (*contra novos haereticos!*): "Non omnes, qui Evangelium . . . recipiunt, salvos futuros, sed eos tantum, qui boni fuerint pisces."

3.4 Conclusion: On the Understanding Scribe (13:51-52)

Literature

Otto Betz, "Neues und Altes im Geschichtshandeln Gottes," in idem, *Jesus: Der Messias Israels* (WUNT 42; Tübingen: Mohr/Siebeck, 1987) 285-300.

Dupont, "Nova et Vetera" 2.920-28.

Hoh, "γραμματεύς," 256-69.

Jülicher, *Gleichnisreden* 2.128-33.

Jacob Kremer, "'Neues und Altes': Jesu Wort über den christlichen Schriftgelehrten (Mt 13,52)," in Jacob Kremer, Otto Semmelroth, and Josef Sudbrack, *Neues und Altes* (Freiburg: Herder, 1974) 11-33.

Simon Légasse, "Scribes et disciples de Jésus," *RB* 68 (1961) 321-45, 481-506.

Orton, *Scribe,* 137-76.

Rudolf Schnackenburg, "'Jeder Schriftgelehrte, der ein Jünger des Himmelreichs geworden ist' (Mt 13,52)," in Kurt Aland and Siegfried Meurer, eds., *Wissenschaft und Kirche: Festschrift für Eduard Lohse* (Bielefeld: Luther, 1989) 57-69.

Manlio Simonetti, "Origene e lo scriba di Matteo 13,52," *Vetera Christianorum* 22 (1985) 181-96.

Tilborg, *Leaders,* 131-34.

Dieter Zeller, "Zu einer jüdischen Vorlage von Mt 13,52," *BZ* NF 20 (1976) 223-26.

For *additional literature* see above, III B on Matthew 13.

51 Have you understood all of this?" They say to him: "Yes." **52/** But he said to them: "Therefore every scribe who became (was made) a disciple for the kingdom of heaven is like a house master who brings out of his storeroom new things and old things."

Analysis

Structure

Our text is a short dialogue. Jesus poses a question to the disciples, they answer, and Jesus continues the dialogue with a short parable. That the text functions to conclude the section is clear. Verse 51 refers back to v. 34. The disciples, unlike the people, have understood "all of this" (ταῦτα πάντα). In addition, the important catchword from vv. 13-23, "to understand" (συνίημι), appears again. A parable also concludes Jesus' discourse, but like the first in vv. 3-9 it is not a parable of the kingdom of heaven. The structure is the reverse of that in vv. 3-23. The text begins with a question about understanding and ends with the parable. Verse 52b is reminiscent of 12:35 before the parables discourse.

Redaction and Tradition

Verse 51 is entirely,[1] v. 52 almost entirely, redactional.[2] For two reasons, however, we should not regard v. 52 as a purely redactional creation.[3] For one thing, at least the opposition "new things and old things" (καινὰ καὶ παλαιά) is not Matthean. For another—and this is more important—it is surprising that Matthew now suddenly speaks of the *scribes* after the instruction of the disciples in 13:36-52. At issue was the understanding of the *disciples*, not simply of a few Christians who held a special position! In my judgment that indicates that there is a traditional kernel in v. 52. However, I am not thinking of a parable. The abstract expressions "old things and new things" speak against that view. Why should a house master bring out[4] of his storeroom[5] "new things and old things" instead of produce, wine, grain, clothes, or tools?[6] Thus the image is not obvious in itself. How-

---

1 On συνίημι, ταῦτα πάντα cf. vol. 1, Introduction 3.2; on v. 51b cf. 9:28; 21:16.

2 On ὁ δὲ εἶπεν, διὰ τοῦτο, πᾶς, μαθητεύω, βασιλεία τῶν οὐρανῶν, ὅμοιος, ἄνθρωπος, οἰκοδεσπότης, ὅστις cf. vol. 1, Introduction 3.2. Γραμματεύς is a favorite Matthean term, but it is determined here by the theme. On ἄνθρωπος with the substantive cf. n. 24 on Matthew 13 (above, III B n. 24 on Matthew 13). On ἐκβάλλει ἐκ τοῦ θησαυροῦ cf. 12:35.

3 Thus, e.g., Goulder, *Midrash,* 375; Tilborg, *Leaders,* 133; Gundry, 281; Orton (*Scribe,* 172-73) regards it as a free adaptation of Luke 6:40, 45.

4 Only with wine would "old" make sense, but that is not under discussion here. Thinking of old rags (following Jer 38:11!) is just as farfetched as the suggestion of Walker (*Heilsgeschichte,* 27-29) and Tilborg (*Leaders,* 132) that the *tertium comparationis* here is

the "strange inconsiderateness" (Walker, 29) of the father of the house who mixes new and old.

5 Cf. BAGD, *s.v.,* 1β (differently 13:44!). On the subject matter: According to Krauss (*Archäologie* 1.355-56) Jewish sources report of אוצרות for wine, oil, and produce. A "treasury" is suitable for a temple or a king but not for the father of a house.

6 *Gos. Phil.* 119 (R. McLean Wilson, *The Gospel of Philip* [New York: Harper and Row, 1962] 56) begins with such an image. The house master brings for the children bread, oil, and meat; for the slaves corn and castor-oil (!); for the animals barley and grass; for the dogs bones; and for the pigs acorns. An application of Matt 13:52 to the various gnostic types of people that fits the image better but is secondary!

ever, it probably would make sense to a Jewish scribe that it is his task to open the treasures of wisdom,[7] to pass on the ancient wisdom of the fathers and let it bubble anew,[8] or to transmit the Torah from Sinai and to adapt it himself for his own situation.[9] Thus in this parable the image becomes understandable only on the basis of the referent! Does that mean that a Jewish proverb about the scribes has been changed into a parable? Given the linguistic evidence, Matthew might be responsible for this.[10] But why? For the formal reason that the text this way would be a better conclusion of the parables chapter? Or for hermeneutic reasons, because a parable, unlike a proverb, demands a decoding and forces the readers to think about what "old" and "new" mean? Or was the picture originally more detailed and clearer?

Interpretation

■ **51** Jesus pauses and asks whether the disciples have understood. "Understanding" belongs to their existence. The issue is not that the disciples can transmit the tradition to the church only when they understand;[11] it is that "understanding" means to comprehend with the head what the parables of the kingdom of God have to do with life. Thus understanding is part of bearing fruit.[12] Jesus himself has taught them this understanding. With a final parable he brings the discourse to a close.

■ **52** Here, as, for example, in 6:25 and 18:23, διὰ τοῦτο serves not to give a reason but to affirm,[13] or, even better, to take the idea further: And in this way (*scil.*, by

understanding) it will happen that every scribe. . . . Μαθητεύω is used in Matthew as a transitive verb ("to make disciples," as in 28:19) and perhaps also as an intransitive deponent ("to become a disciple," cf. 27:57); we cannot be certain.[14] The dative τῇ βασιλείᾳ τῶν οὐρανῶν can be a dative of relation[15] or a dative of advantage ("to become a disciple for the kingdom of heaven");[16] here too a decision is hardly possible. It is clear, however, on the basis of the two parallel texts that here also we are to assume the usual meaning "to make disciples" (or "to become disciples") rather than the narrower meaning "instruct" that is also possible.[17] But who is "every scribe who was made a disciple"? Some interpreters think of Jewish scribes who have become followers of the kingdom of God.[18] However, nowhere else do we hear of Christian scribes (who existed in the Matthean community as well as elsewhere in early Christianity)[19] who previously had been Jewish scribes. Furthermore, γραμματεύς originally had an open, nontechnical meaning[20] (= biblically literate). 23:8-12 does not support the idea that those who were knowledgeable in the scriptures constituted a clearly defined class in the church. So we should think of Christian scribes who probably were primarily occupied with the exegesis of the Old Testament, without being able to define exactly who belonged to the group. Some exegetes have thought that we have here a self-presenta-

---

7   Cf. Σιρ 1:24; 20:30; 40:18-19; 41:14; Wis 7:14.

8   "This is clearly . . . the picture of the scribe rather than of a householder" (Orton, *Scribe*, 152). Cf. Σιρ 21:15; 39:6; 50:27 and Dieter Zeller, "Zu einer jüdischen Vorlage von Mt 13,52," 223–226, 225.

9   In *b. Erub.* 21b = Str–B 1.677 Rabbi Chisda interprets the old and the new fruit of Cant 7:14 to mean the Torah and the words of the scribes. Cf. also *m. Yad.* 4:3 (ibid.): the "new" (חדוש) in the House of Study corresponds to the halakah of Moses from Sinai.

10   He likes parables about the οἰκοδεσπότης. Cf. 13:27; 20:1; 21:33 (redaction!); 24:43.

11   Against Trilling, "Amt," 33.

12   Cf. above, III B 2.1 on 13:18 and 23.

13   Euthymius Zigabenus, 420: Οὐκ . . . αἰτιολογικόν, ἀλλὰ βεβαιωτικόν, ἀντὶ τοῦ "Ἀληθῶς."

14   The basic meaning of μαθητεύω is intransitive: "to be a pupil," cf. BDF § 148 (3).

15   Thus most interpreters; cf. Strecker, *Weg*, 192.

16   Actually: disciples of the kingdom of heaven; cf.

27:57. With the transitive μαθητεύω an instrumental dative also is possible.

17   Vulgate: *doctus in regno caelorum*. This translation makes easier an application to the professional theologian: "only the qualified γραμματεύς is like this father of the house, not simply every 'disciple of the kingdom of heaven'" (Trilling, "Amt," 146).

18   Cf. 8:19! Thus, e.g., Origen, 10.14 = GCS Origenes 10.17 (a Jew interprets the scripture only literally as a Jew = γραμματεύς. Cf. on this Manlio Simonetti, "Origene e lo scriba di Matteo 13,52," *Vetera Christianorum* 22 [1985] 183–84); in modern times cf. McNeile, 206; Hoh, "γραμματεύς," 266–68; Dupont, "Nova et Vetera," 922–23, 927 (for the pre-Matthean logion).

19   Matthew 23:34. Christian scribes are mentioned also by Lucian (*Pergr. Mort.* 11).

20   In Greek γραμματεύς is a secretary or an official. In Judaism the סוֹפֵר (same meaning) becomes the scribe after the exile. Later the rabbis referred to themselves not as סוֹפֵר but as חָכָם. Cf. Str–B

tion of the evangelist.[21] The less one regards $\gamma\rho\alpha\mu\mu\alpha$-$\tau\epsilon\dot{\upsilon}\varsigma$ as a technical designation of a vocation, the more one will be able to say that the author *also* was one of these "educated Christians." Matthew 23:8-10, 34 also show that he was interested in Christian teachers. However, we do not have here an individual self-portrait, similar to the way medieval painters portrayed themselves in biblical pictures; the generalizing $\pi\tilde{\alpha}\varsigma$ clearly does not permit that. It is clear that the expression does not simply mean all of the disciples instructed by Jesus as one might expect from the context,[22] but only those among them who were scripture experts.[23] All who have been instructed by Jesus have the task of preaching (Matt 28:19-20), but the scripture experts among them also have another special task.

Matthew compares them with a householder who manages his storeroom. The Christian expert in the scriptures also manages a "treasure."[24] What are the "old" and "new" things in it? Given the traditional meaning of $\gamma\rho\alpha\mu\mu\alpha\tau\epsilon\dot{\upsilon}\varsigma$ ("scribe"), it is most natural to understand the "old" as the Bible and the "new" as Jesus' gospel of the kingdom of God. Thus the "new" corresponds to discipleship for the kingdom of heaven,

the "old" to the most important traditional task of the scribe. That also fits well Matthew's basic theological concern. Since Jesus fulfills the Law and the Prophets (5:17), Matthew is interested in showing the continuity between "old" and "new."[25] According to him, the break between "old" and "new" occurs not in the message but with its recipients, the people of God. In the context this interpretation fits well with the formula quotation of 13:35 where the mysteries of the kingdom of God, which the people only hear while the disciples understand, are said to be "hidden from the beginning." Things which are long decided, which have long existed, which, so to speak, are "primal" are made known in the preaching of Jesus. From the general expression "new things and old things" we cannot decide whether Matthew understood "old things" to refer to the prophetic predictions relating to Christ, for example, the formula quotations, or to the biblical commandments. It is also in keeping with his thinking that "new things" appears first. That corresponds to 5:17 where Jesus himself by virtue of his sending establishes continuity with Law and Prophets and to 5:21-48, where he does not interpret the Torah, but in continuity with it proclaims the will of the Father.[26] That

1.79–80.

21   See, e.g., Hoh, "$\gamma\rho\alpha\mu\mu\alpha\tau\epsilon\dot{\upsilon}\varsigma$," 268; Jacob Kremer, "'Neues und Altes.' Jesu Wort über den christlichen Schriftgelehrten (Mt 13,52)," 11–33, 26 (both are thinking not *only* of Matthew); Simon Légasse, "Scribes et disciples de Jésus," 490; Goulder, *Midrash*, 375–76. Frankemölle (*Jahwebund*, 145–46) says that in writing chapter 13 Matthew added his new parables to the old Markan parables; W. D. Davies (*The Setting of the Sermon on the Mount* [Cambridge: Cambridge University Press, 1966] 233) cites, e.g., the parable of the darnel and the new Matthean *"gemara"* in 13:37-43. Beare (317–18) concludes on the basis of $o\dot{\iota}\kappa o\delta\epsilon\sigma\pi\acute{o}\tau\eta\varsigma$ that Matthew "holds a position of authority."

22   Kingsbury (*Parables*, 126) tends in this direction, similarly Grundmann, 357. This type of interpretation prevails also in the ancient church, where it was self-evident that the "expert in the scriptures" was to be identified with the apostles, the *"scribae et notarii Salvatoris"* (Jerome, 115). Since, on the other hand, the $o\dot{\iota}\kappa o\delta\epsilon\sigma\pi\acute{o}\tau\eta\varsigma$ is like Christ, the idea of the apostolic *"scriba"* is frequently combined with that of the *imitatio Christi*.

23   On the level of the Matthean redaction Dupont ("Nova et Vetera," 926) understands the $\gamma\rho\alpha\mu\mu\alpha$-

$\tau\epsilon\dot{\upsilon}\varsigma$ in terms of understanding the kingdom of God. Because of the meaning of the word $\gamma\rho\alpha\mu\mu\alpha$-$\tau\epsilon\dot{\upsilon}\varsigma$ I do not think that we can ignore the knowledge of scripture as the decisive element.

24   After 12:35 the reader will probably immediately understand $\vartheta\eta\sigma\alpha\upsilon\rho\acute{o}\varsigma$ metaphorically. Whether Matthew here, as in 12:35, thought of their "heart" or whether instead he thought of their knowledge or even of the gospel must remain an open question.

25   That corresponds in substance to the interpretation of "old" and "new" to refer to the two testaments that has determined the church's explanation since Irenaeus *Haer.* 4.9.1. For Irenaeus both are given by the same house father, Christ the Logos.

26   Cf. vol. 1, II A 2.1 on the interpretation on 5:17 and the Summary.

means, at least when compared with rabbinical scripture interpretation, a new accent[27] without thereby consciously eliminating the continuity with the Jewish biblical expert.[28] Thus what is "new" has preeminence, but those who are expert in the scriptures have the special task of combining the "new" with the "old."[29]

> Thus "old" and "new" does not mean the transmitted Jesus tradition and its actualization for the community.[30] This interpretation is, in my judgment, impossible. According to 28:19-20, the proclamation (and thus also the actualization) of the Jesus tradition is the task of *every* disciple, not just of the scribes. Based on Matt 28:20, I also regard it as impossible that Matthew would have put the "new," viz., the application and adaptation of the Jesus tradition, before the "old," viz., the Jesus tradition itself. With the Jesus tradition Matthew does not distinguish between "old" and "new"; decisive for him is that the present proclamation of the exalted lord is none other than that of the "old" commandments of the earthly Jesus.

Summary

The greatest difficulty of our brief text consists in its relationship to the context. Why does the end of the parables discourse speak of the scribe? After the *disciples* have understood Jesus' parables, one expects a concluding sentence of Jesus that speaks of their task. Instead, he speaks of the Christian γραμματεύς, that is, exclusively of the "theologian" and the theologian's *special*

task. We cannot get around this difficulty. Verse 52 is not actually the goal of the entire discourse, although it is admittedly an important additional thought for Matthew. Why is it so important for him? Perhaps because the relationship between the Old Testament and Jesus' story and proclamation is a central concern precisely in his situation following the break with Israel.[31] For that very reason the γραμματεῖς, the "biblically literate," have such an important task in his church. And that is why they are sent out, along with the prophets and sages, on the preaching mission in Israel (23:34).

History of Interpretation

Thus in the history of interpretation our text was interpreted, not incorrectly, as referring to theologians. The interpretation is often followed by a small excursus with implications for the interpreter's present. Above all, the text has stimulated the interpreters to their own reflections in two directions, each of which we will represent here with an example. In view of the theological task, thorough work with the Bible that is the treasure for "old" and "new" was underscored. "Most dreadfully wrong are those who believe that a churchman is sufficiently educated when he can read the Testament in a German translation or a sermon book or can mouth a few Latin, Greek, or Hebrew words but is completely unaware in all other things, above all does not have or want to learn the foundation of speaking but boasts of resolutely despising it." Bullinger pictures such pastors

---

27 Less so when compared with the interpreters of scripture in apocalypticism and in Qumran who with the aid of scripture write new texts and, by means of pesher interpretation, understand the scripture more deeply than it understands itself. Orton (*Scribe*, 77–151) calls attention to this characteristic.

28 That the new appeared first created the occasion in the history of interpretation for traditional Christian prejudices about the Jewish scribes. Cf., e.g., Jülicher, *Gleichnisreden* 2.132: "The γραμματεῖς feared nothing more than innovations; the tradition of the fathers . . . , that was their gods."

29 Therefore, Isa 43:18-19 cannot be the root of our saying (contra Otto Betz, "Neues und Altes im Geschichtshandeln Gottes," 285–300, 288–92), for there the issue is supplanting the "old" with the "new," not their combination. Likewise, there is an important difference in accent between Matthew, who coordinates the "old" with the "new," and texts such as Mark 2:21-22; 2 Cor 5:17; Rev 21:4-5 that

are more likely to contrast "new" and "old" antithetically.

30 Thus, e.g., Schlatter, 450–51; Trilling, "Amt," 33–34; Rudolf Schnackenburg, "'Jeder Schriftgelehrte, der ein Jünger des Himmelreichs geworden ist' (Mt 13,52)," 57–69, 67–68 as a possibility. Davies, Goulder, and Frankemölle, e.g., defend the same hypothesis for Matthew himself; cf. above, n. 21.

31 Cf. vol. 1, II A 2.1 (the conclusion of the excursus on the formula quotation, following 2:23 and Ulrich Luz, "Das Matthäusevangelium und die Perspektive einer biblischen Theologie," *Jahrbuch für biblische Theologie* 4 (1989) 236–38.

at best as swineherds ("*pastores porcorum*").[32] However, when the subject turns to preaching, then the interpreters like to come back to the parables discourse and to interpret it as a homiletic example: "Thus it also is the task of a '*doctor Ecclesiae*' . . . to make the obvious new and the new obvious."[33] In other words, it is the preacher's task to discover what is new in the old and to relate what is new to what is familiar.

Excursus:
The Matthean Parable Interpretation

There are many monographs on the parables of Jesus but practically no literature that has Matthew's interpretation of parables as its subject. Therefore, the following attempt is to be regarded as an initial exploration of an area that deserves further treatment.

1. Overview
There are in the Gospel of Matthew *three blocks of parables*: 13:3-52; 21:28—22:14, and 24:42—25:30. They have been shaped by the evangelist, in each case on the basis of models in the Markan source. Two of these blocks of parables are public discourses of Jesus. They perform an important function in the flow of the Matthean narrative. In chap. 13 the issue is the separation between the people who do not understand and the disciples who receive Jesus' instruction. In 21:28—22:14 the subject is the polemical introit to Jesus' last great judgment discourse to Israel that will then lead to the final separation from the people (24:1-3). In these two blocks the word "parables" appears frequently.[34] For Matthew "parables" are publicly spoken stories that without interpretation from Jesus remain secretive and without obedience remain "unfruitful."[35] Parables as παραβολαί separate disciples from bystanders and insiders from outsiders. Thus "parables" also become an excellent literary way to portray the distinction

between the church and Israel. In both blocks the disciples or Matthew's implicit readers understand *more* than the hearers who are directly addressed by the parables in the story. They also understand the non-understanding of the primary hearers; they interpret it with the eyes of God.

It is different with the third parable block, 24:42—25:30. Here we have a judgment parenesis addressed to the church, beautifully composed in first shorter, then increasingly longer units (24:42-44, 45-51; 25:1-13, 14-30). This block of parables no longer carries the "plot" of the Matthean story forward but is—as a part of the last Matthean discourse—a concluding sermon for the readers in order that *they* draw the correct conclusions.

2. The Parables of the Kingdom of Heaven
It is especially striking how frequently "Kingdom" (βασιλεία) parables appear in Matthew. In Luke the kingdom of God is mentioned only twice as the referent (13:18, 20, cf. 14:15; 19:11), in Matthew ten times (13:24, 31, 33, 44, 45, 47; 18:23; 20:1; 22:2; 25:1). However, there are in Matthew also a considerable number of parables that have not become parables of the kingdom of heaven (cf. 7:9, 24; 11:16; 12:43; 13:3, 52; 18:12; 21:28, 33; 24:32, 43, 45; 25:14). It is our thesis that *the evangelist is responsible for the large number of explicit parables of the kingdom of heaven.* There are two reasons for this. For one thing, most parable introductions have been strongly edited by the evangelist or are completely redactional. The second reason lies in the observation that Matthew designates especially those parables as parables of the kingdom of heaven that correspond to the emphases of his own understanding of the kingdom of heaven:[36] (1) The kingdom of heaven that the righteous will enter is primarily a future reality.[37] Therefore, the parables of the kingdom of heaven are (almost) always eschatological parables in which the issue is the *future* that *God* plans for his world.[38] As a rule, parables exclusively related

---

32 Bullinger, 139A.

33 Brenz, 511 ("*ut . . . κοινά explicet καινῶς*," and "*καινά explicet κοινῶς*").

34 In 13:3-36: eleven times; 21:28—22:14: three times; in the entire gospel only three other times.

35 In Matt 13:3-36 the people do not understand Jesus' stories. In 21:28-22:14, they understand them but do not draw the right conclusions from them (cf. 21:45-46).

36 Cf. vol. 1, I B 1.1 on 3:2, I B 3.1 on 4:17, II on 4:23-25 (excursus), II A 1.2 on 5:3, II A 2.4.2 on 6:33.

37 Thus Margaret Pamment, "The Kingdom of Heaven

According to the First Gospel," *NTS* 27 (1980/81) 211–29. To be sure, she regards the βασιλεία τοῦ θεοῦ by contrast as a present reality, while I assume only a Matthean linguistic variation for different reasons in each case.

38 Therefore, 21:28-32, 33-42 are not parables of the kingdom of heaven; God's final future is not yet thematized in them. It is different in 22:1-14 because of vv. 11-14. Matthew 7:24-27 and 13:3-9 also are not parables of the kingdom of heaven, for they are formulated from a human perspective.

to the present are not parables of the kingdom of heaven in Matthew.[39] (2) It is the life bestowed by God into which the righteous will come through the judgment of the world-judge. Therefore, in the parables of the kingdom of heaven God's future usually has a double aspect. It is life and salvation but against the background of death and judgment. (3) The kingdom of heaven determines the present when people act already now in keeping with it, that is, when they do its righteousness (cf. 6:33). For this reason many parables of the kingdom of heaven are judgment parables that confront the readers with life and death and call to decision.[40] Altogether one may say that there are points of agreement between the Matthean understanding of the kingdom of heaven and the parables of the kingdom of heaven. In addition, "kingdom" is presumably a kind of "password" that designates a text as proclamation of Jesus, similar to the expressions "gospel of the kingdom" (εὐαγγέλιον τῆς βασιλείας) and "word of the kingdom" (λόγος τῆς βασιλείας; 13:19).

Matthew has the tendency as often as possible to designate parables as "parables of the kingdom of heaven." If a parable is not a parable of the kingdom of heaven, there usually are recognizable reasons for it. Either a different referent was transmitted to the evangelist (7:9, 24; 11:16; 13:3, 52; 18:14; 21:28-32; 24:32-33), or (and!) the rhetorical formation prevents the statement of a referent, as happens with parables that are introduced by questions (7:9; 18:12; 24:45) or that end in imperatives (24:33, 44).

These observations lead to an important conclusion. The number of the explicit βασιλεία parables of the pre-Matthean Jesus tradition may have been small. It is problematic to take the parables of Jesus unexamined as the key to Jesus' understanding of the kingdom of God and vice versa as is done especially in research influenced by C. H. Dodd and E. Jüngel.[41]

3. The Methods of Interpretation of Matthean Parables

Under methods of interpretation I understand basic procedures in the production (or reproduction) of the text that Matthew used when writing his parables. Among these are primarily allegory, repetition, reminiscence, memory verse, and inclusion in the macrotext of the entire gospel.

3.1 Allegories[42] and Related Matters

The Gospel of Matthew is regarded as the gospel that most allegorizes the parables.[43] However, the degree of allegory varies greatly; in Matt 13:24-30, 21:33-43, or 22:1-14 it is, for example, very high, in 13:44-45, 18:23-35, or 20:1-16 very low.

3.1.1 The allegorical interpretation often takes place by means of *"conventional" metaphors* with a definite meaning, as, for example, seed, harvest, father, servant, accounting, reward, wedding, etc. They are not innovative for the readers but move in horizons familiar from the Bible and tradition. Jesus has already repeatedly selected conventional metaphors from the repertoire of Jewish tradition and thereby has suggested to his hearers certain associations and applications. Matthew has gone further along this road. He has clarified traditional conventional metaphors and formulated them in allegorical interpretations. He seldom created new allegories; on the whole he is guided in this point by the tradition[44] and, in my judgment, not basically different from Jesus. That corresponds to the communicative function of the

39 Exceptions are 3:44, 45-46 that were taken by Matthew already as parables of the kingdom of God from the tradition.

40 On this basis both 24:45-51 and 25:14-30 would have to be parables of the kingdom of heaven. In 24:45-51 the traditional introduction made that impossible. For 25:14-30 I have no explanation.

41 Dodd, *Parables*; Jüngel, *Paulus,* esp. 135-39.

42 Under allegory I understand not a textual genre but a "rhetorical or poetic process" in the production of the text (Klauck, *Allegorie,* 354; Heinrich Lausberg, *Handbook of Literary Rhetoric* [Leiden: Brill, 1998] § 895, pp. 398–99: τρόπος; *figura sententiae*; Quintilian *Inst. orat.* 8.6.44) in which the level of the words and of the meaning differ but are in continuity with each other by means of metaphors of various kinds

or other linguistic means (e.g., irony, riddle).

43 Cf. Jeremias, *Parables,* 85.

44 Cf. Klauck, *Allegorie,* esp. 357–58. Examples: cf. above, III B 2.2 on the tradition history and source of 13:24-30, 37-43, above, III B 2.1, 13:18-22 on the Matthean interpretation of Markan parables, and vol. 3 on 21:33-46. On the Matthean interpretation of Q parables cf. above, II D 1.3 on 11:19 and vol. 3 on 24:45-51; 25:14-30.

45 That is a unique idea for those who follow Jülicher, but it is not at all unfamiliar to those who know what other scholars have always said in objection to Jülicher on the basis of, among other things, Jewish parables. Tribute should be paid here, e.g., to Paul Fiebig (cf., e.g., *Altjüdische Gleichnisse und Gleichnisse Jesu* [Tübingen/Leipzig: Mohr, 1904] 98–102).

conventional metaphors. They make it possible for narrators to combine with their parables certain intentions of communication that the hearers who live in the same tradition understand, and they make it possible for a tradition-oriented community to arrive at an intersubjective consensus in the interpretation of a parable. In addition, they make it easier to preserve a parable over a longer period of time. The allegory with conventional metaphors is in my view the interpretive method of Matthew that is the most tradition-oriented. Even the later allegorical parable interpretation in the ancient church works by and large with the same conventional metaphors that are given by the Bible—metaphors that it sometimes enlarges and applies to new situations. In my judgment, the conventional metaphors are one of the most important formal connective links between the parable interpretation of Jesus, of Matthew, and of the ancient church.[45]

3.1.2 The so-called *audacious metaphor*,[46] on the other hand, is less prominent in Matthew. Audacious metaphors often make the reality seem alien and teach us to see it in a new light. Along with surprising twists of the story that characterize many of Jesus' parables even when they make use of a familiar subject,[47] audacious metaphors are among the most important innovative features of the parables of Jesus.[48] Here Matthew differs from Jesus, for he has, in my judgment, not created any parables but only passed them on and interpreted them. The reworking of the parable of the great banquet and its connection with the story about the guest without a wedding garment (22:1-14) that may be attributed to the evangelist is the only "audacity" of Matthew to be treated here of which I am aware. However, in Matthew's day Jesus' audacious metaphors have become familiar metaphors that no longer are able to surprise or alienate. People have known for a long time that the kingdom of God is like a mustard seed or that the king is going to invite the people from the highways and fences. Here lies a fundamental problem. The continuing tradition of Jesus' parables robs them of at least some of their effective power. One must ask where in Matthew the innovative, surprising, and alienating potential of Jesus' parables comes to bear.

The two following methods of interpretation are

related to allegory. In contrast to conventional metaphors, they are at least partly Matthean and innovations for the readers.

3.1.3 *Direct insertions of the referent in the image* that reveal what the issue is in the stories are, for example, the invitation of the "evil and good" to the wedding feast in 22:10, the "entering into the joy of the Lord" in the story of the talents (25:21, 23) or—already traditional—the "place" of the evil servant "with the hypocrites" (24:51).[49]

3.1.4 On two occasions Matthew created *new referents of parables*, viz., by giving a salvation-history interpretation to the parable of the two sons (21:31-32) and by changing the advice about exorcisms into a parable (12:43-45).

3.2 Interpretation of the Parables by Inserting Them into the Context

When the Matthean parables receive new potential meaning in comparison with the tradition, it happens first of all by means of the macrotext of the gospel in which they now appear.

3.2.1 The *reminiscences* of other texts point the reader to the meaning of individual parables or intensify their meaning. Thus 13:30, for example, is reminiscent of 3:12; 16:27-28 and 24:31 are reminiscent of 13:41; 18:30, 34 are reminiscent of 5:25-26; 19:21 is reminiscent of 13:44-46; 22:13 is reminiscent of 8:12; or 25:11-12 is reminiscent of 7:23. The readers remember earlier direct statements, or they are reminded of a parable at a later place in the gospel. By the continuous reading of the gospel or by its "rereading" the interpretation of the parables is intensified.

3.2.2 Matthew makes copious use of the *repetition* of motifs as a technique for making the parables illuminate each other. In 13:3-32 the three seed parables interpret each other. Matthew 21:33-43 and 22:1-10 repeat the motif of the sending of the servants; 24:45-51 and 25:14-30 also are "servant" ($\delta o \tilde{v} \lambda o \varsigma$) parables that interpret each other. Double parables have a similar function. Repeated memory verses are akin to the repetitions: thus 24:42; 25:13 ("watch . . ."); 19:30;

---

46 On the audacious metaphor cf. Harnisch, *Gleichniserzählungen*, 125–41.

47 An example: that the farmer of Matt 20:1-15 pays the last day laborers first and then pays all of them the same amount.

48 An example: when the kingdom of God, of all things, is compared with a grain of mustard.

49 Related are: the reference to the destruction of Jerusalem in 22:7 and the references to "weeping and gnashing of teeth" in 22:13, 24:51, and 25:30 to the degree that they are not commentaries by the narrator.

20:16 ("the last will be first . . ."), and repeated formulas (for example, of weeping and gnashing of teeth five times at the end of parables!). Here also the repetition drives home the decisive point.

3.2.3 Most important, however, is the *placement of the parables in the macrotext of the entire gospel*. Matthew repeatedly inserts parables into his story as "companion stories" that interpret for the disciples the course of the narrative (for example, 12:43-45; 13:24-33; 21:28-22:14; 25:1-30).[50] Their beginning point usually corresponds to the "situation" of the story. Jesus preaches in Israel at a time when the image of sowing (13:3-32) dominates the accompanying stories. In the "salvation-history" parables of 21:28—22:14 it is primarily Israel's lack of faith that is interpreted corresponding to the situation at which the Matthean story has arrived. In 25:1-30 the point of view is that of the church, and the perspectives are the judgment, again corresponding to the context. Thus parables and macrotext are associated with each other; in the parables Jesus explains his story to the disciples—and thus to the church—and in so doing he explains to the church its own story on the way from Israel to the Gentiles. The insertion into the macrotext is the most basic interpretive method for the salvation-history tendency of the Matthean parable to which we now turn.

4. The Tendencies of the Matthean Parables
Matthew's parables speak substantively in two main directions, viz., with salvation-history messages and with parenetic messages.

4.1 The Salvation-History Tendency
Among the parables in which Jesus interprets for the disciples his and their story with the aid of "companion stories" are especially 12:43-45; 13:24-33, 37-43, 47-50; 21:28—22:14; 25:14-30. In the service of the salvation-history interpretation are the conventional metaphors (for example, seed, harvest, vineyard, servants, accounting), scattered "audacious" innovations (for example, 22:7 and the surprising conclusion in 22:11-13), reminiscences (for example, in 22:13 of 8:12), and repetitions (for example, the sending of the servants in 21:34-36 and 22:3-6), but especially the insertion into the context of the story of Jesus on

which they comment and which they interpret. The salvation-history parables repeatedly open up for the readers the view of the entirety of the story of Jesus. In the instruction to the disciples in 13:36-52 the horizon already widens to judgment. In 21:28-22:14 the perspective opens progressively. If 21:28-32 dealt only with the rejection of John and Jesus, in the allegory of the evil workers in the vineyard the judgment is announced, and 22:2-14 tells in the parable of the salvation history until the judgment of the world. At the same time those two parables open up the view into the past and include the time of the prophets of the old covenant. Thus the parables open for the disciples the perspective beyond their location in each case and repeatedly let them recognize the meaning and the goal of the entire story. They function in the Matthean story as road signs that make clear to the readers where they are and where the vehicle is headed.

Matthew thus takes up a basic feature of Jesus' parables. If with Jesus himself we can understand his behavior as a "commentary on his parabolic preaching,"[51] with Matthew the parables become "commentaries" on the story of Jesus. In both cases the parable narrator Jesus cannot be separated from the stories told. Christologically it is important for Matthew that Jesus and no one else tells and interprets the parables to the disciples. He thus takes the place of the interpreting angel in apocalyptic visions. As the only teacher, Jesus reveals to the community the knowledge of the story of which he himself is the central point of orientation.

4.2 The Parenetic Tendency
Parenetic parables may have different intentions. They may confront the readers with the basic alternative for or against the kingdom of heaven (for example, 25:1-13), but they may also have quite concrete behavior as their goal (for example, 18:12-14). Many allegories serve to heighten the parenetic feature. That is clear not only in 13:19-23 and in 13:37-39[52] but also elsewhere. When, for example, in the story of the king who settles accounts the main character is a "debtor" ($\dot{o}\varphi\epsilon\iota\lambda\acute{\epsilon}\tau\eta\varsigma$; 18:24, cf. 6:12), when the story of the workers in the vineyard deals with "evil workers" ($\dot{\epsilon}\rho\gamma\acute{\alpha}\tau\alpha\iota\ \dot{\alpha}\rho\gamma\sigma\acute{\iota}$) and wages (20:1-3, 6, cf. 9:37-38; 12:36; 5:12; 6:1-18), when in the

50   Mary Ann Tolbert, *Sowing the Gospel* (Minneapolis: Fortress, 1989) 103: "Third degree narratives."

51   Weder, *Gleichnisse,* 95. Since Jesus explicates in his parables theologically "his own behavior with God's behavior," after Easter the narrator had to become the subject of the narration. Matthew has taken up this basic feature of post-Easter parable interpreta-

tion by using parables of Jesus as methods of interpreting the story of Jesus.

52   Cf. above on the interpretation of those texts.

53   Cf. above on 13:44-46.

54   Paul Ricoeur, "Stellung und Funktion der Metapher in der biblischen Sprache," in *Metapher: zur Hermeneutik religiöser Sprache* (EvTh Sonderheft;

parable of the maidens not only the opposites "fool-ish/wise" ($\mu\omega\rho\acute{o}\varsigma/\varphi\rho\acute{o}\nu\iota\mu\varsigma$; cf. 7:24-27) but also $\gamma\rho\eta\gamma\rho\acute{e}\omega$ and $\check{e}\tau o\iota\mu\varsigma$ (cf. 24:42-44) appear, or when in 24:45-51 the issue is eating, drinking, drunkenness, and beating one's fellow servants, these metaphors come immediately from the world in which the hear-ers live. Allegories repeatedly secure the parable in the life of the hearers. However, reminiscences also serve the parenetic tendency as, for example, when the parables of the treasure and of the pearl are sug-gestive of the story of the rich young man,[53] or when for the readers of 18:23-35 the saying in the Sermon on the Mount about going to the judge (5:25-26) and the petition for forgiveness in the Lord's Prayer (6:12) come alive again and open up the understand-ing of the parable. Corresponding to this feature is the basic trait of Matthean hermeneutics that is visible in 13:3-23. A part of understanding of the parables is bearing the fruit they call for.

In all of that it seems to me that a second basic trait of the parables of Jesus persists. They also were not intended so much to be interpreted as applied. Especially the great parables of Jesus are not *compar-isons* that speak of the kingdom of God and could then be translated into *statements about* the kingdom of God; they are *stories* that deal with life, interpret it anew, and want to be *translated into life*.[54] Matthew has understood and intensified this feature of Jesus' para-bles. To be more precise: He has understood this fea-ture in an imperative sense and thus has sharpened the parables in the direction of parenesis.

4.3 The Relationship Between the Two Tendencies
Our distinction between the salvation-historical and the parenetic interpretation of the Matthean parables is an aid to our understanding. In most of the para-bles both tendencies occur. In many parables with a salvation-history tendency judgment serves as a "hinge" that lets them "turn" into parenesis. Thus most of the salvation-history parables are two-dimen-sional. On the other hand, there are hardly any para-bles that do not in some way begin with the new reality that came about through the story of Jesus. Whether it be the sowing, the great forgiveness of debt, the search for the strayed sheep, entrusting someone with the household (24:45)—in some way almost all Matthean parables take up the new reality

of Jesus even when they do not develop any salvation-history stages or perspectives. Most parables are to be interpreted not on one plane but have two levels of meaning potential.[55]

In this regard we see a surprising similarity between Matthew and the scriptural exegesis in the ancient church. There also the allegorical interpreta-tion primarily served two tendencies: translation into the life of the hearer in the moral interpretation, and the salvation-history knowledge of faith in the allegor-ical and anagogic interpretation. In the scripture interpretation of the ancient church the various meanings of scripture also stand *side by side* and not against each other; they express potentials that one and the same text has. Correspondingly, there are lev-els of understanding. The parables intend at one and the same time to give knowledge and to effect action; understanding is both comprehending and acting (cf. Matt 13:19-23). Since with his parable interpretation Matthew also takes up decisive concerns of Jesus, viz., the reference of the parables to his own activity on the one hand and their translation into life on the other, it follows that there is a continuous line in parable interpretation that leads from Jesus through Matthew to the ancient church. In my judgment, the parable interpretation of the ancient church is on the whole closer to Jesus than is Jülicher's rationalizing and generalizing of the parables. *The Matthean parable interpretation is a bridge between Jesus and the ancient church that can clarify the proximity between the two.*

5. The Matthean Parables as Parables of Judgment
Judgment receives an enormously prominent position in the Matthean parables. This was clear already in the presumably secondary parable of the darnel in which what in Mark 4:29 is the harvest in Matt 13:40-43 becomes separation. The saying about the weeping and gnashing of teeth became the stereotypical end-ing of five parables.[56] Parables of judgment in Matthew almost always have the accent on the nega-tive ending.[57] They want to warn the church. While in the history of the tradition it is often difficult to dis-tinguish exactly between the original form and possi-ble new Matthean formulations in comparison with the parables in Luke's special material, it is notable that on the whole Matthew prefers parables with a

---

Munich: Kaiser, 1974) 70: "The untranslatability (*scil.*, of the parable) into ordinary language is solved only by the *applicatio* . . . in the praxis of life."

55 Here the salvation-historical aspect in a certain way corresponds to what we designated for the entire Matthean story as "indirect transparency," while the

parenetical aspect corresponds to the "direct trans-parency." Cf. above on the summary to chaps. 8–9.

56 Matthew 13:42, 50; 22:13; 24:51; 25:30.

57 Cf. 13:40-43, 49-50 (the righteous are mentioned only briefly in v. 43); 18:32-35; 22:11-13; 24:43 (neg-ative image of the robber); 24:50-51; 25:11-12 (the emphasis is on the foolish maidens); 25:24-30. In

tragic ending or often accentuates the tragic ending.[58]

Thus the parables repeatedly deal with judgment. The two first blocks of parables end with images of the judgment (13:40-43, 49-50; 22:11-14). In the third block of parables, 24:42–25:30, judgment itself is the theme. On the other hand, for the Matthean proclamation of judgment parables are the dominant form of speech. With the exception of a few brief logia (for example, 7:21-23; 10:32-33), Matthew speaks of judgment only in parables. That is especially noticeable in a synchronic reading of chaps. 24–25. Here Matthew reports the end events leading to the gathering of the elect and the lament of the nations (24:29-31) as a direct announcement of Jesus. Then the form of speaking changes abruptly, and at the same time Jesus begins to speak directly to the church *and* to speak in parables. Even the description of what the Son of Man will do with the gathered nations at the end leads to the famous text of the separation of sheep and goats (25:31-46) in such images that people—incorrectly, but not by accident—have repeatedly regarded it as a parable. Form and content thus belong together. Matthew speaks in his parables repeatedly of judgment. And Matthew obviously wants to speak of judgment primarily in parables.

The finding confronts us with serious questions. What does this shifting of the accent to judgment mean theologically? Has Jesus' message been transferred to the ethical, the imperative, perhaps to the "legalistic" area? And what does it mean that the parables become the dominant way of expressing the proclamation of judgment? Does Matthew misuse here a Jesus form of speech? We cannot answer these questions here; we postpone them for the time being.[59]

---

58   the categories of Via (*Parables*, 96) the "tragic" parables are clearly dominant over the "comic" parables.
      Missing in Matthew, e.g., are: Luke 15:8-10, 11-32; 16:1-8; 18:1-8.

59   Cf. the excursus on the Matthean understanding of judgment at 25:31-46.

Literature
See above, III B.

A   The Parables Discourse as Part of the Jesus Story

The narrative interruptions of this discourse (vv. 10-11a, 34-37a) show that what we have in chap. 13, much as is later the case in chaps. 23–25, is first of all in part *story*. It describes how through the instruction of Jesus the disciples learn to understand the people's lack of understanding and the practical goal of the parables. For the disciples it is thus the story of a *path* to understanding. Serving as a negative foil by contrast are the people whose path is a dead end. However, the parables discourse is not a mere stage in the Matthean story. This is shown in the following section, 13:53—16:20, when the story initially continues as if the parables discourse were not even there. Jesus continues to turn to the people; they are not hardened but are open and sympathetic toward Jesus. The separation continues between Jesus and the Jewish leaders, not between Jesus and the people. Not until 16:13-20 is there a certain distance—not hostility—between Jesus and the people.[1] And not until the passion narrative is it clear that the people as a whole reject Jesus' call to the reign of heaven. What then is the meaning of the interruption of the narrative by the parables discourse? Our thesis is: *It condenses and anticipates the story of the entire Gospel of Matthew in a concentrated form.* What will happen in the story of Jesus as a whole is anticipated here and taught to the disciples. In this sense—and not for formal reasons[2]—the parables discourse is the center of the entire gospel.

B   The Parables Discourse as Address

This condensing of the Matthean story in chap. 13 is at the same time an address to the community. This is true in two respects.

1. Israel's lack of understanding is by no means a reason for the church to feel confirmed and comforted. Instead, it has performative power and is itself intended to bring about understanding. Matthew wants to lead the community of disciples to understanding and thus into life precisely by understanding this non-understanding. Part of this understanding is to apply Jesus' word of the kingdom of heaven to oneself and to bear its fruit (cf. vv. 19-23). For the very reason that the people do not do that, it becomes a negative model of warning.

2. Our chapter is also a direct exhortation and demand to the church. It speaks of the fruit, of the future of the kingdom of heaven that is the future of a church on the way, and once more of giving away one's possessions. Above all, the temporal perspective of our chapter extends to the final judgment.[3] The anticipation of the final judgment of the Son of Man is a key, for it is a decisive motor for the conduct of the church. It keeps the church, now separated from Israel, from triumphantly proclaiming itself as God's new people of salvation and from smugly gloating over its greatness and the Gentiles who are streaming to it. It means that the church appears in our chapter only as a church that acts—a church that is called to bear fruit and that itself will be tested in the judgment. The church learns that everything that Jesus teaches in parables about the kingdom of heaven is to be translated into its own life and into its own praxis. That is how it will show that it has understood.

On the Meaning of the Parables Discourse Today

From Matthew's perspective two things are central for today's understanding of the kingdom of God.

1. On the one hand, the kingdom of heaven is clearly something transcendent that will not be revealed until the future. God himself will create it; the church is to listen to Jesus' gospel, to pray (Matt 6:10), and to hope (Matt 26:29).

2. The second basic idea is that of the actively functioning and obedient community of disciples. The future kingdom of the Father, at the beginning of which stands the judgment of the Son of Man Jesus, liberates and encourages the church in the present to active conduct. The Matthean parables of the kingdom of God have performative power. They do not merely teach; they create the obedience[4] that is already part of the kingdom.

---

1   Cf. below, III C 3.3 on 16:13-16 and 16:20.
2   Cf. vol. 1, Introduction 1 (state of research).
3   Cf. the "historical" structural model of Denis, "Parabels" (above, III B, n. 6).

4   Insofar it is correct that du Plessis ("Meaning") and especially Gary A. Phillips ("History and Text: The Reader in Context in Matthew's Parables Discourse," in SBLSP 1983, 415–37 = *Semeia* 31 [1985]

By contrast, precisely these two dimensions of the kingdom of God, its futurity and transcendence on the one hand and the human activity toward it on the other, seem to break apart today. One can act in history toward secular, immanent goals, hopes, or utopias about which people can agree and which they can realize. However, the coming kingdom of God, created by God and not people, appears to bring to an end human history and thus also human activity. Our own understanding of reality, influenced by modern ideas of autonomy and the ability of the human subject to act, collides with a fundamentally different understanding of reality that is foreign to us. We can see that in two examples from the modern influence of the idea of the kingdom of God.

a. *Immanuel Kant* shares with Matthew the idea that he can picture a moral person only as an active person. The kingdom of God begins for him "once the principle of the gradual transition of ecclesiastical faith to the universal religion of reason, and so to a (divine) ethical state on earth, has become general and . . . also *public*."[5] Thus there is nothing transcendent about the kingdom of God, and it is future only in the sense that its establishment is still in the distance. For Kant, however, the freedom to act comes because the kingdom of God in the last analysis is the collective self-realization of moral persons and not a waiting for something wholly other. Human beings themselves execute the divine plan for the world.[6] As a logical consequence, along with the transcendent-future character of the kingdom of God, the idea of unconditional grace also is eliminated for Kant as something that in the final analysis is immoral.[7] In my judgment Kant shows how a transcendent kingdom of God that is not identical with human achievement is inconceivable with the idea of the autonomously acting human subject.

b. On the other hand, for the *history of religions school* the kingdom of God is something completely transcendent—it is the new eon that does not develop historically but breaks suddenly and generally visible into this world as a crisis. The whole arsenal of apocalyptic hopes and concepts of that time is part of it. However, this kingdom of God has experienced the same thing in modern Europe that happened to the historical Jesus of Albert Schweitzer: It was discovered "but passes by our time and returns to its [His] own,"[8] for it is "a transethical reality" and cannot be the basis for any secular activity. At best we can understand historically what the kingdom of God brought for Jesus and others who were able to believe in it. The "prophetic enthusiasm" and "pneumatic ecstasy"[9] connected with its hope mediated to such people confidence and courage. The history of religions school shows how a transcendent and future kingdom of God cannot justify and support action for modern people.

Kant and the history of religions school both call attention to the modern dilemma with regard to the kingdom of God. A coming and transcendent kingdom of God is today, for most people, not a valid expression of their own hopes but an alien religious chipher, a somewhat curiously articulated great dream. The kingdom of God in the sense of a reign of human morality, on the other hand, has been shipwrecked on the historical experiences of our century. Two world wars, the Holocaust, global economic injustice, the threatening destruction of the natural bases of life, and the explosively expanding technology that increasingly dominates humanity instead of liberating it, have removed us so far from Kant's belief in the human being that we probably will agree with him only in one regard: "The actual establishment" of the kingdom of God is "still infinitely distant."[10]

Can the church help here—the church in which in the history of the interpretation of the parables of our chapter the kingdom of God repeatedly has been seen as effective? It seems to me that precisely for those people who today seriously struggle for the great dream of the kingdom of God, the legitimacy

---

111–37) ask for the pragmatic meaning of the chapter. Phillips says (425): "The reader of Matt 13 is manipulated by the narrator into acquiring a cognitive and pragmatic ability to hear and to speak Jesus' parables and to engage in a praxis that produces both word and deed."

5   *Religion*, 113.

6   Cf. Magdalene Bussmann, "Reich Gottes," in Peter Eicher, ed., *Neues Handbuch theologischer Grundbegriffe* (Munich: Kösel, 1985) 4.55.

7   "No thoughtful person can bring himself to believe this (i.e., atonement rendered for him), even though self-love often does transform the wish for a good, for which man does nothing and can do nothing, into a hope" (*Religion*, 107).

8   Schweitzer, *Quest*, 399. [The second expression is not in the ET.—*Trans.*]

9   Weiss, *Proclamation*, 78.

10   Kant, *Religion*, 113.

of combining, indeed identifying, the kingdom of God with the church as was done for centuries in various ways in the interpretation of our texts has become seriously doubtful. What can the kingdom of God have to do with a church that is experienced in a Catholic setting as a domineering and depressing hierarchy or in a Protestant setting as a noncommittal both/and? It is exactly with the church that we experience the chasm between claim and reality as so large. If one were to try today to put the church into the parables of Matthew 13, for many people the appropriate image would not be that of wheat, of the treasure, or of the mustard seed but at best the image of a very stony and barren field that is in urgent need of a deep plowing.[11]

Trajectory for Today

It is obvious that in this situation the parables discourse cannot exercise the same fascination today as does a text like the Sermon on the Mount, although, or perhaps just because, it speaks more clearly of that future perspective that supports the behavior commanded in the Sermon on the Mount. I would like to offer, from the perspective of the Matthean texts, three impulses toward its understanding today.[12]

1. *Reality-defying hope of the suffering.* The kingdom of heaven is a word of hope. Words of hope give strength to those who live from hope. They speak differently to people in distress, for example, to the sick in a hospital, to women and men in a South American slum, or to the little, insecure Matthean community between a hostile Judaism and powerful Gentiles, than they do to people in sated consumer societies who no longer recognize their own need and are not moved by the needs of others. Suffering people are able to conceive powerful images of health, justice, fullness, life, and of the kingdom of God. The primary question here is never whether such images and concepts fit the worldview of

an age; it is whether and how they were and are able to comfort, to encourage, and to move to action. They never have fit into secular prognoses; they were always contrary to reality. A society in which such images have become religious fossils must confront the question whether it truly is so advanced that it no longer needs such images of hope or whether it so effectively keeps at a distance and suppresses its own need and that of others that it has become incapable of understanding and giving voice to images of hope that contradict the facts. *In the comfortable sitting room one cannot understand the hope for the kingdom of God.* The hope for the kingdom of God may be like the petition for bread in the Lord's Prayer;[13] for many in the Western world it is only the active *com*-passion with people in true need that makes it possible for us to have such images. Or it may be enough to open the windows of the comfortable sitting room and to let our own need come to us, that is, to realize with horror what the apocalyptic words of our days, for example, atomic threat, "greenhouse effect," homelessness, the irreversibility and acceleration of technical development, *really* mean.[14]

2. *Committed understanding in the circle of hearing and doing.* Understanding Matthean parables of the kingdom of heaven takes place in a circle formed by stories that create hope, Jesus' instruction, understanding, practical application, and the judgment of the Son of Man, all matters that are spoken of again in the stories. No element can be left out of the circle; it characterizes as a whole the *movement* that the kingdom of heaven unleashes and to which it leads. Understanding the kingdom of heaven is thus for Matthew an integrated process, and it belongs together with faith and life. An understanding that does not become part of this circle does not exist for him. Thus understanding always

---

11   The image is borrowed from Ragaz, *Gleichnisse,* 118.
12   These impulses are, of course, very subjective; some may regard them as somewhat too prophetic, others as somewhat too pathetic. But how shall I do justice to the Matthean interpretation of the parables that consisted in sharpening and applying Jesus' parables to life, e.g., by means of allegory, if as an interpreter I make every effort to bracket out my own life from the business of interpretation? It is good if others offer other impulses; the main thing is that they grasp—also as New Testament scholars—that one cannot do justice to Matthean texts when one

stands *outside* them.
13   Cf. vol. 1, II A 2.3.3 on 6:11 with n. 91. Cf. also the analogous statement on the miracles above, on the significance of the miracle stories at the conclusion of chaps. 8–9: The trajectory of the Matthean miracle stories. They are "wonder-full" in light not of natural laws but of genuinely experienced need.
14   Bloch (*Atheism,* 264 [chap. 43], 344 [chap. 52]) has briefly summarized these conditions in a chapter heading: "Hunger, 'Something in a Dream,' 'God of Hope,' Thing-for-Us."

means that one puts one's own life into this circle and risks one's own life. *One cannot understand the parables of the kingdom of heaven on a couch.* Then the kingdom of God indeed becomes a religious fossil about which one can speak, but on the basis of which one cannot act, because a fossil leaves a person cold. Then acting becomes an autonomous activity that has no divine basis and also no longer has a divine promise. In view of today's apocalypses, that is, in my judgment, a rather hopeless attempt. And then the church becomes a visible entity that, identified with the kingdom of God, becomes false and, separated from it, becomes irrelevant. Matthew probably would say that this way it is *impossible* to understand the parables of the kingdom of heaven.

3. *New images of life.* Speaking in *images* belongs to Jesus' language about the kingdom of God. Images grab people; they engage them; they free them from fixed views about the world; they contain life, yet they do not exhaust this life. Matthew knows this. He knows why he speaks of the kingdom of heaven and of judgment almost exclusively in images. It is a fatal characteristic in the history of the interpretation of the Jesus parables that while they were able to give rise to numerous conceptual interpretations, and in a smaller measure to variations and new accentuations of the old images, they hardly ever led to completely new stories. The surprising images first became old familiar images, then canonical and exegetically interpreted images, and finally imageless doctrines. Could that be why life has largely disappeared from these images? *One cannot understand the parables of the kingdom of heaven by exegesis alone.* To go to school with the sole teacher Jesus means more than learning to repeat his stories exactly (although it means that also!); it means to invent stories oneself—stories as Jesus told them, but one's own stories, filled with hope and life, covered by one's own life. In my judgment, the inability to do that shows something of the power of tradition in Christian history.[15]

---

15   I would like at least to call attention to a successful example of what I mean, viz., the little book of the Chinese theologian Choan-Seng Song, *The Tears of the Lady Meng: A Parable of People's Political Theology* (Geneva: World Council of Churches, 1981). It tells the legend of a suffering Chinese mother who stands up to the power of the emperor because she has a different hope. The story is devised, composed, and sketched on the basis of the cross and is more powerful than an entire work of dogmatics or a multivolume New Testament commentary.

Literature

A. G. van Aarde, "Matthew's Portrayal of the Disciples and the Structure of Mt 13:53-17:27," *Neot* 16 (1982) 21–34.

D. W. Gooding, "Structure littéraire de Matthieu 13,53 à 18,35," *RB* 85 (1978) 227–52.

Xavier Léon-Dufour, "Vers l'annonce de l'Église: Mt 14,1—16,20," in idem, *Études*, 231–54.

Jerome Murphy-O'Connor, "The Structure of Matthew 14–17," *RB* 82 (1975) 360–84.

Matthew 13:53—16:20, the part of the report that follows the parables discourse, contains not only many reminiscences of chaps. 11 and 12[1] but also repetitions. Among them are the two feeding miracles, 14:13-21 and 15:32-39 (cf. 16:8-10); the two confessions of the Son of God, 14:33 and 16:16; the two "withdrawals" of Jesus from the hostile leaders of the people, 14:13 and 15:21 (cf. 16:4); and the two healing summaries, 14:34-36 and 15:29-31 (cf. 14:14). It is precisely because of the many repetitions that 13:53-16:20 is not easily outlined.[2] We propose a subdivision into three sections: 13:53—14:33;[3] 14:34—15:39; 16:1-20. This suggestion is based on Jesus' three withdrawals from the leaders of Israel.[4] On two occasions the formulation, as it was in 12:15, is ἀνεχώρησεν . . . εἰς ("he withdrew . . . to"; 14:13; 15:21). The third time it is: καταλιπὼν αὐτοὺς ἀπῆλθεν ("leaving them, he went away"; 16:4c). Before each of these withdrawals

there is a pericope in which Jesus' opponents are active (14:1-12; 15:1-20; 16:1-4b). Jesus' withdrawals are followed twice by feeding stories (14:13-21; 15:32-39, cf. 16:8-10) and twice by scenes that culminate in a confession of the Son of God by the disciples (14:33; 16:16). The conclusion of the second Son of God confession is a momentous answer of Jesus that is reminiscent of the revelation of the Son at the end of the first main part (11:25-27).

As clear as the nucleus of each section is, in each case the beginning and ending are unclear. Neither between 14:33 and 34 nor between 15:39 and 16:1 is there a caesura. The narrator Matthew wanted to create not "sections," but an uninterrupted narrative thread.[5] Nor does Matthew follow a set scheme in the arrangement of the healing scenes (14:14, 34-36; 15:29-31, cf. 13:58).[6] Matthew 13:53-58 and 15:21-28 have no parallel sections in the entire work. It is clear that initially Matthew simply follows Mark's thread. While he provides it with his own structural characteristics, he does not undertake a thoroughgoing reformation. In 13:53—16:20 he never changes the Markan order of Mark 6:1—8:30 but only omits three pericopes (6:7-13;[7] 7:31-37;[8] 8:22-26).

The individual sections build on one another, carry the action further, and deepen the understanding of the readers. If they look at the characters, they notice the progression of the action. The *disciples* grow in understanding and in their confession of Jesus. The second

---

1   Cf. above, the chart at the beginning of section III.

2   Many suggested arrangements begin with the narrative unit 13:53—17:27. Jerome Murphy-O'Connor ("The Structure of Matthew 14–17," *RB* 82 [1975] 360–84), e.g., divides into two main sections: 13:54—16:4 with 15:10-20 as the "center," and 16:5—17:27 with 17:1-8 as the "center." D. W. Gooding ("Structure littéraire de Matthieu 13,53 à 18,35," 227–52) sees two parallel strands each: 13:53—14:36 par. 15:1—16:12; 16:13—17:21 par. 17:22—18:35. Admittedly, with the many repetitions and with the Matthean tendency to connect rather than to separate different sections of his gospel, every suggested arrangement is somewhat artificial. Nevertheless, these suggested arrangements seem to overlook the main line of the Matthean narrative, viz., from the separation from Israel (12:1—16:20) to the church and its life (16:21-28).

3   Patte (206–7) sees in 13:54-14:36 a main section on the theme of "miracle," which is framed by 13:54-58 and 14:34-36 (few miracles in Nazareth, many in

Gennesaret). However, he overlooks the different "recipients" of these miracles (13:53-58; 14:34-36: the people; 14:15, 22-33: the disciples). His prejudice (never really substantiated!) is that he always asks in his sections for a "theme" and thus dissolves the *narrative* into a sequence of thematic discourses. For him a section then follows on the theme of "Jesus and the Pharisees" (15:1—16:12).

4   This is also the decisive viewpoint of division in Xavier Léon-Dufour, "Vers l'annonce de l'Église," 231–54. I agree in general with his division (cf. 249).

5   Cf. above, II B Structure.

6   Still, a healing scene twice appears with a feeding story.

7   Used already in chap. 10.

8   Replaced by the redactional summary 15:29-31.

confession of the Son of God in 16:16 shows an intensification over the first one in 14:33, for Jesus affirms it and responds to it with a promise. The *opponents of Jesus,* on the other hand, stay where they are. Not only does their demand for a sign in 16:1 show that they have not learned anything since 12:38, but their malice becomes more obvious. Matthew now says clearly that they only want to tempt Jesus. Finally, the *people* have Jesus' attention in our section as they previously did, but they are not included in the process of understanding and confessing. They are challenged to understand (15:10), but they do not react. The final section, 16:13-20, suggests a new opposition between the disciples and the people. While the heavenly Father reveals to the former that Jesus is Son of God, "the people" believe Jesus to be John the Baptist, Elijah, or one of the prophets. Thus it is as if they drop out of the controversy over Jesus between the opponents and the disciples. Unlike Mark, Matthew will direct the call to suffering discipleship in 16:24 only to the disciples. Thus at the end the narrative makes visible that distinction between people and disciples which chap. 13 already anticipated.

The progress of the action also becomes clear elsewhere. In 14:1-12 the death of John is, in a manner of speaking, the continuation of 11:2-6 where John was in prison. The second stilling of a storm in 14:22-33 clearly looks back at the first one in 8:23-27, but it intensifies the experiences of discipleship with the episode of Peter walking on water and ends in a confession. In many ways 15:1-20 recalls 13:3-23 but goes beyond it with a word of judgment to the Pharisees (15:13-14). Verse 15:24 refers

back to 10:5-6, but when the Canaanite woman overcomes Jesus' resistance, the way of salvation to the Gentiles that was still prohibited in the disciples discourse of chap. 10 is announced. Thus even at first reading it becomes clear how the narrative progresses. It is not simply narrative material arranged arbitrarily; it moves toward a goal. While it is full of reprises of earlier motifs, themes, and situations, at the same time it intensifies them and carries them further. The various stories cannot simply be moved around in the macrotext.

Thus our proposed arrangement does not understand the narrative unit in 13:53—17:27 as a single, connected *Peter unit* with three subsections, each of which culminates in a Peter section (14:28-32; 16:16-20; 17:24-27).[9] It is true that Peter plays an extremely important role in 13:53—17:27. He appears in key roles much more frequently than he does in Mark. Furthermore, in the following community discourse he introduces the only narrative interruption (18:21). Not until the passion narrative will he play a similarly important role. On the other hand, there is no narrative progress visible in 13:53—17:27 with regard to the figure of Peter. He appears as one of little faith (14:28-31), as a believer (16:16-18), as a tempter (16:22-23), as a mere questioner (15:15; 17:24), alone and together with others (17:1-4). In my judgment, in 13:53—18:35, where the issue is the origin (13:53—16:20) and the life (16:21—17:27; 18:1-35) of the church, Peter has more the literary function of a connecting link between the various sections.

---

9   Peter F. Ellis, *Matthew: His Mind and His Message* (Collegeville, Minn.: Liturgical Press, 1974) 66–67 ("lead up to Peter"); A. G. van Aarde, "Matthew's Portrayal of the Disciples and the Structure of Mt 13:53-17:27," *Neot* 16 (1982) 21–34. The three subsections are 13:54—14:33; 14:34—16:20; 16:21—17:27. However, the division into the subsections is questionable. Especially in 16:21—17:27 it is not clear how what precedes prepares for the scene with Peter. And why should, e.g., the Peter scene in 17:24-27 be more important than the Peter scenes in 16:22-23 and 17:1-4?

1.1   Jesus Teaches in Nazareth (13:53-58)

Literature

Blinzler, *Brüder.*

Lorenz Oberlinner, *Historische Überlieferung und christologische Aussage: Zur Frage der "Brüder Jesu" in der Synopse* (FB 19; Stuttgart: Katholisches Bibelwerk, 1975) 350–55 and passim.

Frans van Segbroeck, "Jésus rejeté par sa patrie (Mt 13,54-58)," *Bib* 48 (1968) 167–98.

Zahn, *Forschungen,* 227–372.

53   **And it happened when Jesus had finished these parables, he went away from there.**
54   **And he came to his hometown and taught them in their synagogue, so that they were astonished and said:**
   "Where did he get this wisdom and the mighty deeds?
55   **Is he not the carpenter's son?**
   Is not his mother called Mariam and his brothers James and Joseph[1] and Simon and Judas?
56   **And are not all his sisters with us? Where did this one get all this?"**
57   **And they were offended at him. But Jesus said to them: "Nowhere is a prophet despised except in his hometown and in his family."**
58   **And he did not do many mighty deeds there because of their unbelief.**

Analysis   Verse 53 is the redactional conclusion of the parables discourse. It is especially similar to 19:1a, while the astonishment of the Nazarenes at Jesus' teachings is reminiscent of 7:28. The brief story that follows is structured concentrically and chiastically. The questions of the Nazarenes constitute the center with a πόθεν ("where") question at the beginning and at the end (vs. 54c, 56b) and three negative questions in the middle. Verse 54a, b and v. 57a, b constitute the

frame.[2] Verse 58 is superfluous in this concentric structure and acts as a kind of addendum.[3] Notable is the detailed listing of Jesus' mother, brothers, and sisters in the questions of the Nazarenes. Matthew uses it to recall the pericope of Jesus' true relatives (12:46-50) to which the words "and in his family" (v. 57), strange in this context, may also refer. In comparison with Mark 6:1-6 the narrative is somewhat tightened and in its image of Christ slightly "retouched,"[4] but not essentially changed. All the changes are redactional;[5] there are here no "minor agreements" that presuppose a different textual basis than the Markan text known to us.[6] We do not have to deal here with the history of the text prior to Mark; I assume with Gnilka[7] that the recollection of a historical event has been supplemented secondarily with the familiar maxim about the unappreciated prophet (Mark 6:4).

Interpretation

■ 53 The evangelist finishes the parables discourse with his usual concluding phrase. Jesus leaves the lake and comes into his old hometown,[8] Nazareth.

■ 54 He begins to teach there in the synagogue. The use of the possessive pronoun "their" creates distance and indicates that Matthew and his readers no longer regard themselves as belonging to the synagogue community. The hearers are shocked at his teaching as at the conclusion of the Sermon on the Mount (7:28; cf. 22:33). Their skeptical reaction shows that there is nothing positive about their astonishment. In this context "wisdom" refers to the preaching of Jesus; according to Matthean usage, "mighty deeds" always refers to Jesus' healing miracles, many of which have already happened in the Galilean villages (cf. 11:21, 23).

---

1   Some MSS, following Mark, read Ἰωσής or Ἰωσή that corresponds to the Galilean form of the name. Ἰωάννης (א*?) is probably a copyist's error (Metzger, *Commentary,* 34).

2   Cf. the graphic arrangement of the translation and Segbroeck, "Jésus," 184.

3   Segbroeck, "Jésus," 190.

4   Cf. the interpretation of υἱὸς τοῦ τέκτονος and of v. 58.

5   Cf. vol. 1, Introduction 3.2 on v. 54 ἐλθών, ὥστε; v. 55 passive λέγω with names. Verse 56 πᾶς, οὖν, ταῦτα πάντα. On "in their synagogue," cf. vol. 1, Introduction 5.3.

6   Ennulat (*Agreements,* 157–62) calls attention especially to Matthew, v. 55 par. Luke 4:33 (ὁ τοῦ τέκτονος υἱός//υἱὸς Ἰωσήφ) and to Matthew, v. 54 =

Luke 4:15 ἐν τῇ (ταῖς) συναγωγῇ (-αῖς) αὐτῶν. The former is not a minor agreement but only a (different) change at the same place. Luke 4:15 is not parallel to Matt 13:54 (cf. Luke 4:16!) but more likely, as Luke 4:44, inspired by Mark 1:39 (plural συναγωγαί!).

7   *Markusevangelium* 1.228–29.

8   Cf. 4:13. Πατρίς may mean "hometown" or in a broader sense "homeland." As in Mark, Nazareth is not mentioned, but according to 2:23 it must be meant. Jesus would not have to travel to his homeland in the wider sense, since at the lake of Gennesaret he is already there. Thus one cannot, as Segbroeck ("Jésus," 171–79) suggests, refer πατρίς to Galilee as a whole and then generalize ἐδίδασκεν on the basis of 4:23; 9:35.

■ **55** Neither fits the image of a craftsman's son, especially when everyone knows him. Τέκτων ("carpenter") may mean someone who makes things from wood or stone, for example, houses or even tools.[9] In the Gospel of Mark Jesus himself is τέκτων; in Matthew he is called "son of the carpenter." The reasons for the change are not entirely clear. It may be that Matthew in Jewish style[10] simply mentions the father's profession. However, it also may be that mentioning Jesus' profession was disturbing, probably not so much because one was ashamed to have a construction worker as a savior[11] as because the tradition nowhere else knows anything about Jesus working at a profession but has him traveling around the country as an itinerant preacher. Along with the father, Mary is mentioned as the mother of Jesus, here in the Semitic form of the name, "Mariam," as is appropriate for Nazarenes.[12] Matthew says nothing here about the mystery of the virgin birth—not because he wanted to say that his native people "(do not) know the mystery of (his) origin,"[13] but because Jesus' virgin birth is not central for his Christology.[14] Of course, "brothers" and "sisters" must be understood in keeping with the simplest meaning to refer to physical siblings of Jesus;

there is nothing in the text that would lead the readers to understand the terms any other way.[15]

■ **56** Thus the Nazarenes are familiar with the family of Jesus, and they use this familiarity to express their distance from Jesus.

■ **57** They "are offended" at him. This word has a strong meaning for the readers of the Gospel of Matthew. They remember the warning that Jesus had pronounced in 11:6 and the "offenses" (σκάνδαλα) that the Son of Man will remove from their midst at the end of history (13:41). In 15:12 the unbelieving Pharisees will take "offense." Thus the "amazement" of the Nazarenes is clearly interpreted negatively here. In 57b Jesus teaches his fellow citizens once again. He says something to them that is a common experience or even a proverb:[16] No prophet is valued in his hometown or in his family! In Matthew's sense "prophet" expresses an inadequate understanding of Jesus (cf. 16:14; 21:11, 46); with this saying Jesus conforms to the Nazarenes' understanding. The family of Jesus does not participate in his rejection,

---

9   Cf. BAGD, *s.v.*; Schlatter, 455. In favor of a woodworker (e.g., carpenter) is the distinction between τέκτων and οἰκοδόμος in the LXX and in Josephus (cf. Schlatter, 455), the infancy narrative of Thomas 13 = *NTApoc* 1.396 (carpenter who makes plows and yokes) and the *Prot. Jas.* 9.1; 13.1 = *NTApoc* 1.379, 381 (builder who works with the ax). The only thing that speaks for the meaning *mason* is the general consideration that houses were built from mud or stone in Galilee, where there was little wood—i.e., almost nothing at all.

10   References in Schlatter, 455.

11   BAGD, *s.v.* τέκτων refers to Aristoxenus fr. 115 and the *Vita Sophoclis* 1 where the father of Sophocles who was a τέκτων was made into an entrepreneur who owned τέκτονες as slaves. In Matthew's Semitic milieu, where it was taken for granted that rabbis practiced a trade, this was probably not the offensive point; cf. *EDNT* 3 (1993) 342. In the history of interpretation one usually assumed with Augustine (*Cons. ev.* 2.42 = 193) that Jesus, the son of a carpenter, practiced his father's profession until he was thirty years of age. However, cf., e.g., Origen *Cels.* 6.34, 36 = *ANF* 4. 588–89 (Celsus calls Jesus a carpenter; Origen denies that anything like that is in the canonical gospels) or Lapide (289), who lists

Catholic exegetes who claim that Jesus lived in pure contemplation until he was thirty years of age.

12   This is not conclusive proof that Matthew was bilingual, as demonstrated by Luke, who uses this form of the name in a Semitic way almost always in his prologue but almost never elsewhere. Cf., however, vol. 1, Introduction 5.1.

13   Schnackenburg 1.131; similarly already Origen, 10.17 = GCS Origenes 10.21 ("for they thought that he was the son of Joseph and Mary"). However, they correctly understand that Jesus is the son of Mary! Furthermore, according to 1:18-25 for Matthew Jesus really is Joseph's (adopted) son.

14   Cf. vol. 1, I A 1.3 (final paragraph).

15   Of course, ἀδελφός/ἀδελφή may have a figurative meaning in Greek ("colleague, like-minded person, member of the same tribe"); it may also have a religious meaning or be used as a form of address—between friends, collegial, or honorary. There is some evidence for "close relatives" in Semitic languages (biblically: Ernst Jenni, "אח," *Theologisches Handwörterbuch zum Alten Testament* 1 [1971] 100; Jewish references in Blinzler, *Brüder*, 44–45). V. Tcherikower and F. M. Heichelheim ("Jewish Religious Influence in the Adler Papyri," *HTR* 35 [1942] 32–33) note only two isolated cases in Greek

but because Matthew in our story reminds the readers of 12:46-50,[17] ἐν τῇ οἰκίᾳ ("in the house") must be interpreted in light of that text. Thus the family of Jesus stands here indirectly on the side of his unbelieving fellow citizens.

■ **58** A brief comment about Jesus' miracles in Nazareth follows. Matthew, who presents Jesus as sovereign lord and miracle worker, obviously was not happy with the Markan formulation that Jesus was not able to perform miracles in Nazareth (Mark 6:5), and he softened it so that his sovereignty remained untouched.[18] Important for Matthew is Mark's final comment. What showed itself in Nazareth is "unbelief." Just as the faith that the sick people have in Jesus is much more than confidence that the healer can help them in their in need, so "unbelief" (ἀπιστία) also means more than that the Nazarenes do not accept the mighty deeds of Jesus; it means a decision about salvation and destruction.

Summary

The concentrically structured story has a clear central point: the unbelieving and mocking questions of the Nazarenes in vv. 54b-56. The issue is their "offense," their "fall, the rejection."[19] It is no accident that in the macrotext of the gospel Jesus is here in a synagogue for the last time.[20] Our narrative thus takes up what has already happened in the parables discourse with the withdrawal of Jesus into the house. In the context of the Matthean narrative it is still premature. Jesus will still speak often to the people, and they will not reject him but at least listen to him. Thus the Nazarenes anticipate what will later prove true of the entire people—their no to Jesus, their unbelief. Our story thus has the character of a signal for what is to come. It is not accidental that it appears at the beginning of a new main section of the book.[21]

History of Interpretation

In the history of the interpretation of our text, the controversy about *Jesus' sisters and brothers* has proved to be the most difficult and thorny theme. The dominant church thesis was that the reference here is to cousins of Jesus. It is advocated decisively and presumably for the first time by Jerome.[22] He had an ascetic concern for virginity that he also claimed for Joseph.[23] Since Jerome this thesis has been dominant both in Catholic interpretation and, until into the nineteenth century, also in humanist and Protestant exegesis. Prior to and along with Jerome the thesis was advocated, especially in the Greek church, that we have here Joseph's children from a first marriage.[24] In the ancient church Tertullian and later the Roman Helvidius regarded them as children born later to Joseph and Mary.[25] Since the beginning of the nineteenth century this view is advocated again in Protestant exegesis,[26] and today it is taken for

where in a papyrus a "nephew" or "great-nephew" was called ἀδελφός.

16 There are no literal biblical parallels but only the experience, e.g., of Jeremiah with the people of Anathoth (Jer 11:18-23). The closest Hellenistic parallel is in Dio Chrysostom *Or.* 30 (47).6 (of the philosopher); cf. Seneca *Ben.* 3.3.1 (general); Apollonius *Letter* 44 in Philostratus *Vit. Ap.* 2.437; Epictetus *Diss.* 3.16.11 (of the philosopher).

17 Cf. above, Analysis.

18 Matthew gives the substance of the omitted verse, Mark 6:5b, that is in tension with 6:5a.

19 Cf. Segbroeck, "Jésus," 198.

20 France, 232.

21 Origen (10.18 = GCS Origenes 10.23; idem *Hom. 33 in Lucam* = GCS Origenes 9.185) interprets Nazareth spiritually to mean Israel, Capernaum the Gentiles. From the perspective of the gospel's macrotext he is right.

22 *Helv.* 13-14 = NPNF Second Series 6.340 (James and Joseph are identical with the sons of the Mary who is mentioned in 27:56); for additional sources see Zahn, *Forschungen,* 320-25; Blinzler, *Brüder,* 143-44. Cf. also vol. 1, I A 1.3 on Matt 1:25.

23 Jerome *Helv.* 19 = NPNF Second Series 6.343.

24 Since the *Protevangelium of James* 8.3; 9.2; 17.1-2 = *NTApoc* 1.379, 383; *Gospel of Ps.-Matthew* 8.4 = ANF 8.372; *History of Joseph the Carpenter* 2 = ANF 8.388. Further apocryphal sources cited in Zahn, *Forschungen,* 309. Origen (10.17 = GCS Origenes 10.21-22) refers to this thesis as the opinion of a number of people. Especially influential was Epiphanius *Haer.* 77.36 = *PG* 42.696 and the circular letter 78.2-24 = *PG* 42.700-37.

25 For anti-docetic reasons: *Marc.* 4.19 = CSEL 47.482-83; *Carn.* 7 = CSEL 70.208-9. Irenaeus's position is unclear. According to Zahn (*Forschungen,* 319), the opinion of Helvidius is dominant among the simple Christians in the pre-Constantinian church while the more educated ones were more likely to share the thesis advocated above in n. 24.

26 Strauss, *Life,* 143-48.

granted.[27] In Catholic exegesis as well there are today voices that cautiously concur. They are, of course, (still?) rare; in Catholic research an almost incredible caution dominates that makes sense to me only in terms of dogmatics or church politics.[28] The question is delicate because of the dogma of the perpetual virginity of Mary. Philologically it is clear. "The Semitic possibility, that in individual cases" ἀδελφοί/ ἀδελφαί ("brothers/sisters") designate "further relatives, can lead to such a judgment only if this is positively demonstrated in each case."[29] In other words, if as an exception "brothers" or "sisters" is to mean "further relatives" in Greek, that has to be clear from the context. Even ancient church fathers knew to distinguish between brothers and cousins of Jesus.[30] There can never be absolute certainty in historical research, but in this case the historical probability is as high as it possibly can be. The problem stemming

from the perpetual virginity of Mary is not a problem of exegesis but of Catholic dogmatics. As a Protestant observer who views the debate and also the manner in which it is carried out not without concern and anxiety, I can only say that from a biblical perspective the center of faith is not at issue in the question of the brothers and sisters of Jesus.[31] It could be, however, that the center of biblical faith is at issue in the manner in which the Catholic church in this non-central question represents today its dogmatic heritage toward freedom of thought and scholarship.

---

27 Zahn (*Forschungen*) was especially important for the history of research.

28 Examples: Lorenz Oberlinner (*Historische Überlieferung und christologische Aussage: Zur Frage der "Brüder Jesu" in der Synopse* [FB 19; Stuttgart: Katholisches Bibelwerk, 1975]) avoids forming clear judgments about the historical question and concentrates on the evangelists who took the existence of physical brothers of Jesus for granted. Raymond E. Brown (ed., *Mary in the New Testament* [Philadelphia: Fortress, 1978] 72) also leaves the question open. Gnilka (*Markus* 1.234–35) expresses in a sibylline way the opinion that "historically stringently" no assumption can be proven. J. Gilles (*Les "frères et soeurs" de Jésus* [Paris: Aubier Montaigne, 1979] 125) and especially Pesch (*Markusevangelium* 1.322–24 [excursus]) are on this point not only clear but also courageous exceptions. Pesch's defense (*Markus-*

evangelium 1 [3d ed.]: 453–62 [Supplement]) is historically brilliant and clear and is also worth reading as a document of church history and of current history.

29 Opinion of Rudolf Schnackenburg, cited in Pesch, *Markusevangelium*, 1, Supplement to the 3d ed., 1980, 454.

30 Hegesippus especially distinguishes between a cousin = ἀνεψιός (Symeon, son of Cleopas [Eusebius *Hist. eccl.* 4.22.4, cf. 3.32.6]) and the brothers of the Lord = ἀδελφοί (James, Jude [τοῦ κατὰ σάρκα λεγομένου . . . ἀδελφοῦ, Eusebius *Hist. eccl.* 2.23.4; 3.20.1]); further evidence in Pesch, *Markusevangelium* (3d ed.; Supplement) 1.456.

31 Gnilka, *Markus* 1.235: "Such a proof . . . would not be especially important for faith."

1.2 The Death of John the Baptist (14:1-12)

Literature

Lamar Cope, "The Death of John the Baptist in the Gospel of Matthew," *CBQ* 38 (1976) 515–19.

Hugo Daffner, *Salome: Ihre Gestalt in Geschichte und Kunst* (Munich: Schmidt, 1912).

Theissen, *Gospels in Context*, 81–97.

Trilling, "Täufertradition," 45–65.

1 At that time Herod the tetrarch heard the news about Jesus, 2/ and he said to his slaves: "That is John the Baptist. He has been raised from the dead. And therefore the powers are at work in him."

3 For Herod had arrested John, bound him, and put him in prison because of Herodias, the wife of his brother, Philip. 4/ For John had said to him: "You are not allowed to have her." 5/ And he intended to kill him, but he was afraid of the people, because they regarded him as a prophet. 6/ But when Herod had a birthday,[1] the daughter of Herodias danced in (their) midst and pleased Herod. 7/ Therefore he promised with an oath to give her whatever she would ask. 8/ But being directed by her mother she says: "Give me here on a platter the head of John the Baptist." 9/ Then the king was sad, but because of the oath and the guests he commanded that it be given to her. 10/ And he sent (people) and had John beheaded in prison. 11/ And his head was brought on a platter and given to the girl, and she brought it to her mother.

12 And his disciples came, took the corpse and buried it. And they came and reported it to Jesus.

Analysis

Structure

The text is closely linked to the previous text with ἐν ἐκείνῳ τῷ καιρῷ ("at that time") and the catchword δυνάμεις ("powers"). The story itself is artless and very brief. After a short scene describing Herod's reaction to Jesus (vv. 1-2), there follows, as in Mark, a flashback that, to be sure, is not very clearly designated as such. The actual account of the murder of the Baptist is divided into an exposition (vv. 3-5), the

dance scene in which the daughter of Herodias is the most important figure (vv. 6-8), and the scene about the granting of her wish in which the king is the main actor (vv. 9-11). The final note of John's burial by his disciples (v. 12) returns the flashback to the main thread of the Jesus story. Of cross-references and reminiscences within the gospel especially worth mentioning are the reminiscence of 11:4 in v. 12 and the look ahead to 21:46 in v. 5.

Source

Mark 6:14-29 is the only source, a conclusion that is confirmed by the observation that most of the Matthean peculiarities are redaction.[2] Matthew has greatly abbreviated the Markan text, especially Mark 6:15-16, 19-21, 22b, 24-25, 27. In Mark the sending and return of the twelve disciples, 6:7-13, 30, provides the framing action. The flashback in 6:14-29 covers the time of their absence with literary skill. With Matthew, who had reported the sending already in chap. 10, the framework is omitted. That means that a new transition to v. 13 is needed. Matthew creates it by taking over ἀπήγγειλαν from Mark 6:30 and forming from it the notice, reversing the process of 11:4, that the disciples of John "reported" to Jesus. This report is then is the occasion for Jesus' withdrawal to the other shore in v. 13.

The Text as Historical Report

How informed is Matthew about the historical circumstances? The Markan narrative is a popular narrative (that is, neither specifically Christian nor from Baptist circles) that must have originated at some distance from the events and that contains some obviously incorrect statements.[3] Matthew's reworking of the story provides an opportunity to test the level of his information. He has avoided some of the errors of Mark's report, but it is difficult to say where he has deliberately avoided them and where they simply were victims of his tendency to abbreviate. He knows that Herod is "tetrarch" (v. 1),[4] but the correct title obviously is not important to him, since he still calls him "king" in v. 9. In v. 6 he makes of Herod's own

---

1   On the construction cf. BDF § 200 (3). Several MSS substitute a genitive absolute for the mixed construction. The strange "dative absolute" perhaps was caused by the abbreviation of Mark 6:21a.

2   Cf. vol. 1, Introduction 3.2 on ἐν ἐκείνῳ τῷ καιρῷ (v. 1); εἶπεν, παῖς, οὗτός ἐστιν, βαπτιστής (v. 2); ὅθεν (v. 7); φημί, ὧδε (v. 8); λυπέω, κελεύω (v. 9); πέμψας (v. 10); προσελθών, ἐλθών (v. 12). On ἠγέρθη ἀπὸ τῶν νεκρῶν (v. 2) cf. 27:64; 28:7; on v. 5 cf. 21:46; on μεθ' ὅρκου (v. 7) cf. 26:72, on ὁμολογέω (ibid.) 7:23. Strikingly un-Matthean are ἀπέθετο (v. 3) and προβιβάζω (v. 8).

3   Cf. esp. Dieter Lührmann, *Das Markusevangelium* (HNT 3; Tübingen: Mohr/Siebeck, 1987) 114–16, and Theissen, *Gospels in Context*, 81–97. The most important text for comparison is Josephus *Ant.* 18.240–56.

4   Likewise Luke 9:7. Independent redaction by Matthew and Luke is probable in the case of this obvious historical error.

daughter, who also is called Herodias (Mark 6:22),[5] a daughter of his wife without mentioning that her name is Salome. Herodias does not play the prodding role with him that she plays in Mark, and Herod Antipas himself becomes the main negative actor—as with Josephus.[6] He thus *also* achieves a theological goal. The parallel between Jesus (Matthew 2!) and John becomes greater than if John had fallen victim to a purely woman's intrigue. However, the first husband of Herodias is called Philip as in Mark; the Western text tradition first corrected the error.[7] Thus Matthew has an at least rudimentary historical knowledge,[8] but he is not very interested in applying it consistently.

That corresponds to his massive abbreviating that is especially noticeable in this story and to his tendency to omit graphic details. Thus inconsistencies arise on the level of the report that obviously do not bother Matthew, or perhaps he is not even aware of them. According to vv. 1-2 the death of John must have happened sometime earlier, otherwise the opinion could not have developed that the miracle worker Jesus is the risen John. According to vv. 12-13, however, the disciples of John announce to Jesus the death of their master as something that has just happened; then he responds by withdrawing to the other shore of the lake where Herod Antipas no longer rules.[9] Since Matthew does not report a change of location after 13:54-58, if we wanted to be precise, we would have to assume that he left Nazareth by boat. The guests of Herod Antipas are omitted in v. 6a but presupposed as obvious in v. 9. In v. 5, differently from Mark, Matthew emphasizes that Herod wanted to kill John; he says nothing about the dark plans of Herodias (Mark 6:19). Nevertheless, in v. 9 he lets him be "sad" about the girl's request.[10] Thus the result is: Matthew is a narrator who is by no means

uninformed, but on the level of the reported story he has little interest in clarity and coherence.

Interpretation

■ **1-2** Jesus' ruling prince, Herod Antipas, hears about his miracles. The readers who already know his father and his brother from Jesus' infancy narrative (cf. 2:1-12, 16-18, 22) suspect that this means nothing good. Herod believes that Jesus is the resurrected John the Baptist. It is not said how he came upon this idea;[11] the most likely suggestion is that Herod Antipas's bad conscience bothered him, and he was afraid that John had been raised by some miracle worker.[12] In any case, Herod's reaction makes clear that John and Jesus have the same enemies.[13] Jesus and his predecessor belong together, even in the eyes of the evil tetrarch.

■ **3-5** Matthew now tells how John the Baptist lost his life. When it happened is not important for him. Just as Mark does, he inserts his narrative as a flashback. However, that John's death cannot be a distant event follows not only from v. 13 but also from 4:12 and 11:2. Obviously Matthew thought that Jesus' activity thus far has taken place during the time when John was in prison. In the Matthean narrative Herod stands in the foreground. Herodias, the actual evil figure according to Mark, recedes into the background. John had forbidden the prince[14] to marry his brother's wife, because that fell under the prohibition of incest (cf. Lev 18:16; 20:21); the divorces that were actively pursued by the women of the Herodian family according to Hellenistic law naturally were not valid for the Baptist. Herod therefore

5   With Nestle[26], the reading should be ϑυγατρὸς αὐ-τοῦ Ἡρῳδιάδος. Cf. Metzger, *Commentary*, 89–90.
6   Cf. Theissen, *Gospels in Context*, 88.
7   D, lat on v. 3.
8   Cf. also above, II B 2.2 on 8:28-9:1 and below, III C 1.4 on 14:22.
9   Lamar Cope ("The Death of John the Baptist in the Gospel of Matthew," 515–19) therefore wants to understand vv. 3-12 as explanatory parenthesis and connect v. 13 with v. 2. However, the parenthesis is too long and too indistinctly marked for the reader to notice. The reminiscence of Mark 6:30 in v. 12 also speaks against this view.
10   Harmonizing interpreters such as Gundry (287) think that Herod Antipas simply wanted to remove John in a somewhat less spectacular way.
11   It is improbable that the Jewish-Christian readers of Matthew would have attributed to the "evil" Herod any pious ideas such as, e.g., the resurrection of the martyrs or even expectations of an eschatological prophet.
12   Cf. Str–B 1.560 on the Jewish belief in miracles of resurrection.
13   Cf. already 3:7: Pharisees and Sadducees; in addition 11:18-19; 21:23, 32.
14   Imperfect with the nuance of untimeliness. cf. Mayser, *Grammatik* 2/1.137.

wants to kill John (while according to Mark he holds him in a kind of protective custody to protect him from his wife's schemes). Only consideration for the people who believe John to be a prophet (cf. 21:26) keeps him from doing so. As in the following narrative section, the people again play here a positive role. They have a friendly disposition toward John and Jesus. Thus the constellation is the same as it will be in 21:46, where the high priests and Pharisees want to kill Jesus, but fear of the people also keeps them from doing so. At the same time, the catchwords "prophet" and "kill" call attention to the Old Testament tradition of murdered prophets[15] that Matthew frequently uses (5:12; 17:12; 21:33-41; 22:3-6; 23:29-36). Israel's prophets were always persecuted and killed. What happened to them also happens to John and will happen to Jesus. Thus every positive trait disappears from Herod Antipas; he belongs to the worst Jewish enemies of Jesus and his predecessor John.

■ **6-8** At the tetrarch's birthday feast the daughter of Herodias dances in front of the invited men. Matthew does not mention her name; he obviously pictures her as a still unmarried girl (v. 11). Of course, the readers will have their own ideas about the morals at Herod's court when they hear that a princess plays a role in this men's banquet that courtesans ordinarily played.[16] She pleases the tetrarch, and therefore he swears that she may make a wish. That again demonstrates his wickedness. The readers of the gospel know from the Sermon on the Mount what God's will is about the oath (5:33-37). Herod Antipas misuses the name of God in such a way that his oath leads to a crime.[17]

■ **8-11** The girl is prompted by her mother[18] to make the terrible request for the head of John the Baptist. While it makes the king sad, he nevertheless commands that the girl's wish be fulfilled. From this point on he is again the acting agent.[19] The imprisoned John is immediately beheaded, and his head is brought on a platter into the hall, as once the head of Queen Vashti had been in the Esther tradition,[20] and it is given to the girl, who gives it to her mother.

■ **12** The macabre story is finished. The narrator need not comment on it; it speaks for itself. He adds that the disciples of John got the body and buried it. Then they go and tell Jesus what has happened. Matthew is here thinking of 11:4 where the disciples of John returned to John with a message from Jesus. Now it is the other way around: They come from John to Jesus. The two of them, the Baptist and Jesus, belong together for Matthew.[21] They proclaim the same message, suffer the same fate, and have the same opponents. Thus it is for him obvious that John's destitute disciples go to Jesus.

Summary

The story has its meaning in the macrotext of the gospel. The rejection of Jesus in Nazareth is followed by another signal for the future: the death of the forerunner, of the returned Elijah, who precedes Jesus on his own way of suffering. The Son of Man will suffer the same fate as he (17:12). The readers of the Gospel of Matthew know the Deuteronomistic tradition of the disobedience of an Israel that has always persecuted and murdered its prophets. The allusion to them is Matthew's most important interpretive element.[22] What happened is an expression of the disobedience that characterized Israel even in biblical times. Although what Herod Antipas has done is especially horrible, it is not an isolated incident. The story of Jesus' passion will confirm it. Thus the allusion to the tradition of the murder of the prophets makes the death of John so to speak a type and includes it in the Matthean view of salvation

---

15   Cf. here Odil Hannes Steck, *Israel und das gewaltsame Geschick der Propheten* (WMANT 23; Neukirchen-Vluyn: Neukirchener Verlag, 1967), passim.

16   As an illustration cf. the story of Joseph the Tobiad in Josephus (*Ant.* 12.187–89) who falls in love with a dancer at the royal table in Alexandria. Even among the Greeks this scene would be totally unseemly. Cf. Theissen, *Gospels in Context*, 89–95.

17   Μεθ' ὅρκου also in 26:72 at Peter's denial.

18   Προβιβάζω, literally "to cause to come forward," may also be used figuratively: "to instruct" (Deut

6:7 LXX) or "to motivate" (sources in Spicq, *Lexicon*, 3. 179; BAGD, *s.v.*).

19   The executioner who is included by Mark in v. 27 is missing. In this way the murder lies on Herod even more directly than in Mark.

20   *Midr. Esth.* 1.19 (91a) in Str–B 1.683.

21   Cf. vol. 1, I B 1.1 on 3:2, 1.2 on δικαιοσύνη, 3.1 on 4:17, II A 3.2 on 7:19; above, II D 1.2 on 11:11-14, 1.3 on 11:16-19, and below, IV A 2 on 17:10-13; also vol. 3 on 21:23-32 and Trilling, "Täufertradition," 57–61.

22   Trilling, "Täufertradition," 47: "The event . . .

history. That Antipas, who certainly was not a very Jewish son of Herod, here plays the role as it were of the negative forerunner of the Jewish leaders and of the entire people in the passion of Jesus, is not at all fair toward Israel and follows the line of the historical construction in 2:3-4 where the evangelist already had the elder Herod act in harmony with "all Jerusalem."[23]

History of Interpretation

In modern times the unnamed daughter of Herodias has become the colorful figure of Salome who is familiar to us from literature and art. She is, however, not a modern invention but the result of a long development that even begins occasionally in the church fathers.[24]

Little is said about her in the ancient church; Herod or the malice of Herodias is more likely to be in the foreground. When one does speak about Salome, it is her dance that attracts attention. "Where . . . there is a dance, there the devil is involved also. God gave us feet not for dancing, but that we might walk in the right way; not . . . that we jump like camels, but that we form the choral dance with the angels."[25] Sometimes their fantasy is excited passionately, and yet it is horrified by the dance. Ambrose describes the dance in detail ("teasing flirtation, neck twisting, flowing hair") and then continues, "Small wonder that the next step would be a crime against the Deity. For how can modesty exist where there is dancing, shouting and noise making?"[26] A literary high point is the powerful twelfth-century description of Theophanes Ceramaeus:

But when she was in the midst of the tipplers . . . she danced, in a frenzy like a bacchanal, shook her hair, turned shamelessly, stretched out her arms, bared her breasts, kicked her feet high one after the other, uncovered herself in fast bodily movements and perhaps even showed something of what is unmentionable. With an indecent look she attracted the attention of all who were present and with all sorts of movements she shocked the thoughts of the viewers.[27]

That the princess was able to captivate him that way and that he looked so intensively at her movements and her body and yet did so with such resistance and rejection, shows us something of the severity of sexual asceticism and the problems connected with it.

After the patristic interpretation had taken the first step in developing of the figure of Salome, in the late Middle Ages the representatives of secular literature began to make use of the material. Salome now slowly separated herself from the role of the obedient daughter that she had previously played. The decisive literary and artistic treatments of the now independent figure of Salome took place in the age of the Renaissance and of the Reformation. She became the driving force and the "sly serpent" in the sixteenth-century plays about John.[28] Of even more importance than the plays about John, with the early Renaissance Salome's dance became a favorite subject of the visual arts (Filippo Lippi, Ghirlandaio, Botticelli, R. von Weyden, Donatello, Andrea del Sarto).[29] Here a biblical theme became attractive because of its worldliness. The portrait painting influenced by Leonardo da Vinci was a decisive turning point for the portrayals of Salome. Now the classical pictures of mature female beauty appear; whether they represent Judith, Mary, Salome, or Magdalene hardly matters, nor whether the accessory is "a bowl with fruit or a bowl with the severed head."[30] To be mentioned here are, for example, Cesare da Sesto and Bernardo Luini from the Lombardian school and Bartolomeo Veneto and Titian from the Venetian school. This development separated Salome from our story; she became an independent theme of paintings and the sole center of attention.

The literature of the eighteenth and nineteenth centuries brought a similar emancipation of the figure of Salome, not from her story but from the church's evaluation and moral condemnation. The dance can now even be viewed positively. As an example we choose the "Atta Troll" of Heinrich Heine (1841), who begins not with the Bible but with popu-

---

seems only to serve to demonstrate that the murder of a prophet has taken place in Israel."

23 Cf. vol. 1, I A 2.1 on 2:3.

24 Mrs. Isabelle Noth wrote the draft of the following section.

25 John Chrysostom, 48.3 = *PG* 58.489–90.

26 Ambrose *Virg.* 3.6 = Boniface Ramsey, *Ambrose* (New York: Routledge, 1997) 113; cf. the hatred of women by Peter Chrysologus, 158 ("refuse of all wickedness" . . . "entirely effeminated and completely unleashed").

27 *Hom.* 71 = *PG* 132.1065.

28 Daffner (*Salome,* 159) on the play about John by the priest Johannes Aal of Solothurn. Even more important than this important play is another by Hans Sachs of 1550, in which Salome suggests to her mother that she get rid of the Baptist by poison or secret murder ("Tragedia mit 6 personen. Die enthaubtung Johannes," in Adalbert von Keller, ed., *Hans Sachs* [Hildesheim: Olms, 1964] 11.198–212).

29 Daffner, *Salome,* 106–37, 163–82.

30 Daffner, *Salome,* 181.

lar belief in which Herodias (!) is punished by being forced to roam abroad on St. John's night because she has loved John the Baptist:

For she loved him once, this prophet:
It's not written in the Bible . . .

Otherwise there's no explaining
The strange craving by that lady:
Would a woman ask the head of
Any man she does not love?

Maybe John, her love, had somewhat
Vexed her, so she had him shortened
By a head; but when the lady
Saw the dear head on the charger,

Ah, she wept and lost her reason,
And she died of loving-madness.
(Loving-madness? How redundant!
Love is nothing but a madness!)[31]

The high point of the literary portrayal of Salome was reached in 1893 in Oscar Wilde's one-act play, *Salome.*[32] With powerful images Wilde describes Salome's glowing passion for John, lets the reader feel the sultry, oppressive, and charged mood, the redemption at kissing John's lips, the horror that overcomes Herod at the sight so that he has Salome killed. Wilde's drama evoked a great deal of protest, but at the time it was also the occasion for a whole flood of new literary and artistic portrayals of Salome. His portrayal of ecstatic lustful sensuality probably finds its perfection in the opera *Salome* by Richard Strauss that premiered in 1905.

What is theologically significant when material emancipates itself from the Bible and the church's tradition? Perhaps it is not completely accidental that the history of our text's influence revolves around that figure whose name the biblical text does not even mention—around a woman, Salome. While in the biblical text the morally objectionable part of her dance is merely presupposed, the history of the text's influence can demonstrate how in a world influenced by the Bible sexuality and lust were able to be suppressed. And it probably is also not completely accidental that this woman really came alive only when she was emancipated from the Bible. Is the history of the text's influence part of the history of woman's emancipation? No, not to the degree that the portraits of the beautiful woman Salome and the modern figure of the passionately loving Salome are images of women created by men. And yet yes, in the sense that in her an originally anonymous woman became the center of interest, and indirectly yes, in the sense that the history of the text in modern times showed at least the beginnings of a new regard for beauty, dance, and love. Theology should self-critically ask itself why this new regard took place not with but against the church's tradition.

31 Hal Draper, *The Complete Poems of Heinrich Heine: A Modern English Version* (Boston: Suhrkamp/Insel, 1982) 459.

32 Written in French, presumably stimulated by a short story of Flaubert.

1.3 The Feeding of the Five Thousand (14:13-21)

Literature

Marie-Émile Boismard, "The Two-Source Theory at an Impasse," *NTS* 26 (1979/80) 1–17.

Jean-Marie van Cangh, *La multiplication des pains et l'eucharistie* (LD 86; Paris: Cerf, 1975).

Heising, *Botschaft.*

Held, "Matthew," 181–84.

Iersel, "Speisung," 167–94.

Luther, *Evangelienauslegung* 4.218–34.

Frans Neirynck, "The Matthew-Luke Agreements in Mt 14:13-14/Lk 9:10-11 (par. Mk 6:30-34)," *EThL* 60 (1984) 25–44.

Patsch, "Abendmahlsterminologie," 210–31.

Repo, "Fünf Brote," 99–113.

Roloff, *Kerygma*, 251–54.

Ludger Schenke, *Die wunderbare Brotvermehrung* (Würzburg: Echter, 1983), 157–64.

Analysis

13 **But when Jesus heard it, he withdrew from there in a boat alone to a deserted place. And when the crowds heard it, they followed him by land from the cities. 14/ And when he got out, he saw a large crowd. He had compassion on them and healed their sick.**

15 **But when evening had come, the disciples came to him and said: "The place is deserted and the hour is already passed. Send, therefore,[1] the crowds away that they may go into the villages and buy food for themselves." 16/ But Jesus said to them: "They don't need to go away; you give them something to eat!" 17/ But they say to him: "We have here only five loaves and two fish." 18/ But he said: "Bring them to me."**

19 **And he ordered the crowds to lie on the grass. He took the five loaves and the two fish, looked up to heaven, offered the prayer of thanks, broke and gave the loaves to the disciples, but the disciples (gave them) to the crowds. 20/ And they all ate and were satisfied; and they gathered the scraps that were left over, twelve full baskets.**

21 **But the (number of the) ones eating was about five thousand men apart from women and children.**

Structure

The section that now follows consists of three "acts"[2]—an exposition (vv. 13-14) that does not yet have anything to do with the feeding, a conversation between Jesus and the disciples (vv. 15-18), and the actual miracle (vv. 19-20). Verse 21 is not part of the narrative but an additional comment by the narrator. The structure makes clear how most of the weight is on the conversation with the disciples. The beginning in v. 13 is reminiscent of 4:12; in addition, vv. 13 and 15 are connected with the beginning of the following story, vv. 22-23, by means of several catchwords, among them ὀψίας δὲ γενομένης. Again it is clear that consistency in the report is not very important for the narrator, Matthew. He fails to notice that the story about walking on the water that comes immediately after the feeding cannot also take place "when it had gotten late" (vv. 15, 23)! The third "act" of the story, the actual feeding, and the closing observation in v. 21, but not the introduction and the conversation with the disciples,[3] are repeated almost literally in the feeding of the four thousand in 15:32-39.[4]

Sources

Matthew continues with his reworking of Mark 6, and comes now to Mark 6:32-44. He has shortened the Markan story by a third. The abbreviations have the effect of making the story more formula-like; the catchword connections are closer together.[5] Most of the changes from Mark are understandable as Matthean diction.[6] The awkward Markan transition in vv. 30-31 has been omitted, as it also is in Luke. Verse 13 is heavily redactional and offers in the two parts of the verse a beautiful, typically Matthean parallelism. Matthew has already used the Markan comparison of the people with a flock missing its shepherd in 9:36. Decisive is the reworking of the conversation with the disciples in the second act. Matthew introduces it anew (v. 16a, b), omits Mark 6:37b-38b, and thus shortens it by one exchange. In its place he forms a new concluding command of Jesus in direct discourse (v. 18).

---

1   *Οὖν* is text-critically quite uncertain. Is it a Matthe-ism added later, or was it omitted on the basis of the parallels?

2   Fabris, 331–31.

3   Here there are only scattered contacts, primarily in v. 14 with 15:32 and in v. 17 with 15:34 (redaction!).

4   "Special material" of vv. 19b-21 are only: the numbers, ἀναβλέψας εἰς τὸν οὐρανόν, εὐλογήσας, the word for "baskets," and a few insignificant nuances in formulation.

5   In vv. 13 and 15, e.g., ἔρημος τόπος; δίδωμι in vv.

16, 19. Matthew also forms new catchword connections (ἀπέρχομαι in vv. 15-16; ὧδε in vv. 17-18).

6   Cf. vol. 1, Introduction 3.2: v. 13 ἀκούσας δέ, ἀναχωρέω, ἐκεῖθεν, ὄχλοι with ἀκολουθέω. Verse 14 θεραπεύω. Verse 15 (οὖν,) ὄχλοι. Verse 17 δέ, ὧδε. Verse 18 δέ, ὧδε. Verse 19 κελεύω, ὄχλοι. Verse 20 περισσευ-, ὡσεί. Ἄρρωστος (v. 14) is a "leftover" from Mark 6:5, 13 that Matthew does not want to do without. Οὐ χρείαν ἔχουσιν (v. 19) corresponds to 9:12.

The *minor agreements* are especially notable. They are quite numerous here. Several are not easily explainable as independent Matthean or Lukan redaction.[7] Examples: Βρώματα ("food," v. 15/Luke 9:13) is not Matthean redaction nor is the topos of the "following crowd" (v. 13/Luke 9:11) Lukan redaction.[8] The common omissions also are noteworthy. Both evangelists omit Mark 6:31.[9] Both replace or supplement the Markan teaching (Mark 6:34d) with a redactionally formulated comment about Jesus' healing activity.[10] Both omit the same conversational exchange between Jesus and the disciples (Mark 6:37b-38a) and then create a similar transition (17a/Luke 9:13b). In so doing they remove the most crass expression of the disciples' non-understanding in Mark.[11] Both are also silent about the crowd gathering in groups (Mark 6:39b) and about the distribution of the fish (the end of Mark 6:41).[12] In addition, some minor agreements have parallels in the Johannine feeding story.[13] Since the latter does not have a literary dependence on the synoptic traditions, such minor agreements may be preredactional in origin, for example, through the influence of other oral variants of our story. One must assume such variants all the more with a story like ours that was told so often. Thus in this text independent redaction by the evangelists and a "deutero-Markan" written recension of

Mark and an oral tradition different from Mark may all have played a role in producing the minor agreements.

Interpretation

Our story belongs along with that of the wedding of Cana (John 2:1-12) to the so-called gift miracles for which "analogies from experience" hardly exist.[14] It was therefore a classic example for the fruitfulness of D. F. Strauss's "mythic" explanation of gospel narratives.[15] The decisive Old Testament prototype that was transferred to Jesus and that led to the formation of our story was the feeding miracle of Elisha in 2 Kgs 4:42-44.[16] It is not enough, however, simply to explain its origin abstractly as the transfer of certain literary traditions to Jesus. Such a transfer occurs not in a vacuum but in a real situation. It may have been a situation of neediness and hunger. The primal human desire for bread and fullness fits it, and stories about becoming satisfied take on special significance.[17] Add to that certain experiences, viz., the memory of the meals Jesus has had with other people, the common agape meals, and the Lord's Supper in the church.[18] This all took shape in the pre-synop-

---

7   Cf. Marie-Émile Boismard ("The Two-Source Theory at an Impasse," 1–17) and the response from Frans Neirynck ("The Matthew-Luke Agreements in Mt 14:13-14/Lk 9:10-11 [par. Mk 6:30-34]," 25–44). Boismard seeks an explanation that takes into account *all* minor agreements and can find it only in his own (extremely complicated: vol. 1, Introduction 2) synoptic theory. Neirynck advocates for the first two verses the thesis that Matthew and Luke independently edited Mark (not convincing everywhere in my judgment). I would like to avoid trying to explain all minor agreements by the same theory.

8   The first minor agreement cannot be explained by Matthew's dependence on Luke, the second not by Luke's dependence on Matthew. Thus neither is a secondary source; they are independent of each other.

9   That Jesus was not able to eat because of the pressure of the crowd was already omitted by Matthew and Luke from Mark 3:20.

10   In this case I would assume independent redaction as most probable. In vv. 13-14 Matthew follows his own schema of 12:15: Jesus knows—ἀνεχώρησεν ἐκεῖθεν—the crowds follow—healings.

11   Ennulat (*Agreements*, 173–74) sees here a consistent

feature of the post-Markan reworking of Mark that he surmises.

12   Cf. also the absence of καὶ ἀπὸ τῶν ἰχθύων (Mark 6:43 par.).

13   The people follow, John 6:2 par. Matt 14:13 par. Luke 9:11; εἶπεν, John 6:10 par. Matt 14:18 par. Luke 9:14; περισσεύω, John 6:12 par., Matt 14:20 par. Luke 9:17 as well as less clear minor agreements in omissions.

14   Theissen, *Miracle Stories*, 105.

15   Strauss, *Life*, 507–19. In literary terms his interpretation is a gem precisely because it is so strong in content.

16   Strauss, *Life*, 517–18. Strauss (517) already called attention to the manna feedings in Exod 16:11-36 and Numbers 11. Cf. John 6:14, 31.

17   Compare the many images of the fullness of paradise or of Utopia in fairy tales and legends.

18   I am naming here factors and traditions that have played a role in the history of our text's tradition without being able or wanting to make a suggestion about separating out what has had an influence and how it was done. Cf. here Gnilka, *Markus* 1.255–58, 262–63; Bovon, *Lukas* 1.475.

tic textual tradition and in different ways also in the various gospel texts. However, we probably will have to give up here the search for a historical kernel in the sense of a single event, unless one simply wants to affirm it contrary to all verifiable experience.[19]

History of Interpretation

Precisely because the feeding story does not have such a historical kernel but is a symbolic story shaped from reminiscences, needs, experiences, and traditions, it is one of those gospel texts to which in the history of interpretation many experiences and needs of churches and individual interpreters could be attached. There is a wealth of symbolic interpretations that are transparent of the community experiences, and in view of the history of the text's origin they are principally justified. The problem for the interpretation is that precisely because there is no unambiguous historical kernel behind our narrative, it appears to be difficult on the basis of the narrative to raise objections anywhere in the face of the great wealth of symbolic interpretations. Symbolic expressions of human experiences and longings always seem true to the degree that they are authentic. Does that change when they are connected, as here, with the name of Jesus? We turn now to the "symbolic" levels of interpretation of the feeding in the history of interpretation and the experiences, longings, and theological reflections behind them:

a. Until the time of the Reformation and on the Catholic side even later, our text was interpreted allegorically to refer to *salvation history*. The feeding story then expressed the content of faith as a whole. The numbers especially offered rich opportunities. The five loaves corresponded to the five books of Moses,[20] the two fish to the prophets and writings[21] or to the books of Joshua and Judges.[22] The twelve baskets corresponded to the twelve apostles.[23] Thus Jesus changed the Torah and the prophets into new spiritual food[24] that is presented to the people in the wilderness, that is, in the gentile country far away from God.[25] In a similar direction is the modern distinction between a feeding for Jews (Mark 6:32-44) and a feeding for Gentiles (Mark 8:1-10) on the level of the Markan redaction.[26]

b. Since the ancient church, a *moral* interpretation of our text has also endured. It draws primarily on Jesus' conversation with the disciples and claims that Jesus wants to overcome the disciples' greed and to get them to share.[27] Jesus, says a poor Central American farmer impressively, shows "that with a little we can do a lot."[28] Or: the few loaves and fish that the disciples have show how simply and frugally Christians should live.[29]

c. *Social* is what we might call a third type of interpretation that emphasizes God's care of the *body*. God is concerned not only for people's spiritual well-being, but "Jesus who had come to feed the souls feeds the bodies also."[30] The text forms an answer to the petition for bread in the Lord's Prayer.[31] While the numerous medieval legends of miraculous feedings by saints rarely make direct use of our story, they

19 Those who do not want to agree with Rudolf Otto (*Kingdom,* 347–48) that Jesus was an irresistible charismatic who could even fill empty stomachs may read Paulus (2.266–78) or Schweitzer (*Quest,* 376–77). The former advocates the thesis that the example of Jesus' philanthropic and sensible generosity was infectious; the latter assumes an eschatological sacrament that was effective in many ways but did not satisfy hunger.

20 See, e.g., Jerome, 121; Strabo, 134. The boy of John 6:9 can then easily be interpreted as Moses. Another explanation is that of an external, sensual word of scripture (for the five senses) in, e.g., Origen, 11.2 = GCS Origenes 10.35; Luther 4.220 (Sermon on fasting from 1525).

21 Anselm of Laon, 1382; Thomas Aquinas, *Lectura,* no. 1243.

22 Paschasius Radbertus, 518.

23 Jerome, 122–23: "Each of the Apostles . . . fills his basket either so that he will have something from which he can later give food to the Gentiles, or so that he can use the remnants to teach that they were real loaves that . . . were multiplied."

24 He did not create the spiritual food from nothing! The text thus becomes an argument against Marcionites and Manichaeans (John Chrysostom, 49.2 = PG 58.498; Jerome, 122).

25 Origen, 10.23 = GCS Origenes 10.32.

26 Cf. those named in Gnilka, *Markus* 1.304, n. 19. The redactional Markan geography is decisive for this interpretation.

27 See, e.g., Luther 4.222–226 (Sermon from 1532 on John 6). Of course, the rationalistic interpretation has the same intention; cf. Paulus above, n. 19.

28 Cardenal, *Gospel* 2.148.

29 John Chrysostom, 49.1–2 = PG 58.497, 498–499 and the tradition dependent on him.

30 Erasmus, *Paraphrasis,* 85; cf. Calvin 2.147.

31 Günther Dehn, *Der Gottessohn* (3d ed.; Berlin: Furche, 1932) 126; similarly, e.g., Schniewind, 178.

show how important this basic idea was in piety.[32]

d. A fourth, *spiritual* type of interpretation points in precisely the opposite direction. One does not live by bread (alone)! Schmithals says today that bread and fish are "the tangible and tasteable word of the merciful one" and not welfare.[33] Earlier, not only Luther on occasion,[34] but already Thomas Aquinas[35] spoke in a similar way.

e. Between the "social" and the purely "spiritual" interpretations stands the *eucharistic* interpretation. In its modern form it begins primarily with the similarity between Jesus' thanksgiving and breaking of bread (v. 19 par.) and the words of institution of the Lord's Supper.[36] In the ancient church it is marginal.[37] In the Catholic exegesis of the Counter-Reformation, the eulogy or eucharistic prayer of Jesus was interpreted as the effective blessing of the bread analogous to the words of institution in the liturgy of the Mass and the multiplication itself analogous to transubstantiation[38]—an interpretation that evoked strong protests from Protestant exegetes.[39]

f. *Ecclesiological* attempts at interpretation in the wider sense are related to the salvation-history and the eucharistic interpretations. Usually the disciples are the starting point here. In the future they will distribute the goods of Christ as apostles.[40] The ecclesiological interpretation sees the role of the priests or pastors in the Lord's Supper prefigured in the disciples' function as mediators toward the people (end of v. 19).[41] The modern redaction-critical interpretation of Matthew especially understands the disciples' ambivalent attitude toward Jesus as the "little faith" that is characteristic of the Matthean community.[42]

Many of these interpretations played a role already in the New Testament texts or in the preliminary stages in the history of the tradition. When a narrator like Matthew retold our story, he accented certain aspects from the story's traditional potential meaning and let others recede into the background and lie fallow.[43] That need not mean that he wanted to criticize or censor the story. The history of interpretation also took that into account, because it almost never limited itself to *one* biblical version of the text but always saw the gospel texts together and then lifted from their fullness those interpretations that especially corresponded to the interpreter's own situation and church tradition. For that reason it is very difficult here to pose critical questions to the history of interpretation on the basis of the interpretation of a single form of the text. We will try now to trace how Matthew accented our story on the basis of *his* image of Jesus as "God with us."

Interpretation

■ **13-14** The introduction connects the story with the macrotext. For the second time (after 12:15) Jesus withdraws because of the threat from Israel's leaders. The people follow Jesus. Thus they are *still* potentially church[44] and not yet, as was anticipated in chap. 13, lacking in understanding and separated from the disciples. The evangelist has little concern about the details of the report; he neither says where the feeding took place nor

---

32 Examples: Columbanus multiplies bread and beer (*Handwörterbuch des deutschen Aberglaubens* [H. Bächtold-Stäubli, ed., Berlin: de Gruyter, 1927] 8.222); Bishop Richardus feeds three thousand poor with a piece of bread that grows in his hand (in "Abraham a Santa Clara," ibid. 8.223, n. 655).

33 Schmithals, *Markus* 1.326, cf. 323.

34 4.230 (Sermon on John 6 from 1526).

35 *Lectura* no. 1242: "Spirituales escae praeponendae sunt carnalibus."

36 Pregnantly in Iersel, "Speisung," 169–73; Heising, *Botschaft,* 61–65; Patsch, "Abendmahlsterminologie," 212–16 (Matt 15:36 is close to the Pauline report of the institution of the Lord's Supper); Gundry, 294 (not only the disciples but the crowd = the whole church eats the Lord's Supper).

37 Ambrose *In Luc.* 6.94 = BKV 1/21.606–7 speaks of a "hint" at the coming Lord's Supper.

38 I was not able to discover a direct interpretation of the loaves as the bread of the Eucharist. Maldonat

(294–95) interprets the *benedictio* as effective blessing of the bread analogous to Gen 1:22, 28. Lapide (295) regards the *transmutatio* of the bread in Matt 26:26 and here as identical.

39 Luther 4.231 (Sermon from 1524); Musculus, 382–83. Episcopius (88) points out that this interpretation of εὐλόγησεν is possible only in Luke 9:16 where the loaves are mentioned as the object.

40 Musculus, 383.

41 Held, "Matthew," 184–85; Iersel, "Speisung," 192–93; Ludger Schenke, *Die wunderbare Brotvermehrung* (Würzburg: Echter Verlag, 1983) 163 ("disciples as mediators").

42 Cf. below, n. 52.

43 That totally new accents appear in Matthew is unlikely, because he abbreviated the story at almost every point.

44 Cf. vol. 1, II on 4:25.

does he make clear from whence Jesus in v. 14 "comes out." As in 9:36, the mercy of Jesus is the reason for all he will now do. Out of mercy he first of all heals the sick from among the people. That is not a rhetorical embellishment. The mercy of Israel's Messiah for his people is important for Matthew; it can be seen almost always in his healings.[45] Just as fundamental is the disciples' task of healing on their mission.[46] The feeding follows the healings. After the "concrete" healings it is difficult to assume that the feeding has only symbolic or only sacramental character. It is just as much a "concrete" miracle.

■ **15-18** It is introduced with a challenge from the disciples. Since it is already late, Jesus should send the people into the villages to buy food. The expression may show that the people are not primarily the poor who are "burdened by their worry about bread."[47] Matthew takes it for granted that they can buy something for themselves. The more precise formulation,[48] "when it had become late," may betray that he is a city dweller. In the cities it seems to have been more the custom to eat the main meal in the evening.[49] The answer in v. 16 already indicates what Jesus will do. From the beginning he says that the people do not have to leave. Matthew portrays him as the superior, sovereign Lord who commands the disciples to do what is seemingly impossible but knows exactly what he is doing. Matthew replaces the Markan answer of the disciples that sounds almost "impudent," since they never carry around them two hundred denarii, that is, a laborer's wages for two hundred days (Mark 6:37). In Mark it expressed crass non-understanding. The only thing remaining for Matthew in v. 17 is doubt. They have only five loaves[50] and two fish.[51] Thus

he is probably thinking of the "little faith" in his church as well that stands somewhere between trust and despair,[52] even if the word does not appear explicitly until the next story. However, this does not simply mean a spiritualizing. For Matthew concrete questions about such things as food also belong to faith (cf. 6:25-34). The conversation with Jesus in which faith or little faith is revealed takes place again before the actual miracle.[53] Faith is not based on the miracle but hopes and asks for it. Jesus does not respond at all to the disciples' skepticism; he has them bring bread and fish.

■ **19** With a command that again suggests Jesus' sovereignty, the narrator introduces the actual miracle. The reference to the groupings of a hundred and fifty from Mark 6:40 is omitted. If Matthew is responsible for the omission, it shows that the idea of the restitution of the people of God in the wilderness period that is connected with it[54] is not important for him. Jesus takes the bread and the fish, looks up to heaven,[55] speaks the customary word of praise,[56] breaks the loaves, gives them to the disciples, and they give them to the people. With these formulations the Jewish-Christian readers remembered their own family and church meals *and,* at the same time, the Lord's Supper. They understood our story first of all as a report of a miracle that, however, reminded them of something they themselves experienced repeatedly with their Lord: the fellowship of eating and of the Lord's Supper.

Whether our text is intended to remind the readers of the Lord's Supper is admittedly controversial in research. In support of the claim it is argued that Matthew omitted the distribution of the fish (end of Mark 6:41, cf. 43) that does not fit the Lord's Supper.

---

45 By means of ἐλεέω (9:27; 15:22; 17:15; 20:30-31) or σπλαγχνίζομαι (9:36 [after 9:35]; 15:32 [after 15:29-31]; 20:34).

46 Cf. the interpretation of 10:7-8 above, II C 2.1.

47 Schlatter, 467.

48 Ὥρα πολλή (Mark 6:35) is more open as a relative statement of time.

49 Krauss, *Archäologie* 3.30–31.

50 Are the five loaves here meant symbolically? Repo ("Fünf Brote," 109) reminds us that in rabbinic language bread may be a symbol for the Torah (cf. Str-B 2.483–84 under c) so that one might think of the five books of Moses. However, the two fish do not fit this understanding. Nor does 16:5-12 point in this direction.

51 Bread and salted or pickled fish as a side dish are

the normal meal of the common people.

52 Held, "Matthew," 183; Jean-Marie van Cangh, *La multiplication des pains et l'eucharistie,* 146–48. Cf. also above, II B 2.1 on the interpretation of 8:26.

53 Cf. 8:26; 9:22, 28-29 and the interpretations there.

54 Cf. Gnilka, *Markus* 1.260–61.

55 A possible but not customary Jewish prayer gesture. Cf. Str-B 2.246–47.

56 Cf. Str-B 4.613–14, 621, 623. Naturally he does not "bless" the loaves (as in Mark 8:7 and Luke 9:16; Matthew is different). In a Jewish milieu God is praised, the food is not blessed.

57 Cf. esp. Iersel, "Speisung," 172–73.

In addition, it is said that "when evening had come" (ὀψίας δὲ γενομένης; v. 15) corresponds to the introduction to the Lord's Supper in Mark 14:17 par. Matt 26:20.[57] Against the view it is argued that Matthew did not omit the fish completely and that the adaptation of his wording to the words of institution is only partial.[58] In my judgment, the alternative Lord's Supper or Jewish meals is wrong. While it cannot be proven that Matthew has deliberately increased the references to the Lord's Supper in comparison to Mark,[59] they were obvious already in the Gospel of Mark, whose non-Jewish-Christian readers *had* to feel reminded of the Lord's Supper,[60] and Matthew did not "censure" them. On the other hand, it seems doubtful to me whether he saw prefigured in the disciples the "table servants" of the Lord's Supper. The fact that the "house father," Jesus, could not break the bread alone for his five thousand "guests" is obvious on the level of the report of the miracle and needs no further explanation.

■ **20** Verse 20 constitutes the conclusion of the story with the demonstration of the miracle. When twelve baskets of fragments are left—κόφινος (a basket for carrying things) is at the same time a measure of volume of about ten liters—it is clear that all the people must have been satisfied, since a miracle had taken place. Nothing here in the text suggests that the number twelve could refer to the twelve disciples. It is even unlikely that Matthew, after omitting Mark 6:40, was thinking of the twelve tribes of Israel.[61]

■ **21** Matthew concludes with a postscript for his readers that gives the number of participants. He makes the Markan statement precise without correcting it. This also shows that he takes seriously the actual miracle,

since one must add women and children to the number of five thousand men who ate.

History of Interpretation

The influence of this concluding notice has an interesting history. While in the tradition of the Greek church's interpretation it is clear that women and children are present,[62] they are excluded in the western interpretation of the ancient church and the Middle Ages. They are unworthy, for example, as "*sexus fragilis et aetas minor*."[63] According to Anselm of Laon the women are "pampered and given to vices."[64] Paschasius Radbertus finds children's play similar to idolatry.[65] Origen is the intellectual father of the eastern and the western interpretations[66] without demonstrating the low points of the western fathers. Since the sixteenth century[67] women and children have been included again to increase the number of participants and thereby the size of the miracle.

Summary

Important for Matthew, who reworked the traditional feeding story by giving it his own accents, was the absolute sovereignty of Jesus, who concretely demonstrates his power over illnesses and hunger. It was important for him that the people once more experienced the power and the attention of their Messiah. Also important for him were the disciples for whom this miracle was intended in a special way. They may be of little faith, but they experienced the merciful power of their Lord. They will experience it again (15:32-39) and through such experiences will come to understanding (16:5-12). Behind the disciples stands the church that in its life with the risen Lord, in its common meals, and in the

---

58 In one point (ἔδωκεν) Matthew is even closer to Mark 14:22-23 than to his own report of the institution. Of course! He was familiar with Mark 14:22-23, but he has not yet written his own report. The situation is similar to that of 13:44-46 par. Mark 10:21. Matthew has glanced over Mark in anticipation; cf. also the analysis 2 on 9:27-31. Roloff (*Kerygma*, 253–54), e.g., denies that the text is related to the Lord's Supper. According to him Matthew wants to re-Judaize the Hellenistic feeding narrative of Mark 8:1-9. However, Mark 6:41 is his source here, and he does not need to re-Judaize it!

59 It may be that the end of Mark 6:41 was missing already in the Matthean source; furthermore, Matthew generally tightens the narrative. Ὀψίας δὲ γενομένης in v. 15 may also refer to the usual time

of the evening meal (cf. above, n. 49).

60 Contra Gnilka, *Markus* 1.261–62; Pesch, *Markusevangelium* 1.352–53: The Lord's Supper was for them the only "Jewish" meal they knew.

61 Heising, *Botschaft*, 54; Repo, "Fünf Brote," 103.

62 Euthymius Zigabenus (436) even emphasizes feeding the family!

63 Jerome, 123.

64 1383. Christian of Stavelot, 1383: "instabilis sexus et mutabilis." This interpretation disappears after the Middle Ages.

65 521.

66 Origen, 11.3 = GSC Origenes 10.37–38.

67 Musculus, 384.

Lord's Supper, may also relive something of the miracle that took place back then at the lake.[68] Not important for him were the salvation-history dimensions and the reminiscences of the feeding of Elisha and of the manna that he played down in his narrative.

How is the Matthean text related to the rich palette of "symbolical" interpretations in the history of interpretation? The ecclesiological (f), but also the social (c), and the eucharistic (e) interpretations are relatively close to it. Other levels of interpretation are important in light of the entire synoptic tradition. Among them is the salvation-history interpretation (a) that in its way further develops the biblical references of the traditional feeding story to Elisha and to Israel's wilderness period. The moral interpretation of our text (b) is justified, since the churches in their common meals after Easter continued Jesus' practice of table fellowship. In all of the cases the churches' own experiences with the risen Lord influence and carry on this story about the earthly Jesus. Thus it seems that almost all interpretations are justified somewhere; obviously impossible is only the question of our text's "correct" interpretation. On the contrary, it may be that the multiplicity of the various attempts at interpretation could be an expression of the liveliness of the risen Jesus who continues his previous story in the churches. Thus interpretation in the case of this story means first of all to discover the wealth of experiences in the texts, not to limit it. Only in the case of the "spiritualist" interpretation (d) do I think that it misses the text, at least in the sense that it distracts from God's concrete and physical care of which our text and the experiences of the early churches bear witness.

---

68 Thus interweaving the report of the singular and past miracle of the bread and fish with the experience of the Lord's Supper that makes it "transparent" is designed to anchor the church's present experiences in the past story of Jesus. Cf. Luz, "Jünger," 153.

1.4 Jesus and Peter on the Lake. The First Confession of the Son of God (14:22-33)

Literature

Berg, *Rezeption.*

Georg Braumann, "Der sinkende Petrus," *ThZ* 22 (1966) 403–14.

W. Norman Brown, *The Indian and Christian Miracles of Walking on the Water* (London: Open Court, 1928).

Albert-Marie Denis, "La marche de Jésus sur les eaux," in I. de la Potterie, ed., *De Jésus aux Évangiles* (BEThL 35; Gembloux: Duculot,1967) 233–47.

J. Duncan M. Derrett, "Why and How Jesus Walked on the Sea," *NovT* 23 (1981) 330–48.

Drewermann, *Tiefenpsychologie* 2.27–35.

John Paul Heil, *Jesus Walking on the Sea* (AnBib 87; Rome: Biblical Institute Press, 1981).

Reinhard Kratz, "Der Seewandel des Petrus," *BibLeb* 15 (1974) 86–101.

J. Smit-Sibinga, "Matthew 14:22-33: Text and Composition," in Epp–Fee, *New Testament Textual Criticism,* 15–33.

Stehly, "Boudhisme," 433–37.

22   And immediately he told the disciples to get into the boat and to go ahead of him to the other side while he sent the crowds away. 23/ And he dismissed the crowds and went up on the mountain by himself to pray. But when it had gotten late, he was alone there.

24   But the boat was already many stadia from land. It was battered by the waves, for there was a headwind.

25   But in the fourth watch of the night he came to them, walking on the lake. 26/ But when the disciples saw him walking on the lake they were bewildered and said, "It is a ghost!" And they cried out in fear. 27/ But immediately Jesus[1] spoke to them and said: "Take courage! It is I. Do not be afraid."

28   But Peter answered him and said, "Lord, if it is you, command me to come to you on the waters." 29/ But he said, "Come." And Peter got out of the boat and walked across the waters and came[2] to Jesus. 30/ But when he saw the wind[3] he was afraid and beginning to sink he cried out and said, "Lord, save me!" 31/ But immediately Jesus reached out his hand, seized him, and said to him: "You of little faith! Why did you doubt?"

32   And when they had climbed into the boat, the wind ceased.

33   But those who were in the boat prostrated themselves before him and said, "Truly, you are God's son!"

Analysis

Structure

Verses 22-23 are a transition that closes the feeding narrative and at the same time prepares for what follows. The story is symmetrically structured. Contrasted with the exposition that includes the description of the storm in v. 24 is its stilling in v. 32. Between them appear the two episodes of the disciples' encounter with Jesus walking on the water (vv. 25-27) and of Peter (vv. 28-31). They are closely connected; the "if it is you" ($\kappa\acute{\nu}\rho\iota\epsilon, \epsilon\grave{\iota} \sigma\grave{\nu} \epsilon\hat{\iota}$) of Peter (v. 28) takes up the "It is I" ($\grave{\epsilon}\gamma\acute{\omega} \epsilon\grave{\iota}\mu\iota$) of Jesus (v. 27). The disciples' confession of faith as the concluding sentence (v. 33) wraps up the entire section. The individual sections are closely bracketed by repetitions[4] and oppositions,[5] resulting in a very concise text. The connections to the context are also numerous. The most important of them are the numerous reminiscences of 8:18, 23-27.[6] The beginning reminds the readers of 14:13-15.[7] Jesus' outstretched hand (v. 31) reminds the attentive readers of 12:49. They will be reminded in 16:16 and especially in 27:54 of the confession of the Son of God in v. 33.[8]

Sources

Verses 22-27, 32-33 are a slightly abbreviated reworking of Mark 6:45-52. Important in terms of content are the omission of "and he wanted to pass them by" (end of Mark 6:48)[9] and of the redactional verse Mark 6:52 with its abrupt statement about the disciples' fail-

---

1   *Ὁ Ἰησοῦς* is poorly attested. J. Smit-Sibinga ("Matthew 14:22-33," 25–26) suggests that it was omitted because of a homoeoteleuton (*ΟΙΣΑΥΤΟΙΣ*).

2   *Καὶ ἦλθεν* is often changed to *ἐλθεῖν*: Peter wants to come to Jesus, but he sinks before he does.

3   *Ἰσχυρόν* is later clarification (contra Nestle[26]).

4   *Ἀπολύω τοὺς ὄχλους* (vv. 22-23); *περιπατεῖν ἐπὶ τὴν (τῆς) θάλασσαν (-ης)* (vv. 25-26, cf. 29).

5   *Ἐμβῆναι εἰς τὸ πλοῖον / καταβὰς ἀπὸ τοῦ πλοίου / ἀναβάντων . . . εἰς το πλοῖον* (vv. 22, 29, 32); *φάντασμα ἐστίν / ἐγώ εἰμι* (vv. 26-27); *ἦλθεν πρὸς αὐτούς / ἐλθεῖν πρός σε (Ἰησοῦν)* (vv. 25, 28-29); frightened Peter / sovereign Jesus (vv. 30-31); *ἦν . . . ἐναντίος ὁ ἄνεμος / ἐκόπασεν ὁ ἄνεμος* (vv. 24, 32).

6   Cf. n. 2 on 8:18-27.

7   Cf. above, analysis 1 on 14:13-21.

8   *Ἀληθῶς!*

9   Did Matthew not recognize that the motif comes from Old Testament theophanies (Exod 33:19, 22; 1 Kgs 19:11)?

ure to understand. Most of the other changes are improvements on Mark[10] or reformulations in Matthean diction.[11] Two "minor agreements" with John 6:19[12] are noteworthy. As in 14:13-21,[13] they show the influence of other oral versions of our story.

Peter's walking on the water in *vv. 28-31* is Matthean special material. Is it a redactional creation or a tradition? The close linguistic connections with the remainder of the pericope that reveal no breaks show Matthew as a master of redactional creation. With few exceptions[14] the vocabulary of these verses is redactional,[15] taken from vv. 24-27, or deliberate reminiscence of 8:25-26 and 12:49. However, the Easter scene with Peter and the disciples on the lake in John 21:7-8 speaks for the existence of a tradition. There too Peter jumps into the water while the other disciples stay in the boat. It is conceivable that this episode was reshaped before Matthew or by Matthew on the basis of biblical and other analogies into a story about walking on the water and inserted into the story of Mark 6:45-52. The reshaping makes sense only as the deliberate attempt to make "symbolic" use of a tradition that meant something different. The supposition that a pre-Matthean Peter episode already ended with a Son of God confession[16] cannot be proven. One could argue that on the level of the Matthean macrotext the disciples' confession appears to be a too early anticipation of 16:17-18, but Matthew himself obviously did not regard it as such, otherwise he would have omitted it. He conceived his story in 13:53—16:20 not in linear terms but in terms

of several parallel threads. For him Peter's confession in 16:16 is probably not a first-time confession but the resumption and intensification of this confession by all the disciples.

Interpretation

■ **22** Immediately after the feeding Jesus causes the disciples to get into the boat. The scene is reminiscent of 8:23, but the readers immediately notice the decisive difference. This time Jesus himself is not with them. Matthew does not say where the disciples are to go. It is quite possible that he knew that Bethsaida, where they went according to Mark 6:45, is not close to Gennesaret, where they finally arrive (Mark 6:53). In that case, as elsewhere[17] he removed an obvious error of Mark without, on the other hand, having any interest in a clear geographical course of events.[18]

■ **23** Jesus climbs the mountain alone in order to pray. It is, as in 17:1-8, the place of special closeness to God. It is getting dark.

■ **24** The narrator's place now changes to the boat. It is already many *stadia*[19] away from the land and is "tortured" by the waves. The idea of human suffering that is unavoidable with the word $\beta\alpha\sigma\alpha\nu\iota\zeta\omega$ ("to torture") is probably intentional.[20] Water, storm, and night are symbols of distress, fear, and death, familiar to the church primarily from the language of the Psalms.[21]

---

10   On the absence of Bethsaida in v. 22, cf. below on the interpretation of v. 22. That Jesus was alone (end of v. 23) comes before the distress of the boat on the lake (v. 24) and results in a more compact report. The dragging and partly repetitive Markan v. 50a is omitted or incorporated into the Matthean v. 26; the temporal sequence in v. 26 is better.

11   Cf. vol. 1, Introduction 3.2 on v. 22 $\epsilon\dot{\upsilon}\theta\dot{\epsilon}\omega\varsigma$, $\dot{\epsilon}\omega\varsigma$ $o\dot{\upsilon}$, $\ddot{o}\chi\lambda o\iota$; v. 23 $\dot{\epsilon}\kappa\epsilon\hat{\iota}$; v. 24 $\delta\dot{\epsilon}$; v. 25 $\dot{\epsilon}\pi\dot{\iota}$ with the accusative; v. 26 $\mu\alpha\theta\eta\tau\alpha\dot{\iota}$, $\lambda\dot{\epsilon}\gamma\omega\nu$, $\varphi\dot{o}\beta o\varsigma$ (cf. 28:4); v. 27 $\lambda\dot{\epsilon}\gamma\omega\nu$; v. 33 $\delta\dot{\epsilon}$, $\pi\rho o\sigma\kappa\upsilon\nu\dot{\epsilon}\omega$, $\lambda\dot{\epsilon}\gamma\omega\nu$, $\upsilon\dot{\iota}\dot{o}\varsigma$ $\theta\epsilon o\hat{\upsilon}$. Most of the other changes have to do with cross-references to other texts or catchword repetitions within the text.

12    $\Sigma\tau\alpha\delta\dot{\iota}o\upsilon\varsigma$, $\varphi o\beta$-, cf. v. 24 or v. 26.

13   Cf. above, n. 13 on 14:13-21.

14    $B\lambda\dot{\epsilon}\pi\omega$, $\ddot{\alpha}\rho\chi o\mu\alpha\iota$, $\dot{\epsilon}\pi\iota\lambda\alpha\mu\beta\dot{\alpha}\nu\omega$. Strangely, $\dot{\epsilon}\pi\iota\lambda\alpha\mu$-$\beta\dot{\alpha}\nu o\mu\alpha\iota$ (with $\chi\epsilon\dot{\iota}\rho$, $\beta\lambda\dot{\epsilon}\pi\omega$ and $\pi\epsilon\rho\iota\pi\alpha\tau\dot{\epsilon}\omega$) appear in the omitted miracle story of Mark 8:22-26. Is this a deliberate reminiscence?

15   Cf. vol. 1, Introduction 3.2. Verse 28: $\dot{\alpha}\pi o\kappa\rho\iota\theta\epsilon\dot{\iota}\varsigma$ $\delta\dot{\epsilon}$

+ subject, $\kappa\dot{\upsilon}\rho\iota o\varsigma$, $\kappa\epsilon\lambda\epsilon\dot{\upsilon}\omega$, $\ddot{\upsilon}\delta\alpha\tau\alpha$, v. 29: $\dot{o}$ $\delta\dot{\epsilon}$ $\epsilon\dot{\iota}\pi\epsilon\nu$, $\dot{\epsilon}\pi\dot{\iota}$ with accusative, v. 30: $\delta\dot{\epsilon}$, $\varphi o\beta\dot{\epsilon}o\mu\alpha\iota$, $\lambda\dot{\epsilon}\gamma\omega\nu$, v. 31: $\epsilon\dot{\upsilon}\theta\dot{\epsilon}\omega\varsigma$, $\dot{o}\lambda\iota\gamma\dot{o}\pi\iota\sigma\tau o\varsigma$. On $\kappa\alpha\tau\alpha\beta\dot{\alpha}\varsigma$ cf. 8:1; 28:2; on $\kappa\alpha\tau\alpha\pi o\nu\tau\dot{\iota}\zeta\epsilon\sigma\theta\alpha\iota$ cf. 18:6; on $\delta\iota\sigma\tau\dot{\alpha}\zeta\omega$ cf. 28:17.

16   Gnilka 2.12.

17   Cf. above, II B 2.2 on 8:28-9:1 and III C 1.2 on the text as a historical report.

18   The other explanation is that Matthew no longer mentioned Bethsaida because of the woe in 11:21. However, Jesus goes to Capernaum (cf. 11:23) again; cf. 17:24.

19   One *stadium* = 192 meters.

20    $B\alpha\sigma\alpha\nu\dot{\iota}\zeta\omega$ is (seldom!) used in reference to a thing (BAGD, *s.v.*, 3) but normally in reference to distress, torture, afflictions, human sicknesses. One need not think especially of the agonies of the end-time (cf. Rev 9:5; 12:2).

21   Water: Ps 18:16-17; 32:6; 69:2-3, 15; night: Ps 91:5; 107:10-12; storm: Ps 107:23-32; Jonah 1-2.

■ **25** The fourth watch of the night, that is, the time of morning light from 3:00 to 6:00 AM, is at the same time the biblical time of God's helpful intervention,[22] and for Christians the time of the resurrection of Jesus (cf. 28:1). At this time, Jesus comes to the disciples across the lake. The context of the story makes it completely clear that he walked not along the shore[23] but on the water toward the disciples. We encounter here an image or a supernatural ability that is mentioned often in antiquity. What did the first readers associate with this image?

Background
As is often the case, in the exegesis of this text as well the Old Testament, biblical associations to the walking on the water are put in the foreground. They are, however, not all that numerous. Our text is not about a *passage* through the water. Texts about the passage through the Sea of Reeds (Exodus 14; cf. Joshua 3–4; 2 Kgs 2:7-8; Isa 43:2-3, 16-17, etc.)[24] are not direct parallels. Nor is the text about walking in the depths of the primal ocean (Job 38:16; Sir 24:5, etc.); it is about walking *on* the water. For such an event there are few Old Testament but many extra-biblical analogies. Since the "*interpretatio hellenistica*" of this text is often repressed by ignoring the material, I offer a brief, thematically arranged overview of the ancient parallels from the area of the Mediterranean Sea, without describing the content of the material in detail.[25]
a. Walking on the water is a solely divine ability.

Human beings cannot do it, or they achieve this ability only by means of magic: Gilgamesh Epic 10.71–77 (only the Sun God Shamash can ride over water); Hymn to Shamash e 29–30, 35;[26] *P. Berol.* 5025. 121-22; *P. Leid.* J 395 [= "Hidden Book of Moses"] 7.20–25;[27] Job 9:8 (especially LXX!); Ps 77:20 is uncertain. As "lord of the Sea" and "god," Caligula builds a bridge over the gulf of Puteoli (Josephus *Ant.* 19.5–6)—a sign of his insanity.

b. Sons of God, that is, heroes or "divine men," may also have this divine ability: Hesiod = Ps.-Eratosthenes, fr. 182;[28] (Ps.-)Apollodorus *Bibl.* 1.4[29] (Orion, Son of Poseidon); Apollonius of Rhodes, *Argon.* 1.181-84 (Tityos, Son of Poseidon); Dio Chrysostom, 3.30 (generally "divine humans"); Porphyry *Vit. Pyth.* 29 (the "one who goes through the air," Abaris, a pupil of Pythagoras); Iamblichus *Vit. Pyth.* 19.91[30] (Abaris).

c. Xerxes, who built a bridge over the Hellespont, is celebrated as one who strides over the sea: Isocrates *Panegyricus* 88–89, judged negatively *Sib. Or.* 4.76-79.[31] The memory of his audacity appears again in negative light in Jewish images of Antiochus IV (2 Macc 5:21) and of the Antichrist (*Apoc. Elijah* 33.1).

d. Walking on the sea is completely impossible for human beings;[32] believing such things is ridiculous: Lucian, *Philops.* 13 (implicitly). Elsewhere Lucian tells the "true story" of "people" with cork feet who are able to walk across water (*Ver. hist.* 2.4).

e. Walking on water happens in dreams and is an omen for a good sea journey: Artemidorus *Oneirocr.* 1.5; 3.16; 4.35.[33]

---

22   Cf. Exod 14:24; Ps 46:6; Isa 17:14.
23   Linguistically, ἐπὶ τῆς (τὴν) θαλάσσης (-αν) may also mean "to the sea" (or "at the sea"). A number of older and newer rationalistic reconstructions of our story's oldest kernel latched on to this meaning. Paulus (2.299–318) said, e.g., that it is not a real but a philological miracle that Jesus walked on the water, while Jeremias (*Theology* 87, n. 4) claims that Jesus stood on the shore and stilled the storm. The newest variant of this type of explanation is given by J. Duncan Derrett ("Why and How Jesus Walked on the Sea," 330–48, 333–35, 342–47), who says that the scene takes place on the north shore of the lake at the mouth of the Jordan where the water is shallow.
24   Gustaaf Adolf van den Berg van Eysinga, *Indische Einflüsse auf Evangelische Erzählungen* (FRLANT 4; 2d ed.; Göttingen: Vandenhoeck & Ruprecht, 1909) 54–55.
25   The excellent work of Berg (*Rezeption*) is especially helpful here.

26   ANET 91 = Gilgamesh Epic (E. A. Speiser, trans.): "Only valiant Shamash crosses the sea; Other than Shamash, who can cross (it)?"; ANET 388 = hymn (Ferris J. Stephens, trans.): "Thou does constantly pass over the vast wide seas."
27   Hans Dieter Betz, ed., *The Greek Magical Papyri in Translation* (Chicago: University of Chicago Press, 1986) 6, 195.
28   Hermann Diels, *Die Fragmenta der Vorsokratiker* (6th ed.; Berlin: Weidmann, 1951) 1.40 (no. 182).
29   Richard Wagner, ed., *Mythographi Graeci*, vol. 1 (2d ed.; Leipzig: Teubner, 1926).
30   Translated by Michael von Albrecht (Zurich: Artemis, 1963) 99.
31   Further references in Berg, *Rezeption,* 62, n. 35.
32   Cf. Gilgamesh above at (a); Horapollon *Hieroglyphica* 1.58 in Berg, *Rezeption,* 71.
33   Two references could not be incorporated into these five groups: *Apoc. Elijah* 25.4–5 (only in Paul Riessler, *Altjüdisches Schrifttum ausserhalb der Bibel* [1927; reprinted Darmstadt: Wissenschaftliche

The result of our survey is: In antiquity walking on water was of great interest to people—not only and not primarily the Jews. It was a dream, a fascinating idea. It is impossible for human beings and is reserved for God, unless humans are in a special way sons of God or achieve divine powers by magic—or unless in their audacity they invade dimensions that are reserved for the divine. Thus it is rather clear in what categories the first readers and hearers must have interpreted Jesus' walk on the water—and then also Peter's. We should point out here that in the culture of India, where there are also numerous parallels, the borders between the divine and the human are fluid in a quite different way.[34]

■ **26** The disciples see a figure coming across the water. It is understandable that they think that Jesus is a supernatural being, a ghost. Understandable also is their fear. Everywhere in antiquity,[35] not just in the Bible, fear is a person's natural reaction when an unknown divine reality happens that is beyond human understanding.

■ **27** Now the divine being begins to speak. Ἐγώ εἰμι has no predicate. Jesus does not say that he is this or that[36] but simply: "It is I." On the surface that is a simple reference of the speaker to himself.[37] Thus Jesus "dedemonizes" the ghost by pointing to himself whom the disciples know. Beneath the surface, however, his "It is I" is reminiscent of Yahweh's self-introduction in the Bible.[38] The biblical God had addressed the patriarchs and Israel with "Be not afraid, for I am . . ."[39] The text is thus multidimensional. With "It is *I*" on the surface the disciples are directed to the man Jesus whom they know. And therein they experience something of the biblical God. Thus the later doctrine of two natures that in the

history of interpretation has provided the categories for the understanding of this text as well connects with something in the text that was there from the beginning.[40] From the perspective of the history of religions, the entire text is syncretistic. One might say that Jesus presents himself here in the dress of a Hellenistic hero and with the language of the Old Testament God.

■ **28** Jesus does not yet calm the storm. Instead, Peter answers him. Peter was thus far known to the readers as the first one called (4:18; 10:2). He speaks to Jesus with the disciples' term "Lord" and asks that this Lord should command him[41] to come to him. Now instead of the "god," Jesus, it is the man, Peter, who wants to walk on water. Everybody knows that that is impossible, as impossible as moving mountains (cf. 17:20). This request for something that is impossible reveals Peter's faith, that is, his trust in the one who has all power in heaven and on earth (Matt 28:18).[42] "If it is you" anticipates the doubt that will appear again in his fear on the lake.

■ **29** Jesus gives him the command that he asks for. It is the basis on which Peter can act. That is important for Matthew. The foundation-laying command of Jesus makes human activity possible.[43] This foundation authorizes it and preserves it from self-grandeur. Thus Peter does not attempt to play the role of a guru or magician exploring or demonstrating his supernatural abilities; he obeys his Lord.

■ **30** Then he gets afraid. It is no longer the same fear as that of the disciples in the boat when they encountered the terrifying divine being. It is, instead, the fear of the storm, of the threat, of being insecure. Matthew

---

Buchgesellschaft, 1966]; of the king of peace); Virgil, *Aen.* 7.810 (poetic description of the warlike Camilla).

34 Cf. below, excursus after the interpretation of v. 31.
35 Cf. Horst Balz, "φοβέω κτλ," *TDNT* 9 (1974) 194.
36 Most of the Old Testament ἐγώ εἰμι statements have a predicate and are statements of self-introduction. Cf., e.g., Gen 15:1 ("I am your shield"); 26:24 ("I am the God of your father Abraham") and Berg, *Rezeption*, 282–305.
37 Cf., e.g., LXX 2 Βασ 2:20; 15:26.
38 Hebrew הוּא אֲנִי, Greek ἐγώ εἰμι. Cf., e.g., Deut 32:39; Isa 41:4; 43:10; 45:18-19; 48:12; 51:12. The formulation in Hebrew and Greek is not always identical. "Fear" and storm are theophany motifs (cf. Exod 19:16; Ezek 1:4, etc.).

39 Μὴ φόβου in connection with ἐγώ εἰμι of the divine self-introduction: Gen 15:1; 26:14; 28:13; 46:3; Isa 41:13, cf. 10; 43:1, 3; *Apoc. Abr.* 9.2–3.
40 Cf., e.g., Albertus Magnus 1.602: Christ shows his divine nature *in potestate*, his human nature *in veritate incidentis*.
41 On the disciples' address κύριος cf. vol. 1, II A 3.2 on 7:21; on κελεύω, 8:18.
42 The interpretation of the ancient church emphasizes Peter's "great zeal." Cf., e.g., John Chrysostom, 50.1 = *PG* 58.505.
43 Augustine emphasizes this very clearly (*Sermo* 76.5 = *PL* 38.481): "Non enim possum hoc in me, sed in te." For Matthew a basic figure of thought: the imperative as indicative!

describes it with words of the passion Psalm 69 [68] vv. 2-3, cf. 15-16. As Peter walks on the "waters," looks at the wind instead of the Lord, and begins to "drown," he "cries": Lord, "save me."[44] The readers, knowing this psalm, pray along with him here. The language of the psalms is their own prayer language. They recognize themselves in Peter and see in the water what threatens them: death, insecurity, unbelief, hostility, sickness, guilt. They know from their own life what it is like when all of these things become overpowering, when one "looks at" the wind and does not listen to the Lord.[45] The images are open, inviting us to put our own experiences into them. It is thus a story about the individual's own experiences in the boat, not those of the entire community. Matthew applies the story of walking on the water not ecclesiologically but to the individual Christian.[46]

■ **31** Jesus reaches out his hand to Peter and speaks to him. On the surface reaching out is necessary so that Peter does not drown. Again there are echoes here of religious[47] and for Matthew probably biblical[48] language so that the gesture says more than what is on the surface. Jesus provides divine protection. Important for Matthew is that this saving presence of God does not mean that no storms appear but that one experiences it *in* the storms. Those who risk obedience and move out from their securities experience it. God's help does not

mean that faith, bright and unthreatened, eliminates life's storms. Once again[49] faith is "little faith," that is, that mixture of courage and fear, of listening to the Lord and looking at the wind, of trust and doubt that according to Matthew remains a fundamental characteristic of Christian existence. That "doubt" is part of faith is important to him, as the repetition of the word in his last text in 28:17 shows. That is not to say that Matthew declared doubt to be an essential characteristic of faith, but neither does he condemn it. What the believer obviously experiences is that it is precisely one's doubt that the Lord receives and overcomes.

The story of Peter walking on the water has a close parallel in the Buddhist Jatakas.[50] A lay brother, while going to a master, came to the edge of a river. The ferry pilot was no longer there. "Driven by joyful thoughts of the Buddha," the brother went across the river. "But when he was in the middle, he saw the waves. Then his joyful thoughts of Buddha weakened, and his feet began to sink. But he evoked again stronger thoughts of Buddha and continued on the surface of the water."[51] The Buddhist text is the closest parallel to Matt 14:28-31 in existence. It shows a characteristic Buddhist quality. One experiences transcendent help not in the help of a personal other but in awakening life within one's self.[52] This story is part of a rich Indian and Buddhist tradition since the *Rig Veda* that deals with levitation or with miraculous river crossings (on foot or by flying) as demonstrations of religious ability, of the power of meditation,

---

44 The words in quotes are from ψ 68.

45 Luther's interpretation (*WA* 38.580) is deeply influenced by the antithesis between seeing and hearing and by Hebrews 11: "Res visibiles tollunt verbum."

46 The main scope of the Matthean story is not christological (thus John Paul Heil, *Jesus Walking on the Sea* [AnBib 87; Rome: Biblical Institute Press, 1981] 84, 97) as in Mark 6:45-52.

47 God saves with his hand in Hellenism too. Cf. Eduard Lohse, "χείρ κτλ," *TDNT* 9 (1974) 425.

48 Cf. ψ 143:7 (salvation from water); further material in Reinhard Kratz, "Der Seewandel des Petrus," 86–101, 90 and nn. 9–11 on 12:46-50.

49 Cf. vol. 1, II A 2.4.2 on 6:30 and above, II B 2.1 on 8:26; below, III C 3.2 on 16:8; IV A 3 on 17:19-20.

50 Stories from the earlier lives of Buddha; according to Stehly ("Boudhisme," 436) they existed as a collection in the fifth century CE, but they contained very many older materials, some of which are found on sculptures from pre-Christian times.

51 *Jataka* 190 quoted in Johannes B. Aufhauser,

Buddha und Jesus in ihren Paralleltexten (KIT 157; Bonn: Marcus und Weber, 1926) 12.

52 The usual Christian description of the contrast would be completely wrong—viz., that the Christian is saved by an encounter with the Other (God!), the Buddhist by himself and his own thoughts.

or of truth claims.[53] Since this is a rich, pre-Christian tradition, it seems to me that an indirect Buddhist influence on the New Testament is entirely possible.[54] Of primary importance, however, is that two such similar stories in two different religions point to a deep convergence of experiences.

■ **32** The story quickly ends. Jesus and Peter get in the boat together, and Jesus stills the storm. Again the miracle of Jesus takes place after the decisive consolation of faith.[55]

■ **33** The disciples fall to the ground and worship Jesus—behavior that is much more conceivable in the "ship of the church" than in a boat on a lake that is still in the midst of a storm.[56] They confess Jesus as God's Son. In so doing they pronounce the christological title[57] that is most important for Matthew and at the same time probably the church's most central confession. There is no reason to doubt that for Matthew this confession is a full and true confession,[58] even though it is singularly close to reports in the Greek world of heroes about sons of gods who walk on the sea. In contrast to Mark, Matthew wants to portray the disciples as believing and understanding persons in spite of all their despair and their need to learn more.

Summary and History of Interpretation

Our story reports how the Christian, represented by Peter, leaves his boat in a concrete venture of obedience and, alone and unsupported in the water, grows beyond himself and thus experiences both his own failure and the Lord's support. It deals with the possibility of exceeding one's own human limitations in faith in the midst of deep despair, fear, misfortune, suffering, and guilt. The decisive question to be put to the text is: How does such an experience of exceeding limits and transcendence happen?

Goethe, who called our story "one of the loveliest legends . . . that I love better than all others," said, "It expresses the noble doctrine that the human person will be victorious in the most difficult enterprise with faith and hearty courage, while he will be lost by the least touch of doubt."[59] He thus speaks only of the human figure. The Buddhist Jataka story answered our question by saying: It comes from thinking of Buddha. It thinks in a category that one might call "immanent transcendence." Eugen Drewermann (in *Tiefenpsychologie*) understands the water as a symbol "of everything in life that in any way can be an experience of insecurity, of the unfathomable, of the abyss: the fear of death, the fear of failure, the fear of meaninglessness, the fear of one's own subconscious drives, the fear of anything that is unfinished, unshaped." What can help us is the "light from the other shore,"[60] that shone in Christ but that can also happen in other people, just as it happened to the Shamans, the Egyptians, etc. in the "eyes (of their) soul" through "holy images" and "instructions in dreams."[61] The three answers have something in common. They transcend the peculiarity of the Christian religion and appear to speak of an experience that is universally human and that has been made under various forms and symbols. Must Christian faith contradict them and point apodictically to Jesus Christ and his story as *the* place where God reveals himself?

Meaning for Today

Our story with its many parallels in the history of religions is an important basic text for pursuing the ques-

---

53 Brown, *Miracles*, 3–29. Important for the New Testament are Mahavagga 1.20.16 in the Vinaya Pitaka of Pali-Kanon (= Brown, ibid., 20), because here the "It is I" of Buddha appears as a response to a disciple's nonrecognition, and the legend of Yasa (Mahavagga 1.7.10 and elsewhere; cf. Brown, ibid., 24) where Yasa overcomes his fear and comes to Buddha by crossing the Varuna. A crossing of a river by Buddha himself is represented as a relief at the eastern gate of the Stupa of Sanchi (from the first two centuries BCE).

54 Thus Richard Garbe, *India and Christendom* (LaSalle, IL: Open Court, 1959) 56–57; Brown, *Miracles*, 69–71; and Stehly, "Boudhisme."

55 Cf. above, II B 4.1 on 9:22 with n. 21.

56 Here too the transparency of the text is clear.

57 Cf. vol. 1, I B 1.2 on 3:17.

58 The church's interpretation frequently, but incorrectly, distinguishes between our confession and that of 16:16 by claiming that here the issue is only Jesus' Messiahship, while in 16:16 it is the true divine Sonship in the sense of the doctrine of the two natures. Cf., e.g., Cajetan (according to Knabenbauer 2.18); Jansen, 140; but also Calvin 2.154.

59 *Conversations of Goethe with Eckermann and Soret* (London: Bell, 1909) 506 (conversation of 12 February 1831).

60 *Tiefenpsychologie*, 30, 31.

61 Cf. *Tiefenpsychologie*, 35.

tion of the so-called absoluteness of the Christian faith. Compared with Matthew's day, the question comes to us in a completely new way, because we know where the parallels came from and can interpret them from their own context. Our text thus becomes an example of the convergence of religious concepts and experiences. We meet here a Christ who is more like Orion and the pre-existent Buddha than the earthly Jesus, who walked the rest of the time with both feet on the ground and not on the water! If we seriously consider that our story is unhistorical and mythologically symbolizes basic early Christian experiences of transcendence, then it is not easy to speak of Christian uniqueness. Did they come together in our text accidentally and externally associated with the name of Jesus? Jesus then would be a contingent vehicle of an experience of God that transcends even him.

In my judgment, we *must* take seriously the parallels in the history of religions in this direction, and we may not interpret them as so much scenery that provides a suitable background for a Christian uniqueness that is then all the more clearly recognizable. There *is* a convergence of religious experiences which we are to understand and gratefully receive. There are human-religious fundamental experiences that are so deeply rooted in the common possession of the human psyche that they are repeatedly verbalized in similar texts. However, there is also a Christian distinctiveness to which I would like to call attention, not to claim superior value but also in gratitude. This distinctiveness becomes visible in the Gospel of Matthew not when our text is read alone but only in the context of the entire story of Jesus. Matthew tells the story of walking on the water as a part of his story of the Son of God in whom God is "with us." He made his way to the "other shore" in obedience to the will of the Father, in love, and in suffering. This way of the Son of God makes clear in *content* what Peter's way on the water looks like. It is not just any way; it is the way of love and obedience. To be sustained by Jesus in the water's abyss does not mean *somehow* to grow beyond oneself and to have experiences of transcendence; it means to yield to Jesus' way of love and then, in an abysmally loveless world, to experience being carried by him. The 39th *Ode of Solomon*—that is, a gnostic "heretical" text (!)—appropriately expressed this concrete "prototype" for the way on the water:

> The Lord has bridged them (*scil.*, the rivers) by his word,
> And he walked and crossed them on foot.
> And his footsteps were standing firm upon the waters, and were not destroyed,
> But they are like a beam of wood that is constructed on truth.[62]
> The "beam of wood that is constructed on truth" is the cross.

---

62   *Odes Sol.* 39.9–10 (James Hamilton Charlesworth, ed. and trans., *The Odes of Solomon* [Oxford: Clarendon, 1973] 136).

2.1   Healings in Gennesaret (14:34-36)

34   And when they had passed over, they came to
land at Gennesaret. 35/ And when the men of
that place recognized him, they sent into that
whole region. And they brought all the sick to
him. 36/ And they asked him just (to be permitted) to touch the fringe of his garment. And all
who touched were saved.

Analysis   The brief crowd scene is divided into a connecting
transition (v. 34) and a healing summary (vv. 35-36).
It sounds familiar to the reader. More than half of the
text takes up earlier formulations (cf. 4:24; 8:16; 9:20-
21). The larger part of the text corresponds to the
source Mark 6:53-56 that is greatly abbreviated. The
central piece, v. 35, which for the most part replaces
Mark 6:54-56a, is clearly redactional in its language
only in its second part.[1] In its first part it takes up language from the feeding story[2] and an unused expression from Mark 1:28.

Interpretation

The story continues without a break after the high point
of the Son of God confession. As is always the case in
Matthew's text, there are no breaks between the individual sections into which today's commentators divide it.[3]
Jesus and his disciples land in Gennesaret. The name is
not documented with certainty as a location.[4] Presumably the fertile plain at the western shore of the lake
north of Magdala is meant. As happened already in 4:24,
Jesus has a wide-ranging effect. The local men[5] permit
all the sick in the area to come. They too expect much of
him. They touch his garment. What the hemorrhaging
woman did earlier (9:20-21) is repeated. All the clouds
seem to have disappeared. It is as if all conflicts have
been blown away. Matthew shows the pious Jew, Jesus,[6]
in the midst of a friendly crowd. Jesus turns to his people and heals all their sick. The many healing summaries
in Matthew[7] show how important Jesus' healing concern
for his people is precisely for the evangelist who elsewhere emphasizes Jesus' commands so much.

---

1   Cf. 4:24; 8:16.
2   Ἄνδρες (v. 21, τόπος (vv. 13, 15).
3   Cf. vol. 1, Introduction 1 and above, the brief excur-
        sus on C (13:53-16:20).
4   Cf. the evidence in Schlatter, 473–74.
5   Ἄνδρες in Matthew means "men" and not "people";
        cf. 14:21. Why only the men? One may say some-
        what pointedly that the women presumably are
        absent "only" for philological reasons, viz., because

of the "linguistic bridge" to 14:21. However, that
shows indirectly that Matthew was hardly aware of
the new position of women in the circle of Jesus or
of the reality that Jesus healed many women.

6   With tassels, i.e., showy decorations on the gar-
        ment; cf. on 9:20.
7   Verses 4:24; 8:16; 9:35; 12:15; 14:14; 15:29-31;
        21:14.

2.2 The Controversy on Clean and Unclean (15:1-20)

Literature
Barth, "Understanding," 85–90.

Berger, *Gesetzesauslegung* 1.272–77, 497–507.

Booth, *Laws of Purity.*

Ingo Broer, *Freiheit vom Gesetz und Radikalisierung des Gesetzes* (SBS 99; Stuttgart: Katholisches Bibelwerk, 1980) 114–22.

Charles Edwin Carlston, "The Things That Defile (Mark 7:14 [sic!] and the Law in Matthew and Mark)," *NTS* 15 (1968/69) 75–96.

Hübner, *Gesetz*, 176–82.

Hummel, *Auseinandersetzung*, 46–49.

Ernst Käsemann, "Matthäus 15,1-14," in idem, *Exegetische Versuche und Besinnungen* (2 vols.; 4th ed. and 2d ed.; Göttingen: Vandenhoeck & Ruprecht, 1965) 1.237–42.

Klauck, *Allegorie*, 260–72.

Helmut Krämer, "Eine Anmerkung zum Verständnis von Mt 15,6a," *WuD* NF 16 (1981) 67–70.

Paschen, *Rein und Unrein.*

Michael Slusser, "The Corban Passages in Patristic Exegesis," in Thomas Halton and Joseph P. Williman, eds., *Diakonia: Studies in Honor of Robert T. Meyer* (Washington, D.C.: Catholic University of America Press, 1986) 101–7.

1   Then Pharisees and scribes come to Jesus from Jerusalem and say:

2   "Why do your disciples transgress the tradition of the elders? For they do not wash their hands when they eat bread." 3/ But he answered and said to them: "Why do you transgress the commandment of God because of your tradition? 4/ For God said: 'Honor the father and the mother,' and 'Whoever speaks evil of father or mother shall die.' 5/ But you say: 'Whoever says to father or mother whatever I owe you is a sacrifice, 6/ may not honor his father.'[1] And (thus) you have annulled the word of God because of your tradition. 7/ Hypocrites! Well did Isaiah prophesy about you saying:

8   'This people honors me with the lips, but their heart is far from me!

9   Vainly do they worship me; They teach as doctrines human commandments.'"

10   And he called the crowd to him and said to them: "Hear and understand.

11   It is not what goes into the mouth that defiles the person, but what comes out of the mouth, that defiles the person."

12   Then the disciples came and said to him, "Do you know that the Pharisees were angry when they heard the word?" 13/ But he answered and said, "Every plant that my heavenly father has not planted will be pulled up. 14/ Leave them! They are blind leaders.[2] But when a blind person leads a blind person, both will fall into the ditch."

15   But Peter answered and said to him: "Explain this[3] parable to us." 16/ But he said: "Are you still without understanding?

17   Do you not understand that everything that goes into the mouth goes into the stomach and is thrown out into the privy?

18   But what comes out of the mouth comes from the heart; that is what defiles the person.

19   For from the heart come evil thoughts, murders, adulteries, fornications, thefts, false testimonies, blasphemies. 20/ That is what defiles the person; but eating with unwashed hands does not defile the person."

Analysis

Structure

This controversy dialogue is quite long. Are we even right in treating it as a single pericope? Or do we have two pericopes that deal one after another (a) polemically with the theme of the tradition of the elders (in vv. 1-9) and (b) thetically-didactically with the theme of purity (vv. 10-20)? Yet the two sections are closely bracketed together. The concluding verse 20b goes back to the hand washing problem (vv. 1-2). Verses 12-14 indirectly continue the polemic against the Pharisees in vv. 1-9. The source analysis will show that these brackets were created by Matthew. Thus we may treat the entire section as a unit.

The polemical first section of *vv. 1-9* consists of an exposition, in which the Pharisees and scribes with the issue of hand washing raise the problem of the tradition of the elders (vv. 1-2), and Jesus' long response dealing with an analogous case and climaxes in a scripture quotation (vv. 3-9). Instead of giving an

---

1   Helmut Krämer, "Eine Anmerkung zum Verständnis von Mt 15,6a," *WuD* NF 16 (1981) 67–70: Οὐ μή with future either means in Greek a very definite negation or as a Semitism (cf., e.g., LXX Lev 19:13; Deut 1:42) a categorical prohibition to strengthen the widespread οὐ with the future in-law texts.

2   Τυφλῶν (thus Nestle[26]) is missing in the best MSS.

The shorter original text is represented by ℵ* B D. It may be that a scribal error first changed τυφλοί to τυφλῶν (K pc sys, c), then τυφλοί was added again.

3   Ταύτην is probably original. The omission could have taken place (a) as an adaptation to Mark, or (b) because the subject is not "this" immediate parable

answer, Jesus exposes the questioners as hypocrites. With its many oppositions this section makes a rough and polemical impression.[4]

The second, thetic-didactic section on true purity begins with an instruction to the crowd (vv. 10-11) that consists of a single logion in antithetical parallelism (v. 11). In v. 12 it makes a transition to instructions for the disciples. The section vv. 12-14, a pronouncement of judgment on the Pharisees (vv. 12-14), is notable because it interrupts Jesus' lesson about purity and deals again with the Jewish opponents but does so only indirectly in the framework of instructions for the disciples. The following instruction for the disciples, vv. 15-20a, explains the logion of v. 11. The structure of this final section is determined by the saying of v. 11 that is being explained. Like the logion, it is divided into a negative (v. 17) and a positive part (vv. 18-20a). The difference in length alone shows the predominance of ethics over the ritual law. In the positive part the expression "from the heart" (ἐκ τῆς καρδίας; v. 18), which makes precise the phrase "come out of the mouth" and at the same time goes back in content to the Isaiah quotation of v. 8, is followed by a sevenfold catalog of vices which carries the weight of the section.

In many ways our controversy dialogue is reminiscent of chap. 13. It also consists of a public instruction and an instruction for the disciples (vv. 1-11; 12-20, cf. 13:1-35, 36-52 and 13:3-9, 10-23). Among the many reminiscences the most important are the catchwords "parable" (παραβολή) and "to understand' (συνιέναι) as well as the polemical Isaiah quotation in both chapters.[5] Thus the division of the content into polemical and thetical parts (vv. 1-9, 10-19) and the formal division into public instruction and instruction for the disciples (vv. 1-11, 12-20) overlap; vv. 12-14 with their indirect polemic do not fit

the framework in any case. Thus several concerns come together in our section: the controversy with Pharisees and scribes over their tradition, the pronouncement of judgment on them, the question about true purity, and the disciples' understanding.

Sources

The main source is Mark 7:1-23. The Matthean changes of Mark's text are relatively minor but often significant in content. They pursue three goals. First of all, Matthew wants to unify[6] the somewhat disordered Markan pericope that has a fresh beginning in v. 14. Second, he reshapes the controversy on the basis of his own understanding of the law that differs from Mark's understanding. And, third, he sharpens the polemic against the Pharisees and scribes. We mention here the most important individual changes.

1. The opponents of Jesus in v. 1 are Pharisees and scribes, not, as in Mark, the Pharisees and only some of the scribes.

2. The Markan explanation of the practice of the Pharisees and "all Jews" in Mark 7:3-4 and the statement of the situation connected with it in Mark 7:2 are omitted. For Matthew's Jewish-Christian readers such an explanation is not necessary; in addition, the problem of cleansing utensils is not an issue in this text. Furthermore, the explanation itself is wrong. It is not true that "all Jews" kept these regulations. That one cleanses oneself by sprinkling after coming in from the market is also incorrect.[7]

3. Matthew reverses the order of two blocks of material, Mark vv. 6-8 (Isaiah quotation) and vv. 9-13 (Corban discussion), and thus creates in vv. 4-9 a thematically unified, clearly structured, and, in comparison to Mark, sharpened[8] controversy that contrasts the "tradition of the elders" and God's Decalogue commandment[9] and climaxes in the Isaiah quotation

---

4 (of the blind guide) but the (previous) parable about defiling.

Παράδοσις τῶν πρεσβυτέρων (ὑμῶν)/ἐντολὴ τοῦ θεοῦ. θεὸς εἶπεν/ὑμεῖς δὲ λέγετε. λόγος τοῦ θεοῦ/παράδοσις ὑμῶν. χείλη/καρδία.

5 On the especially close contacts with 13:3-23 cf. n. 15 there. Verses 12-13 are reminiscent of the parable of the tares. On σκανδαλίζομαι cf. 13:41; on ἐκριζόω cf. 13:29.

6 Dupont, Béatitudes 3.582: "rigoureuse unification."

7 It is not known that the Pharisees after they have been to the market "sprinkle" themselves, their hands, or even what they have bought; it furthermore makes no sense in terms of the ritual law. The Pharisees bathe by immersion when they come back from the market; cf. Booth, Laws of Purity, 200. For

this reason many MSS correct Mark 7:4 to read βαπτίσωνται. Nestle[26] has taken this over as the text, although ῥαντίσωνται as an incorrect statement is presumably the more difficult reading.

8 Especially strange is the new form of Mark, v. 12. The Pharisees and scribes themselves say that one may not honor one's parents.

9 Verse 4: θεός instead of Mark v. 10: Μωϋσῆς.

in vv. 8-9. In the process Mark's repetition in vv. 8 and 9 also disappears.

4. The logion in v. 11 = Mark 7:15 is slightly revised. Ὅ δύναται κοινῶσαι αὐτόν is missing here as it is in v. 17 (= end of Mark 7:18). Οὐδέν is replaced by οὐ. The explicit contrast of "outside" and "inside" is missing here as it is in the entire text.[10]

5. In v. 16 the non-understanding disciples (Mark 7:18) have become *still*[11] non-understanding disciples.

6. Mark 7:19 is almost completely omitted. The double explanation of Mark 7:15 in Mark 7:18-19 and 20-23 thus becomes a simple one. Mark's first, "rationalistic" interpretation according to which Jesus "declared all foods clean" is omitted.[12]

7. The catalog of vices in Mark 7:21-22 is considerably abbreviated, primarily by leaving out those vices that do not directly correspond to Decalogue commandments but frequently appear in the Hellenistically influenced catalogs of vices in the NT letters.[13]

8. In v. 20b Matthew has added a concluding remark that returns to the problem of hand washing.

9. Many generalizing statements in the Markan text are omitted: among them καὶ παρόμοια τοιαῦτα πολλὰ ποιεῖτε from Mark 7:13, the general remark at the end of Mark 7:19, and οὐδέν from Mark 7:15.

10. The most important change, however, is the insertion of the saying about the blind guides in *vv. 12-14*. Verse 14b, c has a parallel in the Sermon on the Plain, Luke 6:39b. As in Luke 6:40 and the parallel Matt 10:24-25,[14] however, it is very doubtful whether the saying stood in Q. In Luke 6:39 it is redactionally introduced and fits poorly into the parenetic context of the Sermon on the Plain. The motif

was proverbial in Hellenism.[15] Most likely Matthew has taken over an oral tradition and connected it with a detailed framework. From him come the new introduction in v. 12a,[16] the question of the disciples in v. 12b,[17] v. 14a,[18] and the new beginning with the question of Peter in v. 15a.[19] The most difficult element to evaluate is the logion in v. 13. Its vocabulary is not altogether Matthean.[20] However, the image of God's planting is familiar from the Bible, and with "to be pulled up" (ἐκριζόω) it is anchored in the macrotext of Matthew[21] so that Matthew might well have formed the logion himself. Thus vv. 12-15 are almost completely Matthean.

The remaining changes of Matthew are less important. They correspond throughout with Matthean style.[22] As in Mark, the OT quotations in vv. 4b and 8-9 correspond literally to the LXX and not to the MT.[23] By changing the order of ὁ λαὸς οὗτος (v. 8a) Matthew is somewhat closer to the LXX than Mark is.

Interpretation

The *main question* that our section poses is what understanding of law and Pharisaic tradition underlies the Matthean treatment. The answers given here are controversial. There are two views on the validity of the ritual law:

1. Matthew distinguishes between the moral law in the Torah that is obligatory for him and the ritual laws that he rejects. He thus is basically close to the Markan position and edits Mark primarily stylistically.[24]

10 Cf. Mark 7:18, 21, 23.
11 Ἀκμήν is a non-Matthean hapax legomenon. Matthew frequently temporally limits the disciples' lack of understanding, but normally he uses οὔπω.
12 Only the reference to the stomach and the privy in v. 17, which has no function in Matthew, reminds readers of it.
13 Cf. the parallels in Pesch, *Markusevangelium* 1.382–83.
14 Cf. above, III C 3.1 on the source of 10:24-25.
15 Cf. 23:16 and the parallels in Klostermann, 133.
16 Matthean are: τότε, προσέρχομαι, λέγω (cf. vol. 1, Introduction 3.2).
17 Only ἀκούσαντες is linguistically Matthean. However, there is also the reference back to 13:19-23.
18 On ἄφετε cf. 3:15; 13:30; on the entire verse cf. 23:13ff, 24.
19 On ἀποκριθεὶς δέ cf. vol. 1, Introduction 3.2; on Peter as spokesman for the disciples see the excur-

sus on 16:13-20, no. 2; on φράσον ἡμῖν τὴν παραβολήν cf. 13:36.
20 On ὁ δὲ ἀποκριθεὶς εἶπεν, πᾶς, πατήρ μου ὁ οὐράνιος cf. vol. 1, Introduction 3.2. Φυτεία is a hapax legomenon in the New Testament.
21 Cf. 13:29.
22 Cf. vol. 1, Introduction 3.2. v. 1: τότε, προσέρχομαι, γραμματεῖς, Φαρισαῖοι, λέγων. Verse 3: ὁ δὲ ἀποκριθεὶς εἶπεν. Verse 5: ὃς ἄν. Verse 7: λέγων. Verse 11: στόμα, οὗτος (after *casus pendens*, cf. 13:19-23). Verses 17-19: στόμα, πονηρός, ἐξέρχομαι. Verse 20: οὗτός ἐστιν, δέ. On ὑποκριτής as address (v. 7), cf. 23:13-29 passim. In v. 11 the parallelism is improved; cf. vol. 1, Introduction 3.1. Παραβαίνω in vv. 2-3 is almost the only non-Matthean expression.
23 Stendahl, *School*, 54–58; Gundry, *Use*, 12–16.
24 Strecker, *Weg*, 30–32 (the Gentile-Christian Matthew contrasts the "observance of ceremonial law" not so much with the OT as with the "Christian" moral

2. He does not fundamentally reject the ritual law, but in concrete cases of conflict he subordinates it to the love commandment and the moral commandments.[25]

Likewise, there are two different views on the question of the "tradition" ($\pi\alpha\rho\acute{\alpha}\delta o\sigma\iota\varsigma$) of the "elders."

a. Matthew regards the Torah as valid but basically rejects the validity of the tradition.[26]

b. He does not reject the validity of the tradition in general but only this Pharisaic tradition. In place of the Pharisaic regulations on hand washing he puts a new, Christian halakah that makes hand washing optional.[27]

Position 1 cannot be combined with position b; position 2, on the other hand, can be combined with a and b.

The controversy comes from various historical and textual *difficulties* that are differently weighed and interpreted.

a. It is not clear what the Pharisaic purity law in the first century was like. We cannot be sure that the later rabbinic system with various degrees of purity was in existence then. What could unclean hands even defile?

b. Historically it is not clear to what degree in the first century the Pharisaic regulations on hand washing were even accepted. Is the controversy about an "*opus supererogatorium*" of an individual Jewish group, or is it about a widespread Jewish practice that seems to be an example for Matthew of the Jewish understanding of the law as such?

c. The logical coherence of the section is not clear. Three different cases are treated, viz., (1) hand washing,

(2) the practice of Corban, and (3) the question about true purity. The Corban question has nothing to do with purity. The question of true purity concerns not the tradition of the elders but the Torah. Only hand washing is concerned with the tradition *and* with purity.

d. Controversial is the Matthean understanding of the law. It is clear that on the whole Matthew has accepted Gentile-Christian, law-free (Mark!) and Jewish-Christian, law-observing (Q and special material) traditions. Where does he himself stand? Every individual interpretation of our text is determined by a general understanding of the law in Matthew. There is no such general understanding that would not have difficulties with individual Matthean texts. Depending on one's general view, one will interpret our text as a key text or as a text with which Matthew somehow had to cope.

e. Mark 7:15-23 is probably the clearest "Gentile-Christian" text in the Gospel of Mark and in my judgment presupposes that the ceremonial law in fact is no longer valid in the Markan community. How should we interpret its treatment by Matthew? Has Matthew basically accepted the intention of Mark 7:15-23 and stylistically tightened the text? Or with his tightening has he changed the intention of the Markan text and so to speak "dammed up" the text? Has Matthew in v. 11 accepted the fundamental meaning of Mark 7:15 without reservation?[28]

f. On the one hand, Matthew seems to have the tendency to limit the controversy and may in this regard be "more Jewish" than Mark. On the other hand, he sharpens the polemic against the Pharisees and scribes and

---

law); Schweizer, 327 (according to Matthew, the *biblical* law "never" wanted "sacrifice or ritual obedience" [cf. the position of Barnabas!]); Walker, *Heilsgeschichte*, 141; Berger, *Gesetzesauslegung* 1.504–6 (Jesus appears as teacher of the law but explains purity in terms of the Decalogue only morally).

25 Bacon, *Studies*, 352–53; Barth, "Understanding," 88–89 (the interpretation of the law in terms of the love commandment de facto breaks through the rabbinic idea of tradition = position 2a); Dupont, *Béatitudes* 3.582; Sand, *Gesetz*, 70; Gnilka 2.26–27.

26 That would be something of a "Sadducean" position. Cf. Schmid, 239; Davies, *Setting*, 104; Guelich, "Not to Annul," 75. (Guelich actually comes close to Strecker but with the difference that according to

him Matthew is concerned not for the *Christian* but for the *biblical* moral law); Ingo Broer, *Freiheit vom Gesetz und Radikalisierung des Gesetzes*, 121, 128 (similar to Guelich).

27 Hummel, *Auseinandersetzung*, 48–49; Hübner, *Gesetz*, 180–81 (Matthew argues rabbinically without saying so: simply with soiled hands no one is a "father of uncleanness").

28 Cf. Barth, "Understanding," 89: "Can (Matthew) have overlooked that 15.11 is directed against the Mosaic law?"

puts them under the judgment of God. How do the two go together?

■ **1** The Pharisees and scribes, Matthew's stereotypical pair of opponents of Jesus,[29] reappear for the first time since 12:38-45. They come from Jerusalem—after 2:3-4 a bad omen for the reader and a "signal" that Jesus' passion is approaching.

■ **2** They accuse Jesus' disciples of ignoring the tradition of the elders. Does "the elders" refer to the first members of the chain of tradition to whom according to *m. Abot* 1.1 Joshua passed on the oral Torah received from Moses? That is hardly to be assumed.[30] Instead, Matthew probably is thinking of the special "laws . . . from the tradition of the fathers" (Josephus *Ant.* 13.297)[31] which the Pharisees, in contrast to the Sadducees, urged on the people. This is confirmed by the "case" with which the story deals, the hand washing before eating that is not part of the biblical ritual law.

■ **3** Jesus prepares for the counterattack. In v. 3 he advocates an aggressive thesis: The Pharisaic traditions stand in opposition to the commandment of God itself. Thus for Matthew the issue is not primarily, as it is for Mark,[32] the problem of human tradition; it is not that *formally* God's commandment and human traditions have different authority and that next to God's commandment *formally* no tradition may be normative. Instead, the issue is a question of content. The tradition of the Pharisees contradicts the *content* of the commandment of God as the example of Corban will show. Therein the Pharisees and scribes "transgress" God's commandment in the name of tradition. Thus the issue is their *behavior*. As always, for Matthew everything is decided by praxis.

Matthew attacks the Pharisees because they violate the content of God's commandment.[33]

What does "your" tradition mean? We should not be too quick to interpret the expression analogous to, for example, "their synagogues" or "their scribes" (for example, 4:23; 9:35; 13:54; 7:29)[34] as "Jewish" tradition in contrast to the church's tradition. Instead, Jesus makes the criticism more pointed. The issue is not the "tradition of the elders" (v. 2) but "your tradition" (v. 3), that is, that of the Pharisees and scribes. That corresponds to the historical situation of his time.

Ritual Hand Washing

Mark 7:1-5 (and perhaps John 2:6) are the earliest references to regular ritual hand washing before eating in Judaism. In the OT only Lev 15:11, a text that is similar in language to Mark 7:2-3, says that a person who suffers a discharge, who according to rabbinic terminology is an originator (אב) of uncleanness, must rinse the hands in order not to pass on the uncleanness by touching others. Otherwise there were regulations about ritual hand washing only for the temple where there was a basin called the "sea," where the priests cleansed their hands and feet before serving at the altar.[35] According to the tractate *Sabbat*,[36] hand washing is among the eighteen things about which Hillel and Shammai agreed, but that is historically very uncertain. In the Mishnah hand washing is regulated into the smallest detail.[37] Even in Talmudic sources, however, one finds the opinion that hand washing is obligatory only after the meals but not before eating.[38] In all probability, hand washing was a special concern of the Pharisees, who tried to enforce the temple laws of ritual purity outside of the temple for the entire land of Israel.[39] According to *t. Demai* 2.11,[40] accepting hand washing is a condi-

---

29 Cf. vol. 1, I B 1.1 on 3:7-10.

30 Had he meant that, Matthew would more likely have said ἀρχαῖοι as he did in 5:21.

31 For rabbinic sources for this expression see Lachs, 245, 247.

32 Mark, who puts the quotation of Isa 29:13 first, structures the entire controversy around this perspective (vv. 7-8). Matthew no longer explores this "potency" of Isa 29:13.

33 Origen, 11.9 = GCS Origenes 10.47: "because of the most necessary commandments of God."

34 In every case it means: those of the *people* of Israel.

35 Josephus *Ant.* 8.86–87. In the same work (12.106) he says that the Bible translators first greeted Ptolemy and then washed their hands in the sea. Cf.

Epiphanius *Ep. Arist.* 305–6.

36 Cf. *m. Šabb.* 1.4; *b. Šabb.* 13b–14b; *y. Šabb.* 1.3d.40 = Str–B 1.696. Cf. in addition *b. Ḥul.* 106a in Str–B 1.697–98.

37 Tractate *Yadayim*.

38 *Y. Ber.* 8.12a.28; *y. Halla* 2.58c.35; *t. Ber.* 5.13 (12) in Str–B 1.697.

39 Jacob Neusner, *Das pharisäische und talmudische Judentum* (Texte und Studien zum antiken Judentum 4; Tübingen: Mohr/Siebeck, 1984) 24–25, 62. The Sadducees, on the other hand, insisted only on purity for the temple, the Essenes on purity for the holy areas of their settlements.

40 Str–B 2.502.

tion for being received into the Pharisaic community. Hand washing is here only an additional measure of the "comrades" in order to prevent defilement by food; basic is submersion in a mikvah (bath by immersion) that alone can purify a body that, for example, from a discharge or some other "father of uncleanness," has become unclean (cf. Lev 15:16, 18). Presumably the Pharisees took a bath by immersion every morning and also upon returning from public places.[41] Montefiore, Neusner, and Booth are in agreement that in the first century hand washing before meals was not yet a general rule; it was a peculiarity of Pharisaic "pietists," while laypersons and rabbis with a traditional view of the law did not observe it. Not until the second century did the Pharisaic observance become generally accepted.[42]

In my view, that allows a more precise historical classification of the Gospel of Matthew. While other Jewish groups, such as the Sadducees and the Essenes, were silenced by the Jewish war, that was not true of the Pharisees and the minority group of Jewish-Christians who were already marginalized within Judaism before 70 CE and now probably were excluded from the synagogue. The Jewish-Christians and the Pharisees, at least in part, had both previously belonged to the peace party. After they survived the catastrophe it is understandable that after 70 CE the struggle between them over who was the true Israel and what was the true interpretation of the law should break out again violently. Matthew 15:1-20 and the entire Gospel of Matthew document this struggle. The Jewish-Christian Matthew experiences with his church how the Pharisees begin to promote their view of the Torah as normative for all of Judaism. Our text was important for him in the struggle against their claims. Thus within Judaism one can define the Gospel of Matthew as one of the few extant documents of anti-Pharisaic reaction in the time after the destruction of the temple.

Thus "your tradition" is probably ambivalent. To the degree that the Matthean church is already excluded

from the Pharisaically dominated synagogue, it designates a demarcation against contemporary Judaism as a whole. That is not a correct description, however, of the way Matthew sees things inwardly. For him the theological controversy about what is "true Israel" goes on. The followers of Jesus, not simply the Pharisees, also claim—in the name of Jesus—to be true Israel. Thus for Matthew, the non-Pharisee and Israelite who believes in Jesus, what is called the "tradition of the fathers" by the Pharisees is "your" special tradition and not the law of God that is for all of Israel. According to his understanding, the Pharisees and the scribes belonging to them come and accuse Jesus that his disciples do not represent the special understanding of the law of the Pharisaic party that contradicts the Torah. Exegetically that means that at least in 15:1-3 it is not the ritual law as such that is at issue for Matthew but a special Pharisaic ritual. He thus is fighting not against the law but for it. In the question of hand washing it is he and not his Pharisaic opponents who represents the traditional interpretation of the Torah. To be sure, Matthew carries on the struggle not on the basis of the traditional interpretation of the Torah but on the basis of Jesus' interpretation, who through his teaching and life has fulfilled the law of Israel.

■ **4** With hand washing it is not immediately evident why one thereby transgresses God's commandment. For this reason Matthew brings another, more evident[43] example, viz., the vows for the temple that are fulfilled at the expense of the parents whom one according to the fourth commandment must honor. The commandments of the Decalogue were considered in Diaspora Judaism,[44] but perhaps in Judaism as a whole,[45] and also in early Christianity as especially central commandments

---

41 Cf. above, n. 7.

42 Montefiore, *Gospels* 1.135–43; Booth, *Laws of Purity*, 202–3. For Neusner (*Das pharisäische und talmudische Judentum*, 90–91) "after the cultic holocaust of the year 70" the people themselves are the "last, even if diminished, sanctuary" where the priestly purity that the Pharisees demanded for everyday life could be practiced—a situation that was especially favorable for the triumph of the basic Pharisaic idea.

43 More evident for the transgression of the will of God! It is not evident, however, that this transgres-

sion takes place in the name of the "tradition of the fathers." Cf. the following excursus on Corban.

44 Philo *Decal.* 18–19 (Decalogue commandments as νόμων . . . κεφάλαια), 175; *Praem. poen.* 2–3; cf. Josephus *Ant.* 15.136; Pseudo-Philo *Lib. ant. bib.* 11, and Berger, *Gesetzesauslegung* 1.262–67.

45 Cf. Berger, *Gesetzesauslegung* 1.267: There are indications that at an early age the Decalogue belonged to the Shema Israel. According to rabbinic sources, that was changed because of the preference of the "Minim" (unbelievers) for the Decalogue. Cf. also Str–B 4/1.190–91.

and as given by God's own hand. The rabbis regarded the Fourth Commandment as a heavy commandment; it was in any case decisive, because it obviously applied to adult children as well and included not only obedience but also support, welfare, and bodily care.[46]

■ **5-6** With their tradition the Pharisees intentionally[47] invalidate this commandment.

Corban

Enough has been written[48] about the Jewish regulations concerning vows and especially about the case indicated here in which children by means of a vow evade the obligation to provide the support that they owe their parents. The Matthean wording[49] corresponds to the Jewish formula for the vow. It is also known that the case of a generational conflict at issue here actually happened.[50] It is controversial whether something dedicated to the temple could still be used by the person who dedicated it.[51] However, the early Christian polemic is not justified. The rabbinic discussions show that the scribes were very much aware of the problem of immoral vows and that they looked for ways to invalidate such vows. However, an invalidation was possible only if the person who made the vow asked for it and if the rabbis agreed that there were valid reasons. The difficulty was that for the rabbis there was not a contradiction on this point between Torah and tradition but between Torah and Torah, viz., the commandment to honor the parents and the inviolability of the vows commanded by God (Num 30:3; Deut 23:24). In other words, the commandment about vows was a part of the Torah, while the deliberations of the rabbis about how one might invalidate immoral vows is to be regarded as among the "traditions of the elders." The difference between the rabbinic and the early Christian traditions of interpretation was that in the latter under no circumstances could the basic commandments of love and of the Decalogue be suspended by a vow, while in the former there were cases in which casuistic solutions were sought.[52] Yet there are also in Judaism impulses pointing in the same direction in which early Christianity went. It is God's own holiness that prohibits immoral vows.[53] Thus if nothing else the evidence of the sources should prohibit ugly Christian feelings of superiority toward Judaism that, unfortunately, appear repeatedly in connection with this passage.[54]

■ **7-9** Jesus' counterattack on the Pharisees and scribes climaxes with a text from the twenty-ninth chapter of Isaiah that is frequently cited in early Christianity.[55] He emphatically calls them "hypocrites," that is, people who talk one way and act another.[56] They talk about obedi-

---

46   *S. Lev.* 19.3 (343a); *t. Qidd.* 1.11 (336) in Str–B 1.706 (feed, clothe, wash, cover, take for a walk, not contradict). *M. Pe'a* 1.1 (Str–B 1.706): For keeping this commandment there are rewards in this world *and* in the coming world, just as there are for works of love and peacemaking.

47   Cf. above, n. 1 and the translation.

48   Especially Zeev W. Falk, "On Talmudic Vows," *HTR* 59 (1966) 309–12; J. Duncan M. Derrett, "*KOPBAN, O ΕΣΤΙΝ ΔΩPON*," *NTS* 16 (1969/70) 364–68 (literature there on 364, n. 2); Pesch, *Markusevangelium* 1.374–75; material in Str–B 1.711–17.

49   Δῶρον is a correct rendering of the Hebrew and Aramaic קרבן (contra Pesch, *Markusevangelium* 1.374). Matthew likes to avoid Aramaisms; cf. vol. 1, Introduction 3.3, n. 98.

50   *M. Ned.* 5.6, cf. 9.1 (in Str–B 1.716).

51   According to *b. Sabb.* 127b use by the dedicating person is forbidden; according to *b. Ned.* 33b–35a the question is solved in different ways.

52   New unforeseeable circumstances, e.g., are a reason for annulling vows: *b. Ned.* 64b; cf. Str–B 1.715.

53   Philo (*Spec. leg.* 2.10–23) prohibits, for the sake of the truthfulness of the oath, all vows from impious motives. In *m. Ned.* 9.1 the "honor of God" is a reason for annulling vows, i.e., vows can be annulled if they would cause a person to sin.

54   Origen (11.9 = GCS Origenes 10.48) (from a "Hebrew"!) already knows that greed (cf. Luke 16:14) was the secret motive of the Pharisees who would have profited (*sic!*) from the donations to the temple. The Swiss (!) A. Schlatter, notorious for repeated anti-Semitic lapses, writes in 1933 (!) that there can be "salvation . . . for Israel only if it is liberated from Pharisaism" (484). Even the German Ernst Käsemann, certainly no blindly obedient man himself, in spite the experiences with his own German history in 1933–45, criticizes the "blind obedience so characteristic of Judaism" ("Matthäus 15,1-14," 239). Too bad!

55   11:5; Rom 9:20; 1 Cor 1:19; cf. Col 2:22.

56   Vol. 1, II A 2.3.1 on 6:2.

ence, but "their heart" is far removed from God's commandment. According to the biblical word, what they say is human doctrine. Does then the antithesis between Torah and "human" tradition become at the end the center of the entire section? The quotation sounds like it, but because it is defined by the preceding Corban discussion in Matthew, in which the issue was not the merely "human" doctrine and practice of the Pharisees and scribes but their doctrine and practice which contradict God's commandment, we should not put the main accent here.[57] As in 13:14-15 it is a biblical word that formulates the accusation. And, as there, the biblical word says more than the text: Not only Israel's leaders but "this people" honors God only with the lips. In the context of Matthew 15 the accusation against the entire nation is still not justified; we have here a signal that points to the end of the Matthean Jesus story.

■ **10** Jesus calls the people together because his instructions that follow have basic meaning for everybody. The entire crowd is called to understand. Through the call to understand and the special instruction of the disciples that follows, the evangelist wants to reemphasize what for him is the fundamentally important reality: Understanding happens in the "'school' of Jesus."[58]

■ **11** The saying of Jesus that now follows is a *crux interpretum* in the Matthean context.

> In *Mark*, 7:15 clearly intended a basic abolition of the distinction between clean and unclean.[59] Mark 7:19 especially makes that unambiguous. Paul probably understood this saying of Jesus in the same way; cf.

Rom 14:14. Its original meaning for Jesus is less clear. Since Jesus elsewhere seems to say that internal purity takes *precedence* over external purity (Matt 23:25-26, cf. 23:23), and since historically the law of purity presumably was relinquished in early Christianity only with the transition to the gentile mission (cf. Acts 10:9-16), it is more probable that Jesus did not basically abandon the purity commandment but only subordinated it on a case-by-case basis to the more weighty commandments, especially the love commandment. In that case, coming from him Mark 7:15 is a sharpened rhetorical formulation that Jewish Christianity (correctly!) understood differently than did Paul or Mark.

With *Matthew* the difficulty is that while he has reworked the Markan text, he did not do so enough that an interpretation different from Mark's would convincingly result. He makes the Markan $\epsilon\dot{\iota}\varsigma$ $\alpha\dot{\upsilon}\tau\acute{o}\nu/\dot{\epsilon}\kappa$ $\tauο\hat{\upsilon}$ $\dot{\alpha}\nu\vartheta\rho\acute{\omega}\pi ου$ more precise by adding $\sigma\tau\acute{o}\mu\alpha$ ("stomach") and thereby makes clear that the issue for him is primarily "sins of the tongue" and food. However, for a Jew food regulations constitute only a part of the purity commandments.[60] Of even more importance is Matthew's avoidance of the exclusive and basically Markan formulation with $ο\dot{\upsilon}δ\acute{\epsilon}\nu$ $\dot{\epsilon}\sigma\tau\iota\nu$ . . . $\hat{ο}$ $δ\acute{\upsilon}\nu\alpha\tau\alpha\iota$ $κοι\nu\hat{\omega}\sigma\alpha\iota$. Thus in Matthew the logion is in part "deprincipled." To be sure, it can hardly be interpreted linguistically as a so-called dialectic negation ("Not so much what goes into a person as . . ."). On the other hand, difficulties arise on the basis of vv. 17-20a if one interprets the logion in the sense of a decisive no to the purity law. The Matthean adaptation of Mark 7:18-19 will show that. The difficulties that arise on the basis of other Matthean texts, for example, of 5:17-19; 8:1-4; 23:23-26, are even greater.

---

57   The Matthean changes in vv. 3-6 also speak against this view, while the wording of the quotation is already set. Against Pesch (*Markusevangelium* 1.373) we also may not say that there was a solid tradition that in the last times "God's commandment . . . will be replaced by human ordinances." Only *T. Abr.* 7.5 presents this contrast.

58   Cf. above, III B 2.1 on 13:18 and 23, III B 3.1 on 13:36, and below, III C 3.2 on 16:11-12.

59   In the history of the word the Jewish-Greek special meaning of $κοι\nu\acute{o}\omega$ = "to profane, make unclean" probably arose in the pre-Maccabean time when the question was debated whether "commonality" between Jews and Greeks could be brought about by identification of the different cults and by abolishing ritual barriers. For the Hellenists among the Jews the word will have had a positive meaning ("to produce commonality"), while the other Jews, per-

haps following a special negative meaning, "common, ordinary," probably gave it a negative meaning ("to make common, to desecrate, to make unclean"). Mark 7:15 takes over the negative usage but in substance reevaluates the Jewish judgment. Cf. Paschen, *Rein und Unrein*, 165–68.

60   Cf. the list of the "centers of uncleanness" in *m. Kelim* 1.1–4, where foods are missing and become unclean only indirectly (by blood when meat is not slaughtered and in any case when consuming corpses). Much more numerous are the cases of secondary uncleanness of foods (through unclean things or people or fluids) that are treated in the Mishna tractates *Toharot* and *Maksirin*. Here the degree of uncleanness is easier. Thus the uncleanness of foods is only a small part of the laws of purity.

Verse 11 remains difficult. I assume that Matthew—probably in the sense of Jewish Christianity before him—did not want to eliminate the purity commandment fundamentally but understood our Jesus saying as a pointed formulation that aims at the *priority* of the love commandment over the purity regulations. On the basis of v. 16 we would have to add that what goes into the mouth defiles not the whole person but only the *stomach*. However, what comes out of the mouth comes from his *heart*, and thus shows that the whole person is unclean. The findings of the entire Gospel of Matthew speak clearly for this interpretation, while the text of vv. 11, 16-20 by itself is not unambiguous. In my judgment, Matthew's attitude toward the purity Torah is like that of Jesus, and it also is not far removed from that of non-Pharisaic Diaspora Judaism for which the moral law was always more important than the ritual law.[61]

In the context of the gospel the basic statement in v. 11 has on the one hand a polemical function against the Pharisees. What defiles them is the teaching that comes from their mouth and abolishes God's commandment. In a polemic against the Pharisees in 12:33-37 the evangelist had already called attention to the unjust words that make the entire tree unusable. Matthew will intensify this polemic in vv. 12-14. On the other hand, the basic statement of v. 11 also has a parenetic meaning for the community. Jesus will speak about it in his instruction for the disciples in vv. 15-20.

■ **12-14** Understandably, the Pharisees, who now are mentioned alone as the most important representatives of Judaism in Matthew's time, react peevishly. Jesus no

longer speaks to them but to the disciples and announces with a picture the judgment of God on the Pharisees. The image of God's planting recalls the nation of Israel or the elect community of salvation.[62] That the Pharisees are not a planting of God, as Jesus' word indirectly indicates, is a slap in the face of their sense of election. The readers of the Gospel of Matthew are remembering the parable of the darnel in the wheat field, where a seed was also growing that did not come from the heavenly father and that will be pulled out by the angels of the Son of Man. Ἐκριζωθήσεται ("will be pulled up") is a *passivum divinum* with an announcement of divine judgment. The disciples are not to have anything more to do with the Pharisees, for they are blind guides (cf. 23:16, 24)[63] in contrast to Jesus who heals the blind.[64] The Pharisees' blindness also consists, according to 23:16-26, in their interpretation of the law that does not know how to distinguish between important and unimportant and thus *completely* misses the will of God. It will end in a catastrophe.[65]

■ **15-16** Similar to 13:10, 36, the disciples ask Jesus through Peter as their spokesman[66] for an explanation of the parable. With his "instruction" Jesus wants to overcome the non-understanding of the disciples who previously still have not understood (cf. 13:18-23, 36-52; 16:9).

■ **17** The most interesting thing about his explanation is what is no longer there from the Markan text. Omitted is that everything that comes from the outside *cannot* defile a person, because it does not go into the heart. Missing is Mark's basic opposition of outside and inside. Matthew says only that the unclean foods that go into a

---

61 Cf., e.g., *Pseudo-Phocylides* 228: Ἁγνεία ψυχῆς οὐ σώματος εἰσι καθαρμοί (dialectic negation?); Philo, *Spec. leg.* 3.208–9 (impurity is primarily injustice and godlessness). If one assumes, however, that Matthew opposes the purity law in the name of the moral law, then he would come close to the position of the "allegorists" whom Philo attacked in Alexandria, of Barnabas, or a position of the ancient anti-Judaism for which the ritual law was a later degeneration of the original imageless monotheism given by Moses (Strabo, *Geogr.* 16.2.37 = C 761).

62 Jer 45:4 and *Ps. Sol.* 14.3–4 come especially close. Additional sources are in Gnilka 2.25.

63 The logion perhaps takes up a Jewish or Pharisaic claim of leadership, cf. Rom 2:19; Josephus *Ap.* 2.41 and Ulrich Wilckens, *Der Brief an die Römer*

(EKKNT 6; 3 vols.; Neukirchen-Vluyn: Neukirchener Verlag, 1978, 80, 82) 1.148, n. 381.

64 Cf. 12:22 with the following protest of the Pharisees, 15:30-31 and the two "doubled" healings of the blind, 9:27-31 and 20:29-34.

65 Gnilka 2.25 with n. 29: "to fall into the ditch" as a biblical image for a catastrophic end.

66 Cf. the excursus on Peter in the Gospel of Matthew, below on 16:13-20.

person go out again, viz., through the intestines as waste. He also does not say that Jesus declared all foods clean (end of Mark 7:19). Of the entire tree of the rationalistic argument against external purity in Mark 7:18-19 only a stump remains in Matthew. In my judgment his omissions are too unified in content for us to describe them simply as stylistic tightening of the material.

■ **18-20a** Verses 18-20a develop the positive side of the "parable." What comes out of the mouth comes from the heart and is thus concerned not merely with the stomach but with the entire person.[67] Matthew puts here two accents: (1) He emphasizes sins of the tongue and thoughts that frame the list of vices.[68] (2) He reduces the Markan catalog of vices and concentrates it on sins against the second tablet of the Decalogue.[69] The second Decalogue tablet, expanded by the addition of "false witness" to Mark, appears in Matthew in the correct order which corresponds to the Hebrew text. As for Philo and other Hellenistic-Jewish writings, the Decalogue is for him the basic expression of God's will. Thus in our text he is not concerned with the abolition of the law but with its fulfillment and at the same time with its new evaluation. For him it is not simply the case that—in biblical tradition—uncleanness is a matter of the whole person.[70] This total understanding is accentuated: Purity is *primarily* a purity of heart, and it expresses itself in words and deeds.

■ **20b** Matthew concludes by returning to the original "case," hand washing. Jesus has not yet even answered the question of the Pharisees and scribes that was posed in vv. 1-2; instead he exposed the questioners as hypocrites. Now the disciples, against whom the question was directed (v. 2), receive the answer. In its language it is connected with v. 11, and it makes clear that the principle of v. 11 applies even for hand washing. Eating with unwashed hands does not defile the person. Why does Matthew add this conclusion? One can give a formal answer. In literary terms the long controversy and didactic conversation needs to be rounded off. One can also

answer in terms of content. One possibility is that Matthew was concerned in this entire controversy *only* with an independent Christian halakah on hand washing, and he directed the entire Markan text toward that end.[71] Then, however, the long dialogue would have been a waste of time. Therefore we must come up with another answer and look at the situation of the Matthean church. In contrast to the Pharisaically dominated synagogue it regards itself as the true heir of Law and Prophets. For Matthew hand washing, just as the question of purity, is a key question in the debate with the Pharisees about what makes Israel Israel. Therefore, much more is at stake with this problem than simply a special halakic question. That is why the entire text is so full of harsh polemics.

> Even with v. 20b at the end we must confess that with no interpretation does it strictly fit the train of thought. If one were to assume that Matthew wants to abolish the ceremonial law in v. 11 (interpretation 1), there would be a lack of clarity in v. 20, for hand washing is not a part of the law but only of the Pharisaic tradition. If, however, one assumes that the issue for Matthew is a precedence of the moral over the ritual (interpretation 2), then v. 20b is too brief. Jesus should say that hand washing is an adiaphoron that one may do as long as it does not keep one from fulfilling the central commandments of God.[72] That Matthew does not say this is in my judgment connected with the reality that from the Pharisaic point of view it was not an adiaphoron but a decisive point for the current controversy where the Jewish-Christians for the sake of the Pharisees had to show their colors.

Summary and History of Interpretation

First of all we recapitulate the difficult structure of the pericope. The Pharisees' question about hand washing is dealt with in two ways. Publicly Jesus polemicizes against how, with the help of the tradition of the fathers, they avoid the will of God (vv. 3-9). The second line of argument in vv. 10-20 expands the problem and deals with the question in terms of its content: Hand washing

---

67 Jerome (131–32) correctly observes that in this anthropology the "animae principale non secundum Platonem in cerebro sed iuxta Christum in corde."

68 $\Delta\iota\alpha\lambda\circ\gamma\iota\sigma\mu\circ\grave{\iota}\ \pi\circ\nu\eta\rho\circ\acute{\iota}/\psi\epsilon\upsilon\delta\circ\mu\alpha\rho\tau\upsilon\rho\acute{\iota}\alpha\iota,\ \beta\lambda\alpha\sigma\phi\eta\mu\acute{\iota}\alpha\iota$. Cf. *1 Enoch* 5.4 (arrogant and harsh words from an impure mouth).

69 Cf. Berger, *Gesetzesauslegung* 1.503.

70 Cf., e.g., Isa 1:16; Hag 2:14; 1QS 3.46; rabbinical references in Rudolf Meyer, "$\kappa\alpha\vartheta\alpha\rho\grave{\circ}\varsigma\ \kappa\tau\lambda$," *TDNT* 3 (1965) 418–23. For a comprehensive presentation of the biblical and Qumran findings see Paschen, *Rein und Unrein*, 17–151.

71 Cf. above, interpretation with n. 27.

belongs to the questions of external purity that do not concern the entire person.

Let us return to the alternative interpretations posed earlier.[73] We have decided—unambiguously on the basis of Matthew's entire text, less clearly on the basis of our individual text—that for Matthew the basic moral commandments of the Decalogue and the truthfulness of speech in any case take precedence over ritual cleanness but that he did not therefore intend to invalidate fundamentally parts of the Torah (= interpretation 2). However, we could not unambiguously determine his view of the oral, postbiblical tradition of the fathers. In my judgment, in this text Matthew is interested neither in basically rejecting the tradition of the elders (interpretation a) nor in basically affirming it and simply substituting his own halakah for the Pharisaic halakah (interpretation b). He spoke of the tradition only polemically, not thematically. That means that we can only say that where the tradition of the elders is in conflict with God's command itself, Matthew categorically rejects it. It is only on the basis of the entirety of his understanding of the law that we can say that Matthew understands Jesus' preaching not as tradition (that is added to the Torah and actualizes it) but as direct proclamation of the will of God that fulfills the Torah from its center (5:17-48). For him, as for Jesus, the value of the individual regulations of the law is decided in each concrete situation on the basis of love as the central commandment. Thus there does not seem to be a place anymore for a tradition in the Jewish sense.

There are in addition two other reasons why this text is important for him. It sharpens the polemic against the Pharisees and scribes up to the announcement of judgment and thus prepares for Jesus' third "withdrawal" (15:21). And it discloses to the questioning disciples the ethical meaning of his parable and leads them to understanding.

The question about the Pharisaic hand washing regulations was settled at an early date by later history that brought the Matthean church into the fellowship of Gentile Christianity. The church's interpretation that wanted to actualize the text thus looked for analogies to the Jewish ritual laws in its own church situation. Are, for example, the church's commandments on fasting correct in the light of Matt 15:11? Here one must distinguish: It is not meat or other foods that are damaging (cf. 1 Tim 4:4) but what is caused by them in the heart: greed, luxury.[74] Thus with fasting it is not a question of avoiding meat but of self-discipline or the exercise of the freedom to abstain. John Chrysostom gives another important application with regard to regulations about sexual abstinence. Not by sexual abstinence in itself is one obedient to God, nor by intercourse in marriage is one disobedient; one bypasses the commandment of Jesus only if one dares not to pray after marital intercourse "even though there is nothing evil in it." That obviously is a problem of his time, while in other things one was "tolerant." "But if you have slandered or blasphemed, . . . do you lift up your hands?"[75] Our text contains a potential meaning that is directed against any ascetic-legal religious regulations that touch a person only externally.

---

72 There is a difference between hand washing and Corban!

73 Above, at the beginning of the interpretation.

74 Origen, 11.12 = GCS Origenes 10.53–54 ($\pi\lambda\epsilon o\nu\epsilon\xi\acute{\iota}\alpha$, making an idol of the stomach, with a reference to Rom 14:23); Lapide, 303 (*gula, luxuria*). Wolzogen (309) formulates very precisely: it is the *mala intentio* that defiles the person.

75 51.5 = 735.

2.3 The Encounter with the Canaanite Woman (15:21-28)

Literature

Dermience, "Pericope," 25–49.

Roy A. Harrisville, "The Woman of Canaan," *Int* 20 (1960) 274–87.

Kasting, *Anfänge*, 109–15.

Simon Légasse, "L'épisode de la Cananéenne d'après Mt 15,21-28," *BLE* 73 (1972) 21–40.

Tino Lovison, "La pericopa della Cananea Mt 15,21-28," *RivB* 19 (1971) 273–305.

Jerome H. Neyrey, "Decision Making in the Early Church," *ScEs* 33 (1981) 373–78.

Sharon H. Ringe, "A Gentile Woman's Story," in Letty M. Russell, ed., *Feminist Interpretation of the Bible* (Philadelphia: Westminster, 1985) 65–72.

Helga Rusche, "Für das 'Haus Israel' vom 'Gott Israels' gesandt," in Horst Goldstein, ed., *Gottesverächter und Menschenfeinde?* (Düsseldorf: Patmos, 1979) 99–122.

E. A. Russell, "The Canaanite Woman and the Gospels (Mt 15,21-28; cf. Mk 7,24-30)," in *Studia Biblica* 1978/2 (JSNTSup 2; Sheffield: Department of Biblical Studies, University of Sheffield, 1978) 263–300.

Theissen, "Sozialkolorit," 202–25. [ET = *Gospels in Context*, 61–80].

Trilling, *Israel*, 99–105.

21 And when Jesus went out from there he withdrew into the region of Tyre and Sidon.

22 And behold, a Canaanite woman from that area came out, cried and said, "Have mercy on me, Lord, Son of David. My daughter is severely demon-possessed." 23/ But he answered her not a word. And his disciples came and asked[1] him and said, "Send her away, for she is crying after us."

24 But he answered and said, "I was sent only to the lost sheep of the house of Israel."

25 But she came, fell down before him, and said, "Lord, help me!" 26/ But he answered and said, "It is not good to take the children's bread and to throw it to the dogs." 27/ But she said, "Certainly, Lord. And (yet) even the dogs eat the crumbs that fall from the table of their masters."

28 Then Jesus answered and said to her, "Woman, your faith is great. Let it be to you as you wish." And her daughter was healed from that hour.

Analysis

Structure

The introductory v. 21 contains another withdrawal of Jesus like those of 12:15 and 14:13. The scene is thus changed from the preceding story. Most noticeably, the persons confronting Jesus abruptly change from the Jewish leaders to a gentile woman. The healing story does not begin until v. 22. Compared with the stylistic structure of healings from a distance,[2] it is striking that the request of the representative and the concluding assurance of healing are very brief (vv. 22, 28 with inclusion: γυνή, θυγάτηρ). The emphasis is on the intervening dialogue and especially on the difficulty in Jesus' fulfilling the request. It takes place in vv. 23-24 in three stages: with Jesus' silence, with the disciples' suggestion that the woman be sent away, and finally with an answer from Jesus that fundamentally justifies the disciples' request. The rejection is so massive that the woman has to repeat her request in v. 25.[3] Jesus' categorical answer in v. 26 is a new impediment. The woman turns this answer around in v. 27 and thus proves her trust. After v. 28 the scene and the characters again change; thus the bracketing of the story in its immediate context is quite weak. There are, however, a number of verbal relationships to the larger context: The address of the woman to Jesus in v. 22 is reminiscent of 9:27. Jesus' answer in v. 24 takes up 10:5-6. The conclusion in v. 28 recalls 8:13.

Sources

The source of our text is Mark 7:24-30; there are no other or secondary sources.[4] Especially in vv. 22-25 and 28 the text has been completely rewritten by Matthew. In these verses the redactional characteristics are extraordinarily heavy.[5] Matthew used here only a few of Mark's words; in addition, one can see the influence of Mark 10:47-48. Thus v. 24 is probably redactional. Since it is part of a completely redactional dialogue, one will regard it not as a traditional

---

1 Ἠρώτουν instead of ἠρώτων: Mixing the paradigms in -αν and -ειν sometimes occurs in the Koine (BDF § 90).

2 Pesch (*Markusevangelium* 1.386) assumes the following topoi: (1) the representative's request, (2) impediment, (3) the representative's expression of trust, (4) assurance and dismissal.

3 Verses 22 and 25: twice ἐλθοῦσα and κύριε.

4 Cf. especially Tino Lovison, "La pericopa della Cananea Mt 15,21-28," *RivB* 19 (1971) 273–305 and Dermience, "Pericope."

5 Cf. vol. 1, Introduction 3.2 on ἰδού, ἀπό, ἐκεῖνος, ἐξέρχομαι, κράζω, λέγων, ἐλεέω, κύριε, υἱὸς Δαυίδ, κακῶς, δαιμονίζομαι (v. 22), δέ, ἀποκρίνομαι, προσελθών, μαθητής, λέγων, κράζω (v. 23), ὁ δὲ ἀποκριθεὶς εἶπεν (v. 24), δέ, ἐλθών, προσκυνέω, λέγων, κύριε (v. 25), τότε, ἀποκριθεὶς εἶπεν, γενηθήτω, θέλω, ἀπὸ τῆς ὥρας ἐκείνης (v. 28). Θυγάτριον (diminutive!) and ἀκάθαρτος are terms that are avoided in Matthew; cf. vol. 1, Introduction 3.3. On οὐκ . . . εἰ μή (v. 23) cf. 12:24; 14:17; [17:21] (always redactional). On οὐκ ἀποκρίνομαι λόγον

saying of Jesus[6] but as a Matthean creation based on the traditional saying in 10:5-6.[7] As is often the case, the Markan secrecy motif (Mark 7:24a) is a victim of the Matthean reconstruction. The Markan exposition that mentions the woman's problem (Mark 7:25a, b) is likewise missing. In Matthew, much more elegantly, the woman comes straight to Jesus and expresses her need directly (v. 22). Verse 28 is newly formulated analogous to 8:13: The exorcism at a distance on behalf of a gentile woman (Mark 7:29-30) has become in Matthew a miracle of faith. In its structure the text is now reminiscent of Mark 10:46-52, where the sick person also asks twice for healing because the people stranding around try to drive him off. The entire Matthean treatment shows a great deal of literary artistry.

History of Interpretation

In the history of our text's interpretation two kinds of interpretation always stand side by side: (a) the salvation-history interpretation and (b) the parenetic-existential interpretation. In the Middle Ages the two were able to be connected by the multiple meaning of scripture.

a. The *salvation-history interpretation* made use of the allegorical method. Its most influential representatives are Hilary and Jerome. Hilary interpreted the Canaanite woman as a proselyte who is pleading for her child, the Gentiles.[8] The healing from a distance corresponds to the situation of the Gentiles. They are saved not by encountering Jesus but through his word.[9] Especially v. 26 is understood allegorically.

The dogs are the Gentiles, the children are Israel. The bread is not real bread but the doctrine, the gospel.[10] The table is the holy scripture.[11] Here it is especially clear how the allegorical interpretation spiritualizes and theologizes the miracle story. Frequently repeated is an inventive and sharp formulation of Jerome to the effect that formerly the Jews were children and the Gentiles were dogs; now it is the other way around.[12] Calvin's formulation is significant and exegetically correct: Our story is a "prelude" of what will be after Easter.[13]

b. The *parenetic-existential interpretation* more strongly reflects the historical and also the confessional changes. In the ancient church, in the Middle Ages, and in the post-Reformation Catholic tradition of interpretation, faith is understood primarily as a virtue. Belonging to it are, for example, modesty, perseverance, reverence, prudence, trust,[14] but especially *humility*. The interpreters saw the strongest expression of the woman's humility at the beginning of v. 27. "The Lord had called her 'dog.' She did not say, 'I am not a dog,' but she said, 'I am one!'"[15] While a medieval interpreter saw masculine virtues in the woman's behavior,[16] for a modern Protestant exegete, the humble acceptance of grace was the essence of the feminine soul.[17] In our time the basic attitude changes. Humble submission is no longer regarded as a virtue. The saying about the children and the dogs is regarded as an "atrocious saying" and the "worst kind of chauvinism,"[18] and it is inconceivable for many that Jesus could have demanded such submissiveness. Fortunately, however, the historical-critical

---

(v. 23) cf. 22:46; 27:14 (LXX: 3 Βασ 18:21; 4 Βασ 18:36; Isa 36:21; 1 Macc 15:35). On v. 24 cf. 10:5-6. Ἀπεστάλην is LXX language (Dermience, "Pericope," 36–38).

6   Thus especially Jeremias, *Promise,* 27–28 (v. 24 is a word of Jesus) and Bultmann, *History,* 38 (v. 24 is a traditional word of Jesus; Mark is secondary by comparison), cf. also Hahn, *Mission,* 55 (v. 24 comes from particularistic Jewish Christianity).

7   Cf. above, II C 2.1 Analysis. Thus already Ernst von Dobschütz, "Matthäus als Rabbi und Katechet," *ZNW* 27 (1928) 339 and again Trilling, *Israel,* 99–100, 105. Frankemölle (*Jahwebund,* 137–39) regards 10:5-6 as also redactional. Strecker (*Weg,* 108, 194–95) follows Bultmann (above, n. 6) and concludes that 15:24 is primary in comparison with 10:5-6.

8   Hilary, 15.3 = SC 258.36.

9   Augustine *Quaest.* 1.18 = 17.

10   Theodore of Mopsuestia fr. 83 = Reuss, 126 (teaching by words and signs); Maldonat, 314 (*evangelica gratia*).

11   Christian of Stavelot, 1390.

12   134; cf. Rabanus, 980; Dionysius the Carthusian, 184. In an anti-Jewish version John Chrysostom *Adv. Jud.* 1.2 = *PG* 48. 843: The Jews who have killed their prophets have degenerated into dogs.

13   2.166. Clearly similar already is Zwingli, 335: Matt 15:24 has a temporally limited meaning.

14   Cf. Lapide, 307; Jerome, 133 (*fides, patientia, humilitas*); John Chrysostom, 52.2 = *PG* 58.520–21 (endurance, prudence, humility).

15   Augustine *Sermo* 77.11, cf. 77.1, 13 = *PL* 38.487, cf. 483, 488–89; Peter Chrysologus *Sermo* 100.4 = CChr.SL 24A.619.

16   Albertus Magnus, 618: "masculinum sibi ingerens animum."

17   Olshausen 534: "Faith and humility are so intimately at one . . . ; they draw the heavenly essence itself down into the sphere of earth. Faith is again obviously seen . . . as a state of mind— . . . as the perfect womanhood of the soul."

18   Beare, 342–43.

exegesis has often relieved him of responsibility for it by declaring the logion to be inauthentic![19]

In the Reformation tradition, *faith* instead of humility becomes the center of the story. Luther especially has interpreted our story in two impressive sermons[20] in terms of faith that believes against all outward appearance. "Christ presents himself here as the heart feels it to be. It thinks there is only *no*, and yet that is not true. Therefore the heart has to turn away from its feelings and must comprehend and hold fast the deep, secret *yes* that is under and above the *no* with solid faith in God's word, as this simple woman does."[21] For most interpreters influenced by the Reformation our story becomes a story of faith[22] even if the accents shift. The obstacles that faith, understood as deed, had to overcome often took the place of the woman's unshakable confidence that expressed itself in prayer.[23] The "classical" interpretation of our story in today's exegesis by H. J. Held, who understands it as an instructive dialogue on the "theme of faith,"[24] belongs to this Protestant tradition of interpretation.

Interpretation

■ **21** We will attempt to trace and to make precise these two interpretations in the text itself. The salvation-history scope becomes clear already in the first verse. After the attacks of the Pharisees and scribes, Jesus withdraws once again. He goes to the region of Tyre and Sidon[25] where he meets a gentile woman who comes out to him. "Canaanite" ($Xαναναῖος$) is not only a biblical expression for "Gentile,"[26] but presumably also the self-designation of the Phoenicians[27] at the time of Matthew.[28] The Syrian Matthew, who perhaps knew Aramaic, would then have replaced the typically "western" designation "Syro-Phoenecian" ($Συροφοινίκισσα$)[29] (Mark 7:26) with his own "local" designation.[30]

But did Jesus according to Matthew really go into gentile country? This is sometimes denied,[31] and it is done for two contradictory reasons: (a) Geographically the city of Tyre at that time covered a large area and extended to Kedesa (less than ten km northwest of Lake Merom). It comprised areas that from the biblical perspective belonged to the Holy Land, viz., to the tribes of Asher, Dan, and Naphthali, and certainly were at the time inhabited by Jews.[32] Thus Jesus may have spent time in the area of Tyre, but in Jewish villages. Viewed biblically he would remain in the "Holy Land." However, the "gentile" expression, "the region of Tyre and Sidon," shows that Matthew was not interested in the idea of the "biblical" Holy Land. (b) Philologically v. 22 could mean that the woman "came out of that region" so that she would have met

19 On the question of authenticity cf. Pesch, *Markusevangelium* 1.390–91.

20 Sermon of 21 February 1524 = *WA* 15.453–57; Sermon on Fasting, 1525 = *WA* 17/2.200–204.

21 Luther 2.510 (= Sermon on Fasting, 1525).

22 Cf., e.g., Bucer, 136; Bullinger, 151. Zinzendorf (2.1030) is impressive: "'Yes Lord! But still.'" One cannot say it more briefly; actually the entire theory of faith is brought together in those three, four words.

23 Cf., e.g., Dickson, 214–15: the story deals with four "trials of faith."

24 "Matthew," 197–200, quote 193.

25 A favorite Old Testament pair of gentile cities. Cf. above 11:21 and II D 2.1 n. 20.

26 Cf. Klauck, *Allegorie,* 274.

27 "Phoenician" is the Greek translation of "Canaanite": $φοῖνιξ$ is Greek and is derived from the adjective $φοῖνος$ = red (Gerhard Wallis, *BHH* 3 [1966] 1465). "Into the Hellenistic period" Canaan designates "the Syrian coast, the area where the *kinachchu,* red purple, is produced, and its back country" (Johannes Hempel, *BHH* 2 [1964] 926). Isa 23:11-12 show that Phoenicia is part of Canaan.

28 According to Augustine (*Expos. ad Rom.* 13 = CSEL 84.162) the *rustici* in Hippos called themselves "Chanani." In Middle Hebrew כְּנַעֲנִי means "Canaanite," "Phoenician," and "merchant" (Jastrow 1.650). "Canaan" as designation of the land is attested on coins of the second century BCE and, according to Otto Eissfeldt ("Phoiniker [Phoinikia]," PW 20/1 [1941] 354), in Philo Byblius.

29 Theissen, "Sozialkolorit," 222. The Carthaginians were Lybophoenicians. Especially from the western (Roman?) perspective, the Phoenicians had to be distinguished from the Carthaginians, who lived closer.

30 It need not be therefore assumed that he was a Phoenician (thus Kilpatrick, *Origins,* 132–33).

31 By, e.g., Manson, *Sayings,* 200; Kasting, *Anfänge,* 113, Simon Légasse, "L'épisode de la Cananéenne d'après Mt 15,21-28," *BLE* 73 (1972) 21–40, 24–26; Terence L. Donaldson, *Jesus on the Mountain: A Study in Matthean Theology* (JSNTSup 8; Sheffield: JSOT, 1985) 132; Schweizer, 330.

32 Albrecht Alt, "Die Stätten des Wirkens Jesu in Galiläa," in idem, *Kleine Schriften zur Geschichte des Volkes Israel* (Munich: Beck, 1953) 2.453–54; A. H. M. Jones, *The Cities of the Eastern Roman Provinces* (2d ed.; Oxford: Clarendon, 1971) 270; Theissen, "Sozialkolorit," 217–19.

Jesus in Galilee and not in the area of Tyre. Then εἰς τὰ μέρη Τύρου καὶ Σιδῶνος would have to mean "in the direction of" the region of Tyre and Sidon. However, that is improbable: Ἀπὸ τῶν ὁρίων ἐκείνων almost certainly refers to γυνή and not to ἐξελθοῦσα.[33] For εἰς it is in any case more natural to assume the ordinary meaning "into."[34]

Thus Jesus temporarily went to the region of the gentile cities Tyre and Sidon, just as in 8:28-34 he went to the land of the Gadarenes in spite of 10:5-6. In the next pericope he will already be back in Israel. Matthew seems to be less interested in the salvation history–geographical problem of the Holy Land than in the persons. Important for him is Jesus' encounter with a gentile woman. As was the encounter with the centurion of Capernaum, it is an exception that Matthew emphasizes as such. This exception, however, has a future.

■ **22** As others who seek healing from Jesus, in her distress the woman cries[35] constantly.[36] That she was a single mother or a widow because she and not, as in 8:5-6; 9:18; 17:14-15, the father of the child "comes out"[37] to Jesus is every bit as unprovable as is the suggestion that she might have been a well-to-do Greek-speaking urbanite.[38] However, Matthew has no interest in either possibility. His statements about the woman are scanty; only her unflinching crying out reveals the magnitude of her distress. Need teaches one to pray. She speaks to Jesus in the biblical language of the psalms,[39] that is, in the language of prayer with which the church is familiar. That makes it possible for the readers to identify with her. "Lord" (Κύριε) is the title with which disciples and supplicants address Christ.[40] By addressing him as "Son of

David" the gentile woman expresses that she is turning to the Messiah of Israel who has already healed many among his suffering people.[41] Thus she knows that Jesus is sent to Israel; and her faith is seen precisely in the fact that she nevertheless cries out to him.

■ **23-24** The disciples attempt to frighten the woman away. They play a negative role as in 14:15; 19:13. Their interpretation of the woman's crying is not very kind; they hear not that she is in distress but that she is following them, bothering them with her crying.

It is understandable that this unkindness did not fit the church's traditional image of the disciples and that people have tried to exonerate them. The ancient church widely interpreted ἀπόλυσον αὐτήν as "free her," that is, "do what she asks."[42] This interpretation had for its part consequences in the history of theology. In the late Middle Ages the interceding disciples became prototypes for the intercession of the saints. The exegesis of the reformers rejected this view and rediscovered the actual meaning of v. 23b. For Luther the text shows that the intercession of the saints is not necessary.[43]

The saying of Jesus in v. 24 is not isolated in the context,[44] but has a rhetorically precise function toward the woman. Jesus intensifies the disciples' rejection of her and gives their unkindness as it were salvation-history "dignity." The lost sheep of the house of Israel[45] are not only the "black sheep" in Israel but the entire people of God to whom Jesus is sent. Verse 24 is formulated as a

---

33 That results from the word order; cf. 4:25; 27:57. Otherwise the verb would come first in Matthew; cf. 14:13; 19:1; 20:29; 24:1. Ἐξέρχεσθαι may well be absolute in Matthew; cf. 9:31; 14:14 (a suggestion of C. Riniker).

34 As in Mark 7:24. Matthew does not suggest here a correction.

35 Cf. 8:29; 9:27; 20:30-31, cf. 21:15.

36 Imperfect!

37 Sharon H. Ringe, "A Gentile Woman's Story," in Letty M. Russell, ed., *Feminist Interpretation of the Bible* (Philadelphia: Westminster, 1985) 70.

38 Theissen ("Sozialkolorit," 211–13) surmises this on the basis of Ἑλληνίς (Mark 7:26) and κλίνη (Mark 7:30).

39 Ἐλέησόν με κύριε: ψ 6:3; 9:14; 26:7; 30:10; 40:5; 85:3; 122:3, etc.

40 Cf. above, II B 1.1 on 8:2.

41 Cf. on 9:27 and the excursus there on the Son of David in Matthew. Of course, we may not ask how the gentile woman knew that Jesus is the Son of David (which is why in the history of interpretation she became a proselyte; cf. above n. 8), but only what Matthew wanted to say with this title.

42 E.g., Hilary, 15.2 = SC 258.34. Cf. also the *Einheitsübersetzung* (Common translation): "Free her (from her worry)." Verse 24 then refuses the disciples' request. Of course, the reason for the disciples' request in the ὅτι clause then becomes quite remarkable.

43 2.504 = Sermon of 21 February 1524.

44 Thus Trilling, *Israel,* 101; Lachs, 248.

45 Epexegetical genitive. Cf. above, II B 2.1 on 10:6.

commissioning word in biblical language solemnly[46] and so fundamentally and exclusively[47] that there is no room left to fulfill the woman's request. The rejection of Gentiles that Jesus formulated in 8:7 in a concrete case here becomes the principle that is derived from his sending by God.[48] It is thus clear that the mission command to go to the Gentiles (28:18-20) will mean a fundamental change in the divine plan.[49] In the hindsight of the Matthean church that has received from the Lord the commission to go to the Gentiles, v. 24 is "historical,"[50] but not therefore surpassed and meaningless. In it the church hears that God remained faithful to his special promises to Israel when he sent the Son of David, Jesus. It also hears that by rejecting Jesus Israel has brought on itself guilt toward God.[51] That he turns to the Gentiles after Easter is a new, unheard-of act of grace on the part of the risen Lord. What Jesus does in our story with the gentile woman is a "signal" of this coming, unheard-of grace of God.

■ **25** Again the woman turns to Jesus and falls on the ground before him in homage (cf. 8:2; 9:18). Again she calls him "Lord," and again she implores him with words from the prayer language of the psalms.[52]

■ **26** Again Jesus refuses her. The interpretation of the image of the dogs and the children oscillates among an excuse that renders the saying harmless and dismisses the insult of the comparison with the dogs,[53] explaining it historically in terms of the social tensions of the area,[54] and indignation over Jesus' narrow-mindedness.[55]

To interpret the image it is important to understand that κυνάριον means not the young or small dog but the dog that is a household pet.[56] House dogs were as widespread and beloved at all social levels in antiquity as at any other time[57]—if we can ignore for a moment the twentieth century and the sometimes exaggerated love of dogs in the first world. Nor was there in Judaism a special hostility to dogs, although there was an obvious fear of the numerous stray dogs.[58] While people sometimes threw food to stray dogs and then chased them away, it was taken for granted that people fed house dogs with table scraps. That is a regular topos in ancient literature.[59]

It is a household image and has nothing to do with the despised wild dogs. Only with the household pet does the contrast between dogs and children make sense. It is thus not an expression of contempt because dogs were especially miserable animals, but only in the sense that the gentile woman is not compared with a child. Mark used it in such a way that he set priorities. The children are fed *first*; later the dogs receive the scraps. That reflects the real circumstances. The woman's answer in Mark 7:28 changed the accent of the image. Even the dogs under the table receive something! Matthew omits Mark 7:27a and with it the relativizing πρῶτον. That corresponds to his fundamental v. 24. In this way the image receives a different accent. The issue is no longer the leftovers of the children's food that the dogs receive later but that children and dogs do not get the same food. Even so the image remains in the framework of the ordinary.[60] In Matthew's text it is obviously

---

46 Cf. n. 21 on 10:5-15.

47 Οὐκ . . . εἰ μή.

48 Ἀπεστάλην: *passivum divinum.*

49 Mark has a different view. Cf. Zenji Kato, *Die Völkermission im Markusevangelium* (EHS 23/252; Bern: Lang, 1986).

50 Strecker, *Weg,* 109.

51 Trilling, *Israel,* 105.

52 Ψ 43:27; 69:6; 78:9; 108:28 (always imperative aorist).

53 See, e.g., McNeile 231: "Half-humorous tenderness"! It is frequently pointed out that κυνάριον is a diminutive. "Little dog" [*Hündlein*] in German, especially in a modern, animal-friendly society, sounds cute.

54 Theissen ("Sozialkolorit," 214–21) calls attention to the social tensions between the dependent, Jewish rural population and the Hellenized, rich urban

population in the region of Tyre.

55 Cf. Beare above, n. 18.

56 BAGD, *s.v.* The usual diminutive is κυνίδιον.

57 F. Orth, "Hund," PW 8 (1913) 2557–58. "Dog" is both an insult and an object of art, animal of the gods and symbol of loyalty. Cf. Will Richter, "Hund," *KP* 2 (1967) 1245–49.

58 Therefore in the Mishnah the dogs are regarded as wild animals (*m. Kil.* 8.6 = Str–B 1.722).

59 Aristotle *Gen. an.* 2.6 = 744b (in the οἰκονομία the best food is given to the free persons, the worst to the pets); Euripides *Cret.* 469 [626] (the scraps for the dogs); Phaedrus *Fabulae* 3.7 [3d ed., Alice Brenot, ed.; Paris: Société d'Édition "Les Belles-Lettres," 1969] (bones from the master's table); Apuleius *Met.* 7.14 (the leftovers for the dogs); Quintilian *Inst. orat.* 8.3.22 (feeding dogs is commendable); Philostratus *Vit. Ap.* 1.19 (as dogs eat

understood allegorically. After the redactional v. 24 one will identify the children with the Israelites[61] and the dogs with the Gentiles, although "dogs" was not necessarily a conventional metaphor for "Gentiles."[62] Only this identification makes the different accent of the image in comparison with Mark understandable. Thus the difference between Jews and Gentiles is a principal one for the Jewish-Christian Matthew; it is not simply the question of when the mission to the Gentiles takes place.

■ 27 The woman agrees with Jesus. To say that the woman designated herself as "dog" is to read into the text a humility that is foreign to it.[63] Instead, she uses the image to contradict Jesus. Some of the children's food is even for the household pets, when the fragments fall from the table of the masters.[64] In spite of being rejected several times the woman is not discouraged, and she maintains her request to the Lord.

■ 28 Jesus finally responds to her. He describes her unconditional confidence, expressed in constantly repeated requests, as faith.[65] As he usually does, Jesus speaks of the faith of the supplicant; she does not speak of her own faith. That is important, for faith means that one has nothing except trust in Jesus. The story ends as does that of the centurion of Capernaum. The request of the woman who has asked without ceasing is granted. Her daughter will get well. The unconditional trust in the Lord and Son of David also includes the concrete experience of healing.

Summary and Meaning for Today

The Matthean community hears the message of the story also for itself. In its own experiences of illness and discouragement it hears what Jesus says about the power of prayer and faith. In addition, after 8:5-13 in the macrotext of the gospel this story means a further salvation-history "signal" for the church that lives among the Gentiles with the task of proclaiming Jesus' message to them: Jesus has not confined God within the borders of Israel, but has let himself be moved by the faith of the gentile woman. For the Matthean community that is separated from Israel, this confirmed by Jesus' example the possibility of seeking a new life and a new field of endeavor among the Gentiles.

Thus the original meaning of our story in fact lies in the direction of the church's two main modes of interpretation, the "salvation-history" and the "parenetic-existential" interpretations. Since they remained rather constant throughout the history of the church, one might think that here the meaning of a text was faithfully preserved once and for all in the history of interpretation. That is, however, not the case. In my judgment the history of interpretation illustrates how one can miss the meaning of a text simply by repeating it and not changing it in a new situation.

a. In a situation in which the gentile church was solidly established and Jewish Christianity had practically disappeared, the *salvation-history interpretation* of our text no longer demonstrated the power of God's love that bursts the borders of Israel; it almost exclusively justified the legitimacy of the church's status quo in history. It no longer opened new doors; it merely injured the Jews who were not present in the church. What might a new "salvation-history" interpretation that preserves something of the explosive power of the old text look like today? The text might receive new power, for example, ecumenically explosive power, if an interpreting church community were ready to try to identify with the Pharisees and scribes from whose territory Jesus withdrew rather than with the Canaanite woman or her daughter as is usually done. For, according to our text, church happens where God responds to human faith, not where an institution calls itself church.

---

the scraps from the table, so Damis collects the precious scraps from the "table" of the divine Apollonius). Cf. the rabbinic parable of the dogs at the banquet of the king in *Midr. Ps.* 4 § 11 (24a) = Str–B 1.724–25 and the story of Jonathan b. Amram in *b. B. Batra* 8a (= Str–B 1.726), a close parallel to our text even in subject matter.

60 Cf. Aristotle, above, n. 59.

61 A conventional metaphor! Cf. Exod 4:22; Hos 11:1; *m. ʾAbot* 3.14 (15); additional material in Eduard Lohse, "υἱός κτλ," *TDNT* 8 (1972) 359–60.

62 While Str–B 1.724–25 gives sources for this usage, at the same time on pp. 722–26 he offers examples for other figurative uses and opinions of dogs. Israel Abrahams (*Studies in Pharisaism and the Gospels* [2 vols.; 1917; reprinted New York: Ktav, 1967] 2.195) correctly protests against this usual distortion in "commentaries on Mt."

63 Cf. above, n. 15.

64 Τῶν κυρίων αὐτῶν can also be explained in terms of the image and does not necessarily presuppose that one shares the expectation of the Jews that they will be masters over the Gentiles in the messianic age.

65 Cf. 8:10, 13; 9:22, 29.

b. With the *parenetic-existential interpretation*, the Reformation discovered anew the deep power of faith of which this story speaks. When, however, this exegetical discovery was passed on, it was in danger of being lost again. The discovery became a doctrine that could be transmitted. Thus in the course of the history of interpretation in Protestantism the *story* that Matthew told became a *doctrine* in narrative form,[66] for example, Jesus' "position on a controversial issue, namely, the Gentile mission,"[67] or the "expression of a historical theological reflection about the meaning of faith."[68] What a loss of reality and experience there is when this story is reduced to a doctrine! If the text here suggests to us a way of getting at its meaning—at odds with a dominant trait of its history of interpretation and in a sense also at odds with the Matthean redaction—it is to take seriously again its shape as *story*. For a story mediates experiences, and one can understand experiences, like stories, only by becoming part of them.

---

66 Cf. Held, "Matthew," 199 (on v. 28): For Mark the fact of the healing is important; in Matthew "the subject is only the fact of faith and its power."

67 Held, "Matthew," 199.

68 Frankemölle, *Jahwebund*, 135.

2.4 Healings and the Second Feeding (15:29-39)

<table>
<tr><td>

Literature

Donaldson, *Jesus*, 122–35.

Lange, *Erscheinen*, 407–15.

Thomas J. Ryan, "Matthew 15:29-31: An Overlooked Summary," *Horizons* 5 (1978) 31–42.

Schottroff, "Volk," 151–57.

Trilling, *Israel*, 132–34.

For *additional literature* see III C 1.3 on Matt 14:13-21.

</td><td>

Analysis

</td><td>

Structure

</td></tr>
</table>

Analysis

Source

29 And when Jesus had gone away from there, he came to the Lake of Galilee. And when he had gone up the mountain, he sat down there.

30 And great crowds came to him who had with them lame, blind, crippled, mute[1] and many others; and they laid them at his feet. And he healed them 31/ so that the crowd wondered when they saw how the dumb spoke, the crippled (became) whole, the lame were walking, and the blind saw. And they praised the God of Israel.

32 But Jesus called his disciples to him and said, "I have compassion on the crowd, because they have already stayed with me three days and have nothing to eat. And I am not willing to send them away hungry lest they lose their strength on the way." 33/ And the disciples say to him, "Where in the desert will we (find) enough bread to satisfy such a large crowd?" 34/ And Jesus said to them, "How many loaves do you have?" But they said, "Seven, and a few small fish."

35 And he commanded the crowd to lie on the ground, 36/ took the seven loaves and the fish, gave thanks, broke them, and gave them to the disciples, and the disciples to the crowds. 37/ And they all ate and were satisfied, and they took up seven baskets[2] full of the leftover fragments. 38/ But the (number of) those who ate were four thousand men without women and children.

39 And he sent the crowds away, got in the boat, and came to the region of Magadan.

Structure

The healing summary of vv. 29-31 and the feeding story that follows in vv. 32-38 constitute a unit.[3] The mountain at the Sea of Galilee is the scene for healings and feeding. Since the people who are fed have already come with the sick in v. 30, there is no introductory remark to the second feeding as there is at Mark 8:1a. The result is a three-part structure similar to 14:13-21. After an introduction with healings (vv. 30-31) there is a detailed conversation with the disciples (vv. 32-34) and then the feeding (vv. 35-38). Two transitional geographical comments frame the entire unit (vv. 29, 39). The introduction and the summary are familiar to the readers. They have heard almost all of it earlier in the gospel.[4] Matthew here wants to evoke a familiar picture of Jesus' activity, and repetitions and reminiscences serve that purpose. The feeding story involves a new beginning to the degree that now Jesus is dealing directly with the disciples and no longer with the people. In the dialogue between Jesus and them it is noteworthy that the introductory statement of Jesus' intention (v. 32) is longer than the entire dialogue that follows (vv. 33-34). Jesus stands at the center. From v. 36 on the actual feeding (vv. 35-38) agrees with 14:19b-21 except for a few words.[5] Again the feeding ends with a crossing (v. 39) that in its formulation is reminiscent of 14:22-23.

For the most part Matthew himself has shaped the introductory healing summary.[6] It takes the place of the healing of the deaf-mute in Mark 7:31-37. Matthew has omitted this healing story with its magical tricks, the miracle worker's foreign words of magic, the command to secrecy, and only slight possibilities for a symbolic interpretation; only a few reminiscences recall it. However, that Matthew has not

---

1 The order of the four adjectives is text-critically very uncertain. There is widespread agreement that χωλούς stands at the beginning. There is no way of deciding between the order of ℵ et al. (= Nestle²⁶) and that of B et al. (= Nestle²⁵).

2 What is meant is a large or small woven basket that, e.g., could be used for food remnants and fish (Pollux *Onom.* 6.94) or grain (Hesychius, *s.v.* = 4/1 [1968] 68).

3 Cf. Trilling, *Israel*, 133.

4 Μεταβὰς ἐκεῖθεν: 12:9; παρὰ τὴν θάλασσαν τῆς Γαλιλαίας: 4:18; ἀνα(βαίνω) εἰς τὸ ὄρος . . . (καθίζομαι): 5:1; 14:23; χωλοί (περιπατέω), τυφλοί (+ βλέπω), κωφοί: 11:5; ὄχλος, θαυμάζω: 9:33; δοξάζω θεόν: 9:8; large crowds streaming together with sick people: 4:24-25; 12:15; 14:35-36; healings of the

blind: 9:27-31, cf. 12:22; healings of the mute: 9:32-33; 12:22; healing of the lame: 9:2-8; healing of a cripple: 12:9-14. In my judgment this rich arsenal of reminiscences makes it impossible with Donaldson (*Jesus*, 119, 131) to find an inclusion between 4:23-5:1 and 15:29-31.

5 "Special material" are: the different numbers, εὐχαριστέω instead of εὐλογέω and σπυρίς.

6 Cf. above, n. 4 on the internal Matthean reminiscences and vol. 1, Introduction 3.2 on μεταβαίνω, ἐκεῖθεν, ὄρος, ἐκεῖ, προσέρχομαι αὐτῷ, ὄχλοι, πολλοί, ἑαυτοῦ, ἕτερος, θεραπεύω, ὥστε, Ἰσραήλ. On ῥίπτω cf. 9:36; 27:5. Τοὺς πόδας αὐτοῦ is an unused "scrap" from Mark 7:25.

created an image of Jesus' activity completely on his own or from his own reminiscences follows from the introductory scene to the Johannine feeding miracle in 6:2-3, where likewise healings by Jesus, his "going up on the mountain," and his "sitting there" are mentioned. Much as with the agreements between Matt 14:13-21 and John 6, we probably are dealing with the influence of oral tradition.[7] The feeding corresponds to Mark 8:1-10.

Matthew shortens his source slightly at the beginning by omitting Mark 8:1a at the end of v. 32, by omitting the superfluous aside that "many of them have come a long way" (Mark 8:3b), and especially by omitting the distribution of fish that Mark relates separately in 8:7. Instead, in vv. 34 and 36 he mentions the fish with the loaves. His procedure is here exactly the same as with the first feeding. Compared with Mark, he strengthens the parallel to the first feeding story in the concluding section, vv. 35-39. His stylistic reworking of the Markan text is minimal.[8]

Interpretation

■ **29** Jesus returns from the gentile territory to the shore of the lake. In contrast to Mark nothing is said about the route he takes. While Matthew knows that Jesus was in gentile Phoenicia, he has no interest in depicting geographically a "journey into gentile country." His excursions beyond the borders of Israel in 8:28-34 and 15:21-28 are exceptions, as are the encounters with individual Gentiles.[9] When he now goes "on the mountain," the formulation leads one to think of the same mountain as in 14:23 or perhaps even 5:1. "The mountain" is the place of God's nearness (14:23; 17:1), sometimes also the "exalted" place where satanic (4:8) or divine (28:16)

power is manifest and the place of teaching (24:3; 5:1). It has no established symbolic meaning.[10]

■ **30-31** The following list of the sick is a summary and reminds the reader of the scenes where Jesus had healed the blind, dumb, lame, or crippled[11] among the people of Israel. The mass healings correspond so much to the previous healings of Jesus in Israel that for this reason alone the often advocated thesis that Jesus here heals Gentiles is impossible.[12] No! Jesus is not doing something here that he has never done before; he helps the sick of God's people Israel as he has always done. Galilee is here not the so-called Galilee of the Gentiles, of the prophetic proleptic reference in 4:15; it is the land in which the activity of Israel's Messiah on behalf of his people took place, the activity about which Matthew has told. Thus once more, for the last time in his gospel, Matthew describes in summary fashion how the Messiah Jesus does good things for his people. The people themselves are suffering; there are many sick who are laid at the feet of Jesus.[13] In spite of the hostility of the Pharisees and scribes, once again all the people come to Jesus, seeking help and in a positive mood. When the text concludes by saying that the people "praised the God of Israel," it suggests the language of the psalms. The liturgical "praised be the God of Israel" presumably was familiar to the Matthean church from its own worship.[14] Jesus thus acts as Israel's healing Messiah on behalf of the God of Israel.

It is difficult to determine how aware Matthew is of the biblical background of this scene or how consciously he has understood Jesus' healing activity in

---

7   Cf. above, n. 13 on 14:13-21.

8   Redactional vocabulary: ϑέλω, μήποτε (v. 32), ὥστε (v. 33), ἐπί with accusative (v. 35), ὄχλοι plural (v. 36), πᾶς (v. 37); cf. vol. 1, Introduction 3.2; on λέγει in the historical present with sayings of Jesus, cf. vol. 1, Introduction 3.1 (end).

9   Correct Bonnard, 234: There are in Matthew only encounters with individual Gentiles and not with the gentile people.

10   Cf. vol. 1, II A 1.1 on 5:1. Donaldson (*Jesus*, passim) thinks that the biblical Zion tradition has thoroughly influenced the text. That is improbable. "The mountain," not the "holy mountain" or "Mount Zion" as in the Bible, is located most of the time in Galilee and in at least two Matthean passages it is definitely *not* Zion (4:8 and 24:3 where

Jesus goes away from Zion "on the mountain").

11   Cf. above, n. 4. Κυλλός is ὁ πεπηρωμένος (mutilated) οὐ μόνον πόδα, ἀλλὰ τὴν χεῖρα (Suidas, 3.210 = Ada Adler, ed., *Suidae Lexicon* [5 vols.; Leipzig: Teubner, 1928–38]). The man with the withered hand in 12:9-14 is a prime example of a κυλλός.

12   Strongly advocated, e.g., by Frankemölle (*Jahwebund*, 117) and Gundry (319) with the main argument that only Gentiles could praise the "God of Israel." On this strange argument cf. below, n. 14.

13   The idea of proskynesis (thus Schottroff, "Volk," 153), as it occurs in a number of healing stories (8:2; 9:18; 15:25), may also be suggested here.

14   Cf. ψ 40:14; 71:18; 105:48; Luke 1:68; Schlatter, 493.

Israel as the fulfillment of eschatological predictions. Behind Mark 7:31-37 stood Isa 35:5-6, a text that also belongs to the general background of Matt 11:5 without being actually quoted. Perhaps one may also think of Isa 29:18, 23, because Matthew has already taken over from Mark a verse of this chapter in 15:8-9.[15] Matthew certainly was aware of the general biblical background. On the other hand, however, he does not assimilate the wording to a certain biblical passage as he does in 11:5, but he summarizes what he himself has reported of Jesus' healings.[16]

■ **32** The second feeding that now follows is also intended to show Jesus' mercy toward the people. Jesus himself takes the initiative and says to the disciples what he in a sovereign manner now "wants" to do. Matthew omits the observation that some of the people came from a distance (Mark 8:3b) because it was superfluous or because he wants to avoid any suggestion that they might be Gentiles,[17] for in the Markan source this second feeding, taking place as it does on the eastern gentile shore of the lake after Jesus' major journey into gentile territory, is probably a feeding of Gentiles. That is certainly not the case in Matthew.[18]

■ **33-34** The disciples' non-understanding questions, taken over from Mark, are more difficult to understand in Matthew, since unlike Mark he is not interested in portraying the disciples as completely lacking in understanding. Matthew simply faithfully reproduces his Markan tradition. Furthermore, in 16:9-10 he will come back to their little faith.

■ **35-37** The feeding itself reminds the readers clearly of 14:13-21. Jesus does again what he has already done once before. While in vv. 36-39a Matthew follows his model, Mark 8:6-10a, somewhat exactly, at the same time

almost his entire text agrees with 14:19b-21. He thereby emphasizes the fundamental meaning of the feeding. Jesus truly eliminates his people's hunger. One can again sense the reference to the Lord's Supper, not merely because Matthew omits Mark 8:7 and, as in 14:19-21, subordinates the fish meal to the bread meal, but also quite simply because he repeats those words from the first feeding that had to remind his readers of the Lord's Supper.[19] It is true that the feeding is not a Lord's Supper but a regular meal with bread and fish, and it is also true that the agreement with the words of institution is not literal.[20] It did, however, remind the church *also* of the Lord's Supper and helped it to understand that something of what is reported here also happened in its own realm of experience.

■ **38** The story's conclusion also is strongly reminiscent of the first feeding; only the numbers and the word for "basket" are different.

■ **39** As after the first feeding, Jesus dismisses the crowd, gets into the boat, and this time comes to the area of Magadan. We know almost as little about its location as we do about the Markan Dalmanutha. Many manuscripts[21] surmise that it means Magdala on the western shore of the lake. In addition, there is an analogy in Josh 15:37 that suggests that Magadan could have been a popular form of the name Magdala.[22]

Summary and History of Interpretation

A summary creates difficulties. Characteristically, our story never has interested exegesis very much. It is often missing in old commentaries, especially when its interpreters were interested primarily in its spiritual content

---

15 Thomas J. Ryan ("Matthew 15:29-31: An Overlooked Summary," 31–42, 38) is of the opinion that Isaiah 29 on the whole determines the basic structure of Matthew 15.

16 If one goes beyond the list of the sick and tries to interpret our scene against the background of general biblical statements concerning the eschatological gathering of the people (thus Donaldson, *Jesus,* 129: Jer 31:10-14; Ezek 34:14, 26-27), one becomes mired in uncontrollable speculations.

17 Cf. Gnilka 2.36.

18 Contra Lohmeyer, 258; Gundry, 321. Cf. above on vv. 30-31.

19 The most important variation is εὐχαριστήσας

instead of εὐλόγησεν. Εὐχαριστήσας appears alongside εὐλογήσας also in the Matthean words of institution. That shows that the two words are synonymous for Matthew (as in general for Jewish Greeks). A reference to the Pauline form of the words of institution (1 Cor 11:24) is not necessary in view of the loose connection to the report of the institution, contra Patsch, "Abendmahlsterminologie," 215.

20 C, L, W, and *l* among others have intensified it in vv. 35-36: λαβών, ἔδωκεν.

21 C, L, Θ, f1, 13, mae bo, *l*, etc.

22 The LXX reproduces Migdal Gad with Μαγαδαγαδ.

and not in the story itself, in which case everything necessary had already been said at 14:13-21. Yet even when one wants to take the story as such seriously in this context, there are problems. Why does Matthew report two feedings? He is not interested in a feeding of the Jews and a feeding of the Gentiles. Obviously there is no advance in the second feeding over the first.

> When the exegetes of the ancient church do not simply ignore this pericope, they offer rather fantastic ideas. They begin, for example, with the different symbolism of the numbers. Here Jesus no longer, as with the five loaves, changes the Old Testament law, but the bread is "the scripture of the New Testament in which the sevenfold grace of the Holy Spirit is revealed and given."[23] The numbers also are used to support the claim that it was a feeding of Gentiles, since the four thousand people come from the four directions.[24] According to Origen the people who were present at the second feeding are better than the people in the earlier story, because here it was not only barley breads as it had been then (John 6:9), and because the smaller amount of fragments shows that they were more receptive.[25] Everywhere the interpreters begin with the differences between the two feedings instead of asking why Matthew has told

so similarly the two stories that were already different in the tradition.

There is really only one answer. Matthew did not want to emphasize the differences. Instead of distinguishing between the two feedings, he wanted to use them as types. He wanted to say that Jesus again and again dealt with his people Israel as is reported in the many healings and in the two feeding stories. He has helped the people this concretely, this physically. He wanted to make that clear once more before he has Jesus turn his attention primarily to the community of disciples. The rejection that Jesus will experience at the end from all Israel is then all the more strange and puzzling. However, he also wanted to say something fundamental for the church. Jesus is present and able to be experienced in the church just as concretely and as physically as he was at the feeding. It happened not just once; it happens repeatedly: in healings, in the church's table fellowship, in the Lord's Supper.

---

23   Strabo, 140; cf. Hilary, 15.10 = SC 258.45.
24   Hilary, 15.10 = SC 258.47.
25   Origen, 11.19 = GCS Origenes 10.68–69.

3.1   Second Demand for a Sign and Jesus' Withdrawal (16:1-4)

Literature

Toshio Hirunuma, "Matthew 16:2b-3," in Epp–Fee, *New Testament Textual Criticism*, 35–45.

Claus Peter März, "Lk 12,54b-56 par Mat 16,2b.3 und die Akoluthie der Redequelle," *SNTU* A 11 (1986) 83–96.

1   **And the Pharisees and Sadducees approached. And to tempt him they asked him to show them a sign from heaven.**

2   **But he answered and said to them, 4/ "An evil and adulterous generation demands a sign, and only the sign of Jonah will be given to it." And he left them and went away.**

Analysis

Textual Criticism

Numerous manuscripts, but not the majority of the Egyptian witnesses and also not all witnesses of the other families, have an addition after v. 2aα: "When it is evening you say, 'It will be good weather, for the sky is red.' And in the morning, 'Today it will rain, for the sky is red and overcast.' You know how to interpret the appearance of the sky, but you cannot [interpret] the signs of the times?" Is this addition original? For the following reasons the answer will most likely be negative.[1]

a. Text-critically the short text is attested by the best manuscripts, but geographically it is heavily weighted toward Egypt; it is missing in the West.[2] The list of the witnesses for the long text is very impressive, especially quantitatively. On the basis of the textual witnesses, in my judgment the short text is to be preferred.

b. In terms of content an argument against the long text is that the weather rule given here, in contrast to the one in Luke 12:54-56, belongs to the most widespread and obvious ones of antiquity.[3] Thus it may have been inserted anywhere. The contents of the short text could have been expanded because the pericope was felt to be too short and colorless.

c. Of only slight importance is the observation that

πυρράζω is a very late verb for which there is evidence only in Byzantine Greek.

An argument for the long text might be that the text was shortened under the influence of the parallels Matt 12:38-40 and Mark 8:11-13. Just as conceivable, however, is a gloss *ad vocem* "sign" (σημεῖον).

If vv. 2aβ-3 is an addition, then it does not come from Q = Luke 12:54-56.[4] That is improbable anyway, since only the structure and very few words agree; above all, Luke mentions other weather rules. There are no traces in Matt 16:2-3 of a Matthean redactional reworking. Matt 16:2-3 presumably originated as a gloss without direct influence from Luke 12:54-56.

Context and Source

The second demand for a sign takes place in Magadan and again without interruption follows the preceding passage. It is connected with the following teaching of the disciples by the pair of opponents, "Pharisees and Sadducees" (Φαρισαῖοι καὶ Σαδδουκαῖοι; cf. vv. 6, 11, 12). Naturally the readers immediately remember the first demand for a sign in 12:38-40 from which the answer to this "evil and adulterous generation" comes (vv. 4a, b = 12:39b, c without τοῦ προφήτου). Mark 8:11-13 is the source. Matthew shortens the Markan pericope by omitting Mark 8:12a and instead of Mark 8:12b chooses his own formulation from 12:39. The other minor changes are redactional.[5] In some details the Q text that stands behind Luke 11:16 also has an influence.

Interpretation

■ **1-2** In content the section brings little that is new; its meaning comes from its position in the context. Jesus probably is alone. His disciples will not meet him again until the other shore (v. 5). Already they have nothing

---

1   Scholarship is divided. The short text is preferred, e.g., by Kurt and Barbara Aland, *The Text of the New Testament* (Grand Rapids: Eerdmans, 1989) 307; Hirunuma, "Matthew 16:2b-3"; Gnilka 2.40–41; Sand, 320. The long text is preferred by, e.g., März ("Akoluthie"), Schnackenburg (1.147), and Albert Huck and Heinrich Greeven (*Synopse der drei ersten Evangelien* [13th ed.; Tübingen: Mohr/Siebeck, 1981]). Most abstain from voting, with Nestle[26].

2   On the distribution among the textual families cf. Hirunuma, "Matthew 16:2b-3," 36.

3   Pliny the Elder *Hist. nat.* 18.78; Aratus *Phaen.*

858–71; cf. Virgil *Georg.* 1.438–56 [patchy morning and evening sky = rain; fiery evening sky = east wind]; Aristotle *Probl.* 4.26.8 = 941a [clear sunset = beautiful weather]. There is the same weather rule ("evening red brings a day most bright, morning red will not last 'til night") north of the Alps. Cf. *Handwörterbuch des deutschen Aberglaubens* 1.55–57; 9 [Supplements] 14–15).

4   Thus März, "Akoluthie," 90–95.

5   Cf. vol. 1, Introduction 3.2 on προσελθών, ὁ δὲ ἀποκριθεὶς εἶπεν, καταλείπω. Matthew likes to use ἐπερωτάω, in comparison with Mark usually a term

more to do with the Jewish leaders;[6] only Jesus exposes himself again to their attack. As in 3:7 with John the Baptist, the Pharisees and Sadducees again appear. The combination is stereotypical in 16:1-12. We may not ask, therefore, why the Sadducees of all people come from Jerusalem to the Lake Gennesaret and whether they had any dealings with Jesus at all. It may be that Matthew, as at the beginning of the first narrative strand in 14:3-12, wanted to underscore the parallel between Jesus and the Baptist. They have the same opponents. The Pharisees and Sadducees, who usually have so little in common, are united against John and Jesus.[7] Their malice is even greater than it was in 12:38-40. Matthew mentions first that behind their question is a malicious, tempting, satanic (cf. 4:1, 3) purpose. From now on that is clear; Matthew will repeat it on several occasions (19:3; 22:18, 35). After two miraculous feedings in which great crowds participated, and after two mass healings, this demand for a sign is unambiguously malicious. The more precise "from heaven" that Matthew adds this time intensifies the request and makes clear that the opponents want not a miracle but a cosmic sign.[8]

■ 4 Jesus can dismiss this demand quickly. He has long since said what is to be said. Jesus' answer is more intense than that of 12:38-45 in its brevity and in its failure to make explicit what the sign of Jonah is. The opponents already know; further words are superfluous. The sign of Jonah, Jesus' dying and rising after three days,[9] will soon become serious. Thus this answer of Jesus is actually breaking off communication. It also makes sense that he now walks away, leaving the Pharisees and Sadducees standing there. He will not see them again until Judea or in Jerusalem (19:3; 22:23).

---

he avoids, for questions by enemies (12:10; 22:23, 35, 46; 27:11, cf. 22:41). On ἐπιδείκνυμι (3,0,1) cf. 22:19; 24:1. On the pairs of Jewish opponents cf. vol. 1, I A 1.1 on 3:7.

6   Cf. Schweizer, 333–34; Gundry, 325.

7   As an analogy, Maldonat (318) points out that anti-Catholicism is the common denominator of Calvinists and Lutherans.

8   Cf. n. 27 on 12:38-45.

9   Cf. above, III A 2.2, Summary: 38-45.

3.2 Warning Against the Teaching of the Pharisees and Sadducees (16:5-12)

5 And when the disciples came to the other side, they had forgotten to take bread. 6/ But Jesus said to them, "Take care and beware of the leaven of the Pharisees and Sadducees!" 7/ But they discussed it among themselves and said, "We have brought no bread."

8 But when Jesus knew it, he said, "Why do you discuss it among yourselves, you persons of little faith, because you have no bread? 9/ Do you not yet understand, and do you not remember the five loaves for the five thousand and how many baskets you gathered? 10/ Or the seven loaves for the four thousand and how many baskets you gathered?

11 How do you not understand that I was not talking to you about bread! But beware of the leaven of the Pharisees and Sadducees!" 12/ Then they understood that he had not said to beware of the leaven (of the loaves)[1] but of the teaching of the Pharisees and Sadducees.

Analysis

Structure

The interpretation of this pericope is difficult. The difficulties are due, in my judgment, to the frequent failure to determine its structure correctly. The problem of the disciples that they do not have bread (v. 5) is taken up again in v. 7.[2] Jesus' warning against the leaven of the Pharisees and Sadducees in v. 6 is repeated word for word in v. 11b. In the first round, vv. 8-10, Jesus turns initially to the disciples' worry about bread. In v. 11 he points back to his warning of v. 6. He repeats it with a sharp negation, and Matthew explains it in the concluding verse 12.[3] Thus after the exposition in vv. 5-6 the section has two themes that are treated one after the other: (1) the disciples' problem, viz., the missing loaves (vv. 7-10); (2) Jesus' warning against the leaven of the Pharisees and Sadducees (vv. 11-12). In the first part vv. 9 and

10 refer back to 14:13-21 and 15:32-39; in the second, νοέω and συνίημι recall the instructions to the disciples of chap. 13 and 15:10-20.

Source

The source is Mark 8:14-21,[4] an artistic and presumably largely redactional pericope.[5] In its vocabulary the Matthean treatment is redactional throughout[6] to the extent that it does not repeat the "internal vocabulary" of the text, as it does in vv. 11-12. Characteristic of the Matthean style are the numerous catchword repetitions: ἄρτος (7 times), προσέχω, ζύμη, λαμβάνω (3 times each), διαλογίζομαι ἐν ἑαυτοῖς (twice), the repetition of the warning (vv. 6, 11), and the attempts at parallelisms (vv. 8, 9). The most important Matthean changes are: (1) The scene does not take place in the boat, as it does in Mark, but on the other shore after the crossing. (2) The unnecessary remark that the disciples had only one loaf in the boat (Mark 8:14b) is omitted. (3) Herod (Mark 8:15) is replaced with the Sadducees (cf. 16:1). Thus the reference back to Mark 3:6 is dropped. (4) Omitted are the Markan references to the disciples' hardened hearts (Mark 6:52) that does not appear in Matthew, and to Israel's failure to see and hear (Mark 4:12) in Mark 8:17b-18. (5) The two unnecessary answers of the disciples at the end of Mark 8:19 and the end of 8:20 disappear. Verses 8b-11 are a compact teaching of Jesus. (6) The short Markan conclusion that ends in an open question is replaced in vv. 11-12 by a longer conclusion that (a) once again emphasizes the warning against the leaven of the Pharisees and Sadducees, (b) communicates what the disciples did not understand, and (c) maintains as a result of the entire conversation that the disciples now understand and indicates how the saying of Jesus was intended. In this way exter-

---

1 Textually ἀπὸ τῆς ζύμης τῶν ἄρτων (B, lat, co, Or, et al.) or . . . τοῦ ἄρτου (C, *l*, sy[p. h], et al.) is better attested. However, the easiest *stemma* is possible for the short reading represented by D, Θ, sy[s], et al. On the one hand, τῶν ἄρτων assured the literal understanding of "leaven." On the other, τῶν Φαρισαίων καὶ Σαδδουκαίων (ℵ, et al.) was added creating a rhetorically clear antithesis. However, if need be one can also assume that ζύμη τῶν ἄρτων was felt to be pleonastic and thus shortened. Result: I am more inclined to favor the short reading.

2 Catchwords ἄρτους, λαμβάνω, vv. 5/7.

3 The keywords Φαρισαῖοι καὶ Σαδδουκαῖοι and ζύμη connect vv. 6, 11, 12.

4 There is no Q saying preserved in Luke 12:1 (B. H. Streeter, *The Four Gospels* [London: Macmillan, 1924] 279, cf. Gnilka, 2. 43) that might have influ-

enced v. 6. Προσέχετε ἑαυτοῖς is a Lukanism. The hypocrisy of the Pharisees corresponds in substance with Luke 20:20; furthermore, Matthew hardly would have let it slip by if he had found it in Q. Instead, we must assume a Lukan reminiscence of the text Mark 8:14-15 that is located in the great omission.

5 Cf. Gnilka, *Markus* 1.309–10.

6 On ἐλθών, μαθηταί (v. 5), δέ, εἶπον with dative, προσέχω, Σαδδουκαῖοι (v. 6), ἐν ἑαυτοῖς, ὀλιγόπιστος (v. 8), οὐδέ, λαμβάνω (vv. 9-10), πῶς with a question for something impossible, περί with the genitive, τότε, ἀλλά (vv. 11-12). Cf. vol. 1, Introduction 3.2. With the exception of διδαχή, the remaining words of the redactional vv. 11-12 are repeated vocables. On διαλογίζομαι ἐν ἑαυτοῖς cf. 21:25 redaction.

nally the Matthean pericope becomes much clearer. (7) The healing of a blind man that follows in Mark 8:22-26 and that symbolizes how the blind eyes of the disciples are opened does not fit in Matthew since the disciples already "see." Therefore it is omitted.

Interpretation

■ **5** Matthew obviously imagined that in 15:39 Jesus had gone to Magadan alone. There he encountered the Pharisees and Sadducees and then left. Now the disciples return to him (without a boat!). They have forgotten to bring provisions. As usual, Matthew has not imagined the geography very precisely.[7] Important for him is the distance from the Jewish opponents that is expressed with πέραν.

■ **6** Now a kind of "broken communication" develops. Instead of taking care of the disciples' problem, Jesus starts to talk about what is on his mind since 16:1-4. He warns the disciples about the "leaven" of the Pharisees and Sadducees with whom he has just been dealing. The disciples, however, are occupied with their problem about provisions and pay no attention to what he says. There is a breakdown in communication. Jesus and the disciples talk past each other.

> "These few verses have always amazed the exegetes," Bonnard writes.[8] Indeed, the logic of the section is strange. The disciples do not have bread. Then Jesus speaks an enigmatic word about leaven. What does this saying have to do with their concern? The disciples do not understand Jesus' saying because he speaks metaphorically. But how does it help in understanding the metaphor when Jesus reminds them of the feedings that involved real bread? If the issue for Matthew was only "that temporarily they had not understood an enigmatic saying,"[9] why then the massive accusation of little faith (v. 8) that elsewhere in Matthew does not mean intellectual misunderstanding?[10] Should the disciples perhaps think that someone who fed five thousand people could also formulate a metaphorical saying? Or it has been

thought that Jesus "in a typically Jewish procedure [!] takes up at random a word from the conversation of his disciples."[11] Did he perhaps hear wrongly and think the disciples had spoken about leaven? Or did the disciples think that Jesus wanted to warn about "accepting bread from the Pharisees and Sadducees"?[12] Was there the danger that the disciples would regard the Pharisees and Sadducees as bakers? Such exegetical exercises obviously result in nonsense. Even less helpful here is theological profundity: Jesus is showing the Palestinian church that "their plight that makes it difficult for them to acquire the natural means of life . . . does not (worry) him," that, on the contrary, he "(sees) therein the call to remain free of Jewish influence."[13] Yet in the feedings of which he reminds the disciples he took quite seriously the lack of the "natural means of life."

■ **8-10** Jesus does not yet explain his own saying; first he responds to the disciples' fear. He recognizes[14] what their problem is and, therefore, scolds them as "of little faith." After the two feedings the disciples could have been confident that Jesus is capable of providing for their needs. If he was able to satisfy five thousand and four thousand, how much more the small circle of disciples! Thus little faith is, here as always, lack of trust in Jesus' creative power. Only in this way do the references in vv. 9-10 to the two feedings make sense. They offer no help in explaining the saying about leaven. In contrast to Mark who is concerned to emphasize the disciples' almost grotesque lack of understanding, vv. 9-10 have their own weight in Matthew. Jesus overcomes the disciples' little faith by reminding them of miracles they have experienced. Therefore, we may not play the (false) bodily needs off against the (true) spiritual ones as often has been done in the history of interpretation. If we interpreted it this way, Jesus would have accused the disciples of falsely worrying about the needs of the flesh,[15] and he would have said that earthly care "distracts from what is

---

7 After 15:39 (Magadan) one now assumes the eastern shore.

8 239.

9 Barth, "Understanding," 114.

10 Sand, 322: "Little faith consists in 'not-yet-understanding.'" That is precisely what it does not mean in Matthew!

11 Bonnard, 239. Which word?

12 Str–B 1.728.

13 Schlatter, 501 (1929 or 2d ed. 1933, at the time of

the economic crisis and of the Aryan laws!).

14 Since διαλογίζομαι ἐν ἑαυτοῖς also may mean "to discuss among themselves," γνούς does not have to mean divine insight into human thoughts, contra Gundry, 326.

15 Luther, WA 38.607: "Preoccupati carnis sensu nunc magis soliciti fiunt pro ventre." Origen, 12.5 = GCS Origenes 10.75: The disciples have indeed gone to the other side but not from the σωματικά to the πνευματικά.

real."[16] However, the Matthean Jesus says that the disciples—in a very physical matter—do not have enough confidence in him.

■ **11-12** Jesus now returns to his own warning. He was talking not about bread but about something quite different,[17] viz., about the leaven of the Pharisees and Sadducees. Thus Matthew returns to the saying about leaven,[18] the interpretation of which remained open in his Markan source, and he repeats it. What he thereby accomplishes is that the disciples do not remain lacking in understanding as in Mark, but, as in 13:11-23, 36-50 and 15:15-20, they come to understanding through Jesus.[19] "Leaven" is an open metaphor that can be used positively[20] as well as, much more frequently, negatively.[21] The *tertium comparationis* is that "a little leaven leavens the whole lump,"[22] that is, leaven's contiguousness. What Mark 8:15 might have meant with the leaven of the Pharisees and of Herod was presumably just as unclear for Matthew as for us. He now gives his interpretation. It means their teaching. The disciples should beware not of leaven in the literal sense—that indeed would be senseless—but of the teaching of the Pharisees and Sadducees. Jesus' impulse of v. 11 has opened for them the metaphorical meaning of his saying.

Summary and History of Influence

The Matthean meaning is clear only in general terms. After his last, decisive withdrawal from Israel that his opponents have compelled, Jesus warns the church fundamentally against the teaching of the Jewish leaders. Since, as is well known, Pharisees and Sadducees represent quite different teachings, Matthew is obviously not interested in their distinctive characteristics but in the big picture. Their teaching is destructive leaven, because it does not agree with the teaching of the "one teacher" (23:8), Jesus. Now that the community of disciples is withdrawing from the rest of Israel,[23] it also must reorient in terms of teaching. That is the issue here.

It is difficult to connect 16:11-12 with other Matthean statements. There is no direct relationship to 12:33-37. There was not a warning against specific *doctrines* of the Pharisees but a warning against their "fruitless" words, that is, words not accompanied by deeds.[24] The relationship to 23:3 is very difficult: "Everything that they say to you do and keep . . ." This verse cannot be harmonized with 16:11-12, but it also cannot be harmonized with the immediately following 23:8, where Jesus is the church's only teacher.[25] The problem was recognized early on. While the church's exegesis generally interpreted the leaven as the Pharisees' interpretation of the law[26] in

---

16 Gnilka 2.44.

17 As far as I am aware, ζύμη never occurs in Greek and Jewish writings as *pars pro toto* meaning bread. On the other hand, the word is open to metaphorical interpretations. Cf. below, nn. 20-21.

18 The only difficulty for the proposed interpretation is in v. 11a. The repetition of νοεῖτε and οὐ περὶ ἄρτων creates the impression that Jesus had assumed a wrong understanding of the *meaning* of v. 6. However, that is presumably overinterpreting, and v. 11a is simply a transition. Νοέω in Matthew is used openly and nonspecifically; the simple repetition of v. 6 in v. 11b also speaks against the idea that Jesus wants to correct a false *interpretation*.

19 Συνίημι means an "intellectual" understanding that refers, as in 13:19-23, 51 and 15:10, to the interpretation of sayings of Jesus. Cf. above, III B 2.1 on 13:23.

20 Luke 13:21; *y. Ḥag.* 1(!), 76c.37 in Str–B 1.728 (leaven as an image for the power of the Torah); *Pereq he-Shalom* in Abrahams, *Studies*, 1.53 (peace is for the world as leaven for the dough). Cf. also n. 61 on 13:31-33.

21 In Judaism the negative valuation probably is indi-

rectly related to the fact that leaven cannot be brought as an offering (Lev 2:11). In Philo leaven is an image for pride (*Q. Exod.* 1.15 on 12.8) or for sensual pleasures (*Q. Exod.* 2.14 on 23.18). For the rabbis leaven later becomes a regular metaphor for the evil instinct (Str–B 4.469, 474 [*b. Ber.* 17a!], 478). Cf. also Plutarch *Quaest. Rom.* 2.289F (the process of fermentation caused by leaven is in reality a decaying).

22 1 Cor 5:6; Gal 5:9—presumably a proverb.

23 Cf. below on 16:13.

24 Strecker (*Weg*, 138-39) differs: he sees in 12:33-37, just as in 15:1-20 and 16:11-12, the abrogation of the Pharisaic ceremonial law and does not take into account 23:3 as a preredactional tradition.

25 Cf. the interpretation of 23:3.

26 From Jerome (137) to Lapide (313). This interpretation was made easy by interpreting the feeding as Jesus "changing" the Mosaic law. Cf. above, the history of interpretation of 14:13-21. In this way vv. 8-10 can also be integrated into a unified train of thought.

order to remind possible "Judaizing" Christians that the Christian understanding of the law is spiritual and not literal,[27] Maldonat recognized already the tension with 23:3 and thought that the leaven must have meant Pharisaic and Sadducean special teachings that went beyond the interpretation of the scriptures they had in common with the Christians.[28] He and others were all the more attracted to this interpretation because the text then served as an excellent warning against heretics whose specialty it was to offer their own characteristic doctrines that went beyond scripture and church dogma. Thus Pharisees and Sadducees became "types" for others, be they Papists, Calvinists, or Lutherans.[29]

Such uses of biblical texts are distressing, whether it is for the Pharisees and Sadducees who are misused as "types," or for the disqualified heretical brothers and sisters whose "devil's doctrine" one wants to avoid. Matthew, whose church after the separation from the synagogue *had* to define itself separately from Judaism, is not innocent. If one seeks in our text a positive potential meaning that runs contrary to this history of interpretation, perhaps one can remember that for Matthew discipleship means again and again going to "school" to Jesus. School with Jesus today could mean dealing critically on the basis of Jesus with the tradition and the church's errors. With Matthew, however, such a Jesus school also means, as Luther formulated it,[30] that Jesus "does not discard" the disciples but that they continue to be carried by him; that is, it means forgiveness.

---

27   Origen, 12.5 = GCS Origenes 10.76; cf. John Chrysostom, 53.3 = *PG* 58.529: The disciples still observed the Jewish purity and food regulations.
28   320.
29   E.g.: Calvin 2.180 (the Papist Antichrist uses theology to establish his kingdom); Maldonat, 320 (the *perniciosi haeretici* are not better than if the devil confessed Christ).
30   *WA* 38.609.

3.3 The Second Son of God Confession and the Promise to Peter (16:13-20)

Literature

Otto Betz, "Felsenmann und Felsengemeinde," *ZNW* 48 (1957) 49–77.

Bornkamm, "Lösegewalt" 2.37–50.

Colin Brown, "The Gates of Hell and the Church," in James E. Bradley and Richard A. Muller, eds., *Church, Word and Spirit: Historical and Theological Essays in Honor of Geoffrey W. Bromiley* (Grand Rapids: Eerdmans, 1987) 15–43.

Rudolf Bultmann, "Die Frage nach dem messianischen Bewusstsein Jesu und das Petrus-Bekenntnis," in idem, *Exegetica*, 1–9.

Idem, "Die Frage nach der Echtheit von Mt 16,17-19," in idem, *Exegetica*, 255–77.

Kenneth L. Carroll, "'Thou Art Peter,'" *NovT* 6 (1963) 268–76.

Claudel, *Confession.*

Cullmann, *Peter,* 159–242.

August Dell, "Matthäus 16,17-19," *ZNW* 15 (1914) 1–49.

Albert-Marie Denis, "L'investiture de la fonction apostolique par 'apocalypse,'" *RB* 64 (1957) 335–62, 492–515.

Dennis C. Duling, "Binding and Loosing: Matthew 16:19; Matthew 18:18; John 20:23," *Forum* 3/4 (1987) 3–31.

Jacques Dupont, "La révélation du Fils de Dieu en faveur de Pierre (Mt 16,17) et de Paul (Gal 1,16)," in idem, *Études* 2.929–39.

J. A. Emerton, "Binding and Loosing—Forgiving and Retaining," *JTS* n.s. 13 (1962) 325–31.

William R. Farmer and Roch Kereszty, *Peter and Paul in the Church of Rome* (New York: Paulist, 1990).

Joseph Fitzmyer, "Aramaic Kepha and Peter's Name in the New Testament," in Ernest Best and R. McLean Wilson, eds., *Text and Interpretation: Studies in the New Testament Presented to Matthew Black* (Cambridge: Cambridge University Press, 1979) 121–31.

Frankemölle, *Jahwebund,* 155–58, 220–47.

Ferdinand Hahn, "Die Petrusverheissung Mt 16,18-19," in Karl Kertelge, ed, *Das kirchliche Amt im Neuen Testament* (Wege der Forschung 439; Darmstadt: Wissenschaftliche Buchgesellschaft, 1977) 543–63.

Harnack, "Spruch," 637–54.

Richard H. Hiers, "'Binding' and 'Loosing': The Matthean Authorizations," *JBL* 104 (1985) 233–50.

Hoffmann, "Petrus-Primat," 94–114.

Hommel, "Tore," 124–25.

Golgotha, 68–77.

Christoph Kähler, "Zur Form- und Traditionsgeschichte von Mt 16,17-19," *NTS* 23 (1976/77) 36–58.

J. Kreyenbühl, "Der Apostel Paulus und die Urgemeinde," *ZNW* 8 (1907) 81–109, 163–89.

Werner Georg Kümmel, "Jesus und die Anfänge der Kirche," in idem, *Heilsgeschehen* 1.289–309.

Künzel, *Studien,* 181–93.

Lambrecht, "Du bist Petrus," 5–32.

Lampe, "Spiel," 227–45.

Joel Marcus, "The Gates of Hades and the Keys of the Kingdom (Mt 16:18-19)," *CBQ* 50 (1988) 443–55.

Maarten J. J. Menken, "The References to Jeremiah in the Gospel According to Matthew," *EThL* 60 (1984) 5–25.

Oepke, "Herrnspruch," 110–65.

Papsttum.

Béda Rigaux, "Der Apostel Petrus in der heutigen Exegese," *Concilium Einsiedeln* 3 (1967) 585–600.

Bernard P. Robinson, "Peter and His Successors: Tradition and Redaction in Mt 16:17-19," *JSNT* 21 (1984) 85–104.

Wolfgang Schenk, "Das 'Matthäusevangelium' als Petrusevangelium," *BZ* NF 27 (1983) 58–80.

Josef Schmid, "Petrus der 'Fels' und die Petrusgestalt der Urgemeinde," in J. B. Bauer, ed., *Evangelienforschung* (Graz: Styria, 1968) 159–75.

Karl Ludwig Schmidt, "Die Kirche des Urchristentums," in *Festgabe für Adolf Deissmann* (Tübingen: Mohr/Siebeck, 1927) 258–319.

Rudolf Schnackenburg, "Das Vollmachtswort vom Binden und Lösen, traditionsgeschichtlich gesehen," in Paul-Gerhard Müller and Werner Stenger, eds., *Kontinuität und Einheit: Für Franz Mussner* (Freiburg: Herder, 1981) 141–57.

Ortensio da Spinetoli, *Il Vangelo del primato* (Brescia: Paideia, 1969).

Thyen, *Studien,* 218–59.

Anton Vögtle, "Messiasgeheimnis und Petrusverheissung: Zur Komposition Mt 16,13-23," in idem, *Evangelium,* 137–170 (first appeared in 1957/58!).

Idem, "Ekklesiologische Auftragsworte des Auferstandenen," in idem, *Evangelium,* 243–52.

Idem, "Das Problem der Herkunft von 'Mt 16, 17-19,'" in idem, *Offenbarungsgeschehen und Wirkungsgeschichte* (Freiburg: Herder, 1985) 109–40.

Max Wilcox, "Peter and the Rock: A Fresh Look at Matthew 16:17-19," *NTS* 22 (1975/76) 73–88.

Literature on Matthew's Image of Peter

Josef Blank, "Petrus und Petrusamt im Neuen Testament," in *Papsttum,* 59–103.

Brown–Donfried–Reumann, *Peter,* 83–101.

Erich Grässer, "Neutestamentliche Grundlagen des Papsttums?" in *Papsttum,* 33–58.

Paul Hoffmann, "Die Bedeutung des Petrus für die Kirche des Matthäus," in Joseph Ratzinger, ed.,

Dienst an der Einheit Düsseldorf: Patmos, 1978) 9–26.

Kingsbury, "Figure of Peter," 67–83.

Mussner, *Petrus und Paulus,* 11–22.

Pesch, *Simon-Petrus,* 96–109, 140–44.

Schnackenburg, "Petrus," 107–25.

Michael J. Wilkins, *The Concept of Disciple in Matthew's Gospel* (Leiden: Brill, 1988) 173–216.

Literature on the History of Interpretation

Klaus Berger, "Unfehlbare Offenbarung. Petrus in der gnostischen und apokalyptischen Offenbarungsliteratur," in Paul-Gerhard Müller and Werner Stenger, eds., *Kontinuität und Einheit: für Franz Mussner* (Freiburg: Herder, 1981) 261–326.

Burgess, *History.*

Fröhlich, *Formen.*

Gillmann, "Auslegung," 41–53.

G. Glez, "Primauté du Pape," *DThC* 13 (1936) 248–344.

Gert Haendler, "Zur Frage nach dem Petrusamt in der alten Kirche," *StTh* 30 (1976) 89–122.

Kasper, "Dienst," 81–104.

Hugo Koch, *Cathedra Petri: Neue Untersuchungen über die Anfänge der Primatslehre* (BZNW 11; Giessen: Töpelmann, 1930).

Ludwig, *Primatsworte.*

Franz Obrist, *Echtheitsfragen und Deutung der Primatsstelle Mt 16,18f in der deutschen protestantischen Theologie der letzten dreissig Jahre* (NTAbh 21/3–4; Münster: Aschendorff, 1961).

Karl-Heinz Ohlig, *Why We Need the Pope* (St. Meinrad: Abbey, 1975).

Joseph Ratzinger, ed., *Dienst an der Einheit* (Düsseldorf: Patmos, 1978).

Peter Stockmeier, "Das Petrusamt in der frühen Kirche," in Georg Denzler et al., eds., *Zum Thema Petrusamt und Papsttum* (Stuttgart: Katholisches Bibelwerk, 1970) 161–79.

Idem, "Papsttum und Petrus-Dienst in der frühen Kirche," *MThZ* 38 (1987) 19–29.

H. Vorgrimmler, "Das 'Binden' und 'Lösen' in der Exegese nach dem Tridentinum bis zu Beginn des 20. Jahrhunderts," *ZKTh* 85 (1963) 460–77.

Wilhelm de Vries, *Der Kirchenbegriff der von Rom getrennten Syrer* (Orientalia Christiana analecta 145; Rome: Pont. Institutum Orientalium Studiorum, 1955).

Idem, "Entwicklung," 114–33.

13 But when Jesus had come into the region of Caesarea Philippi, he asked his disciples and said, "Who do people say that I,[1] the Son of Man, am?" 14/ But they said, "Some (say) 'John the Baptist,' others 'Elijah,' but (still) others, 'Jeremiah or one of the prophets.'" 15/ He says to them, "But you, who do you say I am?" 16/ But Simon Peter answered and said, "You are the Christ, the Son of the living God."

17 But Jesus answered and said to him, "Blessed are you, Simon Barjona, for flesh and blood did not reveal that to you but my father in heaven!

18 And I say to you: You are 'stone' (Peter), and on this 'rock'[2] I will build my church, and the gates of the realm of the dead will not be stronger than it.

19 I will give you the keys of the kingdom of heaven, and what you bind on earth will be bound in heaven, and what you loose on earth will be loosed in heaven."

20 Then he commanded the disciples that they should tell no one that he is the Christ.

Analysis

Structure

The pericope makes a fresh beginning after a change of location. It is divided into three parts: (a) The conversation with the disciples in vv. 13-16. It is clearly structured by Jesus' two parallel questions about people's opinion (v. 13c) and the disciples' own opinion (v. 15). (b) A small discourse of Jesus in vv. 17-19. The formal correspondence of the two predications "you are the Christ . . ." and "you are Peter . . ." in vv. 16 and 18 closely connects it to the preceding part; it is Jesus' answer to Peter's confession. The three sayings of vv. 17, 18, 19 have a certain similarity of form. After an introductory sentence an antithetical or continuing parallelism follows in all of them. All three are determined by the second-person singular; in vv.

---

1   The text with $\mu\epsilon$ is clearly more difficult, because after the insertion of $\tau\grave{o}\nu$ $\upsilon\grave{i}\grave{o}\nu$ $\tau o\hat{\upsilon}$ $\grave{a}\nu\vartheta\rho\acute{\omega}\pi o\upsilon$ (that differs from Mark and Luke) one of the three accusatives is redundant. Supporting the text offered by Nestle[25, 26] are only the uncials ℵ and B, and a few versions and church fathers (without Origen in the Greek!). In my judgment, the insertion of $\mu\epsilon$ is not an adaptation to Mark and Luke; instead, its omission simplifies the redundant text.

2   The wordplay $\pi\acute{\epsilon}\tau\rho o\varsigma/\pi\acute{\epsilon}\tau\rho\alpha$ cannot be imitated in German or English. At that time $\pi\acute{\epsilon}\tau\rho o\varsigma$ was not a personal name (cf. below, Tradition History and Origin of Vv. 18-19, *ad* c) and therefore should not be translated as "Peter." $\Pi\acute{\epsilon}\tau\rho o\varsigma$ clearly means "stone" (= $\lambda\acute{i}\vartheta o\varsigma$), while $\pi\acute{\epsilon}\tau\rho\alpha$ just as clearly means "rock." The play on words is shrewd in Greek, because it plays with various meanings of the same root word.

18-19 future tenses dominate. However, they are formally quite different in detail so that it is better not to speak of a three-stanza poem.[3] Furthermore, the images change.[4] (c) The concluding v. 20 bypasses the promise to Peter to return to his confession in v. 16. It has a surprising effect. Jesus speaks only of the Christ confession, not the Son of God confession, and again addresses all the disciples.

Obviously the pericope has an important function in the entire gospel. It awakens not only memories of 14:2, 5 (v. 14), 14:33 (v. 16), and 13:16-17 (v. 17) but especially of the fundamental text of the revelation of the Son, 11:25-27.[5] And it is a prelude not only to 18:18[6] (v. 19b, c) and the saying in 23:13 about the Pharisees who close the kingdom of heaven (v. 19a) but especially to the basic revelatory scene before the Sanhedrin in 26:61-64.[7] There Peter is present only at a distance (v. 58), and the high priest takes over his role in a strange reversal.

Our text is closely connected to the following pericope, 16:21-28.[8] Taken together the two sections form a chiasm: A disciples conversation or instruction with the Son of Man title provides the framework (vv. 13-15, 24-28). A conversation with Peter with the contrast humans-God follows (vv. 16-19, 22-23), and a renewed address to the disciples constitutes the center (vv. 20, 21-22). An antithetical correspondence is especially obvious in the Peter section. Again Jesus addresses Peter personally (εἶ) but this time not as the rock but as Satan and σκάνδαλον. In addition, our section is especially bracketed with the christologically central passage 17:1-13 with the catchwords

"Son of Man" (υἱὸς τοῦ ἀνθρώπου) and "Son [of God]" (υἱὸς [θεοῦ]), with Elijah and John the Baptist, and with Peter and God's own revelation of Jesus as Son of God.

Source and Redaction

■ **13-16, 20** Mark 8:27-30 is the source for *vv. 13-16, 20*. The treatment is recognizable as Matthean almost throughout.[9] With the end of the great Lukan omission the threefold transmission resumes. That means that the minor agreements between Luke and Matthew also begin again.[10] Two changes of the Markan text are especially noticeable. In v. 13 Matthew moves the Son of Man title up from Mark 8:31, and in v. 14 the people believe Jesus to be the returned Jeremiah. The difficult transition from v. 19 to v. 20 can be explained only in terms of source criticism. After his insertion Matthew returns to the Markan source, but since Mark has a different view of Peter's confession the connection does not fit.

■ **17** *Verse 17* cannot stand alone, because it has no object that states the content of the revelation to Peter. What then originally preceded it? If one regards v. 17 as an old tradition, three answers are possible. (1) Verse 17 (-19) was the original answer of Jesus to Peter's confession that then was repressed in the Markan tradition.[11] The Semitisms that people believed they could recognize here were regarded as decisive for the older age of vv. 17-19. Most interpreters today do not assume the existence of genuine translation Semitisms but of an originally Greek text with biblical coloring.[12] Above all, in the Markan

---

3 E.g.: Jeremias, *Golgotha*, 68–69, Oepke, "Herrnspruch," 151–52, Gnilka 2.47.

4 Cf. below, Tradition History and Origin of Vv. 18-19, (a).

5 Common catchwords are ἀποκαλύπτω, υἱός, πατήρ, οὐρανός/γῆ.

6 In 18:17-18 the saying on binding and loosing also follows the catchword ἐκκλησία.

7 Common catchwords are οἰκοδομέω, τοῦ θεοῦ τοῦ ζῶντος, ὁ Χριστὸς ὁ υἱὸς τοῦ θεοῦ. Cf. τὸν υἱὸν τοῦ ἀνθρώπου.

8 Lambrecht ("'Du bist Petrus,'" 6) speaks of a diptych.

9 Cf. vol. 1, Introduction 3.2 on ἐλθών, δέ (v. 13), μέν - δέ, ἕτερος (v. 14), ἀποκριθεὶς δέ + subject + εἶπεν (v. 17a), τότε, μαθητής (v. 20). On εἰς τὰ μέρη cf. 2:22; 15:21, on the historical present λέγει in sayings of Jesus, vol. 1, Introduction 3.1. Θεὸς ζῶν is biblical language and also widespread in early Christianity (Gnilka 2.59).

10 Most striking is τοῦ θεοῦ after χριστός in v. 16/

11 This thesis used to be widespread among the old representatives of the traditional Matthean priority, but, e.g., Bultmann (*History*, 258) also advocates it.

12 That is true in v. 17 of σὰρξ καὶ αἷμα; cf., e.g., Wis 12:5; 1 Cor 15:50; Gal 1:16; Eph 6:12; Heb 2:14. Βαριωνᾶ is difficult, but Mark 10:46 and Acts 13:6 show that such Semitisms (based on a knowledge of the tradition) can be found in Greek texts. In the LXX Ἰωνᾶς several times stands for the Hebrew יְהוֹחָנָן. Cf. Jeremias, "Ἰωνᾶς," 407. Max Wilcox, "Peter and the Rock: A Fresh Look at Matthew 16:17-19," 73–88, 82) refers to "'Semitisms' . . . of thought rather than of grammar."

Luke 9:20. Here I assume independent (and different!) redaction by Matthew and Luke. Χριστός in the sense of "the anointed (of God)" appears also in Acts 2:36 and 3:18 on the lips of Peter; cf. 4:26. On the basis of the minor agreements Claudel (*Confession*, 225, 245) concludes that Matthew and Luke had access to a pre-Markan text recension. According to him its conclusion is Matt 16:18.

redaction a later deletion of Jesus' answer to Peter's confession would hardly be understandable. Thus here also Mark's usual priority is to be preferred. (2) Or must we assume that an unknown, lost piece of tradition preceded v. 17?[13] A favorite answer is that Matt 16:17-19 is a part of the report of a post-Easter appearance that was not preserved in its entirety.[14] But why was it lost? Or why was only the second part preserved? Such a report climaxing with Jesus' response to a confession would be a formal oddity. Thus this assumption also is difficult. (3) However, then the only remaining possibility is that v. 17 as a response of Jesus to Peter's Markan confession is a later addition. By whom? Is the evangelist or an editor before him responsible for it? Of course, we may not exclude the possibility that expanding the Markan confession of Peter with the confessional title "Son of God" and Jesus' response comes from a pre-Matthean reworking of Mark 8:27-30 in the church. There are, however, several Mattheisms.[15] Above all, the reminiscences of 11:25-27 make the thesis probable that Matthew himself is the author of v. 17.[16] Then he has created v. 17 as a transitional phrase to vv. 18-19.

■ **18-19** In my judgment, *vv. 18-19 and v. 19b, c* are clearly preredactional.[17] In *v. 18* the introduction "and glory to you" (κἀγὼ δέ σοι λέγω ὅτι)[18] but hardly "my church"[19] may come from Matthew. A number of completely non-Matthean linguistic peculiarities show that the logion is traditional.[20] *Verse 19b, c* has an almost completely identical variant in 18:18 and one that is similar in John 20:23—variants that

grant to all the disciples the authority to bind and to loose. That supports the assumption that v. 19b, c was a traditional logion that was originally independent of v. 19a. Can one of the two versions be explained as a redactional reworking of the other? Both the plural and the singular of "heaven" (οὐρα-νός)[21] and both ὃ ἐάν and ὅσος ἐάν[22] may be redactional. The introduction with "Truly, I say to you" (ἀμὴν λέγω ὑμῖν) in 18:18 may (but need not) be redactional. Thus we can make a decision on the priority question only by considering the history of the tradition.

■ *19a* For *v. 19a*, the saying about the keys, we must consider the possibility of a redactional origin. It has no parallel in 18:18 and John 20:23. In the context it is a transitional phrase between v. 18 and v. 19b, c. A transition is necessary, because in v. 19b, c Peter is no longer the foundation of the church but its authorized teacher, and because its opposite in v. 19b, c is no longer Hades but heaven. The future verb form "I will give" (δώσω) corresponds to "I will build" (οἰκοδομήσω) in v. 18. The image of the keys at least associatively takes up the concept of the house and indicates Peter's authority, the content of which is then described in v. 19b, c. "Kingdom of the heavens" anticipates the contrast of "on earth" and "in the heavens" in v. 19b, c. While it is true that the hapax legomenon "keys" (κλείς) speaks against regarding the transitional phrase as redactional, in favor of the Matthean redaction is the observation that we have no evidence in contemporary Judaism for the image

13 Ortensio da Spinetoli (*Il Vangelo del primato*, 28) assumes that Matt 16:13-20 is an "anthology" of Peter texts.

14 Cf. those mentioned below in n. 31.

15 On ἀποκριθεὶς δέ + subject, εἶπον with dative, πατήρ μου ὁ ἐν τοῖς οὐρανοῖς, cf. vol. 1, Introduction 3.2. On οὐκ–ἀλλά, cf. Schenk, *Sprache*, 21. Σίμων as address may be Matthean (cf. 17:25). Βαριωνά remains difficult since Matthew rather avoids Aramaisms (vol. 1, Introduction 3.3, n. 98).

16 Anton Vögtle ("Messiasgeheimnis und Petrusverheissung. Zur Komposition Mt 16,13-23," 137–70, 166–67, 169) advocated this thesis for the first time in very cautious words. It led to a *Monitum* of the Sacred Office in 1961 (Burgess, *History*, 163). Vögtle finds widespread agreement today—among others in Brown–Donfried–Reumann, *Peter*, 89.

17 Especially Wolfgang Schenk ("Das 'Matthäusevangelium' als Petrusevangelium," 58–80, 73–74) and Goulder (*Midrash*, 383–93) disagree.

18 Cf. vol. 1, Introduction 3.2 *s.v.*, κἀγώ, δέ, λέγω.

19 The possessive pronoun μου put first is not markedly Matthean. It appears in Matthew 7 times before the noun and 66 times after the noun. In Mark the ratio is 1 to 29, in Luke 10 to 71. "Church of the Lord" is found again in the *Didache* (9.4; 10.5; without dependence on Matthew). Cf. also below, n. 20.

20 Non-Matthean are: ἐκκλησία for the whole church, the concept of the church as a building, the hapax legomenon κατισχύω, also ἐπί with the dative.

21 It speaks for Matthean redaction in 16:19 that the plural οὐρανοί fits smoothly into the context, while in Matthew 18 only v. 18 has the singular (along with the plural eight times). However, it speaks for the Matthean redaction of 18:18 that in the contrast οὐρανός/γῆ Matthew prefers the singular.

22 On ὃς ἐάν cf. vol. 1, Introduction 3.2; ὅσος ἐάν: 6/2/1, cf. 7:12; 22:9; 23:3.

of opening the kingdom of God;[23] it appears only in Matthew, who speaks frequently of "entering the kingdom of heaven." 23:13, where the scribes and Pharisees close the kingdom of heaven, is the only parallel to our text and sounds as if it is formulated in conscious opposition to it.[24] Thus v. 19a is conceivable (not provable!) as a redactional transitional phrase.[25]

Tradition History and Origin of Vv. 18-19

■ **18-19** According to our deliberations thus far, *vv. 18 and 19b, c* may be two originally separate unrelated logia. The variants support this conclusion. For v. 19b, c they are 18:18 and John 20:23; for v. 18a one may also cite Mark 3:16 and John 1:42. The view is also supported by the fact that the images are not unified. In v. 18 Peter is the foundational rock on which the house of the church is built; in v. 19a he is the man with the keys who, however, unlocks and locks not the church but heaven; and in v. 19b, c he is the rabbi who binds and looses. In v. 18 the church is a building; in v. 19a heaven is a building; v. 19b, c avoids the image of the building altogether. Kähler has attempted to explain the entire text, including v. 17, on the basis of parallels as "investiture of the transmitter of revelation."[26] However, his parallels relate only to the beatitude in the second-person singular; the contexts are in each case quite different. In my judgment there never was an established

schematic form. Result: The two logia must be considered separately.

■ **18** For *v. 18*, the saying about the rock, there are three possible origins. The saying may (1) come from *Jesus*. Today, however, this possibility is increasingly losing supporters.[27] Within approximately thirty years even the picture in Catholic research has changed radically. Today one can hardly say any longer for this text that is so important for the Roman Catholic Church that one's confessional standing determines the results of one's research. The most important argument against the authenticity is the singular occurrence of "my church" in a saying of Jesus.[28] "Church" (ἐκκλησία) appears in the entire synoptic Jesus tradition on only one other occasion, in 18:17 (in the sense of an individual community), so that it is not part of the language of Jesus. It is true, of course, that Jesus has gathered God's people Israel and portrayed it symbolically in the circle of the Twelve and that he might, therefore, basically have spoken of the "assembly" (= קהל) of the people of God that he "builds."[29] In that case, however, one would expect the biblical "assembly of God" or something similar but not "my assembly," for this expression includes the idea of a special community within

---

23 *3 Bar.* 11.2 is later and probably Christian overlay. Earlier is only the general Middle Eastern and ancient idea of heaven as a room or a vault with gates (Joachim Jeremias, "θύρα," *TDNT* 3 [1965] 176–77) and keys (idem, "κλείς," *TDNT* 3 [1965] 744)—a concept that does not fit well with the "kingdom of God" that in the tradition is not primarily spatial.

24 In my judgment βασιλεία τῶν οὐρανῶν in 23:13 is redactional and γνῶσις in Luke 11:52 is Q text. Cf. Polag, *Fragmenta*, 56–57 and vol. 3 on the passage. For additional redactional sayings of εἰσέρχεσθαι in the kingdom of heaven (conceived spatially in Matthew) see vol. 1, Introduction 3.2.

25 Likewise Gnilka 2.56.

26 Christoph Kähler, "Zur Form- und Traditionsgeschichte von Mt 16,17-19," 46–56. His most important parallels are 4 Ezra 10:57; *Jos. Asen.* 16.14; *3 Enoch* 4.9; *Memar Marqah* 2.9 (= John Macdonald, ed., *Memar Marqah: The Teaching of Marqah II* [Beihefte zur Zeitschrift für die alttestamentliche Wissenschaft 84; Berlin: Topelmann, 1963] 72).

27 In the German-speaking Protestant area the last great defenders of authenticity have been Karl Ludwig Schmidt, "Die Kirche des Urchristentums," 258–319, 281–302; Oepke, "Herrnspruch," 148–51,

and Cullmann, *Peter*, 186–99 (with Jesus' farewell meal [Luke 22] as the historical anchor). In the Catholic domain Josef Schmid ("Petrus der 'Fels' und die Petrusgestalt der Urgemeinde," 159–75, 170–75) offers the most forceful recent defense of authenticity. Refutations of authenticity that have become classic are those by Rudolf Bultmann ("Die Frage nach der Echtheit von Mt 16,17-19," 1.281–309, 299–308). Others who advocate authenticity in the Catholic area are, e.g., A. Feuillet, "'Chercher à persuader Dieu' (Gal 1,10)" *NovT* 12 (1970) 356; Léopold Sabourin, *L'Évangile selon saint Matthieu et ses principaux parallèles* (Rome: Biblical Institute Press, 1978) 214–16; Albright-Mann, 195–96.

28 *Mov* is presumably part of the tradition; cf. above, n. 19.

29 On the well-documented Jewish linguistic usage of "building" the community cf. Philipp Vielhauer, *Oikodome: Aufsätze zum Neuen Testament* (ThBü 65; Munich: Kaiser, 1979) 6–8.

or alongside Israel.[30] Jesus gathered the people of God, not the holy remnant of Israel. The expression "my church" (ἐκκλησία μου) is most easily understandable in a situation in which the Christian communities already existed already alongside the Jewish synagogues. The etymology of the name Peter also speaks in favor of a creation by a Greek-speaking church (cf. below).

If one assumes that the saying was *created by the church*, then the saying may either be:

(2) a formation of the *Aramaic-speaking church*. In this case it is popular to think of the first appearance of the Risen One to Peter (Luke 24:34; 1 Cor 15:5)[31] on which occasion the official or honorary name "rock" (Kepha, Peter) might have been bestowed on Simon. Or it comes

(3) from a *Greek-speaking church*. Then one usually thought of Syria, either

(3.1) at the time after the conflict in Antioch[32] when Peter had asserted himself against Paul, or

(3.2) at the late period after the death of the apostles when the reference to them as "rocks" of the tradition became important[33] or when the Syrian church separated from the synagogue.[34] The criteria available for a decision are: (a) historical deliberations, (b) the Semitisms, (c) deliberations on the name Kepha/Peter.

(a): Nothing can be decided on the basis of histori-

cal considerations. While Peter indeed received the first Easter appearance and is for Paul in Gal 1:18 the most important man in Jerusalem in the earliest period, the more one emphasizes his position of primacy in the early church the more difficult it is to understand why he left Jerusalem and at the time of the apostolic council already was only one (and not the first one mentioned!) of several pillars in the structure of the church (Gal 2:9). Peter also played an important role in Antioch. In the retrospective view of the late, post-apostolic period Peter was in any case important as the first apostle.

(b): Nor do the *Semitisms* help much. Even "gates of the realm of the dead" (πύλαι ᾅδου) is more likely a Greek than a Semitic formulation.[35] The play on words with the name Peter is possible in Greek as well as in Aramaic (cf. below).

(c): "Peter" (Πέτρος) did not exist as a pre-Christian Greek name; for an Aramaic name Kepha there is only one uncertain reference.[36] Thus the meaning of the word כֵּיף is decisive for the surname Kepha. As P. Lampe ("Spiel") has shown in a detailed investigation, כֵּיף as a rule means a round stone (stone, gem, hailstone, nugget, also shore) and only seldom, almost only in the Targums under the influence of the Hebrew סֶלַע, does it mean a "rock." Thus Aramaeans initially would have heard "stone" when כֵּיף was used and would have wondered how one can

---

30 Karl Ludwig Schmidt, who is one of the most forceful advocates of our logion's authenticity in our century, understands it as a "special כְּנִשְׁתָּא" in Israel in which the "remnant of Israel" is represented, comparable to the "new covenant" of the community of the Damascus Document ("καλέω κτλ," *TDNT* 3 [1965] 526).

31 See, e.g., Rudolf Bultmann, "Die Frage nach dem messianischen Bewusstsein Jesu und das Petrus-Bekenntnis," 5–7; Strecker, *Weg*, 206–7; Birger Gerhardsson, *Memory and Manuscript* (Uppsala: Acta Seminarii Neotestamentici Upsaliensis, 1961) 267; Künzel, *Studien*, 188–90 (all of whom accept the unity of 17-19); Brown–Donfried–Reumann, *Peter*, 92 (for v. 18); Anton Vögtle, "Das Problem der Herkunft von 'Mt 16, 17-19,'" 109–40, 113–18 (for vv. 18-19); similarly Claudel, *Confession*, 368–69 (basic text of 16:13-16, 18). The parallel of John 21:15-17 (three times Σίμων Ἰωάννου!) speaks for an Easter tradition but not for the first appearance or an old tradition.

32 See, e.g., Pesch, *Simon-Petrus*, 101; Thyen, *Studien*, 232–33; Kenneth L. Carroll, "'Thou Art Peter,'" 268–74, 275–76 (the Antioch church's "declaration of independence" from Jerusalem).

33 See, e.g., Hans von Campenhausen, *Kirchliches Amt*

und geistliche Vollmacht in den ersten drei Jahrhunderten (BHTh 14; Tübingen: Mohr/Siebeck, 1953) 142 (ET = *Ecclesiastical Authority and Spiritual Power in the Church of the First Three Centuries*, trans. J. A. Baker [London: A. & C. Black, 1969]); Hoffmann, "Petrus-Primat," 102–6; Lampe, "Spiel," 243–44; Kähler, "Zur Form- und Traditionsgeschichte von Mt 16,17-19," 36–58, 43–44; Lambrecht, "Du bist Petrus," 25 ("a late text").

34 Schweizer's conjecture (338).

35 Frequently in Greek since Homer, in Hebrew only in Isa 38:10; Sir 51:9. In the OT and in Judaism "gates of death" is more common; cf. Jeremias, "πύλη," 924; Hommel, "Tore." The absence of the article means nothing; many of the Greek references collected by Wettstein (1.430–31) are formulated without the article.

36 From the Elephantine papyri, fifth century BCE! Cf. Joseph Fitzmyer, "Aramaic Kepha and Peter's Name in the New Testament," 121–31, 127. It is unclear whether the name is Aramaic.

build something on a round stone. Only secondarily would they have thought that כֵּיף infrequently can also mean "rock."[37] The play on words is clearer in Greek, since one can play with various vocables.[38] Πέτρος means "stone" and thus is the literal translation of כֵּיף; πέτρα means "rock." That speaks for a Greek play on words, even if it does not convincingly exclude an Aramaic original text. While "Cephas" is widespread in primitive Christianity from early on, it was probably not initially known as a name and certainly not as the name of an office[39] but as a surname.[40] It probably goes back to Jesus.[41] However, its original meaning is unclear.[42] We must begin with the normal meaning of the word, "stone." Peter could mean, for example, "gem,"[43] or it could be an allusion to Simon's decisiveness, hardness.[44] We do not know. What seems clear is only that "Cephas" cannot have had a negative meaning; otherwise the word could not have been accepted so quickly as a proper name. Result: The surname Cephas is old, but Matt 16:18 is not. The verse is probably not the interpretation but a *re*interpretation of the surname Cephas. On the

whole, its derivation from a Greek-speaking community seems probable (as in [3] above).

In my judgment the word most likely has been formulated looking back at Peter's activity as something in the past. The late parallels that speak of the apostles as the foundation of the structure of the church (Eph 2:20; cf. Rev 21:14) speak for this view. The close material parallel in John 21:15-17 in the appendix to the Syrian Gospel of John also speaks in its favor. On the other hand, there is, in my judgment, no polemical note in v. 18, be it against Jerusalem or against Paul's apostolate, that might support an early interpretation. Therefore the word probably came into existence not as a polemic against Paul's claim in Gal 1:16-17 but independently of it.[45] It most likely comes from a time when it became important to look back to the time of the apostles as the foundation-laying time for the church.

■ **19b, c** With the saying about binding and loosing in *v. 19b, c* we must first of all determine whether the plural version of 18:18 or the singular of 16:19 is primary. Scholarship here comes to very different con-

---

37 On the basis of the etymology (כּוּף = to bend, bow) one probably will think initially of freestanding, round rocks (Petra, Sinai, Wadi Ram!) that are hardly a suitable foundation for a building. Cf. Lampe, "Spiel," 232, 235–36.

38 Lampe, "Spiel," 243; Pesch, *Simon-Petrus*, 102. The *Act. Pet.* 23 gives a formally similar etymology in Latin, by the way (Petrus = *paratus*), in a text that is influenced by Matt 16:17-19 but does not take over the etymology of Matt 16:18! Similarly, Optatus of Mileve derives Cephas von κεφαλή (*Libri VII [Adversus Donatianae]* 2.2 = CSEL 26.36).

39 That could be said only on the basis of Matt 16:18!

40 Schmid (248) points out correctly that in Aramaic Πέτρος must have originated as a surname, since proper names were not translated into Greek. It may be that the *status determinatus* of the Aramaic כֵּיפָא also supports this conclusion (suggested by C. Riniker). Paul already understands "Cephas" as a proper name and therefore most of the time uses the transcription Κηφᾶς. Πέτρος is then a surname that quickly became a proper name, similar to Χριστός.

41 Cf. Mark 3:16-17 along with the antiquated Boanerges.

42 An exact analogy is the surname of Aristocles = Platon (Diogenes Laertius, 3.4): He received it from his teacher Dionysius. It was so widespread from the very beginning that the real name Aristocles is hardly known any longer. Its meaning is unknown; Diogenes mentions among other possible reasons

the breadth of his forehead or his style. Lampe ("Spiel," 238, n. 3) correctly reminds us that Simon had to have a surname in order to distinguish him from the "Cananaean" Simon.

43 A suggestion of Pesch, *Simon-Petrus,* 30.

44 Bullinger (156A) derives the German family names "Steiner," "Velser," "Kissling" from the hardness of character.

45 In view of the quite different use of σάρξ καὶ αἷμα and the otherwise only very sparse word similarities, that is in any case most probable. Dependence on Gal 1:16-17 is assumed by J. Kreyenbühl, "Der Apostel Paulus und die Urgemeinde," 163–89, 163–69 (anti-Pauline polemic of the early church) and Albert-Marie Denis, "L'investiture de la fonction apostolique par 'apocalypse,'" 507–9. Jacques Dupont ("La révélation du Fils de Dieu en faveur de Pierre [Mt 16,17] et de Paul [Gal 1,16]," in idem, *Études,* 2.931–35) is critical of the view. Gerhardsson (*Memory and Manuscript* 1961], 270) and Dupont (937) assume conversely that Gal 1:16-17 is dependent on Matt 16:18; cf. Pesch, *Simon-Petrus,* 100. Critical here is Franz Mussner, *Der Galaterbrief* (HThKNT 9; Freiburg: Herder, 1974) 90, n. 60.

clusions.[46] The main argument in favor of 16:19 was that this verse is better anchored in the context. Our tradition-history analysis has shown this argument to be flawed. The main argument for the greater age of 18:18 is that the variant in John 20:23, an almost certainly pre-Johannine saying, is also formulated in the plural. A further argument is that presumably Matt 18:18 was added to 18:15-17 before Matthew.[47] Thus we regard the plural version of Matt 18:18 as older. The saying is a very old early Christian logion that linguistically and conceptually is rooted in Judaism. It expresses the early Christian understanding of the apostle or of the itinerant missionary as an authorized representative of the exalted Son of Man. The closest parallels are the Q logia Luke 10:5-6, 10-11, 13-15 and above all 10:16: "Whoever hears you hears me, and whoever rejects you rejects me, and whoever rejects me rejects the one who sent me." We can hardly determine whether in the traditional logion the thought is originally of doctrinal decisions, legal decisions, or of granting salvation and condemnation, since the formulation is very general ($\H{o}\sigma\alpha$). The parallels from the sending discourse of Q speak in favor of the last choice.

The singular formulation in Matt 16:19 is thus probably secondary. Much speaks in favor of the assumption that if it is Matthew who created the entire context of vv. 17-19, then he is responsible for this also. He probably then created v. 19b, c as a doublet to 18:18. If this is correct,[48] we have gained an important insight. While Matt 16:18-19 probably contains no old material on a "historical" primacy of Peter, *for the evangelist the special position of Peter was obviously important*. One cannot say that Matthew "eliminated" the special position of the prince of the apostles.[49] On the contrary, he has emphasized it.

How he emphasized it must be interpreted in the framework of the Matthean image of Peter.

Interpretation

■ **13** Jesus comes into the area of Caesarea Philippi in the far north of Israel, near the source of the Jordan. He asks the disciples for the "people's" (*Menschen*) opinion about the "Son of Man" (*Menschen*-Sohn). "Son of Man" is emphasized by the play on words and by its appositional position. The play on words expresses distance. The people obviously do not know who in reality is the Son of Man. The effect of the question is heightened by the fact that here for the first time in his narrative Matthew contrasts the reaction of the people to Jesus with that of the disciples. The disciples (and even more so the gospel's Christian readers!) have a pre-knowledge of the "Son of Man," for Jesus himself has told them something about his role (10:23; 13:37, 41). The outsiders had thus far not understood Jesus' public sayings about the Son of Man (11:19; 12:40, cf. 8:20). From this point on until the passion Jesus will no longer speak publicly of the Son of Man. Only in the great trial scene before the Sanhedrin, which we have understood formally as a kind of reversal of our text, will he once more, in response to the high priest's question whether he is the Christ and the Son of God, speak publicly of himself as the Son of Man (26:64). Thus Matthew begins in this passage of his narrative an element that will come to its climax in the final condemnation of Jesus by the leaders of Israel. The title of Son of Man serves here to distinguish the "knowing" disciples from the people.[50]

46   The priority of Matt 16:19 is advocated, e.g., by Bultmann, *History*, 141; Bornkamm, "Lösegewalt," 45–49; Strecker, *Weg*, 223; Trilling, *Israel*, 157–58; Rudolf Schnackenburg, "Das Vollmachtswort vom Binden und Lösen, traditionsgeschichtlich gesehen," 141–57, 151. The priority of Matt 18:18 is advocated, e.g., by Erich Dinkler, "Die Petrus-Rom-Frage," *ThR* NF 27 (1961) 36; Anton Vögtle, "Ekklesiologische Auftragsworte des Auferstandenen," 250–52; Wilhelm Pesch, *Matthäus der Seelsorger* (SBS 2; Stuttgart: Katholisches Bibelwerk, 1966) 42; Hoffmann, "Petrus-Primat," 101; Ferdinand Hahn, "Die Petrusverheissung Mt 16,18-19," 543–63, 557–58; Thyen, *Studien*, 237–38; Claudel, *Confession*, 316–17

47   Cf. analysis of 18:15-20.

48   Concerning the evaluation of this tradition-historical reconstruction: Many of the individual decisions (e.g., for v. 19a as redactional) are very hypothetical, but they mutually support each other and result in a remarkably coherent total picture.

49   Thus Strecker, *Weg*, 206: "eliminates Peter's special position" with 18:18 on the level of the Matthean redaction.

50   For additional material see below, the excursus on 16:21–28:4. "Son of Man" in Matthew's narrative.

■ **14** The disciples report on the people's opinions. Like the scoundrel Herod Antipas (14:2), they think Jesus is the resurrected John the Baptist or Elijah. Jesus is neither of these (cf. 17:12!). Or they think he is Jeremiah—something that we cannot explain with certainty. It is conceivable that there was a popular expectation about Jeremiah's return.[51] Whether this prophet has a special meaning for Matthew, who explicitly quotes Jeremiah in 2:17 and 27:9, must remain uncertain.[52] In any case, the people do not comprehend what Jesus is. It is no accident that Matthew here does not return to the people's question whether Jesus is the son of David (12:23)—that is, to the most positive statement the people have thus far made about Jesus.

■ **15-16** Jesus now asks the disciples for their own opinion. As in 15:15, Peter answers for the disciples.[53] Is Peter *only* speaking here for the disciples? That he is the spokesman for the disciples is supported by the fact that he repeats the church's confession[54] that all the disciples have already said in the boat (14:33) after Jesus walked on the water. It is not a literary blunder on Matthew's part that Peter is not the first to make the Son of God confession.[55] Instead, he has consciously formulated here

and has intentionally let Peter say precisely what the disciples also confessed and what the church confesses. The only difference is that v. 16 is formulated more fully and solemnly. As in 1:17; 2:4; 11:2; 22:42; 26:63, "the Christ" (ὁ Χριστός) is the Messiah of Israel. This Messiah is God's own son in whom the living God acts "with us."[56] "The living God" (Θεὸς ζῶν) is a biblical designation for God that became important as a short formula for faith in Greek-speaking Judaism and in the New Testament, especially in the missionary proclamation. It means the real God who acts in history in contrast to the dead gentile idols.[57] Then there is the full double name "Simon Peter." It is in this form unique; only in 4:18 and 10:2 is "Peter" used as surname immediately after "Simon." The result is a strange phenomenon. The evangelist wants to direct his readers' attention to Peter and his confession, although as their spokesman Peter answers a question directed to all the disciples and does not state a confession that differs from the one that all of them had already made.

■ **17** The beatitude directed only to Peter shows that he is at the center of attention in a very special way. However, it is important to observe once again here that in

---

51 Cf. 2 Macc 15:14-16 (Jeremiah as heavenly intercessor); 5 (= 4) Ezra 2:18 (the return of Isaiah and Jeremiah that, in my judgment, is not a Christian concept); *Prophetarum vitae* 2 = of Jeremiah, 19 *recensio anonyma* (Theodor Schermann, ed. [Leipzig: Teubner, 1907] 74: Moses and Jeremiah are "together until today").

52 Maarten J. J. Menken ("The References to Jeremiah in the Gospel according to Matthew," 5–25, 17–24) has Matthew think of the suffering prophet Jeremiah. However, the people are hardly thinking here of Jesus' suffering, which he will announce only after 16:21 and then only to the disciples.

53 Thus Peter answers *pro multis* (Augustine, *Sermo* 76.1 = *PL* 38.479), similarly Jerome (140) and most ancient and medieval authors. In the Counter-Reformation the accent is changed: Peter answers *tamquam . . . summus Ecclesiae Praeco* (Jansen, 150; cf. Lapide, 315: Peter wanted all of them to take up his confession).

54 The formulation corresponds to the conclusion of the Syrian semeia source in John 20:31; John takes it up in 11:27.

55 Such lapses do not happen to Matthew elsewhere. Schweizer (338) wants to solve the "tension" in the history of the tradition by saying that Matthew can-

not have created vv. 16-17 himself, since with 14:33 he would have robbed Peter's confession of its importance! Rudolf Schnackenburg ("Petrus," 122) distinguishes between the "church's cultic praise" and Peter's "full" confession. Both depend on traditions of the ancient church. According to Euthymius Zigabenus (466), in 14:33 the disciples confess Jesus only as a great miracle worker, while Peter confesses him φύσει as Son of God. Cf. above, n. 58 on 14:22-33.

56 Cf. vol. 1, I A 2.2 on 2:15 and I B 1.2 on 3:17, above, II D 2.2 on "the Son" and below on 17:2-5.

57 2 Macc 7:33; 15:4; 3 Macc 6:28; Bel Θ 24–25; *Sib. Or.* 3.760–63; *T. Job* 37.2; *T. Abr.* 17.11; *Jos. Asen.* 8.5–6; 11:10; *Historicus Callisthenes*, 44 (= Albert-Marie Denis, *Concordance Grecque des Pseudépigraphes d'Ancien Testament* [Louvain-la-Neuve: Université catholique de Louvain, Institut Orientaliste, 1987] 919); 1 Thess 1:9; Acts 14:15; 2 Cor 6:16; Heb 3:12; 9:14; 1 Tim 4:10.

13:16-17 not only Peter but all the disciples were called blessed by Jesus. And the idea that it is not humans[58] but the heavenly father alone who reveals his son to people is also already known to the readers of the gospel from 11:25-30 where, furthermore, it is said openly in a way that includes all the disciples. If v. 17 was created by the evangelist himself, then we must carefully note the similarity to those passages. Nevertheless, there is here a beatitude that in a special way applies to Peter, the first person called to be a disciple, the son of John,[59] as Matthew says in Semitic style. Thus we again encounter the remarkable juxtaposition of the unique bearer of revelation, Peter, whom Jesus called blessed and the Father's revelation that he experiences that is granted to every disciple.

■ **18** In the famous rock saying Jesus ceremonially continues his blessing with a promise to Peter. Much here is difficult and controversial. It seems somewhat clear that Jesus is not bestowing the name of Peter but interpreting it; Peter has had this name for a long time (cf. 4:18; 10:2).[60] It also seems clear that "my church" ($\dot{\epsilon}\kappa\kappa\lambda\eta\sigma\dot{\iota}\alpha$ $\mu o\upsilon$) means the whole church and not simply an individual congregation, for example, in Syria. We draw that conclusion first of all from the fact that Jesus can build only *one* "church" ($\dot{\epsilon}\kappa\kappa\lambda\eta\sigma\dot{\iota}\alpha$) and second from the image of the church as a "building." Behind it stands the idea of the people of God and the biblical language about the house of Israel. Especially in the Qumran texts the community is frequently referred to as the temple, the "holy house,"[61] that the teacher of righteousness builds (4QpPs 37 3.16). In early Christianity the idea of

the church as a building or temple is widespread.[62] We conclude it finally from the macrotext of the gospel. After the evangelist has related in several stages how Jesus and his disciples "withdrew" from Israel, he now announces where the disciples' separation from the people becomes clear—the construction "of his church." For Matthew, who throughout makes his story of Jesus transparent of the story of his church,[63] the issue is now the "founding" of the church. Finally, the basic meaning of the rock is clear from the image. With a rock foundation the church is promised stability and permanence. A house built on rock remains standing (cf. 7:24-25). This corresponds to the basic tendency of the promise of v. 18c, even if this is difficult to interpret. Finally it is clear that Peter has an irreplaceable function in the church. He is the building's ground, different from everything that is then built on it. Related, though not stated, is the idea of the unity of the church that rests on *one* foundation.[64] That much is clear. Unclear are above all two questions.

Rock

1. What is behind the rock that is the foundation of the church as building? From the Jewish tradition there are two possible associations.

> a. There is a personal tradition that is connected to Isa 51:1-2. Abraham is the rock out of which Israel was broken.[65] To be sure, however, the image is not that of a building; only in a single late passage that is probably influenced by Matt 16:18 does Abraham based on Isa 51:1 become the foundation rock.[66] Result: Peter, the "rock," is not the new Abraham.

---

58 $\Sigma\grave{\alpha}\rho\xi$ $\kappa\alpha\grave{\iota}$ $\alpha\grave{\iota}\mu\alpha$: an early Jewish expression (Eduard Schweizer, "$\sigma\acute{\alpha}\rho\xi$ $\kappa\tau\lambda$," *TDNT* 7 [1971] 109) often used by the rabbis where human transitoriness is contrasted with divine omnipotence (ibid., 116).

59 Cf. John 1:42; 21:15-17. The name Jonah scarcely appears in Judaism of the day (Jeremias, "Ἰωνᾶς," 407); however, Ἰωνᾶς appears in the LXX for the Hebrew יְהוֹחָנָן; cf. above, n. 12. The expression has connection neither to the prophet Jonah nor to the difficult בַּרְיוֹנֵי = Zealots (?); cf. Martin Hengel, *The Zealots* (Edinburgh: T. and T. Clark, 1989) 53–55.

60 This also distinguishes our text from the biblical bestowing of a name in Gen 17:5, 15 where a promise is connected with the name change.

61 E.g.: 1QS 8.5-10; 9.6; 11.9; CD 3.19; 1QH 6.26-27; 4QFlor 1.6; Betz, "Felsenmann," 52–53.

62 Cf., e.g., Gal 2:9 (pillars!); 1 Cor 3:9-17; Eph 2:20-22; *Hermas, Vis.* 3.2.4–9 (= 10.4–9); *Sim.* 9.3.1–4.8 (= 80–81).

63 Cf. above on the summary of chaps. 8-9, sections 4-6.

64 Knabenbauer, 2.56.

65 Pseudo-Philo *Lib. ant. bib.* 23.4-5.

66 *Yalqut* 1 § 766 = Str-B 1.733. It is strange that for "rock" the rare loanword פְּטְרָא is used. Lampe (*Spiel*, 243) suggests here with good reasons a Jewish antithesis against Christian $\vartheta\epsilon\mu\acute{\epsilon}\lambda\iota o\varsigma$ and $\pi\acute{\epsilon}\tau\rho\alpha$ statements.

67 *M. Yoma* 5.2 (אֶבֶן . . . שְׁתִיָּה).

68 Which is why Muhammad ascended to heaven from here!

69 For the references see Jeremias, *Golgotha*, 54–58.

b. A widespread temple tradition mentions a "foundation stone," that towers out of the ground in the Holy of Holies.[67] This stone has numerous functions in the Jewish tradition. It is the entrance into the heavenly world.[68] It is at the same time the plug thrown by God himself into the floods at the beginning of the creation of the world to shut off the great flood, and finally it is the stone that seals the world of the dead.[69] These traditions belong to the old Zion traditions of the Jerusalem temple as especially the important text of the cornerstone, Isa 28:14-22, may well show.[70]

Does our text make use of these old Zion traditions? It is a seductive idea, for it would fit well the idea that the church built on the rock Peter is a bulwark against the underworld. However, the devil is in the detail. In these traditions the subject is always a "stone" (אֶבֶן, λίθος), never a "rock." The image of the hostile "gates of Hades" of v. 18 is used there in a completely different way. Based on the Zion traditions the keystone of the dome that holds back the primal flood would have to be the gate of Hades. We never hear it said there that the temple is built on the "foundation stone" in the Holy of Holies. Although such concepts as that of the stone on Zion do not have to be completely logical and coherent, the differences are great. Thus I hardly think that our verse originally was created against this mythological symbolic background.[71] In my judgment, it presupposes only the name Cephas-Peter, the idea of the church as a temple and building, and the tendency of the post-apostolic time to understand the apostles as the foundational figures of the church (Eph 2:20; Rev 21:14). The evangelist, who again takes up the catchword "to build" (οἰκοδομέω) in the framework of his great "reprise" of our text in the trial before the Sanhedrin (26:61), may have seen in the church the new temple

that Jesus builds in three days. Of course, secondary associations with the cosmic stone in the temple that holds back the primal flood cannot be excluded for the evangelist, but neither are they necessary, and they are not at all compatible with the image of the hostile "gates of Hades."[72] They do not appear until the history of interpretation where different traditions were mixed together.[73]

Gates of Hades

2. What does it mean that "the gates of Hades will not overcome it"? We begin with a few linguistic observations. While κατισχύω usually is translated "to have the upper hand, to win the victory" in a way that suggests the image of a struggle,[74] κατισχύω normally has the weaker meaning "to be superior, stronger than."[75] In addition to the literal meaning, "gates" may also mean the area they surround, thus, for example, a city,[76] but not the powers that rule it. "Hades" is the dwelling place of the dead and corresponds to the Hebrew "Sheol" (שְׁאוֹל). To be distinguished from Hades is the place of punishment for evil persons—"hell"—the Gehenna that substantively and linguistically becomes increasingly important in rabbinic Judaism.[77] "Gates of Hades" (πύλαι ᾅδου) is a standard expression that most of the time in the Bible and often in Greek in combination with a verb of motion (such as "to come to the gates of Hades") means death or mortal danger.[78] The philological evidence strongly limits the palette of possible interpretations to which we now turn.

a. The *interpretation that focuses on Peter* relates αὐτῆς ("it") to Peter the rock and not to the church. It understands "gates of Hades" as a symbolic expres-

---

70 Cf. Hans Wildberger, *Jesaja* (BKAT 10/3; Neukirchen-Vluyn: Neukirchener Verlag, 1982) 3.1075–77.

71 Jeremias (*Golgotha*, 69–74) differs: Peter is the cosmic holy rock.

72 It is not the primal flood that threatens in Matt 16:18. Cf. the other image in 1QH 6.24–27. The text is a psalm of a person who has found refuge from the primal flood in the building of the community that God has built on a rock (סלע); there is an association with Isa 28:16-17. Here the gates serve precisely as protection.

73 Cf. Ephraem Syrus, 241–42. A single Jewish reference offers a beautiful example of the merging of traditions. Following Num 23:9, *Exod. Rab.* 15.7 (on 12:2) interprets the patriarchs as a rock (צור) on

which the world rests and associates with it the threat to the world from the primal flood.

74 Itala: *vincent* (along with *praevalebunt*); Peshitta: *chzn = superare*.

75 In Thes. Steph. 4, *s.v.*, this is the basic meaning (there are many references). Cf. also Harnack, "Spruch," 639–40; Hommel, "Tore," 24. Along with part of the Itala the Vulgate translates *praevalebunt*.

76 Jeremias, "πύλη," 925, n. 44. Claudel (*Confession*, 335) attempts to save the meaning "powers of death" with the aid of a Semitism. Unnecessary detours!

77 Str-B 4.1022.

78 Isa 38:10; Wis 16:13; *Ps. Sol.* 16:2; *3 Macc.* 5.51, cf. 1QH 6.24 and the further parallels in Jeremias, "πύλη," 925.

sion for "death." Thus v. 18c promises Peter that he will not die before the parousia. This interpretation of Harnack ("Spruch") can claim not a few of the church's oldest interpretations.[79] It is difficult, however, because αὐτῆς most naturally refers to the closest word ἐκκλησία ("church") and not to the more remote πέτρα ("rock").[80]

b. The *figurative interpretation* understands "gates of Hades" to refer to sin or heresies. It is an interpretation that was widespread in the ancient church and in the Middle Ages.[81] It is a practical application of the text as it often appears in the framework of the "moral" interpretation, and as an *application* it is justified. Philologically it is impossible, because "gates of Hades" means death.

c. The *interpretation in terms of the powers* expands "gates of Hades" with the help of the rhetorical device of the synecdoche (*pars pro toto*) and thinks of the gatekeepers or more plausibly of the "powers of the underworld who are God's enemies who assault the rock." The future κατισχύσουσιν then may (but need not!) be interpreted eschatologically as meaning the tribulations of the end-time.[82] Close parallels are, for example, Rev 9:1-12, where the abyss of hell opens and the locusts of the fifth trumpet attack the people, or Rev 20:3, 7-10, where Satan is released from hell for the last time. This interpretation is popular, but in my judgment it also taxes the "gates of Hades" in a linguistically inadmissible way.

d. In the interpretation of Jesus' promise in terms of *the members of the church*, the issue is their future resurrection. Christ will call his dead to himself, and the gates of Hades will not be able to hold them back,[83] for he himself is risen and now has "the keys of Death and of Hades" (Rev 1:18). While this interpretation is kerygmatically productive, it has the disadvantage that on the basis of v. 18b ἐκκλησία refers to the *building* of the church, that is, to the church as an institution and not to its individual members.

It is easier, in my judgment, to proceed from the intransitive interpretation of κατισχύω in the sense of "to be stronger than," "to have the upper hand." Then the promise of v. 18c speaks of a comparison and not of a struggle.[84] The gates of Hades as the essence of the realm of the dead that humans cannot conquer will not be stronger than the church built on the rock. That means that the church is promised "imperishable permanence as long as this age exists,"[85] for its Lord will be with it always to the end of the age (28:20).

■ **19a** Matthew continues with a new image. What v. 18a expressed "architectonically," v. 19 says functionally. Now Peter's function as a rock is stated. The issue is no longer the church as "building," but the keys to the kingdom of heaven. Whoever has the keys is either the gatekeeper or—what is more probable with several keys—the manager[86] who has authority over his Lord's rooms and buildings. Although the concept of a divine "gatekeeper" is widespread in antiquity,[87] in our text the thought is not of the heavenly gatekeeper Peter of later popular belief but of the authority bestowed on the earthly Peter. In Matthew the coming kingdom of heaven that one "will enter" is just as clearly distinguished from the church as in v. 19b, c heaven is from the earth where Peter is.

■ **19b, c** Of what does Peter's "power of the keys" consist? Verse 19b, c must answer this question. One expects a saying about opening and closing such as Isa 22:22 or Rev 3:7. Instead, the talk is of binding and loosing. What

79   Ephraem Syrus and especially Origen (references in Harnack "Spruch," 641–43); Ambrose *In Luc.* 7.5 = BKV I/21.625; rejected by Jerome (141).

80   In order to avoid this Harnack ("Spruch," 649–52) has stricken v. 18b as a Roman interpolation and thereby made clear the weakness of his interpretation.

81   Origen, 12.12 = GCS Origenes 10.90; Jerome, 141; Ambrose *In Luc.* 6.99 = BKV 1/21.614–15; frequently since then.

82   Jeremias, "πύλη," 927 (quotation; eschatological interpretation), Betz, "Felsenmann," 70–71 (non-eschatological interpretation). Joel Marcus ("The Gates of Hades and the Keys of the Kingdom [Mt 16:18-19]," 443–55) understands the church as the battlefield between the demonic powers coming up

through the gates of Hades and the exalted Christ who guides the church in its decisions through the opened gate of heaven (v. 19a!).

83   Schlatter, 509–10; cf. Cullmann, *Peter,* 207–9.

84   In any case, the "gates of Hades" as a party in the struggle is a strange idea. Maldonat, 327: "Neque . . . solent portae vincere, sed resistere."

85   Schmid, 250; cf. Barth, *CD* 4/2.672–74.

86   Cf. Isa 22:22; *3 Enoch* 48C (appendix) 3–4 (authority over the heavenly palaces) and Joachim Jeremias, "κλείς," *TDNT* 3 (1965) 750.

87   Dell ("Matthäus 16,17-19," 35–38) recalls Helios, the Horae, Dike, Janus, Shamash. In Judaism it is angels (*T. Levi* 5.1; *3 Bar.* 6.13), especially Michael (*3 Bar.*11.2). To be sure, it usually also contains the element of authority.

does this mean? Recollection of binding and loosing spells[88] has led some[89] to think of "binding" demons (cf. Mark 3:27) and (more seldom) of "loosing" demon-possessed people.[90] More likely is the usual interpretation that proceeds from the rabbinic pair אָסַר/הִתִּיר (Aramaic אֲסַר/שְׁרָא). The primary meaning is "forbidding" and "permitting" with a halakic decision of the rabbis,[91] that is, the interpretation of the law. Less frequently, but documented in contemporary sources, a judge's activity is meant. Then "to bind" and "to loose" correspond to "to put in fetters" or "to acquit."[92] Furthermore, it is the rabbinic conviction that God or the heavenly court recognizes the halakic decisions and the judgments of rabbinical courts.[93] Thus not only the concepts "binding/loosing" but the entire saying is rooted in Jewish thought. Our text is presumably thinking of teaching, while in 18:18 the thought is of judging, without the two meanings being mutually exclusive.

■ **19, b, c** This interpretation is confirmed by 23:13, a verse that is simply a counterimage to v. 19a and illuminates it. Here Jesus accuses the scribes and Pharisees of closing off the kingdom of heaven to people. The focus is obviously on their interpretation of the law that is incapable of distinguishing between essential and marginal issues. One may conclude from that text that it is Peter's task to open the kingdom of heaven for people, and to do it by means of his binding interpretation of the law.[94] He is to interpret God's will as Jesus has revealed it in order to lead people into that narrow path at the end of which the narrow gate opens to the kingdom of heaven (cf. 7:13-14). Thus the commandments of

Jesus that Peter proclaims and interprets are the key to heaven. "Simon is" the keeper of the keys and "rock as surety and guarantor of the teaching of Jesus."[95] On this basis it is also correct when many authors see in the perspective of our text the "service of Peter" in the church "in the constant uncompromising advocacy of the teachings of Jesus."[96] To be sure, the general formulation with ὃ ἐάν suggests that one should interpret it as openly as possible and, for example, not fundamentally to exclude the idea of church discipline or forgiveness of sins. It will stand in the foreground in 18:18 because of the context there. Matthew concentrates this authority here on the founding apostle Peter. The issue is the special authority of the apostle who had died a few years earlier in Rome. Nevertheless it is, as 18:18 will show, the authority of every disciple and every community. Again we encounter the overlapping of Peter's historical uniqueness and his role as a model for every disciple.

In the church's interpretation v. 19 was largely related to the sacrament of penance or the excommunication and readmission to the church.[97] Thus exegetically it misses the main emphasis of v. 19. However, it is hermeneutically important, because it proceeds from the total witness of the New Testament, that is, it sees v. 19 together with 18:18 and John 20:23. There are in addition the experiences of the interpreters for whom the church's authority existed primarily in the sacrament of penance. Both of them, recourse to the total witness of the Bible and to one's own experiences, are hermeneutically legitimate. This interpretation is thus an example of how old words can gain new meaning.

---

88 Dell, "Matthäus 16,17-19," 38–46, cf. Dennis C. Duling, "Binding and Loosing: Matthew 16:19; Matthew 18:18; John 20:23," 3–31, 7–8, 21–23.

89 Richard H. Hiers, "'Binding' and 'Loosing': The Matthean Authorizations," 233–50.

90 But what does one do then with the promise that the bound or loosed will also be bound or loosed in heaven? The neuter object ὃ ἐάν also is a bad fit.

91 Str–B 1.739–41.

92 Cf. Isa 58:6; CD 13:9–10; Josephus *Bell.* 1.111; cf. J. Andrew Overman, *Matthew's Gospel and Formative Judaism: The Social World of the Matthean Community* (Minneapolis: Fortress, 1990) 104–6. In later rabbinic terminology there is a source for "to impose the ban" or "to rescind" it: *b. Moᶜed Qat.* 16a = Str–B 1.739.

93 Material in Str–B 1.741–46.

94 In an isolated Jewish reference (*S. Dt.* 32.25 = Str–B 1.741) "to open" and "to close" are also used for doctrinal decisions.

95 Gnilka 2.64.

96 Mussner, *Petrus und Paulus,* 21; similarly Pesch, *Simon-Petrus,* 143–44; Gnilka 2.69; Schnackenburg, "Petrus," 124–25.

97 For the material cf. below on the history of interpretation of 16:19: Consequences for v. 19.

■ **20** With vv. 18-19 the high point of the pericope is reached. In v. 20 Matthew returns somewhat abruptly to the Christ confession of v. 16. As does Mark, he adds to it a command of silence. Differently from Mark, however, it can only have the meaning of maintaining the boundary between the disciples and the people that emerged in vv. 13-16. The knowledge that Jesus is the Christ belongs to the disciples alone. They now constitute the church which also is distinguished from the people.

Excursus:
Peter in the Gospel of Matthew

Literature: Cf. above at the beginning of III C 3.3. Peter seems important in the Gospel of Matthew under two aspects. On the one hand, he is in different ways a model of every disciple or of the disciples as a whole. On the other hand, he is a unique historical figure and plays a singular role.

Overview
No disciple name appears as frequently for Matthew as does Peter. In his gospel he has put Peter in the place of the disciples (15:15; 18:21). He has inserted special traditions that he has connected with the name of Peter or that prior to him were already connected with it (14:28-31; 16:18; 17:24-27). However, he also has done the opposite. He has replaced Peter with the disciples (21:20; 24:3)[98] or omitted him (9:22-23;[99] 28:7). If we compare the evidence with the findings about the sons of Zebedee whom Matthew omitted five or six times but never added, then we must say that Peter obviously does have a special meaning for Matthew. Not just any disciple name could take his place.

Peter as Type I: Spokesman for the Disciples and "Pupil"
Peter's first function is to speak for the disciples. He asks questions for the disciples (15:15; 18:21). Outsiders address him instead of Jesus (17:24). He raises objections and is corrected by Jesus (16:22-23; 19:27-30; 26:33-34). More difficult is the question whether the content of Peter's "role as a

pupil" was intentionally accented by Matthew. Does his name appear perhaps especially with questions about church or the Christian "halakah"?[100] I would like to give a cautiously negative answer to this question. In Peter pericopes the issues are not always "halakic" questions.[101] In the most important "halakic" pericopes in the Gospel of Matthew (for example, 12:1-14; 19:1-9) Peter does not appear. The typical function of Peter the "pupil" is in my judgment more general. However, what is true in all these cases is that as a pupil Peter takes on the typical role of a disciple, for to go to "school" with Jesus is the essence of discipleship. It is noteworthy, however, that this typical role of a disciple is so often transferred to Peter.

Peter as Type II: His Behavior
Peter is typical not only as a "pupil" of Jesus. Peter appears just as important as a paradigm of Christian behavior or misbehavior. He risks believing, and he fails (14:28-31). He confesses Jesus as God's Son and at the same time is afraid of suffering (16:16, 22). As with other disciples, he is not able to stay awake (26:36-46). He denies Jesus with an oath and repents (26:33-35, 69-75). In the process his image sometimes becomes darker than it is in the Markan tradition. In 16:23 he is rebuked with the harsh word σκάνδαλον; in 26:72 he swears a false oath. Sometimes the image becomes lighter. In 26:40 it is not only Peter who is rebuked; in 26:75 he weeps "bitterly."[102] On the whole there is a striking "ambivalence"[103] in Peter's behavior. He is confessor *and* tempter, denier *and* penitent, courageous *and* weak. In all these things he is typical of the disciples as such.

In comparison with Mark we can say that where Peter does not have a typical function as "pupil" or as a paradigm of Christian behavior but simply appears in a story, Matthew can omit him much as he does the sons of Zebedee (9:22-23; 28:7). Only where he has a typical function does he remain as an indispensable part of the story; he may even be added or replaced by "the disciples."

Peter as a Unique Figure
However, Peter also plays a unique role. The relative frequency with which he appears in the

---

98   *Oi μαθηταί* instead of the four disciples Peter, Andrew, James, John.

99   Together with James and John, cf. Mark 5:37.

100 Thus with reference to 16:19; 15:15; and 17:24-27 especially Hummel, *Auseinandersetzung*, 59–60, 63; Gnilka 2.25–26.

101 The issue in 15:15-20 is more than a specifically

Christian halakah on hand washing (contra Hummel, *Auseinandersetzung*, 49). In 18:21-22 as well the issue, unlike 18:15-17, deals with fundamental questions that exceed the halakic perspective—also in 19:27-30.

102 However, that is presumably a pre-Matthean minor agreement.

Gospel of Matthew must be explained. It must especially be explained why he appears so frequently in Matthew 13–18, that is, in the "church-founding part" of Matthew's story.[104] Peter cannot *simply* be a typical disciple.[105] Alone the statistical findings on the synchronous level forbid explaining Peter's special position as an inherited tradition in which Matthew is no longer interested.[106] In 10:2 Matthew had designated Peter as "first" ($\pi\rho\hat{\omega}\tau o\varsigma$). Simply to say here that Peter was the first one called is difficult,[107] because according to 4:18-20 one would have to explain why Andrew is ignored. We interpreted vv. 17-19 as a redactional composition based on individual traditional materials, and we called attention to its position in the macrotext. Peter is important precisely here where the church originates from Israel. Thus it is not enough to speak of Peter as "*Rabbi supremus,*"[108] for in the Matthean story Peter is obviously a singular and unique figure. However, it also is not enough to speak of a "salvation-history" priority of Peter,[109] for his uniqueness is precisely that the "unique" Peter has a typical *function* in the present.

Connecting the Unique and the Typical

There are theological implications when the unique Peter becomes the typical disciple in the Gospel of Matthew. Peter becomes the living expression for the idea that the church constantly is referred back to its historical beginning. Peter, the disciple who questions Jesus, who is instructed and corrected by Jesus, who has his faith experiences with Jesus, who fails Jesus and nevertheless is supported by him, demonstrates that Christian faith always exists only as a return to those experiences that Peter had in a historically unique situation with Jesus. "The unique events during the lifetime of Jesus lay the foundation for what will be repeated continually in the community."[110] The historically unique figure of Peter is "a concrete expression of what for Matthew must belong to the enduring peculiarity of the church: its connection with Jesus."[111] That corresponds to what we surmised

for 16:19 as the center of binding and loosing: promoting the commandments of *Jesus*.

The *Johannine beloved disciple* is an exact parallel to the Matthean figure of Peter. He too, who according to John is beloved by Jesus, lives close to him and knows him, is a model of the typical disciple. And he also is in my judgment a historically unique figure, a witness and bearer of tradition.[112] It is in keeping with the substantive parallelism between the two that Peter and the beloved disciple in the Gospel of John almost always appear together. In my judgment, what the founding apostle Peter meant for Syrian Christianity as a whole, the beloved disciple meant for the Johannine circle in particular, and he did so to an even greater degree. It is quite conceivable that Peter's meaning for the Syrian church as the bearer of tradition and as a model influenced the formation of the texts about the beloved disciple. Thus John could mirror the relationship of his own community to the Great Church in the relationship of the beloved disciple to Peter.[113]

In a broader sense other apostles in the post-apostolic period were seen in a similar way. One may think of the Paul of the Pastoral Epistles. He also is proclaimer and origin of the tradition entrusted to the church and at the same time, as 2 Timothy shows, a model for life. The Lukan image of Paul also shows parallel features. In any case, the Matthean image of Peter belongs to the post-apostolic period and is typical of it.

Why Was It Peter Who Became the Apostolic Founding Figure of the Church?

"Paul" in the Pastoral Epistles or the beloved disciple in the Gospel of John represent at one and the same time a certain theology and piety. Can we say the same thing for Peter in the Gospel of Matthew? We know very little here. In my judgment what we can say is as follows.

a. Peter became the founding figure geographically in the entire church, not only, for example, locally in

---

103 Hoffmann, "Petrus-Primat," 106–7.

104 Cf. above, the final paragraph of C (13:53-16:20).

105 This thesis of Strecker (*Weg,* 205) is even more unusual, because Strecker elsewhere emphasizes the historically unique character of the twelve disciples of Jesus.

106 Cf. Strecker, *Weg,* 206 on 16:19: "It is not significant redactionally as a historicizing statement about a special authority of Peter."

107 Cf. above, the history of interpretation of 10:1-5a with nn. 22–23.

108 Formulation by Gnilka 2.66. Furthermore, accord-

ing to 23:8, Christ and not Peter is *Rabbi unicus.*

109 Kingsbury, "Figure of Peter," 81–82.

110 Schweizer, 344.

111 Hoffmann, "Petrus-Primat," 110.

112 Cf. Rudolf Schnackenburg, *The Gospel According to St. John* (3 vols.; New York: Crossroad, 1987) 3.375–388.

113 Christian Link, Ulrich Luz, and Lukas Vischer, *Sie hielten fest an der Gemeinschaft* (Zurich: Benziger, 1988) 165–68.

Syria or Rome, and theologically in all areas of Christianity, not only, for example, in Jewish Christianity. Here is a relative difference from other founding figures like Paul or the brother of the Lord, James. What is distinctive about the post-apostolic image of Peter is that Peter most clearly becomes the founding figure of the *entire* church. It is not only Matthew who sees him this way but also John 21:15-17 and the Book of Acts. Correspondingly, in contrast to the Johannine beloved disciple the Matthean Peter does not play a special role; he does and is exactly what *all* disciples do and are. Is the Gospel of Matthew under the "patronage" of Peter an ecumenical gospel? It was in any case very quickly received by the entire church.[114] By working the Jewish Christian Q tradition into the Gentile-Christian Gospel of Mark it itself performed an "ecumenical" linking function.

b. Peter did not, in the first instance, become the founding figure of post-apostolic Christianity through his own theology. At most one may point out that Peter, the missionary to Israel and later to Gentiles, probably always played a mediating role in the church and perhaps was influential less because of his own position than because of his function as a bridge between Jewish Christianity and Gentile Christianity. In a word, he harmoniously represented the way of the gospel from Israel to the Gentiles. With Matthew's programmatic openness for the gentile mission that may have played a role at least indirectly. In any case, this also helps explain Peter's meaning for the entire church.

c. It was not exclusively through his leading role in the primitive church that Peter became the church's most important apostolic founding figure. Naturally it was important that the first appearance after Easter was to Peter and that he played a central role in the earliest Jerusalem church. However, it is indeed amazing that there is in the New Testament no detailed report about the first appearance to Peter and that his emerging leading role in the primitive Jerusalem church actually becomes important only in the late Book of Acts.

d. It seems more important to me that Peter became the apostolic founding figure of the post-apostolic period through his connection with Jesus. He differs in this regard from Paul and James, the brother of the Lord. His importance in the later period corresponds largely to the importance of the Jesus tradition in the post-apostolic church.[115] In all synoptic gospels his call as the first disciple is much more important than is the first Easter appearance to him. This is also what Matthew means when immediately after the "founding" of the church (16:18) he speaks of Peter's task to bind and to loose, that is, in a binding way to teach everything that Jesus has commanded (cf. 28:20). According to Matthew Peter is foundational for the church because *Jesus* is foundational.

Peter in Syria

We append a brief look at the special circumstances in Syria from whence Matthew came. Matthew 16:18 and John 21:15-17 are the earliest and most important testimonies for a special role for Peter in Syria. Matthew 16:18 was received earlier in Syria than in other areas of the church. In the Jewish-Christian Pseudo-Clementine *Homilies* 17.18-19, with the help of Matt 16:18, "Peter" as the rock opposes the claim of Paul based only on a vision. "Rock" here refers to Peter as the guarantor and bearer of the tradition. According to the Pseudo-Clementines the *Cathedra Petri* is in Antioch.[116] Matthew 16:17-19 is also received in gnostic Peter texts, although we cannot locate these writings with certainty in Syria. Peter is here the model of the spiritual person and the bearer of the revelation.[117] In later church tradition Peter became the first bishop of Antioch.[118] Writings attributed to Peter play an important role in the Syrian area; the most famous example is the tradition that Bishop Serapion of Antioch (toward the end of the second century) prohibited the reading of the Gospel of Peter in a nearby church because he recognized it as heretical.[119] The passion narra-

---

114 Cf. vol. 1, Introduction 5.6.

115 On this basis one cannot say that "at the end of the New Testament period . . . 'theologically' to a great degree Paul" and not Peter had won out (contra Mussner, *Petrus und Paulus,* 133).

116 Cf. the concluding passages in each case: *Hom.* 20.23 and *Rec.* 10.68-71.

117 Cf. especially the *Acts Pet. 12 Apost.*, NHC VI 8, 35-39, 21 (Peter and the eleven disciples receive the revelation!); *Apoc. Peter*, NHC VII 71, 14-72, 4 (Peter as ἀρχή and type of the bearer of revelation). For additional material see Klaus Berger,

"Unfehlbare Offenbarung. Petrus in der gnostischen und apokalyptischen Offenbarungsliteratur," 261-326, 278-79.

118 Sources compiled by Glanville Downey, *A History of Antioch in Syria from Seleucus to the Arab Conquest* (Princeton: Princeton University Press, 1961) 584-86. The earliest reference is Origen, *Hom. in Luc.* 6 (GCS Origenes 9 [2d ed., 1959] 32).

119 Eusebius, *Hist. eccl.* 6.12.3-6. For additional material see Berger, "Unfehlbare Offenbarung. Petrus in der gnostischen und apokalyptischen Offenbarungsliteratur," 261-326, 274-75.

tive of the Gospel of Peter has close material and structural connections to Matthew.[120] John 21:15-17 and the history of the reception of Matt 16:18 show that the Gospel of Matthew fits the Syrian church landscape influenced by Peter.

Summary

■ **17-19** Matthew inserted his Peter episode into the Markan scene at Caesarea Philippi for two reasons. For one thing, in his "inner" story he now comes to the founding of the church in Israel that is separate from the nation. Jesus wanted the church, and by building it on Peter he has also inaugurated its way from Israel to the Gentiles. However, Peter also has a fundamental meaning directly for the church of Matthew's day. A "Petrine" church is, like Peter, constantly dependent on the teacher Jesus and bound to his teaching. And a "Petrine" church will repeatedly have the experiences that Peter had with Jesus. The issue in our text is especially the church's true confession that Peter has taught the church how to say and that Jesus has affirmed for it. In all these things Peter is fundamental (foundational) for the church. "The *historical* Peter" remains the constant "rock, the fundament for all churches of all times," and he does so because "what continues has its roots in the once-for-all unique event,"[121] in Jesus.

For this very reason, however, this uniqueness could not be continued. The old Protestant thesis so strongly emphasized by Cullmann[122] that Matt 16:17-19 does not envisage a succession of Peter's *office* is much more than simply a Protestant thesis today; it corresponds to the tendency of the text itself. The rock, the foundation, is fundamentally different from what is built on it, the house. The rock remains; the house built on it gets higher. "The idea of a constantly growing foundation is . . . an internal impossibility."[123] That view is confirmed by historical development. While a succession in the sense that office bearers were appointed by apostles in the local churches—for example, elders, bishops, or deacons—is clearly documented by the end of the first century, there is no evidence for a succession of the apostles in their apostolic *office* that is valid for the whole church. The post-apostolic time, including Matthew's church, is aware of officeholders only at the level of the local congregation. Almost all New Testament and post-New Testament references to the apostolic appointment of officeholders refer to local churches.[124]

It is different with the *ministry* of Peter, by which I mean, following Matt 16:16, 19, the public witness to the "unabridged faith in Christ" and the church's constant commitment to the "program of Jesus."[125] The ministry continued after the death of the apostles. In the post-apostolic age it was primarily the apostolic traditions and the living image of the apostles and later the New Testament that "assumed" this ministry. Then in a secondary sense, and based on these traditions, the presbyters and bishops took over the service of this ministry of Peter.[126]

Negatively what this means is that Matthew does not know "something like an '*office* of Peter'"[127] in his church; he *only* knows Peter the disciple of Jesus whose image he has to preserve for his community, because it is the church of Jesus and so that it may remain the church

120 Wolf-Dietrich Köhler, *Die Rezeption des Matthäusevangeliums in der Zeit vor Irenäus* (WUNT 2/24: Tübingen: Mohr/Siebeck, 1987) 437–48; a literary dependency cannot be demonstrated.

121 Cullmann, *Peter,* 242, 217.

122 Cullmann, *Peter,* 224: "The apostles give over to those men the leadership (i.e., of the communities) but not their own apostolic office."

123 Blank, "Petrus und Petrusamt," 83.

124 Cf., e.g., Acts 14:23; *1 Clem.* 42.4–5; 44.1–3; the bishop lists of individual churches from the second century. The only possible exceptions are the apostolic pupils Timothy and Titus in the Pastoral Epistles. How far does the literary fiction there reflect an actual role they played in the whole church? In any case, they do not assume the role of the apostle and sole giver of the tradition, Paul, but they point to him and preserve his heritage.

125 Formulations by Mussner (*Petrus und Paulus,* 137) and Hoffmann ("Petrus-Primat,") 114. Cf. above n. 96.

126 The second-century bishop lists for which we have evidence in various localities were important not for their own sake but in the interest of ensuring the tradition (against Gnosticism!).

127 Contra Franz Mussner, "Petrusgestalt und Petrusdienst in der Sicht der späten Urkirche," in Joseph Ratzinger, ed., *Dienst an der Einheit* (Düsseldorf: Patmos, 1978) 27–45, see p. 33. The italics are mine.

of Jesus. Positively it means that Matthew definitely is thinking of a material continuity, that is, a continuation of the *ministry* of Peter. This is supported not only by Matt 18:18, but especially by Peter's "typical" function which is sustained by the reality that what Peter received as commission from Jesus is of continuing importance for the church.

History of Interpretation

■ **17-19** Can this *ministry* of Peter in our text's "trajectory"[128] also be assumed by a central *office* of Peter? In the history of its influence[129] the interest is concentrated in its reception by the Roman papacy: In large letters verse 18 decorates the dome of St. Peter's Church in Rome. On the basis of the exegesis we can formulate the consensus that "only a qualitative leap leads from the Peter of the Bible to the pope in the Eternal City."[130] The statement condemned by the council fathers of 1870 to the effect that "blessed Peter the Apostle was not appointed the prince of all the Apostles and the visible Head of the total Church Militant; or that the same directly and immediately received from the same our Lord Jesus Christ a primacy of honour only, and not of true and proper jurisdiction,"[131] is still defended today by a large majority of Catholic scholars. However, the difficulties accumulate not only from exegesis. The proof from tradition has become equally difficult, if one

understands tradition to mean in the classical sense taken up again by Vatican II "God's word, which was entrusted to the apostles by Christ the Lord and the Holy Spirit" and handed down by them "to the successors . . . in its full purity."[132] For even in the investigation of the beginnings of the Roman primacy and of the early history of the reception of Matt 16:18 a rupture has occurred that is perpetuated by very large portions of Catholic research.[133] Probably the most important insight is that one must distinguish between the two; only relatively late were the beginnings of the Roman primacy connected with the reception of Matt 16:18. The important points of the interconfessional scholarly consensus are:

1. The Roman congregation laid claim to special authority quite early. *1 Clement* gives evidence for it at a time before there was a monarchical episcopate in Rome.[134] Toward the end of the second century the behavior of the Roman bishop Victor in the Easter controversy demonstrates both Roman claims and their rejection by almost all other bishops.[135] The factors which from the second to the fourth centuries led to the formation of the Roman primacy in the church were quite diverse. Rome was the capital of the empire; the congregation was large and important because of its benevolence; it was an important center of orthodoxy; it

---

128 Brown–Donfried–Reumann, *Peter,* 163.

129 I owe here much to the preparatory work of Andreas Ennulat.

130 Erich Grässer, "Neutestamentliche Grundlagen des Papsttums?" in *Papsttum,* 33–58, 104; cited with approval by Blank ("Petrus und Petrusamt") in *Papsttum,* 104.

131 Vaticanum 1, *Pastor Aeternus* 1 Canon = DS no. 3055 = Geddes MacGregor, *The Vatican Revolution* (Boston: Beacon Press, 1957), "First Dogmatic Constitution on the Church of Christ. Chap. 1: Of the Institution of the Apostolic Primacy in blessed Peter," 187.

132 Vatican 2, *De divina revelatione* 2/9 = *LThK* 13 (1967) 522–23. Walter M. Abbott, ed., *The Documents of Vatican II* (New York: Herder, 1966) 117.

133 Cf., e.g., the "classical" presentation by G. Glez ("Primauté du Pape," *DThC* 13 [1936] 248–344) that leaves open only the question whether the connection of the papal primacy with Rome is a salvation-history necessity or a historical accident, with the

presentations by Karl-Heinz Ohlig, *Why We Need the Pope,* de Vries, "Entwicklung," or Peter Stockmeier, "Papsttum und Petrus-Dienst in der frühen Kirche," 19–29.

134 Ignatius is not aware of a monarchical bishop in Rome as a conversation partner. *Herm., Vis.* 1.4 = 8.3 provides evidence for a presbyterial constitution for Rome. According to Peter Lampe (*Die stadtrömischen Christen in den ersten beiden Jahrhunderten* [2d ed.; Tübingen: Mohr/Siebeck, 1989] 334–41) the strong divisions in the Roman church are the reason for the late formation of a monarchical episcopate in Rome.

135 Eusebius *Hist. eccl.* 5.23–24.

possessed apostolic founders and tombs of apostles, notably the tomb of Peter. In later times especially the political structure of the empire encouraged and required hierarchical structures and a monarchical head of the church as well.

2. In contrast to Matt 16:17, in the early period Matt 16:18 was, so to speak, not received.[136] Almost all the earliest receptions of v. 18 understand Peter typically, that is, as the "ideal" disciple. Except for the gnostic *Apocalypse of Peter* and the gnostic *Acts of Peter and the Twelve Apostles*[137] it was above all Origen who was foundational. He understands Peter as the prototype of the disciple who "comprehended the building of the church in him (*scil.*, the disciple), effected by the word, and (thus) . . . gained strength" (*Cels.* 6.77). In the commentary he says expressly: "Every disciple of Christ who drinks from the spiritual rock Christ (1 Cor 10:4) is rock."[138] Tertullian also interprets the authority given to Peter as the authority of pneumatic people.[139]

3. In the third century the most significant exegesis of our passage is that of Cyprian who sees in Peter the prototype of every bishop. Just as the authority of *all* bishops is derived from the *one* Peter, so the "bishops watch over the Church that we may prove that also the episcopate itself is one and undivided."[140]

4. Not until the third century was the Roman preeminence legitimated with Matt 16:17-19. When it hap-pened for the first time is not clear. Was it already in the early part of the third century? Tertullian polemicizes against an "apostolic man" who for himself and "every church which is akin to Peter" claims the authority to bind and to loose sins like Peter.[141] Is he thinking of Callistus of Rome? That is controversial, although it seems most probable to me. Origen also, who had been in Rome once, polemicizes against those who think "that the whole church is built by God on Peter alone."[142] It is not at all certain that he is thinking of Rome. Bishop Stephanus (254–257) is the first who we unambiguously *know* applied the word of the rock to the Bishop of Rome.[143] We conclude, therefore, that *in all probability Matt 16:17-19 has been used since about the first half of the third century in Rome as secondary legitimation of claims that the Roman community had already raised earlier.*

5. Connecting Matt 16:18 with a legally understood preeminence of Peter and of the idea of his succession by the Roman bishops also was done only with some hesitation. That sort of thing is documented for the first time in the Pseudo-Clementines,[144] but it is done there in connection with the primacy of James. Then one can surmise this connection with Bishop Stephanus, after him with Optatus of Mileve.[145] In the later fourth and fifth centuries the idea of an almost mystically understood identity of the Roman bishop with Peter is often more important than the idea of succession.[146]

---

136 For this reason the verse earlier was regarded as a gloss by some Protestants, most notably Harnack ("Spruch")—incorrectly, of course.

137 Cf. above, n. 117.

138 12.10–11 = GCS Origenes 10.85–88; quotation 12.10 = 86.

139 *Pud.* 21 = ACW 28. 118–22. Further material on the use of Matt 16:18-19 by Tertullian in William R. Farmer and Roch Kereszty, *Peter and Paul in the Church of Rome* (New York: Paulist, 1990).

140 Cyprian *Unit. eccl.* 4–5 = FC 36.98–100 (quotation 5 = 99). In his letters Cyprian even appeals to the figure of Peter to reject Roman claims. In the impressive *Ep.* 71.3 he does so with the reference that Peter submitted to Paul's reasonable arguments and did not "claim anything for himself insolently" (FC 51.264). Still important on the interpretation is the work by Hugo Koch (*Cathedra Petri: Neue Untersuchungen über die Anfänge der Primatslehre*), who paid for his non-papal interpretation of Cyprian in 1912 with the loss of his permission to teach and his

professorial chair.

141 Tertullian *Pud.* 21 = ACW 28.118–22; quotations 119, 120.

142 12.11 = GCS Origenes 10.86. To be sure, the commentary probably belongs to Origen's late writings, while his visit to Rome took place in his early period (Eusebius *Hist. eccl.* 6.14.10).

143 Cyprian *Ep.* 75.17 = FC 51.307. Cyprian's opinion on this: "Aperta et manifesta Stephani stultitia."

144 *Epistula Clementis ad Jacobum* 1–2 = GCS 42.5–6: Peter appoints Clement (!) as bishop in Rome. However, for the Pseudo-Clementines Peter's *cathedra* is in Antioch (above, n. 116).

145 Ludwig, *Primatsworte*, 61–62.

146 For Siricius (384–399) cf. Ludwig, *Primatsworte*, 84–85; for Leo the Great, below, n. 175.

What are the results of these findings? Seen historically, the papal primacy is a *new* institution that resulted from new historical factors. The way was prepared for it in the pre-Constantinian period, and it prevailed in the post-Constantinian age. It proved itself in the West as a defense against political storms and heretical claims. In this sense it is the result of a "development."[147] It remains an open question whether, and if so why, this development can claim any higher theological dignity than other developments in the soil of the ancient church, for example, the development to the autocephalous ecumenical patriarchates. Historically, we must say that the interpretation of Matt 16:18 in terms of the Roman primacy is a *new* interpretation from the third century. It is a later "rereading of scripture,"[148] based on "historical . . . experiences of faith," or, put somewhat more sharply, a "retroactive legitimizing" of a Roman claim to leadership that has developed since the third century.[149] Thus it is in my judgment not an exaggeration to speak with the Catholic dogmatician W. Kasper of a true "legitimation crisis" of the papacy.[150] Since it is alluded to only cautiously in the literature, one is grateful when a Catholic dogmatician, rooted in his church, so openly calls it by name. Is there anything left to do other than to abandon the attempt to legitimate the papacy on the basis of Bible and tradition? Cardinal Newman did it by saying that it is not history but "the Church's use of History, in which the Catholic believes."[151]

But now it is time to mention a completely different difficulty, viz., one that is my own. In this commentary,

as a Protestant struggling with the predominance of "*sola scriptura*," I advocate a hermeneutics of the "trajectory" of biblical texts and repeatedly have made myself the advocate of *new* discoveries of the potential of biblical texts in new situations. The meaning of a biblical text for me consists not merely in the *re*production of its original sense but in the *production* of new meanings in new situations guided by the trajectory of the texts and supported by the totality of the Christian faith.[152] Therefore I also want to be basically open for the new Roman "rereading" of Matt 16:18 that developed in the third to fifth centuries. The self-critical question for me is whether, on the basis of the trajectory of the text, we can even raise critical questions about this interpretation, or whether I simply have to say that the potential meaning of Matt 16:18 is unlimited and that even an interpretation in terms of the pope is one of its possible legitimate developments. The question to be tested here is whether in a hermeneutics of the history of influence and of the production of meaning there is the possibility that scripture can stand in judgment on a church in a way that corresponds to the Reformation's basic principle.[153]

This question is to guide our further deliberations. We must initially remember that the papal primacy in its jurisdictional form was never completely received by the whole church, that is, neither in the East nor in the West, where later the Reformation partially prevailed. Correspondingly, the "papal" interpretation of our text always remained only one among others. Three ways of

---

147 De Vries, "Entwicklung," 132. To be sure, to speak of "New Testament germs" (de Vries) seems questionable in view of Matt 16:18. In my judgment, Luke 22:32 and John 21:15-17 where Peter receives a commission would more readily justify such a statement.

148 Kasper, "Dienst," 85.

149 Heinrich Döring, "Papsttum," in *Neues Handbuch theologischer Grundbegriffe* (1985) 3.318.

150 "Dienst," 83.

151 J. H. Newman, *A Letter Addressed to His Grace the Duke of Norfolk* . . . (London: Pickering, 1875), 105 (cited from Burgess, *History,* 87).

152 Systematically, I am not at all far removed from the position advocated by Joseph Ratzinger in his Münster inaugural lecture: Tradition is "interpretation

of the Christ event . . . on the basis of the Pneuma," and that means "at the same time from the ecclesiastical present," because Christ is alive in the "church which is his body, in which his spirit is active" (Karl Rahner and Joseph Ratzinger, *Offenbarung und Überlieferung* [QD 25; Freiburg: Herder, 1965] 40–41). Only I would not postulate from this a somehow qualitative "more" of a "church theology of the New Testament," of a dogma or a *regula fidei* over the original meaning of the texts (something that Ratzinger [43–48] attempts cautiously and differentiatedly). Instead, for me a *constitutive element of church* is *a constantly open discourse* between a possible original meaning and one's own and other new interpretations.

153 Here, where the issue is the papacy, it is appropriate

interpreting the rock have competed since late antiquity. The first and the third related the text personally to Peter, the second did not.

1. *The "Eastern" interpretation: Peter's confession (or faith) is the church's fundamental rock.* We have seen already that the oldest interpretations of Matt 16:18, especially with Origen and Tertullian, offer the typical interpretation of Peter as a "spiritual Christian."[154] The interpretation of the rock as meaning Peter's faith or his Son of God confession must be regarded as a further development of this oldest "typical" interpretation. It is present already in Origen[155] and then influences all Greek exegesis. Peter's confession "does not belong to Peter alone but happened for all people. By calling his confession a rock, he made it clear that he will build the church on it."[156] The interpretation is based on the context of v. 18. In response to Peter's confession of faith Jesus had called him blessed and gave him the promise of v. 18. This is also the predominant interpretation among the Syrian Jacobites and Monophysites.[157] Through Ambrose, Hilary, and Ambrosiaster it became known in the West[158] and was then advocated in Western interpretation throughout the entire Middle Ages along with the Augustinian interpretation (cf. below).[159] Its intention was not to deny Peter's personal function as the rock; rather it was initially to

interpret and to apply that function. Only where its advocates had to separate themselves from Roman claims was faith or the confession able to take Peter's place as "rock."[160] With an anti-Roman emphasis this interpretation was also advocated by the reformers.[161] However, it would be misleading to describe it as a specifically Protestant interpretation. The Anabaptists for their part advocated it with an anti-Reformation accent. The church is to be built on "one's own free . . . confession" "from the Father's revelation."[162] At the time of the Reformation, this "Eastern" interpretation was the most widespread, that is, the "ecumenical" interpretation of the day.

2. *The Augustinian interpretation: Christ is the fundamental rock of the church.* This interpretation also has its roots in Origen, who for the first time called attention to 1 Cor 10:4 as a parallel,[163] in Tertullian, and in Eusebius.[164] Its real father, however, is Augustine, who repeatedly advocated it: "For the Latin *petra* is not named from Peter but Peter from *petra*." Peter has confessed the rock which is Christ (1 Cor 10:4). "Upon this foundation Peter himself was also built. For indeed no one can lay another foundation besides that which has been laid, which is Christ Jesus (1 Cor. 3:11). In this interpretation Peter is not the rock, but "on account of the primacy of his apostleship (he) served as the representation of this Church."[165]

---

to remember that even the shape of the Protestant national churches of the twentieth century is largely determined by the legitimacy of what actually has happened and not by the Bible. It is simply amazing how painlessly, how matter-of-factly and without discussion one comes to terms with this in the "churches of the scripture."

154 Cf. above, Excursus: Peter in the Gospel of Matthew: Overview, Peter as Type I, and Peter as Type II.

155 Fr. 345 2 = GCS Origenes 12.149; Tertullian (*Praescr. haer.* 22.4–5 = ANF 3.253) understands Peter as the guarantor of the unfalsified and public apostolic tradition.

156 Theodore of Mopsuestia fr. 92 = Reuss, 129; similarly, e.g., Eusebius *Praep. ev.* 1.3.1 = GCS 43/1.10; idem, *Theoph.* 4.11 = GCS 3/2.181–82; John Chrysostom, 54.2 = *PG* 58. 534; Euthymius Zigabenus, 465–66; Theophylactus, 320; for additional Greek representatives of this interpretation see Ludwig, *Primatsworte,* 48–51, 97–104.

157 Wilhelm de Vries, *Der Kirchenbegriff der von Rom getrennten Syrer,* 24–33, 61–67.

158 Ambrose *In Luc.* 6.98 = BKV 1/21.614; Hilary *Trin.* 6.36 = FC 25.206; Ambrosiaster on Eph 2:20 = *PL* 17.380.

159 Examples in Gillmann, "Auslegung," 43–51.

160 In the early period, e.g., in Ambrose (*De Inc. Dom. Sacr.* 4.32 = CSEL 79. 238–39), who suggestively sees for Peter a primacy *confessionis . . . , non honoris, . . . fidei, no ordinis.* Cf. later Faber Stapulensis, 178 = 75 (so that one might not say that Peter himself is the rock, Jesus later called him Satan) and Erasmus (*Adnotationes,* 88 with reference to Origen).

161 See, e.g., Zwingli, 321; Melancthon, Treatise on the Power and Primacy of the Pope = *Book of Concord,* 324.

162 Peter Walpot, *The Great Article Book* 1.93 = Quellen zur Geschichte der Täufer 12 (Gütersloh: Mohn, 1967) 108. The antithesis is directed against the churches of the Reformation with their infant baptism that build their church not on one's own confession but on "godfather, godmother and relatives."

163 12.10 = GCS Origenes 10.86.

164 Tertullian *Marc.* 4.13.6; Eusebius *In Ps.* 17.15 = *PG* 23.173D.

165 *In Joh. ev. tract.* 124.5 = FC 92.89. Further passages in Fröhlich, *Formen,* 151; Gert Haendler, "Zur Frage nach dem Petrusamt in der alten Kirche," 89–122, 114–17.

Augustine was able to interpret this representation impressively: He is "in one moment blessed, in the next Satan," strong and weak, a *figura* of the Christian, even of the office bearer who cannot be perfect according to the demand of the Donatists.[166] Augustine himself regarded this interpretation as an alternative to the Petrine interpretation. It is a new interpretation that is important to him, but he wants to leave the final judgment about it to the reader of his works.[167] Its hermeneutical strength is in any case that it interprets Matt 16:18 on the basis of the entire witness of the New Testament.

Augustine's later readers rendered their judgment. In the Middle Ages the Augustinian interpretation became the dominant interpretation in the West.[168] It obviously proved itself as a convincing expression of Christ piety and made it possible for all imperfect Christians to identify with Peter. I scarcely am aware of a commentary that does not advocate it, either alone or with the "Eastern" interpretation of the rock as faith. That is amazing, for in the medieval commentaries of the West one also expects the "papal" interpretation of Matt 16:18. However, there are only a few scattered traces of it, and that in two different ways. Either the Augustinian interpretation serves as the basis in order to polemicize against the papal interpretation: The pope is not the foundation of the church, but the church is the foundation and the mother also of the pope.[169] Or with theologians friendly to the pope such as Thomas Aquinas one may find the attempt to add the papal interpretation at least secondarily to the christological one: Christ is foundation *secundum se,* Peter only insofar as he confessed Christ.[170] With this distinction Thomas decisively influenced the later Catholic exegesis, and with his "Tract Against the Errors of the Greeks" he also influenced the debates of the nineteenth century. It is

not surprising that the Protestant exegesis took up the Augustinian interpretation and gave it an antipapal accent,[171] but here again it is important that this has not been a special Protestant exegesis. In the tradition of the Reformation it was quite possible to admit that Peter also is a rock, for example, following the "Eastern" interpretation of the rock as faith, at least in the sense that this rock embodied faith and not force.[172] Early on, by the way, it was recognized also in the tradition of the Reformation that *exegetically* Augustine's interpretation does not meet the sense of Matt 16:18 and that the rock promise must be related exclusively to Peter.[173]

3. *The Roman interpretation. Peter and after him the pope is the church's foundation rock.* The most important basic texts from the fifth century are the third and fourth sermons of Leo the Great on the anniversary of his consecration as bishop. What is impressive in them is a genuine Peter piety. The authority of the other apostles rests on Peter and his special authority. "In Peter, therefore, the fortitude of all is reinforced." In Peter also rests the authority of the pope, for everything the pope commands is to be ascribed to Peter's present activity through him. Thus Peter is not in the first instance the "first pope," but as *Petrus vivus*[174] he is present in his successors.[175] It is significant for the succeeding period that the "papal" interpretation of our text is to be found primarily and almost exclusively in decrees.[176] Of special importance are the *Decretum Gelasianum,* because here Matt 16:18 serves as proof that the papal primacy is not of human but divine origin,[177] and the *Decretum Gratianum* from the twelfth century, the original germ of the later *Codex Iuris Canonici.*[178] The papal interpretation first entered Catholic exegesis in the Counter-Reformation, where it marks a genuine change.[179] With the polemics against the Protestant exegesis of

166 *Hom.* 76.3 = *PL* 38.480.

167 *Retract.* 1.20.2 = CSEL 36.97–98.

168 After the preparatory work of Gillmann ("Auslegung"), Fröhlich (*Formen*) deserves the credit for demonstrating this; cf. especially 117–26.

169 Paschasius Radbertus, 560; A. Tostatus, *Commentarii in Matthaeum, Opera 18–24* (Venice: Balleoniana, 1728) 4 (edition of 1596 = *Opera* 21, 169–70, according to Gillmann, "Auslegung," 51).

170 *Lectura* no. 1384.

171 See, e.g., Luther, *WA* 38.618–20; idem, 2.539 ("He wants to have one rock and they [*scil.,* the papists] want to have two"); Calvin 2.188–89; Musculus, 413.

172 Luther 2.537: "If the pope follows him [*scil.,* Peter], then we want to call him a rock too."

173 Impressively, e.g., Episcopius, 98–99; in the Enlight-

enment, e.g., Grotius 2.47.

174 Fröhlich, *Formen,* 114.

175 Cf. especially *Sermo* 4.3–4 = FC 93.27–29; quotation 4.3 = 28.

176 Fröhlich, *Formen,* 117: "Proving the primacy is . . . the only place where it . . . could assert itself against the victorious stream of the competing Augustinian and Eastern interpretations."

177 DS no. 350. Date: 6th century?

178 Cf. Gillmann, "Auslegung," 42–43. Gratianus himself follows Augustine's interpretation.

179 Thomas de Vio Cajetan, *Commentarii in Evangelia* (Venice, 1530), 91; Maldonat, 323–26; Salmeron 3.2 = 4.387–400; Lapide, 316–18; Jansen, 150–51. The most influential person was Robert Bellarmine, *De Romano pontifice* (Sedan, 1619) 1.10–13 = 72–105.

the passage, the exegesis of the ancient church is now rejected. It is said that Augustine, who distinguishes between Peter and *petra* (= Christ), unfortunately did not know Hebrew.[180] Faith cannot be the rock, because Christ explains the name of Peter and with *hanc* points to Peter.[181] Also with the Counter-Reformation began the time of the "papal" interpretation of the church fathers—an interpretation that has not been overcome until this century—who now often were claimed on behalf of Roman positions that they never advocated.[182]

For the present situation of the churches an important question arises from this stage in the history of Matt 16:18. What does it mean for the Catholic and the Protestant churches that the Reformation against which the Counter-Reformation reacted is indirectly responsible for the "papal" interpretation of Matt 16:18? What does it mean that the final victory of the papal over the conciliar principle in the Catholic church and the associated restructuring of the papacy in the nineteenth century at least indirectly is a negative consequence of the Protestant antithesis?

4. *Consequences for v. 19.* The most widespread church interpretation of v. 19 relates it to the forgiveness of sins in the sacrament of penance or to the related issues of excommunication and reinstatement to the church.[183] It is no accident that the interpreters normally saw a priestly authority in v. 19.[184] However, the various interpretations of the rock could lead also to special accentuations of v. 19 that became important in the various confessions:

a) The Augustinian interpretation, which saw in Peter a representative of the church, emphasized that the keys are given to the entire church. "What was given to that individual was given to the church."[185] The interpretation of the Reformation was able to follow Augustine, emphasizing on the basis of 18:15-18 that the ecclesiastical power of the keys also takes place in the *mutua consolatio fratrum* where two or three people are gathered in Jesus' name.[186]

b) On the basis of the interpretation taken over in the Reformation that the rock means Peter's confession it becomes understandable why the reformers also saw the church's power to bind and to loose at work in preaching. "Indeed we know that only the word of God can open the door to life for us." Therefore, "the preaching of the gospel is for the purpose . . . of loosing our bonds."[187] This interpretation was advocated with special clarity in Calvinism, where the private confession was replaced by the "open" confession in the worship service before the sermon. It was attacked by Catholic exegesis.

c) The Catholic exegesis of the day expanded the power to bind and to loose to the reigning power of the pope. The keys are a "sign of the kings and regents, not of the doctors and teachers or preachers."[188] The keys designate the *authoritas gubernandi,* whereby the kingdom of heaven was identified with the church.[189] The Protestant exegetes protested against it because it meant a confusion of the two kingdoms.[190]

What sort of conclusions can we draw from the history of our text's influence? What perspectives result from the biblical text itself for its strongest result, the papacy?[191]

---

180 Lapide, 317.

181 Jansen, 150–51.

182 Cf. the "testimonies" in Robert Bellarmine, *De Romano pontifice,* 76–79; Salmeron 3.2 = 4. 394–97; Maldonat, 325–26.

183 Already Callistus (?) in Tertullian *Pud.* 21 = ACW 28.120–21 interprets it this way. Further examples: Theodore of Mopsuestia fr. 92 = Reuss, 129; Thomas Aquinas *S. th.* Suppl. q.18 a.3; Luther 2.533; Apology 12 = *Book of Concord,* 210; *Catechismus Romanus* 2.5.11; on the post-Tridentine Catholic interpretation cf. H. Vorgrimmler, "Das 'Binden' und 'Lösen' in der Exegese nach dem Tridentinum bis zu Beginn des 20. Jahrhunderts," 462–69. Cf. also above, excursus at the end of the interpretation of v. 19a, b, c.

184 Thus Thomas Aquinas *Lectura* no. 1388–92. As an exception in the history of interpretation Thomas emphasizes the mediation of the priestly *potestas* through the pope (ibid., no. 1393).

185 *Sermo* 149.7 = *PL* 38.802.

186 Luther, *WA* 38.630.

187 Calvin 2.187, cf. idem, *Inst.* 4.6.4.

188 Lapide, 319.

189 Jansen, 151–52.

190 Brenz, 569.

191 I concentrate on the papacy because it is the most important effect of the text. Although I am a Protestant Christian, with all respect for the special character of our sister Catholic church I do not want to be silent here, since we Protestants as members of the future (visible!) *Una Sancta Ecclesia* are also affected by the shape of our sister church. Since this text does not have the same fundamental significance for Protestants, the critical questions must be directed first to the sister Catholic church.

Meaning for Today

The history of interpretation showed the variety of "realizations" of our text in the church's historical experiences. It can be shown that aspects of the basic biblical text are present in *all* patterns of interpretation. Some of the truth of Christian faith is alive in all of them.[192] What that means for me is that *if in the name of one interpretation of our text others are suppressed and disciplined, part of the Christian faith is suppressed.*

> To be sure, the nearness to the biblical basic text is variously constituted and variously great. One sees it in the "Eastern" interpretation in its interest in the apostolic Jesus tradition that is the foundation of the church. One sees it in the Augustinian interpretation on the one hand in the christological basis that incorporates the witness of the *entire* New Testament and on the other hand in the possibility of understanding Peter as the representative of the entire church, also of all its members. The Roman interpretation has taken over from Matt 16:18 at least the idea that Peter himself became the rock of the church. On the basis of the Matthean understanding of Peter I must say, however, that for me Origen's "typical" representation of the historical Peter in *every* disciple appears to be closer to the Matthean text than is the "Roman" representation of Peter in *one* special officeholder, the pope. This interpretation is in my judgment the farthest removed from the text.

The history of interpretation shows that in all patterns of interpretation *contingent historical experiences* of churches and Christians that have determined and shaped the interpretations are visible. This is true not only of the Roman interpretation, which provided a solution to the need of the church for institutional unity in late antiquity, of the church's struggle for independence from the states in the Middle Ages, and also of the fear of the "gates of Hades" that threatened in the nineteenth century;[193] it is true also of other interpretations. It was necessary for the Eastern churches to hold fast to the received foundation of faith in the struggle against the heresies of the fourth to sixth centuries; and preserving the tradition later established their identity

in the world that had become Islamic. Origen's image of the historical Peter who was endowed with spiritual knowledge by the living God was at the same time an eloquent expression of his own existence as an endowed Gnostic in and for the church catholic. Finally, the Augustinian interpretation was closest to the grace piety of "ordinary" Christians. Thus in each case the historically contingent experiences are part of the truth of interpretations of our text. Given this recognition, *I am more than skeptical about the absolute claim that arises when certain historical experiences become the obligatory "ius Divinum."* One can only wish that the wealth and the variety of faith experiences occasioned by our text might become known again in our churches.

> Just as Catholic church historians in recent times are also emphasizing the historical experiences that led to the emergence of the papacy, perhaps as a Protestant "doubter" I might be permitted to ask questions based on the history of the text's influence: Whose experiences actually were they? The question is justified in view of the fact that until the time of the Reformation the "Roman" interpretation was by and large *only* a Roman interpretation, that is, an interpretation of the popes themselves and of their theologians and jurists, while the Augustinian interpretation obviously better reflected the piety of people even in the Western church. Furthermore, in its history the "Roman" interpretation was repeatedly combined in a special way with ecclesiastical claims of power. In view of its history the way of the papal office from a ruling office to a serving office is especially difficult.

Guidelines for an Office of Peter

If we attempt positively on the basis of Matt 16:17-19 and the Matthean image of Peter to formulate guidelines that could serve as an orientation for an ecclesiastical office of Peter, it seems to me to be especially important *that Matthew says nothing about the unique Peter that is not also valid for all the other disciples.* A related factor is the fraternal and nonhierarchical structure of the Matthean church that 18:1-22 and 23:8-11 make especially clear.

---

192 Permit me to quote here the reaction of a concerned Catholic friend that moved me. I do so because as a Protestant Christian I can speak more openly than he. When he read this text, he said: "In all of them? There are also perversions of this text! You are too conciliatory!"

193 "Portae inferi . . . maiore in dies odio undique insurgunt." *Pastor Aeternus* (DS no. 3052) begins with these words. One thinks of revolution, young national states, the threatening loss of the Vatican state, bourgeois-enlightenment-egalitarian ideas! It was the fear of these that shaped the First Vatican Council.

What that means for me is that if in a church the *service* of Peter is concentrated in *one office* of Peter, that is possible only when in this *one* that clearly takes shape which based on Jesus Christ *all* are, *and nothing more*. In other words, *in the perspective of Matt 16:18-19, there may be an office of Peter as a representation of the entire church, but not as its head*.

> On this basis a Protestant outsider will read with special interest what Catholic brothers write about the necessary "communal tendency" of the office of Peter.[194] And he will follow with special pain how Catholic sisters and brothers suffer repression in their own church, not in the service of the church's unity but its uniformity.

Peter, the church's founding figure in the Gospel of Matthew, is at the same time the embodiment of the unity of the *entire* church. Thus it is part of the trajectory of our text that it *pose to all churches the critical question to what extent "offices of Peter" in them serve the unity of the entire church.*

> Catholics and Protestants confront different questions here. Protestant churches are to be asked whether their own experiences of fragmentation since the Reformation do not indicate that in addition to the fundamentals of faith "*offices* of Peter" are necessary that embody a *lived* unity. They are to be asked to what degree the various "offices of Peter" that they have also created, for example, teaching offices such as theological faculties or offices for ecumenical relations, are truly "fundamental" for their churches and not simply incidental. The Catholic church and especially those who hold the papal office of Peter are to be asked what it means for them "that the pope is the greatest obstacle on the way to ecumenism."[195] In a pointed and deliberately Protestant form the question is: Is the pope's ministry of Peter a ministry of Peter for the Roman Catholic *part* of the church or, in the trajectory of our text, a ministry for the *entire* Christian church? Thus far the non-Roman churches, for whom paradoxically it has been precisely their common no to the papal office of Peter that has led them to seek and to find their own way to greater unity, have hardly experienced it in this true sense.[196] It does not have to be this way. If it were different—if we Protestants in our longing for the unity of the church had the experience that we are represented, and not judged, by the pope, much could begin to happen, especially since on the basis of the Bible we are aware of the diversity of possible forms the ministry of Peter might take. We also would not have to reject *iure Divino* a papal *ministry* of Peter that in the service of the Jesus tradition guarantees the unity of the *whole* church. Yet this chapter of the history of the influence of Matt 16:18 has not yet been written.

---

194 Kasper, "Dienst," 95.

195 Paul VI (1967) according to *Papsttum*, 263. The truth of this sentence is confirmed by the fact that today a living unity of the church is often lived and experienced at the grass roots, but the papacy is not included in it.

196 Will the pontificate of John XXIII, who in an unimagined way *represented* the hope of the entire church for unity and who, like the New Testament Peter, became a living example of this unity, someday be continued?

After Jesus has withdrawn from his enemies (16:4) and has intimated the founding of the church (16:18-19), he acts primarily on behalf of the disciples who are transparent of the church. Instructions to the disciples (16:21-28; 17:9-13, 19-20, 22-23, 25-18:35; 19:10-12, 23-20:28) and stories about the disciples (17:1-8, 14-18; 19:13-22) dominate this section. Jesus' opponents, the Pharisees, appear actively only once more (19:3). The crowds also are no longer at the center of attention. On only two more occasions do they play a decisive role as active players (19:2; 20:29-31). Once the crowd appears "passively," a prop on the stage, as it were (17:14); once the people appear, so to speak, "anonymously" as bearers of an action (19:13). Compared with the preceding section and the following section, chaps. 21–25, where again the people and Jesus' opponents will play a central role, our section shows a marked shift in focus. Its content corresponds to this change. The focus now is essentially on questions of the church, its life, its experiences, its order, and its behavior. On the deep level of the Matthean story we have now entered the realm of the church. It is a church that has originated in Israel, is opposed by its leaders, but has not yet separated from Israel.

Like the preceding section, 12:1—16:20, the section is divided into three parts and consists again of two narrative parts (16:21—17:27; 19:1-20, 34) and an accompanying discourse (chap. 18). As there, here too the evangelist follows the structure of the Gospel of Mark, whose main section about discipleship in suffering (Mark 8:27-10:52) he takes up and supplements. He begins with Jesus' first prediction of his suffering to his disciples in 16:21. In 17:12, 22-23 and 20:18-19 Jesus will repeat his predictions of suffering. The predictions fulfill not only a narrative purpose in which they are a leitmotif of this main section, connecting its two narrative parts, and at the same time looking ahead to the last section of the Matthean narrative, chaps. 26–28; they also have a central function theologically, for it is the

story of Jesus, in particular the story of his suffering and dying, that shapes the life of the church which is the main issue in our section. One has seen that already in 5:10-12 and in the disciples discourse of chap. 10, and the introductory section, 16:21-28, will make it clear programmatically.

> I am following here the most widespread "narrative" structural model of the Gospel of Matthew[1] with modifications.[2] If one takes 16:21—28:20 as one single main part and 16:21 as its title,[3] the special character of 21:1—25:46 is not recognized. Here Jesus turns his attention outward to the people and not inward to the disciples; the content is focused not, as in 16:21—20:34, primarily on church questions and the disciples' own suffering but on the controversy with Israel's leaders and the church's final separation from Israel. It is no accident that after 20:17-19 the next prediction of the suffering of the Son of Man does not appear until 26:2. However, 21:1—25:46, as 12:1—16:20, are primarily directed outward and continue the "salvation-history" narrative thread of chaps. 12–16. These two sections are thus a frame around the community section, 16:21—20:34, just as the suffering and resurrection of the Son of Man, first announced in the main section 16:21—20:34 and then reported in chaps. 26–28, is a frame around the predominantly salvation-history part, chaps. 21–25. I would like to emphasize this special character of chaps. 21–25 in my proposed structure. However, I am in agreement with the representatives of the "Markan" structural model that the *narrative* provides the decisive points of view for the structure.

A   Experiences of the Disciples on the Way to Suffering (16:21—17:27)

With 16:21 Jesus turns to the future, to Jerusalem. He looks ahead to his suffering and thus states the leitmotif of the section 16:21—17:27. It is framed by predictions of Jesus' dying and rising (16:21; 17:22-23).[4] In the middle there is an additional prediction of the suffering of the Son of Man (17:12b). Thus the goal of the previously portrayed enmity of Jesus' opponents becomes visible. Into Jesus' predictions of his suffering are

---

1   Cf. vol. 1, Introduction, section 1 (Markan structural model), forcefully advocated by Jack Dean Kingsbury (*Matthew: Structure, Christology, Kingdom* [Philadelphia: Fortress, 1975] 7–25) and David R. Bauer (*The Structure of Matthew's Gospel: A Study in Literary Design* [JSNTSup 31; Sheffield: Almond, 1988] esp. 73–108).

2   Cf. vol. 1, Introduction 1 on the overall structure.

3   Bauer, *Matthew's Gospel*, 108: "16:21 encapsulates the major themes in the material that follows," viz., Jesus' own road to the passion and the instructions to the disciples about their own suffering.

4   Matthew 17:24-27 is not easily incorporated into the structure. Cf. below on the analysis of that section.

inserted "contrapuntally," as it were, the transfiguration story and the story of the healing of the epileptic in which Jesus appears in glory and power.

The transition to the new main section takes place not with a caesura but with a connecting bridge provided by the two chiastically related sections 16:13-20 and 16:21-28.[5] The figure of Peter, who plays a central role in both parts, also provides an important link between the two sections 13:53—16:20 and 16:21—17:27.[6]

---

5   Cf. above on the structure of 16:13-20; below on the structure of 16:21-28.

6   Cf. above, the final paragraph of C (13:53—16:20).

Literature

Gerhard Dautzenberg, *Sein Leben bewahren* (SANT 14; Munich: Kösel, 1966) 68–82.

Friedrich, *Gott im Bruder*, 46–53.

Geist, *Menschensohn*, 127–44.

Martin Künzi, *Das Naherwartungslogion Markus 9,1 par.: Geschichte seiner Auslegung* (BGBE 21; Tübingen: Mohr/Siebeck, 1977).

Marguerat, *Jugement*, 85–100.

Harald Riesenfeld, "The Meaning of the Verb ἀρνεῖσθαι," *ConNT* 11 (1947) 207–19.

For *additional literature* see II C 3.3 on Matt 10:34-39.

21 From that time on Jesus[1] began to show his disciples that he must go to Jerusalem and suffer much from the elders and high priests and scribes and be killed and be raised on the third day. 22/ And taking him aside Peter began to remonstrate with him and said, "(God) be gracious to you, Lord! Certainly that shall not happen to you!" 23/ But he turned and said to Peter, "Get behind me, Satan! You are an offense to me, for you are thinking not of God's (things) but of human (things)."

24 Then Jesus said to his disciples, "If anyone wants to come after me, he shall deny himself and take up his cross and follow me.

25 For whoever wants to save his life will lose it, but whoever loses his life for my sake will find it.

26 For what will a person profit by winning the whole world but losing his life? Or what will a person give in exchange for his life?

27 For the Son of Man will come in the glory of his father with his angels, and then he will repay each according to his conduct.

28 Amen, I say to you: There are some of the ones standing here who will not taste death until they see the Son of Man coming in his kingdom."

Analysis **Structure**

It is best to take vv. 21-28 together, although in v. 24

Jesus begins anew and speaks now to all the disciples, not simply to Peter. In terms of content they are a unit. A single arch extends from the suffering of Jesus through the suffering of the disciples who follow him to the final coming of the Son of Man. The section outlines a perspective of the totality of discipleship. In addition, it is formally a chiastic reversal of the preceding section, 16:13-20,[2] so that it belongs together for that reason as well. In interpreting it one must constantly look back at Peter's confession. It is closely bracketed with the macrotext. Looking backward, vv. 24-25 take up logia from the disciples discourse (10:38-39). Looking ahead, the language of v. 21 is closely connected with Jesus' following predictions of the suffering, especially with 17:22 and 20:17-19. The catchwords "Jerusalem," "to suffer," "to kill" (Ἰεροσόλυμα, πάσχω, and ἀποκτείνω), but also the "elders," "high priests," "scribes" (πρεσβύτεροι, ἀρχιερεῖς and γραμματεῖς) as opponents, point to what is to come. They will occur together again in the passion narrative (27:41, cf. 26:3, 47, 57; 27:1, 3, 12, 20; 28:11-12). Finally Matthew formulates the coming of the Son of Man in judgment (v. 27) with words that will appear again in 24:30 and 25:31.[3] Thus again vv. 21-28, as already vv. 13-20, are a key section, strongly bracketed in the entire gospel, that summarizes in few words the entire future perspective of Jesus and his disciples.

One can also divide this section in three parts. In v. 21 Jesus turns to the disciples as he did in v. 20. As in vv. 16-19, a dialogue with Peter follows in vv. 22-23; vv. 24-28 are addressed to the disciples. Formally they are not a dialogue but a concluding speech of Jesus. Verses 24-26 are three logia that suggest parallelism. Verses 27-28 constitute a solemn conclusion to the discourse. The Son of Man title provides the frame around 16:13-28 (vv. 13, 27-28).

Source

The *source* of our section is Mark 8:31–9:1. The larger and smaller changes are almost all redactional;[4] this is also true of v. 27 that is for the most part a new for-

---

1 Ἰησοῦς Χριστός, ℵ, B, and others (= Nestle[25]) is attested only in Egyptian texts and is probably a secondary addition based on 16:16.

2 Cf. above on the structure of 16:13-20.

3 The connections are to be explained in part by the common Son of Man tradition (between Mark 8:38 and 13:26). In the case of 25:31 we are dealing with a deliberate Matthean formulation that is reminiscent of quite diverse passages (in addition to 16:27, 24:30; also 13:49 and 19:28), contra Friedrich, *Gott im Bruder*, 53.

4 Cf. vol. 1, Introduction 3.2 on v. 21 ἀπὸ τότε, μαθητής, ἐγείρω (but cf. below, n. 6), v. 22 λέγων, κύριε, v. 23 στρέφω (cf. 9:22), v. 24 τότε, v. 25 εὑρίσκω, v. 26 ἐάν, δέ, ἤ, v. 27 μέλλω, γάρ, τότε, ἀποδίδωμι. On ἑκάστῳ κατά (v. 27) cf. 25:15. LXX language (cf. vol. 1, Introduction 3 on Style) are ἵλεως with κύριος (v. 22; cf. 1 Βασ 14:15; 2 Βασ 20:20; 23:17; Amos 7:2; Isa 54:20 etc.; especially frequent in the Jewish-Greek of 2/4 Macc) and the end of v. 27 (cf. ψ 61:13; Prov 24:12, Σιρ 35:22). Not Matthean, but understandable on the basis of the

mulation.[5] Obvious major changes are: (1) In v. 22b
Peter formulates his remonstrances in direct speech.
(2) In v. 23a the other disciples are not mentioned.
(3) The introduction to v. 24b-e is shortened; Jesus
speaks only to the disciples, not to the people. (4) In
v. 27 Mark 8:38 is severely abbreviated. Verse 27b is
not found in Mark. Matthew had already offered the
same logion in 10:32-33 in its Q form; instead of
repeating it here, he de facto creates a new saying.
Verse 27 becomes the immediate basis for vv. 24-26.
(5) Verse 28 is not reintroduced, and it becomes a
Son of Man saying, the kingdom of God becomes the
kingdom of the Son of Man. Thus vv. 27 and 28 come
together. On the whole, the changes firm up the section by comparison with Mark. Some minor agreements are conspicuous. In v. 21 = Luke 9:22 ἀπό
instead of ὑπό with the passive and even "to be raised
on the third day" (τῇ τρίτῃ ἡμέρᾳ ἐγερθῆναι) might
come from a deutero-Markan recension of the text,[6]
while the omission of the Markan redactional "and of
the gospel" (καὶ τοῦ εὐαγγελίου) in v. 25 = Luke 9:24
more likely comes from the influence of the Q recension or Matthean redaction.

Tradition History and Origin
On the *tradition history* and *origin* of the individual
sayings cf. the analysis of 10:37-39.[7] The question of
the origin of the "saying about the appointed time" in
v. 28 = Mark 9:1 is especially difficult. These days it is
usually rejected as a saying of Jesus and attributed to
the primitive church, much like 10:23 and 24:34 =
Mark 13:30. Yet we are justified in asking whether
such a claim is not an attempt in modern, historical-
critical form to avoid the fact that Jesus was mistaken
in his near expectation. Is the wish to free Jesus from
an error the father of the thought? The saying is not a
great deal different from the word of comfort in
10:23 that may have come from Jesus. The difference
is merely that here the near expectation plays a more
central role. On the other hand, the early Christian
prophetic sayings in 1 Cor 15:51-52 and 1 Thess 4:16-
17 confirm that there actually were dominical sayings

created in primitive Christianity that looked for an
appointed end in the near future. As a matter of honesty we will have to leave the question open.

Interpretation
■ **21** After the command to silence in v. 20 that made of
the disciples insiders with special knowledge which the
people did not have, Jesus announces to them his suffering and his resurrection. Thus he now deepens the disciples' special knowledge. The announcement is
completely open, no longer a secret as it was in 12:40,
but it is meant only for the disciples.[8] The Matthean
introduction is relatively extensive, for the prediction of
suffering is no longer Jesus' direct response to Peter's
confession as it was in Mark; instead, Jesus begins a new
instruction. Since he will repeat it several times leading
up to his arrival in Jerusalem (17:12, 22-23; 20:17-19),
Matthew says, "From that time Jesus began . . ." He uses
"to show" (δεικνύειν), because "to teach" (διδάσκω;
Mark 8:31) for him means primarily ethical instruction;[9]
one should not theologically overload this rare word.[10]
"Mast" (δεῖ) indicates the divinely decreed necessity that
Jesus must suffer and die. Nevertheless it is planned by
the Jewish leaders of their own free will and with their
own malice for which they bear full responsibility. God's
plan and human responsibility are no more mutually
exclusive in Matthew than they are elsewhere in the New
Testament and in Judaism. Jesus is aware of this plan.
His announcement already anticipates in broad strokes
the entire passion narrative. The passive verbs show that
it is not he who is the acting agent but the Jewish leaders
or, in the final analysis, God. Nevertheless the passion
narrative will show that Jesus is also active. He goes the
way assigned him as God's obedient Son. His approaching suffering and his resurrection will now overshadow
the progress of the Matthean story.

redactional interpretation, are: in v. 21 the avoided
terms (vol. 1, Introduction 3.3) ἤρξατο (but cf.
4:17), δεικνύειν, Ἱεροσόλυμα, and the additions οὐ
μὴ ἔσται σοι τοῦτο and σκάνδαλον εἶ ἐμοῦ in vv.
22-23. Cf. the interpretation on these verses.

5   Strecker (*Weg*, 27–28) regards v. 27b as preredactional. However, v. 27b is not a quotation from a
biblical text (that was influenced by Hebrew); it is a
Greek ad hoc formulation in biblical language.

6   Although ἀπό appears frequently in Matthew, it is
not redactional in this usage. Τῇ τρίτῃ ἡμέρᾳ
ἐγερθῆναι is not Lukan, but it corresponds to the

kerygmatic language of early Christianity. Cf. 1 Cor
15:4 and Ennulat, *Agreements*, 190. Mark 10:34 is
changed in a similar way.

7   See above, II C 3.3, also on the "original meaning"
of 10:38; in addition Gnilka, *Markus* 2.12–14,
22–23.

8   The omission of Mark 8:32a is not a correction; it is
the omission of something that is clear for Matthew
anyway.

9   Cf. vol. 1, II on 4:23-25: Excursus on Preaching,
Teaching, and Gospel in Matthew, with n. 2.

10 We may, e.g., not think on the basis of Rev 1:1 of

■ **22** Peter takes Jesus to himself[11] and rebukes him. Ἵλεως σοι is presumably biblical language[12] and is to be understood as a less forceful form of "God forbid!" or "May God prevent it!"[13] Why does Peter want to protect Jesus from suffering? Is he guided by a Jewish Messianic understanding according to which the Messiah is a political military figure?[14] Or is Matthew simply thinking here "in human terms," since Peter's pain is understandable, because he loves Jesus and does not want him to die?[15] Seldom, however, can we demonstrate such considerations for Matthew. Since in vv. 24-26 Jesus teaches about suffering in discipleship, as with Mark he probably understood Peter's protest not simply as a protest against Jesus' suffering but also as a protest against the disciples' own suffering—and that of the church. Then Peter is here also the spokesman for the disciples, just as he formulated his confession in v. 16 with the words of the disciples' and church's confession. As a disciple he lives in the ambivalence of trust and doubt, of confessing and fear of the consequences of this confessing, and of betrayal and remorse (26:69-75).[16] The issue is not that Peter is worse than the other disciples,[17] because, for example, he will deny Jesus, no more than in 16:16-19 he was better than they.

■ **23** Jesus' reaction to this rebuke is extremely sharp. "Get behind me, Satan" (Ὕπαγε . . . Σατανᾶ) is reminiscent of the last temptation in 4:10 where Jesus rejected the world rule offered by the devil. "Offense" (σκάνδαλον)[18] is a strong word and means in substance the occasion for sin. Presumably the expression is biblically ceremonial and formulated by Matthew in direct con-

trast to the rock that Peter was in 16:18.[19] There Jesus had called Peter "rock" for the sake of what not flesh and blood but the heavenly father had revealed to him. Here he is an "offense," because he strives for the human rather than for the divine. Verses 17-18 and 23 define the fundamental opposition between God and humans. It is by God's gift that Peter is a rock; it is from his own thinking that he is an "offense." Thus his objection serves as a type or model. When confronted with suffering Peter thinks like a "human being"—rationally, egoistically, perhaps even from human love. Jesus responds with a sharp antithesis. These human standards have no validity before God. His message to humans is solely and alone the call to a radically understood discipleship. Ὀπίσω μου presumably already indicates that. It is reminiscent of 4:19, looks ahead to v. 24, and assigns to Peter the only possible place: behind Jesus.

History of Interpretation

■ **22-23** I would like to call attention especially to two interpretations, because they capture the depth of this fundamental opposition between God and humans. *Calvin* contrasts Peter's well-meaning intentions with Jesus' harsh answer and asks why Jesus has such a harsh outburst. His answer is that while the lusts of the flesh are indeed difficult to rule, there is "no more ravening beast than the wisdom of the

the communication of eschatological mysteries.

11 For the popular translation "took him aside," BAGD *s.v.* mentions no certain New Testament sources except our text and Mark 8:32, and no secular sources at all.

12 Cf., e.g., 2 *Βασ* 20:20; 23:17; 1 Chr 11:19; Hebrew חלילה. Cf. also Str-B 1.748.

13 However, the Greek parallels literally mean: May God be gracious. Cf. Sophocles *Oed. Col.* 1480 and the inscriptions in Allen, 181.

14 Cf. Bonnard, 248.

15 Thus, e.g., Jerome, 144 (*de pietatis affectu veniens*). A "friendly" interpretation may be supported by προσλαβόμενος that emphasizes the fellowship. Søren Kierkegaard (*Works of Love* [Princeton: Princeton University Press, 1946] 90) formulates

impressively: Not an ungodly but "the best and most kindly man, humanly speaking, must be offended at Him" and must first learn "what love is, divinely understood."

16 The Catholic J. Blank ("Petrus und Petrusamt," 101) formulates pointedly, but in substance correctly, that Peter is seen here as *simul iustus et peccator.*

17 As stated, e.g., by Plummer, 234: "A primacy of evil rather than of good."

18 Cf. nn. 23–24 on 13:36-43. The word is also used of persons in 13:41.

19 It is quite conceivable that Matthew—not the pre-Matthean redaction that did not yet have σκάνδαλον—is determined by Isa 8:14, where Aquila reads στερεὸν σκανδάλου (Field, 446). The suggestion is supported by Rom 9:33 and 1 Pet 2:8 (as one

flesh."[20] On this basis he arrives at his interpretation of self-denial. It is for him the "chief sum of the Christian life" and the gateway to the way of the cross. It consists first of all of seeing that human reason is no longer "the person's master" and no longer "has dominance over morals."[21] Thus for Calvin "self-denial" stands in radical opposition to every shrewd Christian adjustment to the circumstances, and it belongs to what on the basis of the Sermon on the Mount we called radical "'contrasting signs' of the kingdom of God" that the church of Christ must pose.[22] *Kierkegaard* contrasts God's absoluteness with human reason even more impressively:

> At the absolute the understanding stands still. The contradiction which arrests it is that a man is required to make the greatest possible sacrifice to dedicate his whole life as sacrifice—and wherefore? There is indeed no wherefore. "Then it is madness," says the understanding. There is no wherefore, because there is an infinite wherefore. But whenever the understanding stands still in this wise, there is the possibility of offense. If now there is to be victorious advance, faith must be present.[23]

Interpretation

■ **24-25** The suffering of Jesus and the discipleship of suffering belong inseparably together. From the Gospel of Mark Matthew had learned that it is truly possible to understand Jesus only by following him in suffering (cf. Mark 8:31-34; 9:30-37; 10:32-45). He himself formulated the principle that simply saying "Lord, Lord" will not help in the judgment of the Son of Man (7:21). Instead, what matters is obedience. In 13:19-23 he made it clear that "understanding" and "bringing fruit" belong together. In Matthew's sense Peter has probably "understood" who Jesus is, but he is not ready to live this understanding. Therefore Jesus now says—only to the disciples and not, as in Mark, also to the people—what the consequences are of his way of suffering. In the process Matthew initially repeats the sayings about the discipleship of the cross and about losing one's life that he had already used at the conclusion of the disciples discourse in 10:38-39. He does this not accidentally, because they

stood in his two main sources,[24] but because they are fundamentally important. It is clearer in v. 21 than in 10:38[25] that he is thinking in terms of Christ. He is thus not concerned with replacing an ideal of life that sees happiness as the freedom from suffering with a desire for suffering or asceticism; his sole concern is the disciples' Christ-likeness which costs them something. It is also clear that suffering is not passive acceptance but an active form of life: "If anyone wants . . ." ($\epsilon \check{\iota} \ \tau\iota\varsigma \ \vartheta\acute{\epsilon}\lambda\epsilon\iota$ . . .). As in 10:39, the saying about losing one's life calls attention to the reality that martyrdom is the final pinnacle of discipleship of the cross without being its condition. Life will be given to the follower of Jesus on the other side of death. The prior carrying one's cross, on the other hand, is not focused on martyrdom but is understood comprehensively and means all suffering on behalf of the cause of Jesus. In Matthew's understanding the positive meaning of "bearing the cross" is orienting oneself to Jesus as the model for life and knowing the experience of being borne by the exalted Lord. At the beginning of discipleship stands the call to deny oneself that Matthew here, unlike 10:38, takes over from the Gospel of Mark. That means a conscious decision—a "contradiction against one's own vital interests"[26]—in turning to Christ.

Self-Denial

Ἀπαρνεῖσθαι in connection with the reflexive pronoun ἑαυτόν is a new linguistic creation in Mark 8:34. The basic meaning of the verb ἀρνέομαι is "to say no," "to refuse." The compound verb ἀπαρνεῖσθαι is intensive or identical in meaning to the simple verb. In a religious sense, with reference to gentile gods, the simple verb was used almost exclusively in Hellenistic Judaism.[27] In the synoptic tradition it is rooted in the logion about confessing (Luke 12:8-9) and in the story of Peter's denial (Mark 14:66-72). "To deny oneself" was presumably created as a counterformulation to "to deny Christ." Since the expression is new, only the context in Mark (and Matthew) can determine its meaning. It refers to the negative side of what is positively expressed with "to confess

---

witness) that also know this wording.

20   2.193.
21   *Inst.* 3.7.1.
22   Cf. vol. 1, in the summary of II A 2.2.5 (on 5:38-42) and the last page of vol. 1.
23   *Training,* 121.
24   Matthew 16:27, different from 10:32-33, shows that

he also can avoid doublets.

25   Cf. above, II C 3.3 on Jesus' understanding of 10:38.
26   Pesch, *Markusevangelium* 2.59.
27   Harald Riesenfeld, "The Meaning of the Verb ἀρνεῖσθαι," 207–19, 210–11; Spicq, *Lexicon,* 1.202.

Christ" or "to follow." Thus it is not a general ascetic ideal. To what, however, must one say "no"? The imperative aorist that is striking when used along with ἀκολουθείτω[28] could indicate that it is a single act at the beginning of an ongoing way to the cross, thus, for example, a baptismal promise. In the Markan as in the Matthean context it probably means the decision no longer to make one's own life principle "wanting-to-save-one's-life" (Mark 8:35a) and to abandon one's own "I standpoint."[29] Mark 8:36 appears to indicate that it involves giving up the "winning" of possessions. Thus suffering and the willingness to renounce go together.[30]

The call to "self-denial" in connection with our logion has had a rich history that we will not trace here in detail.[31] It was often combined with an ego- and world-denying asceticism. In a standard Catholic ethical work produced in the second half of our century, the "mortification of the imagination, of the feelings, of the emotions, and the senses" was still decisive for the "voluntary acceptance of renunciation and affliction."[32] More recently one seems to have repressed this problematic heritage of Christian tradition, at least in theology if not necessarily everywhere in church praxis.[33] Only a quarter of a century later in a standard ecumenical ethical work "self-denial" is not even mentioned, and scarcely anything is said about the entire area of a *special* Christian lifestyle or

a *special* ethic of the Christian church that is different from the world. Christian ethics here knows that it must answer "before the forum of critical reason" and aims at "universality."[34] The change in direction is truly fundamental,[35] and in view of the way a completely secular lifestyle of a once-Christian society is taken for granted it is alarmingly conforming to me. In this situation in which the number of religious people with which a Christian tradition hostile to body and life must cope is rapidly diminishing, I have no desire to join in the general chorus about this tradition which is such a burden on us. Instead, as an exegete who at the same time is an advocate of his texts for the present, I would like to remind us of the substance that Matthew meant. "Self-denial . . . is not suicide, for there is an element of self-will even in that. To deny oneself is to be aware only of Christ and no more of self, to see only him who goes before and no more the road which is too hard for us." This deliberate decision for a different orientation of life that is not focused on the ego is fundamental for all gospels. It is not a matter of practicing Christian laws or ascetic self(!)-perfection but of an alternate form of life that is not oriented toward the ego and that is made possible only by being bound to Jesus, that is, in discipleship and in the *community* of the followers he

---

28 Grammatical parallels in Mayser, *Grammatik* 2/1.149–50.

29 Drewermann, *Markusevangelium* 1.581. He formulates significantly that "self-denial" stands not against "self-finding," but against the externally perhaps aggressive but finally fearful self-preservation of those who live fixated on their own ego. Good also is Bovon, *Lukas* 1.483: ". . . to bring to light one's actual, sober, fragile ego in relation to Christ."

30 Erich Fromm's distinction "to have or to be" (*To Have or to Be* [New York: Harper & Row, 1976]) has a great deal to do with the issue here. Cf., e.g., pp. 155–57 (in the 1981 Bantam paperback edition). Fromm wants to remind us here that while the lifeform that is identified with self-denial and the way of the cross is demanded by Jesus and is made possible through fellowship with him, it is at the same time more than a mere Christian specialty; it is rather the possibility of "finding life" in the full sense of the word (cf. v. 25).

31 Cf. above, II C 3.3 on the history of interpretation of 10:38-39 and Louis Beirnaert, *LThK* 9 (1964) 630–31.

32 Bernhard Häring, *The Law of Christ: Moral Theology for Priest and Laity* (3 vols.; Westminster, Md.: New-

man, 1966–68) 3.44, 48. Cf. above, II C 3.3 Summary (a) on the trajectory of our text.

33 Drewermann (*Markusevangelium* 1.574–77) offers impressive examples from the practice of marital counseling in his church which declares *every* marriage as indissoluble. Perhaps the problems are somewhat different in a Protestant national church in which the "law of Christ" has paled for a long time. Here it is more likely that the dominant ethos takes possessions and consumerism for granted and, if need be, justifies them as "self-actualization." Matt 16:24 is directed against *this* kind of self-actualization but not against authentic "living" (v. 25!).

34 Anselm Hertz, Wilhelm Korff, Trutz Rendtorff, and Hermann Ringeling, eds., *Handbuch der christlichen Ethik* (2 vols.; Gütersloh: Mohn, 1979) 1.6. Missing in the index is not only "self-denial," but also, e.g., "Sermon on the Mount," "prayer," or "monasticism." Is that accidental? Yet see now Christofer Frey, *Theologische Ethik* (Neukirchener Arbeitsbücher; Neukirchen-Vluyn: Neukirchener Verlag, 1990), *s.v.* "Bergpredigt" (esp. 10ff., 15ff., 159ff.).

35 Contrast Calvin's interpretation (above, nn. 20–21), which begins by saying that human reason is not neutral but as "wisdom of the flesh" is an instrument of its desire for life.

has created.[36] One presupposes that such a life is voluntary, free of any church coercion; the twice-used θέλειν in vv. 24-25 presumably indicates a potential meaning of our text for the present. However, a "Christianity [which] has ceased to be serious about discipleship" and "can no longer see any difference between an ordinary human life and a life committed to Christ"[37]—which has become almost commonplace at least in Protestant national churches—probably stands about where Peter stood according to v. 22 and will also have to hear what Peter heard in v. 23.

■ **26** Verse 26a substantiates v. 25. The logion that was taken over from Mark and scarcely changed presupposes the experience that obviously one can win the whole world and lose one's life. "Winning the whole world" (κερδαίνειν τὸν κόσμον) is to be taken quite literally.[38] One may earn enormous amounts of money and then suddenly be dead. "Why does he (scil., the greedy person) insist on gathering when the gatherer cannot last?"[39] This experience is graphically portrayed in the story of the rich farmer (Luke 12:16-21) and also documented elsewhere.[40] In its formulation the second saying, v. 26b, sounds like ψ 48:8-9.[41] In its content, however, the issue here is not, as it is there, that no one is rich enough to redeem himself from God, but, as in related Greek proverbs, that there is nothing that can be exchanged, no equivalent (ἀντάλλαγμα) for life. Life is more than all the gold; it is the most precious thing there is.[42] Thus when speaking of self-denial, Matthew's

main concern is saying no to striving for possessions. That is in keeping with the central position that the warning against wealth has for him.[43] Unlike the Greek texts, however, the issue is precisely not that earthly life is the highest of all goods. Instead, for him "life" (ψυχή) transcends earthly life. The future tenses are real and refer to the coming judgment. In the final sense only the judge of the world will grant or withhold life. At the end of the way to the cross on which the disciples of Jesus are going, Jesus himself will receive them as world-judge.

■ **27** Therefore, he turns to the Son of Man who will come with his angels and judge the world. Matthew speaks of the judgment with a biblical expression but not with an actual quotation.[44] He speaks, of course, of the judgment on human behavior that the evangelist will describe in 25:31-46 in greater detail. The use of the abstraction πρᾶξις (behavior), that is more likely to be avoided by the LXX, is unusual in comparison with the tradition. It may be that Matthew chooses this expression because the context speaks primarily not of the disciples' active "deeds" (ἔργα) but of their active suffering.[45]

History of Interpretation

The exegesis of the Reformation, especially the Lutheran exegesis, had its difficulties with this understanding of judgment. In Matthew it is the commu-

---

36 Cf. Ulrich Luz, "Selbstverwirklichung? Nachdenkliche Überlegungen eines Neutestamentlers," in Friedrich de Boor, ed., *Selbstverwirklichung als theologisches und anthropologisches Problem* (Halle: Martin Luther Universität Halle-Wittenberg, 1988) 132–52.

37 Quotations from Bonhoeffer, *Cost*, 77–78.

38 Ζημιόω also frequently has a financial meaning and means "to fine someone" or in a passive sense "to be fined, to pay a fine, to suffer financial loss" (LSJ, s.v. 2.1).

39 Gregory the Great 32.5 = *PL* 76.1236.

40 Cf. Sir 11:18-19; Menander fr. 301 = Theodor Kock, ed., *Comicorum Atticorum Fragmenta* (Leipzig: Teubner, 1888) 3.85; Job 2:4.

41 Ἄνθρωπος, δώσει, τῆς ψυχῆς αὐτοῦ. Cf. Gerhard Dautzenberg, *Sein Leben bewahren*, 71–74.

42 Homer *Il.* 9.401 (οὐ γὰρ ψυχῆς ἀντάξιον); Anacreon *Od.* 23 (= *Griechische Lyrik* [Weimar: Aufbau, 1976] 163); Aeschylus *Pers.* 842 (riches are of no use to the dead); Pollux 3.113 (τὴν ψυχὴν ἂν ἀνταλλάξας τοῦ χρυσίου). Wettstein 1.434:

"*Sententia proverbialis.*"

43 Cf. vol. 1, II A 2.4.1 on 6:19-24 (Analysis); on 6:24; 2.4.2 on 6:25-34 (Summary) and above, III B 3.2 on 13:44-46 and the text mentioned there.

44 The language is reminiscent of: ψ 61:12; Prov 24:12; Σιρ 35:22. Cf. *1 Enoch* 45.3; 69.26–29; Rom 2:6; Rev 2:23 (usually formulated with ἔργα).

45 This is a suggestion from S. Schwarz. Πράσσω is not only behavior; it also includes a person's experiences. The verbal abstract πρᾶξις can also (seldom) have the nuance "faring well or ill" (LSJ, s.v. IV). While ἔργον usually designates the (concluded) deed, πρᾶξις is more likely to refer to the process of acting in a very open sense; cf. the translation "behavior."

nity of disciples against whom the coming judgment is directed.[46] How does it relate to justification *sola gratia*? Luther distinguishes between person and works: "Not the works (*opera*) but the agent (*operans*) will receive a reward. But the agent is the one who before the work is either good or evil." "However, Christ speaks here not of justification but of his judgment seat in which he will judge the righteous and the ungodly. Thus he teaches here not how we become righteous but how in the case of the righteous and the unrighteous it is to be decided whether they were righteous or unrighteous."[47] This creates difficulties for us. Either justification by grace alone has no longer any effect in the last judgment, or it eliminates the judgment based on works for the Christians who are justified. Brenz "solves" the problem, for example, in the latter sense by saying that according to works all are not only judged, but condemned, because all are sinners. However, "those who believe in Christ will be preserved," "for even if they are sinners, they have, because they believe in Christ, the forgiveness of sins in Christ."[48] That is not how Matthew thinks. The conclusion of his final discourse, 24:37–25:46, which speaks of the judgment of the Son of Man on the works of the church, makes completely clear that in the judgment the "disciples" can actually lose their life.

It is notable that Matthew does not perceive the coming "judgment based on behavior" as threat and terror, even when it is directed at the church. That will become clear at the very latest in v. 28. The issue there is its temporal proximity, and this is a comfort for the church. How does that happen? We can only indirectly infer an answer from the text. Matthew gives one indication by speaking of following Jesus. The coming world-judge–Son of Man Jesus is the one who even now is with the disciples, instructing them, going before them into suffering and the resurrection, calling them blessed, again calling them to "follow him" when they fail, and also being with them as the exalted one "always until the end of the world" (28:20). The judgment loses its terror, because the expected Son of Man is no other than *Jesus* whom the church knows and who throughout the story

has gone the same way they will go.[49] The other clue is in the little word "father." The God whose glory the Son of Man will reveal is none other than the father of whom Jesus spoke and who hears the prayers of the church (cf. 6:7-13).

■ **28** The view of the judgment of the Son of Man ends with a solemn word of comfort. The comfort consists in the announcement that the coming of the Son of Man is so imminent that "some of the ones standing here" will still experience it. Matthew has formulated the saying of Mark 9:1 that he had received as a saying of the Son of Man and thus related it to v. 27. It obviously did not matter to him that the coming "kingdom of God" thus became the coming "kingdom of the Son of Man," in spite of the tension that is created with 13:38, 41. An even greater problem is that the coming of the Son of Man is temporally determined as in 10:23 and 24:34. He is coming while "some" of the first generation are still alive.

History of Interpretation

It is difficult to say to what degree the many reinterpretations in the history of interpretation[50] are a sign that the problem was recognized. It is more likely that the widespread interpretation of the kingdom of God as the church, the gnostic and later Origenistic search for a deepened, "spiritual" sense of the text, and the immediate proximity of the transfiguration pericope[51] did not even let the problem surface. In the Gospel of Thomas those who understand the words of the living Jesus will not taste death.[52] Origen also interpreted the saying spiritually to refer to the spiritual person's vision of the glorious and all-surpassing word of God.[53] The most widespread interpretation in the Eastern and Western church related the saying to the transfiguration whereby then "some" referred to Peter, James, and John.[54] In addition, since the time of Gregory the Great there is the interpretation supported by Matt 13:36-43 that the βασιλεία means the church, its mission and great-

---

46 Cf. 7:21-27; 13:36-43, 47-50; 24:37-25:30. Marguerat (*Jugement*, 87) points out that judgment is precisely *not* part of the missionary preaching.

47 *WA* 38.646, 645.

48 Brenz, 581.

49 Cf. the excursus on judgment in vol. 3.

50 Cf. Künzi, *Markus 9,1.*

51 Mark may already have seen an anticipation of the βασιλεία in the story of the transfiguration; cf. Gnilka, *Markus* 2.27.

52 Logion 1; cf. logia 18, 19.

53 12.33 = GCS Origenes 10.146.

54 See, e.g., John Chrysostom, 56.1 = *PG* 58.549; Cyril of Alexandria *Matt.* (= *PG* 72.365–474) 424–25;

ness.[55] Since the Reformation, or even since the Middle Ages, there is the added interpretation in terms of the resurrection of Jesus[56] or his ascension.[57] The Reformation took over the previous interpretations. With the Enlightenment came the first attempt at a "historical" interpretation, understanding the saying to refer to the destruction of Jerusalem.[58] Often these interpretations were connected with the interpretation of the parousia, and then it was suggested that transfiguration, resurrection, ascension, etc. foreshadowed the distant parousia "typologically."[59] Reimarus was the first to say in passing that our logion speaks not of the distant but of the near parousia.[60] Since the nineteenth century claiming that the word was not a genuine saying of Jesus[61] has been a favorite way of avoiding the recognition that Jesus was in error.[62]

Why was Matthew able to pass on this saying about a fixed time and regard it as a word of comfort, even though more than a half century after Jesus and after the death certainly of most of the apostles he must have had difficulties with its formulation? The close connection with the saying about the judgment of the Son of Man in v. 27 and his other sayings about a fixed time speak against the idea that Matthew saw the fulfillment of this prediction in the story of the transfiguration. There he speaks neither of the Son of Man nor of his "coming." The difficulty exists not only with Matthew. There are in early Christianity and also in contemporary Judaism similar sayings.[63] For various reasons we surmise that Matthew himself expected the end to be near.[64] That makes it more understandable why our Jesus logion for him was an actual word of comfort, but it solves the problems no more than it does at 10:23. In my judgment

an aporia remains here as well as there. Matthew faithfully preserved the Jesus tradition even when he was able to accept it only it in its trajectory.

Summary

Our section is one of the most important texts of the gospel. The second part of the "diptych,"[65] Matt 16:13-28, does not offer a "didactic collection" of important christological statements[66]—Matthew does not lay out a christological "doctrine." Instead, he makes Peter's christological confession part of life. To that degree our text is a parallel to 7:21-23 where Matthew made clear for the first time that confession without praxis is worthless. To that degree it is also a parallel to the disciples discourse of chap. 10, where the issue was that the disciples accept Jesus' task and reflect Jesus' lifestyle and his suffering. As there, the issue is that living and suffering in conformity to Christ is the decisive *nota ecclesiae*. Thus this text also leads from Christology to ecclesiology that belongs constitutively to Christology. It also corresponds to 11:28-30, that call of the savior who "translates" into life the revelation given by God to the Son and to his own. And it has its hermeneutical parallels in chap. 13, where it became clear that understanding Jesus' instruction and the fruits of the word belong together. Christologically Matthew expresses it in such a way that he frames Peter's confession of the *Son of God* with a section that speaks of the *Son of Man*. If for Matthew the issue with Peter's Son of God confession was Jesus' uniqueness which only the Father can reveal, with the Son of Man the issue is the way which the future judge of the world with his own followers has to *go* through humility,

---

Hilary, 17.1 = SC 258.62; Augustine *Sermo* 78.1 = *PL* 38.490; Zwingli, 326–27; Maldonat, 339.

55 32.7 = *PL* 76.124. Similarly, e.g., Bede, 80; Strabo, 143; Musculus, 422.

56 As, e.g., Luther, *WA* 38.649; Calvin 2.196; Bucer, 164.

57 Dionysius the Carthusian, 193.

58 See, e.g., Lightfoot 2.422 (on Mark 9:1); Wettstein 1.434.

59 Cf. Künzi, *Markus 9,1,* 188–89.

60 "Concerning the Intention of Jesus and His Teaching," in *Reimarus,* 215–18 (II § 38).

61 Künzi (*Markus 9,1,* 105–12) mentions, among others, F. C. Baur, H. A. W. Meyer, C. H. Weisse, O. Pfleiderer, H. J. Holtzmann.

62 Loisy (2.18, 28) differs. He says that Mark 8:31 par.

is not genuine, but Mark 9:1 par. may correspond to the expectation of Jesus.

63 Apart from 10:23, cf. 24:34 par.; 1 Cor 15:51-52; 1 Thess 4:16-17; 4 Ezra 4:26, 7:28. 4 Ezra is contemporary with Matthew and is evidence for the near expectation. John 21:18-23 reveals the difficulties with such expectations.

64 Cf. vol. 3 on the interpretation of chap. 24.

65 Cf. above, III C 3.3 n. 8.

66 Geist, *Menschensohn,* 161.

hostility, suffering, and resurrection and in which his disciples participate. For Matthew here is the key to life. Thus neither an ecclesiastical teaching office nor a theological faculty can be the judge of what a true confession to the Son of God is but only the Son of Man who judges the *praxis* of the confessing disciples.

Excursus:
The Son of Man in the Gospel of Matthew

Literature

Colpe, "ὁ υἱὸς τοῦ ἀνθρώπου," 459–61.
Geist, *Menschensohn.*
Joseph Fitzmyer, *A Wandering Aramean* (Missoula: Scholars Press, 1979) 143–60.
Hare, *Son of Man,* 113–82.
Kingsbury, "Figure of Jesus," 3–36.
Idem, "The Title 'Son of Man' in Matthew's Gospel," *CBQ* 73 (1975) 193–202.
Lange, *Erscheinen,* 188–211.
Marguerat, *Jugement,* 67–83.
Mogens Müller, *Der Ausdruck "Menschensohn" in den Evangelien* (Acta theologica Danica 17; Leiden: Brill, 1984) 104–23, 189–200.
Idem, "Mattaeusevangeliets messiasbillede: Et forsog at bestemme Mattaeusevangeliets forstaelse af Jesu messianitet," *SEÅ* 51–52 (1986/87) 168–79.
Theisohn, *Richter,* 156–201.
C. Weist, "Wer ist dieser Menschensohn? Die Geschichte der Exegese zum Menschensohn-begriff" (Diss., Vienna, 1972).

Survey

The Matthean Son of Man sayings are not equally distributed throughout the gospel. A rough survey shows that they are missing in the Sermon on the Mount and that they appear occasionally beginning in 8:20. Between 16:13 and 17:22 they are somewhat clustered (six logia). An even stronger cluster appears at the end of the gospel between 24:27 and 26:64 (twelve logia). Further observations are to be made at the surface level of the

text. Prior to 16:13 most of the Son of Man sayings are addressed to the people and/or the opponents of Jesus (8:20; 9:6; 11:19; 12:8, 32, 40) and less frequently to the disciples (10:23; 13:37, 41). After 16:13 Jesus speaks about himself as the Son of Man only to the disciples (twenty times). Only in the last passage, 26:64, does he speak publicly once more of the Son of Man.[67] In terms of content, if we begin provisionally with the traditional rough division of the Son of Man sayings into sayings about the presently active, the suffering and rising, and the coming Son of Man,[68] then one can say that, except for the final trial scene in 26:64, Jesus never speaks publicly of the coming Son of Man. Nor does he speak of the suffering and rising Son of Man except in the paradoxical sign of Jonah of 12:40. Thus only the sayings about his present activity, almost all of which occur in the first part of the gospel, are public.[69] Relatively frequently the Son of Man references appear in polemical texts (9:6; 11:19; 12:8, 32, 40). Jesus speaks of the suffering, dying, and rising of the Son of Man in chaps. 17, 20, and 26 (with the exception of 12:40). He speaks of his coming in judgment in a concentrated way in 24:27–25:31 (seven times), but even before that he repeatedly intimates it to the disciples (10:23; 13:41; 16:27-28; 19:28). Thus the distribution of the Son of Man sayings throughout the Gospel of Matthew is in terms of their content not accidental.

Sources

For the most part Matthew takes over the Son of Man sayings from his sources Mark, Q, and the special material. A corresponding observation is that the expression "Son of Man" appears only in sayings of Jesus, never in narrative texts and, unlike "Son of God," "Lord," or "Son of David," never as direct address or confession. Grammatically, therefore, "Son of Man" is never the predicate,[70] but very frequently it is the subject. Thus very many Son of Man sayings make statements about what Jesus (= the Son of Man) does or suf-

---

67 Therefore, "Son of Man" is not, in contrast to the confessional title "Son of God," "'public' in character" (thus Jack Dean Kingsbury, "The Title 'Son of Man' in Matthew's Gospel," *CBQ* 73 [1975] 193–202, 201). While it is correct that Jesus with the help of this term describes "his relationship to the world" (ibid.), he does so to the disciples and only in small part directly to the world. "Public" is at the very least quite open to misunderstanding!

68 In terms of tradition history this rough division is

(to a degree!) correct, but it no longer reflects the Matthean understanding. Cf. below on the Son of Man in Matthew's narrative.

69 An exception is 20:28. The same thing is true for Mark.

70 Matthew 13:37 in the framework of the allegorical interpretation is an exception.

fers, but a Son of Man saying is never used to say who Jesus is.[71] Matthew omits no Son of Man saying from his sources, but in a few individual cases he substitutes "I" for ὁ υἱὸς τοῦ ἀνθρώπου (5:11; 10:32, cf. 16:21).[72] On the other hand, he creates additional Son of Man sayings redactionally, and he does so from all three "groups," but most frequently they are sayings about the coming activity of the Son of Man (13:41; 16:28; 24:30a; 25:31).[73]

Traditional Meaning
a. For an average Syrian in Matthew's day the expression ὁ υἱὸς τοῦ ἀνθρώπου would be strange and not understandable. It never appears in Greek in everyday language. For those who knew Aramaic—and that is inconceivable neither for the readers nor for the evangelist in Syria—there existed in everyday language the usually undetermined[74] term בַּר אֱנָשׁ in the sense of "a person, somebody" which, although infrequently, also could be used in connection with the first-person singular in the sense of "I as human," "a human being [thus also I]."[75] But the Christian, always doubly determined, expression ὁ υἱὸς τοῦ ἀνθρώπου is not a literal translation of that term and it must have been strange even to someone who spoke Aramaic. Thus on the level of everyday language ὁ υἱὸς τοῦ ἀνθρώπου was always a very spe-

cial, strange, and correspondingly mysterious expression.

b. In the biblical and Jewish religious tradition Dan 7:13 is the "basic text" ("one *like a* son of man"). Demonstrably Matthew deliberately made use of Daniel 7 for some Son of Man sayings. In 24:30 and 26:64 he has assimilated the Markan text he received to Dan 7:13-14[76] and thus strengthened the biblical reminiscence. A reminiscence of Dan 7:13-14 is also probable in 28:18-19. All other sayings about the coming Son of Man are not verbally connected to Daniel 7. Neither in my judgment can a direct literary influence of the similitudes of the Book of Enoch on Matthew be demonstrated.[77] However these findings are to be explained in the history of the tradition, this means that for Matthew and his readers their knowledge of the Son of Man was deepened with the aid of the Book of Daniel but did not primarily originate there.[78]

c. Who the "Son of Man" is Matthew and his readers know instead from Christian tradition. In it the expression is consistently doubly determined—a feature that gives it the character of a titular designation of an individual person.[79] From Christian tradition also comes the relatively fixed scope of the words and motifs that characterize

---

71 Kingsbury, "Figure of Jesus," 22–27.
72 The reverse is true after 16:13.
73 With 19:28 it is very unclear whether it is a traditional Son of Man saying or (what in my judgment is more likely) not. Of the remaining new formations, 13:37 and 16:13 are hardly to be associated with a certain "time," while in content 26:2 follows other sayings about the "handing over" of the Son of Man.
74 In Geza Vermes' list in Black, *Approach*, 310–28, there are only very scattered references for determined בַּר נָשָׁא and, of course, none for double determination.
75 Colpe, "ὁ υἱὸς τοῦ ἀνθρώπου," 403–4; more cautiously Joseph Fitzmyer, *A Wandering Aramean*, 152–53.
76 Ἐπὶ τῶν νεφελῶν τοῦ οὐρανοῦ (Mark: ἐν or μετά).
77 Thus Theisohn, *Richter*, 158–82, 198–200 for 13:40–43; 19:28; 25:31. In my view, however, Theisohn is able to make probable only the congruence of motifs and not literary dependence; cf. Hare, *Son of Man*.
78 I agree with Mogens Müller (*Der Ausdruck "Menschensohn" in den Evangelien*, 89–154) that the direct influence of Daniel 7 on Matthew (and Mark) is quite limited. One can draw different conclusions

about the history of the tradition. One may, e.g., assume with Müller that Jesus made use of the nontitular Aramaic expression for "someone, a human being" and that the church interpreted this usage in some passages on the basis of the LXX text of Daniel 7. However, along with the majority of German-speaking research one may assume that the church (or in my judgment Jesus) drew on an expectation of an eschatological Son of Man that had long since become independent of Daniel 7. Then Jesus' self-designation as "'the' Son of Man" is within Judaism a parallel to *1 Enoch* 70–71 and, in a sense, to the similitudes. This question is not significant for the interpretation of the Matthean usage.

79 As a rule the expression is used with the definite article in the similitudes of *1 Enoch* (cf. Matthew Black, *The Book of Enoch or I Enoch* [SVTP 7; Leiden: Brill, 1985] 206–7). The determination may be connected linguistically with the titular character and with the fact that Daniel 7 is applied "messianically" ("this [= the one mentioned in Daniel 7] Son of Man"). The dating of the similitudes continues to be controversial. In my judgment they are witnesses for a non-Christian "messianic" interpretation of Daniel 7 that is parallel to the Son of Man expecta-

both the sayings about the suffering and rising of the Son of Man[80] and those about his coming.[81] Such a solid field of words and motifs, like the constant double determination of the expression, must come from oral Christian tradition. We can conclude, therefore, that Matthew's Christian readers already knew many of the Son of Man sayings they already found in the gospel from the church's tradition. If they also were familiar with the sayings source or the Gospel of Mark, which is in my judgment possible but certainly was not the case with all of them, then that is all the more true. Thus *Matthew can presuppose a pre-knowledge among his readers*. This pre-knowledge came not primarily from the Book of Daniel or from Jewish tradition but from the traditional Son of Man sayings of Jesus. "Son of Man" was thus for them not an essentially meaningless expression with which Jesus referred to himself,[82] nor was it simply inherited from apocalyptic Messianic and judgment expectations;[83] it was a piece of "Christ talk" that was filled with reminiscences.[84] Among the reminiscences of the "Son of Man" for them was everything that Jesus had said about himself in his Son of Man sayings that were passed on. That means that at the first Matthean Son of Man saying the readers already knew that this Son of Man would die, rise, sit at the right hand of God, and come again as judge of the world. And the author Matthew knew that his readers knew this.[85]

"Son of Man" in Matthew's Narrative

The evangelist uses the expression in 9:6; 11:19; 12:8, 32, 40 in polemics of Jesus against his Jewish *oppo-*

nents. Did they understand what connotations Jesus (and the church!) associated with this expression? The answer to this question becomes possible through the macrotext of the gospel, and it must be: no. There is direct proof for that in the case of the "sign of Jonah." There the "Son of Man" is for them "that deceiver" (27:63).[86] An answer is also possible in the case of 12:8, for the Pharisees decide to destroy the Son of Man (12:14). At any rate, it is clear in the case of 11:19 and 12:32, for in both cases "this generation" speaks "a word against the Son of Man." In 8:19-20 "Son of Man" is combined with a reference to his homelessness which his followers must share in order to be able to understand him. Whatever the opponents of Jesus may have understood, they did not accept his claim that is connected with the expression "Son of Man." It corresponds to that reality that Matthew obviously and quite deliberately has Jesus speak only to his disciples about the future fate, about the resurrection, the exaltation, and the parousia of the Son of Man for judgment.[87] Only in 26:64 in the last Son of Man saying does he speak publicly to the high priest and his judges. There, however, it is too late. The Son of Man announces judgment on his judges, and they do not notice it. The high priest tears his garments—something that in the opinion of the evangelist and his readers he should do but certainly not because Jesus has blasphemed (26:65-66). A ghostly enigmatic, "Johannine" scene! Thus the expression "Son of Man" in general serves to constitute and to manifest the break between Jesus' opponents and the disciples. The disciples (or the readers of the gospel) here know more than Jesus' opponents do. They know into what abyss the latter are going

---

tion that the circles around Jesus (and John the Baptist?) presuppose.

80 Παραδίδωμι (5), ἐγείρω (3), χείρ (2). In parentheses are the number of occurrences in the corresponding Matthean logia.

81 Ἔρχομαι (7), δόξα (4), ἄγγελοι (4), καθίζω/κάθημαι (3). The word ἄγγελοι does not come from Dan 7:9-13. Especially the redactional saying in 25:31 contains almost all of these expressions and is thus a kind of summary of the Matthean concept of the coming of the Son of Man.

82 Thus the thesis of Hare (*Son of Man*) who for his part is influenced by, among others, Ragnar Leivestad ("Der apokalyptische Menschensohn ein theologisches Phantom," *ASTI* 6 [1968] 49–105).

83 Tödt (*Son of Man*, 92–94) and Marguerat (*Jugement*, 71) interpret in this direction. They emphasize in different ways "the strengthened connection with apocalyptic tradition" (Tödt, 92).

84 For Hare (*Son of Man*, 123–24, 181), on the other hand, "Son of Man" is a self-designation of Jesus which for the Matthean readers has no hidden connotations resulting from apocalyptic tradition or from Semitic thinking. Its significance is certainly "not trivial," but "an elevated term pointing to the mystery of Jesus' destiny" (ibid., 181–82). However, Hare wants to say no more than this. "Son of Man" remains for him a type of surname of Jesus, the original meaning of which was forgotten.

85 This is a classic example for how important reflection about the "implied reader" can be for understanding a text.

86 While they address Pilate as κύριος!

87 That may be related to the fact that in the "public" Sermon on the Mount in 5:11 Matthew replaces the Son of Man title with "I" and does not even use it in 7:21-23.

because they do not accept the claim of the Son of Man.[88] There is in the Gospel of Matthew a mystery of the Son of Man Jesus that arises through the narrative structure and that needs to be accented only occasionally by means of explicit commands to keep it secret (16:20; 17:9). The mystery is not that Jesus is the Son of Man; it is that only his disciples know that he is Son of God and know about the transfiguration, the coming resurrection and exaltation of the Son of Man and about his coming as judge.

We now turn to the perspective of the *disciples and readers*. They have a foreknowledge about the Son of Man Jesus. They know what it means that it is precisely the Son of Man who later is exalted to heaven and will come again as judge who does not have a home on earth (8:20) and is reproved by "this generation" as a glutton and a drunkard (11:19). In the figure of the disciples the readers experience how this knowledge came about. Jesus repeatedly took his disciples who followed him aside and taught them about his future suffering, dying, and rising. Thus they learned that he (or God) and not his enemies directed the story of his suffering. He comforted them (10:23; 16:28; 19:28) or warned them (13:41; 16:27; 24:37-44; 25:31-46) by pointing to his coming in judgment as Son of Man. It is true that in Matthew there is a special accent on the future coming of the Son of Man Jesus in judgment. He has especially elaborated the warning to the church. The resumption of 24:30-31 in 25:31-32 makes of the entire intervening section 24:32—25:30 a pointed parenetic application of the coming of the Son of Man announced in 24:29-31. In addition, with 13:40-43 and 25:31-46 Matthew goes beyond the mere Son of Man logia and gives suggestive and graphic *descriptions* of the judgment the Son of Man.[89]

At the same time the entirety of Jesus' instruction makes it clear that "Son of Man" by no means designates only the lord of judgment. *Instead, Jesus speaks of the "Son of Man" when he speaks of his story and his way.* As the Son of Man Jesus is the one who is homeless, who is despised, who has authority, who is handed

over and killed, who is risen, who is exalted, and who will come for judgment.[90] Thus Matthew also knows the exalted Son of Man. He speaks of him not only in the traditional saying of 26:64 but in substance also in 28:18. Not only the earthly one, but also the exalted one, exercises through his church the authority to forgive sins and to use the Sabbath for human well-being (9:6, 8; 12:1-8).[91] Correspondingly, in some of the sayings the evangelist created it is no longer possible to assign them clearly to one of the traditional "groups" of sayings: The "Son of Man" sows not only during his earthly activity but also as the exalted one through his disciples (13:37-41); his "Kingdom" ($\beta\alpha\sigma\iota\lambda\epsilon\acute{\iota}\alpha$) will not only be revealed in the future (16:28, cf. 25:31, 34), but it already determines in the present the whole world (13:41, cf. 11:27; 28:18). Jesus is Son of Man in his total activity (16:13). "Son of Man" is thus first of all a "*horizontal*" title with which Jesus describes his way through history in contrast to the confessional title "Son of God" that contains a "vertical" element. God himself reveals Jesus as the Son of God (1:22-23; 2:15; 3:17; 11:27; 16:17; 17:5) and the human response to this revelation is the Son of God confession. In the second place, "Son of Man" is also a *universal* title[92] that designates Jesus' path to the rule and judgment over the whole *world*, in contrast to the title "Son of David," which has a more limited scope and illuminates exclusively Jesus' relation to his people Israel.

A View of the History of Interpretation

In *Eph*. 20.2 Ignatius already combines the Son of Man Christology with the Son of God Christology of the confession of Rom 1:3-4 and thus arrives at the antithesis of "Son of Man" and "Son of God." It is a prelude to the ancient church's interpretation in terms of the doctrine of the two natures.[93] With him "Son of Man" is already the incarnate human being Jesus, the Son of David according to the flesh.[94] It is a long way from Matthew to Ignatius, who knew him but may not have loved him very much. Nevertheless a bridge is recognizable.[95] If in Matthew "Son of

---

88 This makes it again clear how poorly 12:32 fits into Matthew's theology. Cf. above, III A 2.1 on Matthew's understanding of that word.
89 Tödt, *Son of Man,* 78.
90 Similarly Kingsbury, "Figure of Jesus," 30–32.
91 Geist (*Menschensohn,* 340, 411) says not incorrectly that Son of Man in Matthew also has an ecclesial dimension.
92 Geist, *Menschensohn,* 368.
93 On the further development cf. Colpe ("ὁ υἱὸς τοῦ ἀνθρώπου," 476–77) and, differently, the excellent work by Weist ("Menschensohn") that surveys the

entire history of exegesis.
94 In characteristic difference from the genuinely gnostic usage where "Son of the man" (genealogically understood!) means the Son of the *God* Anthropos and thus Jesus' heavenly origin; cf. Colpe, "ὁ υἱὸς τοῦ ἀνθρώπου," 474–76.
95 Contra Weist ("Menschensohn," 30) who claims a merely formal reception of the concept of the Son of Man from the New Testament but without "being filled with New Testament contents."

Man" indicates "horizontally" the path Jesus takes through history to his rule as judge of the world and if, by contrast, "Son of God" provides the vertical perspective—thus lets Jesus be seen, as it were, with divine eyes—then the new version of this Christology in Ignatius and in the later ancient church indicates indeed a transformation of the Matthean statements but a transformation that in my judgment preserves more of Matthew's thought than does the Johannine transformation that identifies the Son of Man with the Son of God who came down from heaven. Later the expression "Son of Man" was understood not only in terms of the incarnation but also in terms of the birth of Jesus from Mary that according to the church's exegesis Daniel 7 already foresaw.[96] Thus Jesus was basically Son of Man with regard to his human nature. One was able to integrate the New Testament statements about the majesty of the Son of Man—for example, the statements concerning the coming judge of the world—on the basis of the *communicatio idiomatum.*[97]

---

96   See, e.g., Justin *Dial.* 76.1 (virgin birth); 100.3 (likewise, and Jesus as the second Adam); Irenaeus *Haer.* 3.16.3 (incarnation), 5 (ability to suffer); Tertullian *Marc.* 4.10.6–16 (Daniel predicts the virgin birth).

97   Weist ("Menschensohn," 68–69, 88–91) shows this with special impressiveness for Thomas Aquinas and J. Gerhard.

Literature

Baltensweiler, *Verklärung.*

George Henry Boobyer, *St. Mark and the Transfiguration Story* (Edinburgh: T. and T. Clark, 1942).

F. H. Daniel, "The Transfiguration (Mk 9:2-13 and Parallels)" (Diss., Vanderbilt, 1976) 97–157.

Erich Dinkler, *Das Apsismosaik von S. Apollinare in Classe* (Wissenschaftliche Abhandlungen der Arbeitsgemeinschaft für Forschung und Lehre des Landes Nordrhein-Westfalen 29; Cologne: Westdeutscher Verlag, 1964).

Donaldson, *Jesus,* 136–56.

Matthias Eichinger, *Die Verklärung Christi bei Origenes: Die Bedeutung des Menschen Jesus in seiner Christologie* (Vienna: Herder, 1969).

André Feuillet, "Les perspectives propres à chaque Évangéliste dans les Récits de la transfiguration," *Bib* 39 (1958) 281–301.

Geist, *Menschensohn,* 144–62.

Georges Habra, *La transfiguration selon les Pères Grecs* (Paris: Éditions S.O.S., 1973).

Adolf von Harnack, "Die Verklärungsgeschichte Jesu, der Bericht des Paulus (1 Kor 15,3ff) und die beiden Christusvisionen des Petrus," SPAW.PH (1922) 62–80.

Lange, *Erscheinen,* 415–36.

McGuckin, *Transfiguration.*

Ulrich B. Müller, "Die christologische Absicht des Markusevangeliums und die Verklärungsgeschichte," *ZNW* 64 (1973) 159–93.

Frans Neirynck, "Minor Agreements Matthew-Luke in the Transfiguration Story," in idem, *Evangelica: Gospel Studies* (Frans van Segbroeck, ed.; BEThL 60; Louvain: Peeters, 1982) 797–810.

Christoph Niemand, *Studien zu den Minor Agreements der synoptischen Verklärungsperikopen* (EHS 23.352; Frankfurt: Lang, 1989).

Johannes Maria Nützel, *Die Verklärungserzählung im Markusevangelium* (fzb 6; Würzburg: Echter Verlag, 1973) 275–88.

Onasch, *Idee.*

Sigfred Pedersen, "Die Proklamation Jesu als des eschatologischen Offenbarungsträgers," *NovT* 17 (1975) 241–64.

Harald Riesenfeld, *Jésus transfiguré* (Copenhagen: Munksgaard, 1947).

M. Sabbe, "La rédaction du récit de la transfiguration," in *La venue du Messie* (RechBib 6; Louvain: Desclée de Brouwer, 1962) 65–100.

Gertrud Schiller, *Ikonographie der christlichen Kunst* (5 vols.; Gütersloh: Mohn, 1966–80) 1.155–61.

I. Turowski, "Geschichte der Auslegung der synoptischen Verklärungsgeschichte in vornizänischer Zeit" (Diss., Heidelberg, 1966).

1   **And after six days Jesus takes Peter, James, and his brother John and leads them privately to a high mountain. 2/ And his figure changed[1] before them. And his face shone like the sun, and his clothing became white as light. 3/ And behold, Moses and Elijah appeared to them and talked with him. 4/ But Peter answered and said to Jesus, "Lord, it is good that we are here. If you want, I will make three huts here, one for you, one for Moses, and one for Elijah." 5/ While he was still speaking, behold, a bright cloud overshadowed them, and behold, a voice (came) and said, "This is my beloved Son in whom I was well pleased. Listen to him!" 6/ And when the disciples heard it they fell on their face and became very fearful. 7/ And Jesus came to them, touched them, and said, "Rise,[2] and do not be afraid." 8/ But when they lifted their eyes they saw no one except him, Jesus alone. 9/ And when they were coming down from the mountain, Jesus commanded them and said, "Tell no**

---

1   *Μεταμορφοῦσθαι* = Latin *transfigurari* is translated literally in most European languages (e.g., English "transfigure"). Since the Bible translations of the Reformation period (Luther, Zurich Bible, but also Eck and Emser) the German translation *"verkleren"* [to glorify, be radiant, be in ecstasy] or *"erkleren"* [to explain, declare] has prevailed. In Middle High German this word had the double meaning of *"erläutern"* (= *declarare,* to elucidate) and *"erhellen"* (= *dilucidare,* to illuminate, light up); cf. Matthias Lexer, *Mittelhochdeutsches Handwörterbuch* (Stuttgart: Hirzel, 1979) *s.v.* The Bible translations are determined in content by the idea of a body of light; in the Gospel of John, Luther is able to translate δοξάζω with *"verkleren"* (7:39; 12:16 and frequently). In today's German usage this word has been secular-

ized ("he looks radiant"); for this reason we avoid it in our translation. Cf. Friso Melzer, *Der christliche Wortschatz der deutschen Sprache* (Lahr: Kaufmann, 1951) 475–76. The linguistic history of the word "*Verklärung*" [transfiguration] itself shows how much we Westerners have lost the understanding of this story.

2   It is difficult to capture in translation the similarity in sound between ἐγέρθητε and ἐγερθῇ (v. 9).

one (anything about the) vision until the Son of Man is raised from the dead."

10   And the disciples asked him and said, "Why then do the scribes say that Elijah must come first?" 11/ But he answered and said, "Elijah indeed is coming and 'will restore everything.' 12/ But I say to you that Elijah has already come, and they have not recognized him, but they did with[3] him whatever they wanted. Thus the Son of Man will also suffer by them." 13/ Then the disciples understood that he spoke to them about John the Baptist.

Analysis   **Structure**

The pericope consists of the transfiguration story (vv. 1-9) and an appended discussion with the disciples (vv. 10-13). Although the partners in the conversation here seem to be "the" disciples and not simply the three disciples of v. 1, there is the impression of a single pericope. The disciples' question in v. 10 is tied to the transfiguration scene with the appearance of Elijah. Verse 9b, the announcement of the resurrection of the Son of Man, and v. 12, the announcement of his suffering, parallel one another. Verse 9 functions as a hinge between the two parts. The verse serves both as the conclusion of the transfiguration, corresponding to going up the mountain in v. 1, and as the transition to the discussion with the disciples.

The first part, the transfiguration story, shows traces of a chiastic structure. Corresponding to one another antithetically are: the ascent and descent from the mountain (vv. 1, 9), the transfigured Jesus in the company of Moses and Elijah, and Jesus alone, without them (vv. 2-3, 7-8). At the center is the voice of God (vv. 5-6).[4] It is obviously for Matthew also in substance the most important element, as the detailed reaction of the disciples demonstrates. Thus in contrast to the other Synoptics, he has clearly made the *audition* (and not the vision of the transfigured one!) the center of his story. The second part, the conversation of vv. 10-13, begins with a question from the disciples about the Jewish expectation of the return of Elijah. Jesus' answer consists of three parts.

First he confirms the Jewish expectation with words from the Bible (v. 11). Then he interprets it in his own words on the basis of what has actually happened (v. 12a, b). And finally he adds an announcement of the suffering of the Son of Man (v. 12c). Since that is something for which he had not been asked, the emphasis lies on this "extra." The concluding v. 13 corresponds to the introductory question of v. 10.

Once again the pericope is, as the preceding ones, very closely bracketed with its context. The connections backward to 16:13-23 are especially close. As in 16:14, Elijah appears. As in 16:16, 22, Peter is the speaker. As in 16:16-17, the subject is the Father's revelation of Jesus' sonship. As in 16:20, the disciples are to remain silent about what they have heard. The two Son of Man sayings in vv. 9b and 12c together correspond to the prediction of the suffering in 16:21. The entire pericope has the effect of a narrative "reprise" of 16:13-23.[5] Furthermore, the heavenly voice in v. 5 is identical with that of 3:17 in the baptism story. The "high" mountain is reminiscent of 4:8. John's suffering has already been mentioned in 11:12-14; 14:3-12. Our text also looks forward to the passion and Easter story. The points of connection in vv. 5-6 with the centurion's Son of God confession under the cross in 27:54 include not only οὗτος . . . υἱός but also the bystanders' fear (ἐφοβήθησαν σφόδρα). In the pericope of the empty tomb there appears not only the key word ἐγείρεσθαι ("to be raised") but also the address μὴ φοβεῖσθε ("do not be afraid") and the motif of the white garment (28:3-7).[6] There are also points of contact with the Gethsemane pericope.[7] It is further important that in the concluding pericope of Matt 28:16-20 there are references again not only to the mountain and the Son (28:16) but also (the only other place in the Gospel of Matthew) to Jesus' "coming to them" (28:18). Thus the points of contact with the passion and Easter story are numerous.

---

3   Ἐν is likely the original text since it is missing in Mark. It is not a Semitism but a formulation that is also possible in Greek with the meaning "to do something with someone." Cf. BAGD, *s.v.* ἐν, 2.

4   The Markan and Lukan versions are different. There it is the concluding high point.

5   Donaldson (*Jesus,* 153–54) says that Matt 17:1-9 is a demonstration of the revelation of Matt 16:16-17 in a "dramatic fashion."

6   In v. 2, D and others have strengthened the connection to 28:3: λευκὰ ὡς χιών.

7   As already in Mark. In Matthew the Gethsemane

pericope is the only other pericope in which Jesus is alone with the three disciples. A new catchword in comparison with Mark is ἐγείρεσθαι (v. 7; 26:46). Both pericopes conclude with a reference to the suffering of the Son of Man (v. 12b, 26:45b).

Source

The source is Mark 9:2-13. The most important Matthean change in the *transfiguration story* is the addition of vv. 6-7, telling of the disciples' fear and how Jesus raises them up. With the addition of vv. 6-7 our story gains a new conclusion that is positive for the disciples. Linguistically the addition comes from the pen of the evangelist;[8] however, it may be that in his copy of Mark the motif of the disciples' fear, which is very strange in Mark 9:6b, had been moved to a more suitable later place.[9] The common omission of the reference to the fuller in Mark 9:3b is also framed by a series of smaller agreements[10] so that a deutero-Markan recension is a possibility as the source for Matthew. However, we cannot be certain; many minor agreements in this text may be independent redaction.[11] The remaining unimportant differences between Matthew and Mark are almost always the result of Matthean redaction.[12]

Matthew has significantly changed the *conversation with the disciples*. He omits the disciples' lack of understanding in Mark 9:10 and thus relates the disciples' question in v. 10 immediately to the saying of Jesus in v. 9b. The suffering of the Son of Man appears no longer in Jesus' question (Mark 9:12b) but in his answer (v. 12c). The two references to fulfilling the scripture (Mark 9:12bα and the end of 9:13) are missing. Matthew has added the sentence about the understanding of the disciples in v. 13, much as in 16:12. On the whole the somewhat chaotic conversation in Mark has become much clearer in the Matthean version. The special vocabulary of the section is almost completely redactional.[13]

Interpretation

The transfiguration narrative is difficult to interpret. It contains a multitude of possible associations and reminiscences of biblical and Jewish materials, but there is no key in the tradition that completely unlocks it. Repeatedly there are individual statements that do not fit a certain background or a certain expectation or that fit several of them. Thus one has the impression that the transfiguration story is distinctively "of manifold meanings." A related factor is that its origin and the oldest history of its tradition are hidden. Matthew has worked on the story redactionally and also integrated it into his macrotext. The result is the creation of new accents without excluding the traditional possibilities of interpretation.

Tradition

We will begin by attempting to trace the interpretive horizons that were present in the tradition. They correspond to the types of interpretation of the traditional story found in the more recent research that, admittedly, do not appear in pure form but are overlapping.

a. The transfiguration story is reminiscent of the *Exodus tradition* and especially of *Moses*. Moses goes up the cloud-covered Mount Sinai with Aaron, Nadab, and Abihu. On the seventh day God calls him out of the cloud to himself (Exod 24:1, 9, 15-16). The exhortation "listen to him" (ἀκούετε αὐτοῦ) spoken at the

---

8   Redactional may be: ἀκούσας, μαθητής, πίπτω, πρόσωπον (26:39!), φοβέομαι, σφόδρα (27:54!), προσέρχομαι, ἄπτω, ἐγείρω, cf. vol. 1, Introduction 3.2. Πίπτω ἐπὶ πρόσωπον, φοβέομαι σφόδρα, μὴ φοβεῖσθε and ἐπαίρω τοὺς ὀφθαλμούς are LXX expressions.

9   Along with the identical but differently located ἐφοβήθησαν, the finite form ἐπεσκίασ(ζ)εν αὐτοὺς in v. 5 par. Luke 9:34 is a notable minor agreement. The differently formulated introductory genitive absolute (ibid.) is probably redactional in Matthew but not necessarily in Luke.

10   The omission of τόν, μόνους (Mark 9:2), and στίλβοντα (Mark 9:3; πρόσωπον v. 2 par. Luke 9:29; the change in the order of Moses and Elijah.

11   Frans Neirynck ("Minor Agreements Matthew-Luke in the Transfiguration Story," 797–810) advocates this for all minor agreements; a deutero-Markan recension for a part of the minor agreements is advocated by Ennulat (*Agreements*, 200–208) and the detailed work by Christoph Niemand (*Studien zu den*

Minor Agreements der synoptischen Verklärungsperikopen; a special tradition for Luke is assumed by Tim Schramm, *Der Markusstoff bei Lukas* (SNTSMS 14; Cambridge: Cambridge University Press, 1971) 136–39. The number of the minor agreements in Matt 17:1-9 is extremely high (fourteen).

12   Cf. vol. 1, Introduction 3.2 on λάμπω, πρόσωπον (both only weakly redactional, but cf. 13:43!), δέ, ἰδού, μετά, ἀποκριθεὶς δέ + subject, εἶπον, κύριε, εἰ θέλεις, ὧδε, αὐτοῦ λαλοῦντος (taken over from Mark 5:35; cf. 12:46; 26:47), λέγων, ἐντέλλομαι (only weakly redactional), ἕως οὗ, ἐγείρω. The hapax legomenon ὅραμα that occurs twenty-four times in the LXX Daniel as well as elsewhere is also not Matthean. The evidence for φῶς, φωτεινός is not clear.

13   Cf. vol. I introduction 3.2 on μαθητής, οὖν, ὁ δὲ ἀποκριθεὶς εἶπεν, μέν - δέ, οὕτως, μέλλω, τότε,

end by the heavenly voice also is reminiscent of Moses the prophet (cf. Deut 18:15). When Moses descended from Sinai, his face was radiant (Exod 34:29-35); he also had experienced a kind of transformation. Does the transfiguration story want to show Jesus as a new Moses, perhaps as the eschatological end-time prophet?[14] However, neither the Son of God title nor the fact that in v. 3 the old Moses appears in heavenly form along with Elijah fits this interpretation. A number of details also do not fit Exodus 24.[15] The transformation of Moses in Exodus 34 is also something different. It became visible after God had spoken with him, and it did not immediately end, while Jesus' transformation took place before God spoke and was only temporary. The cloud calls attention not only to the Sinai scene but beyond that is a widespread biblical symbol for God's presence. Not only did it cover Sinai; it accompanied Israel on its wilderness journey, lay over the tent of meeting (Exod 40:34-38), and filled the temple (1 Kgs 8:10-11). In short, our story doubtless contains reminiscences of the Sinai traditions, but it cannot be understood exclusively on that basis.

b. According to a Jewish tradition the cloud also lay over *Mount Moriah* when Abraham sacrificed his "beloved Son" Isaac (Gen 22:2, 12, 16).[16] That is a second biblical story our scene might recall. Especially the "beloved Son" of the heavenly voice is reminiscent of the sacrifice of Isaac and not of Moses on Sinai.[17] On the whole, however, this story is quite different from the transfiguration of Jesus; all the other features of the Moriah narrative do not fit.

c. The transfiguration story is reminiscent of an *inthronization*. It seems to me that our most important parallel here is not the ancient Egyptian inthronization ceremony with its three stages of the exaltation and endowment of the god-king with heavenly life, his presentation before the heavenly powers, and the transfer of power,[18] although it has also been employed for the understanding of other New Testament texts.[19] If we apply it to our text, there are difficulties. While the transfiguration of Jesus (v. 2) could correspond to the first stage, the exaltation and endowment with heavenly life, Jesus' encounter with the heavenly figures, Moses and Elijah, is not a presentation before heavenly powers. The third stage, the transfer of power to the king, does not occur at all in the transfiguration story. We are on safer ground if we think of Ps 2:7, which stands behind the heavenly voice of v. 5. It is a psalm that comes from the enthronement ritual of the Jerusalem kings and that was a major influence on the New Testament Son of God Christology. In the early confession of Rom 1:3-4 Jesus' "inthronization" as Son of God was connected with the resurrection (cf. Acts 13:33-34). It meant at the same time Jesus' exaltation and his association with divine spirit and power. The voice of God in v. 5 is especially to be interpreted against this background. In my judgment this explains why later in the *Apocalypse of Peter* the "transfiguration" was associated with Jesus' ascension.[20] Then, of course, the conclusion of the story in Matthew becomes especially conspicuous. Instead of the heavenly world-ruler, suddenly only "Jesus alone" is left (v. 8), who speaks to his disciples of the suffering of the Son of Man. Other motifs also, such as the mountain or the cloud, can be integrated into this view only with great effort,[21] while others, such as the six days and Peter's

συνίημι, βαπτιστής. The future ἀποκαταστήσει corresponds to Mal 3:23 (LXX). On ἐπιγινώσκω cf. vol. 1, II A 3.2 on 7:15-23, n. 3. Unusual is πάσχω ὑπό (16:21 ἀπό).

14   Pesch, *Markusevangelium* 2.76–77 and Davies, *Setting,* 50–56. Strauss (*Life,* 544–46) speaks of a direct transfer of Moses characteristics to Jesus.

15   The "transformation" of Moses in Exodus 34 became visible after God had spoken with him, and it continued. However, Jesus was "transformed" first and then only temporarily. Moses was accompanied not only by the three companions but also by seventy elders, and then he stepped alone into the cloud.

16   *Tg. Yer. I* on Gen 22:4; *Qoh. Rab.* 9.7 § 1 (= Freedman-Simon 8.231).

17   Cf. David Flusser, *Jesus* (New York: Herder and Herder, 1969) 95–97.

18   Especially Ulrich B. Müller ("Die christologische Absicht des Markusevangeliums und die Verklärungsgeschichte," 159–93, 185–87) following

Eduard Norden (*Die Geburt des Kindes* [3d ed.; Darmstadt: Wissenschaftliche Buchgesellschaft, 1958] 116–28).

19   Its aftereffects have been seen in the Fourth Eclogue of Virgil and in the christological hymn of 1 Tim 3:16. According to Philipp Vielhauer ("Erwägungen zur Christologie des Markusevangeliums," in idem, *Aufsätze zum Neuen Testament* [ThBü 31; Munich: Kaiser, 1965] 199–214) it determines the Christology of Mark; the three stages are Mark 1:9-11; 9:2-8; 15:39.

20   *Ethiopic Apoc. Pet.* 15–17 = NTApoc 2.680–83.

21   For the mountain Donaldson (*Jesus,* 147) remembers Zion as the place of Yahweh's throne and the inthronization of the Judean king. For ἐπισκιάζειν by the cloud Eduard Norden (*Die Geburt des Kindes,* 92–97) recalls the miraculous birth of the child of the gods. However, nothing is said here about a birth.

huts, cannot be integrated at all.

d. For many scholars the transfiguration story has been reminiscent of the *Feast of Tabernacles*.[22] The obvious point of contact is in the "huts" ($\sigma\kappa\eta\nu\alpha\acute{\iota}$) that Peter wants to build for the three heavenly men. Furthermore, the Feast of Tabernacles begins on the sixth day after the Day of Atonement (cf. v. 1 with Lev 23:27, 34). However, the points of contact are sparse.[23] Above all, the heavenly beings do not even respond to Peter's suggestion about building huts. We probably cannot make these huts the basis of an interpretation.

e. Our story recalls Jewish and Christian future hopes, especially the *transformation into the future resurrection body*. These reminiscences are important for vv. 2-3. Paul and Jewish apocalyptists (1 Cor 15:51-52;[24] *2 Apoc. Bar.* 49.2-3; 51.3, 5, 9-12) speak of a future transformation into an eschatological body of glory. The righteous will have white garments and radiant faces in the new world (cf. Dan 12:3; *1 Enoch* 62.15-16; 4 Ezra 7:97 [face like the sun]; *2 Apoc. Bar.* 51.3).[25] However, these points of contact are not specific. A glorious appearance and white garments are general characteristics of belonging to the heavenly world; cf., for example, the angels. Associations with future hopes are also awakened by the figure of Elijah, who according to Mal 3:23 and Sir 48:10 is to come to restore Israel. Occasionally one has also thought of the reappearance of Moses.[26] On the whole, the returning Elijah is the forerunner, while the "historical" Moses is the prototype of the Messiah; hardly ever do they appear together in purely Jewish

texts. One sees nothing in our story of the tasks and functions that according to Jewish expectation they will have at the end of time. They appear simply as representatives of the heavenly world and speak with the transfigured Jesus. Fittingly, both are believed in Judaism to have been carried up to heaven.[27] In short, the associations with eschatological hopes for the future which our text permits are not specific. There are features that *also* can be interpreted eschatologically, and with the appearance of Elijah the disciples were also confronted with Jewish future hopes (v. 10). However, these are at the same time also generally "heavenly" features. Today, therefore, most have abandoned the previously popular interpretation of our story as an anticipated parousia.[28]

Result: The transfiguration story given to Matthew is a "polyvalent" story that permits several possibilities of association. The most important are the features taken over from the Sinai theophany (a above) and the inthronization idea (c). Jesus is enthroned as Son of God and revealed on the new "Sinai." The other possibilities of association we have outlined are more likely (cf. b, e), or even clearly (cf. d), marginal. Our story is a very independent, unique, christological legend that by no means was created by the simple transfer of other motifs and images to Jesus. Matthew changed it by giving it a different conclusion with vv. 6-7 and the close connection with vv. 10-13.

---

22 See, e.g., Harald Riesenfeld (*Jésus transfiguré*), who interprets the Feast of Tabernacles on the basis of the ancient Near Eastern enthronement festival as the Mowinckel school understood it; Baltensweiler, *Verklärung* (cf. below n. 80).

23 Daube (*New Testament*, 30–32) reminds us that in Aramaic the hut is מְטַלְלְתָא ("roofing"), derived from the verb טלל = to cover. In Aramaic the word is often used for the presence of the Shekinah or the "cloud of glory" and can be rendered in Greek with ἐπισκιάζω. To be sure, the image then is not correct. In vv. 4-5 it is not the "roofing," i.e., the hut, that the cloud of light "covers." HbrMt also thinks of the Shekinah or the tent of meeting; there σκηνή is translated with מִשְׁכָּן (not סכה). We are far removed here from the idea of the Feast of Tabernacles. Cf. also below, n. 35.

24 To be sure, Paul uses the "Hellenistic" verb μετα-μορφοῦσθαι quite differently; cf. Rom 12:2; 2 Cor 3:18.

25 Further references in Str–B 1.752–53.

26 Joachim Jeremias, "Μωϋσῆς," *TDNT* 4 (1967) 856.

27 On Moses' assumption into heaven, which in Judaism probably was a rather widespread idea that, however, eventually did not prevail, cf. Josephus *Ant.* 4.320–23; for (sparse) later Jewish references see Str-B 1.753–54, and Klaus Haacker and Peter Schäfer, "Nachbiblische Traditionen vom Tod des Mose," in Otto Betz, Klaus Haacker, and Martin Hengel, eds., *Josephus-Studien: Untersuchungen zu Josephus, dem antiken Judentum und dem Neuen Testament: Otto Michel zum 70 Geburtstag gewidmet* (Göttingen: Vandenhoeck & Ruprecht, 1974) 166–74. On the *Assumption of Moses*, which in my view is a positive witness for this (name and 10:12!), cf. Egon Brandenburger in *Apokalypsen* (JSHRZ 5; Gütersloh: Mohn, 1974), 61–62.

28 George Henry Boobyer, *St. Mark and the Transfiguration Story*.

Matthew

■ **1** We turn now to the Matthean level where what initially interests us is the Matthean interpretation of the *figure of Christ*. Jesus leads the three disciples up a "high mountain." The recollection of 4:8-10 is clear, where on a high mountain Satan offered world rule to the Son of God.[29] Jesus has gone not the Satanic way of world dominance but the way of obedience laid out for him by God. He has encountered hostility in Israel, and the way to death is laid out for him (16:21). At this point in his story Matthew designs a positive counterimage to 4:8-10. The transfiguration is also a contrasting image to the life of Jesus in hiddenness, homelessness, and hostility.

■ **9** In v. 9 he designates this image with an apocalyptic expression[30] as ὅραμα, as a "revealed vision." He does so in the interest not of the modern historical concern to explain our story in terms of a "mere" vision but of the theological concern that seeing the glorified Jesus is a "vision" granted by *God*, not simply an ordinary part of the disciples' life with Jesus. At issue is a special revelation of God that, contrary to everyday experiences, discloses the truth about Jesus from God's perspective.

■ **6-7** Matthew stylizes this vision in the way the apocalyptic seer in the Book of Daniel received revelation. After seeing the "vision" and hearing the "voice," Daniel, full of terror, "falls on his face"; but the angel "touches" him, "wakes him up," and says, "do not be afraid" (Dan 8:16-17; 10:9-12, 16-19).[31]

■ **2** But what is the content of this revelation? It is a vision of Christ in the future glorious appearance of the Risen One. Just as "his face shone like the sun," the righteous will some day shine in the kingdom of the Father (13:43). His garments become white like light. White is the angel's garment on Easter morning (28:3); and the cloud out of which God himself speaks (v. 5) is full of light.

■ **3** It is probable that Moses[32] and Elijah here do not represent the Law and Prophets, as older[33] and more recent[34] exegesis assumed. The end of v. 5 = Deut 18:15 is more reminiscent of the prophet Moses than of the lawgiver; and why should Elijah be *the* typical prophet? As was the case already in the tradition, they are simply representatives of the heavenly world.

■ **5** And all of this is interpreted by God himself, who is present in the cloud with his bright power and who overshadows the three heavenly figures.[35] He speaks as a voice out of the cloud of light and presents Jesus as his Son. Matthew repeats here the voice at the baptism (3:17) and thus elevates Jesus above Moses and Elijah, who are now no longer mentioned.[36] The readers of the gospel know that the Son of God[37] is the one "with" whom God has acted in a unique, special way (1:18-25; 2:15; 3:17). He is the one who rejected satanic rule and was obedient to his Father in a unique way (4:1-11). They sense that he is the one to whom God has given all dominion and all knowledge (11:27). They will soon experience that he is the Son of Man whom obedience to the Father will lead into suffering and into death (17:12). It is he whom the divine voice and the vision granted to the disciples reveal in his true Easter glory.

---

29   Matthew 16:23 was already reminiscent of the same section 4:8-10.

30   Cf. above, n. 12.

31   Cf. in addition Ezek 1:28-2:2; *1 Enoch* 14.14, 25; 15.1; Rev 1:17.

32   That Moses is placed first can be explained (as in Luke) with the restoration of the "historical" order.

33   See, e.g., *Didascalia* 26 = Achelis-Flemming, 129; Jerome, 148; John Chrysostom, 56.1 = *PG* 58.550 (Moses testifies against the Jews who accuse Jesus of violating the law). The disappearance of Moses and Elijah is often interpreted to mean that now the time of Law and Prophets is past (since Jerome, 150).

34   See, e.g., Sigfred Pedersen, "Die Proklamation Jesu als des eschatologischen Offenbarungsträgers," 241–64, 255, 259; André Feuillet, "Les perspectives propres à chaque Évangéliste dans les Récits de la transfiguration," 281–301, 293; Lange, *Erscheinen*, 426.

35   Ἐπεσκίασεν αὐτούς: perhaps in deliberate contrast to the tent of meeting (Exod 40:34-35) or the Jerusalem temple (1 Kgs 8:10-11), which Moses or the priests are not permitted to enter as long as the divine cloud "overshadows" it.

36   Already Marcion has emphasized αὐτοῦ: listen to *him*, not Moses or Elijah (Tertullian *Marc.* 4.22.1 = CSEL 47.491). Without knowing who their ancestor was in this regard, many have repeated the idea: e.g., Calvin 2.201–2; Lapide, 336 ("non Mosen, qui iam abijt"). The text does not say that, although it emphasizes only Jesus as the Son. Correctly Strabo, 144: Moses and Elijah are *servi*.

37   Cf. vol. 1, I B 1.2 on 3:17 (Son of God).

And it is no accident that our pericope is linked not only to the story of Easter morning (28:3-7) but also to the concluding epiphany of Jesus on the Galilean mountain (28:16, 18-19). Thus the heavenly voice which for Matthew is the center of the story directs the readers formally to the macrotext of the gospel that explains who the Son of God is. In terms of content this is of great significance. It is the story of the chosen one, of the obedient one, the suffering and risen one that reveals the Son of God, not alone and not primarily his heavenly glory that is seen only here on the mountain. It is he whom the disciples are to *hear*. In the narrative the "listen to him" (ἀκούετε αὐτοῦ) of the divine voice is, as it were, God's finger pointing down from the mountain. Below, on the level of everyday life, the Son of God will proclaim to his disciples the will of the Father and the gospel of the kingdom. It is important for Matthew that he will speak to them of the suffering of the Son of Man right after the transfiguration on the mountain (vv. 11-12). It is just as important as the fact that after this "high point" on the mountain the three disciples will next appear together in the Gethsemane scene, that is, at the absolute "low point" of the story of Jesus (26:37).

■ **4** Matthew also interprets the *disciples' perspective* quite intentionally. Peter, again the disciples' spokesman, overwhelmed by seeing the heavenly figures, wants to build "huts." The thought is not of the tabernacles of the festival, nor is it scarcely of the heavenly mansions for the righteous (cf. *1 Enoch* 41.2; John 14:2). Either it means, quite simply, dwellings for the heavenly guests,[38] in which case Peter wants to receive the heavenly beings in an inappropriate, earthly way. That heavenly beings should live in tents on mountains is an impossible thought![39] Or he is thinking of heavenly beings dwelling on the mountain, in the same way that the Shekinah resided in the temple or in the holy city (cf. Ezek 37:27; Zech 2:14; Rev 21:3).[40] In that case he would like to keep the heavenly beings on this mountain. May we surmise even more? As in 16:22, does he want to protect Jesus

from suffering in Jerusalem?[41] Matthew leaves it open. Unlike Mark, he is not interested in blaming Peter.[42]

■ **5-6** Instead, the presence of God develops on this mountain its own dynamic, and it simply ignores Peter's suggestion. The cloud seizes the three heavenly beings, while the disciples remain outside with their thoughts of huts and hear only the voice. It is so powerful that they fall on the ground in fear. It is the divine glory and truth that throws them to the ground and instills fear in them.

■ **7-8** And now they *experience* the personal attention of the Son of God. They still have their faces to the ground from terror over the encounter with the divine when someone touches them, lifts them up, and takes away their fear. It is no longer the heavenly transformed Jesus who does this but the one whom they can see without terror, Jesus "alone," in his human form. In this form Jesus encounters the disciples.

■ **9** While coming down from the mountain he commands them to be silent about their mountain experience until his resurrection. As in 16:20, the command to silence serves to define the boundaries against outsiders. The revelation on the mountain is granted only to the disciples, who as a special group are contrasted with the people. It is temporarily in effect until the resurrection again sheds light on the character of the mountain experience. It is a part of the anticipated Easter glory; therefore one can understand and proclaim it only on the basis of Easter. Easter includes the way to the passion. That the Son of Man is the Son of God in the glory that was revealed on the mountain is only right and true when the Son of God as Son of Man in humiliation has gone the way of suffering. Now Jesus will speak to the disciples about this; they are to "listen to him" (v. 5b). Both aspects belong together in the Matthean image of Jesus, so that the "huts" where the divine dwells are erected in the low places and not on the high mountaintops that only a few disciples reach.

■ **10-13** Thus the theological meaning of the disciples' conversation in vv. 10-13 also becomes clear. Verse 10

---

38 Gaechter (568) correctly points out that according to Arab custom every eminent guest among the Bedouins gets his own tent.

39 Impressively later Proclus of Constantinople *Orationes* 8.3 = *PG* 65.769: "a tent for Christ who with me stretched out the heavens?! A tent for him who with me laid the foundations of the earth?! . . . A

tent for Adam who has no father, and for the God who has no mother?!"

40 Cf. above nn. 23, 35.

41 Impressively John Chrysostom, 56.2 = *PG* 58.552: Jesus will certainly be on the mountain, and no one will learn where he is.

42 Mark 9:6 is omitted. In v. 4 Matthew adds a pious εἰ

relates back to the whole transfiguration pericope. The disciples have seen on the mountain the transformed Son of God Jesus and Elijah, and they now remember the Jewish expectation that Elijah must come "first," that is, before the end.[43] The readers in Matthew's church may also have been thinking that Jewish enemies were able to use this expectation as an argument against Jesus' messiahship: Since Elijah has not yet returned, Jesus cannot be Messiah and Son of God.[44] In his answer in v. 11 Jesus first takes up the Jewish expectation and formulates it "biblically" with the words of Mal 3:23 (LXX). As there, $\dot{\alpha}\pi o\kappa\alpha\tau\alpha\sigma\tau\acute{\eta}\sigma\epsilon\iota$ appears in the future tense. Did Matthew think that Elijah would appear again before the parousia of Jesus?[45] That is improbable, since the order of the two returns of Elijah in vv. 11-12 would then be reversed. The future tense is probably only adaptation to the biblical wording and understood from the temporal standpoint of the prophet Malachi.[46] In v. 12a, b Jesus contrasts the prediction of the scripture with the fulfillment that is emphatically formulated as his own word. Malachi's prediction has already been fulfilled with the coming of John the Baptist.[47] The disciples already know that the Baptist is the returned Elijah (11:10, 14). In v. 13 Matthew recalls this once more and thus again makes clear how it is through the "instruction" of Jesus that the disciples come to understanding. Contrasted with them are the Jewish opponents who "have" not "recognized" who John was and "did with him what they wanted."[48] However, the center of Jesus' instruction is in v. 12b: The Son of Man Jesus must also go the same way of suffering that John the Baptist went.[49]

Thus in this instruction after the transfiguration on the mountain Jesus points out that the way to the mountain where the Risen One again will meet them can only be a way through suffering that is the consequence of the Son's obedience to the Father. At the end of the way, the cross, God will be present with his signs (27:51-53), and the centurion will recognize Jesus as Son of God (27:54). And then, after Easter, on the mountain, God will grant all power to his Son (28:16-20). John the Baptist already has gone the way through suffering. Jesus and his disciples will have to travel it. Christologically the risen Son of God, whose glory the disciples were able to sense on the mountain, and the suffering Son of Man, whose way to Jerusalem lies before them, must remain together.[50]

History of Interpretation

The transfiguration story has had an especially intensive influence in the Greek and Russian church.[51] It is closely identified with the Feast of Metamorphosis that has been celebrated in the East since the sixth century and is among the twelve great church festivals.[52] The most

---

$\vartheta\acute{\epsilon}\lambda\epsilon\iota\varsigma$ to Peter's proposal.

43   For a survey of the Jewish material see Str–B 4.779–98.

44   Demonstrated by Justin *Dial.* 49.1

45   Justin *Dial.* 49.2. Many of the church's interpreters (e.g., John Chrysostom, 57.1 = *PG* 58.559–60) think that at his second parousia Elijah will especially convert unbelieving Israel. The Reformation exegesis abandons the thesis of the *duplex Elia* (Thomas Aquinas, *Lectura* no. 1447) and advocates the interpretation given above. See, e.g., Calvin 2.204.

46   Similar future tenses, e.g., are in 1:23 and 12:18-21.

47   Since the "restoration" in light found in the later rabbinic expectations included, among other things, the restoration of the purity of Israel, of peace, of the proclamation of the true halakah, and the preaching of repentance (Str–B 4.792–97), one could well combine the Baptist's activity with it.

48   It does not bother Matthew that it was not the scribes who killed John; he includes them in the common negative front of Jesus' Jewish opponents.

49   Cf. above, II D 1.2 on 11:11-14, II D 1.3 on 11:16b-19d, and III C 1.2 summary on the parallel between the fate of the Baptist and the fate of Jesus.

50   Cf. the excursus on 16:21-28, no. 4.

51   On the history of the early interpretation cf. Matthias Eichinger, *Die Verklärung Christi bei Origenes: Die Bedeutung des Menschen Jesus in seiner Christologie,* and I. Turowski, "Geschichte der Auslegung der synoptischen Verklärungsgeschichte in vornizänischer Zeit" (with purely dogmatic interest in the relationship of history and revelation). Georges Habra (*La transfiguration selon les Pères Grecs*) examines the post-Nicene fathers (systematically constructed; for the most part it is only with difficulty that one can recognize his sources as interpretations of the text of Matthew 17) as does McGuckin (*Transfiguration*) (with text examples reproduced in detail).

52   In the Western church the transfiguration belongs only to the lesser festivals (6 August).

important witnesses of the history of our text's influence are the festival sermons of the Metamorphosis[53] and, along with them, the theme's artistic representations in icons, murals, and pictures.[54] Onasch is of the opinion that the "transfiguration" has something of the same central meaning for the Eastern church that the idea of justification has for the West.[55] However, "transfiguration" means not our story, Matt 17:1-13, but the mystical and hope-filled participation of the believers in the reality of Christ's resurrection, precisely what our story symbolizes. The sermons and icons are important, because they are able to incorporate both levels which were fundamental for the Matthean story—the christological level of the revelation of the glory of Christ and the level of the disciples who share in the power of the metamorphosis. By looking at the history of the text's influence we will see that only when both levels are related to each other—only when the readers of this text let Jesus lead them to the mountain and again back down from the mountain does an understanding become possible which is appropriate to the text itself.

1. According to the opinion of the interpreters, the *christological* issue is the revelation of the *deity* of Christ. "He led them up the mountain in order to show them the divine glory." The prophets Moses and Elijah had not previously known Jesus' humanity and so they rejoiced, but for the apostles the deity of Jesus was something new.[56] John Chrysostom writes, "he opened a little of his deity and showed them the divinity within."[57] On the mountain "the entire Trinity appears . . . , Christ the Son in glorious form; the Father in the voice . . . , the Holy Spirit in the cloud of light that overshadowed them." In formulating it

this way Luther takes up the church's entire interpretation.[58] He thinks thereby not of a direct revelation of the deity that, of course, is not bodily and thus not available to the senses; what is revealed is only a "derived" glory that "passes over" to him "as when the air is illuminated by the sun."[59]

2. However, the christological statements never remained an abstract doctrine; the church's interpreters always highlighted in various ways what we have called the disciples' perspective in Matthew. Unlike the evangelist, however, they spoke not only of the disciples' terror in the presence of the divine but also of their own participation in the transfiguration. They were interested not simply in the transfiguration of Christ but in a certain way also in their own *transfiguratio* that *consistit in configuratio cum Christo*.[60] A Reformed thinker, Musculus, formulates: "We too must share in it, for the kingdom of Christ is in us. Thus his majesty and glory must shine in us also."[61] The festival of the Metamorphosis is the festival of Christ and at the same time our festival as well—the festival of the future "deification of nature, of its transformation into a better condition, of its ecstasy and of its ascent from the natural to the supernatural."[62] Thus one also understood the transfiguration story as a model of an experience of the believers, and one could speak of their ascent up the mountain, their experience on the mountain, and their renewed descent. The apsis mosaic of San Apollinare in Classe in Ravenna (seventh century) expresses it symbolically. Portrayed here is not only the transfigured Christ (in the form of a cross) with Elijah and Moses and the apostles (in the form of lambs) but also the local saint, Apollinaris, in the posture of prayer and the congregation in the form of lambs. Does that

---

53 Of primary importance are Ephraem Syrus, *Speech on the Transfiguration* = BKV 1/37.184–95; Pseudo-John Chrysostom *In transfigurationem* = PG 61.713–16; Proclus of Constantinople *Orationes* 8 = PG 65.763–72; Cyril of Alexandria *Hom. div.* 9 = PG 77.1009–16; Basileios of Seleucia *Or.* 40 = PG 85.451–62; Timothy of Antioch *In crucem et in transfigurationem* = PG 86.255–66; John of Damascus *Homilae in transfigurationum* = PG 96.545–76; Andreas of Crete *Oratione* 7 = PG 97.931–58; Pantaleon of Constantinople *Oratione* 2–3 = PG 98.1247–60; Gregorios Palamas *Homilae* 34–35 = PG 151.423–49; from the West, Leo the Great *Sermo* 51 = FC 93.218–24. McGuckin (*Transfiguration,* 172–235) offers selected translations.

54 Cf. Gertrud Schiller, *Ikonographie der christlichen*

Kunst 1.155–61. On the *metamorphosis* as a basic element of the entire phenomenon of icon painting cf. Onasch, *Idee der metamorphosis,* 45–65.

55 Onasch, *Idee der metamorphosis,* 7.

56 Ephraem Syrus, *Speech on the Transfiguration,* 5.7 = BKV 1/37.185 (quotation), 187.

57 *Hom.* 21 = PG 63.700.

58 *WA* 38.660–61, cf. Strabo, 144.

59 Thomas Aquinas *S. th.* 3, q.45, a.2 corpus. The scholastics speak of the *claritas* as a "*dos*" of the body of glory, that "*dispensative*" shines in Christ, as "*divinitatis . . . index*" (Lapide, 330).

60 Lapide, 331.

61 424.

62 Andreas of Crete *Oratione* 7 = PG 97.933.

change the perspective of the text?[63] I think that, as with Matthew, it depends on *how* the experiences on the mountain are related to the descent from the mountain into the "plain."

a. The *ascent up the mountain* includes a renunciation of earthly cares and desires. The mountain is the "mountain of wisdom," and what is at stake in the six days is "looking no more at what is visible and . . . loving the world no more."[64] What is at stake is "leaving the dust for the dust, transcending the body of humility and stretching out to the high and divine mirror of love and thus seeing what is not seeable."[65] Especially influential here was the Lukan version of the text, because in Luke 9:28-29 Jesus goes up the mountain with the disciples in order to pray. The ascent consists in frequent and intensive prayer, for "prayer is the transformation of the soul."[66]

b. The statements about what happens *on the mountain* are very reserved. It is a spiritual, *mystical experience*. Much is said by Origen. The issue is "building huts" not externally but "in oneself for the word of God." The issue is that the bright cloud which is the Spirit "protects, enlightens and shines on . . . the righteous."[67] They are reserved, because the fathers in general were well aware that Christ's transfiguration on the mountain was an anticipation of eschatological glory[68] and that such experiences are possible in this life only fragmentarily. Thus one of the most impressive transfiguration texts speaks of the end-time when the believers will have the form of angels and will be united eternally with Christ:

[We will be] filled in holy contemplations of his visible theophany that shines on us with brilliant rays as on the disciples in that most divine metamorphosis. From him we share in the enlightenment of the mind in a sense that is free of passion and matter and in the unification that transcends the spirit. . . . But for the present, as far as we have the possibility, we depend on appropriate symbols for the divine.[69]

Maximus the Confessor speaks of the present revelation of the disciples: "Even before the end of their earthly life [the disciples moved] from the flesh to the spirit." They "learned mystically that the splendor of his face . . . that transcends the power of all eyes is a symbol of his divinity that transcends all understanding, or intelligence, or essence, or knowledge."[70] These, however, are not physical experiences; the Greek exegesis always emphasized that the light of the figure of Jesus and of his garments was not a natural light.[71] The "light from Tabor" became a center of the piety of the late-medieval mysticism of the Hesychasts. For them Christ has not two but three hypostases.[72] The first is the divine light that he is in the kerygma of the gospel and through which at all times he transforms the people who "put on the divine splendor from above and are transformed into the likeness of the glory of the Lord whose face on the mountain today [!] shone as gloriously as the sun."[73] Greek iconography often expressed it by showing rays of light emanating from the transfigured Christ.

c. The *descent from the mountain* was thus not incidental, because time and again here, as probably with Matthew also, there are insights into the limitations of "mountaintop experiences." Origen himself, whose regard for the spirituality of the spiritually perfect is by no means minimal, says, "Jesus did not do what Peter wanted," but "came down from the mountain to those who could not go up it and see his transfigura-

---

63 Erich Dinkler (*Das Apsismosaik von S. Apollinare in Classe,* 87–103) interprets the entire mosaic strongly eschatologically. The cross is the eschatological victory sign (Constantine!), the lambs are to be understood in terms of Revelation 7. If this is correct, then the time difference between present and eschaton is the decisive barrier against a direct presence of the believers with the glorified Lord. They see the future but are not yet there. However, the interpretation of the mosaic is controversial.

64 Origen 12.37.36 = GCS Origenes 10.153, 151.

65 John of Damascus *Hom. in trans.* 10 = PG 96.561.

66 Lapide, 331.

67 Origen 12.41, 42 = GCS Origenes 10.163, 165.

68 Cf. above, n. 54 on 16:21-28 on the connection with 16:28 in the church's exegesis. Thus the connection between transfiguration and parousia is on the whole stronger in the exegesis of the church than it is in Matthew himself, where 16:28 is not developed in this direction.

69 Pseudo-Dionysius Areopagita *De divinis nominibus* 1.4 = PG 3.592.

70 *Ambiguorum Liber* = PG 91.1128.

71 "If he had been shining as the sun, the disciples would not have fallen on the ground, for they saw the sun every day" (John Chrysostom *Hom.* 21 = PG 63.700).

72 McGuckin, *Transfiguration,* 119, 232.

tion, so that they might at least see him as they are capable of seeing him."[74] Leo the Great and many with him understand the entire mountain episode as a source of strength for those who later must go the way of the cross and in contrast to Peter they emphasize that in the "temptations of this life" it is more important to ask "for patience than for glory."[75] Peter is sharply censured, not merely because he had completely forgotten his other nine companions,[76] but because it is his task to build the church on earth and not a hut on the mountain.[77] Especially impressive here is the conclusion of one of Augustine's sermons:

> Come down, Peter! . . . Proclaim the word! Keep at it in season and out of season. Convict. Admonish. . . . Work. Perspire. Endure torture. . . . Come down in order to work on earth, to serve on earth, to be despised, to be crucified on earth. Life comes down to be killed; bread comes down to be used up; the way comes down to become exhausted underway; the spring comes down to run dry. And you refuse to work? Do not seek what is yours. Have love. Proclaim the truth. Then you will come to eternity where you will find certainty![78]

The modern exegesis of our text leads us into a different world. It asks not how hearers and readers participate in this story; it primarily asks historical questions about the origin of our story. Either it explains it externally, for example, from a meeting of Jesus with two followers at sunrise on a foggy morning, when the sleepy disciples did not completely understand what was happening.[79] Or it explains it psychically as a vision the disciples had before or after Easter.[80] Or one explains it in terms of the history of ideas and dresses the transfigured Jesus, for example, with the garments of Moses or of a king.[81] While I would by no means dispute such interpreta-

tions, what they have in common is that they experience the story as alien and try to rationalize this strangeness.

It is surprising by contrast how vivid our story is in the exegesis of the church and how relevant it is to life. Why is that? The interpreters of the ancient church always interpreted a story such as ours as participants. They saw themselves and their readers in the disciples, wandered with them up the mountain and back down, experienced what happened there and were moved by it. In the exegesis we established that our narrative contains a christological perspective and a disciples perspective that are woven together and interrelated. The interpreters of the ancient church knew that from the beginning, because they themselves were present in the story of Jesus and heard it in terms of their own life perspective. The doctrine of the fourfold meaning of scripture helped them to combine these perspectives methodologically, whereby as a rule the christological perspective or faith appeared in the allegorical interpretation—the disciples perspective or their own life in the moral interpretation. Our story shows in an exemplary way the hermeneutic fruitfulness of the fourfold meaning of scripture.[82]

Summary

Once we have understood this, we also understand that the transfiguration story ultimately deals with the relationship between special religious experience and everyday life and suffering. Matthew was also there on the mountain; he too shared the longing for a shining face and a white garment that moved the later Greek exege-

---

73 Gregorios Palamas *Hom.* 35, *PG* 151.437.
74 Origen 12.41 = GCS Origenes 10.163–64.
75 *Sermo* 51.5 = FC 93.221–22.
76 Dionysius the Carthusian, 197.
77 Ephraem Syrus (above, n. 53) 8 = 188; Proclus of Constantinople *Orationes* 8.2 = *PG* 65.768.
78 *Sermo* 78.6 = *PL* 38.492–93.
79 Paulus, 2.539–43.
80 Since Johann Gottfried Herder, "Vom Erlöser der Menschen," in idem, *Werke*, vol. 19 (Bernhard Suphan, ed.; Berlin: Hempel, 1880) 180. More recently, forceful advocates of the vision hypothesis are, e.g., Adolf von Harnack, "Die Verklärungsgeschichte Jesu, der Bericht des Paulus (1 Kor 15,3ff) und die beiden Christusvisionen des Petrus," 62–80, 73–80 (vision of Peter during the

life of Jesus); Eduard Meyer, *Ursprung und Anfänge des Christentums*, vol. 1: *Die Evangelien* (6th ed.; Darmstadt: Wissenschaftliche Buchgesellschaft, 1962) 152–57; Baltensweiler, *Verklärung*, 87–90 (a vision on the occasion of a Feast of Tabernacles, when Jesus inwardly overcame the temptation of a political messianic ideal).
81 Cf. above, Tradition b and c.
82 Since it speaks of the future life in glory, it also opens up the possibility of an anagogic interpretation.

sis. He did not regard the mountaintop as an illusion or a projection. However—and this is probably where he differs from the great majority of Greek exegesis—he also knew that an *encounter* with God which lifts the person up only happens when one is addressed by "Jesus alone," without heavenly glory and attendants. Unlike Luke 9:34, he did not take the disciples into the cloud. According to him what is decisive for the disciples takes place not on the mountain but afterwards. To say it once more in the language of a Greek: "For if he had not become like us, who among us could endure the God who breaks out from above, and who could endure his radiant, unspeakable glory that probably no created being can endure?"[83]

---

83   Cyril of Alexandria, 425.

Literature

Hermann Aichinger, "Zur Traditionsgeschichte der Epileptiker-Perikope Mk 9,14-29 par Mt 17,14-21 par Lk 9,37-43a," *SNTU* A 3 (1978) 114–43.

Gerhard Barth, "Glaube und Zweifel in den synoptischen Evangelien," *ZThK* 72 (1975) 269–92.

Günther Bornkamm, "Πνεῦμα ἄλαλον," in idem, *Geschichte und Glaube* (BEvTh 53; Munich: Kaiser, 1971) 2.21–36.

Jean Duplacy, "La foi qui déplace les montagnes (Mt 17,20; 21,21 et par.)," in André Barucq, ed., *À la rencontre de Dieu: Mémorial Albert Gelin* (Bibliothèque de la Faculté Catholique de Théologie de Lyon 8; Le Puy: Mappus, 1961) 272–87.

Frankemölle, *Jahwebund,* 21–27.

Ferdinand Hahn, "Jesu Wort vom bergeversetzenden Glauben," *ZNW* 76 (1985) 149–69.

Held, "Matthew," 187–92.

Hans Klein, "Das Glaubensverständnis im Matthäusevangelium," in Ferdinand Hahn and Hans Klein, eds., *Glaube im Neuen Testament: Studien zu Ehren von Hermann Binder anlässlich seines 70. Geburtstags* (Biblisch-theologische Studien 7; Neukirchen-Vluyn: Neukirchener Verlag, 1982) 29–42.

Erna Lesky and Jan Hendrik Waszink, "Epilepsie," *RAC* 5 (1962) 819–31.

Léon Vaganay, "Les accords négatifs de Matthieu-Luc contre Marc. L'épisode de l'enfant épileptique (Mt 17,14-21; Mc 9,14-29; Lc 9,37-43a)," in idem, *Le problème synoptique. Une hypothèse de travail* (Bibliothèque de théologie 3/1; Paris: Desclée, 1954) 405–25.

Josef Zmijewski, "Der Glaube und seine Macht," in Josef Zmijewski and Ernst Nellessen, eds., *Begegnung mit dem Wort: Festschrift für Heinrich Zimmermann* (BBB 53; Bonn: Hanstein, 1980) 81–103.

Zumstein, *Condition,* 435–43.

14   And when they came to the crowd,[1] a man came to him, fell on his knees before him 15/ and said, "Lord, have mercy on my son, because he is moonstruck and sick,[2] because he often falls into the fire and into the water. 16/ And I brought him to your disciples and they were not able to heal him."

17   But Jesus answered and said, "O unbelieving and perverse generation! How long shall I be with you? How long shall I endure you? Bring him here to me." 18/ And Jesus rebuked him, and the demon came out of him, and from that hour the boy was healed.

19   Then the disciples came to Jesus in private and said, "Why were we not able to cast it out?" 20/ But he says to them, "Because of your little faith. For amen, I say to you: If you have faith as a mustard seed, you will say to this mountain 'Move over there,' and it will move, and nothing will be impossible for you."[3]

Analysis

Structure

The pericope consists of three parts: exposition (vv. 14-16), healing (v. 18), and the concluding discussion with the disciples (vv. 19-20). It picks up on v. 16 and in Matthew is not an extension as in Mark but the goal of the entire text. The most important keyword is οὐκ ἠδυνήθη . . . ("not able") in vv. 16 and 19; cf. οὐ . . . ἀδυνατήσει ("nothing . . . impossible") in v. 20. The reproach in v. 17 interrupts the connection. The text is not connected to the immediate context either backward or forward. The final logion in v. 20 is important for Matthew, for he takes it up again in 21:21.

Sources

a. Verses 14-18: In comparison with Mark 9:14-27 the text has shrunk to a good third of its size. The Markan introduction, Mark 9:14-17a, has almost completely disappeared. From Mark 9:20-25a Matthew takes over only a part of the description of the illness in Mark 9:22. He brings it in earlier in v. 15 in place of Mark 9:18a. The healing in v. 18 is considerably shortened in comparison with Mark 9:25b-27. It is by no means unusual for Matthew to shorten miracle stories, but here it is quantitatively striking. The special problem is that Luke 9:37-43 omits about the same parts of the Markan story, even though the Lukan text has a completely different scope than does the Matthean text. In Luke the focus is on the healing by the word of Jesus; in Matthew this is only the prelude to teaching the disciples about their faith. There are three possible explanations.

1. Matthew and Luke have independently redacted Mark's text.[4] The difficulty of this thesis is that the agreements between Matthew and Luke are quite numerous and do not simply include common omis-

---

1   Genitive absolute without genitive: BDF § 423 (6).

2   Nestle[26] reads πάσχει instead of ἔχει. Although the idiomatic expression κακῶς ἔχειν is the *lectio facilior,* the weight of the manuscripts must be determinative. The MSS group C, D, W, f¹, ¹³, *l,* supported by parts of the Latin and Syriac tradition, is less weighty. Furthermore, it is these witnesses that offer

3   v. 21 that is certainly secondary. Cf. the variant readings ποιήσωμεν in v. 4 and ἀπιστία in v. 20. V. 21 is a secondary addition based on Mark 9:29 in the Western, Byzantine, and small parts of the Egyptian tradition.

4   See, e.g., Allen, 190; Gnilka 2.105.

sions. In my judgment some of the positive agreements can scarcely be explained as redaction.[5] The Matthean abbreviations of the long miracle story, Mark 9:14-27, may still be understandable,[6] but in my view the Lukan omissions are no longer understandable.[7] Result: I find it improbable that Matthew and Luke here used the Markan text as we have it.

2. Matthew and Luke used an older variant of Mark 9:14-29 as a source or a secondary source that in particular did not include the Markan discussion of faith.[8] If in Mark 9:14-27 not only vv. 14-17 but also vv. 23-24 should be largely redactional (which in my judgment is improbable), then the Matthean/Lukan source is closely related to Mark's source. When formerly Mark 9:14-29 was often understood as the literary combination of two healing stories,[9] one of which contrasted Jesus and the incompetent disciples while the other contained the faith motif, it was thought that Matthew and Luke had used only one of Mark's two sources. I tend to be skeptical of all attempts to decompose the story of Mark 9:(14) 17-27, which in my view is quite colorful but not contradictory.[10] Then one can only surmise that a rather firmly established oral tradition has influenced Matthew and Luke.[11] This hypothesis is almost always possible when there are minor agreements, and almost never provable.

3. Matthew and Luke used a deutero-Markan recension of Mark 9:14-29 that shortened and simplified the Markan text.[12] The difficulty with this thesis is not only that one would have to assume an unusual and radical redaction by deutero-Mark, but also that Matthew takes from Mark 9:20-24 part of v. 22, while Luke takes v. 20a.[13] In my judgment this thesis is supported not by our text but by its probability with many other texts. Result: Choosing between the second and third hypotheses is not possible for me and perhaps not necessary. We may assume, for example, a redacted Markan text *and* the influence of oral tradition. In any case, Matthew himself intensively reworked the text.[14] Most importantly, he has made the real center of the story the discussion with the disciples that is handed down in Mark 9:28-29 as an addition.

b. In *vv. 19-20* Matthew has replaced the Markan "exorcism recipe" (Mark 9:29) with the saying about the faith that moves mountains. His source was presumably the saying about faith as a mustard seed from Q = Luke 17:6[15] that has a variant in Mark 11:23. Matthew has partially adapted it to Mark 11:23

---

5   Verse 16 par. Luke 9:40 καὶ οὐκ ἠδυνήθησαν. Would Luke have replaced one of his favorite words, ἰσχύω? On the whole v. 17a agrees with Luke 9:41a. Did two evangelists independently of one another add καὶ διεστραμμένη according to Deut 32:5 (LXX) without following the wording of this passage for the rest of the text?

6   That is true also for the omission of Mark 9:23-24, the discussion about faith in which Matthew is interested. "After the first prediction of the passion, there is no further mention of the faith of those who ask Jesus for help" (Hans Klein, "Das Glaubensverständnis im Matthäusevangelium," 29–41, 32) but only of the faith of the disciples. Cf. 20:29-34 in contrast to 9:27-31!

7   Luke's focus was on the miracle itself! Why would he have shortened this miracle so radically by, among others things, omitting the actual exorcism in Mark 9:25b-26? Cf. Luke 4:33-37; 8:26-39 as contrasting examples.

8   See, e.g., Léon Vaganay, "Les accords négatifs de Matthieu-Luc contre Marc. L'épisode de l'enfant épileptique (Mt 17,14-21; Mc 9,14-29; Lc 9,37-43a)," 405–25 (source: a Greek Ur-Matthew); Schweizer, 351–52; Roloff, *Kerygma,* 147; Theissen, *Miracle Stories,* 136.

9   See, e.g., Bultmann, *History,* 211–12; Günther Bornkamm, "Πνεῦμα ἄλαλον," 2.21–36, 24; Schweizer, *Mark,* 187.

10 Cf. Pesch, *Markusevangelium* 2.86, 95.

11 Bovon, *Luke* 1.507–8.

12 Hermann Aichinger, "Zur Traditionsgeschichte der Epileptiker-Perikope Mk 9,14-29 par Mt 17,14-21 par Lk 9,37-43a," 114–29, 117–29; Ennulat, *Agreements,* 208–13.

13 Hypothesis no. 2 can avoid this difficulty in assuming that Matthew and Luke were, along with the old variant, also familiar with our text of Mark 9:14-27.

14 Redactional are: v. 14 προσέρχομαι, ἄνθρωπος with the participle; v. 15 λέγων, κύριε + ἐλεέω, κακῶς v. 16 προσφέρω, θεραπεύω v. 17 ἀποκριθεὶς δέ + subject, μετά with the genitive, ὧδε; v. 18 θεραπεύω, παῖς, ἀπὸ τῆς ὥρας ἐκείνης; cf. vol. 1, Introduction 3.2. On γονυπετέω (v. 14) cf. 27:29; on σεληνιά-ζομαι (v. 15) cf. 4:24; ἐξέρχομαι + ἀπό (v. 18) appears redactionally four times.

by replacing[16] the image of the mulberry tree with the more common one of the mountain.[17] The other changes in the text are also redactional.[18] The logion itself is a conditional announcement[19] in prophetic style that probably comes from Jesus.

Interpretation

■ **14-18** Matthew reports this miracle story concisely. Except for our story, only the story of the Gadarene demoniac (8:28-34) has been as massively abbreviated. Obviously Matthew did not particularly like exorcisms,[20] for in our story he avoided all indications that the sick boy was possessed until he had to mention it (v. 18!).[21] Thus instead of the narrative which is so colorful in Mark, we have only the naked narrative skeleton. Jesus comes to the crowd (v. 14), the father brings his moonstruck son (v. 15), Jesus casts out the demon (v. 18). In addition, there are the father's statement about the disciples' inability that prepares for vv. 19-20 and the prophetic reproach of v. 17.

Some observations about the story itself: The external circumstances are related with little precision. Based on the context, "they came" (ἐλθόντων) in v. 14 should refer to Jesus and the three disciples who were on the mountain of transfiguration, but v. 16 speaks not of the remaining nine disciples but only of "the disciples." The crowd is almost the only element that is still present in Matthew and Luke from the detailed Markan introduc-

tion; it is probably needed because of the reproach directed to the "unbelieving generation" (v. 17). Like other suppliants, the father addresses Jesus as "Lord" and in the solemn style of the psalms asks for mercy for his son.[22] Matthew says nothing of the demon's rage.[23] The only indication of the mortal danger of the illness is that the boy frequently falls into fire or water when he has his seizures. That the disciples could not heal the boy (v. 16) is important; it prepares for the concluding verses 19-20. Matthew notes the healing quite briefly and in a formulaic way (cf. 8:13; 9:22; 15:28).

> Moon sickness is *epilepsy*, the "holy illness" that according to a widespread view in antiquity could be caused by the moon goddess Selene and be connected with the phases of the moon.[24] In antiquity epilepsy was explained either as a supernatural phenomenon—as "being possessed" (ἐπιληψία) by a divine power (= "ἱερὰ νόσος") or by demons—or in medical literature as a natural illness that "does not seem to be more divine or holy than other illnesses."[25] Mark 9:14-29 par. holds the demonological

---

15 Luke 17:1-6 may be a Q context. Note how close the parallels are in Matthew: 18:6-7, 15, 21-22; 17:20.

16 Thus Emanuel Hirsch, *Frühgeschichte des Evangeliums*, vol. 2: *Die Vorlagen des Lukas und das Sondergut des Matthäus* (Tübingen: Mohr/Siebeck, 1941) 154; Zmijewski, "Glaube," 87–88.

17 "To move mountains" was a proverbial saying in Judaism for impossible things; cf. Str-B 1.759. Thus the Markan image of the mountain is probably secondary to the "original" Q version.

18 Cf. vol. 1, Introduction 3.2 on τότε, προσέρχομαι, εἶπον, λέγω in the historical present, ὀλιγοπιστ-, ἀμὴν γὰρ λέγω ὑμῖν, ἐάν, ἐρῶ, μεταβαίνω, ἐκεῖ. Διὰ τί is redactional four times (Schenk, *Sprache*, 176); the hapax legomenon ἀδυνατέω takes up the keyword δύναμαι.

19 Conditionalizing by means of a conditional clause or a participle + announcement; cf., e.g., Isa 1:19; Jean Duplacy, "La foi qui déplace les montagnes (Mt 17,20; 21,21 et par.)," 272–87, 281; Sato, "Q," 121, 124.

20 Böcher ("Magie," 11–24) notes a general reduction of magical elements in Matthew.

21 Again Matthew has little concern for the external course of events. He does not notice that in v. 18a Jesus actually "rebukes" the sick boy, because he has not yet mentioned the demon whom he, of course, has in mind.

22 Cf. vol. 1, Introduction 4.2.1 and 9:28; 15:22; 20:30-31.

23 In contrast to Luke 9:39 he does not add to the description his own description of the illness; cf. Bovon, *Luke* 1.510.

24 For references see Klostermann on this passage; also Erna Lesky and Jan Hendrik Waszink, "Epilepsie," 819–31, 820–21.

25 Hippocrates *De morbo sacro* 1 (excerpts of the important writing are printed by Lührmann, *Markusevangelium*, 274–79).

view. In the history of interpretation Origen[26] represents an important turning point. As the first to confront the natural, medical explanation of illness on the basis of the biblical text, he expressly rejects it by appealing to scripture. Origen's influence was substantial;[27] the medical explanation of epilepsy lost ground after late antiquity. Saints replaced physicians.[28] On the other hand, there was also potentially positive meaning in the biblical story. Illnesses such as epilepsy do not conform to the human image willed by God, and the struggle against it takes place with the will of Christ and by his power.[29]

■ **17** In this brief narrative only v. 17 provides an almost irritating "foothold." Verse 17 is irritating, because instead of a response to the father's request it contains a double complaint from Jesus in biblical style about "this unbelieving and perverse generation."[30] To whom does that refer? The context most naturally suggests the disciples, since mention has just been made of their failure.[31] However, nowhere in his entire gospel does Matthew call the disciples "this generation." In v. 20 he speaks in conscious distinction not of their "unbelief,"[32] but of their "little faith."[33] Primarily, however, the generalizing "generation" ($\gamma\epsilon\nu\epsilon\acute{\alpha}$) would not be at all appropriate if Jesus were speaking only of a few people. Since in v. 14 the crowd is mentioned anyway, as in the other passages[34] we probably should understand the expression to refer to Jesus' Jewish contemporaries, that is, to the crowd. The Gospel of Matthew as a whole will show that the behavior of "this generation" is typical: Israel has already shown with the prophets that it was always "unbelieving" and "perverse" (cf. 23:34-36). The two "how long" questions become significant in the context

of the entire gospel. In 23:37-39 Jesus will announce that he will leave Jerusalem and the temple. In 24:1-2 he will do that and will speak to the disciples on the Mount of Olives about, among other things, the catastrophe coming over Israel. In addition there is a redaction-critical observation. The first of the two questions is "How long will I be *with you?*" Here Matthew has changed the Markan $\pi\rho\grave{o}\varsigma$ $\acute{\nu}\mu\tilde{\alpha}\varsigma$ to $\mu\epsilon\vartheta$' $\acute{\nu}\mu\tilde{\omega}\nu$ and thus created a reference to his Immanuel Christology (1:23; 28:20)[35] which frames his entire gospel. "Jesus, the Emmanuel, the $\mu\epsilon\vartheta$' $\acute{\nu}\mu\tilde{\omega}\nu$ $\acute{o}$ $\vartheta\epsilon\acute{o}\varsigma$, . . . threatens his withdrawal that is identical with God's withdrawal."[36] Thus v. 17 is a "signal" that points to the coming judgment on Israel. In literary terms the function of this notably irritating foothold in our story is not so much on the surface level of what is reported but on its deeper level where the issue is the separation of the Jesus community from Israel and God's judgment on Israel. The clearest indication of that is that "this generation" has not done anything here that warranted Jesus' rebuke. As in 13:10-15 Matthew is thinking not of concrete guilt on the surface of his story but in general of Israel's unbelief.

■ **19-20** The narrative does not reach its goal until vv. 19-20 where the issue is the disciples' inability to cast out the demon. Does the disciples' question refer only to the story of Jesus back then? If so it would be difficult to understand why Matthew would have changed the Markan answer and replaced it with a reference to the disciples' little faith—an expression that for him is always directed at the church's concrete situation. At the beginning of the disciples discourse Jesus had given the twelve

26   13.6 = GCS Origenes 10.193.
27   Cf. Franz Joseph Dölger, "Der Einfluss des Origenes auf die Beurteilung der Epilepsie und Mondsucht im christlichen Altertum," in idem, *Antike und Christentum* (Münster: Aschendorff, 1934) 4.101–7.
28   Hans Jorg Schneble, *Krankheit der ungezählten Namen* (Bern: Huber, 1987) 60–67. In Germany St. Valentine (of Terni), in France John (usually the Baptist) became the patron saints against epilepsy.
29   Cf. Owsei Temkin (*The Falling Sickness: A History of Epilepsy from the Greeks to the Beginnings of Modern Medicine* [2d ed.; Baltimore: Johns Hopkins, 1971] 170–72) on Arnald of Villanova and Paracelsus.
30   Deut 32:5: $\gamma\epsilon\nu\epsilon\acute{\alpha}$ $\sigma\kappa\delta\lambda\iota\grave{\alpha}$ $\kappa\alpha\grave{\iota}$ $\delta\iota\epsilon\sigma\tau\rho\alpha\mu\mu\acute{\epsilon}\nu\eta$; cf. 32:20-42. On the lament with "how long" cf. Num 14:27. For further passages see Pesch,

Markusevangelium 2.90.
31   Thus Held, "Matthew," 191; Zumstein, *Condition,* 439.
32   As with the people of Nazareth in 13:58.
33   Ἀπιστία, the reading of the *textus receptus,* is an adaptation to v. 17.
34   Cf. 11:16 (and the interpretation there); 12:39, 45; 16:4; 23:36; 24:34. Deut 32:5 also refers to the people.
35   Cf. vol. 1 on 1:23.
36   Frankemölle, *Jahwebund,* 26.

disciples the authority and the task to heal sick and to cast out demons (10:1, 8). We interpreted this commission as a real task that was fundamentally valid for the church.[37] From 7:22 we know that miracles continued to happen in the church, even in questionable ways. Thus we interpret the disciples' question against the background that in Matthew's charismatic community sometimes the experiences of healing did not happen.[38] The churches behind the Gospel of Mark probably had similar problems, as Mark 9:28-29 demonstrates. There, just as in James 5:13-16, intensive prayer is decisive for the success of a healing.

The answer given by Matthew is more basic than the Markan answer. It consists of an answer from the evangelist himself and the traditional Jesus saying about mustard seed faith. His own answer is: Failure in healing is an expression of little faith. Little faith is, as in 6:30, 8:26, 14:31, and 16:8,[39] faith that has become discouraged and lacks trust in God's miraculous help. Thus Matthew does not think that healings and exorcisms are special experiences that sometimes happen and sometimes do not. He is much more "enthusiastic" and regards healings and exorcisms as experiences that are an essential part of faith. Where they are absent, faith has not lived up to its potential. "Little faith" *must* be overcome by actually laying claim to the power of Jesus. To his own answer Matthew adds the logion about the faith that can move mountains—a saying so important for him that he transmitted it twice (cf. 21:21). It contrasts "little faith" with "faith like a mustard seed," obviously a faith that is also "little." At first glance the distinction is confusing.[40] What is meant?

> Often the interpreters were inclined to put forward their own understanding of faith under the signature of the vague "faith as a mustard seed." The point with

the mustard seed is then not that it is small but that it has a strong, sharp taste.[41] Or the issue is the "faith that . . . is aware of its own ungodliness (Rom 4:5)."[42] Or it is faith "that is based completely on God and that shares in his power."[43] We should not overinterpret. In the traditional Jesus saying of Luke 17:6 the comparison of faith with a mustard seed serves to contrast what is incomprehensibly small, viz. faith, with what is incomprehensibly large, viz., what faith effects, that is, the uprooting of a sycamore tree with its giant roots. Thus the issue is not a special "mustard seed faith," but faith as such. In Matthew also it is related not to little faith but to moving a mountain. Here also we must beware of overinterpretations. While there are biblical statements that say that God in his saving future will level mountains (but not move them!) (Isa 40:3-5, 49:11, Zech 14:10), "to uproot" or "tear out mountains" is a widespread Jewish hyperbole for "to do something impossible" that could be applied in quite different ways.[44] Contrary to a popular interpretation, in my judgment the issue in the logion is not that faith will participate "in God's creative activity" or in the "miracle of eschatological renewal,"[45] but much more simply that seemingly impossible things are promised to faith. What things? There is no reason to think that even Jesus is not thinking also of miracles in this saying.[46]

In v. 20 Matthew contrasts faith with little faith. To believe means to trust in Jesus that he "can do that" (9:28) or that "nothing will be impossible for you." While for Matthew too all members of the church are "believers" (18:6), faith comes into its own when the issue is miracles and extraordinary proofs and experiences. Venture, prayer, obedience on the one side and the unrestricted power of Jesus on the other side constitute faith. Faith means departure, prayer, venture, laying claim to the unrestricted power of Immanuel that is promised to the church (28:20). And since, according to Matthew, this power is repeatedly available in concrete miracles that by no means are *only* symbolic, that means that the miracle

37 Cf. above, II C 2.1 on 10:7-8.
38 Likewise Zumstein, *Condition*, 439.
39 Cf. vol. 1 on 6:30 and the interpretation above on 8:26, 14:31, 16:8.
40 Many of the church's exegetes followed the example of Jerome (153) who on the basis of 1 Cor 13:2 (πᾶσαν τὴν πίστιν) made of the mustard seed faith a "great" faith! Then the philological problems and the problems of content become "solvable"!
41 Thus Augustine *Joh. ev. tract.* 40.8 = FC 88.131.
42 Schniewind, 195.
43 Zmijewski, "Glaube," 98.

44 Str–B 1.759. Biblically it comes the closest to Isa 54:10.
45 See, e.g., Eduard Lohse, in Hans-Jürgen Hermisson and Eduard Lohse, *Faith* (Nashville: Abingdon, 1978) 123; Ferdinand Hahn, "Jesu Wort vom bergeversetzenden Glauben," 149–69, 166.
46 That would best fit the reality that in the synoptic tradition the root "faith" appears primarily in connection with miracles.

in this text is not simply irrelevant and designed to introduce a teaching, even though Matthew so radically abbreviated it. Instead, it is a central question of faith for the evangelist that miraculous healings actually happen in the church.

Summary and History of Interpretation

It is here at the very latest that the *reality* question becomes a burning issue. Faith has never moved mountains! Nor does it normally heal epileptics and other sick people. It is amazing how almost two thousand years of interpreting a biblical saying have succeeded in ignoring this problem. The apostles would have had no convincing reason to move mountains is John Chrysostom's opinion.[47] Calvin thinks that the issue is to be "temperate" and to wish only "what the Lord promises."[48] Again we encounter the familiar thesis that miracles were especially necessary at the beginning of the church's history but not later.[49] It is claimed that the "eccentricity" of the expression shows that the issue is not "grotesque" miracles like moving mountains, but "participating in God's omnipotence" is "related to the concern of faith."[50] A lovely, gloriously general formulation! But what is the concern of faith? According to Matthew it is obviously precisely healing the sick or other *extraordinary* claims on God's power. According to him that is precisely the way faith is distinguished from little faith.

We are certainly justified in raising questions here. If complete faith were manifested only in the ability to perform miracles, it also would be true that "the more we grow in faith and trust, the more we (also) grow in this ability."[51] Or conversely: The less we have the ability to perform miracles, the more we must conclude that we are far from full faith and from God. What is *promised* to faith comes dangerously close here to a power that one possesses. Paul is more theologically advanced on this point when he consistently understands healings as χαρίσματα, that is, as gifts that a free God grants to the church, not to every believer. Not everyone who is unable to do miracles is of little faith. Matthew may think too enthusiastically. Still, his voice should be heard in our churches today which not only often understand charismatic experiences as (at best!) somewhat extreme additions to faith rather than its essence but that beyond that often have forgotten how to lay claim to God as a power for achieving things that appear impossible. Then faith changes nothing; it simply lets God of necessity become the authority that sanctions what is and gives people the strength to be satisfied with what is "possible."

---

47   57.3 = *PG* 58.562.
48   Calvin 2.210.
49   Luther, *WA* 38.665. Cf. above, nn. 39, 69 on 10:5-15.
50   Gerhard Ebeling, *Dogmatik des christlichen Glaubens* (Tübingen: Mohr/Siebeck, 1979) 2.464.
51   Lapide, 339.

Literature

Thompson, *Advice,* 16–49.

22 **But when they gathered in Galilee Jesus said to them, "The Son of Man will be delivered into the hands of men, 23/ and they will kill him, and on the third day he will be raised." And they became very sad.**

Analysis After the healing of the epileptic Matthew moves immediately to the prediction of the passion. In its formulation it is reminiscent of 16:21. Verses 20:18-19 will then take up the previous announcements of suffering. The source is Mark 9:30-32. Matthew has shortened the detailed introduction of Mark 9:30b-31a and has substituted the disciples' sadness for their lack of understanding (Mark 9:32). Linguistically the treatment is primarily, but not completely, redactional.[1]

Interpretation

The Matthean introduction is difficult. Συστρέφεσθαι is frequently documented with the meaning "to gather."[2] However, why did the disciples gather when, according to v. 19, they are already with Jesus?[3] Is this one of the frequent cases of narrative carelessness? The reference to Galilee is also not all that simple. Matthew probably knows that Caesarea Philippi is not in Galilee, so he now has Jesus return there. Perhaps he is also thinking already of 19:1. Jesus will soon leave Galilee for the last time and go to Jerusalem. Galilee is important for Matthew as the place of Jesus' activity (4:12), as the place where the disciples were called (4:18), and as the place where the church began (28:16). Thus he who in v. 24 will once again mention "Jesus' city" Capernaum (cf. 4:13) in vv. 22 and 24 draws a large arc back to the beginning of his story. Jesus' activity in his land of Galilee will soon come to an end.

The announcement of the suffering itself is short and terse. Unlike δεῖ ("must"; 16:21), μέλλει ("will be") indicates not the necessity but the imminence of Jesus' dying and rising. The contrast between "Son of Man" [*Menschen-sohn*] and "human beings" [*Menschen*] emphasizes the paradox. Jesus, about whose future majesty as Son of Man–world-judge the disciples know (16:27-28), will be delivered into the hands of human beings. As 16:21, 20:18-19, and the passion narrative show, "human beings" means Jesus' Jewish opponents and the Romans. Παραδίδωμι ("to deliver") is a word familiar to the readers of the gospel that has christological connotations. Verse 10:4 ("Judas Iscariot, who also delivered him") shows that Matthew is thinking of readers who know the story of the passion. Unlike Mark, Matthew does not say that the disciples did not understand Jesus' word. Since for Matthew "understand" is more likely to mean something "intellectual,"[4] he must be more precise than Mark. The disciples "understood" quite well what Jesus said, but they cannot accept what they understand. Therefore, they became very sad.[5] Their refusal to accept is reminiscent of Peter's reaction in 16:22-23; it contrasts with the clarity and decisiveness with which Jesus himself looks ahead to his dying.

Summary

Mark interpreted his second prediction of the passion "existentially" with the pericope of the disciples' dispute about rank (Mark 9:33-37). On the one hand, Matthew has expanded this pericope into his community discourse and thus emphasized its ecclesiological relevance, while on the other hand with the short text about the temple tax (vv. 24-27) he separated it from the announcement of the suffering. Thus the announcement of the suffering is isolated and is correspondingly difficult to interpret. In the macrotext of the gospel it points

1   Linguistically Matthean are δέ, μέλλω, ἐγείρω, λυπέω, σφόδρα; cf. vol. 1, Introduction 3.2. Τῇ τρίτῃ ἡμέρᾳ ἐγερθήσεται corresponds literally to 20:19 and almost literally to 16:21 (Mark is different in each case), ἐλυπήθησαν σφόδρα to 18:31. Verse 22a is not Matthean, especially the hapax legomenon συστρέφομαι.

2   References in LSJ, *s.v.* IV; for Jewish and biblical references see Thompson, *Advice,* 17–18. An alternative meaning is "to press together" (around a leader, as a compact group; for references see LSJ, *s.v.* V).

Semantically this nuance is not clearly separated from "to gather" and is therefore also possible. Impossible is "move about together" (McNeile, 257). That would correspond to ἀναστρεφομένων and thus to the correction of the MSS C, D, W, Θ, *l*, f[13], etc., that were also somewhat confused by the text's "difficult" reading.

3   Certainly not because they had been separated from him since 17:1 (thus Bonnard, 263). Cf. v. 19!

4   Cf. above, III B 2.1 on 13:23.

5   Correctly Gnilka 2.113: "embarrassed denial." Cf. 19:22; 26:22.

ahead to the enigma of the passion. There the Son of Man is delivered to hostile people, abandoned by the "grieving" disciples, and will go his way alone to the end. However, God will raise the Son of Man on the third day and give him all power in heaven and on earth. The ancient commentators already noticed that the disciples appear not to react at all to the announcement of the resurrection. It is as if it disappears from view.[6] Here obviously there are limits to the human ability to understand. One can only experience the miracle of the resurrection; one cannot understand it in advance.

6   It is also misunderstood in 16:21 and in the parallel 20:19. Cf. Origen, 13.9 = GCS Origenes 10.206; Jerome, 154.

Literature

Richard J. Cassidy, "Matthew 17:24-27—A Word on Civil Taxes," *CBQ* 41 (1979) 571–80.

David Daube, *Appeasement or Resistance?* (Berkeley: University of California Press, 1987) 39–58.

Derrett, *Law* 1.247–65.

David E. Garland, "Matthew's Understanding of the Temple Tax (Matt 17:24-27)," in *SBLSP* (1987) 190–209.

Horbury, "Temple Tax," 265–86.

Simon Légasse, "Jésus et l'impôt du Temple (Mt 17,24-27)" *ScEs* 24 (1972) 361–77.

Liver, "Half-Shekel Offering," 173–98.

Sara Mandell, "Who Paid the Temple Tax, When the Jews Were Under Roman Rule?" *HTR* 77 (1984) 223–32.

Rudolf Meyer, "Der Ring des Polykrates, Mt 17,27 und die rabbinische Überlieferung," *OLZ* 40 (1937) 665–70.

Montefiore, "Jesus," 60–71.

Thompson, *Advice*, 50–68.

Vollenweider, *Freiheit*, 171–77.

Eino Wilhelms, *Die Tempelsteuerperikope Mt 17, 24-27 in der Exegese der griechischen Väter der alten Kirche* (Suomen eksegeettisen seuran julkaisuja 34; Helsinki: Kirjapaino, 1980).

Analysis

24   **But when they came to Capernaum the collectors of the double drachma approached Peter and said, "Does your teacher not pay the double drachma?" 25/ He says, "Yes."**
And when he came into the house, Jesus went before him and said, "What do you think, Simon? From whom do the kings of the earth collect toll or taxes? From their sons or from strangers?" 26/ But when he said, "from strangers," Jesus said to him, "Then the sons are free. 27/ But so that we do not give them offense, go to the lake, cast the hook, and take the first fish that comes up. And when you open its mouth you will find a stater. Take it and give it to them for me and for you."

Structure

The pericope consists of two scenes—the conversation between the tax collectors and Peter (24-25aα) and the conversation between Jesus and Peter in the house (25aβ-27). In the latter Jesus does almost all of the talking. He takes the initiative and gives the answers. Subordinated with a genitive absolute,[1] Peter is little more than a prop on the stage. Had Peter not already given the tax collectors an affirmative answer in v. 25aα, the pericope could end with v. 26, which appears to suggest a basically negative attitude on the part of Jesus toward the temple tax. Thus the fish miracle which is announced to Peter the fisherman in v. 27 and makes the payment of the tax possible is necessary for the pericope to become a unit. The actual miracle is not reported. The pericope is very brief and is formulated with a surprising number of participles. It is not bracketed with the context.

Source

The statement of the situation in v. 24 and the house in v. 25 correspond to Mark 9:33 and probably are taken over from there. Yet the location in Capernaum also fits the pericope, or the temple tax was collected in the place of residence (of Peter and Jesus).[2] Was the story's traditional location in Capernaum the occasion for Matthew to insert it at Mark 9:33, even though it created a disturbing interruption between the announcement of the suffering of Jesus and its ecclesiological application to the church in chap. 18? In any case it would have fit even worse in chaps. 4 and 8–9, chapters that also take place in Capernaum. The story itself contains numerous Mattheisms,[3] but also numerous peculiarities and hapax legomena,[4] that were dictated only in part by the content. They are usually attributed to the oral tradition that Matthew received. That cannot be proven, but neither is there reason to contradict it.

---

1   Thus probably the original text in v. 26 that was frequently changed and later expanded by dittography.
2   Cf. vol. 1, I B 3.1 on 4:12-17 ("Origin").
3   On ἐλθών (four times redactional as a genitive absolute), δέ, προσέρχομαι, λαμβάνω, εἶπον, διδάσκαλος as a designation of Jesus by outsiders (cf. 9:11), λέγει (historical present), λέγων, τί + dative + δοκεῖ, ἔφη + dative and subject, ἄρα γε, σκανδαλ-, πορευθείς, βάλλω, εὑρίσκω, ἐκεῖνος, λαβών, and the large number of participles cf. vol. 1, Introduction 3.1 and 3.2. On the address "Simon" alongside "Peter" cf. 16:16-17; on the ques-

tion with τίς and subject before it (v. 25) cf. 16:15. Βασιλεῖς τῆς γῆς is LXX language; cf. Strecker, *Weg*, 200. On the house as the place of the instruction of the disciples cf. 13:36. For Gundry (356) the pericope is entirely redactional.

4   Δίδραχμον and στατήρ (note the change!), τελέω (in this meaning), προφθάνω, ἀλλότριος, ἐλεύθερος, ἄγκιστρον, ἀνοίγω τὸ στόμα (in this usage).

Tradition History

Formally the story is very unusual. Its beginning is suggestive of a controversy story; in the second scene a teacher-student conversation takes place; it ends with the announcement of a miracle. Nevertheless, in its present form it is a unity. Peter's positive answer in v. 25aα requires that somehow Jesus will have a positive attitude toward the temple tax. Thus we cannot simply explain the entire v. 27 as a secondary addition to vv. 24-26.[5] At the same time we must ask whether the negative-sounding answer of Jesus in vv. 25b-26 is not older than the remaining scene.[6] The double scenery of vv. 24-25aα and vv. 25aβ-27 could speak in favor of such a conclusion. However, this is no more than a possibility. Deliberations about the historical situation and about the interpretation must supplement the tradition-history speculation.

The Temple Tax

It is clear that at issue is the Jewish half-shekel or double drachma tax for the support of the temple and not a civil Roman tax.[7] The half-shekel tax was to be paid annually by each free adult Israelite, excluding women, slaves, and children. It served to pay the expenses of the temple cult. Our main sources of information are the first two sections of the Mishnah tract *Seqalim* that, to be sure, contains the rabbinic theory about the tax that was no longer collected

after the destruction of the temple.[8] Historically three things are clear: (1) It is a relatively late assessment, documented only in late biblical texts,[9] that originally was not a regular tax. (2) After the destruction of the temple the Romans established in its place the so-called *fiscus Iudaicus,* a tax of equal amount that all the Jews in the empire had to pay to the Jupiter Capitolinus (Josephus *Bell.* 7.218).[10] (3) Contrary to a widespread misunderstanding, the emperor Nerva did not abolish this special tax but only the *Fisci Iudaici calumnia,* that is, the fact that one could be forced to pay it on the basis of a denunciation.[11]

Historically, when and to what degree the temple tax became an obligatory annual tax for all Jews is controversial. The older view assumed that it had long been taken for granted in the time of Jesus, both in the diaspora and in the land of Israel. Recently considerable doubts have been expressed about this thesis.[12] In Qumran the basic biblical passage Exod 30:11-16 was interpreted to mean that the temple tax was paid by each Israelite only once in his lifetime (4Q 159:6-7).[13] Above all, however, several sources show us that the Sadducean priesthood obviously rejected it, and not, as was maliciously claimed, because the priests did not want to pay it for selfish

---

5 See, e.g., Kilpatrick, *Origins,* 41–42; cf. Roloff, *Kerygma,* 118; Schweizer, 356; Gnilka 2.114. Vollenweider (*Freiheit,* 173–74) would like to regard only the fish motif as secondary (perhaps v. 27aβb), but its fairytale-like quality (cf. below on the interpretation of vv. 24-27) is not reason enough for such a conclusion.

6 Thus Bultmann, *History,* 34–35. The contrary thesis, that vv. 25b-26 are a later addition (suggested by Frankemölle, *Jahwebund,* 175), is in my judgment unthinkable. Verse 27 does not follow v. 25a.

7 Thus many church interpreters (cf. history of interpretation) and recently Richard J. Cassidy, "Matthew 17:24-27—A Word on Civil Taxes," 571–80. There is no evidence for such a tax in Palestine.

8 *M. Seqal.* 8.8. For additional material see Str–B 1.760–70.

9 The oldest text is Neh 10:32-33 (the people of rank, Levites, priests, and pious commit themselves to pay annually 1/3 shekel for the expenses of the temple cult); later the basic passage is Exod 30:11-16 (provision for each Israelite who is capable of military service to pay a half-shekel of silver as כֹּפֶר [ransom] for his life). According to the commentators this text is postexilic and refers to a one-time assess-

ment. Whether 2 Chr 24:6, 9 refer to Exod 30:11-16 or to Exod 25:1; 38:25 is controversial; here it is a one-time assessment for the restoration of the temple.

10 Josephus mentions explicitly: "wherever they lived . . . , the sum they had previously paid into the temple at Jerusalem."

11 Cf. the well-known coin inscription from the time of Nerva. Suetonius (*Domitianus* 12) reports on the *calumnia:* Under Domitian, based on denunciations both uncircumcised σεβόμενοι and Jews who were no longer practicing but circumcised were forced to pay the *fiscus.* Thus under Domitian the tax created problems for all Jewish and Gentile Christians but beginning with Nerva only for law-observant Jewish Christians and practicing Jews. Dio Cassius (66.7.2) maintains the later status quo: practicing Jews must pay.

12 Liver, "Half-Shekel Offering," 185–90 (fundamentally); Horbury, "Temple Tax," 277–82 (balanced); Sara Mandell ("Who Paid the Temple Tax, When the Jews Were under Roman Rule?" 223–32) even assumes that only the Pharisees paid the temple tax (an exaggerated view in my judgment; the evidence cited below in n. 18 is completely ignored).

reasons (*m. Seqal.* 1.4).[14] Instead, the Sadducees were basically of the opinion that the Tamid sacrifice should be paid voluntarily.[15] That is how it had been done earlier; in the Persian and Hellenistic periods the king was mainly responsible for the expenses of the cult.[16] That the sources from Persian times (1, 2 Chronicles, Tobit, also *Jubilees*) say nothing about the temple tax indirectly confirms that it was voluntary. When was this practice changed? There are good reasons to assume that it took place in the time of Alexandra Salome (76–67 BCE).[17] The Pharisees probably wanted the cult expenses to be paid with clean money by Israelites, while the Sadducees were followers of the traditional regulation. Then the annual temple tax would have been required of all Jews from the middle of the first century BCE. This explains why on the one hand quite diverse sources indicate that the Diaspora delivered large sums to the temple,[18] and also why after 70 the Romans established the *fiscus Iudaicus* as something that was to be taken for granted for *all* Jews in the entire empire. On the other hand, at the time of Jesus the people still remembered the Sadducees' earlier opinion and

probably also were familiar with the Essenes' different practice. We also know that in Israel, and especially in Galilee, conditions were not the best for paying the temple tax.[19] Thus the tax collectors' question directed to Peter or to the Jewish-Christian church was a genuine question.

Origin

It is out of the question that the text, vv. 24-27, comes from the time after the destruction of the temple and deals with the problems the church faced in the time of Domitian with the *fiscus Iudaicus*.[20] Both the voluntary nature of the tax implied by v. 24 and the example of vv. 25-26 that would have made Christians "sons" of the gentile "kings of the earth," speak against this view.[21] Thus the text must originate in a Jewish-Christian community prior to the year 70. There is no way of knowing anything about where it originated and was passed on.[22] In my judgment that the tax collectors direct their question to Peter, that is, to the disciples' spokesman, speaks compellingly for concluding that the entire apophthegm is a creation of the church.[23] Thus the church is being

13 DJD 5 (1968) 7. Controversial is whether the passage reflects an old ordinance or is a specifically Qumran compromise between faithfulness to the law and the "illegitimate" temple cult. Schürer-Vermes (2.271, n. 52) is of the latter opinion. However, the first thesis better fits Exod 30:11-16 and the other historical data.

14 Str-B 1.762 (in the name of Johanan ben Zakkai).

15 *B. Menaḥ.* 65a; scholion on *Meg. Taʿan.* in Liver, "Half-Shekel Offering," 189.

16 Ezra 6:8-12 (Darius); 7:15-18 (Artaxerxes: donations of the king + voluntary contributions of the Diaspora); Josephus *Ant.* 12.140–41 (Antiochus III); 2 Macc 3:3 (Seleucus IV); cf. 1 Macc 10:39-40 (Demetrius gives the high priest the gentile region of Ptolemais for defraying the expenses of the cult).

17 Cf. *Meg. Ta an.* 1 = (Riessler, 346) and Sean Freyne, *Galilee from Alexander the Great to Hadrian 323 BCE to 135 CE* (Wilmington, Del.: Glazier, 1980) 279.

18 Philo *Spec. leg.* 1.76–77 (annual tribute); cf. *Rer. div. her.* 186 (Egypt); Josephus *Ant.* 18.312–13 (Babylonia); *m. Seqal.* 2.1. Other references cannot be related unambiguously to the temple tax.

19 Sean Freyne (*Galilee from Alexander the Great to Hadrian BCE to 135 CE*, 280) calls attention to *m. Ned.* 2.4 (the Galileans are not familiar with the Hebe [= half-shekel tax] at the temple hall) and to the fact that pilgrimages to Jerusalem did not take place regularly. A general, not specifically Galilean reference is *Mek. Exod.* 19.1 = Jakob Winter and August Wünsche, *Mechiltha: ein tannaitischer Midrasch zu Exodus*

(Leipzig: Hinrichs, 1909) 192 (the subjection of Israel to foreigners after 70 is, according to Johanan ben Zakkai, the punishment for refusing to pay the temple tax).

20 Many assume this to be the *Sitz im Leben* of the present version: e.g., Kilpatrick, *Origins*, 42; Davies, *Setting*, 390–91 (vv. 24-27 a "Gemara" on the ἄνθρωποι of vv. 22-23); Montefiore, "Jesus," 66–67; Walker, *Heilsgeschichte*, 101–3 (the Christians are the "free persons," who for missionary reasons, in order not to irritate the kings, pay the tax).

21 Wolzogen (324) already formulates as a counterargument against the prevailing interpretation: Then Christ and the disciples would have to be sons of Caesar!

22 That the stater was worth two double drachmas only in Damascus and in Antioch is one of the tenaciously held apocrypha of NT scholarship; cf. vol. 1, Introduction, n. 184. A στατήρ is a measurement of weight that earlier corresponded to two, in New Testament times to four, Attic or Ptolemaic drachmas. Cf. Frederic W. Madden, *Coins of the Jews* (London: Trübner, 1881) 293–94.

23 Derrett (*Law*), Montefiore ("Jesus," 67–68), and Horbury ("Temple Tax," 282–86) trace the entire pericope (in part without v. 27αβb) back to Jesus.

addressed, and again it is being taught in the figure of Peter by the "only teacher" Jesus. Peter's compromising attitude also fits well with what we know about Peter's attitude after Easter (cf. Gal 2:11-13).[24] The caution of the community that does not want to offend the Jews (v. 27a) presupposes that the temple tax had become generally accepted, and it fits well the general situation of Palestinian Jewish Christianity before the Jewish war.

For the saying in vv. 25-26 that points in a different direction (assuming that it always dealt with the temple tax)[25] there are two possibilities. It can (a) come from a Jewish-Christian community critical of the cult that had already fundamentally separated itself from the temple cult and that in its "no" to the cult understood itself as the true sons of God.[26] One would have to think of a church such as the church of the letter to the Hebrews that, however, lived in a Jewish environment and adapted to its environment, as vv. 24 and 27 show. Then one may regard vv. 25-26 as historically and traditionally older, in which case a church that knew itself to be free from the ceremonial law later adapted to its Jewish environment, for example, in the time before the Jewish war when the pressure to conform became stronger. Or one may regard the entire pericope as equally original, in which case a church which inwardly knew it was free from the ceremonial law outwardly conformed. However, as the interpretation will show, the historical situation also permits us (b) to trace the logion back to Jesus.

Interpretation: The Church, Jesus

■ **25-26** The rhetorical question in vv. 25-26 uses a traditional image.[27] "From whom do the secular kings take tribute[28] or tax?[29] From their sons or from strangers?" A "king of flesh and blood" is the favorite subject of rabbinic parables.[30] The image is not completely clear. In all probability "sons" literally means royal princes. Then the "strangers" (ἀλλότριοι) are, in a somewhat unusual formulation, all those who do not belong to the royal family.[31] The image is almost absurd and therefore self-evident. It would not occur to anyone that royal princes would pay taxes and tribute.[32] It has also been suggested that the thought is that Roman citizens, unlike the subjected "foreigners," did not pay head and real estate taxes and often were also excused from assessments.[33] This interpretation fits ἀλλότριοι ("strangers") better but is improbable, because υἱός ("son") in connection with a person is not a general concept of belonging but leads one to expect a literal understanding.[34]

---

24 Schnackenburg 2.166.

25 Of course, we do not *know* this on the basis of vv. 25b-26 alone. However, the logion never could have been handed down without a statement of its theme. The simplest assumption is that the theme remained the same and in vv. 24-27 was simply rephrased by the church and adapted to the changed situation.

26 Cf. Vollenweider, *Freiheit*, 175.

27 Formally similar are Matt 7:3-4 and 10:29.

28 Indirect taxes. Horst Balz (*EDNT* 2 [1991] 287) speaks of customs or usage taxes or tolls.

29 The Roman term for the Greek φόρος = tribute, direct tax. What is meant is the *tributum soli* and the *tributum capitis*; cf. Schürer-Vermes 1.401-2.

30 Cf. the splendid collection of Ignaz Ziegler, *Die Königsgleichnisse des Midrasch beleuchtet durch die römische Kaiserzeit* (Breslau: Schottlaender, 1903). To be sure, I did not find an exact parallel.

31 The contrast "child or son—foreigner" is unusual; normal is the contrast "nation (Israel)—foreigners." Cf. in any case Josephus *Bell.* 7.266: ἀλλότριοι—οἰκειότατοι. Princes are frequent in rabbinical parables; cf. Ziegler, *Die Königsgleichnisse des Midrasch beleuchtet durch die römische Kaiserzeit*, 391-453.

32 The parable in *b. Sukk.* 20a = Str-B 1.771 uses the same idea. A king voluntarily pays toll. Cf. also 1 Sam 17:25: The king releases the family of his son-in-law from paying taxes.

33 On the freedom from taxes for Romans (and Italians) since the first century BCE cf. Joachim Marquardt, *Römische Staatsverwaltung* (Leipzig: Hirzel, 1876) 2.173. In 6 CE the census had led to the rebellion of the Galilean Judas; cf. Josephus *Bell.* 2.118. Cf. also the importance as a symbol of freedom of the remission of taxes granted the Maccabees by the Seleucids at various times (e.g., 1 Macc 10:31; 11:35-36; *Meg. Ta an.* 6 = Riessler, 346; for other cities and territories, Mommsen, *Römisches Staatsrecht*, 737-38). Roman citizens were not excused from local and provincial tolls in general but very often on the basis of treaties or restrictions in privileges granted to the cities. Cf. Mommsen, *Römisches Staatsrecht*, 691-92; Schürer-Vermes 1.373-74 with nn. 94-97.

34 While it is true that Semitic "son" is a "broader term of association" (Georg Fohrer, "υἱός κτλ," *TDNT* 8 [1972] 345, cf. 345-47; Eduard Lohse, ibid., 358-59; Eduard Schweizer, ibid., 365), it is then connected with another designation; cf. 8:12 υἱοὶ τῆς βασιλείας.

However, moving from the image to the referent is difficult. If one interprets (a) vv. 25-26 as a saying of a Jewish-Christian community that is critical of the cult, it is a programmatic explanation of fundamental theological importance. Then the issue is "Jesus' freedom toward the temple, the Sabbath, the whole law of Moses."[35] It is more than a mere criticism of a single regulation. This is true not because with the temple tax that supports it the "temple cult as such is called into question";[36] instead it comes from the image of the freedom of the sons. "Sons" are the Christians, because their relationship to the "king" is no longer based on a cult where one pays taxes like the "strangers." "The eschatological filial relationship replaces the temple and suspends the cultic law at its very center."[37] Then it is not analogous to the freedom from assessments that the Jewish priests claimed for themselves,[38] because the Jewish Christians have never claimed a central place for themselves *in* the temple as the priests had done. Instead, for them it was Jesus' unique atoning sacrifice (Rom 3:25) and the heavenly priesthood after the order of Melchizedek that replaced the temple cult. Then one *could* still participate in the cult and become "to the Jews as a Jew" (1 Cor 9:20) as Paul's example shows (cf. Acts 21:23-26). That, however, was an act of freedom for the sake of the gospel or in order not to give offense. Many exegetes have also known wherein this fundamental freedom is

rooted. "The confession of Jesus' death and resurrection," of which the preceding prediction of the passion spoke, "provides . . . the basis for the disciples' freedom."[39] Or in a different variant: Jesus does not pay, but it is not "because he is a Galilean, but because he is 'the Son.'"[40] The "ancestors" of such interpretations are initially Paul (Gal 3:24-27, 4:6-7; Rom 8:14-15) and then in the history of theology primarily the great allegorists of the ancient church, Cyril and Hilary.[41] Our text then would be an offshoot of the circle around Stephen that was critical of the cult.[42] In my judgment this interpretation is possible, but it creates major difficulties. Verses 25-26 would then never explicitly state the main issue, viz., the idea of a spiritual temple and cult, and it would thus remain open to misunderstanding. In addition, there are major difficulties in harmonizing such an interpretation with an understanding of the law that takes seriously that the Matthean Jesus came to fulfill the law even in its iotas and accent marks (5:17-19).[43]

Therefore I would like (b) to propose a different possible interpretation of vv. 25-26. In the Judaism of that day "sons" can be a regular metaphor for the Israelites.[44] If one understands it this way, the saying raises a new argument in the internal Jewish controversy about the temple tax. The Israelites are like sons and belong to God's family. Therefore the temple should not be run on a system that is appropriate for kings of the world

---

35 Schniewind, 176.

36 Vollenweider, *Freiheit,* 175. Contrary examples: Sadducees and Essenes.

37 Vollenweider (*Freiheit,* 176) citing Mark 14:58; reinterpreting the temple to mean the church may go back to the Jerusalem primitive church. Similarly Gnilka 2.116 ("the church has gained a new relationship to God that is no longer . . . bound to the temple") and Grundmann, 410.

38 David Daube (*Appeasement or Resistance?,* 39–47) thinks that Jesus claims "priestly status" for himself and for those who belong to him (47). Cf. the debate in *m. Šeqal.* 1.3.

39 Frankemölle, *Jahwebund,* 176.

40 Schmid, 266. Cf. David E. Garland, "Matthew's Understanding of the Temple Tax (Matt 17:24-27)," 206: "As God's son, Jesus should never have been obligated to pay a tax imposed by his Father . . . Jesus lays claim to a status for which no Israelite qualified. He presumes to be above the law."

41 Cyril of Alexandria *In Joh.* 2.5 = *PG* 73.309: "We do not think one should serve the lord of all things ταῖς ἔξωθεν δωροφορίαις," but in the Spirit and in truth; Hilary, 17.11 = SC 258.70: "Ut ostenderet legi se non esse subiectum et ut in se paternae dignitatis gloriam contestaretur."

42 Gnilka 2.118. Schweizer, 357: "complete and fundamental freedom of the church from the Jewish Temple community."

43 It does not cause great difficulties for those who assume that for Matthew the ceremonial law is abolished and that texts such as 5:18-19 are only meaningless traditions; cf. vol. 1, II A 2.1 on 5:17-19.

44 Georg Fohrer and Eduard Lohse, "υἱός κτλ," *TDNT* 8 (1972) 351–53, 354–55, 359–60.

toward foreigners but never for a father toward his children.[45] Thus understood, the saying may well come from Jesus. On the one hand it fits Jesus' relationship to God. God's fatherhood is at the center of his piety. On the other hand it is in keeping with Jesus' relatively reserved attitude toward tithing (cf. 23:23 par.). Driving the money changers from the temple (Mark 11:15-17) may also be important here, since they were necessitated by the temple tax that had to be paid in shekels that could not be transported from the Diaspora.[46] In a wider sense Jesus' answer is in keeping with the reserved, even hostile, attitude toward the temple that appeared occasionally in Galilee.[47] It may be that the Galilean Jesus in practice represented the old position of the Sadducees that the donations to the temple should be voluntary, but he did so for different reasons. He opposed a practice that had been introduced by the Pharisees, but he did not oppose the Torah—a Torah that in the opinion of many contemporary Jews did not speak at all of an obligation to pay an annual temple tax. He demands for the poor of Galilee the freedom from this obligation to contribute annually a large amount of money to the distant temple in Jerusalem, but he did not advocate freedom from the cultic law. This interpretation of the logion is also possible. It has the advantage that the logion says explicitly everything that it means. It fits well in the pre-Matthean Palestinian Jewish Christianity that still regarded itself as part of Israel and not in an exclusive sense as God's "sons." It is an interpretation that stands on its own without drawing on Paul. It is understandable that a Jesus community that still understood

itself to be part of Israel paid the temple tax to keep peace. That is the sense of the entire apophthegm, vv. 24-27, to which we now turn.

Church

■ **24-27** Those who collect the double drachma tax do not ask what Jesus thinks about the cultic law and the temple; they ask about his attitude toward the temple tax. Peter gives the tax collectors an unqualified affirmative answer that likely reflected the practice of the Jewish-Christian churches before the destruction of the temple. However, what follows is surprising. In the house Jesus, whose miraculous knowledge is suggested here quite incidentally, anticipates a further question from Peter and instructs Peter about his own attitude toward the temple tax. It no longer determines the church's behavior. In the entire apophthegm vv. 25-26 simply prepare for v. 27 and are handed down by the church as a reminder that its own practice is a compromise for the sake of peace and love but not a position on something that is fundamental, viz., faithfulness to the Torah.[48] Thus the present pericope climaxes in v. 27, the announcement of the miracle of the coin or jewelry in the fish that is familiar from various popular tales.[49] Why was it taken up here? Certainly the memory of the poverty of Jesus and of the circle of disciples plays a role. And certainly the fisherman Peter provides an appropriate occasion for a fish story.[50] Important also was the confidence that God or the Lord provides for the church's material needs, even if it is in a quite unex-

---

45 Apart from the regular metaphor "son," no allegorical interpretations of the image are necessary as, e.g., with the "foreigners."

46 Cf. *m. Seqal.* 1.3; 2.1.

47 Cf. Gerd Theissen, "Jesus' Temple Prophecy: Prophecy in the Tension Between Town and Country," in idem, *Social Reality,* 97–106.

48 This too is not un-Jewish. In a similar way the rabbinate "tolerantly" ruled *post festum* that "for the sake of the ways of peace" pledges should not be exacted from priests who refused to pay the temple tax (*m. Seqal.* 1.3).

49 Herodotus 3.42; Strabo 14.1.16 (ring of Polycrates); *Gen. Rab.* 11 (8b) = Str–B 1.614; *b. Sabb.* 119a = Str–B 1.675 (pearl in the fish as reward for celebrating the Sabbath or the Day of Atonement); *b. B. Batra* 133b (a fish with a pearl is sold to the temple treasury). For additional Jewish references see Rudolf Meyer, "Der Ring des Polykrates, Mt 17,27 und die rabbinische Überlieferung," 665–70, 668–69 and Ginzberg, *Legends* 4.171, 6.300 (about Solomon). Derrett (*Law,* 259, n. 2) offers Indian parallels. For many parallels from fairy tales and legends see Reinhold Köhler, *Kleinere Schriften,* vol. 2: *Zur erzählenden Dichtung des Mittelalters* (Weimar: Felber, 1900) 208–9 (usually as the story of a lost piece of jewelry, often with magical power). Compared to the parallels, Matt 17:27 is a notably independent variant, primarily because a coin is in the fish's *mouth.*

50 Thus Peter does not play an important role in this text as the first apostle or as the only one for whom Jesus pays.

pected way.[51] Much as in the late Lukan version of the legend of Peter's call in Luke 5:1-11, in our legend Jesus' knowledge and authority become an essential scope.[52] Not only is Jesus the Lord also of the fish; even the amount of money needed is exact. Important also for the church is the miraculous foreknowledge of Jesus, who already knew miraculously in v. 25 what Peter had been asked out in front of the house. That also makes understandable why the pericope was handed down even though the temple tax no longer existed and even though with its "successor," the tax for the *fiscus Iudaicus*, in view of the imperial pressure one no longer had a choice about whether to pay or not.

Matthew

What is *Matthew's* interest in our story? The temple tax no longer existed in his time. The good relationship with the synagogue was already destroyed. Our text is the document of a former solidarity[53] that had been overtaken by history. If Matthew himself regarded the annual double drachma tax as a commandment of the Torah, our text bears witness to Jesus' actual fulfillment of the law on his own authority. If Matthew still knew that the double drachma tax is not a commandment of the Torah but belongs to the "tradition of the fathers," then he showed how even such traditions could be accepted occasionally for the sake of love. And of course he also reveals joy that Jesus looks into and rules not only hearts but also nature. However, I no longer see a current *Sitz im Leben* for this text in the time after 70. Matthew has transmitted it out of faithfulness to the tradition.

History of Interpretation

The most important influence of the text came from a misinterpretation for which there is early evidence.[54] The double drachma tax was understood as a civil tax because, among other reasons, the "kings of the earth" and the technical terms τέλος and κῆνσος appeared in the text. Then the text could be connected with Mark 12:13-17 and Rom 13:1-7 and made to speak of the obligation that Christians had to be subordinated to the state and to pay taxes not de jure but de facto.[55] Interpretations from the Reformation were especially able to use this text as proof for the doctrine of two kingdoms. Human beings, consisting of body and soul, are subject to the magistrate as far as the body is concerned, while the spirit obeys the spirit of God. Christ, "who was completely spiritual," gives an example here for the external subordination under secular authority.[56] Luther understood the civil taxes as "guest money," since people are "guests" in the kingdom of the world.[57] That Christ, "the only Son of God," "became a servant with the others of his own free will" could be used as an argument both against the early Anabaptists, who did not want to have anything to do with the state, and also against the Catholic church,[58] which in the late Middle Ages obviously appealed to this text to support its claim of freedom from civil taxes for the clergy.[59] While in the interpretations of the reformers there were still clear limits to the claims of the "kingdom of the world," those limits later receded into the background. Then the only remaining issue in our text was that Christ "by means of an amazing miracle and his memorable example affirmed the obedience that is due the political magistrate."[60]

Humanistic exegesis discovered again what especially the Eastern church was still partly aware of, viz., that our text spoke not of civil taxes,[61] but of the cul-

51 Protestant interpretation was able to find its work ethic in v. 27. Cf. already Brenz, 593–94: The fisherman Peter acquires the money for the taxes by fishing, a farmer from the field, a merchant from trade. Paulus (2.614–15) states that the fisher Peter "found" the stater by selling the fish. The issue is thus diligent "work at one's trade" (Holtzmann, 262) or the "blessing of industry" (K. Hase according to Meyer, 301). The early bird catches the worm!

52 Cf. Jerome, 155: "Quid primum mirer . . . nescio utrum praescientiam an magnitudinem Salvatoris." John Chrysostom 58.2 = *PG* 58.567: Jesus is God and Lord over everything, even over the sea.

53 Simon Légasse, "Jésus et l'impôt du Temple (Mt 17,24-27)," 361–77, 372: In Matthew's day this now "outdated" story becomes a parable that recom-

mends "une attitude conciliante vis-à-vis des Juifs."

54 Irenaeus *Haer.* 5.24.1.

55 See, e.g., Origen, 13.10 = GCS Origenes 10.207; Jerome, 184–85.

56 Zwingli, 331–32.

57 *WA* 38.667.

58 Calvin, 2.238.

59 One does not find this in commentaries. Lapide (342) speaks of *nonnulli Canonistae* and resists their claim.

60 Benedictus Aretius, *Commentarii in Domini nostri Jesu Christi Novum Testamentum* (Paris: Ioannem le Preux, 1607) 158.

61 Grotius, 2.74–75; Wolzogen, 324 (cf. above, n. 21); Episcopius, 109–10.

tic temple tax. Protestant exegesis accepted this insight more slowly than did Catholic exegesis, not primarily because the text was abandoned as an argument for Christian loyalty to the state, but because one thus lost an argument against the privileges of Catholic clerics.[62]

When one began with the Jewish temple tax, old christological interpretations of our text again surfaced. The accents could vary, depending on whether one emphasized the freedom of the Son (vv. 25-26) or the voluntary payment of the temple tax for the sake of peace. Peter, who so quickly affirmed the question of the collectors, obviously was not yet convinced of the deity of Jesus, says Ishodad of Merv, for "God never takes tribute from his Son who is a partner in his kingdom."[63] Or one could emphasize the by no means un-Matthean idea that the incarnate Son of God "'came not to dissolve the law but to fulfill it'"

and therefore paid the tax that the law required.[64] It is of more than passing interest for determining the standpoint of especially German-speaking Protestant exegesis that as a rule it was easy for it to emphasize v. 26 and the freedom of Jesus and his sons, because for it the issue was cult and law,[65] while its Protestant ancestors were troubled by Jesus' freedom and preferred to emphasize with v. 27 his voluntary submission, because they related the text to taxes and the claims of the state. A good example of the way dogmatic and other premises influence exegesis!

---

62   Calovius (339–40) complains about the way Grotius was treated by the Jesuits!
63   Ishodad of Merv, *The Commentaries*, ed. M. D. Gibson (Horae Semiticae 5; Cambridge: Cambridge University Press, 1911) 1.70.

64   Cyril of Alexandria fr. 211 = Reuss, 222.
65   Cf. above, nn. 37, 39–40, 42.

Literature

Pierre Bonnard, "Composition et signification historique de Matthieu 18," in idem, *Anamnesis: recherches sur le Nouveau Testament* (Cahiers de la Revue de théologie et de philosophie 3; Geneva: Revue de théologie et de philosophie, 1980) 111–20.

Raymond E. Brown, *The Churches the Apostles Left Behind* (New York: Paulist, 1984) 138–45.

Kähler, "Kirchenleitung."

Légasse, *Jésus*, 32–36, 51–72, 104–19, 215–31.

Ingrid Maisch, "Christsein in Gemeinschaft," in Lorenz Oberlinner and Peter Fiedler, eds., *Salz der Erde–Licht der Welt: Exegetische Studien zum Matthäusevangelium: Festschrift für Anton Vögtle zum 80. Geburtstag* (Stuttgart: Katholisches Bibelwerk, 1991) 239–66.

Ernest R. Martinez, "The Interpretation of οἱ μαθηταί in Matthew 18," *CBQ* 23 (1961) 281–92.

Wilhelm Pesch, "Die sogenannte Gemeindeordnung Mt 18," *BZ* NF 7 (1963) 220–35.

Idem, *Matthäus.*

Rossé, *Ecclesiologia.*

Rudolf Schnackenburg, "Mk 9,33-50," in *Synoptische Studien: Alfred Wikenhauser zum siebzigsten Geburtstag am 22. Februar 1953* (Munich: Zink, 1953) 184–206.

Schweizer, *Matthäus,* 106–15.

Thompson, *Advice.*

Thysman Raymond, *Communauté et directives éthiques: La catéchèse de Matthieu* (Recherches et Synthèses: Section d'exégèse: 1; Gembloux: Duculot, 1969) 74–82.

Trilling, *Hausordnung.*

Idem, *Israel,* 106–23.

Léon Vaganay, "Le schématisme du discours communautaire à la lumière de la critique des sources," *RB* 60 (1953) 203–44.

Zimmermann, "Struktur," 4–19.

Zumstein, *Condition,* 386–421.

H. C. van Zyl, "Structural Analysis of Mt 18," *Neot* 16 (1982) 35–55.

Position in the Gospel

Matthew's fourth discourse is also his shortest. It is not immediately clear that it is to be a discourse, since, unlike the clear introductions to the other discourses (5:1-2; 10:1, 5a; 13:1-3a; 23:1), nothing in 18:1-4 leads the readers to expect a major address. The discussion with the disciples in vv. 1-4 is expanded into a discourse by means of a succession of additional explanations from Jesus.[1]

It is not clear what led the evangelist to insert a discourse here, since it destroys the carefully balanced sequence of Mark's three predictions of the passion. Nor is the discourse set off by the surrounding narrative as well as are the other discourses. That Matthew wanted to follow the model of the Pentateuch by creating five discourses of Jesus is, of course, a primary consideration. It is one of the fundamental principles underlying his reworking of Mark's gospel. In all probability the reasons for his insertion of the discourse at precisely this point are primarily external. It is time for a discourse, since the narrative section that began with 13:53 is already longer than any earlier narrative section in Matthew. Furthermore, since at this point Mark had added a collection of sayings to two narrative pericopes (9:33-40), this was a good opportunity to insert a discourse. In addition, 19:1 provides a break in the narrative. Jesus is leaving Galilee for the final time; the multitudes are going to be with him again.

Matthew omits the pericope of the strange exorcist (Mark 9:38-40), since it does not fit thematically in a context that deals with relationships within the community. Furthermore, he has already used Mark 9:40 in 12:20 in reverse order. It may also be that the content of the pericope disturbs him, since in 7:22 he describes the false prophets with language that describes the behavior of the strange exorcist.[2] The understanding of the church in Mark 9:38-40 is probably too loose for Matthew.[3] He is able to omit *Mark 9:41*, because he has already offered the logion in 10:42.[4] In addition, chap. 18 is concerned not with the treatment of wandering charismatics but with relationships within the community. Matthew omits

---

1   There is little reason to join Thompson (*Advice,* 16) in regarding the pericope on the temple tax in 17:24-27 as the first section of chap. 18. Matthew 18:1 introduces a new beginning and new conversation partners, the disciples.

2   Common to Matt 7:22 and Mark 9:38-39 are the words: Τῷ (σῷ) ὀνόματι (σου) δαιμόνια (ἐκβάλλειν),

τῷ ὀνόματι (δύναμιν, ποιεῖν).

3   Cf., e.g., Pesch, *Matthäus,* 62: Mark 9:38-40 is "too tolerant"; Schweizer, *Matthäus,* 110: In 7:22-23 and 24:11-12 Matthew is opposing false prophets; he would never have been that open toward people who were not members of the church.

4   Verse 5, on the other hand, is not a genuine parallel

the logion about salt (*Mark 9:49-50*), because he has already used the Q version of the saying in 5:13.

Structure

An outline of the discourse is not easily discernible. Possible clues to its structure are: (a) the narrative insertion in vv. 21-22; (b) the reference to βασιλεία τῶν οὐρανῶν in vv. 1, 3-4, and 23; (c) catchwords that appear in more than one pericope but which do not characterize the entire discourse[5]—παιδίον (vv. 2-5), ἐν μέσῳ (vv. 2, 20), ὄνομα (vv. 5, 20), εἷς τῶν μικρῶν τούτων (vv. 6, 10, 14), ὁ πατήρ μου ὁ ἐν οὐρανοῖς (vv. 10, 14, cf. 19, 35), ἐάν (vv. 12-19, eleven times),[6] ἀφίημι (vv. 12, 21, 27, 32, 35), ἁμαρτάνω (vv. 15, 21), and ἀδελφός vv. (15, 21, 35); and (d) the similar verses 6 and 10 (to give offense to or to despise the little ones), 10 and 14 (the closeness of the little ones to the Father), and 14 and 35 (two sides of the same comparison with the heavenly Father). No outline of the material takes into account all of these features.

The various proposals divide the discourse into either two parts or three parts. In the former case the break occurs between vv. 20 and 21 (the narrative insertion)[7] or between vv. 14 and 15 (a division by content: first a section on the "little ones," then a section on the "brothers").[8] A division into three parts begins with a section dealing with humility vis-à-vis the little ones (vv. 1-9) followed by a section on forgiveness (vv. 10-22). The parable (vv. 23-35) would then make up the third section.[9] However one divides the discourse, it is clear that Matthew is not interested in clear divisions. In every case catchwords tie the sections together. Verses 21-22 are obvious transitional verses, since they look back to vv.

12-14, while at the same time they introduce vv. 23-35.

In my judgment, the narrative insertion with Peter's question in v. 21 is the most obvious feature to be considered. The section of the discourse that follows in vv. 21-35 summons the members of the church to forgiveness. The structure of the earlier section is less clear. The introductory scene with the small child (vv. 1-5) is followed by two pericopes that deal with the proper attitude toward other church members. One should not cause them to stumble (vv. 6-9), and one should forgive them (vv. 10-14). The rule of excommunication that then follows in vv. 15-18 resumes the theme of vv. 6-9; at the same time it continues the theme of forgiveness from vv. 12-14. The concluding vv. 19 and 20 emphasize the vertical dimension by speaking of the disciples' relationship to the Father and to the exalted Lord. They are conspicuous in a discourse that deals elsewhere with the horizontal dimension of community, yet they are not merely an afterthought. They are reminiscent both of the basic Immanuel motif (cf. 1:23)[10] and of the motif of answered prayer that plays a key role in the Sermon on the Mount (cf. 6:7-8; 7:7-11). Verses 19-20 are thus central to the discourse.[11] At its midpoint Matthew speaks of God's promised presence and directs the reader's attention to what is above. The function of the key vv. 19 and 20 in this address is thus similar to that of vv. 24-25 in Matthew 10.

---

	to 10:40, since nothing is said there about accepting children.
5	Léon Vaganay ("Le schématisme du discours communautaire à la lumière de la critique des sources," *RB* 60 [1953] 203–44) has subjected these keywords to a thorough examination. Behind Matthew 18 and Mark 9 he sees an Aramaic original whose context was only partially preserved in the Greek versions. His thesis has not found general acceptance.
6	Along with still more widely corresponding cases to which the numerous parallelisms point: γένηται (vv. 12-13), ἀκούσῃ (vv. 15-16), παρακούσῃ (v. 17, twice), and δήσητε/λύσητε (v. 18).
7	See, e.g., Thompson, *Advice*, 239–40, 244: a disciples section—a Peter section; Radermakers, 235–36.
8	This is the most common division of the chapter.

Pesch (*Matthäus*, 15–16, 50) has been influential here. He has found "two didactic pieces," in Matthew 18, viz., "on the true worth of the 'children and the little ones'" and on "true brotherliness." Others who offer similar divisions are Gnilka 2.119–20; Patte, 247, 252; Davies-Allison 2.750–51.

9	Trilling (*Hausordnung,* 19–65, and *Israel,* 106) offers a somewhat different arrangement. Following the "basic demand" in vv. 1-5 there are three "individual demands" in vv. 6-14, 15-20, 21-35. H. C. Van Zyl's outline ("Structural Analysis of Mt 18," 35–55) is similar.
10	Cf. vol. 1, Summary on 1:24-25.
11	Cf. especially Gerard Rossé (*Ecclesiologia*) and Gnilka (2.120): Verse 20 is the "secret midpoint" of the address.

The discourse is addressed to the disciples (vv. 1-3, 10, 12, 18-19, 35) or to Peter as their representative (vv. 21-22).[12] Although formulated in the second-person singular, the rule of excommunication in vv. 15-17 is clearly addressed to all the disciples. It is they with whom the readers primarily identify. There is no basis in the discourse for suggesting that the evangelist intended to speak only to a particular group of readers such as, for example, the leaders of the church.[13]

Sources

Matthew uses the same method in this discourse that he uses in chapters 10, 13, 23, 24–25. To a foundation from the Gospel of Mark (Mark 9:33-37, 42-47 = vv. 1-9) he adds Q material and his own special material. From the sayings source he takes Q 17:1-4 = vv. 6-7, 15, 22. The parable of the unmerciful steward (vv. 23-35) and possibly the parable of the lost sheep as well (vv. 12-13) come from his own material. In my judgment he had them only in oral form.[14]

Theme

The theme of the discourse has been described in various ways. It is customary to speak of a *Discourse on the Church*[15] with the theme of "church order."[16] Trilling speaks of "rules for God's household."[17] Grundy offers the superscription "brotherliness in the church."[18] In contrast to the first foundation-laying ecclesiological discourse in chapter 10 that dealt with the mission of the church, that is, with the church's relationship to the world, the issue in this second foundation-laying ecclesiological discourse is church solidarity and the preservation of community. My title is thus "community discourse,"[19] and I hope that with this choice I have been able to define the content that the two main sections of the chapter have in common.

---

12   Cf. the excursus above, III C 3.3 on Peter in the Gospel of Matthew.

13   For Kilpatrick (*Origins,* 79) and Jeremias (*Parables,* 40) Matthew 18 is a "major instruction for the leaders of the churches," a thesis that correctly is almost universally rejected. Neither in the context of the main section (16:21–20:34) nor in the address itself is there anything to suggest that not all members of the church are addressed. Ernest R. Martinez ("The Interpretation of οἱ μαθηταί in Matthew 18," 281–92) argues that beginning in 10:1-4 the disciples are the Twelve and that they represent the leaders of the church. Matthew's terminology, however, is the same both before and after 10:1-4.

14   Cf. below, IV B 1.3 on the analysis of 18:10-14 and IV B 2.2 on the analysis of 18:23-35.

15   Sand, *Gesetz,* 363; Schnackenburg 2.167; cf. Fabris, 381.

16   Grundmann, 411.

17   The title of his book: *Hausordnung Gottes.* Except for 16:18, however, Matthew nowhere has the idea, so important elsewhere in the New Testament, of the church as a house or a temple.

18   358. Cf. Gnilka 2.119: "On the little ones and the brothers."

19   Similarly Kähler, "Kirchenleitung," 142; Ingrid Maisch, "Christsein in Gemeinschaft," 239–66 = this title.

The structure of this first section is not easily discernible. The text speaks first of παιδία ("children"; vv. 2-5), then of μικροί ("little ones"; vv. 6-14), and finally, beginning with v. 15, of ἀδελφοί ("brothers"). Verses 2-5 are generally instructive. I read them as a kind of statement of principle that is important for the entire discourse. After v. 5 direct address dominates the text, but the persons addressed appear to change. Verses 6-7 appear to be directed to those who lead others astray and vv. 8-9 to those who are in danger of being led astray, while vv. 10-14 appear to be directed to the rest of the church. It is more difficult to determine the underlying tendency of the section. In vv. 6-9 and 15-18 the issue appears to be separation from sinners, while in vv. 5, 10-14, and 21-22 it appears to be their acceptance. The question facing the interpreter is: What relationship do the two themes have to one another? Does the section offer a coherent development of a single idea, or do two different lines of thought simply exist side by side? The text gives few clues concerning how the author understands the logical sequence of the sections. The impression is that Matthew simply strings together from his sources individual units that deal with life in the church. Such a conclusion leaves the interpreter somewhat unsatisfied. Only a careful analysis of the text can clarify its central issue—viz., how separation and exclusion are related to acceptance and forgiveness.

1.1 The Fundamental Principle: A Return to Humbleness (18:1-5)

Literature

John Dominic Crossan, "Kingdom and Children: A Study in the Aphoristic Tradition," *Semeia* 29 (1983) 75–95.

Dupont, *Béatitudes* 2.161–215.

Idem, "Ἐὰν μὴ στραφῆτε καὶ γένησθε ὡς τὰ παιδία (Mt 18,3)," in idem, *Études*, 2.940–50.

Ragnar Leivestad, "ΤΑΠΕΙΝΟΣ-ΤΑΠΕΙΝΟΦΡΩΝ," *NovT* 8 (1966) 36–47.

Barnabas Lindars, "John and the Synoptic Gospels: A Test Case," *NTS* 27 (1981) 287–94.

Peter Müller, *In der Mitte der Gemeinde: Kinder im Neuen Testament* (Neukirchen-Vluyn: Neukirchener Verlag, 1992).

Daniel Patte, "Jesus' Pronouncement About Entering the Kingdom like a Child: A Structural Exegesis," *Semeia* 29 (1983) 3–42.

John W. Pryor, "John 3:3.5: A Study in the Relation of John's Gospel to the Synoptic Tradition," *JSNT* 41 (1991) 71–95.

Vernon K. Robbins, "Pronouncement Stories and Jesus' Blessing of the Children," *Semeia* 29 (1983) 43–74.

Rudolf Schnackenburg, "Grossein im Gottesreich: Zu Mt 18,1-5," in Ludger Schenke, ed., *Studien zum Matthäusevangelium: Festschrift für Wilhelm Pesch* (SBS; Stuttgart: Katholisches Bibelwerk, 1988) 269–82.

Wolfgang Stegemann, "Lasset die Kinder zu mir kommen," in idem and Willy Schottroff, eds., *Traditionen der Befreiung: Sozialgeschichtliche Bibelauslegungen*, vol. 1: *Methodische Zugänge* (Munich: Kaiser, 1980) 114–44.

Hans R. Weber, *Jesus and the Children* (Geneva: World Council of Churches, 1979).

David Wenham, "A Note on Mark 9:33-42/Matt 18:1-6/Luke 9:46-50," *JSNT* 14 (1982) 113–18.

For *additional literature* on the church discourse see above, IV B.

1 **In that hour the disciples came to Jesus, saying, "Who then is the greatest in the kingdom of heaven?" 2/ And calling a child to him, he put it in their midst 3/ and said, "Amen, I say to you, if you do not turn and become like children, you will not enter the kingdom of heaven. 4/ For whoever will humble himself like this child is the greatest in the kingdom of heaven. 5/ And whoever receives even one such child in my name receives me. . . ."**

Analysis

Structure

The discourse begins with an apophthegm. In response to a question from the disciples (v. 1) Jesus offers first an object lesson (v. 2) and then an answer that eventually becomes a longer address (vv. 3-20). In a strict sense Jesus' answer lies in v. 4, where the final clause parallels exactly the disciples' question in v. 1. Verse 3 thus functions as preparation. Jesus refers to the object lesson with the child and then in a solemn amen pronouncement says something about which the disciples have not even asked. The first four verses constitute a formally compact, expanded *chreia*.[1] Verse 5 sounds as if it has been added. Scholarship is divided whether it belongs to our section or is already part of the following section. Verse 6, how-

---

1   Along with John Dominic Crossan ("Kingdom and Children: A Study in the Aphoristic Tradition,"   75–95, 77–80) and Vernon K. Robbins ("Pronouncement Stories and Jesus' Blessing of the Children,"

ever, takes up a new subject, the question of offenses. New also is the catchword μικροί. While the sentence structure of v. 5 is similar to that of v. 6, the contents of the two verses are not parallel. In my judgment it is therefore better to connect v. 5 with vv. 1-4 and to understand it as an addition to the answer of Jesus given in v. 4. Matthew thus stays within the limits given him by Mark.

Source

The source is Mark 9:33-37. The Markan pericope consists of two *chreiai*. In vv. 33-35 the first *chreia* consists of a complex introduction and a Jesus saying that formally does not correspond to the disciples' question in exact detail. Verses 36-37 constitute a second, somewhat incomplete *chreia* which, without actually naming the disciples, assumes that it is they who are addressed. It consists of a symbolic act and a gnome. Matthew has completely reworked the Markan text. He has merged the two Markan *chreiai* into a single apophthegm[2] by omitting most of the first one (Mark 9:33-35).[3] Matthew's introduction in v. 1 is almost totally redaction.[4] In Matthew the disciples simply pose a general question to Jesus as teacher. Matthew takes over Mark's introduction to the second *chreia* in v. 36 almost word for word.[5] Between it and the Jesus logion of Mark 9:37 (= v. 5) he inserts vv. 3-4, which for him are the point of the apophthegm.

A comparison with Luke 9:46-48 reveals a series of notable so-called minor agreements—viz., the omission of Mark 9:33-34a, 35 and of ἐναγκαλισάμενος αὐτὸ in Mark 9:36b along with the positive agreement of ὃς ἐὰν δέξηται . . . παιδίον in Matt 18:5 and Luke 9:48. In the case of Mark 9:33-35 it is likely that this small apophthegm is a redactional creation,[6] while the second apophthegm, Mark 9:36-37, is probably pre-Markan tradition. Matthew and Luke obviously shortened their Markan text in light of the oral tradition they remembered. Matthew frequently omits references to Jesus' emotions.[7] The appearance of the verb immediately following ὃς ἐὰν is normal for both Matthew and Luke.[8] That Matthew and Luke edited Mark independently of one another is further confirmed by the fact that they both improve Mark's clumsy double *chreia*, but they formulate Jesus' actual response to the disciples' discussion differently and at different places (Matt 18:4; Luke 9:48c).[9] Thus the best explanation of the evidence here is still the simple two-source theory without the assumption of an additional recension.[10]

The most difficult source-critical problem of our section is the issue of the *origin of vv. 3-4*. There are two basic theories. Either Matthew inserts Mark 10:15 at this point and then omits it later in his gospel,[11] or the verse is independent of Mark and represents the earliest version of a logion[12] that was widespread in

---

43–74, 48–51), following ancient rhetoric (cf. Quintilian *Inst. orat.* 1.8.4), I define *chreia* as a pregnantly formulated simple sentence (or action) about a particular historical person that is used in instruction. Simple *chreiai* can be used in the instruction in different ways. They can be expanded, e.g., by the addition of dialogue or novelistic elements. For an expanded *chreia* I use here the term "apophthegm."

2   Matthew 18:1-5 did not originate, therefore, as an expanded *chreia* but as the combination of two *chreiai*.

3   The introduction, vv. 33-34, which possibly is Mark's own redaction, is very clumsy. Matthew is going to use the logion of Mark 9:35 two more times in a similar form (20:26-27; 23:11).

4   Cf. vol. 1, Introduction 3.2 on ἐκείνη + ὥρα, προσέρχομαι, λέγων, ἄρα, βασιλεία τῶν οὐρανῶν.

5   On προσκαλεσάμενος cf. the redactional 10:1 and 15:32.

6   Mark used the logion 10:43-44 that he had received through the tradition to create a short apophthegm in keeping with his basic idea of discipleship as the way of suffering; cf. Gnilka, *Markus* 2.55; Lührmann, *Markusevangelium*, 165–66.

7   Cf. Mark 1:43 par. Matt 8:3 par. Luke 5:13; Mark 3:5 par. Matt 12:12 par. Luke 6:10; Mark 7:34 par. Matt

15:30; Mark 10:21 par. Matt 19:21 par. Luke 18:22.

8   Twenty-one times in Matthew; nine times in Luke.

9   Luke 9:48c is independent of Matt 18:4, contra David Wenham ("A Note on Mark 9:33-42/Matt 18:1-6/Luke 9:46-50," 113–18, 113–114), who assumes a common tradition for them.

10   Cf. Ulrich Luz, joint reviewer with W. R. Farmer, "The Minor Agreements of Matthew and Luke against Mark and the Two-Gospel Hypothesis," in Georg Strecker, *Minor Agreements: Symposion Göttingen* (GThA 50; Göttingen: Vandenhoeck & Ruprecht, 1991, 1993) 217–18; contra Ennulat, *Agreements*, 214–17. Since Matt 18:3-4 is missing in Luke, it is unlikely that Luke used Matthew.

11   Robert H. Gundry, *Mark: A Commentary on His Apology for the Cross* (Grand Rapids: Eerdmans, 1993) 360; Trilling, *Israel*, 108; especially Dupont, *Béatitudes* 2.168–71.

12   Barnabas Lindars, "John and the Synoptic Gospels: A Test Case," 287–94; Schweizer, 361; Davies-Allison 2.756–57.

early Christianity.[13] The clear influence of Matthew's editorial hand in our logion speaks for the first theory.[14] Its parenetic form is also typical of Matthew. That all other early Christian variants of the logion do not speak of "receiving the kingdom" as does Mark and are thus closer to Matthew speaks for the second theory.[15] Unlike Matt 18:3, Mark 10:15 shows no evidence of editorial changes, and it is possible that Mark found the logion in its present form and inserted it into his pericope about blessing the children (Mark 10:13-14, 16). In short, it is possible, but not certain, that instead of Mark 10:15 Matthew used a variant of the logion about becoming a child that he was familiar with from oral tradition.[16] It would still be the case, however, that in a tradition-history sense Mark 10:15 is the earliest version of the logion available to us.[17]

Verse 4 can be explained relatively easily. The logion is an abbreviated variant of 23:12 par. Luke 14:11. Verse 4b is an editorial repetition of the question of the disciples in v. 2.[18]

Interpretation

■ **1** "In that hour" is one of the temporal linkages appearing frequently in Matthew that suggest the uninterrupted flow of the narrative without necessarily implying a direct connection with the immediately preceding unit (cf. 3:1; 12:1; 14:1). As in 13:36 and 24:3 the disciples come to Jesus and pose a question that becomes the point of departure for a longer discourse. Matthew has omitted Mark's reference to the argument among the disciples. What lies behind their question is of no concern to him, nor is he interested in portraying the disciples as sinful or guilty of a false desire for glory.[19] They pose rather a general question[20] that Jesus uses as the occasion for a discourse about basic principles. We need not necessarily look, therefore, for a particular concrete situation in the church that Matthew was addressing with his fourth discourse.[21] The disciples ask on general principles who the greatest[22] is in the kingdom of God. Μέγας ("great") implies position and honor; the greatest in a kingdom are the governors and ministers.[23] The question does not indicate whether the focus is on the disciples' present position (as in Mark and Luke) or on their position in the coming kingdom of heaven. It is Jesus' answer in v. 3 that reveals that the latter is the primary concern.[24]

■ **2-3** Initially, instead of answering their question, Jesus does something unexpected. He calls a child and puts it in their midst. Then he begins a formal explanation that

13　Cf. John 3:3, 5; *Gos. Thom.* 22, 46; *Hermas, Sim.* 9.29 = 106.3.

14　Cf. vol. I, Introduction 3.2 under ἀμέν [λέγω ὑμῖν], ἐάν, γίνομαι ὡς, εἰσέρχομαι εἰς τὴν βασιλείαν τῶν οὐρανῶν. Our verse is based on the pattern of the verse 5:20 that is also editorial. A more difficult case is στραφῆτε that does indeed appear in Matthew on two other occasions in editorial material (always aorist passive) but not, as in this case, with a metaphorical meaning. The plural ὡς τὰ παιδία is in keeping with the direct address to the disciples.

15　Thus Paul Joüon, "Notes philologiques sur les évangiles," *RechSR* 18 (1928) 347–48. Jeremias (*Theology*, 155) is of the opinion that στραφῆτε καὶ γένησθε corresponds to the iterative Hebrew שוב + verb and could be a Semitism in the sense of "to become a child again." However, Dupont's careful rebuttal ("στραφῆτε") has demonstrated that this thesis is almost certainly false, since in the LXX שוב is never translated with στρέφω, and its Semitic equivalents do not have the meaning of "again."

16　A similar claim is made by John W. Pryor, "John 3:3.5: A Study in the Relation of John's Gospel to the Synoptic Tradition," 71–95.

17　Matt 18:3 is strongly editorial. The two Johannine versions (independent of Matthew?) are filled with baptismal theology. In Mark 10:15 the βασιλεία appears as pure gift, an understanding that fits well with the original beatitudes in Luke 6:20-21. It may be that Matthew, on the other hand, took over and reworked an already ethical version of the logion much as he did in his beatitudes 5:5, 7-9.

18　On οὗτος at the beginning of the clause cf. Schenk, *Sprache*, 386. On ὅστις, οὖν, ὡς see vol. 1, Introduction 3.2. Ὡς τὸ παιδίον τοῦτο connects the traditional saying with the context.

19　The apostles' φιλοδοξία (Theophylactus, 337) is not the main problem for Matthew. He is even less concerned about the question that later interpreters posed—viz., whether the apostles might be guilty of a deadly sin (Maldonat, 359).

20　Ἄρα can appear in a question that arises out of what has preceded. However, the particle can also serve simply "to enliven the question." Cf. BAGD, *s.v.* ἄρα, 2 and 24:45.

21　This is Thompson's basic thesis (*Advice*). According to him, vv. 5-9 especially show that the evangelist is dealing with a "divided community."

22　Comparative instead of superlative in popular language: BDF §§ 60, 244.

23　Cf. Esth 10:3; 1 Macc 7:8.

also does not answer the disciples' question. They had simply posed a general question, but Jesus' answer is directed specifically at them: "If *you* do not turn and become like children . . ." Jesus suddenly raises the issue of their own lives. The answer contains the form of a word about entering the kingdom of heaven that is especially popular with Matthew. It is also noteworthy that for the moment the question of the best places in heaven is no longer under consideration. Simply entering the kingdom of heaven itself presupposes a fundamental transformation of conventional life. For Matthew "turning" is not a *terminus technicus* for "conversion."[25] The expression is important, however, because in its metaphorical sense it is unusual. Jesus demands of his disciples a fundamental change. To become like children is obviously a kind of existence that is out of the ordinary. To become like children is a paradox, since it is impossible for those who are no longer children to become children again. What does it mean that one is to do something that is impossible—that contradicts what by nature is possible?[26]

History of Interpretation

Since the text does not explicitly say what is characteristic of children, it is not surprising that every age to a great degree has read into the text its own understanding of what a child is. In the process a fundamental change in the meaning of the text seems to have prevailed throughout most of the history of the text's interpretation. For the most part the interpreters ask not what children *are* like; they ask instead what children *should* be. More often than not they read the text as if it said: "Become like good, well-behaved children." The following examples illustrate how the ideal child has been understood in different ages.

Frequently innocence,[27] gentleness,[28] and simplicity[29] are emphasized. In obvious distinction from the apostles, children are "not inquisitive; they do not strive for empty glory; they are not haughty; they are free of malice and rivalry, ambition, conflict and . . . stubborn passion."[30] According to Hilary "they follow their father, love their mother, do not know how to think evil of their fellow humans, have no interest in wealth, are not impudent, do not hate, do not lie, believe what they are told, and regard whatever they hear as true."[31] The ascetic Origen says that children who have had no sexual experiences are for the most part free of "passions, and weaknesses, and sicknesses of the soul."[32] Basil is of the opinion that they "do not talk back, do not quarrel with the teacher, but rather accept instruction docilely."[33] Luther emphasizes that a child accepts the punishments meted out by its parents,[34] Zwingli that children do not hold a grudge. (Revenge is the prerogative solely of the governing authorities.)[35] Calvin underscores the humility of children that is worthy of imitation,[36] Brenz that children trust their parents,[37] Olshausen their unpretentiousness.[38] For Goethe "the seeds of all the virtues, all the powers" are in children.[39] Zinzendorf emphasizes that just as a child wants to be nursed and to be carried by its mother, so Christ will take him in his arms and put to death everything in him that is obstinate.[40] Hymn composers call the faithful to be "devout and joyful like children," or they encourage

24 That corresponds to the future orientation of the kingdom of heaven elsewhere in Matthew; cf. above, the excursus on the interpretation of Matthew's parables, 2, in III B 3.4. The disciples' question is the same question asked by the mother of the sons of Zebedee in 20:21, and it reflects the view common in Judaism that there are different degrees of honor in the afterlife. Cf. Str–B 1.249–50; 4.1131–32, 1138–40; Dalman, *Words*, 113–15. Matthew is also aware of this idea; cf. 5:19, 11:11.

25 For that Matthew usually uses the root μετανο-.

26 Kierkegaard, *Training*, 3/4: "To *be* a child . . . when one actually is one, is easy; however, to become one *again*—this again is what is decisive."

27 Jerome, 156–157; Leo the Great *Sermo* 37.3 = FC 93.161.

28 Leo the Great *Sermo* 37.3 = FC 93.161.

29 John Chrysostom 58.2 = *PG* 58.568–569; Desiderius Erasmus, *Opera Omnia*, vol. 6: *Novum Testamentum, cui, in hac Editione, subjectae sunt singulis paginis Adnotationes* (1705; reprint Hildesheim: Olms, 1962) 94.

30 Euthymius Zigabenus, 497.

31 Hilary, 18.1 = SC 258.74.

32 13.16 = GCS Origenes 10.220.

33 Basil *Regulae brevius* no. 217.

34 2.588 = a sermon from 1533.

35 334.

36 2.214.

37 596.

38 578.

39 *The Sufferings of Young Werther*, Book 1, June 29 (Bayard Quincy Morgan, trans.; New York: Ungar, 1957) 42.

40 1122, 1129.

the church: "Let us be childlike, not quarreling on the way."[41] Matthew 18:3-4 was an important text for Leo Tolstoy. In children "he discovered the human originality of Jesus' love of neighbor"; before they are trained in any way they are figures of innocence and love. In them there is hope; they "acknowledge no difference between their own and other nations."[42] For Franz Rosenzweig children incorporate hope—a trust in the future.[43]

Finally, a few examples from our own century: It is important "to become undemanding, like children."[44] Well-behaved children are "dociles et confiants, ils acceptent d'être instruits et d'obéir."[45] A child "is aware that it is little" and accepts it.[46] A child is "open to learning new ideas" and "out of gratitude (or fear) for security they accept what those who are larger and stronger can give them."[47] In the history of the interpretation of this text children are exemplary children of their fathers. Only infrequently do exegetes remember that actual children can be quite different.[48]

The history of interpretation shows how easily the interpretations are conditioned by the interpreters' images of children and especially how often they read into our text patriarchal ideals about raising children without being aware of what they are doing. "Like children" has been regarded as empty space that the exegetes have been only too willing to fill in terms of their own relationship to children. We must ask whether the text actually intends to be that vague, or whether it does not instead presuppose a quite clear understanding of "child." It is thus important to ask what connotations the text presupposes for readers in that day.

Interpretation

■ **4** Our starting point is the explanatory v. 4. The point of comparison between children and the disciples is paraphrased as ταπεινόω ("to humble," "make low"). The first association here for the readers is the smallness of children. Ταπεινός can mean "little." The primary meaning of the root ταπεινο-, however, is "low" or "humble." One who is low is insignificant, impotent, weak, and lives in poor circumstances. Given this meaning of the word, we need to take a brief look at the social world of that day.

> It is important to remember here the negative social situation of children in antiquity. Children were not full human beings with their own integrity but incomplete (νήπιοι) beings who needed to be trained; that is, they were not yet grown.[49] Judaism often regarded them negatively as beings not yet capable of making judgments. "Morning sleep and midday wine and children's talk and sitting in the meeting houses of the ignorant people put a man out of the world" (m. ʾAbot 3.11).[50] That, as is well known, the words παῖς and παιδίον can also mean "slave," says a great deal about the legal standing of children, who were subject to the unlimited authority of their fathers.[51] The point of comparison for our logion is thus first of all children's physical size, then also their powerlessness and their low social standing.

41   *Evangelisches Gesangbuch* 482, 5 (Matthias Claudius, "Der Mond ist aufgegangen"); ibid., 393, 7 (Gerhard Tersteegen, "Kommt Kinder, lasst uns gehen").

42   The first quote comes from a review by C. Münch; the second from Leo Tolstoy, "The Gospel in Brief," in *The Works of Leo Tolstoy* (London: Humphry Milford, 1933) 11.223. Tolstoy's novel *Resurrection* is especially important for his use of Matthew 18; see below on the history of interpretation of 18:21-22. For Matt 18:3-4 of special importance are two narratives for which our text serves as a motto: "Wer hat recht?" in L. Tolstoy, *Späte Erzählungen* (J. Hahn, trans. and ed.; Stuttgart, 1976, 195–216), and the delightful short story "Little Girls Are Wiser Than Men"—a story about adults who quarrel and children who, after a silly falling out, immediately play with each other again. See *The Works of Leo Tolstoy* (London: Humphrey Milford, 1928) 13.184–86.

43   *The Star of Redemption* (trans. from the 2d ed. of

1930; New York: Holt, Rinehart and Winston, 1971) 347.

44   Klostermann, 148.

45   Lagrange, 347.

46   Schniewind, 196.

47   Schweizer, 363, 362.

48   A number of interpreters see children in a more negative light, but they do so for theological reasons such as, e.g., the idea that children are not free of original sin (e.g., in Musculus, 442–43).

49   Peter Müller, *In der Mitte der Gemeinde: Kinder im Neuen Testament,* 162.

50   Cf. the triad often appearing in Jewish texts: "deaf mutes, feeble minded, children" (*m. Erub.* 3.2; *m. B. Qam.* 4.4; 6.2, 4); "women, slaves, children" (*m. Šeqal.* 1.3; *m. Sukk.* 2.8; 3.10).

51   Unlike τέκνον that underscores the relationship of the child to its parents.

Disciples who are like children are thus small, insignificant, and without power. Something of that sense is expressed in the following verses when for Matthew the "little" church members are caught in a snare (vv. 6-9), or when they lose their way and are as helpless as a lost sheep (vv. 12-13). What does it mean then when Matthew speaks in v. 4 of a freely chosen "lowliness" (ταπειώσει ἑαυτόν)? In the New Testament the root ταπεινο- is usually translated with the sense of humility or modesty, yet that can hardly be its meaning for Matthew.[52] The root word means the entire condition of lowliness, not merely the inner attitude of humility. Only seldom does ταπεινός appearing by itself mean "humble" in the Jewish Greek of that day and in New Testament Greek;[53] more often it means "lowly." As with the gnome in 23:12, "whoever humbles himself will be exalted," our text refers both to the external conditions and to the internal attitude.[54] In a general sense, to become low voluntarily is to reverse completely one's previous standards of thought and action and to orient one's life to a different order and to new standards.[55] While the disciples' lowliness *also* includes the attitude of humility, it involves much more than an inner stance. One must work at the practice of lowliness.[56] It is expressed, for example, by extending hospitality to children (v. 5), by loving the "little ones" as brothers and sisters (vv. 10-14), by being willing to forgive without limitations (vv. 21-22), by giving up one's own possessions out of love for one's neighbor (19:16-21), and above all by renouncing hierarchical honors (23:8-10) and by serving (20:26-28; 23:11). To such a life the kingdom of heaven is promised.[57]

■ **5** Verse 5 is loosely related to the preceding verses. "One such child" (ἓν παιδίον τοιοῦτο) alludes more likely to v. 2 than to vv. 3-4; it is an actual child who is being received. Unlike the similar statement in 10:40 where the context suggests hospitality toward wandering charismatics, here it is left open whether the thought is of homeless and orphaned children or in a figurative sense also of receiving children who have a home.[58] On the one hand, v. 5 is an initial parenetic concrete example of what it means to become low. It is a call to solidarity and love. Those who are "low" like a child have the ability to live in community. On the other hand, however, the verse is a promise that Christ himself is present in the children. Verse 20 again clearly speaks of the presence of Christ in the church, and in 25:31-46 the idea of the presence of Christ in "little persons" is further developed.

Summary

Much as the evangelist earlier began the Sermon on the Mount with his ethically reformulated beatitudes, he begins his fourth discourse with a basic demand of the

---

52 In part the following comments correct what I said above on the interpretation of 11:29.

53 Ragnar Leivestad, "ΤΑΠΕΙΝΟΣ-ΤΑΠΕΙΝΟΦΡΩΝ," 36–47, 43, 46) cites only *T. Gad* 5.3 and the Christian gloss on *T. Dan* 6.9. In 11:29 the evangelist calls special attention to the inner dimension of lowliness, i.e. humility, by adding τῇ καρδίᾳ. The term used for the inner attitude in the New Testament letters is ταπεινόφρων or ταπεινοφροσύνη.

54 Luke relates them in 14:11 to the seating order at a banquet, in 18:14 to the tax collector's humility before God. The rabbinic sources *Lv. r.* 1.5 (105c = Str–B 1.774; from Hillel), *b. Erub.* 13b, 35 (from the school of Hillel), ᾽*Abot R. Nat.* 11, *Der. Er. Zut.* 9 (all cited in Str–B 1.921) underscore the inner aspect of lowliness, modesty, and humility.

55 Milan Machovec, *Jesus für Atheisten* (Stuttgart: Kreuz, 1972) 119.

56 When Musculus (443) emphasizes that *humilitas non tollit officia* so that, e.g., a slave owner only needs to change his spirit (*animum*), his view reflects the perspective of the Reformation's doctrine of the two kingdoms but not that of Matthew.

57 That v. 4b takes up the comparative formulation of v. 1 reveals that Matthew does not reject the Jewish idea of different places in heaven. On the other hand, the parallel between "entering the kingdom of heaven" (v. 3) and "to be the greatest in the kingdom of heaven" (v. 4) shows that he does not attribute much importance to it.

58 But neither is the issue receiving persons who metaphorically are "children"—i.e., the neglected members of the church or "average Christians" (Bonnard, 268; Gundry, 266 [quotation]; France, 271). In the NT παιδία is used only as direct address but never as a direct designation of church members.

Christian life that involves a completely new standard of judgment.[59] To be a Christian is to turn the world's standards upside down. The greatness to which one is to aspire is measured not in such things as power, influence, and money; one is rather to submit to lowliness, scorn, poverty, humility, and service. The guiding principle of one's life must be different from that which is customary among the rulers of the Gentiles (20:25) or among the Pharisees (23:6-7).[60] The concrete examples of lowliness in the remaining texts of our chapter show that living well together, forgiveness, and love are upper-most in Matthew's mind. His primary concern is the church whose character must be determined by the principle of littleness. In v. 1 the disciples had asked about which individual is the greatest in the kingdom of heaven. As the entire chapter will show, however, Jesus summons them to behavior that is appropriate to the kind of family life that is characterized by lowliness. Such consciously chosen lowliness stands under the promise of the kingdom of heaven. What that promise consists of is not stated in the text; Matthew simply repeats in v. 4 the wording of the disciples' question.

---

59 Trilling, *Hausordnung,* 19; Rossé, *Ecclesiologia,* 63. Kähler ("Kirchenleitung," 142–43) correctly emphasizes the character of v. 4 as a fundamental statement, but it is not simply a matter there of the Christians' "self-understanding."

60 In Matthew the Pharisees become a negative stereotype. Later interpreters have been even more extreme in this regard. According to Schlatter (543), e.g., "the effort to be 'great' permeated all of Pales-tinian piety." Schlatter's own evidence (545) contradicts that kind of statement.

1.2 Warning Against the "Snares" (18:6-9)

Literature

Alphonse Humbert, "Essai d'une théologie du scandale dans les Synoptiques," *Bib* 35 (1954) 1–28.

Juan Mateos, "Análisis semántico de los lexemas ΣΚΑΝΔΑΛΙΖΩ/ΣΚΑΝΔΑΛΟΝ," *Filología Neotestamentaria* 2 (1989) 57–92.

Otto Michel, "μικρός κτλ," *TDNT* 4 (1967) 648–59.

Jacques Schlosser, "Lk 17,2 und die Logienquelle," *SNTU* A 8 (1983) 70–78.

Stählin, "σκάνδαλον κτλ."

For *additional literature* on the church discourse see above, IV B.

6	**But whoever causes one of these little ones who believe in me to fall, for him it would be better to have an ass's millstone hung around his neck and to be drowned in the deepest sea.**
7	**Woe to the world because of[1] the 'snares'! It [is][2] indeed necessary that the 'snares' come, but woe to [that] person through whom the 'snare' comes!**
8	**But if your hand or your foot causes you to fall, cut it off and throw it from you. It is better[3] for you to enter into life maimed or lame than to be cast into eternal fire with two hands or two feet.**
9	**And if your eye causes you to fall, pluck it out and throw it from you. It is better for you to enter into life one-eyed than to be thrown into the hell of fire with two eyes.**

Analysis

Structure

Verse 6 begins as did v. 5, yet it appears to introduce a new element. The new key word that connects the following four sayings is σκανδαλίζειν ("cause to fall," three times; also three times "snare," σκάνδαλον). In addition, the attention is now on "little ones" rather than on children. The section consists of four sayings. Verses 6 and 8-9 contain so-called Tov-sayings[4] which are introduced with a relative or conditional clause followed by an imperative. Verses 8-9 are also expanded with comparative clauses. These two logia, which appeared earlier in 5:29-30, have parallel structures. There is no clear structure to v. 7, nor can one find a logical connection among the separate sayings in vv. 6-9. Difficult especially is the transition from v. 7 to vv. 8-9.

Sources

Mark 9:42-43, 45, 47 serves as the basis for vv. 6, 8-9; Q 17:1b for v. 7. It is not always easy to recognize Matthew's editorial contributions. He has drastically shortened the Markan text. The two logia about the hand and the foot (Mark 9:43, 45) have been merged into one. In *v. 6* (= Mark 9:42) κρεμασθῇ and καταποντισθῇ could be redaction.[5] There is no linguistic reason for saying the same for εἰς ἐμέ and the unique ἐν τῷ πελάγει.[6] In his careful analysis Schlosser has demonstrated that a Q variant of the logion Mark 9:42 probably lies behind Luke 17:2. There is no evidence that it influenced Matthew, yet that would explain why in *v. 7* the evangelist makes use of the immediately preceding verse Q 17:1. It is possible that Matthew himself created the Semitizing woe pronounced on the world in v. 7a.[7] In v. 7c he expanded the Q text with τῷ ἀνθρώπῳ (ἐκείνῳ) from Mark 14:21 (cf. Matt 26:24). The other variations from Luke 17:1b are difficult to explain. In *vv. 8-9* the Q version of 5:29-30[8] influences especially the introductory lines (εἰ δὲ ἡ χείρ σου . . . σκανδαλίζει σε, ἔκκοψον αὐτ[ὸ]ν καὶ βάλε ἀπὸ σοῦ). The reduction of the three Markan sayings to two also agrees with the Q text. Matthew is responsible for αἰώνιος and

---

1   Instead of a genitive of the cause Matthew offers a Semitic formulation (מִן . . . ל אוֹי); cf. Rev 8:13. For examples see Schlatter, 549; BDF §176 (1).

2   It is difficult to determine whether ἐστίν and ἐκείνῳ belong to the text.

3   Using an adjective + מִן or וְל א in place of the comparative is Semitic style. Cf. Beyer, *Syntax*, 80, n. 1; Black, *Approach*, 117.

4   On the form cf. Graydon F. Snyder, "The Tobspruch in the New Testament," *NTS* 23 (1976/77) 117–20. Tov-sayings begin in Hebrew with טוֹב or נוֹחַ. The conditional introduction and the comparison are not essential to the genre.

5   Cf. 14:30; 22:40.

6   The term used with the genitive τῆς θαλάσσης is not only unique in the New Testament; it also appears in the entire literature of antiquity only in works that are influenced by Matthew. However, the combination פילנוס דימא is frequently found in Jewish texts in which פילנוס is a common loanword. Cf. Jastrow, *s.v.* פילנוס and Samuel Krauss, *Griechische und lateinische Lehnwörter im Talmud, Midrasch und Targum*, 2 vols. (Berlin: S. Calvary, 1898–99) 2.444. It is very close to Aramaic and thus quite conceivable for a Syrian like Matthew.

7   Although that is linguistically difficult to prove. Only κόσμος is Matthean; ἀπό appears frequently in Matthew. Cf, vol. 1, Introduction 3.2.

8   Cf. vol. 1, II A 2.2.2 on 5:27-30 (Analysis).

$\pi \nu \rho \acute{o} \varsigma.$[9] The Markan text is additionally abbreviated by the omission of the superfluous verse 9:46.

Interpretation

■ **6-9** The following section is exceedingly difficult. Although Matthew has intensively revised it, the text still cannot be arranged smoothly into a train of thought. A major difficulty is that the roles of the persons addressed appear to change. In vv. 8-9 people are addressed who are in danger of being led into temptation. Thus in the terminology of v. 6 they are the "little ones." In v. 10 that follows people are addressed who might be contemptuous of these little ones. In vv. 6-7 there is no direct address. It is simply left to the readers to decide how they fit in the text and with whom they want to identify. Do they belong to the "little ones who believe in me"—that is, to those who might be led astray? If so, then they hear vv. 6-7 primarily as a word of comfort. Those who would cause them to fall stand under God's "woe" and will be judged. Or do they belong to those who might mislead others? In that case the text is primarily a word of warning. They themselves are threatened with judgment.

Also difficult is the transition from vv. 1-5 to vv. 6-7. Are the "little ones" identical with the "children" of v. 5? Such an identification is linguistically possible,[10] but one is at a loss then to explain the change in terminology. Or does $\mu \iota \kappa \rho o \acute{\iota}$ refer back to vv. 3-4 so that the "little ones" are those who have become lowly like a child? In either case it is not clear why a statement about leading the little ones astray appears at the beginning of the discourse on community. What does that have to do with becoming lowly? The train of thought is extremely fragmented. Matthew appears not to have been able to subordinate different traditions under a clear concept of his own.

Perhaps that is why he abbreviated Mark 9:42-50 so radically.

■ **6** There are hardly suitable translations for the verse's keywords, the verb $\sigma \kappa \alpha \nu \delta \alpha \lambda \acute{\iota} \zeta \epsilon \iota \nu$ and the substantive $\sigma \kappa \acute{\alpha} \nu \delta \alpha \lambda o \nu$.

The root meaning of $\sigma \kappa \acute{\alpha} \nu \delta \alpha \lambda o \nu$ is "snare." It seldom appears with a figurative meaning in Hellenistic sources, but the LXX offers numerous examples of such usage. We have no instances of the causative verb $\sigma \kappa \alpha \nu \delta \alpha \lambda \acute{\iota} \zeta \omega$ ("cause to fall") that are not dependent on the LXX. Matthew is fond of the root, because it makes his language sound biblical. Frequently the Old Testament texts still contain the image of the root meaning "snare," but sometimes the image is no longer recognizable. Such is the case in the New Testament where $\sigma \kappa \acute{\alpha} \nu \delta \alpha \lambda o \nu$ is connected with $\pi \acute{\epsilon} \tau \rho \alpha$ ("rock"). Then the translation "offense" is appropriate. However, the root contains much more than is suggested by the weak expression "offense/to offend"; it speaks of something that is destructive of a human life or the life of the people of God.[11] Another popular translation, "seduction" or "to seduce," is inappropriate, because in the popular mind it is usually associated with sexual seduction, and that is not a prominent meaning in the biblical examples.[12] I have thus chosen the literal translations "snare" and "to cause to fall," even though the image of the snare is nowhere explicit in the Matthean texts, and even though for that reason this translation sounds stranger to modern ears than the words $\sigma \kappa \acute{\alpha} \nu \delta \alpha \lambda o \nu$ and $\sigma \kappa \alpha \nu \delta \alpha \lambda \acute{\iota} \zeta \omega$ sounded to the Greek-speaking readers who were familiar with them from the Bible.

For Matthew "cause to fall" ($\sigma \kappa \alpha \nu \delta \alpha \lambda \acute{\iota} \zeta \omega$) is connected with rejecting Jesus (11:6; 13:57; 15:12; 26:31, 33) and apostasy (13:21; 24:10). That he is thinking here also of leading people into apostasy is obvious, since the little ones are described as "those who believe in me."[13] Of course, in Matthew apostasy is not simply a matter of

---

9 In Matthew $\alpha \grave{\iota} \acute{\omega} \nu \iota o \varsigma$ is always connected with $\zeta \omega \acute{\eta}$ or with $\pi \tilde{\nu} \rho$. On $\gamma \acute{\epsilon} \epsilon \nu \nu \alpha$ $\tau o \tilde{\nu}$ $\pi \nu \rho \acute{o} \varsigma$ cf. 5:22.

10 "Little one" can mean "child" in both Greek and Hebrew. Cf. BAGD, *s.v.* $\mu \iota \kappa \rho \acute{o} \varsigma$, 1, b; Jastrow, *s.v.*; Michel, "$\mu \iota \kappa \rho \acute{o} \varsigma$," 650.

11 Cf., e.g., Josh 23:12-13; Judg 2:3; Ps 105:36 LXX; Hos 4:17; Wis 14:11.

12 It appears with this meaning only in Sir 9:5 and *Ps. Sol.* 16.7.

13 E.g., Stählin, "$\sigma \kappa \acute{\alpha} \nu \delta \alpha \lambda o \nu$," 351–52; Alphonse Humbert, "Essai d'une théologie du scandale dans les Synoptiques," 1–28, 10; Grundmann, 416; Schnackenburg 2.169; cf. Thompson, *Advice,* 119. Cf.

L. Michael White ("Crisis Management and Boundary Maintenance: The Social Location of the Matthean Community," in David Balch, ed., *Social History of the Matthean Community* [Minneapolis: Fortress, 1991] 226), who points out that the term in Matthew is often connected with the church's boundaries vis-à-vis Judaism or with apostasy.

embracing false doctrine, since it expresses itself in concrete deeds that do not correspond to the will of God (cf. 7:21-23).[14]

Thus the readers are to think of the act of seducing people to sin that has such catastrophic consequences for the seducer that it would be better for that person to be drowned on the high seas with a giant millstone around his or her neck.[15] An "ass's millstone" is the upper stone, usually made of basalt, of a Greco-Roman mill that is turned by an ass, or by a horse, or even by slaves. It is in the shape of a double funnel or hopper. The grain is poured into the upper funnel, while the lower funnel rests on the cone-shaped lower stone of the mill. The stone is usually narrow in the middle so that from a distance it looks somewhat like an hourglass. The Greek word for this upper millstone is ὄνος.[16] To be thrown into the depth of the ocean with such a stone around one's neck is a hyperbolic image for a gruesome fate from which there is no escape. The image suggested itself both because the millstone is a common metaphor for a heavy weight[17] and because drowning on occasion at least was a method used to execute criminals.[18] It is an allusion to the final judgment. Even that kind of horrible fate is better than what awaits a "person of snares" in the final judgment.

Still to be explained is the expression "one of these little ones who believe in me." Matthew found it in Mark 9:42, and it became such an important term for him that he used it several times in his gospel (10:42; 18:6, 10, 14; cf. 25:40, 45). It was not a fixed designation for Christians.[19] The most difficult question is whether "these little ones" are a particular group in the church[20] or

---

14 In 13:41 the σκάνδαλα are thus the "ones who do lawlessness."

15 An analogy (suggested by C. Münch), that does not necessarily imply a connection to Matt 18:6-9, is offered by the trial of Socrates (Plato *Ap.* 24b, c). Socrates, who is guilty of leading the youth astray (διαφθείρω), is punished by death.

16 Hesychius *s.v.* = Maurice Schmidt, *Hesychius of Alexandria* (Athens: Georgiades, 1975) 3.209: ὁ ἀνώτερος λίθος τοῦ μύλου, in contrast to the μύλη, the lower millstone. Pollux (*Onom.* 7.19; 10.112) speaks of the ὄνος ἀλέτων = mill ass = μυλονικός (*P. Lond.* 335.7 in Moulton-Milligan, *s.v.* μύλος). One can find descriptions of such mills in Dalman, *Arbeit* 3.230-35 with an illustration; Krauss, *Archäologie* 1.95-97; Marquardt, *Privatleben* 2.421-23.

17 The closest parallels are Rev 18:21 and *b. Qidd.* 29b = Str-B 1.778: "A millstone around his neck [the reference is to a wife!] and he is to be occupied with the Torah?" For other references see ibid.

18 Catapontism appears as punishment or revenge for tyrants (Plutarch *Moralia* [II] 257D; Polybius 2.60.8), as an especially gruesome punishment (Suetonius *Aug.* 67; Diodorus Siculus 14.112; Josephus *Ant.* 14.450), or as punishment for a terrible crime (Diodorus Siculus 16.35). Since the corpse was not buried, it was regarded by Jews as well as by Greeks as an especially barbaric form of execution.

19 The term is used as a designation for church members in the gnostic *Apocalypse of Peter* (NHC VII) and in the *Second Apocalypse of James* (NHC V). Eduard Schweizer ("Christianity of the Circumcised and Judaism of the Uncircumcised," in Robert Hamerton-Kelly and Robin Scroggs, eds., *Jews, Greeks and Christians: Religious Cultures in Late Antiquity: Essays in Honor of William David Davies* [Leiden: Brill, 1976] 247-48) and Graham N. Stanton (*A Gospel for a New People: Studies in Matthew* [Louisville, Ky.: Westminster/John Knox, 1993] 273-74) appear to assume that there is a sociological continuity between Matthew's church and that of the gnostic *Apocalypse of Peter,* since in the latter work there also appears an ascetic church of "little ones" that is antihierarchical. However, the continuity between Matthew and the *Apocalypse of Peter* is not sociological but literary. The gnostic author uses the church's Gospel of Matthew, attacks the leaders of the orthodox church, and hopes to win for himself the "little ones" (NHC VII 78, 20; 79, 19; 80, 1 and 11)—i.e., members of the church who for a while are deceived by their leaders (80, 1-15). Cf. Klaus Koschorke, *Die Polemik der Gnostiker gegen das kirchliche Christentum* (NHS 12; Leiden: Brill, 1978) 80-83. Similarly the *Second Apocalypse of James* also regards the "little ones" as potential Gnostics (NHC V 54, 26ff.).

20 Zahn (568) speaks of a special "class of disciples." Based on 10:42 Légasse (*Jésus,* 83-85) thinks of the ordinary Christians who have only their faith in Jesus, while Jürgen Roloff ("Das Kirchenverständnis des Matthäus im Spiegel seiner Gleichnisse," *NTS*

whether the expression refers to all of its members.[21] In 10:42 the contrast with the prophets and the righteous suggested that the little ones were ordinary Christians who were not included in those special groups.[22] In our text the readers will most likely understand the expression in terms of vv. 3-4. "The little ones who believe in me" are disciples who have become lowly like a child and who therefore are so precious in God's sight that they will be the greatest in the kingdom of heaven. The expression is thus a programmatic shorthand for what Christians are and should be. Similar to the way in which the members of the church as "the poor in spirit" (5:3) are simultaneously humble and blessed,[23] as little ones they are insignificant in the eyes of the world but, as vv. 10-14 again will show, in God's eyes they are infinitely important. Thus the answer to the question whether the term "little ones" here refers to all Christians or to a special group is: All Matthean Christians are little ones to the degree that they affirm this insignificance and practice it as humility and love.

Thus not all Christians are little ones, but they all can become little. By using the term three times in our chapter (vv. 6, 10, 14), the evangelist reminds his readers that they are to orient their lives down and not up. They are to want to be not great, as, for example, prophets and righteous persons are (10:41), not rabbis, fathers, or masters (23:8-10). They are to be small, as children are. In God's eyes these persons who are intentionally little are important beyond measure. It is for this reason—and not because as simple Christians they are easily led

astray—that seducing them is so terrible.

We return to our initial question: To whom is v. 6 addressed? Most readers of Matthew's gospel will not have read the verse as a warning.[24] Who among the possible readers of the gospel who believe in Jesus and who are called by him to the life of humility would recognize that a warning against setting a snare for a believer is directed at them? It is more likely that the verse is a comfort for the readers who understand themselves as little ones. Their seducers will come to a horrible end in the final judgment.[25]

■ **7** Verse 7 appears to confirm this understanding. With a double cry of woe the evangelist reinforces for his church what has been said. In the Gospel of Matthew σκάνδαλα ("snares") always refers to persons.[26] Matthew is thinking of those persons who threaten the world into which the Son of Man has sown his seed and which is his kingdom (13:38; 28:18). For him the church is a part of the world that is the kingdom of the Son of Man. It is not itself evil, but it contains evil which the Son of Man will someday remove and destroy (13:40-43). In 24:10-12 it is somewhat clearer that Matthew is thinking of the false prophets whose coming Jesus has already predicted and about whom he has already warned the church in 7:15-23.[27] These "snares" must come, since according to apocalyptic expectation evil must prevail in the final days before the coming of the Son of Man. Unfortunately, we do not learn any more about the concrete situ-

---

38 [1992] 342) thinks of "the simple, non-itinerant church members."

21   In the latter case τῶν πιστευόντων εἰς ἐμέ is an attributive addition that explains the term τῶν μικρῶν τούτων. In the former and grammatically more difficult case we would have to understand the term as a partitive genitive: "these little ones among those who believe in me." It is difficult to determine with any certainty what the term means in Mark 9:42.

22   Cf. above, II C 3.4 on 10:42.

23   Cf. vol 1, II A 1.2 on 5:3. Cf. also νήπιοι in 11:25.

24   This is the way Jürgen Roloff (*Die Kirche im Neuen Testament* [GNT 10; Göttingen: Vandenhoeck & Ruprecht, 1993] 147–48) reads the verse. He claims that Matthew warns wandering charismatics whose

view he himself largely shares that they should not give offense to the resident Christians.

25   To be sure, in its deep structure the text itself contains a "snare" of which Matthew probably was not aware. He does not define when leading astray a brother or sister Christian becomes a "snare" which endangers that person's life. A number of readers will remember from the Sermon on the Mount that a single abusive word spoken against a brother can bring one into the hell of fire (5:21–22). It could easily happen that one could cause a brother or sister to commit such an offense. To that degree sensitive and alert Christian readers can read the text as a warning after all. With the σκάνδαλα, however, Matthew is thinking not of these readers but of the

ation to which our text speaks.[28] The verse ends with a pointed repetition of the warning. Judgment is pronounced on the seducers.

History of Interpretation and Summary

Thomas Aquinas has written an impressive *quaestio "de scandalo"*[29] that aptly underscored what is special in our text. He carefully distinguishes between seductions that lead to a deadly sin and those that lead to a sin that can be forgiven. He also makes a distinction between those that one consciously and intentionally does and those that one causes through no fault of one's own. It is no accident that he almost completely ignores our text in Matthew. It is also noticeable how little the deliberations of later interpreters have to do with Matthew's "snares" (σκάνδαλα). They make the anthropological argument, for example, that evil is simply part of human nature,[30] or they claim that at the very least pardonable sins are unavoidable even for the righteous. They speak of human freedom[31] or of divine discipline.[32] They ask how then one is to avoid such offenses, when they are so inevitable.[33]

Matthew appears to be aware of none of these concerns. He makes no distinction between "snares" and lesser seductions. He is interested only in warning the disciples against every impulse to evil. As in other texts, there is here no middle ground. In light of the unequivocal will of the Father there are for him no pardonable sins and no forgivable seductions. An unconditional, ethical severity runs throughout his book—a severity that corresponds to his radical understanding of the uncon-

ditioned will of God as it is expressed, for example, in the antitheses of the Sermon on the Mount. It is a severity that goes hand in hand with the perspective of the coming judgment of the Son of Man in which there will be only yes or no—only participation in the heavenly wedding banquet of the son of the king or weeping and gnashing of teeth (cf. 22:11-13). Thus the double woe that Jesus pronounces in v. 7 also is not the woe of the heavenly philanthropist[34] mourning his world; it is the anticipated woe of the world-judge.

Matthew's intention is thus to shake up Christians by confronting them with the severity of the last days. Are not the divergent anthropological and pedagogical reflections of later interpreters more humane than his rigid black-and-white perspective? For Matthew there is obviously such a thing as absolute evil in the world, yet can we define and avoid this evil as clearly as Matthew demands here?

Interpretation

■ **8-9** Following his source in Mark, Matthew adds to the warning against seducers a direct warning to the members of the church who are in a position to be seduced. While he repeats the sayings about severing one's hand and eye that he has already used in 5:29-30 in connection with the second antithesis, he applies them differently. In the context of the second antithesis, Matt 5:29-30 is a warning against sexual seduction. Here the thought is more likely of a challenge to the little ones to avoid all contact with people who want to destroy their faith.[35] The application in Matthew 5:29-30 is similar to

---

false prophets to whom he never speaks directly. Cf. below, n. 27.

26   Cf. above, III B 3 (on 13:41) and IV A 1 (on 16:23).

27   Note that vv. 6-7 are formulated in the third person. As is the case with the false prophets in 7:15-20 and 24:11, the corrupters are not directly addressed. Thompson (*Advice,* 120) works from the assumption that in Matthew's day "the scandal was an actual problem." Schweizer (*Matthäus,* 110) thinks that there were in Matthew's church "progressive and more likely conservative groups." He reads the situation of Romans 14–15 and 1 Corinthians 8–10 into the text. Pesch (*Matthäus,* 32) thinks of the poor in an urban church who, e.g., are disadvantaged at the Lord's Supper as in 1 Cor 11:17-22. Gundry (362) knows that Matthew's church had antinomistic

leaders. Unfortunately, we know only that the "snares" for Matthew do not represent a Christian position so that he could have debated with them as Paul did with the "strong." They were, rather, part of the evil powers of the last days.

28   On the false prophets cf. vol 1, II A 3.2 on 7:15-23 and below, V B 1 on 24:10-12.

29   *S. th.* 2/2, q.43.

30   Origen, 13.23 = GCS Origenes 10.242-43.

31   Lapide, 347.

32   "The offenses make one . . . more vigilant, more circumspect, more cautious" (John Chrysostom, 59.1 = *PG* 58.575).

33   John Chrysostom, 59.1 = *PG* 58.574.

34   Cf. Theophylactus, 337.

35   One often sees the continuing influence of the

rabbinic parallels that relate hands and eyes to sexual sins.[36] Our text, on the other hand, is closer to Hellenistic parallels that compare the radical separation from bad friends or from evil in general to the work of a physician who may have to amputate parts of a body.[37] That the hyperbole of severing a body part refers to real incidents—on the one hand to actual judgments against adulterers or violent persons,[38] on the other to a physician's practice—intensifies the power of the images and the urgency of the exhortation.

It is not easy to fit this section into the rest of chap. 18. What does it have to do with the becoming lowly of vv. 3-4 which stands as a heading over the chapter? How does it relate to what follows? Cutting off one's body parts fits most naturally with the excommunication of the unrepentant brother in 18:17, even though the hyperbole is formulated much more radically than is the church regulation of vv. 15-17. Yet it does not fit well with the image of seeking the lost sheep in vv. 12-14 and even less so with the idea of forgiving seventy-seven times in vv. 21-22. It is as if there were two different melodies in our chapter that are not in harmony. We will need to explore further how they relate to each other.

---

36   Str-B 1.302–3. For additional material see J. Duncan M. Derrett, "Law in the New Testament: *Si scandalizaverit te manus tua abscinde illam* (Mk 9:42) and Comparative Legal History," in idem, *Studies in the New Testament* (Leiden: Brill, 1977) 1.4–31.

interpretation of Origen (13.24 = GCS Origenes 10.245–46), who combines our text with the Pauline idea of the body of Christ (1 Corinthians 12). One then has to think of the excommunication of members of the church; e.g. Klostermann, ad loc.; Pesch, *Matthäus*, 32; Alexander Sand, *Das Matthäusevangelium* (Erträge der Forschung 275; Darmstadt: Wissenschaftliche Buchgesellschaft, 1991) 368–69.

37   Helmut Koester ("Mark 9:43-47 and Quintilian 8.3.75," *HTR* 71 [1978] 151–53) cites Quintilian's famous parable of the physician who must amputate diseased members of the body. Quintilian applies it to bad friends and relatives. In the Socratic tradition the physician's amputation of a part of the body is compared with the separation from unreason: Xenophon *Mem.* 1.2.55; Plato *Symp.* 205e; Aristotle *Eth. eud.* 1235a; cf. Sextus *Sent.* 13.273 (Henry Chadwick, ed., *The Sentences of Sextus* [Cambridge: Cambridge University Press, 1959]). For further sources for this image see vol. 1, II A 2.2.2, n. 50.

38   Cf. vol 1, II A 2.2.2, n. 46.

1.3 The Search for the Lost (18:10-14)

Literature

Sasagu Arai, "Das Gleichnis vom verlorenen Schaf—eine traditionsgeschichtliche Untersuchung," *Annual of the Japanese Biblical Institute* 2 (1976) 111–37.

E. F. F. Bishop, "The Parable of the Lost or Wandering Sheep. Mt 18:10-14; Luke 15:3-7," *ATR* 44 (1962) 44–57.

Catchpole, "Schaf," 89–101.

Cramer, "Mt 18,10b," 130–46.

J. Duncan M. Derrett, "Fresh Light on the Lost Sheep and the Lost Coin," *NTS* 26 (1979/80) 36–60.

Dupont, "Implications" 2.647–66.

Idem, "Parabole" 2.624–46.

Robert C. Gregg, "Early Christian Variations on the Parable of the Lost Sheep," *Duke Divinity School Review* 41 (1976) 85–104.

Jean Héring, "Un texte oublié: Matthieu 18,10" in *Aux sources de la tradition chrétienne: Mélanges offerts à M. Maurice Goguel* (Neuchâtel: Delâchaux & Niestlé, 1960) 95–102.

Merklein, *Gottesherrschaft,* 186–92.

Antonio Orbe, *Parábolas Evangélicas en San Ireneo* (BAC; Madrid: Editorial Católica, 1972) 2.117–81.

William L. Petersen, "The Parable of the Lost Sheep in the Gospel of Thomas and the Synoptics," *NovT* 23 (1981) 128–47.

Franz Schnider, "Das Gleichnis vom verlorenen Schaf und seine Redaktoren," *Kairos* 29 (1977) 146–54.

Manlio Simonetti, "Due note sull' angelologia Origeniana. I. Mt 18,10 nell interpretazione di Origene," *Rivista di cultura classica e medioevale* 4 (1962) 165–79.

For *additional literature* on the church discourse see above, IV B.

10   **See that you do not despise one of these little ones! For I say to you: Their angels always see in heaven my father's face in heaven.[1]**

12   **What do you think? If a man has a hundred sheep and one of them goes astray, will he not leave the ninety-nine on the mountains and go and look for the one that is lost? 13/ And if he happens to find it, amen, I say to you: He rejoices over it more than over the ninety-nine who did not go astray. 14/ Thus it is not the will before your[2] father in heaven that one of these little ones should perish.**

Analysis

Structure

Verses 10 and 14, both of which speak of "one of these little ones" and of the "father in heaven," frame the short parable of the sheep gone astray. These keywords also connect our section to its context (cf. vv. 6, 19, and 35). Unlike its parallel in Luke 15:4-7, the parable is an argument in a debate rather than a narrated story. It consists of two conditional clauses, each of which is introduced with ἐάν ("if"). The first is followed in v. 12 with a rhetorical question that the readers themselves must answer, the second in v. 13 with a pronouncement in the form of an authoritative amen saying. The section begins by posing a question to the readers: "What do you think?" The so-called parable is thus a dialogue between the author and his implied readers in which he tries to win their agreement.[3] Its theme is given by the three appearances of πλανᾶσθαι ("go astray"). After the solemn amen saying in v. 13, its application in v. 14, which makes no further reference to the shepherd's joy, is surprising. Verse 14 appears to refer more to the behavior of the shepherd described in v. 12 than to his joy.

Sources

The closing word in *v. 14* is clearly redactional,[4] a judgment that is confirmed by the difficulty of the transition to v. 14 from v. 13, where the subject is the shepherd's joy over finding the sheep. The closing verse speaks not of the shepherd's joy but of his efforts. Much less clear is v. 10. Although some exegetes regard the entire verse as editorial,[5] it has a

---

1   Verse 11, included in the Western and Byzantine manuscript tradition, is: "The Son of Man came to save the lost." It approximates Luke 19:10 and fits well with the content of the traditional parable of the lost sheep, but text-critically it is clearly secondary. That v. 11 also appears in HbrMt, is a clear indication of how late this text is. See Howard, 89.

2   Is μου or ὑμῶν the preferred reading in v. 14? Although μου is supported by good witnesses (among others, B and Θ), the parallels in vv. 10 and 35, both of which have μου, suggest that an original ὑμῶν was adapted to the parallels.

3   Trilling (*Israel,* 112) calls it a "short mashal" that formally is related to 5:14b-16; 12:11, 33-34; 15:13-14.

4   Cf. vol 1, Introduction 3.2 on οὕτως, θέλημα, ἔμπροσθεν, πατὴρ ὁ ἐν τοῖς οὐρανοῖς, μικροί. Based on Luke 15:4, 6, ἀπόληται was part of the tradition.

5   Thus Gundry, 364. Redactional are ὁρᾶτε μή (9:30, 24:6; in the papyrii cf. Moulton-Milligan, 455; BDF § 461 [1] and n. 2), ἐν οὐρανοῖς (cf. 5:45; 12:50; 18:14; 19:21), γάρ, λέγω ὑμῖν, πρόσωπον, πατήρ; cf. vol 1, Introduction 3:2.

number of elements that are not Matthean.[6] I assume with the majority, therefore, that Matthew connected the traditional logion in v. 10b with the section on the little ones by means of the redactional v. 10a.

The parable of the lost sheep in *vv. 12-13* appears also in Luke 15:4-7 and in *Gos. Thom.* 107. Was it in Q? Common to Matthew and Luke is the core of the exposition (v. 12 in Matthew; v. 4 in Luke) and the reference to the joy over the one sheep that is greater than that over the ninety-nine (v. 13; v. 7 in Luke's application). The most important distinctive element in Luke is the detailed description of how the shepherd finds the sheep, carries it on his shoulders, comes home, calls together his friends and neighbors, and invites them to share his joy (Luke 15:5-6). The interpretation in Luke 15:7 is different from that in Matt 18:14 but it too is editorial. The motif of joy, merely suggested by Matthew in v. 13, becomes in Luke the focus of the parable, and Luke formulates it in his own distinctive way as joy in heaven over a single repentant sinner.[7]

A decision about Matthew's distinctive features is not always easy. In addition to the concluding v. 14, it is clear that the introduction τί ὑμῖν δοκεῖ is editorial.[8] Matthean is the verb πλανάομαι (instead of ἀπόλλυμαι) in vv. 12-13 that corresponds not only to the content of Matthew's reinterpretation but also to biblical language.[9] Casting the text in the form of a

debate is probably Matthean along with the frequent ἐάν clauses in 18:12-17. It may be that ἐπὶ τὰ ὄρη is also editorial; the expression appears frequently in the LXX.[10] The most difficult question is whether the graphic description of the behavior and the joy of the shepherd is Luke's secondary elaboration or whether Matthew has shortened his source. I lean toward the second option. Matthew's abbreviations are the result of the way he reformulated the text. Unlike most interpreters,[11] I am of the opinion that the detailed narrative in vv. 5-6, which linguistically is not typically Lukan, is earlier.[12]

It is an open question whether the parable existed in Q. The language that Matthew and Luke have in common is limited almost exclusively to formulations that are necessary for the basic structure of the narrative, and neither text offers a compelling reason for locating the parable in Q. In Q it presumably would have appeared with the parable of the lost drachma,[13] in which case Matthew then would have omitted the latter parable. The most frequently used argument to support such a view is that, unlike a sheep, a coin cannot go astray, and Matthew therefore could not have applied the parable of the drachma to errant church members.[14] The argument, however, is not very convincing, since Matthew's primary interest is in the search for what has been lost, and the woman with the coin could have illustrated the point quite well. It

---

6   Unique in Matthew is the LXX expression διὰ παν-τός (105 times in the LXX!) and the concept of personal angels who see God's face (cf. below on guardian angels). Seeing God's face is a biblical concept; cf. Eduard Lohse, "πρόσωπον κτλ," *TDNT* 6 (1968) 777–78.

7   Lukan are μετανοέω/μετάνοια, ἁμαρτωλός, χρείαν ἔχειν.

8   Cf. 17:25; 21:28; 22:17, 42; 26:66.

9   Vol. 1, Introduction, 3.2. In combination with πρό-βατον, πλανᾶσθαι appears six times in the LXX.

10   Ἐπὶ τὰ ὄρη appears twenty-eight times in the LXX, in particular in Jer 27:6 in connection with sheep (πρόβατα ἀπολωλότα ἐγενήθη ὁ λαός . . . ἐπὶ τὰ ὄρη); Ezek 34:6, 10, 13, 16.

11   See, e.g., Adolf von Harnack, *Sprüche und Reden Jesu: Beiträge zur Einleitung in das Neue Testament* (Leipzig: Hinrichs, 1907) 2.65–66; Bultmann, *History,* 171; Schulz, *Q,* 387–88; Weder, *Gleichnisse,* 172, who claims that the oldest core consists of the basic elements of Luke 15:4 and Matt 18:13; Norman Perrin, *Rediscovering the Teaching of Jesus* (1967; reprinted New York: Harper & Row, 1976) 99; Dupont, "Parabole," 638; Merklein, *Gottesherrschaft,* 188; Arland Dean Jacobson, *The First Gospel: An Introduction to Q* (Sonoma: Polebridge, 1992) 225–26

(Jacobson thinks, however, that the style of the rhetorical question could be secondary). The most popular argument for the secondary character of Luke 15:6 is that, while v. 6 fits with the companion parable of the lost drachma, it does not fit with the parable of the lost sheep, since the shepherd would have returned the sheep to the flock instead of taking it into his house. Thus, e.g., Légasse, "Jésus," 57; Catchpole, "Schaf," 93; Dupont, "Parabole," 637. The argument is, in my judgment, rather weak. Why may the shepherd not live near the flock or first go home with the sheep?

12   With Lührmann, *Redaktion,* 115; Lambrecht, *Treasure,* 43–44.

13   Catchpole, "Schaf," 91–92.

14   E.g., Catchpole, "Schaf," 91–92; Jacobson, *The First Gospel,* 227.

15   Or as the Gnostic who is seeking his true self that is hidden in the world. Cf. Wolfgang Schrage, *Das Verhältnis des Thomas Evangeliums zur synoptischen Tradition und zu den koptischen Evangelienübersetzungen* (Berlin: Töpelmann, 1964) 196.

16   Thus William L. Petersen ("The Parable of the Lost Sheep in the Gospel of Thomas and the Synoptics," *NovT* 23 [1981] 128–47), who claims that the greatest sheep is the people of Israel for whom God has

438

seems more likely to me, therefore, that Matthew and Luke obtain this parabolic material from the oral tradition independently of each other.

Tradition History and Origin

Does *Gos. Thom.* 107 help with the reconstruction of the original version of the text? There the parable is a parable of the kingdom of God in which the sheep that has gone astray is the "greatest." The joy of the shepherd and his neighbors when the sheep is found (Luke 15:6) is not portrayed; the parable ends with a reference to the shepherd's efforts and his great love for the sheep. The shepherd can be understood as Christ who seeks the Gnostic who is lost in the world of matter.[15] The absence of Luke's v. 6 makes it possible for the gnostic narrator to create a linear narrative focused on the point of the redeemer's love for the Gnostic. If that corresponded to the original form of the parable, we would have to look for a new point for the original version. Did it perhaps speak of God's love for the lost sheep of Israel?[16] The issue is complicated. I find it more likely, therefore, that the shepherd's joy, which leaves its mark on the second part of both the Matthean and Lukan accounts (Matthew v. 13; Luke vv. 5-6), belongs to the original point of the parable. Thus the earliest version of the parable is probably best preserved in Luke 15:4-6, and in all probability the parable goes back to Jesus.

Interpretation: Jesus

In explaining the original meaning of the parable we will need to keep two things in mind. The first is that the image of sheep and their good and evil shepherds comes from the repertoire of biblical images with which all of Jesus' hearers were familiar. Jesus uses conventional metaphors designed to evoke particular associations. The sheep are reminiscent of the members of Israel as the people of God.[17] Shepherds are her political and religious leaders[18] or even God himself as the leader of the nation and its individual members.[19] Closely related to our parable is especially Ezek 34:1-16 where the issue is Israel's unworthy shepherds who have been feeding only themselves so that the sheep have been scattered over the mountains with no one to search for them. By contrast God promises that he himself will be Israel's shepherd and that he will seek the lost sheep and find pasture for them on the mountains of Israel.[20]

The second consideration is that it is difficult to understand Jesus' parable separate from his own mission to the people of Israel.[21] It is designed not to convey a general truth such as "finding makes you happy" or to make a general theological statement about "God's love for each individual sinner,"[22] but to help its hearers understand the "signification du comportement de Jésus."[23] Behind Jesus' activity stands God, the good shepherd, who rejoices over Israel's lost when they permit themselves to be found by Jesus' message of the king-

---

the greatest love. However, it would hardly have occurred to readers familiar with the Bible, who immediately understand "sheep" to refer to Israel, that the ninety-nine sheep could be gentile nations. Furthermore, why should Israel be the only sheep that strayed? Sasagu Arai ("Das Gleichnis vom verlorenen Schaf—eine traditionsgeschichtliche Untersuchung," 111–37, 130–31) assumes that the oldest layer of the parable included only Luke 15:4, and he interprets the parable in terms of Jesus' activity in Israel.

17   Cf., e.g., 1 Kgs 22:17; Isa 13:14; 40:11; 53:6; Jer 31:10; 50:6-7; Zech 11:4-17; 13:7; Pss. 79:13; 95:7; 100:3 and above, II C 2.1, n. 21.

18   Cf., e.g., Isa 44:28; Jer 3:15; 23:1; 50:6; Mic 5:4; Zech 10:2; 11:6; 13:7.

19   Of the nation: Gen 48:15; 49:24; Isa 40:11; Jer 31:10; Ezek 34:12; Ps 80:2; cf. Pss 79:13; 95:7; 100:3. Of individuals: Ps 23:1-3; cf. Ps 119:176.

20   We must leave open the question to what degree Jesus was able to make use of existing stories in his

selection of the actual material. Of special importance is a legend about Moses who was looking for a runaway goat from Jethro's herd of sheep. See *Exod. Rab.* (68b) in Str–B 2.209. Cf. J. Duncan M. Derrett, "Fresh Light on the Lost Sheep and the Lost Coin," *NTS* 26 (1979/80) 36–60, 43. Philo and Josephus appear to be not yet familiar with the legend. Cf. in addition the parable of the herdsman from whose herd an animal ran off into the camp of a non-Israelite (*Gen. Rab.* 86 [55b] = Str–B 1.785). Farther removed is the parable of the missing sheep in *Peseq. R. Kah.* 2.8. See Thoma-Lauer, *Gleichnisse,* 115. For all of these cases a precise dating is next to impossible.

21   Especially emphasized by Dupont, "Parabole," 638–46 and "Implications," 658–66.

22   Jülicher, *Gleichnisreden* 2.331. Cf. Manson, *Sayings,* 284.

23   Dupont, "Implications," 665.

dom of God.[24] The question "who among you" seeks the assent of the hearers. Jesus compares his own behavior with that of a shepherd who, when a sheep is lost, of course[25] looks for it, and behind the comparison is the image of the God of Israel to whom the Bible bears witness as a good shepherd of his people. Thus Luke's application of 15:7 did not do a bad job of capturing the original focus of the parable. The special biographical situation that Luke created for the parable in 15:1-2 in which Jesus defends his own activity against the Pharisees also portrays the relation between the parable and its narrator.

Interpretation: Matthew

The history of the parable's transmission and interpretation is a model of how emphasizing different perspectives can lead to the discovery of multiple new meanings. The evangelist Matthew understands the parable parenetically. No longer is the emphasis "on the joy of the shepherd; now it is on his searching as a model."[26] The members of the church are to behave as the shepherd did. In the service of this new perspective are the intro-

ductory v. 10, the rhetorical question in v. 12, and the new application in v. 14.

■ **10** "Do not despise one of these little ones!" $Kαταφρονεῖν$ is a relatively open verb for "despise" that can also have the nuances of "to disregard" or "not to be concerned with."[27] In contrast to v. 6, the readers can no longer regard themselves as little ones; now they are addressed as persons who may well despise the little ones. Does that mean that the little ones here (unlike v. 6 but as in 10:42) are a special group of Christians[28]— viz., the despised, the obscure, the unlettered, the spiritually distraught,[29] the recently baptized,[30] or the simple people such as, for example, John Chrysostom's urban audience whom he forcefully addresses as "a blacksmith, a cobbler, a peasant, a dunce"?[31] Yes and no! The diversity in the roles offered the readers is part of the strategy of the text that addresses the entire church. Thus among the readers there could be those who look down on others when, for example, they are in a position of importance as the leaders of the church. Others are not respected in the church, either because they are insignificant socially or in their status in the church, or because

---

24 Cf. Catchpole, "Schaf," 99.

25 Thus the parable does not intend to portray an "utterly foolish" behavior of a shepherd (thus Perrin, *Rediscovering*, 100, and Hare, 212). This impression comes from the fact that the narrative does not say what the shepherd did with the other ninety-nine sheep—whether he first drove them into a pen (cf. E. F. F. Bishop, "The Parable of the Lost or Wandering Sheep. Mt 18:10-14; Luke 15:3-7," 44–57, 49–50), or whether he asked other shepherds to watch over them (cf. Jeremias, *Parables*, 133–34). The concern is really unnecessary, however, since every parable is an abbreviated story that omits unnecessary details. Of course it is possible that the shepherd drove his sheep into a pen; that would be when he noticed that one was missing. But that is a detail that is not important for the purpose of the parable. Furthermore, the introductory question, "what man of you" (Luke 15:4), presupposes that every good shepherd will act as the shepherd of the parable did.

26 Jeremias (*Parables*, 40).

27 It is not synonymous with $σκανδαλίζω$; it is much weaker.

28 The meaning cannot be children in the sense of v. 5. Such an interpretation is no longer possible after

the change from $παιδία$ to $μικροί$ in vv. 5-6. We might at most consider it for a pre-Matthean original version of v. 10 that we are scarcely able to reconstruct. This interpretation was especially popular after the Reformation when the angels were regarded as the guardian angels of children. Luther believes that it is proper and necessary to preach about the good guardian angel of children who wears a white robe and sits at the child's crib (2.606–7). Since the post-Reformation period our text also was used to justify infant baptism. See, e.g., Bullinger, 175A; Brenz, 599; more recently Jean Héring, "Un texte oublié: Matthieu 18,10," 95–106, 101–2.

29 Episcopius, 112.

30 Theodore of Heraclea, no. 105 = Reuss, 86.

31 John Chrysostom, 59.4 = *PG* 58.579.

they have chosen to be little (vv. 3-4); they can be objects of contempt. Although they are not directly addressed here, they can claim the promise that their angels will see God's face. "To see the face of" God is an expression that probably originated in the language of the court,[32] but already in the Bible it has become religious and cultic language.[33] It expresses a familiarity with God that is normally not available to humans in a direct sense. Verse 10b is thus both a reinforcement of the warning against those who despise the little ones as well as a word of comfort to these who are of infinite worth.

Guardian Angels

The text presupposes an understanding of guardian angels that, when compared with contemporary Judaism, demonstrates unique features. The idea that people have a guardian angel that accompanies them throughout life is part of a widespread conceptual world and is related to such ideas as the ancient Persian belief in Fravashis,[34] the Roman idea of *genius*,[35] and the Greek idea of the *daimon* that accompanies people.[36] In the biblical-Jewish cultural world the concept of guardian angels that are not allied with individuals or of guardian angels of special, distinguished persons is relatively old.[37] The idea that each individ-

ual has a personal guardian angel is widespread for the first time in rabbinic Judaism, but these guardian angels live on earth and do not belong to the highest class of angels, which, according to the widely held view, are the only ones who see God's face.[38] The most likely bridge to the view found in our text that individuals have personal angels in heaven would be the idea that the individual guardian angels from time to time ascend to heaven in order to report to God on their charges or to intercede for them, or the idea that the guardian angels will be present at the last judgment.[39] The view in our text is thus by no means common in Judaism. We should not conclude, however, that it offers an intentional contrast to Jewish thought.[40]

History of Interpretation

■ **10** Our verse has an interesting history. It became a locus classicus of Christian angelology as well as *the biblical proof text for the Christian belief in personal guardian angels.*

Of course, *concepts of guardian angels* are widespread in the ancient church even as they are among the Jews, Greeks, and Romans. They did not originate with texts such as Matt 18:10 or Acts 12:15, although these texts confirmed them and legitimated them in

---

32 On seeing the king's face cf. 2 Kgs 25:19 LXX; Esth 1:14; 4:11.

33 Cf., e.g., Gen 32:31 (Penuel!); Exod 33:20, 23 (Moses is not able to look on God's face); Pss 41:3 LXX (in the temple) and 104:4 (in a general religious sense, with $\delta\iota\grave{\alpha}\ \pi\alpha\nu\tau\acuteo\varsigma$).

34 Cf. Georg Widengren, *Die Religionen Irans* (Religionen der Menschheit; Stuttgart: Kohlhammer, 1965) 21–24.

35 Cf. Kurt Latte, *Römische Religionsgeschichte* (Handbuch der klassischen Altertumswissenschaft 5/4; 2d ed.; Munich: Beck, 1960) 103–7.

36 Especially important are Plato *Phaedr.* 107d; *Resp.* 617d–621b; Menander fr. 550 (*CAF 3*); the Stoic, Marcus Aurelius, 5.27. On the entire concept cf. M. P. Nilsson, *Geschichte der griechischen Religion* (Handbuch der klassischen Altertumswissenschaft; 2d ed.; Munich: Beck, 1961) 2.210–13.

37 Ps 91:11–13; further sources in Gnilka 2.131. On the angels of individuals see Gen 24:7, 40; 48:16 (Jacob); *Lib. ant. bib.* 59.4 (David); Tob 5:4-15, 22 (Raphael with Tobit); *T. Jos.* 6.7 (Abraham); *t. Sabb.* 17.2–3 (136) = Str–B 1.781 (guardian angels of the righteous while traveling).

38 *1 Enoch* 100.5 (guardians of the righteous); *b. Šabb.*119b; *Tg. Yer. I* on Gen 24:7; *b. Ḥag.* 16a (two

ministering angels accompany people); *Tanch.* 99a (interpretation of Ps 91:11); *Midr Qoh.* 10:20 (49b): a hierarchy of guardian angels—cherub—seraph; only the seraph appears before God; sources in Str–B 1.781–83. Str–B 1.783–84 cites sources in which ministering angels do not see God. On the tasks of the guardian angels cf. Str–B 3.437–39. *T. Adam* 4 lists the complete hierarchy of angels. Personal guardian angels are the lowest; only the "thrones, cherubim, and seraphim" see God. In the New Testament Acts 12:15 and Heb 1:14 assume the existence of personal guardian angels.

39 *Adam and Eve* 33 (while the angels of Adam and Eve worshiped God in heaven, Satan took advantage of their absence); *3 Bar.* 12–13 (at the last judgment the angels bring baskets with the deeds of the righteous and unrighteous); *2 Enoch* 19.4, long recension (the individual angels write down human deeds "before the face of the Lord"). The rabbinic sources are in Str–B 3.439.

40 According to Str–B 1.783 and Michel ("μικρός," 651, n. 15) this is a recurring claim in the commentaries. It furthermore has a precursor in the history of interpretation: Calovius (344–45) criticizes Grotius (2.83), who cited Jewish ideas about angels.

a secondary way. The prevailing concept, for which Matt 18:10 probably became the primary biblical proof text, was that every individual, beginning at birth, has a personal guardian angel.[41] Less frequent is the idea that one has a guardian angel only after one's baptism[42] or that a person is followed by not one but two angels, a good one and an evil one.[43] Interesting, and not at all Matthean, is Origen's idea that only the little one whose soul is incomplete has a guardian angel, while "God himself helps those who are more complete."[44] In the classic angelologies of Dionysius the Areopagite and Thomas Aquinas our text plays no role or, in the latter case, a subordinate role. Thomas's primary interest is in the heavenly beings as such, their existence and their nature, and he speaks only secondarily of their tasks among human beings. As with the rabbis, he regards the guardian angels as among the lesser angels. Matthew 18:10, far from providing evidence to the contrary, simply proves that the guardian angels of the little ones are the highest of the lesser angels.[45]

It is with the reformers that the picture first changes. While Luther does not doubt the existence of guardian angels, he questions the Catholic claim that the highest angels are not concerned about the little ones.[46] Calvin, on the other hand, doubts that Matt 18:10 justifies the conclusion that individual persons have their own guardian angels.[47] As a conse-quence, the Reformed thinkers for the most part rejected the concept of individual guardian angels as early as the seventeenth century,[48] while the belief survived somewhat longer among the Lutherans.[49] In the Enlightenment there is an increasing tendency to interpret our text symbolically.[50] In modern usage the term guardian angel, at least in the Protestant parts of northern Europe, has become little more than a figure of speech used especially with reference to children. The catechism of the Catholic church, on the other hand, maintains not only the existence of angels as an article of faith but also the existence of individual guardian angels.[51]

It must be asked, of course, whether even in north-ern Europe we are seeing today the beginning of a movement in the other direction. One indication of such a movement might be the explosion of esoteric piety that has led to renewed attention to ideas of angels and guardian angels. "Angels represent a point of contact between the human and the divine worlds. They are characterized as independent, spiritual beings of light created by God. Guardian angels play a special role. Not only do they protect human beings; they also promote their spiritual growth and conceptual ability without limiting their free will."[52]

---

41 See, e.g., *Opus imperfectum* 40 = 854; Dionysius the Carthusian, 205; Maldonat, 361; at birth: Jerome, 159; Thomas Aquinas *S. th.* 1, q.133, a.4.

42 Origen, 13.27 = GCS Origenes 10.254.

43 Origen *Hom. in Lucam* 35.3 = GCS Origenes 9.197–98; cf. *Hermas, Man.* 6.2.1 = 36.1.

44 *Hom. in Num.* 24:3 = GCS Origenes 7.231–32.

45 *S. th.* 1, q.113, a.3 ad 1.

46 "While they see the Father's face without ceasing, nevertheless they watch over the child who is dirty and bathes and the servant who woos Rebecca on behalf of Isaac. God's angels are household servants and nursery maids" (2.609 = Sermon from 1531); cf. Walter von Loewenich, *Luther als Ausleger der Synoptiker* (Forschungen zur Geschichte und Lehre des Protestantismus 10/5; Munich: Kaiser, 1954) 241.

47 2.218, with references to other biblical texts. Cf. also *Inst.* 1.14.7. However, according to Knabenbauer (2.122) Cajetan is also obviously skeptical about individual guardian angels.

48 According to information from Th. Mahlmann (Marburg) and J. Bauer (Göttingen), J. J. Heidegger and F. Turettini reject the idea with clear antipapal polemics, while the enlightened Cocceian J. Braun (*Selecta Sacra* I [1700] §141) already engages in a sharp polemic against the *superstitiosi*.

49 According to Th. Mahlmann and J. Bauer, the idea of special individual guardian angels is defended into the middle of the eighteenth century. The first clear rejection comes from Johann Georg Walch, *Einleitung in die dogmatische Gottesgelehrtheit* (2d ed., Jena: Crokers, 1757), vol. 7 § 21.

50 On the beginning cf. above, n. 48. Paulus (2.650) interprets the text to refer to the people who look after the children; cf. also de Wette, 108. According to Cramer ("Mt 18,10b") even early Syrians interpreted the angels of Matt 18:10 symbolically as the Holy Spirit (Afrahat) or as the prayers of the little ones (Ephraem). The motive for these interpretations, however, was not a problem with the idea of angels but the concern to take seriously God's invisibility.

51 Catechism. This is the title of no. 328. On guardian angels no. 336; on Matt 18:10 cf. nos. 329, 337 (ET: *Catechism of the Catholic Church* [Chicago: Loyola University Press, 1992]).

52 From a report by Marianne Kappeler and Pascal Mösli. Cf. Günther Schiwy, *Der Geist des neuen Zeitalters* (Munich: Kosel, 1987) esp. 56ff.; T. L. Taylor, *Warum Engel fliegen können–Lichtvolle Kontakte mit unseren Schutzgeistern* (Munich, 1990).

It is clear that Matt 18:10 provides a biblical witness for the idea of individual guardian angels. It is equally clear for me that the idea has its roots in an outdated worldview. I am of the opinion that a modern interpretation of Matt 18:10 can simply try to take seriously the *substance* of the concern expressed in the language of an earlier age—viz., God's special concern for the little ones, for the humble and despised—while abandoning the concrete idea of guardian angels, since it is no longer self-evident to the modern mind.

■ **12-13** As his next argument designed to prevent contempt for the little ones, Matthew introduces his version of the parable of the lost sheep. In so doing he shifts the accent from the little ones (v. 10) to the sheep that have gone astray. A clear distinction is made between "go astray") ($\pi\lambda\alpha\nu\acute{\alpha}o\mu\alpha\iota$) and "to be lost" ($\alpha\pi\acute{o}\lambda\lambda\nu\sigma\vartheta\alpha\iota$). The latter refers to the ultimate loss of salvation, the former to fundamentally flawed behavior before God[53] that may result in the loss of salvation but does not of necessity do so.[54] In the context of the entire chapter the readers will most likely think of people who have fallen victim to the "snare" ($\sigma\kappa\acute{\alpha}\nu\delta\alpha\lambda o\nu$) that leads to sin (v. 6). The introductory formula "what do you think" ($\tau\acute{\iota}\ \acute{\nu}\mu\hat{\iota}\nu$ $\delta o\kappa\epsilon\hat{\iota}$) is designed to provoke the readers to answer the question for themselves.

In Matthew the parable itself consists of two argumentative statements introduced by "if" ($\acute{\epsilon}\acute{\alpha}\nu$), each of which has its own independent importance. The first sentence emphasizes the shepherd's behavior. He drops everything and, appropriate to the unlimited value of the little ones, goes in search of the one who has gone astray. The formulation "if a man has" ($\acute{\epsilon}\grave{\alpha}\nu\ \gamma\acute{\epsilon}\nu\eta\tau\alpha\acute{\iota}$ $\tau\iota\nu\iota\ \acute{\alpha}\nu\vartheta\rho\acute{\omega}\pi\omega$) with the following rhetorical question invites the readers to become involved in the story by asking themselves where and for whom they are called to act in the same way that this "certain man" acts on behalf of the sheep. Nothing in the parable suggests that only certain readers (such as, for example, the church's leaders) might be addressed.[55] At the same time, however, Matthew's text strengthens the connections to the original biblical text in Ezekiel 34.[56] Thus not only does the shepherd serve as a human model for appropriate behavior in the church; behind him stands God, who is searching for his people who have wandered away.

The second $\acute{\epsilon}\acute{\alpha}\nu$ sentence, v. 13, also reflects the experiences of the readers. Since it is uncertain whether one will be able to find a brother or a sister who has gone astray, the sentence begins with the uncertain "if . . . has" ($\acute{\epsilon}\grave{\alpha}\nu\ \gamma\acute{\epsilon}\nu\eta\tau\alpha\iota$).[57] In view of the parenetic application in v. 14, the shepherd's joy is superfluous. Would it be a case of overinterpreting the parable to suppose that many readers who were familiar with the traditional version of the parable and for whom in addition the similarity to Ezekiel 34 was reminiscent of the heavenly shepherd would think here of God who rejoices over the sinner who has been found? In my judgment the parable in Matthew is by no means one-dimensional; it has harmonic tones.[58]

■ **14** Still, as is clear in the newly formulated, strongly Semitizing application of v. 14, the dominant impulse of Matthew's interpretation is parenetic. There Matthew speaks of the "will" of the heavenly father rather than of

---

53   In biblical and Jewish sources $\pi\lambda\alpha\nu\acute{\alpha}\omega$ is often used metaphorically for Israel with reference to Yahweh or idolatry or the worship of images. Cf. Herbert Braun, "$\pi\lambda\alpha\nu\acute{\alpha}\omega$," *TDNT* 6 (1968) 234–35, 237. In Jewish sources it is often used with reference to the time before the end (ibid., 241); cf. Matt 24:4-5, 11, 24.

54   Albertus Magnus, 673: "Errans ovis non est perdita, sed est in via perditionis."

55   The idea is appealing, of course, that the church's "shepherds" could be especially affected by the image of the shepherd. Cf. Raymond E. Brown, *The Churches the Apostles Left Behind* (New York: Paulist, 1984) 139. In early Christian circles "shepherd" was a widespread metaphorical designation for the function of the leaders of the church such as, e.g., pres-

byters (cf. Acts 20:28; Eph 4:11; 1 Pet 5:2). We do not know whether there were leaders in Matthew's church who especially identified with the function of the shepherd. We can only be certain that both the general warning in v. 10 and the parable of the shepherd were not *only* addressed to obvious office bearers in the church.

56    $\acute{E}\kappa\zeta\eta\tau\acute{\eta}\sigma\omega\ \tau\grave{\alpha}\ \pi\rho\acute{o}\beta\alpha\tau\acute{\alpha}\ \mu o\nu$ (v 10); $\acute{\epsilon}\pi\grave{\iota}\ \tau\grave{\alpha}\ \acute{o}\rho\eta$ $\acute{I}\sigma\rho\alpha\acute{\eta}\lambda$ (v 13); $\zeta\eta\tau\acute{\eta}\sigma\omega\ .\ .\ .\ \tau\grave{o}\ \pi\lambda\alpha\nu\acute{\omega}\mu\epsilon\nu o\nu$ (v 16); cf. vv 4, 6.

57   Thompson, *Advice,* 164.

58   It is an oversimplification, therefore, when Strecker (*Weg,* 149) states that "Jesus' demand" here does not "presuppose a prior forgiveness from God." Cf. also ibid., n. 2.

what is "well pleasing," a common Jewish expression[59] that would have corresponded to 11:26.[60] Since it is not the will of the heavenly father that one of these little ones should perish (ἀπόληται) in the final judgment, the members of the church are called to love, forgiveness, and to receiving the lost back into the community. And since in the entire section 18:6-14 the little ones do not constitute a special, sociologically separate group of Christians, the text also implies that no one can be absolutely certain that he or she will not go astray. Yet this implication is also one of our section's unspoken harmonic tones, as is the idea of divine forgiveness.

History of Interpretation

■ **12-14** The interpretation of our parable has had a rich history, especially in the ancient church.[61] First, there was Christian Gnosticism, for which our text was a key text. The church's allegorical interpretation, which later came to dominate, both appropriated and rejected the gnostic interpretation. The parenetic interpretation, for which Matthew was the first representative, in general played a secondary role in the church's interpretation.

The Gnostic Interpretation

According to the church fathers, Simon Magus, who later came to be regarded as the "arch heretic," already offered an interpretation of our parable. For him the lost sheep was Helena, the prostitute from Tyre who was the incarnation of the primal mother, the "first idea" that had become matter, while he, her savior, was the good shepherd.[62] Related to this interpretation is that of the Valentinians, who regarded the lost sheep as Achamoth—that is, the divine wisdom that had fallen out of the divine pleroma into

lower matter. This wisdom is in turn the "mother" of the Gnostics who prefigures their way.[63] Mark, the Gnostic, uses the numbers in the parables of the lost drachma and the lost sheep in a complicated system of numerical speculation that in my judgment assumes that the ninety-nine sheep represent the heavenly pleroma, while the lost sheep is the fallen eon that has been captured by matter.[64] *Gospel of Thomas* 107 would fit in well with this idea, if we may understand the "great sheep" as the Gnostic who has gone astray and has been brought to knowledge by Christ. The Gnostics interpret the parable allegorically, in other words, in terms of humanity's fundamental destiny or in terms of the drama of salvation in its entirety that is represented on the one hand by Christ the redeemer and on the other hand by the part of the divine pleroma that has been captured by matter.

The Church's Allegorical Interpretation

One finds several of the orthodox interpretation's basic motifs as early as Irenaeus. The shepherd is the Logos; his descent from the mountains is his incarnation; and the lost sheep, as Irenaeus claims against the Gnostics, is his own creature.[65] Tertullian emphasizes against the Docetics that the lost sheep was saved along with its body.[66] In Origen all of the basic elements of the church's classical interpretation are present. The good shepherd is the redeemer; the sheep are the entire "rational creation," whereby the ninety-nine left behind on the mountains are the angels; the sheep that is saved below in the "valley of tears" is the Adamic humanity. The descent of the shepherd from the mountains (*ex Trinitate descendit!*) is the incarnation.[67] This interpretation is repeated throughout the entire history of interpretation with only minor variations,[68] and it is not fundamentally

59 Cf. above, II D 2.2, n. 57.
60 In Matthew the Father's "will" is always used ethically to refer to something demanded of human beings rather than to refer to what God will do. This meaning is further strengthened by ἔμπροσθεν that in Matthew clearly is used with the sense of πρό.
61 Robert C. Gregg ("Early Christian Variations on the Parable of the Lost Sheep," 85–104) gives a brief overview of the Ante Nicene period. The early sources are discussed more thoroughly by Antonio Orbe, *Parábolas Evangélicas en San Ireneo*, 2.117–81.
62 Irenaeus *Haer.* 1.24.2; Hippolytus *Ref.* 6.19.
63 Irenaeus, *Haer.* 1.8.4.
64 *Haer.* 1.16.1. Somewhat different are the numerical speculations in Irenaeus *Haer.* 2.24.6 and in the *Gos.*

Truth, NHC I 31, 35–32, 16. Here the lost sheep is probably the fallen Gnostic whose finding restores the ninety-nine to the "correct" whole number of one hundred.
65 Irenaeus *Haer.* 3.19.3; *Epid.* 33.
66 *Carnis* 34.1–2 = CSEL 67. 73–74.
67 Origen *Hom in Gen.* 2.5 = GCS Origenes 6. 34; cf. *Hom in Num.* 19.4 = GCS Origenes 7.184; *Cels.* 4.17.
68 A few examples from the wide selection available are: Jerome 160 (with a reference to Phil 2:6-7); Apollinaris of Laodicea no. 89 = Reuss, 28; Hilary, 18.6 = SC 258.80; Gregory *Hom* 34.3 = *PL* 76.1247–48; Peter of Laodicea, 204 (Phil 2:6-7!); Paschasius Radbertus, 615–16; Christian of Stavelot, 1409; Anselm of Laon, 1407 (Phil 2:6-7); Dionysus bar Salibi, 299.

different from the gnostic interpretation. Here as there the parable is regarded as a representation of the drama of salvation. Here as there all can see themselves in the lost sheep so that the parable becomes for everyone an encounter with the redeemer.

The Parenetic Interpretation

The basis of this approach lies in an interpretation that is offered by several of the church's exegetes as an alternative to the previous interpretation. The hundred sheep are to be understood not as all "rational creatures," but as human beings, so that ninety-nine refers to the righteous and the one sheep to the unrighteous.[69] Then, on the basis of this interpretation, direct parenetic applications are possible. Origen applies the parable to the leaders of the church: "You are a shepherd (*'pastor es'*); you see the Lord's sheep hanging over a precipice and in danger of falling. Will you not run to them? . . . Do we not want to follow the example of the teacher-shepherd?"[70] The *Didascalia* addresses the bishops who have been favored "with the face of Christ" and challenges them to care for all—those who have not sinned as well as the sinners.[71] For John Chrysostom, who uses the text as a criticism of all-consuming greed, it is addressed to all members of the church.[72] Theodoret summarizes the entire first part of the chapter (becoming like a child, giving no offense, and seeking the weak and the shabby) with one sentence: "It is not enough to be satisfied with your own salvation."[73]

In the third-century controversy over the restoration of lapsed Christians our text became a significant force in church history. Cyprian appeals to our text when he wants to receive back into the church those who have "fallen." "Although the Lord, having left the ninety-nine whole, sought the one wandering and weary and, having found it, He Himself carried it back on his shoulders, we not only do not seek out the weary, but we hinder them when they come."[74] On the other hand, the Montanist Tertullian, who

obviously has to defend himself against such an interpretation, struggles with the text. He escapes the dilemma by appealing to the historical situation in Jesus' day. Jesus was able to speak of receiving Gentiles but not of restoring Christians to fellowship, since in his day there were as yet no Christians.[75]

New Accents

For the most part the modern interpretation of the parable has followed traditional lines with only an occasional appearance of a new theological insight. For Luther the parable becomes a visible expression of *sola gratia*: "We are the lost sheep. . . . The sheep cannot help itself. . . . The sheep does not go looking for its Lord; the Lord goes looking for the sheep. . . . Christ the Lamb takes the sheep on his shoulders; it is thus, and not the other way around. He must carry the sheep, and then it comes to the right place. It walks not on its own legs, but on those of the shepherd."[76] For liberal theology the parable becomes the center of the proclamation of Jesus: "God the father is . . . *eo ipso* merciful"; for him "the highest consideration" is "the eternal worth of the individual soul."[77]

Summary

Once again the potential meaning of a biblical text has in the course of the history of its interpretation given rise to a wealth of meanings. Is any of these interpretations false? On the basis of its original meaning is there any point at which we must reject a given development? It is a difficult question to answer, especially since the New Testament itself shows that the original parable contains different possibilities. There is already in Jesus' use of the parable a reference to his own activity that was richly explored later in the christological interpretation of the shepherd. The parenetic impulse that was especially important for Matthew did not any more constitute an absolute rejection for him of the idea of the love of God than it did in later interpretations. Even the

---

69 As a variant reading in Jerome, 160; Thomas Aquinas, *Lectura* no. 1511; Maldonat, 363; Lapide, 350; Jansen, 164.

70 *Hom. in Josh* 7.6 = GCS Origenes 7.333–34.

71 6 (= Achelis-Flemming, 27); 7 (= Achelis-Flemming, 32-33; quotation p. 33).

72 59.7 = *PG* 58.582–84.

73 In Cramer, "Mt 18,10b," 146.

74 *Ep.* 55.15 = FC 51.142–43.

75 *Pud.* 7 = ACW 28.68–72. Earlier the Catholic Tertullian had interpreted the text much differently in *Paen.* 8 = ACW 28.29–30.

76 3. 227–28 (from a sermon from 1524 on Luke 15).

77 Holtzmann, *Theologie* 1.220–21, 229–30. Quotations from 221, 230.

gnostic interpretation of the text should not be rejected altogether. Of course, the strict separation between the "mountains" of the heavenly pleroma and the valley of tears of the material world in which the sheep has gone astray is not in the New Testament,[78] yet it is important to remember that the entire interpretation of the church that sees the text as an allegorical portrayal of the mystery of the redemption of Adamic humanity itself draws on Gnosticism. It is precisely the christological and allegorical interpretation of the church that is indebted for many of its most important insights to the gnostic "heresy."

Over and over we see that the text is interpreted from the center of each interpreter's understanding of Christ and thus from the entirety of the biblical witness. For Matthew this center was Christ the Cosmocrater who gives God's commandments to the church. In the interpretation of the ancient church—especially that of the Eastern church—it was the incarnate Christ of Phil 2:6-7.[79] For Luther it was the redeemer who carries the lost sheep on his shoulders without any conditions.[80] Interpreters similarly read the parable in such a way that they saw themselves in it, whether as part of the Adamic humanity that the sheep represents or, as in Luther's case, by directly identifying with the sheep. The story thus became an expression of the interpreter's own basic faith experience.

If anything, it is the legitimacy of Matthew's own parenetic interpretation that might be called into question. Is it not so far removed from the attitude of Jesus that the parable becomes legalistic?[81] I think not.

Matthew's parenesis makes it possible for "little ones"— church members who have gone astray—to experience the searching love of God in a concrete way in the church. It also keeps the members of the church who are at work seeking the lost "little ones" from doing so with the secret arrogance of "big ones," who themselves make no mistakes and who are the infallible guardians of the truth. In a church that is fundamentally a *corpus permixtum* there can only be "little ones" and persons who are forever unsure of themselves. Such insight can lead to the kind of love that is the fruit of a true interpretation of a biblical text.[82]

Another question deals with the relation between Matthew's appeal for forgiveness and acceptance and the perfectionistic character of his church that is on the road to perfection (cf. 5:20, 48). It is noteworthy that the "perfectionist" Matthew became the major witness for the "liberal" Cyprian and not for the "perfectionist" Tertullian. Are there in Matthew two opposing tendencies? Does the exhortation to be prepared to forgive destroy the severity of the moral demand? The question brings us to the fundamental theological question of our chapter—a question that becomes concrete in the next pericope: How can Matthew, who urges the members of his church to be willing to forgive without end, affirm the church discipline of which he himself speaks in vv. 15-17?

---

78 Nor do the gnostic numerical speculations have any basis in the text. Contrasting one and ninety-nine is a typically Jewish way of saying "few" and "many." Cf. Str–B 1.784–85.

79 Cf. above, nn. 67–68.

80 Cf. above, n. 76.

81 Weder, *Gleichnisse*, 176.

82 Cf. Luz, *Matthew in History*, 91–96.

1.4 On Brotherly Admonition and on Prayer (18:15-20)

Literature

Garhard Barth, "Auseinandersetzungen um die Kirchenzucht im Umkreis des Mattäusevangeliums," *ZNW* 69 (1978) 158-77.

Gustav Adolf Benrath, "Busse," *TRE* 7 (1981) 452-73.

Bornkamm, "Lösegewalt," 37-50.

José María Bover, "Si peccaverit in te frater tuus . . . Mt 18,15," *EstBib* 12 (1953) 195-98.

Brooks, *Community,* 99-107.

José Caba, "El poder de la petición communitaria (Mt 18,19-20)," *Greg* 54 (1973) 609-54.

Timothy R. Carmody, "Matthew 18:15-17 in Relation to Three Texts from Qumran Literature (CD 9:2-8, 16-22; 1QS 5:25-6:1)," in Maurya P. Horgan and Paul J. Kobelski, eds., *To Touch the Text: Biblical and Related Studies in Honor of Joseph A. Fitzmyer* (New York: Crossroad, 1989) 141-58.

Catchpole, "Reproof," 79-89.

Paul Christian, "Was heisst für Matthäus: 'In meinem Namen versammelt' (Mt 18,20)?" in Wilhelm Ernst, Konrad Feiereis, and Fritz Hoffmann, eds., *Dienst der Vermittlung: Festschrift zum 25-jährigen Bestehen des Philosoph.-Theol. Studiums im Priesterseminar Erfurt* (EThSt 37; Leipzig: St. Benno, 1977) 97-105.

David Daube, "A Missionary Term," in idem, *New Testament,* 352-61.

J. Duncan M. Derrett, "'Where Two or Three Are Convened in My Name . . .': A Sad Misunderstanding," *ExpT* 91 (1980) 83-86.

Walter Doskocil, *Der Bann in der Urkirche: Eine rechtsgeschichtliche Untersuchung* (Munich: Zink, 1958).

David Flusser, "'I Am in the Midst of Them' (Mt 18:20)," in idem, *Judaism and the Origins of Christianity* (Jerusalem: Magnes, 1988) 515-25.

Goran Forkman, *The Limits of the Religious Community* (Lund: Gleerup, 1972).

Jean Galot, "'Qu'il soit pour toi comme le païen et le publicain,'" *NRTh* 96 = 106 (1974) 1009-30.

García-Martínez, "Represión," 23-40.

Heinz Giesen, "Zum Problem der Exkommunikation nach dem Matthäus-Evangelium," in idem, *Glaube und Handeln* (EHS 23/205; Frankfurt: Lang, 1983) 1.17-83.

Hunzinger, "Bann II," 161-67.

Idem, "Die jüdische Bannpraxis im neutestamentlichen Zeitalter" (Diss., Göttingen, 1954).

Idem, "Spuren pharisäischer Institutionen in der frühen rabbinischen Überlieferung," in Gert Jeremias, Heinz-Wolfgang Kuhn, and Hartmut Stegeman, eds. *Tradition und Glaube: Das frühe Christentum in seiner Umwelt: Festgabe für Karl Georg Kuhn zum 65. Geburtstag* (Göttingen: Vandenhoeck & Ruprecht, 1971) 147-56.

Georg Korting, "Binden oder Lösen," *SNTU* A 14 (1989) 39-91.

James L. Kugel, "On Hidden Hatred and Open Reproach: Early Exegesis of Leviticus 19:17," *HTR* 80 (1987) 43-61.

John H. Leith and Hans-Jürgen Goertz, "Kirchenzucht," *TRE* 19 (1990) 173-91.

Christoph Link, "Bann V," *TRE* 5 (1980) 182-90.

Horacio Lona, "'In meinem Namen versammelt': Mt 18,20 und liturgisches Handeln," *Archiv für Liturgiewissenschaft* 27 (1985) 373-404.

Lührmann, *Redaktion,* 111-21.

Marchand, "Matthieu 18,20."

May, "Bann IV," 170-82.

Rudolf Pesch, "'Wo zwei oder drei versammelt sind auf meinen Namen hin . . .' (Mt 18,20)," in Ludger Schenke, ed., *Studien zum Matthäusevangelium: Festschrift für Wilhelm Pesch* (SBS; Stuttgart: Katholisches Bibelwerk, 1988) 227-44.

Victor C. Pfitzner, "Purified Community—Purified Sinner," *Australian Biblical Review* 30 (1982) 34-55.

Bernhard Poschmann, *Paenitentia secunda. Die kirchliche Busse im ältesten Christentum bis Cyprian und Origenes* (Theophaneia 1; Bonn: Hanstein, 1940).

Béda Rigaux, "'Lier et délier,'" *La Maison-Dieu* 117 (1974) 86-135.

Joseph Sievers, "'Where Two or Three . . . ': The Rabbinic Concept of Shekinah and Matthew 18:20," in Asher Finkel and Lawrence Frizzell, eds., *Standing Before God: Studies on Prayer in Scriptures and in Tradition with Essays: In Honor of John M. Oesterreicher* (New York: Ktav, 1981) 171-82.

Hendrik van Vliet, "No Single Testimony" (Diss., Utrecht, 1958).

Anton Vögtle, "Ekklesiologische Auftragsworte des Auferstandenen," in idem, *Evangelium,* 243-52.

L. Michael White, "Crisis Management and Boundary Maintenance: The Social Location of the Matthean Community," in David Balch, ed., *Social History of the Matthean Community* (Minneapolis: Fortress, 1991) 211-47.

Zimmermann, "Struktur," 4-19.

For *additional literature* on the community discourse see above, IV B.

15	But if your brother sins against you,[1] go and reprove him with just the two of you alone. If he hears you, you have gained your brother.

16	But if he does not listen to you,
	take one or two with you
	      so that 'every word might be confirmed by the
	      statement of two or three witnesses.'

17	But if he refuses to listen to them,
	tell it to the church.
	But if he refuses to listen even to the church,
	      let him be to you as the Gentile and the tax
	      collector.

18	Amen, I say to you:
	Whatever you bind on earth shall be bound in
	      heaven,
	and whatever you loose on earth shall be loosed
	      in heaven.

19	Again I say to you:[2] If two of you agree on earth[3] about anything they ask, it will happen to them from my father in heaven,
20	for where two or three are assembled in my name there I am in their midst."

Analysis

Structure

The expressions "Amen, I say to you" (ἀμὴν λέγω ὑμῖν; v. 18) and "again I say to you" (πάλιν λέγω ὑμῖν; v. 19) divide the section into three subunits. That there is no visible logical relationship among them makes the interpretation of the text especially difficult. Features appearing in more than one section are the use of "if" (ἐάν) to begin a clause (vv. 15a, b, 16, 17a, b, 19, cf. 18a, b) and the number "two" (δύο; vv. 16, 19, 20).[4] Between vv. 17 and 18 the persons addressed change. As was the case in vv. 8-9, vv. 15-17 speak to the individual church member.

a. The church rule in *vv. 15-17* consists of five sentences in the style of casuistic law, although they are not completely parallel. Verse 15a also constitutes the exposition. Verse 15b stands out as the only one of the five that reckons with a positive result. Verses 16-17 constitute a series of increasing intensity in which

a negative result is assumed in each case.[5] Verse 16 is expanded with a biblical quotation.

b. The transition from vv. 15-17 to the double logion about binding and loosing in *v. 18* is smooth. Since the readers of necessity will understand binding and loosing as a reference to the church's behavior toward the sinner of vv. 15-17, v. 18 is easily understood as the Lord's sanction of the church's action.

c. *Verses 19-20* appear to introduce a new theme, yet the ἐάν clause connects v. 19 to vv. 15-17, and the contrast between ἐπὶ τῆς γῆς and ἐν οὐρανοῖς provides a link to v. 18. We will thus regard the two verses as having a close relationship to vv. 15-18 and not as constituting a special unit. Still, the use of πάλιν to link vv. 18 and 19 leaves open the question of the logical relationship between them. One of the difficulties in the interpretation of our text is created by the need to construe a logical connection between vv. 18 and 19 for this reason as well as because of its concluding position and the brevity of its apodosis.

Sources

The parallel in Luke 17:3-4, a hortatory wisdom saying, corresponds to vv. 15a and 22. The consensus is that the saying existed in Q and that Luke preserves the Q text reasonably well. Matthew adds the redactional v. 21, while the intervening verses are inserted into the Q text. The main questions are: Who is responsible for the insertions? What role did Matthew play in the formulations? The great uncertainty about both questions adds to the difficulty of interpreting the text.

a. In the opinion of most exegetes *vv. 15-17* are neither the original Q text,[6] nor Matthew's editorial creation,[7] nor a special tradition that is completely independent of Q;[8] they constitute rather an expansion of Q prior to Matthew in, for example, Q^Mt.[9] Matthew's share of the special vocabulary is by no

---

1   Εἰς σέ is omitted by the most important Egyptian witnesses. With José María Bover ("Si peccaverit in te frater tuus . . . Mt 18,15," 195–98) et al. I argue for the longer text, since it is found in all text families. Matthew takes the wording from Q 17:4. The omission in many MSS probably was influenced by Luke 17:3. (According to the opposing hypothesis εἰς σέ was added under the influence of v. 21.) The decision has important consequences for our understanding of the section, and it is regrettable that it must remain so uncertain.

2   Text-critically, ἀμήν is not well supported.

3   The indicative future is not only supported by the better witnesses text-critically than is the subjunctive aorist; after ἐάν was used seven times with the subjunctive aorist in vv. 12-17, it is clearly the more difficult reading. Cf. Moulton–Howard–Turner 3.116; BDF § 373 (3).

4   Note the graduation: ἕνα ἢ δύο, δύο, δύο ἢ τρεῖς.

5   Matthew 5:21-22 is similar in form. Cf. 5:34-36; 10:40-42; 23:8-10, 20-22.

6   Catchpole, "Reproof."

means sufficient to justify regarding all three verses as redactional.[10] At most the quotation from Deut 19:15 in v. 16b might be redactional.[11]

b. An important question for the interpretation of the text is whether Matthew found *v. 18* and vv. 15-17 already connected or whether he himself attached v. 18 to vv. 15-17. Since ἀμὴν λέγω ὑμῖν can be both tradition and redaction, the opinion of exegetes depends almost completely on whether they regard as original the singular form of the binding and loosing saying in 16:19 or the plural version in 18:18. Those who regard v. 18 as a new version of an originally singular form of the saying will more likely attribute its insertion in our text to Matthew as well.[12] Those who, as I do, regard the plural form, which is also transmitted in John 20:23, as the oldest[13] can easily believe that vv. 15-18 constitute a unit prior to Matthew.[14] This latter view makes it easier to live with the apparent tension between vv. 15-18 and vv. 12-14 and 21-22, where it is not anticipated that sinners will be excluded even in heaven. Apart from such observations based on the contents of the verses, however, there are no arguments one way or the other, and the

most honest thing to do is to recognize how hypothetical are all of our conclusions here.

c. With regard to *vv. 19-20* the questions are somewhat easier. Here again we can reckon with the possibility of several redactional insertions into the text without attributing both verses in their entirety to Matthew.[15] It is possible (although we can say no more than that) that prior to Matthew v. 20 was added to support the promise of v. 19. The term "again" (πάλιν), a favorite Matthean expression, could indicate that it was Matthew who first added this double logion to the "church order" of vv. 15-18, but such a conclusion is by no means certain.[16]

Origin

The expanded church rule of vv. 15-17 probably originated in a Jewish Christian community that still regarded itself as part of Israel and that had not yet embraced the gentile mission. For its members the terms "Gentiles and tax collectors" still refer to people with whom one did not associate.[17] Verse 18 probably came from the church rather than from Jesus,

---

7   Gundry, 367–70.

8   Thus especially the (essentially English) representatives of the source "M." See, e.g., Streeter, *Gospels*; Manson, *Sayings*; García Martínez, "Represión," 36. Brooks (*Community*) regards vv. 15-17 as an expansion of Q and attributes only vv. 18-20 to "M."

9   See, e.g., Lührmann, *Redaktion*, 112–13; Bornkamm, "Lösegewalt," 38; Zumstein, *Condition*, 387–88; Davies-Allison 2.781–87.

10   Cf. vol. 1, Introduction 3.2 on δέ, ὕπαγε, ἐάν, ἀδελφός (little specifically), παραλαμβάνω (outside of 1:18–2:23 it is scarcely redactional), εἷς, ἤ, δύο ὥσπερ. Non-Matthean are ἐλέγχων, μεταξύ κτλ. (instead of κατ᾽ ἰδίαν), παρακούω, ἐκκλησία (here different from 16:18 where it has the meaning of assembly). We are familiar with the appearance of ἐθνικός and τελώνης together from the traditional logion in 5:46-47. The usage contradicts Matthew's open attitude toward Gentiles.

11   This conclusion is supported by the fact that the quotation is based on the text of the LXX that has a special affinity to A. Cf. Stendahl, *School*, 138–39. It is found in the New Testament, however (2 Cor 13:1; 1 Tim 5:19), and in the Jewish tradition it is so common (cf. below, n. 32) that it could have been inserted at any stage of the tradition. In any case, from a tradition-history perspective it may be secondary, since it disrupts the series of five ἐάν clauses. The two or three witnesses do not fit with ἔτι ἕνα ἤ δύο, because the brother who is being confronted is not a witness!

12   E.g., Zimmermann, "Struktur," 18; Lange, *Erscheinen*, 131; Gnilka 2.136; Davies-Allison 2.787.

13   See above, III C 3.3 on the tradition history and origin of 16:19b, c.

14   Simarly, e.g., Pesch, *Matthäus*, 42; Zumstein, *Condition*, 388–89. The change from singular to plural need not be a problem, since v. 18 refers not only to "you," but also to the "one or two" brothers of v. 15b or to the "church" of v. 17. Cf. also 5:33-37; Q 13:34-35; for Matthew cf. 5:39; 6:1-2, 22-24; 7:1-6; 23:25-26.

15   Among favorite Matthean words from vol. 1, Introduction 3.2 are: πάλιν, λέγω ὑμῖν, δύο, the contrast οὐρανός-γῆ (ἐπὶ τῆς γῆς 2–4 times redactional), ὃς ἐάν, πατήρ, ἐν οὐρανοῖς, γάρ, συνάγω, ἤ, ἐκεῖ, ἐν μέσῳ. On ἐμὸν ὄνομα cf. 19:29. Completely non-Matthean are συμφωνέω, the hapax legomenon πρᾶγμα, γενήσεται (instead of γενηθήτω), the attraction of the relative pronoun, συνάγω (perfect elsewhere only in 22:41 and 27:17) referring to the disciples, οὗ connected with ἐκεῖ. Noteworthy also is that Matthew has used ἐν μέσῳ rather than μετά with the genitive as he did in 1:23 and 28:20.

16   Wilhelm Pesch ("Die sogenannte Gemeindeordnung Mt 18," *BZ* NF 7 [1963] 220–35, 228) thinks, e.g., that vv. 15-20 were a unit before Matthew. Goulder (*Midrash*, 400–401) refers to 1 Cor 5:4 where in connection with excommunication reference is made to an assembly (συνάγω) as well as to the name and the presence of the Lord.

17   Their judgment in v. 17b is not at all typical of

but it is very old.[18] At the most v. 19 might go back to Jesus but without the justification in v. 20 that is likely a secondary addition.[19] It may be that v. 20 originated after Easter, since it most naturally refers to the presence of the risen Lord in his church.

Interpretation

Verses 15-18 fit awkwardly in the context. Verses 12-14 spoke of the shepherd who searches for the lost sheep, and the following text (vv. 21-22) is going to say that one should forgive seventy-seven times. Yet the subject of our text is exclusion from the church—excommunication. Verses 19-20 appear to have no connection either to vv. 15-18 or to vv. 21-22. Verses 15-18 are also in tension with other texts in Matthew's gospel. How do they compare with the prohibition of judging in 7:1-2 and with Matthew's understanding that the church as *corpus permixtum* is a place where good and evil exist side by side until the judgment (13:37-43, 49-50; 22:11-14)? Not a few exegetes see here a tension that can scarcely be resolved,[20] and herein lies the major problem for understanding our text.

There are four basic ways of solving the problem.

1. Verses 15-18 speak not of excommunication from the church but of *winning the lost back to the church.* Galot is the most consistent representative of this interpretation, which I designate here as the *grace model.* According to Galot the text speaks not of exclusion but of the "réconciliation fraternelle." All three conversations with the sinner serve this end. He

argues that ἐλέγχειν means not *reprove* or *accuse* but "raisonner" "pour le convaincre." That the sinner should be "to you as the Gentile and the tax collector," does not mean that one should break off all fellowship, since Jesus was especially gracious to the Gentiles and the tax collectors.[21] At the very least it is here that this interpretation reveals how absurd it is. Other exegetes, while not going this far, emphasize that vv. 15-17 describe not an expulsion from the church but an interpersonal problem between two individuals.[22] Of course, in support of such an interpretation are the likely original reading εἰς σέ in v. 15 and the repeated personal pronoun in the second person (σου, σοι) but not the reference to the assembly of the church in v. 17.

2. The second attempt to solve the problem regards excommunication as an "extreme option" that does not reflect the "law of life under which the church lives as a whole."[23] It is thus possible only in a *borderline case.* I call this interpretation, therefore, the *borderline case model.* According to this model the church's actual law of life is the law not of exclusion but of the forgiveness that is required in the surrounding verses 10-14 and 21-22. The goal of this model is an appeal to the members of the church, or its leaders, to abandon the law of love only in exceptional cases. Such an exception might be a capital sin that is so serious that it can no longer be forgiven.[24] Verses 19-20 provide excellent support for this interpretation, if we can understand the logical link that is missing between vv. 18 and 19 to be that "all acts of

---

Jesus. Unlike 5:46-47, here there is no alienating effect. Cf. vol. 1, II A 2.2.6 on 5:43-48, n. 11.

18 Cf. above, III C 3.3 on the tradition history and origin of 16:19c.

19 José Caba ("El poder de la petición communitaria (Mt 18,19-20)," 609–54, 620) concludes that v. 19 originated from a combination of 7:7 and 21:22.

20 Cf. C. G. Montefiore (*Gospels* 2.681) who regards the text as "scarcely consistent"; Ortensio da Spinetoli (*Matteo: Il vangelo della chiesa* [Commenti e studi biblici; 4th ed.; Assisi: Cittadella editrice, 1983] 503) wonders whether Matthew has forgotten chap. 13; Garhard Barth, "Auseinandersetzungen um die Kirchenzucht im Umkreis des Mattäusevangeliums," 158–77, 174–75; Fabris, 391.

21 Galot, "Qu'il soit pour," 1014 (quotation), 1018 (quotation), 1023–24.

22 E.g., Paul Gaechter, *Die literarische Kunst im Matthäusevangelium* (SBS 7; Stuttgart: Katholisches Bibelwerk, 1965), 599; Thompson, *Advice,* 184, 201;

Bonnard, 275; Catchpole, "Reproof," 87; Gundry, 368.

23 Bornkamm, "Lösegewalt," 42. This suggested solution is the most widespread. Even Gnilka (2.139) claims that Matthew "shifts . . . the accent from a legal concept to a pastoral-ecclesiological concern." We need not abandon church law here that readily.

24 Kähler, who makes this suggestion, points out that the infrequently used word ἁμαρτάνω appears again in 27:4 in connection with the death of Judas ("Kirchenleitung," 140–44). The warning against σκανδαλίζειν in vv. 6-7 could speak for this interpretation, but what shall we say then about vv. 21-22 where ἁμαρτάνειν appears for a third time? Here Matthew requires forgiveness, and he gives an answer that contradicts Kähler. Of possible importance is the reference to the unforgivable sin against the Spirit in 12:31-32—a logion that, to be sure, is hardly understandable in its Matthean context. Cf. above, III A 2.1 on Matthew's understanding of 12:31-32.

discipline [are] undergirded by the group's prayer."[25] Then God will at least have the last word on the extreme option of excommunication. On the other hand, v. 18 is creates a problem for this view, since it gives heavenly sanction to what appears to be only an outside possibility.

3. G. Rossé offers an interesting solution. For him the key to the problem is v. 20. This verse, which speaks of the presence of Jesus in his church, is to be understood against the background of Old Testament *covenant theology*.[26] For that reason I call it the *covenant theology model*. On the one hand, within the covenant relationship established by Christ, forgiveness and the presence of the Lord are promised to the church. On the other hand, the covenant idea means that offenses against the Father's will are especially serious, since they call into question the covenant relationship.[27]

4. The fourth possibility is simply to leave the contradictions as they are without trying to impose an underlying theological idea on them. Here Matthew is seen as a redactor of various traditions who felt obligated to include in his gospel, "in the least inhospitable context he could find,"[28] his own church's rule of excommunication. Since this view of necessity surrenders any hope of a coherent interpretation of the content of Matthew's collected traditions, I call it the *inconsistency model*. It poses a serious question to a fundamental methodological (and theological) exegetical postulate. Exegetes almost always assume, consciously or unconsciously, that a text has a logical consistency that is capable of being grasped with our modern categories so that they can interpret it. Thus they often fall prey to the temptation to read a meaning into the text if need be. I do not believe that we have to do without an overarching meaning of the entire text in this case, but the question that this approach forces us to face remains fundamentally important.

The exegesis will show to what degree these four approaches to the text are valid.

■ **15** Ἁμαρτάνω is an open word that thus far has not been defined in any special way in the Gospel of Matthew. In the context the readers relate the word on the one hand to "to cause to fall" (σκανδαλίζω; vv. 6, 8-9), and they know that sin is something that is serious. On the other hand they relate it to the sheep that has gone astray; then they know that sins can be forgiven. The text speaks specifically of the *brother's* sin. Those who are addressed are expected to take the initiative, not because they have official responsibility for the way the members of the church conduct their affairs but because they are directly affected by the brother's sin ("against you"; εἰς σέ). Yet the "sin" that one member of the church has committed against another is not a private matter about which the church is not concerned. It is a biblical, Jewish, and early Christian conviction that every sin affects the entire church. Presumably the purpose of the private conversation is to protect the brother's feelings; without witnesses present he will not be embarrassed. The primary meaning of ἐλέγχω here is "to take to task, to call to account," since hovering in the background is Lev 19:17 with the Niphal of יכח (= "to reprove," instead of "anger"). However, as the reference to the "witnesses" shows, the basic meaning "to convict" is not far removed. Leviticus 19:17, appearing just before the command to love one's neighbor in Lev 19:18, has a long history of interpretation in Judaism, the essence of which is that the public admonition of an Israelite brother is an expression of the love of one's neighbor and of solidarity within the people of God.[29] Such a brotherly admonition can have a positive result: Then "you have won your brother." The figurative sense

25   Trilling, *Hausordnung*, 56.
26   Rossé, *Ecclesiologia*, esp. 93, 109–10. Cf. Lona, "In meinem Namen," 387–88. In large part Rossé follows Frankemölle (*Jahwebund*, esp. 24–37), who has discovered the fundamental christological and theological statements of Matthew's gospel in the μεθ' ὑμῶν of 1:23 and 28:20.
27   Jesus' commands are not just any commands; they are "esigenze del Regno" (Rossé, *Ecclesiologia*, 110).
28   C. J. A. Hickling, "Conflicting Motives in the Redaction of Matthew," *Studia Evangelica* 7 (TU 126; Berlin: Akademie-Verlag, 1982) 259.
29   On the Jewish reception of Lev 19:17 cf. James L. Kugel, "On Hidden Hatred and Open Reproach: Early Exegesis of Leviticus 19:17," 43–61. Sir 19:13-17 is an important witness for the wisdom reception, but cf. esp. *T. Gad* 6.3–7: "If a man sin against thee, speak peaceably to him . . . and if he repent and confess, forgive him. . . And though he deny it and yet have a sense of shame when reproved, give over reproving him. For he who denieth may repent so as not again to wrong thee. . . . And if he be shameless and persist in his wrong-doing, even so

of κερδαίνω with humans as the object is uncommon in both Greek and biblical sources,[30] but it appears twice as a term used in the early Christian mission (1 Cor 9:19-22; 1 Pet 3:1). Matthew is probably thinking primarily of the restoration of the sinner to the people of God or to the church.

■ **16** A conversation with witnesses is the next step only when the private conversation is not successful. Why are the witnesses present? Since they are eyewitnesses of the conversation rather than of the accused brother's sin, their purpose cannot be to testify later in the assembly of the church about his deed. Deuteronomy 19:15 is thus not introduced in the sense of the biblical text. The two witnesses are used differently, however, not only in the New Testament,[31] but also in Judaism. In rabbinic texts an especially important task of the witnesses is to warn the offender about his deed[32] and thus to make it as difficult as possible to condemn him, since only someone who has been warned by several witnesses can later be legally condemned.[33] It is not clear whether they serve a similar purpose in our text or whether, as others have surmised, they are to strengthen the brother's admoni-

tion, so that the ῥῆμα here meant not "content," but quite literally the "word" of admonition.[34]

■ **17** The church rule does not envisage the possibility of a further positive outcome of this conversation. If the second attempt also fails and the sinner does not respond,[35] as a last resort the matter is to be brought before the entire church. To treat someone as a tax collector and Gentile does not mean final condemnation, but from the perspective of Jewish Christians who are faithful to the Torah it does mean that one has nothing more to do with him. For all practical purposes that means not only breaking off all private contact between two individuals but expulsion from the church.[36] While there is no mention of the possibility that the sinner at a later date will be readmitted to the church or saved in the final judgment, as Paul envisages, for example, in 1 Cor 5:5 and 2 Cor 2:7-10, it is in my judgment probable.[37] Nor is anything said in any detail about how the expulsion is carried out. That no church officials are mentioned here of course does not mean that there were none in Matthew's church. Still, it is noteworthy that our text speaks to the brother who is affected. There is also

---

forgive him from the heart" (ET: R. H. Charles, *The Apocrypha and Pseudepigrapha of the Old Testament* [Oxford: Clarendon, 1913] 2.341–42). A phenomenal text! In Qumran cf. esp. CD 7.2–3; 9.2–3; 13.18. Str–B 1.787–90 quotes impressive rabbinic sources on the history of Lev 19:17, some of which are genuine parallels to Luke 17:3-4. The most important NT sources (without direct reference to Lev 19:17) that portray reprimanding as a sign of genuine brotherliness are Gal 6:1; 1 Thess 5:14; 2 Tim 2:25. Cf. *Did.* 15.3-4.

30 David Daube ("A Missionary Term," 352–61) surmises that behind the term lies the Hebrew שכר or the Aramaic אגר for which there is some (scarce!) evidence with a figurative meaning. *Faute de mieux,* that is the best possible explanation.

31 Cf. Matt 26:60; 2 Cor 13:1; cf. John 8:17-18.

32 *M. Sanh.* 5.1; 8.4; 10:4; *m. Mak.* 1.8–9; *m. Soṭa* 1.1–2 (all in Str–B 1.790). *Mek. Exod.* on 21:12. Hendrik van Vliet ("No Single Testimony," 54–55) offers further sources.

33 1QS 6.1 follows its admonition concerning individual reproof with the statement based on Lev 19:17: "Also, let no cause be brought before the Many (i.e., the church assembly), by one man against another, unless reproof has been made before witnesses"

(ET: André Dupont-Sommer, *The Essene Writings from Qumran* [Geza Vermes, trans.; Cleveland: World, 1962] 84–85). The statement is in keeping with the rabbinic witnesses cited in n. 32.

34 Thompson, *Advice,* 183; Gnilka 2.137. Schweizer's pastoral concern is commendable, but it has no basis in the text when he says (371) that they are "to protect the sinner; the admonisher may well be wrong, or someone else may find the right words when he cannot."

35 Παρακούω (to overhear, to hear what is not intended for one's ears, to hear incompletely, to hear incorrectly) in several late Greek and LXX texts means "not to hear, to disobey." Cf. BAGD *s.v.*

36 For Galot, "Qu'il soit pour," 1021–28 the second-person singular address offers essential support for his interpretation in the sense of the "grace model." But why should the private break in relations between two individuals be decided in the church assembly and then confirmed in heaven? The second-person singular address is already given in the history of the tradition. Σοι simply functions to establish this consistent address rhetorically in v. 17 as well.

37 Can we with Hunzinger ("Bann II," 165) arrive at that conclusion based on the reference to "loosing"

no place for office bearers in the discussion of vv. 1-14, which is consistently directed to the church.

Expulsion from the Church

People can be expelled from religious groups and sects but not from national groups or churches that include the entire population. Our verses have no parallels, therefore, in texts that deal with the nation of Israel. There can be no such thing as an expulsion from the nation of Israel for someone who is born a Jew. Nor does the synagogue ban for which there is evidence from the Talmudic period serve as an actual parallel.[38] Like excommunication in the Catholic church it is a disciplinary measure designed both to bring the sinner to repentance and to establish the authority of the synagogue. Since the third century Judaism has drawn a distinction among a reprimand (נְזִיפָה), the light, thirty-day ban (נִדּוּי), and the more severe ban that is of unlimited duration (חֵרֶם). It is a distinction that does not appear in earlier sources.[39] Whether a synagogue ban existed in the first century, as Hunziger still thought,[40] is regarded as unlikely today. The rabbis are aware, however, of a process similar to that of Matt 18:15-17 that is not related to an expulsion. When a sinner asks for forgiveness from the one against whom he has sinned, he should first do it privately. Then, if he receives no forgiveness, he should do it with witnesses.[41] Of course, there is no church gathering here as a third stage.

There are, however, genuine parallels to our process of expulsion in the groups (viz., the Pharisees and the Essenes), which in the period before the destruction of the temple argued with one another about the meaning of true Israel. From the perspective of the sociology of religion they are "sects" every bit as much as are the Jewish-Christian churches, since they are exclusively minority groups that people join by choice and that control the reception of new members and the exclusion of unworthy members with a normative self-definition.[42] From the fact that there were conditions for membership in the Pharisaic Chaburah (association) we can indirectly conclude that members might also be expelled from the group.[43] We know more about the Qumran community. The complicated regulations about both temporary and definitive expulsions from the Qumran community that we find in the *Manual of Discipline* (1QS 6.24–7.25) give no indication of a process that takes place in stages. It is probable, however, that an admonition before witnesses was necessary before one member could bring charges against another member before the entire assembly (1QS 6.1; CD 9.3–4).[44] It is true, of course, that in these two texts and in Matthew the context is different in each case. In 1QS 5, 6 the issue appears to be promotion or demotion in the community's hierarchy; in CD 9 we are dealing with a legal proceeding. Thus Qumran probably has a disciplinary process that takes place in two or three[45] stages but not one that results in expulsion. In spite of the similarities in certain details, therefore, it is unlikely that direct connections or borrowings exist between Matthew's church and Qumran.[46]

---

in v. 18? *Did.* 15.3 (perhaps based on our text?) already places limits on excluding a member from the church: No one should speak with a person who has sinned against another "until he repents."

38   Str–B 4.293-333 gives an overview of the texts.

39   Cf. Hunzinger, "Bannpraxis," 52–61, 66–67.

40   The evidence cited by Hunzinger ("Bannpraxis," 24–33) and Goran Forkman, *The Limits of the Religious Community,* 93–97) is questionable.

41   *Y. Yoma* 8.45c.19; *b. Yoma* 87a (in Str–B 1.796).

42   Cf. Max Weber, *Economy and Society* (Berkeley: University of California Press, 1978) 1204–5 and below, on the meaning of the community discourse today, the excursus on "sect" under no. 2.

43   According to *t. Demai* 3.4, a tax collector cannot belong to a Pharisaic brotherhood. Str–B 2.506 offers similar sources. According to Claus-Hunno Hunzinger ("Spuren pharisäischer Institutionen in der frühen rabbinischen Überlieferung," in Gert Jeremias, Heinz-Wolfgang Kuhn, and Hartmut Stegeman, eds., *Tradition und Glaube: Das frühe*

Christentum in seiner Umwelt: Festgabe für Karl Georg Kuhn zum 65. Geburtstag [Göttingen: Vandenhoeck & Ruprecht, 1971] 153–55; "Bann II," 163) the נִדּוּי of the later period developed from the Pharisaic practice of exclusion.

44   CD 9.2-8 is an interpretation of Lev 19:17-18. 1QS 5.24-25 is reminiscent of Lev 19:17.

45   1QS 5.25 and 6:1 come the closest to reflecting a process in three stages in which the first stage is a private admonition, the second takes place with witnesses, and the third is a discussion in the presence of "many," i.e., in the church assembly, while CD 9.3 appears to be aware only of the admonition before witnesses.

46   As differences García Martínez ("Represión," 37–38) cites especially the decidedly "private" character of the first stage of admonition and the decisive role of the Mebaqqer in Qumran. Furthermore, according to Plato (*Ap.* 26a) Socrates alludes to a similar Greek custom: Before one brings someone to trial, one reprimands the person in private. (The

Finally, there are similar cases of expulsion in the New Testament. The most important parallels are the Pauline text about the expulsion of the fornicator that is closely related to our text (1 Cor 5:1-5)[47] and the text about the expulsion of the member who insulted Paul (2 Cor 2:5-11). In 2 Thess 3:14-15 the reprimand is explicitly mentioned. Office bearers who are responsible for the excommunication do not appear until later in the Pastoral Epistles (1 Tim 1:20; Titus 3:10; cf. 1 Tim 5:19-21; 3 John 10).

■ **18** It is possible that the saying about binding and loosing in v. 18 was already part of the unit in the tradition prior to Matthew. We will begin, however, by interpreting it for itself and ask what our verse means with "binding" and "loosing." Three factors are important for the interpretation: (1) the parallel in 16:19 which the readers already know; (2) the immediate context; and (3) the spheres of association already attached to the two concepts in the Jewish tradition.

Concerning (1): In 16:19 the accent lay on the disciples' instructional decisions, and in support of this interpretation we can cite numerous Jewish texts that use the pair of terms הִתִּיר/אָסַר (Aramaic שְׁרָא/אֲסַר) in the sense of "to forbid" and "to permit."[48]

Concerning (2): However, this meaning does not fit in our context. The word refers to every disciple who forgives or "retains" sins and to the church assembly. It grants the highest authority to its decisions. "Binding" and "loosing" refer here not to teaching or interpreta-tion but rather to judicial decisions, and in the context they must have the meaning of "retaining" or "forgiving" sins.

Concerning (3): The Jewish parallels that point in such a direction are scarce.[49] Nevertheless, in my judgment they are sufficient to justify understanding the text this way. When they forgive or retain, the disciples bind heaven, that is, God, not only in the present but also in his verdicts in the final judgment.[50] Verse 18 gives the decisions of the church and its members about which vv. 15-17 speak an unprecedented authority that can scarcely be surpassed. Thus the saying's *application* here is different from that in 16:19—a situation that is quite possible with a legal principle formulated in such a universal way and introduced with the general ὃ ἐάν or ὅσα ἐάν. We should not, however, speak of different *meanings*. It follows that, of the four types of interpretation about which we initially spoke, a pure grace model is, in light of v. 18, impossible.

We have thus explained the logion of v. 18 for itself, but we have not yet understood it in the context of 18:12-22. Here the question is: What is the significance of this strongly judicial saying that offers heavenly confirmation even to the church's decision not to forgive in a context that speaks of seeking the lost and of unlimited forgiveness? Is it for Matthew really a borderline case? The history of the text in the major churches reveals

---

reference is from C. Münch.) Such a parallel also shows that we need not assume that 18:15-17 was directly and exclusively dependent on Qumran.

47 Cf. above, n. 16.

48 Cf. above, III C 3.3 on 16:19 with n. 91.

49 Josephus *Bell.* 1.111 (to be thrown into jail, to be released from jail); *b. Moʿed Qat.* 16a in Str–B 1.739 (to impose and suspend the ban, third century); *T. Yer. II* on Gen 4:7 (to loose and retain [נטר] sins in the coming world; unfortunately, this close parallel does not use the word "bind"). 1 Kings 8:31–34 gives a biblical example for connecting human and divine forgiving/retaining. The two words are also used with a remote meaning in magic and in exorcisms. Cf. above on 16:19 with nn. 88–90; Davies-Allison 2.635–36. A basic meaning of the Hebrew/Aramaic אסר is "to imprison." The Aramaic שְׁרָא often has the meaning "to forgive" (Jastrow, *s.v.* 2). In Greek δέω and λύω can also be understood metaphorically in various ways. According to LSJ, *s.v.*, δέω also means confinement

through success or sadness or, in general, impedi-ment. According to LSJ, *s.v.*, λύω also means the suspension of laws, the rebuttal of arguments, transgressing commandments, making good on one's mistakes, and, of course, quite frequently, release from prison. Otto Michel ("Binden und Lösen," *RAC* 2 [1954] 374) refers to the legal use of the term in the Latin authors that is perhaps most important for the history of interpretation. *Obligatio* is liability for a contractual debt, while *solutio* is release from that liability.

50 That follows from the realistically understood periphrastic divine future. Cf. Davies-Allison 2.638.

51 *Did.* 15:3. *Ep. Apost.* 48–49 = NTApoc 1.226 connects Matt 18:15-20 with the warning about listening to slanders.

another possibility of resolving this tension. The churches understand Matt 18:15-18 in terms of excommunication—an excommunication that they enlist in the service of a disciplinary ministry to sinners—that is, one might say in the ministry of grace (that, to be sure, is often a hidden grace). This type of interpretation that for all practical purposes lies behind the practice of excommunication or a church ban in the major churches and that is also articulated in the history of interpretation we might designate the *discipline model*.

History of Interpretation

■ **15-18** 1. In the observable Christian churches of the *early period* we occasionally find indications that Matt 18:15-18 was used to justify a practice of expulsion that was similar to that of the Matthean church.[51] Then in the centuries *following the Constantinian transition* there were major changes in the history of the church that influenced the interpretation of Matt 18:15-18. On the one hand, in the major church excommunication became more and more an instrument of discipline. It served to lead the sinner to remorse and to penitence.[52] A related development is the practice of distinguishing among degrees of excommunication that resulted in the Middle Ages in the distinction between an *excommunicatio maior* (= anathema) and an *excommunicatio minor*.[53] On the other hand, beginning in late antiquity, especially under the influence of the Celtic churches, public church penance became less important, and private confession and penance took its place. The "minor" excommunication—that is, the exclusion from communion of persons guilty of deadly sins—now became part of the discipline of confession and penance. The much less frequent "major" excommunication, on the other hand, was public; it involved a rupture between the community and the sinner, and increasingly it had secular consequences for the person involved (banishment from the court, the loss of the rights of a citizen, etc.).

From early on the word about binding and loosing (v. 18) was used with reference to the sacrament of confession.[54] Since an admonition of public offenders with only two or four people present makes little sense, the "brotherly admonition" of Matt 18:15-16 moves into the larger context of the church's pastoral care in the practice of confession. The view gradually prevailed that Matt 18:15-18 applied only to hidden sins and not to public offenses.[55] The text-critically controversial εἰς σέ (v. 15) was able to be understood as a reference to the private character of the sins in question.[56] Thus for the interpreters of our text the discretion with which the sinner was treated played a major role. The private conversation keeps the sinner from being humiliated in public.[57] Under no circumstances is the brother who confronts the sinner to become a *proditor*—that is, someone who publicly broadcasts his brother's sin.[58] Matthew 18:15-18 is thus de facto divorced from public excommunication. Since pastoral care in the major church was primarily a function of the priests and monks, it was questioned whether "brotherly admonition" is a command for them alone or for all Christians. The answer was that it applies to everyone insofar as brotherly admonition is an expression of the love of one's neighbor; the laity, however, is not involved in punishment.[59]

2. With the *Reformation* came an energetic protest against the mixing of spiritual and secular power that had existed in the late Middle Ages. For Luther the Catholic church's excommunication, which quite often was connected with such things as the confiscation of property, banishment, the release of an excommunicated person's subjects from their oath of allegiance, was nothing more than what the imperial ban should be. For this reason he affirms the "minor ban," the church's exclusion of a member from communion but decidedly rejects the "major," secular ban.[60] The other reformers followed him in this regard. One can trace in all of their statements of principle strong reservations against any mixing of the two realms.[61] The tragedy of the Reformation was that it was unable to preserve the basic idea of distin-

---

52 Cf. John Chrysostom 60.1 = *PG* 58.585. He instructs "exclude them, so that they do not go in themselves." The Council of Lyon (1245) states: "Medicinalis sit excommunicatio" (in May, "Bann IV," 176).

53 May, "Bann IV," 170–76.

54 Cf. above on 16:17-19, n. 183.

55 Origen, 13.30 = GCS Origenes 10.263; Dionysius the Carthusian, 208–9; Thomas Aquinas *S. th.* 2/2 q.33, a.3 corpus; Calvin 2.227; idem, *Inst.* 4.12.6. 1 Timothy 5:20 became the basic biblical text for the procedure to follow in the case of public sins.

56 Dionysius the Carthusian, 207.

57 Origen *Hom. in Lv.* 3.2 = SC 286.126; Augustine *Sermo* 82.8 = *PL* 38.511; John Chrysostom 60.2 = *PG* 58.586; Jerome, 161; Bede, 84; Dionysius bar Salibi, 300. Cf. also Wolzogen, 328.

58 Augustine *Sermo* 82.7 = *PL* 38.510.

59 Thomas Aquinas *S. th.* 2/2, q.33 a.1; a.3 corpus.

60 Martin Luther, sermon on the ban, 1520, *WA* 6.63–65; idem, *WA* 47.281–283; cf. idem, Smalcald article 9 = BSLK 456–457 = *Book of Concord*, 314.

61 Calvin *Inst.* 4.11.1, 4; on Zwingli cf. Ulrich Gäbler, *Huldrych Zwingli: His Life and Work* (Philadelphia: Fortress, 1986) 103–5.

guishing between spiritual and secular authority that corresponded to the doctrine of the two kingdoms. Since "public" sins such as adultery, drunkenness, murder, or heresy always and above all were matters that affected public order, that is, the state, almost everywhere in the areas where the churches of the Reformation were dominant there arose consistories or councils of elders responsible for overseeing public morality and enforcing the appropriate ecclesiastical and civil punishments. For the most part they were appointed by the state or, in the cities, by the city council. For its part the admonition based on Matt 18:15-17 had its place then in the area of personal pastoral care and was separate from public church discipline.

It is thus clear why the main features of the interpretation of Matt 18:15-17 are largely the same in both confessions. The traditions of both confessions on the interpretation of our text gave special attention to the pastoral concern in the text. One is to forget the injustice that one has received and think instead of the brother's injury.[62] The issue is not atonement, but loving admonition—not one's own victory, but the brother's salvation.[63] In both confessions there is agreement that in the case of public offenses charges should be brought immediately without a prior brotherly conversation. The sole dissent should have arisen in the interpretation of ἐκκλησία ("church"). It is not surprising that the Catholic interpreters, both before and after the Reformation, almost always speak here of officeholders; surprising are the few notable exceptions where Catholic interpreters remind us of the church assembly.[64] It is more amazing that most Protestant interpreters understand ἐκκλησία as referring without question to pastors or elders.[65] Only a small number of interpreters notice that v. 17 refers to the entire church assembly.[66]

Calvin, who in other instances was such a brilliant exegete, avoided this insight by "historicizing" the text back into the life of Jesus and understanding "church" as referring to the synagogue.[67]

3. Only in small, *manageable communities,* among them *monastic communities,* was the Matthean rule actually practiced in the way the evangelist intended. It plays a major role in the long and short rule of Basil.[68] According to the *Regula Benedicti,* a stubborn, disobedient, or proud brother is to be warned twice by his superior in secret prior to a public reprimand. The expulsion which then follows can have varying degrees of severity, yet it is always accompanied by the abbot's pastoral concern. Corporal punishment and permanent expulsion from the order are used only as a last resort.[69]

Our text takes on a similar importance for the *radical churches of the Reformation.* The point of departure for the Anabaptists is the same as that for the reformers, viz., the strict separation between the church's power of the keys and the state's power of the sword. "Now the ban, as it is ordered in the churches of Christ, and the sword, as it is ordered in the world, are as different as evening and morning. They are as incompatible as life and death. Therefore, they may not be joined together."[70] Unlike the reformers, however, the Anabaptists were able to maintain this principle. As early as 1524 Konrad Grebel argues in his letter to Thomas Münster that one should not defend the gospel with the sword, nor should one kill those whom one expels according to the rule of Jesus.[71] Article 2 of the Schleitheim articles of Michael Sattler says of the ban that is to be executed according to Matt 18:15-17 that it is not a question of life and death but of who may participate in the Lord's Sup-

62 Jansen, 165.

63 John Chrysostom 60.1 = *PG* 58.583; Wolzogen, 329. Especially impressive is Augustine, *Sermo* 82.3 = *PL* 38.507: "Si amore tui id facis, nihil facis. Sie amore illius facis, optime facis."

64 Hilary, 18.7 = SC 258.82; Jerome, 161 (*multi*); Anselm of Laon, 1408 (the priest carries out only the actual excommunication); Erasmus, *Paraphrasis,* 100.

65 Calvin 2.229; Bucer, 149; Bullinger, 175 (*dic . . . praesidentibus*); Calovius, 348 (the pastors); Beza, 81 (with an open polemic against the interpretation that involves the entire church; according to him the church must be an aristocracy).

66 Episcopius, 115; Wolzogen, 329.

67 2.229; Beza, 81 (both argue that, as in Judaism, a

"sanhedrin" must exercise the central authority in the church).

68 Long rule, 36; short rule 3.9.47, 261 (Frank, 161–62, 199, 202, 222, 335). Matthew plays a major role for Basil. He recommended a public reprimand and expulsion not only for the monasteries but also for the churches. Cf. Klaus Koschorke, *Spuren der alten Liebe: Studien zum Kirchenbegriff des Basilius von Caesarea* (Paradosis 32; Freiburg: Universitätsverlag, 1991) 158–81.

69 *Regula Benedicti* 23–28 = von Balthasar, *Ordensregeln,* 217–20.

70 Peter Walpot, *The Great Article Book* 4.36 = *Quellen zur Geschichte der Täufer 12: Glaubenszeugnisse oberdeutscher Taufgesinnter* (Gütersloh: Mohn, 1967) 253.

per.[72] The two 1527 works of Baltasar Hubmaier, "On Fraternal Admonition" and "On the Christian Ban," became fundamental documents for the Anabaptist churches.[73] They are important because they make a clear connection between church discipline and believers' baptism. Church discipline is meaningless for people who have been baptized without their knowledge and who have not consciously affirmed the church's self-definition on the basis of which they are expelled.[74] A church discipline based on Matthew 18 has remained an important part of the life of the church in Baptist communities,[75] as it later became in such groups as Congregational, Methodist, and Pietistic communities.[76]

4. It is well known that church discipline has gradually disappeared in the *modern age,* especially in the churches of the Reformation. The main reason is probably that the state has become secularized and that the churches have lost much of their influence over the people of independent conscience who remain members only because of tradition. Excommunication thus became de facto irrelevant, and it also increasingly disappeared from the exegesis of Matt 18:15-18. H. Grotius is not at all enamored of the idea of excommunication; he does not think that that is what Christ was talking about.[77] The Armenian Episcopius states: "It is not the church but the individual who binds."[78] The early Rationalist Wolzogen limits the church's power to bind and loose to those sins committed against the church rather than against God.[79] The Lutheran Rudolph Sohm, for whom the true church is the invisible church, says about our text: There is "no governmental act, no 'ban,' no act at all of the assembly (ekklesia). Instead, it is incumbent on the individual Christian (singular 'you') to regard the one who refuses to hear the voice of God as excluded from the community of Christians *ipso jure*."[80] Thus for him the gift of binding and loosing can have nothing to do with legal decisions, only with the word of God.[81]

These references to the history of the text's interpretation and its continuing influence reveal that a church discipline based on Matt 18:15-18 can be practiced only in a church that is like Matthew's church. It is a discipline that is possible in small, manageable congregations whose members choose to belong. Where such a church becomes a large church into which its members are born and which may even include an entire nation, this practice of church discipline changes. In such a case Matt 18:15-18 has a new *Sitz im Leben* in the church's discipline, or one might say that it loses its *Sitz im Leben.*

71   In Leland Harder, ed., *The Sources of Swiss Anabaptism: The Grebel Letters and Related Documents* (Scottsdale, Pa.: Herald, 1985) 290.

72   William R. Estep Jr., ed., *Anabaptist Beginnings (1523–1533): A Sourcebook* (Bibliotheca Humanistica & Reformatorica 16; Nieuwkoop: de Graaf, 1976) 101.

73   In *Baltasar Hubmaier, Theologian of Anabaptism,* ed. and trans. H. Wayne Pipkin and John H. Yoder (Scottsdale, Pa.: Herald, 1989) 372–85, 409–25.

74   "Where water baptism is not given according to the order of Christ, there it is impossible to accept fraternal admonition from one another in a good spirit. For no one knows either who is in the church and who is outside" (*Baltasar Hubmaier,* 385). Hubmaier thus recognized the decisive truth that in the final analysis "church discipline" is an absurdity in a church to which its members do not belong of their own free will.

75   Christian Neff gives a survey of the history of the ban in Baptist churches in his article "Ban," in the *Mennonite Encyclopedia* (Hillsboro, Kans.: Mennonite Brethren Publishing House, 1955) 1.219–223.

76   For the Congregationalists cf. the explanation by Savoy, 19–22 = *Kirchen der Welt* 11.207 (church discipline is the business of the churches, not of the synods). For the Brethren cf. Donald F. Durnbaugh, ed., *The Church of the Brethren: Yesterday and Today* (Elgin, Ill.: Brethren Press, 1986) 52, 74, 94. On Spener's distinction between church discipline and the discipline of public morals cf. Paul Grünberg, *Philipp Jakob Spener,* vol. 2: *Spener als praktischer Theologe und kirchlicher Reformer* (Göttingen: Vandenhoeck & Ruprecht, 1905) 122–27.

77   Nevertheless: "Quamquam ad ean (sc. excommunicationem) ex hoc . . . loco non absurde argumentum duci posse non negaverim" (2.92).

78   Episcopius, 115.

79   Wolzogen, 330. According to him only the apostles had the complete power to bind and loose.

80   Rudolf Sohm, *Wesen und Ursprung des Katholizismus* (1912; reprinted Darmstadt: Wissenschaftliche Buchgesellschaft, 1967) 42.

81   Rudolf Sohm, *Kirchenrecht* (reprinted Munich: Duncker & Humblot, 1923) 1.37–38. Exegetically Holtzmann (265) is more accurate here when he sees in Matthew's understanding of church discipline and the power of the keys "the dawning age of the Catholic church."

Interpretation

■ **19** To the general principle of v. 18 the evangelist adds once again (πάλιν) a formally structured principle. If two persons agree[82] about anything[83] for which they are praying,[84] it will "happen" for them. The idea is not so much that common prayer is more important than individual prayer; it is that those who are praying agree in what they are praying for. Two is the minimum number of people who can agree or disagree about anything. The answer to prayer thus depends on the relationship among the various members of the church. Purely self-centered requests will not be granted.

Why does the evangelist add to vv. 15-18 this verse which gives the impression of introducing something new? The close grammatical connection to vv. 15-18 indicates that he sees a connection between the contents of the two texts, vv. 15-18 and vv. 19-20. Is the answering of community prayer for him the basis of the authority to bind and to loose even for heaven?[85] Or is he saying that there are limits to the absolute authority promised to the church in v. 18 in the sense that this authority is not the church's possession but something that it exercises only in prayer?[86] He does not say. Of course, for him and his readers everything he has said since v. 12 deals with prayer: looking for the errant brother, trying to "win" him, even breaking off relations with him. Indeed, all of the church's "binding" and "loosing" was probably accompanied by prayer. In this sense the reference to prayer probably for him does not so much limit the church's authority to bind and to loose as it describes and justifies it. Thus v. 19 indicates what the basis is for the power promised to the church in v. 18. It originates in God, is rooted in prayer, and remains dependent on God.[87] Verse 19 implies a retreat from "retaining" to "forgiving," a preference for "loosing" over "binding," and thus an anticipation of vv. 21-22 only in the sense that the church naturally will pray not for the destruction but for the salvation and the return of erring brothers and sisters. The reference to prayer makes clear once again that for Matthew binding and loosing is a matter for the church and not for individual office bearers.

■ **20** Verse 20 ends the section with a final argument that expands the concrete situation of v. 19. The presence of the risen Lord is promised not only for those who pray but for any two or three who come together for the sake of Jesus. Once again two or three are minimum numbers. In a rhetorically effective way the small number underscores how great is the promise that the risen Lord will be in their midst. Of all the statements in the text v. 20 covers the widest area. Far from being a superfluous addition, therefore, it is the christological center of the entire chapter.[88] Εἰς τὸ ἐμὸν ὄνομα corresponds to the biblical and Jewish expression לְשֵׁם, "for the sake of," "with reference to [the name]."[89] In addition, the readers will certainly think of the name of Jesus that they invoke and in which they pray. That association, along with the verb "to gather," will also make the readers think of the church's worship gatherings without

---

82   *Gos. Thom.* 48 says more pointedly: "If two make peace with each other . . ."

83   Πρᾶγμα is a general term and is by no means a *terminus technicus* for "legal matter." When the reference is to a legal matter (as, e.g., in the case of 1 Cor 6:1) the context must clearly indicate as much.

84   Αἰτέω means initially "to request" and only secondarily "to pray." After 6:8 and 7:7, however, the readers must assume that our context is referring to prayer; cf. 21:22. Derrett's interpretation is impossible, therefore, when he understands πρᾶγμα as a lawsuit, αἰτέω as the human request for the payment of a monetary debt, and συνάγω (v. 20) as an agreement between two opponents in a trial (J. Duncan M. Derrett, "'Where Two or Three Are Convened in My Name . . .': A Sad Misunderstand-

ing," 83–86). Our text is concerned not with the harmonious working out of agreements in trials and the heavenly blessing that is bestowed on such compromises but with sinners and the answering of prayers.

85   In that case we would expect a γάρ.

86   But then we would expect a δέ.

87   "C'est dans la prière que doit être tranché le désaccord avec le frère" (Marguerat, *Jugement,* 434).

88   Frankemölle, Jahwebund, 29; Rossé, *Ecclesiologia,* 98; Gnilka 2.135

89   *M. ʾAbot* 4:11 is an especially close parallel: "Any assembling together that is for the sake of Heaven (לְשֵׁם שָׁמַיִם) shall in the end be established, but any that is not for the sake of Heaven shall not in the end be established."

requiring that one think exclusively of formal worship.[90] The readers will also be reminded of the presence of Immanuel in their lives which is so important for Matthew's Christology (1:23), although the expression "in their midst" (ἐν μέσῳ) certainly does not help that recollection.[91] Of possible importance also are the widespread and relatively early Jewish statements about the presence of the Shekinah among human beings. The Shekinah is present not only when ten men constitute a minyan and study the Law,[92] but also when there are only two of them, or even only one[93]—indeed, wherever there are righteous persons.[94] The statement about the presence of the risen Lord Jesus in his church that is so basic for Matthew's Christology is rooted in Jewish thought, and we should not claim with some sort of theological finesse that these declarations about Christ are superior to the rabbinic statements about the presence of the Shekinah.[95]

Our verse belongs to the "high" christological statements of the New Testament. Without in any way identifying Jesus with God personally and ontologically, functionally the statement describes Jesus as acting precisely where according to biblical and Jewish belief God himself acts.[96] In 28:20, the final verse of the gospel, Matthew takes up once again the statement of v. 20. There one can finally see how important this verse is for his understanding of the church.

History of Interpretation

■ **19-20** The two verses became very important in the history of interpretation.[97] It is difficult to organize or to evaluate the streams of interpretation, and my selection in the following list is somewhat subjective.

1. The presence of Christ in his church was translated into the language of the ancient church's *Christology.* God incarnate is not only present where his visible body is.[98] He is neither only in heaven nor only on earth; he is omnipresent and active as God's Logos among his believers.[99] Since the believers gathered in prayer are at the same the time the body of Christ, he can even be understood to be present by being identical with them.[100] The transition from Matthew's Immanuel Christology to the trinitarian Christology of the ancient church is unusually easy. The ancient church's Christology proved to be an exceptional vessel for making understandable Matthew's basic christological affirmation about the identity of the earthly Jesus with the exalted Lord and about the exalted one's continuing presence on earth.

---

90 That is Lona's concern ("In meinem Namen"). See esp. 389–90, 401–2.

91 Perhaps the purpose of ἐν μέσῳ is to call attention back to the beginning of our main section (18:1-20), viz., to the child in the midst of the disciples (v. 2) that indirectly is reminiscent of Christ (cf. v. 5).

92 *M. ʾAbot* 3.6; *Mek. Exod.* on 20:24 (80b); cf. *b. Sanh.* 39a: Where ten are gathered, the Shekinah is present.

93 *M. ʾAbot* 3.2, 6.

94 *Midr. Ps.* 90 § 10 (196a). All sources cited in nn. 92–94 are in Str–B 1.794–95.

95 J. Weiss (352) is happy that "the heavenly Lord himself," "the living person Jesus" takes the place "of the incomprehensible 'glory' that exists separate from God" in Judaism. His joy over the "more personal, more inward, and more joyful" new religion is primarily a statement about him. Schweizer (374) contrasts the two or three with the ten adult men needed for a synagogue worship service (minyan!). According to *m. ʾAbot* 3.2, 6 (above, n. 93), however, the Shekinah does not depend on the minyan. David Flusser ("'I Am in the Midst of Them' (Mt 18:20)," 515–25, 518) argues in a similar fashion.

96 That is especially true of early Jewish Christianity that applied biblical statements about the κύριος to Jesus. On Matthew's "high" Christology cf. Ulrich Luz, "Der Antijudaismus im Matthäusevangelium als historisches und theologisches Problem. Eine Skizze," *EvTh* 53 (1993) theses 1.3.2, 4.3.1, and 4.3.3–4.

97 On the early history of interpretation prior to Cyprian cf. Lona, "In meinem Namen," 390–400. On the history of the interpretation of v. 20 cf. Marchand, "Matthieu 18,20."

98 Origen *Cels.* 2.9 = ANF 4.433.

99 Origen *Comm in Rom.* 8.2 = *PG* 14.1161–63; Cyril of Alexandria *In Joh.* 9 on 13:33 = *PG* 74.155–58. From here there are, of course, direct lines to the later Lutheran ubiquity doctrine—not, however, to the Reformed theologians.

100 Marchand, "Matthieu 18,20," 212–13.

2. That only *two or three* believers are required for Christ to be present among them was something of a problem for many who were accustomed to the larger, institutional dimensions of the church. For many commentators such groups were too small, since they would be in danger of becoming sects. Cyprian asks: "How . . . can someone agree with anyone when he himself does not agree . . . with the body of the church?"[101] Officeholders felt discriminated against. Ignatius of Antioch, who presumably was familiar with our passage, says: "If the prayer of one or two has such might, how much more has that of the bishop and of the whole Church!" (*Eph.* 5.2) Tertullian sounds a completely different note: Two or three are a church, even if they are only laypersons.[102] Occasionally in the ancient church one finds the special interpretation that two or three refers to Christian marriage.[103] Later interpreters often emphasize the significance of this promise for the entire church. If the prayer on which only two people agree is granted, how effective then must be the prayer on which many priests agree, or even regional synods and councils?[104] Of course, that is not at all what Matthew is thinking. For him the church lives in the fraternal, manageable local church. Its character is determined neither by hierarchies nor by the number of its members.[105]

3. *Where* is Christ present with the two or three who are gathered? Catholic ecclesiastical interpretation points first of all to formal worship.[106] Is the promise of v. 20 also valid elsewhere? Is it valid, for example, for the Christian life of a monastic order?[107]

Time and again throughout the history of interpretation there have been suggestions in this direction, such as when Basil in his rules ties the presence of the exalted Lord to obedience;[108] when the gathered three are interpreted as "faith, love, hope"; or when Nicholas of Lyra in his *Postilla* adds "united in love" to "gathered."[109] What is probably the best expression of this idea is the third verse of the medieval song *Ubi caritas est vera, Deus ibi est* which paraphrases Matt 18:20.[110] Matthew has broadened the scope of our passage in the concluding summary verse 28:20. Expanding the promise of the presence of Jesus to include all of the church's functions that are performed in his name is in keeping with Matthew's Christology, which places so much emphasis on mission, community, love, and suffering as characteristics of the church.

4. Our passage especially is designed to encourage the practice of public prayer among brothers and sisters.[111] However, many interpreters have been more interested in the *individual, personal prayer* of the Christians who are perfect. One first sees this emphasis clearly in the gnostic reception of Matt 18:20: "Where there are two or one, I am with him."[112] This concern is supported later by the allegorical interpretation that, beginning with Origen, interpreted the agreement of the two (or three) as the agreement of body, spirit, and, if needed, soul.[113] Such an interpretation misses the decisive concern of the text.

5. As was the case in the interpretation of 7:7-11, the *unconditional promise that prayer will be answered* has created difficulties with our text as well. It has

101 *Unit. eccl.* 12 = FC 36.107–8.

102 *Cast.* 7.3 = ANF 4.54.

103 See, e.g., Clement of Alexandria *Strom.* 3.10 (68.1) = FC 85.298. "Three" includes then the couple's child.

104 John Chrysostom *Adv. Jud.* 3.3 = *PG* 48.865; Cyril of Alexandria *Ep.* 55 = *PG* 77.291–94 (in both cases applied to the Council of Nicæa); Pope Colestin *Epist.* 18.1 = *PL* 50.505 (applied to the Council of Ephesus); Gregory the Great *Epist.* 9.106 = *PL* 77.1031 (= 1032).

105 Aretius, 164: "Disce: Ecclesiam veram non constitui ex turba multa seu pauca."

106 *Catechism* no. 1088; DS[36] no. 2297 = *Encyclical Mediator Dei* from 1947; *The Constitution on the Sacred Liturgy of the Second Vatican Council,* chap. 1.7.

107 Cf. Paul Christian, "Was heisst für Matthäus: 'In meinem Namen versammelt' (Mt 18,20)?" 97–105.

108 *Regula fusius* 5; *Regula brevius* 225 = Frank, 96, 315–16.

109 Dionysius bar Salibi, 301; Dionysius the Carthusian, 210 (in love and grace); Nicholas of Lyra without marginal numbers ("*caritate uniti*"). Cf. Jürgen Moltmann, *Church,* 123 (in apostolate, in the sacraments, and in the fellowship of the brethren).

110 The text is in Marchand, "Matthieu 18,20," 467–69. The song has become important once again in the liturgy of Taizé: *Songs & Prayers from Taizé* (Chicago: GIA Publications, 1991), no. 49.

111 Cf. Calvin 2.231–32. According to *Inst.* 4.1.9, Matt 18:20 is a *promise for the visible church.*

112 *Gos. Thom.* 30. The conjectural original form of the saying in *P. Oxy.* 1.23ff (NTApoc 1.109) speaks only of "one."

113 Origen 14.3 = GCS Origenes 10.278–80; cf. Jerome, 162–63; Peter of Laodicea, 206.

been argued that God answers prayers not unconditionally but only when those who pray ask for wholesome things, when they themselves are worthy, and when they do not pray out of a desire for revenge.[114] Naturally, we can regret the moralizing of an unconditional promise of God that is given with such interpretations, but we should also recognize that this distortion of the text comes from the real-life experience that God often does not grant requests, and not only when the prayers are selfish and are not supported by the community. We must take seriously this experience that almost never is stated explicitly in the history of the interpretation of the text.

This difficulty brings us then to the most difficult question related to the content of our text. For whom is the promise valid that Christ will be with two or three who gather in his name? As early as Cyprian the opinion was expressed that the promise could not apply to schismatics. Does Christ countenance private conventicles outside the church? With his promise Christ certainly does not want to "separate the people from the church" that he has created and established![115] Theophylactus observes: "Annas and Caiaphas also were in agreement!"[116] What about the situation when churches pray against each other in the name of Christ? Is it enough with the Protestants to appeal to the word of God that is the basis of every true Christian community? Maldonat argues, not without justification, that such an appeal is not enough, since God's word is ambiguous and must be interpreted; that is why we must have church councils.[117] Clearly it is easy for all who regard themselves as Christians to lay claim to the promise of Matt 18:20 for themselves, but it is difficult to agree (συμφωνέω!) on criteria that keep groups and confessions from making absolute claims on their own behalf based on this promise.[118] In my judgment, it is especially important to remember here that v. 20 intends to be

understood as a marvelous *divine* assurance, but we are not justified in using divine assurances and promises to strengthen our own claims to legitimacy.

Summary

■ **15-20** Our interpretation began with the tension between the church discipline of vv. 15-17 and the encouragement to practice unlimited forgiveness and to seek the lost (vv. 12-14, 21-22). None of the possible interpretations that we initially cited[119] appears to be entirely adequate. We saw that Matthew actually understood his rule of excommunication to be exactly that. He did not simply take it over as part of the tradition; he consciously made it an integral part of his text—a factor that speaks against the "grace-model." The rule is located in the center of his chapter on community. It is prepared by vv. 6-7, underscored by v. 18, and made more intense by vv. 19-20. For Matthew, therefore, it is probably more than a "borderline case" that contradicts the church's real "ethos" and that he accepts against his will. Against the "discipline model" that underlies the dominant church's excommunication is the fact that the text nowhere speaks of discipline or training. Avoiding those persons who are as tax collectors and sinners and seeking the lost stand side by side without any connection. The "covenant theology model" might have some legitimacy, since Matthew in his Immanuel Christology is indeed influenced by the biblical understanding of God's presence among his people—a concept that in the broadest sense can be described as "covenant." But remembering that grace and judgment exist side by side in a similar way in the Bible[120] does not yet solve the question of how the two are related to each other.

Thus the problem remains: How does one reconcile the instruction about the brotherly conversation that

---

114 John Chrysostom *Hom in Act*. 37.3 = *PG* 60.265–66 (he mentions prayers for the world, for the church, for peace, for the needy); Euthymius Zigabenus, 508 (one must be κατὰ τοὺς ἀποστόλους); Dionysius bar Salibi, 301; Wolzogen, 331 (one is not to pray for wealth, honor, or physical power).

115 *Unit. eccl.* 12 = FC 36.107–8.

116 Theophylactus, 344

117 Maldonat, 369.

118 In his reflection on our text Karl Barth (*CD* 4/2.699–706) mentions several such absolutes: conversation focused on a common creed, mutual

recognition as baptized and as brothers and sisters, being able to celebrate the Eucharist together, and common prayer.

119 Cf. above at the beginning of the section on Interpretation and on v. 18.

120 Not expelling members, since such activity is hardly compatible with the idea of a nation.

might well result in expelling someone from the church with the ethos of unending searching for sinners and of forgiving? Must we simply live with the contradiction and settle for an "inconsistency model"? I would moderate the contradiction somewhat and at the same time describe it with greater precision by saying that an expulsion from the church is necessary only when a sinner refuses to ask for forgiveness—an understanding that may be tacitly assumed in vv. 21-22.[121] We must also more sharply define the contradiction between Matt 18:15-18 and Matthew's basic idea of the church as *corpus permixtum* (13:37-43, 47-50; 22:11-14). In my judgment, that righteous and unrighteous persons exist together in the church does not mean that it should abandon the effort to realize the law of the love of Christ in its midst.[122] Thus the attempt to exclude the sinner (vv. 15-17) does not in itself contradict the thrust of the idea of the *corpus permixtum*. However, the claim of v. 18 that one can bind heaven with such an exclusion does contradict Matthew's conviction that only the Son of Man can judge (13:40-43, 49-50).[123]

Matthew does not eliminate these tensions. He can say neither that the church's binding is meaningless nor that it limits the love that Jesus commands. He can say neither that the church should dispense with binding and loosing nor that its activity restricts the sovereignty of the Son of Man and world-judge.[124] Nor did he subordinate the church's activity to a divine plan of discipline that would have permitted him to portray all binding and loosing as finally an expression of God's love.[125] This tension is understandable when one looks at the origins of the material. The rule of vv. 15-17 that originated in the early church and its supporting saying about binding and loosing in v. 18 reflect the situation of the beginning institutionalization of the Jesus community which had to distinguish itself from the majority

society which did not believe in Jesus. Verses 21-22 and also 12-14, on the other hand, go back to Jesus himself and are not originally concerned with the problem of institutionalization. Thus Matthew provides for the church neither a harmonious collection of rules for action nor a compact ideological pattern with which it could legitimate its actions. There is in vv. 15-20 no systematic integration of the various lines of thought. One might regret the situation and attribute it to the evangelist's incompetence, but I do not think that we do justice to the text simply by regretting what it contains. Matthew did something different: He connects the binding and loosing in vv. 19-20 with prayer and thus brings all human activity under the power, the promise, and the grace of God. These two verses are key verses for the entire chapter. With them Matthew suggests (but only suggests!) that the tensions in which the church lives are to be carried to God in prayer and are to be lived in the promise of the presence of Christ. He remains the church's Lord and foundation.

■ **18:1-20** Nevertheless, I would like to go beyond Matthew and say a few things about the relative value of the various instructions that make up the totality of Matt 18:1-20. Central for Matthew are the basic law of love (5:43-48; 7:12; 22:34-40) and the universal mission command (28:19-20). The leading motif of the chapter is "becoming small" (18:3-4) in the service of the community. From that perspective seeking the lost, "loosing," and forgiving (vv. 5, 10, 12-14, 15, 21-22) take precedence over pruning (vv. 8-9), "binding," and expelling (vv. 16-17). That the church should come to regard someone "as the Gentile and the tax collector" can be at most the consequence of the church's action; it can never be its goal. The church's judgment that the "snares" and the corrupters are subject to the "woes" of Jesus the world-judge can never be an act with final

---

121 Thus Calvin (2.234) clarifies on vv. 21-22: According to Luke 17:3-4 the command of unlimited forgiveness applies for the sinners who show remorse. According to Calvin, one cannot forgive others directly. One can, however, be free of hate toward them in the sense of loving one's enemy. That is in fact what Luke 17:3 says (ἐὰν μετανοήσῃ). In Matt 18:21-22 it is not explicitly stated; nevertheless Matthew will have understood vv. 21-22 as connected to v. 15 and not in opposition to vv. 16-17.

122 Cf. above on the ethical interpretation of Matt 13:36-43: III B 3.1 Summary and Ethical Interpretations.

123 The exclusiveness implied by "as the Gentile and tax collector" also is in tension with the inclusiveness of loving one's enemy (5:43-48).

124 Nevertheless, v. 18 approaches such a view and is for that reason a troublesome statement. At the very least, v. 18 is somewhat "inconsistent" within the totality of Matthew's theology.

validity; it can only be an expression of love for the little ones who have been led astray. In that sense these activities are indeed "borderline cases" for the church,[126] and its "binding" must occur in the hope that someday it will be "loosed" in heaven.

> In its model of the two stages the Syrian *Book of Stages* expresses the superiority of forgiving as follows: "Just as sucking milk is torture for an adult and bread causes an infant to choke, the smallest commands differ from perfection. In eternity, however, no one will be exalted because of the command, 'Turn your brother over to the church and regard him as a Gentile,' and no one will achieve perfection who is not able to 'forgive him seven times seventy,' and 'regard him higher than yourself.'"[127]
> Unlimited love is thus the more perfect way.

Matthew does not think in terms of two stages. He thinks rather of perfection as a *way* that the disciples of Jesus are to go.[128] On this way they all remain together in solidarity until the judgment of the Son of Man to which they all will be subjected. For Matthew, on the way of perfection the wandering charismatics will be bound in solidarity with resident disciples and those who have given up their possessions with those who have retained their property,[129] just as the righteous will be with those who err and who are led astray. I think that in this sense the seven times seventy forgiving is for Matthew closer to perfection than is the rule of church discipline in vv. 15-17. Paul thought in a similar way when in 1 Cor 6:1-11 he set the church's court of arbitration and the renunciation of legal claims side by side as two Christian possibilities that are by no means of equal value and when in 1 Cor 5:5 he suggests as a final possibility the salvation of the member who is excluded from the church.

Meaning for Today

Our reflections cannot end here. Our survey of the history of the interpretation of the text has demonstrated that in earlier centuries the institution of excommunication underwent numerous changes in the major churches, that it sometimes degenerated into an ecclesiastical or governmental instrument of power, and that it today has largely disappeared in Protestantism, while in Catholicism, at least in northern Europe, it retains little meaning for the masses of church members. That is by no means to say that our modern churches in Matthew's sense have come any closer to the better way of Matt 18:10-14 and 21-22—the way of forgiveness. The history of interpretation shows that brotherly admonition that includes the possibility of a church ban was able to be combined with the forgiveness of sins by means of integration into the community only in small, manageable communities that were not organized along authoritarian-hierarchical lines. Both realities *together* were regarded as essential for the life of a living Christian community. It is no accident that Luther also found a place for the rule of Matthew 18 in his vision of the congregation of those who "seriously want to be Christians and who confess the gospel with hand and mouth" that he outlined in his well-known foreword to the "German Mass."[130]

There are also similar voices from later periods.[131] Most notably, in the church struggle Dietrich Bonhoeffer

---

125 In view of the history of the interpretation we should probably be thankful to Matthew for this. Often enough church officials have justified excommunications and expulsions with such a concept of discipline and have thereby obscured and cemented their own claims to power.

126 Cf. above, the four basic types of interpretations (point 2).

127 *Liber Graduum* 11.5 = 281ff.; cf. 2.6 = 39–40; 4:1-2 = 83–90; 5:10 = 117–18; 11:3 = 277–78; 19:23, 25 = 491–92, 495ff.

128 Cf. Ulrich Luz, *The Theology of Matthew* (Cambridge: Cambridge University Press, 1995) 55–56. Admittedly, this also is an external attempt at systematizing Matthew's statements that has merely tried to get behind the formulation of the "way of righteousness" (Matt 21:32). Perhaps it best captures what Matthew intended but did not explicitly state.

129 Cf. above, C on the addressees of the disciples discourse (9:36—11:1).

130 *Deutsche Messe*, in Otto Clemen, ed., *Luthers Werke in Auswahl*, 4 vols. (Berlin: de Gruyter, 1950–59) 3.296–97.

131 Cf., e.g., Alexander Schweizer (*Pastoraltheologie oder die Lehre von der Seelsorge* [Leipzig: Hirzel, 1875] 118), who claimed that "the more the powerful state churches free themselves from their attachment to the state and become smaller, more free (i.e., more independent) communities, the more . . . church discipline [will] be restored, even to the establishment of excommunication, and the pastoral care appropriate to it will accompany it."

made a thorough study of the question of church discipline and reflected on its theological necessity: "Forgiveness can never be preached authoritatively without the concrete preaching of repentance and judgment." Such preaching requires the key of loosing and binding, although the latter is subordinate to the former. That which is holy must not be squandered. "What protects the gospel is the preaching of repentance that calls sin sin and declares the sinner guilty."[132] Only the church which identifies wrong can forgive it. "But such (church) discipline is not to establish a church of the perfect; but . . . (it) is a servant of the precious grace of God."[133] The demanding community to which Matthew introduces the readers in our chapter lives in just this kind of unexpected grace that lays claim on one's life. To such a living community belongs the truth that clearly defines boundaries (vv. 15-17), the love that occasionally violates the boundaries (vv. 10-14, 21-22), and, finally, prayer to the one who is lord and judge (vv. 19-20), who with his presence draws the church into the movement between truth and love. One must live with the tensions that result from such a situation. To eliminate these tensions in the institutional church would be fatal, both in a Protestant "church for all" in which in the name of (cheap!) grace the danger exists that nothing will matter anymore, as well as in a Catholic "true church" in which grace is always in danger of becoming the instrument of an ecclesiastically administered discipline.[134] In this tension the guiding principle must be the love that sometimes simply may not turn a blind eye to sin.

> When with Bonhoeffer and others I regard the clear naming of sin, untruth, and wrong as fundamental for the church, I do not mean to say that our modern national churches should reintroduce a church discipline. These days adults are leaving the churches on their own initiative without the churches having to exclude them. The question is: Why? If they are leaving because in their "self-centered unfaith"[135] they recognize the boundaries of the truth to which the church bears witness and that they are consciously abandoning, their action is legitimate. If, however, in the churches the truth is as relative and as vague as it is elsewhere, then people are leaving the church not because they can no longer affirm the truth it proclaims but because churches that have no identity are simply superfluous. In that case it is not only the church discipline that the churches have lost; it is also their churchness. When, however, the church represents in word and deed the truth by which it is constituted, in my judgment an excommunication is scarcely necessary, since in the modern world its adult members themselves perform the function that in earlier days "excommunication" as a disciplinary instrument was designed to do. Either they identify with the church, or they leave it.

---

132 "Schlüsselgewalt und Gemeindezucht," in idem, *Gesammelte Schriften*, vol. 2: *Kirchenkampf und Finkenwalde: Resolutionen, Aufsätze, Rundbriefe, 1933 bis 1943* (Munich: Kaiser, 1960) 369–81. Quotations, 370–71.

133 Bonhoeffer, *Cost,* 288.

134 My Catholic partner, P. Hoffmann, asks: In the history of our attempts to overcome the tension between Jesus' radical message of love and the church's institutionalization, have we not at the same time, time and again, tried to domesticate the radical message of Jesus? "The question is: Can Jesus' ethic even live in an institution? M. Weber's observation that 'bureaucracy and brotherliness are mutually exclusive' is true also in the question of forgiveness." Where it is "administered, it cannot exist. You might say that the church falls into the trap that it itself has set."

135 Gerhard Ebeling, *Kirchenzucht* (Stuttgart: Kohlhammer, 1947) 26.

2.1 Unlimited Forgiveness (18:21-22)

Literature

Israel Abrahams, "God's Forgiveness," in idem, *Studies* 1.139–49.

Idem, "Man's Forgiveness," in idem, *Studies* 1.150–67.

21 **Then Peter came and said to him: "Lord, how often will my brother sin against me, and I will forgive him? Up to seven times?" 22/ Jesus says to him: "I do not say to you seven times but seventy-seven times.[1]**

Analysis A narrative interlude introduces the brief *chreia* that follows. Peter, the pupil, approaches Jesus and poses a question that refers back to v. 15a (ἁμαρτήσῃ εἰς σέ). Jesus' answer is direct and to the point; it cannot stand alone, and it is not a gnome with universal validity.[2] The form is not that usually found in a *chreia* of Jesus, because Matthew completely reformulated the Q text that he found in Q 17:3-4. He made use of only a few terms from the Q text (ἁμαρτάνω εἰς [σέ], ὁ ἀδελφός [σου], ἑπτάκις, ἀφήσω), and he did so in a different place. From these words Matthew created his own *chreia* with his own Jesus logion[3] that is even more demanding than the Q text—a text that we can no longer reconstruct with precision.[4]

Interpretation

■ **21** Peter's question leads to the theme of the second part of the address—forgiveness. Are there limits to forgiveness? With "will sin against me" (ἁμαρτήσῃ εἰς ἐμέ) Matthew's purpose is not to limit the question primarily to interpersonal sins;[5] it is, rather, to revisit the formulation of v. 15 and to strengthen what was said there. The sevenfold forgiveness that Peter suggests is by no means trivial. Seven is the traditional number of perfection.[6] That Peter suggests forgiving seven times does not mean, therefore, that he wants to grant his brother only a limited forgiveness.[7] Instead, the sense of Peter's question is: "Is perfect forgiveness expected of me?"

■ **22** Jesus could simply have answered yes, but his answer calls for even more perfection. The most perfect, boundlessly infinite, countlessly repeated forgiveness is demanded of Peter.[8] The answer that Matthew attributes to Jesus cannot be surpassed. It is programmatic rather than pragmatic. It is possible that the evangelist is thinking of Gen 4:24; otherwise there is no explanation for

---

1   There are two possible translations: "77 times" and "7 × 70" (without "times" added). Linguistically, the first version is not completely correct, since in the case of composite numerical adverbs the ending -ακις always appears with the last number. Cf. Raphael Kühner and Bernhard Gerth, *Ausführliche Grammatik der griechischen Sprache* (2 vols.; 3d ed.; Munich: Hueber, 1963) 1.637. The second is even less correct, since there is no substantive (e.g., "sins") after the multiplied cardinal number 70 × 7 = 490, or in response to the questioning ἑπτάκις one would likewise expect a numerical adverb. The same lack of clarity is in the LXX text of Gen 4:24, the text on which v. 22 is likely based (Hebrew: 77; there are no numerical adverbs in Hebrew). Along with BAGD, *s.v.* ἑβδομήκοντα and Moulton–Howard–Turner 1.98; 2.175, I prefer the first translation, since I am not inclined to attribute to the LXX a mistranslation.

2   The sentence is even shortened, because it presupposes the question.

3   Matthean are τότε, προσέρχομαι, Peter as spokesman for the disciples, εἶπεν with dative, κύριε as a disciple's address, ἕως as preposition, λέγει in words of Jesus. Cf. vol. 1, Introduction, end of 3.1, 3.2 along with above, in III C 3.3 the beginning of the excursus on Peter. Strange is the Semitizing avoidance of the conditional clause in the question in v. 21. Actually the question should

be: How many times must I forgive, *if* my brother sins against me?

4   That there was a Q text, therefore, is based not on agreement in the wording but on the sequence: Luke 17:1-2 = Matt 18:6-7; Luke 17:3-4 = Matt 18:15, 21-22; cf. Luke 17:5-6 = Matt 17:19-20. It is possible that Luke preserves the sentence construction. In Q there were three parallel ἐάν clauses with an imperative as the main clause. Already in Q the third ἐάν clause was longer than the others, and it was expanded by Luke with καὶ ἑπτάκις ἐπιστρέψῃ πρὸς σὲ λέγων μετανοῶ.

5   Cf. Theophylactus, 344: The text deals only with interpersonal sins, for only the priest can forgive sins against God.

6   Cf. Karl Heinrich Rengstorf, "ἑπτά κτλ," *TDNT* 2 (1964) 627–28, 631 (esp. Lev 16:19; 2 Sam 12:6 LXX).

7   Cf. John Chrysostom, 61.1 = *PG* 58.587 (Peter intended to do something great); Olshausen (591) refers to "the imperfect moral culture of Peter."

8   Cf. Euthymius Zigabenus, 509: ἄμετρον, διηνεκές, ἀεί; Maldonat, 370: "magis infinitum"; "innumerabiliter innumerabilibus (vicibus)."

the unusual formulation of the number seventy-seven.[9] If there the issue was limiting the revenge that hangs over the bloody deeds of the descendants of Cain and Lamech, here it is the abolition of revenge altogether. In the church Jesus' rule of radical forgiveness is in effect.

History of Interpretation

Jesus' answer in v. 22 is formulated as a fundamental principle. As was the case with the prohibition against judging (7:1-2) or against swearing (5:33-37), it pays little attention to the practical questions that it raises. Human experience is that forgiveness that is unconditioned and endlessly repeated, that can be taken for granted, simply encourages evil people.[10] Thus in the ancient church and in Catholic interpretation one frequently finds a concern for the responsible use of the sacrament of penance that should not be dispensed indiscriminately.[11] At the very least remorse is required.[12] Otherwise in extreme cases forgiveness would be granted to persons who do not even ask for it.[13] Augustine and many others emphasize the necessity of ecclesiastical discipline "with words and, if necessary, also with whipping."[14] In his monastic communities Basil regards obedience to the abbot, who grants forgiveness, as the precondition for the willingness to forgive.[15] Pastoral concerns also play a major role in the traditional interpretation of the Reformation. Calvin asks: "Should we believe every expression of remorse?" His clear answer is: No, "penitence is a holy thing"[16] that one should not take lightly. Such concerns based on experiences that must be taken seriously appear to be far removed from the absolute principle of v. 22.

The Reformation's tradition makes still another factor clear: Secular authorities may not forgive sins; they must punish them.[17] Can our verse then even apply to magistrates and to fathers of families? Frequently the authority of Matt 18:22 is limited to the kingdom of Christ, or the limited *vocatio specialis* of a judge or a father is contrasted with the *vocatio generalis* that every Christian has.[18] As is the case with many of the commandments of the Sermon on the Mount, there is in the Reformation's interpretation the danger that forgiving seventy-seven times, since it is something that judges, politicians, and fathers cannot do, becomes simply an inner attitude. One can imagine no greater protest against this kind of interpretation than the attitude of Leo Tolstoy, who chose Matt 18:21-22 as the motto for his novel *Resurrection*. The novel's hero, Nekhlyudov, comes to the conclusion that precisely in the area of justice the only valid action is unlimited forgiveness. His experiences with the Russian legal system and Russian prisons (which arguably are not different from other legal systems and prisons) led him to the conclusion that they are ruled by injustice rather than justice. The only possible principle is that of Matt 18:22, "because there are none who are not themselves guilty, and therefore none who can punish or reform."[19]

Summary

As in his earlier discourses Matthew has introduced this fourth discourse as a discourse on the kingdom of God (18:1), and it is probably no accident that he formulates Jesus' rule about unlimited forgiveness as a basic principle without reservation and without regard for so-called reality. In that regard Tolstoy is closer to Matthew than are the reformers or those Catholics who permit Jesus' principle of forgiveness to be so obscured by the discipline of penance that it is almost unrecognizable. For

---

9   Even in the ancient church there was already disagreement whether the number was to be understood as seventy-seven (thus Tertullian *Or.* 7 = ANF 3.684; Origen 14.5 = GCS Origenes 10.282–83; Augustine *Cons. ev.* 2.12 = 94) or as 490 (thus *Didascalia* 11 [Achelis-Flemming, 66]; Jerome, 163; Hilary, 18.10 = SC 258.84 and the majority).

10   According to Calvin (2.234), always forgiving is damaging. Musculus (451) feared that too much forgiveness would encourage sin and that not enough would fail to do justice to brotherly love. For him Peter's suggestion finds the middle ground.

11   Maldonat, 370.

12   Anselm of Laon: We are not charged "passim peccata dimittere, sed poenitentiam agenti."

13   Tertullian (*Marc.* 4.35) is the first to state that, while one cannot forgive persons who do not seek forgiveness, one should not inwardly resent their sin.

14   *Sermo* 83.7 = *PL* 38.518; Jansen, 167; Lapide, 357.

15   *Regula brevius* 15.

16   2.235.

17   Luther 2.628–29.

18   Brenz, 609–10.

19   Leo Tolstoy, *Resurrection* (London: Oxford, 1899), part 3, section 28.

Matthew, unlimited forgiveness in the mutual relationships of sisters and brothers is the perfect way, the better way, that was intended by Jesus.[20] He also knows, however, that perfection is not a law, and certainly it is not a standard by which one can measure others; it is, rather, a goal toward which the church is traveling with its Lord. That in daily life one is to focus on this rule of perfection and apply it in the life of the church does not mean that one no longer distinguishes between good and evil since everything is forgiven anyway. Or, stated exegetically: One is neither simply to subordinate Jesus' rule of forgiveness to the church's discipline of penance, nor beyond the church's judgments about good and evil to create an ideal space in which everything is forgiven and therefore nothing matters. One is, rather, to demonstrate the forgiveness that Jesus requires precisely *in* the church that makes distinctions between good and evil. The addition of vv. 21-22 does not negate vv. 15-18; one must, rather, live with the tension between the two texts.

---

20   Cf. above, IV B 2.1: Summary 18:1-20.

2.2 The Unmerciful Debtor (18:23-35)

Literature

Martinus C. de Boer, "Ten Thousand Talents? Matthew's Interpretation and Redaction of the Parable of the Unforgiving Servant (Matt 18:23-35)," *CBQ* 50 (1988) 214–32.

Breukelman, "Erklärung," 261–87.

Broer, "Parabel," 145–64.

Thomas Deidun, "The Parable of the Unmerciful Servant," *BTB* 6 (1976) 203–24.

Derrett, *Law*, 32–47.

Christian Dietzfelbinger, "Das Gleichnis von der erlassenen Schuld," *EvTh* 32 (1972) 437–51.

Erlemann, *Bild Gottes*, 76–92.

Fiedler, *Sünder*, 195–204.

Harnisch, *Gleichniserzählungen*, 253–71.

Jülicher, *Gleichnisreden* 2.302–14.

Linnemann, *Parables*, 105–13, 173–79.

Reiser, *Jesus*, 273–81.

Scott, *Hear*, 267–80.

Spicq, *Dieu*, 55–63.

Sugranyes de Franch, *Études*.

Weber, "Alltagswelt," 161–82.

Idem, "Vergeltung oder Vergebung? Mt 18,23-35 auf dem Hintergrund des 'Erlassjahres,'" *ThZ* 30 (1994) 124–51.

Weder, *Gleichnisse*, 210–18.

Weiser, *Knechtsgleichnisse*, 75–104.

For *additional literature* on the church discourse see above, IV B.

23 Therefore the kingdom of heaven is like a king who wanted to settle accounts with his slaves. **24/** And when he began the reckoning, one was brought[1] to him, a debtor of ten thousand[2] talents. **25/** And when he was not able to pay, the lord commanded that he be sold along with his wife and his children and everything he had and that he be repaid. **26/** Therefore the slave fell to the ground and said, 'Have patience with me, and I will pay you everything.' **27/** And the lord of that slave had compassion and released him and forgave him the loan.

28 But as he was going out that slave found one of his fellow slaves, who owed him a hundred denarii, and he seized him and choked him and said, 'Pay everything that[3] you owe.' **29/** The fellow slave fell to the ground, therefore, and said, 'Have patience with me, and I will pay you.' **30/** But he did not want (that) but went away and threw him into prison until he should pay what he owed.

31 When, therefore, his fellow slaves saw what had happened, they were indignant, and they went and told their lord everything that had happened. **32/** Then his lord summoned him and said to him, 'You wicked slave! I forgave you that entire debt because you pleaded with me. **33/** Should you not have had mercy on your fellow slave even as I had on you?' **34/** And his lord was angry and delivered him to the torturers until he should pay everything he owed.

35 My heavenly father will do the same to you, if you do not forgive, each one his brother, from your heart."[4]

Analysis

Structure

The material is loosely connected with the previous section. As elsewhere, διὰ τοῦτο is a corroborative transition.[5] It is primarily the concluding v. 35 that relates our story to the context (cf. vv. 10, 14, 19, 21). The story is concise and artistic. The introduction in v. 23 consists of the statement of the subject and an exposition that reads like a title. The conclusion in v. 35 formulates the point of the parable. Between them appear three scenes[6] with changing locations[7] and main characters. The first scene takes place between the king and his slave (vv. 24-27), the second between the slave and his fellow slaves (vv. 28-30), the third once again between the king and his slave (vv. 31-34). Each of the three scenes begins with a narrative introduction (vv. 24-25, 28, 31). Then in the first and second scenes the debtor involved speaks first with gestures and words that are almost identical: πεσὼν οὖν . . . λέγων μακροθύμησον ἐπ᾽ ἐμοί, καὶ . . . ἀποδώσω σοι (vv. 26, 29). In the third scene, where the

---

1   In spite of its weaker witnesses (B, D) the hapax legomenon προσήχθη may well be more original than the typically Matthean προσηνέχθη.

2   The reading πολλῶν (ℵ, co) and "hundred" (c) probably are designed to correct the absurdly large amount.

3   BAGD, *s.v.* εἰ VII. The translation "if you are guilty/indebted" is possible, but it assumes that the first slave does not even know for certain whether there are outstanding debts.

4   Most witnesses, esp. *Byz.*, add τὰ παραπτώματα αὐτῶν and thus strengthen the similarity to 6:14-15.

5   Cf. above, III B 3.4 on 13:52.

6   Observed already by Calvin 2.235. Cf. Breukelman, "Erklärung," 262–63.

7   Verse 28: ἐξελθών, v. 31: ἐλθόντες.

8   Θέλω, συναίρω, δοῦλος (ἐκεῖνος), ὀφείλω, ἀποδίδωμι, κύριος, πεσών, μακροθύμησον ἐπ᾽ ἐμοί, ἀφίημι, σύνδουλος, τὰ γενόμενα, παρακαλέω.

9   *Clearly redactional,* according to vol. 1, Introduction 3.2, in v. 23 are: διὰ τοῦτο, ὁμοιόω, βασιλεία τῶν οὐρανῶν, ἄνθρωπος + attributive (in parables cf. 13:45, 52; 20:1; 22:2); v. 24: δέ, εἷς as an indefinite pronoun; v. 25: δέ, κελεύω, πάντα ὅσα (cf. 13:46);

debtor has lost any possibility of further action, the lord immediately pronounces the word that decides his fate (vv. 32-33). Each scene closes by describing what the creditor does with the debtor (vv. 27, 30, 34). In the first and third scenes the verses 27 and 34 are antithetical: καὶ σπλαγχνισθείς (ὀργισθείς) . . . ὁ κύριος . . . ἀπέλυσεν (παρέδωκεν) αὐτόν. The lord thus chooses in v. 34 the negative course of action from which, to the readers' surprise, he let himself be dissuaded in v. 27. Now his behavior parallels that of the slave toward his fellow slave in v. 30, although admittedly the wording is identical only at the conclusion (ἕως . . . ἀποδῷ . . . τὸ ὀφειλόμενον). Thus the story is well composed throughout. The frequent repetition of words strengthens the impression of conciseness.[8] Our story's style also creates a concise and artistic effect. It is composed in polished Koine. Almost all the sentences begin with a participial construction. The most important exception in v. 30a (ὁ δὲ οὐκ ἤθελεν) is conspicuous. At that point the narrative takes a final, tragic turn of events. Only upon second reading does the reader notice that the key word βασιλεύς in v. 23 never appears again. Other than that, however, there are no breaks or uneven elements in the story.

Sources

The text contains throughout a high percentage of Matthew's favorite terms.[9] For the most part the words that are not Matthean are given by the narrative material.[10] The preference for participial constructions, aorists, and direct address is also Matthean,[11] leading several interpreters to surmise that the entire story is Matthew's creation.[12] Against that view is the fact that the story speaks of a king only in the introduction and that after v. 25 the reference is exclusively to the "lord." Furthermore, several terms are not Matthean.[13] I am of the opinion, therefore, that Matthew put into written form a story that previously had been transmitted orally, as he also did with several other parables.[14]

Tradition History

It is amazing that a number of exegetes are tempted to decompose a story that is so concise and that so thoroughly reveals the hand of the evangelist. What are their reasons? There are basically two different types of decomposition.

a. The "major" decomposition. According to several exegetes the original story ended with v. 30.[15] In their view the intention of the story is to lead the readers to the conclusion that the behavior of the slave who has experienced such great love is incomprehensible. What follows in vv. 32-34 may "no longer

---

v. 26: πεσών with προσκυνέω (cf. 2:11), οὖν, λέγων; *v. 27*: δέ, ἐκεῖνος; *v. 28*: ἐξελθών, δέ, ἐκεῖνος, λέγων; *v. 29*: πεσών, οὖν, λέγων; *v. 30*: δέ, ἀπελθών, ἕως (conjunction); *v. 31*: ἰδών, οὖν, ἐλυπήθησαν σφόδρα (cf. 17:23; 26:22), ἐλθών, διασαφέω (only in Matthew; cf. 13:36); on the entire verse cf. 28:11; *v. 32*: τότε, λέγει (historical present), πονηρός, ἐκεῖνος; *v. 33*: ἐλεέω, κἀγώ; *v. 34*: ἕωι οὗ; *v. 35*: οὕτως, πατήρ μου ὁ οὐράνιος, ἀδελφός. *Possibly redactional* are, *v. 23*: θέλω, συναίρω λόγον μετά (cf. 25:19); *v. 24*: the unnecessary genitive absolute (cf. vol. 1, Introduction 3.1), ἄρχομαι (cf. 20:8), συναίρω, τάλαντον; *v. 25*: ἀποδίδωμι, the unnecessary genitive absolute, πιπράσκω (cf. 13:46; 26:9), κύριος; *v. 26*: πᾶς, μακροθυμέω ἐπί (appears only in Jewish Greek: twice in the LXX, *Apoc. Ezra, T. Job*, not in Philo and Josephus); *v. 27*: σπλαγχνισθείς (cf. 20:34), κύριος, ἀπολύω, ἀφίημι (leading word in 18:12-35); *v. 28*: εὑρίσκω, εἷς with genitive, σύνδουλος (cf. 24:49), κρατήσας (cf. 14:3; 22:6; 26:57 [partial redaction], πνίγω (cf. 13:7), ἀποδίδωμι; *v. 29*: σύνδουλος, μακροθυμέω ἐπί, ἀποδίδωμι; *v. 30*: θέλω, βάλλω, ἀποδίδωμι; *v. 31*: σύνδουλος, κύριος, (πάντα) τὰ γενόμενα (cf. 28:11); *v. 32*:

προσκαλεσάμενος [five times redactional]; *v. 33*: ἔδει (cf. 25:27), σύνδουλος, ὡς; *v. 34*: ὀργισθείς (cf. 22:7), κύριος, παραδίδωμι, ἀποδίδωμι, πᾶς; *v. 35*: ποιέω, ἐὰν μή, ἀφίημι, ἕκαστος (four times, of which about three are redactional).

10 Δοῦλος, ὀφειλέτης, μυρίοι, γυνή, τέκνον, ὀφείλω, ἑκατόν, δηνάριον, φυλακή.

11 Cf. vol. 1, Introduction 3.1.

12 Goulder, *Midrash*, 404; Breukelman, "Erklärung," 287; Gundry, 371–72.

13 *Verse 24*: Προσάγω is a hapax legomenon; *v. 25a*: ἔχω = to be capable; δάνειον = a hapax legomenon in the NT; *v. 29*: παρακαλέω; *v. 30*: ἀλλά; *v. 34*: βασανιστής = a hapax legomenon in the NT; *v. 35*: ἀπὸ τῶν καρδιῶν ὑμῶν (ἀπὸ καρδίας is a LXX expression, but it is always singular and always without the article, even when used with a plural possessive pronoun).

14 Cf. on 13:44-50 above, the Analysis of III B 3.2 and 3.3; on 20:1-16 below, IV C 4; vol. 3, V A 2.4 on 22:1-14; V B 2.6 on 25:1-13.

15 Fiedler (*Sünder*, 197–99) claims that for the master to rescind his earlier kindness goes beyond the limits of the parabolic image. Weder (*Gleichnisse*, 211)

be said, because it relativizes . . . God's mercy."[16] However, the thoroughgoing and uniform editorial reworking of the story speaks against isolating individual verses. In my judgment, the negligible variations in vv. 32-33 make sense on the synchronic level of Matthew's narrative.[17] Since above all, however, the hearers will want to know how the king in his sovereign authority is going to react to the unmerciful slave's "change of roles"[18] in vv. 28-30, at v. 30 the story is not yet complete.

b. The "minor" decomposition. Secondary or editorial according to other exegetes is v. 34, the description of how the lord turns his debtor over to the torturers.[19] According to this view the parable thus ends with the "stylistically appropriate"[20] rhetorical question of v. 33. Yet the character of v. 34 is not noticeably more Matthean than is the rest of the text. Furthermore, after the lord's clear word against the evil slave, "every hearer" will ask, "'What is going to happen to him?'"[21] The question becomes even more legitimate when one considers that the symmetry of the three scenes requires a final description of the creditor's reaction. Thus the story is not complete at v. 33. Several exegetes also regard not only v. 34 but also v. 31 as an editorial addition.[22] Yet there are no especially clear redactional reasons for eliminating the verse, and in the three-part structure of the entire parable it is indispensable. It is furthermore important for the communication with the hearers, since they will react to the first two scenes much as the fellow slaves do.

One cannot resist making an observation based on methodological principles about these attempts to reconstruct the history of the tradition lying behind the parable. In my judgment we have here a classic example of how theological premises influence tradition-historical reconstruction. There is a clear attempt to distance Jesus from the idea of judgment. Is this a case of using tradition history to judge the validity of an idea?

Back to the decomposition of our text: The thoroughgoing and uniform editorial formulation of the text permits us to designate something Matthean or secondary only when there are additional reasons for so doing. Such is the case in several places. Verse 35 is connected with the entire chapter, viz., with vv. 10, 14, 15, 19, 21 through the catchwords "heavenly father," "to forgive," "brother" ($\pi\alpha\tau\grave{\eta}\rho$ . . . $\acute{o}$ $o\mathring{v}\rho\acute{\alpha}\nu\iota o\varsigma$, $\mathring{\alpha}\phi\acute{\iota}\eta\mu\iota$ and $\mathring{\alpha}\delta\epsilon\lambda\phi\acute{o}\varsigma$). This verse may well be redaction in spite of "from your heart" ($\mathring{\alpha}\pi\grave{o}$ $\tau\hat{\omega}\nu$ $\kappa\alpha\rho\delta\iota\hat{\omega}\nu$ $\mathring{v}\mu\hat{\omega}\nu$). Verse 23a may also be redaction, since not only does it correspond verbatim to the Matthean introduction to a parable in 22:2a; with "Kingdom of heaven" it also refers back to vv. 1-4. I also think that both the one-time reference to the "king" in v. 23 and the truly royal sum of ten thousand talents in v. 24 may also come from Matthew's hand.[23] Admittedly, there are no inconsistencies in the narrative itself that would justify such a conclusion. "Lord" ($K\acute{v}\rho\iota o\varsigma$) is an appropriate designation for a king,[24] and the exorbitant, royal sum of ten thousand talents serves as an effective contrast to the one hundred denarii (v. 28). However, in 22:2 Matthew also changed the "a man" ($\mathring{\alpha}\nu\vartheta\rho\omega\pi\acute{o}\varsigma$ $\tau\iota\varsigma$) of Luke 14:15 to "a (human) king" ($\mathring{\alpha}\nu\vartheta\rho\omega\pi o\varsigma$ $\beta\alpha\sigma\iota\lambda\epsilon\acute{v}\varsigma$), and in 25:15-30 as well it is probably the evangelist who changed the traditional minas to talents. We can no longer say with sufficient clarity how many other narrative elements, for exam-

---

argues that what is reported in vv. 32-34 "is unbecoming in a lord whose word is trustworthy."

16   Weder, *Gleichnisse*, 215; Ernst Fuchs's judgment ("Das Zeitverständnis Jesu," in idem, *Zur Frage nach dem historischen Jesus* [Tübingen: Mohr/Siebeck, 1960] 361) is even sharper: vv. 32-34 "hardly do justice to the gracious nobility itself."

17   Weder, *Gleichnisse*, 211: Instead of $\sigma\pi\lambda\alpha\gamma\chi\nu\acute{\iota}\zeta o\mu\alpha\iota$, $\delta\acute{\alpha}\nu\epsilon\iota o\nu$, $\pi\rho o\sigma\kappa\upsilon\nu\acute{\epsilon}\omega$, vv. 32-33 have $\mathring{\epsilon}\lambda\epsilon\acute{\epsilon}\omega$, $\mathring{o}\phi\epsilon\iota\lambda\acute{\eta}$, $\pi\alpha\rho\alpha\kappa\alpha\lambda\acute{\epsilon}\omega$. Cf. below on vv. 32-33.

18   Harnisch, *Gleichniserzählungen*, 256.

19   Perrin, *Rediscovering*, 125; Harnisch, *Gleichniserzählungen*, 261–62 (v. 34 places the sovereign actor in conflict with his graciousness); Broer, "Parabel," 156–57 (the issue is the servant's behavior, not his fate); Merklein, *Gottesherrschaft*, 132 (with reservation); Gnilka 2.144–45.

20   Harnisch, *Gleichniserzählungen*, 261. In the parallel texts, however, the sovereign actor's action either

had already been told (Matt 20:13-15; Luke 15:31-32), or as in our text it is told after the rhetorical question (Matt 25:26, 28).

21   Weiser, *Knechtsgleichnisse*, 91.

22   E.g., Weiser, *Knechtsgleichnisse*, 85–86; Merklein, *Gottesherrschaft*, 237; Zumstein, *Condition*, 410.

23   Cf. Martinus C. de Boer ("Ten Thousand Talents? Matthew's Interpretation and Redaction of the Parable of the Unforgiving Servant [Matt 18:23-35]," 218–30). He suggests (228) that the original figure was ten thousand denarii instead of ten thousand talents. Then the story could be about a "tax collector" who as a local small businessman leased the right to assess taxes and had a subleasor (thus Weber, "Alltagswelt," 167–69).

24   Documented by Sugranyes de Franch, *Études*, 31–32.

ple, the debtor's proskynesis in v. 26, Matthew also added.

We do not know more about stages of the tradition prior to Matthew. The simplest assumption is that the narrator Matthew took over the parable's basic structure from the church's tradition with no changes. There is no reason to question the general assumption that the parable originated with Jesus.

Interpretation

■ **23** There is little in the parable's imagery that is difficult to understand. The kingdom of heaven is like a king.[25] The familiar metaphor "king" of necessity would make Jewish hearers and readers think of God.[26] "Settling accounts"[27] is also a commonly used metaphor that suggests the idea of judgment.[28] Δοῦλος can intentionally mean any kind of slave, since it was not unusual that slaves were entrusted with financial matters. In biblical-Jewish usage the term suggested religious connotations of persons who "serve" God. In order to escape the absolute antithesis between parables and allegories that has dominated parable research since Jülicher, it is important that we recognize these associations that would have been self-evident for Jesus' hearers and Matthew's readers.[29] In creating parables all Jewish

tellers of parables, including Jesus, expected their hearers to associate certain meanings with the words they used.

■ **24-27** The first debtor owes the king ten thousand talents. The hearers will have been struck by the size of the figure.[30] Many of them will have concluded that the story is about some sort of dignitary—perhaps a minister or a major tax collector[31]—so that the amount remains somewhat plausible.[32] Nothing more is revealed about the matter; further details on the subject are not necessary for understanding the story. Important is only that the hearers scarcely will have identified with a person from these social classes.

"Debtor" and "to owe" are terms that easily suggest religious connotations. For Jesus' Aramaic-speaking hearers the word חוֹבָא has both meanings—monetary debt and sin. The Greek-speaking readers of the Gospel of Matthew knew the Lord's Prayer (cf. 6:12). The debtor is unable to repay his debt, which of course does not mean that he was entirely without means.[33] The king commands that he and his family be sold in order to cover at least some of his loss from the proceeds.[34]

---

25 On the parable's introduction see above, n. 1 on 13:24.

26 Erlemann, *Bild,* 85–86. Cf. below, n. 74.

27 Συναίρω λόγον appears frequently in the papyri (Spicq, *Dieu,* 55, n. 1; BAGD, *s.v.,* συναίρω).

28 Cf. *m. ʾAbot* 3.1, 4.22, 29; Reiser, *Jesus,* 125–27, 301, n. 202; Erlemann, *Bild,* 157–58; Str-B 1.640 (metaphorically understood rendering account); 4.10 (heavenly ledger); Luke 16:1-8; 19:12-27; related is the metaphor of reward.

29 On the conventionalized metaphors cf. above, III B 3.4 in the excursus on the Matthean interpretation of parables, 3.1.1.

30 Thompson, *Advice,* 213. In Greek μύριοι is the highest possible number, while τάλαντον is the coin with the highest possible value. In this sense Clement of Alexandria (*Paed.* 2.10 [115.4] = FC 23.188) speaks of a single garment for ten thousand talents.

31 For sources for δοῦλος with this meaning see BAGD, *s.v.* δοῦλος, 2; Spicq, *Dieu,* 55, n. 2.

32 By comparison: 2 Macc 5:21 (Antiochus plunders 1,800 talents from the temple); Josephus *Ant.* 12.176 (the Tobiad Joseph offers 16,000 talents for the privilege of taxing Coele Syria and Phoenecia); 14.72 (Pompey finds 2,000 talents in the temple);

17.318-20 (the annual tax income of the tetrarchies of Philip, Herod Antipas, and Archelaus are 100, 200, and 600 [according to *Bell.* only 400] talents, respectively); Polybius, 21.26 (the richest man in Greece, Alexandros, possesses more than 200 talents); Plutarch *Anton.* 56 (Cleopatra brings 20,000 talents to Antony at Ephesus); Jerome *Dan.* 11.5 = *PL* 25.560 (Ptolemy Philadelphus's annual income is 14,800 talents); according to 3Q15 the Essenes had more than 6,000 talents hidden in Israel (Spicq, *Dieu,* 55–56, n. 4).

33 Obviously the king can still sell his possessions.

34 Jeremias (*Parables,* 211, n. 13) states that the price of a slave ranged from five hundred to two thousand denarii.

Which legal terms are assumed here is hotly debated. *Selling debtors into slavery* is permitted in both Hellenistic and Roman law, but over time the practice was limited.[35] According to Exod 22:2 (only?) thieves were to be sold into slavery.[36] In Jewish law the sale of a Jew to Gentiles is not permitted.[37] A man is forbidden to sell his wife[38] and, according to some texts, also his sons.[39] More common than the sale of debtors as slaves was the practice of *imprisoning debtors*,[40] the purpose of which was to compel the debtors' relatives and friends to ransom them, that is, to pay the debt.[41] In the East debtors were normally thrown into prison, but beginning in the third century there were efforts, especially in Egypt, to limit the practice that was becoming widespread.[42] The practice of imprisoning debtors does not occur in Jewish law,[43] which, of course, does not mean that it did not exist in Hellenized Palestine. Thus the readers will most likely have thought of this story's king as a gentile king—not because they wanted to distance themselves as Jews from the conditions portrayed in the parable but because in the world of their experience most of their earthly kings were Gentiles.[44]

The debtor prostrates himself before the king in the *proskynesis* that is customary in the East before both rulers and gods.[45] He asks for a reprieve, for patience.[46] The readers will have smiled at his glib assurance that he will repay *everything*. Given the large amount of money involved, either they dismissed his promise as simply a rhetorical embellishment,[47] or they looked forward to finding out what such a "great one"—for example, someone who had bought the right to collect taxes—would do to swindle his way into that much money. However, the story takes a surprising turn of events. The king has mercy on the slave, releases him, and forgives his large debt.[48] The slave himself would never have dared to ask for so much.[49] The amount of the gift is fantastic for both the readers of the gospel and for Jesus' hearers. Today we could express it only in the millions, or even

35   On the Hellenistic laws cf. Sugranyes de Franch, *Études*, 61–62, 119–24; W. L. Westermann, "Sklaverei," PWSup 6 (1914) 931; Hans G. Kippenberg, *Religion und Klassenbildung im antiken Judäa* (SUNT 14; Göttingen: Vandenhoeck & Ruprecht, 1978) 141–42; On the very severe ancient Roman law cf. Max Kaser, *Das römische Zivilprozeßrecht* (Handbuch der klassischen Altertumswissenschaft 10/3–4; Munich: Beck, 1966) 101–4 (there the first measure is private imprisonment for debt; if after a certain time the debtor is not redeemed, he is sold into slavery).

36   There are indications, however, that debtors were actually sold: 2 Kgs 4:1; Isa 50:1; Amos 2:6, 8:6; Neh 5:2, 5.

37   Josephus *Ant.* 16.3: Prior to the time of Herod a thief could not be sold to non-Jews.

38   *M. Soṭa* 3.8; *t. Soṭa* 2.9 (295) = Str-B 1.798. But what happened to women and children whose men were sold into slavery for the payment of debt?

39   Cf. Str-B 1.798.

40   Hans G. Kippenberg, *Religion und Klassenbildung im antiken Judäa*, 142–44; Sugranyes de Franch, *Études*, 60–62, 113–18.

41   Cf. above, n. 35; see also Josephus *Bell.* 2.273 (about Albinus): Left in the prisons are only people too poor to pay.

42   Sources cited in Sugranyes de Franch, *Études*, 115–18. The most impressive is an edict of Tiberius Alexander from 68 CE that permitted imprisonment only in the case of debts to the public treasury (Wilhelm Dittenberger, *Orientis graeci inscriptiones selec-*

tae [2 vols.; 1903–5; reprinted Hildesheim: Olms, 1970] 2 no. 669 = 394).

43   Reiser, *Jesus*, 275, n. 63.

44   Thus I do not think that the contrast between Jew and Gentile is important in this parable. (Of a different opinion is Scott, *Hear*, 271, 274–78.) We do not even know whether the two debtors were Jews or Gentiles.

45   With προσεκύνει Matthew wants to direct the readers' attention to God.

46   In the LXX μακροθυμέω becomes a description of God who withholds his wrath (among other places Exod 34:6; Ps 7:12 LXX; 85:15 LXX). It is conceivable that this expression also evoked theological associations from Matthew's readers.

47   Klostermann (153) calls it an "emergency promise."

48   Δάνειον is simply a different way of saying ὀφειλή that is appropriate here because v. 27 is formulated from the king's perspective. Hesychius (*s.v.* = 1.460) notes δάνειον and ὀφείλημα as synonyms. Pollux (*Onom.* 3.84) places ὀφείλειν and δανείζεσθαι side by side. The explanation that they simply are different ways of saying the same thing is much simpler than the complicated suggestions of Derrett and Weber. Derrett (*Law*, 39–40) claims that the king first translated the errant minister's debt into a loan, which he then forgave. That suggestion, however, reads more into the text than it says. Weber ("Vergeltung oder Vergebung? Mt 18,23-35 auf dem Hintergrund des 'Erlassjahres,'" 124–51) sees in δάνειον an allusion to Deuteronomy 15, the OT text on the year of release where the word appears

billions. The verb "to forgive" ($\mathring{\alpha}\varphi\acute{\iota}\eta\mu\iota$) also is capable of more than one meaning and suggests a religious dimension.[50]

■ **28-30** A second scene follows in which the "great one" whose debt has been forgiven goes out and comes across a "fellow slave,"[51] who owes him a comparatively small amount of money. It is about one six hundred thousandth of the figure that has just been forgiven him[52]— an amount that even a poor farmer could scrape together in the course of a year. The "great one" seizes him and chokes him, something that was socially unacceptable even if not all that unusual.[53] That the "great one" seizes and chokes the "little one" with his own hands suggests to the readers that he has lost control of himself, and it does not bode well for the rest of the story. The "little one" now does exactly what the "great one" did earlier with the king.[54] He asks his creditor for time to repay the debt—a request that, in view of the small amount involved, is not unrealistic. But the "great one" will hear nothing of it. He has his fellow slave thrown into prison, or he takes him there himself. He does not sell him to get his money, not because he is compassionate but because the amount owed is less than

the price of a slave, and according to Jewish law he thus is not allowed to sell him.[55] The "great one's" behavior is thus brutal but by no means unusual. If the readers are particularly scandalized by his behavior, it is because they have heard in vv. 24-27 of the unprecedented forgiveness of his debt. Because of what happened earlier, the normal brutality of life is seen as something that is truly shocking. The earlier events of vv. 24-27 thus change the readers' eyes. It is now clear why the amount owed by the "great one" had to be so exorbitant. It was not to portray the protagonist as a minister, a tax official, or a major entrepreneur; it was to demonstrate how scandalous was the refusal to forgive such a small debt after such a great one had been forgiven.[56]

■ **31-34** The other slaves, having seen it all, resent what has happened, and their feelings are doubtless those the hearers are intended to have.[57] They go to their lord and tell him in no uncertain terms[58] what has happened, thus setting the stage for the third scene. The lord does not even demand an explanation from his slave; he addresses him immediately as "evil slave." The readers thus realize that judgment has already been passed on him. The way the lord reminds the slave that he has for-

---

frequently. The other conceptual connections between Matt 18:23-35 and the OT laws on the year of release are so general that in my judgment the thesis is not convincing.

49   There were, of course, numerous examples of the forgiveness of taxes, debts, etc. However, the sources gathered by Weber ("Alltagswelt," 177–78) show that it usually happened on special occasions, such as a coronation, or for special persons, as in the case of a reward for special loyalty, rather than, as in our story, simply because of the debtor's need, and of course the amount forgiven was not this large.

50   The verb is used in Greek sources as well as in biblical sources for the remission of sins (BAGD, s.v., 2).

51   The term is consciously chosen in order to indicate that they belonged to the same class and thus should share a sense of solidarity.

52   An Attic talent corresponded to six thousand drachmas = denarii.

53   Cf. Pollux *Onom.* 3.116 ($\mathring{\alpha}\gamma\chi\omega\nu$ $\tau o\grave{\upsilon}\varsigma$ $\chi\rho\acute{\eta}\sigma\tau\alpha\varsigma$, $\mathring{\alpha}\pi o\pi\nu\acute{\iota}\gamma\omega\nu$ $\tau o\grave{\upsilon}\varsigma$ $\mathring{o}\varphi\varepsilon\acute{\iota}\lambda o\nu\tau\alpha\varsigma$); Lucian *Dial. mort.* 2 (22).1; Plautus *Poenulus* 789–90; Aristophanes *Eq.* 775 ($\sigma\tau\rho\acute{\varepsilon}\beta\lambda\omega\nu$, $\mathring{\alpha}\gamma\chi\omega\nu$, $\mu\varepsilon\tau\alpha\iota\tau\tilde{\omega}\nu$); *m. B. Batra* 10.8 (someone is censured for choking a debtor in the street). Almost all sources reveal a negative attitude

toward such behavior.

54   Only the proskynesis is missing; this time the "creditor" is a human being.

55   In Judaism the sale of a debtor into slavery was possible only when the debt was at least equivalent to the price of the slave (*Mek. Exod.* 22:2 [95b]; *b. Qidd.* 18a = Str–B 1.797; further sources in Str–B 4.700–701).

56   In the history of interpretation (since John Chrysostom, 61.1 = *PG* 58.589) usually the exceeding greatness of human guilt toward God (= ten thousand talents) is contrasted with human guilt toward other human beings (= one hundred denarii). This interpretation misses Matthew's point, since for him it is the "great one's" unforgiven debt toward his *fellow slave* that is decisive for his relationship to God.

57   Both in the LXX (as a translation of חרה = to be angry) and in Greek sources (cited by Spicq, *Dieu*, 59, n. 2) $\lambda\upsilon\pi\acute{\varepsilon}o\mu\alpha\iota$ can be stronger than "to mourn" and can express the combination of "tristesse . . . indignation . . . et dégoût" (ibid.).

58   $\Delta\iota\alpha\sigma\alpha\varphi\acute{\varepsilon}\omega$, a word that appears in late LXX texts, means: to say point-blank, to make clear.

given his "entire debt," ten thousand talents, is rhetorically effective. Now he will demand that the debt be paid in full—"that entire debt" ($\pi\hat{\alpha}\nu\ \tau\grave{o}\ \overset{\circ}{o}\varphi\epsilon\iota\lambda\acute{o}\mu\epsilon\nu o\nu$).[59] It will not have especially bothered the readers that in so doing the king rescinded the word that he had earlier given the "great one." Thanks to the narrative's strategy, readers are on the side of the "little one," and it meets with their approval when the king bases his own behavior on "the behavior of the servant toward his fellow servant"[60] and judges the "great one" as he himself has judged (cf. 7:1b).[61] They also will not be especially bothered that the king has the "great one" tortured—a practice that had been customary in Israel since Herod.[62] Torturing debtors who had been sold into slavery was one way of compelling relatives and friends to purchase the tortured person's freedom. It is conceivable that some of Matthew's readers were reminded of the torments of hell described in apocalyptic texts—a train of thought that may well not have been unintended by the narrator.[63] In any case it is clear as the narrative progresses that, although the parable does not say so explicitly, it is doubtful that the "great one" with the large debt that he must now pay in full will ever be released from prison.

■ **32-33** However, the most important verses of the final scene are vv. 32-33, since here the narrator speaks indirectly to the readers through the mouth of the king. Here he reveals the thinking that underlies the entire parable. The slave should have imitated the king in granting mercy. Theologically the *imitatio Dei* stands in the background here (cf. 5:48; Luke 6:36). The narrator

intentionally replaces the "secular" word $\sigma\pi\lambda\alpha\gamma\chi\nu\acute{\iota}\zeta o\mu\alpha\iota$ with the Bible word $\overset{\circ}{\epsilon}\lambda\epsilon\acute{\epsilon}\omega$ that can call up associations in the readers' minds with biblical statements about God's mercy. Observant readers of the gospel will also be reminded of the fifth beatitude in Matt 5:7.

What is the parable's point? We must first of all attempt to understand it apart from Matthew's application in v. 35. The issue is the behavior of the "great one" toward the "little one" and the lord's judgment on the former. His behavior will be "incomprehensible" for the parable's hearers and readers.[64] Why? The kind of behavior that was ordinarily taken for granted becomes intolerable in the light of God's overpowering forgiveness. In that sense the parable's first scene, which describes this forgiveness, is indispensable for formulating the point of the parable. It is God's overpowering forgiveness alone that makes the "great one's" behavior evil. Such an observation will make sense to the hearers, since God's forgiveness is not simply an external matter; it is a power that overwhelms and transforms the whole person.[65] Precisely for that reason the king's harsh reaction, far from confusing the hearers,[66] will elicit their support and understanding. The final judgment, with which the parable ends and which evokes certain associations from the hearers, thus functions not as a meaningless threat. It is comprehensible precisely because the "great one's" behavior remains incomprehensible. When the hearers apply this judgment to their own lives, it clearly has ethical consequences. If in their confrontation with Jesus they have experienced God's overpowering and unexpected forgiveness so that the "great one's"

59 $\Pi\hat{\alpha}\sigma\alpha\ \overset{\text{'}}{\eta}\ \overset{\circ}{o}\varphi\epsilon\iota\lambda\acute{\eta}$ and $\pi\hat{\alpha}\nu\ \tau\grave{o}\ \overset{\circ}{o}\varphi\epsilon\iota\lambda\acute{o}\mu\epsilon\nu o\nu$ correspond to each other. The lord thus completely rescinds his forgiveness of the debt. Ὀφειλή is an uncommon word in the Bible, but it appears frequently in the papyri (Moulton-Milligan, *s.v.*)
60 Weder, *Gleichnisse*, 211, n. 8.
61 I thus do not think, as Scott does, that the readers are disturbed because their dependable order falls apart when the king appears to violate his word (*Hear*, 277–78): "If a king can take back his forgiveness, who is safe?" The "order" is destroyed only for the "great one," and the readers are disturbed only if in some way they have identified with him. Yet that is precisely what the parable's narrative strategy prevents.
62 Josephus *Bell.* 1.548; On torture in connection with

personal executions in general cf. Sugranyes de Franch, *Études*, 62–63; Spicq, *Dieu*, 60, n. 2; Reiser, *Jesus*, 275, n. 64.
63 Βασαν- referring to the torments of hell: Rev 14:10-11, 20:10; Luke 16:23, 28; cf. Matt 8:29. Jewish sources: 2 Macc 7:17; Wis 3:1; *4 Macc.* 9.9, 12:12; *1 Enoch* 10:13; 22:11; 25:6 [Greek]; *T. Abr.* 12.18 (with βασανισταί!); cf. 4 Ezra 7:67, 9:12-13.
64 Weder, *Gleichnisse*, 214.
65 Dan O. Via (*Self-Deception and Wholeness in Paul and Matthew* [Minneapolis: Fortress, 1990] 131) states it well: The king's forgiveness is "a power for a new kind of life," an "enablement." For that reason grace may "not be fruitless" (Gnilka 2.147) in the lives of the hearers.
66 Scott, *Hear*, 278; cf. above, n. 61.

behavior makes no sense to them while God's judgment makes sense, then they should and will act differently than did the "great one."

This description of the point implies various *demarcations*. Our story is not simply a *parable "about the forgiveness of guilt."*[67] Its focus is on the second and third scenes. And we certainly are not to individualize the grace that is the parable's indispensable presupposition and to understand it generally as the gift "of time that is radically liberated from the weight of the future."[68] The issue is rather very concretely the "ordinance of mercy."[69] It is forgiveness and a new relationship with one's fellow human beings. We also *do not have here a "parable about the Last Judgment"* in the sense that it is intended simply as an *"admonition with a warning"* in light of an impending judgment.[70] The first scene is not totally irrelevant![71] The parable's view is certainly ethical, but its ethic is not unconditioned.[72] Indeed, the "final" judgment, that is, the "settling of accounts," has long since begun. The hearers who have experienced something of God's unexpected forgiveness in their encounter with Jesus are in the midst of a process of settling accounts, the conclusion of which will be the final judgment. Finally, we do *not* have in our parable the neoorthodox concern for *the novelty of the new covenant.*[73] It is true that behind our parable lies the concrete and demanding experience of grace in one's encounter with Jesus, but this experience is not portrayed as antithetical to the Jewish experiences of forgiveness.[74] It is Matthew, not Jesus, who understood this parable as a parable of the kingdom of God, and for Matthew the will of God which is proclaimed in the world in light of the kingdom of God is definitely not contrary to the Law and the Prophets.

■ **35** In the final verse the evangelist presents his own view, which builds on v. 34 and takes up the language and substance of 6:14-15. Now it becomes explicitly clear that the parable speaks of God and the forgiveness of sins. Matthew thus interprets the parable's conventional metaphors allegorically without treating the entire parable as an allegory.[75] He speaks to the "brothers," that is, the church. Judgment is pronounced on the church when it does not practice forgiveness among its members. The direct address grabs the readers' attention. Suddenly they see that in their own lives they may well play the role of the unmerciful "great one" from whom they were feeling so estranged while they were listening to the parable. Thus once again a Matthean discourse ends with a threat of judgment (cf. 7:26-27; 13:49-50; 24:37—25:46). Again, corresponding to the ecclesiastical

---

67 The title of Dietzfelbinger's article cited above in the literature on this section.

68 Harnisch, *Gleichniserzählungen,* 269. Cf. Christian Dietzfelbinger, "Das Gleichnis von der erlassenen Schuld," 437–51, 451 ("a gift of time"). Harnisch and Dietzfelbinger arrive at this interpretation which neglects the parable's concrete character because they ignore the parable's "stock metaphors" out of a (false!) fear of allegorical insertions.

69 Linnemann, *Parables,* 112–13.

70 Cf. Jeremias, *Parables,* 213.

71 The scene's content is important for the parable, and it is not simply a rhetorical device to provoke "the indignation of the fellow slaves" or of the readers (Jülicher, *Gleichnisreden* 2.312).

72 Those persons are thus right who emphasize that the point of the parable can emerge only from the connection of all three scenes. Cf., e.g., Merklein, *Gottesherrschaft,* 239.

73 Thomas Deidun ("The Parable of the Unmerciful Servant," 215) speaks of "the concrete urgency and essential novelty of the new dispensation."

74 A glance at the Jewish parallels reveals the similarity: *b. Ros Has.* 17b = Str–B 1.425–26 (a parable in which the king forgives his debtor his debt and his insult and challenges him to do the same with his neighbor); *Ex. r.* 31 (91b) = Str–B 1.800–801 (a parable in which the moneylender has long since forgiven the debt); *Tanch. emur* 178a = Str–B 1.798–99 (a parable in which a city is unable to pay its exorbitant tax, and the king remits the debt); *Pesiq. R. Kah.* 14:7 = Thoma-Lauer, *Gleichnisse,* 222 (a parable about a goldsmith whose debt is paid); *S. Zuta* on Num 27:17 (cited by Fiedler, *Sünder,* 203): God led Israel out of Egypt on the condition that it would not demand payment on its sins but would forgive them; cf. *S. Deut.* § 210 on 21:8). Parallels also exist in the parenetic tradition. Cf., e.g., *T. Zeb.* 7.2 (from what God gives you show compassion and pass it on); similarly *Ps. Phocylides* 29. Broer ("Parabel," 162–63) offers other sources.

75 Even if Matthew may have added such metaphors (e.g., "king"), he remains basically within the framework of Jesus' parable. Nor has the church's interpretation in the case of this parable distanced itself fundamentally from its original character. For the most part only individual features, and hardly ever all of them, were allegorized. Maldonat (371) explains it in a theory of parables. There are *necessariae . . . parabolae partes* that can be interpreted allegorically, and *emblemata . . . ornatum . . . et exple-*

model of the *corpus permixtum* (13:37-43, 49-50; 22:11-14), it is also the church—indeed, it is precisely the church—that stands under judgment. Although in the parable God's forgiveness precedes human forgiveness, for Matthew in the final judgment divine forgiveness presupposes human forgiveness. A similar point was made in the Lord's Prayer (6:12 [ἀφήκαμεν Aorist!], 14-15) and in 5:23-24.[76] The final statement that literally says "from your hearts" indicates that the forgiveness of sins involves not merely that one is outwardly reconciled with one's brothers and sisters but also that one affirms them completely.[77] In spite of the peculiar plural, it may also be reminiscent of Israel's basic commandment, the Shema Israel (Deut 6:5; cf. Matt 22:37).[78] Brotherly forgiveness is no incidental matter, and unkindness among persons is a sin of no little importance. Both of them lie at the heart of one's relationship to God.

Does this view not change the parable's original "line of argument into its opposite" by reducing it to a simple warning?[79] Even those who regard v. 34 as secondary need to take the question seriously. I prefer to speak not of a change but of a different emphasis in the story. In my judgment the ethical character of the parable is not new with Matthew; from the beginning it was a part of this story which is about making grace real in everyday life. What is new in Matthew that was not there for Jesus is the way the context limits the rule of forgiveness to Christian sisters and brothers. Above all, however, it is Matthew's interpretation alone that emphasizes v. 34. It is an emphasis that intensifies the parable's parenetic dimension. For Matthew the Father's future, perhaps threatening activity appears to be more important than his saving activity of the past. Does the idea of judgment become an independent reality here? Does the idea of judgment negate grace's reliability? Is what Matthew says

here really different from or more than Sir 28:2: "Forgive your neighbor's wrong, then your sins will be forgiven when you pray" or more than Jas 2:13: "Judgment will be without mercy to the one who does not do mercy"? Does Matthew's emphasis offer more than a common parenesis: If you don't forgive, you won't be forgiven? The fundamental question is whether one can still experience the judging "Father" of Matt 18:35 as the same Father who through Christ forgives human guilt in unending love.

History of Research

It is a question that dominates the history of interpretation that on the whole treats our parable as something of a stepchild.

> The reason commentaries on our parable are so meager is that on the surface its meaning appears to be clear and not to need any explanation,[80] while at the same time it provides little basis for an allegorical-savation-history interpretation. It was not until the Middle Ages that it was interpreted allegorically. The first servant was then described as the Jewish people, the second as the Gentiles. The torturers could have been the angels of judgment or even the destroyers of Jerusalem, Vespasian and Titus.[81] Yet this type of interpretation appears to have disappeared even before the end of the late Middle Ages.

For several of the church's interpreters the fundamental question has been: Can God, who has forgiven all human sins, rescind this act of grace? The few interpreters in the early church who concerned themselves with the question saw no problem here. The early Antiochian, Apollinaris of Laodicea, refers to Rom 11:29 ("irrevocable are God's gifts of grace") and says simply: "(human) wickedness is capable even of nullifying this word."[82] Similarly, we can read in Augustine that "sins that have been forgiven return when there is no broth-

---

tionem adjecta that cannot be allegorized. He regards vv. 25 and 31, e.g., as emblematic.

76 Cf. vol. 1, II A 2.3.3 on 6:12.

77 That is well stated in the Catholic *Catechism*, no. 2843: "Everything depends on the whole 'heart.' We are not able to forget a guilt completely. Yet the heart that is open to the Holy Spirit permits the injury to become compassion and purifies the memory by letting the debt become an intercessory prayer."

78 Berger, *Gesetzesauslegung* 1.77.

79 Weder, *Gleichnisse*, 217–18. This thesis is often pro-

posed with less radical claims. Cf., e.g., Linnemann, *Parables*, 107; Zumstein, *Condition*, 408.

80 *Juxta letteram non est aliqua difficultas* (Dionysius the Carthusian, 210).

81 Cf. with varying degrees of detail Bede, 84; Strabo, 117; Rabanus, 1013–15; Anselm of Laon, 1410–11; Dionysius the Carthusian, 210–12 (christological, ecclesiological, anthropological, but no salvation-history allegory).

82 No. 92 = Reuss, 29.

erly love."[83] It was in the Middle Ages that people first wrestled with the problem at a deeper level. Albertus Magnus notes that the reappearance of sins that have been forgiven "appears to contradict the righteousness of God that does not punish excessively (*ultra condignum*)." He then discusses the opinion of the "ancients" according to which certain mortal sins negate prior forgiveness, and he formulates in opposition to this view his own thesis that what leads to divine judgment is not the ongoing consequence of earlier sins but the present *deformitas ingratitudinis*—that is, not remaining in grace.[84] Thomas Aquinas brings together both opinions: "Thus because of ingratitude (*ratione ingratitudinis*) the sins previously forgiven return through subsequent mortal sins."[85] Later orthodox Catholic and Protestant dogmatic theology has followed him in this view.[86] In this way God's righteousness is at least formally satisfied.

Such considerations appear to be foreign to the interpretations of the reformers who assume that it is possible to lose God's grace. Calvin rejects the scholastic solution and says that people who punish harshly as did the first slave are unworthy of God's mercy.[87] In the midst of a forceful sermon, the thrust of which is that the forgiveness of sins that comes through Christ applies to one's entire life even after baptism, Luther is able to say immediately: "Thus we should remain in the Lord Christ when we have sinned and not turn away from him; otherwise, we will lose the forgiveness of our sin."[88] The reformers appear not to think much of the scholastic theological solution of the problem. Their interpretations connect clear assertions that God's forgiveness precedes all human behavior and is its immovable foundation[89] with the recognition that God is independent of his own grace and can even retract it. Both realities must stand side by side. God's freedom is not something that one can theologically manipulate.

Summary

For Matthew also it is clear that God's forgiveness can be lost through human unkindness so that one's earlier guilt returns. "If that were not possible, this discourse of Christ would have no persuasive power."[90] What meaning then does grace have for him? Is it still the determining factor so that his message of judgment is a reminder that the *gift* of grace negates neither God's freedom nor human freedom? Or is it in the final analysis no longer the determining factor? In that case the Matthean parable would be a serious threat, since it is possible for God to retract his grace. Is judgment for Matthew a concept that aids in the exercise of grace?[91] Or is judgment the determining idea, since human beings can never completely depend on grace? With its strong editorial emphasis on imminent judgment our parable does not permit an unambiguous assertion. While our story makes judgment understandable and clear, judgment still remains a threat that also hangs over the heads of the disciples who are addressed in the community discourse. We will have to reserve an answer to the question for a comprehensive portrayal of Matthew's understanding of judgment.[92]

---

83   *Bapt. Don.* 1.12.20 = *PL* 43.120.
84   Albertus Magnus, 683–84.
85   *S. th.* 3, q.88, a.2 corpus.
86   Cf., e.g., Maldonat, 372; Lapide, 358–59; Jansen, 169; Häring, *Law* 1.467; on the Protestant side with minor variations, e.g., Calovius, 251; Wolzogen, 333.
87   2.114.
88   Martin Luther, "Matth 18-24 in Predigten ausgelegt, 1537–1540," *WA* 47.310. Cf. his statement in a sermon from 1524 (2.627): "If you want to be lazy, you will fall out of this [i.e., Christ's] kingdom"; ibid.: "if anyone misuses the grace he has received . . . the result is eternal damnation."
89   Forgiveness is "the fruit that follows our faith, and not a work with which we can earn the forgiveness of sins" (2.640; a sermon from 1528).
90   Episcopius, 116.
91   In his excellent "new version" of this parable, the world-famous short story "A Spark Neglected Burns the House," Leo Tolstoy tells of two farmers whose initially meaningless quarrel escalates until half of the village burns down. This judgment is, however, a penultimate judgment. Because of the conflagration the farmer, Ivan, says to his father: "Forgive me, father; I am guilty before you and before God." It leads to a new beginning. In Matthew it appears to be the end. Cf. *The Works of Leo Tolstoy,* vol. 13: *Twenty Three Tales* (London: Humphrey Milford, 1928) 83–101.
92   Cf. the excursus on Matthew's understanding of judgment in vol. 3 following 25:31-46.

In the structure of the Gospel of Matthew there are a number of similarities between the second and fourth discourses. Externally, the disciples discourse (chap. 10) and the community discourse are the two shortest discourses. They, and only they, are both directed exclusively to the disciples. They have similar structures. Each has at its center a central christological affirmation (10:24-25; 18:19-20). Both deal basically with the church. It is true, of course, that that is all they have in common, since they deal with the church from different perspectives. If chap. 10 dealt with the disciples' mission, authority, sending, and experiences, chap. 18 deals with their relationships among themselves. In brief one could say that chap. 10 speaks of the church in the world, that is, of the church's external dimension, while chap. 18 speaks of the church's life, that is, of its internal dimension. Once again[1] we will try to summarize the discourse in terms of several basic characteristics that according to Matthew make the church the church.

1. According to Matthew the church's fundamental attribute is *community*, lived and experienced. The entire discourse is about community and not about some such thing as "church order." That is not only true for Matthew; almost everywhere in the New Testament the church is characterized as lived and experienced community.[2] However, by building a particular discourse around the theme of community, Matthew focuses attention in a special way on this basic feature. When the church is not community, it is not the church.

2. For Matthew the key to a life capable of community is *lowliness* (vv. 3-4). Such lowliness requires a change of one's orientation; the renunciation of power, rank, wealth, and self-promotion; the recognition of one's own fallibility and lack of security; taking seriously the other members of the family and always reaching out to them;

and direct communication. Lowliness as the key to community life means critically questioning all hierarchical church structures.

> It is noteworthy that in Matthew 18 it is always the disciples who are addressed and that they can assume different roles.[3] Office bearers never appear. It does not follow, however, that there were no officeholders in Matthew's church or members who held special positions such as scribes (13:52), prophets (10:41; 23:34), itinerant charismatics ("righteous," 10:41), or even elders who regard themselves as shepherds of the church.[4] If there were such offices in the church, overcoming the claims to power that accompany them becomes the program of Matthew 18, as the programmatic grammalogue μικροί ("little ones") reminds us.[5] Yet the church rule of vv. 15-17 also reveals that brotherhood, sisterhood, and community were not simply empty words. When the brotherly admonition in v. 15 is initiated by the offended church member, and when no officials are mentioned in connection with the assembly which in v. 17 excludes the sinner, that is not merely a hypothetical description; it must have reflected the reality in Matthew's church. This view is supported by the open statements about prayer and the assembly of "two or three" in the name of Jesus (vv. 19-20) which sharply contrast with what we later read in Ignatius about the need to have a bishop present. Thus in Matthew's church overcoming authority structures in the church with the idea of community is more than a theoretical postulate.

3. According to Matthew 18 there are *boundaries to church membership* that are marked out by sinful deeds, especially by causing church members to stumble (vv. 6-9) and by refusing to forgive (vv. 31-35) but not by false *doctrine*.[6] These boundaries are revealed at the last judgment (vv. 6-7; 34-35). The expulsion from the church which Matthew's community knows serves to remind the members of these boundaries, not to minimize or to

---

1 Cf. above, The Basic Message of the Disciples Discourse following II C 4.

2 Cf. e.g. 1 Corinthians 12–13; Rom 12:9–13:10; Eph 4:1-16; John 15:1-17; 1 John 4:16-21 or the summaries in Acts 2:42-47 and 4:32-35 as condensations of Luke's description of the church.

3 Viz., the roles of those who are threatened by the σκάνδαλα, those who despise the "little ones," the sheep who go astray, the brothers who have been injured, those who pray in the community, those who are called to forgive and who are threatened with judgment.

4 Cf., however, the frequently mentioned πρεσβύτεροι τοῦ λαοῦ which may be a distinguishing term (26:47, 27:1 and elsewhere) as well as above, IV B 1.3, n. 55.

5 Cf. above on 18:6. A similar purpose lies behind 23:8-10.

6 Cf. 7:21-23; 24:10-12 (hate and lack of love).

7 Cf. above on 18:12-13 on the implicit theological dimension of the parable of the shepherd and the fundamental behavior of the king in vv. 23-27.

8 Cf. 5:48. It is only the line of "seeking" and "forgiv-

eliminate sin but to recognize and name it. Matthew does not say when in the eyes of the Son of Man and world-judge a sin involves a "falling" ($\sigma\kappa\alpha\nu\delta\alpha\lambda\acute{\iota}\zeta\varepsilon\sigma\vartheta\alpha\iota$) from which there is no recovery.

4. In the perspective of Matthew 18 a fundamental characteristic of the church is that it time and again *bursts the boundaries* that it is compelled to draw. With regard to the behavior of the church members, therefore, seeking the lost (vv. 12-14) is more important than is eliminating $\sigma\kappa\acute{\alpha}\nu\delta\alpha\lambda\alpha$ ("snares"), and unending and unlimited forgiveness (vv. 21-22) is closer to the perfection that the father desires than is "brotherly admonition" or expulsion from the church. What corresponds to God's own behavior[7] which is the fundamental model of perfection[8] is only searching, not eliminating—only forgiving, not earthly "binding."

5. Essential to Matthew's understanding of community is that in the perspective of Matthew 18 *it is not possible to distinguish between a sin against a sister or a brother, that is, a sin against the community, and a sin against God.* Thus human relationships also cannot be of less value than is one's relationship to God. Just as in Matt 5:21-48 it is in loving that perfection is revealed,[9] in Matthew 18 it is precisely despising the little ones and refusing to forgive one's fellow members that evokes God's judgment.

6. *Christologically,* in Matthew 18 Jesus appears as the teacher who reminds his disciples of the father's forgiveness that they have experienced and who above all challenges them to reorient their lives fundamentally toward the little ones, the community, and forgiveness. He appears in the center of the chapter as the one who accompanies his church and who is present in it, even where only two or three are together in his name (vv. 19-20). He thus appears as the earthly and as the exalted one.[10]

7. As was the case with the Sermon on the Mount and the parabolic discourse, the chapter ends with the *judg-ment idea.* In our chapter it serves to underscore the injunction to love. Indirectly the idea of judgment relativizes v. 18, which historically has had such a great influence. God will sit in judgment on his disciples, that is, the church, as well and will ask them why, when they have been granted unlimited forgiveness, they have bound others instead of loosing them.

On the Meaning of the Community Discourse Today

As was the case with Matthew 10, Matthew 18 is a basic ecclesiological text. When in conclusion I try once again to express its meaning in terms of the present situation, naturally my own northern European, Protestant situation is dominant. Every such attempt is contextual and, of course, also subjective. It is to be understood as a contribution to a dialogue on the *meaning* of the Gospel of Matthew today. On the basis of Matthew 18 I find two points are significant.

1. *Community as a fundamental characteristic of the church.* When contrasted with what our modern northern European churches actually are, the almost self-evident basic New Testament assertion that the church is a community of persons living in fellowship with the exalted Christ (cf. 18:20!) is shattering. This fundamental Matthean designation contradicts not only what our European, Sunday-morning-worship state churches *are*; it also contradicts the way our churches ecclesiologically *understand* themselves.

> In the history of theology "church" has seldom been defined in terms of community. Once the "community of the saints" (for example, in the *Confessio Augustana*) regarded itself as constituted solely by word and sacrament, it no longer was concerned about what constituted the "community" of these saints. The "saints" were reduced to hearers of the word and recipients of the sacraments.[11] When in the First Vatican Council the church understood itself as a hierarchically structured institution, its existence as church in no way depended on how community was

---

9   ing" that also corresponds to the prohibition of a final separation before the last judgment in the basic texts 13:37-43, 49-50 and 22:11-14.

Cf. vol. 1, II A 2.2 (8. The antitheses in the framework of Matthean theology), II A 2.2.6 on 5:48, and Summary. Cf. also no. 3 of the history of interpretation of 22:34-40 and the analysis of 23:13-33 on the relationship between love of God and love of neighbor.

10   On the identity between the earthly and the exalted Lord that is fundamental for Matthew's Christology cf. vol. 1, I A 1.3 on Matt 1:23 and below, vol. 3 on Matt 28:20.

11   Cf. *Confessio Augustana* 7 and 8 = BSLK, 61–62 = *Book of Concord,* 32–33. From the rudimentary statements about the community of saints in *CA* 7, *CA* 8 can immediately move to the validity of the sacra-

experienced and lived in this institution.[12] Even in the second Vaticanum's Constitution on the Church, which describes the church as "people of God," at most only peripheral attention is paid to the individual, visible congregation in which community alone actually can be lived and experienced. Dogma has scarcely ever had anything to say about "community" as the church's defining characteristic, for example, about love as the most important *nota ecclesiae*. From the perspective of the Jesus movement and the New Testament, this deficiency is extraordinary, and its only explanation can be that the Jesus communities of the New Testament age became "churches" in the sociological sense of the word—that is, they became mediators of salvation—cultic and training institutions for an entire society.

It is therefore not surprising that the basic, ecclesiological eighteenth chapter of Matthew is among the texts that have led a shadowy existence in ecclesiology. Our text has played an essential role neither for reflection about the nature of the church nor for canon law. Even in the religious orders and in the free churches which grew up in opposition to the major churches of the Reformation, it seems to me that only individual sections of the chapter have become important, especially vv. 15-17, but never Matthew 18 as an entire chapter.

Only recently has the idea of community again begun to play a more important role for ecclesiology. On the Protestant side Bonhoeffer's *Sanctorum Communio* offers important initiatives that attempt to overcome not only the typical Protestant diastasis between invisible and visible church but also the alternative between an institution (= church) and an association (= sect) as formulated by Max Weber and Ernst Troeltsch.[13] Bonhoeffer said that "the church is a community *sui generis,* a community of spirit and love," and on the basis of his understanding of the church he tried to move beyond the distinction between church and sect that the sociology of religion had created.[14] His initiatives have once again confronted theology with the question of the ecclesiological meaning of community. Liberation theologians have discovered the critical power of the idea of community to question ecclesiastical authority structures.[15] In the congregational renewal movement the "fraternal life" is once again understood as a basic *nota ecclesiae*, whereby on the Protestant side one is clear that it is never a *nota* of the institution of the church.[16] H. J. Kraus strongly emphasizes the character of the church as community, because he is concerned to ensure that "the category of religion" does not "take over the primitive Christian table-fellowship" and reduce faith to an "ecclesiastically sanctioned private Christianity."[17] On the Catholic side M. Kehl, for example, bases his ecclesiology on the idea of community.[18] Outside Europe experiences in the base

---

ments in a church that for all practical purposes is a society of non-saints.

12 This is illustrated by the design for a constitution on the church of the First Vatican Council that conceives of the church from the top down in terms of Ephesians 4. It is no accident, therefore, that in its concluding chap. 10 it states in direct contradiction to Matthew 18 that the church "is a society of unequals" (NR no. 394).

13 Cf. below, no. 2.

14 *The Communion of Saints* (New York: Harper & Row, 1963) 185.

15 Cf. Leonardo Boff (*Church: Charisma and Power: Liberation Theology and the Institutional Church* [New York: Crossroad, 1985] 119): "Sacred power lies within the entire community"; Jürgen Moltmann, *Church*, 316: "The expression 'brotherliness' surmounts the language of rule and privilege"; Elisabeth Schüssler-Fiorenza gave her collection of ecclesiological studies the programmatic-Matthean

title *Discipleship of Equals* (New York: Crossroad, 1993).

16 Cf. F. Schwarz and C. A. Schwarz, *Theologie des Gemeindeaufbaus* (3d ed.; Neukirchen-Vluyn: Neukirchener Verlag, 1987) 117–48. The quotation is from p. 125.

17 Hans-Joachim Kraus, *Reich Gottes, Reich der Freiheit* (Neukirchen-Vluyn: Neukirchener Verlag, 1975) 388–96. The quotations are from pp. 388–90.

18 Medard Kehl (*Die Kirche: Eine katholische Ekklesiologie* [Würzburg: Echter Verlag, 1992] 51) states that as a community of believers the church is a "sacrament of God's *communio*." Paul Hoffmann (*Das Erbe Jesu und die Macht in der Kirche* [TTB 213; Mainz: Matthias-Grünewald, 1991] esp. 70ff., 92ff., 122ff.) makes important contributions in this direction.

19 In the Federal Republic of Germany and in Switzerland this development is already (1993) visible in several cities such as Basel or Hamburg. Especially the situation in the former German Democratic

communities of South America have sparked renewed interest in the question of community.

In the process Matthew 18 has remained largely undiscovered as a fundamental ecclesiological text, even though it could give some indication how a church that understands itself in terms of community is a church. In my judgment the experience of community offers a right way of appropriating grace and conduct. In a community in which persons are accepted and in which God's love is experienced in human love, grace is concrete and is something that can be experienced. At the same time it is true that in a community that does things in common and that bears the actions of the individual, Jesus' commandments are something other than individual Christian duties—that is, something other than "laws." In this way Matthew 18 sheds light on a dimension of the church that in my judgment is equal to word and sacrament and superior to every juridical church structure.

2. *The message of Matthew 18 for a national church in transition to a new social form.* Today our northern European national churches are facing a transition to a post-Christian society in which they doubtless will constitute a minority.[19] It is in my opinion unavoidable that in such a society they are going to be divorced from the state. At the moment they offer a mixed picture. On the one hand they (still!) provide for the religious needs of the entire population with rituals. Because of their tradition they are held in high regard out of proportion to their numbers, and they have a corresponding influence. On the other hand they appear to contain a number of active minorities, movements, communities, and groups that to a degree both compete with one another and complement each other. In this situation I would like to ask what impulses the community discourse can give for the form of our churches both today and in the future.[20]

We choose as our point of departure the common distinction between "church" and "sect" which has been important for the sociology of religion since Ernst Troeltsch and Max Weber. The question is: At the end of the Constantinian age are our national churches, which in sociological terms originated as sects, facing an epoch in which, in sociological terms, they will become sects again? Above all: In view of their biblical (in our case Matthean) heritage should they welcome this development, or should they try to prevent it? As is well known, according to Troeltsch[21] the New Testament is the legitimate root both of the Christian communities that are sects and of the major churches. He emphasizes especially the lines that lead from Paul to the major churches and from Jesus or the Synoptic Gospels to the sects. In an age in which the end of the national churches is in sight it is important, therefore, to ask what contribution the Gospel of Matthew has to make to this discussion.

> When I use the term "sect" in this context, I use it in a value-neutral sense as a category of the sociology of religion. It is not easy to do so in the present ecclesiastical and cultural situation on the European continent, since the term "sect" is constantly loaded with negative connotations. It is associated on the one hand with a theological value judgment. In contrast to "church," "sect" is involved with schism and heresy.[22] On the other hand it is associated with a philosophical value judgment from the Enlightenment: "Sect" means intolerance and fanaticism. Unlike the United States and England, where a variety of Christian denominations influence one's perception, on the European continent with its state-church structures largely intact it is extremely difficult to accept an open concept of sect as defined by the sociology of religion. As a result, it is much more difficult in this part of the world than it is in the Anglo-Saxon world for theology to be open not only to Ernst Troeltsch's heritage as a sociologist of religion but

---

Republic shows that it is not possible to reverse the exodus from the church which during the socialist period was encouraged with moderate pressure (but for the most part no longer exists) and to restore the conditions of a state church.

20 Cf. on the Sermon on the Mount vol. 1, II A History of Interpretation and the conclusion following II A 3.4: (a) The form of the church.

21 *The Social Teaching of the Christian Churches* (2 vols.; Chicago: University of Chicago Press, 1981) 1.340–43.

22 However, etymologically *secta* is related to *sequor* or

sector (to follow, to go after) and not to *seco* (to cut). See Karl Ernst Georges, *Ausführliches Lateinisch-Deutsches Handwörterbuch* (8th ed.; Hannover: Hahnsche Buchhandlung, 1988) 2.2559, and Günther Kehrer, *Einführung in die Religionssoziologie* (Darmstadt: Wissenschaftliche Buchgesellschaft, 1988) 158.

also to the New Testament heritage to the degree that it alludes to "sect." I intend, therefore, to avoid the term "sect" as a theological, largely pejorative concept, since in my judgment it is almost always used to legitimate one's own form of church and to keep one from hearing those biblical texts that get in the way of such self-justification.

Loosely following Max Weber, Ernst Troeltsch, Bryan Wilson, and Robin Scroggs,[23] I find the following typical characteristics of a sect useful for the study of early Judaism and primitive Christianity: (1) Sects are relatively small and identifiable groups.[24] (2) They possess a constituent and compulsory self-definition, and (the two go together) they tend to make exclusive claims for the truth they espouse.[25] (3) Membership in sects is by choice; one joins a sect and, unlike the member of a "church," is not born into it.[26] (4) As a rule they have a procedure for expelling members.[27]

(5) Most sects are relatively elitist—that is, they strive for ethical purity among their members, and they tend to be radical and perfectionistic.[28] (6) They demand total involvement from their members, and they constitute an intensive community.[29] (7) As minorities they are somewhat distant from the ruling classes of their society.[30]

Along with Wilson I would not try to define a sect's attitude toward the world, since there are here a number of varieties.[31] It is not necessary that sects be apocalyptic or chiliastic; that was not the case even in primitive Christianity.[32] Nor would I try to define a sect's leadership structure; here also there are quite different possibilities ranging from authoritarian-hierarchical to familial-democratic forms.[33] It seems to me that it would be difficult to draw a sharp distinction between "sects" and "denominations," since as a rule a denomination is the form of a sect established

---

23 Max Weber, *Economy,* 1204–11; Troeltsch, *Social Teaching* 1.331–43; Bryan R. Wilson, *Religious Sects: A Sociological Study* (New York: McGraw-Hill, 1970); Robin Scroggs, "The Earliest Christian Communities as Sectarian Movement," in Jacob Neusner, ed., *Christianity, Judaism and Other Greco-Roman Cults: Studies for Morton Smith at Sixty* (SJLA 12/2; Leiden: Brill, 1975) 1–23.

24 Troeltsch (*Social Teaching* 1.331) and Weber (*Economy,* 1204) emphasize on this point that groups whose members join of their own free will of necessity give up any claim to universality.

25 Weber (*Economy,* 1204); Troeltsch (*Social Teaching* 2.998): "confessing churches"; Wilson (*Sects,* 26): "sole possessor of true doctrine, of appropriate ritual and of warranted standard of rectitude"; 29: "exclusive commitment"; 29–34. Related to this characteristic is the factor that from the point of view of the history of religions sects appear only in religions that have a founder, so that a group can define itself only in terms of a tradition that is determinative for a religious community. Cf. Kurt Rudolf, "Wesen und Struktur der Sekte," *Kairos* 21 (1979) 250–51.

26 Troeltsch, *Social Teaching* 1.339; Wilson, *Sects,* 28; Scroggs ("Communities," 6, 20). For this reason sects frequently pressure people to convert.

27 Weber (*Economy,* 1204–5) speaks of community as a "device for selection" or weeding out. Cf. Wilson, *Sects,* 27. In contrast to the primarily "disciplinary" exclusions in major churches, the criteria tend to be severe.

28 Troeltsch (*Social Teaching* 1.336, 339) speaks of "a select group of the elect." He also emphasizes (ibid., 2.993, 1000) the ethical character of sects in con-

trast to the "grace character" of churches. Weber (*Economy,* 1204) speaks of an "aristocratic group" and of an "association of persons with full religious qualification." Wilson speaks of "exemplary conduct" and of "worthiness" or "merit" (*Sects,* 28–30).

29 Troeltsch, *Social Teaching* 1.331. Wilson (*Sects,* 26) speaks of a "complete and conscious allegiance of its members" and states that "this 'us' is set over against all others." Scroggs ("Communities," 6, 20) refers to "total commitment" and an intense family feeling (6, 14–15).

30 Troeltsch, *Social Teaching* 2.993, 995, 998. By contrast, the church, according to Troeltsch (ibid., 2.1007–8), is always identified with the "secular poor." Cf. Wilson (*Sects,* 231–33), who speaks of the formation of sects as social compensation. Scroggs ("Communities," 9ff.) calls primitive Christianity a protest movement and speaks (4–5, 16–17) of the rejection of the establishment's worldview.

31 In pp. 37–40 he identifies them as conversionist (= missionary), revolutionist (= expecting a completely different kingdom of God), introversionist (= retreating from the world), manipulatist (= manipulating the world with esoteric or occult agents), thaumaturgical, reformist, or utopian.

32 Following Troeltsch (*Social Teaching* 2.993, 995, and elsewhere) Scroggs ("Communities," 20–21) regards the apocalyptic character as a determining characteristic of primitive Christian sects.

33 In my opinion Weber (*Economy,* 1208) is one-sided in emphasizing the affinity of the sects for democracy.

over a long term that has found its fixed structure and its place in a society.[34] Important distinctions between a sect and a denomination remain the stronger minority character of a sect, its greater distance from a society's centers of power, and its stronger tendency toward rigorism and exclusivity. Finally, I see no reason to identify opposition to or even separation from a majority (= church) as constitutive of a sect. Such a separation is only possible where there are such churches—for example, not in the United States and in antiquity, but in Judaism prior to the consolidation of the rabbinic movement.

To begin with, in this open sense the Matthean church, along with all other New Testament churches and, for example, the Essenes,[35] is to be regarded as a "sect." A number of the "characteristics of a sect," for example, its relative smallness or its distance from the centers of social power, were not things that the Matthean church chose for itself. To that degree such characteristics are not theologically significant. Other "characteristics of a sect" exhibited by the Matthean church are more likely to correspond to what the Matthean church intended in fulfillment of its mission—for example, its binding self-definition which it received from Jesus, its membership by choice, the total involvement of its members, and the intensive community. In my judgment such "characteristics of a sect" have an ongoing importance as a model for our churches today.

Let us try then to draw on Matthew 18 in our search for a biblically based form for our churches as "sects" in an approaching, post-Constantinian era. What strikes me as being of the greatest interest here is that Matthew 18 contains elements that have the potential for breaking out of the Matthean church's character as a sect. The lead motif of "lowliness" includes the idea that no one, not even a "little one," is absolute in relation to others; one must over and over be considerate of others. Forgiveness includes the rigorous questioning of what lies behind one's own binding activity. Alongside the tendency toward exclusivity Matthew 18 requires an openness that is directly related to the church's own self-definition—that is, to the command of Jesus. Alongside elite tendencies is the knowledge that one is oneself at all times in danger and in need of forgiveness. The community discourse of Matthew 18 thus requires that a Christian community have the character of a sect, and at the same time it have a power that transcends that character. In my judgment it is the ongoing influence of Jesus, the "only teacher," that keeps the Matthean church from becoming an elite sect closed in on itself. Thus Matthew 18 opens an important perspective for national churches that probably in the future will become "sects" in the sociological sense, whether or not they want it to happen or will even acknowledge it when it does happen. The important question then will be whether they succeed in preserving Matthew's lowliness motif and in remembering that they themselves are endangered and are not absolute.

34   H. Richard Niebuhr's *The Social Sources of Denominationalism* (1929; reprinted Hamden, Conn.: Shoe String Press, 1954) is basic for distinguishing between sects and denominations.

35   On the question whether the Pharisees can be called a sect cf. vol. 3, V A 4.2.7 on the excursus on the scribes and Pharisees, specifically 2.1 and 2.3.2.

Literature

Rolf Busemann, *Die Jüngergemeinde nach Markus 10* (BBB 57; Bonn: Hanstein, 1983).

Warren Carter, *Households and Discipleship: A Study of Matthew 19–20* (JSNTSup 103; Sheffield: JSOT, 1994).

The concluding section of the main division that deals with Jesus' activity in the church (16:21—20:34) is introduced with a geographical reference. Jesus leaves Galilee and is on the way to Judea (19:1). The readers already know that Jesus must go up to Jerusalem, the city of suffering (16:21). He and those around him have already gathered in Galilee for a procession to the Holy City (17:22).[1] They know, therefore, that Jesus is leaving Galilee for good. The next geographical statement appears in 20:17 prior to the next prediction of the passion. The third follows in 20:29 at the conclusion of this section, when Jesus has already left Jericho and is not far from Jerusalem. The prediction of the passion in 20:18-19 stands substantively, though not textually, in the middle of the section. The shadow over Jesus darkens; the disaster draws near.

The multitudes that follow Jesus are mentioned only at the beginning (19:2) and at the end (20:29). In the first section of the text Jesus' most important opponents, the Pharisees, also reappear to tempt him as they did in 16:1. They also announce to the readers the major debates that await Jesus in Jerusalem. Otherwise the entire section can be described as instructions to the disciples. Scenes in which outsiders are present (cf. 19:3-9, 13, 16-22; 20:20-21) also become occasions for teaching the disciples. Beyond this general characteristic, however, there is no apparent systematic arrangement of the scenes, which themselves are formally different and are of varying lengths. Nor does the section have an overarching theme.[2] Still, there are certain points of emphasis. In the first part (chap. 19) two ethical issues are dealt with that are important for the life of the church, marriage and possessions. In the middle part (20:1-16; cf. 19:16-30) Jesus speaks repeatedly of the question of the reward that awaits his disciples. The concluding part (beginning with 20:17) is clearly focused on the coming suffering and its consequences for the disciples.

---

1   Following Shemuel Safrai (*Die Wallfahrt im Zeitalter des zweiten Tempels* [Forschungen zum jüdisch-christlichen Dialog 1; Neukirchen-Vluyn: Neukirchener Verlag, 1981] 121–27), Donald Verseput notes that pilgrims normally traveled to Jerusalem in large groups and claims that the difficult συστρε-φομένων in 17:22 could be understood as such a gathering ("Jesus' Pilgrimage to Jerusalem and Encounter in the Temple: A Geographical Motive in Matthew's Gospel," *NovT* 36 [1994] 109–14). If 17:22 in fact indicates that Jesus' disciples constituted such a group of pilgrims, then the readers know that the journey to the city of death has already finally been determined.

2   Patte (263) finds the theme of this section in the issue of human evil, whereby the catchword is *hardness of heart*, but he needs to find a "theme" everywhere. Cf. above, III C, n. 3. Warren Carter

(*Households and Discipleship: A Study of Matthew 19–20*) understands Matthew 19–20 as a kind of Matthean *Haustafel* with the themes of marriage, children, possessions, and slavery (20:17-28) that radically changed the traditional, hierarchical household structures. However, "possessions" is not really a *Haustafel* theme. In any case, there is no place in this concept for Matt 20:1-16, 29-34.

Literature on vv. 3-9 and the entire text

Allison, "Divorce," 3–10.

Berger, "Hartherzigkeit," 1–47.

Craig L. Blomberg, "Marriage, Divorce, Remarriage and Celibacy: An Exegesis of Mt 19:3-12," *Trinity Journal* 11 n.s. (1990) 161–96.

Marcus Bockmuehl, "Matthew 5:32; 19:9 in the Light of Prerabbinic Halakah," *NTS* 35 (1989) 291–95.

Henri Crouzel, "Le texte patristique de Matthieu 5,32 et 19,9," *NTS* 19 (1972/73) 98–119.

David Daube, *New Testament,* 71–86.

Derrett, *Law,* 363–88.

Albert Descamps, "Les textes évangéliques sur le mariage," in idem, *Jésus et l'église: Études d'exégèse et de théologie* (BEThL 77; Louvain: University Press: Peeters, 1987) 510–83.

Jean Duplacy, "Note sur les variantes et le texte original de Matthieu 19,9," in idem, *Études de critique textuelle du Nouveau Testament* (BEThL 78; Louvain: University Press: Peeters, 1987) 387–412.

William A. Heth and Gordon J. Wenham, *Jesus and Divorce: The Problem with the Evangelical Consensus* (Nashville: Nelson, 1984).

Michael W. Holmes, "The Text of the Matthean Divorce Passages: A Comment on the Appeal to Harmonizations in Textual Decisions," *JBL* 109 (1990) 651–64.

Armin Kretzer, "Die Frage: Ehe auf Dauer und ihre mögliche Trennung nach Mt 19,3-12," in Helmut Merklein and Joachim Lange, eds., *Biblische Randbemerkungen: Schülerfestschrift für Rudolf Schnackenburg zum 60. Geburtstag* (2d ed.; Würzburg: Echter Verlag, 1974) 218–30.

B. C. Labosier, "Matthew's Exception Clause in the Light of Canonical Criticism: A Case Study in Hermeneutics" (Diss., Westminster Theological Seminary, 1990).

Corrado Marucci, *Parole di Gesù sul divorzio* (Aloisian 16; Brescia: Morcelliana, 1982) 250–311.

Idem, "Clausole Matteane e critica testuale," *RivB* 38 (1990) 301–25.

Francis J. Moloney, "Matthew 19:3-12 and Celibacy: A Redactional and Form Critical Study," *JSNT* 2 (1979) 42–60.

B. E. Morgan, "The Synoptic Pericopes Concerning Divorce and Remarriage: An Exegetical and Hermeneutical Study" (Diss., Fort Worth, 1987) 73–149.

Kurt Niederwimmer, *Askese und Mysterium* (FRLANT 113; Göttingen: Vandenhoeck & Ruprecht, 1975) 42–58.

B. J. Schaller, "Genesis 1.2 im antiken Judentum" (Diss., Göttingen, 1961).

Hans Joachim Schoeps, "Restitutio principii als kriti-
sches Prinzip der nova lex Jesu," in idem, *Aus frühchristlicher Zeit* (Tübingen: Mohr/Siebeck, 1950) 271–85.

van Tilborg, *Leaders,* 117–26.

Angelo Tosato, *Il matrimonio nel giudaismo antico e nel nuovo Testamento* (Rome: Biblical Institute Press, 1976).

François Vouga, *Jésus et la loi selon la tradition synoptique* (Le Monde de la Bible 17; Geneva: Labor et Fides, 1987) 89–106.

Gordon J. Wenham, "Matthew and Divorce: An Old Crux Revisited," *JSNT* 22 (1984) 95–107.

Idem, "The Syntax of Matthew 19:9," *JSNT* 28 (1986) 17–23.

For *additional literature* see vol. 1, II A 2.2.3 on 5:31-32.

Literature on vv. 10-12

Bauer, "Mt 19,12," 253–62.

Blinzler, "Εἰσὶν εὐνοῦχοι," 254–70.

Idem, "Justinus Apol. 1,15,4 und Matthäus 19,10-12," in Albert Descamps, ed., *Mélanges bibliques en hommage au R. P. Béda Rigaux* (Gembloux: Duculot, 1970) 45–55.

Burchill, "Evangelical Counsels," 68–134.

Constantin Daniel, "Esséniens et eunuques (Matthieu 19,10-12)," *RevQ* 6 (1967) 353–90.

Jean Galot, "La motivation évangélique du célibat," *Greg* 53 (1972) 731–58.

Gamba, "Eunuchia," 243–87.

Antonio García del Moral, "'Los eunucos que a sí mismos se hicieron tales por el reino de los cielos' (Mt 19,12). ¿Para ocupar los puestos de responsabilidad y servico?" *Cultura Biblica* 38 (1981) 171–98.

Harvey McArthur, "Celibacy in Judaism at the Time of Christian Beginnings," *AUSS* 25 (1987) 163–81.

Quentin Quesnell, "'Made Themselves Eunuchs for the Kingdom of Heaven' (Mt 19:12)," *CBQ* 30 (1968) 335–58.

Sand, *Reich Gottes.*

Segalla, "Il testo," 121–37.

Donald W. Trautman, *The Eunuch Logion of Matthew 19:12: Historical and Exegetical Dimensions as Related to Celibacy* (Pontificia Studiorum Universitas: Officium Libri Catholici; Rome: Catholic Book Agency, 1966).

And it happened when Jesus finished these words he went away from Galilee and came into the region of Judea across the Jordan. 2/ And great multitudes followed him, and he healed them there.

And Pharisees came to him to test him, and they said: "Is a man[1] permitted to dismiss his wife for any cause?" 4/ But he answered and said: "Have you not read that the creator[2] 'from the beginning made them male and female'?" 5/ And he said: "'Therefore a man shall leave father and mother and shall connect with his wife, and the two shall become one flesh.' 6/ Thus they are no longer two but one flesh. What therefore God has brought together a person shall not separate." 7/ They say to him: "Why then did Moses command to give a certificate of divorce and to dismiss [her]?" 8/ He says to them: "In view of your hard-heartedness Moses permitted you to divorce your wives. But from the beginning it has not been so. 9/ But I say to you that whoever dismisses his wife, not for fornication, and marries another commits adultery."[3]

The disciples say to him: "If this is the way it is for a man with his wife, it is good not to marry." 11/ But he said to them: "Not all grasp this[4]

word but (only those) to whom it has been given. 12/ For there are eunuchs who were born that way from a mother's womb, and there are eunuchs who were castrated by humans, and there are eunuchs who have castrated themselves because of the kingdom of heaven. Whoever is able to grasp it, let him grasp it."

Analysis

Structure

The section consists of three parts. *Verses 1-2* provide a summarizing scene. Surrounded by crowds, Jesus is on the road from Galilee to Judea, healing as he goes. The second scene, *vv. 3-9*, falls into two parts, vv. 3-6 and 7-9, each of which is introduced by a question from the Pharisees. Both parts of Jesus' answer contain a clear reference to the "beginning"—that is, to creation ($\dot{\alpha}\pi'\ \dot{\alpha}\rho\chi\hat{\eta}\varsigma$, vv. 4, 8b). The emphasis is of central importance for Matthew, since it raises the answer to a level of which the questioners had not even thought. Jesus refers to creation that fundamentally does not allow for divorce. In his first answer he speaks only of creation and completely ignores the Pharisees' question about the legitimate grounds for divorce. Thus in v. 7 they are forced to refer to the

---

1   Is $\dot{\alpha}\nu\vartheta\rho\dot{\omega}\pi\omega$, missing in the most important representatives of the Alexandrian text type (ℵ, B, et al.), original? Although $\dot{\alpha}\nu\vartheta\rho\omega\pi o\varsigma$, as the substantive most frequently used by Matthew after $\Ἰ\eta\sigma o\hat{\upsilon}\varsigma$ could have been added, in my judgment it belongs to the text, since the short text is an almost exclusively Egyptian reading.

2   The choice is between $\kappa\tau\dot{\iota}\sigma\alpha\varsigma$ and $\pi o\iota\dot{\eta}\sigma\alpha\varsigma$. Since the former is a Matthean hapax legomenon and the latter could be adapted to the following $\dot{\epsilon}\pi o\dot{\iota}\eta\sigma\epsilon\nu$, the former is clearly the preferred reading.

3   The text of v. 9 is uncertain. A number of ancient witnesses are more closely related to Matt 5:32, especially almost all of the fathers, as Henri Crouzel ("Le texte patristique de Matthieu 5,32 et 19,9," 98–119) points out. However, the forms of accommodation to Matt 5:32 are quite different. The problem is that in the diversity of accommodations no clearly defined text stands out. In place of the one verb $\mu o\iota\chi\hat{\alpha}\tau\alpha\iota$ at the end of the entire verse (ℵ, D, L, some of the Latin, Coptic, and Syrian texts) many of the witnesses have two main verbs, either $\pi o\iota\epsilon\hat{\iota}\ \alpha\dot{\upsilon}\tau\dot{\eta}\nu\ \mu o\iota\chi\epsilon\upsilon\vartheta\hat{\eta}\nu\alpha\iota$ and $\mu o\iota\chi\hat{\alpha}\tau\alpha\iota$ (among others, P[25] and B) or $\mu o\iota\chi\hat{\alpha}\tau\alpha\iota$ twice (among others, some of the Latin and Syrian witnesses). In Θ and other Syrian witnesses the "Markan" variants and Matt 5:32b are almost completely combined. Each of the four text types is further divided into subgroups. The textual evidence is thus very complicated. The only clear thing is that $\mu\dot{\eta}\ \dot{\epsilon}\pi\dot{\iota}$

$\pi o\rho\nu\epsilon\dot{\iota}\alpha$, found in neither Mark nor Matt 5:32, is original (with ℵ, L, Θ, C*, many Syriac witnesses, et al.). After the thorough studies of Jean Duplacy ("Note sur les variantes et le texte original de Matthieu 19,9," 387–412) and Corrado Marucci (*Parole di Gesù sul divorzio,* 250–311), it seems probable to me that the shortest text with only one verb (offered by ℵ, L, and, with variants, by other representatives) is the oldest. (Concurring are Nestle[26] and Metzger, *Commentary,* 47–48; Michael W. Holmes ["The Text of the Matthean Divorce Passages: A Comment on the Appeal to Harmonizations in Textual Decisions," 661–63] offers a contrary view.) It is at the same time the "most Markan" text, without being completely identical with Mark 10:11. This text was then either adapted to Matt 5:32, or expanded by means of Matt 5:32b, or both. There is no clearly recognizable basis for the content of the many changes; they are all accommodations to the parallels.

4     $To\hat{\upsilon}\tau o\nu$ is missing in, among others, B, f[1], and several minor text witnesses. Is its omission the *lectio arduor,* since without $\tau o\hat{\upsilon}\tau o\nu$ it would be not at all clear about which word Jesus speaks? Yet the manuscript evidence for $\tau o\hat{\upsilon}\tau o\nu$ is so much better (perhaps cited even by Justin!) that we must regard it as original. To me the easiest explanation is a mechanical omission based on a homoioteleuton (-$o\nu$ appears three times). This text-critical variant is also

biblical justification of divorce. Jesus' second answer is reminiscent of the third antithesis in 5:31-32 and contains three parts: He devalues the Moses text that the Pharisees have cited; he refers once again to the original state of creation; and finally in v. 9 he summarizes the will of God in a basic statement of principle. Only incidentally does he respond to the question of the Pharisees posed in v. 3 about the "cause" (αἰτία [μὴ ἐπὶ πορνείᾳ]). The manner in which Jesus avoids the Pharisees' question makes an impression of sovereignty.

Finally, the concluding scene, *vv. 10-12*, consists of a question of the disciples that with the catchword αἰτία is loosely connected to the question of the Pharisees in v. 3 and that is followed by Jesus' answer. The content surprises the readers, since in vv. 3-9 Jesus had not intended to discourage marriage. Jesus answers with a logion (v. 11), with a supporting enigmatic word in three parts, each of which is introduced by "they are" (εἰσίν; v. 12a-c), and with a summons to pay attention (v. 12d). The enigmatic saying of v. 12a-c is framed by the double appearance of "to grasp" (χωρέω). The logical structure is not immediately apparent.

Sources
In *vv. 1-2*, the first scene, the evangelist uses Mark 10:1. The rest is redaction, whereby along with the closing formula of his discourses Matthew makes use of expressions from the summary of 4:24-25 and from other texts.[5] *Verses 3-9* are a thorough reworking of Mark 10:2-9. Of Matthew's changes the following four are the most important: (1) Matthew includes Mark 10:11 in his public instruction. He obviously sees no reason why Mark should have made it an instruction for the disciples. (2) He omits Mark 10:12, which shares the Hellenistic-Roman assumption that the wife can also divorce her husband.[6] (3) In v. 3 Matthew changes the Pharisees' introductory question in view of the exception clause of v. 9. Is divorce permitted *for any cause?*[7] (4) Above all, however, Matthew rearranges the controversy story in a way that makes it much clearer. In response to the Pharisees' question Jesus first formulates his basic thesis with a word from the creation story (vv. 4-5) and draws his conclusions from it (vv. 6a, b). Then he answers a Pharisaic objection (vv. 7-8). Finally he summarizes his own position once again (v. 9) in a way that incidentally answers the Pharisees' original question (v. 3). Matthew lets Jesus first cite scripture before he brings him into apparent conflict with Moses. The other, smaller changes are more or less clearly redactional.[8] It is not necessary to assume the existence of another source alongside Mark as is frequently done under Streeter's influence.[9]

---

	of major importance for the meaning of the text. Cf. below on the interpretation of v. 11.
5	From 4:24-25 are: ἐθεράπευσεν, καὶ ἠκολούθησαν αὐτῷ ὄχλοι πολλοί, Γαλιλαία, Ἰουδαία, πέραν τοῦ Ἰορδάνου. Cf. in addition 8:1, 12:15, 14:13. In addition, clearly redactional are: μετῆρεν (cf. 13:53), ἀπό, ἐκεῖ, avoiding πάλιν when it has no earlier reference, and avoiding compositions with συν- (cf. vol. 1, Introduction 3.2, 3.3, and n. 92). Difficult is only the omission of καί before πέραν τοῦ Ἰορδάνου.
6	The discussion among Bernadette Brooten, Eduard Schweizer, and Hans Weder over the divorce rights of the Jewish woman offers little for our problem. It does not really matter how much upper-class Jewish women in the time of Jesus claimed this right; under normal circumstances Jewish women did not have it. (Bernadette J. Brooten, "Konnten Frauen im alten Judentum die Scheidung betreiben?" *EvTh* 42 [1982] 65–80; Eduard Schweizer, "Scheidungsrecht der jüdischen Frau? Weibliche Jünger Jesu?" *EvTh* 42 [1982] 294–300; Hans Weder, "Perspektive der Frauen?" *EvTh* 43 [1983] 175–78; Bernadette J. Brooten, "Zur Debatte über das Scheidungsrecht der jüdischen Frau," *EvTh* 43 [1983] 466–78).
7	Linguistically the Matthean character cannot be established with certainty. Κατά with the accusative

	in the sense of "in agreement with" could be Matthean. (According to Sheret ["Examination," 143] it appears six times.) Πᾶς is a favorite of Matthew. Αἰτία (three times in Matthew, once in Mark, and once in Luke) appears elsewhere only in v. 10 and 27:37.
8	On προσέρχομαι αὐτῷ, λέγων, ἀναγινώσκω, εἶπον, οὖν, λέγω + the historical present, δέ, οὗτος cf. vol. 1, Introduction 3.2. On avoiding ἐπερωτάω cf. vol. 1, Introduction 3.3. In v. 4 ὁ κτίσας is influenced by κτίσεως. While δοῦναι (v. 7) replaces the LXX wording of Deut 24:1, it is also occasioned by the same verse of the Bible. Verse 5 is expanded according to the LXX version of Gen 2:24, but the quotation is not literal. Γέγονεν (v. 8b) appears redactionally four to five times in Matthew; the inserted sentence v. 8b is central for Matthew's theology of marriage and corresponds to 24:21. I regard the substance of the unchastity clause of v. 9 as the tradition of the Matthean church (cf. vol. 1, III A 2.1 on the interpretation of 12:36-37); its insertion with μὴ ἐπί comes from Matthew's hand.
9	Streeter, *Gospels*, 259. Cf. recently, e.g., Abel Isaksson, *Marriage and Ministry in the New Temple: A Study with Special Reference to Mt. 19:3-12 and 1 Cor. 11:3-16* (Lund: Gleerup, 1965) 75–92; van Tilborg,

It is not easy to make a decision about vv. *10-12*. Linguistically, v. 12a-c and the summons to attention of v. 12d are clearly tradition.[10] Linguistically, v. 10 is equally clearly redaction.[11] A decision about v. 11, which plays a key role for the traditional-historical reconstruction, is the most difficult. I regard the entire verse as redactional.[12]

Tradition History and Origin

Verses 3-9 are not at issue in a commentary on Matthew;[13] here we are dealing only with vv. 11-12. Especially Blinzler has argued that vv. 11-12 are preserved in their entirety in an earlier form in Justin *1 Apol.* 15.4. He claims that v. 11a originally stood after v. 12c in Justin's form (πλὴν οὐ πάντες τοῦτο χωροῦσιν).[14] I do not find the thesis convincing, since in *1 Apol.* 15.1-3 Justin offers Jesus' sayings on marriage in what is clearly Matthew's sequence and in a wording that reflects Matthew's editorial hand (Matt 5:28, 29, 32 = 19:9) and in 15.4 also appears to presuppose Matthean redaction.[15] It is likely, therefore, that the traditional logion consisted only of v. 12a-c. Most people trace this logion back to Jesus. It is in keeping both with his own unmarried life and with his followers' temporary rejection of family life and sexual activity.

Interpretation

■ **1-2** Matthew concludes the community discourse with his customary formula ending (cf. 7:28; 11:1; 13:53; 26:1). Jesus now leaves Galilee for the last time and comes into the region of Judea. The readers thus become aware of the impending major conflict in Jerusalem. The isolated "across the Jordan" (πέραν τοῦ Ἰορδάνου) is difficult. Since it is improbable that Matthew is thinking here of the Roman administrative region of Judea, which included Perea[16] after the death of Agrippa I, there are only two possibilities. Either he understands it with ἦλθεν as a later designation of the route (he went . . . beyond the Jordan), or he is ignorant of the geographical-historical circumstances.[17] Contrary to Mark's account, the (Galilean?) crowds follow Jesus. They are potentially church.[18] Jesus heals the people as in 4:23-24; 8:16; 9:35; 12:15; 14:14; 15:30; cf. 21:14. It is an important comment for Matthew. Since the crowds follow him at the end of our section in connection with a healing story, it provides a framework around the entire section chaps. 19–20. Jesus, the healing Messiah, remains faithful to his mission to all the people until the end.

■ **3** The Pharisees now approach Jesus and question him in order to tempt him. The readers are reminded of 16:1 and have a foreboding that something sinister is going to happen. Matthew changes Mark's question to: Is it lawful to dismiss one's wife for any cause?[19] The question probably reflects the way the issue was debated between the schools of Hillel and Shammai.[20] Matthew, however, attaches no importance to their debate. He is not concerned with the historical schools of Pharisees at the

---

Leaders, 122–23. For Dungan (*Sayings*) the text provides evidence for the Griesbach hypothesis.

10　Redactional are γάρ, οὕτως, ὅστις, ἄνθρωπος, βασιλεία τῶν οὐρανῶν (cf. vol. 1, Introduction 3.2), precisely not the major words of v. 12.

11　Redactional could be the expressions λέγουσιν αὐτῷ οἱ μαθηταί (cf. 9:28; 13:51; 15:33; 20:22, 33), εἰ (Schenk, *Sprache*, 220), ἄνθρωπος, μετά, συμφέρω (cf. vol. 1, Introduction 3.2). Αἰτία, ἄνθρωπος, γυνή, γαμέω are occasioned by the context.

12　Redactional are: ὁ δὲ εἶπεν αὐτοῖς, λόγος (cf. vol. 1, Introduction 3.2); on οὐ πᾶς . . . ἀλλά cf. 7:21 and Schenk, *Sprache*, 21; on οἷς δέδοται cf. 13:11. Χωρέω is difficult. Perhaps the word came from v. 12d.

13　Cf. Gnilka, *Markus* 2.70; Pesch, *Markusevangelium* 2.124–25.

14　Blinzler, "Εἰσὶν εὐνοῦχοι," 264–67 and "Justinus *1 Apol.* 15.4 und Matthäus 19,10-12," 51–55.

15　Βασιλεία τῶν οὐρανῶν. Cf. in addition Arthur Bellinzoni, *The Sayings of Jesus in the Writings of Justin Martyr* (NovTSup 17; Leiden: Brill, 1967)

60–61; Wolf-Dietrich Köhler, *Die Rezeption des Matthausevangelium in der zeit vor Irenaus* (WUNT 2/24; Tübingen: J. C. B. Mohr, 1987) 230.

16　Along with Galilee!

17　This is more probable. Cf. vol. 1, I B 1.1, n. 5 on 3:1. By contrast, in 4:25 Matthew correctly distinguishes between Judea and the Transjordan area. The difference shows that Matthew has little interest for geographical questions.

18　Cf. vol. 1, on 4:25.

19　Linguistically κατὰ πᾶσαν αἰτίαν can mean two different things: (a) "for just any reason" (negation: not for just any reason); thus BDF § 275 (2); or (b) "for any reason at all" (negation: not for any reason; thus Moulton–Howard–Turner 2.199 with n. 3). Linguistically either is possible, but the first possibility fits better with the exception clause of v. 9.

20　According to *m. Giṭ* 9.10; *b. Giṭ* 90a; *y. Giṭ* 9.50d. 29; *S. Deut.* 24:1 § 269 (= Str-B 1.313–14) the schools of

time of Jesus. He simply describes "the" Pharisees as wanting to tempt Jesus. His purpose in so doing is undoubtedly to suggest that the Pharisees' question was not genuine—indeed, that their motives were malicious (cf. 22:18, 35). In addition, Matthew obviously lets them formulate their question in such a way that its implied "liberal" attitude toward divorce is far removed from Jesus' more severe view of marriage.[21] The wording of the question and Matthew's description of it as "tempting" thus reveals to the readers that the Pharisees are far removed from God's will and are satanic (cf. 4:1, 3). His treatment of the Pharisees here thus corresponds to his usual practice of not distinguishing among the various Jewish groups. He simply denounces all of them as Jesus' opponents.

■ **4-6** Jesus therefore completely ignores their question. Instead, he refers to the scriptures: "Have you not read?" It is these scriptures, after all, that he wants to fulfill with his mission and with his teaching (5:17). More than

that, he refers to God himself and to the "beginning" ($\dot{\alpha}\rho\chi\acute{\eta}$) of Gen 1:1.[22] By referring to the word of the creator and by using the formula "from the beginning" ($\dot{\alpha}\pi'$ $\dot{\alpha}\rho\chi\hat{\eta}\varsigma$) he emphasizes the special authority of the following words. Unlike the rabbinic exegesis,[23] but like the Qumran community, Jesus understands Gen 1:27 in terms of marriage.[24] It is possible that this exegesis presupposes the Jewish concept found in both Philo and the rabbis that God created the primal human being of Genesis 1 androgynous.[25] Woman and man are thus intimately bound because it is only together that they are human in the fullest sense of the word.[26] The quotation from Gen 2:24 that Matthew takes special pains to insert[27] fits in with this understanding. Man and woman will be "one flesh." The word expresses the unity of man and woman that is experienced in their sexual activity.[28] Verse 6 draws a summarizing conclusion from the quota-

---

Hillel and Shammai argue about the interpretation of עֶרְוַת דָּבָר in Deut 24:1. The school of Hillel emphasizes "something" (דָּבָר) and arrives at a lenient standard for divorce—e.g., even when one is simply dissatisfied with one's wife (Akiba, *S. Deut.* 24.1 § 269 = Str-B. 1.313). Shammai's school emphasizes the "scandalous" (עֶרְוָה) and arrives at a more severe standard for divorce, conceivably only in the case of adultery. Josephus dismisses his wife μὲ ἀρεσκόμενος αὐτῆς τοῖς ἔθεσιν (*Vit.* 426) and observes laconically in *Ant.* 4.253 that there are many possible grounds for divorce. Philo is critical of divorces that take place simply because of the man's mood (*Spec. leg.* 3.79–82) but is aware that there are many grounds for divorce (3.30). It is clear from what both of them have to say that (a) a liberal practice of divorce was widespread and that (b) the grounds for divorce was a subject of debate. For further information on the Jewish divorce law see Gnilka, *Markus* 2.76–78.

21 The Pharisees do not ask, e.g.: "Are there legitimate grounds for divorce?" If Matthew does implicitly refer to the dispute between the schools of Hillel and Shammai, he does so by letting "the" Pharisees state Hillel's position in the form of a question and by thus emphasizing their distance from Jesus.

22 Cf. Isa 48:16; 63:16; Hab 1:12; Sir 24:9; fr. *Jub.* 4.15; 12.26; *As. Mos.* 1.13; 12.4. Often the expression ἀπ' ἀρχῆς refers biblically to creation or to the beginning of salvation history. Occasionally, however, its time is indefinite.

23 Cf. Str–B 1.801–2.

24 CD 4.21 (against polygamy and against divorce).

25 In my judgment Daube (*New Testament*, 72–83), B. J. Schaller ("Genesis 1.2 im antiken Judentum," 94–95, 153–54), and Derrett (*Law*, 372–80) have demonstrated this thesis convincingly. Cf. Philo, *Leg. all.* 2.13; *Op. mun.* 76.134; and the sources in Str–B 1.801–2. Daube (*New Testament*, 83–85) attributes this meaning to Mark, but his reasons are not convincing.

26 According to *b. Yeb.* 63a and *Gen. Rab.* 17.11d = Str–B 1.802, the rabbis of the third century understand the text this way. Augustine's understanding here (*Civ. D.* 14.21–23 = NPNF 2.278–80) is important for subsequent interpretation: Gen 1:27-28 indicates that procreation belongs to the perfect humanity of paradise and thus is not under original sin; sexual activity is sinful only when "shame of lust" is part of the process (23 = 279).

27 The unclear καὶ εἶπεν probably presupposes Jesus as the speaker rather than God, who then would be the "author" of the scriptural quotation. While the latter is possible for Matthew, it is elsewhere expressly stated (e.g., 1:22; 2:15). In either case the insertion of the words adds weight to the scriptural quotations. The quotation from Gen 1:27 is now isolated and is thus pronounced. After reading it the readers must refocus. The quotation from Gen 2:24 is emphasized with its own introduction.

28 Cf. Philo *Op. mun.* 152: as two halves of a being. That Paul in 1 Cor 6:16 and the author of Eph 5:31

tions and concludes with a word of Jesus.[29] It is God himself who has brought the marriages together;[30] therefore human beings should not dissolve them.

■ **7-8** The Pharisees object: But Moses commanded that we give a certificate of divorce! It is immediately clear where the evangelist is headed. The word of Moses opposes the creator's act (v. 4). The readers are reminded of 15:2-4 where the tradition of the elders is contrasted with God's command. In 22:24, 31 Matthew will also contrast the word of Moses with God's word. The readers wonder what is going to happen, since they know that for Jesus the word of Moses and the word of the creator cannot contradict one another (cf. 5:17). How will Jesus solve the problem? Verse 8 offers the solution. While the Pharisees refer to Moses' commandment (ἐνετείλατο), Jesus speaks simply of Moses' permission (ἐπέτρεψεν)—of a concession in light of[31] the people's disobedience and "hard-heartedness."[32] In contrast to the Markan text, where Jesus speaks of a commandment of Moses and the Pharisees speak of permission, Matthew reverses the verbs. In so doing he does not directly contradict Deut 24:1-4, since what is "commanded" or forbidden there is only a man's remarriage with his ex-wife who in the meantime has been divorced again. Divorce is merely presupposed.[33] Matthew does, however, contradict the entire Jewish interpretation that understands this institution of divorce not only as a valid legal institution but also as Israel's exclusive privilege.[34] Divorce can even be an obligation for the man, especially when his wife is sexually unfaithful.[35] For Matthew, however, the word of Moses as a simple concession is not of equal value with the creator's word.

Verse 8b takes up v. 4 once again in a way that underscores the inferiority of the Torah of Moses. Alongside the substantive contradiction that compels Matthew to regard Moses' commandment as having only relative value there appears a formal principle: What is old has fundamentally a prior claim to truth over what is younger. This principle was widespread in that day.[36] It is an essential presupposition for ranking material within the Torah that begins with Mark 10:2-9 par. We stand here at a point of departure with Judaism. The mainstream of Jewish interpretation has fundamentally rejected any distinction between the will of the creator and a commandment of Moses. For the rabbis the entire Torah comes from God. Whoever attributes even a single verse only to Moses has despised the word of God.[37] The Torah—in its entirety!—belongs to the preexistent realities that were with God before the world was created.[38] The same is true for Philo. While for him nature is the "oldest ordinance" (*Abr.* 6), it is perfectly codified by Moses.

---

indirectly or directly relate the quotation to the cosmic body of Christ also shows that what is meant is a real union resulting in a new reality. The rabbinic exegesis regarded Gen 2:24 as the basis for marriage regulations for Gentiles = Noachians. Cf. *b. Sanh.* 57b–58b.

29   To which 1 Cor 7:10 probably alludes.

30   In Greek ζεύγνυμι and συζεύγνυμι frequently refer to lovers and to married persons. Cf. BAGD, *s.v.* The concept that God himself ordains marriages is widespread among the rabbis. Cf. Str–B. 1.803–4.

31   Πρός with the accusative can mean here: (1) against (opposition), (2) tending toward (result or purpose), or (3) regarding, with respect to. Only the context and the content enable us to make a decision. The first possibility makes no sense; a certificate of divorce does not serve to combat hard-heartedness. The second interpretation is quite possible in terms of a theory of stubbornness (cf. Schenk, *Sprache,* 420), but in light of 13:13 (cf. above, III B 2.1 on the interpretation of 13:13) it is improbable.

32   Σκληροκαρδία is a biblical, especially wisdom, term that in general refers to the inner dimension of sin, particularly against God. It reflects an unwillingness to repent, being closed to God, stubbornness. Cf. Berger, "Hartherzigkeit," passim.

33   But not only conceded!

34   Cf. Str–B 1.312, 805.

35   *T. Soṭa* 5.9 (302); *b. Giṭ.* 89a–90b; *m. Ketub.* 7.6; *b. Yeb.* 63b; *b. Erub.* 41b (all cited in Str–B 1.315–17). Cf. *Tg. Yer. I* Deut 22.26; 1QapGen 20.15 (Abraham asks of God that Sarah not be "taken away from him" through impurity).

36   On the classical period cf. Peter Pilhofer, ΠΡΕΣΒΥΤΕΡΟΝ ΚΡΕΙΤΤΟΝ (WUNT 2/39; Tübingen: Mohr/Siebeck, 1990). On Palestinian Judaism cf. Max Küchler, *Schweigen, Schmuck und Schleier* (Novum Testamentum et Orbis Antiquus 1; Göttingen: Vandenhoeck & Ruprecht, 1986) 21–30.

37   *B. Sanh.* 99a = Str–B 1.805.

38   Str–B 2.353–57.

Are there *Jewish tendencies in the direction of this sort of distinction between the creator's will and Moses' commandment?* There is the Jewish statement that God added the Prophets and the "Writings" to the Torah because of the people's sin.[39] That, however, is not to say that these parts of the Tanak were inferior or even false. It is furthermore a common Jewish conviction that God wrote only the Decalogue with his own hand.[40] Jewish also is the statement that the angels participated in the giving of the Torah on Sinai (cf. Gal 3:19). But that happened precisely "to honor the Torah"[41] and not to denigrate it. All in all, the basic conviction about the Torah's preexistence was a barrier to devaluing the law of Moses. There are, in my judgment, only four genuine "bridges" to our text.

1. The first bridge consists of several prophetic texts that are critical of parts of the Torah. The most important is the difficult statement in Ezek 20:25-26 that God gave the people bad laws in response to their sins.[42] As far as I can see there is no evidence that this text played a significant role in Jewish interpretation; it was tempered in the Targum.[43] The texts Amos 5:25 and Jer 7:22-28 are related to Ezek 20:25-26. Both speak of Israel's early period before it had a cult; the Jeremiah text refers to Israel's obstinacy (7:26; ἐσκλήρυναν τὸν τράχηλον αὐτῶν).

2. The second bridge is a basic principle of Jewish interpretation according to which early Torah material carries greater weight than what comes later.[44] Here too the principle does not mean that an individual Torah is rejected.

3. The third bridge is the distinction between חוֹבָה ("obligation") and רְשׁוּת ("free choice"). But neither is there here the attempt to devalue those commandments that are not obligatory.[45]

4. There is, finally, an analogous process in Hillel's institutionalization of the *prozbol*—that is, the reservation of the right not to forgive a debt in the Sabbath year. This reservation was needed so that people would agree to lend money and, in the words of the Mishnah, because the people "transgressed what is written in the law" (*m. Šeb.* 10.3). Both the divorce commandment and the *prozbol* are commandments that are needed "for the sake of the world's order."[46] The rabbis regarded both commandments positively, because they demonstrate that God does not require from humans what is beyond their capacity. At the time of Moses and of Hillel the Torah is a living reality that must be adapted to human needs. Except for rabbinic Judaism's positive regard for such changes, the main difference is that for the rabbis Hillel does not have Moses' authority.

These "bridges" cannot obscure the reality that the suspension of the law of Moses in our text is far removed from the mainstream of Jewish Torah interpretation.

---

39 Cf. esp. *b. Ned.* 22b (a late statement from the fourth century): If Israel had not sinned, it would have received only the Torah and the book of Joshua. Remotely relevant are also the statements that in the messianic age part of the Torah as well as the Prophets and the Kethuvim will no longer be needed, since there will be no more sin (Str–B 1.246–47).

40 Str–B 4.437–43.

41 *Pesiq. R.* 21 (103b) = Str–B 3.554.

42 Of course, Ezekiel is thinking concretely only about the literally understood commandment of the sacrifice of the firstborn. Cf. Walther Zimmerli, *Ezekiel: A Commentary on the Book of the Prophet Ezekiel* (2 vols.; Hermeneia; Philadelphia: Fortress, 1979–83) 1.411–12.

43 In the *Tg. Jonathan* on Ezek 20:25 it is not God but the rebellious Israelites who make bad laws. Cf. Berger, "Hartherzigkeit," 45. Berger's work offers a wealth of material and demonstrates (contrary to his intention) that there scarcely was a connection between the OT statements about Israel's stubbornness and statements critical of the Law in Judaism.

44 The rabbinic principle, which was by no means undisputed, was: בַּמִּקְרָא קוֹדֶם בַּמַּעֲשֶׂה כָּל־הַקּוֹדֶם (what precedes in the biblical text precedes also in reality). Cf., e.g., *Pesiq. R.* 23.4 = 116–17 (circumcision appears in Exod 19:5 before the Decalogue). For further sources see Wilhelm Bacher, *Die exegetische Terminologie der jüdischen Traditionsliteratur,* vol. 1: *Die bibelexegetische Terminologie der Tannaiten* (1899; reprinted Darmstadt: Wissenschaftliche Buchgesellschaft, 1965) 112, and Hans Joachim Schoeps, "Restitutio principii als kritisches Prinzip der nova lex Jesu," 272.

45 Sources in Bacher, *Die exegetische Terminologie der jüdischen Traditionsliteratur,* vol. 1: *Die bibelexegetische Terminologie der Tannaiten* 1.58–59; van Tilborg, *Leaders,* 121; Abel Isaksson, *Marriage and Ministry in the New Temple: A Study with Special Reference to Mt. 19:3-12 and 1 Cor. 11:3-16* (Lund: Gleerup, 1965) 121. It is precisely this background that underscores the difference with Matt 19:7-9. Jesus is not of the opinion that the certificate of divorce is a matter of personal discretion; he refers only to the case of πορνεία.

46 *M. Giṭ.* 4.3

The real parallels to Matt 19:7-8 lie not in Judaism but in Christianity. Paul regards the law that is 430 years younger as less fundamental than the promise; indeed, it is a principle that in a sense contradicts the gospel (Gal 3:17). It is important for him that Abraham's faith was more important for his righteousness than was his circumcision (Rom 4:9-10), since therein lies his meaning for *all* believers. Paul speaks of the entire Torah the same way that Matthew speaks of the special case of the commandment about the certificate of divorce. At the same time that means that the distinction between the original, pure will of God and the later, conflicting law of Moses cannot serve as a basic principle for unlocking Matthew's entire understanding of the law. Fundamental for Matthew, rather, is the idea that Jesus came to fulfill the Law and the Prophets (5:17-19). From the Jesus tradition he took the idea of the distinction between God's will as creator and the law of Moses and used it in this special case to relate the pure will of the creator (or of Jesus) to an Old Testament Torah that openly contradicted it. In this way he had also been able to understand the third antithesis as fulfilling the law rather than as abolishing it. A similar thought is the contrast in 15:2-9 between the will of God and the tradition of the elders.

History of Interpretation

In my judgment, other Christian parallels are already part of the history of the interpretation of our text. It became the fundamental text for the understanding of the law of the Gnostic Ptolemaeus. With the aid of Matt 19:6, 8 and Matt 15:4-9 he was able to distinguish between human laws, among them the law of Moses and the traditions of the elders, and the divine law that itself is not equally valuable in all its parts.[47] In Jewish Christianity then—especially in the Pseudo-Clementines, which are strongly influenced by

Matthew—the entire cultic law is understood as a "concession" of Moses in light of the people's sin.[48] Justin and Irenaeus regarded it in much the same way.[49] Thus for the later church our text was an aid in dealing with the question of the validity of the Mosaic law.

■ **9** The word of Moses, interpreted by Jesus, is followed by Jesus' own word which is introduced by "but I say to you" (λέγω δὲ ὑμῖν; similarly 5:32). As in the Sermon on the Mount the divorce prohibition here belongs to the public teaching of Jesus that the disciples are someday to proclaim to all peoples. For Jesus divorce is absolutely forbidden except in the case of πορνεία—a term that refers to every form of inappropriate sexual activity on the wife's part, especially adultery.[50] That the possibility of divorce is now granted immediately following the unqualified reference to the divine order of creation and the dismissal of Deut 24:1-4 as simply Moses' concession to Israel's sin runs contrary to the flow of the text. Matthew will simply have attributed to Jesus his own church's practice. Indirectly, however, a theological concern of the evangelist is clear, even though he does not explicitly state it. If there is indeed one case in which divorce is possible and that thus requires a certificate of divorce, it is obvious that Jesus did not annul the law of Moses but that even in this case he fulfilled it. Thus in Matthew's church even the regulation about the letter of divorce in Deut 24:1-4—in comparison to the order of creation only an "iota" in the law—is taken seriously.

In the exegesis of v. 9 there are two difficult questions for which the text itself does not provide an answer.

1. Does the exception "not for fornication" (μὴ ἐπὶ πορνείᾳ) mean that the husband of an unchaste wife *may* terminate his marriage[51] or that he *must* divorce

47 Epiphanius *Haer.* 23.4.3–14.
48 *Ps.-Clem. Rec.* 1.36: Moses *concessit* sacrifice as long as it is offered to God.
49 Justin *Dial.* 18.2; 46.5–7; Irenaeus *Haer.* 4.15.1–2.
50 Cf. vol. 1, II A 2.2.3 Matthew on πορνεία.
51 According to Phillip J. Sigal ("The Halakhah of Jesus of Nazareth According to the Gospel of Matthew" [Diss., Pittsburgh, 1979] 114) divorce is not required; based on the Jewish principle there is the legal possibility of waiving one's right to divorce. However, Matt 1:18-25 contradicts this view. According to 1:19, "righteous" Joseph saw no

legal possibility of not divorcing Mary; he saw only the possibility of dismissing her secretly. According to Matthew it took the intervention of an angel to permit Joseph not to divorce Mary. Cf. Allison, "Divorce."
52 Cf. the sources cited above in n. 35. In my judgment Marcus Bockmuehl ("Matthew 5:32; 19:9 in the Light of Prerabbinic Halakah," 291–95) has demonstrated that it is plausible that a prerabbinic halakah existed that required divorce in the case of adultery. Matthew 1:19 also supports this view. In the rabbinic view a husband is forbidden to have sexual

her? The Jewish parallels that interpret divorce in the case of adultery as a requirement[52] and the earliest Christian history of the reception of the Matthean clause[53] both speak for the second possibility.[54]

2. Does the exception "not for unchastity" refer only to the first part of Jesus' command, viz., to divorce, or does it refer also to the second part, viz., to remarriage? In the former case there is a general prohibition of a second marriage; in the latter case v. 9 permits the second marriage of a man who has divorced his wife because of adultery. We are confronted with the classic alternative of the history of interpretation that is constituted on the one side by the Catholic prohibition of a second marriage and on the other by the possibility of such a marriage granted by Erasmus and the Orthodox and Protestant interpretation.[55] The wording of v. 9 offers no basis for a decision one way or the other. At the very least the possibility appears to remain open that a man who has divorced his wife on the justifiable grounds of adultery may marry another. Matthew 5:32 was clearer on this point. From the prohibition expressed there against marrying a divorced woman one could arrive indirectly, by expanding the prohibition to

divorced men, at the impossibility of a second marriage following divorce.[56]

There is much to be said for interpreting 19:9 as 5:32. (a) If we understand "and marries another" ($\kappa\alpha\grave{\iota}$ $\gamma\alpha\mu\acute{\eta}\sigma\eta$ $\breve{\alpha}\lambda\lambda\eta\nu$) as a general prohibition of remarriage for the divorced man, then 5:32b and 19:9 complement one another. The prohibition of remarriage for a divorced man in 19:9 corresponds to the prohibition in 5:32 against marrying a divorced woman.[57] (b) The almost unanimous history of interpretation in the ancient church speaks for the "Catholic" interpretation.[58] This "hard" interpretation of v. 9, which completely alters the Jewish divorce law, makes the negative reaction of the disciples in v. 10 more understandable. If that is the case, then the "divorce" of the wife in the case of adultery is for all practical purposes a "separation."[59] The situation is similar for Hermas, who categorically forbids a second marriage and designates as $\mathring{\alpha}\pi o\lambda\acute{v}\epsilon\iota\nu$[60] "separation" without the possibility of a new marriage.[61]

It is thus clear that the view of marriage in Matthew's church, in spite of the introduction of the unchastity clause, probably is not essentially different from that of Jesus. Jesus declares divorce to be fundamentally inimi-

---

intercourse with his wife if she has engaged in illicit sexual activity (*S. Deut.* 24.1 § 269 = Str–B 1.313; *m. Soṭa* 5.1 = Str–B 1.321).

53 *Hermas, Man.* 4.1.4–8 = 29:4-8 (here, to be sure, with the possibility that the wife repents and returns to the husband). For further sources see vol. 1, II A 2.2.3 on 5:32, n. 47.

54 Ἐπέτρεψεν is not necessarily a counterargument. While it is true that according to v. 8 divorce is generally a "concession" of Moses, the exception clause of v. 9 appears within a commandment of Jesus.

55 Cf. vol. 1, II A 2.2.3 where I discussed the history of interpretation of 5:31-32.

56 Cf. vol. 1, A 2.2.3 on the history of interpretation, the Catholic position. A number of witnesses have inserted the prohibition of Matt 5:32b into v. 9 (cf. above, n. 3). The most likely possibility (but it is no more than a possibility) is that the manuscripts that omit καὶ γαμήσῃ ἄλλην permit a man who is divorced because of his wife's adultery to enter a second marriage with a woman who has not been divorced (thus in different ways, e.g., in f¹, P²⁵, B, and C*).

57 Thus especially Jacques Dupont, *Mariage et divorce dans L'Évangile* (Bruges: Desclée de Brouwer, 1959) 75–157).

58 Cf. vol. 1, II A 2.2.3, nn. 51–53.

59 Here the conversation with my Catholic partner P. Hoffmann is a dialogue with reversed fronts. While I, the Protestant, am inclined *exegetically* to the "Catholic" position, the Catholic P. Hoffmann, along with many other Catholic exegetes and moral theologians, represents the opposing "Erasmic" position. He writes: "In both versions the clause nullifies the rule of Jesus 'remarriage = adultery' that is elsewhere valid. That is to say, however, that where adultery has occurred, remarriage is not automatically adultery."

60 While ἀπολύω is not the usual term for "divorce," it is possible. 1 Εσδρ 9:36; *Les Grotte de Murrabb at* no. 115.4 = DJD 2.248. The word also appears the same way in the use of our logion in *Hermas, Man.* 4.1.6–7 (= 29.6–7). Thus in Hermas ἀπολύω does not mean "to separate" in the sense of the *separatio tori et mensae*; instead it derives this meaning from the context.

61 In all of his publications Gordon J. Wenham ("Matthew and Divorce: An Old Crux Revisited," 95–107, and "The Syntax of Matthew 19:9," 17–23) argues on behalf of this thesis that 19:9 is a summarizing and abbreviated version of 5:31-32. I do not find this argument convincing, since 5:32b deals

493

cal to God; for him marriage is for a lifetime. Matthew and his church do not negate this principle of Jesus; they simply are convinced, in agreement with a widespread Jewish halakah, that there is one case in which the husband may not maintain the marriage—viz., the case of his wife's unchastity or adultery. In such a case the husband must send his wife away. This Matthean possibility of separation, however, is completely different from the Jewish divorce whose purpose is to make remarriage possible. Even for the rigorous Jewish representatives of Shammai's school, adultery destroys a marriage, and the partners are free to remarry.[62] For Matthew and his church marriage is part of the created order and reflects "Adam's" primal existence (Gen 1:27), and as such it may not be annulled. It remains indissoluble, even when the husband must send his wife away because of unchastity.

Jesus and the Essene Understanding of Marriage

Jesus' view of marriage and the view of the Matthean church that he influenced are thus similar to the Essene understanding. Outside the Essene community there are only scattered tendencies in the direction of marriage for life. The most important text here is Mal 2:10-16. It may be that in Judaism only the Essenes required marriage for life in a programmatic sense. It is relatively certain that the biblical basis of marriage for them was Gen 1:17; 7:9; and Deut 17:17 (CD 4:2-5:2).[63] It is also certain that some among the Essenes regarded marriage for the propagation of children as an obligation (Josephus Bell. 2.160-61). What is controversial is whether the inner group of Essenes was celibate. In his thorough eyewitness report Josephus speaks of their "lack of respect"

($\dot{\upsilon}\pi\epsilon\rho o\psi\acute{\iota}\alpha$) for marriage (Bell. 2.120–21) but not of celibacy. He does that only in the more abbreviated report in Ant. 18.21.[64] Present-day Qumran scholarship is split on the issue. According to some, the residents of Qumran were committed to the principle of celibacy in contrast to the Essenes who lived in the land of Israel outside the cloister.[65] Others are of the opinion that it is inconceivable that a Jewish group faithful to the Torah would have fundamentally rejected the obligation to marry. For them the "disrespect" for marriage about which Josephus speaks is due to the fact that for all practical purposes the strict purity regulations required the wives of the Qumran Essenes to live outside the "cloister" and that probably the majority of the men in the cloister were still unmarried or were widowers or even divorced men who thus could not marry again.[66] In any case, a look at the Essenes reveals that with their understanding of lifetime marriage and their prohibition against remarriage they constituted a legitimate parallel to Matt 19:3-9. Whether the Qumran Essenes can also be cited as a parallel to a strict celibacy in the sense of Matt 19:12 is much more uncertain.

Meaning for Today

As a Protestant exegete I am confronted with a difficult situation. The exegesis shows that in all probability (one cannot say more than that) the Catholic practice of refusing divorce while allowing the partners to have separate living arrangements comes the closest to Matthew's intention. Unfortunately, in all probability Jesus also did not resist trying "to regulate matters of the

---

with the divorced woman, while 19:9b speaks to the divorced man.

62   Characteristically, the rabbis advise against a second marriage not on principle but for pragmatic reasons. Cf. Str–B 1.320–21.

63   CD 4.21 speaks of the lifetime of the man (בחייהם) rather than of the lifetime of the woman. (A different judgment is in vol. 1, II A 2.2.3, n. 14 where along with many others I conjectured the existence of a scribal error.) In the pre-Qumran Temple Scroll, on the other hand, only polygamy is forbidden the king; remarriage after the death of his first wife is permitted (11QT 57.17–19).

64   The reports of Philo (Apology = Eusebius Praep. ev. 8.11.14) and Pliny (Hist. nat. 5.17) that presuppose that the Essenes were basically celibate have less

value, since they are not the reports of eyewitnesses.

65   Thus most recently Elisha Qimron, "Celibacy in the Dead Sea Scrolls and the Two Kinds of Sectarians," in Julio Trebolle Barrera and Luis Vegas Montaner, eds., The Madrid Qumran Congress: Proceedings of the International Congress on the Dead Sea Scrolls, 18–21 March 1991 (Studies on the Texts of the Desert of Judah 11/1; Leiden: Brill, 1992) 287–94. According to Qimron the Qumran Essenes regarded Jerusalem as their "camp" where sexual activity was forbidden (cf. CD 12.1–2). This prohibition was not in effect for the other Essene settlements.

66   Thus most recently Hartmut Stegemann, The Library of Qumran: On the Essenes, Qumran, John the Baptist and Jesus (Grand Rapids: Eerdmans, 1998) 193–98.

heart by means of laws,"[67] but decisively established a fundamental principle.[68] The usual practice in Protestant churches, which appears to set no limits on multiple church weddings, is far removed from this principle. Our text is strikingly unmodern and is at odds with a landscape that is characterized on the one hand by the demand for individual fulfillment and by experiments with new forms of cohabitation and on the other hand by marital difficulties and high rates of divorce.

As a biblical scholar and theologian shall I wag a scolding finger and advocate returning to our beginnings? I cannot do that without first acknowledging that the times have really and irrevocably changed. Marriage based on love between two adults has taken the place of an arranged marriage involving juveniles. The socially isolated nuclear family has taken the place of life in a larger extended family. The average human life span is about double that of antiquity; thus the average length of a marriage has also at least doubled.[69] Modern history is a history of increasing individualization that we cannot and may not reverse. As a consequence, people bring different and higher expectations to marriage today. Furthermore, in Jewish, ancient, and Christian-European history, marriage is at the very least one of the more subtle institutions of patriarchal domination, and it is our task to overcome this domination. For all of these reasons many people today no longer regard marriage for life as a self-evident institution. It is viable only when two people choose it and want it to be so.

In this context the Matthean texts on marriage are of little help. They presuppose a reality of marriage that differs from our own. They are formulated from a male point of view, address only male hearers, and are therefore one-sided and partisan—a reality that is clear when they ignore the situation of divorced women[70] or when they completely ignore the husband's adultery. In Matthew it appears that only women commit adultery and only men divorce. It is true that the texts take a step in the direction of equality by considerably sharpening the standards for men, but their goal is not the equal treatment of husband and wife, even in the sense of contemporary Hellenistic society. Thus the experiences and difficulties of modern people, including persons involved in pastoral care, receive little attention in Matthew's texts on marriage.

That observation brings me to a second point. As an exegete I cannot speak a word of warning on behalf of the texts without also posing critical questions to the texts themselves. Does Jesus really take seriously the social and psychological situation of his contemporaries? (I am thinking here primarily, but not solely, of the situation of the divorced woman.) Is Matthew's fear that the old and new husband will be defiled by a wife's extramarital sexual activity more than a relic of Jewish-priestly purity concerns?[71] Has Jesus really considered the implications for marriage of what was for him the central reality—God's love for all people, including disadvantaged women? The legalistic description of every divorce and of every marriage of divorced persons as adultery can become a dangerous generalization and is in danger of ignoring the actual person.

If Jesus' prohibition of divorce is not to remain an ascetic or a Qumran-like remnant in his proclamation, we must understand it in the context of his total activity. We cannot speak of Jesus' prohibition of marriage, for example, without telling the story of the adulteress in John 7:53-8:11. Only in this way can we ensure that Jesus' principle, encompassed is it were in divine and human love, becomes a good law. We must, however, also remember that the earliest Christians were remarkably flexible in dealing with Jesus' principle and were not reluctant to adapt and to change it. Among such changes is not only Matthew's exception-clause but also Paul's regulations for mixed marriages (1 Cor 7:12-16), and especially Hermas's insistence that women and men (!) who have committed adultery be permitted to return to their spouses if they are repentant (*Hermas, Man.* 4.1.7–8 = 29.7–8). This last change is the most notewor-

---

67   Contra Drewermann, *Markusevangelium* 2.95.
68   Cf. vol. 1, II A 2.2.3 on 5:32, Jesus.
69   Eugen Drewermann (*Das Matthäusevangelium: Bilder der Erfüllung,* 3 vols. [Olten: Walter, 1992–95] 2.461, 473) has drastically and impressively demonstrated the historical changes in the "created order" of marriage.

70   Cf. vol. 1, II A 2.2.3 on 5:32b.
71   *S. Lv.* 21.7 (379a) = Str–B 1.3: A priest may not marry a divorced woman; *m. Yeb.* 6.4–5 = Str–B 1.3: A high priest may not even marry a widow.

thy, since it reflects Jesus' spirit of unlimited forgiveness. Its tension with Deut 24:4, and probably also with Matthew, is palpable.

In my judgment, therefore, when we want to formulate the meaning of the divorce prohibitions for the present day, we must look at the center and at the whole of the New Testament. It seems to me that the Catholic divorce law, close as it is to the substance of Matthew's position, does not do justice to the New Testament at an essential point. In the New Testament we can see precisely with Jesus' prohibition of divorce an amazing process of adaptation and change for which even Matt 5:32 and 19:9 give evidence. Catholic ecclesiastical law, on the other hand, has for the past thousand years no longer taken into consideration the changed human situation, so that the early Christian principles have ossified into statements of law.

On the other hand, it is clear from the New Testament that not all institutions are relative and situationally conditioned. There are good and divinely ordained orders, and among them are especially marriage and family. When I try to think through this reality in terms of the middle of the New Testament, I do not simply want to distinguish between "orders of creation" and other institutions; I would rather ask to what degree an institution might be a vessel for the center of New Testament ethics, the "law of Christ" (Gal 6:2)—viz., for love.[72] Thus in terms of the New Testament I do not want simply to sanctify marriage as a Christian principle; I want to understand it as an exceptional instrument of love.[73] Can the monogamous marriage based on trustworthi-

ness and a long-term commitment[74] still be—or perhaps one should say, again be—such an exceptional instrument of love? In my judgment this is the critical question that the New Testament poses to the troubled churches in a completely open society, be they tradition-bound or almost totally open to change.

History of Interpretation

■ **10-12** The conversation with the disciples which follows in vv. 10-12 is important in the history of the church, because it is one of the classic texts for the "evangelical counsel" concerning the single life, and it plays a major role in the discussion of celibacy. A number of modern Catholic interpreters use the text to claim that celibacy is grounded in the gospel:

> The celibacy desired by Jesus has nothing to do with the ideal of abstinence. . . . (It) is not based on a low view of sexuality or of marriage. . . . Its goal is to ensure that all of one's energy will be devoted to the Kingdom of God . . . (Those who choose celibacy) have a high regard for marriage . . . and they willingly forego it so that they can be claimed by a kingdom that invites them to leave everything in order to follow Christ.[75]

In order to be authentic, celibacy must be a sign of the "effective dynamic" of the kingdom of God; it must be preceded by "the overwhelming experience" of "the presence of the Lordship of God."[76] Only infrequently these days do Catholic interpreters still use our text as a basis for the permanency of celibacy, overcoming sexual desires, or the elevated position of the unmarried life "in the hierarchy of values" in the kingdom of God.[77]

---

72   I am not able, therefore, to find the theological basis of the indissolubility of monogamous marriage in the created order as do Matt 19:4 and Mark 10:6, and I have reservations about one marriage for life as a "created order" as is done, e.g., on the Protestant side by Emil Brunner (*The Divine Imperative* [Philadelphia: Westminster, 1947] 340–50), Werner Elert (*The Christian Ethos* [Philadelphia: Muhlenberg, 1957] 93), Helmut Thielicke (*Theological Ethics* [Grand Rapids: Eerdmans, 1981] 3.104–5, 108–9); and, on the Catholic side, e.g., by M. Kaiser, in Joseph Listl, Hubert Müller, and Heribert Schmitz, eds., *Handbuch des katholischen Kirchenrechts* (Regensburg: Pustet, 1983) 730–31; *Catechism* nos. 1603–5, 1660. Such an understanding always appeals to Matt 19:3-9 (exegetically accurately, of

course), but we may isolate this text from the entirety of the New Testament.

73   I have for marriage, therefore, an understanding similar to that of Thomas Aquinas for the gospel counsels of the single life and of poverty. Cf. below, IV C 3 nn. 97–99. In my judgment marriage and the single life are equally "instruments of perfection" or charismata.

74   Thus not a solitary marriage for life!

75   Jean Galot, "La motivation évangélique du célibat," *Greg* 53 (1972) 731–58, 756–57.

76   Segalla, "Il testo," 137; Francis J. Moloney, "Matthew 19:3-12 and Celibacy: A Redactional and Form Critical Study," 42–60, 53.

77   Gamba, "'Eunuchia,'" 262, 265 (quotation), 283–84.

Protestant interpreters show an amazing lack of interest in this text.

In the ancient church Matt 19:11-12 played only a minor role, and then primarily to justify sexual abstinence. It was not until the Middle Ages that these verses became the cardinal text for the "evangelical counsel" concerning chastity (1). The reasons for the ancient church's reserve toward Matt 19:11-12 lie in its aversion to eunuchs[78] and in the necessity of resisting a literal interpretation of the text. Our text led Origen and others to castrate themselves.[79] A more general reason for the church's reserve was the desire to resist the exaggerated ascetic tendencies that Matt 19:11-12 occasioned. The church's "virgins" were not regarded as persons who were especially perfect and whose place in heaven is superior to that of God's other sons and daughters.[80] Even the spiritual interpretation of our text is an attempt to avoid a literal understanding and to resist ascetic tendencies (2). The text played a larger role later in the time of the Reformation, when it was caught up in the swirl of interconfessional polemics about the value of monastic vows and of celibacy (3).

Most of the church's interpreters anticipate the modern exegetical insight that *the third type of eunuch is to be interpreted symbolically*. All three types practice abstinence. In the first two cases, however, their abstinence is natural or necessary; only the third kind of abstinence is a gift of grace (*per gratiam*) or a virtue (*virtuosa*),[81] since according to Clement of Alexandria a true eunuch is not the one who is not capable of sexual intercourse but the one who does not desire it.[82] Most widespread has been the figurative interpretation in the sense of sexual asceticism. We find it, for example, in the Gnostics or in the Syrian itinerant ascetics, the "virgins" of the pseudo-Clementine letters.[83] However, many people in the mainstream church also understand Matt 19:12 as recommending sexual abstinence.[84] For Augustine it is the "priceless pearl" for which the disciples sacrifice everything.[85] In order to place limits on asceticism the church's interpreters are often cautious with our text, and they frequently emphasize that "it is not for everybody." Both Clement of Alexandria and his gnostic opponent Valentine warn against compulsive sexual asceticism based on our text.[86] The church's official monasticism is also very cautious about an exaggerated sexual asceticism.[87] Early on it is clearly stated that virginity is not a command for everybody.[88] Reflecting this caution, one understood Matt 19:12 to be recommending virginity rather than requiring it.[89] To be sure, it was not until the High Middle Ages that chastity based on Matt 19:12 became one of the three

---

78 Even today eunuchs cannot become clerics. The decree of the Council of Nicæa, based on Lev 21:20-21 and Deut 23:1-2 (DS[36] No. 128a) remains valid today (*Codex iuris canonici* canon 1041 No. 5).

79 On Origen cf. Eusebius *Hist. eccl.* 6.8.1–3. On others in the ancient church who castrated themselves cf. Bauer, "Mt 19,12," 257–58. On the ancient church's caution cf. ibid., 261–62. Since the eighteenth century Matt 19:12 has also been interpreted literally by the Russian sect of the Skoptsy, who saw in castration the only way to enter the kingdom of heaven.

80 Thus Ps.-Clement *Ep. ad virg.* 1.4. Cf. Cyprian *De habitu virginum* 23 = *PL* 4.475–76.

81 Dionysius the Carthusian (214) who represents the "normal exegesis" in a brief, pregnant form. Cf. John Chrysostom (62.3 = *PG* 58.599) who claims that the issue is removing evil thoughts.

82 *Paed.* 3.4 (26.3) = FC 23.221.

83 Clement of Alexandria *Strom.* 3.1 (1.4) = FC 85.256 (Basilidians); ibid., 3.13 (91.2) = 313 (Julius Cassianus); Ps.-Clement *Ep. ad virgines* 1.1.

84 Characteristic examples, e.g., are Tertullian *Mon.* 3 = ANF 4.60; John Chrysostom *Virg.* 49.7 = SC 125.280, 282. Ambrose *Vid.* 13 = 75 = *PL* 16.257–58.

85 *Conf.* 8.1 = FC 21.198.

86 *Strom.* 3.1 (2.1) = FC 85.256 (Valentine: Those who struggle day and night against sexual temptation and who are always afraid that they will not be able to resist it are better off avoiding the celibate life); 3.6 (45–52) = FC 85.284–91 (Clement). In this context Clement also shares the information, based on Phil 4:2, that Paul was also married (*Strom.* 3.6 [53.1–2] = FC 85.289). This idea was circulated widely in the reformers' polemic against celibacy (cf. below, n. 100). Bauer ("Mt 19,12," 262) offers further evidence for a polemic against an ascetic interpretation of 19:12.

87 Matt 19:12 appears neither in Basil's rules nor in the Benedictine rules. Cf. Burchill, "Evangelical Counsels," 248.

88 John Chrysostom *In Tit* 1.2 = *PG* 62.666; ibid. *In 1 Cor.* 21.5 = *PG* 61.176; Afrahat, 18.9 = Bert, 297. Often Matt 19:12 is cited in connection with Matt 19:21.

89 Since Ambrose *Exhort. virg.* 3.17–18 = *PL* 16.341–42; ibid. *Vid.* 13.75 = *PL* 16.257–58; cf. Jerome *Jov.* 1.12 (= 256–57) = *PL* 23.238. Later the connection became important with Paul's advice in 1 Cor 7:25.

classic "evangelical counsels," that are instruments of love's perfection.[90] Occasionally Matt 19:12 has also been connected with the idea of reward and payment.[91] Relating "because of the Kingdom of heaven" (διὰ τὴν βασιλείαν τῶν οὐρανῶν) to the eschatological kingdom of heaven with an instrumental sense has resulted in a disastrous interpretation. Virginity is then a means for achieving the kingdom of heaven.[92]

To be sure, sporadically, especially in Greek exegesis, all three eunuch types have been interpreted allegorically. This approach made it possible to apply the text to areas other than marriage and abstinence. To be a eunuch then generally means not to be able to bear fruit.[93] The natural eunuchs, for example, can be those who by nature are good.[94] Those who have been castrated are, for example, the ones who have been led astray by false teachers and philosophers or, in a positive sense, the ones who have been led to understanding and good works by human teachers.[95] Those who have become eunuchs for the sake of the kingdom of God, for example, are the ones who have come to understanding simply by reading the Word of God.[96] Understood this way, v. 12 can even be useful in Protestant exegesis, since even for married persons there is the possibility of castrating one's self and serving the gospel.[97] Here the allegorical interpretation provides an exegetical escape from the text.

Since the *Reformation* the main issue for the interpretation of the text has been what value one should put on unmarried life. The interpretations influenced by the Reformation have been less than enthusiastic about it. There are in reality very few people to whom God has given sexual abstinence.[98] The reformers warn against hasty monastic vows[99] and emphasize freedom, claiming that the unmarried life in reality is not a *praeceptum*; it is only a *permissio*.[100] It is also emphasized that sexual abstinence is for the purpose of serving the apostolic task and that it therefore was intended primarily for the apostles and not for Christians of all times.[101]

The Catholics mount a sharp attack against this Protestant caution. They claim that chastity is not simply a condition; it is a virtue that has a tremendous value all its own.[102] It is specious to point out that most people do not have the gift of abstinence; one must be worthy of such gifts of God, "because only through experience can someone know whether he has the gift of chastity."[103] Historically it was significant that the Council of Trent, relying on 1 Corinthians 7 and Matt 19:12, continued to maintain that virginity is "better and happier" than marriage.[104] Still, with all of the controversy the agreement on at least one point demonstrates that we are dealing here not with dramatically opposing positions but with different emphases. Even the Catholics agree that

---

90 Cf. below, IV C 3 on the history of interpretation, no. 2.

91 By and large this development took place slowly. An example is Christian of Stavelot, 1414 (in addition to eternal life the virgins receive *condigna retributio*).

92 Maldonat, 387: "Ad regnum coelorum promerendum," with an appeal to Origen, Hilary, Chrysostom, Euthymius; and the *Opus imperfectum*. Lapide (366), on the other hand, understands *propter regnum coelorum* in the usual Protestant sense: "ut expeditiores sint ad praedicandum Evangelium."

93 Clement of Alexandria *Strom.* 3.15 (99.1) = FC 85.318: A "eunuch" is someone who "is sterile in relation to truth."

94 Gregory of Nazianzus *Or.* 37.20 = *PG* 36.305; Peter of Laodicea, 213 (those who by nature are rational); HbrMt = Howard, 95 (those who have not sinned).

95 In a negative sense, Origen 15.4 = GCS Origenes 10.358; Jerome ad loc. Basilides the Gnostic (in Clement of Alexandria *Strom.* 3.1 [1.4] = FC 85.256) has a somewhat different understanding: "Hypocrites" are those who are ascetic in order to show off). In the positive sense see Gregory of Nazianzus *Or.* 37.20 = *PG* 36.305; Euthymius Zigabenus, 520; Theophylactus, 353.

96 Origen, 15.4 = GCS Origenes 10.358; Euthymius

Zigabenus, 520.; Theophylactus, 353 (those who instruct themselves).

97 Calovius, 360.

98 Luther 2.651: "They are scarce people. One will not find one in a thousand."

99 Calvin 2.248–49; *Inst.* 4.13.17.

100 Bullinger, 180A; Brenz, 617: "Non est legem ponere, sed libertatem concedere."

101 The view is formulated most clearly by Zwingli, who claims that the apostles are unmarried because they have so much work to do for the kingdom of God (316). Zwingli makes Paul into the prototype (in the positive sense) of the Protestant pastor or professor of theology who "tot . . . laboribus fatigatus totque periculis exercitus, raro apud uxorem erat," "tametsi uxorem haberet." One wonders whether an "evangelical counsel" would not be justified in such a case (but not that of Matt 19:12)!

102 Maldonat, 387: The Calvinists say that celibacy, like fasting, is in and of itself neither good nor bad. Should we say the same thing about the immoderation that is the opposite of fasting? Lapide (366) calls celibacy "virtus . . . , suique victoria" and continues: "mentem attolit ad celestia meditanda . . . ex hominibus facit Angelos."

103 Maldonat, 387 (my translation).

abstinence is a gift of God rather than an accomplishment, and they like to quote Augustine: "Domine, da quod iubes, et iube quod vis. Iubes continentiam, da continentiam."[105]

Interpretation

Given the history of interpretation, the main question for exegesis is to what degree and in what sense vv. 11-12 can serve as the basis for monastic or priestly celibacy. It is precisely this question that is once again controversial. We have essentially two opposing types of interpretation that relate vv. 11-12 to the context in completely different ways. Their main difference lies in the way they understand the λόγος οὗτος of v. 11. What is this word that not everyone can grasp?

1. The representatives of the traditional *"celibacy interpretation"*[106] as a rule relate v. 11 to the following logion, v. 12a-c. They read the text as if a colon followed v. 11. The two logia that speak of "grasping" (vv. 11, 12d) provide a framework around the eunuch saying. Verses 10-12 constitute then a relatively self-contained unit that, after the section on marriage is concluded, deals with a new subject, with a different way—the way of the unmarried life. According to this view, v. 10 is a transitional verse. The disciples think that if monogamy "is enforced that severely, it is better to avoid marriage." Jesus, who must "have been irritated at the disciples' naive statement, lets it . . . stand" and "uses it as a welcome occasion to make a saying" that "has little to do with" what was said in vv. 3-9.[107] Indeed, *in this interpretation the disciples' comment in v. 10 can carry even greater weight. It can be the "word" (λόγος) to which Jesus refers.*[108] In this case with his comment he affirms it, limiting its scope, while at the same time surpassing it with his reference to the kingdom of heaven. In either case v. 12c

carries special weight. Not only are there people who are born eunuchs or who are eunuchs because of human intervention; there are also "eunuchs" for the sake of the kingdom of God, and that is something worth "grasping"!

2. The representatives of the "marriage interpretation"[109] relate "this word" (λόγος οὗτος) back to v. 9. Only those persons can "grasp" this word of Jesus about divorce to whom God has granted it. The representatives of this interpretation say that v. 9 is so difficult because a separation caused by unchastity is not, as it is for the Pharisees and the rest of Judaism, for the purpose of making remarriage possible. Instead, the divorced partners must remain unmarried. The disciples' indignation may not have been very noble, but at least they understood what was at stake. Jesus says that only those persons have room for this word for whom God makes that possible. Verse 12 serves as justification (γάρ): There are eunuchs for the sake of the kingdom of heaven! Verse 12d then summons the hearers once again to make room for the word of Jesus prohibiting the remarriage of separated persons. This interpretation attributes no independent importance to v. 12. Verses 10-12 are a Matthean addition that serves to underscore Jesus' word about the sanctity and indissolubility of monogamous marriage.

Matthew

■ **10-11** Let us try to interpret the text on Matthew's level. With v. 10 the Pharisees appear to have disappeared;[110] Jesus is talking to the disciples. After he has just spoken so highly of marriage in vv. 3-9, their comment that it would be better to remain single seems rather inappropriate. It is not clear why they prefer not to marry. Is it because one must remain single if the first

104 DS[16] 1810.
105 Lapide (365) following Augustine (*Conf.* 6.11).
106 Its classic representative is Blinzler, "Εἰσὶν εὐνοῦχοι." Schmid (279–80) has been very influential. D. W. Trautman's special examination (*The Eunuch Logion of Matthew 19:12: Historical and Exegetical Dimensions as Related to Celibacy*) is also worth mentioning. On the Protestant side Kurt Niederwimmer (*Askese und Mysterium*, 54–58) is especially helpful. Allison ("Divorce," 5–6) is the most recent representative of this view.
107 Quotations in Wellhausen, 96–97.
108 Thus Allen, 205; B. Weiss, 337; Gamba, "'Eunuchia,'" 257; Craig L. Blomberg, "Marriage, Divorce, Remarriage and Celibacy: An Exegesis of Mt 19:3-12," 161–96, 184.
109 A forerunner of this interpretation is Zahn, 584. Dupont (*Mariage*, 161–220) is its most important "father." Other important representatives are Quentin Quesnell ("'Made Themselves Eunuchs for the Kingdom of Heaven' [Mt 19:12]," 335–58) and Burchill ("Evangelical Counsels," 92–134).
110 That Matthew does not mention their departure shows one more time how little he is interested in his narrative's superficial coherence. Cf. above, III C 1.2 on the analysis of 14:1-12.

marriage fails? Or is it because Jesus' command is too severe for them? It is clear that the wife's perspective again is no more a factor here than it is in the entire pericope.[111] Usually αἰτία is interpreted in terms of the Latin *causa*: If that's the way it is for a man and a woman . . .[112] Jesus does not reprove the disciples for their comment; he says: "Not everyone has room for this word." Χωρέω (literally: "to make room," "contain") can mean intellectual understanding. It may be, however, that Matthew, who ordinarily uses συνιέναι for "understanding," gives it a broader meaning that includes agreement and willing obedience.[113] Λόγον with the demonstrative pronoun τοῦτον referring to what has preceded, which probably was already in the original text, most likely refers to what has been said.[114] But to what exactly? In my judgment, the word of the disciples is not an option since, first of all, nowhere else in the Gospel of Matthew is a statement of the disciples given that importance.[115] In the second place, it is in tension with the word of Jesus in vv. 3-9 that spoke of valid marriage rather than of the unmarried life. In the third place, the disciples' comment bases the desirability of sexual abstinence on the difficulties of marriage and not on the kingdom of heaven, as will be the case in v. 12. Thus the λόγος may be v. 9 or possibly even all of vv. 3-9. In my judgment, in a society that understood the sense of divorce essentially to be to make remarriage possible and that regarded divorce as a privilege granted to Israel (that is, to Israel's men) but not to the Gentiles, that kind of harsh reaction from the men who were affected is completely understandable, without concluding from the absence of a

rebuke from Jesus that the evangelist or his implied readers approved of it. The disciples' reaction gives Jesus an occasion to expand his "word" (λόγος; v. 9). It is obvious from their masculine, human reaction that not every man is capable of making room for Jesus' marriage halakah in his own life. That requires a special grace of God.[116] Obviously, as v. 12 shows, the difficulty lies in the sexual abstinence that Jesus demands after the first marriage "for the sake of the kingdom of God."[117]

■ 12 Thus far our interpretation has clearly tended in the direction of the second of the alternatives that we have outlined above. However, its difficulties become obvious when we come now to v. 12, which Matthew adds in support of what has been said. At first glance the verse does not fit badly in the context. In pre-Christian sources "eunuchs" are not simply unmarried persons.[118] According to rabbinic texts, they can also be married; they simply are not able to beget children.[119] In that sense it is quite appropriate to compare with eunuchs those members of the church who have to divorce their wives because of adultery and who are not free to remarry and to produce children with a new wife. Thus those who by grace remain unmarried out of obedience to Jesus' command are "eunuchs for the sake of the kingdom of heaven." At the same time, however, it becomes clear that v. 12a-c does not justify v. 11 very well.[120] The distinction between the "eunuchs for the sake of the kingdom of heaven" and the "normal" eunuchs has no relevance, if from v. 9 on the text has been talking about remaining unmarried for the sake of the kingdom of God; in this use of the logion 12a and

---

111 Cf. Lagrange, 373: "L'expression respire la mauvaise humeur de l'homme, habitué à traiter la femme à sa guise." Lohmeyer (282) is of the opinion that the comment applies equally well to a Don Juan and to a misogynist.

112 There is no real evidence for this Latinism, and the reference back to v. 3 is superficial, because the meaning of αἰτία is different. Still, there is no real alternative to this interpretation.

113 Χωρέω with the infinitive means "to be able." (For sources see Dupont, *Mariage,* 178.) In the case of arrangements or terms it means "to accept" (see LSJ, *s.v.*).

114 The backward-looking demonstrative pronoun οὗτος, which in the NT has largely replaced the forward-looking ὅδε, sometimes can also look forward.

But in the almost formulaic connection with λόγος in Matthew οὗτος *always* refers to what has preceded: 7:24, 26, 28; 19:1, 22; 26:1; 28:15.

115 That is, however, the case with words of Jesus. Cf. 13:11, the closest parallel to 19:11!

116 Δέδοται is *passivum divinum,* as in 13:11. The conversation with the disciples about possessions in 19:23-26 has a similar progression. Cf. the reference to the grace of God in v. 26.

117 The possible analogy in Qumran (above, n. 66) could show that such cases were not infrequent.

118 It is more the case that this meaning of the word resulted from Matt 19:12. From Athenagoras on (*Suppl.* 33) παρθενία and εὐνουχία are synonyms.

119 *M. Yeb.* 8.4 = Str-B 1.806. *B. Yeb.* 80b (= ibid.) compares the eunuch from birth with the barren wife.

12b are superfluous. The expression "because of the Kingdom of heaven" ($\delta\iota\grave{\alpha}\ \tau\grave{\eta}\nu\ \beta\alpha\sigma\iota\lambda\epsilon\acute{\iota}\alpha\nu\ \tau\hat{\omega}\nu\ o\mathring{v}\rho\alpha\nu\hat{\omega}\nu$) refers only very obliquely to the grace about which v. 11b spoke; v. 12 points in a direction different from that of v. 11b. Furthermore, Jesus based his prohibition of divorce not on the kingdom of God but on the order of creation. And, finally, it is more likely that Jesus' statement that there "are" ($\epsilon\mathring{\iota}\sigma\acute{\iota}\nu$) eunuchs for the sake of the kingdom of God poses sexual abstinence as a general possibility while Matthew, on the other hand, is talking about what a particular group of people—viz., the married men who are separated from their wives—with the help of God's grace *must* do. For precisely this reason he emphasizes the point once more with v. 12d. Those who henceforth are to live without sexual activity should seize this possibility also.

The interpretation of this text as an addition to the marriage command of v. 9 (= type b, above) may correspond to Matthew's intention, but the logion of v. 12 goes beyond the earlier verse. Our source analysis corresponds to this conclusion. Verse 12 is a traditional logion that may come from Jesus, one which Matthew obviously made use of in a specific way, perhaps narrowing its scope. But what is its original meaning? Of course, to answer that question we must completely ignore its present context.[121]

Jesus

The logion lists three different groups of eunuchs. Jesus makes use of a common Jewish division. The group of eunuchs "from the mother's womb"[122] corresponds to the rabbinic סָרִיסֵי חַמָּה (eunuchs of the sun) or to the סָרִיסֵי שָׁמַיִם (eunuchs of heaven), while the group who are made eunuchs by people corresponds to the rabbinic סָרִיסֵי אָדָם (eunuchs of men).[123] The first group shows that not only castrated persons are regarded as eunuchs but also those who are naturally impotent. Eunuchs are universally despised and ridiculed, especially in Judaism, because they cannot fulfill God's command to beget children.[124] In addition, people castrated by human hands have a bad reputation, because in heathen cults (for example, Cybele, Dea Syria) there were castrated priests, while in Judaism there was a strong prohibition of castration.

Now after the mention of these two well-known groups of eunuchs there is a surprise in the logion's third part. A new, unknown group of eunuchs appears— viz., those who castrate themselves because of the kingdom of God. Of what kind of people could that be a description in Jesus' surroundings? We hear nothing of actual castration in the Jesus movement. It is probable, however, that John the Baptist, Jesus himself, and some of his disciples were not married.[125] The other disciples, as long as they are on the road with Jesus, do not live with their families. They are not eunuchs (סָרִיסִים) in the rabbinic sense of the word. Jesus' married disciples did not live permanently without their wives. Jesus and John the Baptist chose to remain unmarried without being eunuchs in the physical sense. It was regarded as strange

---

120 Sand (*Reich Gottes*) also observes that this interpretation takes seriously the sequence of vv. 9-11 but does not do justice to v. 12. According to him, therefore, v. 11 refers back to v. 9. However, he understands v. 12 not as justifying v. 11, but as going beyond it. He claims that the "inconvenience" of the severe marriage instruction (v. 10) points "to the even greater challenge to forgo marriage" (54, 58–59; quotation, 59). But he ignores $\gamma\acute{\alpha}\rho$, and he leaves the reference back to v. 9 hanging in the air.

121 Moloney ("Matthew 19:3-12," 43–52) also assumes that both types of interpretation have their place in the tradition history: interpretation a with Jesus and interpretation b with Matthew.

122 A biblical expression: Judg 16:17; Job 38:8; Pss 21:10 (LXX) and 70:6 (LXX); Isa 49:1.

123 Str-B 1.805–7.

124 According to Deut 23:1-2 eunuchs are not permitted in the cultic community, but according to Isa 56:3-5 and Wis 3:14 things will be different in the future. According to Josephus (*Ant.* 4.290–91) one should avoid eunuchs who cannot fulfill the command to beget children and who have feminine souls and bodies. On the ridicule of and disrespect for eunuchs in the Roman world cf. Hug, "Eunuchen," PWSup 3.453–54. Lucian (*Eun.* 6) gives an example of that kind of ridicule: Eunuchs should be excluded from temples and public events. Such creatures with a mixture of man and woman are $\mathring{\epsilon}\xi\omega$ $\tau\hat{\eta}\varsigma\ \mathring{\alpha}\nu\theta\rho\omega\pi\epsilon\acute{\iota}\alpha\varsigma\ \phi\acute{v}\sigma\epsilon\omega\varsigma$.

125 According to the Montanist Tertullian, all of the apostles except Peter were unmarried (*Mon.* 8 =

that the men in the Jesus community gave up their married life.[126] It is possible that hostile opponents insulted them as "eunuchs"—that is, as riffraff who were no better than the priests of Cybele and heathen courtiers.[127] In that case Jesus took up this pejorative term for that very reason and formulated a logion not about unmarried persons (ἄγαμοι, παρθένοι) but about "eunuchs."[128] Of course, then εὐνουχίζω is to be understood figuratively, and it means to commit oneself to the unmarried life or to sexual asceticism.[129] These new-styled "eunuchs" make their decision because of the kingdom of God. Διά can mean "because of" or "for the sake of." The logion leaves open the question whether the "eunuchs" have given up their sexual life in order to enter the kingdom of God or because they are motivated by the kingdom of God. However, the open formulation "there are eunuchs," which declares that renouncing marriage and sexual life is not appropriate for everybody, speaks more for the second interpretation.

Yet even then the question remains: Why do people who have been grasped by the kingdom of God give up their married life? Do they only do it so that they can travel with Jesus and proclaim the kingdom of God?[130] Or so they will not be distracted from their work for the kingdom of God by concern for their family?[131] Or because people who have been grasped by the kingdom of God in "indescribable joy" can give their hearts nei-ther "to money and possessions" nor to family and marriage?[132] We don't really know. It seems to me that it would be most helpful to remember that according to Jesus in the kingdom of God resurrected persons "will neither marry nor be given in marriage" (Mark 12:25)—a view that in Judaism at that time was possible but not necessarily self-evident.[133] Did a certain understanding of the kingdom of God thus influence Jesus' own celibate way of life and his disciples' decision to forgo family life? If so, then it is more likely that he came out of an ascetically inclined branch of Judaism to which John the Baptist also belonged.[134] There is a general similarity with the Qumran community, which on the one hand had a strict view of marriage, yet on the other hand also neglected marriage. On the whole, we know here very little, not even whether Jesus' ascetic tendencies belonged to his roots in John the Baptist which he later partly overcame with his return to the land of Israel. In any case, it is important that Jesus, much as was later the case with Paul, did not require his followers to remain unmarried. While his logion refers positively to the existence of people who because of the kingdom of God forgo the married life, it does not call upon people to do so.[135]

ANF 4.65). Tertullian (*Mon.* 17 = ANF 4.72) refers to John the Baptist as a "eunuch of Christ."

126 Begetting sons is an obligation for Jewish men (*m. Yeb. 6.6*), and early marriage was normal—at age 18 for men and at sexual maturity for women. Harvey McArthur ("Celibacy in Judaism at the Time of Christian Beginnings," 177–80) comes to the conclusion that occasionally men may have married at an age older than 25. Single rabbis were absolutely an exception. Except for the oft-quoted Simeon ben Azzai (*m. Yeb. 8.7*), there is only one other very uncertain reference: Hanina (*b. Qidd.* 29b). Thus figures such as John the Baptist, Bannus (Josephus *Vit.* 11), Jesus, or Paul may have attracted attention. Whatever the situation may have been with the Essenes of Qumran (cf. the excursus above [on 19:9] on Jesus and the Essene understanding of marriage), the reports of Josephus and Philo shows that their unmarried lifestyle, alleged or actual, attracted the attention of outsiders, but it was very marginal in the Essene writings.

127 Thus Blinzler's attractive conjecture ("Εἰσὶν εὐνοῦχοι," 268–69).

128 Even if the choice of εὐνοῦχος/εὐνουχίζω was occasioned by a hostile insult, that of course says nothing about how long the unmarried life would last. While eunuchs in the first two groups are permanently disqualified for marriage, it can be a different matter for the "eunuchs because of the kingdom of God," as the example of Peter shows.

129 The aorist indicates a single decision. He does not say whether it is valid for one's entire life. One can compare the hyperboles in 5:29-30 and 18:8-9.

130 1 Cor. 9:5 speaks against such a view.

131 An attitude that would correspond to 1 Cor 7:32-35.

132 Blinzler, "Εἰσὶν εὐνοῦχοι," 263. It is an attractive interpretation, but it has a fundamental flaw. Why should love and sexuality not be compatible with the kingdom of God?

133 Cf. below on 22:30.

134 We know very little about such a branch. The rabbis are aware that Moses lived a celibate life after meet-

Meaning for Today

Thus the later church appropriately identified our Jesus logion with the charisma of celibacy. But this interpretation cannot be attributed to the evangelist, Matthew. By applying the old word of Jesus to the innocently divorced who may not enter a second marriage, Matthew has reduced its scope. And even in terms of Jesus' understanding we can justify a voluntary celibacy understood as a charisma but not the priestly celibacy required by the church. It also seems to me that it is not possible to find in our word justification for lifelong celibacy. Understanding celibacy as the state of perfect control of sexual concupiscence and even relating it to the celebration of mass, or relating priestly celibacy to the eschatological wedding of Christ with the church, is far removed from our logion.[136] Above all, it contradicts our logion when one makes of it a *command* that is required for certain workers in the kingdom of God— viz., the priests. To this degree Matt 19:12 provides a great deal of potential for criticizing the present Catholic practice of requiring priestly celibacy. But basically the Catholic interpretation is right when, based on Matt 19:12, it understands the voluntary unmarried life as a way of life that is influenced by the kingdom of God in a special way and thus has its own special chance and grace.[137]

Matthew 19:12 poses to Protestant Christians the question why they are so unwilling to experience something that for Jesus and for many Christians after him was good and helpful, simply because of their fear of anything that appears to be Catholic. In connection with our text Kierkegaard described the reality of his own church with the formula "civic rectitude." What is Christian in it is added simply as a "seasoning" to enhance the enjoyment of the secular. There is nothing left of the "possibility of offense," to which for him belongs among other things the alternative to the "normal," married way of life that Matt 19:12 opens up.[138]

---

ing God (*b. Šabb.* 87a. For further sources see Allison ["Divorce," 6, n. 18] and Brooks [*Community*, 108]). It was said of Elijah, about whose family we hear nothing in the Bible, that he did not marry (Ginzberg, *Legends*, 6.316; Tertullian *Mon.* 8 = ANF 4.65).

135 Cf. Segalla ("Il texto" 124), who says that Jesus does not praise celibacy; he simply "defends a fact." Sand (*Reich Gottes*, 76) speaks of a "legitimizing word" that provides protection for unmarried persons.

136 Appropriately, the most recent Catholic documents on priestly celibacy no longer make the former claim; instead, celibacy is understood as "a precious gift given by God to his Church" and as a "positive enrichment of the priesthood" (John Paul II, apostolic writing *Pastores dabo vobis*, 25 March 1992, no. 29 [ET by United States Catholic Conference, p. 76]). But why is this "precious gift" and this "enrichment" of the priesthood (which obviously is not an essential attribute of the priesthood) made a requirement for the priesthood of the Latin church? "Whoever is able to grasp it, let him grasp it."

137 To be sure, substantive questions remain to be addressed to Jesus. The ascetic tendencies that did exist in Judaism still do not provide a reason for elevating the unmarried life over marriage. The reference to the absence of marriage in the resurrection (Mark 12:25) is temporally conditioned. Comments that justify an unmarried life with the special task that the kingdom of God brings are situational, and they can appear quite different in other situations. The conversation that we would like to have here with Jesus is difficult, since in the final analysis we simply do not know why one would forgo marriage for the sake of the kingdom of God.

138 *Training,* 113–14.

Literature

Daube, *New Testament*, 224–46.

Jeremias, *Infant Baptism*.

Gerhard Krause, ed., *Die Kinder im Evangelium* (Stuttgart: Klotz, 1973).

Andreas Lindemann, "Die Kinder und die Gottesherrschaft," *WuD* NF 17 (1983) 77–104.

Ingetraut Ludolphy, "Zur Geschichte der Auslegung des Evangelium Infantium," in Erdmann Schott, ed., *Taufe und neue Existenz* (Berlin: Evangelische Verlagsanstalt, 1973) 71–86.

Réne Péter, "L'imposition des mains dans l'Ancien Testament," *VT* 27 (1977) 48–55.

Wolfgang Stegemann, "Lasset die Kinder zu mir kommen," in idem and Willy Schottroff, eds., *Traditionen der Befreiung: Sozialgeschichtliche Bibelauslegungen*, vol. 1: *Methodische Zugänge* (Munich: Kaiser, 1980) 114–44.

Strobel, "Kindertaufe," 7–69.

For *additional literature* see above, IV C on Matthew 19–20.

13

Then children were brought to him so that he might lay his hands on them and pray (for them). But the disciples rebuked them. 14/ But Jesus said: "Permit the children, and do not prevent them from coming to me, for the kingdom of heaven belongs to such ones." 15/ And after he had laid his hands on them he went away.

Analysis

That a small section on children follows the comments on marriage does not mean that the two sections are part of a catechism or a household code (*Haustafel*).[1] The short pericope is more tightly composed than is Mark 10:13-16. The logion in Mark's v. 15, which interrupts the flow of the pericope, is omitted since Matthew had already used a variant in 18:3. The formally closed little story is framed by the expression "lay hands upon" (τὰς χεῖρας ἐπιθεῖναι) in vv. 13 and 15. The conclusion, following Mark 10:17, relates how Jesus went away. Unlike the case in Mark, Jesus does not rebuke the disciples,[2] nor does he take the children in his arms.[3] Using some of Mark

10:16, Matthew replaces Mark's ἅψηται with the laying on of hands and prayer, formulations that were not especially typical for him. The other changes are linguistically Matthean.[4]

Interpretation

■ **13-15** Children are brought to Jesus, perhaps by their parents; we are not told. Jesus is to bless them and pray for them. That is the way Matthew interprets the Markan request that Jesus touch the children. In contrast to παῖδες, παιδία are small children. According to Hippocrates, they are under seven years of age.[5] The expression "lay hands upon" is biblical; the LXX uses it to refer to quite different ritual practices—for example, the "laying" of hands on the sacrificial animal (for example, Lev. 1:4 and frequently), or at Joshua's "ordination" (Deut 34:9),[6] or the "laying on" of hands in the case of parental blessing.[7] It may be that there was in Judaism at the time of the New Testament the custom that scribes blessed children and that Matthew could have used that custom as a pattern. However, that remains very uncertain.[8]

Infant Baptism in the New Testament?

Whether Matthew also has a Christian practice in mind is hotly debated. In both the history of interpretation and in the modern discussion the debate is centered on the question of *infant baptism*. The main exegetical argument for infant baptism was the expression "do not prevent" (μὴ κωλύετε; v. 14), which is reminiscent of the question about hindrances to baptism in Acts 8:36.[9] The connection is very weak. While it is true that Luke's preferred word κωλύω ("to prevent") appears in Acts three times in connection with baptism (8:36; 10:47; 11:17), in none of the cases is hindrance to baptism the issue.[10] The debate about infant baptism that was initiated by the publications of Joachim Jeremias appears to have

---

1   Jeremias, *Infant Baptism*, 50: a "catechism" on Mark 10:1-31; Warren Carter, *Households and Discipleship: A Study of Matthew 19–20* (JSNTSup 103; Sheffield: JSOT, 1994): a *Haustafel*.

2   Cf. on 19:10-11, 27; 20:20-21.

3   As Mark 9:36 par. Cf. above, IV B 1.1 on the source of 18:1-5, with n. 7.

4   Cf. vol. 1, Introduction 3.2 on τότε, προσφέρω, βασιλεία τῶν οὐρανῶν, πορεύομαι, ἐκεῖθεν.

5   According to Philo *Op. mun.* 105.

6   Hebrew סמך. Cf. Daube, *New Testament*, 225–29; Réne Péter, "L'imposition des mains dans l'Ancien

Testament," 49–53. Behind the term is the concept of a transfer of power from one person to another so that the result is a "substitute."

7   The only evidence for this usage is Gen 48:14-18, where the term is שׁלח or שׁית.

8   The evidence for this usage is very late: *Soph.* 18.5 = Str–B 2.138 (blessing by the scribes); *Siddur Sephat Emeth* 44 = Str–B 1.808 (blessing by the parents).

9   Oscar Cullmann, "Spuren einer alten Taufformel im Neuen Testament," in idem, *Vorträge und Aufsätze 1925-1962* (Tübingen: Mohr/Siebeck, 1966) 525.

demonstrated that there is no convincing reference in the New Testament to a baptism of small children.[11] First Corinthians 7:14 is clear evidence to the contrary. The roots of Christian baptism in the baptism of John would tend to speak against a baptism of small children,[12] while the analogies to mystery religion initiations clearly speak against such a practice.[13] It is true, of course, that older children were regarded as "of age" relatively early in antiquity.[14] In the course of the second century the baptism of older children appears to have been widespread, but the baptism of infants remained the exception probably to the end of the century.[15] Most people probably regarded infants as sinless and thus not in need of baptism.[16]

Thus in my judgment the formulations of our text were hardly determined by the ritual of infant baptism. That is not to say, however, that there were no connections between the text and a liturgical practice; it is simply the blessing rather than the baptism of children that we are dealing with. The evidence for such a conclusion is not the verb "to prevent" but the repeated expression "to lay hands upon." The biblical sources often refer to a rite (but not to the same rite).

A rite also lies behind Acts 13:3, where the reference likewise is to laying on of hands and prayer. Naturally, it cannot be proven that there was a rite of blessing children in Matthew's church, but I am almost certain that in primitive Christianity children were present at the church's regular worship. If the earthly Jesus called them to come to him, the churches that transmitted our text will scarcely have kept them away from the presence of the exalted Lord.[17]

The disciples try to keep the people with their children away from Jesus. Matthew has no interest in why they do it; he also omits Jesus' rebuke. His only concern is Jesus' reaction: Do not prevent them, because the kingdom of heaven belongs to such as these. The readers of the Gospel of Matthew understand this word of Jesus in terms of 18:1-5. Thus Matthew initially is thinking of real children as in 18:2, 5 and also 21:15-16. They are close to Jesus and are permitted to be with him. Presumably this conscious attention to children was especially characteristic of Jesus; there are no history-of-

---

Of course, Acts 8:36 is the *only* place where κωλύω is used this way.

10   Critically against Cullmann, "Spuren," 525–28.

11   Jeremias, *Infant Baptism*. Cf. George Raymond Beasley-Murray, *Baptism in the New Testament* (1962; reprinted Grand Rapids: Eerdmans, 1973) 306–59. Kurt Aland, "Die Stellung der Kinder in den frühen christlichen Gemeinden—und ihre Taufe," in idem, *Neutestamentliche Entwürfe* (ThBü 63; Munich: Kaiser, 1979) 198–232; Gerhard Barth, *Die Taufe in frühchristlicher Zeit* (Biblisch-theologische Studien 4; Neukirchen-Vluyn: Neukirchener Verlag, 1981) 137–45; Ferdinand Hahn, "Kindersegnung und Kindertaufe im ältesten Christentum," in Hubert Frankemölle and Karl Kertelge, eds., *Vom Urchristentum zu Jesus: für Joachim Gnilka* (Freiburg: Herder, 1989) 497–507, and especially the careful study by Strobel, "Kindertaufe." Only Andreas Lindemann ("Die Kinder und die Gottesherrschaft," 97–101) assumes that discussions about the baptism of children constituted the *Sitz im Leben* of Mark 10:13-16.

12   Especially proselyte baptism, in which presumably small children were also baptized, is not the source of Christian baptism; Jewish believers in Jesus were also baptized! Even in Gentile Christianity it appears to have had little influence on Christian baptism.

13   There is evidence that children from seven to eleven years of age were initiated into the mysteries. See Strobel, "Kindertaufe," 26–27. For other sources see Walter Burkert, *Antike Mysterien: Funktionen und Gehalt* (3d ed.; Munich: Beck, 1994) 54, with n. 114.

14   On Hellenism cf. n. 13. On Judaism cf. Strobel ("Kindertaufe," 27–28) and *m. ʾAbot* 5.21. Jewish children begin reading the Bible at five years of age and the Mishnah at age ten. They are obligated to keep the commandments at the age of sexual maturity (13). See, in addition, Str-B 2.144–47.

15   Only *Mart. Pol.* 9.3, Justin (*1 Apol.* 15.6), and Irenaeus (*Haer.* 2.22.4) refer to the baptism of small children (not necessarily of infants). Infant baptism first appears to be the standard practice with Hippolytus and Origen (Strobel, "Kindertaufe," 13–15). Aristides (*1 Apol.* 15.6) speaks of the baptism of older children who are able to make their own decision. According to Celsus (Origen *Cels.* 3.44 = ANF 4.481–82), many παιδάρια belong to the church. Strobel ("Kindertaufe," 23–43) assumes that in the second century children often belonged to the church at an age when they themselves were capable of learning and making distinctions, although there was no required minimum age for such membership.

16   Cf. e.g., Aristides, *Apol.* 15.11. For further sources see Aland ("Die Stellung der Kinder in den frühen christlichen Gemeinden—und ihre Taufe," 214–15, and Strobel, "Kindertaufe," 23. On Judaism cf. Albrecht Oepke, "παῖς, κτλ.," *TDNT* 5 (1967) 646–47.

17   Strobel, "Kindertaufe," 58–59.

religions analogies.[18] This attention remained important for the churches. However, τοιούτων ("such ones") indicates that the issue is not merely children in the literal sense; beyond them it is all who are "little," who are looked down on as unimportant, and also those who lay claim to the kingdom of heaven's reversal of power and become poor in spirit (5:3) and humble as a child (18:3-4). They too receive Jesus' blessing.

History of Interpretation

Of greatest interest in the history of our text's interpretation is its function as a major biblical proof text for infant baptism. How important the text continues to be in this regard becomes clear not in the exegeses, but in the baptismal liturgies where it or the parallel text Mark 10:13-16 still appears with great frequency.[19] By contrast, in the history of interpretation for centuries this use of the text was quite marginal. While it was believed that the text did justify the baptism of children, it was seldom used that way.[20] Of greater importance was the parenetic interpretation—that is, the call to adults to become like children: to become simple, unassuming, humble, innocent, not impressed by externals, etc.[21] In the history of interpretation little attention is paid to the children themselves. Only occasionally does the parenetic interpretation include the call to give special attention to the training of the children to whom Jesus gave his attention.[22] There is also an occasional call to parents to pray for their children and to bring them frequently to the priests for blessing.[23] Our text first became important as a biblical justification for infant baptism for the reformers in their controversies with the Anabaptists.

In a 1525 sermon on our text Luther did not yet have to defend the baptism of children. Instead, he was concerned to show that children already have their own faith.[24] It is different in his sermons on Matthew 18–24 from the years 1537–40, where he reacts sharply against the Anabaptists. In response to the argument that children could not yet believe because they do not yet have reasoning powers, he emphasizes that this is precisely the advantage that children have. With them the reason that overwhelms the Bible with its intelligence "flees away . . . to Babylon."[25] In his Matthew commentary Zwingli conducts a polemic against the Anabaptists, who fail to recognize that Jesus uses the children as a model for adults.[26] Calvin argues from the center of Reformation faith and claims that infant baptism is an especially expressive "figure of the free forgiveness of sins."[27] However, his main exegetical argument for infant baptism in his long discussion in *Inst.* 4.16 is not Matthew 19 but Old Testament circumcision. Since the Reformation references to infant baptism appear regularly not only in Protestant[28] but also in many Catholic commentaries.[29] In contrast, the Anabaptist Peter Walpot emphasizes that baptism is of no value apart from faith. To the children who cannot yet believe, Christ grants the kingdom of God without faith and without

---

18 Even the so-called rediscovery of the child in Hellenism (cf. Oepke, "παῖς, κτλ.," 640–41) is, in my judgment, invalid.

19 Examples: *Agende für die Evangelische Kirche der Union 2: Die kirchlichen Amtshandlungen* (Witten: Luther, 1964) 14–15; *Agende für Evangelisch-lutherische Kirchen und Gemeinden 3/1* (Hannover: Lutherisches Verlagshaus, 1988) 26–27; *Agende für die Evangelische Kirche von Kurhessen-Waldeck 3: Amtshandlungen* (Kassel: Presseverband Kurhessen-Waldeck, 1975) 203–4 (references from M. Josuttis). The situation is different on the Catholic side to the degree that the *Rituale Romanum*, which was in effect until the Second Vatican Council, did not envisage the reading of a scripture for the baptism of children. The *Ordo Baptismi Parvulorum* of 1969 envisages a service of the word for which Mark 10:13-16 is suggested as a text (information from Th. Egloff, Liturgisches Institut Zürich).

20 The earliest source is Tertullian *Bapt.* 18, where this understanding is presupposed, although Tertullian is speaking precisely against early baptisms. Otherwise Ludolphy ("Geschichte," 74) has been able to cite only two sources from the ancient church: *Const. ap.* 6.15.7 = Franz Xavier Funk, *Didascalia et Constitutiones Apostolorum* (Paderborn: Schöningh, 1905) 339, and Innocent I *Ep.* 30.5 = DS[36], 219.

21 Apollinaris of Laodicea no. 96 = Reuss, 32; John Chrysostom, 62.4 = *PG* 58.600–601; Dionysius the Carthusian, 215; *Opus imperfectum* 22 = 805. Cf. also above, IV B 1.1 on the history of interpretation of 18:1-2.

22 Basil, *Regulae brevius* no 292 = 260–61.

23 *Opus imperfectum* 22 = 805; cf. Maldonat, 388.

24 2.654–60.

25 *WA* 47.326–337, quote from 331.

26 437.

27 2.252.

28 E.g., in Bullinger, 181; Bucer, 156; Musculus, 456; Aretius, 170; Brenz, 619; Wolzogen, 336.

29 Maldonat, 389; Valdés, 333–34; S. Barrasas in Ludolphy, "Geschichte," 83, n. 36; Lapide, 367–68.

baptism.[30] In short, the use of our text in the exegesis of the Reformation and the post-Reformation period to support infant baptism is a classic case of using a biblical text as a "secondary legitimation" of an institution that had existed for a long time without any biblical basis.

It was not until the Enlightenment that the interest in infant baptism diminished, at least in the interpretation of our text.[31] In our century it has for the most part disappeared from the exegesis of Matt 19:13-15 par. Even Cullmann and Jeremias, the last two great representatives of the view that infant baptism was practiced in the New Testament period, emphasize that our text does not speak explicitly of it; it merely presupposes the baptism of children.[32] Thus on this point the exegesis of the text has moved on.

Meaning for Today

Thus the history of interpretation illustrates how little a biblical text can accomplish against the weight of tradition and liturgy, even in the Protestant churches of the word. It is exegetically certain that Matt 19:13-15 does not provide a basis for infant baptism, and it is probable that the New Testament does not justify the practice. It is rather historically a result of the changing social character of the church in the New Testament period. The most that could be said is that it is indirectly a consequence of the New Testament proclamation of grace.[33] As an exegete I would like to ask of our churches greater—and that means public—honesty toward the bib-

lical text. It is a misuse of the Bible when priests and pastors against the best exegesis use our texts without commentary at infant baptisms and thus continue to contribute to the entrenchment of a possibly unbiblical baptism of children, and when church officials often actually require such behavior. The biblical texts cannot defend themselves against such a practice, and it is the task of the exegetes to do that on their behalf.

However, what positive conclusions can we draw from our text? I am not interested here in entering the lists on behalf of an unrepeatable blessing or presentation of small children by the church, although (perhaps!) there was such a practice in the Matthean church. As an unrepeatable act, especially in churches that in other regards do not practice blessing, it would be little more than a substitute for infant baptism. However, in the perspective of our text I would like first of all to encourage our churches to include children, not only in separate rooms and on separate occasions but also precisely in our main corporate worship—and to include them not as passive participants who it is hoped will keep quiet but as persons who *as children* help shape our worship and make it more spontaneous, lively, and in a positive sense perhaps somewhat more chaotic. In the second place I would like to encourage our churches to rediscover the reality of blessing not only for children but also for others—and to do that not merely in corporate worship.

---

30 *The Great Article Book* (c. 1577) = *Quellen zur Geschichte der Täufer 12: Glaubenszeugnisse oberdeutscher Taufgesinnten* (Gütersloh: Mohn, 1967) 75–76.

31 For an overview see Ludolphy, "Geschichte," 77–78.

32 Cullmann, "Spuren," 529; Jeremias, *Infant Baptism*, 49.

33 And, in my judgment, an illegitimate one. That the baptized infant in no way can *experience* the divine grace, which is every bit as concrete as that water makes one wet, is in my judgment the main argument against this kind of "further development" of the New Testament. It is, after all, not the parents who are baptized!

Literature

Barth, *CD* 2/2.613–30.

Burchill, "Evangelical Counsels," 135–231.

Clement of Alexandria, Τίς ὁ σωζόμενος πλούσιος (GCS 17 = GCS Clemens Alexandrinus 3.157–91). (ET: ANF 2.591–604 or G. W. Butterworth, trans. [Loeb Classical Library; 1919; reprinted Cambridge: Harvard University Press, 1960].)

Claude Coulot, "La structuration de la péricope de l'homme riche et ses différentes lectures (Mc 10,17-31; Mt 19,16-30; Lc 18, 18-30)," *Revue des Sciences Religieuses* 56 (1982) 240–52.

Peter Eicher, "Die Befreiung zur Nachfolge: Zur Geschichte des 'reichen Jünglings,'" in idem, ed., *Karl Barth, Der reiche Jüngling* (Munich: Kosel, 1986) 13–66.

Jesús García Burillo, "El ciento por uno (Mc 10,29-30 par): Distoria de las interpretaciones y exégesis," *EstBib* 36 (1977) 173–203; 37 (1978) 28–55.

Richard Webb Haskin, "The Call to Sell All: The History of the Interpretation of Mark 10:17-23 and Parallels" (Diss., Columbia University, 1968).

Rudolf Hoppe, "Vollkommenheit bei Matthäus als theologische Aussage," in Lorenz Oberlinner and Peter Fiedler, eds., *Salz der Erde–Licht der Welt: Exegetische Studien zum Matthäusevangelium: Festschrift für Anton Vögtle zum 80. Geburtstag* (Stuttgart: Katholisches Bibelwerk, 1991) 141–64.

John Paul II, *The Splendor of Truth: Veritatis Splendor: Encyclical Letter August 6, 1993* (Washington, D.C.: United States Catholic Conference, 1996) 12–45.

A. F. J. Klijn, "The Question of the Rich Young Man in a Jewish-Christian Gospel," *NovT* 8 (1966) 149–55.

Simon Légasse, *L'appel du riche: Marc 10,17-31 et parallèles. Contribution à l'étude des fondements scripturaires de l'état religieux* (Verbum Salutis. Collection Annexe; Paris: Beauchesne, 1966) 113–214.

Eduard Lohse, "'Vollkommen sein.' Zur Ethik des Matthäusevangeliums," in Lorenz Oberlinner and Peter Fiedler, eds., *Salz der Erde–Licht der Welt: Exegetische Studien zum Matthäusevangelium: Festschrift für Anton Vögtle zum 80. Geburtstag* (Stuttgart: Katholisches Bibelwerk, 1991) 131–40.

Ulrich Luck, "Die Frage nach dem Guten," in Wolfgang Schrage, ed., *Studien zum Text und zur Ethik des Neuen Testaments: Festschrift zum 80. Geburtstag von Heinrich Greeven* (BZNW 47; Berlin: de Gruyter, 1986) 282–97.

Martin Luther, "Die Zirkulardisputation über das Recht des Widerstandes gegen den Kaiser. Mt 19,21, 9. Mai 1539" (*WA* 39/2.34–91).

Michael Mees, "Das Paradigma vom reichen Mann und seiner Berufung nach den Synoptikern und dem Nazaräerevangelium," *Vetera Christianorum* 9 (1972) 245–65.

José O'Callaghan, "Examen crítico de Mt 19,24," *Bib* 69 (1988) 401–5.

Per foramen acus: Il cristianesimo antico di fronte alla pericope evangelica del "giovane ricco" (Studia Patristica Mediolanensia 14; Milan: Vita e Pensiere, 1986).

du Plessis, *ΤΕΛΕΙΟΣ*.

J. A. Rustad, "Matthew's Attitude Towards the Law in Mt 19:16-22" (Diss., Concordia Seminary in Exile, 1976).

Thea Vogt, *Angst und Identität im Markusevangelium* (NTOA; Göttingen: Vandenhoeck & Ruprecht, 1993) 142–83.

E. Yarnold, "*Τέλειος* in St. Matthew's Gospel," *Studia Evangelica* 4 (TU 102; Berlin: Akademie, 1968) 269–73.

Literature on 19:28

Broer, "Ringen," 148–65.

Fred W. Burnett, "Παλιγγενεσία: Matt 19:28: A Window on the Matthean Community," *JSNT* 17 (1983) 60–72.

J. Duncan M. Derrett, "Palingenesia (Matthew 19:28)," *JSNT* 20 (1984) 51–58.

Jacques Dupont, "Le logion des douze trônes (Mt 19,28; Lc 22,28-30)," in idem, *Études* 2.706–43.

Friedrich, *Gott im Bruder,* 53–66.

Geist, *Menschensohn,* 238–45.

Hampel, *Menschensohn,* 140–51.

Marguerat, *Jugement,* 460–72.

Reiser, *Jesus,* 258–62.

Christian Riniker, "Die Gerichtsverkündigung Jesu" (Diss., Bern, 1991) 406–17.

Heinz Schürmann, *Jesu Abschiedsrede Lk 22,21-38: III. Teil einer quellenkritischen Untersuchung des Lukanischen Abendmahlsberichts* (NTAbh 20/5; Münster: Aschendorf, 1957) 37–54.

David C. Sim, "The Meaning of παλιγγενεσία in Matthew 19,28," *JSNT* 50 (1993) 3–12.

Theisohn, *Richter,* 153–74.

Anton Vögtle, *Das Neue Testament und die Zukunft des Kosmos* (KBANT; Düsseldorf: Patmos, 1970) 156–66.

For *additional literature* see above, IV C on Matthew 19–20.

16 And behold, one came to him and said, "Master, what good thing must I do to have eternal Life?" 17/ But he said to him, "Why do you ask me about the Good? There is one who is good. But if you want to enter into life, keep the commandments." 18/ He said to him, "Which ones?" And Jesus said, "These: 'You shall not kill, you shall not commit adultery, you shall not steal, you shall not bear false witness, 19/ honor the father and the mother,' and 'you shall love your neighbor as yourself.'" 20/ The young man says to him, "All these things have I kept. In what[1] am I still deficient?" 21/ Jesus spoke to him, "If you want to be perfect, go, sell your possessions and give (them) to the poor, and you will have treasure in (the) heavens, and (come) hither and follow me." 22/ But after the young man had heard the word,[2] he went away grieving, for he had many possessions.

23 But Jesus said to his disciples, "Amen, I tell you that a rich man hardly will enter the kingdom of heaven. 24/ Again I say to you, it is easier for a camel[3] to go through[4] the eye of a needle[5] than for a rich man to enter the kingdom of God." 25/ But when the disciples heard it they were exceedingly astonished and said, "Who then can be saved?" 26/ But Jesus looked at them and said, "This is impossible with human beings but with God everything is possible."

27 Then Peter answered and said to him, "See, we have left everything and have followed you. What then will we have?" 28/ But Jesus said to them, "Amen, I say to you, in the regeneration, when the Son of Man has sat on the throne of his glory, you who have followed me will yourselves also sit on twelve thrones and will judge the twelve tribes of Israel. 29/ And everyone who for the sake of my name has left houses, or brothers, or sisters, or father, or mother,[6] or children, or fields will receive a hundredfold[7] and will inherit eternal life. 30/ But many who are first will be last, and last first.

Analysis

Structure

The demarcation of the text is somewhat arbitrary at the end, since vv. 27-30 serve to prepare for 20:1-16. On the one hand, the four verses are connected to vv. 16-26 with the catchwords "to follow" (ἀκολουθέω; vv. 21, 27-28) and "eternal life" (ζωὴ αἰώνιος; vv. 16, 29). In addition, Peter and the disciples offer a positive contrast to the young man. On the other hand, the question "What then will we have?" (v. 27) introduces the theme of reward, the treatment of which does not reach a preliminary conclusion until 20:16. Without a new narrative beginning, 20:1-16 follows seamlessly on 19:27-30. The repetition of v. 30 in 20:16 shows that the two sections are related.

The entire section vv. 16-30 consists of three parts.[8] It begins with Jesus' meeting with the young man (*vv. 16-22*), which itself is subdivided into three parts by

---

1   The translation "what do I still lack?" (BAGD, *s.v.* ὑστερέω, 1c) is imprecise, or even wrong, since ὑστερέω is constructed with the genitive. Τί is a kind of accusative of general reference. Cf. BDF § 154.

2   Is τοῦτον a secondary reading from B and several other Egyptian and Western witnesses that adds precision? Or is the simple τὸν λόγον (C, D, Θ, lat, sa, bo, et al.) adaptation to Mark?

3   There is scarcely any evidence for the reading κάμιλος = ship's rigging in Matthew (limited almost entirely to the Armenian and Georgian translations). There is somewhat more evidence for the reading in Luke 18:25 (additionally only in S and several minuscules).

4   Many witnesses follow Luke and replace διελθεῖν with εἰσελθεῖν. Several then omit the following εἰσελθεῖν for stylistic reasons. Cf. the summary by José O'Callaghan, "Examen crítico de Mt 19,24," 401-5, 402-4.

5   We have a choice of three largely synonymous words, all of which generally mean "hole": τρῆμα (e.g., an opening for the handle of a rudder on a ship [Pollux *Onom.* 1.88] or the hole bored in a stone so that it could be worn as decoration [Moulton-Milligan, 641]), τρύπημα (literally "that which

is bored," e.g., the opening of a pipe [Pollux *Onom.* 4.70]), and τρυμαλιά (the scarcest of the three words, in the LXX it appears five times with πέτρα as "crevice"). The reading τρυμαλιά, offered by C, K, Θ, and many other witnesses came probably from Mark, τρῆμα, offered by ℵ and B, from Luke. It is likely that Matthew's original is τρύπημα.

6   While ἢ γυναῖκα is well attested by ℵ, C, W, Θ, *l*, f13, lat, sy, sa, bo, mae, etc., it is possible that it was taken over from Luke 18:29. Cf. Metzger, *Commentary*, 50.

7   Ἑκατονταπλασίονα (= Mark) is better attested than πολλαπλασίονα, which was taken over from Luke 18:30.

8   In his suggestion of a concentric structure with v. 24a as the middle Claude Coulot ("La structuration de la péricope de l'homme rich et ses différentes lectures [Mc 10,17-31; Mt 19,16-30; Lc 18, 18-30]," 240–52, 249) completely ignored this simple fact.

its three questions, and is framed with an introduction (v. 16a) and a conclusion (v. 22). Jesus then instructs the disciples about wealth (*vv. 23-26*) and is interrupted by the disciples' amazed reaction (v. 26). Peter's question (v. 27), which introduces the third part (*vv. 27-30*), summarizes what the young man should have done—viz., leave everything and follow Jesus. Then on behalf of the disciples Peter poses the question about reward that corresponds to the young man's question about eternal life. Jesus responds with two statements that are related to the question (vv. 28-29) and a final general gnome whose interpretation will involve several problems.

Source

Mark 10:17-31 is the source of our text. In Matthew's reworking of the Markan text almost all of his changes correspond to his own style.[9] With the change from the good person to the good thing Mark's v. 18 is better integrated into the text.[10] The command to love one's neighbor (v. 19b) and the idea of perfection (v. 21) are added. The questioner is made a νεανίσκος (vv. 20, 22).[11] That Jesus loved the young man is omitted (Mark 10:21a) as is Mark's somewhat awkward v. 24 which speaks of the difficulty of entering the kingdom of God at all. The logion about the twelve thrones (v. 28aβ, b) is, except for the introduction "Amen, I tell you," new when compared with Mark. Quite unusual are the "smaller agreements" with Luke. Most of them are to be explained simply as independent Matthean and Lukan redaction,[12] although it is difficult to explain their great number.[13]

The Logion About the Thrones (v. 28aβ, b)

There is a parallel to this logion in Luke 22:28-30. The two logia begin quite differently, but there is a great deal of agreement in their conclusions. Unlike most critics, I am not inclined to assign the word to the sayings source, since in both Matthew and Luke it is completely isolated from other Q texts.[14] We can only guess what its place in Q might have been. It is more likely that Matthew and Luke took it from the oral tradition in different versions. Attempts at literary-critical or tradition-critical reconstructions have not led to any clear results, and I offer here only my own view. In Luke the ideas of judging the twelve tribes and of eating in the kingdom of God are not related. The word may already have been in an expanded version when Luke took it over. Although it is not certain, it may be that Matthew added the introductory "(you) who have followed me" (οἱ ἀκολουθήσαντές μοι). Probably the hapax legomenon παλιγγενεσία was part of the tradition.[15] It is difficult to know what to think about "when the Son of Man has sat on the throne of his glory" (ὅταν καθίσῃ ὁ οἱὸς τοῦ ἀνθρώπου ἐπὶ θρόνου δόξης αὐτοῦ), since the expression is repeated with almost identical words in 25:31. Are both texts redactional, or is 25:31 a redactional imitation of our text? It is almost impossible to decide, but the possibility that Dan 7:9 is behind the "thrones" of the judging disciples[16] encourages me to see in our logion an original Son of Man saying. In its Matthean version the second part

---

9 Cf. vol. 1, Introduction 3.2 on ἰδού, προσελθὼν αὐτῷ εἶπεν (v. 16), εἰ + θέλω, εἰσέρχομαι, τηρέω (v. 17), λέγω + historical present, δέ, θημί (v. 18), λέγω + historical present (v. 20), εἰ θέλεις (v. 21), δέ, ἀμὴν λέγω ὑμῖν, βασιλεία τῶν οὐρανῶν (v. 23), πάλιν, δέ (v. 24), ἀκούσας δέ, μαθητής, λέγων, ἄρα (v. 25), δέ (v. 26), τότε, ἀποκριθεὶς εἶπεν, ἄρα, ἔσται (v. 27), δέ, ἀκολουθέω (v. 28), πᾶς ὅστις (v. 29). On ἐρωτάω (v. 17) cf. 15:23; 16:13; 21:24 (redactional in each case). Ἔτι (v. 20) is redactional in about four other places. On τέλειος (v. 21) cf. 5:48. On τὰ ὑπάρχοντα (v. 21) cf. 25:14. On σφόδρα cf. above on 17:6, 23; 18:31.

10 Of course, "there is one who is good" is still in v. 17b, reminiscent of Mark 10:18, and is without much relation to the context.

11 Νεανίσκος appears only here in Matthew, but it is missing in the parallels to Mark 14:51 and 16:5.

12 The following agreements are compatible with the redaction of both evangelists, or they make sense because of difficulties in the Markan text: the omis-

sion of μὴ ἀποστερήσῃς (Mark 10:19 par.) that is not in the OT, the insertion of ἔτι (Matt 19:20/Luke 18:22), the omission of Jesus' emotions (ἠγάπησεν, στυγνάσας) (Mark 10:21-22 par.), and the omission of Mark 10:24. I find it more difficult to understand the drastic reduction of the introduction in Mark's v. 17 par. and the omission of διδάσκαλε (Mark 10:20 par.) that would have been appropriate for Matthew (cf. 8:19).

13 Ennulat (*Agreements*, 222–34) counts forty agreements!

14 Cf. vol. 1, II A 2.1 on 5:18 and II A 2.2.3 on 5:32; above, II D 1.2 on 11:12-13; IV B 1.3 on 18:12-14; vol. 3 on 22:1-10 and on 25:14-30.

15 Matthew would have used an expression that was not as Greek: ἐν τῇ συντελείᾳ τοῦ αἰῶνος or ἐν τῷ αἰῶνι τῷ μέλλοντι (cf. 12:32).

16 In *Tanch.* B Lev. קדשים § 1 (36a) = Str-B 4.1103) at the judgment the thrones of Dan 7:9 are erected on which Israel's great figures will join God in judging the Gentiles. Revelation 20:4 shows that such con-

of the logion—that is, the reference to the twelve thrones—may be traditional.[17] Does an original version of this logion go back to Jesus? With great caution (we can speak with any confidence only of its second half) I am inclined to say yes to the question, especially since there is no reference to the church, and the twelve are related only to the people of Israel.[18] If that is correct, then this is the only place that reveals what significance the circle of the twelve had for Jesus.

Interpretation

Matthew's version of the story of the rich man, who here for the first time becomes a "young man," contains an emphasis that became very important for the history of the church—viz., the concept of perfection (v. 21). This emphasis permits us to pose two basic questions that the interpretation of our text must answer. (1) What does the perfection that Jesus demands of the rich man in v. 21 have to do with keeping the commandments? (2) Are the "perfect" a particular group of people who then will receive a special reward (v. 28)? Or, asking the question from the other direction: To what degree does what Jesus says to the rich man (vv. 16-21) apply to all disciples (vv. 23-30)?

■ **16-17** A man comes to Jesus and asks him about the "good thing" that he must do to achieve eternal life. The question is in the biblical tradition. The good is the will of God that is preserved above all in the law.[19] The theme of the section is thus stated. At issue is what is necessary "to enter the kingdom of heaven" (v. 23).[20] Jesus rejects the man's question. What is good is a matter of common knowledge. He who alone is "good"–viz., God himself[21]–has decreed it in his law.[22] Thus Jesus does not have something to add to what to this point in Judaism has been regarded as the essence of the good. Instead, he fulfills the Law and the Prophets (5:17). For this reason he refers the questioner to the Torah.

■ **18-19** The question "Which ones?" permits Jesus to enumerate several commandments from the second

---

cepts can be quite old. Cf. Jacques Dupont, "Le logion des douze trônes (Mt 19,28; Lc 22,28-30)," in idem, *Études* 2.736–37; Broer, "Ringen," 157–58.

17 The probability is greater that Luke omitted δώδεκα because Judas's betrayal had just been predicted in 22:21-23.

18 Along with Hampel (*Menschensohn,* 148–51), Reiser (*Gerichtspredigt,* 249–50), and Christian Riniker ("Die Gerichtsverkündigung Jesu," 409–12). The closest parallel from Jesus material is Matt 9:37-38 which speaks of the disciples as coworkers in the harvest.

19 Cf. Deut 30:15; Amos 5:14; Mic 6:8; and Ulrich Luck, "Die Frage nach dem Guten," 282–97, 285–97. For rabbinic Judaism the question about the good is identical with the questions about the Law. *M. ʾAbot* 6.3: "Good is naught else than the Law."

20 The supposition is popular that Matthew changed the address "Good Teacher" for dogmatic reasons, because it bothered him that Jesus rejected the divine title "good" (cf. n. 21). It is more likely that the opposite is true. That Jesus rejected a title that belongs only to God would have been a sign of his genuine piety for a Jewish-Christian like Matthew. Cf. 23:9. It is more likely that what bothered Matthew was that an outsider who addresses Jesus as διδάσκαλε connects it with this exalted title. He was especially able to shorten the Markan pericope, however, because he avoided a secondary theme.

21 The history of the interpretation of this text has

had to deal with christological problems, primarily because the text of the Vulgate and of the *textus receptus* follow Mark. While the text was an effective argument against the Gnostics (the Father, Creator, and Lawgiver is by essence good; cf. Ps.-Clement *Hom.* 18.1–3; Irenaeus *Haer.* 4.12.3), it appeared to agree with the Arian view that the Father is good in essence, the Son only *per participationem* (according to Thomas Aquinas, *Lectura* no. 1581). Countless authors take issue with it, among them Ambrose (*In Luc.* 8.65–67 = BKV 1/21.500–502) and the so-called Arian *Opus imperfectum* 33 = 806–7. Of course, for the Orthodox interpreters as the second person of the Trinity Christ was also in essence "good."

22 Thus Jesus is not saying: You should have asked God instead of me about the good (thus Berger, *Gesetzes-auslegung* 1.445). The suggestion is nonsense, since Jesus himself is the one who fulfills the law and interprets it authoritatively. Of course one should ask him!

tablet of the Decalogue. The wording is similar to that of Matthew's Bible, the LXX,[23] but in the order of the commandments he follows the Hebrew Bible and his own antitheses (5:21-30). The commandment to honor one's parents, which Matthew, like Mark, adds to the list of commandments from the second tablet, was regarded as a social command in Judaism as well.[24] In 15:1-11 Matthew had expressly interpreted it as such. In these commandments of everyday life it is important to honor the one who alone is good. To the commandments of the Decalogue Matthew adds the commandment to love one's neighbor, found in Lev 19:18, which he regards as a "great" commandment (22:36-39).[25] His readers will be reminded of the antitheses that Jesus had concluded with the love of one's enemy that surpasses the love of one's neighbor, and with the reference to God's perfection (5:43-48).

■ **20** For the first time Matthew introduces the questioner as a "young man" (νεανίσκος). A νεανίσκος is a young man who is probably less than thirty years of age.[26] Why does Matthew make him a νεανίσκος? For one thing, it will have been historically true that especially young people broke with their families and gave

away their possessions in order to follow Jesus as itinerant charismatics.[27] For another, in this way Matthew is able to use the stages of human life in a play on words. The young man must become a grown, mature man (= τέλειος).[28]

He explains to Jesus that he has kept all the commandments. Matthew does not have Jesus challenge this claim, unlike the version of our story in the Gospel of the Nazarenes preserved by Origen,[29] and unlike countless later commentators.[30] What did he and his readers think of the man's answer? Whoever is aware of the Sermon on the Mount knows that the commandments of the second tablet, but especially the love command, are so demanding that it is impossible to check them off casually as fulfilled. Nevertheless, Matthew will have taken him seriously and regarded him in a positive light, because in his own way the man is looking for the "better righteousness" (cf. 5:20).[31] He asks Jesus what commandments he has yet to keep. Thus as a Jew he presupposes that the good consists of numerous commandments that one is obligated to keep.

■ **21** Jesus does not even reject this understanding. Instead, on the surface he accepts it by giving the young

---

23 Οὐ with the future instead of μή with the subjunctive. Matthew omits μὴ ἀποστερήσῃ, which does not come from the Bible.

24 Berger, *Gesetzesauslegung* 1.287–89.

25 Cf. the similar arrangement in *Didache* 1–2. There Lev 19:18 is the fundamental commandment which is the basis for the other commandments.

26 According to Diogenes Laertius (8.10) one is a νεανίσκος between the ages of 20 and 40, according to Philo *Op. mun.* 105, between 21 and 28; in earlier years one was a μειράκιον, later an ἀνήρ. In *Cher.* 114 the order is: βρέφος, παῖς, ἀντίπαις, ἡβῶν, μειράκιον, πρωτογένειος (a youth with his first beard), νεανίας, τέλειος ἀνήρ.

27 Cf. above, II C 3.3 on 10:35. Cf. also the parallels and n. 53. It is easy to forget that at least the earliest primitive Christianity may have been largely a "youth religion." Cf. Gerd Theissen, "'We Have Left Everything . . .' (Mark 10:28): Discipleship and Social Uprooting in the Jewish-Palestinian Society of the First Century," in idem, *Social Reality,* 91–92.

28 Cf. Philo *Cher.* 114 (above, n. 26) and Eph 4:13; E. Yarnold, "Τέλειος in St. Matthew's Gospel," 269–73, 272–73.

29 There Jesus refers to his great wealth and the many poor and hungry people whom he has not helped

(Origen, 15.14 = GCS Origenes 10.389). A. F. J. Klijn ("The Question of the Rich Young Man in a Jewish-Christian Gospel," 149–55) has demonstrated that this version of the story is based on Matthew.

30 The interpreters were divided whether the young man had really kept the law. Many said yes, primarily because according to Mark 10:21 Jesus loved the man. He may have been greedy, but he was no hypocrite (John Chrysostom, 63.1 = PG 58.603; Basil, "Homily Against the Rich" 1 = BKV 1/47.240–41). According to Euthymius Zigabenus (524) he has kept the commandments outwardly by not harming anyone. Along with the *Gospel of the Nazarenes* and Jerome (169–70, *mentitur*), others have reacted more negatively to him. The judgment on him is consistently negative when he becomes an allegorical embodiment of the Jewish people (e.g., Hilary 19.6 = SC 258.96; *Opus imperfectum* 33 = 808), and in the Protestant interpretation, when he represents the type of person who is justified by works (e.g., Luther, *WA* 47.339–40.345 [here he becomes a Pharisee]; Calvin 2.255–58). Brenz (626) is especially cute: There Jesus no longer loves the young

man an additional commandment that he must keep in order to be "perfect." He must sell his possessions—an action that is connected with the invitation to discipleship.

Perfection

What is perfection? There is more than meets the eye in this play on the stages of human life. "Perfection" is of fundamental importance for Matthew. His understanding of the term is not that of the Greeks for whom perfection is a human ideal in the sense of true knowledge and true virtue.[32] Matthew is rooted rather in the biblical, Jewish tradition. Here τέλειος stands for תָּמִים and means "complete," undivided obedience to God. Christian, especially Protestant, interpretation is quick to explain that Matthean perfection is to be understood qualitatively and not quantitatively, in contrast to the Qumran Essenes who are concerned that the members of the sect with God's help keep the entire intensified law. It is thus claimed that in Matthew's sense to be perfect is not to follow a path "that eventually leads to perfection"; rather, "whoever becomes a disciple of Jesus, that one is perfect."[33] For understanding Matthew's use of τέλειος Old Testament texts in particular are cited which underscore the undividedness of obedience to God (for example, 1 Kgs 11:4). However, such an approach grasps only part of Matthew's understanding of perfection. In my judgment, our text and the parallel text 5:48[34] show that three points are important for Matthew.

1. There is doubtless a qualitative element in perfection that is intimated in both texts by love. Those persons are perfect who understand God's commandment in the sense of love of enemy and of neighbor as an unbounded, indivisible demand and who act accordingly (cf. 5:43-48). In this sense for Matthew for the young man to give up his possessions as he was challenged to do was a radical expression of the love command that for Jesus knows no boundary.[35] In the first place, therefore, perfection is love.[36]

2. But there is also a quantitative element in perfection. To become perfect is to go beyond what is normal and customary. It is to embark on a way that reflects something of God's otherness and of Jesus' own radical life. That is what was meant in 5:20 with περισσεύσῃ . . . πλεῖον, and that is what the *Didache*, a work influenced by Matthew, means with the "whole yoke of the Lord" (6:2). In this sense the young man's quantitative question was justified when he asked what he was still lacking.[37] For this reason Jesus gives him a commandment that makes love concrete and radical. Thus perfection is in the second place complete obedience. In this case it is giving up one's possessions for the sake of the poor.[38]

3. Finally, perfection is a matter of complete attachment to Jesus that is expressed in our text with the call

---

man; instead, he ridicules him for giving such a childish answer.

31 Unlike the *Gospel of the Nazarenes,* the Synoptics do not initially say that the man was rich (which might cast suspicion on his assurance that he has kept the love commandment).

32 To be sure, the understanding of τέλειος in Greek philosophy may have offered an important point of contact, since perfection there is connected with the question of the good. Cf. Plato *Phileb.* 61a, 67a. On Stoicism see Rudolf Hoppe, *Der theologische Hintergrund des Jakobusbriefes* (FzB 28; Würzburg: Echter, 1977) 29–31.

33 Eduard Lohse, "'Vollkommen sein.' Zur Ethik des Matthäusevangeliums," 131–40, 134–40, quotation 139. On the understanding of תָּמִים in the Qumran texts cf. Gerhard Delling, "τέλος κτλ," *TDNT* 8 (1972) 73; Paul Johannes du Plessis, *ΤΕΛΕΙΟΣ,* 104–15.

34 Cf. vol. 1, II A 2.2.6 on 5:48.

35 In the *T. Iss.* 5.2 the commandment to love one's

neighbor is connected with concern for the poor. *B. Ber.* 61b = Str-B 1.817 understands giving away one's possessions to be implied by the *Shema.*

36 Ceslas Spicq, *Agape dans le Nouveau Testament* (Paris: Gabalda, 1958) 1.36–37; du Plessis, *ΤΕΛΕΙΟΣ,* 172–73. On the classical ecclesiastical interpretation cf. below, nn. 96–100.

37 James 1:4 also demonstrates these two elements of perfection: τέλειοι καὶ ὁλόκληροι ἐν μηδενὶ λειπόμενοι.

38 This is the emphasis of all those authors who interpret 19:21 in the sense of a *consilium evangelicum* and a double morality. See, e.g., Holtzmann, 268, Montefiore, *Gospels* 2.695–96, Ernst Bammel, "πτωχός κτλ," *TDNT* 6 (1968) 903.

"follow me" (ἀκολούθει μοι) and in Matthew 5 by prefacing the entire Sermon on the Mount with the call of the disciples (4:18-22). Thus in the third place—and this is the most important element—perfection is a matter of following Jesus.[39] The reference to discipleship as the heart of perfection makes something else immediately clear. For Matthew "perfection" is not the highest stage of the Christian life, a position to which only a few, "better" Christians are called.[40] Discipleship for Matthew is not something that is reserved for only a few special Christians; it is rather the key to being a Christian at all.[41] Thus the young man is called to a perfection to which all are called. It is not the "decisive alternative" to the "legalistic righteousness . . . of Judaism."[42] It is rather the heightening of this righteousness by the one who came to fulfill the Law and the Prophets (5:17).

All are called to be perfect. Here "if you want" (εἰ θέλεις) does not mean, any more than it does in v. 17, that the man is free to ignore the following commandment. The surrendering of possessions of which Jesus now speaks is no more optional than is discipleship or the love of one's enemy.[43] From Matthew's perspective the Catholic attempts to understand v. 21 as "counsel" or as the requirement of a "work that exceeds one's duty" (opus supererogationis)[44] appear as a form of moderation or adaptation. For the evangelist the demand to give up one's possessions is a fundamental demand that applies to everyone.[45] He is also far removed from the claim so popular in the history of interpretation, especially in Protestantism, that the young man was an exceptional case whose special problem was that he was too

attached to his money.[46] The contrasting image of the disciples in v. 27 makes clear that discipleship means leaving everything—even houses and lands. But not all members of Matthew's church were itinerant charismatics; it was certainly the case that most of them were resident members who offered hospitality to the wandering charismatics (10:40-42). Thus Matthew probably understands the demand to give up one's possessions neither as a law for everyone nor as advice for a few but as an appeal to all to go this way as far as possible, because giving away one's possessions is a "focal instance" of love.[47] Under no circumstances does he understand this intensification of love as something harmless, as if it were enough not to cling to one's wealth and to dispense a few crumbs from one's own excess. For him the treasure in heaven and the treasure on earth are mutually exclusive (cf. 6:19-21). "The money question raises the issue of one's own humanity."[48]

■ 22 The rich young man understands at least that much, and for that reason he goes away sorrowful.[49]

Matthew and Wealth

The criticism of wealth in the Gospel of Matthew has Jewish roots. The basic *traditions* are: (1) The Old Testament and Jewish conviction that personal property brings with it social responsibility—a conviction which, for example, is important for many prophets and for Deuteronomy and also is found frequently in early Judaism.[50] (2) Fundamental also is the negative attitude toward wealth that is evident in apocalyptic groups which themselves lived in the dark shadows of life. Wealth is part of the evil of this eon.[51] (3) Important finally is a Jewish understanding of conversion.[52]

---

39   Barth, "Understanding," 99.

40   Thus Klostermann (158) with a reference to the *consilia evangelica*. He claims that Matthew prepares the way for "the ethic of emerging Catholicism."

41   Cf. vol. 1, Summary at conclusion of I B 3.2 on 4:18-20.

42   Contra Hoppe, *Der theologische Hintergrund des Jakobusbriefes*, 159.

43   Correctly emphasized by Simon Légasse, *L'appel du riche: Marc 10,17-31 et parallèles: Contribution à l'étude des fondements scripturaires de l'état religieux*, 206–7, 212–13. Indirectly the context (vv. 16, 23-26) makes it clear that the man will now miss his chance at eternal life.

44   Dionysius the Carthusian, 216.

45   Cf. vol. 1 on 6:19-34, immediately following the cen-

ter of the Sermon on the Mount, esp. Summary at the conclusion of II A 2.4.1 and commentary on 6:34-35. On 8:19-20 cf. above, II B 2.1; on 10:7-8, II C 2.1; on 13:22, III B 2.1; on 13:44-46, III B 3.2; on 16:26, IV A 1.

46   Cf. below, nn. 102, 125–27.

47   Burchill, "Evangelical Counsels," 221–24, 230 ("focal instance").

48   Quotation from vol. 1, II A 2.4 on 6:21: "Bei der Frage nach dem Geld steht das Menschsein auf dem Spiel."

49   Erich Fromm formulates it well on v. 22 in his distinction between having and being: "In the New Testament, joy is the fruit of giving up having, while sadness is the mood of the one who hangs onto possessions" (*To Have or To Be?* [New York: Harper &

The most important *parallels* are the rejection of personal property in the Torah-faithful Qumran community (1QS 6.19–20; 7.6–7, 24–25; 9.8–9) and the itinerant Cynic philosophers.[53] Direct or indirect contacts with Qumran are, of course, possible; contacts with the itinerant Cynic philosophers cannot be proven, but neither can they be excluded. The motives for rejecting property vary. In Qumran the issue is the purity of the possessions of the community of those who have distanced themselves from the "men of deceit" (1QS 9.8). In the case of the Cynics it is a matter of the wise man's freedom.[54] With the followers of Jesus the rejection of possessions is based on the kingdom of God and on the love associated with the kingdom of God.[55] *Historically* Matthew's church is influenced by the wandering charismatics and by Jesus' radical rejection of possessions. The fundamental identification of the church with these radical followers of Jesus[56] meant that their traditions became important for the church on its way to "perfection." An additional factor was the experience made time and again in the missionary preaching and in the life of the churches that the "deceit of wealth" was probably the most important impediment to unconditional obedience to the word of Jesus (cf. 13:22; 16:24-26). The rich man's refusal may well have been a common experience for the church.

■ **23-26** A conversation with the disciples follows that with the rich man. Matthew's version is shorter than that of his Markan source, primarily because he omits Mark 10:24, which speaks of how difficult it is for everyone to enter the kingdom of God. Thus our text speaks *only* of the problem of riches, and it offers no possibility for expanding the discussion to include a general human problem. The disciples whom Jesus addresses here—and thus by implication Matthew's readers—are in an ambivalent situation with regard to this problem. On the one hand, it is clear from the expression "a rich man" in v. 23 and from Peter's question in v. 27 that they are not among the rich. On the other hand, even they are shocked by Jesus' harsh word about the camel and the eye of a needle. Obviously the issue is difficult also for them. This ambivalence will correspond to the situation of Matthew's church. On the one hand, nowhere in the Gospel of Matthew do we get the impression that there were actual rich people in the church. On the other hand, it is probable that most of the members of Matthew's church did not give away their possessions (cf. 13:22), and in the case of the itinerant charismatics there obviously was the problem of receiving payment for preaching and healing (10:8-9). Thus perhaps even the readers had reason to be shocked.

In other regards the conversation with the disciples largely follows its source. What is important for Mark is important also for Matthew. The basic idea is that there is a fundamental tension between worldly possessions and the coming kingdom of God.[57] Jesus' word about

---

Row, 1976] 105; cited according to the 1981 Bantam edition).

50   Cf. e.g., Job as a friend of the poor (*T. Job* 9–15); Philo *Fug.* 28–29; *2 Enoch* 42.8–9; 50.5–51.2 (giving one's possessions for the poor for the sake of the coming eon); 63.1–4. In addition see the rabbinic sources in Str-B 1.817–18; 4.537ff.

51   *1 Enoch* 46.4–7; 94–104 passim.

52   Cf. 2 Esdr 13:54; *Pesiq.* 178b = Str-B 1.817; *Jos. Asen.* 12.12; 13.2–8.

53   The most important parallels to our text are Crates, who lived without possessions for the sake of his own inner freedom (Diogenes *Ep.* 9 = Abraham J. Malherbe, ed., *The Cynic Epistles* [Sources for Biblical Study 12; Missoula: Scholars Press, 1977] 102; Diogenes Laertius 6.87) and the conversion of a young man (μειράκιον) in Diogenes *Ep.* 38.4–5 = Malherbe, 162. Cf. in addition Epictetus *Diss.* 2.14.18–24 (but here without any surrender of property), Philostratus *Vit. Ap.* 6.16 (the νεανίσκος Neilos gives his possessions to his relatives and becomes a gymnosophist [naked Brahmin]); Lucian *Pergr. Mort.* 15 (Peregrinus as a philosopher claims to be a second Crates); Philo *Vit. cont.* 13 (the Therapeutae are free of possessions). For additional material see F. Gerald Downing, *Jesus and the Threat of Freedom* (London: SCM, 1987) 83–95.

54   "Crates, the son of Crates, sets Crates free" (Diogenes *Ep.* 9 = Malherbe, 102).

55   By contrast, Crates leaves his property not to the poor but to the city. In the ancient church's interpretation of Matt 19:21 it is repeatedly emphasized that one's money should be given to the poor and not to one's own relatives or children (e.g., Jerome *Ep.* 130.14 = NPNF second series 6.262). It was not until later that the monastic orders and the church became the "heirs" of the poor.

56   Cf. on Matthew 10, II C (4. The Addressees) and Summary: The Basic Message of the Disciples Discourse.

57   Of course, βασιλεία τῶν οὐρανῶν (v. 23) and βασιλεία τοῦ θεοῦ (v. 24) are variants of the same

the camel and the eye of a needle is also true for him in all of its harshness. The opposites are proverbial[58] and they refer to the largest possible animal and the smallest possible opening.[59] Verses 25-26, which in the Markan source emphasize God's grace with regard to the needle's eye, are if anything toned down in Matthew. Ἀλλ᾽ οὐ παρὰ θεῷ is missing so that the entire weight is no longer on the biblical-sounding concluding clause παρὰ δὲ θεῷ πάντα δυνατά. Instead, both parallel clauses—"with men this is impossible" and "with God all things are possible"—carry equal weight. Thus that with God everything is *possible* probably does not necessarily mean for Matthew that he will *actually* break the rule about the camel and the eye of a needle.

■ **27-29** With v. 27 the disciples move to the foreground. Their spokesperson, Peter, asks a question not contained in Mark about the heavenly reward of those who, like the disciples, have left everything and have followed Jesus. Since for Matthew, himself a Jew and a disciple of Jesus, the idea of a heavenly reward is self-evident (cf. 5:12, 46; 6:1-18; 10:41-42; 20:1-16), Peter does not need to be rebuked for his question. Jesus' answer consists of two different words whose relationship to one another is dif-

ficult to determine. The logion v. 28aβ, b which has been inserted into Mark's text speaks of the twelve who will play a special role with the Son of Man as co-judges over the twelve tribes. When v. 29 begins with πᾶς ὅστις, on the other hand, it appears to speak in a more general sense of the reward that everyone will receive. Does the text speak, therefore, of a special reward that the apostles or the "perfect," that is, the itinerant charismatics, will receive among the disciples? Much speaks against this thesis. Peter speaks for all the disciples and not just for a special group among the disciples.[60] All Christians, and not only some of them, understand themselves to be followers of Jesus. In v. 29 Matthew omitted precisely those Markan elements that most easily could have been understood in terms of the new life in settled communities.[61] Of course, the traditional logion v. 28aβ, b does speak of a special position of the twelve in the final judgment. But since for Matthew the twelve "back then" represent the present disciples of Jesus,[62] presumably for him the emphasis is not that the twelve apostles will receive a reward that differs from that of all other later Christians.[63] Instead, he understands vv. 28 and 29 together. That the twelve will sit on

---

formula, as the sequence of δυσκόλως and εὐκοπώτερον and the repetition of εἰσέρχεσθαι clearly demonstrate. Armin Wouters's attempt (". . . *wer den Willen meines Vaters tut*": *Eine Untersuchung zum Verständnis vom Handeln im Matthäusevangelium* [BU 16; Regensburg: Pustet, 1992] 60–61, 91–101) to distinguish between them by claiming that βασιλεία τοῦ θεοῦ refers to the present kingdom and βασιλεία τῶν οὐρανῶν to the future kingdom is completely impossible. Our text makes quite clear that Matthew, who frequently, but not always, conforms to the contemporary language of the synagogue (cf. "βασιλεία τῶν οὐρανῶν" in vol. 1, I B 1.1 on 3:1-12), does use it in connection with new theological concepts.

58   Cf. Str-B 1.828.

59   Gnilka, *Markus* 2.88. The occasional transcription of κάμηλος into its homonym κάμιλος (a ship's rigging or rope) assimilates the imagery of the hyperbole but does not weaken it. The eye of a needle is now contrasted with the thickest of all "threads." Much better known even today is the identification of the needle's eye with a city gate in Jerusalem for which there is evidence since the High Middle Ages (in the *Glossa ex Anselmo* in Thomas Aquinas, *Catena,* 288 [ET: 2.670]; Paschasius Radbertus, 665;

Anselm of Laon, 1415). There never was such a city gate in Jerusalem. This interpretation clearly is designed to make the hard word of Jesus more acceptable. Even more interesting than this new interpretation itself is the question why it has remained so popular.

60   Cf. above, the excursus on Peter in the Gospel of Matthew in III C 3.3.

61   "Houses . . . and lands, with persecutions."

62   Cf. Luz, "Jünger," 142–46, 151–52 and above, II C (4. The Addressees).

63   Not even in the form that the apostles are promised a special position that they will receive in the new eon and not here, as suggested by Fred W. Burnett ("Παλιγγενεσία: Matt 19:28: A Window on the Matthean Community," 60–72, 64–65) in order to reconcile a contradiction with 18:1-5; 20:20-28; 23:8-12 of which Matthew is not even aware.

64   The idea of v. 28 is one of the Jewish and Christian concepts available to Matthew according to which the righteous (Wis 3:8; *1 Enoch* 38.5; 91.12; 95.3; cf. 1QpHab 5.3), or the entire nation of Israel (*Jub.* 24.29; *1 Enoch* 90.19; cf. Dan 7:22), or the Christian community (1 Cor 6:2-3; Rev 20:4?) will participate in the final judgment. That Matthew is also familiar with such concepts is clear in 25:40, 45 where the

the thrones is for him a special form of the "hundred-fold" that is promised to all.[64]

■ **28** Verse 28 offers several exegetical difficulties. It is not clear what Matthew means with the hapax legomenon παλιγγενεσία. Clearly the Greek-sounding term[65] refers not to the "rebirth" of the individual (as in Titus 3:5) but to the eschaton. Beyond that, however, the text gives no indication what is meant. It seems to me that the most likely possibility is the resurrection of the dead,[66] more in the sense of the eschatological restoration of the twelve tribes[67] or the re-creation of the world.[68] The "throne of glory" may mean the throne of God[69] on which the Son of Man will sit. Together with the Son of Man the twelve apostles will "judge" Israel on their thrones. That κρίνω could mean "to rule" is a philological fiction that is clearly false,[70] even though it has enjoyed near-universal acceptance since H. Grotius,[71] who may have been the first to suggest it. That the evangelist is not interested in the concept of judgment in any detail is clear from the fact that in 25:31 he can recall our verse even though there it is not the twelve apostles but the "least of the brothers" who are present at the judgment of the Son of Man, and it is not

the twelve tribes of Israel but "all the nations" (πάντα τὰ ἔθνη) who are judged. Our context is not interested in what may have been a polemical element in earlier stages of the tradition—viz., that it is Israel and not the Gentiles that the twelve judge.[72] In the Matthean context the logion is simply a word of promise. In view of what they have to give up in the present, the twelve are promised an incredible exaltation that is out of all proportion to their present sacrifice. The "hundredfold" of v. 29 is but a natural extension of this promise.

■ **29** Matthew has taken over this second promise in abbreviated form from the Gospel of Mark. He no longer speaks of the new fellowship and the community property that already in this eon will be granted to all who have given up their families and their possessions.[73] He no longer shares Mark's concern for overcoming the individual's anxiety by means of community solidarity.[74] Matthew is interested only in the eternal reward which, while he does not describe it in detail, he does characterize with the biblical-sounding "a hundredfold" (ἑκατονταπλασίονα).[75] A difficult question is why, unlike Luke's gospel, the wife (and husband!) is missing from the list of family members who must be left behind. Matthew

---

world-judge refers to "these" the least of his brothers. Obviously they are understood to be present.

65 The word is used by the Stoics as a designation of the renewal of the world after the ἐκπύρωσις and is then applied to the fate of the individual soul, e.g., in the mysteries. There is no direct Hebrew or Aramaic equivalent.

66 This usage is supported by Philo *Poster. C.* 124; *Cher.* 114; *Leg. Gaj.* 325, where the word is almost a technical term in this sense. J. Duncan M. Derrett, who holds to this interpretation, assumes that the Hebrew equivalent is תְּחִיָּה, the Pharisaic-rabbinic term for the resurrection of the dead ("Palingenesia [Matthew 19:28]," 51–58, 53).

67 Thus, e.g., Anton Vögtle, *Das Neue Testament und die Zukunft des Kosmos,* 165–66. Of course, this concept is presupposed in Matt 19:28. It is questionable, however, whether it can be expressed simply by παλιγγενεσία without any modifying word. Still, cf. Josephus *Ant.* 11.66 ("restoration" of Israel after the Exile).

68 This is the most common interpretation. David C. Sim ("The Meaning of παλιγγενσεία in Matthew 19,28," 3–12, 7–12) cites Matt 5:18 and 24:35 as evidence that Matthew also is familiar with this hope which had been known since Trito-Isaiah. Cf. Philo

Vit. Mos. 2.65 (restoration of the world after the flood).

69 As in Jer 14:21; 17:12; Dan 3:54 LXX; Wis 9:10, etc. The expression fits with Matthew's preference for biblical language. A literary relation to the parabolic addresses of *1 Enoch* such as Theisohn (*Richter,* 152–201) suggests cannot be demonstrated.

70 It comes from confusing the *historical* fact that in Israel judges ruled and kings judged with the *semantic* meaning of κρίνω. None of the evidence that BAGD, s.v. κρίνω, 3bβ offers to support this meaning says what is claimed for it.

71 2.125. Still, Grotius clearly speaks of a *tralatio,* i.e., of a transferal of meaning.

72 Broer ("Ringen," 159–64) emphasizes this meaning for the tradition.

73 With the plural οἰκίας Matthew makes it clear that he is thinking of leaving property and not one's family (as perhaps Mark means).

74 Thus the impressive psychological interpretation of Mark 10:17-31 offered by Thea Vogt, *Angst und Identität im Markusevangelium,* 173–83.

75 Cf. 2 Sam 24:3 LXX; 1 Chr 21:3.

simply follows Mark's text here, and it may be that he was thinking that new converts frequently must make a break with their parents (cf. 10:35, 37), while Christian married couples may not have been at all unusual, even as missionaries.[76]

■ **30** The logion about the many who are first who will be last and vice versa brings the thought to a close for the time being. It is clear from the context that one is thinking of the great reversal in the last judgment. But who are the first, and who are the last? The context suggests as the most likely possibility that the "last" could be the disciples who in the present leave everything and who one day will judge Israel, while among the "first" are people like the rich man of vv. 16-22. But Matthew does not say that, and when he limits the statement to "many" ($\pi o \lambda \lambda o i$) instead of saying simply "the first," the readers are puzzled. For this reason another interpretation frequently has been suggested, viz., that Matthew concludes by warning the Christians who become confident about their future heavenly position. But Matthew also does not say that directly. "As readers we are puzzled and cannot resolve the ambiguity of this verse."[77] So what is meant? It seems to me that Matthew has left it open intentionally, because he wants his readers to move on to the next section of the text with this open question.

Summary

It is time to attempt to give an exegetical response to our two basic questions.[78] (1) For Matthew the perfection that Jesus demands of the rich man is not something that lies beyond the Old Testament commandments; it is, rather, their perfect fulfillment in the sense of the antitheses of the Sermon on the Mount and the love command. According to Matthew, Jesus has come not to eliminate the Law and the Prophets, not even to add something to them, but to fulfill them (5:17). (2) Accordingly, the "perfect" are not a special group within the church. All of the church's members are called to the way of perfection. As was the case with the antitheses of the Sermon on the Mount, the appeal to abandon one's possessions in a life of following Jesus is directed to the entire church. Matthew is undoubtedly aware that he is not going to make itinerant charismatics of the entire church. For him also, therefore, the appeal to live without possessions is not a Christian law; it is rather a call to do as much as possible at this focal point of faith.

History of Interpretation

Our text has seriously engaged the church's interpreters. In much the same way as with the interpretation of the antitheses of the Sermon on the Mount, basic theological decisions of the most important epochs of the church's history that still influence us today are visible in the history of the interpretation of this text. Unfortunately, for long stretches of this interpretation Ernst Bloch is right when he says that the church has "widened that aperture [*scil.*, the eye of the needle] considerably" in order to make it easier for the rich to enter the kingdom of heaven and for the church to live with this text.[79]

1. Matt 19:21 as a Commandment for Everyone

For the interpreters of the ancient church it is initially clear that the command of Christ in v. 21 is to be taken literally and that it applies to everyone. Origen tells the rich to share their possessions with the poor so that they will profit from their prayers.[80] John Chrysostom says expressly that it is not enough to despise wealth inwardly; one must do something and support the poor.[81] The bishop and monastic founder, Basil, is especially forceful in demanding of all that they give away their possessions. According to him Matt 19:21 applies even to the fathers of families with children: Are children to be an excuse for not keeping God's commandments?[82] Jesus' word to the young man is for him "a commandment that is obligatory for all Christians."[83] Wealth, understood as what exceeds the basic necessities of life, is for Basil a contradiction of the highest commandment of the love of neighbor which has the goal of economic equality among people.[84]

76   Cf. 1 Cor 9:5.

77   Patte, 273.

78   See above, Interpretation.

79   Bloch, *Atheism*, 125.

80   15:17 = GCS Origenes 10.397.

81   63:2 = *PG* 58.605. Similarly Jerome, 170.

82   *Hom.* 7 (Against the Rich) 7 = BKV 1/47.253–54.

83   Koschorke, *Spuren*, (par. 32) 77.

84   A. Persic, "Basilio: Una sola chiamata per tutti i christiani," in *Per foramen*, 182.

85   That is clear when the Emperor Julian ridicules the Christians by suggesting that one could smooth their way into the kingdom of heaven by relieving them of their property (Julian *Epistulae* 115 [Joseph

However, both Origen and John Chrysostom already reveal the *tendency to moderate* the radical command of Jesus. One should give at least *some* of one's possessions to the poor. As the church evolved the ancient ideal of the itinerant charismatics who lived without possessions could not be maintained.[85] The emphasis was increasingly placed on the right *attitude* toward one's possessions with the claim that Jesus does not say that it is impossible, only that it is difficult, for rich people to enter the kingdom of heaven.[86] Hilary recommends moderation in dealing with possessions. He claims that possessions themselves are not bad; they become bad when they are used to hurt others.[87] In any case one is to avoid greed, the love of wealth.[88]

2. The Development to the Consilium Evangelicum

It was also understood, however, that for Jesus perfection was characterized not by the moderate use of possessions but by their absolute rejection.[89] In the increasingly compromised Catholic imperial church hermits or monastic communities attempted to take seriously the commandment to be perfect, which included the total rejection of possessions.[90] The best-known examples of a complete rejection of possessions on the basis of Matt 19:21 are the Egyptian Antonius in the ancient church and Peter Waldo in the Middle Ages.[91] Our text was equally important for the Franciscans. In both versions of the Franciscan rule Matt 19:21 is the first biblical text cited.[92] The coexistence of the medieval church with hermits, orders, and popular movements of the poor mirrored in a different form the coexistence of itinerant charismatics and resident disciples in primitive Christianity.

Matthew 19:21 thus became the counsel that only a few are capable of following. The term *consilium*

appeared early in connection with Matt 19:21,[93] even though the actual church teaching of the three *consilia evangelica*—poverty (Matt 19:21), chastity (Matt 19:12), and obedience = discipleship (Matt 19:21)— did not appear until the Middle Ages. According to this doctrine there are two different kinds of calling in the Christian church—one for perfection and the other for everyday living.[94] The medieval exegesis cited two callings that existed already among the followers of Jesus. Alongside the apostles, who left everything, were Nicodemus, Gamaliel, and Joseph of Arimathea.[95] God has richly poured out his mercy on the "perfect," whom he has called to the *vita apostolica* of poverty and chastity, even as he did on the prodigal son.[96] The entire system is effectively presented by Thomas Aquinas. According to him perfection consists *essentially* in the love of God and of others as it is formulated in the divine law. But it exists *instrumentally* in the counsel to poverty and to the unmarried life, since both counsels address essential hindrances to love.[97] With Thomas it is important that the perfect are not simply identical with the calling of the *religiosi*; it is important for everyone to strive for perfection, whereby the evangelical counsels are an important help.[98] Voluntary poverty is not itself perfection; it is rather *via* and *praeambulum* to perfect love.[99] What Matthew and Thomas have in common is that they speak of perfection as a *way* that it is important to go.

Sometimes, although not explicitly in the case of Thomas, to the idea of the two "callings" is connected the idea of a special reward for those who are perfect. One finds allusions to it in the heavenly treasure of v. 21 or, less frequently, in v. 28.[100]

This framework for the interpretation of Matt 19:16-22 remains valid Catholic doctrine. Later

Bidez and Franz Cumont, eds.; Paris: "Les Belles Lettres," 1922]).

86 "Non impossibilitas . . . sed raritas demonstratur" (Jerome, 171); cf. Ephraem, 15.5 = 267; Euthymius Zigabenus, 525 (for a rich person it is difficult; for a greedy person impossible).

87 19:9 = SC 258.98.

88 Since Irenaeus *Haer.* 4.12.5.

89 Jerome (170), with a reference to Ananias and Sapphira.

90 Cf. *Liber Graduum* 14.2 = 327–28.

91 Athanasius *Anton.* 2 = NPNF Second Series 4.196; Anonymous of Laon in Kurt-Victor Selge, *Die ersten Waldenser* (Arbeiten zur Kirchengeschichte 37/1; Berlin: de Gruyter, 1967) 231–32.

92 *Regula non bullata* 1 and *Regula bullata* 2 in von Balthasar, *Ordensregeln,* 287, 314.

93 Ambrose *Vid.* 12 = *PL* 16.256; Augustine *Sermo* 86.2, 8–9, 14 = *PL* 38.524, 527, 530; further sources in Burchill, "Evangelical Counsels," 29–36.

94 Eusebius *Dem. ev.* 1.8.3 = GCS 23.39.

95 Christian of Stavelot, 1417.

96 Bernard of Clairvaux *Sermones de diversis* 27.3 = *PL* 183.613.

97 *S. th.* 2/2 q.184, a.3.

98 *S. th.* 2/2 q.186 a.2 (*Non tenetur habere perfectam caritatem, sed tenetur ad hoc tendere*). Voluntary poverty is an *effecax exercitium* for perfect love (a.3).

99 *Lectura* no. 1595.

100 In, e.g., Dionysius the Carthusian, 217; Dionysius bar Salibi, 309; Maldonat, 396; Lapide, 374 (on v. 28); Jansen, 180 (on vv. 28-29). Cf. above, IV C 1, n. 91.

exegetes frequently cited it, and the Catholic church's catechism has reaffirmed it.[101]

3. Clement of Alexandria

Clement's homily on Matthew 19 (Τίς ὁ σωζόμενος πλούσιος) has the purpose of demonstrating that rich persons can indeed be saved. For Clement, understanding the text in terms of outwardly giving away one's possessions instead of in terms of the soul from which the love of possessions, anxiety, and worries about the earthly life must be banned, is superficial.[102] The real threat to salvation is not wealth but one's emotions, for salvation does not depend on externals. The rich man who "is a slave of his possessions and . . . [carries] them about in his soul" can be far from salvation, but the same can be true of the poor man with his passions. One should aspire not to poverty but to poverty of spirit according to Matt 5:3.[103] Thus one must be concerned to "detach yourself from the alien possessions that dwell in your soul, in order that you may become pure in heart and may see God."[104] Wealth, however, is an adiaphoron; of itself it is neither good nor bad. Instead of abandoning it, one should make of it an instrument of righteousness.[105] Of course, Clement expresses tendencies that *also* appear in other interpretations of our text in the ancient church,[106] but he takes them further than almost all other interpretations. It is not without reason that E. Troeltsch says that of all the writings of the ancient church this sermon is "the most favorable toward wealth" and "one of the most sensible works from the economic point of view."[107]

4. The Allegorical Interpretation

The allegorical interpretation of our text was initiated by Origen, programmatically developed by Hilary, and then continued to be of influence in the Middle Ages. It separated the text from the problem of wealth even more radically. While Origen understood the rich man symbolically as someone who owns many evil works,[108] Hilary contributed to the development of an allegorical interpretation involving salvation history. The rich man embodies Judaism, which claims to hold only to the law. Jesus confronts it with the challenge to abandon this shadow of the truth and at the same time to share the law with the Gentiles (= the poor).[109] In the Middle Ages a number of interpreters represented this type of interpretation. Notable among them were the *Opus imperfectum* and Paschasius Radbertus.[110] For Paschasius Radbertus salvation for the Jews depended solely on works and not on faith.[111] With such an extreme thesis this type of interpretation belongs, along with that of Clement, to the precursors of the Protestant exegesis. This approach gave rise to impressive interpretations of v. 24. The camel was often understood as a reference to the Gentiles, since it is a wild animal.[112] Then the needle's eye might mean such things as the narrow gate of Matt 7:12-13,[113] confession,[114] or the passion of Christ.[115]

5. The Protestant Interpretations

With the Reformation our text became the object of an intense interconfessional controversy that influenced almost all interpretations. The interpretations of all the reformers are amazingly similar. They are directed against the "evangelical counsels," since the counsels embody the attempt to earn life through one's own effort—an attempt that characterized not only monasticism in a special way but in their view also the entire papal church.[116] The Protestant interpreters understood Jesus' commandment to the young man to sell his possessions as a concrete expression of the love commandment—that is, as commandment and not as counsel. The middle of God's

---

101 Cf., e.g., Fritz Tillmann, *Die Idee der Nachfolge Christi* (Handbuch der katholischen Sittenlehre 3; 4th ed.; Düsseldorf: Patmos, 1953) 199–200; Catholic *Catechism*, nos. 2052–54.

102 2.2 = ANF 2.591, Loeb 273–75; 11.2 = ANF 2.594, Loeb 291–93.

103 15.2 = ANF 2.595, Loeb 301; 16.3 = ANF 2.595, Loeb 303 (quotation); 18.5 = ANF 2.596, Loeb 307; 17.5 = ANF 2.595–96, Loeb 305.

104 19.3 = ANF 2.596, Loeb 309 (quotation).

105 15.3 = ANF 2.595, Loeb 301; 14.3 = ANF 2.595, Loeb 299.

106 Cf. esp. L. F. Pizzolato, "Una società cristiana alle prese di un testo radicale: l´esegesi della pericope nella Chiesa latina post-cosstantiniana," in *Per foramen*, 264–328.

107 Troeltsch, *Social Teaching*, 184, n. 58.

108 15.18 = GCS Origenes 10.399.

109 19.5–8 = SC 258.94–98.

110 *Opus imperfectum* 33 = 805–16; Paschasius Radbertus, 658–67.

111 Paschasius Radbertus, 659.

112 Hilary, 19.11 = SC 258.100; *Opus imperfectum* 33 = 810. Paschasius Radbertus (665) thinks of Gentiles because of Isa 60:6.

113 *Opus imperfectum* 33 = 812.

114 Paschasius Radbertus, 665.

115 Augustine *Quaest.* 112.

116 Luther, *WA* 47.349; Calvin 2.255. In a similar way the Reformers simply identified, incorrectly, the ethic with double standards with Catholic interpretation of the Sermon on the Mount. Cf. vol. 1, II A

law which is valid for all people is not something that is merely external; it is rather that one "should not love anything" more than God and that one therefore should love one's neighbor as oneself.[117] Of course, in this radical sense the man could not keep the law; indeed, no one can keep it. Thus Jesus' conversation with him in no way intended to lead him to meritorious works; it was designed rather as a "preschool" that would "lead him to righteousness by grace" in the sense of the *usus elenchticus legis* (the use of the law in order to convict).[118] His greed reveals a false view of himself—his striving for a righteousness based on works.[119] Thus the rich man becomes the prototype of the godless person.[120] It is clear that the essence of the text cannot lie in the sale of possessions; indeed, such an action would once again be a work and might even be an expression of "pure boastfulness."[121] Luther says pointedly that Christ himself did not sell his goods and his clothes but ate and drank.[122] In his theses on Matt 19:21 Luther turns the text upside down and claims that Christ's commandment is precisely not to leave everything and like the monks to live "on handouts from others," but in the sense of the second tablet of the law "(to) earn, keep, protect, and manage everything" so that one not become a thief and robber—indeed, if need be as "a citizen of this world" to defend one's own possessions. Thus to care for one's own family with one's own possessions corresponds to the commandments of the second tablet and is a commandment of faith. To leave them would be a sin. For Luther the only situation in which one may disregard the commandments of the second tablet and may abandon everything is when one must do it for the sake of the first tablet—for confessional reasons of faith, when a non-Protestant government forces one to deny one's faith.[123] It scarcely would be possible to misunderstand more the poverty commandment of our text. Out of the thesis that Jesus gives a commandment instead of counsel one has created for all practical purposes a prohibition.[124]

6. The Post-Reformation Interpretations

These offer little that is new. The possibility of a special, monastic way had been destroyed once and for all. As Protestant, middle-class domesticity came to dominate, the interest in our text waned. The teacher Olshausen makes of the Prostestant *usus elenchticus legis* an example of the savior's admirable pastoral skill in dealing with the young man.[125] The ambitious youth should have let Jesus lead him "to self awareness and thus to a right relationship" to the savior.[126] The claim is firmly repeated that his was a special case, a special command for an especially miserly person, a *personale praeceptum* that has no more general validity than does the command to Abraham to sacrifice Isaac.[127] Thus the text no longer makes any claims on the reader, for who is so miserly that the text needs to speak to him? Finally, for Max Weber the radical demand to give away one's possessions, along with the Sermon on the Mount, becomes the essence of the principled ethic that one can follow only "completely or not at all"—an ethic for saints whose deeds are "completely irrational" and are only

---

The Sermon on the Mount, 4: On the History of Interpretation of the Sermon on the Mount.

117 Luther, *WA* 47.350.
118 Calvin 2.255.
119 Calvin, *Inst.* 4.13.13; Zwingli, 349–50.
120 Luther, *WA* 47.356.
121 Calvin 2.257.
122 Luther, *WA* 47.353.
123 Luther, "Zirkulardisputation," theses 8, 14 (quotation), 24 (quotation), 30 (quotation), 26–27, 21 = 39–40; German edition = 44–46. The thrust of the disputation is that, while one need not defend one's possessions from the governing authority, one should do so against the pope, who is a robber and a thief and not a legitimate secular authority. Melancthon (193) puts it sharply: To give away the family's possessions is not *supra legem* but *infra legem*. On the contrary, it is a *praeceptum* to make use of the family's possessions to help whomever one can help.
124 The interpretation of the Spaniard de Valdés

(334–44) is in many ways comparable to the main lines of the Protestant interpretations. He also describes the rich man as an example of self-righteousness whom Jesus wants to lead to the experience of grace. Is there some Protestant influence here?
125 734–35. Cf. de Wette (115), who claims that Jesus wants to lead a representative of works-righteousness "to a better self-awareness and to the consciousness of his ethical weakness."
126 Zahn, 590–92.
127 Since Calvin, *Inst.* 4.13.13 (near the end); Bucer, 157 (*personale praeceptum*); Bullinger, 182 (*speciale experimentum*, referring to Abraham); Musculus, 458; cf. Dickson, 259.

of "exemplary value," since they cannot be demanded of everyone. As a politician's maxim and as a requirement for everyone Matt 19:21 would be irresponsible and senseless.[128]

Meaning for Today

The history of the interpretation of the text continues to influence our present. In *Protestantism* it has been almost exclusively a history of displacement and delusion. As a consequence our purpose here must be to recover our text as a text that deals with a rich man and with wealth. We Protestants must learn that anew and why for Jesus and early Christianity there was clearly a fundamental tension between the kingdom of God and wealth. We must learn again that a central issue of faith is how one deals with money. While it is true that "if . . . we give away all our possessions, that act is not in itself" the obedience that discipleship requires "for we might then be choosing a[n alternative!] way of life for ourselves,"[129] it is more important today to learn the opposite truth—viz., that the obedience of discipleship must fundamentally change the way we deal with our own money, because money governs the world, and following Jesus is love's protest against this "government." Furthermore, it seems to me that we Protestants also must reconsider whether, in addition to an average, middle-class Christianity, there should not be special, radical forms of Christian love and commitment that, while not required of everyone, can be "recommended" to individuals—forms that are important for everyone, since they remind us of the kingdom of God of which Jesus spoke and that bring into question the power of money.[130] In the light of our text we would have to consider anew, creatively and imaginatively, just how such alternative expressions of love might look today. But it is my opinion that any concrete suggestion that does not lead to changes in both

personal and ecclesiastical finances simply ignores the text. Here it is especially clear that any present understanding of a biblical text must include practical application—that, in other words, a merely verbal, abstract understanding that excludes one's own existence from the claims of the text is no genuine understanding.

To the *Catholic church,* on the other hand, whose "official" interpretation of the text as an "evangelical counsel" does a better job of preserving its potential meaning, we would have to ask how it effectively deals with the danger of a division of Christians into two classes—"normal" and "special" believers, among whom are the clergy, monks, nuns, and the hierarchy.[131] Time and again in its history there has been the tendency to turn "instruments" of perfection for everybody into the "evangelical counsels" that are the preconditions of perfection for a few.[132] In this way the two-tiered system of Christians has been solidified, and the evangelical counsels have become laws for the few. It is probable, however, that Matthew is thinking not of two levels of discipleship but of a way of life in which everyone does as much as is possible. He views itinerant charismatics and resident disciples, persons without possessions and propertied persons who are responsible for them, not separately but together.

Let me take this occasion to refer to two interpretations of our text from this century, a Protestant and a Catholic, which have in common that each of them in much of what it says swims against the stream of the dominant interpretation in its own church. It seems to me that *Karl Barth*'s interpretation is significant, because it makes clear how God's reign and the surrender of one's possessions belong together. Surrendering one's possessions as an act of love shows "that you have them, and not they you,"[133] and it thus witnesses to the reality that *God* "has" the person— indeed, that God has the person both as a free

---

128 Max Weber, "Politik als Beruf," in idem, *Gesammelte Politische Schriften* (2d ed.; Tübingen: Mohr/Siebeck, 1958) 538, 540.

129 Bonhoeffer, *Cost,* 74.

130 Cf. Fyodor Dostoievsky, *The Brothers Karamazov,* book 1, chap. 5 (Constance Garnett, trans.; New York: Random House, n.d.). Alyosha Karamazov stands before the church and considers the statement, "Give all that thou hast to the poor and follow Me, if thou wouldst be perfect." Alyosha says to himself: "I can't give two roubles instead of 'all,' and only go to mass instead of 'following Him.'"

131 My Catholic partner, Paul Hoffmann, adds: and how they come to terms with the tension between "individual poverty" and the "wealth of the cloisters and the church."

132 For this reason Karl Rahner speaks of the call of everyone, including married persons, to a *single* perfection ("On the Evangelical Counsels," in idem, *Theological Investigations* [New York: Herder & Herder, 1971] 8.140–46).

133 Barth, *CD* 2/2.620.

human being and as his partner in covenant. Thus living without possessions as an expression of the love of neighbor is not, as with Luther, a special case of obedience to the first tablet of Commandments; it is rather its supreme case. The second interpretation is that offered by *John Paul II* in his encyclical *Veritatis Splendor*. In this interpretation he dispenses with the distinction between "commandment" and "counsel" and between beginners and those who are perfect, and he understands the "summons" of Matt 19:21 as a summons to *everyone* to love one's neighbor. All are called to perfect love "whose standard is God alone."[134] The encyclical emphasizes with notable

clarity that such a summons to all involves freedom (and, in my judgment, also excludes any legalistic requirement of "evangelical counsels"!).[135] Both of the interpretations energetically call attention to the power of God cited in v. 26 which, according to Karl Barth, is the "hinge"[136] of the entire text and is the only thing which can enable our churches to abandon the rigid structures that have grown out of the text and thus to regain the text.

---

134 John Paul II, *Veritatis Splendor*, no. 18, 31–32.

135 John Paul II, *Veritatis Splendor*, nos. 13, 24, pp. 21–24, 38–40. To be sure, I would draw different conclusions from the encyclical's systematic approach than does the pope. In my judgment, the *law* (and not the "counsel") of celibacy for priests contradicts the call to perfection in freedom for all—the call that the pope sees in Matt 19:16-22 in

an impressive way. Or is there for this call a special perfection alongside the general perfection?

136 Barth, *CD* 2/2.625.

Literature

Paul Billerbeck, "Das Gleichnis von den Arbeitern im Weinberg Mt 20,1-16 und die altsynagogale Lohnlehre," in Str–B 4.484–500.

Bornkamm, "Lohngedanke," 69–93.

Ingo Broer, "Die Gleichnisexegese und die neuere Literaturwissenschaft: Ein Diskussionsbeitrag zur Exegese von Mt 20,1-16," *Biblische Notizen* 5 (1978) 13–27.

Ignacio R. Cóbreces, "Los obreros de la viña. Elementos midráshicos en la parábola de Mt 20,1-16," *Studium* 30 (1990) 485–505.

J. Duncan M. Derrett, "Workers in the Vineyard: A Parable of Jesus," *JJS* 25 (1974) 64–91.

Christian Dietzfelbinger, "Das Gleichnis von den Arbeitern im Weinberg als Jesuswort," *EvTh* 43 (1983) 126–37.

Jean Duplacy, "Le maître généreux et les ouvriers égoistes (Mt 20,1-16)," *BVC* 44 (1962) 16–30.

Jacques Dupont, "La parabole des ouvriers de la vigne (Mt 20:1-16)," *NRTh* 79 (1957) 785–97.

Idem, "Ouvriers de la onzième," 16–26.

John H. Elliott, "Mt 20:1-15: A Parable of Invidious Comparison and Evil Eye Accusation," *BTB* 22 (1992) 52–65.

Erlemann, *Bild*, 93–114.

D. L. Gragg, "The Parable of the Workers in the Vineyard and Its Interpreters: A Text-Linguistic Analysis" (Diss., Emory University, 1990).

Harnisch, *Gleichniserzählungen,* 177–200.

Wilfrid Haubeck, "Zum Verständnis der Parabel von den Arbeitern im Weinberg (Mt 20,1-15)," in idem and Michael Bachmann, eds., *Wort in der Zeit: Neutestamentliche Studien: Festgabe für Karl Heinrich Rengstorf zum 75. Geburtstag* (Leiden: Brill, 1980) 95–107.

Joseph H. Heinemann, "The Conception of Reward in Mt 20, 1-16," *JJS* 1 (1948/49) 85–89.

Heinemann, "Status," 263–325.

Hezser, *Lohnmetaphorik.*

Jeremias, *Parables,* 33–38, 136–139.

Jülicher, *Gleichnisreden* 2.459–71.

Lambrecht, *Treasure,* 69–88.

C. L. Mitton, "The Workers in the Vineyard," *ExpT* 77 (1965/66) 307–11.

Ekkehard Mühlenberg, "Das Gleichnis von den Arbeitern im Weinberg (Mt 20,1-16) bei den Vätern," in Herbert Eisenberger, ed., *EPMHNEYMATA: Festschrift für Hadwig Hörner zum sechzigsten Geburtstag* (Heidelberg: Winter, 1990) 11–26.

Johannes M. Nützel, "'Darf ich mit dem Meinen nicht tun, was ich will?' (Mt 20,15a)," in Lorenz Oberlinner and Peter Fiedler, eds., *Salz der Erde–Licht der Welt: Exegetische Studien zum Matthäusevangelium: Festschrift für Anton Vögtle zum 80. Geburtstag*

(Stuttgart: Katholisches Bibelwerk, 1991) 267–84.

Antonio Orbe, *Parábolas Evangélicas en San Ireneo* (BAC; Madrid: La Editorial Católica, 1972) 1.411–60.

de Ru, "Conception," 202–22.

Ludger Schenke, "Die Interpretation der Parabel von den 'Arbeitern im Weinberg' (Mt 20,1-15) durch Matthäus," in idem, ed., *Studien zum Matthäusevangelium: Festschrift für Wilhelm Pesch* (SBS; Stuttgart: Katholisches Bibelwerk, 1988) 245–68.

Jacques Schlosser, *Le Dieu de Jésus* (LD 129; Paris: Cerf, 1987) 213–33.

Schnider, "Gerechtigkeit," 88–95.

Schottroff, "Solidarity," 129–47.

Michael Theobald, "Die Arbeiter im Weinberg (Mt 20,1-16). Wahrnehmung sozialer Wirklichkeit und Rede von Gott," in Dietmar Mieth, ed., *Christliche Sozialethik im Anspruch der Zukunft* (Studien zur theologischen Ethik 41; Freiburg: Herder, 1992), 107–27.

Weder, *Gleichnisse,* 218–30.

Karl Weiss, *Die Frohbotschaft Jesu über Lohn und Vollkommenheit: Zur evangelischen Parabel von den Arbeitern im Weinberg* (NTA 12/4–5; Münster: Aschendorff, 1927).

Reinhold Zwick, "Die Gleichniserzählung als Szenario: Dargestellt am Beispiel der 'Arbeiter im Weinberg' (Mt 20,1-15)," *Biblische Notizen* 64 (1992) 53–89.

1 For the kingdom of heaven is like a house master who early in the morning went out to hire workers for his vineyard. 2/ And after he agreed with the workers for a denarius for the day, he sent them into his vineyard. 3/ And when he went out about the third hour he saw others standing idle in the marketplace, 4/ and he said to those, 'You also go into the vineyard, and I will give you what is just.' 5/ And they went. And when he went out again about the sixth and the ninth hour, he did the same thing. 6/ And about the eleventh he went out and found others standing and said to them, 'Why are you standing around here all day doing nothing?' 7/ They say to him, 'No one hired us.' He says to them, 'You also go into the vineyard.'

8 And when evening had come the lord of the vineyard says to his steward, 'Call the workers, and give them their pay, beginning with the last up to the first.' 9/ And when the ones from the eleventh hour came, they each received a denarius. 10/ And when the first came, they thought that they would receive more; and each of them also received a denarius. 11/ But when they received it, they complained about the house master 12/ and said, 'These last ones worked one hour, and you made them equal to us who

have borne the burden of the day and the heat.'
13/ But he answered and said to one of them,
'My friend, I do not do you an injustice. Did you
not agree with me for a denarius? 14/ Take what
is yours and go. I want to give (the same) to this
last one as to you. 15/ Or[1] may I not do what I
want with what is mine? Or is your eye evil,
because I am good?'
16/ Thus the last will be first and the first last."[2]

Analysis

Structure

The parable is related loosely to the preceding material; it serves as a kind of justification ($\gamma\acute{\alpha}\rho$). A detailed theme is lacking. Instead, there is simply one who acts in a sovereign manner—the "house master" with whom the kingdom of heaven is compared. Then the narrative begins immediately. Verse 1b begins with the first-time designation ($\acute{\alpha}\mu\alpha\ \pi\rho\omega\acute{\iota}$) which introduces the first part of the narrative. It consists of four sequences[3] of unequal length, each of which, starting with the second, begins with "he went out" ($\grave{\epsilon}\xi\epsilon\lambda\vartheta\acute{\omega}\nu$), plus a time designation (vv. 3a, 5b, 6a). Since the individual scenes are stereotypically Matthean,[4] it is that much easier for the readers to recognize how the scenes differ from one another. Only in the first scene does the house master make an agreement ($\sigma\upsilon\mu\zeta\omega\nu\acute{\epsilon}\omega$) with the day laborers over their wages. In the second he simply promises "what is just." In the case of the workers who are recruited at the eleventh hour he does not even mention the wage anymore. Thus the readers are anxious to find out what the house master is going to pay the various groups. Those who are recruited at the sixth and ninth hours are mentioned only in passing ($\grave{\epsilon}\pi o\acute{\iota}\eta\sigma\epsilon\nu$ $\grave{\omega}\sigma\alpha\acute{\upsilon}\tau\omega\varsigma$). They are not important for the narrative; they merely heighten the drama. It is the workers recruited at the eleventh hour who are important. For one thing, their recruitment does not follow the

three-hour pattern that has been dominant up to this point. For another, they are emphasized with the brief dialogue in vv. 6-7. Thus the readers have a special interest in what is going to happen to them.

The second part of the narrative begins with a new time designation ("and when evening had come"; $\grave{o}\psi\acute{\iota}\alpha\varsigma\ \delta\grave{\epsilon}\ \gamma\epsilon\nu o\mu\acute{\epsilon}\nu\eta\varsigma$, v. 8).[5] It consists of two scenes. In the shorter first scene (vv. 8-9) the lord turns his attention to the last recruited workers and orders that they be paid.[6] It is reported briefly and without comment that each of them receives a denarius. The readers' tension is only partly resolved, however, since this payment requires some sort of explanation. In addition the readers wonder about the expression "beginning with the last up to the first," which on the surface appears to be superfluous and whose meaning they initially do not understand. The second, much longer scene of vv. 10-15 carries the weight of the narrative. It involves the house master and the "first ones," who now come to be paid, and who also receive a denarius (v. 10). They are, of course, not satisfied with their pay, and they protest loudly and pointedly (vv. 11-12). With "agree for a denarius" ($\delta\eta\nu\alpha\rho\acute{\iota}o\upsilon\ \sigma\upsilon\nu\epsilon\phi\acute{\omega}\nu\eta\sigma\alpha\varsigma$) the lord's concluding answer (vv. 13-15) refers to the initial agreement (v. 2), and with "I do not do you an injustice" ($o\grave{\upsilon}\kappa\ \grave{\alpha}\delta\iota\kappa\hat{\omega}$ $\sigma\epsilon$) it takes up the theme of justice that has already been anticipated with "what is just" ($\delta\acute{\iota}\kappa\alpha\iota o\nu$; v. 4). In this parable, which thus far has contained only brief fragments of dialogue, the response appears to be unusually long, and as a result it carries significant weight. It consists of two statements in the first person ($o\grave{\upsilon}\kappa\ \grave{\alpha}\delta\iota\kappa\hat{\omega}$, v. 13b; $\vartheta\acute{\epsilon}\lambda\omega$, v. 14b), each of which is justified with a rhetorical question (vv. 13c, 15a) and concludes with a final statement (vv. 14a, 15b). The first final statement is a command, the second a question. Since the lord speaks personally to one of the

---

1　The $\mathring{\eta}$ is well attested, and in my judgment it belongs to the text. Perhaps it was omitted to keep it from being read with the following $\mathring{\eta}$ as "either . . . or."

3　Numerous MSS of the later *textus receptus* add here, somewhat inappropriately, according to 22:14: "For many are called, but few are chosen."

3　Reinhold Zwick ("Die Gleichniserzählung als Szenario: Dargestellt am Beispiel der 'Arbeiter im Weinberg' [Mt 20,1-15]," 64 [1992] 53–89) compares the entire parable with the scenario or script ("treatment") of a film, with the individual scenes corresponding to film sequences. This comparison describes the form of the parable better than does the popular comparison with a drama that is divided into acts and scenes.

4　Three times $\grave{\epsilon}\xi\epsilon\lambda\vartheta\acute{\omega}\nu$, four designations of the time with $\pi\epsilon\rho\acute{\iota}$, four times $\epsilon\grave{\iota}\varsigma\ \tau\grave{o}\nu\ \grave{\alpha}\mu\pi\epsilon\lambda\hat{\omega}\nu\alpha$ (two of them with $\grave{\upsilon}\pi\acute{\alpha}\gamma\epsilon\tau\epsilon$), twice $\grave{\epsilon}\sigma\tau\hat{\omega}\tau\alpha\varsigma$, twice $\grave{\epsilon}\sigma\tau\eta\kappa\acute{\epsilon}$-$\nu\alpha\iota$ with $\grave{\alpha}\rho\gamma o\acute{\iota}$, twice $\mu\iota\sigma\vartheta\acute{o}o\mu\alpha\iota$.

5　The division of the parable into three parts (vv. 1-7, situation; vv. 8-10, crisis; vv. 11-15, solution) represented, e.g., by Schnider ("Gerechtigkeit") or Harnisch (*Gleichniserzählungen*) is based on the literary genre of drama and not on external characteristics of the text.

6　The steward is only an auxiliary figure who permits the lord to call attention to the particular mode of payment. He does not appear as a person who acts independently.

members of the group, the impression is strengthened that he is speaking directly to the readers—a feature that makes the final question of v. 15b especially compelling. Nothing more is said about a reaction of the day laborers; the "crisis" in the narrative is not resolved.[7] Thus the individual readers must themselves answer the final question of v. 15b which is formulated with "you." The concluding v. 16 brings the parable's application introduced by the stylistic οὕτως. It is a variation of the word about the last and the first with which the readers are already familiar from 19:30. It takes up the idea of the second part of the parable, where in v. 8 the two most important groups of workers are designated as "first" and "last" (πρῶτοι and ἔσχατοι).

With the exception of v. 16, the entire parable gives the impression of being compact, and it is artistically narrated throughout.

Source

As is the case with most of the major units of special Matthean material, our parable has a number of features that are stylistically Matthean.[8] The evangelist must have played a major role in their (first?) written formulation and in their narrative formation. That, on the other hand, the parable is not a new redactional creation is clear from the fact that the application in v. 16 makes use of only one of its secondary motifs, viz., the sequence in the payment from v. 8, but does not take up its main point, viz., the identical payment and the rationale that the house master gives for his behavior.

Tradition History

As is the case with almost all Matthean parables, one can scarcely decompose this compact story. Clear only is that Matthew added the concluding v. 16; it connects the parable with 19:30 and fits awkwardly with the subject matter of the parable. Since the parable's introduction in v. 1a is Matthean,[9] it was probably created by the evangelist. It remains open, therefore, whether the parable was a story about the kingdom of God prior to Matthew. I regard it as most likely that it did not begin with any kind of "theme"; Jesus simply told a story. For the rest of the parable one cannot discover any secondary insertions. The few attempts made in this direction have only weak support.[10] We can proceed on the assumption, therefore, that the narrative framework of this parable is quite old. Since its contents fit well with Jesus' affirmation of outsiders, poor, and sinners in light of the kingdom of God, hardly anyone has suggested that it does not come from Jesus.[11]

Interpretation

To repeat an oft-quoted statement of Adolf Jülicher, our story appears to be a "gospel *in nuce*."[12] It is remarkably close to Paul, since it deals with "the limits of works in view of the . . . mercy of God,"[13] with the "incomprehensible disturbance of the habitual" by the grace that

---

7 Christian Dietzfelbinger, "Das Gleichnis von den Arbeitern im Weinberg als Jesuswort," 126–37, 128.

8 Matthean are (cf. vol. 1, Introduction 3.2) in *v. 1*: ὅμοιος, γάρ, βασιλεία τῶν οὐρανῶν, ἄνθρωπος with an attribute, οἰκοδεσπότης, ὅστις, perhaps ἅμα (cf. 13:29), ἐξέρχομαι; *v. 2*: μετά, δέ, ἡμέρα, on ἐκ with the price cf. 27:7; ἐξελθών, ὥρα, ἄλλος, ἕστηκα, ἀργός (cf. 12:36); on περί with a time designation cf. 27:46; *v. 4*: ἐκεῖνος, ὑπάγω, καὶ ὑμεῖς (cf. Schenk, *Sprache*, 314), ὅς ἐάν; *v. 5*: δέ, ἀπέρχομαι, πάλιν, ἐξελθών, ὥρα, ὡσαύτως (cf. 21:36); *v. 6*: δέ ἐξελθών, εὑρίσκω, ἄλλος, ἑστώς, ὧδε, ἀργός; *v. 7*: ὑπάγω, καὶ ὑμεῖς; *v. 8*: ὀψίας δὲ γενομένης, κύροις τοῦ ἀμπελῶνος (cf. 21:40), καλέω, ἀποδίδωμι, μισθός, ἀπό - ἕως; *v. 9*: ἐλθών, δέ, λαμβάνω; *v. 10*: ἐλθών, λαμβάνω, perhaps πλεῖον; *v. 11*: λαμβάνω, κατά with gen., οἰκοδεσπότης; *v. 12*: λέγων, οὗτος, ὥρα, ποιέω, ἡμέρα; *v. 13*: ὁ δὲ ἀποκριθεὶς . . . εἶπεν, εἷς, ἑταῖρε, οὐχί (cf. 5:46-47; 6:25; 13:55-56; 18:12); *v. 14*: ὑπάγω, θέλω, δέ, οὗτος; *v. 15*: θέλω, ἤ, ποιέω, ἀγαθός/πονηρός, ἐν used

instrumentally (Schenk, *Sprache*, 240–41); on ὀφθαλμὸς πονηρός cf. 6:23; perhaps ἐγώ. Not Matthean are the hapax legomena μισθόω, ἐπίτροπος, ἴσος, βάρος, καύσων (possibly Matthean as a LXX word), and ἀδικέω.

9 Cf. esp. 13:52 and the other ἄνθρωπος parables 13:24; 18:23; 22:2, 11, 25:14.

10 For Crossan (*Parables*, 112–14) the original parable ends with v. 13, among other reasons because v. 15 is a recapitulation of 19:17. For Scott (*Hear*, 286–87), following Via (*Parables*), it ends with v. 14a.

11 Along with "Leaven" and "Good Samaritan" it passed the test in the U.S. "Red Letter Edition" with the highest possible score (*The Parables of Jesus: Red Letter Edition* [Sonoma, Calif.: Polebridge, 1988] 104).

12 *Gleichnisreden* 2.471. Cf. Jeremias, *Parables*, 139: "the core of Jesus' vindication of the gospel" of "God's goodness."

13 Jüngel, *Paulus*, 164.

makes clear to people that they "are intent on their own security and self-assertion."[14] Of course, our story's "gospel *in nuce*" was the gospel from a Protestant rather than from a Catholic perspective. That is clearly expressed in the case of Günther Bornkamm, who says in his important article on the concept of reward in the New Testament that the parable bears witness to "the miracle of divine righteousness and mercy against the background of the human understanding of righteousness, reward, and achievement" and that it separates "finally the idea of recompense from the idea of earning." Every "human claim shatters on the freedom and the greatness of God's grace."[15] Even earlier H. J. Holtzmann had said: "This remarkable parable deals a death blow to the concept of reward by making use of it" and by letting concepts such as reward and achievement "sink under the weight of a religious idealism to which all reward no longer appears as legal recompense but only as a gift, as overflowing grace, as the reward of grace."[16] Finally, for Joachim Jeremias two worlds are at odds in this parable: "the world of merit, and the world of grace; the law is contrasted with the gospel."[17] Modern Catholic exegesis agrees by and large with this Protestant understanding of the parable, albeit with more cautious and less exuberant words.[18]

History of Interpretation in the Modern Period

Today this interpretation influences both of the major Western confessions. It has its roots in the Reformation and in the Protestant liberal theology which was heavily influenced by German idealism. A look at the history of the parable's interpretation in the modern period should sharpen our view. Anticipating this part of the history of interpretation is all the more possible since the Reformation meant a new beginning for the interpretation of Matt 20:1-16.

The Interpretation During the Reformation

As early as 1517 Luther saw in our parable the distinction between those in the church who serve in order to get a reward, such as priests and monks, and those humble persons of the eleventh hour who would like to work if "only someone would find them worthy and would hire them."[19] In his later interpretations v. 16 is increasingly emphasized. Those who do not arrogantly presume that they have earned the penny receive everything, while those who regard themselves as the first workers and want to earn more will be last, and they lose everything.[20] No persons are so exalted before God that they have nothing to fear, and no persons are so low that they are beyond hope. It is rather true for everyone "that they look not to the penny, but to the graciousness of the house father, that is equal and all the same over persons high and low . . . over saints and sinners."[21] Thus the Pauline statement is true that the gospel makes all persons equal (Rom 3:23).[22] Calvin also claims that Jesus speaks here not of the price for human work but of the richness of God's graciousness on behalf of human beings apart from works.[23] Especially important for him is the idea of the freedom of God, who is obligated to no one, but who in his grace calls whom he will.[24]

Interpretations after the Reformation continually refer to the difference between reward and the grace freely given for those who "know that they have

---

14 Harnisch, *Gleichniserzählungen*, 190–91.

15 Bornkamm, "Lohngedanke," 88.

16 Holtzmann, *Theologie* 1.261.

17 *Parables,* 139.

18 Important on the idea of reward is Wilhelm Pesch's differentiated monograph, *Der Lohngedanke in der Lehre Jesu* (Münchener theologische Studien 1/7; Munich: Zink, 1955) esp. 9–12. Also important is Josef Schmid's 1956 commentary that is quite free of Catholic dogmatic thought. See esp. pp. 283–94. Since its appearance Catholic interpretations frequently emphasize the "order of grace" against the "connection between achievement and reward." Cf. Wolfgang Trilling, *The Gospel According to St. Matthew* (2 vols.; Herder and Herder, 1969) 2.125; Gnilka 2.182 ("grace's free choice" versus "self-promotion" [cf. Calvin and n. 24!]); Schnackenburg

2.188–89.

19 Sermon from 1517 (*WA* 1.132–34). Quotation according to Luther 2.674. The distinction is reminiscent of one of Tauler's sermons that distinguishes between those who work externally in the vineyard and the others who are concerned not with approval and profit but solely with love for God (Susannah Winkworth, *The History and Life of the Reverend Doctor John Tauler with Twenty-Five of His Sermons* [London: Allenson, n.d.], 262).

20 2.679 (sermon from 1523).

21 *WA* 17/2.141 (collection of sermons on fasting, 1525).

22 2.677 (Sermon from 1523).

23 *Inst.* 3.18.3.

24 2.267.

earned nothing."[25] Bucer compares the workers of the eleventh hour with the good thief on the cross who was in no position to achieve any more works and who had nothing except his repentance.[26] For J. Valdés what characterized the workers of the last hour is that in their case faith is added to external works, while the protesting workers act out of self-love.[27] According to Brenz the heart of the parable is the opposition between law and gospel. In his view the people of the law who work from early morning "trust in their own efforts and merits, murmur against the lord," and thus become last.[28] In the exegesis of the Reformation the distinction between the workers hired earlier and those hired later, all of whom receive the same reward, thus becomes an absolute difference between works-persons who demand to be paid for their accomplishments and persons of faith who know that they have no claims before God. Only the latter will receive grace from God. In the process v. 16 becomes the key verse for understanding the text.

From the Difference Between Gospel and Law to the Anti-Jewish Interpretation

The Reformation's antithesis between "works people" and "faith people" quickly combined with the traditional salvation history interpretation[29] according to which the workers hired initially are the Jews between Adam and Jesus, while the workers of the last hour are the Gentiles called by Jesus.[30] This traditional interpretation thus takes on a harshly *anti-Jewish tendency*. A good example is Brenz's interpretation. For him the agreement about the denarius is a *pactum legis*. The Jews work all day for a reward, but since no one can keep the law, they fail to reach their goal. Thus what God owes them at the end of the day is not the denarius of eternal life but his curse. "What they have earned is that he leaves them behind in their blindness."[31] Now instead of receiving the same reward, they are the last, that is, they are condemned, because they have relied on their own merits instead of on God's grace.

This is the ground in which has grown the principal difference between the gospel "of God's joyful giving" and "Jewish arithmetic" or "arrogant Pharisaic meritocracy,"[32] which in subtle or massive ways has influenced a large part of especially the German-language exegesis. A pregnant example is Billerbeck's influential excursus on the "doctrine of rewards in the ancient synagogue." Here the axiomatic distinction between the gospel of Jesus and the Jewish doctrine of rewards based on the law is combined with the Wellhausen school's idea of decline. The Jewish "rewards compulsion" thus results from the fact that the synagogue was unable to maintain the original biblical conviction of the reward of grace.[33] This anti-Judaism is a consequence of systematizing the rabbinic statements that were spoken in different times, in quite different situations, and to quite different hearers. It is well known that those who wish to do so can systematize them in just about any conceivable way. Such a systematic approach says little about the authors of the statements, but in this case it says a great deal about Billerbeck.[34]

The Liberal Interpretation

It is likely that *Kant* and the idealistic ethic of duty had a significant influence on today's dominant understanding of our text, although I am not aware of any direct statement from him on Matt 20:1-15. For Kant the "drudging and mercenary faith (*fides mercenaria, fides servilis*)" of the positive religions was not saving, because it is not a free disposition of the heart and thus is not moral.[35] Under Kant's influence, in the nineteenth century the decisive message of the parable becomes the need to overcome the heteronomy that is part of the idea of reward. F. C. Baur understands the kingdom of God as a progressive realization of God's will on earth and sees in the parable of the workers the idea that "everything in the kingdom of God is such a free gift that one can only act with a receptive attitude."[36] According to H. Weinel the parable is designed to break through the idea of reward and to teach that God judges people

25 E.g., Musculus, 468 (quotation); Calovius, 376.
26 159.
27 Valdés, 354.
28 Brenz, 642
29 Cf. below, History of Interpretation: Ancient Church.
30 Cf. below, n. 101.
31 Brenz, 639–40.
32 Jülicher, *Gleichnisreden* 2.471, 466.
33 Str–B 4.490–95. For a critical evaluation cf. H. Heinemann, "The Conception of Reward in Mt 20, 1-16," 85–89

34 More differentiated is Pesch's presentation in *Der Lohngedanke in der Lehre Jesu*, 81–106. Quite good, in my judgment, is Moore, *Judaism* 2.89ff.
35 *Religion Within the Limits of Reason Alone* 3.1.7 (1934; reprinted New York: Harper & Row, 1960) 106; cf. also 4.1.1 = 149–51.
36 *Vorlesungen über neutestamentliche Theologie* (reprinted Darmstadt: Wissenschaftliche Buchgesellschaft, 1973) 72; cf. 71.

not by their deeds but by their "will to work" or by their "resolve to do what is good."[37] Even sharper is the opinion of H. J. Holtzmann that "this remarkable parable destroys the concept of reward" with the idea of the reward of grace. It is a forward-looking text in a world in which "autonomy and theonomy compete with one another."[38] The parable of the workers reveals "a higher point of view," while texts like Luke 14:12-14 or 16:1-13, 19-31 reflect not "the style of Jesus," but "the coarser attitude of a Jewish disciple who misrepresents the master."[39] For P. Billerbeck the eleventh-hour laborers are positive figures, not only because they correspond to the type of believer influenced by the Reformation thinkers but also because they act morally, since "it is simply a person's duty to work without any thought of reward." The eleventh-hour laborers act morally, because they work without thought of reward, "simply because the house master needs them," and they leave "everything else up to his sense of fairness." The other workers, on the other hand, show by their complaining "that they did not work for the sake of the house master."[40] Here the Neoprotestant ideal of the Christian who acts morally is combined with the bourgeois ideal that has crept into the text of the workers who do their duty without consideration of reward. Günther Bornkamm summarizes that because of the "influence of the idealistic ethic as well as the stand against Catholic theology and practice . . . in modern Protestantism we have lost the Bible's idea of reward . . . , much to our detriment."[41]

The Catholic Exegesis
In the face of this interpretation the Catholic exegesis of Matt 20:1-16 was in a difficult position. While it initially further developed the salvation-history and parenetic interpretation of the ancient church,[42] it was increasingly forced by the Protestants to defend the traditional Catholic doctrine of reward. For this reason the problem of the idea of reward comes to dominate the Catholic exegesis. From the days of the ancient church, interpreters had used the "many dwelling places" of John 14:2 to introduce into the interpretation of Matt 20:1-16 the idea of diverse merits and degrees of reward.[43] In his interpretation Thomas Aquinas speaks of the "one salvation for all," but of varieties of participation in it.[44] It is difficult to find such varieties in the text of Matt 20:1-16. More recently Lapide, for example, tried to circumvent the idea of equal reward by claiming that there are different denarii; the Jews had a silver or bronze denarius, while the Christians had one of gold.[45] He solved the problem of the identical reward much as Thomas had done by saying that *generice et abstracte* all will have the same eternal life but that there are in heaven degrees of nearness to God.[46]

Another problem is posed by the fact that in our story unequal work is equally rewarded. Gregory of Nazianzus had already indicated that God also takes into consideration one's clear will and good intentions. Furthermore, since those who came late worked without a firm agreement about their wages and did not complain about the lord, they compensated for their missing works with their greater faith.[47] We can read in a medieval text that one's inner fervor and *recta intentio* are rewarded.[48] Later someone like Maldonat can say that many righteous people work as much in a short time as others do during their entire life.[49] A modern attempt to achieve a balance between a doctrine of recompense and equal reward goes back to Gregory of Nazianzus and claims that God looks not on the actual work done but on the "inner willingness to work and to

37 Heinrich Weinel, *Biblische Theologie des Neuen Testaments* (4th ed.; Grundriss der theologischen Wissenschaft 3/2; Tübingen: Mohr/Siebeck, 1928) 119.
38 Holtzmann, *Theologie* 1.261–62.
39 Paul Wernle, *Jesus* (2d ed.; Tübingen: J. C. B. Mohr, 1916) 69–70.
40 Str-B 4.485–87.
41 Bornkamm, "Lohngedanke," 70.
42 Cf. below, History of Interpretation: Ancient Church.
43 The comparison of the two texts appears for the first time in Tertullian *Mon.* 10.9 (6) = CSEL Tert. 4.64. Cf. Ekkehard Mühlenberg, "Das Gleichnis von den Arbeitern im Weinberg (Mt 20,1-16) bei den Vätern," 12–13.

44 *Lectura* no. 1640. Cf. also his attempt to combine God's righteousness with his grace. In the process Matt 20:1-16 moves to the side of grace (*S. th.* 1, q.23 a.6, esp. ad 3).
45 Lapide, 380. Cf. 383.
46 Lapide, 382.
47 Gregory of Nazianzus *Or.* 40.20 = SC 358.240.
48 Dionysius the Carthusian, 223. Cf. the liberal interpretation of Weinel, *Biblische Theologie des Neuen Testaments.*
49 Maldonat, 407. Cf. the Jewish parable of Rabbi Bun below, n. 90.

sacrifice" that lies behind it.[50] All of these examples show that the fundamental statements of Matt 20:1-16 can hardly be reconciled with the traditional Catholic doctrines about recompense and reward.

Thus the basic intention of the Protestant interpretation of Matt 20:1-16 has prevailed and has been adopted by both confessions. It is based more on v. 16 than on the entire parable. The history of interpretation has demonstrated how temporally conditioned this understanding of the parable has been. It has been formed by the fundamental theological categories of the Reformation of the sixteenth century and by the spirit of bourgeois liberalism and anti-Judaism. For this reason an exegetical examination of this "Protestant" consensus is necessary that will focus on two major points: (1) the understanding of reward and (2) the relationship of our parable to Judaism.

Interpretation: Jesus

■ **1** Jesus tells the story of an owner of a vineyard who is looking for day laborers in the marketplace. His hearers are familiar with the scene from their own daily lives. Many midsized and large farms were cultivated in those days by day laborers who were cheaper for an employer than slaves were, since he did not suffer losses when they were sick or when they died.[51] The workday began at sunrise.[52] The hearers will have understood the house

master to be the proprietor of a midsized operation, because he himself comes to hire his day laborers; the owner of a large acreage more likely would have lived in the city and have had a manager who lived on the land. There probably were many day laborers. It is true that we have little direct evidence for unemployment in Israel at that time,[53] but it is likely that it was always present in this land of emigration, all the more in a time in which small farmers were gradually being displaced. A denarius was the customary wage for a day's work.[54] Since the Mishnah calculates that a person needs a minimum of 200 denarii per year in order to exist,[55] this income presupposes that a day laborer was able to find work at least 200 days in a year and that he furthermore did not have to support a family. One denarius could buy 10 to 12 small, flat loaves of bread; 3 to 4 denarii 12 liters of wheat (from which one could make about 15 kilograms of bread) or a lamb; 30 denarii a slave's garment; 100 denarii an ox.[56] In view of these prices the day laborers had a hard life.[57]

■ **2-5** The farmer makes a—presumably oral—agreement with the day laborers[58] and sends them into his vineyard. The hearers may have accepted it when he comes to hire new workers at the third hour, that is, around nine o'clock,[59] but that it happens two more times is unusual and grabs their attention. Some have offered the expla-

---

50   Karl Weiss, *Die Frohbotschaft Jesu über Lohn und Vollkommenheit: Zur evangelischen Parabel von den Arbeitern im Weinberg*, 75.

51   For this reason Terentius Varro advises that as a precaution one should hire day laborers in unhealthy areas and for heavy work (*Res rustica* 1.17.2-3). On the difficult social conditions of day laborers cf. in general Hezser, *Lohnmetaphorik*, 57–91; Schottroff, "Solidarity," 132–35; Ben David, *Talmudische Ökonomie*, 65–69; David A. Fiensy, *The Land Is Mine: The Social History of Palestine in the Herodian Period* (Lewiston, N.Y.: Mellen, 1991) 85–90.

52   Str–B 1.830.

53   Josephus (*Ant.* 20.219-20) speaks of unemployment in Jerusalem after work is completed on the temple. That people are still standing idly in the marketplace during the afternoon (Matt 20:6) is also evidence of unemployment.

54   Tob 5:15-16. For the rabbinic sources see Ben David, *Ökonomie*, 376, n. 338; Str–B 1.831; Heine-

mann, "Status," 275–77; Heszer, *Lohnmetaphorik*, 81. In addition, one frequently received a meal. Meir, e.g., had a higher wage as scribe, Hillel a lower one as day laborer (Str–B 1.831).

55   Ben David, *Ökonomie*, 292–93.

56   *M. Šeb.* 8.4; *m. Šeqal.* 4.9; *m. Menaḥ.* 13.8; *m. Arak.* 6.5; See the price lists in F. M. Heichelheim, "Roman Syria," in Tenney Frank, ed., *An Economic Survey of Ancient Rome* (6 vols.; Baltimore: Johns Hopkins, 1933–40) 4.121–257, there 183–88.

57   That is proverbial even in prophetic times: "He who earns wages puts them into a bag with holes" (Hag 1:6).

58   Str–B 1.830-31; Hezser, *Lohnmetaphorik*, 67–71.

59   The day was divided into twelve hours that began at sunrise and were of varying lengths, depending on the time of year (Krauss, *Archäologie* 2.421).

530

nation that the grapes were being harvested and that they needed to be gathered before the fall rains,[60] but the text leaves open the question whether the day laborers were harvesting grapes in the fall or whether, for example, they had to weed the vineyard in the spring. It has no intention of making the farmer's strange behavior plausible; instead, it wants its hearers to wonder about this farmer who does such a bad job of planning. They also are wondering about the wages that the farmer will pay. "What is just" leaves everything wide open and raises the suspicion of a possible conflict.

■ **6-7** It is both surprising and unusual that the farmer hires more workers at the eleventh hour. Formally the eleventh hour falls out of the previous three-hour pattern. Such an action makes no sense if for no other reason than the time it will take to get to the vineyard—time for which the farmer must pay.[61] The narrative pauses to spend a moment with these last workers. The lord asks them why they are standing around doing nothing.[62] They answer with the "banality" that no one has hired them. Of course no one has; the farmer can see that they are unemployed! The brief dialogue makes it possible for the hearers to spend a moment with these men who have been left without work. What kind of people are they? Are they too old, or are they sick people whom no one wanted? Did they miss their chance for work because they overslept? The narrator answers none of these questions. He simply wants the hearers to pay special attention to these last workers.

What lies behind the scenes of the narrative fiction for the hearers? Those who are familiar with the Bible are likely to think of Israel when they hear of the "vineyard." As the narrative progresses, however, they are not permitted to pursue that idea. The owner of the vineyard is suggestive of God for two reasons. For one thing, the biblical tradition suggests it,[63] so that the readers understand Jesus' story within the framework of God's relationship to his people. For another, the parable uses well-known images. There are numerous stories in the rabbinic tradition about farmers or the owners of houses who put day laborers to work in their garden and then pay them wages that are the occasion for critical questions.[64] However, the Jewish parallels differ from Matt 20:1-15. They do not speak of a vineyard, nor do they relate that the farmer hires the day laborers at different times. Thus even if the hearers should be familiar with Jesus' repertoire as a teller of stories, this story is still original. It awakens tension and amazement and does not permit an easy understanding of its metaphors.

■ **8-9** The wages are paid at sundown, just as the Bible and the Jewish tradition anticipate.[65] The word "wages/reward" [German: *Lohn*] again directs the hearers' attention to God who will reward the righteous in the future life.[66] In v. 8 the "house master" ($o\mathring{\iota}\kappa o\delta\epsilon$-$\sigma\pi\acute{o}\tau\eta\varsigma$) suddenly becomes the "lord of the vineyard" ($\kappa\acute{\upsilon}\rho\iota o\varsigma\ \tau o\mathring{\upsilon}\ \mathring{\alpha}\mu\pi\epsilon\lambda\mathring{\omega}\nu o\varsigma$)—another element that makes it easy for the readers to think of God. The narrator here introduces the figure of the steward that nowhere else plays a role in the parable. The steward appears only for the sake of the Lord's unusual order that in paying the

---

60 Thus Jeremias, *Parables*, 136 and Flusser, *Gleichnisse*, 34.

61 Hezser, *Lohnmetaphorik*, 69.

62 Ἀργός (= inactive) can mean "unemployed" or "lazy." The narrative does not indicate whether the farmer's question is an indirect reproach and the answer of the idlers is a weak excuse (thus Jeremias, *Parables*, 136), or whether both the question and answer are "genuine." The answers of the exegetes who fill this gap in the text in various ways depending on their own social position demonstrate how the text engages its readers.

63 Isa 5:1-7; Ps 80:9-15; Jer 12:10; cf. Hos 2:15; Amos 9:13-14; Cant 1:6.

64 Hezser (*Lohnmetaphorik*, 301–10) has collected the (for the most part late) Jewish parables with related images. On my use of the comparisons cf. the sum-

mary below. The most important are the two early statements of Rabbi Tarfon in *m. ʾAbot* 2.15–16: "The day is short and the task is great and the labourers are idle and the wage is abundant and the master of the house (בַּעַל הַבַּיִת) is urgent. . . . If thou hast studied much in the Law much reward will be given thee, and faithful is thy taskmaster who shall pay thee the reward of thy labour . . ." [ET Danby, 449]. The text shows that as early as the Tannaitic period expressions such as "house master," "reward/wage," "work," "laborer" were used metaphorically quite naturally.

65 Lev 19:13; Deut 24:14-15. Hezser (*Lohnmetaphorik*, 76–80) offers numerous Jewish sources.

66 It was self-evident to rabbinic Judaism that the reward would not be paid until the eschaton (*m.*

workers he should begin with the last.[67] In the story this order makes it possible for the workers who had been hired first to see what the others receive; otherwise the controversy portrayed in vv. 11-15 could not have happened. On the level of the narrative the hearers' attention is aroused. They are now expecting something unusual to happen. And, in fact, it does! That the last workers, to whom the farmer had promised nothing at all, should receive an entire denarius, is completely unexpected,[68] and it contradicts what one logically would expect from an employer.[69]

■ **10-15** Now it is finally the turn of the first workers hired.[70] They think that they are going to receive more, as indeed the readers probably also expect. But each[71] of them also receives only one denarius. They protest, and in so doing they make the readers aware of the normal standard of fairness. The house master has arbitrarily damaged the basic principle of justice[72] by treating those who have worked only one hour the same as those who have endured the burden and the heat of the day.[73] The narrator gives them a chance to make their case in detail, since what they have to say is not simply self-serving and must be taken seriously.[74] That suggests that he especially has his hearers in mind and that he wants to speak to what he assumes their concerns will be.[75] As at the end of the parable of the prodigal son (Luke 15:25-32) here also after the action is completed an extended conversation clarifies the point. The house master turns to a spokesman of the first group and addresses him in a

---

ʾAbot 2.16) [conclusion]. For further sources see Str–B 4.491, 494–95; Weder, *Gleichnisse,* 223, nn. 70–71.

67 Jeremias (*Parables,* 35–36 and 137) interprets ἀπόδος τὸν μισθόν as "pay them all their wages" and ἀρξάμενος ἀπὸ τῶν ἐσχάτων as "including the last." The emphasis on ἀρξάμενος at the beginning speaks against such a reading. The simple article in no way implies that the *full* wage is meant after the farmer previously had not specifically stated what the "just" wage would be. Thus the hearers still wonder what is going to happen.

68 J. Duncan M. Derrett ("Workers in the Vineyard: A Parable of Jesus," 64–91, 75–77) is of a different opinion. According to him the farmer acts as one would expect and in conformity with the law by paying his day laborers "as an unemployed person" ([כְּפוֹעֵל בָּטֵל] *m. B. Meṣ.* 2.9; 5.4; *m. Bek.* 4.6; *b. B. Meṣ.* 31b, 68a, b. For further sources see Ben David, *Ökonomie,* 377, n. 360; J. H. Heinemann, "Status," 278–83). But we do not know precisely what kind of reward that was. Only two cases are somewhat similar to the behavior of the kind-hearted farmer of Matthew 20. Should through no fault of the employee the work be discontinued or not require as much time as was anticipated, in certain conditions the entire wage must be paid (*b. B. Meṣ.* 76b, 77a), but that does not parallel our text. More important is Josephus *Ant.* 20.120. Upon the completion of the temple, artisans who were laid off were paid an entire day's wage, even if they had worked only one hour. However, this was a special arrangement designed to keep unemployed artisans in Jerusalem quiet and to reduce the temple treasure that had become too large. On the whole we are left with what the story itself says: The farmer's behavior was incomprehensible and surprised everyone.

69 A good example is the parallel from Diodorus Siculus 4.20.2–3 noted by Hezser, *Lohnmetaphorik,* 85: During the course of her work, a pregnant day laborer gives birth to a child. She lays it in the bushes and continues to work so that she will not lose her wages. The child's crying catches the attention of the overseer, who asks the worker to stop working. She refuses to do so, however, because she is determined to get her entire wage. Finally, because of her persistence, she convinces the overseer, and he pays her an entire day's wage.

70 There is no more mention of the workers hired in the third, sixth, and ninth hours. The narrator used them in the first part of the parable only to heighten the tension and to emphasize how astonishing was the farmer's behavior toward the last workers.

71 Ἀνά replaces the distributive numbers that are missing in Greek, and it can also appear before substantives. Cf. BAGD, *s.v.* ἀνά, 3. On the article before prepositions cf. BDF § 266 (1).

72 In Greek ἴσος/ἰσότης is a fundamental dimension of justice. Cf. Rudolf Hirzel, *Themis, Dike und Verwandtes* (Leipzig: Hirzel, 1907) 228–320, 421–23. That the first workers in the name of justice protest against "equality" may be intentional irony.

73 In the LXX καύσων is the hot, desert wind that blows from the east.

74 This is seen not only when the first workers claim an additional payment but also when they challenge the house master's justice. The narrator also could have had them say something egotistical.

75 It is true that with this parable Jesus especially had potential critics in mind and that he took them seriously by "allowing room in the parable for the eval-

friendly, condescending tone as "friend" (ἑταῖρε).[76] He first defends his behavior on the basis of the formal justice that the spokesman himself had claimed. He has paid what they had agreed; beyond that they have no legitimate claim. Thus in his own way he has satisfied the principle of "equality": The reward must correspond to the effort (*m. Abot* 5.23). The protester can take what he has coming to him and go home![77]

The farmer also defends his behavior by referring to the right of an owner to do what he wants with[78] his property.[79] The narrator obviously expects his hearers to agree not only with the first principle but also with the second.[80] At the very end the farmer poses a personal question that at the same time reveals the real motive for his behavior. He himself is good,[81] although he is not obligated to act that way. Is it jealousy that prompts the protest of the one who speaks for those hired first? This is the question which the farmer asks in such a rhetorically effective way with the help of the standard metaphor of the "evil eye."[82] It is also the question the narrator would like to leave with his hearers.

Summary

How are we to describe the sense of this story? Based on v. 15, the interpreters are in agreement that it has to do with God's graciousness—a graciousness that finds its concrete expression in the life of Jesus. As the farmer dealt with the last workers, so Jesus deals with those who by normal standards have no claim on God. In the name of God he affirms the sinners, who do not keep the law; the women and the poor, who for various reasons cannot keep the law in its entirety; the sick, who are excluded from the community; and the unlettered *am ha aretz*, who are ignorant of the law. Since the parable not only *tells* about God's graciousness but also offers an interpretation of Jesus' behavior in narrative form, it is a part of the *experience* of the divine graciousness that people have with Jesus.[83] Later, therefore, Matthew is justi-

---

uation of his listeners" (Linnemann, *Parables,* 27). It is wrong, however, implicitly and exclusively to regard these critics as Pharisees as do many interpreters (including Jülicher, *Gleichnisreden* 2.466–67; Jeremias, *Parables,* 38; de Ru, "Conception," 209–10; Wilfrid Haubeck, "Zum Verständnis der Parabel von den Arbeitern im Weinberg (Mt 20,1-15)," 95–107, 101–02) as if an external and formal understanding of the divine righteousness belonged in a special way to the Pharisees' image of God (and not rather to the Christian image of Pharisees!) and as if everyone could not have reacted in the same way as did the first workers!

76 Ἑταῖρε is, e.g., what a commander would call his soldiers, the designation of a pupil, a friend, a subordinate. For the sources see Karl Heinrich Rengstorf, "ἑταῖρος," *TDNT* 2 (1964) 699.

77 The first workers are not thereby "thrown out," nor is there the thought of a catastrophe comparable to 22:11-13 and 25:11-12, 26-28. There is merely the simple assertion that the speaker has received the justice that he is demanding and that he can therefore go (ὑπάγω as in v. *4*) (contra Via, *Parables,* 153–54).

78 Presumably ἐν is to be understood instrumentally.

79 Cf. Plato *Leg.* 922d. Cf. e: "If what is mine belongs to me, may I not then give it to whom I wish?" The issue is the freedom of a testator to divide his possessions among his heirs. The owner's absolute power not only to use his possessions, but also even to destroy them, corresponds also to the view of Roman law (Max Kaser, *Das römische Privatrecht* [2d ed.; Handbuch der Altertumswissenschaft 10/3.3.1; Munich: Beck, 1971] 1.125).

80 For Schottroff ("Volk," 184) the verse is an example of how "little people speak in the language of their masters" and take over their worldview, in this case the idea of an owner's absolute power over his property.

81 Naturally Matthew's readers remember 19:17 so that ἀγαθός underscores the allegorical understanding of the house master as God.

82 Behind the metaphor of the "evil eye" there is, of course, the magical concept of the "evil look" for which John H. Elliott ("Mt 20:1-15: A Parable of Invidious Comparison and Evil Eye Accusation," 52–65) has contributed a great deal of material. However, in the biblical-Jewish tradition the "evil eye" has long since become a standing metaphor for greed or envy. Cf. vol. 1, II A 2.4.1 n. 44 on 6:23.) The situation is similar in Latin, where envy is *invidia*.

83 Cf. Weder (*Gleichnisse,* 227, 229), who says that the parable becomes "the event of God's graciousness" and "the explication of his (*scil.* Jesus') behavior."

fied in designating this story as a parable of the kingdom of heaven that Jesus both proclaimed and embodied.

Describing the parable's scope in negative terms is somewhat more difficult. What is the parable's target? It is certainly not the case that God's graciousness and justice are regarded antithetically as opposites. Instead, the story portrays the miraculous graciousness of a farmer who does all that justice requires of him.[84] Nor does the parable treat grace and reward as opposites. On the contrary, the grace shown toward the last workers is precisely that they receive their *reward*, purely as a matter of grace. The parable is most likely directed against human efforts to link God's justice and God's graciousness in such a way that one becomes the standard for the other. In that case either God *may* no longer be gracious, since the principle of justice forbids it, or he *must* be gracious to all, since the principle of equality dictates that all have an equal claim to graciousness. Thus the parable is focused on a just God's *freedom* to be gracious. It does not offer a new system of unmerited graciousness that will take the place of the normal standards of a justice that grants to all what they have earned.[85] Instead, the standard values are "disrupted"[86] by the appearance of God's love, and they thereby lose their deadly universal validity. "I came not to call the righteous but sinners" (Mark 2:17).[87] This description of Jesus' activity neither denies nor excludes the righteousness of the righteous. It simply brings God to those who need him, the sinners.

Finally, the scope of the parable includes a new attitude toward one's neighbor which the experience of grace makes possible. Those who make God's justice the dominant principle and do not permit his graciousness to appear alongside it are incapable of solidarity. With his direct question in v. 15 the owner of the vineyard makes the "spokesman" aware that the *principle* of achievement leads to arrogance toward those who have earned less and envy toward those who have earned more or who have been rewarded unjustly. Part of the parable's point—not as the result of a theoretical insight but as a practical consequence of one's own experience—is a new sense of solidarity with those who are not well off but to whom God is gracious.[88]

How is our parable related to the Jewish understanding of reward and grace? One can, of course, find a number of statements in rabbinic texts that presuppose a calculating attitude toward reward that more than corresponds to the attitude of the spokesman for the workers who were hired first.[89] It is also true that most of the rabbinic parables which can be compared with Matt 20:1-16 because of their similar imagery either suggest that, contrary to outward appearances, the various workers who received the same wage actually did the same work,[90] or they speak of unequal pay for unequal work.[91]

---

84 For this reason Michael Theobald ("Die Arbeiter im Weinberg [Mt 20,1-16]: Wahrnehmung sozialer Wirklichkeit und Rede von Gott," 120) describes the scope of the parable as "more than just."

85 Thus D. L. Gragg, "The Parable of the Workers in the Vineyard and Its Interpreters: A Text-Linguistic Analysis," 112-25.

86 The formulations are based on Harnisch, *Gleichniserzählungen*, 177, 188. Jüngel is right, therefore, when he says that the issue in our parable is "the limits of works in light of the graciousness of God that is taking place" (*Paulus*, 164). De Ru says that the idea of reward is not negated, but God's graciousness "surpasses all calculation" ("Conception," 210-11).

87 The parable of the two sons in the vineyard (Matt 21:28-31) has a similar thrust: "Tax collectors and harlots will enter the kingdom of God before you" (21:31). Of course, in that narrative the emphasis lies on the first son's obedience; in 20:1-15 nothing is made of the fact that the last day laborers (just as

all the others!) actually did go into the vineyard.

88 Correctly emphasizing the parenetic dimension are Lambrecht (*Treasure*, 78: Understanding the lord's behavior involves total agreement with him), Dupont ("Ouvriers," 25-26: The first workers must acknowledge the last workers as brothers), and Schottroff ("Solidarity," 138, 144-45: The parable is designed to teach solidarity).

89 Amply documented by Str–B 4.490-95.

90 *Y. Ber.* 2.5c.15 and parallels = Str–B 4.492: A laborer who worked for only a short time and then took a long walk with the king receives the same wage as the others. The story refers to Rabbi Bun who in the twenty-eight years of his life mastered more Torah than others do in one hundred years.

91 *S. Lv.* 26.9 (450a) = Str–B 4.493: Israel is like a reliable worker who receives a higher wage than do the others. *Dt. r.* 6 (203a) and parallels = Str–B 4.497-98: The workers do not know how much they will be paid for working under different trees, and their pay varies. The point is that keeping different com-

Alongside these texts, however, are others which insist that one should not obey the law for the sake of a reward[92] and that every reward from God is a gift of grace.[93] Also important are the numerous statements about repentance which emphasize that repentance is possible anytime, even to the last moment before death, and that it always is able to save.[94] The coexistence of God's distributive justice alongside his surprising, incalculable grace that we find in Matt 20:1-15 corresponds to the rabbinic view of the two מדות (measures) that are found in God—judgment and mercy—that give reason for hope but at the same time prohibit all calculation.[95] This concept provides the setting for a Jewish text that well summarizes Matt 20:1-15. God showed Rabbi Jose ben Halafta the treasures with which the righteous will be rewarded in heaven. But there was among them a large treasure for those "who have nothing" of which God said: "To those who have I give from their reward, but to those who have nothing I give from this treasure." The biblical text on which the source is based is Exod 33:19: "I am gracious to whom I am gracious" (cf. Rom 9:15).[96] Here also God's grace is grounded in his freedom.

Matthew 20:1-15 is thus not a text that fundamentally goes beyond the Jewish thinking about rewards and establishes by contrast a new religious principle, that of *sola gratia*. Furthermore, there is a great deal of diversity among the Jewish statements about reward; they do not all say the same thing.

Matthew 20:1-15 presents a sharply accentuated view of one pole of the Jewish image of God that is filled with tension and richly diverse. With the parable of the laborers in the vineyard Jesus speaks of God's grace without changing the axiom of God's justice. Such a change is a later development of the proclamation of Jesus. While it lies *in the perspective* of our text, it is not directly contained in it. It developed in Paul and certainly in the Reformation and occasioned among other things the transition from the idea that all the laborers received the same reward to the idea that those who have nothing are rewarded by grace, while the first workers who depend on their works lose their salvation and, because of their "self-love," miss the kingdom of God.[97] This Protestant interpretation that currently dominates the field has made v. 16 pivotal for the text. However, in accentuating the verse it also changed its emphasis. If reward by grace becomes the sole principle, the danger arises that people can lay claim to it. "Pardonner, c'est son métier!" (Voltaire). The Reformation did not intend that God should be misused this way, but it has not always been able to avoid it.

Matthew

In the history of our parable's interpretation it has frequently found new applications. A first example is the way Matthew himself applies it.

■ **16** By inserting the parable here Matthew wanted to elucidate further the saying about the first and the last with which the previous pericope had ended (19:30). For

---

mandments results in different rewards. Hallel-Midrash (in Erlemann, *Bild*, 109) says that God is *not* like a king who pays a lazy worker and an energetic worker the same wage.

92 Fundamental is the saying of Antigonus of Soko in *m. ʾAbot* 1.3: "Be not like slaves that minister to the master for the sake of receiving a bounty." Almost proverbial is the expression that one should not use the "crown" (= the Torah) simply for one's own advantage (*m. ʾAbot* 1.13; 4.5). For further sources see Str-B 4.496–97 and Moore, *Judaism* 2.95–99.

93 Among the parables with related images we can cite here are *Midr. Ps.* 26.3.109a and parallels = Hezser, *Lohnmetaphorik,* 307–9: A king who pays a full wage to a lazy servant is praised. For evidence of the idea of reward as a gift of grace see Str-B 4.489–90.

94 Simeon bar Yohai: If someone was a scoundrel his entire life and repents at the very last, God receives him (*t. Qidd.* 1.14–15 [337] and parallels = Str-B 1.166). For further sources see Moore, *Judaism* 1.520–34.

95 On the two measures cf. Efraim Elimelech Urbach, *The Sages: Their Concepts and Beliefs* (2 vols.; Jerusalem: Magnes, 1975) 1.448–61. On the complementary character of justice and grace in rabbinic Judaism cf. Moore, *Judaism* 1.392–98.

96 *Tanch.* B (on Exodus) 9:3 § 16 (Hans Bietenhard, trans., *Midrasch Tanhuma B: Rabbi Tanhuma über die Torah, genannt Midrasch Jelammedum,* 2 vols. [Bern: Lang, 1980–82] 1.413).

97 Zwingli, 353: "philautia et sui ipsius operumque propriorum aestimatio."

this reason he concludes the parable by repeating the saying in a slightly modified form. "Thus [that is, in the way the parable describes] the[98] last will be first and the first last." The order, which differs from that of 19:30, corresponds to the parable when it speaks first of the "ascent" of the last (vv. 8-9) and then of the "descent" of the first (vv. 11-15). Thus v. 16 serves to summarize the parable. However, John Chrysostom already observed that it appears not to offer a very good summary: "The Lord indicates there (that is, in vv. 1-15) that everyone can count on the same reward, not that some are excluded while others are admitted."[99] What v. 16 actually should say, based on the parable, is that the last will be *like* the first.[100] With this final verse Matthew takes up not the central idea of equal pay but the description in v. 8 of the sequence in which the wage is paid ("beginning with the last up to the first"). Does this mean that he misunderstood the parable? Has he replaced the idea of equal pay for all laborers with that of the reversal of positions in the eschaton?

This difficulty is related to another problem. Of whom is the evangelist thinking when he refers to the "first" and the "last"? The suggestion that he is thinking of the Jews and Gentiles in a framework of salvation history has received wide acceptance.[101] In that case, that "the first will be last" is probably to be understood in the sense of the statement of 21:43 that the kingdom will be taken from Israel. The most that can be said for this interpretation is that the metaphor "vineyard" appears again in 21:28, 33-41. But neither the context 19:27-30; 20:20-23, that deals with the *disciples'* reward, nor the parable itself, which in no way says that the "first" will have their denarius taken from them, points in this direction. It is more probable, therefore, that we should understand the "first" and the "last" to be members of the church. This suggestion is supported by the probable use at Matthew's level of ἐργάται to mean Christian laborers in the kingdom of God (cf. 9:37-38; 10:10). However, much as we have already seen in 19:30, there are still two possible applications. Is Matthew with the parable trying primarily to comfort the "little ones" (18:1-14), for example, the latecomers, the unimportant, or the resident Christians in the local churches in the face of the important members of the church, the apostles, the scribes, or the itinerant charismatics by assuring them that these others will have no advantage in the coming kingdom of heaven—indeed, that they will be last?[102] Or is he instead trying to warn the "great ones," saying to them that they will have no privileges in the kingdom of heaven, even if they have worked harder in the vineyard of the church than have the others?[103] The latter is not improbable, for Matthew is clearly aware of the problems that arise when disciples become great and famous (cf. 18:1-9; 23:8-12).[104] Still, it seems to me that a

---

98 *Oi* instead of πολλοί (19:30), since the statement is a general principle that can be derived from 20:1-15.

99 John Chrysostom, 64.3 = *PG* 58.612.

100 As Thomas Aquinas (*Lectura* no. 1648) suggests as a possibility: "Novissimi primis aequabuntur."

101 See, e.g., Jülicher, *Gleichnisreden* 1.470; Jacques Dupont, "La parabole des ouvriers de la vigne (Mt 20:1-16)," 785–97, 790; Scott, *Hear*, 285 (Pharisees/disciples); Fabris, 421; Gundry, 399; Ignacio R. Cóbreces, "Los obreros de la viña: Elementos midráshicos en la parábola de Mt 20,1-16," *Studium* 30 (1990) 485–505, 487 (Jewish Christians/Gentile Christians).

102 See, e.g., Dupont, "Ouvriers de la onzième," 19; Patte, 278; Ludger Schenke, "Die Interpretation der Parabel von den 'Arbeitern im Weinberg' (Mt 20,1-15) durch Matthäus," 245–68, 267–68 (the rich are the last and are to be comforted); Johannes M. Nützel, "'Darf ich mit dem Meinen nicht tun, was ich will?' (Mt 20,15a)," 267–84, 283 (encouragement in the sense of 19:25-26).

103 The interpretation "critical of the church" is represented, e.g., by Schweizer, 395; Schottroff, "Solidarity," 142–43; Harnisch, *Gleichniserzählungen,* 199 (pronouncement of judgment on the church); Schnider, "Gerechtigkeit," 95; Lambrecht, *Treasure,* 83; Hezser, *Lohnmetaphorik,* 257–58.

104 The addition to v. 16 in C, D, W, Y, etc. also understands it this way. Cf. above, n. 2.

choice between the two alternatives is no more possible here than it was in 19:30. The statement remains ambiguous, and how it is applied depends on whether given readers identify with the laborers hired first or with those who are the very latest. In all probability Matthew intentionally leaves here an opening into which his readers can project themselves, depending on the group to which they assign themselves.

Understanding the "first" and the "last" as referring to church members does not mean, in my judgment, that we must accuse Matthew of surrendering the idea of "equal reward" in favor of the idea of a reversal of positions. In 19:16, 29 Matthew simply spoke of "eternal life" and of "hundredfold." In 20:20-23 he will explicitly reject the idea of a special reward for apostles. We may surmise, therefore, that this basic idea is also important for him in our parable.[105] He probably understood v. 16 to be a rhetorically exaggerated warning in the sense of 18:3-4 and 23:12 without thinking of differing heavenly rewards in the sense of a reversal of positions in the eschaton.

History of Interpretation: Ancient Church

In addition to Matthew's use of our parable the history of interpretation has contributed two further applications, both of which date from quite early in the ancient church and to a degree are still known in the churches today.

> a. Since Irenaeus (*Haer.* 4.36.7) the parable has been given a *salvation-history* allegorical interpretation. The workday came to represent world history. The farmer as a rule stood for the trinitarian God, the denarius for the eternal life that is granted to all believers, the vineyard for the church, the marketplace for the world, the heat of the day for its temptations, and occasionally the steward for Christ. Since Origen[106] the various hours of the day have been firmly connected with stages of salvation history. The morning hour corresponds to Adam's period, the third hour is the time of Noah, the sixth that of Abraham, the ninth that of Moses, and finally the eleventh that of Christ, who calls the Gentiles into the vineyard.[107] As a rule the relation between the last workers, that is, the Christians, and the earlier ones, that is, the Jews, was not understood to mean that the Jews lost their salvation but that they "have been saved in second place, after the Gentiles."[108]
>
> b. Alongside this allegorical interpretation in salvation-history terms there has been since Origen[109] an *individual*-allegorical interpretation that in later times was passed on as a *moral interpretation*. Here the "day" is the individual's life span. Many people are Christians from birth, others from their early youth or adulthood. Still others do not come to Christ until old age or just before their death.[110] Often this interpretation is found in quite direct statements such as a word of comfort for those who have come late to baptism, the call to decision for those who are indecisive, the admonition for veteran church workers not to let up in their work. On the other hand this understanding of the text obviously was used as an argument for postponing baptism until one's deathbed; Gregory of Nazianzus was forced to argue against such a use of the text.[111]

Neither application is Matthean. The former is reminiscent of the salvation-history parable of the vineyard in 21:28-43; the latter has no roots in Matthew whatever. There is thus no direct exegetical basis for either. The first interpretation was occasioned by the need for a fundamental theological reflection about the relationship of the Christian church to pre-Christian salvation history. In the case of the second application, what led to the new interpretation was a new experience in the history of the church, viz., the presence of new converts alongside veteran church members and the baptism in

---

105 Marguerat (*Jugement*, 470–72) especially emphasizes that in the context of 19:16—20:28 the red thread is "l'égalité des salaires."

106 15.32 = GCS Origenes 10.446-8.

107 Thus, e.g., Jerome, 175; Cyril of Alexandria no. 226 = Reuss, 228–30; Augustine *Sermo* 87.4 (5) = *PL* 38.533; Hilary, 20.6 = SC 258.108; Gregory the Great *Hom. in ev.* 19.1 = *PL* 76.1154; *Opus imperfectum* 34 = 819; Bede, 88; Christian of Stavelot, 1422; Thomas Aquinas, *Lectura* no. 1626; Dionysius the Carthusian, 221.

108 *Opus imperfectum* 34 = 822.

109 15.36 = GCS Origenes 10.456-58.

110 In, e.g., Jerome, 175; Gregory of Nazianzus *Or.* 40.20 = GCS 358.240–43; Basil *Regula brevius* no. 224 (Frank, 315); John Chrysostom, 64.3 = *PG* 58.613 (comfort for those who were baptized late); Augustine *Sermo* 87.5 (7) = *PL* 38.533; Gregory the Great, *Hom. in ev.* 19.2–3 = *PL* 76. 1155–56.

111 *Or.* 40.20 = SC 358.240.

the same church of children, adults, and persons on their deathbeds. While neither of these interpretations has a direct biblical basis, they have done no more than what Matthew himself tried to do. They related an old, established text to a new situation because of their fundamental experience that the living Christ who spoke through the biblical parable also wants to speak to the people of later times through his word. Thus both of these new interpretations are justified by the process that is going on inside the Bible itself. Out of the old text they produced new possibilities of meaning and in so doing demonstrated that the text was not an antiquated, foreign word but a living word of God. Whether they are faithful to the direction laid down by Jesus in his parable or to the middle of the New Testament witness must be determined by their concrete application in each individual case.

17 **And when Jesus went up to Jerusalem[1] he took the twelve[2] aside and said to them on the way, 18/ "Behold, we are going up to Jerusalem, and the Son of Man will be delivered to the chief priests and scribes, and they will condemn him to death, 19/ and they will deliver him to the Gentiles to mock and to scourge and to crucify, and on the third day he will be raised."**

Analysis Our text is a brief prediction of the stages of Jesus' approaching suffering formulated in simple sentences. The twelve appear only as hearers. The source is Mark 10:32-34, and Matthew has shortened[3] and only slightly reworked it. The changes from Mark can be easily understood as Matthean redaction.[4]

Interpretation

Verse 17 marks the beginning of the final section of Matthew 19-20. Jesus is already on the way to Jerusalem.[5] What in 16:21 was announced is now already reality; the end is near. Jesus takes the twelve aside. His announcement of the Son of Man's[6] approaching death and resurrection is part of his instructions to the disciples; his Jewish opponents and the crowds are not aware of it.[7]

Unlike Mark 10:32-34 the narrator is interested only in Jesus, not in the disciples. The entire focus is on the way Jesus is to go. Since this way is part of God's plan, its

stages are framed by two *passiva divina* "will be delivered," "will be raised" ($\pi\alpha\rho\alpha\delta o\vartheta\eta\sigma\epsilon\tau\alpha\iota$, $\dot\epsilon\gamma\epsilon\rho\vartheta\eta\sigma\epsilon\tau\alpha\iota$); between them appear the individual stages of Jesus' suffering. Now that the time is near, the announcement describes them in some detail rather than in summary form as in 16:21 and 17:22. More clearly than in Mark the main human actors are the Jewish high priests and scribes.[8] Only their activity is described with finite verbs "will condemn," "will deliver" ($\kappa\alpha\tau\alpha\kappa\rho\iota\nu o\hat\upsilon\sigma\iota\nu$,[9] $\pi\alpha\rho\alpha\delta\acute\omega$-$\sigma o\upsilon\sigma\iota\nu$). Again unlike Mark's account, what the Romans do—viz., mock, spit, and crucify—is only the consequence or goal of the evil behavior of the Jewish leaders ($\epsilon\iota\varsigma$ $\tau\acute o$). This prediction of the passion already reveals, therefore, something of Matthew's understanding of the passion. That the scribes will play only a minor role in the passion in comparison with the Pharisees and elders does not concern Matthew.[10] Since all Jewish groups reject Jesus, the opposing groups are interchangeable. Jesus' detailed prediction reminds the readers of the gospel of the passion narrative that they already know from the Gospel of Mark. They visualize Jesus as he is handed over to the high priests (cf. Mark 14:10-11, 18, 41-44), as he is tried and condemned to death (Mark

---

1 Although $\mu\acute\epsilon\lambda\lambda\omega\nu$ $\delta\grave\epsilon$ $\dot\alpha\nu\alpha\beta\alpha\acute\iota\nu\epsilon\iota\nu$ $\acute I\eta\sigma o\hat\upsilon\varsigma$ sounds Matthean, it is not well enough attested by B and a few translations to be regarded as original. Metzger (*Commentary*, 51) suggests that there has been a topographical emendation. Since Jesus has not been in Jericho, he is simply "about" to go up to Jerusalem. However, see below, n. 5.

2 The simple $\delta\acute\omega\delta\epsilon\kappa\alpha$ is better attested than $\delta\acute\omega\delta\epsilon\kappa\alpha$ $\mu\alpha\vartheta\eta\tau\acute\alpha\varsigma$. I am assuming that Matthew has taken over Mark's text here and that later copyists inserted the $\mu\alpha\vartheta\eta\tau\alpha\acute\iota$ that is common elsewhere in Matthew (cf. 10:1; 11:1; 26:20).

3 The description of the feelings of Jesus' companions and followers in the introduction to Mark's narrative in 10:32 is missing, as is the summary at the end of Mark 10:32 in anticipation of the prediction of the passion. In the prediction itself the catchword $\dot\epsilon\mu\pi\tau\acute\upsilon\omega$ is missing (but not in 26:67 and 27:30).

4 The typical Markan expression $\kappa\alpha\tau'$ $\iota\delta\acute\iota\alpha\nu$ appears in Matthean redaction also in 14:23. $\Sigma\tau\alpha\upsilon\rho\acute o\omega$ is redactional also in 23:34; 26:2; 27:35. It appears in 26:2 and 27:31 in connection with $\epsilon\iota\varsigma$ $\tau\acute o$. Matthew avoids $\pi\acute\alpha\lambda\iota\nu$ when it does not have a direct antecedent. Cf. vol. I, Introduction 3.3. In all three announcements of the passion $\tau\hat\eta$ $\tau\rho\acute\iota\tau\eta$ $\acute\eta\mu\acute\epsilon\rho\alpha$ with

$\dot\epsilon\gamma\epsilon\acute\iota\rho\omega$ replaces Mark's $\mu\epsilon\tau\grave\alpha$ $\tau\rho\epsilon\hat\iota\varsigma$ $\acute\eta\mu\acute\epsilon\rho\alpha\varsigma$ $\dot\alpha\nu\alpha\sigma\tau\hat\eta\nu\alpha\iota$. Cf. above, IV A 4, n. 1 on 17:22-23.

5 $\dot A\nu\alpha\beta\alpha\acute\iota\nu\omega$ (= Hebrew עלה) is *terminus technicus* for the journey to Jerusalem and does not mean that Jesus must already be on the actual ascent from Jericho to Jerusalem.

6 On the term $\upsilon\iota\grave o\varsigma$ $\dot\alpha\nu\vartheta\rho\acute\omega\pi o\upsilon$ in connection with the way of Jesus cf. the excursus above, IV A 1, nos. 4, 5.

7 On Matthew's "Son of Man secret" cf. the excursus above, IV A 1, no. 4, and Ulrich Luz, "The Son of Man in Matthew: Heavenly Judge or Human Christ," *JSNT* 48 (1992) 12–16.

8 Again an example of the stereotypical enumeration of Jewish opponents in groups of two. Cf. vol. 1 on 3:7-10: Jewish Groups. By omitting the article before $\gamma\rho\alpha\mu\mu\alpha\tau\epsilon\acute\upsilon\sigma\iota\nu$ Matthew more closely identifies the two hostile groups.

9 $K\alpha\tau\alpha\kappa\rho\acute\iota\nu\omega$ does not appear in Matthew's scene before the supreme council, but it does appear in Mark 14:64. Matthew here has Mark's passion narrative in mind.

10 They appear only in 26:57 and 27:41.

14:64), as he is delivered to the Romans (Mark 15:1), mocked (Mark 15:20), scourged (Mark 15:15),[11] and crucified (Mark 15:20-39). It is thus clear from the prediction of the passion not only that the implied reader of the Gospel of Matthew is already familiar with the passion narrative but also that Matthew's story is not designed to create tension. Jesus and the readers know what is coming. Jesus can enter his suffering out of obedience to God; in the reading of chap. 26 the readers of the gospel will deepen their understanding of what they already know.[12] The catchword "crucify" appears for the first time and reveals the ultimate goal of the evil strategy of the Jewish leaders (cf. 26:2; 27:26, 31). Yet announcing the crucifixion is not the final objective of Jesus' prediction. God who has set all of this in motion will again intervene. He will raise Jesus on the third day, as the churches believe (cf. 1 Cor 15:4) and as Matthew himself will tell (28:1-15).

The focus is thus on Jesus the Son of Man, his approaching fate, and God's plan for him. The text is only indirectly interested in the disciples to the degree that they know that they also one day will be "handed over" (cf. 10:17-22) and that they also must go the way of the cross (cf. 10:38; 16:24-26). The following section deals with their suffering.

---

11 Only here the order does not agree!
12 In the terminology of Seymour Benjamin Chatman, since the readers know the story they must all the more pay attention to the discourse (*Story and Discourse: Narrative Structure in Fiction and Film* [Ithaca: Cornell University Press, 1978]).

Literature

H. A. Brongers, "Der Zornesbecher," *OTS* 15 (1969) 177–92.

Kenneth Willis Clark, "The Meaning of *[KATA]KϒPIETEIN*," in idem, *The Gentile Bias and Other Essays* (NovTSup 54; Leiden: Brill, 1980) 207–12.

Hampel, *Menschensohn*, 106–10, 302–42.

Paul Hoffmann and Volker Eid, *Jesus von Nazareth und eine christliche Moral* (QD 66; 2d ed.; Freiburg: Herder, 1975) 186–230.

R. Le Déaut, "Goûter le calice de la mort," *Bib* 43 (1962) 82–86.

Simon Légasse, "Approche de l'épisode préévangélique des fils de Zébédée (Marc 10,35-45)," *NTS* 20 (1973/74) 161–77.

Jürgen Roloff, "Anfänge der soteriologischen Deutung des Todes Jesu (Mk 10,45 und Lk 22,27)," in idem, *Exegetische Verantwortung in der Kirche: Aufsätze* (Göttingen: Vandenhoeck & Ruprecht, 1990) 117–43.

David Seeley, "Rulership and Service in Mark 10:41-45," *NovT* 35 (1992) 234–50.

Peter Stuhlmacher, "Existenzstellvertretung für die Vielen (Mk 10,45. Mt 20,28)," in Rainer Albertz et al., eds., *Werden und Wirken des Alten Testaments: Festschrift für Claus Westermann* (Göttingen: Vandenhoeck & Ruprecht, 1980) 412–27.

20 **Then the mother of the sons of Zebedee came to him, knelt, and asked him for something. 21/ But he said to her, "What do you want?" She says to him, "Say that these my two sons may sit one on your right and one on your left in your kingdom." 22/ But Jesus answered and said, "You do not know what you ask. Can you drink the cup that I will drink?" They say to him, "We can." 23/ He says to them, "You will indeed drink my cup, but to sit at my right and left is not mine to give, but (it is for those) for whom it has been prepared by my father."**

24 **When the ten heard it, they became angry at the two brothers.**

25 **But Jesus called them to him and said, "You know that the rulers of the Gentiles lord it over them and the great ones have power over them.**

26 **It shall[1] not be so with you. No, with you whoever wants to be great shall be your servant,**

27 **and with you whoever wants to be first shall be your slave,**

28 **as the Son of Man came not to be served but to serve and to give his life as a ransom for many."[2]**

Analysis **Structure**

The section is divided into two parts, viz., one introduced by the question of the mother of the Zebedees (vv. 20-23), and a second introduced by the disciples' indignation (vv. 24-28). The first subunit is a conversation that begins with a question of Jesus to the mother and ends with his definitive answer. It contains in v. 22 a remarkable break. The mother of the sons of Zebedee had asked a question, but Jesus' answer is directed not to her but to her two sons. The second subunit consists only of an address from Jesus; the disciples' indignation is not expressed in direct speech. This address begins with two sentences about the authority of the great and powerful among the Gentiles (vv. 25-26a). It is followed by two opposing statements, chiastically structured,[3] that suggest how it is to be different "with you" (vv. 26b-27) and a concluding comparison of these opposing sentences with the behavior of the Son of Man, Jesus (v. 28). Thus in this section Jesus has not only the first and last words; he also has the most important and longest word. From the beginning to the end he is the defining figure.

Source

The source, Mark 10:35-45, is only slightly modified. The three most important changes are: (1) Instead of the Zebedees it is their mother who poses the question about the best places in heaven (vv. 20-21). With this change Matthew creates a difficulty for himself, because Jesus' answer in vv. 22-23 is still directed to

---

1 Unlike Mark 10:43, in Matthew we should read ἔσται here. As in the two cases that follow, the future has an imperative meaning (BDF § 362).

2 D and a few other Western witnesses have here an extensive addition: "But you should endeavor to become greater from what is small and smaller from what is great. When you come and are invited to a banquet, do not take the places of honor, lest someone come who is better known than you, and then the host, when he comes, says to you, 'There is room for you down there,' and you are shamed. But if you take a lesser place, and someone comes who

is less important than you, the host will say, 'Move up the table,' and this will be advantageous for you." The text is a secondary variant of Luke 14:8-11 with a new introduction. It provides a transition to vv. 26-28.

3 In vv. 25c/26b μεγάλοι and μέγας are corresponding terms, and κατεξουσιάζω and εἶναι διάκονος are antithetical. In vv. 25b/27 ἄρχοντες and πρῶτος are matching, while κυριεύω and εἶναι δοῦλος are antithetical.

the disciples.[4] (2) The mother is initially silent (v. 20b); she does not have the courage to speak until Jesus asks the question. Thus in vv. 20-28 Jesus has both the first and last words. (3) Matthew omits Mark's two references to the approaching baptism of death (vv. 38-39).[5] He has also omitted the logion in Q 12:49-50 that has a similar content. In both cases we can only speculate about his reasons.[6] On the whole it is not easy to understand the changes in Mark's text, and the theory of Markan priority has a difficult time with this pericope. However, since almost all of the other small changes are easily understood as Matthean[7] (which would not be the case for Markan changes, if we were to assume the priority of Matthew), it is likely that here also the priority belongs to Mark.

Interpretation

To a large extent vv. 20-28 sound like a reprise of some of the evangelist's important themes with which the readers are already familiar. The question about a special reward in heaven was already posed in 19:28 with the logion of the twelve thrones, and in 20:1-16 it received a negative answer. The metaphor of the "cup" (vv. 22-23) reminds the readers of the prediction of the passion in vv. 17-19. The rule that the disciples are to become "servants" and "slaves" (vv. 26-27) is reminiscent of the content of the introduction to the community discourse in 18:1-4, although with different language. The readers are by no means surprised when a reference to

the Son of Man follows in v. 28, since the Son of Man was already mentioned in v. 18. For the most part, therefore, the text takes up and expands familiar themes, and in so doing it reflects the repetitive style of Matthew, the teacher.[8] It is precisely because the readers of our section bring with them a great deal of prior understanding and their own insight from their reading of the gospel thus far that the evangelist can limit himself to adding a few emphases to the Markan text.

■ **20-23** Why the mother comes to Jesus in place of the sons remains a mystery. Most interpreters say that Matthew wanted to avoid having the apostles James and John ask an impossible question. That may be right, but it would mean that Matthew was not very consistent. Since from v. 22 on Jesus is talking to the sons, it is easy to surmise that they had sent her on ahead and that they in reality were using her.[9] In all probability, however, we have here but one more example that the narrator Matthew has little interest in external consistency. Are there other explanations? The mother of the Zebedees is mentioned again in 27:56 where Matthew either has identified her with Salome (Mark 15:40) or has replaced Salome with her.[10] When we read the two texts together, they suggest that Matthew imagines that Zebedee's wife

---

4   According to Elaine Mary Wainwright (*Towards a Feminist Critical Reading of the Gospel According to Matthew* [BZNW 60; Berlin: de Gruyter, 1991] 256) Jesus' answer in vv. 22-23 is clearly directed at the mother *and* the sons, a claim that is improbable, since v. 23 speaks of sitting at the left and the right and thus only of the martyrdom of the sons. Matthew probably is simply following here Mark's text.

5   The Byzantine text and a few witnesses from other families reintroduce both of them, but the readings are clearly secondary.

6   Is the statement too easily misunderstood, since in the meantime βαπτίζω has become *terminus technicus* for Christian baptism? Gnilka (2.189) assumes that Matthew wanted to avoid a Greek image, but I do not find the suggestion convincing in view of the evidence for biblical usage in the translations of the Bible collected by Gerhard Delling ("Βάπτισμα βαπτισθῆναι," in idem, *Studien zum Neuen Testament und zum hellenistischen Judentum* [Göttingen:

Vandenhoeck & Ruprecht, 1970] 243–44).

7   Cf. vol. 1, Introduction 3.2 on τότε, προσέρχομαι, μετά, προσκυνέω (v. 20), οὗτος (v. 21), ἀποκριθεὶς δὲ . . . , μέλλω (v. 22), πατήρ μου (v. 23), δέ (v. 25), ὥσπερ (v. 28). On introducing the mother of the Zebedees cf. 27:56, on Jesus' βασιλεία cf. 16:28. On the historical present of λέγω cf. vol. 1, Introduction 3.1. According to vol. 1, Introduction 3.3. ἄρχομαι (Mark 10:41) is a term that Matthew avoids.

8   Cf. above, III, on 12:1–16:20. The technique of repetition is especially obvious in 16:21–20:34 with the predictions of the passion and in 16:21–26:64 in the Son of Man sayings.

9   A view expressed as early as Augustine (*Cons. ev* 2.64 = 226) and Jerome (177) and after them by many medieval and later authors. (Jerome attributes to the woman both *affectus pietatis* and *error muliebris*!) It is also known in the East (e.g., Theophylactus, 364).

10   The comparison with 9:9 par. Mark 2:13, where

was a follower of Jesus on the way to Jerusalem.[11] Matthew does not portray her in a negative light. She pays homage to Jesus on her knees, and initially she does not speak—behavior that favorably sets her apart from the somewhat impudent request of the two sons in Mark that implies that Jesus simply must grant their wish.[12] She does not speak until Jesus encourages her to do so. Her request for the places of honor for her sons in Jesus' coming heavenly kingdom is not all that unusual, since they belong to the inner circle of disciples (17:1; cf. 26:37).[13] The right-hand seat is the best; the seat on the left is generally regarded as less honorable,[14] but that is not a factor in our text. At the same time, however, for the readers her request is an example of the disciples' false striving for earthly greatness (cf. 18:1-2). After 19:30—20:16 they know that according to Jesus there are no special privileges in the kingdom of heaven.

Jesus waves the disciples aside; he cannot grant their request. Initially he does not say why; instead, he responds with a surprising counterquestion that changes the subject:[15] "Can you drink the cup that I will drink?" Much as he did on the mount of transfiguration (cf. 17:9-13) Jesus leads the Zebedees directly into the depth of life. Suffering and death are something that is in their future and that *they* will have to endure. "Cup" is a metaphor that since the time of the prophets usually means God's judgment.[16] Its meaning is not hard and fast, however, and it can also refer to a person's "fate" or in a more narrow sense to death.[17] After 20:18-19 the readers have almost certainly understood the cup in the last sense. Boldly and courageously the Zebedees claim that they most certainly can go through martyrdom with Jesus. It is likely that the readers reacted with skepticism to this confident affirmation. They know the story of the passion and know that the disciples ran away on that occasion. They are also familiar with Peter's denial and his vigorous protest that proceeded it (Mark 14:29-31). Presumably they furthermore know nothing of John's later martyrdom.[18] However, their verbal willingness to go through martyrdom is of no use to the sons of Zebedee, since it is not Jesus' place to grant the places of honor at his side. They are for those for whom God himself has prepared them and to whom only he can give them.[19] One simply has no claims before God.

Matthew *replaces* "Levi" with "Matthew" (cf. above, II B 3.2), suggests that we cannot exclude the possibility of a similar change in 27:56. In that case we would have here as well as in 27:56 evidence that Matthew or his church had a special interest in this woman.

11   Cf. Elaine Mary Wainwright (*Towards a Feminist Critical Reading of the Gospel According to Matthew*, 255.

12   Θέλομεν ἵνα ὃ ἐὰν αἰτήσωμέν σε ποιήσῃς ἡμῖν.

13   The readers are also thinking of 19:28.

14   The seat at the right hand is for the crown prince (Josephus *Ant.* 6.235). On the street the teacher walks in the middle with the older pupil to his right and the younger to his left (*b. Yoma* 37a = Str–B. 1.835). For further sources see Pesch, *Markusevangelium* 2.156.

15   As he does in 18:3. Cf. above, IV B 1.1.

16   Cf. esp. H. A. Brongers ("Der Zornesbecher," 177–92) and Leonhard Goppelt, "πίνω κτλ," *TDNT* 6 (1968) 149–53.

17   *T. Abr.* A 16; *Tg. Yer. I, Tg. Yer. II,* and *Tg. Neof. I* on Gen 40:23; *Tg. Neof.* on Deut 32:1. Cf. R. Le Déaut, "Goûter le calice de la mort," 82–86, 84–85; Simon Légasse, "Approche de l'épisode préévangélique des fils de Zébédée (Marc 10,35-45)," 161–77, 164; *Asc.*

Isa. 5.13; *Mart. Pol.* 14.2 (the cup of Christ).

18   Tertullian (*Praescr. haer.* 36) is the first to know that John was dipped in boiling oil, but that no harm came to him, and that he died a natural death at an advanced age. Why, therefore, does Matthew (as does Mark) have Jesus confirm for both Zebedees their future martyrdom (τὸ μὲν ποτήριόν μου πίεσθε)? Were they also aware of a tradition about John's martyrdom? Or was it enough that they remembered the martyrdom of James? Or is the focus rhetorically only on the concluding sentence (τὸ δὲ καθίσαι, etc.)? Or is the entire statement ironic?

19   The sentence is expanded over Mark 10:40, but it is still incomplete. The Latin tradition corrected the situation by inserting a *vobis* (vg and it except for d and q. H clarifies by transposing: *meum non est dare vobis.* Cf. Adolf Jülicher, *Itala I: Mattäus-Evangelium* [Berlin: de Gruyter, 1938]). Then the text would mean: It is not my place to give the seats of honor to you (*scil.* because others will be more worthy than you); it is rather my place to give them to those for whom my father has prepared them (viz., to the most worthy). With this explanation one not only maintained the principle that reward would always

History of Interpretation

With its idea of subordination v. 23 was difficult for the later church, because it appeared to be a trump card in the hand of the Arians.[20] Augustine's only defense is the dogmatic assertion: "What has been prepared by His Father has also been prepared by the Son Himself, because He Himself and the Father are one."[21] Another dogmatic solution of the difficulty was relating v. 23 to Christ's human nature.[22] The breakthrough on behalf of the original meaning of the text did not come until the early Enlightenment. The Cartesian Wolzogen points out that nowhere in the scripture does Christ or the Holy Spirit predestine; it is the Father alone who does it. "It follows that Christ is not the highest God."[23] As a matter of fact it would never have occurred to Matthew, who identified Jesus functionally (Immanuel) if not exactly ontologically with God, that making Christ subordinate to the Father (cf. also 24:36)—a relationship that for him was self-evident—in any way might damage his majesty.

Interpretation

■ **24-27** The other ten disciples become angry at the sons of Zebedee, even though the latter had been rebuffed by Jesus. With their jealousy do they show that they are cut from the same mold as the other two? Wanting to be great on earth or by means of religious compensation in the beyond (18:1) obviously is characteristic not merely of a few; it is found in all disciples of Jesus. Jesus sees what is going on inside them and calls them to come to him. He refers to the gentile rulers and to the power elite around them. Unfortunately, we cannot answer with certainty the important question whether in vv. 25-27 Jesus contrasts the servant character of the church in a broad sense with all worldly authority or in a narrow sense with only evil and tyrannical authority. That v. 25 speaks of the rulers of the Gentiles[24] could speak for limiting the meaning to "negative" authorities. In the final analysis we must leave open the question whether the two verbs κατακυριεύω and κατεξουσιάζω ("lord it over" and "have power over") have a neutral or a negative meaning—that is, whether they mean "to rule, to exercise authority" or "to oppress, to exercise might."[25] In my judgment, however, the decisive argument for the broad interpretation is that the following rules in vv. 26-27 are not simply designed to correct the abuse of power that can happen with worldly rulers. The issue for Jesus is not that such common excesses of worldly authority as repression or the unjust use of power should not happen in the church but that there simply is not to be in the church any "being great" and "being first" at all. It is probable, therefore, that vv. 25-27 fundamentally contrast the world's authority structure and the church's service structure.[26]

Διάκονος ("servant") appears for the first time in our text. Its root form appears scarcely at all in the Bible. In profane Greek διακονέω ("to serve") initially means personal service at the table and can then also be used in a more general sense.[27] In contrast to κύριος ("master"), δοῦλος means "slave," that is, someone who is subordinate and not free. The readers already are familiar with the word because they are δοῦλοι of the Lord Jesus (10:24-25). Now they are also to serve one another as slaves in the church. All of this means a fundamentally new orientation that turns normal ways of evaluation

---

be paid according to merit; one also eliminated the irritating "Arian" subordination. Cf. the history of interpretation. It appears frequently among the fathers: e.g., Ambrose *Fid.* 5.6.80–84 = CSEL 78.246–47; Bede, 89; Dionysius the Carthusian, 225; Maldonat, 418.

20 Cf. Ambrose *Fid.* 5.5.55 = CSEL 78.238.
21 *Trin.* 1.12 (25) = FC 45.37.
22 Zwingli, 354.
23 Wolzogen, 346.
24 After v. 19 the readers here also may well have understood ἔθνη to mean "Gentiles."
25 In compound verbs κατα- can carry various nuances of meaning—among others, a perfective meaning (to do something to the end) or also a negative meaning (to do something in a bad sense). Cf.

Moulton–Howard–Turner 2.316. Κατακυριεύω has almost the same meaning as the simple κυριεύω and in the LXX it can be used both with a negative nuance of enemies as well as in a positive sense of people or even of God. To be sure, Kenneth Clark's study ("The Meaning of *[KATA]KYPIETEIN*," 207–12) clearly speaks against a negative interpretation. BAGD (s.v. κατεξουσιάζω) translates the seldom-appearing verb in a negative sense ("tyrannize over someone"). However, the few sources given there only partially support the negative nuance. The question plays a major role in the interpretation after the Reformation. Cf. below on the history of interpretation.

26 David Seeley ("Rulership and Service in Mark 10:41-45," 234–50, 234–45) compares Mark 10:41-45 with

upside down, just as did the challenge in 18:1-4 to become "little" like children.[28] One can sense something of the "common" thinking even in the way the counter-sentence is formulated: "If someone wants to be great among you . . ." The issue, however, is not to present a new way to greatness—a more noble way than that of authority and power; it is rather that the desire to be great is itself to be eliminated, since even the most subtle desire for greatness for oneself corrupts genuine service. For this reason Jesus speaks in paradoxes: "Whoever wants to be great" shall become small and give up the idea of greatness. Thus the purpose of the two ὃς ἐάν ("whoever") sentences of vv. 26-27 is not to show the church a new way of becoming great but to call her away from her natural desire and to turn this desire upside down. In this way—and only in this way—the church can be a counterculture to the world. After 18:1-4 Matthew is now saying this for the second time.[29]

History of Interpretation

For the exegetes of the Reformation and the post-Reformation period vv. 24-27 constituted a special crux. In our verses a fundamental difference between state and church appears to be expressed that led the Anabaptists to the conviction that "it is not appropriate for a Christian to serve as a magistrate."[30] The verses created difficulties for the reform-minded exegetes. They had no problem emphasizing with strong words—against the Catholic prince bishops—that "the office of a shepherd is so unlike that of a prince" that it is impossible for one person to hold both of them.[31] However, Luther already emphasizes that our text confirms rather than rejects secular government.[32] Protestant and Catholic exegetes were in

agreement that our text speaks not of Christian princes but of heathen rulers who governed their subjects as tyrants.[33] According to Bucer the magistrates even "serve" in a special way.[34] Brenz is of the opinion that one and the same person can be prince and bishop, "etsi difficillimum est."[35] But what then is the difference between the Protestant ruling prince who at the same time held the office of a bishop and a Catholic prince bishop or even the regent of the church-state, the pope, whom Lapide cites in this context as exemplary, since he calls himself "servus servorum Dei"?[36] The Protestant exegetes' approval of an episcopacy whose members also exerted governing authority in matters of state clearly colored their view of this text. In the interpretation influenced by the new symbiotic relationship between state and church the text's view of the fundamental difference between the authority structures in the state and the non-authority structures in the church had no chance of being heard. Given this interpretation it is not surprising that wherever the Protestants were the dominant church they had the fatal tendency well into our century to take over for the church almost every form of civil authority structure (monarchical, parliamentary, or even the "*Führer* principle"). By contrast it is gratifying to find, at least in an "opposition figure" like Wolzogen, precisely what in my judgment the text wants to say. There is a fundamental difference between the structure of the church and secular authority as such, not merely unjust authority that is perverted by arrogance and ambition. "To exert power over nations . . . to demand obedience from them, belongs to the nature and essence of authority; that is, however, the direct opposite of what Christ here requires of the apostles, namely, lowliness and submission. If, therefore, this is what Christ com-

---

the Hellenistic traditions about the good ruler, who is a servant and benefactor of his subjects (e.g., in Musonius Rufus or Dio Chrysostom *Or.* 1.3) and with the Cynic-Stoic traditions about the wise ruler. However, the wholesale contrast to "the" rulers of the Gentiles in Matt 20:25 par. probably shows that our saying does not reckon with the existence of the good rulers and views worldly authority in general in a negative light. Presumably the Jesus tradition is not familiar with the traditions cited by Seeley.

27 Jürgen Roloff, "Anfänge der soteriologischen Deutung des Todes Jesu (Mk 10,45 und Lk 22,27)," 117–43, 131.

28 The statement of the Sophist Callicles in Plato *Gorg.* 491e gives a good example of the "normal" evaluation: "How can a person become happy (εὐδαίμων)

who serves (δουλεύων) anyone else?"

29 He will say it a third time in 23:8-12.

30 Schleitheim Confession, Article 6 = William R. Estep Jr., ed., *Anabaptist Beginnings (1523–1533): A Sourcebook* (Bibliotheca Humanistica & Reformatorica 16; Nieuwkoop: de Graaf, 1976) 103.

31 Calvin, *Inst.* 4.11.2.

32 2.685–86.

33 Cf., e.g., Musculus, 473; Lapide, 390; Jansen, 186 with a reference to the negative sense of the prefix κατα.

34 Bucer, 161A.

35 Brenz, 671.

36 Lapide, 390–91.

mands . . . it follows that he himself abolishes authority."[37]

■ **28** The order that is to prevail in the church corresponds to what the Son of Man himself has done (ὥσπερ). His activity is the model to which the church must orient itself. However we may solve the difficult tradition-history and -historical questions that this word poses, it is clear in the Matthean context that the Son of Man saying in v. 28 is not a foreign element that is incidental to the text; it is the high point of an organic train of thought that begins (v. 18) and ends (v. 28) with the suffering of the Son of Man. For Matthew, "Son of Man" is a self-designation of Jesus that includes all of his activity—his earthly activity, his death, and his future exaltation.[38] The earthly activity of the Son of Man is described in v. 28b with "to serve" (διακονέω). Perhaps the readers think initially of Jesus' "table service" in the feeding stories or later in the Eucharist; in a broader sense they probably think of his healings. Beyond that he will "give his life" as it were as the final and highest act of his service (v. 28c). Jesus had already said this to his disciples on several occasions in the gospel, along with the idea that surrendering one's life must be the consequence of service also for them (10:38-39; 16:24-26). The only new element here is that Jesus interprets his death. He is λύτρον for many.

> In connection with this passage numerous questions are raised today about the nature and meaning of Jesus' atoning death, but there is little in Matthew that provides an answer for the questions. In the context of the Gospel of Matthew v. 28 is an isolated verse that is somewhat paralleled only in 26:28 and that furthermore Matthew takes over from Mark word for word. Λύτρον appears only here in the gospel. It means "ransom"; it is, for example, the price paid for the release of slaves,[39] or in the LXX it is the ransom money paid in the place of capital punishment (Exod

21:30 is but one of its frequent appearances). From the many New Testament concepts of atonement and redemption the idea that the believers are redeemed by Christ (1 Cor 6:20; 7:23 [τιμή instead of λύτρον]) comes the nearest to what might be meant here.[40] Matthew will hardly have been thinking here of an individual biblical text, certainly not of Isa 53:10-12, a text that has scarcely any common vocabulary with Matthew and that also has no particular meaning elsewhere for Matthew.[41] Thus the precise meaning of the statement remains relatively indefinite. For Matthew the idea of a ransom or "substitute" is probably less important here than the radical nature of Jesus' service. Jesus took his service to others so seriously that he gave his own life for "many."[42]

Summary and Meaning for Today

Jesus speaks to the sons of Zebedee not about their heavenly positions of honor but about their future death. Once again he calls the disciples' attention to the complete reversal of all worldly authority structures in the church. Thus he gives the church a fundamental orientation—an orientation that is downwards, toward service. In the final analysis it is the orientation that gets its bearings from his own way—the way of the Son of Man. For Matthew the church's service structure means abandoning every authority structure in the church.

What does that mean for the church's legal structure? In the history of the church, texts such as 20:24-28 or 18:1-4 have almost never been understood as a basis for canonical law. They have had scarcely any effect outside the area of individual behavior. None of the major churches is in its structure a church of "service" in Matthew's sense. In my judgment that is not merely to be explained as a disavowal of the church's origins and as conformity to worldly forms of authority. The problem lies deeper. In a church that is oriented downwards,

---

37 Wolzogen, 347.

38 Cf. the excursus on the Son of Man, no. 4, above, IV A 1.

39 Spicq, *Lexicon* 2.426–27.

40 One can compare also 1 Tim 2:6 (ἀντίλυτρον), Tit 2:14 (λυτρόω), 1 Pet 1:18 (λυτρόω). However, the content of the concept is quite vague in all of these texts. Even less precise is ἀπολύτρωσις, which can become a general term for "redemption."

41 Above all, the central catchword λύτρον does not appear there. Cf. Peter Stuhlmacher, "Existenzstellvertretung für die Vielen (Mk 10,45. Mt 20,28),"

412–27, 417–18; Hampel, *Menschensohn*, 317–25. On Isa 53 in Matthew cf. above on 8:17. This is not the place to speak of all possible biblical instances of pre- and early forms in the tradition history of the logion.

42 We are not to understand πολλοί (without the article) inclusively in the sense of "everyone," as has been done since Joachim Jeremias (*The Eucharistic Words of Jesus* [London: SCM, 1964], 179–82). The thought here is of the church.

toward service, and not upwards, toward power, should there even be structures, "superior" and "lower," pastors/priests and "laypersons"? Should there even be an institutionalized church "government"? It would appear that some form of authority is unavoidable in an institutionalized church. Is not every act of "service"—especially when it is combined with competence, knowledge, or a special charismatic gift—also a use of power and authority? It is right that a church has never actually tried to base its constitution on this guideline of Matthew (and of Jesus!). Much more frequently our text has been used (often not even consciously) to obscure or to "rename" authority that was and is a very present reality in the church. We do not do justice to the text, however, when those who (often almost alone!) do the talking in the church humbly refer to themselves as "ministers," or when he who is "first" ($\pi\rho\hat{\omega}\tau\sigma\varsigma$) in the church humbly calls himself *servus servorum Dei*. Is the guideline that Jesus and Matthew give us utopian? Developing a legal constitution for the church that would be a "service constitution" is in any case a task that all denominations must take seriously.[43]

---

43   Cf. the important reflections in Barth, *CD* 4/2.690–695.

Literature

Burger, *Davidssohn*, 72–74.

Held, "Matthew," 219–23.

For *additional literature* see above, the excursus on the Son of David in Matthew in II B 4.2.

29   **And as they were going out from Jericho, a great crowd followed him. 30/ And behold, two blind men who were sitting beside the way and who had heard that Jesus was passing by cried out and said, "Have mercy on us, Son of David!"[1] 31/ But the crowd rebuked them, that they should be silent. But they cried out louder and said, "Have mercy on us, Lord, Son of David!" 32/ And Jesus stood still, called them, and said, "What do you want me to do for you?" 33/ They say to him, "Lord, that our eyes may be opened!" 34/ But Jesus, filled with compassion, touched their eyes, and immediately they saw again and followed him.**

Analysis   **Structure**

The narrative of the healing of the two blind men brings chaps. 19–20 to a close. The Matthean story of Jesus has now arrived at the final stage before Jerusalem. At the same time it forms the transition to the new main section, chaps. 21–25. In the following chapter Matthew will make use both of the healing of the blind and the acclamation "Son of David" (21:9,

14-15). The narrative has a clear structure. Verse 29 provides the place and the setting. In the exposition of vv. 30-31 attention is focused on the two blind men who are sitting by the way as Jesus passes by. In spite of the crowd's interference they call out twice (ἔκραξαν λέγοντες -μεῖζον ἔκραξαν λέγοντες) and with almost identical words ask for Jesus' mercy (ἐλέησον ἡμᾶς, υἱὸς Δαυίδ, the second time intensified with κύριε). The conversation with Jesus, who stops to talk with them, follows in vv. 32-33.[2] Verse 34 tells of the healing that Jesus performs out of mercy (σπλαγχνισθείς) in response to the request of the blind men. The blind men now follow Jesus just as the crowds had in v. 29.

Source

Matthew had already told a freer version of this story in 9:27-31. This time he remains closer to his source, Mark 10:46-52. As is often the case in his miracle stories, a number of details are omitted, especially from Mark 10:49-50, because Jesus calls the blind men to come to him directly, without the crowd's mediation.[3] In v. 29 Matthew simplifies Mark's confusing geographical statements that speak first of going into, then of leaving Jericho; Jesus has already been in Jericho.[4] Matthew assimilated his two versions of the story to each other only moderately. The most important example of such assimilation is that in both cases

---

1   The text of the two requests in vv. 30-31 is uncertain. In v. 30, along with the important witnesses ℵ, D, Θ, f¹³, et al., I read the short text. The addition of κύριε probably was influenced by vv. 31, 33. In v. 31 the "liturgical" κύριε ἐλέησον is not original, although the language of the psalms (ἐλέησον ἡμᾶς κύριε: Ps 122:3 LXX; cf. 6:2 LXX; 9:13 LXX; 30:9 LXX; 85:3 LXX), in spite of its weaker attestation, probably is.

2   Στάς is in opposition to παράγει.

3   Other elements omitted are: the disciples of Mark 10:46, who play no role in the story; the designation "beggar"; the reference to Jesus as Ναζαρηνός in v. 47 which after 2:1-12 is only partially accurate for the Bethlehemite, Jesus; the mantle and the springing up in v. 50; the catchword "way" (of suffering) in v. 52 that is so important for Mark.

4   Luke also simplifies them but in a different way. According to Luke 18:35 the story takes place while Jesus is entering Jericho. The passage is a good indication that Matthew and Luke do not know each other. In the history of interpretation this difficulty led to a centuries-long discussion about whether Jesus healed a blind man at Jericho once, twice, or three times. According to Augustine (*Cons. ev.* 2.65 [125–26]), the normal view held by most of the

church fathers was that there were two healings, one when Jesus entered Jericho and one when he left. The difficulty that Matthew speaks of two blind men while in Mark there is only one, Bartimaeus, was solved by explaining that Mark mentioned only the better-known of the two men. Relatively infrequently there also appears the view that there were three healings of blind men (Origen, 16:12 = GCS Origenes 10.510. To support this view Origen appeals to verbal inspiration!); Calvin (2.278) and his intimate enemy Maldonat (420–21, who incorrectly cites Theophylactus) represent in full agreement the view that all three stories go back to the same event. This view quickly became dominant, but not everywhere, as the modern fundamentalist commentary by Gerhard Maier (*Matthäus-Evangelium* [2 vols.; Bibel-Kommentar; Neuhausen: Hänssler, 1979–80] 2.139–40) shows.

he speaks of the healing of two blind men who are nameless.[5] Taken together, however, with his new narratives he develops two potential meanings that were inherent in Mark 10:46-52. In 9:27-31 he tells the story as a story of faith, while in 20:29-34 he omits the faith motif. The climax of the story is that Jesus heals by touch ($ἅπτω$) without saying anything.[6] With the strange use of $ὄμμα$ ("eye") in v. 34 it may be that he wants to allude to the story of Mark 8:22-26 that he has omitted.[7] On the whole Matthew here remains closer to his Markan source than he does in 9:27-31.[8]

Interpretation

■ **29-31** Jesus leaves Jericho.[9] The last stage of the way to Jerusalem is under way. He is surrounded by the crowd which follows him and is potentially the church.[10] Two blind men appear. The readers remember how Jesus has already healed the blind on earlier occasions (9:27-31; 12:22; 15:30-31; cf. 11:5). They also remember what Jesus has said about the crowds that do not see (13:13-14) and their blind leaders (15:14). Out of their own biblical-Jewish tradition they are furthermore aware that there is not only physical blindness; there is also a blindness of the heart and of the thoughts.[11] They will also understand this story metaphorically. They themselves

are people who sit by the roadside and urgently and incessantly cry for mercy[12] to Jesus who wants to pass them by.[13] Like these blind men, they also should not let anyone keep them from crying to Jesus. The blind men call out to the Son of David, the helping and healing Messiah of Israel. With this title Matthew situates this title in his macrotext. Jesus is the Messiah awaited by Israel, who heals the sick of his people and who soon will enter the Holy City in the name of the Lord (21:5, 8). He will receive there, however, a divided reception and, as 13:13-14 already indicated, he will ultimately be rejected by the "blind" Pharisees and scribes (cf. 23:16-26).[14] The appearance of "Lord" ($κύριε$) in the second cry for help not only intensifies the prayer; it also makes the identification easier for the readers, since this is what they call the exalted Jesus.[15]

■ **32-34** The twice-shouted request of the blind men makes Jesus, who was about to pass them by, stop in his tracks.[16] He calls them to come to him. They make their request concrete: Jesus should open their eyes! Jesus does that by touching them. This gesture, emphasized by Matthew, shows that the healing is by no means to be understood *only* metaphorically.[17] The Matthean miracle

---

5 Cf. above, II B 4.2 with nn. 5–6.

6 For Held ("Matthew," 224–25), who interprets Matthew's miracle stories paradigmatically, the "faith story" of 9:27-31 is more Matthean, while 20:29-34 only rudimentarily shows the Matthean interpretation of his miracle stories. Our interpretation attempts to exhibit the meaning of 20:29-34 in its own right.

7 Common catchwords are $ἅπτω$, $ὄμμα$, $ἀναβλέπω$. On the Matthean "wastebasket" from which Matthew continually pulls out formulations and motifs of Markan texts that he has omitted cf. above, II B 4.3 with n. 3 and below, V A 3.1, n. 8.

8 The other minor changes are linguistically Matthean. Cf. vol. 1, Introduction 3.2 on $ἀκολουθέω$ mit $ὄχλων$ (v. 29), $καὶ ἰδού$, $λέγων$ (v. 30), $δέ$, $λέγων$, $κύριε$ mit $ἐλεέω$ (v. 31), $κύριε$ (in the mouth of persons imploring help; cf. above, II B 1.1 on 8:2), $ἀνοίγω$ (as 9:30) (v. 33), $σπλαγχνίζομαι$, $δέ$, $ἅπτω$ (as 9:29), $εὐθέως$ (v. 34). $Παράγων$ was suggested by Mark 2:14 = Matt 9:9 or 9:27. On $μεῖζον$ cf. Schenk, *Sprache*, 222. $Ἀνοίγω$ with $ὀφθαλμοί$ is LXX language.

9 For information about Jericho in that day see Gnilka, *Markus* 2.109.

10 Cf. vol. 1, II on 4:25.

11 Sources in Wolfgang Schrage, "$τυφλός κτλ$," *TDNT* 8 (1972) 276–78, 281–82, 284–86.

12 $Ἐλέησον$ ($κύριε$) is reminiscent of the language of the psalms and perhaps of the language of the church's own worship. Cf. vol. 1, Introduction 4.2.1 and above, II B 4.2 on 9:27 and III C 2.3 on 15:22.

13 It is easier to identify with two nameless blind men than with a blind beggar whose name and whose father's name are known.

14 Cf. the excursus Son of David above, II B 4.2.

15 Thus $υἱὸς Δαυίδ$ refers to the past, while $κύριε$ makes the situation present. Cf. Roloff, *Kerygma*, 133–34.

16 $Παράγει$ (v. 30) is opposed to $στάς$. Ernst Lohmeyer's attempt, based on OT texts (Exod 33:19, 22!), to understand Jesus as an "epiphanial sign" is more wistful than to the point ("Und Jesus ging vorüber," in idem, *Urchristliche Mystik* [2d ed.; Darmstadt: Gentner, 1958] 70–79; quotation is from 78).

17 Healings also take place in Matthew's church. Cf. 10:8; 17:19-20; above, the summary of chaps. 8–9, no. 4 and IV A 3 on 17:19-20.

stories remain, rather, reports of something that happened in the life of Jesus. It is precisely this potential meaning of Mark 10:46-52 that our text accentuates. It is emphasized that *back then* two blind men who called out to Israel's Messiah were given the light of sight once again physically by the touch of Jesus. It is only as a report about an actual healing that this story becomes transparent[18] for the experiences of the readers who have been granted sight by Jesus.[19] Jesus did this as an act of mercy, similar to the way that out of mercy he gave his people bread and sent messengers to them (14:14; 15:32; 9:36). After their healing, the two who have been granted their sight join the crowd that is following Jesus.

Summary

In the macrotext of the story of Matthew our text turns from the large section about Jesus' activity in the church that has risen in Israel (beginning with 16:21) back to the main thread of the narrative: the activity of Israel's Messiah among his people. With the last of many healings of the blind he calls attention once again to the great light that "the people who sat in darkness" saw (4:16), and at the same time he prepares for the final activity of the Son of David Jesus in Jerusalem (cf. 21:9, 15-16). Indirectly he also prepares for the hostile reaction of the leaders of the people who remain blind leaders (15:14; 23:16-26) and who are going to kill Jesus, who is the light. Thus our story stands at an important transition in Matthew's narrative. At the same time, however, the story is basic for the readers' own experiences when they ask for their Lord's mercy and in following him thank him for their own "sight."

History of Interpretation

In the ancient church and in the Middle Ages the healing of the two blind men was interpreted allegorically. Understood allegorically it no longer told of the Jesus of that day who healed two blind men. Instead, it proclaimed the present God-man Jesus who saves believers from the world's blindness. Jericho is the world.[20] Based on the Hebrew it was often said that Jericho (יְרִחוֹ) is the city of the moon (יְרֵחַ) that receives its light not from itself but from elsewhere, from the sun.[21] The incarnate man Jesus "passes by"; the passing by refers to his birth, his life, and his death—in short, to his humanity. The point is that in the passing by we meet the deity; it is what "stands still," what is unchanging, in the midst of the world's impermanence.[22] The God Jesus who stops where he is frees the world from its blindness. Our text thus becomes, as it were, in the form of language the husk of the meeting with the one who is true God and at the same time is human. "Seeing" is then faith, the enlightening that comes through "the doctrine of preaching."[23] In this thought-system the "blind" can be interpreted in different ways.

a. Viewed from a *salvation-history* perspective they can be Judah and Israel who are waiting for their messiah, about whom they know only that he will be a descendent of David.[24] Others have thought of the two blind men as the two most important Jewish groups, the Sadducees and the Pharisees.[25] Still others thought of the Gentiles, the descendants of Ham and Japheth,[26]

---

18 On the transparency of the Matthean miracle stories cf. above, the summary of chaps. 8–9, nos. 5–6.

19 Appropriate to the transparency of the story, syc adds to the end of v. 33 "and we see *you*."

20 See, e.g., Origen, 16.9 = GCS Origenes 10.503; Augustine *Quaest.* 1.28 = 22; Ishodad of Merv, 79.

21 See, e.g., Gregory the Great *Hom in ev.* 2.2 = *PL* 76.1082; Rabanus, 1033.

22 "Temporalia enim transeunt, aeterna stant" (Augustine *Quaest.* 1.28 = 23. Cf. idem, *Sermo* 88.10 [9].15 [14] = *PL* 38.544, 547). Gregory the Great *Hom in ev.* 2.6 = *PL* 76.1084: "According to his human nature he had to be born, grow, die, rise, move from one place to another," that is, pass by.

23 Jerome, 180; Augustine *Sermo* 88.4 = *PL* 38.541 (seeing in the sense of Matt 5:8); Gregory the Great

Hom in ev. 2.8 = *PL* 76.1085 (seeing Jesus with the eye of the spirit); Albertus Magnus, 710 (the quotation).

24 See, e.g., Origen, 16.10 = GCS Origenes 10.505 (they did not see the true Logos in the Law and the Prophets); 12 = ibid., 511; Theophylactus, 368.

25 See, e.g., Jerome, 180–81 (for him the multitudes are the haughty Gentiles); Bede (89) and Rabanus (1033) as a possibility.

26 Hilary, 20.13 = SC 258.118; Ambrose *In Luc.* 8.80 = BKV 1/21.511; *Opus imperfectum* 36 = 832 as a possibility.

or of the two parts of the church, Jews and Gentiles, who are hindered from coming to faith by the "crowd," that is, at the time of the apostles by the Jews, later by the "Gentiles who persecuted [the Christians] more harshly and severely."[27]

b. But the two blind men frequently were also interpreted as referring to the *individual person*. According to the impressive sermon of Gregory the Great on Luke 18:31-43, the two blind men represent the members of the human race who through the presence of the redeemer receive light that enables them to travel on the way of life.[28] The "multitudes of persons of the flesh" then represents the lusts and the desires that trouble us in our prayers.[29] Human beings must recognize that they are blind and must ask Christ to open their inner eyes.[30] Thus our text describes how Christ "heals with his touch the spirit that has been blinded with worldly desires" and gives light "that we may follow in his steps."[31]

This allegorical interpretation is impressive and hermeneutically productive. It demonstrates how the current understanding of Christ—in this case the doctrine of the two natures—can become the key to understanding the text. Thus the present, living Christ speaks through the text that in this way becomes something more than simply the report of something in the past. It reveals to the believing readers the salvation-history situation in which they live, and it reveals to them their own experiences that they have made with the living Christ. At the very latest one can see here how close the allegorical interpretation is to what the evangelist himself did with the story of the healing of blind Bartimaeus which had come to him in his tradition. He integrated it into his story of Jesus which relates how Jesus, the Messiah of Israel, became the light of the Gentiles. And he makes it transparent for the believers' own experience of receiving sight in their meeting with Christ. Far from being an exegetical aberration, the allegorical interpretation of the ancient church thus incorporates much of the substance of what the text says. Nor is it an aberration in worldview, viz., a regrettable concession to the Greek spirit in exegesis. It is at least an initial attempt at reading the Bible christologically—an attempt to discover the deity of Jesus in the human story and in the human text of the Bible.[32] In this regard the ancient church's interpretation of vv. 29-34 is exemplary.

---

27 Augustine *Sermo* 88.11 (10) = *PL* 38.544–45; Bede, 89–90 (quotation on 90) as a possibility.

28 2.1 = *PL* 76.1082.

29 2.3–4 = *PL* 76.1083 (quotation 3 = 1083); Thomas Aquinas, *Lectura* no. 1676; Albertus Magnus, 711 (quotation).

30 Valdés, 362.

31 Erasmus, *Paraphrasis,* 110.

32 Cf. Luz, *Matthew in History,* chap. 5.

11.16	187		9.8	515	11.227	25
11.18	181		11.6	163	12.106	329
12.1-2	494		11.9	362	12.140-41	415
13.9-10	365		3Q15	471	12.176	471
13.18	452		4Q159		12.187-89	307
1QapGen			6-7	414	13.294	173
20.15	490		4QFlor		13.297	329
20.28-29	203		1.6	362	14.72	471
22.16	162		1.8	268	14.450	433
1QH			4QpNah		15.136	330
2.9	164		3.5	163	16.3	472
2.11-12	142		4QpPs		17.135-36	77
2.21	142		37 2.14	142	17.318-20	471
2.25-29	142		37 3.16	362	18.21	494
3.6	21		4QTestim.		18.28	152
3.13-16	21		15–17	112	18.85-87	216, 217
6.22-24	21		11QMelch	134	18.113-14	10
6.24-27	363		11QPsᵃ		18.240-56	305
6.24	363		21.11-17	157	18.312-13	415
6.26-27	362		11QPs		19.5-6	319
7.4	21		154.4	163	20.97-99	134, 217
7.26-33	157		154.7	163	20.120	532
8.31	21		11QT		20.219-20	530
13.14	139		15.17-19	494	20.264	162
18.12-13	139				*Ap.*	
18.16	139		*Murrabbaᶜat*		2.41	333
18.23	139		no. 115.4 =		*Bell.*	
1QpHab			DJD 2.248	493	1.111	365, 454
2.6	142				1.548	474
2.7	148		**d / Other Jewish Literature**		2.97	471
5.3	516				2.118	416
12.4	164		Josephus		2.120-21	494
1QS			*Ant.*		2.124-26	78
3.13—4.26	255		4.253	489	2.125	77
3.46	334		4.290-91	501	2.134	77
5–6	453		4.320-23	397	2.160-61	494
5.24-25	453		6.166	48	2.168	152
5.25	453		6.168	48	2.259-62	134, 216
6.1	452, 453		6.235	543	2.273	472
6.19-20	515		8.47	221	2.405	40
6.24—7.25	453		8.86-87	329	2.407	40
7.6-7	515		8.354	95	2.570	40
7.24-25	515		9.85	262	3.437	43
8.5-10	362		9.214	219	6.426	42
9.6	362		11.66	517	7.100	25
9.8-9	515		11.145-47	112	7.218	414

f / New Testament

Colestin
Epist. 18.1 — 460

Const. Ap.
6.15.7 — 506

Cyprian
Ep.
54.3 — 272
55.15 — 445
55.25 — 272
58.3-4 — 105
59.5 — 103
66.4 — 120
71.3 — 371
75.17 — 371
Hab. virg.
21 — 239
Unit. eccl.
4–5 — 371
6 — 206
12 — 460, 461

Cyril of Alexandria
404
fr.
103 — 29
105 — 35
113 — 34
123 — 101
125 — 105
126 — 110
128 — 116
136 — 139
139 — 143
148 — 159
150 — 173
156–57 — 207
163 — 221
211 — 420
226 — 537
Ep.
55 — 460
Hom. div.
9 — 401
Hom. 41 in Luc.
239

Matt.
424–25 — 386
In Joh.
2.5 — 417
9 — 459
Third Letter to Nestorius
110
Trin.
11 — 159

Cyril of Jerusalem
Cat.
3.6 — 139
4.7 — 159
4.7 — 156
6.6 — 156
7.15 — 113

Didache
1–2 — 512
8.1 — 36
9.5 — 356
10.5 — 269, 356
11.4 — 119, 120
11.5-6 — 78
11.7 — 208
11.8 — 210
11.9 — 78
11.12 — 78
12–13 — 62
12.1 — 119, 120
13.1 — 75
15.3-4 — 452
15.3 — 453, 454

Didascalia
6 — 445
11 — 466
13 — 73
21 — 218
26 — 185, 398

Dionysius Areopag.
279, 442

Ep. Apost.
48–49 — 454

Ephraem Syrus
Commentaire de l'Évangile
Concordant ou Diatessaron
44, 226, 259,
363, 364,
401, 403, 519
Sermo
8 — 279
148 — 279

Epiphanius
circular letter
78.2-24 — 303
Haer.
23.4.3-14 — 492
37.7.6 — 88
77.36 — 303

Epistula Clementis ad Jacobum
1–2 — 371

Ethiopic Apoc. Pet.
15-17 = NTApoc
2.680-83 — 396

Eusebius
Ctr. Marc.
1.1.6 — 156
Dem. ev.
1.8.3 — 519
Hist. eccl.
2.23.4 — 304
3.20.1 — 304
3.30 — 14
3.32.6 — 304
4.22.4 — 304
5.18.7 — 79
5.23-24 — 370
6.8.1-3 — 497
6.12.3-6 — 368
6.14.10 — 371
In Ps.
17.15 — 373
Praep. ev.
1.3.1 — 373
8.11.14 — 494

ἀρκετός
95[1]
ἀρνέομαι
100[17], 104[58], 383
ἁρπάζω
137, 140, 141[52]
ἄρρωστος
310[6]
ἄρτι
41[8], 137, 137[6], 269[26]
ἄρτος
349, 349[1, 2], 351[18]
ἀρχαῖος
329[30]
ἀρχή
368[117], 486, 489,
489[22]
ἀρχιερεύς
380
ἄρχω
151[4], 179[6], 318[14],
381[4], 469[9], 532[67],
542[7]
ἄρχων
39, 39[1], 40[2], 41, 41[7],
[12], 541[3]
ἀσθένεια
13[5]
ἀσπάζομαι
71[9]
αὐξάνω
257[7], 262
ἀφίημι
26, 27[7, 9], 206, 327[18],
422, 468[8], 469, 470,
476
ἀφορίζω
281, 281[2]

βάλλω
13, 27[6], 107, 107[1],
267[5], 268[12], 281[2, 3],
283[21], 413[3], 431,
469[9]
βαπτίζω
326[7], 542[6]

βαπτιστής
396[13]
Βαριωνά
355[12]
βάρος
526[8]
βασανίζω
8[6], 318, 318[20]
βασανιστής
469[13]
βασιλεία
9[15], 32, 63, 67, 137,
137[10], 139, 198[9],
204[64, 65], 231[24],
232[26], 237, 250[154],
267[5], 268[12], 275[4],
285[2], 286, 290,
357[24], 386, 386[51],
391, 422, 425[4], 468[9],
488[10, 15], 498, 501,
504[4], 510[9], 515[57],
526[8], 542[7]
βασιλεύς
89, 268[12], 413[3], 469,
470
βαστάζω
13[5], 14, 108
βεβηλόω
180[19]
βιάζω
137, 140, 140[36], 141
βιαστής
137, 140, 141[45], 141
βλαστάνω
253, 253[12]
βλασφημέω
202[46]
βλασφημία
334[68]
βλέπω
236, 238[20], 318[15],
343[4]
βρυγμός
267[5], 268[12]
βρῶμα
311

Γαλιλαία
343[4], 487[5]
γαμέω
488[11], 493
γέεννα
432[9]
γενεά
129, 148[34, 35], 213,
214[7], 215, 218[47],
408, 408[30]
γεννητός
137[10]
γένος
282[6], 283
γῆ
28[14], 29, 39[1], 41[8],
46, 71[10], 82[97], 107[1],
156, 158[12], 217[41],
355[5], 356[21], 413[3],
448, 449[15]
γίνομαι
8[6], 11, 123[3], 151,
158[12], 218[47], 310,
315, 315[59], 336[5],
422[6], 426[15], 438[10],
443, 449[15], 468[8],
487[8], 525, 526[8]
γινώσκω
155[1], 156[1], 164,
165[88], 168[112], 169,
180[20], 190[5], 237,
246, 350[14]
γνῶσις
357[24]
γονυπετέω
406[14]
γραμματεύς
16, 214[2], 285[2], 286,
286[17, 18, 20], 287,
287[23], 288, 327[22],
380, 539[8]
γράφω
137[9]
γρηγορέω
293

γυνή
41[8], 137[10], 336, 339,
469[10], 488[11]

δαιμονίζομαι
13, 23, 23[1, 3], 50[6],
199[19], 336[5]
δαιμόνιον
421[2]
δαίμων
198[10]
δάνειον
469[13], 470[17], 472[48]
δείκνύω
381, 381[4]
δένδρον
258
δεσμωτήριον
130[2]
δέχομαι
119, 119[2], 425
δέω
422[6], 454[49]
δηνάριον
469[10], 525
διάβολος
268[11], 269[16]
διακονέω
544, 546
διάκονος
541[3], 544
διαλογίζομαι
349, 349[6], 350[14]
διαλογισμός
334[68]
διαπεράζω
1[2], 15, 23
διασαφέω
469[9], 473[58]
διαστέλλομαι
41[8]
διαστρέφω
506[5]
διατάσσω
123, 123[3]

διαφέρω
103[47]

διδάσκαλος
16, 17, 31[4], 95[3], 96,
214[2], 413[3], 510[12],
511[20]

διδάσκω
123[3], 233, 237[9],
301[8], 381

διδαχή
349[6]

δίδραχμον
413[4]

δίδωμι
165[81], 181[28], 215,
218[47], 237, 243[74],
246, 310[5], 314[58],
345[20], 356, 385[41],
487[8], 488[12]

δίκαιος
119, 119[2], 238[20],
267[5], 268[12], 281,
281[2], 283, 525

δικαιοσύνη
246[106]

διστάζω
318[15]

διώκω
85[10]

δοκέω
413[3], 438, 443

δόξα
390[81], 510

δοξάζω
343[4], 393[1]

δουλεύω
96[12], 545[28]

δοῦλος
10[17], 95[3], 96,
97[22], 468[8], 469[10],
471, 471[31], 541[3],
544

δύναμαι
27[6], 46, 505, 506[5]

δύναμις
151, 216, 305, 421[2]

δυνατός
516

δύο
46, 448[4], 449[10, 15]

δυσκόλως
516[67]

δύω
39[2]

δώδεκα
66, 123, 511[17], 539[2]

δῶμα
101[24]

δωρεάν
70

δῶρον
6[16], 331[49]

ἑβδομήκοντα
465[1]

ἐγείρω
26[2], 27[6], 41[8, 11, 12],
187[15], 220[60], 305[2],
380, 380[4], 381[6],
390[80], 394, 394[2, 7],
411[1], 539, 539[4]

ἐγκρύπτω
263, 265[4]

ἐγώ εἰμι
317, 317[5], 320, 320[36]

ἐθνικός
449[10]

ἔθνος
73, 74, 75, 85, 85[6],
89, 89[38], 190, 193[37],
268, 517

εἶπον (λέγω)
28[13], 31[5], 179[6], 186[5],
214[3], 224[2], 230,
236[7], 253[10], 268[13],
285[2], 305[2], 311[13],
318[15], 326[4], 327[20],
336[5], 344[8], 347[5],
349[6], 355[9], 396[12],
407[18], 413[3], 448,
449, 465[3], 487[8],
510[9], 526[8]

εἰρήνη
107, 110

εἷς
422, 448[4], 449[10],
449[15], 526[8]

εἰσέρχομαι
41[8, 11], 70, 357[24],
426[14], 510[9], 516[57]

εἰσπορεύομαι
41[8]

ἕκαστος
380[4]

ἑκατόν
469[10]

ἐκβάλλω
23[1], 39[1], 50[6], 64[5],
192[17, 22], 198, 198[10],
202[50], 285[2], 421[2]

ἐκεῖθεν
31[4], 46[3], 123[3], 190[5],
311[10], 504[4]

ἐκζητέω
443[56]

ἐκκλησία
355[6], 356[20], 358,
362, 449[10], 456

ἐκκόπτω
431

ἐκριζόω
326[5], 327, 333

ἐκτείνω
224, 225[13]

ἐλαφρός
157[7]

ἐλέγχω
449[10], 450, 451

ἐλεέω
31[3], 34, 49,
314[45], 336[5], 339[39],
406[14], 469[9], 470[17],
474, 548, 548[1],
549[8]

ἔλεος
31[3], 52, 174[154]

ἐλεύθερος
413[4]

ἐμβαίνω
1[2], 15, 16[2, 9], 233[6],
317[5]

ἔμπορος
275[4], 278

ἔμπροσθεν
99[4], 158[12], 437[4],
444[60]

ἐναγκαλίζομαι
425

ἐναντίος
317[5]

ἐνθύμησις
199[21], 200[23]

ἐντέλλομαι
395[12], 490

ἐντολή
326[4]

ἐξέρχομαι
46, 50[6], 233[4], 281[2],
327[22], 336[5], 339,
406[14], 468[7], 525,
525[4], 526[8]

ἔξεστιν
178, 179, 186[3]

ἐξομολογέω
158[10, 12], 162[53, 56],
163[70]

ἐξουσία
10, 26, 27[6], 28, 28[14],
69, 75, 165[81]

ἐξώτερος
9

ἐπαίρω
395[8]

ἐπερωτάω
186[6], 347[5], 487[8]

ἐπιβλέπω
138 [23]

ἐπιγινώσκω
31[4], 156[1], 157[5], 167,
396[13]

ἐπιείκεια
175

ἐπικαλέω
96[14]

καθαρίζω
4[1], 5, 6
καθεύδω
43[26], 253, 256[43]
καθίζω
281, 343[4], 390[81],
510, 543[18]
κάθημαι
147[21], 151[8], 233[2],
390[81]
καινός
285
καιρός
23[3], 24, 24[16], 157,
169, 305, 305[2]
κακῶς
336[5], 405[2], 406[14]
καλέω
526[8]
καλός
281, 281[1]
κάμιλος
509[3]
κάμινος
267[5], 268[12]
καρδία
173, 217[41], 237[15],
326, 326[4], 429[53],
469[9, 13], 470
καρπός
65[11], 243[74], 253[10, 12]
καταβαίνω
151, 151[2], 318[15]
καταβολή
265, 265[4]
καταδικάζω
180[20], 202[52]
κατακαίω
256, 267[1]
κατακρίνω
220[62], 539
κατακυριεύω
544
καταλείπω
299, 347[5]

καταποντίζω
318[15], 431
κατασκηνόω
257[2]
καταφρονέω
440
κατεξουσιάζω
541[3], 544
κατισχύω
356[20], 363, 364
καύσων
526[8], 532[73]
κελεύω
16[2, 3], 305[2], 310[6],
318[15], 320[41], 468[9]
κερδαίνω
385, 452
κῆνσος
419
κήρυγμα
215
κηρύσσω
71[5], 99, 123[3]
Κηφᾶς
359[40]
κλαίω
145
κλαυθμός
11[28], 267[5], 268[12]
κλείς
356
κοινόω
332[59]
κοπάζω
16[9], 317[5]
κοπιάω
171[126], 172
κόπτω
145, 145[8]
κόσμος
265[2], 267[11], 385,
431[7]
κόφινος
315
κράβατος
27[6]

κράζω
39[2], 46, 336[5], 548
κράσπεδον
41[8]
κρατέω
41[11], 187[15], 469[9]
κραυγάζω
194, 194[47]
κρεμάννυμι
431
κρίνω
517
κρίσις
129, 182[43], 190, 192,
193, 194, 194[39], 213
κρύπτω
157[5], 265[4], 275[5]
κτίσις
486[2], 487[8]
κυλλός
344[11]
κῦμα
16[2]
κυνάριον
340, 340[53]
κυριεύω
541[3], 544[25]
κύριος
2, 5, 5[3], 6[10], 8[6], 16,
16[2, 7], 18, 39, 46[3],
48, 95[3, 5], 96, 101[26],
158[10, 12], 253[10], 317,
318[15], 320[41], 336[5],
339[39], 341[64], 380[4],
390[86], 395[12], 406[14],
459[96], 465[3], 468[8],
469, 470, 526[8], 531,
548, 548[1], 549,
549[12, 15]
κωλύω
504, 505[9]
κώμη
91[9]
κωφός
39, 50[7], 134, 343[4]

λαλέω
39[1], 230, 233, 233[4],
224, 224[2], 237[9],
257[3], 395[12]
λαμβάνω
14, 14[10], 114, 119,
119[2], 186[6], 345[20],
349, 349[2, 6], 413[3],
526[8]
λάμπω
395[12]
λαός
50[5], 327, 438[10], 478[4]
λέγω
5[3], 8[6], 16[9], 31, 31[4],
32, 32[13], 36[2], 39[2],
46, 46[3], 50, 50[5], 61,
64[4], 84, 85[10], 86[15],
98[4], 145, 151[8],
180[19], 198, 202[50],
214[2], 253[10], 268[13],
301[5], 318[15], 326[4],
327[16], 427[16], 336[5],
344[8], 349[6], 356,
356[18], 380[4], 395[12],
406[14], 407[18], 413[3],
425[4], 437[5], 448,
449[15], 465[3], 468,
469[9], 487[8], 492,
510[9], 542[7], 548, 549[8]
λεπρός
5
λευκός
394[6]
λίθος
354[2], 363
λόγος
13, 71[9], 198, 211,
237[15], 257[6], 290,
326[4], 336[5], 469[9],
471[27], 509[2]
λυπέω
305[2], 411[1], 469[9]
λύτρον
546, 546[41]

λυτρόω
546⁴⁰
λύω
422⁶, 454⁴⁹

μαθητεύω
156, 285², 286,
286¹⁶
μαθητής
15, 16⁶, ⁹, ¹⁰, 26, 31,
31⁴, 32¹⁶, 63, 66,
66⁵, 119, 123, 123³,
224², 230, 236⁷,
237¹⁵, 268¹³, 318¹¹,
336⁵, 349⁶, 355⁹,
365⁹⁸, 380⁴, 395⁸,
488¹¹, 510⁹, 539²
μακροθυμέω
468, 468⁸, 472⁴⁶
μαλακία
66⁵
μᾶλλον
140⁴⁴
μανθάνω
32²¹, 156, 156³,
157⁶, 174
μαρτύριον
6, 85⁶, 89
μαστιγόω
85, 89³⁹
μάχαιρα
110³⁸, ³⁹
μέγας
137¹⁰, 181, 181³⁷,
182, 426, 541³, 548,
549⁸
μέλλω
136³, 380⁴, 395¹³,
411, 411¹, 510¹⁵,
542⁷
μένω
151
μερίζω
198⁹
μεριμνάω
85

μέρος
339, 355⁹
μέσος
281¹, 422, 449¹⁵, 459
μεταβαίνω
23³, 123³, 186⁶,
343⁶, 407¹⁸
μεταμορφόω
393¹, 397²⁴
μετανοέω
151, 438⁷
μετάνοια
438⁷
μεταξύ
449¹⁰
μηδείς
41⁸, 46
μήτηρ
107, 224, 225¹⁶,
228¹
μικρός
62, 120⁷, 137¹⁰,
139, 139²⁸, 422,
424, 425, 432,
434²¹, 437⁴,
440²⁸
μισθός
119, 119², 526⁸,
532⁶⁷
μισθόω
525⁴, 526⁸
μοιχαλίς
214³, 217
μοιχάομαι
486³
μοιχεύω
486³
μόνος
8⁴, 41⁸, 119, 119⁶,
122²⁸, 179
μυρίος
469¹⁰, 471³⁰
μυστήριον
237, 237¹⁰
μωρός
163⁶⁶, 293

νεανίσκος
510, 510¹¹, 512,
512²⁶
νεκρός
19, 19³⁴, ³⁷
νεφέλη
389⁷⁶
νήπιος
162, 163⁶⁶, 164, 169,
171, 172, 172¹³⁵,
434²³
νῖκος
192, 192²²
Νινευίτης
215
νοέω
349, 351¹⁸
νόμος
180¹⁹, 257⁶
νόσος
13, 66⁵, ⁶, 407
νότος
220⁶⁴

ξηραίνω
41⁸, 186⁶

ὁδός
71⁶, 179
ὀδούς
267⁵, 268¹²
οἰκία
33²⁶, 39¹, ², 41⁸, 46³,
233¹, 303, 517⁷³
οἰκιακός
95, 97²¹ 107
οἰκοδεσπότης
95⁵, 286¹⁰, 287²¹, ²²,
526⁸, 531
οἰκοδομέω
355⁷, 356, 363
οἶκος Ἰσραήλ
73²¹
οἰνοπότης
149³⁷

ὀλιγόπιστος
16, 16², 318¹⁵, 349⁶
ὄμμα
549⁷
ὅμοιος
230, 231²², 275⁴,
285², 526⁸
ὁμοιόω
231²², ²⁴, 468⁹
ὁμολογέω
100¹⁷, 104, 104⁵⁸,
105, 305²
ὄνομα
66⁷, 90, 119, 119²,
192²¹, 421², 422,
449¹⁵, 458
ὄνος
433
ὅραμα
395¹², 398
ὁράω
23³, 26, 26¹ 27⁶, 31⁴,
33²⁹, 41⁸, 46, 60⁴,
64³, 132¹⁷, 136¹,
179⁶, 214², 236,
437⁵, 469⁹
ὀργίζω
469, 469⁹
ὅρκος
305², 307¹⁷
ὄρος
5¹, 343⁶, 438, 438¹⁰,
443⁵⁶
οὐαί
153
οὐράνιος
469⁹, 470
οὐρανός
9, 16, 98⁴, 136², 156,
158¹², 163⁷⁰, 216²⁴,
224², 231²⁴, 232²⁶,
236⁷, 253¹⁰, 275⁴,
285², 286, 310⁴,
327²⁰, 355⁵, 356,
356¹⁵, ²¹, 389⁷⁶, 422,
425⁴, 437⁴, 448,

πρεσβύτερος
326[4], 380, 478[4]

πρόβατον
71[3], 85, 438[10], 443[56]

προβιβάζω
305[2], 307[18]

προσάγω
468[1], 469[13]

προσέρχομαι
8[6], 16, 16[9], 36[2], 41[8],
46[3], 230, 236[7],
237[15], 253[10], 268[13],
305[2], 327[16], 336[5],
343[6], 347[5], 395[8],
406[14], 407[18], 413[3],
425[4], 465[3], 487[8],
510[9], 542[7]

προσέχω
88[25], 349, 349[4, 6]

πρόσκαιρος
249[137]

προσκαλέω
66[5], 425[5], 469[9]

προσκυνέω
39[2], 41[8], 318[11], 336[5],
469[9], 470[17], 472[45],
542[7]

προσλαμβάνω
382[15]

προσφέρω
13, 27[6], 39[2], 50[3, 6],
199[19], 406[14], 468[1],
504[4]

προσφωνέω
147[21]

πρόσωπον
138[22], 395[8], 437[5]

προφήτεια
237[12]

προφητεύω
137, 137[7], 237[15]

προφήτης
119, 119[2], 136[1], 214,
238[20], 347

προφθάνω
413[4]

πρῶτος
66[8], 68, 68[24], 69,
253[10], 367, 526, 541[3]

πτωχός
134

πύλη
358, 363

πῦρ
267[5], 268[12], 281,
432, 432[9]

πυρράζω
347

πωλέω
98[3], 275[4], 278[40]

πῶς
178[3]

ῥάβδος
71[6], 77[51]

ῥαντίζω
326[7]

ῥῆμα
211, 452

ῥίπτω
64, 64[3], 343[6]

σάββατον
178, 179, 186[3]

σαγήνη
281, 282

Σαδδουκαίος
347, 349[1, 3, 6]

σαπρός
281

σάρξ
355[12], 359[45], 362[58]

Σατανᾶς
382

σέβω
414[11]

σεισμός
16[10], 20

σεληνιάζομαι
406[14]

σημεῖον
216, 216[24], 219

σήμερον
151, 151[7]

Σιδών
339

Σίμων
356[15]

σῖτος
253, 256

σκανδαλίζω
135, 177, 237[15],
326[5], 431, 432,
440[27], 450[24], 451,
479

σκάνδαλον
218, 268[12], 269,
269[23, 24], 302, 366,
381[4], 382, 382[19],
431, 432, 434[25], 435,
443 479

σκεῦος
205

σκηνή
397[23]

σκληροκαρδία
490[32]

σκότος
9

σκύλλω
64[2]

σοφία
149[43], 163[70]

σοφός
158[12], 163[66]

σπείρω
250[154], 252, 257[4]

σπέρμα
252, 257[4]

σπλαγχνίζομαι
5, 5[4], 64[3], 314[45],
469, 470[17], 474, 548,
549[8]

σπουδή
140[44]

σπυρίς
343[5]

στάδιον
318[12]

στατήρ
413[4], 415[22]

σταυρός
114, 114[62], 115

σταυρόω
539[4]

στόμα
327[22], 332, 413[4]

στρέφω
41[8], 380[4], 426[15]

στυγνάζω
510[12]

συλλέγω
281[1]

συμβούλιον
186[6], 188

συμφέρω
488[11]

συμφωνέω
449[15], 461, 525

συνάγω
253[10], 256, 281,
281[1], 449[16]

συναγωγή
301[6]

συναίρω
468[8], 471[27]

σύνδουλος
468[8]

συνέδριον
88

σύνεσις
163[70]

συνετός
158[12]

συνίημι
228[3], 237[15], 250[146],
285, 285[1], 326, 349,
351[19], 396[13]

συντέλεια
268[11, 12], 510[15]

συντηρέω
36[3]

συντρίβω
191

συστρέφω
411, 411[1]

σφόδρα
394, 395[8], 411[1],
469[9], 510[9]

σχολάζω
221[78]

σώζω
6[2, 10], 20, 39[2], 40,
42[18], 43[22, 23], 116[79]

σῶμα
102

τάλαντον
469[9], 471[30]

ταπεινός
173, 429

ταπεινότης
196

ταπεινοφροσύνη
175 429[53]

ταπεινόω
428, 429

τέκνον
146[11], 428[51], 469[10]

τέκτων
301[6], 302, 302[9, 11]

τέλειος
163[66], 510[9], 512,
513, 513[32]

τελευτάω
41[8]

τελέω
85[10], 86, 86[12], 123[1, 3]

τέλος
90[49], 419

τελώνης
67[9], 449[10]

τέρας
216

τηρέω
510[9]

τίλλω
179[6]

τόπος
310[5], 324[2]

τότε
27[6], 36[2, 3], 64[4],
199[19], 214[2], 253[10],
268[13], 327[16], 336[5],
349[6], 380[4], 395[13],
407[18], 465[3], 469[9],
504[4], 510[9], 542[7]

τρεῖς
448[4], 539[4]

τρῆμα
509[4]

τρίτος
380, 381[6], 539[4]

τροφή
71

τρυμαλιά
509[5]

τρύπημα
509[5]

τυφλός
39, 46[3], 134, 199[19],
325[2], 343[4]

Τύρος
339

ὕδωρ
318[15]

υἱοὶ τῆς βασιλείας
9, 9[15], 267[11], 268,
268[16], 416[34]

υἱός
156, 164, 267[5],
268[12], 301[6], 318[11],
355, 355[7], 394, 416

υἱός τοῦ ἀνθρώπου
17, 99[4], 129, 183[48],
202[46], 216[24], 351[1],
355, 355[7], 389, 510,
539[6]

υἱός Δαυίδ
132[21], 199[19], 336[5],
548, 549[15]

ὑπάγω
8[6], 23[1], 25[19], 275[4],

278[40], 382, 449[10],
525[4], 526[8], 533[77]

ὑπακούω
16[9]

ὑπάρχω
510[9]

ὑπόδημα
71[6], 77[49], 79

ὑποκριτής
327[22]

ὑστερέω
509[1]

φάγος
149[37]

φαίνω
50[5], 253[10]

φάντασμα
317[5]

Φαρισαῖος
214[2], 327[22], 347,
349[1, 3]

φημί
253[10], 305[2], 413[3],
510[9]

φθάνω
204, 204[65, 66]

φιλέω
108[6]

φοβέω
27[6], 60, 93[1], 101[26],
318[15], 320[39], 394,
395[8]

φόβος
318[11]

φορτίζω / φορτίον
157[7], 172

φράζω
327[19]

φρόνιμος
293

φυλακή
469[10]

φυτεία
327[20]

χαλκός
71[6]

Χαναναῖος
336[5]

χαρά
275[4]

χάρισμα
410

χεῖλος
326[4]

χείρ
13, 39[2], 41[7, 11], 186[3,
6], 224, 224[2], 225[13],
318[14], 390[80], 431,
504

χιών
394[6]

χόρτος
253

χρεία
179, 438[7]

Χριστός
130[2], 132, 132[20],
355[7], 359[40], 361

χωλός
134, 343[1, 4]

χωρέω
487, 488, 500[113]

ψευδομαρτυρία
334[68]

ψυχή
102, 116, 116[79, 80],
118, 385, 385[41]

ψυχρός
120, 122, 122[31]

ὧδε
305[2], 310[6], 395[12]

ὥρα
8[6], 39[2], 41[8], 314[48],
336[5], 406[14], 425[4],
526[8]

צֶאֱ
329

3. Subjects

Heil, J. P.
317, 321
Heine, H.
309
Heinemann, J.
134
Heinemann, J. H.
524, 530, 532
Heising, A.
313, 315
Held, H. J.
1, 5, 8, 13, 14, 15,
23, 26, 34, 39, 40,
43, 46, 52, 57, 154,
310, 313, 314, 338,
342, 405, 408, 548,
549
Hempel, J.
338
Hengel, M.
1, 15, 18, 72, 114,
362
Hengel, R.
1
Heppe, H.
55, 126, 207
Herder, J. G. H.
403
Héring, J.
437, 440
Hermaniuk, M.
245
Hertz, A.
384
Heth, W. A.
485
Heuberger, J.
235, 239, 249
Hezser, C.
524, 530, 531, 532,
535, 536
Hickling, C. J. A.
451
Hiers, R. H.
353, 365

Higgins, A. J. B.
98, 99, 213, 214, 219
Hilgert, E.
15, 21
Hill, D.
31, 119, 121, 276
Hill, G. F.
277
Hirsch, E.
407
Hirunuma, T.
347
Hirzel, R.
532
Hoffmann, P.
8, 9, 64, 70, 71, 78,
81, 99, 129, 131,
134, 136, 139, 145,
146, 147, 149, 155,
164, 165, 166, 167,
201, 274, 353, 358,
360, 367, 369, 464,
480, 493, 522, 541
Hoh, J.
285, 286, 287
Holmes, M. W.
485, 486
Holtzmann, H. J.
147, 161, 419, 445,
457, 527, 529
Hommel, H.
353, 358, 363
Hoppe, R.
508
Horbury, W.
413, 415
Houssiau, A.
155, 159
Howard G.
158
Hubmaier, B.
457
Huck, A.
347
Hübner, H.
178, 179, 325, 328

Hull, J. M.
1, 42
Hummel, R.
26, 31, 33, 34, 47,
48, 178, 182, 183,
187, 188, 197, 325,
328, 366
Hunzinger, C.H.
257, 261, 447, 452,
453
Hutter, M.
40, 42

van Iersal, B. M. F.
15, 310, 313, 314
Isaksson, A.
487, 491
Ishodad of Merv
420, 550

Jacobson, A. D.
438
Jansen, C.
68, 79, 159, 174,
194, 322, 361, 374,
375, 445, 456, 466,
477, 519, 545
Jastrow, M.
40, 338, 431, 432,
454
Jenni, E.
96, 302
Jeremias, J.
8, 10, 72, 86, 103,
114, 141, 146, 147,
158, 161, 162, 164,
192, 205, 213, 217,
219, 220, 235, 240,
241, 242, 243, 252,
253, 254, 260, 267,
277, 280, 290, 303,
319, 337, 353, 355,
357, 358, 362, 363,
364, 397, 423, 426,
440, 471, 475, 504,
505, 507, 524, 526,

527, 531, 532, 533,
546
John XXIII
377
John of Damascus
401, 402
John Paul II
503, 508, 523
Jones, A. H. M.
338
Joüon, P.
426
Jülicher, A.
38, 95, 145, 147,
197, 203, 220, 222,
235, 243, 244, 248,
252, 253, 257, 269,
275, 277, 281, 282,
285, 288, 290, 439,
468, 475, 524, 526,
528, 533, 536, 543
Jüngel, E.
252, 253, 261, 280,
282, 290, 526, 534

Kähler, C.
353, 358, 421, 423,
429, 450
Käsemann, E.
99, 197, 200, 212,
325, 331
Kahlmeyer, J.
15, 21
Kaiser, M.
496
Kant, I.
173, 296, 528
Karlstadt, A.
136, 144
Kaser, M.
472, 533
Kasper, W.
354, 372, 377
Kasting, H.
71, 74, 336, 338

601

Werner, M.
92
Wernle, P.
160, 529
Westermann, W. L.
472
de Wette, W. M. F.
166, 197, 207, 218,
521
Wettstein, J. J.
18, 20, 25, 33, 76,
88, 96, 215, 221,
358, 385
White, K. D.
235, 241
White, L. M.
432, 447
Widengren, G.
441
Wikenhauser, A.
32
Wilde, O.
309
Wilckens, U.
162, 333
Wilcox, M.
355
Wildberger, H.
363

Wilhelms, E.
413
Wilkens, W.
228, 229, 246, 256,
265
Wilkins, M. J.
354
Wilson, B.
482
Wilson, R. M.
285
Wink, W.
129, 132, 139
Winter, J.
165, 415
Winter, P.
155, 156
Wolzogen, J. L.
28, 160, 183, 184,
221, 335, 415, 419,
455, 456, 457, 461,
477, 506, 544, 546
Wouters, A.
516
Wrede, W.
191

Wrege, H.-T.
197
Wünsche, A.
165, 415
Wyclif, J.
175

Yarnold, E.
508, 512

Zahn, T.
32, 33, 73, 91, 133,
173, 209, 221, 301,
303, 304, 433, 499,
521
Zeller, D.
8, 9, 98, 99, 101,
145, 146, 147, 285,
286
Zieglar, I.
416
Ziesler, J. A.
36, 37
Zimmerli, W.
491

Zimmermann, H.
421, 447, 449
Zinzindorf, N.
80, 113, 170, 174,
272, 280, 338, 427
Zmijewski, J.
405, 407, 409
Zumstein, J.
70, 76, 87, 155, 245,
405, 408, 409, 421,
449, 470, 476
Zwick, R.
524, 525
Zwingli, H.
14, 30, 43, 68, 79,
80, 82, 90, 102, 104,
105, 175, 183, 184,
207, 209, 220, 222,
223, 227, 238, 239,
269, 274, 337, 373,
387, 419, 427, 455,
498, 506, 521, 535,
544
van Zyl, H. C.
421, 422

Designer's Notes

In the design of the visual aspects of *Hermeneia*, consideration has been given to relating the form to the content by symbolic means.

The letters of the logotype *Hermeneia* are a fusion of forms alluding simultaneously to Hebrew (dotted vowel markings) and Greek (geometric round shapes) letter forms. In their modern treatment they remind us of the electronic age as well, the vantage point from which this investigation of the past begins.

The Lion of Judah used as visual identification for the series is based on the Seal of Shema. The version for *Hermeneia* is again a fusion of Hebrew calligraphic forms, especially the legs of the lion, and Greek elements characterized by the geometric. In the sequence of arcs, which can be understood as scroll-like images, the first is the lion's mouth. It is reasserted and accelerated in the whorl and returns in the aggressively arched tail: tradition is passed from one age to the next, rediscovered and re-formed.

"Who is worthy to open the scroll and break its seals. . . ."
Then one of the elders said to me
"weep not; lo, the Lion of the tribe of David,
the Root of David, has conquered,
so that he can open the scroll and
its seven seals."
Rev. 5:2, 5

To celebrate the signal achievement in biblical scholarship which *Hermeneia* represents, the entire series will by its color constitute a signal on the theologian's bookshelf: the Old Testament will be bound in yellow and the New Testament in red, traceable to a commonly used color coding for synagogue and church in medieval painting; in pure color terms, varying degrees of intensity of the warm segment of the color spectrum. The colors interpenetrate when the binding color for the Old Testament is used to imprint volumes from the New and vice versa.

Wherever possible, a photograph of the oldest extant manuscript, or a historically significant document pertaining to the biblical sources, will be displayed on the end papers of each volume to give a feel for the tangible reality and beauty of the source material.

The title-page motifs are expressive derivations from the Hermeneia logotype, repeated seven times to form a matrix and debossed on the cover of each volume. These sifted-out elements will be seen to be in their exact positions within the parent matrix.

Horizontal markings at gradated levels on the spine will assist in grouping the volumes according to these conventional categories.

The type has been set with unjustified right margins so as to preserve the internal consistency of word spacing. This is a major factor in both legibility and aesthetic quality; the resultant uneven line endings are only slight impairments to legibility by comparison. In this respect the type resembles the handwritten manuscripts where the quality of the calligraphic writing is dependent on establishing and holding to integral spacing patterns.

All of the type faces in common use today have been designed between AD 1500 and the present. For the biblical text a face was chosen which does not arbitrarily date the text, but rather one which is uncompromisingly modern and unembellished so that its feel is of the universal. The type style is Univers 65 by Adrian Frutiger.

The expository texts and footnotes are set in Baskerville, chosen for its compatibility with the many brief Greek and Hebrew insertions. The double-column format and the shorter line length facilitate speed reading and the wide margins to the left of footnotes provide for the scholar's own notations.

Kenneth Hiebert

Category of biblical writing,
key symbolic characteristic,
and volumes so identified.

1
Law
(boundaries described)
 Genesis
 Exodus
 Leviticus
 Numbers
 Deuteronomy

2
History
(trek through time and space)
 Joshua
 Judges
 Ruth
 1 Samuel
 2 Samuel
 1 Kings
 2 Kings
 1 Chronicles
 2 Chronicles
 Ezra
 Nehemiah
 Esther

3
Poetry
(lyric emotional expression)
 Job
 Psalms
 Proverbs
 Ecclesiastes
 Song of Songs

4
Prophets
(inspired seers)
 Isaiah
 Jeremiah
 Lamentations
 Ezekiel
 Daniel
 Hosea
 Joel
 Amos
 Obadiah
 Jonah
 Micah
 Nahum
 Habakkuk
 Zephaniah
 Haggai
 Zechariah
 Malachi

5
New Testament Narrative
(focus on One)
 Matthew
 Mark
 Luke
 John
 Acts

6
Epistles
(directed instruction)
 Romans
 1 Corinthians
 2 Corinthians
 Galatians
 Ephesians
 Philippians
 Colossians
 1 Thessalonians
 2 Thessalonians
 1 Timothy
 2 Timothy
 Titus
 Philemon
 Hebrews
 James
 1 Peter
 2 Peter
 1 John
 2 John
 3 John
 Jude

7
Apocalypse
(vision of the future)
 Revelation

8
Extracanonical Writings
(peripheral records)